THE JERUSALEM TALMUD
THIRD ORDER: NAŠIM
TRACTATES *SOṬAH* AND *NEDARIM*

STUDIA JUDAICA

FORSCHUNGEN ZUR WISSENSCHAFT DES JUDENTUMS

HERAUSGEGEBEN VON
E. L. EHRLICH UND G. STEMBERGER

BAND XXXI

WALTER DE GRUYTER · BERLIN · NEW YORK

THE JERUSALEM TALMUD
תלמוד ירושלמי

THIRD ORDER: NAŠIM
סדר נשים
TRACTATES *SOṬAH* AND *NEDARIM*
מסכתות סוטה ונדרים

EDITION, TRANSLATION, AND COMMENTARY

BY

HEINRICH W. GUGGENHEIMER

WALTER DE GRUYTER · BERLIN · NEW YORK

ISBN 978-3-11-068117-8
e-ISBN (PDF) 978-3-11-089182-9

This volume is text- and page-identical with the hardback published in 2005.

Library of Congress Control Number: 2020942830

Bibliographic information published by the Deutsche Nationalbibliothek
The Deutsche Nationalbibliothek lists this publication in the
Deutsche Nationalbibliografie;
detailed bibliographic data are available on the Internet at http://dnb.dnb.de.

© 2020 Walter de Gruyter GmbH, Berlin/Boston

Printing and binding: CPI books GmbH, Leck

www.degruyter.com

Preface

The present volume is the seventh in this series of the Jerusalem Talmud, the second in a five volume edition, translation, and Commentary of the Third Order of this Talmud. The principles of the edition regarding text, vocalization, and Commentary have been spelled out in detail in the Introduction to the first volume. The text in this volume is based on the manuscript text of the Yerushalmi edited by the Academy of the Hebrew Language, Jerusalem 2001.

The extensive Commentary is not based on emendations; where there is no evidence from manuscripts or early prints to correct evident scribal errors, the proposed correction is given in the Notes. In response to a suggestion by a reviewer, for each paragraph the folio and line numbers of the text in the Krotoschin edition are added. It should remembered that these numbers may differ from the *editio princeps* by up to three lines. It seems to be important that a translation of the Yerushalmi be accompanied by the text, to give the reader the possibility to compare the interpretation with other translations.

Again I wish to thank my wife, Dr. Eva Guggenheimer, who acted as critic, style editor, proof reader, and expert on the Latin and Greek vocabulary. Her own notes on some possible Latin and Greek etymologies are identified by (E. G.).

Contents

Introduction to Tractate Sota   1

Chapter 1, המקנא

Halakhah 1	7
Halakhah 2	22
Halakhah 3	36
Halakhah 4	41
Halahkah 5	47
Halakhah 6	52
Halakhah 7	54
Halakhah 8	60
Halakhah 9	69
Halakhah 10	71

Chapter 2, היה מביא מנחתה

Halakhah 1	79
Halakhah 2	91
Halakhah 3	104
Halakhah 4	106
Halakhah 5	110
Halakhah 6	112
Halakhah 7	123

Chapter 3, היה נוטל את מנחתה		
Halakhah 1		126
Halakhah 2		134
Halakhah 3		137
Halakhah 4		141
Halakhah 6		156
Halakhah 7		159
Halakhah 8		168
Halakhah 9		172
Chapter 4, ארוסה		
Halakhah 1		178
Halakhah 3		184
Halakhah 4		186
Halakhah 5		190
Halakhah 6		194
Chapter 5, כשם שהמים		
Halakhah 1		198
Halakhah 2		206
Halakhah 4		225
Halakhah 5		230
Halakhah 6		234
Halakhah 7		238
Chapter 6, מי שקינא		
Halakhah 1		245
Halakhah 2		248
Halakhah 3		254
Chapter 7, אילו נאמרין		
Halakhah 1		263
Halakhah 2		269

Halakhah 3	273
Halakhah 4	277
Halakhah 5	289
Halakhah 6	297
Halakhah 7	303

Chapter 8, משוח מלחמה

Halakhah 1	308
Halakhah 2	311
Halakhah 3	313
Halakhah 4	330
Halakhah 5	334
Halakhah 6	338
Halakhah 9	344
Halakhah 10	347

Chapter 9, עגלה ערופה

Halakhah 1	351
Halakhah 2	360
Halakhah 3	366
Halakhah 4	368
Halakhah 5	369
Halakhah 6	383
Halakhah 7	387
Halakhah 8	389
Halakhah 9	390
Halakhah 10	390
Halakhah 11	394
Halakhah 12	398
Halakhah 13-14	401
Halakhah 15	408
Halakhah 16	410
Halakhah 17	415

Introduction to Tractate Nedarim	421

Chapter 1, כל כינויי נדרים

Halakhah 1	425
Halakhah 2	448
Halakhah 3	453
Halakhah 4	458

Chapter 2, אלו נדרים

Halakhah 1	463
Halakhah 2	467
Halakhah 3	470
Halakhah 4	473
Halakhah 5	478

Chapter 3, ארבעה נדרים

Halakhah 1	481
Halakhah 2	482
Halakhah 3	498
Halakhah 4	499
Halakhah 6	503
Halakhah 7	506
Halakhah 10	508
Halakhah 12	509
Halakhah 14	512

Chapter 4, אין בין המודר

Halakhah 1	519
Halakhah 2	522
Halakhah 3	528
Halakhah 4	532

Halakhah 5	535
Halakhah 6	536
Halakhah 7	538
Halakhah 8	539
Halakhah 9	540

Chapter 5, השותפין

Halakhah 1	569
Halakhah 3	574
Halakhah 4	576
Halakhah 6	577
Halakhah 7	579
Halakhah 8	579
Halakhah 10	580

Chapter 6, הנודר מן המבושל

Halakhah 1	583
Halakhah 2	588
Halakhah 3	591
Halakhah 4	602
Halakhah 5	607
Halakhah 7	615
Halakhah 8	617
Halakhah 10	619
Halakhah 11	623
Halakhah 12	625

Chapter 7, הנודר מן הירק

Halakhah 1	627
Halakhah 2	630
Halakhah 3	633
Halakhah 4	639

Halakhah 5	644
Halakhah 6	648
Halakhah 7	654
Halakhah 9	657
Halakhah 11	658

Chapter 8, קונם יין

Halakhah 1	629
Halakhah 3	637
Halakhah 4	640
Halakhah 5	641
Halakhah 6	643
Halakhah 7	645
Halakhah 11	648
Halakhah 12	653
Halakhah 13	652

Chapter 9, רבי אליעזר

Halakhah 1	654
Halakhah 2	661
Halakhah 3	665
Halakhah 4	666
Halakhah 5	669
Halakhah 6	672
Halakhah 9	674
Halakhah 10	676
Halakhah 11	677

Chapter 10, נערה מאורסה

Halakhah 1	679
Halakhah 2	686
Halakhah 3	689

Halakhah 5	690
Halakhah 6-7	692
Halakhah 10	699

Chapter 11, אילו נדרים

Halakhah 1	710
Halakhah 3	721
Halakhah 4	725
Halakhah 6	729
Halakhah 7	731
Halakhah 8	732
Halakhah 9	733
Halakhah 11	735
Halakhah 12	737
Halakhah 13	737

Indices

Index of Biblical Quotations	743
Index of Talmudical Quotations	
Babylonian Talmud	747
Jerusalem Talmud	750
Tosephta	751
Other Talmudic Sources	752
Index of Greek, Latin, Hebrew, and Arabic, Words	752
Author Index	753
Subject Index	755

Introduction to Tractate Soṭah

The Tractate received its name from the topic of its first part, the rules concerning the wife suspected of adultery, *Num.* 5:11-31. The title, שׂוֹטָה "the deviant", is derived from v. 12, "if a man's wife deviates and is unfaithful to him," when in fact the case treated is one where the wife is not proven to have been unfaithful but only is suspected of adultery. From the biblical formulation the rabbis concluded that for a simple suspicion the husband cannot demand that his wife cleanse herself by undergoing the Temple ceremony, but must present to the local court *prima facie* evidence of adultery so that the court can refer him to the Temple. The evidence required by the rabbis is (1) a formal warning of his wife by the husband delivered before witnesses, and (2) testimony that the wife had a secret rendez-vous with her presumed paramour. The wife cannot be presumed guilty since there are no witnesses to adultery but she cannot be considered innocent either since her indiscretion was proved. Therefore the procedure is a mixture of elements that presume innocence and others which presume guilt. In any case, the biblical procedure is not a medieval ordeal since the procedure is clearly labelled as free of danger for the innocent. In Chapter 9, it is reported that the Temple procedure fell into disuse while the Temple was still standing. Therefore, the discussion is purely theoretical.

A reasoned non-rabbinic treatment of the biblical text is: H. Ch. Brichto, *The case of the SŌṬÁ and a reconsideration of biblical "law"*, HUCA 46, 1975, 55-70. The interpretation of the language of "impurity" used in the biblical and talmudic texts as equivalent for "prohibited act" is explored in: מתתיהו כהן, מושגי טומאה וטהרה בלשון המקרא ויחסם למושגי איסור והיתר בלשון חכמים. בית מקרא כה ד [קלה] תשנג, 1993 ע' 289-306.

The first Chapter discusses the proofs which the husband has to provide to gain the right to bring his wife to the Temple. Since a husband is under the obligation to divorce an adulterous wife, the witnesses to the wife's indiscretion establish the fact that the wife is temporarily forbidden to her husband until she is cleared by the Temple procedure. (Since rabbinic law prohibits testimony for or against a close relative, and a person is closely related to himself, neither husband nor wife nor paramour can testify in court about this matter.) If the wife refuses to undergo the procedure, she must be divorced for cause. In a later Chapter the corollary is established that a husband who has witnesses to his warnings and to his wife's indiscretion but is unwilling or unable to bring his wife to the Temple must divorce her, but for all monetary aspects of the divorce he then is the guilty party. One of the conditions of the Temple procedure is that the husband be free of sin (v. 31). This implies that if the husband has marital relations with his wife while she is temporarily forbidden to him, the procedure becomes inactive and he becomes the guilty party in the divorce. The next topic discussed in the Chapter details the procedings in the Temple leading up to the core of the procedure. Then both Mishnah and Gemara turn to a series of homilies on the principle "measure for measure" of God's justice.

The second and third Chapters deal with the sacrificial aspects of the Temple procedure, and the rituals to be followed to have the suspected wife swear that she was not unfaithful and drink the water containing dust and the dissolved ink from the scroll on which the officiating priest wrote the oath. Then the Mishnah describes the action of the water on a guilty wife, which in the Talmud is interpreted to mean that the adulteress dies, difficult to read into the Mishnah. (Philo, *The Special Laws III*, 62, holds that the woman becomes chronically ill of dropsy; this may be the Sadducee interpretation. Brichto identifies the sickness as spurious pregnancy.) Connected with this is a discussion whether any merits of the wife's may avert the bad consequences of her actions. Since the procedure involves a flour offering and in biblical law flour offerings of priests are treated differently from the offerings of female members of priestly families, there follows a general discussion of the legal differences in the status of men and women.

The fourth Chapter deals with those cases in which the woman is prevented from undergoing the Temple procedure (even if she would be willing) and the cases in which she is considered the guilty party in the ensuing divorce, as well as the consequences of indiscretions of wives of people disabled from going to court permanently (such as a deaf-mute) or temporarily (such as a prison inmate).

The fifth Chapter contains only one statement regarding the suspected wife, viz., that the action of the water on the wife is identical with the action of the water on the paramour. This is a statement of R. Aqiba derived from Scripture. The rest of the Chapter treats unrelated statements by R. Aqiba derived from Scripture.

The sixth Chapter returns to the topic of the first and discusses in detail the extent of the *prima facie* evidence the husband has to present to the court or, if the husband prefers to go to divorce court, the evidence necessary to deprive the wife of her divorce settlement.

The seventh Chapter contains only one statement regarding the suspected wife to the effect that the Temple procedure can be conducted in any language the wife understands. The rest of the Chapter discusses which religious procedures may be conducted in the vernacular and which require the use of Hebrew, with most of the Chapter treating the latter case.

The last two Chapters describe two cases in which the Hebrew language is mandatory. Chapter Eight is an extensive exegesis of *Deut.* 20:1-9; Chapter Nine describes the ceremony of the calf used to expiate an unsolved murder (*Deut.* 21:1-9). The second part of that chapter notes that during the last decades of the Second Temple, the ceremony of the calf was abolished because of the increase in unsolved murders, and the ceremony of the suspected wife ceased because of the preponderance of misbehaving husbands. This is followed by a litany of evils increasing from Temple times to the wars with the Romans and their aftermath. The last Mishnah probably is a Talmudic addition ending with the statement that the Messiah can only appear if the situation in the world is absolutely unbearable. The other statements of that Mishnah in the two Talmudim are very different, but since the Babli (and Tosephta) versions are quoted in the Yerushalmi, their source must be Galilean.

Chapters Seven and Nine are interesting for a study of the hermeneutical rules, which are given in forms different from the formulation in *Sifra* and the Babli.

The text of the Yerushalmi *Soṭah* is reasonably well established since we have two manuscripts, the Leiden ms. and the Rome ms. of the first Order. For a few chapters, there also are Genizah fragments which derive from an archetype different from the two complete mss. A list of manuscript readings and the deviations of the Žitomir-Wilna text from the *editio princeps* appears in the Wilna edition of the early 1920's (Reprint Jerusalem 1969).

המקנא פרק ראשון

משנה א: (fol. 16a) הַמְקַנֵּא לְאִשְׁתּוֹ רִבִּי אֱלִיעֶזֶר אוֹמֵר מְקַנֵּא עַל פִּי שְׁנַיִם וּמַשְׁקֶה עַל פִּי עֵד אֶחָד אוֹ עַל פִּי עַצְמוֹ. רִבִּי יְהוֹשֻׁעַ אוֹמֵר מְקַנֵּא עַל פִּי שְׁנַיִם וּמַשְׁקֶה עַל פִּי שְׁנַיִם.

Mishnah 1: If a man declares his jealousy[1] to his wife, Rebbi Eliezer says, he declares his jealousy in front of two [witnesses] and takes her to drink[2] by the testimony of one witness or his own testimony[3]. Rebbi Joshua says, he declares his jealousy in front of two [witnesses] and takes her to drink by the testimony of two [witnesses][4].

1 If a man suspects his wife of infidelity, he may subject her to the ordeal described in *Num.* 5. Since the ordeal involves a sacrifice and it is forbidden to bring profane food into the Temple precinct, the wife has to be warned in due form not to associate with the man the husband suspects to be his wife's paramour. His right to bring his wife to the Temple can be established only by the testimony of two witnesses of good standing.

2 I. e., he takes her to the Temple precinct for the ordeal.

It will be explained later that from the moment the husband establishes his right to submit his wife to the Temple ordeal, any intercourse with her is forbidden to him until she is cleansed by the ordeal. This means that without a Temple, the wife will be forbidden after the jealousy was declared and the husband has to divorce his wife and can never take her back. If he can establish the fact that she was alone with another man after being duly warned, the divorce would be the wife's fault and no payments would be due at the time of the divorce.

3 In the interpretation of the Mishnah, R. Eliezer holds that once the wife was warned in due form, the fact

that she had a tête-à-tête with the suspect does not need a formal proof; the husband can declare to the priest in the Temple that he saw the two together.

4   R. Joshua requires that both the warning to the wife and the fact of a subsequent tête-à-tête have to be established in a form acceptable to the priests' court in the Temple.

(fol. 16b) **הלכה א**: הַמְקַנֵּא לְאִשְׁתּוֹ כול׳. כְּתִיב וְעָבַר עָלָיו רוּחַ קִנְאָה וְקִנֵּא אֶת אִשְׁתּוֹ וגו׳. שֶׁלֹּא יְקַנֵּא לָהּ לֹא מִתּוֹךְ שְׂחוֹק וְלֹא מִתּוֹךְ שִׂיחָה וְלֹא מִתּוֹךְ קַלּוּת רֹאשׁ וְלֹא מִתּוֹךְ מִתּוּן. אֶלָּא מִתּוֹךְ דָּבָר שֶׁל אֵימָה. עָבַר וְקִינֵּא לָהּ בְּאֶחָד מִכָּל־הַדְּבָרִים הַלָּלוּ. מַה אִתְאָמְרַת. לְמִצְוָה. לְעִיכּוּב. אִין תֵּימַר לְמִצְוָה. קִינוּיוֹ קִינּוּי. אִין תֵּימַר לְעִיכּוּב. אֵין קִינּוּיָיו קִינּוּי. אַתְיָיא כְהָדָא. כָּל־מָקוֹם שֶׁנֶּאֱמַר חוּקָּה תּוֹרָה מְעַכֵּב.

Halakhah 1: "If a man declares his jealousy to his wife," etc. It is written[5]: "A spirit of jealousy overcame him and he declared his jealousy to his wife;" this implies that he should not declare his jealousy jokingly, or in the middle of a conversation, or lightly, or in a friendly manner[6] but in a way that inspires fear. If he transgressed and declared his jealousy in one of the aforementioned ways: was this said as an obligation or as a necessity? If you say as an obligation, his declaration of jealousy is valid[7]. If you say as a necessity, his declaration of jealousy is invalid. This is resolved referring to the statement[8]: Anywhere "law" or "teaching" is mentioned, it is an absolute necessity.

5   *Num.* 5:14.

6   The witnesses to the declaration of jealousy must be able to testify that the wife could not possibly have had the impression that the husband was less than absolutely serious.

7   While he did not do what he was supposed to do, his dereliction would not invalidate his declaration.

8   Accepted also in the Babli, *Menaḥot* 19a. Any procedure that is described as תּוֹרָה or חֻקָּה in the Torah

must be executed to the letter or it is invalid; quoted also in *Soṭah* 2:3 (18a), *Pesaḥim* 7:2 (34b).

It follows that for the Yerushalmi, any declaration of jealousy that is not executed in a spirit of gravity is invalid.

(16b, line 22) הַקֵּינוּי. רְבִּי יהוֹשֻעַ אָמַר בְּשֵׁם רְבִּי לִיעֶזֶר. חוֹבָה. רְבִּי יְהוֹשֻעַ אָמַר רְשׁוּת. אָמַר רְבִּי לֶעָזָר בֶּן רְבִּי יוֹסֵי קוֹמֵי רְבִּי יָסָא. אַתְייָא דְרְבִּי לִיעֶזֶר כְּבֵית שַׁמַּי וּדְרְבִּי יְהוֹשֻעַ כְּבֵית הִלֵּל. דְּרְבִּי לִיעֶזֶר כְּבֵית שַׁמַּי. דְּבֵית שַׁמַּי אוֹמְרִים. לֹא יְגָרֵשׁ אָדָם אֶת אִשְׁתּוֹ אֶלָּא אִם כֵּן מָצָא בָהּ עֶרְוָה. מָצָא בָהּ דְּבָרִים כְּאוּרִין. לְגָרְשָׁהּ אֵינוֹ יָכוֹל שֶׁלֹּא מָצָא בָהּ עֶרְוָה. לְקַייְמָהּ אֵינוֹ יָכוֹל שֶׁמָּצָא בָהּ דְּבָרִים כְּאוּרִין. לְפוּם כֵּן הוּא אוֹמֵר. חוֹבָה. וְהָא תַנֵּי מִשּׁוּם בֵּית שַׁמַּי. אֵין לִי אֶלָּא הַיוֹצְאָת מִשּׁוּם עֶרְוָה. מְנַיִּין הַיוֹצְאָה וְרֹאשָׁהּ פָּרוּעַ וּצְדָדֶיהָ מְפוּרָמִים וּזְרוֹעוֹתֶיהָ חֲלוּצוֹת. תַּלְמוּד לוֹמַר כִּי מָצָא בָהּ עֶרְוַת דָּבָר. אָמַר רְבִּי מָנָא קִייַמְתִּיהָ בְּעֵדִים. וְכָאן שֶׁלֹּא בְעֵדִים.

The declaration of jealousy, Rebbi Joshua said in the name of Rebbi Eliezer, is obligatory[9]; but Rebbi Joshua said, it is optional. Rebbi Eleazar ben Rebbi Yose said before Rebbi Yasa, it turns out that Rebbi Eliezer follows the House of Shammai and Rebbi Joshua the House of Hillel[10]. As the House of Shammai say, a man may not divorce his wife except if he found in her a matter of nakedness[11]. If he found her behavior ugly[12], he cannot divorce her since he found no proof of adultery; he cannot keep her since he found her behavior ugly. Therefore, he says, it is obligatory. But was it not stated in the name of the House of Shammai: Not only that the woman must leave because of incest; from where that she must leave if her head's [hair] is loose, if the side seams of her dress are open, or her arms stripped bare[13]? The verse says, "for he found in her a matter of nakedness." Rebbi Mana said, I confirmed this if there are witnesses, but not if there are no witnesses[14].

9 If the husband has reason to suspect his wife, he has no choice but is obligated to declare his jealousy. In the Babli, 3a, the position of R. Eliezer is ascribed to R. Aqiba and that of R. Joshua to R. Ismael. Since R. Joshua is the greater authority than R. Eliezer and R. Aqiba is greater than R. Ismael, in practice the Babli takes the position opposite to the Yerushalmi.

10 Mishnah *Giṭṭin* 9:11; *Sifry Deut.* #269.

11 Illegitimate nakedness: incest and adultery.

12 "Ugly things" in a moral sense, from which one may presume that she was unfaithful but there is no proof. The Babli uses כעור in the same sense. In *Ketubot* 7:7 (fol. 31c), Babli *Yebamot* 24b/25a an example is given, that the husband comes home and sees a pedlar leave the house and his wife getting dressed. Our sources indicate that in such a case the husband may divorce his wife without paying, claiming the divorce is his wife's fault. It is not mentioned that in the absence of witnesses to the presumed sex act, the House of Shammai prohibit the divorce. This may qualify the entire argument as homiletic.

13 In the Babli, *Giṭṭin* 90a/b, this is a statement of R. Meïr, following the House of Hillel.

14 If there are independent witnesses to the indecent behavior (Note 12), the House of Shammai agree that the husband must divorce his wife; but in the case of a declaration of jealousy they might not permit a divorce except if the ordeal proves the wife guilty.

(16b, line 32) וּדְרִבִּי יְהוֹשֻׁעַ כְּבֵית הִלֵּל. דְּבֵית הִלֵּל אוֹמְרִים. אֲפִילוּ הִקְדִּיחָה תַבְשִׁילוֹ. לְפוּם כֵּן הוּא אוֹמֵר. רְשׁוּת. רָצָה לְקַנְאוֹת יְקַנֶּה. רָצָה לְגָרֵשׁ יְגָרֵשׁ.

"And Rebbi Joshua [follows] the House of Hillel." For the House of Hillel say, even if she burned his food[10]. Therefore, he says it is optional. If he wants to declare his jealousy, he declares his jealousy; if he wants to divorce her, he divorces her[15].

15 Mishnah *Ketubot* 7:6 spells out that the husband can divorce his wife for cause (without payment) if he can prove indecent conduct. If he divorces her because she is a bad cook, he has to pay.

(16b, line 34) וּמַה טַעְמָא דְרַבִּי לִיעֶזֶר. כִּי מָצָא בָהּ עֶרְוַת דָּבָר. עֶרְוָה זוֹ סְתִירָה. דָּבָר זֶה קִינּוּי. דָּבָר דָּבָר. מַה דָּבָר הָאָמוּר לְהַלָּן עַל פִּי שְׁנַיִם עֵדִים. אַף דָּבָר הָאָמוּר כָּאן עַל פִּי שְׁנַיִם עֵדִים. וּמַשְׁקֶה עַל פִּי עֵד אֶחָד אוֹ עַל פִּי עַצְמוֹ. וּמָעֲלָה בוֹ. בִּתְנָאִים שֶׁהָיְתָנָה עִמָּהּ עַל פִּי אֲחֵרִים.

What is Rebbi Eliezer's reason? "For he found in her a word of nakedness.[16]" "Nakedness", that is the rendez-vous[17]. "Word", that is the declaration of jealousy. "Word, word"; just as "word" mentioned there requires two witnesses[18], so "word" mentioned here requires two witnesses. "But he can take her to drink by the testimony of one witness or his own testimony," "she was untrue to him in untruthfulness[19]", about the conditions spelled out to her through the mouth of others[20].

16   *Deut.* 24:1.

17   "Meeting in secret" with another man.

18   *Deut.* 19:15: "By the mouth of two witnesses or three witnesses shall a *word* (fact, circumstance) be confirmed." The argument is based on the second hermeneutical rule (*Sifra* Introduction) that the meaning of words is unchanged from one occurrence to the other.

In the Babli, *Giṭṭin* 90a, this is quoted as the argument of the House of Shammai.

19   *Num.* 5:12. The root מעל denotes the sin of embezzlement or fraud (*Lev.* 5:15, *Num.* 5:6; cf. Arabic نغل) or general mischief (*Lev.* 26:40, *Ez.* 18:24, *Ezr.* 9:4; cf. Arabic سال).

20   In this interpretation, מעל refers to fraud as breach of contract; it does not imply unfaithfulness of the wife, as explained in *Num.* 5:14. Therefore, the breach of contract is that the wife went to a rendez-vous with the man forbidden to her by the declaration of jealousy in front of two witnesses. The clause (*Num.* 5:12) that she breached

her contract *with him* is read to mean that he is empowered to prosecute this breach before the Temple priests.

(16b, line 38) תַּנֵּי. רְבִּי יוֹסֵי בֵּירְבִּי יוּדָה אוֹמֵר מִשּׁוּם רְבִּי לִיעֶזֶר. מְקַנֵּא עַל פִּי עֵד אֶחָד אוֹ עַל פִּי עַצְמוֹ וּמַשְׁקֶה עַל פִּי שְׁנַיִם. נֶאֱמַר כָּאן כִּי מָצָא בָהּ עֶרְוַת דָּבָר. וְאֵין מְצִיאָה בְכָל־מָקוֹם אֶלָּא בְעֵדִים. מַה מְקַיֵּים רִבִּי לִיעֶזֶר דָּבָר. דָּבָר שֶׁהוּא מַרְגִּיל לָבוֹא לִידֵי עֶרְוָה. עַד אֶחָד מַהוּ שֶׁיַּשְׁקֶה. מַה אִם פִּיו שֶׁאֵינוֹ זוֹקְקוֹ לִשְׁבוּעַת מָמוֹן הֲרֵי הוּא מַשְׁקֶה. עֵד אֶחָד שֶׁהוּא זוֹקְקוֹ לִשְׁבוּעַת מָמוֹן לֹא כָל־שֶׁכֵּן. קָרוֹב מַהוּ שֶׁיַּשְׁקֶה. מִי קָרוֹב מִבַּעֲלָהּ. עֵד מִפִּי עֵד מַהוּ שֶׁיַּשְׁקֶה. מַה בֵּינוֹ לְבֵין הַקָּרוֹב. קָרוֹב אַף עַל פִּי שֶׁאֵינוֹ כָשֵׁר עַכְשָׁיו כָּשֵׁר הוּא לְאַחַר זְמָן. עֵד מִפִּי עֵד אֵינוֹ כָשֵׁר לֹא עַכְשָׁיו וְלֹא לְאַחַר זְמָן.

It was stated[21]: "Rebbi Yose ben Rebbi Jehudah says in the name of Rebbi Eliezer, he declares his jealousy by the testimony of one witness or his own testimony; he takes her to drink on the testimony of two witnesses." It is said here: "For he found in her a word of nakedness[16]"; "finding" anywhere has to be validated by witnesses[22]. How does Rebbi Eliezer explain "a word"? A circumstance that brings into the habit of nakedness[23]. May a single witness let him take her to drink[24]? His own testimony can never obligate him to swear in money matters but it will let him take her to drink[25], a single witness who will obligate him to swear in money matters[26] not so much more? May a relative bring her to drink[27]? Who is a closer relative than her husband? May a hearsay witness bring her to drink? What is the difference between him and a relative? A relative may be disabled today but he might be enabled later[27], a hearsay witness is not acceptable either today or later[28].

21 Babli 2b, Tosephta 1:1.

22 Everywhere the Torah uses the expression כִּי מָצָא, כִּי יִמְצָא, "if it happened" the implication is that the

case must be heard before a duly constituted court.

23   A "word (or case, matter) of nakedness" is not nakedness itself.

24   This seems to refer to the first version (the Mishnah) of R. Eliezer's position. The earlier argument (Note 20) showed that the husband is empowered to bring his wife to the Temple on his own testimony; one still needs an argument to permit a single witness to a secluded rendez-vous to allow the husband to bring his wife to the Temple.

25   R. David Fraenckel points out that this sentence is ambiguous. It either can mean that a person's own word in money matters can never bring onto him a biblical obligation to swear, for if he agrees that he owes money he pays and if he disputes the [entire] claim and the other party has neither witnesses nor documents, no oath is due. But it also may mean that a statement of a claimant can never obligate the defendant to swear.

26   *Num*. 35:30: "A single witness should not testify in a death penalty case" is interpreted to mean that in money matters a single witness in support of a claim of money obligates the defendant to swear (Sifry *Num*. 161; the argument here is hinted at in Sifry *Deut*. 188).

27   No relative can be a witness in court in any proceeding. Therefore, it is most irregular that the husband's word should carry any weight in any proceedings.

27   If he is a relative by marriage, he ceases to be a relative if the marriage is dissolved.

28   While a woman may rely on hearsay testimony about her husband's death (*Yebamot* 16:5 ff.), this is an extra-judicial proceeding. In judicial proceedings, hearsay testimony is strictly excluded.

(16b, line 47) מַה טַעֲמָא דְרִבִּי יְהוֹשֻׁעַ. כִּי מָצָא בָהּ עֶרְוַת דָּבָר. דָּבָר זֶה הִקִינוּי. כִּי מָצָא. אֵין מְצִיאָה אֶלָּא בְעֵדִים. וּמְקַנֵּא עַל פִּי עֵד אֶחָד אוֹ עַל פִּי עַצְמוֹ. וּמַעֲלָהּ בּוֹ. בְּקִינוּי. מַה מְקַיֵּים רִבִּי יְהוֹשֻׁעַ עֶרְוָה. עֶרְוָה שֶׁהִיא בָאָה מִכֹּחַ דָּבָר.

What is the reason of Rebbi Joshua[29]? "For he found in her a word of nakedness.[16]" "Word", that is the declaration of jealousy. "For he found"; "finding" has to be validated by witnesses[22]. ("But he can take her to drink by the testimony of one witness or his own testimony," "she was untrue to him in untruthfulness".)³⁰ How does Rebbi Joshua explain "nakedness"? [A prohibition of] nakedness that came because of a word³¹.

29 In the Babli, 2b, the argument attributed to R. Joshua refers to *Num.* 5:13: "There is no witness *against her*", meaning that a single witness to her adultery will make the Temple ceremony superfluous and will make her lose the *ketubah* money otherwise due to her in a divorce, but will not be valid either to prove a declaration of jealousy or a secluded rendez-vous.

30 The sentence in parentheses has been copied in error from the arguments of R. Eliezer.

31 Because of his word, the declaration of jealousy, she becomes forbidden to him even though there is no witness to her adultery.

(16b, line 50) הֱשִׁיבוּ עַל דִּבְרֵי רִבִּי יוֹסֵי בֶּן יוּדָה. אִם כֵּן אֵין לַדָּבָר סוֹף. הַכֹּל מִמֶּנּוּ לְקַנְאוֹת לָהּ בשנים וּלְהָבִיא עֵדִים שֶׁנִּסְתְּרָה וּלְפוֹסְלָהּ מִכְּתוּבָּהּ. אָמַר רִבִּי יוֹסֵי. מַה טִּיבָהּ לְהִיסָּתֵר. אֶלָּא אַתְיָא דִי לָא עַל דְּמַתְנִיתִין. הַכֹּל מִמֶּנּוּ לַקְנוֹת לָהּ מִפִּיו וְלוֹמַר שֶׁנִּסְתְּרָה וּלְפוֹסְלָהּ מִכְּתוּבָּתָהּ. אָמַר רִבִּי מָנָא. אֲפִילוּ כְהָדֵין תַּנָּייָא אַתְיָיא הִיא כְמָאן דָּמַר. מְקַגֵּא לָהּ מֵאָבִיהָ וּמִבְּנָהּ. הַכֹּל מִמֶּנּוּ לַקְנוֹת לָהּ מֵאָבִיהָ וּמִבְּנָהּ וּלְהָבִיא עֵדִים שֶׁנִּסְתְּרָה וּלְפוֹסְלָהּ מִכְּתוּבָּתָהּ. אִין תֵּימַר. מַה טִּיבָהּ לְהִיסָּתֵר. הַתּוֹרָה הִתִּירָהּ לְהִיסָּתֵר. דָּמַר רִבִּי יוֹחָנָן מִשּׁוּם רִבִּי שִׁמְעוֹן בֵּן יוֹחַי. כְּתִיב כִּי יְסִיתְךָ אָחִיךָ בֶּן אִמֶּךָ וגו'. בִּתְךָ בַסֵּתֶר. אִמְּךָ בַּסֵּתֶר. מִתְיַיחֵד אָדָם עִם אִמּוֹ וְדָר עִמָּהּ. עִם בִּתּוֹ וְדָר עִמָּהּ. עִם אֲחוֹתוֹ וְאֵינוֹ דָר עִמָּהּ.

They answered on the words of Rebbi Yose ben Jehudah: If so, there is no end to it. If he is believed, he declares his jealousy (before two) [by himself]³², brings witnesses that she was in a secluded place and disables her from receiving the *ketubah*³³. Rebbi Yose said, what business did she have in a secluded place³⁴? But it refers to the statement in the Mishnah³⁵. Is he believed to declare formally his jealousy and then say that she was in a secluded place and disable her from receiving her *ketubah*? Rebbi Mana said, even for that other Tanna[36] it is [a] valid [objection], following him who says that he may declare his jealousy in respect to her father or her son. Is he believed to declare his jealousy with respect to her father and her son, can he then bring witnesses that she was in a secluded place with them and disable her from receiving her *ketubah*? If you ask, what business did she have in a secluded place? The Torah permitted her to be in a secluded place, since Rebbi Johanan said in the name of Rebbi Simeon ben Iohai, it is written[37]: "If your brother, your mother's son, incites you, etc.," Your daughter, in secret; your mother, in secret; a man may be alone with his mother and dwell with her[38], with his daughter and dwell with her, with his sister but may not dwell with her[39].

32 The text (in parentheses) is an obvious error but it appears also in the Rome ms. The translation [in brackets] is a conjectured emendation.

The problem is that according to R. Yose ben R. Jehudah's version, the husband may state that he had declared his jealousy without the wife having a possibility of disproving his claim. He may then plant witnesses and trick her into being alone with another man in order to divorce her without payment.

33 The marriage contract specifying the monetary obligations of the husband towards his wife and her children. The same argument is given in the Babli, 2b.

34 Being alone with another man is misbehaving. It is stated in Mishnah *Qiddushin* 4:12 that a woman, other than his mother or daughter, may not be alone with man to whom she is not married (unless the latter's wife is close by). Why should the husband not be able to divorce her through her fault?

35 The Mishnah's version of R. Eliezer's position. In R. Yose ben R. Jehudah's version, at least the fact of the wife's misbehavior must be established in court by two witnesses subject to cross-examination. But in the Mishnah's version, two witnesses

are needed only to certify the relatively minor fact of the declaration of jealousy but after that, the husband can deprive the wife of her *ketubah* money simply by stating that she misbehaved. This contradicts all rules of procedure in civil cases. The same argument is given in the Babli, 2b.

36 R. Yose ben R. Jehudah.

37 *Deut.* 13:7. The verse mentions maternal halfbrother, son, daughter, and wife, as persons who may be in a hidden place with him. In the Babli *Qiddushin* 80b, R. Johanan is quoted in the name of R. Ismael, in *Sanhedrin* 21b and *Avodah Zarah* 36b in the name of R. Johanan's teacher R. Simeon ben Yehosadaq.

38 This is not explicit in the verse but is inferred from the involved description of "your brother, your mother's son"; it is spelled out in the Babli, *loc. cit.*

39 She is not mentioned in the verse.

(16b, line 60) עֵדֵי קִינּוּי שֶׁנִּמְצְאוּ זוֹמְמִין לוֹקִין. עֵדֵי סְתִירָה שֶׁנִּמְצְאוּ זוֹמְמִין אַתָּה אָמַרְתָּ לוֹקִין. מַהוּ שֶׁיְּשַׁלְּמוּ. לֹא מִכּוֹחָן הִיא מַפְסֶדֶת כְּתוּבָתָהּ. אוֹ יָבֹא כַּיי דָּמַר רִבִּי בָּא רִבִּי יְהוּדָה בְּשֵׁם שְׁמוּאֵל. אֵין לְמֵידִין דָּבָר מִדָּבָר בְּעֵדִים זוֹמְמִין. וְהָכָא כֵן.

Witnesses of a declaration of jealousy who were found to be false[40] are whipped. About witnesses concerning her being in a secluded place who were found to be false, you say that they are whipped; why should they not pay[41]? It is not through their action that she loses her *ketubah*[42]. Or it might be, following what Rebbi Abba, Rav Jehudah[43], said in the name of Samuel: One does not infer one thing from another in the matter of false witnesses[44]. And here it is so.

40 The technical term "scheming witnesses" derives from *Deut.* 19:19 where it is stated that the penalty inflicted on a false witness shall be the punishment *he schemed* to inflict on the accused. Tractate *Makkot* mainly deals with the case of false witnesses on whom the punishment intended for

their victim cannot be inflicted; in that case they are whipped for committing a sin. Since males cannot be subject to declarations of jealousy, the false witnesses must be whipped.

41 On their testimony, the wife loses her *ketubah*-money.

42 Without testimony which confirms the declaration of jealousy, their testimony is worthless. Since the verse makes no provision for partial guilt, no monetary punishment can be imposed.

43 Reading רַב יְהוּדָה of a parallel quote in *Ketubot* 2:10. He was Samuel's most outstanding student.

44 A possible explanation of this sentence, which appears here and in *Ketubot* 2:10 without discussion, seems to be that one refrains from imposing the punishment of whipping only in cases in which the imposition of another punishment is straightforward.

(16b, line 64) נִסְתְּרָה בֶּגֶד אֶחָד בְּשַׁחֲרִית וּבְגֶד אֶחָד בֵּין הָעַרְבַּיִם. יָבֹא כְהָדָא. נִתְיַחֲדָה עִמּוֹ בִּפְנֵי שְׁנַיִם. צְרִיכָה הֵימֶנּוּ גֵט שֵׁנִי. בְּאֶחָד אֵינָהּ צְרִיכָה הֵימֶנּוּ גֵט שֵׁנִי. בְּאֶחָד בְּשַׁחֲרִית וְאֶחָד בֵּין הָעַרְבַּיִם. זֶה הָיָה מַעֲשֶׂה וְשָׁאַל רַבִּי לְעֶזָר בֶּן תַּדַּאי אֶת הַחֲכָמִים וְאָמְרוּ. אֵין זֶה יִיחוּד. קִינָּא לָהּ בֶּגֶד אֶחָד בְּשַׁחֲרִית וּבְגֶד אֶחָד בֵּין הָעַרְבַּיִם. מֵאַחַר שֶׁהוּא אִישׁ וְהִיא אִשָּׁה אֵין קִינּוּיוֹ קִינּוּי. יָבֹא כְהָדָא. אֵין מְקַבְּלִין מִן הָעֵדִים אֶלָּא אִם כֵּן רָאוּ שְׁנֵיהֶן כְּאַחַת. רַבִּי יְהוֹשֻׁעַ בֶּן קָרְחָה אוֹמֵר. אֲפִילוּ רָאוּ⁴⁵ זֶה אַחַר זֶה. רַבִּי יִרְמְיָה רַבִּי שְׁמוּאֵל בַּר יִצְחָק בְּשֵׁם רַב. מוֹדִין חֲכָמִים לְרַבִּי יְהוֹשֻׁעַ בֶּן קָרְחָה בְּעֵידֵי הַבְּכוֹרָה וּבְעֵידֵי הַחֲזָקָה. רַבָּא בְּשֵׁם רַבִּי יִרְמְיָה. אַף בְּעֵידֵי סִימָנִין כֵּן. מֵהַדָּא פְּשִׁיטָא שֶׁזֶּה אוֹמֵר. רָאִיתִי שְׁתֵּי שְׂעָרוֹת בְּגַבּוֹ. וְזֶה אוֹמֵר. רָאִיתִי שְׁתֵּי שְׂעָרוֹת בְּגַבּוֹ. זֶה אוֹמֵר. רָאִיתִי שְׂעָרָה אַחַת בְּגַבָּהּ. וְזֶה אוֹמֵר. רָאִיתִי שְׂעָרָה אַחַת בְּגַבָּהּ. לָאו כְּלוּם. כָּל־שֶׁכֵּן גַּבּוֹ וְגַבּוֹ. [שְׁנַיִם אוֹמְרִים. רָאִינוּ⁴⁶ שְׂעָרָה אַחַת⁴⁷ בְּגַבּוֹ. וּשְׁנַיִם אוֹמְרִים. רָאִינוּ⁴⁶] שְׂעָרָה אַחַת בִּכְרֵיסוֹ. רַבִּי יוֹסֵי בֵּירַבִּי בּוּן וְרַבִּי הוֹשַׁעְיָה בְּרֵיהּ דְּרַבִּי שַׁמַּי. חַד אָמַר. פָּסוּל. וְחַד אָמַר. כָּשֵׁר. מָאן דָּמַר. פָּסוּל. כְּמֵעִיד עַל חֲצִי סִימָן. וּמָאן דָּמַר. כָּשֵׁר. אֲנִי אוֹמֵר. שֶׁמָּא נָשְׁרוּ. שְׁנַיִם אוֹמְרִים. רָאִינוּ שְׂעָרָה אַחַת בְּגַבּוֹ.⁴⁸ וּשְׁנַיִם אוֹמְרִים. רָאִינוּ שְׂעָרָה אַחַת בִּכְרֵיסָהּ. רַבִּי חַגַּי אָמַר.

דִּבְרֵי הַכֹּל פָּסוּל. רַבִּי בָּא אָמַר. דִּבְרֵי הַכֹּל כָּשֵׁר. רִבִּי יוּדָן אָמַר. בְּמַחֲלוֹקֶת. רִבִּי יוֹסֵי אָמָר. בְּמַחֲלוֹקֶת. אָמַר רִבִּי יוֹסֵי לְרִבִּי חַגַּיי. וְהָא רִבִּי יוּדָן סָבַר כְּוָתִי. אָמַר לֵיהּ. עַל רַבֵּיהּ אֲנָא פְּלִיג. לֹא כָּל־שֶׁכֵּן עֵילָוֵיהּ. אָמַר רִבִּי מָנָא. יָאוּת אָמַר רִבִּי חַגַּיי. אִילוּ שְׁטָר שֶׁהוּא מְחוּתָּם בְּאַרְבָּעָה עֵדִים וְקָרָא עָלוִי עִרְעֵר. זֶה מֵעִיד עַל שְׁנַיִם וְזֶה מֵעִיד עַל שְׁנָיִם. שֶׁמָּא כְּלוּם הוּא. וְאֵין כָּל־חֲתִימָה וַחֲתִימָה צְרִיכָה (אֶלָּא)⁴⁹ שְׁנֵי עֵדִים וָכָה כָּל־סִימָן וְסִימָן צְרִיכָה שְׁנֵי עֵדִים. רִבִּי חֲנַנְיָה יָלִיף לָהּ מִשְּׁנֵי חֲזָקָה. אִילוּ אֶחָד מֵעִיד שֶׁאֲכָלָהּ שָׁנָה רִאשׁוֹנָה וּשְׁנִייָה וּשְׁלִישִׁית.⁵⁰ וְאֶחָד מֵעִיד שֶׁאֲכָלָהּ רְבִיעִית חֲמִישִׁית וְשִׁישִׁית. שֶׁמָּא כְּלוּם הוּא. וְאֵין כָּל־חֲזָקָה וַחֲזָקָה צְרִיכָה שְׁנֵי עֵדִים וָכָה כָּל־סִימָן וְסִימָן צָרִיךְ שְׁנֵי עֵדִים.

If she was seen going to a secluded place by one witness in the morning[51] and by one witness in the evening, it is to be treated like the following: [52]"If she was together alone with him by the testimony of two witnesses, she needs a second bill of divorce from him; if there was a single witness she does not need a second bill of divorce from him. With one witness in the morning and one witness in the evening, such a case happened and Rebbi Eleazar ben Thaddeus[53] asked the Sages, who told him that this is not being together alone.[54]" If he declared his jealousy before one witness in the morning and before one witness in the evening; since he is a man and she is a woman, his declaration is nothing[55]. Or is it to be treated like the following: [56]"One accepts the witnesses' testimony only if they saw it together. Rebbi Joshua ben Qorḥah says, even if they saw it one after the other.[57]" Rebbi Jeremiah, Rebbi Samuel bar [Rav] Isaac in the name of Rav: [58]The Sages agree with Rebbi Joshua ben Qorḥah with regard to witnesses of firstlings[59] and witnesses of squatters' rights[60]. Rebbi Abba in the name of Rebbi Jeremiah. The same holds for testimony regarding signs[61]. In that case, it is obvious if one says, I saw two hairs on his back and the other says, I saw two hairs on his back[62]. If one says, I saw one hair on her back and the other says, I saw one hair on her back, that is nothing; similarly on his back and on his back[63]. If two say, we saw one hair on his back and two others say, we saw one hair on his belly[64]? Rebbi Yose ben Rebbi Abun and Rebbi Hoshaia the son of Rebbi Shammai, one said, it is invalid, but the other said, it is valid. He who says it is invalid considers him as one who testifies to half a sign[65]. He who says it is valid? I say, maybe they were rubbed off[66]. Two say, we saw one hair on his back and two others say, we saw one hair on his belly. Rebbi Haggai said, everybody agrees that this is invalid [testimony]. Rebbi Abba said, everybody agrees that this is valid[67]. Rebbi Yudan said, this is in disagreement; Rebbi Yose said, this is in disagreement. Rebbi Yose said, does not Rebbi Yudan follow my opinion? He answered, I am disagreeing with his teacher, so much more with him[68]. Rebbi Mana said, Rebbi Haggai was correct. If a document was signed by four witnesses and it was disputed[69], if one person verified the signature of two [witnesses] and another that of the other two, is that worth anything[70]? Does not every single signature need two witnesses? And here, every single hair needs two witnesses. Rebbi Hanania learns it from the years of squatting rights. If one [witness] testified that he ate from the property the first, second, and third years and another [witness] testified that he ate from it the fourth, fifth, and sixth, is that worth anything[71]? Does not every single year need two witnesses? And here, ever single hair needs two witnesses.

45 Reading of the Rome ms. and *editio princeps*. Reading of Leiden ms.: באו "they came".

46 Reading of the parallels *Ketubot* 2:4, *Sanhedrin* 3:10. Reading here: זֶה אוֹמֵר. רָאִיתִי "One said, I saw."

47 Reading of the parallel in *Sanhedrin*. Reading here: שְׁתֵּי שְׂעָרוֹת "two hairs".

48 Reading of the parallels *Ketubot* 2:4, *Sanhedrin* 3:10. Reading here: בּוֹ "on him".

49 Reading of Leiden ms.

50 The corrector wrongly deleted this word.

51 And the same witness saw the suspect man going to the same place.

52 Tosephta *Gittin* 5:4; quoted also in Halakhah *Gittin* 7:4.

53 A Tanna whose time cannot be determined with accuracy. He seems to belong to the later Tannaïm.

54 In the Tosephta: "That is only one witness per incident." It implies that also in the case of the straying wife there are no two witnesses for any incident.

55 In the interpretation of S. Eisenstein, the statement should be read as: "*even though* he is *the same* man and she is *the same* woman *morning and evening*, his declaration is worthless." It seems that this author is correct in reading this interpretation into R. Josef Caro's lengthy discussion of this paragraph in *Bet Joseph, Tur Hošen Mišpat* 30(7). The upshoot of the latter's discussion is that since the declaration of jealousy in every case was made in front of only one witness, nobody is expected to take it seriously.

56 From here to the end of the Halakhah the text is found also in the parallels *Ketubot* 2:4, *Sanhedrin* 3:10.

57 Tosephta *Sanhedrin* 5:5, Babli *Sanhedrin* 30a; *Baba Batra* 32a,165a; *Ketubot* 26b, *Gittin* 33b; Yerushalmi *Ketubot* 2:4; *Sanhedrin* 3:10, 4:1. The Babli seems to imply that practice follows R. Joshua ben Qorha and the Yerushalmi text also has to be interpreted in the same way. For R. Joshua ben Qorha the two single witnesses together can testify not to a single misdeed but to a pattern of misbehavior.

58 In the Babli, *Sanhedrin* 30b, essentially the same ruling.

59 Accoding to Rashi, *Sanhedrin* 30b, this refers to a firstling born in the herd of a Jew. The firstling must be given to a Cohen who, in the absence of a Temple, may slaughter and eat the firstling only after it has developed a permanent defect which disables it from ever being a sacrifice

(*Deut.* 15:21-23). Since the Cohen has a monetary interest in seeing the firstling declared defective, the rabbis decreed that (a) causing a defect in a firstling is sinful and (b) the Cohen is disqualified from testifying that the defect was not induced by humans. The Cohen must find two other witnesses but they do not have to testify on the same thing.

60 In a society in which title to real estate is not necessarily established by documents, title to a property can be proven in court by testimony of undisturbed possession during three years supported by a claim of lawful acquisition (as purchase, gift, or inheritance).

61 To testify that the person in question is an adult qualified to transact business. A person is an adult who (a) has reached the age of consent, 12 and 1 day for a female and 13 and 1 day for a male, and (b) shows signs of puberty in the form of two pubic hairs. While the court may have ways of verifying age, it needs testimony about the pubic hair. Growth of hair on any other part of the body is irrelevant. Therefore, in the following, the expression "hair on the back" or "hair on the belly" cannot mean that but must be read as "hair on the extreme right or left of the pelvic area" and "hair at the upper border of the pelvic area [Maimonides, *Hilkhot Edut* 4:7, Meïri *Sanhedrin* (ed. A. Sofer, Jerusalem 1971) p. 131].

62 This is valid testimony even if it is not simultaneous.

63 Since one pubic hair does not make the person an adult, there is no witness who testifies to the person being an adult.

64 The first witness testifies that the person is an adult. The second witness cannot testify that the person is an adult. In a criminal case, his testimony would be inadmissible. In the case before us, he only testifies that the person has more pubic hair than indicated in the first testimony; the question is whether the second witness, following R. Joshua ben Qorḥa, may be admitted to confirm the first testimony. It is obvious that for the rabbis opposing R. Joshua ben Qorḥa there is no testimony at all.

65 The argument is accepted in both Talmudim. It says (*Deut.* 19:15): "By the mouth of two witnesses or three witnesses the matter should be established." It follows that a witness for half the matter has no standing in court.

66 He testifies that all he saw was one hair, showing that the two hairs

seen by the previous two witnesses were not permanent hair.

67 Since Rebbi Abba had said earlier that the Sages agree with R. Joshua ben Qorḥa that partial testimony is accepted for signs of puberty, he must hold here that everybody agrees that two partial testimonies can be combined if each part is confirmed by two witnesses.

68 He disagrees with R. Abba and holds that the Sages did not accept R. Joshua ben Qorḥa's opinion in this case. In the Babli (*Sanhedrin* 30b), R. Abba holds that the Sages accepted R. Joshua ben Qorḥa's opinion only for questions of real estate.

69 It is claimed that the document is a forgery. In that case, the signatures of the witnesses on the document must be verified by two witnesses (or by comparison with another document signed by the same witness and which had been certified as genuine by some court of law.)

70 That argument seems to be incongruous here. It refers to the reading of the parallels in *Ketubot* and *Sanhedrin*: "One [witness] said, I saw one hair on his back and *another said, I saw one hair on his belly.* Rebbi Abba said, everybody agrees that this is valid. Rebbi Ḥaggai said, everybody agrees that this is invalid [testimony]." However, the problem with this reading is that this kind of testimony has already been rejected (Note 63). The argument of R. Mana II (a student of R. Yudan) must refer to the text given here.

71 While every witness testifies that the person in possession today was undisturbed in his possession for three years, this is not the testimony required by the court. (This case cannot be compared with that of informal testimony referred to in Mishnah *Yebamot* 15:5, where concurrent inference from diverging statements is accepted.)

(fol. 16a) **משנה ב:** כֵּיצַד מְקַנֵּא לָהּ. אָמַר לָהּ בִּפְנֵי שְׁנַיִם אַל תְּדַבְּרִי עִם אִישׁ פְּלוֹנִי וְדִבְּרָה עִמּוֹ עֲדַיִין מוּתֶּרֶת לְבֵיתָהּ וּמוּתֶּרֶת לוֹכַל בַּתְּרוּמָה. נִכְנְסָה עִמּוֹ לְבֵית הַסֵּתֶר וְשָׁהֲתָה כְּדֵי טוּמְאָה אֲסוּרָה לְבֵיתָהּ וַאֲסוּרָה לוֹכַל בַּתְּרוּמָה. וְאִם מֵת חוֹלֶצֶת וְלֹא מִתְיַיבֶּמֶת.

Mishnah 2: How does he declare his jealousy? If he said to her in front of two [witnesses]: Do not speak with the man X, and she spoke with him, she still is permitted to her house[72] and to eat heave[73]. If she enters a hidden room together with him and remains there long enough for impurity[74], she is forbidden to her house[72] and forbidden to eat heave; if he dies she needs *ḥaliṣah* but cannot be married in levirate[75].

72 To sleep with her husband.

73 If her husband is a Cohen, she is not desecrated.

74 The minimal time needed to start intercourse, for the genitals to touch; cf. *Yebamot* Chapter 4, Note 59.

75 If the husband dies childless before the situation is resolved, she cannot be permitted to the levir since she was forbidden to the husband. But since she was not divorced, she cannot be free to marry outside the family without the formality of *ḥaliṣah*.

(fol. 16c) **הלכה ב**: כֵּיצַד הוּא[76] מְקַנֵּא לָהּ כול'. סוֹף דָּבָר עַד שֶׁתְּדַבֵּר עִמּוֹ. הָא אִם נִסְתְּרָה עִמּוֹ וְלֹא דִיבְּרָה אֵין סְתִירָתָהּ כְּלוּם. דְּרוּבָהּ[77] אָתָא מֵימוֹר לָךְ. אֲפִילוּ דִיבְּרָה עִמּוֹ וְלֹא נִסְתְּרָה אֲדַיִין הִיא מוּתֶּרֶת לְבֵיתָהּ וּמוּתֶּרֶת לוֹכַל בַּתְּרוּמָה. לָשׁוֹן נָקִי הוּא מַתְנִיתִין. אַל תִּתְיַיחֲדִי עִם אִישׁ פְּלוֹנִי.

Halakhah 2: "How does he declare his jealousy," etc. Does this mean only, until she talks with him? That would imply, if she went to a secluded place with him without talking, that going to a secluded place would count for nothing[78]? It comes to tell you more: Even if she talked to him but was not with him in a secluded place, she still is permitted to her house and to eat heave, since the Mishnah uses chaste language: Do not be alone with Mr. X[79].

76 All quotes from the Mishnah in this Halakhah follow the text of the Babylonian Mishnah. This shows that the Mishnah in the Yerushalmi was

shortened in transmission.

77 Reading of the Rome ms. Leiden ms: דיברה, induced by the words nearby.

78 Since only talking to Mr. X was forbidden to her. That conclusion seems to be ridiculous.

79 From the start, the husband did not say "do not talk" but "do not be alone". The Babli, 5b, holds that even if the husband says "talking", it is interpreted as meaning "being alone in a hidden room"; cf. *Tosafot* 5b, *s. v.* הא.

(16c, line 30) מַהוּ שֶׁיְקַנֵּא לָהּ מִשְּׁנֵי בְנֵי אָדָם כְּאַחַת. רִבִּי יוּדָן אָמַר. בְּמַחֲלוֹקֶת. מָאן דָּמַר. מְקַנֵּא לָהּ מֵאָבִיהָ וּמִבְּנָהּ. מְקַנֵּא לָהּ מִשְּׁנֵי בְנֵי אָדָם כְּאַחַת. רִבִּי יוֹסֵי בָעֵי. מְקַנֵּא לָהּ מִמֵּאָה בְנֵי אָדָם. אָמַר רִבִּי יוֹסֵי בֵּי רִבִּי בּוּן. אָמַר לָהּ. אַל תִּיכָּנְסִי לְבֵית הַכְּנֶסֶת. נִכְנֶסֶת.

May he declare his jealousy with respect to two men together? Rebbi Yudan said, that is in dispute. He who says that he may declare his jealousy with respect to her father and her son[80], [says] that he may declare his jealousy with respect to two men together. Rebbi Yose asked: May he declare his jealousy with respect to a hundred men[81]? Rebbi Yose ben Rebbi Abun said to him: If he said to her, do not enter the synagogue, she enters[82].

80 Cf. Note 37.

81 On Mishnah *Qiddushin* 4:12, which states that a woman may be alone with two other men, the Yerushalmi notes: "That is, if they are decent men. But if they are amoral, she should not be alone even with a hundred simultaneously." R. Yose denies that anybody may hold that a man cannot declare his jealousy simultaneously with regard to two men.

82 It depends on the circumstances. If the husband wants to prohibit any social interaction to his wife, she may force a divorce through his fault (*Ketubot* 7:5, fol. 31b, line 46; Babli 72a).

עִמּוֹ. אָמַר רִבִּי מָנָא. לֹא אָמַר אֶלָּא עִמּוֹ. הָא זֶה אַחַר זֶה לֹא.(16c, line 34)
רִבִּי אָבִין אָמַר אֲפִילוּ זֶה אַחַר זֶה. מִכָּל־מָקוֹם יֵשׁ רַגְלַיִם לַדָּבָר. לַפְּלַטְיָה
בַלַּיְלָה. לְחוּרְבָּה בַּיּוֹם. לִמְבוֹאוֹת אֲפֵילוֹת בַּיּוֹם.

"With him.[83]" Rebbi Mana said, it only said "with him." Therefore, not one after the other[84]. Rebbi Abin said, even one after the other since anyhow it is obvious[85]: On a road[86] during the night, in a ruin during daytime, in dark passageways during daytime.

83 This refers to the Mishnah which states "If she enters a hidden room together with him".

84 If they are witnesses that she and her paramour entered at different times, the husband has no case.

85 The Mishnah forbids her to her husband any time she was together with her paramour in any more or less hidden place; examples are given.

86 Greek πλατεῖα "open place".

(16c, line 36) שָׁאֲלוּ אֶת בֶּן זוֹמָא. מִפְּנֵי מָה סְפֵק רְשׁוּת הַיָּחִיד טָמֵא. אָמַר לוֹן.
סוֹטָה מָהִיא. אָמְרוּ לֵיהּ. רְשׁוּת הַיָּחִיד. אָמַר לוֹן מָצִינוּ שֶׁהִיא אֲסוּרָה לְבֵיתָהּ.
מִילֵּיהוֹן דְּרַבָּנִן פְּלִיגִין. דָּמַר רִבִּי זְעִירָא רִבִּי יָסָא בְּשֵׁם רִבִּי יוֹחָנָן. קְטַנָּה
שֶׁזִּינְּתָה אֵין לָהּ רָצוֹן לְהֵיאָסֵר עַל בַּעֲלָהּ. וְהָא תַנִּינָן. כָּל־שֶׁאֵין בּוֹ דַעַת לִישָּׁאֵל
סְפֵיקוֹ טָהוֹר. הָא אִם יֵשׁ בּוֹ דַעַת לִישָּׁאֵל סְפֵיקוֹ טָמֵא. בְּרַם הָכָא. אַף עַל פִּי
שֶׁיֵּשׁ בּוֹ דַעַת לִישָּׁאֵל סְפֵיקוֹ טָהוֹר. מִפְּנֵי מָה סְפֵק רְשׁוּת הָרַבִּים טָהוֹר. אָמַר
לוֹן. מָצִינוּ שֶׁהַצִּיבּוּר עוֹשִׂין אֶת פִּסְחֵיהֶן בְּטָהֳרָה בְּשָׁעָה שֶׁרוּבָּן טְמֵיאִין. מַה
טוּמְאָה יְדוּעָה הוּתְּרָה לְצִיבּוּר. קַל וְחוֹמֶר סְפֵק טוּמְאָה.

[87]"They asked Ben Zoma: Why is a doubt in a private domain considered impure[88]? He said to them: Where is the suspected wife? In a private domain[89]. He said to them, we find that she is forbidden for her house[90]." The words of the rabbis disagree, since Rebbi Ze'ira, Rebbi Yasa said in the name of Rebbi Johanan: An underage girl who whored has no

will to be forbidden to her husband[91]. But did we not state:[92] "In any case where there is no mind to be asked, the doubtful case is pure[93]"? Therefore, if there is a mind to be asked, the doubtful case is impure. But here, even while there is a mind to be asked, the doubtful case is pure![94]

[87]"Why is a doubt in a public domain considered pure? He said to them: We find that the public prepare their Passah [as in] purity when most of them are impure[95]. If known impurity was permitted in public[96], so much more for a case of doubtful impurity."

87 An extended text in Tosephta *Taharot* 6:17.

88 This is a question about ritual impurity, not the moral impurity of the straying wife. But since adultery is called "impurity" in the paragraph of the straying wife (*Num.* 5:13,14,19,20, 27,28,29), the rules of ritual impurity and of moral impurity must be identical. The undisputed rule is that if a question arises in matters of ritual impurity it must be resolved by a presumption of impurity in a private domain but of purity in the public domain (cf. Babli, *Soṭa* 28a/b, *Avodah Zarah* 37b, *Ḥulin* 9b). The argument presented by the Tosephta is rejected by the Babli in *Soṭa* in the name of R. Aqiba; in *Avodah Zarah* and *Ḥulin* the rule is accepted as an old tradition devoid of scriptural basis. Cf. Tosafot *Soṭa* 28b, *s. v.* מכאן.

89 A place adequate for intercourse must by definition be private. As the preceding examples show, the definition of "private place" for all kinds of impurity are different from the rules of "private place" in civil matters and regarding the Sabbath (*Shabbat* Chapter 1).

90 In her intimate relations with her husband, she is considered an adulteress even though there remains a doubt whether she actually committed adultery in the hidden room.

91 In the Babli, *Yebamot* 33b, the formulation is: The seduction of a minor girl is rape. The rape victim is explicitly cleared from the guilt of adultery in *Num.* 5:13.

The Medieval authorities make it difficult to understand the position of the Babli in this matter. According to R. Abraham ben David in his glosses to the Code of Maimonides (*Issure Bi'a* 3:2, *Sota* 2:4), the Babli accepts the opinion of the Yerushalmi. Maimonides holds that the underage girl is forbidden to her husband. As usual, he gives no reason for his decision. In the opinion of Don Vidal de Tolosa, approved by Joseph Caro, this is not because of the girl but because the husband forbade her on himself as stated in *Ketubot* 9a for any case in which the husband accuses his wife of infidelity. In the case of an underage girl, this refers only to a girl married off by her father, whose marriage in valid by biblical standards, cf. *Yebamot* 1, Note 118.

92 Mishnah *Taharot* 3:6.

93 Even in a private domain.

94 The argument of the Tosephta is rejected since the minor can tell what happened even if she legally has no will (or at least the seducer could in theory be asked.)

95 If most of Israel are impure, the public service in the Temple is performed in impurity. The only private sacrifice which has the status of a public offering is the Passah lamb (Mishnah *Pesaḥim* 7:6).

96 This is a matter of dispute in the Babli (e. g. *Yoma* 6b), whether for public sacrifices the rules of impurity are *pushed aside* or *eliminated*. Following the first opinion, the invasion of impurity has to be held to a minimum. This opinion is not found in the Yerushalmi. In the second opinion, the one expressed here, the rules of impurity are disregarded; it is *as if impurity were purity*. Under the influence of the Babli, the commentators unanimously emend "in purity" to "in impurity" and even J. Sussman here indicates a corruption. The emendation is totally unnecessary.

(16c, line 45) תַּמָּן תַּנִּינָן כָּל־הָעֲרָיוֹת עָשָׂה בָהּ אֶת הַמְעָרָה כְגוֹמֵר וְחַיָּיב עַל כָּל־בִּיאָה וּבִיאָה. הֶחֱמִיר בְּשִׁפְחָה שֶׁעָשָׂה בָהּ אֶת הַמֵּזִיד כְּשׁוֹגֵג. רִבִּי יִרְמְיָה רִבִּי בָּא בַּר מָמָל בְּשֵׁם רַב. שִׁכְבַת זֶרַע עַד שֶׁיִּפְלוֹט. הָכָא כְּתִיב שִׁכְבַת זֶרַע וְהָכָא כְּתִיב שִׁכְבַת זָרַע. הָכָא אַתְּ אָמַר שִׁכְבַת זֶרַע עַד שֶׁיִּפְלוֹט. וְהָכָא אַתְּ אָמַר כֵּן. אָמַר רִבִּי יוֹסֵי. שַׁנְיָיה הִיא דִכְתִיב וְנִסְתְּרָה וְהִיא נִטְמָאָה. כֵּיוָן שֶׁנִּסְתְּרָה הַתּוֹרָה קְרָאָהּ טְמֵאָה. בְּרַם הָכָא שִׁכְבַת זֶרַע עַד שֶׁיִּפְלוֹט. לֵיי דָא מִילָּה כְּתִיב שִׁכְבַת זֶרַע. לְשִׁיעוּרִין. כְּהָדָא דְתַנִּי. וְנִסְתְּרָה וְהִיא נִטְמָאָה. כַּמָּה הִיא

סְתִירָה. כְּדֵי טוּמְאָה. כַּמָּה הִיא כְּדֵי טוּמְאָה. כְּדֵי בִיאָה. וְכָמָּה הִיא בִיאָה. כְּדֵי הֶעֱרָיָיה.

There[97], we have stated: "In all matters of incest, He made him who touches[98] equal to him who completes and one is guilty for each single intercourse[99]. He was more stringent with the slave girl since in her case He treated the intentional as unintentional." Rebbi Jeremiah, Rebbi Abba bar Mamal in the name of Rav: "Flow of semen," until he ejaculates[100]. Here is written "flow of semen", and here is written "flow of semen.[101]" Here[102], you say "flow of semen" until he ejaculates. And here[103], you say so? Rebbi Yose said, there is a difference, for it is written[104]: "She was hidden and became impure." From the moment she was hidden, the Torah calls her "impure". But here[102], "flow of semen," until he ejaculates. For what reason is written[103] "flow of semen"? For measures[105], as it is stated[104]: "She was hidden and became impure"; what is counted as hiding[106]? Time to become impure. What is the time for impurity? Time for intercourse. What is the time for intercourse? Time for 'touching'[98].

97 Mishnah *Keritut* 2:4. "Incest" always includes adultery.

98 The man whose genital touches the woman's. This is a technical term, cf. *Yebamot* Chapter 6, Note 11.

99 This refers to the rules concerning a slave girl (*Lev.* 19:20-22) who according to some opinions is partially manumitted (cf. Babli *Keritut* 11a.). The Babli's tradition eliminates the rules from practical importance by restricting them to a girl living with a Hebrew slave. Since the institution of Hebrew slaves was abolished with the Babylonian exile, never to be reinstituted, the frequent discussions of the rules are purely theoretical. However, in *Sifra Qedošim Pereq* 5(1), at least one opinion describes the slave girl engaged to a free man in the expectation of her manumission.

As a slave, the girl can not marry and therefore she is free to have guiltless sex with any man not a Jew (cf. *Terumot* Chapter 8, Note 347). Upon manumission, she becomes a free Jewish woman and able to contract a valid marriage with any Jew who is not a priest. She is permitted to live with a Hebrew slave (*Ex.* 21:4). Since her relationship with the slave is not a marriage, her affair with another man is not adultery. From the man's side, the affair with the slave girl is the only sin which can be atoned for by a sacrifice if committed intentionally. A purification sacrifice is possible only for inadvertent sins; the relation with the semi-free girl can be atoned for by a reparation sacrifice. (An intentional sin can only be cleansed by God's mercy in response to repentance.) For inadvertent sins, a purification sacrifice is due for each single transgression; one reparation sacrifice covers the entire affair.

100   *Lev.* 19:20: "If a man sleep with a woman by flow of semen . . ." The intercourse of a free man with the slave girl is not punishable unless there was an ejaculation.

101   In the case of the straying wife, *Num.* 5:13 reads: "A man slept with her with flow of semen." Nevertheless, the wife becomes impure and forbidden to her husband already if her paramour's penis touches her genitals. This seems to contradict our principle that equal expressions used in different circumstances must have equal meanings.

102   In the case of the slave girl.

103   In the case of the straying wife.

104   *Num.* 5:13.

105   To measure how long the wife must be hidden together with her paramour to be impure and subject to the ordeal. In another connection this is quoted in the Babli, 2b.

106   Babli 4a. The Babli discusses why all these expressions have to be used.

(16c, line 52) כַּמָּה הִיא הָעֲרָיָיה. רַבִּי לִיעֶזֶר אוֹמֵר. כְּדֵי חֲזִירַת דֶּקֶל. רַבִּי יְהוֹשֻׁעַ אוֹמֵר. כְּדֵי מְזִינַת הַכּוֹס. בֶּן עַזַּי אוֹמֵר. כְּדֵי לִשְׁתוֹתוֹ. רַבִּי עֲקִיבָה אוֹמֵר. כְּדֵי גִילְגּוּל בֵּיצָה. רַבִּי יוּדָה בֶּן בָּתֵירָה אוֹמֵר. כְּדֵי לִגְמִיתַת שָׁלֹשׁ בֵּיצִים מְגוּלְגָּלוֹת זוֹ אַחַר זוֹ. רַבִּי אֶלְעָזָר בֶּן פִּינְחָס אוֹמֵר. כְּדֵי שֶׁיִּקְשׁוֹר גִּירְדִּי אֶת הַנִּימָה. מִנְיָימִין אוֹמֵר. כְּדֵי שֶׁתּוֹשִׁיט יָדָהּ וְתִטּוֹל כִּכָּר לֶחֶם מִן הַסַּל. אַף עַל פִּי שֶׁאֵין רְאָיָיה לַדָּבָר זֵיכֶר לַדָּבָר יֵשׁ. כִּי בְעַד אִשָּׁה זוֹנָה עַד כִּכַּר לָחֶם וגו'. אָמַר

רִבִּי יוֹסֵי. כָּל־אִילֵּין שִׁיעוּרַיָּיא לְאַחַר הַתָּרַת הַסִּינָר. אָמַר רִבִּי יוֹחָנָן. כָּל־אֶחָד וְאֶחָד בְּעַצְמוֹ שִׁיעֵר. וּבֶן עַזַּי נָשָׂא אִשָּׁה מִיָּמָיו. אִית דְּבָעֵי מֵימַר. נִתְחַמֵּם. וְאִית דְּבָעֵי מֵימַר. בָּעַל וּפִירֵשׁ. אִית דְּבָעֵי מֵימַר סוֹד יי לִירֵיאָיו וּבְרִיתוֹ לְהוֹדִיעָם.

[107]"How long is 'touching'? Rebbi Eliezer says, [time needed] to walk around a date palm[108]; Rebbi Joshua says, to mix a cup [of wine][109]; Ben Azai says, to drink it[110]; Rebbi Aqiba says, [time needed] rolling an egg[111]; Rebbi Jehudah ben Bathyra says, to sip three rolled eggs one after the other; Rebbi Eleazar ben Phineas[112] says, [time needed] for the weaver to bind a thread; Miniamin[113] says, that she can stretch out her hand and lift a loaf of bread from the basket. And though there is no proof, at least there is a hint: 'For a whoring woman up to a loaf of bread.'[114]" Rebbi Yose said, all these measurements [of time] are after she removes her underpants[115]. Rebbi Johanan said, each of them judged by his own experience[116]. But did Ben Azai ever marry[117]? Some want to say, he had an erection. But some want to say, he was married and gave it up[118]. Some want to say, "the secret of the Eternal is for those who fear Him, to inform them about His covenant.[119]"

107   This *baraita* exists in several versions: Babli 4a, *Sifry Num.* 7, *Sifry Zuṭa* 13, Tosephta 1:1, *Tanḥuma* and *Tanḥuma Buber Naśo; Num. rabba* 9(6).

108   In Babli and *Sifry, Sifry Zuṭa*: R. Ismael.

109   In Babli and *Sifry, Sifry Zuṭa*: R. Eliezer.

110   In Babli and *Sifry, Sifry Zuṭa*: R. Joshua. In the Tosefta: Ben Azai says, mixing a cup to drink it.

111   In Babli and *Sifry, Sifry Zuṭa*: Ben Azai says, to fry an egg. The Tosephta, which ascribes the statement to R. Aqiba, also has: to fry an egg. The usual explanation of לגלגל is: To boil an egg softly so it can roll when taken out of its shell. A soft-boiled chicken egg is considered the egg which is most quickly prepared for

human consumption [Rashi in Babli *Šabbat* 80b, cf. Yerushalmi 8:7 (fol. 11b line 70)].

Babli and *Sifry, Sifry Zuṭa* have an additional entry: R. Aqiba says, to sip one (soft-boiled) egg.

112   In Babli and Tosephta: R. Eleazar ben Jeremiah. This reading is suspect since this name is not reported anywhere else in talmudic literarture while R. Eleazar ben Phineas is quoted several times. Because of the dependence of the Tosephta on the Babli [cf. Epilogue in the author's edition of *Ma'aser Šeni, Hallah, Orlah, Bikkurim* (SI 23)], Babli and Tosephta cannot be considered as two independent sources.

This and the following entries are missing in *Sifry*.

113   A student of R. Aqiba. In *Babli, Tanḥuma, Tanḥuma Buber, Sifry Zuṭa*: Polemon. Babli, Tosephta, and the *Tanḥumas* have another entry: Ḥanin ben Phineas says, that she may extract a splinter from her mouth (in *Tanḥuma*: Rebbi Ḥanin, *Tanḥuma Buber*: Ḥanan)

114   Prov. 6:26.

115   Meaning and etymology of the word סינר are in doubt. The translation follows *Arukh* (s. v. סנר I) and Rashi (*Šabbat* 92b): "Small pants which she wears for decency". {This meaning may be compared with Arabic سِنَّر "armor".} Maimonides (Commentary to *Šabbat* 10:4), following a Gaonic commentary (B. M. Levin *Oṣar HaGeonim Šabbat, Oṣar HaPerušim* p. 51): "sash". It is reported in *Megillah* 4:1 (75a, line 30) that from the time of the return from Babylonia, Jewish women wore a *sinār*; according to Rashi's tradition they wore gowns and under them pants from the hips to the knees; according to Maimonides they wore long pants and a sash covering their legs front and back down from the hips. Maimonides's interpretation is the source of the acceptation in modern Hebrew: Apron. {Cf. Greek συνωρίς, -ίδος, ἡ, "pair of horses", also "pair of anything (fetters, manacles)", referring to a *pair* of sashes or pants? (E. G.)}

R. Yose's remark makes all the examples given meaningless for practical applications.

116   Babli 4b.

117   What does he know about sex? He is the example of a man studying 24 hours a day, not having time for anything else.

118   This contradicts the story in the Babli, *Ketubot* 63a, that he was engaged to R. Aqiba's daughter who wanted to marry him after he had become the time's most outstanding

scholar but that he died before he had attained that goal.

119 *Ps.* 25:14.

(16c, line 64) תַּנֵּי. רְבִּי אוֹמֵר. שָׁלֹשׁ טוּמְאוֹת אֲמוּרוֹת בַּפָּרָשָׁה. אַחַת לַבַּעַל וְאַחַת לַבּוֹעֵל וְאַחַת לַתְּרוּמָה. לַתְּרוּמָה. מָצִינוּ אִשָּׁה שֶׁהִיא אֲסוּרָה לְבֵיתָהּ וּמוּתֶּרֶת בַּתְּרוּמָה. לָמָּה לֹא. אִילּוּ בַת כֹּהֵן שֶׁנִּשֵּׂאת לְיִשְׂרָאֵל וְנֶאֶנְסָה שֶׁמָּא אֵינָהּ מוּתֶּרֶת לְבֵיתָהּ וַאֲסוּרָה לֶאֱכוֹל בַּתְּרוּמָה. לֹא מָצִינוּ אִשָּׁה שֶׁהִיא אֲסוּרָה לְבֵיתָהּ וּמוּתֶּרֶת לוֹכַל בַּתְּרוּמָה. אָמַר רִבִּי אָבִין. אִיתְאָמְרַת. אַחַת לַבַּעַל וְאַחַת לַבּוֹעֵל וְאַחַת לַיָּבָם. אָמַר רִבִּי יוֹסֵי בֵּירִבִּי בּוּן. מַתְנִיתִין אָמְרָה כֵן. וְאִם מֵת חוֹלֶצֶת וְלֹא מִתְיַיבֶּמֶת.

It was stated[120]: Rebbi said, three times is "impurity" said in the paragraph[121], one for the husband, one for the paramour[122], and one for heave[123]. For heave? Do we find that a woman is forbidden to her house[72] and permitted to eat heave? Why not? If the daughter of a Cohen was married to an Israel and raped, is she not permitted to her house[124] but forbidden heave? We never find that a woman is forbidden to her house and permitted to eat heave[125]! Rebbi Abin said, it was said: One for the husband, one for the paramour, and one for the levir[126]. Rebbi Yose ben Rebbi Abun said, the Mishnah says so: "If he dies she needs *ḥaliṣah* but cannot be married in levirate."

120 In the Babli, 28a, and in *Sifry Zuṭa* (*Naśo* 14), in the name of R. Aqiba. A complementary version, that three times "if she was not impure" is mentioned to permit her to her husband, presumed paramour (after the husband's death), and heave, is in *Sifry Num.* 19.

121 According to Rashi, once each in *Num.* 5:14, 27, 29.

122 That she could not marry him even if divorced or widowed.

123 If she is married to a Cohen or is the childless daughter of a Cohen married to an Israel, who on becoming a widow would otherwise be permitted

heave. Any woman who ever slept with a man whom she could not marry on the spot (even if raped) is desecrated and permanently barred from priestly status since she cannot "return to her father's house as in her youth" (*Lev.* 22:13). Since a married woman cannot marry another man without a divorce, an adulteress is automatically desecrated.

124   Since the Israel has no sacred status, his relation to his wife is not changed if she is raped.

125   If A implies B it does not follow that B implies A. Therefore, the example given as objection is irrelevant. Since the wife cannot live with her husband until she is cleared from the accusation of adultery, she cannot eat heave until she is cleared.

126   If the husband died childless after his wife was in a hidden place with another man and before she was cleared of the suspicion of adultery.

(16c, line 70) תַּנָּא רִבִּי יַעֲקֹב בַּר אִידִי קוֹמֵי רִבִּי יוֹנָתָן. וְאַתְּ כִּי שָׂטִית תַּחַת אִישֵׁךְ. פְּרָט לָאוֹנָסִין. מַה אַתְּ שְׁמַע מִינָהּ. אֲמַר לֵיהּ. מַה תַּחַת אִישֵׁךְ לִרְצוֹן. אַף כָּאן לִרְצוֹן.

Rebbi Jacob bar Abin stated before Rebbi Jonathan: "'If you deviated from under your husband.'[127] This excludes rape." How do you understand this? He said to him: Just as she is "under your husband" by her consent, so also in this case by her consent.

127   *Num.* 5:20. The *baraita* is not quoted elsewhere. The other sources point out that the raped wife is expressly excluded by v. 13: "And she was not kidnapped" (*Sifry Num.* 7).

(16c, line 73)[128] סוֹטָה כְּשֵׁם שֶׁהִיא אֲסוּרָה לַבַּעַל כֵּן אֲסוּרָה לַבּוֹעֵל. כְּשֵׁם שֶׁהִיא אֲסוּרָה לְאָחִיו שֶׁלַּבַּעַל כָּךְ הִיא אֲסוּרָה לְאָחִיו שֶׁלַּבּוֹעֵל. יָכוֹל כְּשֵׁם שֶׁעָרַת סוֹטָה אֲסוּרָה לְאָחִיו שֶׁלַּבַּעַל כָּךְ[129] אֲסוּרָה לְאָחִיו שֶׁלַּבּוֹעֵל. נִישְׁמְעִינָהּ מִן הָדָא. הָאִשָּׁה שֶׁהָלַךְ בַּעֲלָהּ לִמְדִינַת הַיָּם וּבָאוּ[130] וְאָמְרוּ לָהּ. מֵת בַּעֲלִיךְ. הֲוִיא[131] לָהּ יָבָם וְיִבְּמָהּ וָמֵת. וְאַחַר כָּךְ בָּא בַעֲלָהּ. אָסוּר בָּהּ וּמוּתָּר

בְּצָרָתָהּ. אָסוּר בָּהּ וּמוּתָּר בְּאֵשֶׁת אָחִיו. וְאֵשֶׁת אָחִיו לֹא כְצָרַת סוֹטָה הִיא. הֲדָא הִיא אֲמָרַת[132] שֶׁצָרַת סוֹטָה מוּתֶּרֶת לְאָחִיו שֶׁלַּבּוֹעֵל. אָמַר רִבִּי יוּדָן.[133] אַתְיָיא כְרַבָּנָן דְּתַמָּן. דָּמַר רִבִּי הִילָא. תַּנֵּיי[134] תַמָּן. כָּל־הָעֲרָיוֹת אֵינָן צְרִיכוֹת גֵּט[135] חוּץ מֵאֵשֶׁת אִישׁ בִּלְבָד. רִבִּי עֲקִיבָה אוֹמֵר. אַף אֲחוֹת אִשְׁתּוֹ וְאֵשֶׁת אָחִיו. בְּרַם כְּרַבָּנָן דְּהָכָא. רִבִּי חִייָה[136] בְשֵׁם רִבִּי יוֹחָנָן. הַכֹּל מוֹדִין בְּאֵשֶׁת אָחִיו שֶׁהִיא צְרִיכָה הֵימֶנּוּ גֵט מִשּׁוּם הִילְכוֹת[137] אֵשֶׁת אִישׁ קָנָה בָהּ. עֶרְוָה הִיא. וְעֶרְוָה[138] פּוֹטֶרֶת צָרָתָהּ. אָמַר רִבִּי חִינְנָא.[139] אֲפִילוּ כְרַבָּנָן דְּהָכָא אַתְיָא הִיא. בָּהּ קָנְסוּ. וְלֹא קָנְסוּ בְיוֹרְשֶׁיהָ. אָמַר רִבִּי חֲנַנְיָה בְּרֵיהּ דְּרִבִּי הִלֵּל. אִין כְּרַבָּנָן דְּתַמָּן. יְהֵא מוּתָּר בָּהּ. רִבִּי זְעִירָא[140] בְשֵׁם רִבִּי יוֹחָנָן. צָרַת סוֹטָה אֲסוּרָה וְצָרַת גְּרוּשָׁה מוּתֶּרֶת. רִבִּי יַעֲקֹב[141] בְשֵׁם רִבִּי יוֹחָנָן. כָּל־הַצָּרוֹת מוּתָּרוֹת חוּץ מִצָּרַת סוֹטָה. שְׁמוּאֵל אָמַר. גְּרוּשָׁה עַצְמָהּ מוּתֶּרֶת לְבֵיתָהּ. מָהוּ פְלִיג. בְּגִין דַּהֲווֹן עָסְקִין בְּצָרוֹת לֹא אִדְכָּרִין גְּרוּשׁוֹת. צָרַת סוֹטָה לָמָּה הִיא אֲסוּרָה. רִבִּי יוֹחָנָן אָמַר. מֵרֵיחַ עֶרְוָה נָגְעוּ בָהּ. רַב אָמַר. מִפְּנֵי שֶׁכָּתוּב בָּהּ טוּמְאָה כָּעֲרָיוֹת.

[128]Just as the woman accused of infidelity is forbidden to her husband, so she is forbidden to her paramour. Just as she is forbidden to her husband's brother, so she is forbidden to her paramour's brother. I might think that just as the co-wife of a woman accused of infidelity is forbidden to her husband's brother, so she should be forbidden to her paramour's brother. Let us hear from the following: "A woman's husband went overseas; they came and told her that her husband had died, and she had a levir here; he married her in levirate and died. Then her husband returned. She is forbidden to him but her co-widow is permitted to him; she is forbidden to him but his brother's wife is permitted to him." Is his brother's wife not like the co-wife of a woman accused of infidelity? That means that the co-wife of a woman accused of infidelity is permitted to her paramour's brother. Rebbi Judan said, this follows the rabbis there, as

Rebbi Hila said, one states there, for incestuous relationships no divorce is needed except for a married woman; Rebbi Aqiba says also from his wife's sister. But following the rabbis here? Rebbi Ḥiyya in the name of Rebbi Joḥanan: everybody agrees that his brother's wife needs a bill of divorce from him because of the rule of a married wife. She is forbidden by the incest rules, and an incest-prohibited woman frees her co-wife. Rebbi Ḥinenah said, it is accepted even according to the rabbis here. They fined her but not her heirs. Rebbi Ḥananiah, the son of Rebbi Hillel, said, according to the rabbis there, she should be permitted to him[63]. Rebbi Ze'ira in the name of Rebbi Joḥanan, the co-wife of a woman accused of infidelity is forbidden, the co-wife of a divorcee is permitted. Rebbi Jacob [bar Aḥa] in the name of Rebbi Joḥanan: All co-wives are permitted except the co-wife of a woman accused of infidelity. Samuel said, the divorcee herself is permitted to her house. Does he disagree? Since they were discussing co-wives they did not mention divorcees. Why is the co-wife of a woman accused of infidelity forbidden? Rebbi Joḥanan said, they touched this case because it looks like adultery. Rav said, because impurity is written there parallel to incest prohibitions.

128 Text from Yebamot 10:1, Notes 49-67.
129 In Yebamot: בך תהא.
130 In Yebamot: באו.
131 In Yebamot: והיה. The text here cannot be original.
132 In Yebamot: הדא אמרה, the standard expression.
133 In Yebamot: יודה. The reading here is preferable.
134 In Yebamot: דאמר ר' הילא ותניי.
135 In Yebamot: ממנו גט.
136 In Yebamot: ר' אחייה אמר.
137 In Yebamot: הלכה.
138 In Yebamot: ערוה.
139 In Yebamot: חנניה.
140 In Yebamot: זעירה.
141 In Yebamot: ר' יעקב בר אחא.

משנה ג: אֵילוּ אֲסוּרוֹת לוֹכַל בַּתְּרוּמָה הָאוֹמֶרֶת טְמֵיאָה אֲנִי לָךְ וְשֶׁבָּאוּ עֵדִים שֶׁהִיא טְמֵיאָה. וְהָאוֹמֶרֶת אֵינִי שׁוֹתָה וְשֶׁבַּעֲלָהּ אֵינוֹ רוֹצֶה לְהַשְׁקוֹתָהּ וְשֶׁבַּעֲלָהּ בָּא עָלֶיהָ בַּדֶּרֶךְ. כֵּיצַד הוּא עוֹשֶׂה לָהּ. מוֹלִיכָהּ בְּבֵית דִּין שֶׁבָּאוּתוֹ הַמָּקוֹם וּמוֹסְרִין לוֹ שְׁנֵי תַלְמִידֵי חֲכָמִים שֶׁמָּא יָבוֹא עָלֶיהָ בַּדֶּרֶךְ. רַבִּי יְהוּדָה אוֹמֵר בַּעֲלָהּ נֶאֱמָן עָלֶיהָ. (fol. 16a)

Mishnah 3: The following are prohibited from eating heave[142]: One who says, I am impure for you[143], and where witnesses proved that she is impure[144], and one who refuses to drink[145], and one whose husband refuses to let her drink[146], and one whose husband slept with her on the trip[147]. What does he have to do: He brings her to the court at his place and they give him two scholars to prevent him from sleeping with her on the trip. Rebbi Jehudah says, her husband is believed about her.

142 A Cohen's wife (or the Cohen's daughter who is the childless widow of a Non-Cohen) who is desecrated by adultery; cf. also Note 123.

143 I. e., she says that she slept with another man; there is no difference in this respect whether she committed adultery or was raped.

144 Witnesses to the act of adultery.

145 She maintains her innocence, even though two witnesses attested that she met the man against whom she was warned in a secluded place, but refuses to submit to the ordeal. She remains permanently forbidden to her husband and is permanently excluded from eating consecrated food.

146 Two witnesses attested that she met the man against whom she was warned in a secluded place; therefore, she is disabled from eating heave. She can regain her priestly status only by being cleansed by the ordeal. Since it is written (*Num.* 5:15): "This husband has to bring his wife," without him appearing before the court of the Temple there can be no ordeal and no rehabilitation.

147 *Num.* 5:31 is read as meaning: If the husband is blameless, then this woman has to bear her sin. It follows that if the husband is not blameless [in sexual matters of any kind], the ordeal becomes inactive. Since the *Sotah* is

forbidden to her husband, if he sleeps with her before she is cleansed by the ordeal he is not blameless and the innocence of his wife can never be proven.

(fol. 16d) **הלכה ג**: אֵילוּ אֲסוּרוֹת מִלֶּאֱכֹל בַּתְּרוּמָה כול'. מַתְנִיתִין לֹא כַמִּשְׁנָה הָרִאשׁוֹנָה. דְּתַנִינָן תַּמָּן. בָּרִאשׁוֹנָה הָיוּ אוֹמְרִים. שָׁלֹשׁ נָשִׁים יוֹצְאוֹת וְנוֹטְלוֹת כְּתוּבָה. הָאוֹמֶרֶת. טְמֵיאָה אֲנִי לָךְ. שָׁמַיִם בֵּינִי וּבֵינָךְ. וּנְטוּלָה אֲנִי מִן הַיְהוּדִים. אָמַר רִבִּי אָבִין. וַאֲפִילוּ תֹאמַר כַּמִּשְׁנָה הָאַחֲרוֹנָה. מִכָּל־מָקוֹם יֵשׁ רַגְלַיִם לַדָּבָר.

Halakhah 3: "The following are prohibited from eating heave," etc. Our Mishnah does not follow the earlier Mishnah, as we have stated there[148]: "Three [kinds of] women leave[149] and collect their *ketubah*: One who says, I am impure for you[150], [or] Heaven is between you and me[151], [or] I am separated from the Jews[152]." Rebbi Abin said, even if you say following the later Mishnah, does not the affair have likelihood[153]?

148 Mishnah *Nedarim* 11:12.
149 The court would force the husband to divorce her.
150 A woman married to a Cohen who says that she was raped. Then she is forbidden to him not because of any fault of hers; therefore, she collects the entire amount promised her. The later Mishnah, in a change of practice, requires that the woman prove her case; if she cannot do that, she remains permitted to her husband and permitted to eat heave (because the later authorities suspected that a woman might invent the story of the rape to force a divorce). This contradicts the Mishnah here which states that a woman claiming to have been raped is permanently desecrated.
151 She claims that he is impotent and unable to have satisfactory intercourse; the truth in these intimate matters is known only to Heaven. In the later practice, the rabbi has to negotiate a settlement between the parties.
152 She made a vow forbidding to herself any sexual relation with any

Jew. In the later practice, this is considered a "vow of deprivation" which the husband may annul (*Num.* 30:14). He may annul his part, live with her, and let her be forbidden to all other Jews.

153   The situation here cannot be compared to the one described in *Nedarim*. The woman is forbidden to eat heave only after she was warned before witnesses and nevertheless was in a secluded place according to the testimony of two witnesses. It is a credible inference, even if there is no proof, that she had relations with her paramour.

(16d, line 21) תַּנֵּי. מִבַּלְעֲדֵי אִישֵׁךְ. פְּרָט לְשֶׁקֶּדְמָה שִׁכְבַת זֶרַע אַחֶרֶת לְאִישֵׁךְ. אָמַר רִבִּי אִילָא. כְּעִנְייָן שֶׁנֶּאֱמַר מִלְּבַד עוֹלַת הַבּוֹקֶר. וְהָא תַנִּינָן. כְּשֵׁם שֶׁהַמַּיִם בּוֹדְקִין אוֹתָהּ כָּךְ הֵן בּוֹדְקִין אוֹתוֹ. כְּשֵׁם שֶׁהִיא אֲסוּרָה לַבַּעַל כָּךְ הִיא אֲסוּרָה לַבּוֹעֵל. כְּשֵׁם שֶׁהִיא אֲסוּרָה לְאָחִיו שֶׁלַבַּעַל כָּךְ הִיא אֲסוּרָה לְאָחִיו שֶׁלַבּוֹעֵל. כְּשֵׁם שֶׁהַמַּיִם בּוֹדְקִין אוֹתָהּ עַל כָּל־בִּיאָה וּבִיאָה שֶׁהִיא מְקַבֶּלֶת אֶת בַּעֲלָהּ לְאַחַר הַבּוֹעֵל כָּךְ הֵן בּוֹדְקִין אוֹתוֹ. רִבִּי אָבִין בְּשֵׁם רִבִּי הִילָא. כָּאן בְּיוֹדֵעַ כָּאן בְּשֶׁאֵינוֹ יוֹדֵעַ.

It was stated[154]: "'Except your husband,[155]' which excludes that other semen preceded your husband's[156]. Rebbi Hila said, parallel what has been said, 'except the morning elevation offering.[157]' But did we not state: "Just as the water examines her, so the water examines him. Just as she is forbidden to her husband, so she is forbidden to her paramour"[158]? Just as she is forbidden to her husband's brother, so she is forbidden to her paramour's brother[159]. Just as the water examines her for every intercourse in which she receives her husband after [she had slept with] her paramour, so it examines him[160]? Rebbi Abin in the name of Rebbi Hila: Here, if he knows, there, if he does not know[161].

154   The same statement in Babli *Yebamot* 58a, *Sota* 24b.

155   *Num.* 5:19.

156   If the affair with her paramour

preceded her current marriage, the ordeal will be ineffective.

157 Num. 28:23. While this verse is written at the end of the list of holiday sacrifices, it is obvious that the daily sacrifice precedes all others, Therefore, מִלְבַד means really "after". Similarly, מִבַּלְעֲדֵי אִישֵׁךְ should be translated: "after your husband". (In *Sifry Num.* 13, *Sifry Zuṭa* 20, the verse is interpreted in two other, much different, ways.)

158 Mishnah 5:1.

159 This sentence is an intrusion from the preceding text, Note 128, induced by the similarly formulated Mishnah.

160 This *baraita* assumes that the ordeal is effective if the husband slept with his wife after she committed adultery. But the Mishnah excluded this case!

161 The ordeal is effective if she committed adultery before the husband even became aware of a possible affair. He is not free from sin only if he sleeps with his wife after officially charging her and receiving notice that she was alone with her paramour.

(16d, line 28) רִבִּי חִייָה בַּר יוֹסֵף שָׁלַח בָּתַר אִיתְּתֵיהּ. אָמַר. יַסְקוּן עִמָּהּ תְּלַת תַּלְמִידִין. שֶׁאִם יִפָּנֶה אֶחָד מֵהֶן לְצוֹרְכּוֹ תִּתְיַיחֵד עִם שְׁנַיִם. וְהָא תַּנִּינָן. וּמוֹסְרִין לוֹ שְׁנֵי תַלְמִידֵי חֲכָמִים שֶׁמָּא יָבוֹא עָלֶיהָ בַּדֶּרֶךְ. אָמַר רִבִּי אָבִין. וּבַעֲלָהּ. הֲרֵי שְׁלֹשָׁה. אַף הוּא שָׂכַר לָהּ בַּיִת וְהָיָה מַעֲלֶה לָהּ מְזוֹנוֹת וְלֹא הָיָה מִתְיַיחֵד עִמָּהּ אֶלָּא בִּפְנֵי בָנֶיהָ. וְקָרָא עַל עַצְמוֹ הַפָּסוּק הַזֶּה יָגַעְתִּי בְאַנְחָתִי וּמְנוּחָה לֹא מָצָאתִי.

[162]Rebbi Ḥiyya bar Yosef sent after his wife. He said, three students should accompany her, so that if one has to absent himself for his needs, she should still be with two of them. But did we not state[163]: "And they give him two scholars to prevent him from sleeping with her on the trip"? Rebbi Abin said, with her husband that makes three[164]. [165]{Also he rented a house for her and looked after her upkeep but was never alone with her except in presence of her children. He applied to himself the verse: "I exercised myself in my worry but found no rest[166]".}

162 The same text in *Ketubot* 2:10. Copied in *Num. Rabba Naśo* 9(38), a text of doubtful antiquity.

163 In the Mishnah here, which requires only two chaperones.

164 In Mishnah *Qiddušin* 4:12 it is stated that a woman may be alone with two men, but not with a single man who is not her husband or close relative. The anecdotal fact told here is stated in the Babli, 7a, as a legal precept by R. Ḥiyya bar Yosef's teacher Rav.

165 These sentences make no sense here; they are copied from *Ketubot*, where they refer to Mishnah 2:10, that in a city conquered by an enemy army all women, in absence of testimony to the contrary, are considered raped and, therefore, all wives of Cohanim are prohibited to their husbands. It is reported that R. Zachariah ben Haqqaṣab, who was a priest, testified that his wife's hand did not leave his own from the moment the Roman army entered Jerusalem until it left, but he was rebuked and told that nobody may testify in his own behalf. The *baraita* notes that he refused to divorce her.

166 *Jer.* 45:3.

(16d, line 33) תַּנֵּי. רִבִּי יוּדָה אוֹמֵר. בַּעֲלָהּ נֶאֱמָן עָלֶיהָ מִקַּל וָחוֹמֶר. וּמַה אִם הַנִּדָּה שֶׁחַיָּיבִין עָלֶיהָ כָּרֵת הֲרֵי הוּא נֶאֱמָן עָלֶיהָ. זוֹ שֶׁאֵין חַיָּיבִין עָלֶיהָ כָּרֵת אֵינוֹ דִין שֶׁיְּהֵא נֶאֱמָן עָלֶיהָ. אָמְרוּ לוֹ. לֹא. אִם אָמַרְתָּ בְּנִידָּה שֶׁיֵּשׁ לָהּ הֶיתֵר לְאַחַר אִיסּוּרָהּ. תֹּאמַר בְּזוֹ שֶׁאֵין לָהּ הֶיתֵר לְאַחַר אִיסּוּרָהּ. וְאוֹמֵר מַיִם גְּנוּבִים יִמְתָּקוּ וגו'. אָמַר לָהֶן רִבִּי יְהוּדָה. גְּזֵירַת הַכָּתוּב הִיא. וְהֵבִיא הָאִישׁ אֶת אִשְׁתּוֹ אֶל הַכֹּהֵן וגו'. אָמְרוּ לוֹ. וּבִלְבַד בְּעֵדִים.

It was stated[167]: "Rebbi Jehudah says, her husband is believed about her by an argument *de minore ad majus*. Since he is believed about her when she is menstruating[168], when he would be subject to extirpation because of her, but for this one[169] he is not subject to extirpation because of her, is it not logical that he should be believed about her? They said to him, no. If you mention the menstruating, she will be permitted after being forbidden, what can you say about this one who may not be permitted after being forbidden[170]? And it says, "stolen waters are sweet"[171]. Rebbi Jehudah said to them, it is a decree of the verse: "The man shall bring his wife to the priest"[178], etc. They said to him, only with witnesses[179].

167 *Sifry Num.* 8, *Num. Rabba* 9(38); a more elaborate text in Babli 7a, Tosephta 1:1.

168 The menstruating woman is forbidden to her husband on penalty of extirpation (*Lev.* 20:18). Nobody requires chaperones during the time the wife is forbidden to her husband.

169 A wife suspected of adultery (and even a proven adulteress) is forbidden to her husband but no penalties are specified.

170 If she is found guilty, she will be permanently forbidden and he will be forced to divorce her.

171 *Prov.* 9:17. She is more attractive forbidden than permitted.

178 *Num.* 5:15.

179 General statements in verses are never interpreted to override the general principles of administration of justice. Since relatives cannot testify for or against a person, the husband cannot testify for himself, just as he cannot testify against his bride whom he accuses of prenuptial adultery (*Deut.* 22;14).

(fol. 16a) **משנה ד:** הָיוּ מַעֲלִין אוֹתָהּ לְבֵית דִּין הַגָּדוֹל שֶׁבִּירוּשָׁלַם וּמְאַיְּימִין עָלֶיהָ כְּדֶרֶךְ שֶׁמְּאַיְּימִין עַל עֵידֵי נְפָשׁוֹת וְאוֹמְרִין לָהּ בִּתִּי הַרְבֵּה יַיִן עוֹשֶׂה. הַרְבֵּה שְׂחוֹק עוֹשֶׂה. הַרְבֵּה יַלְדוּת עוֹשָׂה. הַרְבֵּה שְׁכֵנִים הָרָעִים עוֹשִׂים. אַל תַּעֲשִׂי לִשְׁמוֹ הַגָּדוֹל שֶׁנִּכְתַּב בִּקְדוּשָׁה שֶׁיִּימָּחֶה עַל הַמַּיִם וְאוֹמְרִים לְפָנֶיהָ דְּבָרִים שֶׁאֵינָהּ כְּדַי לְשָׁמְעָן הִיא וְכָל־מִשְׁפַּחַת בֵּית אָבִיהָ.

Mishnah 4: They bring her to the Supreme Court in Jerusalem[180] where they try to instill fear in her, as they try to instill fear in witnesses in capital cases[181], and say to her[182]: My daughter, much does wine cause, much does joking cause, much does youth cause, much do bad neighbors cause. Do not cause the Great Name, which will be written in holiness, to be erased by water[183], and they mention in front of her things that neither she nor any of her paternal family should hear.

180 Galilean Amoraim in the Babli, 7b, try to give a reason to this statement: Every procedure characterized as *Torah* (*Num.* 5:30) must be supervised by the supreme court, cf. *Deut.* 17:11.

181 Mishnah *Sanhedrin* 4:5.

182 Tosephta 1:6.

183 The Babli text: Do it for the Great Name, Which will be written in holiness, that It should not become erased by water.

The verse requires that the curses contained in the paragraph *Num.* 5:11-31 be written on a scroll and erased by holy water. While the exact text to be written is a matter of controversy among scholars living 2 generations after the destruction of the Temple, all agree that some verses containing the Divine Name must be written.

הלכה ד: הָיוּ מַעֲלִין אוֹתָהּ לְבֵית דִּין הַגָּדוֹל שֶׁבִּירוּשָׁלַםִ כול׳. כְּשֵׁם שֶׁמְּאַייְמִין עָלֶיהָ שֶׁתַּחֲזוֹר בָּהּ כָּךְ מְאַייְמִין עָלֶיהָ שֶׁלֹּא תַחֲזוֹר בָּהּ. וְאוֹמְרִין לָהּ. בִּתִּי. אִם טְהוֹרָה אַתְּ. דְּבָרִיא לָךְ שֶׁאַתְּ טְהוֹרָה. עִמְדִי עַל בּוּרְייֵךְ. שֶׁאֵין הַמַּיִם הָאֵילוּ דוֹמִין אֶלָּא לְסַם יָבֵשׁ שֶׁהוּא נָתוּן עַל גַּבֵּי בָשָׂר חַי וְאֵינוֹ מַזִּיקוֹ. מָצָא שָׁם מַכָּה הִתְחִיל מְחַלְחֵל וְיוֹרֵד. (fol. 16d)

Halakhah 4: "They bring her to the Supreme Court in Jerusalem," etc. [184]Just as they instill fear in her that she should change her mind, so they instill fear in her that she should not change her mind, and say to her: My daughter, if you are pure, if it is clear to you that you are pure, insist on what is clear to you, since this draught is only like solid poison which if given on healthy skin does no harm; only if it finds there a wound it starts to dissolve and penetrate.

184   Tosephta 1:6, Babli 7b; *Num. rabba* 9(42). In *Sifry Num.* 12, this is a (minority) statement of R. Ismael.

(16d, line 44) רִבִּי זְבַדְיָה חַתְנֵיהּ דְּרִבִּי לֵוִי מִשְׁתָּעֵי הָדֵין עוֹבְדָא. רִבִּי מֵאִיר הֲוָה יָלִיף דְּרִישׁ בִּכְנִשְׁתָּא דְחַמָּתָא כָּל־לֵילֵי שׁוּבָּא. וַהֲוָה תַמָּה חָדָא אִיתְּתָא וְיָלִיפָה שְׁמָעָא קָלֵיהּ. חַד זְמָן עָנֵי דָרִישׁ. אָזְלַת בָּעֲיָת מֵיעוֹל לְבֵיתֵיהּ. וְאַשְׁכָּחַת בּוּצִינָא מִי טָפֵי. אָמַר לָהּ בַּעֲלָהּ. הֵן הֲוַיְתָה. אָמְרָה לֵיהּ. מִישְׁמְעָא קָלֵיהּ דְּדְרוֹשָׁא. אָמַר לָהּ. מִכָּךְ וָכָךְ דְּלֵית הַהִיא אִיתְּתָא עָלְלָה לְהָכָא לְבֵייתָהּ עַד זְמָן דְּהִיא אָזְלָה וְרָקְקָה גּוֹ אַפּוֹי דַּדְרוֹשָׁה. צָפָה רִבִּי מֵאִיר בְּרוּחַ הַקּוֹדֶשׁ וַעֲבַד גַּרְמֵיהּ חָשַׁשׁ בְּעֵיינֵיהּ. אָמַר כָּל־אִיתְּתָא דְּיַדְעָה מִילְחוֹשׁ לְעֵיינָא תֵּיתֵי תִילְחוּשׁ. אָמְרִין לָהּ מְגִירָתָא. הָא עַנְיֵיתֵיהּ. תֵּיעֲלִין לְבֵיתֵיהּ עַבְדִּי גַרְמֵיךְ לַחֲשָׁה לֵיהּ וְאַתְּ רָקְקָה גּוֹ עֵיינֵיהּ. אָתַת לְגַבֵּיהּ. אָמַר לָהּ. חֲכָמָה אַתְּ מִילְחוֹשׁ לְעֵיינָא. מֵאֵימָתֵיהּ עֲלֵיהָ אָמְרָה לֵיהּ. לֹא. אָמַר לָהּ. וְרוֹקְקִין בְּגַוָּיהּ שֶׁבַע זִימְנִין וְהוּא טַב לֵיהּ. מוֹ דְּרָקְקַת אָמַר לָהּ. אָזְלִין אָמְרִין לְבַעֲלֵיהּ. חַד זְמָן אָמְרַת לִי. וְהִיא רָקְקָה שִׁבְעָה זִימְנִין. אָמְרוּ לוֹ תַלְמִידָיו. רַבִּי. כָּךְ מְבַזִּין אֶת הַתּוֹרָה. אִילוּ אָמְרַת לוֹ. לֹא הֲוֵית מַיְיתֵי לֵיהּ וּמַלְקִין לֵהּ סַפְסְלֵיהּ וּמַרְצִיִין. וּמְרַצְיֵיהּ לֵיהּ לְאִיתְּתֵיהּ. אָמַר לוֹן. וְלֹא יְהֵא כְבוֹד מֵאִיר כִּכְבוֹד קוֹנוֹ. מָה אִם שֵׁם הַקּוֹדֶשׁ שֶׁנִּכְתָּב בִּקְדוּשָׁה אָמַר הַכָּתוּב שֶׁיִּימָּחֶה עַל הַמַּיִם בִּשְׁבִיל לְהַטִּיל שָׁלוֹם בֵּין אִישׁ לְאִשְׁתּוֹ. וּכְבוֹד מֵאִיר לֹא כָּל־שֶׁכֵּן.

185Rebbi Zevadiah186, the son-in-law of Rebbi Levi, reported the following happening. Rebbi Meïr used to preach in the synagogue of Hamata187 every Friday evening. There was a woman who used to hear him. Once he extended his sermon. She went and wanted to come to her house but found the light had gone out. Her husband asked her, where have you been? She said to him, to hear the preacher's voice. He said to her, so and so[188], that this woman will not enter here into her house unless she went and spat into the preacher's face. Rebbi Meïr saw this in the holy spirit[189] and faked pain in his eyes. He said, any woman who knows charms for the eye should come and do the charm. Her neighbors said to her, this answers your needs. Go to your house, represent yourself as a sorceress and spit in his eye. She came to him; he asked her, do you know to make a charm for the eye? In her fear of him, she said no. He said to her, if you spit into it seven times, he will feel better. After she had spat, he said to her: Go, and tell your husband, you said to me once, but she spat seven times! His students said to him, so does one denigrate the Torah? If you had ordered about him[191], would we not have brought him, whipped him on the footstool, and make him agree[191] to make up with his wife? He said to them, the honor of Meïr should not be greater than that of his Maker. Since the verse says that the Holy Name, written in holiness, should be erased by the water in order to make peace between husband and wife, the honor of Meïr not so much more?

185 A copy of this text in *Num. rabba* 9(19); a retelling in a different Aramaic dialect in *Lev. rabba* 9(9), a short version in Hebrew *Deut. rabba* 5(14).

186 In *Num. rabba* 9(19): R. Zachariah. This is the correct name as attested to by all other quotes of his statements (cf. *Peah* 8, Note 151).

187 The hot springs of Tiberias.

188 An oath formula, cf. 2S. 19:14.

189 In *Lev. rabba* 9(9), he was informed by the Prophet Elijah.

190 In *Num. rabba* 9(19): לון "to us".

191 In *Num. rabba* 9(19) ומרעיין instead of ומרציין, "one makes his wife pleasing to him." On the face of it, that might be the better text. However, the text here might be a slightly corrupt pun if one reads ומרציין for ומרצעיין, "one treats him with leather straps until he asks his wife for forgiveness" since ע had become silent in Galilean Aramaic.

(16d, line 62) וְאוֹמְרִים לְפָנֶיהָ דְּבָרִים שֶׁאֵינָהּ כְּדַיי לְשָׁמְעָן הִיא וְכָל־מִשְׁפַּחַת בֵּית אָבִיהָ. כְּגוֹן מַעֲשֵׂה רְאוּבֵן בְּבִלְהָה. וּמַעֲשֵׂה יְהוּדָה בְתָמָר. אֲשֶׁר חֲכָמִים יַגִּידוּ. אֵילּוּ רְאוּבֵן וִיהוּדָה. וְלֹא כִחֲדוּ מֵאֲבוֹתָם. וּמַה שָּׂכָר נָטְלוּ עַל כָּךְ. לָהֶם לְבַדָּם נִתְּנָה הָאָרֶץ וְלֹא עָבַר זָר בְּתוֹכָם. כְּשֶׁבָּא מֹשֶׁה לְבָרְכָן. יְחִי רְאוּבֵן וְאַל יָמֹת. וְזֹאת לִיהוּדָה.

"And they mention in front of her things that neither she nor any of her paternal family should hear," etc. [192]For example, what happened between Reuben and Bilhah[193], or what happened between Jehudah and Tamar[194]. [195]"If Sages tell," these are Reuben and Jehudah, "they do not hide before their fathers." What rewards did they take for this, "to them alone the Land was given; no stranger passes in their midst." When Moses came to bless them, "Reuben may live and not die,[196]" "and that for Jehudah[197]".

192 A more detailed homily in the Babli, 7b.
193 Gen. 35:22.
194 Gen. 38:13-26.
195 Job 15:18-19. These verses are explained as referring to Reuben and Jehudah who confessed their sins, in Gen. rabba 57(3), [Num. rabba 13(6)]; Babli *Makkot* 11b; Yerushalmi *Megillah* 4:11 (fol. 75c).
196 Deut. 36:6.
197 Deut. 36:7: "Listen, o Eternal, to Judah's voice."

(16d, line 66) רִבִּי חִזְקִיָּה בְּשֵׁם רִבִּי אָחָא. רִבִּי חִייָה דָּרִישׁ שָׁלֹשׁ מִקְרָאוֹת לְשָׁבַח. וַתֵּשֶׁב בְּפֶתַח עֵינַיִם. וְאִיפְשַׁר כֵּן. אֲפִילוּ זוֹנָה שֶׁבַּזּוֹנוֹת אֵינָהּ עוֹשָׂה כֵן. אֶלָּא שֶׁתָּלַת עֵינֶיהָ לַפֶּתַח שֶׁכָּל־הָעֵינַיִם מְצַפּוֹת לוֹ. אָמְרָה לְפָנָיו. רִבּוֹן כָּל־הָעוֹלָמִים. אַל אֵצֵא רֵיקָם מִן הַבַּיִת הַזֶּה. דָּבָר אַחֵר. בְּפֶתַח עֵינַיִם. שֶׁפָּתְחָה לוֹ אֶת הָעֵינַיִם. שֶׁאָמְרָה לוֹ. פְּנוּיָה אֲנִי וּטְהוֹרָה אֲנִי. וְעָלַי זָקֵן מְאֹד וגו'. ישכיבון כְּתִיב. שֶׁהָיוּ הַנָּשִׁים מְבִיאוֹת קִינֵּיהֶן לְטַהֵר לְבָתֵּיהֶן וְהָיוּ מַשְׁהִין

אוֹתָן. הַקָּדוֹשׁ בָּרוּךְ הוּא מַעֲלֶה עֲלֵיהֶן כְּאִילוּ הֵן שׁוֹכְבִין אוֹתָן. אָמַר רִבִּי תַּנְחוּמָא. הֲרֵי הִיא דּוּ מְקַנְטֵר לוֹן. לָמָּה תְבַעֲטוּן בְּזִבְחִי וּבְמִנְחָתִי. אִין תֵּימַר. עֲבֵירָה חֲמוּרָה יֵשׁ כָּאן. מַבְרִיהָן מִן הַחֲמוּרָה וּמְקַנְתְּרָן בַּקַּלָּה. וְלֹא הָלְכוּ בָנָיו אַחֲרָיו וַיַּטּוּ אַחֲרֵי הַבָּצַע. שֶׁהָיוּ נוֹטְלִין מַעֲשֵׂר וְדָנִין. אָמַר רִבִּי בְּרֶכְיָה. מַבְרַכְתָּא קָיְתָה עוֹבֶרֶת. וְהָיוּ מַנִּיחִין צָרְכֵיהֶן שֶׁלְּיִשְׂרָאֵל וְהָיוּ הוֹלְכִין וְעוֹסְקִין בִּפְרַקְמַטְיָא.

Rebbi Ḥizqiah in the name of Rebbi Aḥa: Rebbi Ḥiyya explains three verses as praise. [198]"She sat at the entrance to the source." Is that possible? Even the most depraved prostitute would not do that[199]. But she lifted her eyes to the door to which all eyes are looking[200]. She said before Him: Master of the Universe, let me not leave this family empty-handed. Another explanation, "at the entrance to the eyes", that she opened his eyes saying, I am unmarried and pure.

"And Eli was very old,[201]" "they would make them lie" is written[202]. That women would bring them their bird-sacrifices to be purified for their houses but since they were dragging their feet[203], the Holy One, praise to Him, found them guilty as if they had slept with them. Rebbi Tanḥuma said, here, he needles[204] them: [205]"why do you disregard my slaughter-sacrifice and my flour-sacrifice?" If you say that they committed a serious crime, why should he absolve them from the serious crime and needle them for a minor one?

[206]"But his sons did not follow in his ways and turned after lucre." That they took tithe but remained judging[207]. Rebbi Berekhia: A camel-caravan came by, they put aside the needs of Israel and were going and attending to business affairs[208].

198 The parallel to the entire section is in *Ketubot* 13:1 (fol. 35b/c). A different version, in the name of other authors, in Babli 10b, *Gen. rabba* 85(8). One of the Babli's authors identifies the place as העינם (Jos. 15:34).

199 To try to sleep with a man not in a room.

200 Usually identified, cf. *Berakhot* 4, Note 234.

201 *1S.* 2:22-23. The same explanation in Babli *Šabbat* 55b; more in detail *Midrash Samuel* 7(4).

202 The masoretic text reads יִשְׁכְּבוּן [Eli's sons] would lie [with the women assembled before the Tent]. A sacrifice of birds is required for a woman healed from prolonged flux to be permitted again to her husband (*Lev.*

15:29) and also for a woman after childbirth (*Lev.* 12:8).

203 Unnecessarily preventing them from sleeping with their husbands.

204 Greek κεντρόω, cf. *Berakhot* 3, Note 96.

205 *1S.* 2:29.

206 *1S.* 8:3. Similar explanations in Babli *Šabbat* 56a.

207 As Levites, Samuel's sons were entitled to tithe. The Yerushalmi faults them for creating an appearance of conflict of interest; in the Babli, there is one opinion that they exacted tithes for themselves, when the farmer should have had full freedom to give the tithe to any Levite of his liking.

208 Greek πραγματεία "business, affairs, work".

(fol. 16a) **משנה ה:** אִם אָמְרָה טְמֵיאָה אֲנִי שׁוֹבֶרֶת כְּתוּבָּתָהּ וְיוֹצְאָה. אִם אָמְרָה טְהוֹרָה אֲנִי מַעֲלִין אוֹתָהּ לְשַׁעֲרֵי הַמִּזְרָח לְשַׁעֲרֵי נִיקָנוֹר שֶׁשָּׁם מַשְׁקִין אֶת הַסּוֹטוֹת וּמְטַהֲרִין אֶת הַיּוֹלְדוֹת וּמְטַהֲרִין אֶת הַמְצוֹרָעִין. וְכֹהֵן אוֹחֵז בִּבְגָדֶיהָ אִם נִקְרְעוּ נִקְרָעוּ וְאִם נִפְרְמוּ נִפְרָמוּ עַד שֶׁהוּא מְגַלֶּה אֶת לִבָּהּ וְסוֹתֵר אֶת שְׂעָרָהּ. רִבִּי יְהוּדָה אוֹמֵר. אִם הָיָה לִבָּהּ נָאֶה לֹא הָיָה מְגַלֵּהוּ. וְאִם הָיָה שְׂעָרָהּ נָאֶה לֹא הָיָה סוֹתְרוֹ.

Mishnah 5: If she said, I am impure, she breaks her *ketubah* and leaves[209]. If she said, I am pure, one brings her to the Eastern gate, the

Nikanor gate, for there one lets the suspected wives drink[210], and one purifies the woman after childbirth, and the persons healed from skin disease[211]. A Cohen seizes her garment[212], if it tears it tears, if it frays it frays, until he uncovers her breast[213], and he destroys her hairdo. Rebbi Jehudah says, if her breast was beautiful, he did not uncover it, if her hair was beautiful, he did not undo it[214].

209   The court immediately has a bill of divorce executed for the husband and annuls her husband's obligations towards her as specified in the *ketubah*.

210   It is mentioned repeatedly that the woman has to stand "before the Eternal", i. e., at a place at which the entrance to the Temple can be seen. It follows from Mishnah 3:4 that the procedure is not executed within the gate but in the women's courtyard close to the gate or at least in the sanctified inner part of the gate.

211   Both the woman after childbirth and the person healed from skin disease are forbidden to "enter the Sanctuary" before their sacrifices have ben offered. Therefore, all their transactions have to be executed in the profane part of the gate, in view of the Temple entrance.

212   According to Rashi and Maimonides, he seizes her neckline.

213   The next Mishnah shows that this means "until the top of her breasts starts to be uncovered."

214   According to him, only those women can be uncovered who are too ugly to inspire any sexual ideas in men who are watching. In the Babli, 8a, Rava quotes a legal principle that a man aroused by one woman will not attack another woman even though he himself knew that this is untrue in reality (*Ketubot* 65a).

(fol. 17a) **הלכה ה**: אם אָמְרָה. טְמֵיאָה אֲנִי. שׁוֹבֶרֶת כְּתוּבָתָהּ וְיוֹצְאָה כול'. כְּתִיב וְהֶעֱמִיד הַכֹּהֵן אֶת הָאִשָּׁה לִפְנֵי י'. זֶה שַׁעַר נִיקָנוֹר. כָּל־מָקוֹם שֶׁנֶּאֱמַר לִפְנֵי י' זֶה שַׁעַר נִיקָנוֹר. כְּתִיב אִם יֶחֱטָא אִישׁ לְאִישׁ וגו'. רִבִּי חִייָה בַּר בָּא וְרִבִּי יְהוֹשֻׁעַ בֶּן לֵוִי. רִבִּי חִייָה בַּר בָּא פָּטַר קְרְיָיה בַּבּוֹעֵל. וְרִבִּי יְהוֹשֻׁעַ בֶּן לֵוִי

פָּטַר קִרְיָיה בָּאִשָּׁה. רִבִּי חִייָה בַּר בָּא פָּטַר קִרְיָיה בַּבּוֹעֵל. הָהֵן זָן וּמְפַרְנֵס וְאַתְּ אָתֵי עַל דַּעְתָּהּ. וְרִבִּי יְהוֹשֻׁעַ בֶּן לֵוִי פָּטַר קִרְיָיה בָּאִשָּׁה. הָהֵן זָן וּמְפַרְנֵס וְאַתְּ תָּלִית עֵינַיִם עַל חוֹרָן.

Halakhah 5: "If she said, I am impure, she breaks her *ketubah* and leaves," etc. It is written: "The Cohen shall put the woman before the Eternal[215]", that is the Nikanor gate[216]. Everywhere it is said "before the Eternal", that means the Nikanor gate. [217]It is written: "If a man sin against a man.[218]" Rebbi Ḥiyya bar Abba and Rebbi Joshua ben Levi. Rebbi Ḥiyya bar Abba explains the verse about the paramour, Rebbi Joshua ben Levi explains the verse about the woman. Rebbi Ḥiyya bar Abba explains the verse about the paramour: That one feeds and sustains and you come to enjoy yourself. Rebbi Joshua ben Levi explains the verse about the woman: That one feeds and sustains and you turn your eyes to another.

215 *Num.* 5:18.

216 In ritual matters, the Nikanor gate is the entrance to the courtyard of the Tent of Meeting. In *Sifry Num.* 17, the statement is "before the Eternal", which means in the East.

217 An explanation why an ordeal must be performed in the Temple, based on Tosephta 1:4 (S. Lieberman in *Tosefta kiFshutah Soṭa* 1, line 19.)

218 *1S.* 2:25. As R. David Fraenckel has noted, it seems that this verse is out of place and should be replaced by *1K.* 8:31-32 which is quoted in Tosephta 1:4, combined with *Num.* 5:27,28 as support that the ordeal of the suspected wife is to be held in the Temple: "If a man sin against his neighbor and causes a curse to be put on him ... and You will hear in Heaven and will judge Your servants to declare the criminal guilty to turn his way on him [her belly will extend and her genitals shrink] and to clear the just to reward him for his just behavior [if the woman was not impure but pure, she will be declared innocent and be blessed with seed.]"

(17a, line 11) וּמְבַזִּין עַל הַסָּפֵק. אָמַר רִבִּי שִׂמְלַאי. בְּכָל־מָקוֹם שֶׁאַתְּ מוֹצֵא
זְנוּת אַתְּ מוֹצֵא אַנְדְּרוֹלְמוֹסִיָּה בָּאָה בָּעוֹלָם.

Does one shame out of a doubt[219]? Rebbi Simlai said[220], anywhere one finds whoring, mass destruction[221] comes to the world.

219 If the woman was innocent, she would have been debased without cause.

220 In Midrashic sources, the text reads: "anywhere one finds whoring, mass destruction comes to the world and kills good and bad." *Gen. rabba* 27:10, *Lev. rabba* 23:9, *Num. rabba* 9(41).

221 The etymology of אנדרולמוסיה is not known. In *Gen. rabba*, Arukh reads אנדרומוסיא. While here the meaning could be "human plague", which could be *$\dot{α}νδρολοιμός$ (Levy), there is another series of sayings mentioning a king who makes war on a rebellious province and causes there אנדרולמוסיה Jastrow proposes *$\dot{α}νδρολημψία$ "robbery of men". (Cf. $ανδρολημψία$ "seizure of foreigners in reprisal for the murder of a citizen abroad" (*Lex ap. D* 23.82) (E. G.)}. In *Gen. rabba* 32(14): "A parable of a king who ordered his דורלומסיא in a province and saved his friend by jailing him." (Following Fürst in *Tanḥuma Buber*, vol. 2, p. בא, Note 24, the word דורמוסיות, דורמוסיאות, found in other Midrashim, is not a shortened form of אנדרולומסיה)

(17a, line 12) קִרְיָיא אָמַר. מַקְרִין וְאַחַר כָּךְ מְבַזִּין. וּמַתְנִיתָא אָמְרָה. מְבַזִּין
וְאַחַר כָּךְ מַקְרִין. אָמַר רִבִּי אִילַי. מִכֵּיוָן דִּכְתִיב וְהֶעֱמִיד וְהֶעֱמִידָהּ וְכִי יוֹשֶׁבֶת
הָיְיתָ. אֶלָּא מַחְמַת עֲמִדָה הָרִאשׁוֹנָה הָיָה פּוֹרֵעַ אֶת רֹאשָׁהּ.

The verse said, one recites and after that one shames[222]. But the Mishnah says, one shames and then one recites? Rebbi Hila said, because the verse says, "he makes stand, he makes her stand[223]"; did she ever sit[224]? But because of the first stand he uncovers her hair[225].

222 V. 17 indicates that as a first step, the Cohen prepares the curse-draught. After that (v. 18) he uncovers the woman's hair. But in the Mishnah,

the preparation of the draught is late (2:2). The recitation of the curses can start only after the draught is prepared.

223 *Num.* 5:18,16.

224 It is forbidden to sit down in the Temple precinct (for everybody except kings of the Davidic line).

225 The text vv. 17-20 is explanatory, not prescriptive. The uncovering of the hair is a consequence of her coming to the Temple. For a coherent parallel (non-rabbinic) reading of the text, cf. the paper by H. C. Brichto, mentioned in the Introduction.

(17a, line 12) מִחְלְפָה שִׁיטָתֵיהּ דְּרַבִּי יוּדָן. תַּמָּן הוּא אָמַר. הָאִישׁ מְכַסִּין אוֹתוֹ מִלְּפָנָיו. וְהָאִשָּׁה מִלְּפָנֶיהָ וּמִלְּאַחֲרֶיהָ. וְהָכָא הוּא אָמַר הָכֵין. תַּמָּן מִכָּל־מָקוֹם לְמִיתָה הִיא מְתוּקֶּנֶת. בְּרַם הָכָא שֶׁמָּא תִּימָּצֵא טְהוֹרָה וְיִתְגָּרוּ בָהּ פִּירְחֵי כְהוּנָה. מִחְלְפָה שִׁיטָתְהוֹן דְּרַבָּנָן. תַּמָּן אִינּוּן אָמְרִין. הָאִישׁ נִסְקַל עָרוֹם וְאֵין הָאִשָּׁה נִסְקֶלֶת עֲרוּמָה. וְהָכָא אִינּוּן אָמְרִין הָכֵין. תַּמָּן וְאָהַבְתָּ לְרֵעֲךָ כָּמוֹךָ. יָבוֹר לוֹ מִיתָה קַלָּה שֶׁבְּקַלּוֹת. בְּרַם הָכָא וְנִיוָּסְרוּ כָּל־הַנָּשִׁים וְלֹא תַעֲשֶׂינָה כְּזִימַּתְכֵינָה.

226The argument of Rebbi Jehudah seems inverted. There227, he says: "One covers a man in front and a woman front and back.228" And here, he says so? There, she goes to her death anyhow, but here, maybe she will be found to be pure and the young priests would attack her229. The argument of the rabbis seems inverted. There230, they say: "A man is stoned naked but no woman is stoned naked." And here, they say so? There, "you shall love your neighbor as yourself," choose for him the easiest death231. But here, 232"all women should be taught and not do as your whoring."

226 A parallel in Sanhedrin 6:8 (fol. 23c, line 17). Similar arguments in the Babli, 8a, *Sanhedrin* 45a.

227 Mishnah *Sanhedrin* 6:5, speaking about people executed by stoning. According to R. Jehudah, they are

clothed in rectangular sheets of cloth.

228   But the majority holds that a woman is stoned only fully clothed. Therefore, R. Jehudah seems unconcerned that men should get bad ideas in seeing her.

229   This is an explicit statement of R. Jehudah 1:7.

230   Mishnah *Sanhedrin* 6:5, *Soṭa* 3:9.

231   Since in rabbinic tradition a person is "stoned" by being pushed down from a high cliff (Mishnah *Sanhedrin* 6:6), his chances of being killed instantly are greater if his fall is not cushioned by clothing. In the Babli, this is not considered a complete answer; the question is whether shame or suffering is worse.

232   Ez. 23:48.

(fol. 16a) **משנה ו:** הָיְתָה מְכוּסָה בִלְבָנִים מְכַסָּהּ בִּשְׁחוֹרִים. הָיוּ עָלֶיהָ כְּלֵי זָהָב וְקַטְלָיוֹת נְזָמִים וְטַבָּעוֹת מַעֲבִירָם מִמֶּנָּה כְּדֵי לְנַוְּלָהּ וְאַחַר כָּךְ מֵבִיא חֶבֶל מִצְרִי וְקוֹשְׁרוּ מִמַּעֲלָה מִדַּדֶּיהָ וְכָל־הָרוֹצֶה לִרְאוֹת בָּא וְרוֹאֶה חוּץ מֵעֲבָדֶיהָ וְשִׁפְחוֹתֶיהָ מִפְּנֵי שֶׁלִּיבָּהּ גַּס בָּהֶן. וְכָל־הַנָּשִׁים מוּתָּרוֹת לִרְאוֹתָהּ שֶׁנֶּאֱמַר וְנִוַּסְּרוּ כָּל־הַנָּשִׁים וְלֹא תַעֲשֶׂינָה כְּזִמַּתְכֵינָה.

Mishnah 6: If she was clothed in white, he[233] covers her in black. If she wore gold jewelry, chains[234], nose rings and finger rings, he removes them from her in order to make her ugly. After that[235] he brings an Egypt rope and binds it higher than her breasts. Anyone who wants to look may come and see, except for her male and female slaves because she feels superior to them. All women are permitted to see her[236], as it was said: "[232]"all women should be taught and not do as your whoring."

233   The presiding Cohen.

234   Semitic plural of Latin *catella*.

235   Obviously not after he removed her rings but immediately after he tore her garment (Mishnah 5).

236   The Babli, 8b, changes that into

an obligation of all women present in the Temple area to come and see. This is unknown to the Yerushalmi.

(fol. 17a) **הלכה ו**: הָיְתָה מְכוּסָה בִלְבָנִים וכו'. מַתְנִיתִין בְּשֶׁאֵינָן נָאִין לָהּ. אֲבָל אִם הָיוּ נָאִין לָהּ לֹא בְדָא.

Halakhah 6: "If she was clothed in white," etc. Our Mishnah [assumes that] they are not fitting her. But if they are fitting her, it does not apply[237].

237 If the woman looks better in black than in white clothes, one leaves her in her white ones. The Babli, 8b, in this case requires that she be given a bad looking garment.

(17a, line 24) מֵבִיא חֶבֶל מִצְרִי. וְלָמָּה חֶבֶל מִצְרִי. אָמַר רִבִּי יִצְחָק. לְפִי שֶׁעָשְׂתָה כְּמַעֲשֵׂה מִצְרַיִם. רִבִּי יִרְמְיָה בָּעֵי. חֶבֶל הַמִּצְרִי מְעַכֵּב. כְּפִיפָה מִצְרִית מְעַכֶּבֶת. מִשֶּׁל מִי הֵן בָּאִין. יָבֹא כַיי דָּמַר רִבִּי. דְּרִבִּי אָמַר. אֲמַת הַמַּיִם וְחוֹמַת הָעִיר וּמִגְדְּלוֹתֶיהָ וְכָל־צוֹרְכֵי הָעִיר בָּאִין מִשְּׁיָרֵי הַלִּשְׁכָּה. וְהָכָא כֵן.

"He brings an Egyptian rope." And why an Egyptian rope? Rebbi Isaac said, because she behaved in an Egyptian way[238]. Rebbi Jeremiah asked: Does the Egyptian rope prevent, does the Egyptian basket prevent[239]? Who pays for them? That one follows what Rebbi said, for Rebbi said[240] that the water supply[241], the city wall and its towers[242], and all public works in the city[243] are paid with the excess of the Temple treasury[244]. The same holds here.

238 The chapter on the incest prohibitions, *Lev.* 18, starts out: "You should not act in the way of the Land of Egypt". Therefore, all infractions of the rules of sexual purity are called "Egyptian ways" even though the prohibition of adultery belongs to the "natural law" obligatory for all of

mankind, even though the latter is formulated as a positive commandment (*Gen.* 2:24): "Therefore, a man has to abandon his father and his mother (prohibition of incest in direct line) and cling to his wife (but not to another man's wife nor to a male)."

239 If her garment was not fastened by a rope or if her flour-offering was not presented in a basket woven from palm leaves, is the ceremony invalid? Since neither of these details is mentioned in the verse, it should be obvious that the answer is no. In the Babli, 8b, this is the explicit deduction, based on the Mishnah, ascribed to Rav Huna, two generations before R. Jeremiah.

240 Mishnah *Šeqalim* 4:2.

241 The open water canal which crosses the Temple yard from North to South.

242 The part bordering on the Temple Mount.

243 On the Temple Mount and its surroundings; e. g., the public *miqwaot*.

244 Any money left on the first of Nisan from the Temple Tax (half a sheqel) of the previous year could no longer be used for the service of the next year. Since it was sanctified public money, it could only be used for the needs of the Temple district other than sacrifices.

(fol. 16a) **משנה ז**: בְּמִידָּה שֶׁאָדָם מוֹדֵד בָּהּ מוֹדְדִין לוֹ הִיא קִישְּׁטָה אֶת עַצְמָהּ לָעֲבֵירָה וְהַמָּקוֹם נִיוְולָהּ. הִיא גִילְּתָהּ אֶת עַצְמָהּ לָעֲבֵירָה הַמָּקוֹם גִּילָה עָלֶיהָ. הַיָּרֵךְ הִתְחִילָה בָּעֲבֵירָה תְּחִילָּה וְאַחַר כָּךְ הַבֶּטֶן לְפִיכָךְ תִּלְקֶה הַיָּרֵךְ תְּחִילָה וְאַחַר כָּךְ הַבֶּטֶן. וּשְׁאָר הַגּוּף לֹא פָלֵט.

Mishnah 7: By the measure a person measures one measures him. She adorned herself for sin, therefore the Omnipresent[241] made her ugly. She bared herself for sin, therefore the Omnipresent laid her bare. The genitals were first in sin and after that the belly; the genitals should be punished first and then the belly[246], while the remainder of the body does not escape[247].

245 For הַמָּקוֹם as a name of God, cf. H. Guggenheimer, *The Scholar's Haggadah*, Northvale NJ 1995, pp. 206, 268-269.

246 Num. 5:21: "When the Eternal will make your genitals shrink and your belly extend." (In the event, v. 27, the order is reversed.) J. C. Brichto (*loc. cit.* Note 225) identifies the symptoms as pseudocyesis, spurious pregnancy.

247 Rabbinic tradition (Mishnah 3:4/5) holds that the guilty woman dies from the draught. This is not in the Biblical text.

הלכה ז: בְּמִידָּה שֶׁאָדָם מוֹדֵד בָּהּ מוֹדְדִין לוֹ כול'. תַּנֵּי בְשֵׁם רִבִּי (fol. 17a) מֵאִיר. בְּמִידָּה שֶׁאָדָם מוֹדֵד בָּהּ מוֹדְדִין לוֹ. מַאי טַעֲמָא. בְּסַאסְּאָה. בְּסָאָה סָאָה. אֵין לִי אֶלָּא סָאָה. מְנַיִין לְרַבּוֹת תֶּרְקָב וַחֲצִי תֶּרְקָב וַחֲצִי קַב וְרוֹבַע וְתוֹמָן וַחֲצִי תוֹמָן וְאוּכְלָא. תַּלְמוּד לוֹמַר כִּי כָל־סְאוֹן סוֹאֵן בְּרַעַשׁ. רִיבָּה כָאן סְאוֹת הַרְבֵּה. אֵין לִי אֶלָּא דָבָר שֶׁהוּא שֶׁלְּמִידָּה. מְנַיִן לִפְרוּטוֹת קְטַנּוֹת שֶׁהֵן מִצְטָרְפוֹת לְחֶשְׁבּוֹן מְרוּבֶּה. תַּלְמוּד לוֹמַר אַחַת לְאַחַת לִמְצוֹא חֶשְׁבּוֹן. בְּנוֹהַג שֶׁבָּעוֹלָם אָדָם נִכְשַׁל בַּעֲבֵירָה שֶׁחַייָבִין עָלָיו מִיתָה בִּידֵי שָׁמַיִם. מֵת שׁוֹרוֹ אָבְדָה תַרְנְגוֹלָתוֹ נִשְׁבְּרָה צְלוֹחִיתוֹ נִכְשַׁל בְּעֶצְבָּעוֹ. וְהַחֶשְׁבּוֹן מִתְמַצֶּה. דָּבָר אַחֵר. אַחַת מִתְאָרְעָה לְאַחַת וְהַחֶשְׁבּוֹן מִתְמַצֶּה. וְכַמָּה הוּא מִיצוּי חֶשְׁבּוֹן. עַד אַחַת.

Halakhah 7: "By the measure a person measures one measures him," etc. [248]It was stated in the name of Rebbi Meïr: By the measure a person measures one measures him[249]. What is the reason? בְּסַאסְּאָה[250], *seah* for *seah*. Not only a *seah*, from where a three-*qab*[251], half a three-*qab*, half a *qab*, a quarter [*qab*], a *toman*[252], half a *toman*, or an *ukla*[253]? The verse says, "for all that is in a *seah*, breaks the *seah* noisily[254];" he added many *seot* here. Not only things that can be measured, from where that small coins add up to a large bill? The verse says, "one to one, to find the bill.[255]" It happens in the world that a person stumbles in a sin for which one would be punished by death by the hands of Heaven. His ox dies, his hen is lost, his flask breaks, and he hurts his finger, by that the bill is paid in full. Another explanation: One is filled into the next and the bill is established. And what is the fulfillment of the bill? Once[256].

248 Tosephta 3:1, Babli 8b. *Midrash Tehillim* 81(2), *Num. rabba* 9(23).

249 The maxim "measure for measure" is found many times; e. g. Babli *Šabbat* 105b, *Megillah* 12b, *Sanhedrin* 90a, *Sifry Num.* 106 (cf. Halakhah 9), *Mekhilta dR. Ismael* (ed. Horovitz-Rabin) pp. 78,81,131; *Gen. rabba* 9(13), *Ex. rabba* 25(13) [shortened 9(9)]; *Tanḥuma Noaḥ* 13, *Wa'era* 14, *Bešallaḥ* 2,4, *Tazria'* 6; and very frequently in the Gaonic literature.

250 *Is.* 27:8.

251 A *seah* is a Roman *urna*, 12.85 l. The *seah* contains 6 *qab* (κάβος); a *terqab* is half a *seah* (Gaonic Commentary to Mishnah *Kelim* 12:3;

misinterpreted as תְּרִיקַב "two *qab*" in Graetz, *Geschichte der Judäer*[4] vol. 3, p. 443.)

252 A *toman* is $1/_8$ *qab*, identical to a Roman *hemina*, Greek ἡμίνα, $1/_2$ *sextarius*.

253 In the Babli עוכלא, a quarter *toman*, a Roman *acetabulum*, 6.6 cl. Qalir (*Silluq Šabbat Šeqalim*) calls it כלה and reports that it is slightly less than a hundredth of a *seah*.

254 *Is.* 9:4.

255 *Eccl.* 7:27. This is the end of the Tosephta and the parallel in the Babli.

256 This explanation is the opposite of the first, that many small sins add up to one huge bill presented to a man by the Heavenly court.

(17a, line 39) תַּנֵּי בְשֵׁם רִבִּי מֵאִיר. כְּשֵׁם שֶׁיֵּשׁ דֵּיעוֹת בְּמַאֲכָל וּבְמִשְׁתֶּה כֵּן יֵשׁ דֵּיעוֹת בָּאֲנָשִׁים. יֵשׁ לְךָ אָדָם זְבוּב נוֹפֵל לְתוֹךְ כּוֹסוֹ וְהוּא נוֹטְלוֹ וְזוֹרְקוֹ וְשׁוֹתֵהוּ. זֶה כִּשְׁאָר כָּל־הָאָדָם שֶׁהוּא רוֹאֶה אֶת אִשְׁתּוֹ מְדַבֶּרֶת עִם שְׁכֵינֶיהָ וְעִם קְרוֹבֶיהָ. אוֹ יֵשׁ לְךָ אָדָם שֶׁפּוֹרֵחַ זְבוּב עַל גַּבֵּי כוֹסוֹ וְהוּא נוֹטְלוֹ וְשׁוֹפְכוֹ וְאֵינוֹ טוֹעֲמוֹ. זֶה הוּא חֵלֶק רַע בָּאֲנָשִׁים שֶׁנָּתַן עֵינָו בָּהּ לְגָרְשָׁהּ. וְיֵשׁ לְךָ אָדָם זְבוּב שׁוֹכֵן עַל כּוֹסוֹ וְהוּא נוֹטְלוֹ וּמֵנִיחוֹ כְּמוֹת שֶׁהוּא. זֶה פַּפּוֹס בֶּן יְהוּדָה שֶׁנָּעַל אֶת הַדֶּלֶת בִּפְנֵי אִשְׁתּוֹ. אָמְרִין לֵיהּ. נְהִיגִין הֲווֹן אַבְהָתָךְ כֵּן. יֵשׁ לְךָ אָדָם מֵת לְתוֹךְ כּוֹסוֹ

וְהוּא נוֹטְלוֹ וּמוֹצְצוֹ וְשׁוֹתֵיהוּ. זֶה הָרָשָׁע שֶׁהוּא רוֹאֶה אֶת אִשְׁתּוֹ לִבָּהּ גַּס בַּעֲבָדֶיהָ לִבָּהּ גַּס בְּשִׁפְחוֹתֶיהָ וְהוּא מְצֻוֶּה עָלֶיהָ לְגָרְשָׁהּ. שֶׁנֶּאֱמַר וְיָצְאָה מִבֵּיתוֹ וְהָלְכָה וְהָיְתָה לְאִישׁ אַחֵר. הַכָּתוּב קְרָאוֹ אַחֵר שֶׁאֵינוֹ בֶן זוּג שֶׁלָּרִאשׁוֹן. שֶׁהוּא הוֹצִיא אֶת אִשְׁתּוֹ מִשּׁוּם עֶרְוָה וַהֲלָהּ נִכְשַׁל בָּהּ. אִם זָכָה הוּא לַשָּׁמַיִם הֲרֵי הוּא מְגָרְשָׁהּ. וְאִם לָאו סוֹף שֶׁהִיא קוֹבַרְתּוֹ. שֶׁנֶּאֱמַר אוֹ כִי יָמוּת הָאִישׁ הָאַחֲרוֹן. רָאוּי הָיָה זֶה לְמִיתָה שֶׁהָאִשָּׁה הַזֹּאת הִכְנִיס לְתוֹךְ בֵּיתוֹ.

[257]It was stated in the name of Rebbi Meïr: Just as there are opinions in eating and drinking, so opinions are [varied] among men. There is a man, if a fly falls into his cup, he takes it out, throws it away and drinks. That is like a normal man who sees his wife talking to her neighbors and relatives[258]. Or you have a man who if a fly flies over his cup, takes it, pours [the contents] out, and does not taste them. That is a bad human attitude because he thinks of divorcing her[259]. Or you have a man who, if a fly sits on his cup, takes it and leaves [the cup] untouched. That is Pappos ben Jehudah who locked his wife in. They said to him, did your forefathers behave like this[260]? Or you have a man who finds a dead fly in his cup, takes it, licks it, and drinks. That is the wicked one who sees that his wife is overbearing with her slaves and slave-girls[261], where he would be commanded to divorce her[262], as it is said: "She left his house and went and married another man." The verse called him *other* because he is not of the class of the first who expelled his wife because of a sexual transgression and the other one stumbled over her[263]. If Heaven gives him credit, he will divorce her; otherwise, at the end she will bury him as it is said, "or if the latter man dies." That man deserves to die since he brought that woman into his house.

257 Parallels in Babli *Giṭṭin* 90a/b; Tosephta 5:9, *Num. rabba* 9(8).

258 Males. (In one version of the Tosephta, קְרוֹבוֹתֶיהָ "female relatives" but S. Lieberman comments on it as קְרוֹבֶיהָ without remark.) It may be that this refers to the case where the wife talks overly long to her male neighbors.

259 Just as the fly did not touch the cup, the wife did nothing wrong; the husband simply looks for an excuse to divorce her without paying.

260 This Aramaic sentence is a commentary of the Talmud; it is not in the other sources.

261 This argument (not found in the Babli, but found in Tosephta and Midrash) seems to contradict the statement of Mishnah 6 that every woman is supposed to feel superior to her slaves. The meaning here seems to be that she has no inhibitions to appear in undress before her slaves.

262 The other sources have a long list of indecent behavior of the wife that should force the husband to divorce her; cf. Mishnah *Ketubot* 7:6.

263 In the Babli, 6a, this interpretation is part of the legal argument that a woman formally accused by her husband cannot be married in levirate after the husband's death.

(17a, line 54) שְׁמוּאֵל אָמַר. פּוֹרְשִׁים מִן הַמְזַנָּה וְאֵין פּוֹרְשִׁין מִבֵּיתָהּ. וְאָתְיָיא כָּיי דָּמַר רִבִּי יוֹחָנָן. אֵשֶׁת אִישׁ שֶׁזִּינְתָהּ הַוְולָדוֹת לַבַּעַל. מִפְּנֵי שֶׁרוֹב בְּעִילוֹת מִן הַבַּעַל.

Samuel[264] said, one separates from the whoring woman but not from her house. This parallels what Rebbi Joḥanan said: [265]"If a married woman committed adultery, her children are her husband's since most of the intercourse was with the husband."

264 In the Babli, 27a, Samuel is reported saying that it is better to marry a woman of questionable character born of a woman of good character than to marry the daughter of a possible adulteress. The opinion attributed to Samuel here is that of R. Joḥanan in the Babli.

265 Tosephta *Yebamot* 12:8, quoted as tannaïtic text in the Babli, 27a.

HALAKHAH 7

(17a, line 56) כָּתוּב אֶחָד אוֹמֵר לַצְבּוֹת בֶּטֶן וְלַנְפִּיל יָרֵךְ. וְכָתוּב אֶחָד אוֹמֵר. וְצָבְתָה בִטְנָהּ וְנָפְלָה יְרֵיכָהּ. וְכָתוּב אֶחָד אוֹמֵר. בְּתֵת ייִ אֶת יְרֵכֵךְ נוֹפֶלֶת וְאֶת בִּטְנֵךְ צָבָה. מִקְרָא אֶחָד מַכְרִיעַ שְׁנֵי מִקְרָאוֹת. אָמַר רִבִּי מָנָא. כָּאן לְמַעֲשֶׂה וְכָאן לִתְנַייָן. אָמַר רִבִּי אָבִין. וַאֲפִילוּ תֵּימַר. כָּאן וְכָאן לְמַעֲשֶׂה כָּאן וְכָאן לִתְנָאִין. לַצְבּוֹת בֶּטֶן וְלַנְפִּיל יָרֵךְ. לַבּוֹעֵל. וְצָבְתָה בִטְנָהּ וְנָפְלָה יְרֵיכָהּ. לָאִשָּׁה. הַדַּעַת מַכְרַעַת. יָרֵךְ הִתְחִילָה בָּעֲבֵירָה תְּחִילָה וְאַחַר כָּךְ הַבֶּטֶן. לְפִיכָךְ תִּלְקֶה הַיָּרֵךְ תְּחִילָה וְאַחַר כָּךְ הַבֶּטֶן. וּשְׁאָר הַגּוּף לֹא פָלַט. רִבִּי אָבָּא בְּרֵיהּ דְּרִבִּי פַּפֵּי עָבַד לָהּ אַפְטָרָה. מָה אִם מִידַּת הַפּוֹרְעָנוּת מְעוּטָה אֵבֶר אֶחָד לוֹקֶה וּשְׁאָר כָּל־הָאֵבָרִים מַרְגִּישִׁין. מִידַּת הַטּוֹבָה הַמְרוּבָּה עַל אַחַת כַּמָּה וְכַמָּה.

One verse says: "For swelling of the belly and shrinking of the genitals," another verse says "her belly will swell and her genitals shrink", and another verse says "when the Eternal will make your genitals shrink and your belly swell."[266] Does one verse weigh more than two verses? Rebbi Mana said, here for the act, there conditional[267]. Rebbi Abin said, you may even say in both cases for the act, in both cases as a condition. "For swelling of the belly and shrinking of the genitals" for the adulterer[268]. "Her belly will swell and her genitals shrink", for the woman. Reason decides, "the genitals were first in sin and after that the belly; the genitals should be punished first and then the belly, while the remainder of the body does not escape." Rebbi Abba the son of Rebbi Pappeus used this as conclusion of a sermon: Since for [heavenly] punishment, which is meted out sparingly, one limb is smitten and all limbs hurt, in the case of [heavenly] benefices, which are given out in abundance[269], [may we] not [expect] so much more!

266 In *Num.* 5:22,27, the belly is mentioned before the genitals but in v. 21 the order is inverted.

267 *Num.* 5:22,27 is a description of

what will or did happen; v. 21 is a curse formula conditional upon the woman having sinned.

268 The infinitives in the sentence are gender neutral. The ordeal indirectly also affects the presumed adulterer, Mishnah 6:1. In the Babli, 27a, this is a conclusion of Rebbi.

269 Babli 11a; extensive discussion in *Tosephta* 4:1.

(fol. 16b) **משנה ח:** שִׁמְשׁוֹן הָלַךְ אַחַר עֵינָיו לְפִיכָךְ נִיקְרוּ פְלִשְׁתִּים אֶת עֵינָיו. אַבְשָׁלוֹם נִתְגַּוָּה בִשְׂעָרוֹ לְפִיכָךְ נִתְלָה בִשְׂעָרוֹ. לְפִי שֶׁבָּא עַל עֶשֶׂר פִּילַגְשֵׁי אָבִיו לְפִיכָךְ נִיתְּנוּ בוֹ עֶשֶׂר לוֹנְכִיּוֹת שֶׁנֶּאֱמַר וַיָּסוֹבּוּ עֲשָׂרָה נְעָרִים נוֹשְׂאֵי כְלֵי יוֹאָב. וּלְפִי שֶׁגָּנַב שָׁלֹשׁ גְּנֵיבוֹת לֵב אָבִיו וְלֵב בֵּית דִּין וְלֵב יִשְׂרָאֵל לְפִיכָךְ נִתְקְעוּ בוֹ שְׁלֹשָׁה שְׁבָטִים שֶׁנֶּאֱמַר וַיִּקַּח שְׁלֹשָׁה שְׁבָטִים בְּכַפּוֹ וַיִּתְקָעֵם בְּלֵב אַבְשָׁלוֹם.

Mishnah 8: [270]Simson followed his eyes, therefore the Philistines pierced his eyes. Absalom beautified himself with his hair, therefore he was hung by his hair. Because he came to his father's ten concubines, therefore ten lances[271] were put into him, as it was said[272]: "Ten squires, Joab's weapons carriers, surrounded him." And because he stole three steals[273], his father's opinion, the court's opinion, and Israel's opinion, therefore three staves were stuck into him, as it was said[274]: "He took three staves in his hand and stuck them into Absalom's heart."

270 This Mishnah is somewhat extended in the Babli, very much enlarged in Tosephta 3:15-16. It is a direct continuation of the first sentence of the preceding Mishnah.

271 Hebraized plural of Greek λόγχη "lance".

272 2S. 18:15.

273 In Mishnah mss. of the Maimonides tradition: שֶׁגָּנַב שְׁלֹשָׁה לְבָבוֹת "he stole three minds"; "misleading" is called "stealing the heart" (*Gen.* 31:20). Cf. also *Mekhilta dR. Ismael, Masekhta deŠirah*, Chap. 6.

274 2S. 18:14.

HALAKHAH 8

הלכה ח: שִׁמְשׁוֹן הָלַךְ אַחַר עֵינָיו כול'. תַּנֵּי. רִבִּי אוֹמֵר. לְפִי שֶׁתְּחִילַת קַלְקָלָתוֹ בְּעַזָּה לְפִיכָךְ עוֹנְשׁוֹ בְּעַזָּה. וְהָכְתִיב וַיֵּרֶד שִׁמְשׁוֹן תִּמְנָתָה. אָמַר רִבִּי שְׁמוּאֵל בַּר נַחְמָן. דֶּרֶךְ נִישּׂוּאִין הָיוּ. (fol. 17a)

Halakhah 8: "Simson followed his eyes," etc. [275]It was stated: Rebbi says, because he started going astray at Gaza, therefore his punishment was at Gaza. But is it not written: "Simson descended into Timna[276]"? Rebbi Samuel bar Naḥman said, that was a formal marriage[277].

275 Tosephta 3:15, [Num. rabba 9(24)]; anonymous Babli 9b, *Mekhilta dR. Simeon bar Ioḥai* p. 74.

276 Jud. 14:1. Gaza is mentioned only v. 16:1.

277 Marriage is mentioned in Timna, a prostitute in Gaza. It is presumed that the girl from Timna was converted following the rules so that the marriage was not sinful.

כָּתוּב אֶחָד אוֹמֵר וַיֵּרֶד שִׁמְשׁוֹן תִּמְנָתָה. וְכָתוּב אֶחָד אוֹמֵר הִנֵּה חָמִיךְ עוֹלֶה תִמְנָתָה. רַב אָמַר. שְׁתֵּי תִמְנִיּוֹת הָיוּ. אַחַת שֶׁלִּיהוּדָה וְאַחַת שֶׁלְּשִׁמְשׁוֹן. רִבִּי סִימוֹן אָמַר. תִּמְנָתָה אַחַת הִיא. וְלָמָּה כָתַב בָּהּ עֲלִייָה וִירִידָה. אֶלָּא שֶׁל יְהוּדָה עַל יְדֵי שֶׁהָיְתָה לְשׁוּם שָׁמַיִם. לְפִיכָךְ כָּתַב בָּהּ עֲלִייָה. וְשֶׁלְּשִׁמְשׁוֹן עַל יְדֵי שֶׁלֹּא הָיְתָה לְשֵׁם שָׁמַיִם כָּתַב בָּהּ יְרִידָה. אָמַר רִבִּי אַייְבוּ בַּר נַגְּרִי. כְּגוֹן הָדָא בֵית מַעֲיָין שֶׁיּוֹרְדִין בָּהּ מִפְלַטְתָהּ וְעוֹלִין בָּהּ מַטִיבֶּרְיָה. (17a, line 69)

[278]One verse says, "Simson descended into Timna", and another verse says, "behold, you father-in-law ascends to Timna[279]." Rav said, there were two Timnot, one of Jehudah and one of Simson. Rebbi Simon said, there was only one Timna(ta). Why does it mention decent and ascent? But in the case of Jehudah, because it was in the name of Heaven, ascent is written. In the case of Simson, because it was not in the name of Heaven, descent is written. Rebbi Ayvu bar Naggari said, for example

like Bet Ma'on[280] to which one descends from Palatatha and ascends from Tiberias.

278 Babli 10a, with different names. *Num. rabba* 9(24), the Yerushalmi version.

279 *Gen.* 38:13.

280 Reading of *Num. rabba* 9(24).

(17b, line 1) כְּתִיב וַיָּבוֹאוּ עַד כַּרְמֵי תִמְנָתָה. אָמַר רַב שְׁמוּאֵל בַּר רַב יִצְחָק. מְלַמֵּד שֶׁהָיוּ אָבִיו וְאִמּוֹ מַרְאִין לוֹ כַּרְמֵי תִמְנָתָה זְרוּעִים כִּלְאַיִם וְאוֹמְרִים לוֹ. בְּנִי. כְּשֵׁם שֶׁכַּרְמֵיהֶן זְרוּעִין כִּלְאַיִם. כָּךְ בְּנוֹתֵיהֶם זְרוּעוֹת כִּלְאַיִם. וְאָבִיו וְאִמּוֹ לֹא יָדְעוּ כִּי מֵיְיָ הִיא כִּי תֹאֲנָה הוּא מְבַקֵּשׁ מִפְּלִשְׁתִּים. אָמַר רִבִּי לֶעְזָר. בְּשִׁבְעָה מְקוֹמוֹת כְּתִיב לֹא תִתְחַתֵּן בָּם. אָמַר רִבִּי אָבִין. לֶאֱסוֹר שִׁבְעָה עַמָּמִין. וְהָכָא הוּא אָמַר הָכֵין. אָמַר רִבִּי יִצְחָק אִם לַלֵּצִים הוּא יָלִיץ.

[281]It is written: "They came to the vineyards in direction of Timna.[282]" Rav[283] Samuel ben Rav Isaac said, this teaches you that his father and mother were showing him the vineyards in direction of Timna sown in several kinds and saying to him: My son, just as their vineyards are sown with several kinds so their daughters are sown with several kinds[284]. "And his father and mother did not know that this was from the Eternal, that he was looking for a pretext from the Philistines." Rebbi Eleazar said, In seven places it is written: "Do not contract marriage with them.[285]" Rebbi Abun said, to prohibit seven peoples[286]. And here, it says so[287]? Rebbi Isaac said, "if he scoffs about the scoffers.[288]"

281 *Num. rabba* 9(24).
282 *Jud.* 14:5.
283 The title has to be "Rebbi".
284 They are children of adultery. *Jud.* 14:4.

285 That verse is only in *Deut.* 7:3. But the prohibition of Canaanite women is also in *Ex.* 34:16. Outside the Pentateuch, the prohibition is mentioned *Mal.* 2:11, *Ezra* 9:2,12,14;

Neh. 10:31.

286 The seven Canaanite tribes enumerated in *Gen.* 15:20-21. Philistines are not mentioned in that list.

287 It is not obvious what the remark means. According to R. David Fraenckel, since Simson's relations with Philistine women were not forbidden, why was he punished? According to R. Moses Margalit, since all non-Jewish women are forbidden in the interpretation of pentateuchal law in *Mal., Ezra, Neh.,* how can it be said that his first marriage was (*Jud.* 14:4) "from the Eternal"?

288 *Prov.* 3:34. According to R. David Fraenckel, since at least Simson's relations with the Gazean prostitute and Dalilah were illegitimate, he deserved punishment.

(17b, line 7) כְּתִיב וַתָּחֶל רוּחַ יי לְפַעֲמוֹ בְּמַחֲנֵה דָן בֵּין צָרְעָה וּבֵין אֶשְׁתָּאוֹל. תְּרֵין אֲמוֹרִין. חַד אָמַר. בְּשָׁעָה שֶׁהָיְתָה רוּחַ הַקּוֹדֶשׁ שׁוֹרָה עָלָיו הָיוּ פְסִיעוֹתָיו כְּמִצָּרְעָה לְאֶשְׁתָּאוֹל. וְחָרָנָה אָמַר. בְּשָׁעָה שֶׁהָיְתָה רוּחַ הַקּוֹדֶשׁ שׁוֹרָה עָלָיו הָיוּ שַׂעֲרוֹתָיו מַקִּישׁוֹת כְּזוּג וְקוֹלָן הוֹלֵךְ כְּמִצָּרְעָה לְאֶשְׁתָּאוֹל. וַיְבָרְכֵהוּ יי. רַבִּי הוּנָא בְּשֵׁם רַבִּי יוֹסֵי. שֶׁהָיְתָה תַּשְׁמִישׁוֹ שָׁוָה לְכָל־אָדָם. וְאִינְקַמָה נְקַם אַחַת מִשְּׁתֵי עֵינַיי מִפְּלִשְׁתִּים. אָמַר רַבִּי אָחָא. אָמַר לְפָנָיו. רִבּוֹנוֹ שֶׁלְעוֹלָם. תֶּן לִי שְׂכַר עֵינִי אַחַת בָּעוֹלָם הַזֶּה וּשְׂכַר עֵינִי אַחַת מוּתְקֶנֶת לִי לֶעָתִיד לָבוֹא. כָּתוּב אֶחָד אוֹמֵר. וַיִּשְׁפֹּט אֶת יִשְׂרָאֵל אַרְבָּעִים שָׁנָה. וְכָתוּב אֶחָד אוֹמֵר. וְהוּא שָׁפַט אֶת יִשְׂרָאֵל עֶשְׂרִים שָׁנָה. אָמַר רַבִּי אָחָא. מְלַמֵּד שֶׁהָיוּ הַפְּלִשְׁטִים יְרֵאִים מִמֶּנּוּ עֶשְׂרִים שָׁנָה לְאַחַר מוֹתוֹ. כְּדֶרֶךְ שֶׁהָיוּ יְרֵאִים מִמֶּנּוּ עֶשְׂרִים שָׁנָה בְּחַיָּיו.

It is written[289]: "The spirit of the Eternal started to ring in him in the encampment of Dan, between Ṣor'a and Eshtaol." Two Amoraïm. One said, when the holy spirit was resting on him, his steps were as from Ṣor'a to Eshtaol. The other said, when the holy spirit was resting on him, his hairs were tolling like a bell and their sound went as from Ṣor'a to Eshtaol.

"The Eternal blessed him[290]". Rebbi Huna in the name of Rebbi Yose:

That his sex life was that of anybody[291].

"I shall revenge *one* revenge of my two eyes from the Philistines.[292]" Rebbi Aḥa said, he said before Him: Master of the Universe! Give me the reward of one of my eyes in this world and the reward of the other eye be prepared for me in the World to Come.

One verse says[293]: "He judged Israel for forty years." And another verse says[294]: "He had judged Israel for twenty years." Rebbi Aḥa said, this teaches that the Philistines were afraid of him twenty years after his death as they were afraid of him during his lifetime.

289 Jud. 13:25.
290 Jud. 13:24.
291 In the Babli, 10a, that his sex organ was of normal size even though otherwise he was a giant.
292 Jud. 16:28. The statement is also in *Num. rabba* 9(24).
293 This should be *Jud.* 15:20, but, as already Tosaphot (*Šabbat* 55b, *s. v.* מעבירם) noted, all texts and versions have "twenty years". David Qimḥi, following the reading of the parallel in *Num. rabba* 14(21), in his commentary to *Jud.* 16:31, reads "twenty years" in the text here and quotes R. Aḥa as explanation of the duplication of the notices in 15:20, 16:31. While our text here is confirmed by the Rome ms., "40 years", Qimḥi's reading as supported by *Num. rabba* (whose first part probably is Provençal) can be taken as testimony for the Provençal text.
294 *Jud.* 16:31.

(17b, line 19) אַבְשָׁלוֹם נִתְנַוֶּה בִשְׂעָרוֹ. רִבִּי חֲנִינָה אָמַר. בַּחֲרוּבִית גְּדוֹלָה הָיָה. יָכוֹל בְּכִידוֹן. רִבִּי בִּיבִי בְשֵׁם רִבִּי יוֹחָנָן. כְּדֵין כְּדָיוֹן[295] הָיָה עָשׂוּי.

"Absalom beautified himself with his hair." Rebbi Ḥanina said, it[296] was like a large carob tree. Should I think like a javelin[297]? Rebbi Bibi in the name of Rebbi Joḥanan: It was made like this and like that.

295 Most moderns read בַּדִּין בַּדִּין "in batches" with *Midrash Samuel* 13[7],27[5] against the testimony of both mss. and the *editio princeps*; cf. the commentary of R. David Fraenckel.

296 The hair.

297 That he wore a pigtail.

(17b, line 21) אָמַר רִבִּי חֲנִינָה. כַּד סְלָקִת לְהָכָא נְסָבִת אֵיזוֹרֵהּ דִּבְרִי וְאֵיזוֹרָא דְחַמוֹי מִקְפָא כּוֹרְתָא דְחָרוּבִיתָא דְּאַרְעָא דְיִשְׂרָאֵל וְלָא מָטוּן. וּקְצִית חַד חָרוּב וּנְגַד מְלֹא יָדוֹי דְּבַשׁ.

²⁹⁸Rebbi Ḥanina said, when I immigrated here, I took my son's belt and the belt of my father-in-law²⁹⁹ to measure around a young carob tree of the Land of Israel and it was not enough. I cut one carob pod and it filled my hand with honey.

(17b, line 24) אָמַר רִבִּי יוֹחָנָן יָפֶה סִיפְסוּף שֶׁאָכַלְנוּ בְיַלְדוּתֵינוּ מִפְּנְקְרִיסִין שֶׁאָכַלְנוּ בְזִקְנוֹתֵינוּ. דִּי בְיוֹמוֹי אִישְׁתַּנֵּי עָלְמָא.

Rebbi Joḥanan said, the second quality fruit we ate in our youth tasted better than the peaches we ate in our old age, because during his lifetime the world changed.

(17b, line 25)אָמַר רִבִּי חִייָא בַּר בָּא. בְּרֹאשׁוֹנָה הָיְתָה סְאָה אַרְבֵּלִית מוֹצִיאָה סְאָה סוֹלֶת סְאָה קֶמַח סְאָה קֵיבָּר סְאָה סוּבִּין סְאָה מוּרְסָן. וּכְדוֹן אֲפִילּוּ חֲדָא בַחֲדָא לָא קַיְימָא.

Rebbi Ḥiyya bar Abba said, one *seah* of Arbel grain did yield one *seah* of fine flour, one *seah* of white flour, one *seah* of dark flour, one *seah* of bran, one *seah* of coarse bran. But today, we do not even get one for one.

298 The following paragraphs are from *Peah* Chapter 7, Notes 71-75. They are added here only because of the mention of a carob tree. Cf. also Babli *Baba Batra* 91b, *Ketubot* 112a.

299 That is a bad corruption. In the text of *Peah*: חֲמֹרִי "my donkey".

(17b, line 28) כְּתִיב וּכְאַבְשָׁלוֹם לֹא הָיָה אִישׁ יָפֶה בְּכָל־יִשְׂרָאֵל לְהַלֵּל מְאוֹד. יָכוֹל בַּכֹּל. תַּלְמוּד לוֹמַר מִכַּף רַגְלוֹ וְעַד קָדְקֳדוֹ לֹא הָיָה בוֹ מוּם. כְּתִיב וְלוֹ הָיָה בֵן וּשְׁמוֹ שָׁאוּל בָּחוּר וָטוֹב וְאֵין אִישׁ מִבְּנֵי יִשְׂרָאֵל טוֹב מִמֶּנּוּ. יָכוֹל בַּכֹּל. תַּלְמוּד לוֹמַר מִשִּׁכְמוֹ וּלְמַעְלָה גָּבֹהַּ מִכָּל־הָעָם. אֲבָל בְּאַבְנֵר מַהוּ אוֹמֵר. הֲלוֹא תֵדְעוּ כִּי שַׂר וְגָדוֹל נָפַל בַּיּוֹם הַזֶּה מִיִּשְׂרָאֵל. וְאַבְנֵר לָמָּה נֶהֱרָג. רִבִּי יְהוֹשֻׁעַ בֶּן לֵוִי וְרִבִּי שִׁמְעוֹן בֶּן לָקִישׁ וְרַבָּנָן. רִבִּי יְהוֹשֻׁעַ בֶּן לֵוִי אָמַר. עַל יְדֵי שֶׁעָשָׂה דָמָן שֶׁלַּנְּעָרִים שְׂחוֹק. יָקוּמוּ נָא הַנְּעָרִים וִישַׂחֲקוּ לְפָנֵינוּ. רִבִּי שִׁמְעוֹן בֶּן לָקִישׁ אָמַר. עַל יְדֵי שֶׁהִקְדִּים שְׁמוֹ לְמוֹ שֶׁלְּדָוִד. הָדָא הוּא דִכְתִיב וַיִּשְׁלַח אַבְנֵר מַלְאָכִים אֶל דָּוִד תַּחְתָּיו לֵאמוֹר לְמִי אָרֶץ. כָּתַב. מִן אַבְנֵר לְדָוִד. וְרַבָּנָן אֲמְרִין. עַל יְדֵי שֶׁלֹּא הִנִּיחַ לְשָׁאוּל לְהִתְפַּיֵּיס מִדָּוִד. הָדָא הוּא דִכְתִיב וְאָבִי רְאֵה גַּם רְאֵה אֶת כְּנַף מְעִילְךָ בְּיָדִי. אָמַר לֵיהּ. מַה אַתְּ בְּעֵי מִן גַּלְגּוֹי דְהָדֵין. בְּסִירָה הוּעֲרַת. וְכֵיוָן שֶׁבָּאוּ לְמַעֲגָל אָמַר לוֹ. הֲלוֹא תַעֲנֶה אַבְנֵר. גַּבֵּי כְּנָף אָמַרְתָּ בְּסִירָה הֶעֱרַת. חֲנִית וְצַפַּחַת. בְּסִירָה הֶעֱרַת. וְיֵשׁ אוֹמְרִים. עַל יְדֵי שֶׁהָיְתָה סִפֵּק בְּיָדוֹ לִמְחוֹת בְּנוֹב עִיר הַכֹּהֲנִים וְלֹא מִיחָה.

[300]It is written[301]: "No man in Israel was beautiful like Absalom, to be very much praised." I could think, in everything. The verse says, "from his foot sole to the top of his forehead[302]". It is written[303]: "He had a son whose name was Saul, select and good, no one of the Children of Israel was better than he." I could think, in everything. The verse says, "from his shoulder on he was higher than all the people." But about Abner, what is written[304]? "You should know that a leader and great man fell today in Israel." [305]Why was Abner killed? Rebbi Joshua ben Levi, Rebbi Simeon ben Laqish, and the rabbis. Rebbi Joshua ben Levi said, because he made fun of the lives of his squires as it is said (*2Sam.* 2:14): "Let the squires get up and play before us." R. Simeon ben Laqish said, because he prefaced his name before that of David; that is what is written (*2Sam.* 3:12) "Abner

sent messengers to David the underling, saying: Whose is the land?" He wrote: From Abner to David. The rabbis say, because he did not let Shaul make peace with David. That is what is written (*1Sam.* 24:5): "My father, see, but see the corner of your coat in my hand!" He said to him, what do you want from the prattling of this one, it was torn off by thorns. But when they came to the circle, he said to him (*1Sam.* 26:14): "Can you answer, Abner?" About the corner, you said it was torn off by a thorn; were spear and pitcher cut off by a thorn? But some say, because he had it in his power to intervene for Nob, the city of priests, and he did not intervene.

300 Parallels in *Midrash Samuel* 13, 27; *Num. rabba* 9(29); *Tanḥuma Buber Ḥuqqat* 8, *Tanḥuma Ḥuqqat* 4; Babli *Sanhedrin* 49a.

301 2S. 14:25.

302 But his hair was questionable.

303 1S. 9:2.

304 2S. 3:38.

305 To the end of the paragraph, this is from *Peah* 1:1, Notes 176-179. The question asked is, why did Providence let Abner lose his usual caution when dealing with Joab. The presumed argument between Saul and Abner is explained in detail in the commentary by R. Ḥananel (Kairuan, early 11th Cent.) to *Sanhedrin* 49a, quoted in *Arukh* (*s. v.* בור ז) as Yerushalmi text; but clearly it is a paraphrase. (Printed on the margin of the Wilna Babli).

(17b, line 42) וּלְפִי שֶׁגָּנַב שָׁלֹשׁ גְּנֵיבוֹת. לֵב אָבִיו. וְלֵב בֵּית דִּין. וְלֵב אַנְשֵׁי יִשְׂרָאֵל. לֵב אָבִיו. דִּכְתִיב וַיְהִי מִקֵּץ אַרְבָּעִים שָׁנָה. כָּל עַצְמוֹ שֶׁלְדָוִד לֹא מָלַךְ אֶלָּא אַרְבָּעִים. וְכָא הוּא אָמַר הָכֵין. אֶלָּא בְּשָׁעָה שֶׁשָּׁאֲלוּ יִשְׂרָאֵל מֶלֶךְ. כִּי נֶדֶר נָדַר עַבְדֶּיךָ. אָמַר לֵיהּ. וּמַה אַתְּ בָּעֵי כְדוֹן. אָמַר לֵיהּ. כְּתוֹב חַד פִּיתָּק דִּתְרֵין גּוּבְרִין דְּנִסְבִּינוֹן עִמִּי. אָמַר לֵיהּ. אֱמוֹר לִי לְמָאן דְּאַתְּ בָּעֵי וַאֲנָא כָּתוּב. אָמַר לֵיהּ. כְּתוֹב לָהּ סְתָם וַאֲנָא לְמָאן דִּבְעֵי אֲנָא נָסֵב. אֲזַל וּצְמַת לֵיהּ תְּרֵין תְּרֵין

גּוּבְרִין. עַד דְּצָמַת לֵיהּ מָאתָן גּוּבְרִין. הָדָא הוּא דִכְתִיב. וְאֶת אַבְשָׁלוֹם הָלְכוּ מָאתַיִם אִישׁ מִירוּשָׁלַם קְרוּאִים וְהוֹלְכִים לְתוּמָּם. קְרוּאִים מִדָּוִד. וְהוֹלְכִים לְתוּמָּם. מֵאַבְשָׁלוֹם. וְלֹא יָדְעוּ כָּל־דָּבָר. מֵעֲצַת אֲחִיתוֹפֶל. רִבִּי הוּנָא בְּשֵׁם רִבִּי אָחָא. וְכוֹלְהוּ רָאשֵׁי סַנְהֶדְרִיּוֹת הָיוּ. וְכֵיוָן דְּחָמוֹן מִילַּיָּיא אָתְיָין לִידֵי חִילּוּפִין. אָמְרִין. רִבּוֹן כָּל־הָעוֹלָמִים. נִפְּלָה נָא בְיַד דָּוִד וְאַל יִפּוֹל דָּוִד בְּיָדֵינוּ. שֶׁאִם אָנוּ נוֹפְלִין בְּיַד דָּוִד הֲרֵי הוּא מְרַחֵם עָלֵינוּ. וְאִם חַס וְשָׁלוֹם יִפּוֹל דָּוִד בְּיָדֵינוּ אֵין אָנוּ מְרַחֲמִים עָלָיו. הוּא שֶׁדָּוִד אָמַר. פְּדֵה בְשָׁלוֹם נַפְשִׁי מִקְּרָב לִי כִּי בְרַבִּים הָיוּ עִמָּדִי. וְלֵב בֵּית דִּין. וַיֹּאמֶר אַבְשָׁלוֹם מִי יְשִׂימֵנִי שׁוֹפֵט הָאָרֶץ וגו'. וַיַּעַשׂ אַבְשָׁלוֹם כַּדָּבָר הַזֶּה. וְלֵב אַנְשֵׁי יִשְׂרָאֵל. וַיְנַגֵּב אַבְשָׁלוֹם אֶת לֵב אַנְשֵׁי יִשְׂרָאֵל.

[306]"And because he stole three steals, his father's opinion, the court's opinion, and Israel's opinion." His father's opinion, as it is written[307]: "It was after forty years." David himself did not rule more than forty years, and here, it says so? But it is from the time that Israel demanded a king[308]. "For your servant made a vow[309]." He said to him, what else do you want? He said to him, write me a tablet that two men should go with me. He said to him, tell me whom you want and I shall write. He said to him, write it to open and I shall take whom I want. He wrote it open. He went and added two people each until he had added 200 people. That is what is written[310], "with Absalom went 200 invited people from Jerusalem, going in their simplicity." Invited, from David. Going in their simplicity, of Absalom. "They did not know anything," of Aḥitophel's counsel. Rebbi Huna in the name of Rebbi Aḥa: They all were presiding judges. Then they saw the things. They went to change sides. They said: Master of all universes: Let us fall in David's hand and do not let fall David in our hands! For if we fall in David's hand, he will have mercy on us. But if, Heaven forbid, David would fall in our hands, we would not

have mercy on him. That is what David said[311], "He saved me in peace from my confidant, for the majority were with me!"

"The court's opinion". "And Absalom said, who would make me the judge of the land.[312]" "So Absalom would act.[313]"

"And Israel's opinion." Absalom insinuated himself with the men of Israel.[313]"

306 The text is copied in *Num. rabba* 9(29).
307 2S. 15:7.
308 Babli *Temurah* 14b; ascribed to R. Joshua. The source is *Seder 'Olam* Chapter 14; cf. the extensive commentary in the author's edition (Northvale NJ, 1998), p. 139.
309 2S. 15:8.
310 2S. 15:11.
311 Ps. 55:19; cf. *Midrash Tehillim* 55[4].
312 2S. 15:4.
313 2S. 15:6.

(fol. 16b) משנה ט: וְכֵן לְעִנְיַן הַטּוֹבָה מִרְיָם הִמְתִּינָה לְמֹשֶׁה שָׁעָה אַחַת שֶׁנֶּאֱמַר וַתֵּתַצַּב אֲחוֹתוֹ מֵרָחוֹק. לְפִיכָךְ נִתְעַכְּבוּ לָהּ כָּל־יִשְׂרָאֵל שִׁבְעָה יָמִים בַּמִּדְבָּר שֶׁנֶּאֱמַר וְהָעָם לֹא נָסַע עַד הֵאָסֵף מִרְיָם.

Mishnah 9: [314]Similarly, for good deeds. Miriam waited for Moses one hour as it is said[315]: "His sister stood by from afar." Therefore, all of Israel stayed put for her for seven days in the prairie as it is said[316]: "The people did not travel until Miriam was taken in."

314 This Mishnah and the next are reproduced and extended in Tosephta Chap. 4, *Mekhilta* בשלח פתיחתא
315 *Ex.* 2:4.
316 *Num.* 12:15.

הלכה ט: וְכֵן לְעִנְיַן הַטּוֹבָה. מִרְיָם הִמְתִּינָה לְמֹשֶׁה שָׁעָה אַחַת. (17b, line 59)
שֶׁנֶּאֱמַר וַתֵּתַצַּב אֲחוֹתוֹ מֵרָחוֹק וגו'. לְפִיכָךְ נִתְעַכְּבוּ לָהּ יִשְׂרָאֵל שִׁבְעַת יָמִים
בַּמִּדְבָּר. שֶׁנֶּאֱמַר. וְהָעָם לֹא נָסַע עַד הֵאָסֵף מִרְיָם. אָמַר רִבִּי יוֹחָנָן. פָּסוּק זֶה
בְּרוּחַ הַקּוֹדֶשׁ נֶאֱמַר. וַתֵּתַצַּב אֲחוֹתוֹ. רָאִיתִי אֶת יי נִצָּב עַל הַמִּזְבֵּחַ. אֲחוֹתוֹ.
אֱמוֹר לַחָכְמָה אֲחוֹתִי אָתְּ. מֵרָחוֹק. מֵרָחוֹק יי נִרְאָה לִי. לְדֵעָה. כִּי מָלְאָה
הָאָרֶץ דֵּעָה אֶת יי. מַה יֵּעָשֶׂה לוֹ. כִּי לֹא יַעֲשֶׂה יי אֱלֹהִים דָּבָר כִּי אִם גָּלָה
סוֹדוֹ אֶל עֲבָדָיו הַנְּבִיאִים.

Halakhah 9: "Similarly, for good deeds. Miriam waited for Moses one hour as it is said[315]: 'His sister stood by from afar' etc. Therefore, [317]Israel stayed put for her for seven days in the prairie as it is said[316]: 'The people did not travel until Miriam was taken in.'" [318]Rebbi Johanan said, the entire verse was said in the language of inspiration: "His sister *stood by*," "I saw the Eternal *standing* on the altar.[319]" "His *sister*," "say to wisdom: you are my *sister*.[320]" "*From far*", "*from far* away the Eternal appeared to me[321]." "To *know*", "for the earth will be full of the Eternal's *knowledge*.[322]" "What will be *done* with him", "because the Eternal will not *do* anything unless He uncovered His counsel to His servants, the prophets.[323]"

317 This version corresponds to the Mishnah in the Babli.
318 *Ex. rabba* 1:26. A similar homily is in the Babli, 11a.
319 *Am.* 9:1.
320 *Prov.* 7:4.
321 *Jer.* 31:2.
322 *Is.* 11:9.
323 *Am.* 3:7.

(fol. 16b) **משנה י**: יוֹסֵף זָכָה לִקְבּוֹר אֶת אָבִיו וְאֵין בְּאֶחָיו גָּדוֹל מִמֶּנּוּ שֶׁנֶּאֱמַר וַיַּעַל יוֹסֵף לִקְבֹּר אֶת אָבִיו. מִי לָנוּ גָדוֹל מִיּוֹסֵף שֶׁלֹּא נִתְעַסֵּק בּוֹ אֶלָּא מֹשֶׁה. מֹשֶׁה זָכָה בְעַצְמוֹת יוֹסֵף וְאֵין בְּיִשְׂרָאֵל גָּדוֹל מִמֶּנּוּ שֶׁנֶּאֱמַר וַיִּקַּח מֹשֶׁה אֶת עַצְמוֹת יוֹסֵף עִמּוֹ. מִי גָדוֹל מִמֹּשֶׁה שֶׁלֹּא נִתְעַסֵּק בּוֹ אֶלָּא הַקָּדוֹשׁ בָּרוּךְ הוּא שֶׁנֶּאֱמַר וַיִּקְבֹּר אוֹתוֹ בַגָּיְא. וְלֹא עַל מֹשֶׁה בִּלְבַד אָמְרוּ אֶלָּא עַל כָּל־הַצַּדִּיקִים שֶׁנֶּאֱמַר וְהָלַךְ לְפָנֶיךָ צִדְקֶךָ כְּבוֹד לִי יַאַסְפֶךָ.

Mishnah 10: Joseph had the merit to bury his father and none of his brothers was greater than he, as it is said: "Joseph ascended to bury his father.[324]" Who would be greater than Joseph? Only Moses could occupy himself with him. Moses had the merit to take Joseph's bones and no one in Israel was greater than he, as it is said: "Moses took Joseph's bones with him.[325]" Who would be greater than Moses? Only the Holy One, Praise to Him, could occupy himself with him, as it is said: "He buried him in the valley[326]." Not only about Moses was this said but about all the just, as it is said: "Your righteousness will precede you, the glory of the Eternal will gather you in.[327]"

324 *Gen.* 50:7.
325 *Ex.* 13:19.
326 *Deut.* 34:6. Another tradition, *Sifry Num.* 32, in the name of R. Ismael counts this verse as one of the three instances where אותו does not mean "him" but "himself".
327 *Is.* 58:8.

(17b, line 67) **הלכה י**: יוֹסֵף זָכָה לִקְבּוֹר אֶת אָבִיו וְאֵין בְּאֶחָיו גָּדוֹל מִמֶּנּוּ כול׳. אָמַר רִבִּי יִצְחָק. כְּבוֹד חַי הָעוֹלָמִים הָיָה עִמָּהֶן. כְּתִיב וַיָּבוֹאוּ עַד גּוֹרֶן הָאָטָד. וְכִי יֵשׁ גּוֹרֶן לָאָטָד. אָמַר רִבִּי שְׁמוּאֵל בַּר נַחְמָן. חִיזַּרְנוּ בְּכָל־הַמִּקְרָא וְלֹא מָצִינוּ מָקוֹם שֶׁשְּׁמוֹ אָטָד. אֶלָּא מַהוּ אָטָד. אֵילוּ הַכְּנַעֲנִים שֶׁהָיוּ רְאוּיִין לִידּוֹשׁ כְּאָטָד. וּבְאֵי זוֹ זְכוּת נִיצּוֹלוּ. בִּזְכוּת וַיַּרְא יוֹשֵׁב הָאָרֶץ הַכְּנַעֲנִי אֶת הָאֵבֶל בְּגוֹרֶן הָאָטָד. וּמַה חֶסֶד עָשׂוּ עִמּוֹ. רִבִּי אֶלְעָזָר אָמַר. אֵיזוֹרֵיהֶם הִיתִּירוּ. רִבִּי

שִׁמְעוֹן בֶּן לָקִישׁ אָמַר. קִישְׁרֵי כְתֵפֵיהֶן הִתִּירוּ. רַבָּנָן אֲמְרִין. זָקְפוּ קוֹמָתָן. אָמַר רִבִּי יוּדָן בַּר שָׁלוֹם. הֶרְאוּ בְאֶצְבַּע וְאָמְרוּ אֵבֶל כָּבֵד זֶה לְמִצְרָיִם. וּמַה אִם אֵילוּ שֶׁלֹּא עָשׂוּ חֶסֶד לֹא בִידֵיהֶן וְלֹא בְרַגְלֵיהֶן רָאוּ מַה פָּרַע לָהֶן הַקָּדוֹשׁ בָּרוּךְ הוּא. יִשְׂרָאֵל שֶׁהֵן עוֹשִׂין חֶסֶד בִּידֵיהֶן וּבְרַגְלֵיהֶן עִם גְּדוֹלֵיהֶן וְעִם קְטַנֵּיהֶן עַל אַחַת כַּמָּה וְכַמָּה.

Halakhah 10: "Joseph had the merit to bury his father and none of his brothers was greater than he," etc. [328]Rebbi Isaac said: The glory of the Lifegiver of the Worlds[329] was with them. It is written: "They came to the threshing place of the brambles.[330]" [331]Since when does the bramble-bush have a threshing place? Rebbi Samuel ben Naḥman said, we checked in all of Scripture and did not find a place called "brambles". What are "brambles"? These are the Canaanites who should have been threshed like brambles. By which merit were they saved? By the merit of: "The inhabitants of the land, the Canaanites, saw the mourning at the threshing place of the brambles.[332]" What act of kindness did they do for him? Rebbi Eleazar said, they unbelted[333]. Rebbi Simeon ben Laqish said, they undid the knots on their shoulders[334]. The rabbis said, they stood up[335]. Rebbi Yudan bar Shalom said, they pointed with their fingers and said, "a heavy mourning is that for Egypt". [336]Now these who did no act of kindness with their hands or feet; look what the Holy One, praise to Him, did reward them with; Israel who are used to do acts of kindness with their hands or feet for their great and their little ones, [they deserve] so much more!

328   *Gen. rabba* 100(7).
329   The Sephardic pronunciation חַי follows Maimonides (*Hilkhot Yesode Hatorah* 2:9). Ashkenazic pronunciation follows the Biblical חֵי (*Dan.* 13:7). The Worlds are this world,

the World to Come, and all other possible worlds He created.

330   Gen. 50:10.

331   The same question, in the framework of a different sermon, in the Babli, 13a.

332   Gen. 50:11.

333   As a sign of mourning, to stay in their houses.

334   Also a sign of mourning, not to appear in their togas.

335   They translate "the inhabitants of the land" as: "those sitting on the earth".

336   The entire paragraph is a sermon in honor of the local burial society.

(17c, line 4)³³⁷ אָמַר רִבִּי אַבָּהוּ כָּל־אוֹתָן שִׁבְעִים יוֹם שֶׁבֵּין אִיגְרוֹת לְאִיגְרוֹת כְּנֶגֶד שִׁבְעִים יוֹם שֶׁעָשׂוּ הַמִּצְרִיִּים חֶסֶד עִם אָבִינוּ יַעֲקֹב.

Rebbi Abbahu said, these seventy days between letters and letters³⁷⁸ correspond to the seventy days in which the Egyptians performed kindness with our father Jacob³⁷⁹.

337   Line 1 in the *editio princeps*. This sermon is an appendix to the preceding one; also found in *Gen. rabba* 100.

378   Between Haman's letters on Nisan 13 (*Esth.* 3:12) and Mordokhai"s letters of Sivan 23 (*Esth.* 8:9). If the months are alternatingly of 29 and 30 days, there are exactly 70 days between the dates.

379   Gen. 50:3.

(17c, line 5) כְּתִיב וַיְקוֹנֵן דָּוִד אֶת הַקִּינָה הַזֹּאת וגו' וַיֹּאמֶר לְלַמֵּד לִבְנֵי יְהוּדָה קָשֶׁת. לֹא מִסְתַּבְּרָה דְלָא. לְלַמֵּד בְּנֵי יְהוּדָה מִי הָיָה. אֶלָּא אָמַר דָּוִד. כֵּינָן שֶׁהַצַּדִּיקִים מִסְתַּלְּקִים הַשּׂוֹנְאִין בָּאִין וּמִתְגָּרִין בְּיִשְׂרָאֵל. הֲלֹא הִיא כְתוּבָה עַל סֵפֶר הַיָּשָׁר. תְּרֵין אֲמוֹרִין. חַד אָמַר. זֶה סֵפֶר בְּרֵאשִׁית. וְחָרָנָה אָמַר. זֶה חוּמָשׁ הַפְּקוּדִים. מָאן דְּאָמַר. זֶה סֵפֶר בְּרֵאשִׁית. נִיחָא. וּמָאן דְּאָמַר. זֶה חוּמָשׁ הַפְּקוּדִים. מַה מִלְחָמָה הָיְתָה שָׁם. וּבְנֵי יִשְׂרָאֵל נָסְעוּ מִבְּאֵרוֹת בְּנֵי יַעֲקָן מוֹסֵרָה שָׁם מֵת אַהֲרֹן. וְכִי בְּמוֹסֵירוֹת מֵת אַהֲרֹן. וַהֲלֹא בְּהֹר הָהָר מֵת. הֲדָא

הִיא דִּכְתִיב וַיַּעַל אַהֲרֹן הַכֹּהֵן אֶל הֹר הָהָר וַיָּמָת שָׁם. אֶלָּא כֵּיוָן שֶׁמֵּת אַהֲרֹן וְנִסְתַּלְּקוּ עֲנָנֵי הַכָּבוֹד וּבִיקְשׁוּ הַכְּנַעֲנִים לְהִתְגָּרוֹת בְּיִשְׂרָאֵל. הָדָא הִיא דִּכְתִיב וַיִּשְׁמַע הַכְּנַעֲנִי מֶלֶךְ עֲרָד יֹשֵׁב הַנֶּגֶב כִּי בָא יִשְׂרָאֵל דֶּרֶךְ הָאֲתָרִים. מַהוּ דֶּרֶךְ הָאֲתָרִים. שָׁמַע שֶׁמֵּת אַהֲרֹן הַתַּיָּיר הַגָּדוֹל שֶׁלָּהֶן שֶׁהָיָה תָר לָהֶן אֶת הַדֶּרֶךְ. בּוֹאוּ וְנִתְגָּרֶה בָהֶן. וּבִיקְּשׁוּ יִשְׂרָאֵל לַחֲזוֹר לְמִצְרַיִם וְנָסְעוּ לַאֲחוֹרֵיהֶן שְׁמוֹנֶה מַסָּעוֹת. וְרָץ אַחֲרָיו שִׁבְטוֹ שֶׁלְּלֵוִי וְהָרַג בָּהֶן שְׁמוֹנֶה מִשְׁפָּחוֹת. אַף הֵן הָרְגוּ מֵהֶן אַרְבַּע. הָדָא הִיא דִּכְתִיב לְעַמְרָמִי לְיִצְהָרִי לְחֶבְרוֹנִי לְעוּזִּיאֵלִי. אֵימָתַי חָזְרוּ. בִּימֵי דָוִד. הָדָא הִיא דִּכְתִיב יִפְרַח בְּיָמָיו צַדִּיק. אָמְרוּ. מִי גָרַם לָנוּ כָּל־הַדָּמִים הַלָּלוּ. אָמְרוּ. עַל שֶׁלֹּא עָשִׂינוּ חֶסֶד עִם אוֹתוֹ צַדִּיק. וְהָלְכוּ וְקָשְׁרוּ לוֹ הֶסְפֵּד וְגָמְלוּ לַצַּדִּיק חֶסֶד. וְהֶעֱלָה עֲלֵיהֶם הַכָּתוּב כְּאִילּוּ מֵת שָׁם וְנִקְבַּר שָׁם. שֶׁגָּמְלוּ לַצַּדִּיק חֶסֶד.

It is written[380]: "And David sang this elegy", etc., "and said: To teach the people of Judah archery." Is it reasonable that he had to teach the people of Judah, who was he[381]? But David said, when the just have disappeared, the haters come and attack Israel. "Is that not written in the book Yashar?" Two Amoraïm. One says, that is the book of Genesis. But the other said, that is the fifth of Numbers[382]. The one who said, this is the book of Genesis, is understandable[383]. But the one who said, that is the fifth of Numbers, what war is reported there? [384]"The Children of Israel travelled from the springs of Bene-Yaʻaqon to Mosera; there Aaron died[385]." Did Aaron die at Mosera? Did he not die on Mount Hor? That is what is written: "Aaron the Cohen ascended Mount Hor and died there.[386]" But when Aaron died and the clouds of glory disappeared, the Canaanites desired to attack Israel. That is what is written: "The Canaanite, the king of Arad, dweller in the Southland, heard that Israel came by the way of the scouts.[387]" What is "the way of the scouts"? He heard that Aaron died, the great scout, who did scout the way for them[388]. They came and attacked them. Then Israel wanted to return to Egypt and travelled eight stations backward. The tribe of Levi ran after them and killed eight families from them[389]. They also killed four of their families. That is what is written: "The Amramite, the Yiṣharite, the Ḥebronite, the Uzielite.[390]" When were they re-established? In David's time. That is what is written: "In his days, the just will blossom[391]". They said, what caused us all this bloodshed? They said, because we did not perform kindness for that just man. They went and organized a eulogy and performed kindness for that just man. The verse considers it as if he died and was buried there where they performed kindness for that just man.

380   2S. 1:17-18.

381   Instead of מי היה, the Rome ms. reads צחי, probably a corruption. The problem is that (1) the mention of Jehudah in a dirge about the slain of Benjamin is somewhat out of place, and (2) that David, who had a magic bow (*Ps.* 18:35), long ago was a teacher of archery. "He" refers to David.

382   In the Babli, *Avodah Zarah* 25a, R. Johanan identifies the book Yashar with Genesis, R. Eleazar with Deuteronomy. In the Babli, the book of Yashar is *not* a book of wars. "Fifth" is the standard rabbinic name for any one of the five books of the Pentateuch.

383   Since it records the victory of Abraham over the kings of the East.

384   From here to the end of the paragraph, the text is also in *Yoma* 1:1, fol. 38b.

385   *Deut.* 10:6.

386   *Num.* 33:38.

387   *Num.* 33:40. The same interpretation is in the Babli, *Roš Haššanah* 3a. Cf. also *Num. rabba* 19(11), *Tanḥuma Buber Ḥuqqat* 42, *Tanḥuma Ḥuqqat* 18; *Threni rabbati* 1(64); *Tosephta* 11:1; *Sifry Num.* 82.

388   Since Aaron was responsible for the Ark which was the pathfinder (*Num.* 10:33).

389   In the catalog of families in *Num.* 26, 8 families are missing compared to the enumeration of grandsons of Jacob in *Gen.* 46: 5 from

Benjamin and 1 each from Simeon, Gad, and Asher.

390   1Chr. 26:23, an isolated verse seemingly without connection to what comes before and after. This is interpreted to mean that David took care to re-establish these families after they had been decimated. The only levitic family missing in the list of *Num. 26* is *Šim'î*.

391   *Ps.* 72:2.

(17c, line 25) עמוֹ. רִבִּי קְרִיסְפָּא בְּשֵׁם רִבִּי יוֹחָנָן. עִם נַפְשָׁךְ אַתְּ עָבַד. אָמַר רִבִּי חָמָא בַּר חֲנִינָא. מָשָׁל לְמֶלֶךְ שֶׁהָיָה מֵשִׂיא אֶת בְּנוֹ. וּבָא אֵיפַּרְכוֹס לִטְעוֹן בָּאַפִּרְיוֹן וְלֹא הָנִיחוּ לוֹ. אָמַר הַמֶּלֶךְ. הָנִיחוּ לוֹ. לְמָחָר הוּא מֵשִׂיא אֶת בִּתּוֹ וַאֲנִי מְכַבְּדוֹ בְּמַה שֶׁכִּיבְּדָנִי. כַּכָּתוּב אָנֹכִי אֵרֵד עִמְּךָ מִצְרַיְמָה וְאָנֹכִי אַעַלְךָ גַם עָלֹה. מַה תַלְמוּד לוֹמַר גַם עָלֹה. אוֹתְךָ אֲנִי מַעֲלֶה וּשְׁאָר כָּל־הַשְׁבָטִים אֲנִי מַעֲלֶה. מְלַמֵד שֶׁכָּל־שֵׁבֶט וְשֵׁבֶט הֶעֱלָה עַצְמוֹת רֹאשׁ שִׁבְטוֹ עִמוֹ.

"With him[325]". Rebbi Crispus in the name of Rebbi Johanan: You do it for yourself[392]. Rebbi Hama bar Hanina: A parable of a king who was marrying off his son. There came a prefect[393] to carry the litter[394], and they did not admit him. The king said, let him; tomorrow he will marry off his daughter and I can honor him the way he honored me. As it is written[395]: "I shall descend with you to Egypt and I shall bring you up, also ascending." Why does the verse say, "also ascending"? I shall bring you up and the other tribes also I shall bring up. That teaches that every tribe brought the bones of their ancestor with them[396].

392   Moses brought Joseph's coffin *for himself*, that God would do for him what he did for Joseph.

393   Greek ἔπαρχος.

394   In which the bride was carried to the wedding ceremony; the organizers thought that being a litter carrier was beneath the dignity of the

prefect.	396 A slightly different interpretation in *Gen. rabba* 94(6).
395 Gen. 46:4.	

(17c, line 31) תַּנֵּי בְּשֵׁם רִבִּי יוּדָה. אִילוּלֵי הַדָּבָר כָּתוּב לֹא הָיָה אִיפְשָׁר לְאוֹמְרוֹ. מְלַמֵּד כְּשֶׁמֵּת מֹשֶׁה הָיָה מוּטָל עַל כַּנְפֵי הַשְּׁכִינָה כְּאַרְבַּעַת מִיל מִנַּחֲלַת בְּנֵי רְאוּבֵן עַד נַחֲלַת בְּנֵי גָד. שֶׁמֵּת בְּנַחֲלַת בְּנֵי רְאוּבֵן וְנִקְבַּר בְּנַחֲלַת בְּנֵי גָד. וּמְנַיִין שֶׁמֵּת בְּנַחֲלַת בְּנֵי רְאוּבֵן. שֶׁנֶּאֱמַר וּבְנֵי רְאוּבֵן בָּנוּ אֶת חֶשְׁבּוֹן וְאֶת אֶלְעָלֵה וְאֶת קִרְיָתַיִם וְאֶת נְבוֹ. וּכְתִיב עֲלֵה אֶל הַר הָעֲבָרִים הַזֶּה הַר נְבוֹ וּמוּת בָּהָר אֲשֶׁר אַתָּה עוֹלֶה שָׁמָּה. וּמְנַיִין שֶׁנִּקְבַּר בְּנַחֲלַת בְּנֵי גָד. שֶׁנֶּאֱמַר וּלְגָד אָמַר בָּרוּךְ מַרְחִיב גָּד וגו׳ כִּי שָׁם חֶלְקַת מְחוֹקֵק סָפוּן. וְהַקָּדוֹשׁ בָּרוּךְ הוּא הָיָה אוֹמֵר. וַיֵּתֵא רָאשֵׁי עָם. וּמַלְאֲכֵי שָׁרֵת הָיוּ אוֹמְרִים. צִדְקַת יי עָשָׂה. וְיִשְׂרָאֵל הָיוּ אוֹמְרִין. וּמִשְׁפָּטָיו עִם יִשְׂרָאֵל. אֵילּוּ וָאֵילּוּ הָיוּ אוֹמְרִים. יָבוֹא שָׁלוֹם יָנוּחוּ עַל מִשְׁכְּבוֹתָם הוֹלֵךְ נְכוֹחוֹ.

[397]It was stated in the name of Rebbi Jehudah: If it had not been written, it would have been impossible to say: This teaches us that when Moses died, he was lying on the wings of the *Shekhina*[398] about four miles, from the inheritance of the tribe of Reuben to the inheritance of the tribe of Gad, since he died in the inheritance of the tribe of Reuben and was buried in the inheritance of the tribe of Gad. From where that he died in the inheritance of the tribe of Reuben? Because it was said, "the tribe of Reuben built Ḥešbon, Elaleh, Qiryatayim, and Nebo.[399]" And it is written[400]: "Ascend this 'Abarim mountain, the Mountain of Nebo, and die on the Mountain up which you will climb." And from where that he was buried in the inheritance of the tribe of Gad? For it was said[401]: "To Gad he said, praised be He Who enlarges Gad, etc. For there the part of the lawgiver is hidden." The Holy One, praise to Him, added: "He came at the head of the people." The angels of the service said, "he executed the

justice of the Eternal", and Israel were saying, "and His laws with Israel.[402]" All together were saying: "[403]May he come in peace, may they rest on their couches, he goes in His pleasure."

---

397 Tosephta 4:8; Babli 13b, *Sifry Num.* 106.

398 The Divine presence on Earth. Parallels about the burial of Moses, cf. *Sifry Deut.* 355,357, *Midrash Tannaïm* p. 224; *Abot dR. Nathan* (Schechter) A 12, B 25; *Bet ha-Midrasch* (Jellinek) vol. 1 p. 115, vol. 6 p. 71.

399 *Num.* 32:38.

400 *Deut.* 32:49.

401 *Deut.* 33:20-21.

402 Since one cannot assume that Moses praised himself.

403 *Is.* 57:2. A fitting end of a sermon of consolation of mourners.

היה מביא את מנחתה פרק שני

(fol. 17c) **משנה א:** הָיָה מֵבִיא אֶת מִנְחָתָהּ בִּכְפִיפָה מִצְרִית וְנוֹתְנָהּ עַל יָדֶיהָ כְּדֵי לְיַגְּעָהּ. כָּל־הַמְּנָחוֹת תְּחִילָּתָן וְסוֹפָן בִּכְלֵי שָׁרֵת. וְזֶה תְחִילָתָהּ בִּכְפִיפָה מִצְרִית וְסוֹפָהּ בִּכְלֵי שָׁרֵת. כָּל־הַמְּנָחוֹת טְעוּנוֹת שֶׁמֶן וּלְבוֹנָה וְזוֹ אֵינָהּ טְעוּנָה לֹא שֶׁמֶן וְלֹא לְבוֹנָה. כָּל־הַמְּנָחוֹת בָּאוֹת מִן הַחִטִּים וְזוֹ אֵינָהּ בָּאָה אֶלָּא מִן הַשְּׂעוֹרִים. מִנְחַת הָעוֹמֶר אַף עַל פִּי שֶׁהִיא בָּאָה מִן הַשְּׂעוֹרִים הִיא בָּאָה גֶרֶשׂ וְזוֹ הָיְתָה בָאָה קֶמַח. רַבָּן גַּמְלִיאֵל אוֹמֵר כְּשֵׁם שֶׁמַּעֲשֶׂיהָ מַעֲשֵׂה בְהֵמָה כָּךְ קָרְבָּנָהּ מַאֲכַל בְּהֵמָה.

Mishnah 1: He[1] brought her flour offering in an Egyptian palm-leaf basket and then puts it on her hands to tire her out. All flour offerings are from start to finish in a Temple vessel except this which at the start is in an Egyptian palm-leaf basket and at the end in a Temple vessel[2]. All flour offerings need oil and incense except this one which needs neither oil nor incense[3]. All flour offerings come from wheat except this one which only comes from barley. The 'omer flour offering, even though it comes from barley, comes as roasted kernels but this one comes as flour. Rabban Gamliel said, since she behaved like an animal so her offering is animal feed.

1 The husband; *Num.* 5:15. The volume of the offering was $1/10$ of an *epha* or about one US Gallon. Cf. also Chapter 1, Note 239.

2 All other offerings must be in a Temple vessel when given to a Cohen to be processed. It is true that the *sotah*-offering also must be in a Temple

vessel once the Cohen takes it, but as long as the Cohen is still occupied with the preliminaries it may not be in a Temple vessel.

3   This is not quite correct; the offering of the poor sinner (*Lev.* 5:11) is likewise without olive oil and incense.

הלכה א: הָיָה מֵבִיא אֶת מִנְחָתָהּ כול׳. כְּתִיב וּבְיַד הַכֹּהֵן יִהְיוּ מֵי הַמָּרִים הַמְאָרְרִים. מֵעַתָּה כְּדֵי לְיַגְּעָהּ. אֶלָּא כְּדֵי לְהַטִּיל אֵימָה עָלֶיהָ. (fol. 17d)

Halakhah 1: "He brought her flour offering," etc. It is written[4]: "In the Cohen's hand shall be the spell-inducing bitter water." Is that to tire her out? Rather to inspire her with fear.

4   *Num.* 5:18. The verse requires that the offering be in the woman's hands all the time the water is in the Cohen's hand.

(17d line 7) מִנְחָתָהּ. מְלַמֵּד שֶׁהִיא קְדֹשָׁה לִשְׁמָהּ. כְּשֵׁם שֶׁהִיא קְדֹשָׁה לִשְׁמָהּ כָּךְ הִיא קְדֹשָׁה לִשְׁמוֹ. וְתַנֵּי רִבִּי חִייָה וּפְלִיג. לִיקְרַב כָּלִיל יְכוֹלָה אֵינָהּ מִפְּנֵי שׁוּתְפוּתָהּ שֶׁל אִשָּׁה. לֵאָכֵל אֵינָהּ יְכוֹלָה מִפְּנֵי שׁוּתְפוּתוֹ שֶׁלָּאִישׁ. אָמַר לֵיהּ. הַקּוֹמֶץ קָרֵב לְעַצְמוֹ וְהַשִּׁייָרִים קְרֵיבִין לְעַצְמָן. וְאַתְּ אָמַר. מִנְחָתָהּ. וְאֶלָּא מַה דְּאִישְׁתָּעֵי קִרְייָא אִישְׁתָּעֵי מַתְנִיתָא. וְהֵבִיא אֶת קָרְבָּנָהּ עָלֶיהָ.

"Her flour-offering." Does that mean that it is sanctified in her name[5]? Just as it is sanctified in her name, so it is sanctified in his name[6]. Rebbi Hiyya stated and disagreed[7]: "It[8] cannot be brought completely because of the participation by the wife. It cannot be eaten because of the participation by the husband." He said to him, the handful[9] is brought separately and the remainder is brought separately[10]. And you say, "her flour offering"? But the expression used by the verse is used by the Mishnah: "He shall bring *her flour-offering* for her.[11]"

5 A flour-offering in order to be valid must be offered by a Cohen in a Temple vessel on behalf of its owner (Mishnah *Menaḥot* 1:1). The Mishnah notes that "he (the husband) brings her (the wife's) flour-offering." Does this mean that the offering is to be offered only on her behalf?

6 It must be brought in both their names.

7 He does not disagree here at all; he supports the previous opinion. The text is from Halakhah 3:7 (fol. 19b line 37) where R. Ḥiyya disagrees. Cf. Tosephta 2:6.

8 If a Cohen suspects his wife of adultery, the flour-offering cannot be burnt as a Cohen's offering (*Lev.* 6:16) and cannot be eaten as the wife's offering (*Lev.* 6:9).

9 Of any flour-offering, a handful of the flour (with the incense) has to be burned on the altar and, normally, the rest is eaten by the Cohanim within the Temple enclosure (*Lev.* 6:7-11).

10 This is a matter of dispute; R. Ḥiyya disagrees with the opinion that the remainders which cannot be eaten by the Cohanim have to be dispersed on the ashes but holds that they have to be burned as a kind of fuel (Halakhah 3:7, Babli 23a).

11 *Num.* 5:15.

(17d line 12) בַּעֲלָהּ מַהוּ שֶׁיַּפְרִישׁ עָלֶיהָ חוּץ מִדַּעְתָּהּ. [מִכֵּיוָן שֶׁיֵּשׁ לוֹ שׁוּתָפוּת בְּמִנְחָה מַפְרִישׁ עָלֶיהָ חוּץ מִדַּעְתָּהּ.]¹² אַחַר מַהוּ שֶׁיַּפְרִישׁ עָלֶיהָ חוּץ מִדַּעְתָּהּ. יָבֹא כַּיֵי דְרַבִּי יוֹחָנָן. [דְּרַבִּי יוֹחָנָן אָמַר]¹² אַרְבָּעָה מְחוּסְרֵי כַּפָּרָה מַפְרִישִׁין עֲלֵיהֶן שֶׁלֹּא מִדַּעְתָּן. וְאֵילוּ הֵן. הַזָּב וְהַזָּבָה וְהַמְצוֹרָע וְהַיּוֹלֶדֶת. שֶׁכֵּן אָדָם מַפְרִישׁ עַל בְּנוֹ הַקָּטָן וְהוּא נָתוּן בַּעֲרִיסָה. נִיחָא זָב וְזָבָה וּמְצוֹרָע. וְיוֹלֶדֶת וְיֵשׁ קְטַנָּה יוֹלֶדֶת. לֹא כֵן אָמַר רַבִּי רְדִיפָא רַבִּי יוֹנָה בְּשֵׁם רַב חוּנָא. עִבְּרָה וְיָלְדָה עַד שֶׁלֹּא הֵבִיאָה שְׁתֵּי שְׂעָרוֹת הִיא וּבְנָהּ מֵתִים. מִשֶּׁהֵבִיאָה שְׁתֵּי שְׂעָרוֹת [הִיא וּבְנָהּ חַיִּים. עִבְּרָה עַד שֶׁלֹּא הֵבִיאָה שְׁתֵּי שְׂעָרוֹת וְיָלְדָה מִשֶּׁהֵבִיאָה שְׁתֵּי שְׂעָרוֹת]¹³ הִיא חָיָה וּבְנָהּ מֵת. מַאי כְדוֹן. שֶׁכֵּן אָדָם מַפְרִישׁ עַל בִּתּוֹ קְטַנָּה מִכֵּיוָן שֶׁהֵבִיאָה לוֹ כְּבָר יָצְאָת מֵרְשׁוּת אָבִיהָ. אֶלָּא שֶׁכֵּן אָדָם מַפְרִישׁ עַל אִשְׁתּוֹ חֵרֶשֶׁת. וְכָאן סוֹטָה קְטַנָּה אֵין אַתְּ יָכוֹל. דָּמַר רַבִּי זְעִירָא רַבִּי יָסָא בְּשֵׁם רַבִּי יוֹחָנָן. קְטַנָּה שֶׁזִּינְתָה אֵין לָהּ רָצוֹן לְהֵיאָסֵר עַל בַּעְלָהּ. וַחֲרֶשֶׁת אֵין אַתְּ יָכוֹל.

דִּכְתִיב וְאָמְרָה הָאִשָּׁה אָמֵן אָמֵן. אָמַר רִבִּי אָבִין. מִכֵּיוָן דִּכְתִיב וְשָׂמַחְתָּ אַתָּה וּבֵיתֶךָ וְהוּא מְעַכֵּב מִלְשָׂמוֹחַ עִמָּהּ. מַפְרִישׁ עָלֶיהָ חוּץ מִדַּעְתָּהּ.

May her husband dedicate for her without her knowledge? Since he is a partner in the flour offering, may he dedicate for her without her knowledge? May another person dedicate for her without her knowledge[14]? It comes following what Rebbi Joḥanan said, as Rebbi Joḥanan said, for the four who need cleansing[15] others may dedicate without their knowledge; these are the following: Man or woman [healed from] genital discharges, one [healed from] scale disease, and the woman after childbirth; since a father may dedicate for his small son who is lying in a crib[16]. One understands man or woman [healed from] genital discharges or [healed from] scale disease, but a woman after childbirth? May a minor give birth?   [17]Did not Rebbi Redifa, Rebbi Jonah, say in the name of Rebbi Hila: If a woman became pregnant and gave birth before she grew two hairs, she and her son will die. After she grew two hairs, she and her son will live. If she became pregnant before she grew two hairs and gave birth after she grew two hairs, she will live but her son will die. How is the situation? Since a man may dedicate for his underage daughter[18]. Since she grew [pubic hair] she already left his power[19]. But it must be since a man may dedicate for his deaf-mute wife. Here, in the case of the suspected wife, the case of the minor does not apply [20]since Rebbi Ze'ira, Rebbi Yasa said in the name of Rebbi Joḥanan: An underage girl who whored has no will to be forbidden to her husband. The case of the deaf-mute does not apply since it is written[21]: "The woman shall say: Amen, amen." Rebbi Abin said, since it is written[22]: "You shall enjoy together with your house," and he is the cause that he cannot enjoy with her, he may dedicate without her knowledge[23].

12 From the Rome ms., missing in Leiden ms.

13 From the Rome ms. and the parallel in *Yebamot*, Chapter 1; Notes 153-154. Missing in Leiden ms.

14 In case the first question is answered in the affirmative, there is a second question to be answered.

15 Anyone whose own body was the source of impurity, when he is pure again cannot enter the Temple precinct unless he first brought a sacrifice of cleansing: The woman after childbirth (*Lev.* 12:6-8), the person healed from scale disease (*Lev.* 14:1-32), and the persons healed from genital discharges (*Lev.* 15:14-15,29-30).

16 Who could have been afflicted with scale disease and, if female, with a discharge at birth mimicking menstruation.

17 Text from *Yebamot* 1:2, Note 153.

18 Therefore, he should be able to dedicate for his wife who also is dependent upon him.

19 Even without growing pubic hair, if he married her off she is emancipated from him. If she is not married, she cannot be a suspected wife.

20 This statement is from Chapter 1, Note 91.

21 *Num.* 5:22. The answer of the wife is a requirement that cannot be waved, cf. Chapter 1, Note 8. Therefore, a mute woman cannot undergo the ordeal. The Babli concurs, 27b, quoted in *Num. rabba* 9(18).

22 *Deut.* 14:26. "A man's house" always means his wife. For example, since the High Priest must purge his sins and those of his house on the day of Atonement (*Lev.* 16:17), an unmarried High Priest cannot officiate.

23 Since he cannot enjoy himself if his wife is forbidden to him, she cannot hinder him in the preparations for her rehabilitation. This answers the original question for the husband. At the same time, R. Abin disagrees with R. Joḥanan and holds that only the husband may dedicate the purgation offering of the woman after childbirth without her knowledge since he has a direct interest in it. While the woman after childbirth is permitted to her husband once she is recovered and

pure, she cannot enjoy the holiday sacrifices with him as long as her sacrifice has not been handed over to the Temple personnel.

(17d line 26) רִבִּי אָחָא בְּשֵׁם רִבִּי אִילָא. אֵינוֹ מַפְרִישׁ עָלֶיהָ עוֹלַת הָעוֹף אֶלָּא חַטָּאת הָעוֹף. מִפְּנֵי שֶׁהִיא מַכְשַׁרְתָּהּ לֶאֱכוֹל בַּזְּבָחִים. תַּנֵּי. אֵינוֹ מַפְרִישׁ עָלֶיהָ אֶלָּא דָבָר שֶׁהוּא מַתִּירָהּ לָהּ בְּזֶה. אָמַר רִבִּי יוֹסֵי. אֵין לָךְ אֶלָּא זֶה. תַּנֵּי. מַה זֶה מְעַכְּבָהּ מִלֶּאֱכוֹל בַּזְּבָחִים. מְעַכְּבָה הִיא מִלֶּאֱכוֹל בַּזְּבָחִים. וּמִכֵּיוָן שֶׁהוּא מְעוּכָּב מִלִּשְׂמוֹחַ עִמָּהּ. כְּמִי שֶׁהוּא מְעַכְּבָהּ מִלֶּאֱכוֹל בַּזְּבָחִים. תַּנֵּי. אֲפִילוּ הַקָּפַת נְזִירוּת עַל רֹאשָׁהּ מְעַכְּבָהּ הִיא מִלּוֹכַל בַּזְּבָחִים. מִכֵּיוָן שֶׁהִיא מְנֻוֶּלֶת וְהוּא מְעוּכָּב מִלִּשְׂמוֹחַ עִמָּהּ. כְּמוֹ שֶׁהוּא מְעַכְּבָהּ מִלּוֹכַל בַּזְּבָחִים.

Rebbi Aḥa in the name of Rebbi Ila: He may not dedicate for her the bird elevation offering, only the bird purification offering because the latter enables her to eat family sacrifices[24]. It was stated: He may dedicate for her only something that enables her to eat family sacrifices. Rebbi Yose said, that[25] is all. It was stated: Just as that disables her from eating family sacrifices, so she disables others from eating family sacrifices; since he is hindered from enjoying with her it is as if he disabled her from eating family sacrifices[26]. It was stated: Even by the shearing of her head[27] she hinders him from eating family sacrifices. Since she is ugly[28] and he is hindered from enjoying with her it is as if he disabled her[29] from eating family sacrifices.

24 This speaks about the woman after childbirth whose husband is poor and can afford only two birds as purgation offering. It is asserted here that the husband on his own can only dedicate a sacrifice in which he has a direct interest, as stated by R. Abin. Mishnah *Keritut* 6:4 notes that only the purification offering enables her to eat family sacrifices. The elevation sacrifice also may be paid by him but only with his wife's knowledge.

25 The offerings of the woman after childbirth.

26 In all cases, those whose impurity was produced by their own body and the suspected wife, where the husband cannot enjoy a holiday without having seen to it that her sacrifice has been presented in good order, any dereliction on his part to remove her disability is put on the same level as his hindering her from eating sacrifices. Therefore, it is his duty to bring these sacrifices and he does not need his wife's consent for the dedication.

27 The wife made a vow to be a *nazir* who may not drink any wine and the husband did not use his right to free her from any vow of self-punishment. As long as she is forbidden to drink wine, he cannot fully enjoy the holiday with her. Therefore, after she has cut her hair, the husband can dedicate the three offerings due from the *nazir* (*Num.* 6:14) without the knowledge of his wife (according to R. Ila only the family sacrifice which permits the wife to drink wine.)

28 Because of her long hair.

29 By not having vetoed her vow he is responsible for the problem.

(17d line 33) תַּנֵּי. רִבִּי יוּדָה אוֹמֵר. מֵבִיא אָדָם עַל יְדֵי אִשְׁתּוֹ כָּל־קָרְבָּן שֶׁהִיא חַיֶּיבֶת. אֲפִילוּ אָכְלָה חֵלֶב וַאֲפִילוּ חִילְלָה שַׁבָּת. וְכֵן הָיָה רִבִּי יוּדָה אוֹמֵר. פְּטָרָהּ. אֵינוֹ חַיָּיב בָּהּ. שֶׁכֵּן הוּא כוֹתֵב לָהּ. וְאַחֲרָן דִּי אַתְיָן לִי עֲלָךְ מִן קַדְמַת דְּנָא.

[30]It was stated in the name of Rebbi Jehudah: A person brings for his wife any sacrifice she is obligated for, even if she ate suet or desecrated the Sabbath. Also, Rebbi Jehudah says, once he divorces her, he is no longer obligated for her, for *he* writes to *her*[31] "any other obligations that come *to me because of you* from earlier times."

30 From *Yebamot* 15:3, explained there in Notes 43-45. The words in Italics are changed in gender from the text in *Yebamot*: The text here refers to the obligations the husband takes upon himself at the time of marriage; the text in *Yebamot* refers to the receipt the divorcee writes upon delivery of the divorce settlement.

31 While he is married, he is liable

also for sacrifices she was obligated to before marriage. Upon divorce, all his obligations cease.

(17d line 36) וְהָתַנֵּי. סֵדֶר מְנָחוֹת כָּךְ הִיא. מְבִיאִין מִתּוֹךְ בֵּיתוֹ בִּכְלִי כֶסֶף וּבִכְלִי זָהָב. וּרְאוּיָה לִיקָּרֵב בִּכְלִי שָׁרֵת.

Was it not stated[32]: "The order of flour offerings is the following: One brings from his house in silver or gold vessels." These would be acceptable as Temple vessels[33].

32   The objection is to the Mishnah which states that "all flour offerings are from start to finish in a Temple vessel" when the *baraita* (Tosephta *Menaḥot* 1:16) states that flour offerings are brought in private vessels to the Temple and only there transferred to Temple vessels.

33   If they were dedicated together with the flour, no other vessels would be necessary. But an Egyptian palm leaf basket is never acceptable as a Temple vessel. The same question and answer in the Babli (14b).

(17d line 38) תַּנֵּי רַבִּי שִׁמְעוֹן בֶּן יוֹחַי. מִפְּנֵי מַה אָמְרוּ. כָּל־הַחַטָּאוֹת וְהָאֲשָׁמוֹת שֶׁבַּתּוֹרָה אֵין טְעוּנִין נְסָכִים. שֶׁלֹא יְהֵא קָרְבָּנוּ שֶׁלַחוֹטֵא נִרְאֶה מְהוּדָּר. הֵתִיבוּן. הֲרֵי חַטָּאתוֹ וַאֲשָׁמוֹ שֶׁלַמְצוֹרָע. אִין תֵּימַר שֶׁאֵינוֹ חוֹטֵא. הָאָמַר רִבִּי יִצְחָק. זֹאת תִּהְיֶה תּוֹרַת הַמְצוֹרָע. זֹאת תּוֹרַת הַמוֹצִיא שֵׁם רָע. אָמַר רִבִּי לָא[34]. מִכֵּיוָן שֶׁנִתְיַיסֵּר וּכְתִיב וְנִקְלָה אָחִיךָ לְעֵינֶיךָ כְּמִי שֶׁאֵינוֹ חוֹטֵא.

Rebbi Simeon bar Ioḥai stated[35]: Why did they say that no purification[36] or reparation sacrifices need wine offerings? That the sacrifice of a sinner should not be magnificent. They objected: There are the purification and the reparation offerings of the scale-diseased[15]. If you say that he is no sinner, did not Rebbi Isaac say: "That shall be the instruction for the scale-diseased," this is the instruction for the slanderer[37]! Rebbi Hila said, since he was made to suffer and it is written³⁸ "that your brother should [not] be contemptible in your eyes," he is as if he had not sinned.

34 Reading of the Rome ms. Leiden: ליה "to him".

35 The Babli, 15a, quotes a more detailed statement by R. Simeon bar Iohai: Why is the sinner let off cheaply in that he saves the expenses for wine, flour, and oil, required for all other private sacrifices?

36 The idea is that חטאת should be considered as "sin offering". It seems more likely that the root חטא basically means "to cleanse". The noun חֵטְא then means "cleansable sin", i. e., inadvertent sin, in contrast to פֶּשַׁע "crime, intentional sin", for which no Temple ritual is available (cf. Babli *Temurah* 15b). The sacrifices of the persons needing purge from impurity (Note 15) shows that "sin offering" is not a primary meaning of our word. An intentional sin can be expiated only by death or by God's grace following sincere repentance.

37 Taking apart the word מצו-רע. In the Babli (mentioned 15a, main source *Arakhin* 16a), R. Johanan holds that scale-disease is a punishment for (1) calumny, (2) homicide, (3) perjury, (4) incest, (4) haughtiness, (5) robbery, (6) envy.

38 *Deut.* 25:3. It is to be noted that in Arabic one of the meanings of both roots צרע and צָרַע, corresponding to the Hebrew צרע "having scale-disease", is "to humble oneself".

(17d line 41) רִבִּי יוֹחָנָן בְּשֵׁם רִבִּי יִשְׁמָעֵאל. מַה מִנְחַת מִנְחַת. מִנְחַת שֶׁנֶּאֱמַר לְהַלָּן שְׁעוֹרִין אַף כָּאן שְׂעוֹרִין. אָמַר רִבִּי לְעֶזָר. נֶאֱמַר כָּאן אָבִיב וְנֶאֱמַר בְּמִצְרַיִם אָבִיב. מַה אָבִיב הָאָמוּר בְּמִצְרַיִם שְׂעוֹרִים אַף כָּאן שְׂעוֹרִין. רִבִּי עֲקִיבָה אָמַר. נֶאֱמַר לַצִּיבּוּר. הָבֵא בִיכּוּרִים בַּפֶּסַח וַהֲבֵא בִיכּוּרִים בָּעֲצֶרֶת. אִם מָצִינוּ שֶׁמִּמִּין שֶׁהַיָּחִיד מֵבִיא חוֹבָתוֹ מִמֶּנּוּ הַצִּיבּוּר מֵבִיא בִיכּוּרִים בָּעֲצֶרֶת. מֵאֵי זֶה מִין הַיָּחִיד מֵבִיא חוֹבָתוֹ. מִן הַשְּׂעוֹרִין. אַף הַצִּיבּוּר לֹא יָבִיא אֶלָּא מִן הַשְּׂעוֹרִין. אִם תֹּאמַר. מִן הַחִיטִּין. אֵין שְׁתֵּי הַלֶּחֶם בִּיכּוּרִין.

Rebbi Joḥanan in the name of Rebbi Ismael: [39]"Flour offering of, flour offering of." Since "flour offering of" said there is of barley, here also it is of barley. [40]Rebbi Eliezer said, it says here "milky white[41]" and it says in Egypt "milky white[42]". Since "milky white" mentioned in Egypt refers to barley, here also it refers to barley. Rebbi Aqiba said, it was said to the public, bring first fruits on Passover and bring first fruits on Pentecost[43]. [44]If we find that from the kind a private person brings his obligatory offering[45] the public bring their first fruits on Pentecost. From which kind does the private person bring his obligatory offering? From barley! Also the public should bring only from barley. If you say from wheat, the Two Breads[46] would not be first fruits.

39 This sentence is also quoted in Halakhah 3:1. The argument refers to *Lev.* 2:14, where "a flour offering of first fruits" is mentioned which is identified as the *'Omer* offering (*Lev.* 23:9-14), traditionally brought from barley (since early in spring there is no wheat ready). The argument attempts to show that the offering mentioned in *Lev.* 2:14 must be the *'omer* offering of barley. The argument of R. Ismael is quoted only here because it cannot be sustained. The basis of the argument is the position that a word used in the legal parts of the Torah can only have one meaning. Since the construct form *"flour offering of"* used for the ritual of the suspected wife (*Num.* 5:15,16,18) refers to barley, it is concluded that the *"flour offering of* first fruits" also must refer to barley. The problem is that the construct state is also used in *Lev.* 2:7, 6:14,16; *Num.* 4:16, 28:8 clearly referring to wheat offerings.

40 A slightly garbled version of a text dealing with the same problem, preserved in *Sifra Wayyiqra Paršata* 13(4). The reading *Liezer* for the first Tanna mentioned here, as against *Lazar* as suggested by the text, follows the reading of *Sifra*. Since this Tanna is mentioned before R. Aqiba, a reading of *Lazar* would refer to R. Eleazar ben 'Arakh.

41 *Lev.* 2:14, a word used in the description of the offering of first

fruits. For the translation of אביב as "milky white", see J. Milgrom, *Leviticus 1-16*, 1991, pp. 192-194.

42   *Ex.* 9:31, referring to barley.

43   During or after the Holiday of Unleavened Bread (depending on the interpretation of the term "after the Sabbath") the *'Omer* offering is required as "first harvest" (*Lev.* 23:9-14).

Pentecost is described as "holiday of first fruits" (*Num.* 28:26).

44   This text is slightly garbled. A more intelligible text is in *Sifra* (but one cannot exclude the possibility that the text in *Sifra* is Amoraic and has been edited to make it more intelligible) and the Babli, *Menaḥot* 68b:

רִבִּי עֲקִיבָה אוֹמֵר. נֶאֱמַר לַצִּיבּוּר. הָבֵא בִיכּוּרִים בַּפֶּסַח וַהֲבֵא בִיכּוּרִים בָּעֲצֶרֶת. כְּמָה מָצִינוּ שֶׁמִּמִּין שֶׁהַיָּחִיד מֵבִיא חוֹבָתוֹ מִמֶּנּוּ יְהֵא הַצִּיבּוּר מֵבִיא בִיכּוּרָיו בָּעֲצֶרֶת. אַף מִמִּין שֶׁהַיָּחִיד מֵבִיא חוֹבָתוֹ מִמֶּנּוּ יְהֵא הַצִּיבּוּר מֵבִיא בִיכּוּרָיו בַּפֶּסַח. מֵאַי זֶה מִין הַיָּחִיד מֵבִיא חוֹבָתוֹ. מִן הַשְּׂעוֹרִין. אַף הַצִּיבּוּר לֹא יָבִיא אֶלָּא מִן הַשְּׂעוֹרִין. מִן הַחִיטִּין. אִם תֹּאמַר. אֵין שְׁתֵּי הַלֶּחֶם בִּיכּוּרִים.

Rebbi Aqiba says: It was said to the public, bring First Fruits on Passover and bring First Fruits on Pentecost. *As* we find that, from the kind a private person brings his obligatory offering the public has to bring their First Fruits on Pentecost, *also from the kind a private person brings his obligatory offering the public brings their First Fruits on Passover.* From which kind does the private person bring his obligatory offering? From barley! Also the public should bring only from barley. If you say, from wheat, the Two Breads are not First Fruits.

45   The only *obligatory* flour offerings of a private person are the purification offering of the poor (*Lev.* 5:11) and the offering for the suspected wife. The *voluntary* offerings of a private person are all high quality wheat.

46   Two wheat breads made from sour dough to be presented to the altar but not burned, *Lev.* 23:17. These are called "First Fruits". If the *'Omer* offering, whose nature is not specified in the verse, were to be brought from wheat, the Two Breads would not be baked from "First Fruits".

(17d line 49) תַּמָּן אָמַר רִבִּי יוֹנָה. חִילְקָה לִשְׁנַיִם. טְרַגִיס לִשְׁלֹשָׁה. טִיסְנֵי לְאַרְבָּעָה. רִבִּי יוֹסֵי בֵּי רִבִּי בּוּן בָּעֵי. מִכָּן וָהֵילַךְ קְמָחִים הֵן. אֵין צָרִיךְ לָבוֹר אֶת הַסּוֹלֶת מִתּוֹכָן.

There, said by Rebbi Jonah: "*Halica*[47], into two parts. *Tragos*[48], into three. *Tisana*[49], into four." Rebbi Yose ben Rebbi Abun asked: From there on, is it coarse flour[50]? One does not have to sift out the fine flour from in between[51].

47 J. Levy, supported by H. L. Fleischer, sees in חילקה Latin *alica, halica* "groats of spelt". This is confirmed by the (Galilean) spelling חליקה of the Rome ms. The spelling חילקה is Babylonian; cf. S. Lieberman, *Tosefta ki-Fshutah Nedarim*, p. 456. He explains that R. Jonah derives חילקה from the Hebrew root חלק "to split" and טרגיס, pronounced *trayis* from Latin *tres* or Greek τρεῖς.

The Mishnah, *Makhširin* 6:2, mentions "spelt groats, *tragos, tisana*" as manufactured products; R. Jonah defines these trade names. In the Babli, *Mo'ed Qatan* 13b, R. Jonah's definition is described as Babylonian; the Galilean definition of חילקה given by Rav Dimi is בונתא, explained by the commentary ascribed to Rashi as "spelt for chewing" and by "Rashi's commentary" edited by E. Kupfer as "shelled spelt", confirming the determination as *halica*.

48 Greek τράγος, "spelt (or other grains); goat". Latin *tragos, tragum* "porridge".

49 Latin "barley groats, pearl barley; barley water"; originally Latin *ptisana*, Greek πτισάνη, "peeled barley, barley gruel".

50 The offering of the suspected wife is defined (*Num.* 5:15) as "coarse barley flour". Is it enough if the kernels are broken into at least five parts or does there have to be a real grinding process? The question is not answered.

51 The presence of a few finely ground pieces of barley does not invalidate the offering if it is recognizable as coarse flour by the naked eye.

משנה ב: (fol. 17c) הָיָה מֵבִיא פְּיָילֵי שֶׁלְחֶרֶשׂ חֲדָשָׁה וְנוֹתֵן לְתוֹכָהּ חֲצִי לוֹג מַיִם מִן הַכִּיּוֹר. רַבִּי יְהוּדָה אוֹמֵר רְבִיעִית. כְּשֵׁם שֶׁהוּא מְמַעֵט בַּכְּתָב כָּךְ הוּא מְמַעֵט בַּמַּיִם. נִכְנַס לַהֵיכָל וּפָנָה לִימִינוֹ וּמָקוֹם הָיָה שָׁם אַמָּה עַל אַמָּה וְטַבְלָה שֶׁלְשַׁיִשׁ וְטַבַּעַת הָיְתָה קְבוּעָה בָהּ כְּשֶׁהוּא מַגְבִּיהָהּ נוֹטֵל עָפָר מִתַּחְתֶּיהָ וְנוֹתֵן כְּדֵי שֶׁיֵּרָאֶה עַל פְּנֵי הַמַּיִם שֶׁנֶּאֱמַר וּמִן הֶעָפָר אֲשֶׁר יִהְיֶה בְּקַרְקַע הַמִּשְׁכָּן יִקַּח הַכֹּהֵן וְנָתַן אֶל הַמָּיִם.

Mishnah 2: He[52] brought a new[53] earthenware bowl[54] and filled it with half a log[55] of water from the laver; Rebbi Jehudah says, a quarter [log][56]. (Just as he[57] shortens the writing so he decreases the amount of water.) He[52] entered the Temple building and turned right. There was a place there, one cubit square, where a handle was fastened to a marble plate. He lifted it, took dust from under it, and put it so that it was seen on the water, as it was said[58]: "From the dust which will be on the ground of the Temple the Cohen shall take and put on the water."

52 The officiating priest.
53 The text of the Yerushalmi is also the text of most Mishnah mss. The word is missing in the Babli mss.
54 Greek φιάλη.
55 0.27 l. Cf. Mishnah *Kelim* 17:11.

55 A quarter log is the rabbinic minimum for any liquid used in any ceremony.
57 Rebbi Jehudah; cf. Mishnah 3.
58 *Num.* 5:17.

הלכה ב: (fol. 17d) הָיָה מֵבִיא פְּיָילֵי כול'. תַּנֵּי חֲדָשָׁה. מַתְנִיתִין דְּרַבִּי אֱלִיעֶזֶר. דְּתַנִינָן תַּמָּן. הָיָה מֵבִיא פְּיָילֵי שֶׁלְחֶרֶשׂ חֲדָשָׁה. מָאן תַּנָא חֲדָשָׁה. רַבִּי לְעָזֶר. דְּהוּא דָרִישׁ לָהּ. אֶל כְּלִי חֶרֶשׂ עַל מַיִם חַיִּים. מַה מַּיִם שֶׁלֹּא נַעֲשָׂה בָהֶן מְלָאכָה. אַף כְּלִי חֶרֶשׂ שֶׁלֹּא נַעֲשָׂה בוֹ מְלָאכָה. נִיחָא תַמָּן דְּהוּא דָרִישׁ אֶל כְּלִי חֶרֶשׂ עַל מַיִם חַיִּים. הָכָא מָה אִית לָךְ. אָמַר רִבִּי יוֹחָנָן. דּוּ סָבַר כְּרִבִּי יִשְׁמָעֵאל. תַּנֵּי. מֵי כִיּוֹר. רַבִּי יִשְׁמָעֵאל. אוֹמֵר מֵי מַעְיָן. וַחֲכָמִים מַכְשִׁירִין

בְּכָל הַמֵּימוֹת. וְהָא דְּרַבִּי לְעֶזֶר כְּרַבִּי יִשְׁמָעֵאל בַּמַּיִם. וְרַבִּי יִשְׁמָעֵאל כְּרַבִּי אֶלְעֶזֶר בִּכְלִי חֶרֶשׂ. אַשְׁכָּח תַּנֵּי. רַבִּי יִשְׁמָעֵאל אוֹמֵר. בִּכְלִי חֶרֶשׂ חֲדָשָׁה. אִית תַּנָּיֵי תַּנֵּי. בִּכְלִי חֶרֶשׂ לֹא בְּמַקֵּידָה. אִית תַּנָּיֵי תַּנֵּי. אֲפִלּוּ בְּמַקֵּידָה. הָווֹן בָּעֵי מֵימַר. מָאן דָּמַר. בִּכְלִי חֶרֶשׂ לֹא בְּמַקֵּידָה. רַבִּי לְעֶזֶר. מָאן דְּאָמַר אֲפִלּוּ בְּמַקֵּידָה. רַבָּנָן. כּוּלָּהּ רַבָּנָן. מָאן דָּמַר בִּכְלִי חֶרֶשׂ לֹא בְּמַקֵּידָה. בְּשֶׁנִּיטַל רוּבָּהּ וּמִיעוּטָהּ קַיָּים. וּמָאן דָּמַר. בְּמַקֵּידָה. בְּשֶׁנִּיטְלָה מִיעוּטָהּ וְרוּבָהּ קַיָּים.

Halakhah 2: "He brought a bowl," etc. It was stated: "A new one.[59]" Our Mishnah follows Rebbi Eliezer[60], as we have stated there[61]: "He brought a new earthenware bowl." Who stated "a new one"? Rebbi Eliezer! Since he explains: "Into an earthenware vessel on fresh water.[62]" Just as the water had no prior use, so the earthenware vessel should not have had any prior use. It is understandable there because he explains: "Into an earthenware vessel on fresh water;" but what may one say here[63]? Rebbi Johanan said, because he[64] agrees with Rebbi Ismael. It was stated: From the wash basin[65]. Rebbi Ismael says, water from a fountain. But the Sages approve of all kinds of water[66]. Therefore, Rebbi Eliezer holds with Rebbi Ismael about the water and Rebbi Ismael with Rebbi Eliezer about the earthenware vessel. It was found stated: Rebbi Ismael says, into a new earthenware vessel. Some Tannaïm state: Into an earthenware vessel but not into a *maqqēdah*[67]. Some Tannaïm state: Even into a *maqqēdah*. They[68] wanted to say, he who says, into an earthenware vessel but not into a *maqqēdah*, is Rebbi Eliezer[69] but those who say, even into a *maqqēdah*, are the rabbis. It all is the rabbis'. He who says, into an earthenware vessel but not into a *maqqēdah*, if most of it was removed but a small part was left; he who says, even into a *maqqēdah*, if a small part was removed but most of it was left[70].

59 In the Babli, 15b, this is attributed to R. Ismael. The statement is not mentioned in the Midrashim. The quote seems to imply a Mishnah text similar to that of the Babli.

60 The argument is mentioned in his name in *Sifra Meṣorah Pereq* 1(4).

61 Mishnah *Nega'im* 14:1, referring to the purification of the person healed from skin disease.

62 *Lev.* 14:5, speaking of the slaughtering of one of the two birds used in the purification rite. "Live" water is running water from a fountain or natural stream.

63 The argument is irrelevant for the ritual of the suspected wife. In the Babli, the connection is made by R. Ismael's rule of *gezerah šawah*: If the meaning of "earthenware vessel" was determined to include "new", the same meaning applies everywhere. The Yerushalmi rejects this application to the names of vessels of common use.

64 R. Eliezer.

65 From which the priests draw the water for their ablutions; cf. *Ex.* 30:17-21. The statement is also anonymous in *Sifry Num.* 10, *Sifry zuṭa Naśo, Num. rabba* 9(12); cf. *Targumim* to *Num.* 5:17. In the Babli, 15b, it is attributed to R. Joḥanan in the *editio princeps*, impossible in a Tannaïtic text, and to R. Ismael in the Munich ms., contradicting the next statement there. In the Babli text quoted in the 12th Century *Sefer Yereïm* 460 (ed. S. Z. Halberstam), the statement is missing; this is the only consistent Babli text, defining this *baraita* as differing from the Mishnah.

66 The last two statements are also in the Babli, 15b. The statement by R. Ismael requires the water to be brought from outside the Temple precinct (the Giḥon source); the rabbis permit the water to be drawn also from the water canal crossing the temple courtyard or from one of the *miqwaot* in the Temple area.

67 From the context (here, and in *Sifra, loc. cit.*) it follows that the word describes a somehow defective or incomplete clay vessel. Ben Jehudah in his *Thesaurus* (p. 3662) quotes several proposed interpretations without giving his own opinion. As a Semitic word, the root is נקד, "exhibiting spots", but cf. Greek μαγίς, -ίδος, ἡ, "kneading trough, pan, plate"; Latin *magis, -idis*, or *magida -ae*, "dish, platter, kneading trough".

68 Some members of the Academy.

69 Since it may be assumed that "a new vessel" means: not a defective one.

70 A broken vessel is acceptable if it represents the major part of a

complete vessel. This statement is not in the Babli; since the Babli requires a new vessel (or at least one renewed by firing), it will reject a broken one.

(17d line 64) אִית תַּנָּיֵי תַנֵי. בִּכְלִי חֶרֶשׂ. לֹא בִּמְפוּחָם. אִית תַּנָּיֵי תַנֵי. אֲפִילוּ בִּמְפוּחָם. הָווֹן בָּעֵיי מֵימַר. מָאן דָּמַר. בִּכְלִי חֶרֶשׂ לֹא בִּמְפוּחָם. רִבִּי לְעָזָר. מָאן דָּמַר. אֲפִילוּ בִּמְפוּחָם. רַבָּנָן. כּוּלָּהּ דְּרַבָּנִין. מָאן דָּמַר. בִּכְלִי חֶרֶשׂ לֹא בִּמְפוּחָם. רַבָּנִין. וּמָאן דָּמַר אֲפִילוּ בִּמְפוּחָם. רַבָּנָן.

Some Tannaïm state: "In an earthenware vessel", not if it is sooty. Some Tannaïm state: "In an earthenware vessel", even if it is sooty. They wanted to say, he who says "in an earthenware vessel", not if it is sooty, is Rebbi Eliezer, but he who says, "in an earthenware vessel", even if it is sooty, follows the rabbis. All is of the rabbis: He who says "in an earthenware vessel", not if it is sooty, follows the rabbis, and he who says, "in an earthenware vessel", even if it is sooty, follows the rabbis[71].

71 A clean vessel is prescribed but an infraction of this rule does not invalidate the procedure. The Babli disagrees, 15b, and declares a sooty vessel unacceptable under any circumstance as long as the soot has not been removed by firing the vessel. Since the statement in the Babli is attributed to Rava who is described as knowledgeable in the rules of the Yerushalmi, the statement in the Babli is a direct polemic against the Yerushalmi.

(17d line 68) תַּמָּן תַּנִינָן. אֵזוֹב שֶׁהִזָּה בּוֹ כָּשֵׁר לְטַהֵר בּוֹ אֶת הַמְצוֹרָע. רִבִּי אִימִּי בְּשֵׁם רִבִּי לֶעְזָר. זוֹ לְהוֹצִיא מִדִּבְרֵי רִבִּי לְעָזָר. דְּתַנֵּי. הִזָּה בּוֹ עַל הַחַטָּאת פָּסוּל לַמְצוֹרָע. הִזָּה בּוֹ עַל הַמְצוֹרָע פָּסוּל לַחַטָּאת. אָמַר רִבִּי יוֹסֵי. וַהֲלֹא קַל וָחוֹמֶר הוּא. מָה אִם הַמְצוֹרָע שֶׁאֵין הַמְלָאכָה פּוֹסֶלֶת בּוֹ הִזָּה בּוֹ עַל הַחַטָּאת פָּסוּל לַמְצוֹרָע. חַטָּאת שֶׁהַמְלָאכָה פּוֹסֶלֶת בָּהּ הִזָּה בָּהּ עַל הַמְצוֹרָע אֵינוֹ דִין שֶׁיְּהֵא פָסוּל לַחַטָּאת.

There[72], we have stated: "A hyssop which was used to sprinkle is acceptable [to be used] to purify the sufferer from skin disease[73]." Rebbi Immi in the name of Rebbi Eleazar[74]: That [was stated] to exclude the opinion of Rebbi Eliezer[75], as it was stated[76]: If he sprinkled with it for purifying, it is disqualified for the sufferer from skin disease. If he sprinkled with it for the sufferer from skin disease, it is disqualified for purifying. [77]Rebbi Yose said, would that not be an argument *de minore ad majus*? Since for the sufferer from skin disease, for whose ceremony use does not disable, if he sprinkled with it for purifying, it is disqualified for the sufferer from skin disease; purifying, for whose ceremony use does disable, if he sprinkled with it for purifying, is it not logical that it should be disqualified for purifying?

72 Mishnah *Parah* 11:8. The hyssop was used to sprinkle water mixed with ashes of the red cow to cleanse a person defiled by the impurity of the dead. From the biblical expression (*Num.* 19:9) מֵי נִדָּה חַטָּאת הִיא "sprinkling water, it is purifying", the water is called in Talmudic terminology מֵי חַטָּאת or simply חַטָּאת "purifying (water)". Cf. also Note 36.

73 Hyssop alone is required for purifying (from the impurity of the dead) (*Num.* 19:18); for the cleansing from skin disease it is used among other things (*Lev.* 14:6).

74 The Amora, ben Pedat.

75 Tosephta *Nega'im* 8:2: "A hyssop acceptable for purifying is acceptable for the sufferer from skin disease. If he used it for sprinkling to purify it is still acceptable for the sufferer from skin disease. Rebbi Eliezer says, the cedar wood, hyssop, and crimson strip mentioned in the Torah (*Lev.* 14:6) cannot have been previously used for any purpose."

The prohibition of prior use is spelled out in the Torah for the red cow only (*Num.* 19:2). By rabbinic tradition, the prohibition is extended to the water used for purifying as explained at length in Mishnah *Parah*. R. Eliezer extends the prohibition to anything used in any ritual of purification by hyssop and water.

76 This *baraita* is not quoted in any other source; the Tosephta quoted in the preceding Note shows that the source of the *baraita* is the school of R. Eliezer.

77 The argument presented here is intended to show an error in the position of R. Eliezer. The argument of R. Yose (ben Ḥalaphta) is not found in any other source.

The argument goes as follows: Everybody agrees that the rules of purification from skin disease are not as stringent as those from the impurity of the dead. If using hyssop for purifying from the impurity of the dead would disqualify it as instrument for purifying from skin disease, one must require that one hyssop cannot be used for several people defiled by contact with a corpse. But is was general practice that the Temple provided a purification service where a person was standing in a window and was sprinkling continuously on the people walking by below, always using the same hyssop (Mishnah *Parah* 11:4); no dissent by R. Eliezer is recorded. Therefore, practice must follow the Mishnah, not R. Eliezer.

(18a line 7) הִזָּה בּוֹ עַל הַמְצוֹרָע זֶה. מַהוּ שֶׁיְּכַשֵּׁר לִמְצוֹרָע אַחֵר. מַה דָּמַר כָּשֵׁר. הָדָא רִבִּי יוּדָה וְרִבִּי לְעָזָר מוֹדֵי בֵיהּ. וּמַאן דָּמַר פָּסוּל. הָדָא לֵית רִבִּי יוּדָה וְרִבִּי לְעָזָר מוֹדֵיי בֵיהּ. תַּנֵּי. אָמַר רִבִּי יוּדָה. שַׁבָּתִי הָיְתָה וְהָלַכְתִּי אַחֲרֵי רִבִּי טַרְפוֹן לְבֵיתוֹ. אָמַר לִי. יְהוּדָה בְנִי. תֶּן לִי סַנְדָּלִי. וְנָתַתִּי לוֹ. וּפָשַׁט יָדוֹ לַחֲלוֹן וְנָתַן לִי מִמֶּנָּה מַקֵּל. אָמַר לִי. יְהוּדָה בְנִי. בְּזוֹ טִיהַרְתִּי שְׁלֹשָׁה מְצוֹרָעִין וְלָמַדְתִּי בּוֹ שֶׁבַע הֲלָכוֹת. שֶׁהִיא שֶׁלַּיַּבְּרוֹת. וְרֹאשָׁהּ טָרֵף. וְאוֹרְכָהּ אַמָּה. וְעוֹבְיָהּ כִּרְבִיעַ כֶּרַע מִיטָה. אַחַת לִשְׁנַיִם וּשְׁנַיִם לְאַרְבָּעָה. וּמַזִּין וְשׁוֹנִין וּמְשַׁלְּשִׁין וּמְטַהֲרִין. בִּפְנֵי הַבַּיִת וְשֶׁלֹּא בִּפְנֵי הַבַּיִת. וּמְטַהֲרִין בִּגְבוּלִין.

If he used it to sprinkle on the sufferer from skin disease, is it acceptable to use it for another sufferer from skin disease? If somebody said it is acceptable, Rebbi Jehudah and Rebbi Eleazar[78] will agree with him. But with him who said, it is disqualified, Rebbi Jehudah and Rebbi Eleazar will disagree. It was stated[79]: Rebbi Jehudah said, it was my

Sabbath[80] and I followed Rebbi Tarphon to his house. He said to me, Jehudah, my son, give me my sandals. I gave them to him. He reached with his hand to the window and gave me a stick[81] from there. He said to me, Jehudah, my son, with this one I cleansed three sufferers from skin disease and I taught with it seven practices. That it is *yabrut*[82], on its head is a leaf[83], it is one cubit long, its width is about one fourth that of a bed's leg (split one into two and two into four)[84], and one sprinkles and repeats and does it a third time[85], and one purifies when there is a Temple and when there is no Temple, and one purifies in the countryside[86].

78 No R. Eleazar (one of the Tannaïm, ben Pada or ben Shamua') is mentioned in any of our other sources as joining R. Jehudah in this controversy.

79 Tosephta *Nega'im* 8:2, *Sifra Meṣora'* (13).

80 It seems that in the Academy of R. Tarphon, the students had to serve their teacher on the Sabbath, taking turns.

81 Hyssop does not grow solid stems. Therefore, this must refer to the cedar branch used in the ceremony. It is to be assumed that cedar and hyssop, mentioned in parallel in the verse (*Lev.* 14:6), follow parallel rules.

82 In the Tosephta אברית, in *Sifra* ברות. The exact kind of cedar mentioned is not known. Since Mishnah *Parah* 11:6 states that any kind of hyssop known by a qualifying adjective is invalid (examples given are: blue hyssop, Roman hyssop, desert hyssop), R. Tarphon insists that any tree of the cedar family qualifies even if its trade name does not even contain the word "cedar".

83 A cedar stick without any green needles is invalid.

84 Even a very thin branch will do.

85 This answers our question.

86 Even though the final purification rite which gives access to the Sanctuary presupposes a Sanctuary, the preliminary rite which re-integrates the sufferer from skin disease into society (*Lev.* 14:1-9), while requiring the services of a Cohen such as R. Tarphon, is independent of the Temple

service. While R. Tarphon was old enough to have served in the Temple, R. Jehudah was born after its destruction.

(18a line 13) מִי. יָכוֹל מַרְאֶה מַיִם. תַּלְמוּד לוֹמַר אָרָךְ. אוֹ אָרָךְ. יָכוֹל מַרְאֶה דִּיוֹ. תַּלְמוּד לוֹמַר מִי. הָא כֵיצַד. מַרְאֶה מַיִם וּמַרְאֶה אָרָךְ. שִׁיעֲרוּ חֲכָמִים חֲצִי לוֹג מַיִם מִן הַכִּיוֹר. וְהָא תַנֵּי. רִבִּי יוּדָה אוֹמֵר. רְבִיעִית. רִבִּי יוּדָה כְּדַעְתֵּיהּ. דְּתַנִּינָן. כְּשֵׁם שֶׁהוּא מְמַעֵט בִּכְתָב כָּךְ הוּא מְמַעֵט בַּמַּיִם.

"Water[87]", I could think it should look like water. The verse says, "dust"[88]. Or "dust", I could think it should look like ink. The verse says, "water". How is that? The looks of water and the looks of dust[89]. The Sages estimated half a *log* of water from the wash basin. But did we not state[90]: "Rebbi Jehudah says, a quarter [log]". Rebbi Jehudah follows his particular way, as we have stated: "Just as he shortens the writing so he decreases the amount of water."

87 *Num.* 5:17: מֵי הַמָּרִים הַמְאָרֲרִים.
88 A translation (Arabism) of the word עָפָר "dust"; cf. Arabic ارض.
89 The dust should be a powder on the clear water.
90 In the Mishnah.

(18a line 17) תַּמָּן תַּנִּינָן. אַף הִיא עָשְׂתָה טַבְלָה שֶׁלִּזְהָב שֶׁפָּרָשַׁת סוֹטָה כְּתוּבָה עָלֶיהָ. שֶׁבְּשָׁעָה שֶׁהַחַמָּה זוֹרַחַת הָיוּ הַנִּיצוֹצִים מְנַתְּזִין מִמֶּנָּה וְהָיוּ יוֹדְעִין שֶׁזָּרְחָה הַחַמָּה. מַה הָיָה כָתוּב עָלֶיהָ. רֵישׁ לָקִישׁ אָמַר בְּשֵׁם רִבִּי יַנַּאי. אָלֶף בֵּית הָיָה כוֹתֵב עָלֶיהָ. וְהָא תָאנֵי. בִּכְתָב שֶׁכֵּן כֵּן כְּתִיב שֶׁכֵּן. לֹא מְעוֹבֶּה וְלֹא מֵידַק אֶלָּא בֵּינוֹנִי. פָּתַר לָהּ בְּאָלֶף שֶׁבּוֹ מֵאָלֶף שֶׁבּוֹ בְּבֵית שֶׁכֵּן מִבֵּית שֶׁכֵּן. תַּנֵּי רִבִּי הוֹשַׁעְיָא. כָּל־פָּרָשַׁת סוֹטָה הָיְתָה כְּתוּבָה עָלֶיהָ. שֶׁמִּמֶּנָּה הָיָה קוֹרֵא וּמְתַרְגֵּם כָּל־דִּיקְדּוּקֵי הַפָּרָשָׁה. וְלָמָּה מַיִם וְעָפָר וּכְתָב. מַיִם. מִמָּקוֹם שֶׁבָּאת. עָפָר. לְמָקוֹם שֶׁהִיא הוֹלֶכֶת. כְּתָב. לִפְנֵי מִי שֶׁהִיא עֲתִידָה לִיתֵּן דִּין וְחֶשְׁבּוֹן.

There[91], we have stated: "Also she made a golden plate with the paragraph of the suspected wife written on it." When the sun rose, sparks were reflected on it and one knew that the sun had risen[92]. What was written on it? Rebbi Simeon ben Laqish[93] said in the name of Rebbi Yannai: Alef-Bet was written on it[94]. But did we not state: In the script there it was written here, not heavy, not thin, but average[95]. Explain "the Alef there" by "from the Alef there"[96]; "the Bet there" by "from the Bet there". Rebbi Hoshaia stated: The entire paragraph of the suspected wife was written there, and from it he was reading and explaining all details of the paragraph[97]: Why water, dust, and writing? Water, from the place she came; dust, the place she goes to; writing, before Whom she will have to be accountable in the future.

91 Mishnah *Yoma* 3:10, speaking of Queen Helena of Adiabene.

92 The golden tablet was fixed on the Eastern wall of the Temple building.

93 The short form ריש לקיש is a Babylonism.

94 Single letters were written on the tablet, each letter being the first of its word. (Cf. P. Kahle, Masoreten des Westens, II, pp. 88-95).

95 The suspected wife's scroll had to be written in the way the letters were on the queen's tablet, not ornamental and not in *italics*. The questioner thought that the entire tablet had to be copied as it was written; then an abbreviated version would be impossible.

96 For each letter one copies the entire word. The first sentence of the scroll would read on the tablet as

אם ל ש א א ו ל ש ט ת א ה ט מ ה ה ה

which would be copied as

אם לא שכב איש אתך ואם לא שטית טומאה תחת אישך הנקי ממי המרים המאררים האלה

where every first letter was copied exactly from the tablet and the rest of the word added in the same style of script.

97 While writing, the Cohen explained the text homiletically to the suspected wife, as explained in the next

paragraph, so that she would understand the meaning of the ceremony.

(18a line 26) תַּמָּן תַּנִּינָן. עֲקַבְיָה בֶּן מְהַלַלְאֵל אוֹמֵר. הִסְתַּכֵּל בִּשְׁלֹשָׁה דְבָרִים וְאֵין אַתָּה בָא לִידֵי עֲבֵירָה. רִבִּי אַבָּא בְּרֵיהּ דְּרַב פַּפֵּי וְרִבִּי יְהוֹשֻׁעַ דְּסִיכְנִין בְּשֵׁם רִבִּי לֵוִי. שְׁלָשְׁתָּן דָּרַשׁ עֲקַבְיָא מִפָּסוּק אֶחָד. וּזְכוֹר אֶת בּוֹרְאֶךָ. בֵּירְךָ. בּוֹרְךָ. בּוֹרְאֶךָ. בֵּירְךָ. מִמָּקוֹם שֶׁבָּאתָה. בּוֹרְךָ. לְמָקוֹם שֶׁאַתָּה הוֹלֵךְ. בּוֹרְאֶךָ. לִפְנֵי מִי שֶׁאַתְּ עָתִיד לִיתֵּן דִּין וְחֶשְׁבּוֹן.

[98]There[99], we have stated: "Aqabiah ben Mehallalel says, consider three things and you will not commit any transgression." Rebbi Abba ben Rav Pappaeus and Rebbi Joshua from Sikhnin in the name of Rebbi Joshua ben Levi: All three Aqabiah derived from the same verse[100]: "Remember your Creator," your fountain, your cavern, your Creator[101]. Your fountain, from where you came. Your cave, to where you are going. Your Creator, before Whom you will have to be accountable in the future.

98   *Lev. rabba* 18(1); cf. *Abot dR. Natan*, A 19, B 32; *Derekh Ereṣ* 3 in the name of Ben Azai.

98   Mishnah *Abot* 3:1: Aqabiah ben Mehallalel says, consider three things and you will not commit any transgression: Know from where you came, where you are going, and before Whom you will be held accountable in the future. From where you came, from a stinking drop. Where you are going, to a place of dust, worms, and vermin. Before Whom you will be held accountable in the future, before the King over emperors and kings, the Holy One, praise to Him."

100   *Eccl.* 12:1.

101   Based on three possible vocalizations of the biblical בראך. The vocalization בּוֹרְאֶךָ instead of the masoretic בֹּרְאֶיךָ is the manuscript's.

(18a line 31) שְׁלֹשָׁה דְּבָרִים צְרִיכִין שֶׁיְּהוּ לִשְׁמָהּ. וְכָתַב לָהּ. וְעָשָׂה לָהּ. אוֹ חוּפְשָׁה לֹא נִיתַּן לָהּ. שְׁלֹשָׁה דְּבָרִים צְרִיכִין שֶׁיְּהוּ נִרְאִין. אֵפֶר פָּרָה. וַעֲפַר סוֹטָה. וְרוֹק יְבָמָה. תַּנֵּי רִבִּי יִשְׁמָעֵאל. אַף דַּם צִפּוֹר מְצוֹרָע. אָמַר רִבִּי זְעִירָא. שִׁיעֲרוּ לוֹמַר. אֵין דַּם צִפּוֹר קְטַנָּה בָּטֵל בִּרְבִיעִית. וְלֹא דַם צִפּוֹר גְּדוֹלָה מְבַטֵּל אֶת הָרְבִיעִית. כְּהָדָא דְתַנֵּי. בְּדָם. יָכוֹל בְּדָם וַדַּאי. תַּלְמוּד לוֹמַר מַיִם חַיִּים. אִי מַיִם חַיִּים. יָכוֹל שֶׁיְּהוּ כוּלָן מַיִם חַיִּים. תַּלְמוּד לוֹמַר דָּם. הָא כֵיצַד. מַיִם חַיִּים שֶׁדַּם הַצִּיפּוֹר נִיכָּר בָּהֶן. שִׁיעֲרוּ חֲכָמִים. רְבִיעִית. רִבִּי פְּדָת בְּשֵׁם רִבִּי יוֹחָנָן. מֵי סוֹטָה נִפְסָלִין בְּלִינָה. רִבִּי אָחָא בְּשָׁם רַב אָבִינָא. כָּל־שֶׁאֵין מִמֶּנּוּ לַמִּזְבֵּחַ אֵין הַלִּינָה פוֹסֶלֶת בּוֹ.

Three things have to be executed in the name [of the woman][102]. "He shall write *for her*.[103]" "He shall execute *for her*.[104]" "Or manumission was not given *to her*.[105]" [106]Three things have to be seen: The ashes of the cow[107], the dust of the suspected wife[108], and the spittle of the sister-in-law[109]. Rebbi Ismael stated: Also the blood of the bird for the sufferer from skin disease[110]. Rebbi Ze'ira said, the Sages estimated that the blood of a small bird becomes negligible in a quarter [log] and the blood of a large bird does not render a quarter [log of water] negligible[111]. As it was stated[112]: "In the blood[113]", should that be only blood? The verse says, "fresh water". If fresh water, should that be all fresh water? The verse says, "in the blood". How is this? Fresh water in which the bird's blood is recognizable. The Sages estimated, a quarter [log]. Rebbi Pedat in the name of Rebbi Johanan: The water of a suspected wife becomes disqualified by staying overnight[114]. Rebbi Aha in the name of Rebbi Abina: Nothing of which the altar has no part becomes disqualified by staying overnight[115].

102   A similar text in Tosephta *Giṭṭin* 2:7.

103   *Deut.* 24:1, speaking of a bill of divorce. The document has to be written *for her*, otherwise it is invalid (Mishnah *Giṭṭin* 3:2, *Sifry Deut.* 269, quoted many times in both Talmudim).

104   *Num.* 5:30. The Cohen has to conduct the ceremony of the suspected wife for that particular woman, otherwise it is invalid. The Babli (18a) refers this only to the scroll which is to be written for the woman, which has to be written and erased with that particular person in mind.

105   *Lev.* 19:20, speaking of a slave girl. The document of manumission has to be executed for the particular slave girl. This requirement is then extended in the Tosephta to the manumission of male slaves.

106   Babli 16b; Tosephta 1:8; *Sifry Num.* 11, *Sifry Zuṭa Naśo*; *Num. rabba* 9(13).

107   Some ash has to be visible on the water used to purify from the impurity of the dead.

108   As described in the Mishnah.

109   *Deut.* 25:9, in the ceremony of *ḥalîṣah*; cf. Mishnah *Yebamot* 12:6.

110   *Lev.* 14:5; the healed patient has to be purified by being sprinkled with spring water mixed with the blood of a bird.

111   Taking exactly one quarter *log* (135 dl, cf. Note 55) will prevent any problems.

112   *Sifra Meṣora' Pereq* 1(5); Babli 16b.

113   *Lev.* 14:6. The Cohen has to dip the hyssop and a living bird "in the blood of the slaughtered bird on the flowing water". The "fresh water" is in a vessel but was taken from a spring. The blood of the slaughtered bird is on the fresh water in the vessel. The simple meaning of the verse, that the bird's blood must form a layer on the fresh water, obviously cannot be meant.

114   Following the opinion that the water has to be taken from the water basin in the Temple. Any water taken from there and sanctified in a temple vessel belongs to the service of that day; once the day has passed (which in the Temple is counted from dawn to dawn), its service cannot be made up (cf. *Sukkah* 4:7). But according to the opinion that the water may come from outside sources, the position of R. Joḥanan could be explained. However, R. Joḥanan holds everywhere that practice follows the anonymous Mishnah (*Yebamot* 4:11, Note 177; Babli *Ḥulin* 43a).

115   R. Joḥanan will hold that water

in the basin is for the altar in the water offering on Tabernacles (*Sukkah* 4:7). The problem is not discussed in the Babli; Maimonides (*Soṭah* 4:12) follows R. Joḥanan as the overriding authority.

(18a line 40) וּמִן הֶעָפָר. יָכוֹל מִן הַמּוּנָח¹¹⁶ לְקוּפָה. תַּלְמוּד לוֹמַר אֲשֶׁר יִהְיֶה בְּקַרְקַע הַמִּשְׁכָּן. אוֹ אֲשֶׁר יִהְיֶה בְּקַרְקַע הַמִּשְׁכָּן. יָכוֹל עַד שֶׁיַּחְפּוֹר בַּדֶּקֶל. תַּלְמוּד לוֹמַר אֲשֶׁר יִהְיֶה. הָא כֵיצַד. אִם אֵין שָׁם מֵבִיא וְנוֹתֵן שָׁם. אָמַר רִבִּי אָבִין. יָכוֹל לֹא יְהֵא כָשֵׁר עַד שֶׁיַּחְפּוֹר בַּדֶּקֶל. תַּלְמוּד לוֹמַר אֲשֶׁר יִהְיֶה. מִכָּל מָקוֹם. הַמִּשְׁכָּן. לְרַבּוֹת הַמִּשְׁכָּן וְנוֹב וְגִבְעוֹן וְשִׁילוֹ וּבֵית הָעוֹלָמִים.

"And from the dust.¹¹⁷" One could think, from what lies in a chest. The verse says, "which will be on the floor of the Sanctuary". If "which will be on the floor of the Sanctuary", one could think only that he has to dig with a pick-axe¹¹⁸, the verse says "which will be". How is that? If there is nothing there, one brings and puts it there. ¹¹⁹Rebbi Abin said, "which will be on the floor of the Sanctuary", one could think [the dust] qualified only if he digs with a pick-axe, the verse says "which will be". From anywhere. "The Sanctuary", that includes the Tabernacle, Nob, Gibeon, Shilo, and the Eternal House¹²⁰.

116 Reading of the Rome ms., already noted by R. Moses Margalit. Leiden ms. and *editio princeps*: מן המזבח לקופה "from the altar into a chest".

117 *Num.* 5:17: "And from the dust which will be on the floor of the Sanctuary, the Cohen has to take and put on the water." The parallel version in the Babli, 15b, [and *Num. rabba* 9(13)], is formulated differently.

118 This דקל is not Aramaic "date palm" but the equivalent of Mishnaic דקר "pick-axe" by a change of liquids.

119 R. Abin reformulates the preceding argument from a slightly different angle. His polemic is directed against a *baraita* preserved only in the Babli (15b, bottom; variant readings in the critical edition p. רלו) which requires the dust to be prepared outside, brought inside, and spread on the floor of the Sanctuary.

120 The order given here is also in the Munich ms. of the Babli. The historic order would be: the Tabernacle, Shilo, Nob, Gibeon, and the Eternal House (the Temple which in rabbinic tradition cannot be replaced by a Sanctuary at any other place, Mishnah *Zebaḥim* 14:8.)

משנה ג: בָּא לוֹ לִכְתּוֹב אֶת הַמְּגִילָה מֵאֵי זֶה מָקוֹם הוּא כוֹתֵב. אִם לֹא שָׁכַב אִישׁ אוֹתָךְ וְאַתְּ כִּי שָׂטִית תַּחַת אִישֵׁךְ וגו'. וְאֵינוֹ כוֹתֵב וְהִשְׁבִּיעַ הַכֹּהֵן אֶת הָאִשָּׁה בִּשְׁבוּעַת הָאָלָה. וְכוֹתֵב יִתֵּן יְ"יָ אוֹתָךְ לְאָלָה וְלִשְׁבוּעָה בְּתוֹךְ עַמֵּךְ בְּתֵת יְ"יָ אֶת יְרֵכֵךְ נוֹפֶלֶת וְאֶת בִּטְנֵךְ צָבָה. וּבָאוּ הַמַּיִם הַמְאָרְרִים הָאֵלֶה בְּמֵעַיִךְ לַצְבּוֹת בֶּטֶן וְלַנְפִּל יָרֵךְ. וְאֵינוֹ כוֹתֵב וְאָמְרָה הָאִשָּׁה אָמֵן אָמֵן. (fol. 17c)

Mishnah 3: Then he starts writing the scroll. From where does he start writing? (*Num.* 5:19) "If no man has lain with you, . . ." (*v.* 20) "but if you deviated from under your husband," etc. He does not write (*v.* 21) "the Cohen has to administer the oath of curse to the woman," but he writes "may the Eternal make you a curse and a swear-word among your people when the Eternal will make your hips diminish and your belly inflate." (*v.* 22) "This curse-water would come into your intestines to inflate belly and diminish hips." He does not write (*v.* 22) "the woman shall say, Amen, Amen."

הלכה ג: בָּא לוֹ לִכְתּוֹב אֶת הַמְּגִילָה כול'. רִבִּי קְרִיסְפָּא אָמַר. אִיתְפַּלְגוּן רִבִּי יוֹחָנָן וְרֵישׁ לָקִישׁ. חַד אָמַר מַשְׁבִּיעַ וְאַחַר כָּךְ כּוֹתֵב. וְחָרָנָה אָמַר. כּוֹתֵב וְאַחַר כָּךְ מַשְׁבִּיעַ. הֲווֹן בָּעֵי מֵימַר. מָאן דָּמַר. מַשְׁבִּיעַ וְאַחַר כָּךְ כּוֹתֵב. הֵיךְ מַה דְּהוּא קִרְיָיא. וְהִשְׁבִּיעַ וְכָתַב. וּמָאן דָּמַר. כּוֹתֵב וְאַחַר כָּךְ מַשְׁבִּיעַ. כְּדֵי לִסְמוֹךְ שְׁבוּעָה לְהַשְׁקָיָיה. אִית תַּנָּיֵי תַנֵּי. בֵּין תְּנַיִין בֵּין שְׁבוּעוֹת מְעַכְּבִין. אִית תַּנָּיֵי תַנֵּי. שְׁבוּעוֹת מְעַכְּבוֹת. תְּנָיִין אֵינָן מְעַכְּבִין. הֲווֹן בָּעֵי מֵימַר. מָאן דָּמַר. בֵּין תְּנָיִין בֵּין שְׁבוּעוֹת מְעַכְּבִין. אִית לֵיהּ חוּקָה תּוֹרָה מְעַכֵּב. (fol. 18a)

וּמָאן דָּמַר. שְׁבוּעוֹת מְעַכְּבוֹת וּתְנָיָין אֵינָן מְעַכְּבִין לֵית לֵיהּ. עוֹד הוּא אִית לֵיהּ. אֶלָּא שֶׁאֵינָן עַל הַסֵּדֶר. וְאַתְיָן אִילֵּין פְּלוּגָתָא כְּהָדֵין פְּלוּגָתָא. מָאן דָּמַר. בֵּין תְּנָיָין בֵּין שְׁבוּעוֹת מְעַכְּבִין. כְּמָאן דָּמַר. מַשְׁבִּיעַ וְאַחַר כָּךְ כּוֹתֵב. וּמָאן דָּמַר. שְׁבוּעוֹת מְעַכְּבוֹת וּתְנָיָין אֵינָן מְעַכְּבִין. כְּמָאן דָּמַר. כּוֹתֵב וְאַחַר כָּךְ מַשְׁבִּיעַ.

Halakhah 3: "Then he starts writing the scroll," etc. Rebbi Crispus said, Rebbi Johanan and Rebbi Simeon ben Laqish[93] disagreed. One said, he administers the oath and then he writes; the other one said, he writes and then he administers the oath. They wanted to say that he who says, he administers the oath and then he writes, follows what is written in the verse[121] but he who says, he writes and then he administers the oath, to join the oath to the drinking[122]. There are Tannaïm who state: The conditions[123] and the oaths impede; there are Tannaïm who state: The oaths impede, the conditions do not impede. They wanted to say that he who says, the conditions and the oaths impede, holds that "law" and "teaching" impedes[124]; but he who says, the oaths impede, the conditions do not impede, does not agree. Certainly he does agree[125] but they[126] are not [written] in order. It turns out that this disagreement is like the previous disagreement. He who says, the conditions and the oaths impede, agrees with him who says, he administers the oath and then he writes; but he who says, the oaths impede, the conditions do not impede, agrees with him who says, he writes and then he administers the oath.

121 Administering the oath is mentioned in verses 19 and 21; writing the curses is only mentioned in v. 23, followed by the commandment to let the woman drink the water in v. 24. But then the ceremony is interrupted by presenting the flour offering and it is stated (vv. 26, 27) that only after that the water is to be given.

122 The Babli [17b, 19b, quoted in *Num. rabba* 5(45)] solves the problem by requiring that the scroll be written

after the wife has agreed to the oath but before it is administered.

123 All details of the procedure outlined in the verses. The first opinion holds that the entire procedure is invalid if one detail is wrong. The second opinion holds that the procedure becomes invalid only if the water is given before the oath was administered.

124 It is a generally accepted principle (Babli *Menaḥot* 19a) that any biblical precept characterized as חֻקָּה or תּוֹרָה is invalid if not executed to the letter. The procedure of the suspected wife is called תורה in v. 30.

125 Nobody disagrees with the rule expressed in Note 124.

126 The sequence of execution of the ceremony may not follow the sequence of the verses; cf. Mishnah 3:1.

(fol. 17c) **משנה ד:** רִבִּי יוֹסֵי אוֹמֵר לֹא הָיָה מַפְסִיק. רִבִּי יְהוּדָה אוֹמֵר כָּל־עַצְמוֹ אֵינוֹ כוֹתֵב אֶלָּא יִתֵּן לִי אוֹתָךְ לְאָלָה וְלִשְׁבוּעָה בְּתוֹךְ עַמֵּךְ בְּתֵת לִי אֶת יְרֵכֵךְ נוֹפֶלֶת וְאֶת בִּטְנֵךְ צָבָה. וּבָאוּ הַמַּיִם הַמְאָרֲרִים הָאֵלֶּה בְּמֵעַיִךְ וגו'. וְאֵינוֹ כוֹתֵב וְאָמְרָה הָאִשָּׁה אָמֵן אָמֵן.

Mishnah 4: Rebbi Yose says, he does not interrupt[127]. Rebbi Jehudah said[128] he does not write anything but (*Num.* 5:21): "May the Eternal make you a curse and a swear-word among your people when the Eternal makes your hips diminish and your belly swell." (*v.* 22) "This curse-water would come into your intestines . . ." He does not write (*v.* 22) "the woman shall say, Amen, Amen."

127 He requires that verses 19-22 be written in their entirety.

128 He holds that verses 19-20 indicate a preparatory speech by the Cohen, that the valid curses, designated as such, are only in v. 21 and part of v. 22.

(fol. 18a) **הלכה ד**: רִבִּי יוֹסֵי אוֹמֵר לֹא הָיָה מַפְסִיק כּוּל׳. לֵוִי בַּר סִיסִי בְּעָא קוֹמֵי רִבִּי. מְגִילַת סוֹטָה מָהוּ שֶׁתְּטַמֵא אֶת הַיָדַיִם. אָמַר לֵיהּ. הֲרֵי זֶה שְׁאֵלָה. אָמַר רִבִּי יוֹסֵי. אֵינָהּ שְׁאֵילָה. כְּלוּם גָזְרוּ עַל הַיָדַיִם שֶׁיְטַמְאוּ אֶת הַיָדַיִם לֹא מִפְּנֵי קְדוּשָׁתָן. וְזוֹ לִמְחִיקָה נִיתְּנָה. לֹא צוֹרְכָה דְלֹא הוֹאִיל וְנִיתְּנָה לִמְחִיקָה.

Halakhah 4: "Rebbi Yose says, he does not interrupt," etc. Levi bar Sisi asked before Rebbi: Does the suspected wife's scroll defile the hands[129]? He said to him, that is a question. Rebbi Yose[130] said, it is no question. Did they not decree impurity of the hands for books only because of their holiness? And that one has to be erased[131]! One only questions because it had to be erased[132].

---

129 All biblical texts defile the hands by a rabbinic decree, to make it impossible to a fellow of the faithful to study the Bible with food in his hand, to protect the books from mice and other animals found around food; cf. Mishnah *Yadaim* 3, Babli *Šabbat* 14a. The decree applies to any text at least 85 letters long. The impurity of hands, being secondary, would not cause any trouble in the Temple. The Cohen simply would have to wash his hands before handling the cup of water from which the woman drinks.

130 The Amora.

131 The entire scroll has to be erased, including the two instances of the Divine Name which in any other circumstance may not be erased. How can such a text claim holiness?

132 R. Yose's argument is irrelevant. There remain two questions: (1) After the script has been erased, does the sheet retain holiness and must be buried, or may it be re-used for profane purposes? If it retains holiness it induces impurity of the hands. (2) If for some reason the scroll was not erased, for example if the wife admits her infidelity, the scroll has to be buried or otherwise hidden (Mishnah 3:3). The question is whether this is a biblical requirement because of the sanctity of the writing, or rabbinical to make sure the scroll could not be used for any other woman (cf. Note 104). The question remains unanswered; Maimonides (*Abot Haṭum'a* 9:11) disregards the question and follows R. Yose.

(18a line 62) כַּמָּה אוֹתִיּוֹת כָּתוּב בָּהּ וִיהֵא שֶׁלֹּא לְצוֹרֶךְ וִיהֵא חַיָּיב. תַּנֵּי רִבִּי חָנִין. בֵּית שַׁמַּי אוֹמְרִים. אַחַת. וּבֵית הִלֵּל אוֹמְרִים. שְׁתַּיִם. אָמַר רִבִּי הִילַי. טַעֲמוֹן דְּבֵית הִלֵּל כְּדֵי לִכְתּוֹב יָהּ. רִבִּי יוּדָן בָּעֵי. כָּתַב מִפִּיו. וּמָחַק בֶּעָפָר. הָיָה כּוֹתֵב רִאשׁוֹן רִאשׁוֹן וּמוֹחֵק. [תַּנֵּי. רִבִּי אֶלְעָזָר בֶּן שַׁמּוּעַ אוֹמֵר. אֵין כּוֹתְבִין עַל אוֹר בְּהֵמָה טְמֵיאָה. אָמַר רִבִּי שִׁמְעוֹן. מִכֵּיוָן דְּאַתְּ אָמַר. לִמְחִיקָה נִתְנָה. לָמָּה אֵינוֹ כּוֹתֵב.]133 תַּנֵּי. רִבִּי אֶלְעָזָר בֶּן [שִׁמְעוֹן]134 אוֹמֵר. רוֹאֶה אֲנִי אֶת דִּבְרֵי אֶלְעָזָר בֶּן שַׁמּוּעַ מִדִּבְרֵי אַבָּא. שֶׁמָּא תֹאמַר. אֵינוֹ שׁוֹתָה. וְנִמְצָא הַשֵּׁם גָּנוּז עַל אוֹר שֶׁלִּבְהֵמָה טְמֵיאָה.

How many letters have to be written unnecessarily[135] for him to be guilty? Rebbi Ḥanin stated: The House of Shammai say, one; the House of Hillel say, two. Rebbi Hilai said, the reason of the House of Hillel: That he could have written Yah[136]. Rebbi Yudan asked, if he wrote from memory[137], or rubbed it off with dust[138], or wrote one word and wiped it off immediately[139]? It was stated: Rebbi Eleazar ben Shamua said, one does not write on leather from an unclean animal[140]. Rebbi Simeon said, since you said it is written to be erased, why can he not write? It was stated: Rebbi Eleazar ben Simeon said, I prefer the words of Eleazar ben Shamua over my father's words. Maybe she will say: I will not drink. Then the Name would be hidden[141] on leather from an unclean animal.

133 From *editio princeps*, not in the ms.

134 From *editio princeps*. In the ms: שמוע.

135 In a way that makes the text unacceptable; e. g. with one of the proscribed types of ink. Then erasing the Name will be sinful.

Tosaphot (20a) have a completely different reading: כמה ימחק "How much does he have to erase? Rebbi Ḥanin stated..."

136 The shortest divine Name which may not be erased.

137 A Torah scroll written from memory, not from a corrected original,

cannot be used (*Megillah*, Yerushalmi 4:1; Babli 18b). This is a rabbinic requirement.

138 The verse requires erasing with water. The answer to this question is not given; the negative answer is obvious from Note 124.

139 Before the ink has time to dry. That procedure saves much time and work. No answer is given. In the Babli, 18a, the procedure is declared invalid.

140 A Torah scroll must be written on leather or parchment from an animal whose kind could be eaten. This is derived in both Talmudim from the verse *Ex.* 13:9: "That the Eternal's Torah shall be in your mouth."

141 Mishnah 3:3. The matter is one of good behavior, not of a biblical precept.

(18a line 69) הָכָא כְּתִיב סֵפֶר וְהָכָא כְּתִיב סֵפֶר. הָכָא אַתְּ אָמַר. כָּל־דָּבָר שֶׁהוּא כְתָלוּשׁ. וְהָכָא [אַתְּ]142 אָמַר הָכֵין. אָמַר לֵיהּ. שַׁנְיָיה הִיא הָכָא דִכְתִיב בַּסֵּפֶר.

There is written "book", and here is written "book"[143]. There, you say anything which is plucked. And here, you say so? He said to him, it is different here because it is written "in a book"[144].

142 From the Rome ms., missing in the Leiden ms.

143 The divorce document is called "a book of divorce" in *Deut.* 24:1. Mishnah *Gittin* 2:3 states that one may write on anything, e. g. on a leaf which was plucked from its plant; according to some authorities the husband may even write the bill on the horns of a cow and deliver the cow to his wife. But for the document of the suspected wife one requires regular writing leather.

144 *Num.* 5:23. This is more explicit in Mishnah 5, quoted in *Sifry Num.* 16; *Num. rabba* 5(47).

(18a line 71) וְכָתַב. יָכוֹל בִּדְיוֹ וּבְסִיקְרָא וּבְקוֹמוֹס וּבְקַלְקַנְתּוֹס. תַּלְמוּד לוֹמַר וּמָחָה. אִי מָחָה יָכוֹל בְּמַשְׁקִין אוֹ בְּמֵי פֵירוֹת. תַּלְמוּד לוֹמַר וְכָתַב. הָא כֵּיצַד. כְּתָב שֶׁהוּא יָכוֹל לְהִימָחוֹת. וְאֵי זוֹ זוֹ. זוֹ [דְיוֹ]145 שֶׁאֵין בּוֹ קַלְקַנְתּוֹס. וְהָתַנֵּי.

אִם מָחַק מִתּוֹךְ הַסֵּפֶר כָּשֵׁר. תִּיפְתַּר כְּהָדֵין תַּנָּיָא דְתַנֵּי. אָמַר רִבִּי מֵאִיר. כָּל־יָמִים שֶׁהָיִינוּ לְמֵידִין אֵצֶל רִבִּי יִשְׁמָעֵאל לֹא הָיִינוּ נוֹתְנִין קַלְקַנְתּוֹס בַּדִּיּוֹ.

[146]"And he writes". I could think [one writes] with ink, or vermilion, or gum, or copper sulfate[147], the verse says, "he shall wipe off"[148]. If he has to erase, I could think [one writes] with drinks or fruit juice; the verse says, "he shall write"[149]. How is that? Writing that can be wiped off. What is this? This is ink without vitriol. But did we not state: If he wiped off from a Torah scroll it is valid. Explain it following the Tanna who stated: Rebbi Meïr said, all the time we were studying with Rebbi Ismael, we put no vitriol in the ink[150].

145 Reading of the Rome ms., missing in Leiden ms. and *editio princeps*.

146 This is the commentary on Mishnah 5.

147 Greek χάλκανθον. Rashi (*Erubin* 13a) translates Romance *adrement*, Latin *atramentum*. Pliny (*Hist. Nat.* xxxiv.32) writes that the Greeks call *chalcanthum* what in Rome is called *atramentum sutorium*, "blacking for leather".

148 *Num.* 5:23.

149 In the sense of a permanent writing.

150 The Babli (*Erubin* 13a) reports that R. Ismael required that a Torah scroll must be written so that it could serve as the suspected wife's scroll.

(fol. 17c) **משנה ה**: וְאֵינוֹ כוֹתֵב לֹא עַל הַלּוּחַ וְלֹא עַל הַנְּיָיר וְלֹא עַל הַדִּיפְתְּרָא אֶלָּא עַל הַמְגִילָּה שֶׁנֶּאֱמַר בַּסֵּפֶר. אֵינוֹ כוֹתֵב לֹא בַקּוֹמוֹס וְלֹא בַּקַּנְקַלְתּוֹס וְלֹא בְּכָל־דָּבָר שֶׁהוּא רוֹשֵׁם אֶלָּא בַדְּיוֹ שֶׁנֶּאֱמַר וּמָחָה כְּתָב שֶׁיָּכוֹל לְהִימָחוֹת.

Mishnah 5: He does not write on a wooden plank, or on papyrus, or on διφθέρα[151], only on a scroll, as it is said: "In a book[148]". He does not write with gum[152] or vitriol nor with anything leaving a permanent impression except with ink; it is written "he shall wipe off", writing that can be wiped off[146].

151 Greek "hide prepared for writing." The traditional interpretation of the Mishnaic word is "rough parchment; incompletely tanned skin."

152 Latin *commis, gummi*; Greek κόμμι, τό "gum".

משנה ו: וְלָמָה הִיא אוֹמֶרֶת אָמֵן אָמֵן. אָמֵן עַל הָאָלָה. אָמֵן עַל הַשְּׁבוּעָה. אָמֵן מֵאִישׁ זֶה. אָמֵן מֵאִישׁ אַחֵר. אָמֵן שֶׁלֹּא נִטְמֵאתִי וְאִם נִטְמֵאתִי יָבוֹאוּ בִי. אָמֵן שֶׁלֹּא שָׂטִיתִי אֲרוּסָה וּנְשׂוּאָה וְשׁוֹמֶרֶת יָבָם וּכְנוּסָה. רִבִּי מֵאִיר אוֹמֵר אָמֵן שֶׁלֹּא נִטְמֵאתִי אָמֵן שֶׁלֹּא אֶטַּמֵּא. (fol. 17c)

Mishnah 6: Why does she repeat[153]: "Amen Amen"? Amen on the curse, Amen on the oath, Amen from this man, Amen from any other man. Amen that I was not defiled and if I was defiled it should hurt me[154]. Amen that I did not deviate preliminarily married[155] and married, waiting for the levir and taken in[156]. Rebbi Meïr says, Amen that I was not defiled, Amen that I shall not be defiled.

153 In the Bablylonian Mishnah: על מה היא אומרת "What does she imply by repeating". The reference is to *Num.* 5:22.

154 In the Babylonian Mishnah, this sentence comes after the following.

155 Cf. *Yebamot*, Chapter 1, Note 63; *Peah* Chapter 6, Note 46.

156 If the first husband had died childless and the levir brings her to the Temple as his wife. Only R. Aqiba considers sexual relations of the not-yet-married widow a crime. All other authorities will remove the mention of the widow "waiting to be married by the levir".

(fol. 18b) **הלכה ו**: אֵינוֹ כּוֹתֵב לֹא עַל הַלּוּחַ כול'. רִבִּי לֶעְזָר בְּשֵׁם רִבִּי יוֹסֵי בֶּן זִמְרָה. אָמֵן לְקַבָּלָה. אָמֵן לִשְׁבוּעָה. אָמֵן יְיָאָמְנוּ הַדְּבָרִים. אָמֵן לְקַבָּלָה מְסוֹטָה. אָמֵן לִשְׁבוּעָה. לְמַעַן הָקִים אֶת הַשְּׁבוּעָה אֲשֶׁר נִשְׁבַּעְתִּי לַאֲבוֹתֶיךָ וגו'. אָמֵן יְיָאָמְנוּ הַדְּבָרִים. וַיַּעַן בְּנָיָה בֶן יְהוֹיָדָע [הַכֹּהֵן][157] אֶת הַמֶּלֶךְ וַיֹּאמֶר אָמֵן וגו'. אָמַר רִבִּי תַּנְחוּמָא. אֵין מִן הָדֵין אָמֵן שְׁבוּעָה. לֵית שְׁמַע מִינָהּ כְּלוּם. וְיֵידָא אָמְרָה דָא לְעָבְרְךָ בִּבְרִית י"י אֱלֹהֶיךָ וּבְאָלָתוֹ. וְאֵין אָלָה אֶלָּא שְׁבוּעָה. כְּמָה דְתֵימַר. וְהִשְׁבִּיעַ הַכֹּהֵן אֶת הָאִשָּׁה בִּשְׁבֻעַת הָאָלָה.

Halakhah 6[158]: "He does not write on a wooden plank," etc. Rebbi Eleazar in the name of Rebbi Yose ben Zimra[159]: "Amen" [is said] for acceptance, "Amen" for an oath, "Amen", may the words be confirmed. "Amen" [is said] for acceptance, from the suspected wife[160]. "Amen" for an oath: "To keep the oath I had sworn to your forefathers", etc[161]. "Amen", may the words be confirmed[162]: "Benaiah ben Yehoyada (the priest) answered the king and said Amen", etc. Rebbi Tanhuma said, that does not prove that Amen means an oath, it implies nothing[163]. But the following says: "that you pass by the covenant of your God and His curse[164]," because oath means curse, as you say[165]: "The Cohen has to administer to the woman the oath of the curse."

157 Insert by the corrector and accepted in *editio princeps*; missing in the first hand of the ms. and the biblical text. It seems that the corrector identified Benaiah's father with the High Priest Yehoyada who lived 200 years later.
158 In the ms. and *editio princeps*: Halakhah 5.
159 In the Babli, *Šebuot* 36a, this is a statement of R. Yose ben R. Hanina, a younger contemporary of R. Yose ben Zimra. In *Num. rabba* 9(46) the reading is that of the Yerushalmi.
160 *Num.* 5:22.
161 *Jer.* 11:5: "To keep the oath I had sworn to your forefathers to give to them the Land flowing with milk and honey as today; I answered and said, *Amen*, o Eternal."

162   *IK*. 1:36.

163   The verse from Jeremiah only confirms what can be learned from the verse in Kings, that Amen is an affirmation.

164   *Deut*. 29:11. The curse is *Deut*. 28:15-68.

165   *Num*. 5:21. In the Babli, *Šebuot* 35b, this is a tannaïtic statement. In *Sifry Num*. 14 the argument is: From the verse one infers that any oath implies a potential curse on the person taking the oath.

(18b line 9) מְנַיִין לָמְדוּ לְגִילְגּוּל שְׁבוּעָה. מְסוֹטָה. וְאָמְרָה הָאִשָּׁה אָמֵן אָמֵן. אָמֵן עִם אִישׁ זֶה. אָמֵן עִם אִישׁ אַחֵר. עַד כְּדוֹן דְּבָרִים שֶׁהוּא רָאוּי לְהַשְׁבִּיעַ. דְּבָרִים שֶׁאֵינוֹ רָאוּי לְהַשְׁבִּיעַ. אָמַר רִבִּי יוֹסֵי בֵּירִבִּי בּוּן. נִישְׁמְעִינָהּ מִן הָדָא. אָמֵן שֶׁלֹּא סָטִיתִי אֲרוּסָה וּנְשׂוּאָה שׁוֹמֶרֶת יָבָם וּכְנוּסָה. אֲרוּסָה וְשׁוֹמֶרֶת יָבָם רָאוּי הוּא לְהִישָּׁבַע. וְתֵימַר מְגַלְגְּלִין. וְהָכָא מְגַלְגְּלִין.

[166]From where did they learn rollover of oaths[167]? From the suspected wife: "The woman shall say, Amen, Amen"; Amen from this man, Amen from any other man. That refers to subjects he is able to make her swear about[168]. What about subjects he is not able to make her swear about? Rebbi Yose ben Rebbi Abun said, let us hear from the following: "Amen that I was not deviant preliminarily married[155] and married, waiting for the levir and taken in[156]." Can he make her swear when she is preliminarily married or waiting for the levir[169]? Nevertheless one rolls over.

166   This paragraph and the next are also in *Qiddušin* 1:5 (fol. 60d). In the Babli, the parallel is *Qiddušin* 27b.

167   If a person is required to swear, the opposing party can add to the contents of the oath any statement similar to the one which causes the oath to be forced. For example, if a person has a monetary claim on another person for which he has partial proof, enough to force the opposing party to swear, he can add to the text of the oath of disclaimer any other financial claim which he might have

but for which the proofs in his hand are not sufficient to force the defendant to swear. This is the topic of *Qiddušin* 1:5. It is seen in Mishnah 7 that some connection of the additions to the original claim is required.

168   While the husband must specify the name of the man he suspects of an affair with his wife in order to declare his jealousy and bring her to the Temple, he could have named any other man. Therefore, he can add the names of other men to the formula of the oath.

169   Mishnah 4:1 states that there is no declaration of jealousy admitted in these two cases since the ceremony applies only to "a wife under her husband (*Num.* 5:19)". Nevertheless, the husband can force her to swear about her behavior when she was his wife but not under him.

(18b line 14) אִית תַּנָּיֵי תַנֵּי. מַה זוֹ בְּאָלָה וּבִשְׁבוּעָה אַף כָּל־הַנִּשְׁבָּעִין בְּאָלָה וּבִשְׁבוּעָה. וְאִית תַּנָּיֵי תַנֵּי. זוֹ בְּאָלָה וּבִשְׁבוּעָה וְאֵין כָּל־הַנִּשְׁבָּעִין בְּאָלָה וּבִשְׁבוּעָה. הֲווֹ בָּעֵיי מֵימַר. מָאן דָּמַר. [מַה]170 זוֹ בְּאָלָה וּבִשְׁבוּעָה אַף כָּל־הַנִּשְׁבָּעִין בְּאָלָה וּבִשְׁבוּעָה נִיחָא. מָאן דָּמַר. זוֹ בְּאָלָה וּבִשְׁבוּעָה וְאֵין כָּל־הַנִּשְׁבָּעִין בְּאָלָה וּבִשְׁבוּעָה. לְגִילְגּוּל אַתְּ לָמֵד. לְאָלָה וְלִשְׁבוּעָה אֵין אַתְּ לָמֵד. אִית תַּנָּיֵי תַנֵּי. מַה זוֹ בְּאָמֵן וְאָמֵן. אַף כָּל־הַנִּשְׁבָּעִין בְּאָמֵן וְאָמֵן. אִית תַּנָּיֵי תַנֵּי. זוֹ בְּאָמֵן וְאָמֵן. וְאֵין כָּל־הַנִּשְׁבָּעִין בְּאָמֵן וְאָמֵן. הֲווֹ בָּעֵיי מֵימַר. מָאן דָּמַר. [מַזוֹ]171 בְּאָמֵן וְאָמֵן אַף כָּל־הַנִּשְׁבָּעִין בְּאָמֵן וְאָמֵן. נִיחָא. מָאן דָּמַר. זוֹ בְּאָמֵן וְאָמֵן וְאֵין כָּל־הַנִּשְׁבָּעִין בְּאָמֵן וְאָמֵן. כְּלוּם לָמְדוּ גִילְגּוּל שְׁבוּעָה לֹא מִסּוֹטָה. לְגִילְגּוּל אַתְּ לָמֵד. לְאָמֵן וְאָמֵן אֵין אַתְּ לָמֵד.

Some Tannaïm state: Since this one is subject to curse and oath, so also all who have to swear are under curse and oath[172]. Some Tannaïm state: This one is subject to curse and oath, but no others who have to swear are under curse and oath. They[173] wanted to say, the one who said, since this one is subject to curse and oath, so also all who have to swear are under curse and oath, is understandable. The one who said, this one is subject to curse and oath, but no others who have to swear are under curse and oath, can you infer for rollover only but not for curse and oath[174]? Some Tannaïm state: Since this one is subject to Amen, Amen, so also all who have to swear are under Amen, Amen. Some Tannaïm state: This one is subject to Amen, Amen, but no others who have to swear are under Amen, Amen. They[173] wanted to say, the one who said, since this one is subject to Amen, Amen, so also all who have to swear are under Amen, Amen, is understandable. The one who said, this one is subject to Amen, Amen, but no others who have to swear are under Amen, Amen, did one not infer rollover of oaths from the suspected wife? Can you infer for rollover only but not for Amen, Amen[174]?

170 Reading of the Rome ms. Missing in the Leiden ms. and *editio princeps*

171 From the Rome ms. Leiden ms. and *editio princeps*: וז.

172 This is the ninth hermeneutical rule of R. Ismael: "Anything which was in a set and was singled out to teach, was not singled out for itself but to teach about the entire set." The rules of oaths derived from the ceremony of the suspected wife must apply to all members of the set of oaths. The same argument in *Sifry Num.* 14, copied in *Num. rabba* 9(46).

173 The members of the Academy of Tiberias.

174 If one negates the 9th hermeneutical rule, one also has to negate the possibility of rollover of oaths in general. It is reported in Tosephta *Sanhedrin* 7:11 that Hillel, about 100 years before R. Ismael, accepted only seven rules (numbers 1-6, 13). The *baraita* may be genuine but it is not practice.

(18b line 25) אָמַר רִבִּי בָּא בַּר מָמָל. מָאן תַּנָּא שׁוֹמֶרֶת יָבָם. רִבִּי עֲקִיבָה. דְּרִבִּי עֲקוּבָה אָמַר. יֵשׁ מַמְזֵר בִּיבָמָה. אָמַר לֵיהּ רִבִּי אִילַי. מַה אִיכְפַּת לֵיהּ מַמְזֵר גַּבֵּי קִינוּי. הַתּוֹרָה אָמְרָה וְקִנֵּא אֶת אִשְׁתּוֹ. אֲפִילוּ מִקְצָת אִשְׁתּוֹ. אָמַר רִבִּי שַׁמִּי. וְלֹא כֵן אָמַר רִבִּי יַנַּאי. נִמְנוּ שְׁלֹשִׁים וְכַמָּה זְקֵינִים. מְנַיִין שֶׁאֵין קִידּוּשִׁין

תוֹפְסִין בִּיבָמָה. תַּלְמוּד לוֹמַר לֹא תִהְיֶה אֵשֶׁת הַמֵּת הַחוּצָה לְאִישׁ זָר יְבָמָהּ יָבוֹא עָלֶיהָ. שֶׁלֹּא יְהֵא לָהּ הֲוָיָה אֵצֶל אַחֵר. אָמַר לֵיהּ רִבִּי יוֹחָנָן. וְלֹא מַתְנִיתָהּ הִיא. אוֹ לְאַחַר שֶׁיַּחֲלוֹץ לֵיךְ יַבְמֵיךְ. אֵינָהּ מְקוּדֶּשֶׁת. וְהָיָה רִבִּי יַנַּיי מְקַלֵּס לֵיהּ. הַזָּלִים זָהָב מִכִּיס. בְּנִי אַל יָלִיזוּ מֵעֵינֶיךָ. חֲכַם בְּנִי וְשַׂמַּח לִבִּי. תֵּן לְחָכָם וְיֶחְכַּם עוֹד. יִשְׁמַע חָכָם וְיוֹסֶף לֶקַח. אָמַר לֵיהּ רִבִּי שִׁמְעוֹן בֶּן לָקִישׁ. בָּתַר כָּל־אִילֵּין פְּסוּקֵי קִילוּסַיָּיא יָכִיל הוּא פָּתַר לָהּ כְּרִבִּי עֲקִיבָה. דְּרִבִּי עֲקִיבָה אָמַר. יֵשׁ מַמְזֵר בִּיבָמָה. וִיתִיבִינֵיהּ. מַה אִיכְפַּת לֵהּ מַמְזֵר גַּבֵּי [קינוי]177א. הַתּוֹרָה אָמְרָה וְקִנֵּא אֶת אִשְׁתּוֹ. אֲפִילוּ מִקְצָת אִשְׁתּוֹ. שׁוֹמֶרֶת יָבָם שֶׁזִּינָת. רִבִּי לָעֲזָר אָמַר מוּתֶּרֶת לְבֵיתָהּ. רִבִּי יְהוֹשֻׁעַ בֶּן לֵוִי אָמַר. אֲסוּרָה לְבֵיתָהּ. רַבָּנָן אָמְרִין. אָמַר רַב מָנָא. לֹא כֵן אָמַר רִבִּי יַעֲקֹב בַּר אָחָא בְּשֵׁם רִבִּי לָעֲזָר. שׁוֹמֶרֶת יָבָם שֶׁמֵּתָה מוּתָּר בְּאִמָּהּ. בְּגִין דְּתַנִּינָן. זֶה הַכְּלָל. כָּל־שֶׁתִּיבָּעֵל וְלֹא תְהֵא אֲסוּרָה לוֹ לֹא הָיָה מַתְנֶה עִמָּהּ.

Rebbi Abba bar Mamal said, who stated "the one waiting for her levir"? Rebbi Aqiba! For Rebbi Aqiba said, there exists a bastard from a sister-in-law[175]. Rebbi Ilai said to him, why should a bastard be relevant for jealousy? The Torah said: "He shall declare his jealousy to his wife", even a partial wife[176]. [177]Rebbi Shammai said, did not Rebbi Yannai say the following: More than 30 Elders voted, from where that *qiddushin* have no legal effect on a sister-in-law? The verse says, "the wife of the deceased may not belong to any outside unrelated man, her levir shall come to her", that she cannot have any existence with another man. Rebbi Johanan said to him, is that not a Mishnah? "Or after your levir will have performed *ḥaliṣah* with you, she is not preliminarily married." And Rebbi Yannai praised him "those who pour out gold from the wallet," "my son, they should not be removed from your eyes," "get wise, my son, and make me happy", "give to the wise that he shall become wiser," "let the wise listen that he increase in knowledge." Rebbi Simeon ben Laqish said, after all these praises I can explain it following Rebbi Aqiba since Rebbi Aqiba said that there exists a bastard from a sister-in-law! Could he not object: Why should a bastard be relevant for jealousy? The Torah said: "He shall declare his jealousy to his wife", even a partial wife. A woman waiting for her levir who whored, Rebbi Eleazar said she is permitted to her house, Rebbi Joshua ben Levi said she is forbidden to her house[178]. What do the rabbis say? Rebbi Mana said, did not Rebbi Jacob bar Aha say in the name of Rebbi Eleazar, if a woman waiting for her levir died, her mother is permitted to [the levir][180], since we have stated: "This is the rule: He cannot stipulate about any intercourse she could have had and would not be forbidden to him.[181]"

175 Cf. *Yebamot*, Chapter 1, Note 30; Babli *Y ebamot* 92a. R. Aqiba declares as a bastard any child from a union not explicitly permitted.

176 Since the widow of a childless man cannot possibly marry any man but her levir (unless she is released by the latter), and she can be married by the levir without any ceremony, she may be considered as engaged to be married by him.

177 This text is from *Yebamot* 1:1, explained there in Notes 93-101.

177א From the text in *Yebamot*. The text here (in both mss. and the *editio princeps*) reads קידושין, which clearly is wrong since the child of a preliminarily married woman from another man is a bastard.

178 "Her house" is really her future house, that of her levir. This is the answer to the question asked if we follow R. Eleazar.

The opinion of R. Joshua ben Levi is in the Babli ascribed to Rav Hamnuna (*Yebamot* 81a,92b,95a,96a; *Gittin* 80b; *Sota* 18b.) In the last source, the decision that practice does not follow Rav Hamnuna is explicitly attributed to Yerushalmi sources.

180 Since a man is forbidden to marry his deceased wife's mother, even if the wife died while being only preliminarily married to him, it follows

that the one waiting for her levir is unrelated to the levir for R. Eleazar. She is unable to be unfaithful to him and the question of R. Ilai cannot be asked.

181 Mishnah 7. R. Abba bar Mamal is correct in the tradition of R. Eleazar. For him, only R. Aqiba could let the levir include a question about the time between the first husband's death and his marriage.

(18b line 42) מַה תַּנָּא הָדָא מַתְנִיתָא. לֹא רַבָּנָן וְלֹא רִבִּי עֲקִיבָה. אֶלָּא כֵינִי. מָאן דָּמַר. מוּתֶּרֶת לְבֵיתָהּ. דְּרַבָּנָן דְּלֹא כְרִבִּי עֲקִיבָה. וּמָאן דָּמַר. אֲסוּרָה לְבֵיתָהּ. רִבִּי עֲקִיבָה דְּלֹא כְרַבָּנָן. אָמַר רִבִּי יַנַּאי. שׁוֹמֶרֶת יָבָם שֶׁזִּינָת מוּתֶּרֶת לְבֵיתָהּ. וְתַנֵּי כֵן. וְנֶעֱלַם מֵעֵינֵי אִישָׁהּ. וְלֹא מֵעֵינֵי יְבָמָהּ. רִבִּי יַעֲקֹב בַּר זַבְדִּי בְּשֵׁם רִבִּי אַבָּהוּ. מַעֲשֶׂה הָיָה וְכֹהֶנֶת הָיְיתָה וְהִתִּירוּהָ לְבֵיתָהּ. אָמַר רִבִּי יוֹסֵי בֵּי רִבִּי בּוּן. אַף לֹא מַכּוֹת אֵין בָּהּ.

How could one state this Mishnah[182]? Not the rabbis nor Rebbi Aqiba! But it is as follows. He who says that she is permitted to her house [follows] the rabbis against Rebbi Aqiba[183]. He who says that she is forbidden to her house [follows] Rebbi Aqiba against the rabbis[184]. Rebbi Yannai said, a woman waiting for her levir who whored is permitted to her house[185]. One had stated this: "It was hidden from her husband's eyes[186]," not from her levir's eyes. Rebbi Jacob bar Zavdi in the name of Rebbi Abbahu: It happened, she was the wife of a Cohen, and they permitted her to her house. Rebbi Yose ben Rebbi Abun said, no whipping is involved.

182 Mishnah 7, just quoted. In the tradition of the Babli and of the independent Mishnah mss., Mishnah 7 is part of Mishnah 6. Then one has a real problem, since in our interpretation Mishnah 6 is R. Aqiba's and Mishnah 7 the rabbi's.

183 Then Mishnah 7 has to be separated from Mishnah 6 as in the Yerushalmi text.

184 There is no problem; Mishnah 7 is part of Mishnah 6.

185 R. Yannai is the one who in the preceding paragraph had stated that a woman waiting for her levir is unable to contract a marriage outside the family. He will also hold that contracting such a marriage is a criminal act since that is formulated as a prohibition in *Deut.* 25:5. As R. Yose bar Abun notes here, the prohibition covers only marriage, not extramarital relations.

186 *Num.* 5:13. This *baraita* is not found in any other source. In a later paragraph, the expression quoted is interpreted to mean that a blind man cannot declare his jealousy and in *Sifry Num.* 7 that if the husband ever had looked the other way he never again could invoke the procedure of the suspected wife.

(18b line 48) לא שֶׁהָיָה רִבִּי מֵאִיר אוֹמֵר. הַמַּיִם בּוֹדְקִין אוֹתָהּ לְמַפְרֵעַ.

Not that Rebbi Meïr was saying that the water checks her outside of its time[187].

187 This refers to the statement in the Mishnah that the husband may stipulate that the wife swear not to be unfaithful in the future. Tosaphot (18a) has a fuller version: לא שֶׁהָיָה רִבִּי מֵאִיר אוֹמֵר. הַמַּיִם בּוֹדְקִין אוֹתָהּ מֵעַכְשָׁיו אֶלָּא הַמַּיִם פְּקוּדִים בָּהּ לִכְשֶׁתִּטַּמֵּא הַמַּיִם בּוֹדְקִין אוֹתָהּ לְמַפְרֵעַ. "Not that Rebbi Meïr was saying that the water checks her *now but that the water is deposited in her body and if she would be defiled the water would check her* retroactively." This is very close to the text of a *baraita* in the Babli (18b) and is suspect against the testimony of both mss.

The usual meaning of למפרע is "retroactively (in time); in inverse order (of an arrangement)". Since, as noted by J. Levy in his Dictionary in the name of H. L. Fleischer, מפרע seems to be an Arabism and Arabic פרע means both ascending and descending, the translation of מפרע chosen here is "not in time (possibly earlier, possibly later)." Then the longer text would be unnecessary and the meaning is clear: The water will have no effect any time a sin was not committed. In the Tosephta (2:2), the reading is: That even after 20 years the water may reawake and check her out.

(18b line 49) תּוֹרַת הַקְּנָאוֹת. תּוֹרַת הָעוֹלָמִים זוֹ. אֵין הָאִשָּׁה שׁוֹתָה וְשׁוֹנָה. אָמַר רִבִּי יוּדָה. הֵעִיד נְחֶמְיָה אִישׁ שִׁיחִין אֶת רִבִּי עֲקִיבָה. הָאִשָּׁה שׁוֹתָה וְשׁוֹנָה. אָמַר רִבִּי עֲקִיבָה אֲנִי אֲפָרֵשׁ. מֵאִישׁ אֶחָד אֵין הָאִשָּׁה שׁוֹתָה וְשׁוֹנָה. מִשְּׁנֵי אֲנָשִׁים הָאִשָּׁה שׁוֹתָה וְשׁוֹנָה. וַחֲכָמִים אוֹמְרִים בֵּין מֵאִישׁ אֶחָד בֵּין מִשְּׁנֵי אֲנָשִׁים שׁוֹתָה וְשׁוֹנָה. כּוֹרְכְּמִית תּוֹכִיחַ. שֶׁשָּׁתָת וְשָׁנַת וְשִׁילְּשָׁה לִפְנֵי שְׁמַעְיָה וְאַבְטַלְיוֹן מֵאִישׁ אֶחָד.

"The teaching about jealousies[188]". This is a teaching of the Temple. [189]A woman does not drink and repeat. Rebbi Jehudah said, Nehemiah the ditch-digger testified before Rebbi Aqiba that a woman drinks and repeats. Rebbi Aqiba said, I shall explain. From one husband a woman does not drink and repeat, from two husbands a woman drinks and repeats. But the Sages say she drinks and repeats[190] whether from one husband or from two husbands. Korkemit shall prove it, who drank and repeated and did it a third time from one husband before Shemaia and Abtalyon[191].

188 Num. 5:29. The text seems to be a composition of two different texts. In *Sifry zuṭa* [also similarly in *Num. rabba* 5(51)] one reads: "'*This* is the teaching about jealousies'; the jealous husband may express his jealousy in Shiloh and in the Eternal House (cf. Note 120). I could think, also at a local altar? The verse says: *This*." The argument is obsolete since it is generally accepted doctrine that after the building of the Temple no local altar was permitted. The question arose since v. 15 requires the husband to bring his wife *to the Cohen*, perhaps not necessarily to the Tabernacle. But since the dust has to be taken from the floor of the Sanctuary, an altar without Sanctuary is excluded. The special emphasis of *this* indicates that no substitute for the Tabernacle is acceptable.

189 In the Babli, 18b, the text of this *baraita* reads: "'*This* is the teaching about *jealousies*', which teaches that a woman drinks and repeats (from the several jealousies). Rebbi Jehudah says

this (a singular), a woman does not drink and repeat. Rebbi Jehudah said, Neḥemiah the ditch-digger testified before Rebbi Aqiba that a woman drinks and repeats and we accepted his testimony from two husbands but not from one husband. But the Sages say that a woman *does not* drink and repeat whether from one husband or from two husbands." The Babli has a complicated explanation to harmonize the anonymous first source (which has to represent the opinion of the majority, the Sages) with the contradictory statement at the end.

The text of *Num. rabba* 5(51), is clearly an explanation of the position of the Babli.

190 In the Rome ms: "*A woman does not* drink and repeat." This text, which eliminates the disagreement with the Babli, is in contradiction to the following.

191 In Mishnah *Idiut* 5:6 she is called Karkemit the libertine (the freedwoman). It is unclear whether at the end there is a difference between the two Talmudim since it is not stated whether Korkemit was repeatedly accused of relations with the same man.

(18b line 54) תַּמָּן תַּנִּינָן. אֵין מַשְׁקִין אֶת הַגִּיּוֹרֶת וכול׳. וַחֲכָמִים אוֹמְרִים. מַשְׁקִין. מַה אֲנָן קַיָּימִין. אִם בְּיִשְׂרָאֵל שֶׁנָּשָׂא גִיּוֹרֶת. כְּבָר כְּתִיב. בְּנֵי יִשְׂרָאֵל. לֹא גֵרִים. אִם בְּגֵר שֶׁנָּשָׂא בַת יִשְׂרָאֵל. כְּבָר כְּתִיב וְהֵבִיא הָאִישׁ אֶת אִשְׁתּוֹ אֶל הַכֹּהֵן. אֶלָּא כֵן אֲנָן קַיָּימִין. בְּגֵר שֶׁנָּשָׂא גִיּוֹרֶת. וּמָה טַעֲמָא דְּרַבִּי עֲקִיבָה. בְּנֵי יִשְׂרָאֵל. לֹא גֵרִים. מַה טַעֲמוֹן דְּרַבָּנָן. וְאָמַרְתָּ אֲלֵיהֶם. לְרַבּוֹת כָּל־הַכָּתוּב בַּפָּרָשָׁה. וּמַה כְּתִיב בַּפָּרָשָׁה. וְשָׁכַב אִישׁ אוֹתָהּ. שְׁכִיבָתָהּ אוֹסַרְתָּהּ. בַּעֲלָהּ מְקַנֵּא וּמַשְׁקֶה.

There, we have stated[192]: "One does not make the proselyte drink, etc. But the Sages say, one makes her drink." Where do we hold? If about an Israel who married a proselyte, it already is written[193]: "The sons of Israel" (not proselytes)[194]. If about a proselyte who married a Jewish girl, it already is written[195]: "The man has to bring his wife to the Cohen." But we must hold about a proselyte who married a proselyte. What is the reason of Rebbi Aqiba[196]? "The children of Israel", not proselytes. What is the reason of the Sages? "You shall say to them[197]", to add everything written in that paragraph. What is written in that paragraph? "A man slept with her". His[198] lying with her makes her forbidden, then her husband declares his jealousy and makes her drink.

---

192   Mishnah *Idiut* 5:6: "He (Aqabia ben Mehallalel) said: One does not make the proselyte or the freedwoman drink, but the Sages say, one makes her drink."

193   *Num.* 5:12. The text is addressed to all Jewish men.

194   This text is an intrusion from the later statement but is also found in *Num. rabba* 9(34). The text quoted by R. Abraham ben David of Posquières (Ravad) in his commentary to *Idiut* has the order inverted and then the clause makes sense: אִם בְּגֵר שֶׁנָּשָׂא בַת יִשְׂרָאֵל. כְּבָר כְּתִיב. בְּנֵי יִשְׂרָאֵל. לֹא גֵרִים. אִם בְּיִשְׂרָאֵל שֶׁנָּשָׂא גִיּוֹרֶת. כְּבָר כְּתִיב וְהֵבִיא הָאִישׁ אֶת אִשְׁתּוֹ אֶל הַכֹּהֵן. "If about a proselyte who married a Jewish girl, it already is written: 'The sons of Israel', not proselytes. If about an Israel who married a proselyte, it already is written: 'The man has to bring his wife to the Cohen.'" Ravad declares his text to be difficult; the Babli, 26a, explicitly rejects the inference from "the sons of Israel".

195   *Num.* 5:15. Any Jewish man is included, even if he is not the son of an Israel.

196   This is clearly in error; it must be Aqabia, not Aqiba; correctly in the text quoted by Ravad and in *Num. rabba*. Aqabia had no rabbinic title.

197   *Num.* 5:12; the text is addressed to everybody who has to hear the commandments, including the proselytes; argument approved in the Babli, 26a.

198   In Ravad's text: Another man's lying...

וְנֶעְלַם מֵעֵינֵי אִישָׁהּ. פְּרָט לְסוּמֵא שֶׁאֵין לוֹ עֵינַיִם. הוּא סוּמֵא (18b line 61)
הִיא סוּמָה. מַתְנִיתָא דְּרַבִּי יוּדָן. פּוֹטְרוֹ מִכָּל־מִצְוֹת הָאֲמוּרוֹת בַּתּוֹרָה.

"It was hidden from her husband's eyes[199]", that excludes the blind man who has no eyes[200]. It is the same for the blind man and the blind woman. This *baraita* follows Rebbi Jehudah who frees him from all obligations in the Torah[201].

199 *Num.* 5:13.
200 *Tanḥuma Naśo* 7, *Tanḥuma Buber Naśo* 11 (Note 62); *Sifry Num.* 7, *Sifry zuṭa Naśo; Num. rabba* 9(36); Babli 27a (the only other source which also includes the blind wife).
201 Quoted also in Babli *Qiddušin* 31a. Since some of the great Babylonian authorities were blind (Rav Sheshet and Rav Yoseph), practice does not follow R. Jehudah. (Nevertheless, Maimonides disqualifies the blind man from the ceremony of the suspected wife).

(fol. 17d) **משנה ז**: הַכֹּל שָׁוִין שֶׁאֵינוֹ מַתְנֶה עִמָּהּ קוֹדֶם לְשֶׁנִּתְאָרְסָה וְלֹא מִשֶּׁנִּתְגָּרְשָׁה. נִסְתְּרָה לְאַחַר וְנִיטְמֵאת וְאַחַר כָּךְ הֶחֱזִירָהּ לֹא הָיָה מַתְנֶה עִמָּהּ. זֶה הַכְּלָל. כָּל־שֶׁתִּיבָּעֵל וְלֹא הָיְתָה אֲסוּרָה לוֹ לֹא הָיָה מַתְנֶה עִמָּהּ.

Mishnah 7: Everybody agrees that he may not stipulate with her about before she was preliminarily married or about after she was divorced[202]. If she was secluded after that[203], became impure[204], and after that he took her back, he cannot stipulate with her. This is the rule: He cannot stipulate about any intercourse she could have had and would not be forbidden to him[181].

202 He cannot ask her to swear that she did not have any intercourse while not being married to him.
203 After the divorce. *Deut.* 24:2-4 prohibits the first husband from remarrying his divorcee if she had married another man after her divorce (*Deut.* 24:2: "She went and became another's [wife]".) Remarrying a wife who was promiscuous after divorce but not otherwise married is not forbidden.
204 Unmarried intercourse is

punishable as harlotry according to some authorities (*Yebamot* 6:5, Note 107; Babli *Yebamot* 61b; *Sifra Emor Pereq* 1).

(fol. 18b) **הלכה ז**: הַכֹּל שָׁוִין שֶׁאֵין מַתְנֶה עִמָּהּ עַל קוֹדֶם שֶׁנִּתְאָרָסָה וְלֹא מִשֶּׁנִּתְגָּרְשָׁה כול'. אָמַר רִבִּי יַנַּאי. פְּשִׁיטָא שֶׁאָדָם מוֹחֵל עַל קִינּוּיוֹ. גֵּירַשׁ כְּמוֹ שֶׁמָּחַל. הֵיךְ עֲבִידָא. קִינֵּא לָהּ וְנִתְגָּרְשָׁה וְהֶחֱזִירָהּ וְנִסְתְּרָה. אִין תֵּימַר. גֵּירַשׁ כְּמוֹ שֶׁמָּחַל. צָרִיךְ לְקַנּוֹת לָהּ פַּעַם שְׁנִיָּיה. אִין תֵּימַר. גֵּירַשׁ כְּמוֹ שֶׁלֹּא מָחַל. אֵין צָרִיךְ לְקַנּוֹת לָהּ פַּעַם שְׁנִיָּיה. אֲבָל אִם קִינֵּא לָהּ וְנִסְתְּרָה וְיָדַע בָּהּ. וְגֵירְשָׁהּ וְהֶחֱזִירָהּ וְנִסְתְּרָה. שָׁתָת וְלֹא בָדְקוּ אוֹתָהּ הַמַּיִם טְהוֹרָה הִיא. אִי מֵאַחַר שֶׁאֵין הַמַּיִם בּוֹדְקִין אֶת הָאִשָּׁה שֶׁהִיא אֲסוּרָה לִבְעִיתָהּ טְמֵיאָה הִיא.

Halakhah 7: "Everybody agrees that he may not stipulate with her about before she was preliminarily married or about after she was divorced," etc. Rebbi Yannai said, it is obvious that a man may forgive about his jealousy[205]. If he divorced her it is as if he had forgiven. How is that? If he had declared his jealousy, divorced her, took her back, and then she was at a secluded place. If you say, if he divorced her it is as if he had forgiven, he has to declare his jealousy a second time. But if you say, if he divorced her it is as if he had not forgiven, he does not have to declare his jealousy a second time. But if he had declared his jealousy, she was at a secluded place and he knew it[206], then he divorced her, took her back, and then she was at a secluded place, if she drank and the water did nothing to her, she is pure. Or maybe that since the water does not check out a woman forbidden to her husband, she might be impure.

205 In the Babli, 25a, this husband may annul his declaration of jealousy only if the wife did not meet her paramour at a secluded place. In the Yerushalmi, *Sanhedrin* 8:6 (fol. 26b, line 33), he may retract his declaration any time before the scroll is erased. In the paragraph here, the argument is as

in the Babli.

206 From that moment on, she is forbidden to him. If he divorces her instead of taking her to the Temple, there is a question whether the divorce annuls the prohibition or not. If the divorce annuls the prohibition, he may take her back and the water will check her out in the future. If the divorce does not annul the prohibition, it is sinful for him to take her back without having her checked out and therefore the entire procedure is invalid since the water acts only if the husband himself is totally free from any sexual misbehavior (*Num.* 5:31).

היה נוטל את מנחתה פרק שלישי

(fol. 18c) **משנה א:** הָיָה נוֹטֵל אֶת מִנְחָתָהּ מִתּוֹךְ כְּפִיפָה מִצְרִית וְנוֹתְנָהּ לְתוֹךְ כְּלִי שָׁרֵת וְנוֹתְנָהּ עַל יָדָהּ. וְכֹהֵן מֵנִיחַ יָדוֹ מִתַּחְתֶּיהָ וּמְנִיפָהּ. הֵנִיף וְהִגִּישׁ קָמַץ וְהִקְטִיר. וְהַשְּׁאָר נֶאֱכָל לַכֹּהֲנִים.

Mishnah 1: He[1] took the flour-offering from the Egyptian palm-leaf basket[2], put it into a Temple vessel and laid that on her hands. The Cohen puts his hands under hers and performs the weave[3]. He weaved, presented[4], took a fistful and put it into the fire. The remainder is eaten by the priests[5].

1   The officiating priest.
2   See Mishnah 2:1.
3   The prescribed movements for the dedication of private offerings. The movements in the six directions (fore and aft, right and left, up and down) are imitated today as the motions of the palm-branch on Tabernacles.
4   Before the altar receives its part, the entire offering in the vessel is presented to the altar at its South-West corner.
5   As are all offerings except those of a priest; cf. *Lev.* 6:7-11.

(fol. 18c) **הלכה א:** הָיָה נוֹטֵל אֶת מִנְחָתָהּ כול'. כְּתִיב וְלָקַח הַכֹּהֵן מִיַּד הָאִשָּׁה אֶת מִנְחַת הַקְּנָאוֹת. וְכִי עַל יָדוֹ הוּא מֵנִיף. וְלֹא עַל יָדָהּ הוּא מֵנִיף. אֶלָּא מִכָּן שֶׁהוּא נוֹטְלָהּ מִתּוֹךְ כְּלִי חוֹל וְנוֹתְנָהּ בִּכְלִי שָׁרֵת וְכֹהֵן מֵנִיחַ יָדוֹ תַּחְתֶּיהָ וּמְנִיפָהּ. וְאֵין הַדָּבָר כָּאוּר. מֵבִיא מַפָּה. וְאֵינוֹ חוֹצֵץ. וּמֵבִיא כֹהֵן זָקֵן. וַאֲפִילוּ תֵימַר.

יָלֶד. שֶׁאֵין יֵצֶר הָרַע מָצוּי לְשָׁעָה. תַּנֵּי רִבִּי חִייָה. סוֹטָה גִידֶמֶת שְׁנֵי כֹהֲנִים מְנִיפִין עַל יָדֶיהָ.

Halakhah 1: "He took the flour-offering," etc. It is written[6]: "The Cohen shall take the jealousy-flour-offering from the woman's hand." Does he perform the weave? Does not she perform the weave[7]? But from here [one understands that] he takes it from a profane vessel and puts it into a Temple vessel. [8]"The Cohen puts his hands under hers and performs the weave." Does the Cohen put his hands under hers? Is that not objectionable[9]? He brings a kerchief[10]. Does that not separate[11]? He brings an elderly Cohen[12]. You may even say, a young man, since bad inclinations do not happen at that hour[13]. Rebbi Ḥiyya stated[14]: If the suspected wife has no hands, two priests weave in her stead.

---

6 *Num.* 5:25: "The Cohen shall take the jealousy-flour-offering from the woman's hand, weave it before the Eternal and present it to the altar."

7 The verse requires that the Cohen perform the weave. But in the case of an animal sacrifice it is required (*Lev.* 7:30) that the individual bringing the sacrifice be the actor: "His hands shall bring the Eternal's gift, the fat on the breast he has to bring, to weave it before the Eternal." In the Babli, 19a, the parallel expressions *his hands, the woman's hand* are taken as proof that the woman has to take part in weaving her gift just as a man has to take part in the weaving of his. The formulation of the Yerushalmi may be interpreted as a question: Since the Mishnah requires the woman to participate and the verse requires the Cohen to perform the weave, how can the Mishnah be justified?

8 The rest of the paragraph is also in *Qiddušin* 1:8 (fol. 61c).

9 In the Babli, this would be written בעור. Is the bodily contact between the Cohen and an otherwise married woman not immoral? It is not directly forbidden since the woman has to be pure to enter the Temple but this makes the situation only worse.

10 Between his and her hands, not to touch the woman.

11 It is a general principle that the Temple service has to be by the priest directly. Since the verse requires the priests to serve in the Temple, they may not wear shoes (even in winter) since then the shoes would be in the Temple, not the Cohen directly. If the Cohen has to perform the weave, his hands cannot be separated from the Temple vessel. If, as indicated in the previous Note, the participation of the woman is implicitly required by the verse, her hands do not count as separation.

12 Presumably he is past all sexual feelings.

13 The fear of the Temple will banish all bad thoughts. The commentaries read the sentence to mean that in the short time needed for the weave, bad thoughts cannot develop. This is obviously false.

14 In *Qiddušin*: R. Ḥiyya stated, it happens (that the Cohen has sinful thoughts). Maybe he implies that since the weaving can be done by two priests for the handless woman, it can be done by two priests for all women. There is no parallel to this *baraita* in any other known source.

(18c line 48) אָמַר רִבִּי יוֹסֵי. בְּכָל־אֲתָר הָדָא הִיא מִילְתָא צְרִיכִין לְרַבָּנָן. מַהוּ מַגִּישׁ. גּוּפָהּ שֶׁלַּמִּנְחָה גוּפָהּ שֶׁלַּכֵּלִי.

Rebbi Yose said: In all cases, the following is an open question for the rabbis: What does he present? The body of the flour offering or the body of the vessel[15]?

15 When the Cohen brings the offering to the altar, does he touch the wall of the altar with the Temple vessel or does he have to turn the vessel so that some of the flour touches the wall? The Babli, 14b, states that the vessel is presented, based on *Lev.* 2:8.

(18c line 49) תְּנוּפוֹת מִנַּיִין שֶׁהֵן קוֹדְמוֹת לַהַגָּשׁוֹת. רִבִּי יִרְמְיָה בְּשֵׁם רִבִּי פְּדָת. מְסוֹטָה לָמְדוּ. אָמַר רִבִּי יוֹסֵי. סוֹטָה לְחִידוּשָׁהּ יָצָאת. וְדָבָר שֶׁהוּא יוֹצֵא לְחִידוּשׁוֹ אֵין לְמֵידִין הֵימֶינּוּ. רִבִּי בּוּן בַּר חִיָּיה שָׁמַע לָהּ מִן הָדָא. זֹאת תּוֹרַת הַמִּנְחָה הַקְרֵב. הֵיכָן הִיא תְּנוּפָה. כְּבָר קָדְמָה. אָמַר רִבִּי יוֹסֵי. תִּיפְתָּר

בִּמְנָחוֹת שֶׁאֵינָן טְעוּנוֹת תְּנוּפָה. וְלֵית שְׁמַע מִינָהּ כְּלוּם. וַיי דָא אֲמָרָה דְּאָמְרִין וְהֵבֵאתָ לְרַבּוֹת מִנְחַת הָעוֹמֶר לָהַגָּשָׁה. וְהִקְרִיב. לְרַבּוֹת מִנְחַת סוֹטָה לָהַגָּשָׁה. וּכְתִיב בַּתְרֵיהּ וְהֵרִים. וְהֵיכָן הִיא תְּנוּפָה. כְּבָר קָדְמָה.

From where that weaves precede presentations[16]? Rebbi Jeremiah in the name of Rebbi Pedat: They learned that from the case of the suspected wife[17]. Rebbi Yose said, the suspected wife is different because of its novelty and one cannot infer from anything that is different because of its novelty[18]. Rebbi Abun bar Ḥiyya understood it from the following[19]: "This is the teaching about the flour offering, present." Where is the weave? It already preceded. Rebbi Yose said, explain it about flour offerings that do not need weaves; you cannot infer anything. Which [verse] says anything? "You shall bring,[20]" to include the *'Omer* flour offering in presentations. "He shall present," to include the suspected wife's flour offering in presentations. It is written after that[21]: "He shall lift a fist full"; where is the weave[22]? It already preceded.

16 Mishnah *Menaḥot* 5:6 states that weave always precedes presentation. One has to wonder about Rashi's Yerushalmi text since in his commentary to that Mishnah he follows R. Jeremiah.

17 Since *Num.* 5:25 clearly prescribes first weave and then presentation.

18 While not in the tannaïtic rules, this is a generally recognized hermeneutical principle in both Talmudim; cf. Babli *Ketubot* 45a,

Sanhedrin 27a. The novelty status of the suspected wife's offering is explained in Mishnah 2:1; therefore, procedural instructions for this offering cannot imply similar instructions for the other flour offerings.

19 *Lev.* 6:7. This paragraph deals with technicalities of all flour offerings, whether they need weaving or not. Any special ceremony for certain offerings must precede the ceremonies common to all offerings.

20 *Lev.* 2:8: "You shall bring the offering made *from these* to the Eternal; the Cohen shall bring it and present it to the altar." "These" are flour and olive oil.

The *baraita* is also quoted in the Babli, *Menaḥot* 60b.

21 *Lev.* 2:9.

22 Which is prescribed for the offering of the suspected wife in *Num.* 5:25..

(18c line 56) תַּמָּן תַּנִינָן. אִילוּ מְנָחוֹת נִקְמָצוֹת וּשְׁיָרֵיהֶן לַכֹּהֲנִים. רִבִּי בָּא בַּר מָמָל וְרִבִּי שמעון בַּר רַב יִצְחָק הֲווֹן יְתִיבִין. רִבִּי בָּא בַּר מָמָל בְּעָא קוֹמֵי רִבִּי שְׁמוּאֵל בַּר רַב יִצְחָק. מִנְחַת הָעוֹמֶר מִנַּיִין שֶׁשְּׁיָרֶיהָ נֶאֱכָלִין. אָמַר לֵיהּ. וְלֹא כֵן אָמַר רִבִּי יוֹחָנָן בְּשֵׁם רִבִּי יִשְׁמָעֵאל. מִנְחַת מִנְחַת. מַה מִנְחַת שֶׁנֶּאֱמְרָה לְהַלָּן מִן הַשְּׂעוֹרִין. אַף כָּאן מִן הַשְּׂעוֹרִין. אַף מִנְחַת סוֹטָה שְׁיָרֶיהָ נֶאֱכָלִין. אַף מִנְחַת הָעוֹמֶר שְׁיָרֶיהָ נֶאֱכָלִין. אָמַר רִבִּי עֲקִיבָה. מִן דְּקַיְימִין קָם רִבִּי בָּא בַּר מָמָל עִם רִבִּי יִרְמְיָה. אָמַר לֵיהּ. חֲמֵית הֵיךְ אַפְרָחֵי הָדֵין דִּידָךְ. מִנְחַת סוֹטָה עַצְמָהּ מִנַּיִין שֶׁשְּׁיָרֶיהָ נֶאֱכָלִין. אַיְיתֵי רִבִּי זְעֵירָא לְרִבִּי יִצְחָק עֲטוֹשַׁיָּא וְתַנָּא לֵיהּ. וְכָל־מִנְחָה בְלוּלָה בַשֶּׁמֶן. מָה אֲנָן קַיָּימִין. אִם בִּבְלוּל שֶׁלַּחִטִּין. כְּבָר הוּא אָמוּר. אֶלָּא אִם אֵינוֹ עִנְייָן לִבְלוּל שֶׁלַּחִטִּין תְּנֵיהוּ עִנְייָן לִבְלוּל שֶׁלַּשְּׂעוֹרִין. וַחֲרֵבָה אָמַר [וַחֲרֵבָה.][23] מָה אֲנָן קַיָּימִין. אִם בְּחָרֵב שֶׁלַּחִטִּים כְּבָר הוּא אָמוּר. אֶלָּא אִם אֵינוֹ עִנְייָן לְחָרֵב שֶׁלַּחִיטִּין תְּנֵיהוּ עִנְייָן לְחָרֵב שֶׁלַּשְּׂעוֹרִין. אָמַר רִבִּי יוֹסֵי. בִּבְלוּל שֶׁלַּחִטִּין וּבְחָרֵב שֶׁלַּחִיטִּין אֲנָן קַיָּימִין. וְלָצוֹרֶךְ אִיתְאָמָרַת. לְכָל־בְּנֵי אַהֲרֹן תִּהְיֶה אִישׁ כְּאָחִיו. הָאִישׁ חוֹלֵק אַף עַל פִּי שֶׁהוּא בַּעַל מוּם. וְאֵין הַקָּטָן חוֹלֵק אַף עַל פִּי שֶׁהוּא תָמִים. אָמַר רִבִּי יוֹסֵי בֵּירִבִּי בּוּן. מִפְּנֵי שְׁרִיבְּתָה תוֹרָה בְּדָבָר אֶחָד אַתְּ מַרְבֶּה אוֹתָהּ לְכָל־הַדְּבָרִים. אֶלָּא אַזְכָּרָה אַזְכָּרָה. מַה אַזְכָּרָה שֶׁנֶּאֱמְרָה לְהַלָּן שְׁיָרֶיהָ נֶאֱכָלִין. אַף אַזְכָּרָה שֶׁנֶּאֱמְרָה כָּן שְׁיָרֶיהָ נֶאֱכָלִין. וְיֵידָא אֲמָרָה דָא. וְהֵבֵאתָ לְרִבּוּת מִנְחַת הָעוֹמֶר לַהַגָּשָׁה. וְהִקְרִיבָהּ. לְרִבּוּת מִנְחַת סוֹטָה לַהַגָּשָׁה. וּכְתִיב בַּתְרֵיהּ וְהַנּוֹתֶרֶת מִן הַמִּנְחָה לְאַהֲרֹן וּלְבָנָיו קוֹדֶשׁ קָדָשִׁים.

There, it was stated[24]: "The following flour offerings have a handful taken and the remainders are eaten." Rebbi Abba bar Mamal and Rebbi [Samuel][25] bar Rav Isaac were sitting together. Rebbi Abba bar Mamal asked from Rebbi Samuel bar Rav Isaac: From where [do we know that] the remainders of the *'Omer* offering are eaten[26]? He said to him: Did not Rebbi Joḥanan say[27] in the name of Rebbi Ismael: "Offering of[28], offering of[29]." Since "offering of" mentioned there[28] is from barley, so also "offering of" mentioned here[29] is from barley. Since the remainders of the offering of the suspected wife are eaten[30], so the remainders of the *'Omer* offering are eaten. Rebbi (Aqiba)[31] said: After they got up, Rebbi Abba bar Mamal was standing with Rebbi Jeremiah. He[32] said to him: Look, how he made your question fly away! From where [do we know that] the remainders of the offering of the suspected wife are eaten[33]? Rebbi Ze'ira[34] brought Rebbi Isaac Aṭoshiyya, who stated for him: "Any flour offering mixed with oil[35]". Where do we hold? If about mixed wheat flour, it already had been said[36]. So if it does not refer to mixed wheat flour, apply it to mixed barley flour. Another [*baraita*] states: "Or dry[35]". Where do we hold? If about dry wheat flour[37], it already had been said. So if it does not refer to dry wheat flour, apply it to dry barley flour. Rebbi Yose said, we deal with mixed wheat flour and dry wheat flour, and it was said for a purpose[38]. "[It] shall belong to all sons of Aaron, to each man as to his brother." A man takes his part even if he is blemished[39]. A minor does not take a part even if he is unblemished[40]. Rebbi Yose ben Rebbi Abun said: Because the Torah added a detail in one case, can you add that in every case? But "remembrance[41], remembrance[42]". "You shall bring,[20]" to include the *'Omer* flour offering in presentations. "He shall present it," to include the suspected wife's flour offering in presentations. It is written after that[43]: "What is left from the offering is most holy for Aaron and his sons."

23 From the Rome ms., missing in the Leiden ms. and *editio princeps*.

24 Mishnah *Menaḥot* 7:1. The list contains the offerings of the *'Omer* and the suspected wife. Such a list is necessary since the flour offerings accompanying an animal sacrifice (*Num.* 15:1-16), as well as the private offerings of a Cohen, are burned completely.

25 This is the correct name. Possibly the name was written ר״ש in a common source of the mss. and was interpreted wrongly by some intermediate scribe.

26 The paragraph of the *'Omer* offering (*Lev.* 23:9-14) prescribes weaving but is silent about anything done after the weaving. It might be concluded that the general rules of the flour offering specified in *Lev.* 6:7-11 do apply. These include that a Cohen has to present the offering to the altar, that he take a handful to the altar to be burned, and that the remainder be eaten under the rules of most holy sacrifices. However, those rules presuppose that pieces of incense are put on top of the offering; this does not apply to the *'Omer* offering. Therefore, the details of the treatment of the *'Omer* offering seem to be undefined.

27 Cf. Chapter 2, Note 39.

28 *Num.* 5:15, "an offering of jealousy".

29 *Lev.* 2:14, "an offering of First Fruits," taken to refer to the *'Omer* offering. These are the only flour offerings referred to in the construct state; this is taken as indication that they follow parallel rules except as indicated otherwise in the biblical text.

30 This is not prescribed in the biblical text but since a handful must be taken to the altar it is accepted that this offering follows the rules of all offerings of which a handful is burned on the altar; cf. Note 26.

31 This attribution is certainly incorrect. Probably one should read "R. Jacob"; one Amora of this name was known as one of the colleagues of R. Jeremiah.

32 Rebbi Jeremiah said to R. Abba bar Mamal.

33 For that offering also, the

handful for the altar is mentioned but nothing else.

34   R. Jeremiah's teacher; he called the specialist for *baraitot* in his academy.

35   *Lev.* 7:10: "Any flour offering mixed with oil or dry shall belong to all sons of Aaron, to each man as to his brother."

36   The list of private flour offerings from wheat flour is in *Lev.* 2:1-10 and there it is emphasized that the remainders have to be eaten by the sons of Aaron.

37   The purification offering of the poor sinner (*Lev.* 5:11-13) is from wheat flour and has to be eaten by the Cohen.

38   The argument of the preceding *baraitot*, which in the Babli (*Menaḥot* 72b) is a pseudo-tannaïtic statement by Ḥizqiah, is irrelevant since the verse teaches important new information for all flour offerings that are eaten (also noted in the Babli).

39   He has a bodily defect which disables him from serving in the Temple (*Lev.* 21:17-19).

40   *Sifra Ṣaw Pereq* 10(9); Babli *Menaḥot* 72b. In *Zebaḥim* 102a it is stated more in detail that the right of a blemished Cohen to eat of the holy food is established in *Lev.* 21 but his right to take part in the distribution of food in the Temple is derived from *Lev.* 6:11 [from *Sifra Ṣaw Pereq* 3(5)]. One really needs *Lev.* 7:10 only to show that a minor cannot claim a part in the distribution (cf. *Šiṭṭa Mequbeṣet*, *Zebaḥim* 102a).

41   *Lev.* 2:9: "The Cohen has to lift its remembrance" which is the fistful of flour with the incense, to be burned on the altar.

42   *Num.* 5:26: "The Cohen has to lift a fistful for its remembrance," speaking of the flour offering of the suspected wife.

43   While in the preceding paragraph the following verse was from the rules of the suspected wife, here the verse is taken from the general rules of a flour offering, *Lev.* 2:10 to imply that every flour offering of which only a fistful is burned on the altar is eaten by the Cohanim.

(fol. 18c) **משנה ב:** הָיָה מַשְׁקָהּ וְאַחַר כָּךְ מַקְרִיב אֶת מִנְחָתָהּ. רַבִּי שִׁמְעוֹן אוֹמֵר מַקְרִיב אֶת מִנְחָתָהּ וְאַחַר כָּךְ מַשְׁקָהּ שֶׁנֶּאֱמַר וְאַחַר יַשְׁקֶה אֶת הָאִשָּׁה אֶת הַמָּיִם. אִם הִשְׁקָהּ וְאַחַר כָּךְ הִקְרִיב אֶת מִנְחָתָהּ כְּשֵׁירָה.

Mishnah 2: He[1] gives her to drink and after that he presents her offering[44]. Rebbi Simeon says, he sacrifices her offering and afterwards gives her to drink as it is said[45]: "After that he shall give the water to the woman to drink." If he gave her to drink and after that sacrificed her offering, it is valid[46].

44 As the Babli (19b) points out, Mishnah 1 only described all the ritual acts to be performed for the flour offering but did not determine the time sequence.

45 *Num.* 5:27.

46 Even for R. Simeon.

(fol. 18d) **הלכה ב:** הָיָה מַשְׁקָהּ וְאַחַר כָּךְ מַקְרִיב אֶת מִנְחָתָהּ כול'. מַה טַעֲמוֹן דְּרַבָּנִין. וּבָאוּ בָהּ. מַה טַעֲמָא דְּרַבִּי שִׁמְעוֹן. וְאַחַר יַשְׁקֶה אֶת הָאִשָּׁה. מַה מְקַיֵּים רַבִּי שִׁמְעוֹן טַעֲמוֹן דְּרַבָּנִין. וּבָאוּ בָהּ. כּוּלְּהוֹן וְלֹא מִקְצָתָן. מַה מְקַיְּימִין רַבָּנָן טַעֲמֵיהּ דְּרַבִּי שִׁמְעוֹן. וְאַחַר יַשְׁקֶה אֶת הָאִשָּׁה אֶת הַמַּיִם. עַל כּוּרְחָהּ שֶׁלֹּא בְטוֹבָתָהּ. מוֹדֶה רַבִּי שִׁמְעוֹן לַחֲכָמִים שֶׁאִם הִשְׁקָהּ וְאַחַר כָּךְ הִקְרִיב מִנְחָתָהּ שֶׁהִיא כְשֵׁירָה. וּמוֹדִין חֲכָמִים לְרַבִּי שִׁמְעוֹן שֶׁאִם הִקְרִיב מִנְחָתָהּ וְאַחַר כָּךְ הִשְׁקָהּ. שֶׁהִיא כְשֵׁירָה. מַה בֵּינֵיהוֹן. מִצְוָה. רַבָּנִין אָמְרִין. מִנְחָה הִיא שֶׁהִיא בּוֹדְקָתָהּ. וְרַבִּי שִׁמְעוֹן אוֹמֵר. הַמַּיִם אֵין בּוֹדְקִין אוֹתָהּ. מַה טַעֲמוֹן דְּרַבָּנָן. מִנְחַת זִכָּרוֹן מַזְכֶּרֶת עָוֹן. מַה טַעֲמֵיהּ דְּרַבִּי שִׁמְעוֹן. וּבָאוּ בָהּ. מַה מְקַיְּימִין רַבָּנָן טַעֲמֵיהּ דְּרַבִּי שִׁמְעוֹן. וּבָאוּ בָהּ. מְלַמֵּד שֶׁהֵן מְחַלְחֲלִין בְּכָל־אֵיבָרֶיהָ. מַה מְקַיֵּים רַבִּי שִׁמְעוֹן טַעֲמוֹן דְּרַבָּנִין. מִנְחַת זִכָּרוֹן מַזְכֶּרֶת עָוֹן. מְלַמֵּד שֶׁכָּל־עֲווֹנוֹת שֶׁיֵּשׁ לָהּ נִזְכָּרִין לָהּ בְּאוֹתָהּ שָׁעָה.

Halakhah 2: "He gives her to drink and after that he sacrifices her offering," etc. What is the reason of the rabbis? "They shall come into her⁴⁷." What is the reason of Rebbi Simeon? "After that he shall give to the woman to drink⁴⁵." How does Rebbi Simeon explain the rabbis' reason, "they shall come into her"? All of them, not part only⁴⁸. How do the rabbis explain Rebbi Simeon's reason, "after that he shall give the water to the woman to drink"? Against her will, without her agreement⁴⁹. Rebbi Simeon agrees with the rabbis that if he gave her to drink and after that presented her offering, it is valid. The rabbis agree with Rebbi Simeon that if he presented her offering and after that gave her to drink, it is valid⁵⁰. What is the difference between them? The commandment. The rabbis say that the flour offering checks her out⁵¹ but Rebbi Simeon says, the water is⁵² what checks her out. What is the reason of the Sages? "A flour offering of remembrance remembering iniquity⁵³." What is the reason of Rebbi Simeon? "They shall come into her⁴⁷,⁵⁴." How do the rabbis explain Rebbi Simeon's reason, "they shall come into her"? This teaches that it shakes all her limbs⁵⁵. How does Rebbi Simeon explain the rabbis' reason, "a flour offering of remembrance remembering iniquity"? This teaches that all iniquities she has committed are remembered at that time⁵⁶.

47 *Num.* 5:24: "The curse-water shall come into her as a bitter one." This is written before the description of the presentation of the flour offering in v. 25.

48 She has to drink the rather small amount of water completely.

49 Cf. Mishnah 3. In the Babli, 19b, this is the position of the rabbis.

50 This statement is not in the Babli. As Tosaphot (19a, s. v. ואחר) points out, the Babli does not object.

51 In the Babli, 20b, this is given as R. Simeon's reason to require sacrificing the offering before the drink.

52 Reading אין as הן, equivalent of Babylonian אינון "they are". Instead of אין, the Rome ms. has היו. The past tense does not agree with the rest of

the text; it should be rejected. Note that there also exists a Babylonian אִין equal to הֵן "yes".

53   *Num.* 5:15.

54   The same explanation as anonymous text in *Sifry Num.* 18; copied in *Num. rabba* 9(18).

55   Cf. Mishnah 4.

56   Before the Heavenly Court which decides about the water's action.

(18d line 20) רַבָּנָן אָמְרֵי. כּוֹתֵב וּמוֹחֵק וּמַשְׁקֶה וּמַקְרִיב. רִבִּי שִׁמְעוֹן אוֹמֵר. כּוֹתֵב וּמַקְרִיב וּמוֹחֵק וּמַשְׁקֶה. כָּל־עַמָּא מוֹדֵיי שֶׁמְּחִיקָה סְמוּכָה לְהַשְׁקָיָה. אֶלָּא דְרַבָּנָן אָמְרֵי. כּוֹתֵב וּמוֹחֵק וּמַשְׁקֶה וּמַקְרִיב. וְרִבִּי שִׁמְעוֹן אוֹמֵר. כּוֹתֵב וּמַקְרִיב וּמוֹחֵק וּמַשְׁקֶה. תַּנֵּי. לְעוֹלָם הִיא יְכוֹלָה לַחֲזוֹר בָּהּ עַד שֶׁלֹּא תִקְרֵב מִנְחָתָהּ. קָרְבָה מִנְחָתָהּ וְאָמְרָה. אֵינִי שׁוֹתָה. מְעַרְעֲרִין אוֹתָהּ וּמַשְׁקִין אוֹתָהּ בְּעַל כּוֹרְחָהּ. כְּרִבִּי שִׁמְעוֹן. בְּרַם כְּרַבָּנָן כְּבָר שָׁתָת. אֲנָן תַּנִּינָן. אֵינָהּ מַסְפֶּקֶת לִשְׁתּוֹת. אִית תַּנָּיֵי תַנֵּי. לֹא הָיְתָה זָזָה מִשָּׁם. מָאן דְּאָמַר. אֵינָהּ מַסְפֶּקֶת לִשְׁתּוֹת. רִבִּי שִׁמְעוֹן. מָאן דָּמַר. לֹא הָיְתָה זָזָה מִשָּׁם. רַבָּנָן.

The rabbis say, he writes, erases, gives to drink, and sacrifices [the flour offering]. Rebbi Simeon says, he writes, sacrifices, erases, and gives to drink. Everybody agrees that erasing immediately precedes drinking; only that the rabbis say, he writes, erases, gives to drink, and sacrifices, while Rebbi Simeon says, he writes, sacrifices, erases, and gives to drink. It was stated: "She may always change her mind as long as her offering was not sacrificed. If her offering was sacrificed and she said 'I do not want to drink' one makes her gargle[56] and forces her to drink". Following Rebbi Simeon. But following the rabbis she already drank[57]. We have stated: "She did not finish drinking[58]". Some Tannaïm state: She did not move from there[59]. He who says, she did not finish drinking, Rebbi Simeon[60]. He who says, she did not move from there, the rabbis[61].

56 The language is from Mishnah 3:3. Since in general ערער means "to protest", it is reasonable to consider the word used here an Arabism, from غرغر "to gargle".

57 The *baraita* can only be from the school of R. Simeon since for the rabbis the offering is sacrificed only after she drank.

58 Mishnah 3:4: The water acted as poison when she was still standing in the courtyard of the Temple.

59 After drinking the water, she had to remain in the courtyard until the fistful of her offering was burned on the altar.

60 Since he was reported to hold that the water is checking her out. In this interpretation, the report in the Mishnah of a disagreement between the rabbis and R. Simeon is followed by an anonymous Mishnah following R. Simeon. This implies (cf. *Yebamot* 4, Note 175, *'Orlah* 2, Note 30) that the Yerushalmi decides that practice follows R. Simeon.

61 Since it was stated in the preceding paragraph that the water is only activated by the burning of the offering on the altar. This reason is given in the Babli for R. Simeon to require the early sacrificing of her offering, cf. Note 51. It shows that the Babli decides that practice does *not* follow R. Simeon.

משנה ג: עַד שֶׁלֹּא נִמְחֲקָה הַמְּגִילָּה אָמְרָה אֵינִי שׁוֹתָה מְגִילָּתָהּ נִגְנֶזֶת וּמִנְחָתָהּ מִתְפַּזֶּרֶת עַל הַדֶּשֶׁן. וְאֵין מְגִילָּתָהּ כְּשֵׁירָה לְהַשְׁקוֹת בָּהּ סוֹטָה אַחֶרֶת. נִמְחֲקָה הַמְּגִילָּה וְאָמְרָה טְמֵיאָה אֲנִי הַמַּיִם נִשְׁפָּכִים וּמִנְחָתָהּ מִתְפַּזֶּרֶת עַל הַדֶּשֶׁן. נִמְחֲקָה הַמְּגִילָּה וְאָמְרָה אֵינִי שׁוֹתָה מְעַרְעֲרִין אוֹתָהּ וּמַשְׁקִין אוֹתָהּ בְּעַל כּוֹרְחָהּ. (fol. 18c)

Mishnah 3: If she said "I shall not drink[62]" before the scroll was erased, her scroll is put away[63] and her offering dispersed on the ashes[64]. Her scroll is not acceptable to be used to make another suspected wife drink[65]. If she said "I am impure" after the scroll was erased, the water is poured out and her offering dispersed on the ashes[66]. If she said "I shall not drink" after the scroll was erased, one makes her gargle and forces her to drink against her will[67].

62 Since she is forbidden to her husband from the moment she was found to have been in a secluded place with her paramour until after she drank the water, by refusing to drink she accepts to be divorced by her husband without any *ketubah* money but without explicitly admitting guilt.

63 Since it was written in holiness and contains the Divine Name, it cannot be destroyed.

64 Since the offering was already dedicated in a Temple vessel, it cannot be returned to profane status. It is put on the ashes taken from the altar.

65 Cf. Halakhah 2:2, Note 104.

66 Since there is no longer any doubt, the water cannot be used, neither can the offering. By her confession of adultery she has to be divorced by her husband, without him having to pay the *ketubah*. On her confession she cannot be prosecuted for adultery because confessions are not acceptable in a court of law since the testimony of close relatives is not admissible and everybody is a relative to himself.

67 Since she caused the Divine Name to be erased, if she does not drink she commits blasphemy.

הלכה ג: עַד שֶׁלֹּא נִמְחֲקָה הַמְּגִילָה כול'. תַּנֵּי. מְגִילָתָהּ נִגְנֶזֶת תַּחַת צִירוֹ[68] שֶׁל הֵיכָל. לָמָּה. בִּשְׁבִיל לְשָׁחֲקָהּ. לוּל קָטָן הָיָה. שָׁם הַמַּיִם נִשְׁפָּכִין. תַּנֵּי. אֵין בָּהֶן מִשּׁוּם קְדוּשָׁה. מַהוּ לִגְבּוֹל בָּהֶן אֶת הַטִּיט. מַה בְּכָךְ. הַמַּיִם נִשְׁפָּכִין.[69] תַּנֵּי. יֵשׁ בָּהֶן מִשּׁוּם קְדוּשָׁה. (fol. 18d)

Halakhah 3: "Before the scroll was erased," etc. It was stated: Her scroll is put away under the hinges of a [gate of] the Temple hall. Why? In order to shred it[70]. A small hollow space was where the water was poured out[71]. It was stated[72]: There is no holiness in it. May it be used to moisten mortar[73]? What should be wrong? It is poured out! It was stated[74]: There is holiness in it.

68   Reading of *editio princeps* and Tosaphot (20a, *s. v.* מגילתה). In ms: צידו "its side". In Tosephta 2:2: טירו.

69   Reading of *editio princeps* and Tosaphot (20a, *s. v.* מגילתה). In ms: נשתכין

70   Tosephta 2:2. The scroll has to be destroyed to avoid its being used again, but this must be done in holiness and without anybody touching the Divine Names.

71   There is no parallel to this statement in any known tannaïtic source; one does not know where this hollow space was. In Babli *Pesaḥim* 34a, the open space between the ramp leading to the top of the altar and the altar is called *lul*; in the parallel Tosephta *Zebaḥim* 7:6 this is called חלון "window" or רבובה, רביכה "hollow with masonry walls." That hollow could not be classified as "small".

72   Tosephta 2:2, referring to the water which no longer is needed.

73   It is sinful to use Temple property for private use. But the water might be used in ongoing repairs on the Temple mount.

74   In another, otherwise undocumented *baraita*. Since it is unknown which of the two *baraitot* represents practice, the unneeded water cannot be used for anything.

(18d line 32) נִמְחֲקָה הַמְגִילָה וְאָמְרָה. טְמֵיאָה אָנִי. הַמַּיִם נִשְׁפָּכִין וּמִנְחָתָהּ מִתְפַּזֶּרֶת עַל גַּבֵּי הַדֶּשֶׁן. הָדָא אָמְרָה שֶׁמִּנְחַת סוֹטָה קָדְשָׁה עַד שֶׁלֹּא תִכָּתֵב הַמְגִילָה. אָמַר רִבִּי יוֹסֵי דְרוֹבָה. תַּנֵּי רִבִּי חִייָה. עַד שֶׁהִיא בַדֶּרֶךְ מִנְחָתָהּ קָדְשָׁה. אָמַר רִבִּי יוֹסֵי בֵּירִבִּי בּוּן. מַתְנִיתִין אָמְרָה כֵן. שֶׁבַּעֲלָהּ בָּעֲלָהּ בַּדֶּרֶךְ.

"If she said 'I am impure' after the scroll was erased, the water is poured out and her offering dispersed over the ashes." This proves that the suspected wife's offering is holy before the scroll is written[75]. Rebbi Yose said, there is more: Rebbi Ḥiyya stated, her offering is holy once she is on her way[76]. Rebbi Yose bar Abun said, our Mishnah states this[77]: "Or if her husband had sexual relations with her on the road."

75   Since following the rabbis the offering is transferred to the Temple vessel only after she drank the water, if her offering is treated as holy but

invalid by being poured over the ashes of the sacrifices, the question arises when the offering acquires the holiness of a Temple offering. The question is obvious even for R. Simeon since it is forbidden to bring profane food into the Temple precinct even though according to him the case of the Mishnah could not arise.

76 From the moment the husband had dedicated the flour, irrespective of the vessel it was brought in.

77 Mishnah 4:2, detailing the cases in which the procedure becomes inactive. If the husband had relations with his wife while she was forbidden to him, he must divorce her since without the Temple procedure she cannot become permitted to him. But because it is his fault that she cannot rehabilitate herself, he has to pay the full amount of his *ketubah* obligation.

(18d line 37) נִמְחֲקָה הַמְּגִילָה וְאָמְרָה. אֵינִי שׁוֹתָה מְעַרְעֲרִין אוֹתָהּ וּמַשְׁקִין אוֹתָהּ בְּעַל כָּרְחָהּ. לָמָה. שֶׁגְּרָמָה לַשֵּׁם שֶׁיִּימָּחֵק. כַּמָּה יִמָּחֵק. תַּנֵּי רִבִּי חָנִין. בֵּית שַׁמַּי אוֹמְרִים. אַחַת. וּבֵית הִלֵּל אוֹמְרִים. שְׁתַּיִם. אָמַר רִבִּי אִילַי. טַעֲמוֹן דְּבֵית הִלֵּל כְּדֵי לִכְתּוֹב יָהּ. אָמַר לוֹ רִבִּי עֲקִיבָה. וְכִי מִפְּנֵי מַה מַשְׁקִין אֶת זוֹ. אִם לְבוֹדְקָהּ. כְּבָר הִיא בְדוּקָה וּמְתוּקֶּנֶת. אֶלָּא סָבַר רִבִּי עֲקִיבָה. הָאוֹמֶרֶת. אֵינִי שׁוֹתָה. כְּאוֹמֶרֶת. אֲנִי טְמֵיאָה לָךְ. וְלֵית לְרִבִּי עֲקִיבָה. מְעַרְעֲרִין אוֹתָהּ לִשְׁתּוֹת עַד שֶׁפָּנֶיהָ מוֹרִיקוֹת וּמַשְׁקִין אוֹתָהּ עַל כּוֹרְחָהּ. אִית לֵיהּ. כְּשֶׁהִתְחִילָה לִשְׁתּוֹת.

"If she said 'I shall not drink' after the scroll was erased, one makes her gargle and forces her to drink against her will." [78]How many letters have to be erased? Rebbi Ḥanin stated: The House of Shammai say, one; the House of Hillel say, two. Rebbi Hilai said, the reason of the House of Hillel: That he could have written Yah. [79]Rebbi Aqiba said to him: But why does one make her drink? If it is to check her out, she already is completely checked out[80]! But Rebbi Aqiba must hold that the one who says "I shall not drink" is as the one who says "I am impure for you"[81]. But does Rebbi Aqiba not agree that "one makes her gargle until her face turned yellow and forces her to drink against her will"? He does, if she started to drink[82].

78   Cf. Chapter 2, Notes 135-136.

79   In a discussion between R. Jehudah and R. Aqiba, quoted in full in Babli 19b, Tosephta 2:3.

80   In the Babli, בדוקה ועומדת "lawfully checked out"; in the Tosephta בדוקה ומנוולת "checked out and degraded".

81   One admits her guilt, the other accepts the consequences as if she were guilty; since the proceedings are extra-judicial, there is no reason to treat the two cases differently.

82   In the Tosephta, following the rabbis who make the entire procedure depend on the burning of the flour offering, R. Aqiba holds that she does not have to drink as long as the offering was not burned. Since for the rabbis the offering follows the drinking, he treats the one who says "I am impure" exactly as the one who pays the fine without admitting guilt. In the Babli, R. Aqiba's argument is explained away: one accepts her statement that she is impure only if made in a self-assured way, when she can be believed; but if she makes the confession while trembling, one suspects that she might be pure but has been intimidated by the procedure and therefore her guilt has not been established. Both sources disagree with the Yerushalmi.

משנה ד: (fol. 18c) אֵינָהּ מַסְפֶּקֶת לִשְׁתּוֹת עַד שֶׁפָּנֶיהָ מוֹרִיקוֹת וְעֵינֶיהָ בּוֹלְטוֹת וְהִיא מִתְמַלֵּאת גִּידִים וְהֵן אוֹמְרִים הוֹצִיאוּהָ הוֹצִיאוּהָ שֶׁלֹּא תְטַמֵּא אֶת הָעֲזָרָה. אִם יֵשׁ לָהּ זְכוּת הָיְתָה תוֹלָה לָהּ. יֵשׁ זְכוּת תּוֹלָה לָהּ שָׁנָה אַחַת יֵשׁ זְכוּת תּוֹלָה לָהּ שְׁתֵּי שָׁנִים יֵשׁ זְכוּת תּוֹלָה לָהּ שָׁלֹשׁ שָׁנִים. מִכָּן אוֹמֵר בֶּן עַזַּאי חַיָּיב אָדָם לְלַמֵּד אֶת בִּתּוֹ תוֹרָה שֶׁאִם תִּשְׁתֶּה תֵּדַע שֶׁהַזְּכוּת תּוֹלָה לָהּ. רִבִּי אֱלִיעֶזֶר אוֹמֵר הַמְלַמֵּד אֶת בִּתּוֹ תוֹרָה מְלַמְּדָהּ תִּפְלוּת. רִבִּי יְהוֹשֻׁעַ אוֹמֵר רוֹצָה אִשָּׁה בְּקַב וְתִפְלוּת. מִתִּשְׁעָה קַבִּין וּפְרִישׁוּת. הוּא הָיָה אוֹמֵר חָסִיד שׁוֹטֶה רָשָׁע עָרוּם אִשָּׁה פְרוּשָׁה וּמַכּוֹת פְּרוּשִׁין הֲרֵי אִילּוּ מְכַלֵּי עוֹלָם.

says "I shall not drink" is as the one who says "I am impure for you"[81]. But does Rebbi Aqiba not agree that "one makes her gargle until her face turned yellow and forces her to drink against her will"? He does, if she started to drink[82].

78 Cf. Chapter 2, Notes 135-136.

79 In a discussion between R. Jehudah and R. Aqiba, quoted in full in Babli 19b, Tosephta 2:3.

80 In the Babli, בדוקה ועומדת "lawfully checked out"; in the Tosephta בדוקה ומנוולת "checked out and degraded".

81 One admits her guilt, the other accepts the consequences as if she were guilty; since the proceedings are extra-judicial, there is no reason to treat the two cases differently.

82 In the Tosephta, following the rabbis who make the entire procedure depend on the burning of the flour offering, R. Aqiba holds that she does not have to drink as long as the offering was not burned. Since for the rabbis the offering follows the drinking, he treats the one who says "I am impure" exactly as the one who pays the fine without admitting guilt. In the Babli, R. Aqiba's argument is explained away: one accepts her statement that she is impure only if made in a self-assured way, when she can be believed; but if she makes the confession while trembling, one suspects that she might be pure but has been intimidated by the procedure and therefore her guilt has not been established. Both sources disagree with the Yerushalmi.

משנה ד: (fol. 18c) אֵינָהּ מַסְפֶּקֶת לִשְׁתּוֹת עַד שֶׁפָּנֶיהָ מוֹרִיקוֹת וְעֵינֶיהָ בּוֹלְטוֹת וְהִיא מִתְמַלֵּאת גִּידִים וְהֵן אוֹמְרִים הוֹצִיאוּהָ הוֹצִיאוּהָ שֶׁלֹּא תְטַמֵּא אֶת הָעֲזָרָה. אִם יֶשׁ לָהּ זְכוּת הָיְתָה תּוֹלָה לָהּ. יֵשׁ זְכוּת תּוֹלָה לָהּ שָׁנָה אַחַת יֵשׁ זְכוּת תּוֹלָה לָהּ שְׁתֵּי שָׁנִים יֵשׁ זְכוּת תּוֹלָה לָהּ שָׁלֹשׁ שָׁנִים. מִכָּן אוֹמֵר בֶּן עַזַּאי חַיָּיב אָדָם לְלַמֵּד אֶת בִּתּוֹ תוֹרָה שֶׁאִם תִּשְׁתֶּה תֵּדַע שֶׁהַזְּכוּת תּוֹלָה לָהּ. רְבִּי אֱלִיעֶזֶר אוֹמֵר הַמְלַמֵּד אֶת בִּתּוֹ תוֹרָה מְלַמְּדָהּ תִּפְלוּת. רְבִּי יְהוֹשֻׁעַ אוֹמֵר רוֹצָה אִשָּׁה בְּקַב

HALAKHAH 4

Halakhah 4: "She does not finish drinking", etc. But did we not think to say "All of them, not part only[88]"? It is as if somebody said, X did not finish drinking when he started shaking[89].

88 Cf. Note 48; it was agreed that the water will not become active until the woman finished drinking.

89 This is a manner of speech meaning "immediately".

(18d line 47) יֵשׁ זְכוּת תּוֹלָה שָׁנָה אַחַת. יֵשׁ זְכוּת תּוֹלָה שְׁתֵּי שָׁנִים. יֵשׁ זְכוּת תּוֹלָה שָׁלֹשׁ שָׁנִים. יֵשׁ זְכוּת תּוֹלָה שָׁנָה אַחַת. מִנְּבוּכַדְנֶצַר. לִקְצָת יַרְחִין תְּרֵי עֲשַׂר. יֵשׁ זְכוּת תּוֹלָה שְׁתֵּי שָׁנִים. מֵאַמְנוֹן. וַיְהִי לִשְׁנָתַיִם יָמִים. יֵשׁ זְכוּת שֶׁתּוֹלָה לְשָׁלֹשׁ שָׁנִים. מֵאַחְאָב. וַיֵּשְׁבוּ שָׁלֹשׁ שָׁנִים אֵין מִלְחָמָה בֵּין אֲרָם וּבֵין יִשְׂרָאֵל. אָמַר רִבִּי יוֹסֵי. נֶאֱמַר. כָּל־אוֹתָן שְׁנֵים־עָשָׂר חוֹדֶשׁ הָיָה עוֹסֵק בְּמִצְוֹת. וְכָל־אוֹתָן שְׁתֵּי שָׁנִים הָיָה עָסוּק בַּתּוֹרָה. וַיֵי דָא אֲמָרָה דָא. וַיֵּשְׁבוּ שָׁלֹשׁ שָׁנִים אֵין מִלְחָמָה בֵּין אֲרָם וּבֵין יִשְׂרָאֵל.

"There is merit which suspends for one year, there is merit which suspends for two years, there is merit which suspends for three years." There is merit which suspends for one year," from Nabuchadneṣar: "At the end of twelve months.[90]" "There is merit which suspends for two years," from Amnon: "It was after two years.[91]" "There is merit which suspends for three years," from Ahab: "They sat for three years when there was no war between Aram and Israel.[92]" Rebbi Yose said, it was said that the entire twelve months he[93] occupied himself with deeds of charity. And all these two[94] years he occupied himself with Torah. That is what it says: "They were in a Yeshiva[95] for three years when there was no war between Aram and Israel."

90 *Dan.* 4:26. It is written in v. 24: Therefore, o king, take my advice: atone for your sins by deeds of charity and for your misdeed by kindness to the poor, then your peace will be prolonged.

In the Babli, 20b, and in *Sifry Num.* 8, this is attributed to R. Ismael as maximum time lag for the water's action.

91 *2S.* 13:23. Absalom managed to kill Amnon two years after the latter had raped Tamar.

92 *1K.* 22:1. Everywhere in talmudic literature is the nameless "king of Israel" of Chap. 22:1-38 identified with Ahab mentioned in vv. 39-40. The three years are counted from the judicial murder of Nabot.

93 Probably referring to Nabuchadneṣar; but in the current text it refers to the first year of Ahab after Nabot's murder.

94 In *Tosaphot*, 20b s. v. יש, the reading is "three years." This reading is slightly suspect since the Babli (21a) accepts only the merit of Torah study as a saving device for Jews (works of charity really being the main vehicle of salvation for Gentiles).

95 A talmudic academy.

(18d line 54) מִנְחַת זִכָּרוֹן כְּלָל. מַזְכֶּרֶת עָוֹן פְּרָט. כְּלָל וּפְרָט אֵין בִּכְלָל אֶלָּא מַה שֶׁבִּפְרָט. אִם אוֹמֵר אַתְּ כֵּן לֹא נִמְצֵאת מִידַת הַדִּין מְקוּפַּחַת. מַה אִם מִידַת הַפּוּרְעָנוּת מְעוּטָה הֲרֵי הִיא מַזְכֶּרֶת. מִידַת הַטּוֹב מְרוּבָּה עַל אַחַת כַּמָּה וְכַמָּה. אֶלָּא מִנְחַת זִכָּרוֹן. יֵשׁ לָהּ זְכוּת. מַזְכֶּרֶת עָוֹן אֵין לָהּ זְכוּת. תַּנֵּי. רִבִּי טַרְפוֹן אוֹמֵר. כָּל־הַזִּכְרוֹנוֹת שֶׁנֶּאֶמְרוּ בַּתּוֹרָה לְטוֹבָה חוּץ מִזּוֹ שֶׁהִיא שֶׁלְּפוּרְעָנוּת. אָמַר לוֹ רִבִּי עֲקִיבָה. אִילּוּ נֶאֱמַר מַזְכֶּרֶת עָוֹן וְשָׁתַק. הָיִיתִי אוֹמֵר כִּדְבָרֶיךָ. הָא אֵינוֹ אוֹמֵר מִנְחַת זִכָּרוֹן אֶלָּא לְטוֹבָה.

96"An offering of remembrance," a general statement; "referring to sin", a detailed statement. If a general statement is followed by a specific one, the general does not mean more than the specific[97]. If you say so, do you not find the argument disadvantaged? If punishment, which is given out sparingly, can refer, then reward, which is given out in abundance[98], should do so much more! But, "an offering of remembrance," if she has merit, "referring to sin", if she has no merit. It was stated: Rebbi Tarphon said, all statements of "remembrance" in the Torah[99] have a good meaning except this one which is for punishment. Rebbi Aqiba said to him: If it only said, "referring to sin", and then was silent, I would agree with your statement. But since it says "an offering of remembrance," this must be for a good [purpose].

96 In different wording, the following two paragraphs are in *Sifry Num.* 8, copied in *Num. rabba* 9(39).

97 The fifth hermeneutical rule of R. Ismael: The only purpose of the offering is to lead to the punishment of the wife should she be found guilty. In the *Sifry*, the argument is in R. Ismael's name.

98 Cf. Halakhah 1:7, Note 269, Babli 11a. Tosephta 4:1 notes that the second of the Ten Commandments defines the measure of reward as at least 500 times the measure of punishment (since "thousands" are at least 2000, the ratio is ≥ 2000/4).

99 All occurences of זכרון in the Pentateuch except *Num.* 5:15,18. R. Tarphon holds with R. Simeon in the next Mishnah that it is preposterous to assume that the procedure has any value if it is inactive in most cases.

(18d line 62) תַּנֵּי. רִבִּי יוּדָה אוֹמֵר בְּשֵׁם רִבִּי לְעָזָר בֶּן מַתְיָה. הֲרֵי הוּא אוֹמֵר וְאִם לֹא נִטְמְאָה הָאִשָּׁה וּטְהוֹרָה הִיא. וְכִי אֵין אָנוּ יוֹדְעִין שֶׁאִם לֹא נִטְמְאָה הָאִשָּׁה שֶׁהִיא טְהוֹרָה. וּמַה תַּלְמוּד לוֹמַר וּטְהוֹרָה הִיא. אֶלָּא סוֹף הַמָּקוֹם פּוֹרֵעַ בָּהּ תַּחַת נִיווּלָהּ. שֶׁאִם הָיְתָה עֲקָרָה נִפְקֶדֶת. יוֹלֶדֶת בְּצַעַר יוֹלֶדֶת בְּרִיוָח. כְּאוּרִים יוֹלֶדֶת נָאִים. שְׁחוֹרִים יוֹלֶדֶת לְבָנִים. קְצָרִם יוֹלֶדֶת אֲרוּכִים. נְקֵיבוֹת יוֹלֶדֶת זְכָרִים. אֶחָד יוֹלֶדֶת שְׁנַיִם. אָמַר לוֹ רִבִּי שִׁמְעוֹן בֶּן לָקִישׁ. אִם כֵּן יֵלְכוּ כָל־הַנָּשִׁים וְיִתְקַלְקְלוּ בִּשְׁבִיל שֶׁיִּפָּקֵדוּ. וְלֵית לְרִבִּי שִׁמְעוֹן וְנִקְּתָה וְנִזְרְעָה זֶרַע אִית לֵיהּ. זֶרַע כָּשֵׁר לֹא זֶרַע פָּסוּל.

It was stated: Rebbi Jehudah says in the name of Rebbi Eleazar ben Matthias: It says, "but if the woman was not impure but was pure[100]."

Would we not know that if she was not impure she was pure? Why does the verse say, "but she was pure"[101]? Only that at the end the Omnipresent rewards her for the abuse, that if she was sterile she will become pregnant[102], [if she] was having difficult births she will have easy ones, [if she] had ugly children she will have good looking ones[103], black ones she will have white ones, short ones she will have tall ones, females she will have males, single children she will have twins. Rebbi Simeon ben Laqish[104] said to him: If it were so then all women should be misbehaving in order to become pregnant! But does Rebbi Simeon not interpret "she will be found innocent and become pregnant with seed"? He does, legitimate seed, not illegitimate[105].

---

100   *Num.* 5:28.

101   In *Sifry Num.* 19, the double expression is justified: R. Ismael holds that she only is permitted to her husband if the procedure had shown her innocence. An anonymous source notes that if she got a divorce after the procedure or her husband died, she was free to marry the man she was suspected of having an affair with; if she was divorced for adultery, the adulterer would be forbidden to her.

The Yerushalmi text is copied in *Num. rabba* 9(50).

102   In the Babli, 36a, and *Sifry Num.* 19, the first clause, about the sterile becoming pregnant, is R. Aqiba's; all the others are attributed to R. Ismael. In the Babli *Berakhot* 31b, the attributions are switched.

103   This clause is missing in the parallels. In Babylonian historical spelling, it would be בעורים.

104   This attribution to a second generation Amora is quite impossible in a tannaïtic text; in the Babli and *Sifry Num.* the argument is R. Ismael's. It seems that the Yerushalmi refers to R. Simeon ben Iohai, quoted in the next sentence.

105   In Halakhah 4:1, a similar (anonymous) argument is quoted to show that a divorcee married to a priest cannot be subjected to the procedure of the suspected wife because even if she was innocent she

could not have legitimate seed from the husband forbidden to her; her children from the priest are desecrated.

(18d line 70) וּבֶן עַזַּאי דְּלֹא כְרִבִּי לְעָזָר בֶּן עֲזַרְיָה. דְּתַנֵּי. מַעֲשֶׂה בְּרִבִּי יוֹחָנָן בֶּן בְּרוֹקָה וְרִבִּי אֶלְעָזָר חַסְמָא שֶׁהָיוּ מְהַלְּכִים מִיַּבְנֶה לְלוֹד. וְהִקְבִּילוּ אֶת רִבִּי יְהוֹשֻׁעַ בִּבְקִיעִין. אָמַר לָהֶן. מַה חִידּוּשׁ הָיָה לָכֶם בְּבֵית הַמִּדְרָשׁ הַיּוֹם. וְאָמְרוּ לוֹ. הַכֹּל תַּלְמִידֶיךָ וּמֵימֶיךָ אָנוּ שׁוֹתִים. אָמַר לָהֶן. אֲפִילוּ כֵן אִי אֶפְשָׁר לְבֵית הַמִּדְרָשׁ שֶׁלֹּא יְהֵא בּוֹ דָּבָר חָדָשׁ בְּכָל־יוֹם. מִי שָׁבַת שָׁם. אָמְרוּ לוֹ. רִבִּי לְעָזָר בֶּן עֲזַרְיָה. וּמַה הָיְתָה פָרָשָׁתוֹ. הַקְהֵל אֶת הָעָם הָאֲנָשִׁים וְהַנָּשִׁים וְהַטָּף. וּמַה אָמַר בָּהּ. הוֹאִיל וְהָאֲנָשִׁים בָּאִים לִלְמוֹד וְהַנָּשִׁים בָּאוֹת לִשְׁמוֹעַ. הַטָּף לָמָּה בָא. אֶלָּא לִיתֵּן שָׂכָר לַמְּבִיאֵיהֶן. אָמַר לָהֶן. אֵין הַדּוֹר יָתוֹם שֶׁרִבִּי אֶלְעָזָר בֶּן עֲזַרְיָה שָׁרוּי בְּתוֹכוֹ.

Ben Azai does not follow Rebbi Eleazar ben Azariah[106], as it was stated[107]: It happened that Rebbi Johanan ben Beroqa and Rebbi Eleazar Hasma were walking from Jabneh to Lydda when they were visiting Rebbi Joshua in Beqiin[108]. He asked them, what was new today in the House of Study? They said to him, we all are your students and drink from your waters. He said to them, even so, it is impossible that there not be a new idea every day in the House of Study. Who stayed there over the Sabbath? They said to him, Rebbi Eleazar ben Azariah. And what was his text? "Assemble the people, men, women, and children.[109]" What did he say about this? Since the men come to learn and the women to hear, why do the children come? It must be to give a reward to those who bring them. He said to them, the generation is not orphaned which counts Rebbi Eleazar ben Azariah among them.

106 R. Eleazar ben Azariah obligates women to listen to the Torah but not to study it.

107 *Hagigah* Babli 3a; Yerushalmi

1:1.

108 In the Babli: פקיעין. The locality is not identified; it cannot be the place of the same name in Galilee.

109 *Deut.* 31:12.

(19a line 3) מַטְרוֹנָה שָׁאֲלָה אֶת רִבִּי לְעָזֶר. מִפְּנֵי מַה חֵטְ[110] אַחַת בְּמַעֲשֵׂה הָעֵגֶל וְהֵן מֵתִים בָּהּ שָׁלֹשׁ מִיתוֹת. אָמַר לָהּ. אֵין חָכְמָתָהּ שֶׁלָּאִשָּׁה אֶלָּא בְפִילְכָהּ. דִּכְתִיב[111] וְכָל־אִשָּׁה חַכְמַת לֵב בְּיָדֶיהָ טָווּ. אָמַר לוֹ הוּרְקְנוֹס בְּנוֹ. בִּשְׁבִיל שֶׁלֹּא לְהָשִׁיבָהּ דָּבָר אֶחָד מִן הַתּוֹרָה אִיבַּדְתָּ מִמֶּנִּי[112] שְׁלֹשׁ מֵאוֹת כּוֹר מַעֲשֵׂר בְּכָל־שָׁנָה. אָמַר לֵיהּ.[113] יִשָּׂרְפוּ דִבְרֵי תוֹרָה וְאַל יִמָּסְרוּ לְנָשִׁים. וּכְשֶׁיָּצְתָה אָמְרוּ לוֹ תַלְמִידָיו. רִבִּי. לְזוֹ דָחִיתָה בְּקָנֶה.[114] לָנוּ מַה אַתָּה מֵשִׁיב. רִבִּי בֶּרֶכְיָה רִבִּי אַבָּא בַּר כַּהֲנָא בְשֵׁם רִבִּי לִיעֶזֶר. כָּל־מִי שֶׁהָיוּ לוֹ עֵדִים וְהַתְרָאָה הָיָה מֵת בְּבֵית דִּין. עֵדִים וְלֹא הַתְרָיָיה הָיָה נִבְדָּק[115] כְּסוֹטָה. לֹא עֵדִים וְלֹא הַתְרָיָיה הָיָה מֵת בַּמַּגֵּפָה. רַב וְלֵוִי בַּר סִיסִי תְּרֵיהוֹן אָמְרִין. זִיבַּח קִיטֵּר נִיסַּךְ הָיָה מֵת בְּבֵית דִּין. טִיפַּח רִיקֵּד שִׂיחֵק הָיָה נִבְדָּק כְּסוֹטָה. שָׂמַח בְּלִיבּוֹ הָיָה מֵת בַּמַּגֵּפָה.

[116]A lady asked Rebbi Eliezer, why did one sin of the golden calf lead to three different kinds of death[117]? He said to her, the wisdom of a woman is only in her spinning rod, as is written: "All wise women span with their hands.[118]" His son Hyrkanos said to him, in order not to give her an answer you made me lose 300 *kor* of tithes every year[119]. He answered him: May the words of the Torah be burned and not be delivered to women! After she had left, his students said to him, rabbi, this one you pushed away with a stick, what do you explain to us? [120]Rebbi Berekhiah, Rebbi Abba bar Cahana in the name of Rebbi Eliezer: Anybody against whom there were witnesses and warning was executed in court[121]. Anybody against whom there were witnesses but no warning was checked similar to a suspected wife[122]. Anybody against whom there were neither witnesses nor warning died from a plague. Rav and Levi bar

Sissi both say: One who sacrificed, burned, and poured out a libation was executed in court[123]. He who clapped his hands, danced, laughed, was checked similar to a suspected wife[124]. If he enjoyed himself silently, he died from a plague[125].

110 Geniza ms: חוטייה. Both spellings are most irregular.

111 Missing in Geniza ms.

112 Geniza ms: ממנו, better fitted to talmudic style.

113 Geniza ms. always: לו.

114 From the Rome and Geniza mss., missing in ms. and *editio princeps*.

115 Geniza ms: היה מת "he died".

116 Babli *Yoma* 66b; *Num. rabba* 9(53).

117 In the aftermath of the sin of the golden calf, it is stated (1) that the Levites killed about 3000 men (*Ex.* 32:28), (2) that the people died of a plague (*Ex.* 32:35), (3) that Moses ground the golden calf into dust, spread it on water and let the people drink, in imitation of the *soṭah* ritual (*Ex.* 32:20).

118 *Ex.* 35:25. R. Eliezer intended to insult the woman who had dared to study Torah (In the Babli, she is called "a wise woman" and her question is dealt with at length by Rashi in his commentary on the Pentateuch). It is not clear whether this represents the general teaching of the House of Shammai or that of R. Eliezer alone.

Since it is common practice to teach Pentateuch and its interpretation to girls it is impossible to understand how Maimonides and Joseph Caro could have R. Eliezer's statement included in their Codes.

119 The lady must have been exeedingly rich if her tithes, given to a Cohen, amounted to 300 *kor* or 9'000 *modii*.

120 In the Babli, this answer and the following one are attributed to "one of Rav or Levi ben Sissi."

121 According to rabbinic theory, nobody can be convicted by biblical standards unless (1) the crime was witnessed by two witnesses of sterling character and (2) criminal intent is proven by two witnesses who testify that the criminal was informed that his intended deed would subject him to prosecution and nevertheless he persisted in his criminal behavior.

122 One has to assume that this procedure was part of the police powers granted to Moses in his position

of king of the Israelites, and that the guilty persons died from the gold water.

123 Since these are acts of Temple worship, as idolatrous practices they are capital crimes (Mishnah *Sanhedrin* 7:6).

124 These are sinful practices if in idolatrous intent but not criminally prosecutable.

125 Since this sin was known only to God, its punishment was by the Hand of Heaven.

(19a line 14) אֵי זֶהוּ[126] חָסִיד שׁוֹטֶה. רָאָה תִינוֹק מְבַעְבֵּעַ בַּנָּהָר. אָמַר. לִכְשֶׁאֲחַלוֹץ תְּפִילַּיי אַצִּילֶנּוּ. עַם כְּשֶׁהוּא חוֹלֵץ תְּפִילָּיו הוֹצִיא זֶה[126] אֶת נַפְשׁוֹ. רָאָה תְאֵינָה בְּכּוּרָה.[127] אָמַר.[126] בְּמִי[128] שֶׁאֶפְגַּע בּוֹ תְּחִילָּה אֶתְּנֶנָּה לוֹ. רָאָה נַעֲרָה מְאוֹרָסָה. וְהָיָה[129] רָץ אַחֲרֶיהָ. הָדָא הִיא דְתַנִּינָן. הָרוֹדֵף אַחֲרֵי חֲבֵירוֹ לְהוֹרְגוֹ. אַחַר הַזָּכוֹר. אַחַר נַעֲרָה מְאוֹרָסָה.

Who is a foolish pious man? He saw a baby struggling in a river[130]. He said, after I take off my phylacteries[131], I shall save him. By the time he takes off his phylacteries, that one is dead. He saw a prime fig and said, I shall give it to the first person I shall meet. He saw a preliminarily married girl and ran after her[132]. That is what we have stated[133]: "If somebody pursues another to kill him, after a male, or after a preliminarily married girl."

126 Missing in Geniza ms.
127 Geniza ms.: בכורית
128 Geniza ms.: לכל מי.
129 Geniza ms.: התחיל "he started to".
130 Really, "making bubbles", because it is drowning. In the Babli, 21b, it is a woman drowning whom he cannot save because it would hurt his salvation if he looked at a woman.

131 Since the phylacteries contain biblical verses, they are holy. He is too ignorant to realize that the commandment to save a life overrides all other commandments except those involving murder, incest and adultery, and idolatry.

132 Since it is a commandment to keep one's word, he brings himself into

a situation in which he can be killed. The Mishnah quoted states that if one observes a person bent on committing a murder, a homosexual rape, or the rape of a preliminarily married girl (*Deut.* 22:23-24), one may kill the attempting murderer or rapist with impunity. If the girl is afraid of him when he presents the fig and runs away, religious law would force him not to run after the girl.

133 Mishnah *Sanhedrin* 8:7: These are the people one may save [from sinning] by killing them: "If somebody pursues another to kill him, or after a male (for homosexual rape), or after a preliminarily married girl [one may kill the perpetrator]; but one who pursues an animal (for sodomy), desecrates the Sabbath, or commits idolatry one may not save by killing him." A bystander can kill a person bent on committing a capital crime only if thereby he saves another human being.

(19a line 19) זֶה שֶׁהוּא מוֹרֶה קַלּוֹת [134.]רָשָׁע עָרוּם. רִבִּי זְרִיקָן בְּשֵׁם רַב הוּנָא. עַל עַצְמוֹ[135] וַחֲמוּרוֹת לָאֲחֵרִים. וְאַתְיָיא כְּהָדָא דְתַנֵּי. כָּל־הָרוֹצֶה לְהַחֲמִיר עַל עַצְמוֹ וְלִנְהוֹג כְּחוּמְרֵי בֵית שַׁמַּי וּכְחוּמְרֵי בֵית הִלֵּל עַל זֶה נֶאֱמַר וְהַכְּסִיל בַּחוֹשֶׁךְ הוֹלֵךְ.[136] כְּקוּלֵּי אִילוּ וָאִילוּ נִקְרָא[137] רָשָׁע. אֶלָּא אוֹ כְדִבְרֵי בֵית שַׁמַּי כְּקוּלֵּיהֶן וּכְחוּמְרֵיהֶן אוֹ כְדִבְרֵי בֵית הִלֵּל כְּקוּלֵּיהֶן וּכְחוּמְרֵיהֶן. הָדָא דְתֵימַר. עַד שֶׁלֹּא יָצְאַת בַּת קוֹל. אֲבָל מִשֶּׁיָּצְאַת בַּת קוֹל לְעוֹלָם הֲלָכָה כְּבֵית הִלֵּל. וְכָל־הָעוֹבֵר עַל דִּבְרֵי בֵית הִלֵּל חַיָּיב מִיתָה. תַּנֵּי יָצְאַת בַּת קוֹל וְאָמְרָה. אֵילוּ וְאֵילוּ דִבְרֵי אֱלֹהִים חַיִּים הֵן. אֲבָל הֲלָכָה כְּבֵית הִלֵּל לְעוֹלָם. וְאֵיכָן יָצְאַת בַּת קוֹל. רַב בִּיבִי בְּשֵׁם רִבִּי יוֹחָנָן. בְּיַבְנֶה יָצְאַת בַּת קוֹל.

"A sly wicked man." Rebbi Zeriqan in the name of Rav Huna: That is one who chooses leniencies for himself and teaches restrictions to others[138]. [139]In this matter, it was stated: "About anybody who wants to take upon himself the stringencies both of the House of Shammai and the House of Hillel it was said: 'The silly one walks in darkness'. The leniencies of both of them, he is called wicked. Only either following the words of the House of Shammai in their leniencies and stringencies, or following the words of the House of Hillel in their leniencies and stringencies." That is, before there came the disembodied voice. But after the disembodied voice was heard, "practice follows the House of Hillel forever." And any who transgresses the words of the House of Hillel is deserving of death. It was stated: There came the disembodied voice and said: "Both of them are the words of the Living God, but practice follows the House of Hillel forever." Where was the disembodied voice heard? Rav Bebai in the name of Rebbi Joḥanan: The disembodied voice was heard at Yabneh.

134 In the Geniza ms: ר׳ זיריקון בש׳ ר׳ חונא "Rebbi Zeriqon in the name of Rebbi Huna". Since R. Zeriqa was a student of Rav Huna and lived a generation before Rebbi Ḥuna, the reading of the text, supported by the Babli, is correct.

135 Geniza ms: לעצמו.

136 The entire clause is replaced in the Geniza ms. by: הרי זה בור "he is a boor".

137 Geniza ms: הרי זה "he is".

138 Babli 21b, as one possibility of many.

139 The same text *Berakhot* Chapter 1, Notes 192-199; *Yebamot* Chapter 1, Notes 256-261. Cf. Babli *Erubin* 6b, 13b.

(19a line 29) אִשָּׁה פְרוּשָׁה. זוֹ שֶׁהִיא יוֹשֶׁבֶת וּמַלְעֶבֶת בְּדִבְרֵי תוֹרָה. וַתֹּאמֶר אֵלַי תָּבוֹא. וַיִּשְׁכַּב עִמָּהּ בַּלַּיְלָה הוּא. אָמַר רִבִּי אַבָּהוּ. כִּבְיָכוֹל הָיָה בַּמַּחֲשָׁבָה. הוּא לְבַדּוֹ הָיָה יוֹדֵעַ שֶׁלֹּא עָלַת עַל דַּעְתָּהּ 140 אֶלָּא בִשְׁבִיל לְהַעֲמִיד שְׁבָטִים.

A predatory woman[141]. That is one who sits and makes fun of the words of the Torah: "She said, you shall come to me . . . and he slept with her that night.[142]" Rebbi Abbahu said, one could think that this was the [divine] intention. He only knew that she was doing this only to produce more tribes.

140 Geniza ms.: על אילא "her intent", a medieval philosophical term, not likely to be original.

141 The Babli has no parallel explanation since it interprets אשה פרושה to mean "a pious woman".

142 Gen. 30:16, Leah buying a night with Jacob from her sister Rachel. R. Abbahu's explanation is slightly more elaborate in *Gen. rabba* 72(4).

(19a line 32) וּמַכַּת פְּרוּשִׁים. זֶה שֶׁהוּא נוֹתֵן עֵצָה לִיתוֹמִים לְהַבְרִיחַ מְזוֹנוֹת מִן הָאַלְמָנָה. כְּהָדָא אַרְמַלְתָּהּ דְּרִבִּי שׁוּבְתַּי הֲוַת מְבַזְבְּזָה בְּנִיכְסַיָּיא. אָתוֹן יַתְמַיָּיא וְקָרְבוֹן לְרִבִּי אֶלְעָזָר. אָמַר לוֹן. וּמַה נַעֲבִיד לְכוֹן וְאַתּוּן שַׁטְיָין. נְפַק כְּתוֹבָה. אָמַר לוֹן. נֵימַר לְכוֹן מֵימַר. עִיבְדוּן גַּרְמֵיכוֹן מְזַבְּנִין. וְהִיא תָבְעָה פּוֹרְנָה וּמוֹבְדָה מְזוֹנָה. עָבְדִין כֵּן. בְּרוֹמְשָׁא אָתַת וְקָרְבַת גַּבֵּי רִבִּי אֶלְעָזָר. אָמַר. זוֹ מַכַּת פְּרוּשִׁין נָגְעוּ בָהּ. יָבוֹא עָלַי אִם נִתְכַּוַּנְתִּי לְכָךְ.

"Hits by the predatory". That is the one who counsels the orphans to hide support from the widow[143]. As the following: Rebbi Sabbatai's widow was wasting the estate. The orphans came before Rebbi Eleazar. He said to them, what can one do for you; you are stupid[144]. Some scribe came out and said to them: I shall tell you what he said: Behave as if you would sell[145] and she will demand her *ketubah*[146] and lose her support. In the evening she came before Rebbi Eleazar. He said, this one was hit by the predatory. It should come over me[147] if I had intended that[148].

143 In the Babli, 21b, this is an opinion of R. Johanan.

144 This is a corruption in the Leiden and Rome mss. (from their common *Vorlage*). The text is better in the Geniza ms: אָמַר לוֹן וּמַה נִיעֲבַד לְכוֹן אֲלָוֵךְ אִימָּה שַׁטְיָיִ מִדְּנַפְקוֹן אָמְרִין לֵי' כְּתוֹבֵיהּ עָמְדוּ עַד גֵּימַר לְכוֹן מַה אָמַר. "He said to them, what can I do for you, your charge is a senile mother. When they left, his scribe told them: stay here until I shall explain to you what he meant."

Occupational names of the measure *pĕ'ōlāh* have been recognized by L. Ginzburg in the Yerushalmi: קְרוֹבָה the liturgical poet, דְּרוֹשָׁה the preacher, כְּתוֹבָה the scribe; all masculine. In the Geniza texts published by M. A.

Friedman, Jewish Marriage in Palestine, Tel Aviv and New York 1981, one finds four כתובא times and כתובה three times.

145 The *ketubah* was a lien on the deceased's real estate. The crooked counsel was that the heirs should loudly declare their intention to sell the real estate, which would force the widow eventually into lengthy court proceedings to recover her lien. The idea was to force the widow into demanding to be paid her *ketubah*, which immediately would terminate her right to support but would allow the heirs to somewhat drag their feet before paying up. The honorable thing would have been to offer the widow to pay her the *ketubah* in a lump sum, in the hope that she would accept the offer. Since then the initiative would be the heirs', the widow's support would have to be paid until the money was delivered in full.

146 Greek φερνή "dowry".

147 An oath formula, "such and such shall come over me if I intended that".

148 He disclaimed authorship of the counsel his (?) scribe had given in his name. It is not reported whether he reversed the transaction.

(19a line 39) חַד תַּלְמִיד מִדְּרַבִּי הָיוּ לוֹ מָאתַיִם חָסֵר דֵּינָר. וַהֲוָה רִבִּי יְלֵיף זְכִי עִימֵּיהּ חָדָא לִתְלַת שְׁנִין מַעֲשַׂר מִסְכֵּינִין. חַד זְמָן עַבְדִּין בֵּיהּ תַּלְמִידוֹי עַיִן בִּישׁ וּמָלוֹן לֵיהּ. אָתָא בְּעֵי מִיזְכֵּי עִימֵּיהּ הֵיךְ מַה דַּהֲוָה יְלִיף. אָמַר לֵיהּ. רִבִּי. אִית לִי שִׁיעוּרָא. אָמַר. זֶה מַכַּת פְּרוּשִׁים נָגְעוּ בּוֹ. רָמַז לְתַלְמִידָיו וְאַעֲלוּנֵיהּ לְקַפֵּילִין וְחַסְרוּנֵיהּ חַד קְרָט. וּזְכָה עִימֵּיהּ הֵיךְ מַה דַּהֲוָה יְלִיף.

[149]A student of Rebbi had 199 denar; Rebbi used to let him receive the tithe of the poor once every three years. His students cast an evil eye on him and completed for him. The next time, when he wanted to let him receive as usual, he said: My teacher, I have the measure. He said, this one was hit by a beast of prey. He gave a hint to his student who took him to a store, made him spend a carat, then he (Rebbi) let him receive as he was used to do.

149 The same text *Peah* 8:8, Notes 112-115; it is referred to in Babli 21b.

149   The same text *Peah* 8:8, Notes 112-115; it is referred to in Babli 21b.

(19a line 44) הוֹסִיפוּ עֲלֵיהֶן בְּתוּלָה צְייְמָנִית וְאַלְמָנָה שׁוֹבָבִית וְתִינוֹק שֶׁהוּא עוֹלֶה לַחֲדָשָׁיו. בְּתוּלָה צְייְמָנִית. מְצַייְמָה אוֹבֶדֶת בְּתוּלֶיהָ. וְאַלְמָנָה שׁוֹבָבִית מִי חֲגָלָה נְסִבַת שֵׁם בִּישׁ. וְתִינוֹק שֶׁהוּא עוֹלֶה לַחֲדָשָׁיו. רִבִּי חִלְקִיָּה בְּשֵׁם רִבִּי סִימוֹן. זֶה שֶׁהוּא גָדוֹל בַּתּוֹרָה שֶׁלֹּא בְּפִירְקוֹ וּמְבַזֶּה גְדוֹלִים מִמֶּנּוּ. אָמַר רִבִּי יוֹסֵי. זֶה שֶׁהוּא בֶן תֵּשַׁע וְאֵיבָרָיו נִרְאִין כְּבֶן שְׁתֵּים עֶשְׂרֵה. וְהוּא בָא עַל אַחַת מִכָּל הָעֲרָיוֹת בַּתּוֹרָה וְהֵן מֵיתוֹת עַל יָדָיו וְהוּא פָטוּר.

They added to these[150] a fasting virgin[151], a neighborly widow, and a child outgrowing his months[152]. A fasting virgin; she pretends to have lost her hymen by fasting[153]. A neighborly widow, by running around[154] she spreads bad reputations. A child outgrowing his months: Rebbi Hilqiah in the name of Rebbi Simon. That is one who is more advanced in his studies than usual for his age and he denigrates those older than him. Rebbi Yose said, that is one nine-years-old who looks like a twelve-years-old. He sleeps with any of the incest prohibitions in the Torah and they are executed because of him but he is free from prosecution[155].

150   To the list of the destroyers of the world.

151   In the Babli (22a): A praying virgin.

152   In the Babli (22a), except the Munich ms.: "a premature baby".

153   But in reality she slept around.

154   The Geniza ms. probably has another reading which, however, is not readable. The translation follows *Arukh*, s. v. חגל.

155   The sex act of a minor less than 9 years old has no legal consequences. If the boy is 9 years and one day old, his sex act counts: if a married woman sleeps with him, she is criminally liable for adultery but he is not responsible since he is a minor. Cf. *Yebamot*, Chapter 3, Note 143.

(fol. 18c) **משנה ח**: רִבִּי שִׁמְעוֹן אוֹמֵר. אֵין הַזְכוּת תּוֹלָה בְּמַיִם הַמָּרִים. וְאִם אַתָּה אוֹמֵר הַזְכוּת תּוֹלָה בְּמַיִם הַמְאָרֲרִים מַדְהֵא אַתָּה אֶת הַמַּיִם בִּפְנֵי כָל־הַנָּשִׁים הַשּׁוֹתוֹת וּמוֹצִיא אַתָּה שֵׁם רַע עַל הַטְּהוֹרוֹת שֶׁשָּׁתוּ שֶׁאוֹמְרִים טְמֵאוֹת הֵן אֶלָּא שֶׁתָּלָת לָהֶן זְכוּת.

Mishnah 5: Rebbi Simeon says, merit does not suspend in the case of the bitter water. If you say that merit suspends in the case of the curse water, you weaken the water in the eyes of all women who drink it and you smear the reputation of the pure women who drank because one would say that they are impure but that merit suspended for them.

משנה ו: רִבִּי אוֹמֵר הַזְכוּת תּוֹלָה בְּמַיִם הַמְאָרֲרִים וְאֵינָהּ יוֹלֶדֶת וְאֵינָהּ מַשְׁבַּחַת אֶלָּא מִתְנַוְּונָא וְהוֹלֶכֶת לַסּוֹף הִיא מֵתָה בְּאוֹתָהּ מִיתָא.

Mishnah 6: Rebbi says, merit suspends in the case of the curse water, but she does not have children[156], does not get better, but degenerates and in the end she dies that death[157].

156 Childbirth is a sign of purity, *Num.* 5:28.
157 Supposing that the (not biblical) symptoms described in Mishnah 4 indicate that she would die immediately after drinking.

(fol. 19a) **הלכה ו**: רִבִּי שִׁמְעוֹן אוֹמֵר. אֵין הַזְכוּת תּוֹלָה בְּמַיִם הַמָּרִים כול'. רִבִּי אוֹמֵר הַזְכוּת תּוֹלָה בְּמַיִם הַמְאָרְרִים כול'. אָמַר רַב הַמְנוּנָא. הַמִּתְנַוְּונָה מוּתֶּרֶת לְבֵיתָהּ. וְאַתְיָא כְהָדָא דְתַנֵּי. רִבִּי שִׁמְעוֹן בֶּן אֶלְעָזָר אוֹמֵר. אֲפִילוּ טְהוֹרָה שֶׁשָּׁתָת סוֹפָהּ שֶׁהִיא מֵתָה בַּתַּחֲלוּאִים רָעִים. מִפְּנֵי שֶׁהִכְנִיסָה עַצְמָהּ לְמִסְפֵּק הַזֶּה הַמְרוּבֶּה.

Halakhah 6: "Rebbi Simeon says, merit does not suspend in the case of the bitter water," etc. "Rebbi says, merit suspends in the case of the curse water," etc. Rav Hamnuna said, the degenerating woman is permitted to her house[158]. This parallels what was stated: Rebbi Simeon ben Eleazar says, even a pure woman who drank will in the end die in great pain because she brought herself into that great doubt[159].

158 In the Bable, 26a, this is a comment of Rav Huna on Mishnah 4:4 that even a Cohen's wife, who would be forbidden to her husband if she was raped, is permitted to her husband after she survived drinking the bitter water. The Babli adds the condition that she not exhibit the features described in the verse, a swollen belly without a pregnancy. That condition is missing in the Yerushalmi.

159 That two witnesses confirmed her being alone with another man. In the Tosephta, 2:3, this is a statement of R. Simeon ben Eleazar in the name of R. Meïr.

(19a line 54) וְאִם לֹא נִטְמְאָה הָאִשָּׁה וּטְהוֹרָה הִיא. זוֹ טְהוֹרָה. לֹא שֶׁבָּאוּ עֵדִים שֶׁהִיא טְמֵיאָה. אִם לֹא נִטְמְאָה הָאִשָּׁה וּטְהוֹרָה הִיא. זוֹ טְהוֹרָה. לֹא שֶׁתָּלַת לָהּ זְכוּת. וְאָתְיָיא כְּמָאן דָּמַר. הַזְּכוּת תּוֹלָה וְאֵינָהּ נִיכֶּרֶת. בְּרַם כְּמָאן דָּמַר. הַזְּכוּת תּוֹלָה וְנִיכֶּרֶת. אָמַר רִבִּי יִצְחָק. כָּאן אָנָן קַייָמִין כְּשֶׁשָּׁתָת וְלֹא בָדְקוּ אוֹתָהּ הַמַּיִם. שֶׁלֹּא תֹאמַר. עֵידֵי שֶׁקֶר הֵן. לְפִיכָךְ לֹא בָדְקוּ אוֹתָהּ הַמַּיִם. אָתָא מֵימַר לָךְ שֶׁאֵין הַמַּיִם בּוֹדְקִין בְּאִשָּׁה שֶׁהִיא אֲסוּרָה לְבֵיתָהּ. אָמַר רִבִּי יוּדָה. וְאָתְיָיא כְּמָאן דָּמַר. הַזְּכוּת תּוֹלָה וְאֵינָהּ נִיכֶּרֶת. וְלָמָּה לֹא הוּכְּרָה מִפְּנֵי שֶׁתָּלַת לָהּ זְכוּת. וְנִקָּה הָאִישׁ מֵעָוֹן. אֵינוֹ חוֹשֵׁשׁ שֶׁמָּא תָּלָה לָהּ זְכוּת. יָכוֹל אַף הִיא לֹא תָחוּשׁ. תַּלְמוּד לוֹמַר וְהָאִשָּׁה הַהִיא תִּשָּׂא אֶת עֲוֹנָהּ. וְאָתְיָיא כְּמָאן דָּמַר. הַזְּכוּת תּוֹלָה וְאֵינָהּ נִיכֶּרֶת.

"And if the woman was not impure but was pure,[160]" this refers to the one who is pure, not that there came witnesses declaring her impure[161]. "If the woman was not impure but was pure," this refers to the one who is pure, not one whose merit suspended [punishment] for her[162]. This follows the one who said that merit suspends and it is not recognizable. But following him who said that merit suspends and it is recognizable[163]?

Rebbi Isaac said, here we deal with one who drank and the water did not test her. It comes to tell you that the water will not test a woman who is forbidden to her house[161,164]. Rebbi Yudan said, this follows the one who said that merit suspends and it is not recognizable. Why was it not recognized? Because merit suspended for her. "The man will be free of sin[165]," he should not worry that maybe merit suspended for her[166]. Should I think that she also should not worry? The verse said, "but that woman shall carry her sin[165]". [This interpretation] follows the one who said that merit suspends and it is not recognizable.

160 *Num.* 5:28.

161 "And if the woman was not impure but was pure, then she will be cleansed and bear children." If she is not impure, it should be clear that she is pure. It is explained that if she was not impure, i. e., if there are no proofs available against her sufficient for a conviction in court, then if she is pure the water will cleanse her and make her fertile. But if her case could be adjudicated in a human court, the Temple should not be used and the water will be just drinking water (cf. Babli 6a).

The Geniza text makes this slightly more clear by quoting: "And if the woman was not impure but was pure, then she will be cleansed."

162 The latter will not experience any change in her fertility status.

163 There seems to be no reason for Rav Hamnuna's position.

164 There is no inference possible on Rav Hamnuna's statement.

165 *Num.* 5:31.

166 The husband who brought his wife to the Temple where the water had no influence on her is free to sleep with her and is told not to worry that she still might be forbidden to him.

משנה ז: (fol. 18c) נִטְמֵאת מִנְחָתָהּ עַד שֶׁלֹּא קָדְשָׁה בַּכְּלִי הֲרֵי הִיא כְּכָל־הַמְּנָחוֹת וְתִיפָּדֶה. וְאִם מִשֶּׁקָּדְשָׁה בַּכְּלִי הֲרֵי הִיא כְּכָל־הַמְּנָחוֹת וְתִישָּׂרֵף. וְאֵלּוּ שֶׁמִּנְחוֹתֵיהֶן נִשְׂרָפוֹת הָאוֹמֶרֶת טְמֵיאָה אֲנִי לָךְ וְשֶׁבָּאוּ לָהּ עֵדִים שֶׁהִיא טְמֵיאָה וְהָאוֹמֶרֶת אֵינִי שׁוֹתָה וְשֶׁבַּעֲלָהּ אֵינוֹ רוֹצֶה לְהַשְׁקוֹתָהּ וְשֶׁבַּעֲלָהּ בָּא עָלֶיהָ בַּדֶּרֶךְ. וְכָל־הַנְּשׂוּאוֹת לַכֹּהֲנִים מִנְחוֹתֵיהֶן נִשְׂרָפוֹת.

Mishnah 7: If her flour offering became impure before it was sanctified in a Temple vessel, it is treated like all other flour offerings and should be redeemed[167]. After it was sanctified in a Temple vessel, it is treated like all other flour offerings and should be burned[168]. The flour offerings are burned[169] in the following cases: One who says, I am impure for you, or that witnesses declared that she was impure; one who refuses to drink, or whose husband does not want to let her drink, or whose husband slept with her on the road. In addition, the flour offerings of women married to Cohanim are burned[170].

167 Its holiness is transferred to a sum of money which then is used to buy a replacement offering. The original offering then becomes profane (Mishnah *Menaḥot* 12:1)..

168 Outside of the holy precinct, on the burning place organized for invalid sacrifices.

169 Even if they are pure and still in the palm-leaf basket.

170 Where it has to be burned is a matter of dispute in the Halakhah.

הלכה ז: (fol. 19a) נִטְמֵאת מִנְחָתָהּ עַד שֶׁלֹּא קָדְשָׁה בַּכְּלִי כול׳. תַּנֵּי. נִטְמֵאת מִנְחָתָהּ עַד שֶׁלֹּא קָדְשָׁה בַּכְּלִי. הֲרֵי הִיא כְּכָל־הַמְּנָחוֹת וְתִיפָּדֶה. מִשֶּׁקָּדְשָׁה בַּכְּלִי. הֲרֵי הִיא כְּכָל־הַמְּנָחוֹת וְתִישָּׂרֵף.

Halakhah 7: "If her flour offering became impure before it was sanctified in a Temple vessel," etc. It was stated: If her flour offering became impure before it was sanctified in a Temple vessel, it is treated like all other flour offerings and should be redeemed; after it was sanctified in a Temple vessel, it is treated like all other flour offerings and should be burned[171].

171 This statement is that of the Mishnah (the one missing word, ואם, is also missing in most mss. of the Babli and of the Maimonides tradition of the Mishnah). The quote seems to be in opposition to statements similar to Tosephta 2:4: "After it was sanctified in a Temple vessel, one has to wait until it spoils and then one takes it out to be burned."

(19a line 67) וְהָאוֹמֶרֶת. טְמֵיאָה אָנִי. לֹא כְחַטָּאת שֶׁמֵּתוּ בְעָלֶיהָ הִיא. וְחַטָּאת שֶׁמֵּתוּ בְעָלֶיהָ יֵלְכוּ הַמָּעוֹת לְיַם הַמֶּלַח. דַּמְיָיא לְאָשָׁם תָּלוּי. אִם לְאָשָׁם תָּלוּי. אֲפִילוּ מִשֶׁקָּדְשָׁה בַכֶּלִי. אָמַר רִבִּי מַתַּנְיָיה. דַּמְיָיא לְאָשָׁם תָּלוּי[172] שֶׁנִּשְׁחַט. דְּתַנִינָן תַּמָּן. אִם מִשֶּׁנִשְׁחַט נוֹדַע לוֹ. הַדָּם יִשָּׁפֵךְ וְהַבָּשָׂר יֵצֵא לְבֵית הַשְׂרֵיפָה.

"One who says, I am impure" Is it not like a purification offering whose owners died? And for a purification offering whose owners died, the money should be thrown into the Dead Sea[172]. It is compared to a hung reparation offering[173]. If it is compared to a hung reparation offering, even if it was sanctified in a Temple vessel[174]! Rebbi Mattaniah said, it is compared to a hung reparation offering that was slaughtered, as we stated there: "If it became clear to him after it was slaughtered, the blood has to be poured out and the meat has to be taken out to the burning place.[175]"

172 From the Rome ms. Word missing in the Leiden ms. by an oversight.

172 The source is found only in parts of the Babli (e. g., *Temurah* 24a) which have no parallel in the Yerushalmi. Since a purification offering makes sense only if its owner is alive; a purification offering whose owner died cannot be used for anything

else and cannot be redeemed. Therefore, it seems that the offering for the woman who declares herself an adulteress should not be burned on the usual spot (where the ashes were from time to time sold by the Temple authorities as fertilizer) but should be thrown into the Dead Sea to make sure no use whatsoever could be made of it.

173   The sacrifice of a person who worries that possibly he could have sinned, *Lev.* 5:17-19. Similarly, the offering of the suspected wife is brought for a case of doubt.

174   This is compared to the reparation offering introduced into the Temple courtyard.

175   It became clear either that an inadvertent sin was committed, and then a purification offering is required, not a reparation offering, or that no sin was committed, and then no offering is required. In the latter case, since the offering was brought for peace of mind, it certainly was the intention of the person to have a valid sacrifice even in case he did not sin. This differs from the case of a sacrifice brought in error which is treated according to the rules of profane animals introduced in error into the Temple; Mishnah *Keritut* 6:1-2. (In the Mishnah, there are dissenting opinions that the hung reparation offering is a valid offering in all cases.)

R. Mattaniah compares transferring the offering into the Temple vessel to slaughtering the animal since the transfer enables the priest to offer a fistful on the alter just as slaughter enables the priest to bring the blood to the altar.

(19a line 71) תַּנֵּי. נִטְמֵאת מִנְחָתָהּ עַד שֶׁלֹּא קָרַב הַקּוֹמֶץ. מֵתָה הִיא וּמֵת בַּעֲלָהּ. הַשִּׁיֵּירִיִּין אֲסוּרִין שֶׁעַל סָפֵק בָּאת מִתְּחִילָּתָהּ. כִּיפְרָה[176] סְפֵיקָהּ וְהָלְכָה לָהּ. בָּאוּ לָהּ עֵדִים שֶׁהִיא טְמֵיאָה. בֵּין כָּךְ וּבֵין כָּךְ מִנְחָתָהּ אֲסוּרָה. מַהוּ בֵּין כָּךְ וּבֵין כָּךְ. בֵּין שֶׁקָּמַץ וּבֵין שֶׁלֹּא קָמַץ. בֵּין שֶׁהִקְטִיר וּבֵין שֶׁלֹּא הִקְטִיר. רִבִּי אִילָא אָמַר. בֵּין שֶׁקָּמַץ וּבֵין שֶׁלֹּא קָמַץ בְּשֶׁלֹּא הִקְטִיר. אֲבָל אִם הִקְטִיר הַשִּׁיֵּירִיִּין מוּתָּרִין.

It was stated: If her offering became impure before the fistful was sacrificed[177]; [178]if she died or her husband died, the rest is forbidden because it was brought from the start to resolve a doubt. Her doubt was atoned for and went away[179]. If there came witnesses declaring that she was impure[180], in any case her offering is forbidden. What means "in any case"? Whether the fistful was taken or not, whether it was sacrificed or not. Rebbi Hila said, whether the fistful was taken or not as long as it was not sacrificed, but if it was sacrificed the rest is permitted[181].

176 Reading of *editio princeps* and the Rome ms. Leiden ms: ספרה "she counted".

177 It is unclear what this sentence implies here. It is obvious that an impure sacrifice is forbidden as sacrifice and as food. In the Babli (note 178), the entire text of the Mishnah is quoted. Therefore, it seems that the sentence is simply a quote from the Mishnah; the note "etc." is missing.

178 Tosephta 2:5 and Babli 6b. There, the text reads: "If her husband or she died before the fistful was sacrificed, the rest is forbidden. But if the fistful was sacrificed and then her husband or she died, the rest is permitted because it was brought from the start to resolve a doubt. Her doubt was atoned for and went away." For most flour offerings, a fistful is offered on the altar, the rest is eaten by the Cohanim under the rules of most holy food.

179 This clause makes more sense in the Tosephta/Babli text, that the rest is permitted to the Cohanim if it became permitted by the rules, i. e., that the fistful was duly put into the fire on top of the altar. It is reasonable that a permitted remainder cannot retroactively become forbidden since the doubt of adultery either was resolved by the procedure or became moot by the death of one of the parties.

180 Tosephta 2:5. Cf. Note 161; then there no longer is any doubt; the procedure becomes inactive and the offering should not be brought.

181 Once it was food for the Cohanim it cannot lose that status except by impurity.

(19b line 1) תַּמָּן תַּנִּינָן. רִבִּי שִׁמְעוֹן אוֹמֵר. מִנְחַת חוֹטֵא שֶׁלַּכֹּהֲנִים נִקְמֶצֶת. וְהַקּוֹמֶץ קָרֵב לְעַצְמוֹ וְהַשִּׁיְירִים קְרֵבִין לְעַצְמָן. וּשְׁנֵיהֶן מִקְרָא אֶחָד דּוֹרְשִׁין.

וְהָיְתָה לַכֹּהֵן כַּמִּנְחָה. רַבָּנִין אֲמָרִין. הֲרֵי הִיא כְמִנְחַת נִדְבָתוֹ. מַה מִנְחַת נִדְבָתוֹ קְרֵיבָה בְּבָלוּל. אַף זוּ קְרֵיבָה בְּבָלוּל. רִבִּי שִׁמְעוֹן אוֹמֵר. הֲרֵי עֲשִׂירִית הָאֵיפָה שֶׁלָּכֹהֵן כַּעֲשִׂירִית הָאֵיפָה שֶׁלַּיִשְׂרָאֵל. מַה עֲשִׂירִית הָאֵיפָה שֶׁלַּיִשְׂרָאֵל נִקְמֶצֶת אַף זוּ נִקְמֶצֶת. אִי מַה זוּ נֶאֱכֶלֶת אַף זוּ נֶאֱכֶלֶת. תַּלְמוּד לוֹמַר וְכָל־מִנְחַת כֹּהֵן כָּלִיל תִּהְיֶה לֹא תֵאָכֵל. אֵילֵין שְׁיָירִים מִשֵּׁם מַה הֵן בָּאִים. מִשֵּׁם קוֹמֶץ מִשֵּׁם שְׁיָירִים אִין תֵּימַר. מִשּׁוּם קוֹמֶץ. אֵינוֹ נוֹתְנָן בַּלַּיְלָה וְאֵינוֹ נוֹתְנָן לְאַחַר מִיתָה וְאֵינוֹ מְחַשֵּׁב לָהֶן. וְאִין תֵּימַר. מִשּׁוּם שְׁיָירִים. נוֹתְנָן בַּלַּיְלָה וְנוֹתְנָן לְאַחַר מִיתָה. מַהוּ שֶׁיְּחַשֵּׁב לָהֶם. נִשְׁמָעִינָהּ מִן הָדָא. רִבִּי שִׁמְעוֹן בֶּן אֶלְעָזָר אוֹמֵר. הַקּוֹמֶץ קָרֵב לְעַצְמוֹ וְהַשִּׁיָירִים מִתְפַּזְּרִין עַל גַּבֵּי הַדֶּשֶׁן. רִבִּי יוֹחָנָן בָּעֵי. מָה אֲנָן קַיָּימִין. אִם בְּדֶשֶׁן שֶׁלַּמַּעֲלָן. כְּבָר אָמַר רִבִּי שִׁמְעוֹן. אֶלָּא אִם אֵינוֹ עִנְיָין לְדֶשֶׁן שֶׁלַּמַּעֲלָן תְּנֵיהוּ עִנְיָין לְדֶשֶׁן שֶׁלַּמַּטָּן. הָדָא אָמְרָה. נוֹתְנָן בַּלַּיְלָה וְנוֹתְנָן לְאַחַר מִיתָה וּמְחַשֵּׁב לָהֶן. אָמַר רִבִּי יוֹסֵי בֵּי רִבִּי בּוּן. אֵינוֹ מְחַשֵּׁב לָהֶן. שֶׁלֹּא הוּכְשְׁרוּ לֹא לַאֲכִילַת אָדָם וְלֹא לַאֲכִילַת מִזְבֵּחַ. רִבִּי בָּא בַּר מָמָל בָּעֵי. הַךְ רִבִּי אֶלְעָזָר בֵּירִבִּי שִׁמְעוֹן בְּשִׁיטַת אָבִיו אוֹ בְּשִׁיטַת חֲכָמִים. אִין בְּשִׁיטַת אָבִיו. יִקְרַב לְמַעֲלָן. אִין בְּשִׁיטַת חֲכָמִים. לֹא יִקְמוֹץ. בְּשִׁיטַת אָבִיו הוּא. רִבִּי שִׁמְעוֹן אוֹמֵר. הֲרֵי עֲשִׂירִית הָאֵיפָה שֶׁלָּכֹהֵן כַּעֲשִׂירִית הָאֵיפָה שֶׁלַּיִשְׂרָאֵל. מַה עֲשִׂירִית הָאֵיפָה שֶׁלַּיִשְׂרָאֵל נִקְמֶצֶת אַף זוּ נִקְמֶצֶת. אִי מַה זוּ נֶאֱכֶלֶת אַף זוּ נֶאֱכֶלֶת. תַּלְמוּד לוֹמַר וְכָל־מִנְחַת כֹּהֵן כָּלִיל תִּהְיֶה לֹא תֵאָכֵל. וּתְהֵא כָלִיל. וְלֹא תֵאָכֵל הִיקְשִׁיתֵיהּ. לֹא הִיקְשִׁיתֵיהּ לְכָלִיל תָּקְטָר.

We have stated there[182]: "Rebbi Simeon says, a fistful is taken from the sinner's flour offering[183] of a Cohen. The fistful is sacrificed separately and the rest is sacrificed separately." Both of them explained the same verse: "It shall be the Cohen's as a flour offering[184]." The rabbis say, it is like his voluntary flour offering. Since his voluntary flour offering is brought entire, that one also is brought entire[185]. Rebbi Simeon says, the tenth of an *epha*[186] of a Cohen is like the tenth of an *epha* of an Israel. Since a fistful is taken from the tenth of an *epha* of an Israel, so a fistful is taken from the tenth of an *epha* of a Cohen. Maybe, since this one is eaten, the other is also eaten[187]? The verse[188] says, "Any flour offering of a Cohen shall be totally burned; it shall not be eaten." The rest, under which category is it brought, under the rules of a fistful or under the rules of remainders[189]? If you want to say, under the rules of a fistful, one cannot bring them during the night, one cannot bring them after death, and he is forbidden to think about them[190]. If you want to say, under the rules of a remainder, one can bring them during the night, one can bring them after death. Is he forbidden to think about them? Let us hear from the following: Rebbi Eleazar ben Rebbi Simeon[191] says, the fistful is sacrificed separately and the rest dispersed over the ashes. Rebbi Joḥanan asked, where are we holding? If the upper ashes[192], Rebbi Simeon already said it. If it cannot refer to the upper ashes, let it refer to the lower ashes[193]. That means, one can bring them during the night, one can bring them after death, and he can think about them[194]. Rebbi Yose ben Rebbi Abun said, he is forbidden to think about them since they are not qualified as food either for humans or for the altar[195]. Rebbi Abba bar Mamal asked: Does Rebbi Eleazar ben Rebbi Simeon follow the rules of his father or the rules of the rabbis? According to the rules of his father, it should be brought on top [of the altar]. According to the rules of the rabbis, why should he take a fistful[196]? He follows his father's rules. Rebbi Simeon says, the tenth of an *epha* of a Cohen is like the tenth of an *epha* of an Israel. Since a fistful is taken from the tenth of an *epha* of an Israel, so a fistful is taken from the tenth of an *epha* of a Cohen. Maybe, since this one is eaten, the other is also eaten? The verse says, "Any flour offering of a Cohen shall be totally burned; it shall not be eaten." Then it should be burned totally! You bound it to "it shall not be eaten"; you did not bind it to "it has to be sacrificed in its entirety.¹⁹⁷"

182 Mishnah *Menaḥot* 6:1. In that Mishnah, the anonymous rabbis hold that the entire offering is burned on the altar in one piece.

183 The flour offering of the very poor person who either refused to testify, was unmindful of his impurity in dealing with the Temple and its appurtenances, or had forgotten an oath he had imposed on himself, *Lev.* 5:11-13.

184 *Lev.* 5:13. Since one speaks of a flour offering, it is diffult to understand why "it should be like a flour offering".

185 Voluntary flour offerings are described in *Lev.* 2:1-11. It is stipulated in *Lev.* 6:16 that no part of a priest's flour offering may be eaten. *Sifra Ṣaw Pereq* 8(5) disagrees with the Yerushalmi; it interprets *Lev.* 6:16 to deal mainly with the Cohen's obligatory offerings and only in a derivative fashion with voluntary offerings.

186 The amount of flour required for the purification sacrifice, *Lev.* 5:11. An *epha* was 3 *seah*.

187 This shows that the offering of a Cohen cannot simply be compared to that of an Israel since the result would contradict biblical precepts.

188 *Lev.* 6:16.

189 This question is about the opinion of R. Simeon. For the rabbis, the offering is brought to the altar in one piece and burned as a sacrifice. But for R. Simeon, since the fistful is brought to the altar as a sacrifice, it makes sense to inquire whether the rest is burned under the same rules or not. If the same rules were to apply, it is difficult to see why there should be two distinct offerings.

190 Sacrifices can be offered in the Temple only between the morning and evening daily sacrifices. Remainders of sacrifices for which blood and fat were offered during daytime can be brought to the altar during the night.

A sacrifice can be brought only during one's lifetime.

In talmudic theory (Mishnah *Zebaḥim* 2:2), a sacrifice is either valid or invalid from the start. Therefore, the biblical prohibitions of פִּגּוּל and נוֹתָר

(*Lev.* 19:5-7) are interpreted to mean that the sacrifice becomes permanently prohibited if any of the prescribed actions in the Temple were executed with the idea that the meat should be eaten out of its allotted time or place. This means that the Cohen, by thinking to eat from the rest of the offering the next day or outside the Temple courtyard while dealing with the fistful taken for the altar, will invalidate the offering. This danger is restricted to the fistful, whose correct treatment will permit the rest to be eaten by the Cohanim. What these think while eating the rest is irrelevant; the only actions which are invalidated by wrong thoughts are those on which something else depends, either that part of the sacrifice becomes permitted as food, or that people are purified or otherwise enabled by it.

191   While both mss. read here "R. Simeon ben Eleazar", the continuation of the paragraph shows that the author must be R. Eleazar ben R. Simeon. The Babli, 23a/b, and the Tosephta, 2:6, read: Rebbi Eleazar ben Rebbi Simeon says, the fistful is sacrificed separately and the rest is dispersed.

192   The ashes on the top of the altar are hot and spreading the offering out means burning it on the altar. If that were the meaning, R. Eleazar's position is that of his father and does not have to be mentioned.

193   The ashes removed from the altar to the floor of the courtyard (*Lev.* 6:2).

194   Anything not destined for the altar cannot permit anything else. Therefore, any wrong intention the Cohen may have while depositing the rest on the ashes is irrelevant; he may think what he wishes. Similarly, since the burning of the fistful permits the consumption (or dispersion) of the remainder by the Cohanim, if the owner of the offering dies after the burning of the fistful it cannot have any influence on the status of the rest.

195   The argument of the previous Note is valid only for the offering of an Israel, for whom the fistful really permits the remainder to the Cohanim. But for the offering of a Cohen, the offering of the fistful according to R. Eleazar ben R. Simon does not permit anything, not even to bring the rest onto the altar. Therefore, the sacrificing of the fistful cannot lift the rules of פגול and נותר for the Cohen's offering.

196   They require that the entire offering be burned, cf. Note 182.

197   R. Eleazar ben R. Simeon

accepts the comparison of the obligatory to the voluntary offering of a Cohen, called "binding (הֶקֵּשׁ) of one verse to the other"; it is only to modify the rule of *Lev.* 6:16, which deals with voluntary offerings, not that of *Lev.* 6:15, which deals with an obligatory offering of another kind.

(19b line 23) אָמַר רִבִּי יוֹסֵי. רָאָה רִבִּי דַעְתּוֹ שֶׁלְּרִבִּי אֶלְעָזָר בֵּירִבִּי שִׁמְעוֹן וְשָׁנָה כְיוֹצֵא בוֹ. רִבִּי בָא בַּר כֹּהֵן בָּעֵי קוֹמֵי רִבִּי יוֹסֵי. וְלָמָּה לִי כְרִבִּי אֶלְעָזָר בֵּירִבִּי שִׁמְעוֹן. אֲפִילוּ כְרִבִּי שִׁמְעוֹן אָבִיו. אָמַר לֵיהּ. אִיכּוּל בְּרֹאשׁ הַמִּזְבֵּחַ וְאֵין שְׂרֵיפָה בְּרֹאשׁ הַמִּזְבֵּחַ. הָתִיב רִבִּי חֲנִינָה קוֹמֵי רִבִּי מָנָא. וְהָא תַנֵּי רִבִּי חִייָה וּפְלִיג. לִיקָרֵב כָּלִיל אֵינָהּ יְכוֹלָה מִפְּנֵי שׁוּתָּפוּת שֶׁלָּאִשָּׁה. לְהֵיאָכֵל אֵינָהּ יְכוֹלָה מִפְּנֵי שׁוּתָּפוּתוֹ שֶׁל אִישׁ. אָמַר לֵיהּ. רִבִּי רָאָה דַעְתּוֹ שֶׁלְּרִבִּי אֶלְעָזָר בֵּירִבִּי שִׁמְעוֹן. וְרִבִּי חִייָה רוּבָה רָאָה דַעְתּוֹ שֶׁלְּרִבִּי שִׁמְעוֹן אָבִיו.

Rebbi Yose said, Rebbi accepted the opinion of Rebbi Eleazar ben Rebbi Simeon and taught accordingly[198]. Rebbi Abba bar Cohen asked before Rebbi Yose: Why Rebbi Eleazar ben Rebbi Simeon? Even following his father, Rebbi Simeon! He said to him, "eating" is on the altar, "burning" is not on the altar[199]. Rebbi Ḥanina objected before Rebbi Mana: Did not Rebbi Ḥiyya disagree: "It cannot be burned completely because of the wife's part[200]; it cannot be eaten because of the husband's part." He said to him, Rebbi accepted the opinion of Rebbi Eleazar ben Rebbi Simeon, the elder Rebbi Ḥiyya accepted the opinion of the latter's father Rebbi Simeon.

198 He holds that the last sentence of the Mishnah can be explained only following R. Eleazar ben R. Simeon.

199 Rabbinic usage follows biblical usage in this case. The burning of sacrifices on the altar is never called "burning", but "eating (by the fire)", cf. *Lev.* 6:3. On the other hand, the burning outside the Temple is always called "burning", cf. *Lev.* 4:12,21; 16:27. If the Mishnah uses the expression "burning", it implies that this cannot be

on the altar.
200 The offering for a Cohen's suspected wife. The first clause is in Tosephta, 2:6. For the intelligible full text of this discussion, cf. Chapter 2:1, Note 7 ff.

משנה ח: בַּת יִשְׂרָאֵל שֶׁנִּישֵׂאת לְכֹהֵן מִנְחָתָהּ נִשְׂרֶפֶת וְכֹהֶנֶת שֶׁנִּישֵׂאת לְיִשְׂרָאֵל מִנְחָתָהּ נֶאֱכֶלֶת. מַה בֵּין כֹּהֵן לְכֹהֶנֶת. מִנְחַת כֹּהֶנֶת נֶאֱכֶלֶת מִנְחַת כֹּהֵן אֵינָהּ נֶאֱכֶלֶת. כֹּהֶנֶת מִתְחַלֶּלֶת וְאֵין כֹּהֵן מִתְחַלֵּל. כֹּהֶנֶת מִטַּמְּאָה לַמֵּתִים וְאֵין כֹּהֵן מִטַּמֵּא לַמֵּתִים. כֹּהֵן אוֹכֵל בְּקָדְשֵׁי קָדָשִׁים וְאֵין כֹּהֶנֶת אוֹכֶלֶת בְּקָדְשֵׁי קָדָשִׁים. (fol. 18c)

Mishnah 8: The offering of an Israel's daughter married to a Cohen is burned[201], the offering of a Cohen's daughter married to an Israel is not burned[202]. What is the difference between a Cohen and a Cohen's daughter? The flour offering of a Cohen's daughter is eaten, that of a Cohen is not eaten. A Cohen's daughter is desecrated, a Cohen is not desecrated[203]. A Cohen's daughter may defile herself for the dead, a Cohen may not defile himself for the dead[204]. A Cohen eats most holy [food], a Cohen's daughter may not eat most holy [food][205].

201 Since it is the husband's money; cf. Chapter 2:1, Note 7.
202 The woman becomes a member of her husband's clan.
203 This is explained in the Halakhah. An illicit marriage bars the wife and her children from ever marrying into the priesthood; a Cohen who divorces his forbidden wife returns to his priestly status.
204 The prohibition of the impurity of the dead is clearly addressed to *the sons of Aaron*, Lev. 21:1.
205 This is a clearly biblical precept; spelled out in *Lev.* 6:11,22; 7:6.

(fol. 19b) **הלכה ח**: בַּת יִשְׂרָאֵל שֶׁנִּישֵּׂאת לְכֹהֵן כול׳. מַה בֵּין כֹּהֵן לְכֹהֶנֶת. מִנְחַת כֹּהֶנֶת נֶאֱכֶלֶת. מִנְחַת כֹּהֵן אֵינָהּ נֶאֱכֶלֶת. דִּכְתִיב. וְכָל־מִנְחַת כֹּהֵן כָּלִיל תִּהְיֶה לֹא תֵאָכֵל. לֹא כֹהֶנֶת. רִבִּי אַבָּהוּ בָּעֵי קוֹמֵי רִבִּי שִׁמְעוֹן בֶּן לָקִישׁ. וְהָא כְתִיב וְכֹהֵן כִּי יִקְנֶה נֶפֶשׁ קִנְיַן כַּסְפּוֹ. מֵעַתָּה כֹהֵן וְלֹא כֹהֶנֶת. מַאי כְדוֹן. וְהַכֹּהֵן הַמָּשִׁיחַ תַּחְתָּיו מִבָּנָיו. אֶת שֶׁבְּנוֹ עוֹמֵד תַּחְתָּיו. יָצָאת זוֹ שֶׁאֵין בְּנָהּ עוֹמֵד תַּחְתֶּיהָ.

Halakhah 8: "The offering of an Israel's daughter married to a Cohen," etc. What is the difference between a Cohen and a Cohen's daughter? "The flour offering of a Cohen's daughter is eaten, that of a Cohen is not eaten." For it is written, "any flour offering of a Cohen shall be total, it should not be eaten[207];" not the Cohen's daugher's. Rebbi Abbahu asked before Rebbi Simeon ben Laqish: Is it not written: "If a Cohen acquire a person with his money[208]," should that apply to a Cohen but not ro a Cohen's daughter? How is that? "The Cohen anointed in his stead, one of his sons;[209]" one whose son fills his place, that excludes her whose son does not fill her place.

207 Lev. 6:16.
208 Lev. 22:11. The verse states that slaves of a Cohen may eat of his sanctified food and we hold (cf. Yebamot 7:1) that the slaves of a Cohen's daughter may eat if and only if she can eat. Should the mention of the masculine form "Cohen" not exclude the daughter of a Cohen. Accepted without discussion in Babli 23b; *Sifra Ṣaw Pereq* 8(4).
209 Lev. 6:15. Verse 16 is an appendix to a paragraph speaking only of the (male) High Priest. The son of a Cohen's daughter belongs to his father's clan, not hers.

(19b line 36) כֹּהֶנֶת מִתְחַלֶּלֶת. וְאֵין כֹּהֵן מִתְחַלֵּל. דִּכְתִיב וְלֹא יְחַלֵּל זַרְעוֹ בְעַמָּיו. אֵין לִי אֶלָּא זֶרַע שֶׁהוּא מִתְחַלֵּל. הִיא עַצְמָהּ מִנַּיִין. וְדִין הוּא. מַה אִם הַזֶּרַע שֶׁלֹּא עָבַר עֲבֵירָה הֲרֵי הוּא מִתְחַלֵּל. הִיא שֶׁעָבְרָה עֲבֵירָה אֵינוֹ דִין

שֶׁתִּתְחַלֵּל. הוּא עַצְמוֹ יוֹכִיחַ. שֶׁעָבַר עֲבֵירָה וְאֵינוֹ מִתְחַלֵּל. לֹא. אִם אָמַרְתָּ בְּאִישׁ שֶׁאֵינוֹ מִתְחַלֵּל בְּכָל־מָקוֹם. תֹּאמַר בְּאִשָּׁה שֶׁהִיא מִתְחַלֶּלֶת בְּכָל־מָקוֹם. הוֹאִיל וְהִיא מִתְחַלֶּלֶת בְּכָל־מָקוֹם דִּין הוּא שֶׁתִּתְחַלֵּל. מַה נַּפְשָׁךְ לוֹמַר. לֹא יָחֵל. לֹא יְחַלֵּל. אַף מִי שֶׁהָיָה כָשֵׁר וְנִתְחַלֵּל.

[210]"'A Cohen's daughter is desecrated, a Cohen is not desecrated.' For it is written: 'He shall not desecrate his seed in his clan.[211]' Not only that he desecrates his seed; from where [that he desecrates] herself[212]? It is a conclusion of an argument. Since the seed who did not commit any sin is desecrated, she, who committed a sin[213], is it not logical that she should be desecrated? He himself gives a counter-argument since he sinned and is not desecrated. No. If you talk about the man who is not otherwise desecrated[214], what can you say about a woman who can be otherwise desecrated? Since she can be otherwise desecrated, it is an argument that she should be desecrated! If you wish[215], you can say, he shall not desecrate - "he shall not repeatedly desecrate,'[216]" even to desecrate one who is enabled.

210 The entire paragraph is from *Sifra Emor Pereq* 2(7-8). For the Babli, 23b, it seems obvious that a woman forbidden to a Cohen becomes desecrated; one only needs a verse to free the Cohen from desecration.

211 *Lev.* 21:15, speaking of the High Priest who married a widow, divorcee, or desecrated woman. The children of such a forbidden union are desecrated in their clan and are permanently barred from any priestly function.

212 A woman who ever slept with a man whom she could not lawfully marry is considered a whore prohibited to a Cohen. By marrying her, he desecrates her permanently.

213 While it is stated two times that a Cohen sins in marrying a woman forbidden to him (*Lev.* 21:7), it is never stated that the forbidden woman sins in letting herself be married by the Cohen. The *Sifra* [*Emor Pereq* 1(12)] derives a warning to her from the

double prohibition in *Lev.* 21:7.

214 He is not permanently desecrated even if he sleeps with a slave girl, a Gentile, or a whore.

215 If you consider the pseudological argument invalid.

216 The root חול, חלל "to desecrate" appears in the Pentateuch also in Hiph'il. The use of the intensive instead of the causative in *Lev.* 21:15 is taken to imply more than one desecration. The Babli, *Qiddušin* 77a, derives different disabilities from the same argument.

(19b line 43) כֹּהֶנֶת מִטַּמְּאָה לַמֵּתִים. רִבִּי דוֹסָא מִמַּלְחִיָּא רִבִּי אָחָא בְּשֵׁם רִבִּי לְעָזָר. כֹּהֶנֶת מוּתֶּרֶת לָצֵאת חוּצָה לָאָרֶץ. מַה טַעֲמָא. אֱמוֹר אֶל הַכֹּהֲנִים. לֹא אֶל הַכּוֹהֲנֹת. דְּלֹכֵן מַה אֲנָן אָמְרִין. הוֹאִיל וְהִיא בְּכְלַל גְּזֵירָה לֹא תֵצֵא. וּתְהֵא בְּכְלַל גְּזֵירָה וְלֹא תֵצֵא. אִם אוֹמֵר אַתְּ כֵּן נִמְצֵאת מַדְחָה פָרָשַׁת טְמָאוֹת.

"A Cohen's daughter may defile herself for the dead." Rebbi Dosa from Malḥiyya, Rebbi Aḥa in the name of Rebbi Eleazar: A Cohen's daughter is permitted to leave the Land[217]. What is the reason? "Say to the Cohanim[218]." Not to the daughters of Cohanim. If it were not so, what would he say? Because she is included in the decree, she cannot leave. Why should she not be included in the decree and be forbidden to leave[219]? If you say so, you push aside the paragraph on impurities[220].

217 A Cohen is prohibited from defiling himself in the impurity of the dead, *Lev.* 21:1-4. By rabbinic decree, a Cohen is forbidden to leave the Land of Israel since the other countries, even disregarding the biblical impurity inherent in them, might be full of unrecognized graves so that the Cohen would automatically incur at least the doubt of contamination by a grave.

218 *Lev.* 21:2: "Say to the Cohanim, the *sons* of Aaron." The prohibitions in this paragraph inherently concern only the males of the family. This is explicit in *Sifra Emor, Introduction*; alluded to in Babli, 23b.

219 Since the prohibition is rabbinic anyhow, how can the extent of the prohibition be measured by biblical standards? It is unlikely that the

prohibition was known before the war of Bar Kokhba. We find king Yannai outside the Land, but he was a Sadducee and opposed to rabbinic prohibitions. But it is reported that R. Eleazar ben Azariah, a Cohen, descendant of Ezra in the tenth generation, went to Rome.

220 Since rabbinic decrees are גדירה, fences around the Law, they should not prohibit what is explicitly permitted in the Pentateuch.

(19b line 48) כֹּהֵן אוֹכֵל בְּקָדְשֵׁי הַקֳדָשִׁים וְאֵין כֹּהֶנֶת אוֹכֶלֶת בְּקָדְשֵׁי הַקֳדָשִׁים. דִּכְתִיב כָּל־זָכָר בַּכֹּהֲנִים יֹאכְלֶנּוּ.

"A Cohen eats most holy [food], a Cohen's daughter may not eat most holy [food]." For it is written (*Lev.* 7:6): "Every male among the Cohanim shall eat it."

(fol. 18c) **משנה ט**: מַה בֵּין הָאִישׁ לָאִשָּׁה. הָאִישׁ פּוֹרֵעַ וּפוֹרֵם וְאֵין הָאִשָּׁה פּוֹרַעַת וּפוֹרֶמֶת. הָאִישׁ מַדִּיר אֶת בְּנוֹ בְּנָזִיר וְאֵין הָאִשָּׁה מַדֶּרֶת אֶת בְּנָהּ בְּנָזִיר. הָאִישׁ מְגַלֵּחַ עַל נְזִירוּת אָבִיו וְאֵין הָאִשָּׁה מְגַלַּחַת עַל נְזִירוּת אָבִיהָ. הָאִישׁ מְקַדֵּשׁ אֶת בִּתּוֹ וְאֵין הָאִשָּׁה מְקַדֶּשֶׁת אֶת בִּתָּהּ. הָאִישׁ מוֹכֵר אֶת בִּתּוֹ וְאֵין הָאִשָּׁה מוֹכֶרֶת אֶת בִּתָּהּ. הָאִישׁ נִסְקָל עָרוֹם וְאֵין הָאִשָּׁה נִסְקֶלֶת עֲרוּמָה. הָאִישׁ נִתְלֶה וְאֵין הָאִשָּׁה נִתְלֵית. הָאִישׁ נִמְכָּר בִּגְנֵיבָתוֹ וְאֵין הָאִשָּׁה נִמְכֶּרֶת בִּגְנֵיבָתָהּ.

Mishnah 9: What is the difference between a man and a woman? A man is dishevelled and with open seams[221], no woman is dishevelled and with open seams. A man can make his son a *nazir*[222], no woman can make her son a *nazir*. A man can shave using his father's vow of *nazir*[223], no woman can shave using her father's vow of *nazir*. A man can betrothe his daughter[224], no woman can betrothe her daughter. A man can sell his daughter[225], no woman can sell her daughter. A man is stoned naked[226], no woman is stoned naked. A man is hanged[227], no woman is hanged. A man is sold for his theft, no woman is sold for her theft.

221 A man afflicted with skin disease must have dishevelled hair and wear clothes open at the seams (*Lev.* 13:45). It is written in v. 44: He is a *man* with skin disease.

222 Mishnah *Nazir* 4:6. The *nazir* is forbidden all grape products, may not cut any hair, and may not defile himself in the impurity of the dead. A father can decree that his underage son be a *nazir* as long as neither the child nor the relatives object. He then is responsible for the cost of all sacrifices due at the end of the *nezirut* period.

223 "Shaving" stands here for the entire ceremony which ends the *nezirut* period, *Num.* 6:13-21. If both father and adult son were *nezirim*, the father had already bought the required sacrifices (one male and one female sheep, and one ram) when he died before using them, the father's dedication is validly transferred to the son.

224 If a man marries off his underage daughter, the marriage is valid by biblical standards. This is derived from *Deut.* 22:16, where the father declares: I gave my daughter to this man as a wife. After the father's death, the widow may only marry off her underage daughter by rabbinic standards. A fully adult daughter must find her own husband.

225 *Ex.* 21:7: "If a *man* sell his daughter as a slave". In rabbinic theory, the institution of Hebrew slavery was bound to that of the Jubilee year. The latter is predicated on the clan holdings of land received under Joshua. Therefore, the Jubilee year should have been disestablished with the first Assyrian deportations of the Ten Tribes.

226 Mishnah *Sanhedrin* 6:3-4.

227 *Deut.* 21:22: "If a *man* was guilty of a capital crime and executed, you should hang *him* on a wooden pole." This refers explicitly to a man.

הלכה ט: מַה בֵּין הָאִישׁ לָאִשָּׁה. הָאִישׁ פּוֹרֵעַ וּפוֹרֵם כּוֹל׳. אִישׁ אֵין לִי אֶלָּא אִישׁ. אִשָּׁה מְנַיִין. תַּלְמוּד לוֹמַר צָרוּעַ. בֵּין אִישׁ בֵּין אִשָּׁה בֵּין קָטָן. אִם (fol. 19b)

כֵּן לָמָּה נֶאֱמַר אִישׁ. לְעִנְיָין שֶׁלְּמַטָּן. הָאִישׁ פּוֹרֵעַ וּפוֹרֵם. אֵין הָאִשָּׁה פּוֹרַעַת וּפוֹרֶמֶת.

Halakhah 9: "What is the difference between a man and a woman? A man is dishevelled and with open seams," etc. "A man[228]". This refers not only to a man; from where for a woman? The verse says, "afflicted with skin disease," whether man, or woman, or minor. If it is so, why is "a man" written? For the next theme[221], "a man is dishevelled and with open seams, no woman is dishevelled and with open seams."

228 *Lev.* 13:44: "A *man* afflicted with skin disease is he, impure is he, the Cohen shall certainly declare him impure if his disease is on his head." A slightly more complete text in *Sifra Tazria' Pereq* 12(1); a shortened text in Babli 23 a, *Keritut* 8b, *Arakhin* 3a.

(19b line 53) הָאִישׁ מַדִּיר וְהָאִישׁ מְגַלֵּחַ. רִבִּי יוֹחָנָן בְּשֶׁם רִבִּי מֵאִיר. עֶשְׂרִים וְאַרְבָּעָה דְּבָרִים מְקוּלֵּי בֵית שַׁמַּי וּמֵחוּמְרֵי בֵית הִלֵּל וְזֶה אֶחָד מֵהֶם. בֵּית שַׁמַּי אוֹמְרִים. אֵין הָאִישׁ מַדִּיר אֶת בְּנוֹ בְּנָזִיר. וּבֵית הִלֵּל אוֹמְרִים. הָאִישׁ מַדִּיר אֶת בְּנוֹ בְּנָזִיר.

"A man can make his son a *nazir*," and "a man can shave". Rebbi Johanan in the name of Rebbi Meïr[229]: In twenty-four matters are the House of Shammai lenient while the House of Hillel are restrictive and that is one of them: The House of Shammai say, a man cannot make his son a *nazir*, but the House of Hillel say, a man can make his son a *nazir*.

229 The Babli (*Sota* 23 b; *Nazir* 25 a/b, 28b, 30a, 61b) and dependent sources [*Num. rabba* 10 (20)] disagree and quote R. Johanan insisting that according to the biblical text, nobody can impose a state of *nazir* on another person but that it is traditional practice (in the words of the Midrash: "going back to Moses on Mount Sinai") that a father may force his son to be a *nazir*,

implying that nobody can dissent.

The same paragraph is found in *Nazir* 4:6, fol. 53c.

(19b line 57) הָאִישׁ מוֹכֵר אֶת בִּתּוֹ. דִּכְתִיב וְכִי יִמְכֹּר אִישׁ אֶת בִּתּוֹ לְאָמָה. הָאִישׁ מְקַדֵּשׁ אֶת בִּתּוֹ. דִּכְתִיב אֶת בִּתִּי נָתַתִּי לָאִישׁ הַזֶּה לְאִשָּׁה וַיִּשְׂנָאֶהָ.

"A man can sell his daughter," for it is written[230]: "If a man sell his daughter as a handmaid. "A man can betrothe his daughter," as it is written[231]: "I gave my daughter as a wife but he hated her."

230 *Ex.* 21:7.

231 *Deut.* 22:16.

(19b line 58) הָאִישׁ נִסְקָל עָרוֹם וְאֵין הָאִשָּׁה נִסְקֶלֶת עֲרוּמָה. דִּכְתִיב וּסְקַלְתָּם אוֹתוֹ. לֹא אֶת כְּסוּתוֹ. רִבִּי חַגַּי בְּעֵי קוֹמֵי רִבִּי יוֹסֵי. וְהָכְתִיב וּסְקַלְתָּם אוֹתָם בָּאֲבָנִים. מֵאַתָּה אוֹתָם. לֹא אֶת כְּסוּתָם. מַאי כְדוֹן. אִישׁ עַל יְדֵי שֶׁאֵין נִיוּוּלוֹ מְרוּבֶּה. לְפִיכָךְ נִסְקָל עָרוֹם. אֲבָל אִשָּׁה עַל יְדֵי שֶׁנִּיוּוּלָהּ מְרוּבֶּה. לְפִיכָךְ אֵינָהּ נִסְקֶלֶת עֲרוּמָה.

"A man is stoned naked, no woman is stoned naked." For it is written[232], "you shall stone him," not his garment. Rebbi Ḥaggai asked before Rebbi Yose: Is it not written[233]: "You shall stone them with stones," does that mean "them but not their garments"? How is that? A man is not greatly degraded by this, so he is stoned naked, but a woman who would be greatly degraded by it cannot be stoned naked[234].

232 There is no such verse. Probably the reference is to *Lev.* 24:14: וְרָגְמוּ אֹתוֹ which means "they shall stone him;" this verse is quoted in *Sifry zuṭa Šelaḥ* 36, Babli *Sanhedrin* 43a.

233 *Deut.* 22:24, speaking of the inhabitants of a city whose inhabitants, men and women, turn to idolatry. If the prior argument were correct, the verse would disprove the Mishnah.

234 There is no biblical source for the statement of the Mishnah. Since a

garment would soften the blows of the stones, the agony of the man to be executed would be prolonged if he were clothed; since he probably would not mind being seen naked, it is to his advantage being executed while naked. But for a woman, the mental anguish of being naked in public would be much greater than the increased physical pain; therefore a woman has to be executed fully clothed.

The Babli *Soṭa* 23b refers to the argument in a very abbreviated way which presupposes the knowledge of the Yerushalmi's argument. The original argument of the Yerushalmi is accepted in the Babli *Sanhedrin* 43a; in 45a the inference is attributed to R. Jehudah who requires that a woman be stoned naked. By contrast, in *Sifra Qedošim Parašah* 10(4), an appropriate verse is quoted, *Lev.* 20:2: "Every *man* in Israel or among the sojourners in Israel who gives of his children to the Moloch shall certainly die, the people of the land shall stone *him* with stone."

(19b line 64) הָאִישׁ נִתְלָה וְאֵין הָאִשָּׁה נִתְלֵת. דִּכְתִיב וְתָלוּ אוֹתוֹ. וְלֹא אוֹתָהּ.

"A man is hanged[227], no woman is hanged." Because it is written, "one shall hang *him*", not her.

(19b line 65) הָאִישׁ נִמְכָּר בִּגְנֵיבוֹ. בִּגְנֵיבוֹ וְלֹא בְּכַפְלוֹ. בִּגְנֵיבוֹ וְלֹא בִּזְמֵימוֹ. בִּגְנֵיבוֹ אֵינוֹ נִמְכָּר וְנִשְׁנֶה. וְאֵין לוֹ עָלָיו דָּמִים. מֵעַתָּה בִּגְנֵיבָה אַחַת אֲבָל בִּשְׁתֵּי גְנֵיבוֹת נִמְכָּר וְנִשְׁנֶה. רִבִּי יִרְמִיָה בָּעֵי. גָּנַב מְשֻׁלָּשׁוּתְפוּת מָה אַתְּ עָבַד לָהּ. כִּגְנֵיבָה אַחַת אוֹ כִּשְׁתֵּי גְנֵיבוֹת. הָיָה גוֹנֵב וּמוֹצִיא בַלַּיְלָה. נֵימַר. אִם יָדְעוּ הַבְּעָלִים בֵּינְתַיִים. שְׁתֵּי גְנֵיבוֹת הֵן. וְאִם לָאו גְּנֵיבָה אַחַת הִיא.

"A man is sold for his theft," for his theft but not for the double restitution[228]. For his theft but not for his perjury[229]. For his theft he is not sold twice. There is only a monetary claim on him. That means, for one theft, but for two thefts he can be sold a second time[230]. Rebbi Jeremiah asked: If he stole from a partnership, how are you treating this? As one theft or as two thefts[231]? If he stole and removed [things] in the night, we would say that if the owners realized [the loss] in the meantime, there are two thefts; otherwise, it is one theft.

228 A parallel to the entire paragraph is in Babli *Qiddušin* 18a. The *baraita* (including its terminology, treating "theft" as masculine) is also in *Mekhilta deR. Simeon bar Ioḥai*, pp. 192-193.

In *Ex.* 22:1 it is stated that if a male thief is killed while digging a tunnel under a house, his killing is self-defense and not punishable. Then in v. 2 it is noted that if he is seen to be unarmed, he cannot be killed but has to repay what he stole and, if he does not have the money, he is sold as indentured servant (for six years). Only in v. 3 follows the rule that the thief has to pay back double of what he took. The sequence of verses makes it clear that the fine remains the obligation of the thief but that he cannot be sold for inability to pay the fine.

229 The perjurer has to be fined the amount the accused would have had to pay if the testimony were truthful (*Deut.* 19:19). Since it is possible that the accused would have had the money to pay, the sale could not have been intended and, therefore, is not a punishment to be imposed.

It is to be noted that in matters of civil law, "man" mentioned in the verse means "adult, man or woman", cf. *Ex.* 21:26, 33; 22:4,9,13. However, in criminal matters one follows the rule אֵין עוֹנְשִׁין מִן הַדִּין, one does not impose punishment by logical argument (but one has to follow the biblical text closely).

230 In the Babli (*loc. cit.*), this is the position of Rava, who often follows the Galilean teaching. Abbai, who represents the Babylonian tradition, allows for at most one sale for multiple thefts from one person. He only permits a second sale for a theft from another victim.

231 The question is not answered since the problem cannot arise before Messianic times (cf. Note 225).

ארוסה פרק רבעי

(fol. 19c) **משנה א**: אֲרוּסָה וְשׁוֹמֶרֶת יָבָם לֹא שׁוֹתָה וְלֹא נוֹטֶלֶת כְּתוּבָּה שֶׁנֶּאֱמַר אֲשֶׁר תִּשְׂטֶה אִשָּׁה תַּחַת אִישָׁהּ פְּרָט לַאֲרוּסָה וְשׁוֹמֶרֶת יָבָם.

משנה ב: אַלְמָנָה לְכֹהֵן גָּדוֹל גְּרוּשָׁה וַחֲלוּצָה לְכֹהֵן הֶדְיוֹט מַמְזֶרֶת וּנְתִינָה לְיִשְׂרָאֵל בַּת יִשְׂרָאֵל לְמַמְזֵר וּלְנָתִין לֹא שׁוֹתָה וְלֹא נוֹטֶלֶת כְּתוּבָּה.

Mishnah 1: A preliminarily married woman[1] or one who waits for her brother-in-law[2] neither drinks nor collects her *ketubah*, since it is said[3]: ". . who will deviate from under her husband," which excludes a preliminarily married woman and one who waits for her brother-in-law.

Mishnah 2: A widow [married to] a High Priest[4], a divorcee[5] or one who received *ḥaliṣah*[6] to a common priest, a female bastard[7] or a Gibeoness[8] to an Israel, or an Israel woman married to a bastard or a Gibeonite, neither drinks nor collects her *ketubah*[9].

1 Cf. D*emai* 4, Note 19.

2 Her husband died childless; she waits to be married by her brother-in-law. In the meantime, the brother-in-law declared his jealousy and brought witnesses that she had an illicit rendez-vous. While a woman waiting for her brother-in-law is unable to marry outside the family without *ḥaliṣah*, her infidelity in her widowhood is not criminal adultery (cf. *Yebamot*, Chapter 2, Note 6). Nevertheless, if a brother-in-law "bespoke" her, she is as if preliminarily married to him and if she violates his demand that she not be with a suspected paramour, he cannot marry her unless she is cleared by the *Soṭah* ritual. Since this is impossible and she has brought the situation on herself by her action, she has to receive *ḥaliṣah*, be divorced, and cannot claim her *ketubah* money.

3 Num. 5:29. "Under her husband" is only a wife living with her husband. In *Sifry Num.* 20 (differently in Babli 24a, attributed to the same authors) there is a discussion on which woman is considered living with her husband.
4 Lev. 21:14.
5 Lev. 21:7.
6 She is a divorcee by rabbinic standards; cf. Mishnah *Yebamot* 2:4.
7 Cf. *Yebamot* Chapter 1, Note 176.
8 Cf. *Yebamot* Chapter 2, Note 72.
9 The Halakhah leaves open the possibility that this latter rule may be a rabbinic decree.

הלכה א: אֲרוּסָה וְשׁוֹמֶרֶת יָבָם כול'. וְיַשְׁקֶינָהּ. גְּזֵירַת הַכָּתוּב הִיא. וְהֵבִיא הָאִישׁ אֶת אִשְׁתּוֹ אֶל הַכֹּהֵן. וְלֹא יְקַנֵּא לָהּ. הַתּוֹרָה אָמְרָה. וְקִנֵּא אֶת אִשְׁתּוֹ. וְקִנֵּא אֶת אִשְׁתּוֹ. אֲפִילוּ מִקְצָת אִשְׁתּוֹ. (fol. 19c)

Halakhah 1: "A preliminarily married woman or one who waits for her brother-in-law," etc. Why can he not make her drink? It is a decision of the verse: "The man shall bring his wife to the Cohen[10]." Then he should not be able to declare his jealousy[11]! The Torah said, "and he declared his jealousy to his wife," "and he declared his jealousy to his wife,[12]" even if she is only partially his wife.

10 Lev. 5:15. A man can bring his wife only if he is living with her.
11 If "his wife" in this paragraph means only the definitively married one, the entire procedure should be impossible for the preliminarily married woman.
12 Lev. 5:14; if the meaning of "his wife" were constant in this verse, the second clause should have read "and he declared his jealousy to her." The woman who is a wife but not a wife in the first sense is the preliminarily married one. Therefore, the second mention of "wife" adds the preliminarily married one as object of jealousy.

(19c, line 25) מַתְנִיתִין דְּבֵית שַׁמַּי. דְּבֵית שַׁמַּי אוֹמְרִים. נוֹטֶלֶת כְּתוּבָּתָהּ וְלֹא שׁוֹתָה. אָמַר רִבִּי יוֹסֵי. תַּמָּן טַעֲמַיְיהוּ דְּבֵית שַׁמַּי. אוֹמֶרֶת. הָבֵיא לִי בַּעֲלִי וַאֲנִי שׁוֹתָה. בְּרַם הָכָא יוֹדַעַת הָיְיתָ שֶׁאֵין אֲרוּסָה שׁוֹתָה. לָמָּה הִכְנִיסָה עַצְמָהּ לְמִסְפֵּק הַמְרוּבֶּה הַזֶּה. בִּשְׁבִיל לְפוֹסְלָהּ מִכְּתוּבָּתָהּ.

Does our Mishnah follow the House of Shammai, since the House of Shammai say, "she takes her *ketubah* but does not drink"[13]? Rebbi Yose said, there the reason of the House of Shammai is that she may say, bring me my husband, then I shall drink[14]. But here, she knew that the preliminarily married cannot drink[15]; why did she bring herself into that great doubt? In order to disqualify herself from receiving her *ketubah*[16].

13 Mishnah 4:3. If the husband died after she was in a secluded place with her paramour but before she could drink.

14 Since the verse requires the husband to bring his wife to the Temple, she can claim that it is not her fault that she could not cleanse herself.

15 It is clear that the House of Shammai also hold that women have to study all the rules (and texts) of the oral law; cf. *Berakhot* Chapter 3, Note 181. If R. Eliezer in Halakhah 3:4 excludes women from the study of Torah, he can mean only the study of the Pentateuch, not that of the oral tradition.

16 For the preliminarily married woman, this refers only to pre-talmudic times, when the *ketubah* was given at the time of *qiddušin*. But later practice was to deliver the document only at the time of the actual marriage (cf. *Ketubot* 5:1).

(19c, line 29) רִבִּי יוּדָה בָּעֵי. כְּמָה דְתֵימַר תַּמָּן. וְקִנֵּא אֶת אִשְׁתּוֹ. וְקִנֵּא אֶת אִשְׁתּוֹ. אֲפִילוּ מִקְצָת אִשְׁתּוֹ. וְדִכְוָותָהּ תַּחַת אִישֵׁךְ. אֲפִילוּ מִקְצָת אִישֵׁךְ. הֵיךְ עֲבִידָה. קִינֵּא לָהּ עוֹדָהּ אֲרוּסָה וּכְנָסָהּ וְנִסְתְּרָה. מַשְׁקֶה אוֹתָהּ עַל קִינּוּיוֹ. קִינֵּא לָהּ עוֹדָהּ שׁוֹמֶרֶת יָבָם וּכְנָסָהּ וְנִסְתְּרָה. מַשְׁקֶה אוֹתָהּ עַל קִינּוּיוֹ. קִינֵּא לָהּ עוֹדָהּ אֲרוּסָה וּכְנָסָהּ וְנִסְתְּרָה וְיָדַע בָּהּ. תֵּצֵא בִּכְתוּבָּתָהּ. וְאִם לָאו תֵּצֵא

בְּלֹא כְתוּבָּה. [קִינֵּא לָהּ עוֹדָהּ שׁוֹמֶרֶת יָבָם וּכְנָסָהּ וְנִסְתְּרָה וְיָדַע בָּהּ. תֵּצֵא בִּכְתוּבָּתָהּ. וְאִם לָאו תֵּצֵא בְּלֹא כְתוּבָּה.] קִינֵּא לָהּ בַּעֲלָהּ וּמֵת וְנָפְלָה לִפְנֵי יָבָם וּכְנָסָהּ וְנִסְתְּרָה. מַשְׁקֶה אוֹתָהּ עַל קִינּוּיוֹ. לֹא קִינֵּא לָהּ בַּעֲלָהּ וָמֵת וְנָפְלָה לִפְנֵי הַיָּבָם וְקִינֵּא לָהּ וְלֹא הַסְפִּיק לִכְנוֹס עַד שֶׁמֵּת וְנָפְלָה לִפְנֵי אָחִיו. אֵינוֹ מַשְׁקֶה אוֹתָהּ. שֶׁלֹּא נָפְלָה לוֹ אֶלָּא מֵחֲמַת אָחִיו הָרִאשׁוֹן. אֲבָל אִם קִינֵּא לָהּ הַיָּבָם וּכְנָסָהּ וָמֵת וְנָפְלָה לִפְנֵי הַיָּבָם וּכְנָסָהּ וְנִסְתְּרָה. מַשְׁקֶה אוֹתָהּ עַל קִינּוּיוֹ.

Rebbi Jehudah asked: As you say, "and he declared his jealousy to his wife," "and he declared his jealousy to his wife,[12]" even if she is only partially his wife, similarly, "under your husband," even if he is only partially your husband[17]. How is that? If he declared his jealousy to her while she was preliminarily married, then he wed her[18], and she went to a secluded place, he makes her drink on the basis of his declaration of jealousy[19]. If he[20] declared his jealousy to her while she was waiting for her brother-in-law, then he[20] wed her, and she went to a secluded place, he makes her drink on the basis of his declaration of jealousy[19]. If he declared his jealousy to her while she was preliminarily married, then he took her in, she went to a secluded place, and after that he had sex with her, she has to leave with her *ketubah*[21]; otherwise[22] she has to leave without *ketubah*. [If he declared his jealousy to her while she was waiting for her brother-in-law, then he took her in, she went to a secluded place, and after that he had sex with her, she has to leave with her *ketubah*; otherwise without *ketubah*.][23] If her husband declared his jealousy and died, she became destined for her brother-in-law who married her, then she went to a secluded place, he makes her drink on the basis of [the first husband's] declaration of jealousy[24]. If her husband did not declare his jealousy and died, she became destined for her brother-in-law who declared his jealousy but did not manage to take her in before he died and she became destined for his brother, the latter cannot make her drink since she became destined for him only because of the first brother[25]. But if her brother-in-law declared his jealousy, took her in, and died, then she became destined for a brother-in-law who took her in, when she went to a secluded place he makes her drink on the basis of his[20] declaration of jealousy.

17 R. Jehudah notes that "under your husband" is repeated (vv. 19,20). Therefore, if the repetition of "his wife" (cf. Note 12) also includes a partial wife (preliminarily married or one who waits for her brother-in-law), the repetition here should also give the partial husband the right to bring his partial wife to the Temple. There is no answer given; R. Jehudah's argument is contradicted by the verse he himself quotes, cf. Chapter 1, Notes 154-156.

18 "He took her in", i. e., he brought her to his house in the final wedding ceremony to live with him.

19 The final wedding activates the prior declaration of jealousy. The Babli agrees, 25a.

20 The brother-in-law.

21 As stated in Mishnah 3:6, the ceremony is ineffective for a woman whose husband had slept with her while she was forbidden to him. Since it is his action that (a) keeps his wife permanently forbidden to him and, (b) prevents his wife from proving her innocence, he as the guilty party is forced to divorce her and to pay the full amount of the *ketubah*.

22 If the husband did not sleep with his wife after she became forbidden to him, he has the choice to divorce her because of her fault, without paying any of his own money.

23 From the Rome ms., probably omitted by the scribe of the Leiden ms. because of the parallel text.

24 Since by biblical standards the brother-in-law's marriage is an automatic consequence of the first husband's death.

25 Since the second brother never became her husband, his declaration is irrelevant to the third brother.

(19c, line 40) תַּמָּן תַּנִּינָן אַיְילוֹנִית וּזְקֵינָה וּשֶׁאֵינָהּ רְאוּיָה לְוֹלֵד לֹא שׁוֹתָה וְלֹא נוֹטֶלֶת כְּתוּבָּה. שֶׁנֶּאֱמַר וְנִקְּתָה וְנִזְרְעָה זָרַע. הָרְאוּיָה לְהַזְרִיעַ זָרַע. יָצְאַת זוֹ שֶׁאֵינָהּ רְאוּיָה לְהַזְרִיעַ זָרַע. הֲתִיבוּן. הֲרֵי אַלְמָנָה לְכֹהֵן גָּדוֹל הֲרֵי הִיא אֵינָהּ רְאוּיָה לְהַזְרִיעַ זָרַע. שַׁנְיָיא הִיא. דִּכְתִיב וְלֹא יְחַלֵּל זַרְעוֹ בְּעַמָּיו. תַּמָּן תַּנִּינָן מַמְזֵר פּוֹסֵל וּמַאֲכִיל. כֵּיצַד. וְהָכָא הוּא אָמַר הָכֵין. אָמַר רִבִּי תַּנְחוּמָא. תַּמָּן וְזֶרַע אֵין לָהּ מִכָּל מָקוֹם. בְּרַם הָכָא זֶרַע כָּשֵׁר. לֹא זֶרַע פָּסוּל. אָמַר רִבִּי יוֹסֵי בֵּירִבִּי בּוּן. כְּלוּם הַמַּיִם בָּאִין אֶלָּא לְהַתִּירָהּ לְבֵיתָהּ. וְזוֹ כֵּיוָן שֶׁנִּסְתְּרָה אוֹמְרִים לוֹ. הוֹצֵא.

There[26], we have stated: "A she-ram[27], an old woman[28], or a sterile one neither drinks nor collects her *ketubah*," as it is said[29]: "She will be declared innocent and bear seed," [this refers to] one able to bear seed; it excludes one who is unable to bear seed. They objected, is there not the widow [married to] the High Priest, is she not able to bear seed[30]? There is a difference, since it is written[31]: "He may not desecrate his seed among his people.[31]" There[32], we have stated: "A bastard disables and enables to eat. How is this?" And here he says so? Rebbi Tanḥuma said, there, "she has no issue" of any kind, but here[33] one requires enabled seed, not disabled seed. Rebbi Yose ben Rebbi Abun said, the water only serves to permit her to her house; but about this one one tells him to divorce once she went to a secluded place[34].

26 Mishnah 4:4; a fuller text in Tosephta 5:4 and Babli 26a as the minority opinion of R. Simeon ben Eleazar; as an alternative explanation in *Sifry Num.* 19.

27 A woman lacking secondary female sex characteristics, cf. *Yebamot*, Chapter 1, Note 65.

28 A post-menopausal woman.

29 *Num.* 5:28.

30 Why is she excluded from drinking (Mishnah 2)?

31 *Lev.* 21:15.

32 Since any child of the widow

will be desecrated, it is not counted as the High Priest's child. Therefore, as far as he is concerned, his wife is unable to bear children.

33 Mishnah *Yebamot* 7:7. An Israel woman widowed from a Cohen may eat heave as long as *any* Jewish descendant of her husband's is alive; a Cohen woman widowed from an Israel may not eat heave as long as *any* Jewish descendant of her husband's is alive.

34 He rejects the earlier attempt to find a biblical source to the rejection of the widow and explains *Lev.* 21:15 as: "He is forbidden to desecrate his seed." The rule excluding the High Priest's widow is rabbinical. If the Temple court refuses to administer the water, the widow remains permanently forbidden to her husband, who therefore is forced to divorce her.

(fol. 19c) **משנה ג**: וְאֵילּוּ לֹא שׁוֹתוֹת וְלֹא נוֹטְלוֹת כְּתוּבָה. הָאוֹמֶרֶת טְמֵיאָה אֲנִי לָךְ וְשֶׁבָּאוּ לָהּ עֵדִים שֶׁהִיא טְמֵיאָה הָאוֹמֶרֶת אֵינִי שׁוֹתָה וְאָמַר בַּעֲלָהּ אֵינִי מַשְׁקֶה וְשֶׁבְּעָלָהּ בַּעֲלָהּ בַּדֶּרֶךְ נוֹטֶלֶת כְּתוּבָה וְלֹא שׁוֹתָה. מֵתוּ בַּעֲלֵיהֶן עַד שֶׁלֹּא יִשְׁתּוּ בֵּית שַׁמַּי אוֹמְרִים נוֹטְלוֹת כְּתוּבָּה וְלֹא שׁוֹתוֹת וּבֵית הִלֵּל אוֹמְרִים לֹא שׁוֹתוֹת וְלֹא נוֹטְלוֹת כְּתוּבָּה.

Mishnah 3: The following cannot drink or collect their *ketubah*: One who says, I am impure for you, or one for whom came witnesses declaring her to be impure[35]; one who says "I will not drink"[36]. But one whose husband refuses to make her drink, or whose husband copulated with her on the road, collects her *ketubah* but does not drink[37]. About those whose husbands died before she would drink, the House of Shammai say, they collect the *ketubah* but do not drink[14], but the House of Hillel say, they neither drink not collect the *ketubah*[38].

35 They are divorced for adultery; in this case no *ketubah* money is due.

36 She accepts the monetary penalty for adultery without admitting guilt.

37 In both cases the husband prevented her from clearing her name; he has to divorce her but must pay. Cf. Note 2.

38 She cannot drink because she has no husband to bring her to the Temple. But having brought her problem on herself by having had a secret rendez-vous, the husband's heirs can tell her to prove her claim to the *ketubah* money by proving her innocence, following the general principle of monetary claims הַמּוֹצִיא מֵחֲבֵרוֹ עָלָיו הָרְאָיָה "the burden of proof is on the claimant" (Yerushalmi *Sanhedrin* 3:9, fol. 21b; Babli *Baba Qama* 46b).

The reading here is that of all Yerushalmi sources and a number of Mishnah mss.; the reading of the Babli here is "either they drink or they do not collect their *ketubah*", but the text is emended in the Babli, *Yebamot* 38b, to conform to the Yerushalmi reading.

הלכה ג: אֵילּוּ לֹא שׁוֹתוֹת וְלֹא נוֹטְלוֹת כְּתוּבָה. הָאוֹמֶרֶת טְמֵיאָה אֲנִי לָךְ כוּל׳. אָמַר רִבִּי יֹאשִׁיָּה. סָח לִי זְעִירָא מִשּׁוּם אַנְשֵׁי יְרוּשָׁלֵם. שְׁלֹשָׁה הֵן שֶׁאִם בִּקְּשׁוּ לִמְחוֹל מוֹחֲלִין לָהֶן וְאֵילוּ הֵן. סוֹטָה וּבֶן סוֹרֵר וּמוֹרֶה וְזָקֵן מַמְרָא כוּל׳. (fol. 19c)

Halakhah 3: "The following cannot drink or collect their *ketubah*: One who says, I am impure for you," etc. Rebbi Joshia said, Ze'ira told me in the name of the people of Jerusalem[39]: In three cases, if they want to forgive, they may forgive. These are: The suspect wife[40], the rebellious son[41], and the rebellious Elder[42], etc.

39 In the Babli (25a, *Sanhedrin* 88a): Ze'ira the Jerusalemite.

40 The Babli explains: The husband may repeal his declaration of jealousy; then there is no case. However, the Babli (25a) restricts this to the time before the wife had a secret rendez-vous whereas the Yerushalmi (*Sanhedrin* 8:6, fol. 26b) lets the husband rescind his action any time before the scroll was erased.

41 Described in *Deut.* 21:18-21;

Sanhedrin Chapter 8.

42 *Deut.* 17:8-12. The Babli in the name of "the colleagues in the South" and the Yerushalmi *Sanhedrin* 8:6 in the name of R. Jehudah ben Bathyra of Nisibis disagree in this case since the authority of the Supreme Court has to be upheld.

(fol. 19c) **משנה ד**: מְעוּבֶּרֶת חֲבֵירוֹ וּמֵינֶקֶת חֲבֵירוֹ לֹא שׁוֹתָה וְלֹא נוֹטֶלֶת כְּתוּבָּה דִּבְרֵי רִבִּי מֵאִיר. וַחֲכָמִים אוֹמְרִים יָכוֹל הוּא לְהַפְרִישָׁהּ וּלְהַחֲזִירָהּ לְאַחַר זְמָן. אַיְילוֹנִית וּזְקֵינָה וְשֶׁאֵינָהּ רְאוּיָה לְוָלָד לֹא שׁוֹתָה וְלֹא נוֹטֶלֶת כְּתוּבָּתָהּ. רִבִּי לֶעֱזָר אוֹמֵר יָכוֹל הוּא לִישָּׂא לוֹ אִשָּׁה אֲחֶרֶת וְלִפְרוֹת וְלִרְבּוֹת מִמֶּנָּה. וּשְׁאָר כָּל־הַנָּשִׁים אוֹ שׁוֹתוֹת אוֹ לֹא נוֹטְלוֹת כְּתוּבָּה.

Mishnah 4: A woman pregnant by another man or nursing another man's [child][43] may neither drink nor collect her *ketubah*, the words of Rebbi Meïr, but the Sages say, he[44] may separate from her and take her back later. A she-ram[27], an old woman[28], or a sterile one, neither drinks nor collects her *ketubah*; Rebbi Eleazar says, he may marry another wife and be fruitful and multiply with her[45]. All other women either drink or cannot collect their *ketubah*[46].

43 A pregnant widow or divorcee is (rabbinically) not permitted to remarry until the baby is weaned.

44 The second husband may live separated from his wife until the baby is weaned and there is no risk that the life of the baby be endangered by another pregnancy and a premature stop of nursing.

45 He takes *Num.* 5:28 as a statement of fact, not a commandment.

46 Since by not drinking they forbid themselves to their husbands; they would have the status of women refusing to live with their husbands who are divorced without payment of the *ketubah* (Mishnah *Ketubot* 5:7).

הלכה ד: (fol. 19c) מְעוּבֶּרֶת חֲבֵירוֹ וּמֵינֶקֶת חֲבֵירוֹ כול׳. לֹא יִשָּׂא אָדָם מְעוּבֶּרֶת חֲבֵירוֹ וּמֵינֶקֶת חֲבֵירוֹ. וְאִם נָשָׂא עָלָיו הַכָּתוּב אוֹמֵר. אַל תַּשֵּׂג גְּבוּל עוֹלָם (אֲשֶׁר גָּבְלוּ רִאשׁוֹנִים)[47] וּבִשְׂדֵי יְתוֹמִים אַל תָּבוֹא. הַנּוֹשֵׂא מְעוּבֶּרֶת חֲבֵירוֹ וּמֵינֶקֶת חֲבֵירוֹ יוֹצִיא וְלֹא יַחֲזִיר עוֹלָמִית. דִּבְרֵי רִבִּי מֵאִיר. וַחֲכָמִים אוֹמְרִים. יָכוֹל הוּא לְהַפְרִישָׁהּ וּלְהַחֲזִירָהּ לְאַחַר זְמָן. וּבְכָל הַדְּבָרִים רִבִּי מֵאִיר קוֹנֵס. נִשְׁמְעִינָה מִן הָדָא. קְטַנָּה שֶׁחָלְצָה תַּחֲלוֹץ מִשֶּׁתַּגְדִּיל. וְאִם לֹא חָלְצָה חֲלִיצָתָהּ כְּשֵׁירָה. רִבִּי מָנָא אָמַר לָהּ סְתָם. רִבִּי יִצְחָק בְּרֵיהּ דְּרִבִּי חִייָה כְּתוֹבָה בְּשֵׁם רִבִּי יוֹחָנָן. דְּרִבִּי מֵאִיר הִיא. דְּרִבִּי מֵאִיר אָמַר. אֵין חוֹלְצִין וְאֵין מְיַיבְּמִין אֶת הַקְּטַנָּה. שֶׁמָּא תִימָּצֵא אַיְילוֹנִית.

"A woman pregnant by another man or nursing another man's [child]," etc. A man should not marry a woman pregnant by another man or nursing another man's [child], but if he did marry her, the verse says about him[48]: "Do not remove the eternal boundaries and do not enter the orphans' field." He who marries a woman pregnant by another man or nursing another man's [child] has to divorce her and should never retake her, the words of Rebbi Meïr, but the Sages say, he[44] may separate from her[49] and take her back later. Does Rebbi Meïr always fine people[50]? Let us hear from the following: [51]"The underage woman who performed *haliṣah* should repeat *haliṣah* once she becomes of age but if she did not repeat it, the *haliṣah* is valid." Rebbi Mana said it without attribution, Rebbi Isaac the son of Rebbi Ḥiyya the scribe[52] in the name of Rebbi Joḥanan[53]: It is Rebbi Meïr who said that one does not perform *haliṣah* or levirate with an underage girl because she might turn out to be a she-ram[54].

47   A meaningless addition of the corrector (from *Deut.* 19:14), printed in *editio princeps*.

48   *Prov.* 23:10.

49   · In the Babli (26a, *Yebamot* 36b), the Sages require a divorce but permit

a remarriage.

50 Since he has no biblical source for his prohibition of remarriage, it is purely a punitive measure against people who flout rabbinic maxims. Does he always prohibit remediation for actions of that kind?

51 *Yebamot* Chapter 12, Notes 103,
107, 108.

52 In *Yebamot*: מטי בה "turns to it". The text here seems original.

53 In *Yebamot*: R. Jonah. The text here seems original.

54 Since R. Meïr accepts the validity after the fact; he does not always refuse remediation.

(19c, line 61) תַּנֵּי. מֵנִיקָה שֶׁמֵּת בַּעְלָהּ לֹא תִינָּשֵׂא עַד עֶשְׂרִים וְאַרְבָּעָה חֳדָשִׁים. דִּבְרֵי רִבִּי מֵאִיר. רִבִּי יְהוּדָה אוֹמֵר. שְׁמוֹנָה עָשָׂר חוֹדֶשׁ. רִבִּי יוֹנָתָן בֶּן יוֹסֵי אוֹמֵר. בֵּית שַׁמַּי אוֹמְרִים. עֶשְׂרִים וְאַרְבָּעָה חֳדָשִׁים. וּבֵית הִלֵּל אוֹמְרִים. שְׁמוֹנָה עָשָׂר חוֹדֶשׁ. אָמַר רַבָּן שִׁמְעוֹן בֶּן גַּמְלִיאֵל. אִם כְּדִבְרֵי הָאוֹמֵר. עֶשְׂרִים וְאַרְבָּעָה חוֹדֶשׁ. מוּתֶּרֶת לְהִינָּשֵׂא לְאַחַר עֶשְׂרִים וְאֶחָד חוֹדֶשׁ. וְאִם כְּדִבְרֵי הָאוֹמֵר. שְׁמוֹנָה עָשָׂר חוֹדֶשׁ. מוּתֶּרֶת לְהִינָּשֵׂא לְאַחַר חֲמִשָּׁה עָשָׂר חוֹדֶשׁ. לְפִי שֶׁאֵין הֶחָלָב נֶעֱכָר אֶלָּא לְאַחַר שְׁלֹשָׁה חֳדָשִׁים.

It was stated[55]: "A nursing woman whose husband died should not remarry[56] until 24 months later, the words of Rebbi Meïr[57]. Rebbi Jehudah says, eighteen months[58]. Rebbi Jonathan ben Yose[59] says, the House of Shammai say 24 months, but the House of Hillel say eighteen months. Rabban Simeon ben Gamliel said, following him who said 24 months, she is permitted to remarry after 21 months; following him who said eighteen months, she is permitted to remarry after fifteen months, since the milk terminates only after three months[60]."

55 Tosephta Nidda 2:2, Babli *Ketubot* 60b.

56 In Tosephta, Babli, and sources dependent on the Babli: לא תינשא ולא תתארס "not remarry, not even preliminarily marry". The Yerushalmi does not mention preliminary marriage.

57 Tosephta Nidda 2:1-3 notes that

the normal period of nursing a baby is 24 months. Therefore, a normal contract for a wet-nurse is for 24 months.

58   He holds that a baby may be weaned after 18 months without danger to his health even under the sanitary conditions of his time.

59   In the mss. of the Babli, R. Nathan bar Yoseph or R. Nathan bar Yose, but in the Gaonic sources mostly R. Jonathan Bar Yose. In *Ma'serot* 5:4, he is called R. Jonathan ben R. Yose and characterized as a student of R. Aqiba.

60   Of a new pregnancy. The baby is not hurt if his mother starts a new pregnancy within three months of the end of his projected nursing period.

(19c, line 67) רִבִּי יַעֲקֹב בַּר אָחָא אָמַר. עֲקַבְיָה שָׁאַל אֶת רִבִּי שִׁמְעוֹן בֶּן לָקִישׁ וְהוֹרֵי לֵיהּ. עֶשְׂרִים וְאַרְבָּעָה חֳדָשִׁים. רִבִּי יִרְמְיָה. עֲקַבְיָה שָׁאַל אֶת רִבִּי חֲנִינָא וְהוֹרֵי לֵיהּ. עֶשְׂרִים וְאַרְבָּעָה חֳדָשִׁים. מָה. תְּרֵין עוֹבְדִין הֲווֹן. חַד בְּשֵׁם רִבִּי חֲנִינָא וְחַד בְּשֵׁם רִבִּי שִׁמְעוֹן בֶּן לָקִישׁ. רִבִּי מָנָא הוֹרֵי. שְׁמוֹנָה עָשָׂר חוֹדֶשׁ וְצָם כָּל־הַהוּא יוֹמָא. רִבִּי מַר עוּקְבָא הוֹרֵי בְּאַרְבְּלִי. עֶשְׂרִים וְאַרְבָּעָה חוֹדֶשׁ. וַאֲפִילוּ מֵת הַתִּינוֹק.

Rebbi Jacob bar Aḥa said, Aqabiah asked Rebbi Simeon ben Laqish who instructed him: 24 months. Rebbi Jeremiah: Aqabiah asked Rebbi Ḥanina who instructed him: 24 months. How? Two cases were there, one in the name of Rebbi Ḥanina and one in the name of Rebbi Simeon ben Laqish. Rebbi Mana instructed: eighteen months, and fasted that entire day[61]. Rebbi Mar Uqba instructed in Arbela: 24 months, even if the baby had died[62].

61   He felt uneasy about his decision even though in general R. Jehudah's opinion is followed in a dispute with R. Meïr.

62   In the Babli, he reports that R. Ḥanina had permitted him to marry after 15 months. The Babli (Note 55) decides on 24 months but permits

immediate remarriage if the baby had died since Jewish women are not suspected to kill their children for a new husband.

(19d, line 2) מוֹדִין חֲכָמִים לְרבִּי אֶלְעָזָר שֶׁאִם הָיוּ לוֹ אִשָּׁה וּבָנִים שֶׁהִיא שׁוֹתָה וְנוֹטֶלֶת כְּתוּבָה. הָיָה לוֹ אִשָּׁה וּבָנִים וּמֵתוּ בֵּין קִינוּי לִסְתִּירָה כְּבָר נִרְאֵית לִשְׁתּוֹת. לֹא הָיָה לוֹ אִשָּׁה וּבָנִים וּמֵתוּ[63] בֵּין קִינוּי לִסְתִּירָה כְּבָר נִרְאֵית שֶׁלֹּא לִשְׁתּוֹת.

The Sages agree with Rebbi Eleazar that if he had [another] wife and children, she drinks and collects her *ketubah*.[64] If he had [another] wife and children but they died between the declaration of jealousy and her secret rendez-vous, she already was eligible to drink[65]. If he did not have [another] wife and children but they died between the declaration of jealousy and her secret rendez-vous, she already was barred from drinking[66].

63   An obvious error but one which appears in both mss.

64   They only hold that the sterile woman cannot be made to drink on the possibility that the husband would at some time in the future marry a child-bearing wife.

65   The status at the time of the declaration of jealousy is determining.

66   This sentence makes no sense. One may conjecture that the original text stated that if the husband acquired a child-bearing wife after declaring his jealousy, it has no influence on the status of his first wife.

(fol. 19c) **משנה ה**: אֵשֶׁת כֹּהֵן שׁוֹתָה וּמוּתֶּרֶת לְבַעֲלָהּ אֵשֶׁת סָרִיס שׁוֹתָה. עַל יְדֵי כָּל־הָעֲרָיוֹת מְקַנִּין חוּץ מִן הַקָּטָן וּמִמִּי שֶׁאֵינוֹ אִישׁ.

Mishnah 5: A Cohen's wife drinks and is permitted to her husband[67]; the wife of a eunuch[68] drinks. One may declare one's jealousy with respect to any incest-'prohibited person[69], except for a minor and a non-man[70].

67 Since she is cleared, she is permitted to her husband who is forbidden to be married even to a rape victim.

68 As Tosaphot point out (26a, *s. v.* אשת סריס), the "eunuch" may be either a person born with defective testicles or a person castrated by chemical means. The verse prohibits only a surgically castrated man to marry into the congregation.

69 Even a person who is entitled to be alone with the wife, such as her father, who is forbidden to her by an incest prohibition.

70 An animal, according to the Babli (26b) and the Rome ms.

(fol. 19c) **הלכה ה**: אֵשֶׁת כֹּהֵן שׁוֹתָה כול׳. דְּלֹכֵן מָה אֲנָן אֲמָרִין. שָׁתַת וְלֹא בֶדְקוּ אוֹתָהּ הַמַּיִם טְהוֹרָה הִיא. אֲנִי אוֹמֵר. הַזְּכוּת תָּלָה לָהּ. נִיחָא כְּמַאן דְּאָמַר. הַזְּכוּת תּוֹלָה וְאֵינָהּ נִיכֶּרֶת. בְּרַם כְּמַאן דָּמַר. הַזְּכוּת תּוֹלָה וְנִכֶּרֶת. אָמַר רַבִּי יִצְחָק. כֵּן אֲנָן קַיָּימִין כְּשֶׁשָּׁתַת וְלֹא הָיוּ הַמַּיִם בּוֹדְקִין אוֹתָהּ. שֶׁלֹּא תֹאמַר. הוֹאִיל וְאֵין הַמַּיִם בּוֹדְקִין בָּאֲנוּסָה אֶלָּא בִּמְפוּתָּה. וְזוֹ אֲנוּסָה הִיא. מָה אֲנוּסָה שֶׁבִּכְהוּנָה כִּרְצוֹן שֶׁבְּיִשְׂרָאֵל. לְפוּם כֵּן צָרִיךְ מֵימַר. מוּתֶּרֶת לְבֵיתָהּ. וּמִנַּיִין שֶׁאוֹנְסִין פּוֹסְלִין בִּכְהוּנָה בְּאֵשֶׁת אִישׁ. מָה אִם שְׁרָצִים הַקַּלִּים עָשָׂה בָהֶן אֶת הָאוֹנֶס כִּרְצוֹן. סוֹטָה חֲמוּרָה לֹא כָּל־שֶׁכֵּן. תַּנֵּי רַבִּי יַעֲקֹב בַּר אִידֵי קוֹמֵי רַבִּי יוֹנָתָן. וְאַתְּ כִּי שָׂטִית תַּחַת אִישֵׁךְ וְכִי נִטְמֵאת. פְּרָט לְאוֹנְסִין. מָה אַתְּ שְׁמַע מִינָהּ. אָמַר לֵיהּ. מַה תַּחַת אִישֵׁךְ לְרָצוֹן. אַף כָּאן לְרָצוֹן. וְהִיא לֹא נִתְפָּשָׂה. [אֲסוּרָה].[71] הָא נִתְפָּשָׂה מוּתֶּרֶת. וְיֵשׁ לָךְ תְּפוּסָה בְּיִשְׂרָאֵל וְהִיא אֲסוּרָה. וְאֵי זוֹ זוֹ. זוֹ שֶׁתְּחִילָּתָהּ בְּרָצוֹן וְסוֹפָהּ בְּאוֹנֶס. וְיֵשׁ לָךְ שֶׁאֵינָהּ תְּפוּסָה בְּיִשְׂרָאֵל וְהִיא מוּתֶּרֶת. וְאֵי זוֹ זוֹ. זוֹ שֶׁתְּחִילָּתָהּ בְּאוֹנֶס וְסוֹפָהּ בְּרָצוֹן. כְּהָדָא אִיתְּתָא אָתַת לְגַבֵּיהּ רַבִּי יוֹחָנָן. אָמְרָה לֵיהּ. נֶאֱנַסְתִּי. אָמַר לָהּ. וְלֹא עָרַב לָךְ

בְּסוֹף. אָמְרָה לֵיהּ. וְאִם יִטְבּוֹל אָדָם אֶצְבָּעוֹ בִּדְבַשׁ וְיִתְּנֶנָּה לְתוֹךְ פִּיו בְּיוֹם הַכִּיפּוּרִים שֶׁמָּא אֵינוֹ רַע לוֹ וּבְסוֹף אֵינוֹ עָרֵב לוֹ. וְקִיבְּלָהּ.

Halakhah 5: "A Cohen's wife drinks," etc. Otherwise, what could we say? She drank and the water had no influence on her; she is pure! I could say, merit suspended for her[72]. That is according to him who says that merit suspends and it is not recognizable. But following him who says that merit suspends and it is recognizable? Rebbi Isaac said, really we deal with the case that she drank and the water had no influence on her; that you should not say since the water has no influence on a rape victim, but only on a seduced woman, this one is a rape victim. But a rape victim in the priesthood is like a willing one for an Israel, therefore it is necessary to say that she is permitted to her house[73]. From where that rape disables a married woman in the priesthood[74]? Since in matters of crawling things, which are a trifling matter, He made forced [impurity] equal to intentional [impurity], in the weighty matter of the deviant not so much more[75]? Rebbi Jacob bar Idi stated before Rebbi Jonathan: "If you deviated from under your husband and became defiled," that excludes rape. How do you understand this? He said to him, just as "under your husband" is by consent, so "if you became defiled" is by consent. "She was not raped", she is forbidden. Therefore, if she was raped, she is permitted[76]. But there is a rape victim which is forbidden for an Israel. Who is that? That is one who started by consent and ended up raped[77]. And there is one who is not a rape victim which is permitted to an Israel. Who is that? That is one who started as a rape victim and ended up consenting[78]. Like that woman who came to Rebbi Johanan and said to him, I was raped. He said to her, but was it not sweet to you in the end[79]?

She said to him, if a person dips a finger into honey and puts it into his mouth on the Day of Atonement, does he not feel bad about it and at the end it is sweet? He accepted her[80].

71   Reading of the Rome ms., missing in the Leiden ms.; probably a copyist's mistake.

72   Cf. Chapter 3, Halakhah 5.

73   The same argument is anonymous in the Babli, 26a.

74   For the Babli, the fact that a raped wife is forbidden to a Cohen is immediately obvious from *Lev.* 21:7 since the definition of a זוֹנָה, usually translated as "prostitute" is (*Sifra Emor Pereq* 1(7) = Babli Yebamot 61b) שֶׁנִּבְעֲלָה בְּעִילַת זְנוּת "who was the object of an unlawful intercourse". The formulation in the passive clearly implies that a rape victim is included.

75   This argument is based on the identity of the word "impurity" used both for ritual impurity (in this case, by touching a dead reptile) and guilt; cf. M. Cohen, מונחי טומאה וטהרה בלשון המקרא וייחסם למושגי איסור והיתר של לשון חכמים, בית מקרא כה,ד [קלה] תשנ"ג, 289.-306. Touching a dead reptile is a minor impurity which can be repaired immediately by immersion in water before sundown. There is no difference between intentional or unintional defilements. By contrast, sexual defilement has far-reaching consequences.

In an elliptic version the argument is in *Sifry Num.* 7. One needs the detailed argument here to understand the text there.

76   This second argument is accepted in the Babli (26a, *Yebamot* 56b).

77   She started playing with another man and ended up being raped against her will. The Babli does not consider this case as one of consensual sex.

78   This case is accepted by the Babli, *Ketubot* 51b.

79   He wanted to forbid her to her (Israel) husband, following the opinion of Samuel's father (Abba bar Abba) who considers rape that in the end is accepted by the victim as consensual sex; Babli *Ketubot* 51b.

80   She is permitted to her husband. This argument is reproduced in the Babli by Rava who is known as a frequent mouthpiece of Yerushalmi arguments. The same argument used in the opposite sense in a tannaïtic statement is in Babli, *Niddah* 45a.

(19d, line 24) וְאַתְּ כִּי שָׂטִית תַּחַת אִישֵׁךְ וְכִי נִטְמֵאת. פְּרָט לְאֵשֶׁת סָרִיס. וַיִּתֵּן אִישׁ בָּךְ אֶת שְׁכָבְתּוֹ. לְרַבּוֹת אֶת הַסָּרִיס. חוּץ מִן הַקָּטָן וּמִמִּי שֶׁאֵינוֹ אִישׁ. [כְּקוֹף].[81]

"If you deviated from under your husband and became defiled,[82]" that excludes[83] a castrate's wife. "And a man ejaculated into you[82]", that includes a castrate. "Except for a minor and a non-man," e. g., an ape.

81 From the Rome ms. which has פקוף, misreading ב.
82 *Num.* 5:20.
83 One would have expected "includes" since her husband has a penis if he is permitted to her (Note 68). Babli 26a, *Sifry Num.* 13 read: "Other than your husband", that includes a eunuch's wife.

(fol. 19c) **משנה ו:** וְאִילּוּ שֶׁבֵּית דִּין מְקַנִּין לָהֶן מִי שֶׁנִּתְחָרֵשׁ בַּעֲלָהּ אוֹ נִשְׁטָה אוֹ שֶׁהָיָה חָבוּשׁ בְּבֵית הָאֲסוּרִין לֹא לְהַשְׁקוֹתָהּ אָמְרוּ אֶלָּא לְפָסְלָהּ מִכְּתָבָּתָהּ. רִבִּי יוֹסֵי אוֹמֵר אַף לְהַשְׁקוֹתָהּ שֶׁכְּשֶׁיֵּצֵא בַעֲלָהּ מִבֵּית הָאֲסוּרִין יַשְׁקֶינָה.

Mishnah 6: For the following the court will declare jealousy: One whose husband had become a deaf-mute, or insane, or was confined in a jail; not to make her drink but to make her ineligible for her *ketubah*[84]. Rebbi Yose says, also to make her drink: When her husband will be freed from jail he should make her drink.

84 Since *Num.* 5:14 requires the husband to declare his jealousy in order to bring her to the Temple. R. Yose requires the presence of the husband only for the trip to the Temple and the ceremony (vv. 15 ff.)

(fol. 19c) **הלכה ו**: אִילּוּ שֶׁבֵּית דִּין מְקַנִּין לָהֶן כול'. בְּנֵי יִשְׂרָאֵל.

Halakhah 6: "For the following the court will declare jealousy," etc. "The children of Israel.85"

84   *Num.* 5:12. Why is a law dealing with the private relations between a man and his wife addressed to the people? To make this a part of public law which falls under the purview of the court. The Babli, 24a, derives the power of the court from the expression איש איש "every man" in v. 12, which includes the incompetent who are dependent on the court.

(19d, line 27) וִיקַנֵּא וְיַשְׁקִינָהּ. גְּזֵירַת הַכָּתוּב הִיא וְהֵבִיא הָאִישׁ אֶת אִשְׁתּוֹ אֶל הַכֹּהֵן. וְלֹא יְקַנֵּא לָהּ. הַתּוֹרָה אָמְרָה. וְקִנֵּא אֶת אִשְׁתּוֹ. וְקִנֵּא אֶת אִשְׁתּוֹ. אֲפִילוּ מִקְצָת אִשְׁתּוֹ.

85Why can he not make her drink86? It is a decision of the verse: "The man shall bring his wife to the Cohen87." Then he should not be able to declare his jealousy88! The Torah said, "and he declared his jealousy to his wife," "and he declared his jealousy to his wife,89" even if she is only partially his wife.

85   This paragraph is copied verbally from Halakhah 1, Notes 10-12, but the meaning is different.
86   Why does the majority not empower the freed or healed husband to make his wife drink?
87   *Num.* 5:15.
88   The court as guardian of the incapacitated man should not be able to do what he himself could not do at the moment.
89   *Num.* 5:14; the court is empowered even if the man is temporarily disabled from acting as a husband.

(19d, line 30) בִּיאַת פְּסוּלִין מִנַּיִין שֶׁהִיא פוֹסֶלֶת. מַה נָן קַיָּימִין. אִם בְּאֵשֶׁת אִישׁ חֲמוּרָה הִיא. אִם בְּאַלְמָנָה לְכֹהֵן גָּדוֹל כְּבָר כָּתוּב וְהֵבִיא הָאִישׁ אֶת אִשְׁתּוֹ

אֶל הַכֹּהֵן. הַצַּד הַשָּׁוֶה שֶׁבָּהֶן אֶת שֶׁזַּרְעוֹ פָּסוּל בִּיאָתוֹ פּוֹסֶלֶת. וְאֶת שֶׁאֵין זַרְעוֹ פָּסוּל אֵין בִּיאָתוֹ פּוֹסֶלֶת. וְאֵילוּ הֵן. בֶּן תֵּשַׁע שָׁנִים וְיוֹם אֶחָד גֵּר עַמּוֹנִי וּמוֹאָבִי אֲדוֹמִי מִצְרִי עֶבֶד מַמְזֵר חָלָל נָתִין כּוּתִי וְגוֹי שֶׁבָּאוּ עַל בַּת כֹּהֵן עַל בַּת לֵוִי עַל בַּת יִשְׂרָאֵל פּוֹסֶלֶת מִן הַכְּהוּנָה. רִבִּי יוֹסֵי אוֹמֵר. כָּל־שֶׁזַּרְעוֹ פָּסוּל בִּיאָתוֹ פּוֹסֶלֶת. וְכָל־שֶׁאֵין זַרְעוֹ פָּסוּל אֵין בִּיאָתוֹ פּוֹסֶלֶת. רַבָּן שִׁמְעוֹן בֶּן גַּמְלִיאֵל אוֹמֵר. כָּל־שֶׁאַתְּ מוּתָּר בְּבִתּוֹ אַתְּ מוּתָּר בְּאַלְמָנָתוֹ. וְכָל־שֶׁאֵין אַתְּ מוּתָּר בְּבִתּוֹ אֵין אַתְּ מוּתָּר בְּאַלְמָנָתוֹ.

From where that the intercourse of a disabled disables[90]? What are we talking about? If about a married woman, there is a serious [offense].[91] If about a widow married to the High Priest, it already is written "The man shall bring his wife to the Cohen.[92]" What is equal between them is: Everybody's intercourse disqualifies those whose descendant would be disqualified[93]. [94]These are: "A child of nine years and one day, an Ammonite, Moabite, Edomite, or Egyptian proselyte, or a bastard, desecrated, Gibeonite, Samaritan, and Gentile who had intercourse with the daughter of a Cohen, a Levite, or an Israel, disqualified her for the priesthood. Rebbi Yose said, everybody's intercourse disqualifies those whose descendant would be disqualified; his intercourse does not disqualify those whose descendant would not be disqualified. Rabban Simeon ben Gamliel says, in all cases, if his daughter is permitted to you, so is his widow; if his daughter is not permitted to you, neither is his widow."

90 Disables a woman of the priestly clan (a wife or a daughter) from eating sanctified food such as heave; cf. *Yebamot* 7:5.

91 Adultery is a capital crime.

92 Cf. Note 87. Mishnah 1 already stated that a forbidden wife is not counted as a wife and we just have established that the intercourse with a man who cannot be legally married

bars a woman from priesthood.

93 The child of the otherwise married woman is a bastard, the child of the widow married to the High Priest is desecrated.

94 This text is from *Yebamot* 7:5, Notes 111-116.

כשם שהמים פרק חמשי

(fol. 19d) **משנה א:** כְּשֵׁם שֶׁהַמַּיִם בּוֹדְקִין אוֹתָהּ כָּךְ הַמַּיִם בּוֹדְקִין אוֹתוֹ שֶׁנֶּאֱמַר וּבָאוּ וּבָאוּ. כְּשֵׁם שֶׁהִיא אֲסוּרָה לַבַּעַל כָּךְ הִיא אֲסוּרָה לַבּוֹעֵל שֶׁנֶּאֱמַר נִטְמְאָה נִטְמְאָה דִּבְרֵי רִבִּי עֲקִיבָה. אָמַר רִבִּי יְהוֹשֻׁעַ כָּךְ הָיָה דּוֹרֵשׁ זְכַרְיָה בֶן הַקַּצָּב. רִבִּי אוֹמֵר שְׁנֵי פְעָמִים הָאֲמוּרִים בַּפָּרָשָׁה אִם נִטְמָאָה נִטְמָאָה אֶחָד לַבַּעַל וְאֶחָד לַבּוֹעֵל.

Mishnah 1: Just as the water checks her out so it checks him[1] out, as it is said, "it will come, it will come". Just as she is forbidden to the husband so she is forbidden to her paramour as it is said, "she was impure, she was impure," the words of Rebbi Aqiba[2]. Rebbi Joshua said, that was the inference of Zachariah the butcher's son[3]. Rebbi said, the two times it said, "she became impure, she became impure," once for the husband and once for the paramour[4].

1 The wife's paramour. It is moreover stated in Halakhah 9:9 (Babli 28a) that the procedure becomes inactive if the husband had ever misbehaved sexually.

2 This will be explained in the Halakhah.

3 An early Tanna, student of Rabban Johanan ben Zakkai.

4 In *Num.* 5:13,14 it is stated twice "she became impure", meaning "she became forbidden"; cf. Chapter 4, Note 75, and the Introduction.

(fol. 20a) **הלכה א:** כְּשֵׁם שֶׁהַמַּיִם בּוֹדְקִין אוֹתָהּ כול'. אֲנָן תַּנִּינָן בָּאוּ בָּאוּ.[5] אִית תַּנָּיֵי תַּנֵּי וּבָאוּ וּבָאוּ. מָאן דָּמַר בָּאוּ בָּאוּ. רִבִּי עֲקִיבָה. וּמָאן דָּמַר וּבָאוּ

וּבָאוּ. רִבִּי יִשְׁמָעֵאל. אֲנָן תַּנִּינָן נִטְמָאָה נִטְמָאָה. אִית תַּנָּיֵי תַּנֵּי וְנִטְמָאָה וְנִטְמָאָה. מָאן דָּמַר נִטְמָאָה נִטְמָאָה. רִבִּי עֲקִיבָה. וּמָאן דָּמַר וְנִטְמָאָה וְנִטְמָאָה. רִבִּי יִשְׁמָעֵאל.

Halakhah 1: "Just as the water checks her out," etc. We stated "they came, they came". Some Tannaïm stated "they will come, they will come". He who said "they came, they came" is Rebbi Aqiba, he who said "they will come, they will come" is Rebbi Ismael. We stated "she became impure, she became impure", some Tannaïm stated "and she became impure, and she became impure". He who said "she became impure, she became impure" is Rebbi Aqiba, he who said "and she became impure, and she became impure" is Rebbi Ismael[6].

---

5   In the Rome ms., באו ובאו. This is Babli style.

6   R. Ismael holds that דִּבְרָה תוֹרָה בִּלְשׁוֹן בְּנֵי אָדָם "the Torah speaks in everyday language" (*Yebamot* 8:1, Note 72; *Nedarim* 1:1; *Šabbat* 19:2; Babli *Berakhot* 31b and 18 other places). This means that any verse containing no linguistic feature noted as an exception in *Gesenius-Kautzsch* must be interpreted following the hermeneutical rules detailed in the introduction to *Sifra*. R. Ismael's argument here is a straightforward application of his rule 3: בנין אב מכתוב אחד "meaning established by one verse". Since both וּבָאוּ (vv. 22,27) and וְנִטְמָאָה (v. 29) [correctly in *Midrash of the 32*

Rules: וְהִיא נִטְמָאָה (vv. 13,14)] are well defined by the first occurrence, the second occurrence has the parallel meaning but refers to a different subject. That this second subject is the suspected adulterer is never indicated in the verse but since he is the only other person possibly being impure in this situation, the transfer of the meanings to him makes sense.

R. Aqiba negates absolutely that "the Torah speaks in everyday language". For him, any *vaw* prefixed to a word has a hidden meaning. [Since his co-student Aquila translated the Torah in this sense "before Rebbis Eliezer and Joshua" (*Megillah* 1:11 fol. 71c, Babli 3a), one may attribute this transformation of the Pentateuch into a book of codes to the tradition of their common teacher Rabban Johanan ben Zakkai.] R. Aqiba is not deterred by the fact that in וּבָאוּ the *vav* is both conjunctive and conversive; any *vav* that is translated even in the LXX by καὶ must indicate a duplication of meaning. If the duplication of subjects were not intended, then Scripture would have found a way to use only באו (or imperfect יבואו) without the *vav*.

The Babli, 28a, takes notice only of the teachings of R. Aqiba.

(20a, line 6) תַּנֵּי בוא ובה. וְכָתוּב כֵּן. כַּיי דָמַר רבִּי אִמִּי בְשֵׁם רבִּי יוֹחָנָן. גּוֹרְעִין לִדְרוֹשׁ מִתְּחִילָתָהּ לְסוֹפָהּ. רבִּי חֲנִינָה בְשֵׁם רבִּי יִרְמְיָה. וַאֲפִילוּ בְאֶמְצַע הַתֵּיבָה. וְיָצַקְתָּ עָלֶיהָ שָׁמֶן. וְיָצַקְתָּ שֶׁמֶן מִנְחָה. לְרַבּוֹת אֶת כָּל־הַמְּנָחוֹת לִיצִיקָה.

It was stated[7], בוא ובה[8]. Is that written? It follows what Rebbi Immi said in the name of Rebbi Johanan: For interpretation, one removes from its beginning to its end[9]. Rebbi Hanina in the name of Rebbi Jeremiah: Even a middle word. "You have to pour oil on." You have to pour oil on a flour offering, to subject all flour offerings to pouring[10].

7 In order to prove that the adulterer is punished by the bitter water just as the adulteress is.

8 A copyist's error makes this expression unintelligible. It must read ובא ובה. Than means that instead of וּבָאוּ בָהּ "they will come into her" (v. 27), the final *vaw* is transferred from the end of the first word to the beginning of the second to read וּבָא וּבָהּ "it will come, and into her", implying that the water will come into somebody and into her, establishing that the presumed adulterer can also be checked out by the water. The technique of transferring letters is accepted not only by the Yerushalmi (also *Nazir* 5:1, 43d line 67; *Horaiot* 1:3, 46a, line 24) but possibly also in the Babli (*Yoma* 48a, *Baba batra* 111b, *Zebahim* 25a, *Bekhorot* 44b).

(Such an argument is quite impossible in a paleo-Hebrew text where the words are separated by a physical divider. The technique of moving letters from the end of one word to the beginning of the following, so much in fashion in modern criticism, presupposes that a change occured at a late time when there were no longer any paleo-Hebrew texts in use.)

9   It really should be "from end to beginning".

10   *Lev.* 1:6: "You have to break it into little pieces and pour oil over it; [because] it is a flour offering", speaking of a pan-fried offering. For some flour offerings it is only specified that oil has to be included, or that oil has to be put on it. From this verse one concludes that "putting on" or "mixing" means "pouring oil over the flour". The argument here proposes to read וְיָצַקְתָּ שֶׁמֶן עָלֶיהָ מִנְחָה instead of וְיָצַקְתָּ עָלֶיהָ שֶׁמֶן מִנְחָה הִיא. This is based on the teaching of R. Aqiba who disregards masoretic accents in all cases (cf. H. Guggenheimer, *The Scholar's Haggadah*, Northvale NJ 1995, pp. 306-307) but in the Babli (cf. Note 8) is strongly opposed by Rava who objects to applying a surgeon's knife to a verse (cf. the explanations of R. Ḥananel in '*Arukh*, s. v. גרע and Rashbam in *Baba batra* 111b, s. v. אלא)

(20a, line 10) הַמְאָרֲרִים. אָמַר רִבִּי תַנְחוּמָא. מִינְיָין הַמְאָרָרִים. כְּנֶגֶד מָאתַיִם וְאַרְבָּעִים וּשְׁמוֹנָה אֵיבָרִים שֶׁיֵּשׁ בָּהּ. וּכְנֶגֶד מָאתַיִם וְאַרְבָּעִים וּשְׁמוֹנָה אֵיבָרִים שֶׁיֵּשׁ בּוֹ.

"The spell acting". Rebbi Tanḥuma said, what is the count of[11] "the spell acting"? It corresponds to the 248 parts of her body and the 248 parts of his body[12].

11   Tosaphot (27b, s. v. כשם) read correctly מנין. The reference is to the (Alexandrinian) custom of using letters as numerals. The count of הַמְאֹרֲרִים is 5+40+1+200+200+10+40 = 496 = 2 · 248.

12   Mishnah *Ahilot* 1:8. A part is either a bone or a vital organ, such as the genitals. No talmudic source, in contrast to medieval rabbinic texts, makes a difference between the number of parts of the male and those of the female.

The implication of the sermon is that the bodies of adulterer and adulteress together bring on the evil spell.

(20a, line 12) וְהָא תַּנִּינָן¹³. כְּשֵׁם שֶׁהַמַּיִם בּוֹדְקִין אוֹתָהּ כָּךְ הַמַּיִם בּוֹדְקִין אוֹתוֹ. כְּשֵׁם שֶׁהִיא אֲסוּרָה לַבַּעַל כָּךְ הִיא אֲסוּרָה לַבּוֹעֵל. כְּשֵׁם שֶׁהִיא אֲסוּרָה לְאָחִיו שֶׁלַבַּעַל כָּךְ הִיא אֲסוּרָה לְאָחִיו שֶׁלַבּוֹעֵל. כְּשֵׁם שֶׁהַמַּיִם בּוֹדְקִין אוֹתָהּ עַל כָּל־בִּיאָה וּבִיאָה שֶׁהִיא מְקַבֶּלֶת אֶת בַּעֲלָהּ לְאַחַר הַבּוֹעֵל כָּךְ הֵן בּוֹדְקִין אוֹתוֹ. הִיא עַל יְדֵי שֶׁדַּרְכָּהּ לֵיאָסֵר בֵּין לוֹ בֵּין לְאַחֵר הִיא נִבְדֶקֶת. אֲבָל הוּא לִכְשֶׁיַּשְׁתֶּה¹⁴ הוּא נִבְדָּק. בָּדְקוּ אוֹתוֹ וְלֹא בָדְקוּ אוֹתָהּ. אֲנִי אוֹמֵר. הַזְכוּת תָּלָה לָהּ. נִיחָא כְּמַאן דָּמַר. הַזְכוּת תּוֹלָה וְאֵינָהּ נִיכֶּרֶת. בְּרַם כְּמַאן דָּמַר. הַזְכוּת תּוֹלָה וְנִיכֶּרֶת. הֲרֵי לֹא הוּכְרָה. אֶלָּא אֲנִי אוֹמֵר. מַיִם מְגוּלִּין שָׁתַת וְנִצְבֵּית. הָכֵין לָא הֲוָון בָּעֵי מִיבְדְּקוּנֵיהּ¹⁵ אֶלָּא כְדוֹן. אֶלָּא אֲנִי אוֹמֵר. עִם אֲחֵרוֹת נִסְתַּר. וְלֹא כֵן סַבְרִינָן מֵימַר. לִכְשֶׁיַּשְׁתֶּה¹⁴ הוּא נִבְדָּק. תִּיפְתָּר שֶׁהָיָה הוּא מֵזִיד וְהִיא שׁוֹגֶגֶת וּבָדְקוּ אוֹתוֹ וְלֹא בָדְקוּ אוֹתָהּ. אֲנִי אוֹמֵר. הַזְכוּת תָּלָה לָהּ. נִיחָא כְּמַאן דָּמַר. הַזְכוּת תּוֹלָה וְאֵינָהּ נִיכֶּרֶת. בְּרַם כְּמַאן דָּמַר. הַזְכוּת תּוֹלָה וְנִיכֶּרֶת. הֲרֵי לֹא הוּכְרָה. אֶלָּא אֲנִי אוֹמֵר. מַיִם מְגוּלִּין שָׁתַת וְנִצְבֵּית. הָכֵין לָא הֲוָון בָּעֵי מִיבְדְּקוּנֵיהּ אֶלָּא כְדוֹן. עִם אֲחֵרִים נִסְתְּרָה. מֵעַתָּה גֵּירֵשׁ יְהֵא מוּתָּר בָּהּ. תִּיפְתָּר שֶׁהָיָה הוּא שׁוֹגֵג וְהִיא מֵזִידָה. וּבָדְקוּ אוֹתָהּ וְלֹא בָדְקוּ אוֹתוֹ. הוּא מֵזִיד וְהִיא שׁוֹגֶגֶת. פְּשִׁיטָה שֶׁהִיא מוּתֶּרֶת לְבֵיתָהּ. גֵּירֵשׁ. מַהוּ שֶׁיְּהֵא מוּתָּר בָּהּ. אִיפְשָׁר לוֹמַר מֵזִיד בָּהּ. וְאַתְּ אָמַר הָכֵין. הוּא שׁוֹגֵג וְהִיא מֵזִידָה. פְּשִׁיטָה שֶׁהִיא אֲסוּרָה לְבֵיתָהּ. גֵּירֵשׁ. מַהוּ שֶׁיְּהֵא מוּתָּר בָּהּ. אִיפְשָׁר לוֹמַר יוֹצֵאת מִתַּחַת יָדוֹ וְאַתְּ אָמַר הָכֵין. וּמִנַּיִין שֶׁהַדָּבָר תָּלוּי בָּהּ. שִׁמְעוֹן בַּר בָּא בְּשֵׁם רִבִּי יוֹחָנָן. כְּתִיב וְאֶל אֵשֶׁת עֲמִיתְךָ לֹא יִתֵּן שְׁכָבְתְּךָ לְזָרַע לְטָמְאָה בָהּ. בָּהּ הַדָּבָר תָּלוּי. אִם הָיְתָה מֵזִידָה אֲסוּרָה. שׁוֹגֶגֶת מוּתֶּרֶת.

Did we not state: "Just as the water checks her out so it checks him out"? ¹⁶Just as she is forbidden to her husband, so she is forbidden to her paramour. Just as she is forbidden to her husband's brother, so she is forbidden to her paramour's brother. Just as the water checks her out for every single intercourse for which she receives her husband after [intercourse with] her paramour, so it checks him out. Since she in general becomes forbidden, whether by him or by another [man], she is checked out[17]. But when he[18] makes [her] drink, he[19] is checked out[20]. If it checked him out but not her, I would say that merit suspends for her[21]. That is according to him who says that merit suspends and it is not recognizable. But following him who says that merit suspends and it is recognizable? Look, she was not recognized! But I could say that she drank uncovered water[22] and it[23] swelled. They should not have her[15] checked out in this way but correctly[24]! But I could say that he was in secret with other women[25]. Did we not think to say, when he makes [her] drink, he is checked out[26]? Explain it that he had criminal intent but she acted in error; then the water checked him out but not her[27]. [[28]If the water checked her out but not him,] I would say that merit suspends for (her) [him][29]. That is according to him who says that merit suspends and it is not recognizable. But following him who says that merit suspends and it is recognizable? Look, she was not recognized! But I could say that she drank uncovered water and her belly swelled. They should not have her checked out in this way but correctly![24] But I could say that she was in secret with other men. Then if he[18] divorced her, she would be permitted to him.[19] Explain it that he acted in error but she had criminal intent; then the water checked her out but not him. If he had criminal intent but she acted in error, then it is obvious that she is permitted to her house[18]. If he[18] divorced her, would she be permitted to him[19]? Is it possible to say that he had criminal intent and you say so? If he acted in error but she had criminal intent, it is obvious that she is forbidden to her house. If he[18] divorced her, would she be permitted to him[19]? Is it possible to say that she left because of him and you say so[30]? From where do we know that all depends on her? Simeon bar Abba in the name of Rebbi Joḥanan: Is is written[31]: "Do not ejaculate semen into your neighbor's wife to be impure through her." It depends on her; if she had criminal intent, she is forbidden, acted in error she is permitted[32].

13 Text of Tosaphot (Note 11): כְּשֶׁם שֶׁהַמַּיִם בּוֹדְקִין אוֹתָהּ עַל כָּל־בִּיאָה וּבִיאָה שֶׁהִיא מְקַבֶּלֶת **מִבַּעֲלָהּ** לְאַחַר הַבּוֹעֵל כָּךְ הֵן בּוֹדְקִין אוֹתוֹ. **וּכְשֵׁם** שֶׁהִיא אֲסוּרָה לְאָחִיו שֶׁלַּבַּעַל כָּךְ הִיא אֲסוּרָה לְאָחִיו שֶׁלַּבּוֹעֵל. הִיא עַל יְדֵי שֶׁדַּרְכָּהּ לֵיאָסֵר בֵּין לוֹ בֵּין לְאַחֵר הִיא נִבְדֶּקֶת. אֲבָל הוּא **לִכְשֶׁתִּשְׁתֶּה** הוּא נִבְדָּק. בָּדְקוּ אוֹתוֹ וְלֹא אוֹתָהּ. אֲנִי אוֹמֵר. הַזְּכוּת תּוֹלָה. נִיחָא **לְמַאן דְּאָמַר**. הַזְּכוּת תּוֹלָה **לָהּ וְאֵינוֹ** נִכֶּרֶת. בְּרַם כְּמַאן **דְּאָמַר**. הַזְּכוּת תּוֹלָה וְנִכֶּרֶת. הֲרֵי לֹא הוּכְרָה. אֶלָּא אֲנִי אוֹמֵר. מַיִם מְגוּלִּין **שָׁתָה וְנִצְבָּה**. הָכֵין לָא הֲוָון **בְּעָיָא** מִבְדְּקוּנֵיהּ אֶלָּא **כְדִין**. אֶלָּא אֲנִי אוֹמֵר. עִם אֲחֵרִים **הָיָה** נִסְתְּרָה. וְלֹא כֵן סַבְרִינַן מֵימַר. **לִכְשֶׁתִּשְׁתֶּה** הוּא נִבְדָּק. תִּיפְתַּר שֶׁהָיָה הוּא מֵזִיד וְהִיא שׁוֹגֶגֶת וּבָדְקוּ אוֹתוֹ וְלֹא בָּדְקוּ אוֹתָהּ. **בָּדְקוּ אוֹתָהּ וְלֹא בָּדְקוּ אוֹתוֹ.** אֲנִי אוֹמֵר. הַזְּכוּת תָּלָה **לֵיהּ**. נִיחָא כְּמַאן **דְּאָמַר**. הַזְּכוּת תּוֹלָה וְאֵינָהּ נִכֶּרֶת. בְּרַם כְּמַאן **דְּאָמַר**. הַזְּכוּת תּוֹלָה וְנִכֶּרֶת. הֲרֵי הוּא לֹא **הוּעַד**. אֶלָּא אֲנִי אוֹמֵר. מַיִם מְגוּלִּים שָׁתָת **וְנִצְבֵּת**. הָכֵין לָא הֲוָה בָּעֵי מִבְדְּקוּנָהּ אֶלָּא **כְדִין**. אֶלָּא אֲנִי אוֹמֵר. עִם אֲחֵרִים נִסְתְּרָה. מֵעַתָּה גֵרַשׁ יְהֵא מוּתָּר בָּהּ. תִּיפְתַּר שֶׁהָיָה הוּא שׁוֹגֵג וְהִיא מֵזִידָה. וּבָדְקוּ אוֹתָהּ וְלֹא בָּדְקוּ אוֹתוֹ. הוּא מֵזִיד וְהִיא שׁוֹגֶגֶת. פְּשִׁיטָא שֶׁהִיא מוּתֶּרֶת לְבֵיתָהּ. גֵּרַשׁ. מַהוּ שֶׁיְּהֵא מוּתָּר בָּהּ. אִיפְשַׁר לוֹמַר מֵזִיד בָּהּ. וְאַתְּ אָמְרַתְּ הָכֵין. הוּא שׁוֹגֵג וְהִיא מֵזִידָה. פְּשִׁיטָה שֶׁהִיא אֲסוּרָה לְבֵיתָהּ. גֵּרַשׁ. מַהוּ שֶׁיְּהֵא מוּתָּר בָּהּ. אִיפְשַׁר לוֹמַר יוֹצְאָה מִתַּחַת יָדוֹ **וְאַתְּ אָמַר** הָכֵין. וּמִנַּיִן שֶׁהַדָּבָר תָּלוּי בָּהּ. שִׁמְעוֹן בֶּן **רִבִּי** אַבָּא בְּשֵׁם רִבִּי יוֹחָנָן. **אָמַר** וְאֶל אֵשֶׁת עֲמִיתְךָ לֹא יִתֵּן שְׁכָבְתְּךָ לְזָרַע לְטָמְאָה בָהּ. בָּהּ הַדָּבָר תָּלוּי. אִם הָיְתָה מֵזִידָה אֲסוּרָה. שׁוֹגֶגֶת מוּתֶּרֶת.

Since Tosaphot in the first Chapter does not quote the Yerushalmi but in the following copies the Yerushalmi frequently, it seems that the printed Tosaphot of the later chapters are from a different author; against E. E. Urbach in בעלי התוספות, ירושלים תשמ"ח

14 Tosaphot לִכְשֶׁתִּשְׁתֶּה "when she will drink (the paramour will be checked out)". This reading implies that the water acts on the paramour at a distance. The text before us could be read either as לִכְשֶׁיִּשְׁתֶּה "when he (the paramour) will drink (on the husband's demand)" or, befitting the context, as לִכְשֶׁיַּשְׁקֶה "if (the husband) will make (the wife) drink". As explained in the Introduction to *Berakhot*, medieval authors are not to be considered as ms. sources, even if the passage is quoted

for itself, not in the course of an argument where paraphrases are common. The reading of Tosaphot is not a reason to question the ms. text.

15 The scribe wrote מבדקוניה. It seems that the ms. before him had מבדקוניה, "to check him out", but the scribe recognized that the masculine was inappropriate and indicated that one should read מבדקונָהּ, "to check her out".

16 The next few sentences are copied from Chapter 1, Note 128. But see the Tosaphot text in which only one sentence from there (and *Yebamot* Chapter 10, Notes 49 ff.) appears.

17 Cf. Mishnah 2:5 that the husband may stipulate that the water check her out not only for adultery with the named respondent but with any man whosoever.

18 The husband.

19 The suspected adulterer.

20 The water is presumed to act at a distance, to make the adulterer's belly swell and his waist disappear. (Cf. Note 14).

21 Cf. Chapter 3, Halakhot 4,5.

22 Water which was left standing uncovered and unattended may contain snake poison, cf. *Terumot* 8:5, in particular Notes 113 ff.

23 Meaning the adulterer's.

24 Reading כדין "correctly" with Tosaphot, against a nondescript כדון "so" in the text. It would be against all rules if water which was left unattended in a vessel were used in the Temple.

25 The accused boy friend was an adulterer but not with that woman.

26 The water acts at a distance only from a woman with whom he actually committed adultery; the explanation attempted in the previous sentence is impossible.

27 If either it was a case similar to date rape or that the adulterer impersonated the husband.

28 Added from Tosaphot, missing in the mss.

29 From Tosaphot text.

30 The Yerushalmi forbids the wife even to the unintentional adulterer; e. g., if she told him that she was single.

31 *Lev.* 18:20.

32 Everything depends on her status; since a rape victim is permitted to her husband, the divorced rape victim is permitted to the rapist but the woman who pretended to be single is forbidden to her boyfriend after her divorce.

משנה ב: בּוֹ בַיּוֹם דָּרַשׁ רַבִּי עֲקִיבָה וְכָל־כְּלִי חֶרֶשׂ אֲשֶׁר יִפֹּל מֵהֶם אֶל תּוֹכוֹ כֹּל אֲשֶׁר בְּתוֹכוֹ יִטְמָא. אֵינוֹ אוֹמֵר טָמֵא אֶלָּא יִטְמָא לְטַמֵּא אֶת אֲחֵרִים לִימַּד עַל כִּכָּר הַשֵּׁנִי שֶׁמְּטַמֵּא אֶת הַשְּׁלִישִׁי.

משנה ג: אָמַר רְבִּי יְהוֹשֻׁעַ מִי יְגַלֶּה עָפָר מֵעֵינֶיךָ רַבָּן יוֹחָנָן בֶּן זַכַּאי שֶׁהָיִיתָ אוֹמֵר עָתִיד דּוֹר אַחֵר לְטַהֵר אֶת כִּכָּר הַשְּׁלִישִׁי שֶׁאֵין לוֹ מִן הַתּוֹרָה שֶׁהוּא טָמֵא וַהֲלֹא עֲקִיבָה תַלְמִידְךָ מֵבִיא לוֹ מִקְרָא מִן הַתּוֹרָה שֶׁהוּא טָמֵא שֶׁנֶּאֱמַר כֹּל אֲשֶׁר בְּתוֹכוֹ יִטְמָא.

Mishnah 2: On the same day[33], Rebbi Aqiba explained: "Any clay vessel into which some of them would fall, all inside shall become impure.[34]" It does not say "is impure" but "shall become impure"[35]; this teaches about the secondarily impure loaf that it defiles the tertiary.

Mishnah 3: Rebbi Joshua said, who would remove the dust from your eyes, Rabban Johanan ben Zakkai, since you were saying that a future generation would purify the tertiary loaf since there is nothing about it in the Torah[36], but behold, your student Aqiba supports it by a verse from the Torah, as it has been said, "everything inside shall become impure."

33 According to the Babli (*Berakhot* 28a), any Mishnah which starts "on the same day" was formulated on the day Rabban Gamliel was deposed. There is no proof that this ever was a Galilean tradition.

34 *Lev.* 11:33, speaking of dead reptiles (which are carriers of original impurity) falling into a clay vessel. In the biblical laws of impurity, no defilement is imparted to a clay vessel touched by impurities from the outside. But if the clay vessel encloses a space that can be covered and something of original impurity enters the space (even before it touches any wall), the entire vessel becomes impure in the first degree. {Degrees of impurity are explained in the commentary to *Demay*, Chapter 2, Note 137.} Therefore, any food inside the vessel becomes impure in the second degree. If that food touches food susceptible to tertiary impurity, the latter becomes impure in

the third degree. Which food can become impure in the third and fourth degrees is a matter of discussion in the Halakhah.

The same verse states that a clay vessel can be purified only by being broken. The shards become pure writing material.

35 Probably he reads יְטַמֵּא "it will defile" in place of יִטְמָא "it shall become impure". Revocalization of the consonantal text is a technique accepted by R. Aqiba, rejected by R. Ismael.

36 He holds that the possibility of tertiary impurity for heave and sacrifices and quaternary for sacrifices is traditional rather than biblical.

The slightly enlarged text is also in *Sifra Šemini Parasha* 7(12).

(fol. 20a) **הלכה ב**: בּוֹ בַיּוֹם דָּרַשׁ רִבִּי עֲקִיבָה כוּל'. רִבִּי יוֹסֵי בֵּי רִבִּי בּוּן אָמַר. רַב וּשְׁמוּאֵל. חַד אָמַר. בֵּין בִּתְרוּמָה בֵין בְּחוּלִין אָמַר רִבִּי עֲקִיבָה. וְחָרָנָה אָמַר. בִּתְרוּמָה אֲבָל לֹא בְחוּלִין. וְלֹא יָדְעִין מָאן אָמַר דָּא וּמָאן אָמַר דָּא. מִן מַה דְּאָמַר רִבִּי יוֹסֵי בְּשֵׁם רִבִּי יוֹנָה. אָמְרִי לָהּ רַב בְּשֵׁם רִבִּי חִייָה רוֹבָא. הַשְּׁלִישִׁי בָּא מֵחֲמַת הַשֶּׁרֶץ. הֲוֵי אוֹמֵר. הוּא דוּ אָמַר. בֵּין בִּתְרוּמָה בֵּין בְּחוּלִין אָמַר רִבִּי עֲקִיבָה. מַתְנִיתָא פְּלִיגָא עַל רַב. אוֹכֵל מַעֲשֵׂר שֶׁהוּכְשַׁר בְּמַשְׁקֶה וְנָגַע בּוֹ טְבוּל יוֹם אוֹ יָדַיִם מְסוֹאָבוֹת. מַפְרִישִׁין מִמֶּנּוּ תְּרוּמַת מַעֲשֵׂר בְּטָהֳרָה מִפְּנֵי שֶׁהוּא שְׁלִישִׁי. וְהַשְּׁלִישִׁי טָהוֹר בְּחוּלִין. פָּתַר לְהָקֵל הוּא. בְּיָדַיִם שֶׁהֵן מִדִּבְרֵיהֶן. וְהָא תַנִּינָן טְבוּל יוֹם. תִּיפְתָּר בִּטְבוּל יוֹם בֵּית הַפְּרָס. אָמַר רִבִּי זְעִירָא. וַאֲפִילוּ תֵימַר. בִּטְבוּל יוֹם דְּבַר תּוֹרָה. שַׁנְיָיא הִיא דִכְתִיב טָהוֹר טָמֵא. טָהוֹר לְחוּלִין מִבְּעוֹד יוֹם וְלִתְרוּמָה מִשֶּׁתֶּחְשָׁךְ. הָתִיב רִבִּי חַגַּיי קוֹמֵי רִבִּי יוֹסֵי. אוֹ נֵימַר. טָהוֹר בְּמַגָּע וְטָמֵא בַאֲכִילָה. אָמַר לֵיהּ. כֵּלִים אֲמוּרִין בַּפָּרָשָׁה. אִית לָךְ מֵימַר גַּבֵּי כֵלִים טְהוֹרִים בְּמַגָּע וּטְמֵאִים בַּאֲכִילָה.

Halakhah 2: "On the same day, Rebbi Aqiba explained," etc. Rebbi Yose ben Rebbi Abun said, Rav and Samuel. One said, Rebbi Aqiba referred to both heave and profane food, but the other referred to heave but not to profane food[37]. But one does not know who said what. Since

Rebbi Yose said in the name of Rebbi Jonah, they said, Rav in the name of the elder Rebbi Ḥiyya: The tertiary comes because of the reptile[38]. This implies that he said that Rebbi Aqiba referred to both heave and profane food[39]. A Mishnah disagrees with Rav: [40]"If tithe food was prepared [for impurity] by a fluid[41] and a *tevul yom*[42] or unclean hands[43] touched it, one may take from it the heave of the tithe in purity because it is tertiary[44], and the tertiary is pure for profane food." He explains that it is a leniency about hands [whose impurity] is rabbinical. But did we not state: "A *tevul yom*"? Explain it by a *tevul yom* from [the impurity] of a broken field[45]. Rebbi Zeïra said, you may even say a biblical *tevul yom*. There is a difference since it is written "pure, impure"[46]. Pure for profane food during daytime and for heave when it gets dark. Rebbi Ḥaggai objected before Rebbi Yose: May we not say: Pure for touch and impure for eating[47]? He answered him, vessels are mentioned in the paragraph! Can you say about vessels that they are pure for touch and impure for eating[48]?

37 The question is whether profane pure food touched by something impure in the second degree remains pure or becomes impure in the third degree.

38 See Note 34. An additional argument, mentioned in Babli 29b, is needed to clarify the statement of R. Aqiba. An original source of impurity is either a "father of impurity" which in touching a pure vessel, person, or food induces primary impurity, or a "grandfather of impurity" creating a "father of impurity" by contact (cf. *Demay*, Chapter 2, Note 137). If a piece of "grandfather of impurity" falls into the clay vessel, the vessel becomes "father of impurity" and the loaf lying in it becomes impure in the first degree. In that case, one has ample biblical references that the loaf is still active in transmitting impurity, generating secondary impurity; the tertiary impurity mentioned by R.

Aqiba is not addressed. Therefore, it is important to state that *Lev.* 11:33 is written in a paragraph dealing with the impurity of dead reptiles which are only "fathers of impurity", inducing impurities that can be washed off by immersion in water. In the entire paragraph, no mention is made of sanctified food. Therefore, the impurity of dead reptiles implies the existence of tertiary impurity of profane food.

39   The Babli, 29a, knows only that Rav holds that tertiary impurity does not exist for profane food. It does not mention any contrary opinion.

40   Mishnah *Tevul Yom* 4:1.

41   Solid food can become impure only if it was in contact with either water or human body fluids under certain circumstances; cf. *Demay* Chapter 2, Note 141.

42   A person who was impure and cleansed himself by immersion in water during daytime. It is explained in *Lev.* 22:6-7 that impurity is removed by immersion in water during daytime "and when the sun disappears he will be pure; afterwards, he may eat sanctified food." (The Babli, *Berakhot* 2a/b, discusses whether וּבָא הַשֶּׁמֶשׁ means "the sun disappears" or "the sun rises"). The *tevul yom* therefore is no longer impure but before sundown he is not pure for sanctified food; cf. *Demay* Chapter 2, Note 138; *Terumot* Chapter 2, Note 51. Since he is forbidden only sanctified food, one may assume that he is pure for profane food. In rabbinical terms, the *tevul yom* after immersion but before sundown is treated as impure in the second degree.

43   Unwashed hands, of an otherwise pure person, are always rabbinically impure in the second degree until washed with at least a *revi'it* (135 cl) of water; cf. *Bikkurim* Chapter 2, Note 4; *Demay* Chapter 2, Note 160.

44   Tithe food in the hand of a Levite is totally profane. The Levite is required to give 10% of the tithe to the Cohen as heave of the tithe, which is sanctified food. While the tithe before the separation of the heave is forbidden as *tevel*, it is not sanctified and any impurity, even secondary, would eliminate the tithe as a source of heave (cf. *Hallah*, Chapter 3, Notes 43-44). If the *tevul yom* may touch tithe from which no heave was given it proves that tertiary impurity does not apply to profane food.

45   A "broken field" is agricultural property of which it is known that it once contained a grave. The position

of the grave is unknown; also it is unknown whether bones from the grave have been dispersed on the field by ploughing. Since there are doubts whether any impurity still exists or where it might be, and it is an open field (where a doubt of impurity is inactive, cf. Chapter 1, Notes 87-96), a person walking over the field is only rabbinically impure.

46 *Lev.* 11:32 has expressions of purity and impurity: "It shall be immersed in water, be impure until evening, and be pure". This implies that a *tevul yom* vessel is both impure and pure; it is according to tradition that one decides in which domain it is pure and in which impure. In 22:6-7, the *tevul yom* person is only forbidden sanctified food in his intermediary state.

47 Since the distinction of the influence of a *tevul yom* on profane or sanctified food is one of interpretation, could one not understand from the verses that the *tevul yom* contaminates any food but is free to touch?

48 The rules of purification in stages by immersion in water (*Lev.* 11:32) deal with vessels, which are inedible.

(20a, line 49) מַתְנִיתָא מְסַייעָא לְרַב. הָרִאשׁוֹן שֶׁבְּחוּלִּין טָמֵא וּמטַמֵּא וְהַשֵּׁנִי פּוֹסֵל וְלֹא מְטַמֵּא וְהַשְּׁלִישִׁי נֶאֱכָל בְּנְזִיד הַדֶּמַע. הָא לַעֲשׂוֹתוֹ דְּמַע אָסוּר וְאָסוּר דְּבַתְרָא. הָרִאשׁוֹן וְהַשֵּׁנִי שֶׁבַּתְּרוּמָה טְמֵאִין וּמטַמְּאִין. וְהַשְּׁלִישִׁי פּוֹסֵל וְלֹא מְטַמֵּא. וְהָרְבִיעִי נֶאֱכָל בְּנְזִיד הַקּוֹדֶשׁ. אִין תֵּימַר. הָא לַעֲשׂוֹתוֹ קוֹדֶשׁ אָסוּר. אַשְׁכָּחַת מֵימַר מִחְלְפָה שִׁיטָתֵיהּ דְּרַב. דָּמַר רִבִּי בָּא בְּשֵׁם רַב. שְׁלִישִׁי בָּא מֵחֲמַת הַשֶּׁרֶץ וְהָרְבִיעִי מוּתָּר לַעֲשׂוֹתוֹ קוֹדֶשׁ. שֶׁלֹא אָמְרוּ רְבִיעִי בַּקּוֹדֶשׁ אֶלָּא בְּקָדְשֵׁי הַמִּקְדָּשׁ מְקוּדָּשִׁין. אָמַר רִבִּי חוּנָה. וְלֹא בִתְרוּמָה אָנָן קַייָמִין. וּתְרוּמָה אָסוּר לַעֲשׂוֹתָהּ קוֹדֶשׁ שֶׁלֹא לְהַמְצִיא בָּהּ תְּקָלָה. וְאָמוּר דְּבַתְרָא. הָרִאשׁוֹן וְהַשֵּׁנִי וְהַשְּׁלִישִׁי שֶׁבַּקּוֹדֶשׁ טְמֵאִים וּמטַמְּאִים. וְהָרְבִיעִי פְּסִיל וְלֹא מְטַמֵּא. וְהַחֲמִישִׁי נֶאֱכָל בְּנְזִיד הַקּוֹדֶשׁ. אִין תֵּימַר. הָא לַעֲשׂוֹתוֹ קוֹדֶשׁ אָסוּר. וְכִי יֵשׁ חֲמִישִׁי בַּקּוֹדֶשׁ. וְאַתְּ אָמַר לֵית כֵּן. וְהָכָא לֵית כֵּן.

A Mishnah[49] supports Rav: "Profane food which is impure primarily is impure and defiles, secondarily it invalidates[50] but does not defile, but the tertiary can be eaten in heave broth.[51]" This implies that it is forbidden to turn it into heave[52]. And it is said[53] after that[54]: "Heave which is impure primarily or secondarily is impure and defiles, tertiarily impure it invalidates but does not defile, but the fourth degree can be eaten in sacrificial broth." If you say that it is forbidden to turn it into sacrificial food, you would find that Rav's statements are contradictory since Rebbi Abba said in the name of Rav: The tertiary comes because of the reptile but the fourth degree can be turned into sacrificial food, because they spoke about fourth degree [of impurity] for sacrifices only for dedicated sacrifices of the Temple[55]! Rebbi Huna said, are we not talking about heave? But it is forbidden to turn heave into sacrificial food in order to avoid accidents[56]! And it was said after that[57]: "Sacrifices which are impure primarily, secondarily, or tertiarily are impure and defile, impurity in the fourth degree invalidates but does not defile, but the fifth degree can be eaten in sacrificial broth." If you say, it is forbidden to turn it into sacrificial food, is there any impurity of the fifth degree in sacrifices[58]? But you say there is not. So here also, there is not.

49   Ṭahorot 2:3.

50   Food whose impurity is contagious is called טמא "impure"; if it cannot be used for any purpose but is not contagious it is called פסול "invalid". Secondarily impure profane food invalidates heave by its touch.

51   The Cohen who eats heave can cook his meal with profane spices that have touched secondarily impure food since secondarily impure profane food is inactive if it touches other profane food.

52   Since it is only permitted to spice heave broth with spices that have touched secondarily impure food, it is implied that the potentially tertiary cannot itself be dedicated as heave.

53   In parallel with the later text, אסור is read as a misspelling for אמור, following all commentators.

54   Ṭahorot 2:4. The Babli, 30a,

quotes Mishnah *Tahorot* 2:2 in which R. Joshua disagrees.

55 Cf. Note 38. It is clear that *Lev.* knows of a status of invalid sacrificial food induced by touching impurity since v. 7:19 requires that sacrificial meat which touched impurity must be burned but is not labelled "impure". In Chapter 11, vessels which touched a dead reptile are called "impure". Therefore, it is established that for sacrifices, anything declared impure in v. 11:33 invalidates sacrifices by its touch. This means that for R. Aqiba in Rav's interpretation, the fourth degree of impurity in the Temple is biblical, but for the rabbis (and for R. Aqiba in Samuel's interpretation) only tertiary invalidity is biblical. (Babli 29b).

56 It is a positive commandment for the Cohen to consume his heave (*Num.* 18:11). Therefore, it is forbidden to expose heave to situations where it could no longer be consumed. But sacrificial food can become invalidated in many ways (such as leaving the Temple precinct, being left overnight, etc.) that would not invalidate heave. Therefore, mixing heave with sacrificial food exposes the Cohen to sinning.

57 *Tahorot* 2:5.

58 Since sacrificial food touching invalid food of the fourth degree remains pure by the definition of invalidity, there can be no reason why profane food prepared by the standards of sacrificial purity could not be dedicated as a valid sacrifice. Therefore, the argument that the Mishnah permits only the addition of profane food one step removed from invalidity to heave but not turning it into heave has no basis in the text and the Mishnah does not support Rav's position.

(20a, line 61) אָמַר רִבִּי יוֹחָנָן. הַשְּׁלִישִׁי בָּא מַחֲמַת שֶׁרֶץ אָסוּר לַעֲשׂוֹתוֹ תְּרוּמָה. בָּעֵי קוֹמוֹי. אֲפִילוּ כְרִבִּי עֲקִיבָה. רִבִּי יוֹסֵי בְּשֵׁם רִבִּי הִילָא. וַאֲפִילוּ כְרִבִּי עֲקִיבָא וְלָמָּה. טְבוּל יוֹם פְּסִיל וְהַשֵּׁינִי פָּסִיל. מַה טְּבוּל יוֹם אֵינוֹ פוֹסֵל אֶת הַחוּלִין מִלַּעֲשׂוֹתָן תְּרוּמָה. אַף הַשֵּׁנִי אֵינוֹ פוֹסֵל אֶת הַחוּלִין מִלַּעֲשׂוֹתָן תְּרוּמָה. רִבִּי יוֹסֵי בְּשֵׁם רִבִּי יוֹחָנָן. שְׁלִישִׁי בָּא מַחֲמַת שֶׁרֶץ אָסוּר לַעֲשׂוֹתוֹ תְּרוּמָה וּמוּתָּר לַעֲשׂוֹתוֹ קוֹדֶשׁ. רִבִּי זְעִירָא בְּעָא קוֹמֵי רִבִּי יָסָא. מְטַמֵּא בַקּוֹדֶשׁ. וְאַתְּ אָמַר אָכֵין. אֲמַר לֵיהּ. מִשּׁוּם מַעֲלָה. אָמַר רִבִּי שְׁמוּאֵל בַּר רַב יִצְחָק. עִיקַר

טוּמְאָתוֹ בַּקּוֹדֶשׁ מִשּׁוּם מַעֲלָה. אָמַר רִבִּי יוֹסֵי. וְלָמָּה הוּא מְטַמֵּא בַּקּוֹדֶשׁ
מִשּׁוּם מַעֲלָה. אָמַר רִבִּי יוּדָן. וַאֲפִילוּ כְּרַבָּנָן דְּאִינּוּן אָמְרִין. אֵין הַשְּׁלִישִׁי
בְחוּלִין. וְלָמָּה הוּא אָסוּר. מְטַמֵּא בַּקּוֹדֶשׁ. מִשּׁוּם מַעֲלָה. אָמַר לֵיהּ רִבִּי יוֹסֵי.
וְלֵית אֲנָן צְרִיכִין שְׁמָעִין לֵיהּ מִן בַּר נָשׁ רַב.

Rebbi Joḥanan said: The tertiary comes because of the reptile[38] but it is (forbidden) [permitted][59] to turn it into heave. They asked before him: Even for Rebbi Aqiba? Rebbi Yose in the name of Rebbi Hila: Even following Rebbi Aqiba. And why? The *tevul yom* makes invalid, secondary impurity makes invalid. Just as the *tevul yom* does not invalidate profane food that it could not be turned into heave[42], so secondary impurity does not invalidate profane food that it could not be turned into heave. Rebbi Yose in the name of Rebbi Joḥanan: The tertiary comes because of the reptile[38], and it is (forbidden) [permitted][59] to turn it into heave but (permitted) [forbidden][60] to turn it into sacrificial food. Rebbi Ze'ira asked before Rebbi Yasa: It defiles sacrifices and you say so[61]? He said to him, because of the distinction[62]. Rebbi Samuel ben Rebbi Isaac said, the source of its impurity is the distinction[63]. Rebbi Yose said, why does it defile sacrifices? Because of the distinction. Rebbi Yudan said, even for the rabbis who say that there is no tertiary in profane food, why is it forbidden? It defiles sacrifices because of the distinction. Rebbi Yose said to him, do we not need to hear this from a great personality[64]?

59 While both mss. read אסור, the following argument shows that it must read מותר.

60 If the first term reads "permitted", this one must read "prohibited", against the testimony of both mss. While a point could be made here to read "permitted", it would involve some twisting of the following argument.

61 Since tertiary impurity induces one of the fourth degree, what is the point in stating that one may not turn tertiary food into sacrifices? It is implied that vegetable sacrifices (flour, wine, oil, and incense) must be prepared by the standards of sacrificial food from the moment they become susceptible to impurity.

62 Except for R. Aqiba in the interpretation of Rav, invalidity of sacrifices of fourth degree impurity is purely rabbinic, to elevate sacrifices one step over heave which has no connection with the Temple; cf. Note 55.

63 This student of Rav and Rav Huna agrees with R. Yasa (Assi), student of Samuel and R. Joḥanan, that impurity of the fourth degree is purely rabbinical.

64 That two fifth-generation Amoraïm have to confirm the consensus of the third generation shows that this purely theoretical statement, almost 300 years after the destruction of the Temple, failed to be accepted popularly. It is defended at length in the Babli, *Ḥagigah* 22a/b.

(20a, line 71) תַּמָּן אָמְרִין. מִמָּה שֶׁקִּילֵס רִבִּי יְהוֹשֻׁעַ אֶת רִבִּי עֲקִיבָה הָדָא אָמְרָה. הֲלָכָה כְיוֹצֵא בוֹ. רַבָּנִן דְּקַיְסָרִין אָמְרִין. לְמִדְרָשׁוֹ קִילְסוֹ. אֲבָל לְמַעֲשֶׂה אֵין הֲלָכָה כְיוֹצֵא בוֹ. דָּמַר רִבִּי אָחָא רִבִּי מַיְישָׁא בְשֵׁם רִבִּי לָעְזָר. לוֹקִין עַל הַשְּׁלִישִׁי שֶׁבְּמַעֲשֵׂה⁶⁵ וַאֲפִילוּ כְרִבִּי עֲקִיבָה. רִבִּי יוּדָן בְּשֵׁם רִבִּי אִילַי. וַאֲפִילוּ כְרִבִּי עֲקִיבָה אֵינָן לוֹקִין. לָמָה. טְבוּל יוֹם פּוֹסֵל וְהַשֵּׁינִי פּוֹסֵל. מַה טְּבוּל יוֹם אֵין לוֹ מַגָּע אֵצֶל הַחוֹלִין. אַף הַשֵּׁינִי אֵין לוֹ מַגָּע אֵצֶל הַחוּלִין. אָמַר רִבִּי אֶלְעָזָר. כְּמִינְיָין הַחוּלִין כָּךְ מִנְיָין הַמַּעֲשֵׂר. וְאַתְיָיא כַּיי דָּמַר רִבִּי יוֹנָה רִבִּי אִימִי בְשֵׁם רִבִּי שִׁמְעוֹן בֶּן לָקִישׁ. בְּכָל חוּלִין אֲנָן קַיָּימִין. וְאָהֵן פִּירְקָא מַעֲשֵׂר אִינּוּן. אָמַר רִבִּי יוֹסֵי. וַאֲפִילוּ רִאשׁוֹן שֶׁבּוֹ אֵינוֹ מְחוּוָר. לֹא אוֹכַל אֵין כְּתִיב כַּאן אֶלָּא לֹא אָכַלְתִּי. מִכֵּיוָן⁶⁶ דִּכְתִיב כְּכָל־מִצְוֹתֶיךָ אֲשֶׁר צִוִּיתָנִי. כְּמִי שֶׁאֵינוֹ מְחוּוָר.

There, they say, because Rebbi Joshua praised Rebbi Aqiba, it implies that practice follows his argument. The rabbis of Caesarea say, he praised him for his ingenuity, but in fact practice does not follow his argument, since Rebbi Aḥa, Rebbi Maisha, in the name of Rebbi Eleazar said, one whips for tertiary [impurity] for tithes[66], even[67] according to Rebbi Aqiba. Rebbi Yudan in the name of Rebbi Hilai: Even according to Rebbi Aqiba one does not whip. Why? The *ṭevul yom* makes invalid, secondary impurity makes invalid. Since the *ṭevul yom* has no touch for profane food[68], also secondary impurity has no touch for profane food[69]. Rebbi Eleazar said, as the count for profane food so is the count of tithes[70]. This corresponds to what Rebbi Jonah, Rebbi Immi, said in the name of Rebbi Simeon ben Laqish: We deal with somebody who ate[71] profane food, and that Chapter deals with tithe[72]. Rebbi Yose said, even its primary [impurity] is not clear. Not "I will not eat" is written, but "I did not eat."[73] Rebbi Abba Mari said, since it is written "following all Your commandments which You commanded me," is it as if it were not clear[74]?

65   While this is the text in both mss., one has to read מַעֲשֵׂר.

66   This refers to the Second Tithe, food that the farmer retains for himself and his family, to be eaten in purity in Jerusalem. On that occasion, he has to declare in the Temple that he "did not separate it while impure" (*Deut.* 26:14; *Bikkurim* 2:2). This implies that Second Tithe becomes desecrated by impurity and must be redeemed. The question is whether eating Second Tithe in any state of impurity is a criminal offense, for which the punishment is whipping. The thesis advanced here is that Second Tithe has a status equal to heave, so that tertiary impurity makes that tithe unusable.

The Babli certainly agrees that the statement of R. Joshua is not an endorsement of the practice since it quotes Mishnah *Tahorot* 2:2 in which R. Joshua disagrees with R. Eliezer whom R. Aqiba follows.

It is always held that first tithe after separation of the heave of the tithe is totally profane in the hand of the Levite, even if consumption is restricted to Levites of good standing.

67   The meaning of this word is

unclear; possibly this is a reflection from "even" in the next sentence.

68 This means that as far as the status of purity is concerned, the touch of a *tevul yom* is totally irrelevant.

69 Since Second Tithe is eaten by the farmer's family, without anything being given to Cohanim or Levites, it cannot have the status of sanctified food.

70 Since for profane food one has only primary and secondary impurity, not tertiary, the same holds for tithes. This contradicts the statement quoted earlier in the name of R. Eleazar.

71 Reading בָּכַל as contraction of בְּאָכַל

72 Chapter 2 of *Tahorot*, which was quoted in the previous paragraph and which details the stages of impurity, mentions only profane, heave, and sacrificial foods. Since the tithes are not mentioned and First Tithe is profane, it is clear that tithes are classified with profane food.

73 *Deut.* 26:14. It is clear that if the farmer ate some Second Tithe in impurity, he cannot make the declaration in the Temple. But this does not imply that eating in impurity is forbidden as a criminal act.

74 Since the verse classifies all that is mentioned there as God's commandments, necessarily the infractions which bar the farmer from making the declaration are criminal acts.

(20b, line 6) רִבִּי אַבָּהוּ בְשֵׁם רִבִּי מָנָא. מִפְּנֵי מַה אָמְרוּ. הַשֵּׁינִי שֶׁבַּחוּלִין מְטַמֵּא מַשְׁקֵה חוּלִין. מִפְּנֵי הַיָּדַיִם. [מַה הַיָּדַיִם]⁷⁵ שֶׁהֵן מִדִּבְרֵיהֶן מְטַמְאוֹת מַשְׁקֵה חוּלִין. שֵׁינִי שֶׁהוּא מִדְּבַר תּוֹרָה לֹא כָּל־שֶׁכֵּן. אִי מַה הַיָּדַיִם סְפֵיקָן לְטַמֵּא אֶת אֲחֵרִים טָמֵא. אַף הַמַּשְׁקִין סְפֵיקָן לְטַמֵּא אֶת אֲחֵרִים טָמֵא. הָתִיב רִבִּי חֲנִינָא לְרִבִּי מָנָא. הֲרֵי אוֹכֶל אוֹכְלִין טְמֵאִין וְשׁוֹתֶה מַשְׁקִין טְמֵאִין סְפֵיקָן לְטַמֵּא אֶת אֲחֵרִים טָמֵא. וְהַמַּשְׁקִין הַיוֹצְאִין מֵהֶן סְפֵיקָן לְטַמֵּא אֶת אֲחֵרִים טָמֵא. וְהָא שֵׁינִי שֶׁהוּא דְּבַר תּוֹרָה סְפֵיקוֹ לְטַמֵּא אֶת אֲחֵרִים טָהוֹר. אָמַר רִבִּי חֲנִינָה קוֹמֵי רִבִּי מָנָא. וְלֹא בִּתְרוּמָה אֲנָן קַיָּימִין. אָמַר לֵיהּ. וַאֲפִילוּ תֵּימַר. בִּתְרוּמָה אֲנָן קַיָּימִין. מַה אִית לֵיהּ טָמֵא יְטַמָּא דְּבַר תּוֹרָה. לֹא רִבִּי עֲקִיבָה.

Rebbi Abbahu in the name of Rebbi Mana[76]: Why did they say that secondarily impure profane food defiles profane fluids[77]? Because of the hands. Since hands, [whose impurity] is rabbinical, defile profane fluids, secondarily impure food, [whose impurity] is biblical, not so much more[78]? Also, since hands, in a case of doubt whether they defiled, impart impurity, so also secondarily impure fluids, in a case of doubt whether they defiled, impart impurity[79]. Rebbi Hanina objected before Rebbi Mana: Look, if somebody eats secondarily impure food and drinks secondarily impure fluids, in a case of doubt whether they defiled, they impart impurity. But secondarily impure foods by biblical standards, in a case of doubt whether they defiled, leave it pure[80]! Rebbi Hanina said before Rebbi Mana[81]: Do we not deal with heave? He said to him, even if you say that we deal with heave; is the one who argues "is impure", "shall become impure"[35] as word of the Torah not Rebbi Aqiba[82]?

75 From the Rome ms., missing in the Leiden ms.

76 R. Mana I.

77 It is a general principle that impure fluids are always primarily impure (cf. Mishnah *Parah* 8:7, *Berakhot* Chapter 5, Note 46; *Demay* Chapter 2, Note 137). This implies that fluids are never just invalid; if they were in contact with impurity, they are always active polluters. This is a rabbinic rule. The sources are discussed in detail in the author's *The Scholar's Haggadah* (Northvale 1995), pp. 230-231.

78 By rabbinic rule, unwashed hands are always secondarily impure. Washed hands remain pure as long as one does not forget about them. The argument here is that the rabbinic institution of impure hands would be incomplete and inconsistent if biblically impure foods did not have the same effect. There is no claim that secondarily impure food defiles fluids to be primarily impure by biblical standards.

79 This statement parallels the formulation everywhere in the Babli that impure fluids of any degree act as

if impure in the first degree.

The entire argument is not relevant for practice, as noted at the end of the paragraph, since Mishnah *Tahorot* 4:2 declares the food that might have been touched by secondarily impure food as pure. This is a sure sign that the argument here follows R. Aqiba.

80 Profane food cannot become impure by secondary impurity. Heave can become impure, but in a public place a doubtful impurity is inactive.

81 He seems to be R. Hanania of Sepphoris arguing before R. Mana II.

82 If secondary impurity is active, it must follow R. Aqiba who equates profane and heave foods in their stages of impurity. For everybody else, the arguments are irrelevant.

(20b, line 16) תַּמָּן אָמְרִין. שְׁתֵּי שְׁאֵילוֹת שָׁאֲלָן חַגַּי הַנָּבִיא. אַחַת הֵשִׁיבוּ אוֹתוֹ כָּרָאוּי וְאַחַת לֹא הֵשִׁיבוּ לוֹ כָּרָאוּי. הֵן יִשָּׂא אִישׁ בְּשַׂר קוֹדֶשׁ בִּכְנַף בִּגְדוֹ. כְּנַף תְּחִילָה. בְּשַׂר קוֹדֶשׁ שֵׁינִי. לֶחֶם וְנָזִיד שְׁלִישִׁי. וְיַיִן וְשֶׁמֶן וּמַאֲכָל רְבִיעִי. וְכִי יֵשׁ רְבִיעִי בַקּוֹדֶשׁ. וַיַּעֲנוּ הַכֹּהֲנִים וַיֹּאמְרוּ לֹא. לֹא הֵשִׁיבוּ אוֹתוֹ כָּרָאוּי. שֶׁיֵּשׁ רְבִיעִי בַקּוֹדֶשׁ. וַיֹּאמֶר חַגַּי אִם יִגַּע טְמֵא נֶפֶשׁ בְּכָל־אֵלֶּה הַיִטְמָא. אִם תִּהְיֶה כְּנַף טְמֵא נֶפֶשׁ וְנָגְעָה בְּכָל־אֵלֶּה. הַיִטְמָא. וַיַּעֲנוּ הַכֹּהֲנִים וַיֹּאמְרוּ יִטְמָא. הֵשִׁיבוּ אוֹתוֹ כָּרָאוּי. דָּמַר רִבִּי יִרְמְיָה רִבִּי חִייָה בְּשֵׁם רִבִּי יוֹחָנָן. קוֹדֶם עַד שֶׁלֹּא גָזְרוּ רְבִיעִי בַקּוֹדֶשׁ שָׁאֲלָן. וְלָמָּה הוּא מְקַלְּלָן. כְּאִינַשׁ דְּבָעֵי עִילָּה עַל חַבְרֵיהּ. וּבֵיתָא מַה אִיכְפַּת לָהּ. לֹא דוּ אָמַר וַאֲשֶׁר יַקְרִיבוּ שָׁם טָמֵא הוּא. כְּמָה דָמַר רִבִּי סִימוֹן בַּר זַבְדִּי. גּוּלְגּוֹלְתּוֹ שֶׁלְּאָרְנָן הַיְבוּסִי מָצְאוּ תַּחַת הַמִּזְבֵּחַ.

There[83], they say: The prophet Haggai asked two questions; one they answered correctly and one incorrectly. [84]"Assume a man carries holy meat in the corner of his garment." The corner is of primary impurity, the holy meat of second degree, bread and soup of third degree, wine, oil, and food of the fourth. Does there exist a fourth degree of impurity for sanctified food? "The Cohanim answered, and said: No." They did not answer correctly, since there is a fourth degree of impurity for sanctified food[85]. "Haggai said, if a person impure by the impurity of the dead would touch all of these, would they be impure?" If the corner would be impure by the impurity of the dead[86] and touched these. Would it be impure? "The Cohanim answered and said, it would be impure." They answered correctly. But Rebbi Jeremiah, Rebbi Hiyya said in the name of Rebbi Johanan: He asked them before they decided about fourth degree [impurity] for sanctified food[87]. Then why did he curse them[88]? As a person who looks for a pretext against his neighbor. What difference does it make for the House? Is that not what he said: "What they are sacrificing there is impure[89]"? That is what Rebbi Simon bar Zavdi said, they found the skull of Ornan the Jebusite[90] under the altar.

83 In Babylonia. However, in the Babli, *Pesahim* 17a, only one verse is discussed and Rav thinks that the question was about fourth degree impurity and the Cohen's answer was wrong but Samuel thinks that the question was about fifth degree and the answer was correct. Modern commentaries on *Haggai* 2:12-13 do not contribute to the understanding of the verses.

84 *Hag.* 2:12. In the verse, the question is הֲיִקְדַּשׁ "is it going to be forbidden as sanctified food?"; cf. Introduction to Tractate *Kilaim*. Sanctified food can be forbidden only if it is either impure or out of its proper place or time. Since the second type of prohibition is not applicable here, the question must be one of impurity.

85 This argument gives biblical status to impurity of the fourth degree but rabbinical to the primary impurity of all impure fluids. Therefore, it belongs to the tradition of R. Aqiba.

86 In that case, the garment of the mourner would have original impurity and the sacrificial meat would be impure in the first degree.

87 In that case, both answers were correct.

88 He really did not curse them but needed the answer "impure" as a starting point of his sermon.

89 *Hag.* 2:14.

89 The original owner of the Temple Mount, *1Chr.* 21:18-26. In *Pesaḥim* 9:1 (fol. 36c), *Nedarim* 6:13 (fol. 39d), *Sanhedrin* 1:2 (fol. 18d), the version is that Ezekias had to postpone the celebration of Passover (*2Chr.* 30:2-3) for a month because Ornan's skull was found under the altar (quoted by Tosaphot, *Sanhedrin* 12a). That version sounds more original.

(20b, line 28) רִבִּי אָחָא בְּשֵׁם רִבִּי אַבָּא בַּר כָּהֲנָא. בִּקְיעִין הָיוּ בְהֵיסֵיטוֹת וְלֹא הָיוּ בְקִיעִין בְּמַדָּפוֹת. הֵן יִשָּׂא אִישׁ בְּשַׂר קוֹדֶשׁ. שְׁאָלָן. טָמֵא מֵת מְטַמֵּא בְהֵיסֵט. וַיַעֲנוּ הַכֹּהֲנִים וַיֹּאמְרוּ לֹא. הֱשִׁיבוּ אוֹתוֹ כָּרָאוּי. שֶׁאֵין טָמֵא מֵת מְטַמֵּא בְהֵיסֵט. שְׁאָלָן. טָמֵא מֵת עוֹשֶׂה מַדָּף. וַיַעֲנוּ הַכֹּהֲנִים וַיֹּאמְרוּ יִטְמָא. לֹא הֱשִׁיבוּ אוֹתוֹ כָּרָאוּי. שֶׁאֵין טָמֵא מֵת עוֹשֶׂה מַדָּף.

Rebbi Aḥa in the name of Rebbi Abba bar Cahana: They were expert in pushings[90] but not expert in slight impurities. [84]"Assume a man carries holy meat," he asked them whether someone impure by the impurity of the dead imparts impurity by pushing. "The Cohanim answered, and said: No;" they answered him correctly. He asked them whether someone impure by the impurity of the dead imparts slight impurity[91]. "The Cohanim answered and said: It will be impure." They did not answer correctly, for the impurity of the dead does not impart slight impurity[92].

90 A person with gonorrhea imparts impurity to anything he moves, even if he never touched it and it was lying on a platform that could never become impure (such as a flat wooden plank.) Cf. *Demay* Chapter 2, Note 163.

91 A person with gonorrhea imparts original impurity to anything he sits on (Lev. 15:10) directly or indirectly. Anything which is above the person becomes impure rabbinically in a "slight impurity"; cf. Mishnah *Zavim* 4:6, *Demay* Chapter 2, Note 162 and J. Levy's long explanation in his Dictionary, vol. 3, s. v. מדף, with H. L. Fleischer's long etymological note, p. 305.

92 Both kinds of impurity are restricted to persons whose own body is the source of the impurity.

(20b, line 33) רִבִּי תַּנְחוּמָא רִבִּי פִינְחָס בְּשֵׁם רִבִּי לֵוִי. עַל הַחֲמִישִׁי בַּקּוֹדֶשׁ שְׁאָלָן. הֵן יִשָּׂא אִישׁ בְּשַׂר קוֹדֶשׁ בִּכְנַף בִּגְדוֹ. כְּנַף תְּחִילָה. וּבְשַׂר קוֹדֶשׁ שֵׁינִי. לֶחֶם וְנָזִיד שְׁלִישִׁי. וְיַיִן וְשֶׁמֶן רְבִיעִי. וּמַאֲכָל חֲמִישִׁי. שְׁאָלָן. וְכִי יֵשׁ חֲמִישִׁי בַּקּוֹדֶשׁ. וַיַּעֲנוּ הַכֹּהֲנִים וַיֹּאמְרוּ לֹא. הֵשִׁיבוּ אוֹתוֹ כָּרָאוּי. שֶׁאֵין חֲמִישִׁי בַּקּוֹדֶשׁ. וְלָמָּה הוּא מְקַלְלָן כְּאֵינָשׁ דְּבָעֵי עִילָּה עַל חַבְרֵיהּ. וּבֵיתָא מָה אִיכְפַּת לֵהּ. וַיֹּאמֶר וַאֲשֶׁר יַקְרִיבוּ שָׁם טָמֵא הוּא. כַּיי דָּמַר רִבִּי סִימוֹן בַּר זְבִיד. גּוּלְגּוּלְתּוֹ שֶׁלְּאָרְנָן הַיְבוּסִי מָצְאוּ תַּחַת הַמִּזְבֵּחַ.

Rebbi Tanḥuma, Rebbi Phineas, in the name of Rebbi Levi: He asked them about the fifth degree of sanctified food. [84]"Assume a man carries holy meat in the corner of his garment." The corner is of primary impurity, the holy meat of second degree, bread and soup third, wine and oil fourth, and the food of the fifth degree. Does there exist fifth degree impurity for sanctified food? "The Cohanim answered, and said: No." They did answer correctly, since there is no fifth degree impurity for sanctified food[85]. Then why did he curse them[88]? As a person who looks for a pretext against his neighbor. What difference does it make for the House? Is that not what Rebbi Simon bar Zavdi said, they found the skull of Ornan the Jebusite[90] under the altar.

(20b, line 40) תַּנֵּי. אָמַר רִבִּי יוֹסֵי. מְנַיִין לָרְבִיעִי בַּקּוֹדֶשׁ שֶׁהוּא פָסוּל. וְדִין הוּא. מָה אִם מְחוּסַּר כִּיפּוּרִים שֶׁאֵינוֹ פָסוּל[93] בִּתְרוּמָה הֲרֵי הוּא פָסוּל בַּקּוֹדֶשׁ. שְׁלִישִׁי שֶׁהוּא פָסוּל בִּתְרוּמָה אֵינוֹ דִין שֶׁיִּפָּסוֹל בַּקּוֹדֶשׁ. הֲרֵי לָמַדְנוּ לִשְׁלִישִׁי מִן הַכָּתוּב. וְלִרְבִיעִי מִקַּל וְחוֹמֶר. הָתִיב רִבִּי יוֹחָנָן. הָאוֹכֶל הַבָּא מֵחֲמַת טְבוּל יוֹם יוֹכִיחַ. שֶׁהוּא פוֹסֵל בַּתְּרוּמָה וְאֵינוֹ פוֹסֵל בַּקּוֹדֶשׁ. רִבִּי חִיָּיה בְּשֵׁם רִבִּי יוֹחָנָן.

אַתְיָיא דְּרִבִּי יוֹסֵי כְּשִׁיטָת רִבִּי עֲקִיבָה רַבּוֹ. כְּמָה דְּרִבִּי עֲקִיבָה אָמַר. יִטְמָא יִטְמָא דְּבַר תּוֹרָה. כֵּן רִבִּי יוֹסֵי אָמַר. יִטְמָא יִטְמָא דְּבַר תּוֹרָה. רִבִּי אַבָּהוּ בְּשֵׁם רִבִּי יוֹסֵי בַּר חֲנִינָה. לֵית רִבִּי יוֹסֵי צָרִיךְ לְהָדֵין קַל וָחוֹמֶר. קִרְיֵי דָרַשׁ רִבִּי יוֹסֵי. וְהַבָּשָׂר אֲשֶׁר יִגַּע. זֶה שֵׁינִי שֶׁנָּגַע בָּרִאשׁוֹן. בְּכָל טָמֵא. זֶה שְׁלִישִׁי שֶׁנָּגַע בַּשֵּׁינִי. לֹא יֵאָכֵל. סוֹף טָמֵא לֹא יֵאָכֵל.

It was stated[94]: "Rebbi Yose said, from where that the fourth degree is disabled in sanctified food? It is an argument. Since one who lacks expiation[95] is not disabled for heave[96] but disabled for sanctified food, it is only logical that third degree [impurity] which is disabled for heave should disable for sanctified food. That means, we learned third degree from a verse[97] and fourth degree from an argument *de minore ad majus*." Rebbi Johanan objected: Food that was touched by a *tevul yom* is a counter-example, because it is disabled in the case of heave but not disabled in the case of sanctified food[98]. Rebbi Hiyya in the name of Rebbi Johanan: Rebbi Yose argues the method of his teacher Rebbi Aqiba. Just as Rebbi Aqiba says "it will be impure", it makes impure by the words of the Torah, so Rebbi Yose says "it will be impure", it makes impure by the words of the Torah. Rebbi Abbahu in the name of Rebbi Yose bar Hanina: Rebbi Yose does not need that argument *de minore ad majus*. Rebbi Yose explains the verse[99]: "Any meat which would touch", that is second degree food because it touched primary impurity; "anything impure", that is third degree food because it touched second degree impurity; "shall not be eaten", the endstage of impurity cannot be eaten.

93 Reading of the Rome ms. Leiden ms. and *editio princeps*: אוכל "food".

94 *Sifra Ṣaw Parasha* 9:2, quoted in *Hagigah* 3:2, fol. 79b; Babli 29b, *Pesahim* 18b/19a, *Hagigah* 24a.

95   If a person whose body was an original source of impurity is healed, he needs immersion in water to be pure and also a ceremony of expiation to be admitted to the Sanctuary and sacrifices (for the person afflicted with skin disease, *Lev.* 14:32; for the persons healed from genital discharges 15:14-15, 29-30; for the woman after childbirth 12:6-8). After immersion in water, the person is totally pure at any place other than the Sanctuary.

96   Tosephta *Ḥagigah* 3:17.

97   In the Mishnah, following R. Aqiba.

98   Tosephta *Ḥagigah* 3:16; *Sifra Emor Pereq* 4(8).

It is proved that sanctified food is not in all respects more restrictive than sacrificial meat. It is remarkable that the Babli does not argue against the thesis of R. Yose since it clearly violates the rule דַּיּוֹ לָבוֹא מִן הַדִּין לִהְיוֹת כְּנָדוֹן "it is enough if inference drawn from an argument be equal to the premiss" (*Baba Qama* 25a). According to this rule, a passive impurity in the minor cannot become an active one in the major. The Yerushalmi knows no such rule; it needs the counter-example of R. Joḥanan. The difference between the Talmudim is that for the Yerushalmi, *de minore ad majus* is a rhetorical device but for the Babli it is part of a meta-logical system (cf. the author's *Logical Problems in Jewish Tradition*, in: *Confrontations with Judaism*, Ph. Longworth, ed., London 1966; pp. 171-196.)

99   A similar interpretation is given as an additional *baraita* in the Babli, cf. Note 94. The authorship of the *baraita* is not indicated in the Babli. The verse quoted is *Lev.* 7:19, the subject of *Sifra Ṣaw Parasha* 9.

(20b, line 50) עַד כְּדוֹן בְּאוֹכְלִין שֶׁנִּיטְמוּ בַּאֲוִיר כְּלִי חֶרֶשׂ שֶׁנִּיטְמָא בְּשֶׁרֶץ. אוֹכְלִין עַצְמָן שֶׁנִּיטְמְאוּ בְּשֶׁרֶץ מְנַיִין. וְדִין הוּא. מַה אִם הַכֵּלִים שֶׁאֵינָן מִטַּמְאִין מֵאֲוִיר כְּלִי חֶרֶשׂ שֶׁנִּיטְמָא בְּשֶׁרֶץ הֲרֵי הֵן מִטַּמְאִין כְּשֶׁרֶץ לְטַמֵּא אוֹכְלִין. [אֳכָלִין שֶׁהֵן מִטַּמְאִין מֵאֲוִיר כְּלִי חֶרֶשׂ שֶׁנִּיטְמָא בְּשֶׁרֶץ אֵינוֹ דִין שֶׁנִּיטַמְּאָן כְּשֶׁרֶץ לְטַמֵּא אֳכָלִין.] 100 עַד כְּדוֹן כְּרַבִּי עֲקִיבָה. כְּרַבִּי יִשְׁמָעֵאל. תַּנֵּי רַבִּי יִשְׁמָעֵאל. וְהַבָּשָׂר אֲשֶׁר יִגַּע בְּכָל־טָמֵא. וְזֶה רִאשׁוֹן שֶׁנָּגַע בְּכָל טָמֵא. לֹא יֵאָכֵל. לְרַבּוֹת אֶת הַשֵּׁנִי. הַשְּׁלִישִׁי מְנַיִין. וְדִין הוּא. וּמַה טְּבוּל יוֹם שֶׁאֵינוֹ

פָּסוּל בְּחוּלִּין הֲרֵי הוּא פוֹסֵל בַּתְּרוּמָה. שֵׁינִי שֶׁהוּא פוֹסֵל בְּחוּלִּין אֵינוֹ דִין שֶׁיִּפְסוֹל בַּתְּרוּמָה. רְבִיעִי בַּקּוֹדֶשׁ מְנַיִין. וְדִין הוּא. וּמָה אִם מְחוּסָּר כִּיפּוּרִים שֶׁאֵינוֹ פוֹסֵל בַּתְּרוּמָה הֲרֵי הוּא פוֹסֵל בַּקּוֹדֶשׁ. שְׁלִישִׁי שֶׁהוּא פוֹסֵל בַּתְּרוּמָה אֵינוֹ דִין שֶׁיִּפְסוֹל בַּקּוֹדֶשׁ. הָא לָמַדְנוּ לָרִאשׁוֹן וְלַשֵּׁינִי מִן הַכָּתוּב. וְלַשְּׁלִישִׁי מִן הַדִּין וְלָרְבִיעִי מִקַּל וְחוֹמֶר. דָּנִין לוֹ דִין מִן הַדִּין. שֶׁיְּהֵא הַכֹּל מְשׁוּעְבָּד לַהֲלָכָה. שֶׁיְּהֵא הַשְּׁלִישִׁי פוֹסֵל בַּתְּרוּמָה וְהָרְבִיעִי בַּקּוֹדֶשׁ.

So far about solid food that became impure in the air space of a clay vessel[34] which had become impure by a reptile[101]. What about solid food that became impure directly from a reptile? Is that not an argument? Since vessels, which cannot become impure in the air space of a clay vessel that became impure by a reptile, become impure by contact with a reptile[102] to defile solid food, [is it not logical that solid food, which becomes impure in the air space of a clay vessel that became impure by a reptile, should become impure by contact with a reptile to defile solid food.] So far, following Rebbi Aqiba. Following Rebbi Ismael? Rebbi Ismael stated: [103]"Any meat which would touch anything impure", that is first degree food which touched any impurity, "shall not be eaten", to add a second degree of impurity. The third degree from where? It is an argument. Since a *tevul yom* who is not disabled for profane food disables heave, it is only logical that a person secondarily impure, who disables profane food should disable heave. The fourth degree for sacrifices from where? It is an argument. Since one who lacks expiation[95] who does not disable heave disables sanctified food[96], it is only logical that third degree [impurity] which disables[104] heave should disable sanctified food. That means, we learned first and second degrees from a verse, the third from an argument and the fourth from an argument *de minore ad majus*. Can one pile argument on argument[105]? Everything is subject to practice, i. e., that third degree disables heave and fourth degree disables sacrifices[106].

100   From the Rome ms., missing in Leiden ms. and *editio princeps*. The Rome ms. everywhere writes rabbinic חרס for biblical חרש.

101   A dead reptile from the 8 kinds enumerated in *Lev.* 11:29-30.

102   Vessels can become impure only from original impurity (a "father" or "grandfather" of impurity, never from derivative impurity.) There is no verse which would indicate otherwise (but in *Pesaḥim* 1:7, fol. 27d, R. Ismael is quoted to the effect that *Lev.* 11:33 also applies to vessels. It may be a veiled reference to the argument presented here.)

103   *Lev.* 7:19.

104   Everywhere here, פוסל "disables" should read פסול "is disabled", except the second occurrence (which infringes on the rules of דיו, Note 98).

105   It is a principle accepted in both Talmudim that at least for any rules of sacrifices and connected matters, most hermeneutical rules cannot be used one after the other; cf. *Yebamot* 8:1, Note 19. A detailed table of legal and illegal combinations, derived from Babli *Zebaḥim* Chapter 5, appears in the author's paper *Über ein bemerkenswertes logisches System aus der Antike*, Methodos 1951, pp. 150-164.

106   *Tosephta Ḥagigah* 3:8. "Practice" here corresponds to "Practice of Moses from Mount Sinai" in the Babli, generally accepted practice whose roots can no longer be ascertained. The status of such practice is more than rabbinic and less than biblical.

(fol. 19d) **משנה ד**: בּוֹ בַיּוֹם דָּרַשׁ רַבִּי עֲקִיבָה וּמָדוֹתָם מִחוּץ לָעִיר אֶת פְּאַת קֵדְמָה אַלְפַּיִם בָּאַמָּה. וּמִקְרָא אַחֵר הוּא אָמַר מְקִיר הָעִיר וָחוּצָה אֶלֶף אַמָּה סָבִיב. אֵיפְשָׁר לוֹמַר אֶלֶף אַמָּה שֶׁכְּבָר נֶאֱמַר אַלְפַּיִם אַמָּה וְאֵיפְשָׁר לוֹמַר אַלְפַּיִם אַמָּה שֶׁכְּבָר נֶאֱמַר אֶלֶף אַמָּה. וְלָמָּה נֶאֱמַר אֶלֶף וְלָמָּה נֶאֱמַר אַלְפַּיִם.

אֶלָּא אֶלֶף אַמָּה מִגְרָשׁ וְאַלְפַּיִם אַמָּה תְּחוּם שַׁבָּת. רִבִּי אֱלִיעֶזֶר בְּנוֹ שֶׁל רִבִּי
יוֹסֵי הַגְּלִילִי אוֹמֵר אֶלֶף אַמָּה מִגְרָשׁ וְאַלְפַּיִם שָׂדוֹת וּכְרָמִים.

Mishnah 4: On the same day[33], Rebbi Aqiba explained: [107]"You shall measure outside the city 2000 cubits to the East," but in another verse it says [108]"outside the city wall, one thousand cubits all around." It is impossible to say 1000 cubits because already it was said 2000 cubits and it is impossible to say 2000 cubits because already it was said 1000 cubits. Why was 1000 said, and why 2000? But 1000 cubits open space[109] and 2000 cubits Sabbath domain[110]. Rebbi Eliezer, the son of Rebbi Yose the Galilean, said: 1000 cubits open space and two thousand fields and vineyards[111].

107 *Num.* 35:5, speaking of the cities to be given to the Levites.

108 *Num.* 35:4.

109 Not for living and not for agriculture.

110 To say that not only for levitic cities but for all cities a belt 2000 cubits wide belongs to the city. Therefore, when it says "Nobody shall leave his place of the Seventh Day" (*Ex.* 16:29), it is implied that on the Sabbath a city dweller may walk in a belt 2000 cubits wide around the city.

111 He holds that the determination of the Sabbath domain as 2000 cubits outside the city wall is rabbinic, but that the belt 2000 cubits wide was given to the Levites and that the outer 1000 cubits were used for agriculture. (Sadducee practice limited walking on the Sabbath to 1000 cubits outside the city, agreeing with R. Eliezer; CD X:21.)

הלכה ה: בּוֹ בַיּוֹם דָּרַשׁ רִבִּי עֲקִיבָה וּמַדּוֹתֶם מִחוּץ לָעִיר וגו'. (fol. 20b) רִבִּי אֱלִיעֶזֶר בְּנוֹ שֶׁל רִבִּי יוֹסֵי הַגְּלִילִי אוֹמֵר. אַלְפַּיִם אַמָּה תְּחוּם עָרֵי הַלְוִיִּם. צֵא מֵהֶן אֶלֶף אַמָּה מִגְרָשׁ. נִמְצָא רְבִיעַ מִגְרָשׁ וְהַשְּׁאָר שָׂדוֹת. רִבִּי יִרְמְיָה רִבִּי שְׁמוּאֵל בַּר רַב יִצְחָק בְּשֵׁם רַב. רְבִיעַ מֵאֶלֶף. אָמַר רִבִּי יִצְחָק. וַאֲפִילוּ תֵימַר. רְבִיעַ מִכָּל־צַד. רְבִיעַ הוּא. מָאן דְּמְרַבַּע אַרְבַּע גַּרְבִּין בָּעֵי אֲשִׁיתְּתֵיסַר. רִבִּי

מָנָא מִשְׁעָר כְּהָדָא לְבֵנָה. רִבִּי אָבָּא מִשְׁעָר כְּהָדָא רְצוּעָה. רִבִּי אוֹשַׁעְיָה מִשְׁעָר כְּהָדָא דִיסְקָרִין. אָמַר רִבִּי יוֹסֵי בֵּירַבִּי בּוּן. חַמְשִׁין עַל חַמְשִׁין בֵּית סְאָה. מֵאַת עַל מֵאַת בֵּית אַרְבַּע סְאִין. כְּהָדָא רֵישׁ גָּלוּתָא אִיטְלַק עִילוֹי חַד טְרִיקְלִין אַרְבָּעִין עַל אַרְבָּעִין דִּימַלְיֵנֵיהּ חִיטִּין. אָתָא לְגַבֵּי רַב הוּנָא. אָמַר לֵיהּ. פַּייְסוּן דְּיִסְבּוּן מִינָךְ עֶשְׂרִין עַל עֶשְׂרִין כְּדוֹן. וְעֶשְׂרִין עַל עֶשְׂרִין בָּתַר זְמָן. וְאַתְּ מִיתְנָגֵר פַּלְגָּא.

"On the same day, Rebbi Aqiba explained: "You shall measure outside the city", etc. Rebbi Eliezer, the son of Rebbi Yose the Galilean, said, 2000 cubits the domain of the levitic cities. Deduct from them 1000 cubits open space, there results one quarter open space and the remainder fields[112]. Rebbi Jeremiah, Rebbi Samuel bar Rav Isaac in the name of Rav: A quarter of 1000[113]. Rebbi Isaac said, even if you say a quarter from every side, it is a quarter. He who wants to make a square from four amphoras needs sixteen[114]. Rebbi Mana estimated it from a brick, Rebbi Abin estimated it from a strip, Rebbi Oshaiah estimated it from a dish[115]. Rebbi Yose ben Rebbi Abun said, 50 by 50 form a *bet se'ah*[116]; 100 by 100 are four *bet se'ah*[117]. As it happened to the Resh Galuta when it was imposed on him[118] to fill a hall of 40 by 40 cubits with wheat. He came to Rav Huna who said to him, negotiate that they should take from you 20 by 20 now and 20 by 20 later; you will earn half[119].

112 This is difficult to understand. A little geometry is needed here (cf. H. Guggenheimer, *Applicable Geometry*, Huntington NY 1977.) Given an oval (a plane convex figure) of area A and perimeter L, the area of the *parallel figure* in distance h, obtained by adding to the figure every exterior point of distance $\leq h$ is

$$A(h) = A + hL + \pi h^2.$$

The excess area of the parallel figure over the original oval is

$$E(h) = hL + \pi h^2.$$

However, if the city has rectangular

shape, in tractate *Erubin* the Sabbath domain is determined as the rectangle whose sides are 2000 cubits from the (straight) walls of the city. In that case, the rectangle defined by lines in distance h has surface area

$$A(h) = A + hL + 4h^2$$

with excess $E(h) = hL + 4h^2$. Let the unit of h be 1000 cubits. In both cases, the condition $E(2) = 4E(1)$ yields $2L = 0$. It follows that $L = 0$: the original oval was a point. The open space is one quarter of the area of the fields only if there is no town; it is a limit case. The parallel text of the entire Halakhah is in *Erubin* 5, fol. 22d; *Makkot* 2:7, fol. 32a.

The Babli, *Eruvin* 56b, explains the problem away by replacing the condition $E(2) = 4E(1)$ by $A(2) = 4E(1)$, computing $A(2)$ by the second formula and $E(1)$ by the first, and assuming $\pi = 3$; clearly recognizing the impossibility of the original statement.

113 This is a radical re-interpretation of the verse: The open space is only 250 cubits wide on each side of the town. Then the problems disappear.

114 A row of length n defines a square of area n^2. For the problem at hand, the remark is irrelevant.

115 Rebbis Mana and Abin derived the second formula of Note 112 by supposing the town walls to form a rectangle; Rebbi Oshaia supposed the town to be of circular shape and derived the first formula. Neither of them accepted the 1:4 ratio.

116 An equivalent statement in Babli *Eruvin* 23b.

117 Since $2 \cdot 2 = 4$.

118 By the government, Parthian or Persan.

119 If the government officials are so ignorant of geometry that they do not realize that only half the surface area will be covered.

(20b, line 74) רִבִּי בָּא בְשֵׁם רַב יְהוּדָה רִבִּי זְעִירָא בְּשֵׁם רִבִּי עוּקְבָא. אֵין מְקַדְּדִין אֶלָּא בְחֶבֶל שֶׁלַחֲמִשִּׁים אַמָּה. רִבִּי זְעִירָא בְּשֵׁם רַב חִסְדַּיי. אֵין מְקַדְּדִין לֹא בְעָרֵי הַלְוִיִּם וְלֹא בִמְקוֹם עֲרִיפָה בַּנַּחַל. נִיחָא כְּמָאן דָּמַר. אֶלֶף אַמָּה מִגְרָשׁ וְאַלְפַּיִים אַמָּה שָׂדוֹת וּכְרָמִים. בְּרַם כְּמָאן דָּמַר. אֶלֶף אַמָּה מִגְרָשׁ וְאַלְפַּיִים אַמָּה תְּחוּם שַׁבָּת. כְּלוּם לָמְדוּ תְחוּם שַׁבָּת לֹא מֵעָרֵי הַלְוִיִּם. לְעִיקָר אֵין מְקַדְּדִין וְלִטְפֵּילָה מְקַדְּדִין.

HALAKHAH 5

Rebbi Abba in the name of Rebbi Jehudah, Rebbi Ze'ira in the name of Rav Uqba: One strip-measures[120] only with a rope of 50 cubits. Rebbi Ze'ira in the name of Rav Ḥisda: One strip-measures neither for the levitic cities nor from the distance for breaking the neck in the wadi[121,122]. This is acceptable for him who says, 1000 cubits of open space and 2000 cubits of Sabbath domain. But for him who says, 1000 cubits of open space and 2000 cubits of fields and vineyards, did they not learn the Sabbath domain from the levitic cities[123]? For the main thing one does not strip-measure; does one strip-measure for the derivative?

120   One determines the distance not on the ground but as if from a plane map of the domain. This means that on an incline one keeps the measuring rope horizontal.

Mishnah *Erubin* 5:4 states that "one measures only with a rope of 50 cubits, no less and no more". The Babli, *Erubin* 58b, disagrees with the Yerushalmi and notes that once one has to strip-measure, i. e. that the rope has to be held horizontally, away from the ground, a rope of 4 cubits is required. From a practical point of view, this seems to be the superior way of measuring. For מקדדין (cf. Arabic قدّ "to make strips"), the Babli has מקדרין.

121   Breaking a calf's neck in a wild place to atone for an unsolved murder, *Deut.* 21:1:9.

122   In the Babli *Erubin* 58b this is a statement by Rav Naḥman in the name of Rav Abba bar Abuh.

123   Since the Mishnah, *Erubin* 5:4, requires that Sabbath domains be measured as one would do on a map, it seems impossible that R. Eliezer ben R. Yose the Galilean accept R. Aqiba's opinion that the extent of the Sabbath domain is fixed in the Torah by the extent of the levitic cities, since the methods of measurement are different in both cases. The Babli, Note 122, gives as reason that for levitic cities and the breaking of the calf's neck one has to measure on the ground, that these are measurements prescribed by the Torah. The obvious inference is that the distance indicated for the Sabbath domain is rabbinic. (The opponents of R. Aqiba hold that the biblical Sabbath distance is the

diameter of the encampment of the Israelites in the plains of Jericho, which in both Talmudim is described as 12 *mīl*, 24 000 cubits; cf. *Šebi'it* 6:1,

Note 28). Therefore, it is permissible to extend the Sabbath domain even of a levitic city further than its political boundaries.

(20c, line 4) וּמְנַיִין שֶׁלֹּא הָיוּ קוֹבְרִין בְּעָרֵי הַלְוִיִם. רִבִּי אַבָּהוּ בְּשֵׁם רִבִּי יוֹסֵי בַּר חֲנִינָה. וּמִגְרְשֵׁיהֶם יִהְיוּ לִבְהֶמְתָּם וְלִרְכוּשָׁם וּלְכָל־חַיָּתָם. לִבְהֶמְתָּם וְלְחַיָּתָם נִתְּנוּ וְלֹא נִיתְּנוּ לִקְבוּרָה.

From where that one does not bury in a levitic city? Rebbi Abbahu[123] in the name of Rebbi Yose bar Hanina: "Their open spaces shall be for their animals, their property, and their lives."[124] They were given for their animals and their lives; the were not given for burial[125].

123 In the Babli, *Makkot* 12a, in the name of R. Abbahu himself.

124 *Num.* 35:3.

125 The cemetery of the Levites has to be on the territory of the surrounding tribe.

(fol. 19d) **משנה ה**: בּוֹ בַיּוֹם דָּרַשׁ רִבִּי עֲקִיבָה אָז יָשִׁיר מֹשֶׁה וּבְנֵי יִשְׂרָאֵל אֶת הַשִּׁירָה הַזֹּאת לַיְיָ וַיֹּאמְרוּ לֵאמֹר שֶׁאֵין תַּלְמוּד לוֹמַר וְלָמָּה תַלְמוּד לוֹמַר לֵאמֹר. אֶלָא שֶׁהָיוּ יִשְׂרָאֵל עוֹנִין אַחֲרָיו שֶׁל מֹשֶׁה עַל כָּל דָּבָר וְדָבָר כְּקוֹרְאִין אֶת הַהַלֵּל אָשִׁירָה לַיְיָ כִּי גָאֹה גָּאָה. לְכָךְ נֶאֱמַר לֵאמֹר. רִבִּי נְחֶמְיָה אוֹמֵר כְּקוֹרִין אֶת שְׁמַע הָיוּ קוֹרִין לֹא כְקוֹרִין אֶת הַהַלֵּל.

Mishnah 5: On the same day[33], Rebbi Aqiba explained: "[126]Then would Moses and the Children of Israel sing the following song to the Eternal to tell." The verse should not have said "to tell"; why does the verse say "to tell"? It was that Israel were repeating after Moses every word, as one reads the *Hallel*[127]: "I shall sing to the Eternal for He is very highly high;" therefore "saying" was said. Rebbi Nehemiah said, they were reciting it as one recites the *Šemaʿ*[128], not as one reads the *Hallel*.

126   Ex. 15:1.
127   *Ps.* 113-118, the holiday songs. The way of recital is described in the Tosephta/Halakhah.

128   The entire recital which starts with "Hear, o Israel," cf. *Berakhot* Chapter 1, Note 1.

(fol. 20c) **הלכה ו**: בּוֹ בַיּוֹם דָּרַשׁ רִבִּי עֲקִיבָה אָז יָשִׁיר מֹשֶׁה וגו'. לְקָטָן שֶׁהוּא מַקְרֵא אֶת הַהַלֵּל בְּבֵית הַסֵּפֶר וְהֵן עוֹנִין אַחֲרָיו עַל כָּל־דָּבָר וְדָבָר. מֹשֶׁה אָמַר אָשִׁירָה. וְהֵן עוֹנִין אַחֲרָיו אָשִׁירָה. מֹשֶׁה אָמַר עוּזִּי וְהֵן אוֹמְרִים עוּזִּי. רִבִּי אֱלִיעֶזֶר בְּנוֹ שֶׁל רִבִּי יוֹסֵי הַגְּלִילִי אוֹמֵר. לְגָדוֹל שֶׁהוּא מַקְרֵא אֶת הַהַלֵּל בְּבֵית הַכְּנֶסֶת וְהֵן עוֹנִין אַחֲרָיו דָּבָר רִאשׁוֹן. מֹשֶׁה אָמַר אָשִׁירָה. וְהֵן עוֹנִין אָשִׁירָה. מֹשֶׁה אָמַר עוּזִּי. וְהֵן עוֹנִין אַחֲרָיו אָשִׁירָה. רִבִּי יוֹסֵי הַגְּלִילִי אוֹמֵר. בְּשָׁעָה שֶׁהָיוּ אֲבוֹתֵינוּ בַיָּם הָיָה עוֹלָל מוּטָּל עַל בִּרְכָּהּ שֶׁלְּאִמּוֹ וְיוֹנֵק מִשְּׁדֵי אִמּוֹ. וְכֵיוָן שֶׁרָאוּ אֶת הַשְּׁכִינָה הִגְבִּיהַּ עוֹלֵל אֶת רֹאשׁוֹ מִבִּרְכָּהּ שֶׁלְּאִמּוֹ וְשׁוֹמֵט הַתִּינוֹק אֶת פִּיו מִדַּדָּהּ שֶׁלְּאִמּוֹ. אַף הֵן פָּתְחוּ אֶת פִּיהֶן בְּשִׁירָה וּבְשֶׁבַח וְאָמְרוּ זֶה אֵלִי וְאַנְוֵהוּ. רִבִּי מֵאִיר אוֹמֵר. אֲפִילוּ עוּבָּרִין מִמְּעֵי אִימּוֹתֵיהֶן הָיוּ אוֹמְרִים שִׁירָה. שֶׁנֶּאֱמַר מִמַּקְהֵלוֹת בָּרְכוּ אֱלֹהִים י֙ מִמְּקוֹר יִשְׂרָאֵל. רִבִּי נְחֶמְיָה אוֹמֵר. בְּשָׁעָה שֶׁעָלוּ אֲבוֹתֵינוּ מִן הַיָּם רָאוּ פִגְרֵי אֲנָשִׁים חַטָּאִים שֶׁהָיוּ מְשַׁעְבְּדִין בָּהֶן בְּפֶרֶךְ בַּעֲבוֹדָה קָשָׁה. וְכוּלָּם פְּגָרִים מֵתִים מוּשְׁלָכִים עַל שְׂפַת הַיָּם. בִּיקְשׁוּ לוֹמַר שִׁירָה וְשָׁרַת עֲלֵיהֶן רוּחַ הַקּוֹדֶשׁ. וַאֲפִילוּ קָטָן שֶׁבְּיִשְׂרָאֵל הָיָה אוֹמֵר שִׁירָה כְּמֹשֶׁה. הָדָא הוּא דִכְתִיב וַיִּזְכֹּר יְמֵי עוֹלָם מֹשֶׁה עַמּוֹ אַיֵּה הַמַּעֲלֵם מִיָּם. אֶת רוֹעֵה הַצֹּאן אֵין כָּתוּב כָּאן אֶלָּא אֶת רוֹעֵי צֹאנוֹ. מְלַמֵּד שֶׁעָשָׂה כוּלָּם רוֹעִים.

Halakhah 6: "On the same day, Rebbi Aqiba explained: "Then would Moses sing," etc. [129]Like a minor who recites the *Hallel* in school and all repeat every word after him[130]. Moses said, "I shall sing[131]", and they repeat after him: "I shall sing". Moses said: "Strength", and they say: "Strength[132]". Rebbi Eliezer the son of Rebbi Yose the Galilean said, like an adult who recites the *Hallel* in the synagogue, and they repeat the first word[133]. Moses said, "I shall sing", and they repeat: "I shall sing". Moses said: "My strength", and they repeat after him: "I shall sing". Rebbi Yose the Galilean says, when our forefathers were in the sea, the toddler was resting on his mother's knees and the baby was suckling from his mother's breast; but when they saw the Divine Glory, the toddler lifted his head from his mother's knees and the baby took away his mouth from his mother's breast; they opened their mouths in song and praise and said, "that is my God and I shall declare Him Beautiful[132]". Rebbi Meïr said, even the fetuses were saying a song from their mothers' wombs, as it is said: "[134]In choirs praise God, the Eternal from the source of Israel." Rebbi Nehemiah said, when our forefathers rose from the sea they saw the corpses of the sinners who had subjected them to hard, forced labor, all of them dead corpses thrown on the sea shore. They wanted to sing and the holy spirit rested upon them. Even the most insignificant in Israel sang the song just as Moses did. That is what is written: "[135]He remembered the days of old, Moses, his people; where is He Who raised them from the sea?" It is not written "the sheeps' shepherd" but "His sheeps' shepherd"; this teaches that He turned all of them into shepherds[136].

129 Tosephta *Soṭah* 6:2-4; Babli 30b/31a. A small part of the text is in *Mekhilta dR. Ismael, Shirah, Parashah* 1 (*Mekhilta dR. Simeon bar Ioḥai*, p. 72, cf. Note 137).

130 The entire class, until they know *Hallel* by heart.

131 *Ex.* 15:1.

132 *Ex.* 15:2.

133 This is prescribed by the Babli,

Sukkah 38b, and retained in the Yemenite *baladī* rite, where the congregation answer *hallelujah* (the first word of *Ps.* 113) at each caesura and end of sentence. The Galilean Amoraic way was for several people to recite the *Hallel*, with each of them saying half a verse (*Berakhot* 8:9 fol. 12c, *Megillah* 1:11 fol. 72a).

134   *Ps.* 68:27. In Mishnaic Hebrew, מָקוֹר means the female womb; cf. *Lev.* 20:18.

135   *Is.* 63:11. The verse ends: "Where is He Who put His Holy Spirit in their midst."

136   Since the first half of the verse equates Moses and His people, the singular of the second clause is taken as collective.

(20c, line 26) מַה תַּלְמוּד לוֹמַר לֵאמֹר. לֵאמֹר לְדוֹרוֹת. רִבִּי אַבָּהוּ בְשֵׁם רִבִּי יָסֵי בֵּירִבִּי חֲנִינָה. כְּהָדֵין פְּסוּקָא. מֹשֶׁה אָמַר אָשִׁירָה. וְהֵן עוֹנִין אַחֲרָיו אָשִׁירָה לַיי כִּי גָאֹה גָּאָה סוּס וְרוֹכְבוֹ רָמָה בַיָּם. מֹשֶׁה אָמַר עָזִּי וְזִמְרָת וְהֵן עוֹנִין אַחֲרָיו עָזִּי וְזִמְרָת יָ'ה. כְּתִיב בִּפְרוֹעַ פְּרָעוֹת בְּיִשְׂרָאֵל בְּהִתְנַדֵּב עָם. הִתְנַדְּבוּ רָאשֵׁי עָם. כְּשֶׁהַקָּדוֹשׁ בָּרוּךְ הוּא עוֹשֶׂה לָהֶן נִיסִים יְהוּ אוֹמְרִים שִׁירָה. הֲתִיבוּן. הֲרֵי גְאוּלַת מִצְרַיִם. שַׁנְיָיא הִיא שֶׁהִיא תְּחִילַת גְּאוּלָתָן. הֲתִיבוּן. הֲרֵי גְאוּלַת מָרְדְּכַי וְאֶסְתֵּר. שַׁנְיָיא הִיא. שֶׁהָיוּ בְחוּצָה לָאָרֶץ. וְאִית דְּבָעֵי מֵימַר. מָרְדְּכַי וְאֶסְתֵּר מִשּׁוּנְאֵיהֶן נִגְאָלוּ. לֹא נִגְאָלוּ מִן הַמַּלְכוּת.

Why does the verse say, "to tell"? To tell to [future] generations. Rebbi Abbahu in the name of Rebbi Yose ben Rebbi Hanina, the entire verse. Moses said, "I shall sing", and they recite after his lead: "I shall sing to the Eternal for He is very highly high; horse and rider He cast into the sea[131]." Moses said: "strength and growth", and they recite after his lead: "strength and growth is Yah[132]".[137] It is written: [138]"When retribution is retributed for Israel, when the people volunteers;" the heads of the people volunteered. When the Holy One, praise to Him, does wonders for Israel, they should sing a song. They objected: There is the redemption from

Egypt! That is something else since it was the beginning of their redemption[139]. They objected. There is redemption of Mardocai and Esther[140]! That is something else since they were outside the Land[141]; some want to say that Mardocai and Esther were freed of their enemies, they were not freed from {Gentile] government[141].

137   In the *Mekhiltot*, this is attributed to R. Eleazar ben Thaddai, a Tanna whose time is difficult to determine and who is never quoted in Yerushalmi sources.   Cf. B.-Z. Wacholder, *The Date of Mekilta de-Rabbi Ishmael*, HUCA 39 (1968), 117-144.

138   *Jud.* 5:2. In rabbinic Hebrew, פרע means "to pay one's debt".

139   Meaning that the Song of the Sea also covers the Exodus, since the latter was confirmed only at the Sea. In the Babli and midrashic literature, *Ps.* 113 is the song of the Israelites during Passover night [*Pesahim* 117a; cf. *Cant. rabba* 1(37), *Mekhilta deR. Ismael, Shirah* 1; *deR. Simeon bar Iohai* p. 71]. Cf. the author's *The Scholar's Haggadah*, pp. 314-319.

140   Who instituted a "day of feasting and joy" but not the recitation of *Hallel, Esth.* 9:22.

141   Babli, *Megillah* 14a.

משנה ו: בּוֹ בַיּוֹם דָּרַשׁ רִבִּי יְהוֹשֻׁעַ בֶּן הוּרְקִנוֹס לֹא עָבַד אִיּוֹב אֶת הַקָּדוֹשׁ בָּרוּךְ הוּא אֶלָּא מֵאַהֲבָה שֶׁנֶּאֱמַר הֵן יִקְטְלֵנִי לוֹ אֲיַיחֵל. וַעֲדַיִין הַדָּבָר שָׁקוּל לוֹ אֲנִי מְצַפֶּה אוֹ אֵינִי מְצַפֶּה לוֹ. תַּלְמוּד לוֹמַר עַד אֶגְוַע לֹא אָסִיר תֻּמָּתִי מִמֶּנּוּ לְמֵד שֶׁמֵּאַהֲבָה עָשָׂה. (fol. 19d)

Mishnah 6: On the same day, Joshua ben Hyrkanos explained that Job served the Holy One, praise to Him, only out of love[142], as it is said[143]: "Behold, even if He will kill me, to Him I pray." But the matter is still in suspense[144], "to Him I look forward" or "I do not look forward to Him".

The verse says, "until I die I shall not remove my innocence from me[145]," this teaches that he did it out of love.

142 His acts represent *amor dei*, not fear of punishment in the World to Come; cf. Mishnah 7.

143 Job 13:15. The *Ketib* is לא איחל, the *Qere* לו איחל. The *Qere* represents the majority of mss. before the Masoretes. The Mishnah shows that the difference of readings existed many Centuries before the Masoretes.

144 Between authenticity of *Ketib* or *Qere*.

145 Job 27:5.

(fol. 20c) **הלכה ז**: בּוֹ בַיּוֹם דָּרַשׁ רִבִּי יְהוֹשֻׁעַ בֶּן הוּרְקָנוֹס כול'. תַּנֵּי בְשֵׁם רִבִּי יְהוּדָה. חַי אֵל הֵסִיר מִשְׁפָּטִי וְשַׁדַּי הֵמַר נַפְשִׁי. שֶׁאֵין אָדָם נוֹדֵר בְּחַיָּיו שֶׁל מֶלֶךְ אֶלָּא אִם כֵּן אוֹהֲבוֹ. מִשּׁוּם רִבִּי נָתָן אָמְרוּ גַּם הוּא לִי לִישׁוּעָה כִּי לֹא לְפָנָיו חָנֵף יָבוֹא.

Halakhah 7: "On the same day, Joshua ben Hyrcanos explained," etc. It was stated in the name of Rebbi Jehudah: "God lives[146] Who removed my lawsuit, and the Ruler made me bitter;" for nobody swears by the King's life unless he loves Him. They said in the name of Rebbi Nathan: "Also He is my help, for insincerity will not come before Him.[147]"

146 Job 27:2. This is an oath formula. Since nobody swears by the life of the king unless he loves the king, the verse supports R. Joshua ben Hyrkanos.

147 Job 13:16; cf. Note 143. The verse following the one in dispute shows that לו is the only consistent reading.

(20c, line 39) כָּתוּב אֶחָד אוֹמֵר וְאָהַבְתָּ אֵת יי אֱלֹהֶיךָ וְכָתוּב אֶחָד אוֹמֵר אֶת יי אֱלֹהֶיךָ תִּירָא וְאוֹתוֹ תַעֲבוֹד. עֲשֵׂה מֵאַהֲבָה וַעֲשֵׂה מִיִּרְאָה. עֲשֵׂה מֵאַהֲבָה. שֶׁאִם בָּאתָה לִשְׂנוֹא דַּע שֶׁאַתְּ אוֹהֵב וְאֵין אוֹהֵב שׂוֹנֶה. עֲשֵׂה מִיִּרְאָה. שֶׁאִם בָּאתָה לִבְעַט דַּע שֶׁאַתְּ יָרֵא. וְאֵין יָרֵא מְבַעֵט.

One verse says, "you shall love the Eternal, your God,[148]" and another verse says, "fear the Eternal, your God, and Him you should serve.[149]"

[150]Act from love and act from fear. Act from love, because if you are tempted to hate, know that you must love and a lover is no hater. Act from fear, because if you are tempted to rebel, know that you must fear and one who fears does not rebel.

148	*Deut.* 6:5.
149	*Deut.* 6:13.
150	From here to the end of the Halakhah the text, with minor variations, is also in *Berakhot* 9:6, Notes 241-255.

(20c, line 42) שִׁבְעָה פְרוּשִׁין הֵן. פָּרוּשׁ שִׁכְמִי. וּפָרוּשׁ נִקְפִּי. וּפָרוּשׁ קִיזַּיי פָּרוּשׁ מַה מַּנְכְּיָיה. פָּרוּשׁ אֲדַע חוֹבָתִי וְאֶעֱשֶׂנָּה. פָּרוּשׁ יִרְאָה. פָּרוּשׁ אַהֲבָה. פָּרוּשׁ שִׁכְמִי. טָעִין מִצְוָתֵיהּ עַל כֵּיתְפֵיהּ. פָּרוּשׁ נִיקְפִּי. אַקֵּיף לִי וַאֲנָא עֲבִיד מִצְוָה. פָּרוּשׁ קִיזַּיי. עֲבַד חָדָא חוֹבָה וְחָדָא מִצְוָה וּמְקַזֵּז הָדָא עִם הָדָא. פָּרוּשׁ מַנְכְּיָיה. מָאן דִּית לִי מַה אֲנָא מְנַכִּי עֲבַד מִצְוָה. פָּרוּשׁ אֲדַע חוֹבָתִי וְאֶעֱשֶׂנָּה. אַיְידֵי חוֹבָתָהּ עֲבְדִית דְּנַעֲבִיד מִצְוָה דִכְוָותָהּ. פָּרוּשׁ יִרְאָה. כְּאִיּוֹב. פָּרוּשׁ אַהֲבָה. כְּאַבְרָהָם. אֵין לָךְ חָבִיב מִכּוּלָּן אֶלָּא פָּרוּשׁ אַהֲבָה כְּאַבְרָהָם.

There are seven kinds of religious people: Religious on the shoulder, religious on credit, religious balancing, religious "what is the deduction," religious "I shall do it when I realize my guilt," religious from fear, religious from love. Religious on the shoulder, he carries his deeds on his shoulder. Religious on credit, "give me credit that I can perform commandments." Religious balancing, he commits one sin and observes one commandment and balances one against the other. Religious "what is the deduction," what I have that is what I am using to deduct for doing a commandment. Religious "I shall do it when I realize my guilt," I committed that sin and therefore I shall do this good deed to counteract it[151]. Religious from fear, like Job. Religious from love, like Abraham. No one is beloved as much as the religious from love, like Abraham.

151 A slightly different list with completely different interpretations in Babli *Soṭa* 22b declares explicitly that the first five are "destroyers of the world." In the Yerushalmi, it is clear that the first five are considered in a negative light but they are still considered better than one who performs no commandments at all.

(20c, line 50) אַבְרָהָם עָשָׂה יֵצֶר הָרַע טוֹב. וּמַה טַעֲמָא. וּמְצָאתָ אֶת לְבָבוֹ נֶאֱמָן לְפָנֶיךָ. אָמַר רִבִּי אָחָא וְהִפְשִׁיר עִמּוֹ וְכָרוֹת עִמּוֹ הַבְּרִית. אֲבָל דָוִד לֹא הָיָה יָכוֹל לַעֲמוֹד בּוֹ וְהָרְגוֹ בִּלְבָבוֹ. מַאי טַעֲמָא וְלִבִּי חָלַל בְּקִרְבִּי.

Our forefather Abraham turned the evil instincts into good ones. What is the reason? (*Neh.* 9:8): "You found his heart trustworthy before You." Rebbi Aḥa said, he compromised, from "concluding a covenant with him." But David could not stand it and killed it in his heart. What is the reason? (*Ps.* 109:22) "But my heart is slain in me."

(20c, line 53) רִבִּי עֲקִיבָה הֲוָה מִתְדַיֵּן קוֹמֵי טוּנוּסְטְרוֹפוֹס הָרָשָׁע. אָתָה עָנָתָא דְקִרְיַת שְׁמַע. שָׁרֵי קָרֵי וְגָחַךְ. אָמַר לֵיהּ סָבָא סָבָא. אוֹ חָרָשׁ אַתְּ אוֹ מְבַעֵט בְּיִיסּוּרִין אַתְּ. אָמַר לֵיהּ תִּיפַּח רוּחֵיהּ דְּהַהוּא גַּבְרָא. לָא חָרָשׁ אֲנָא וְלָא מְבַעֵט בְּיִיסּוּרִין אֲנָא. אֶלָּא כָּל־יוֹמַיי הָיִיתִי קוֹרֵא אֶת הַפָּסוּק זֶה. וְאָהַבְתָּ אֶת יי אֱלֹהֶיךָ בְּכָל־לְבָבְךָ וּבְכָל־נַפְשְׁךָ וּבְכָל־מְאוֹדֶךָ. רְחַמְתֵּיהּ בְּכָל־לִבִּי. וּרְחַמְתֵּיהּ בְּכָל־מָמוֹנִי. וּבְכָל־נַפְשִׁי לָא הֲוַת בְּדִיקָה לִי. וּכְדוֹן דְּמָטַת בְּכָל־נַפְשִׁי וְאָתַת עָנָתָא דְקִרְיַת שְׁמַע וְלָא אַפְלְגִית עֲלֵיהּ. בְּגִין כֵּן קְרֵי אֲנָא שְׁמַע וְגָחַךְ.

Rebbi Aqiba was tortured before the evil Tineius Rufus. There came the time for reciting the *Shema'*. He started to read and laughed. He said to him: Old man, you are either a sorcerer or one contemptuous of suffering. He said to him: The spirit of this man should be blown away; I am neither a sorcerer nor contemptuous of sufferings. But all my life I read this verse (*Deut.* 6:5): "You must love the Eternal, your God, with all your heart, all your soul, and all your force." I loved Him with all my heart. I loved Him with all my money. But whether with all my soul I could not test. But now, when "with all your soul" came, the time of reciting the *Shema'* has arrived and my mind has not wavered, therefore I am reciting and laughing.

(20c, line 61) נְחֶמְיָה עִימְסוֹנִי שִׁימֵּשׁ אֶת רְבִּי עֲקִיבָא עֶשְׂרִים וּשְׁתַּיִם שָׁנָה. הוּא הָיָה אוֹמֵר. אֶתִּים גַּמִּים רִיבּוּיִין. אַכִּין וְרַקִּין מִיעוּטִין. אָמַר לֵיהּ. מַהוּ דֵין דִּכְתִיב אֶת יי אֱלֹהֶיךָ תִּירָא וגו'. אָמַר לֵיהּ. אוֹתוֹ וְאֶת תּוֹרָתוֹ.

Nehemiah from Emmaus served Rebbi Aqiba for 22 years and he taught him "את and גם mean additions, אך and רק mean exclusions." He asked him: What means that which is written (*Deut.* 6:13) "את the Eternal, your God, you must fear." He said to him, Him and His Torah.

(fol. 19d) **משנה ז**: אָמַר רְבִּי יְהוֹשֻׁעַ מִי יְגַלֶּה עָפָר מֵעֵינֶיךָ רַבָּן יוֹחָנָן בֶּן זַכַּיי. שֶׁהָיִיתָ דוֹרֵשׁ כָּל־יָמֶיךָ שֶׁלֹּא עָבַד אִיּוֹב אֶת הַמָּקוֹם אֶלָּא מִיִּרְאָה שֶׁנֶּאֱמַר אִישׁ תָּם וְיָשָׁר וִירֵא אֱלֹהִים וְסָר מֵרָע. וַהֲרֵי יְהוֹשֻׁעַ תַּלְמִיד תַּלְמִידְךָ לִמֵּד שֶׁמֵּאַהֲבָה עָשָׂה.

Mishnah 7: Rebbi Joshua said, who would remove the dust from your eyes, Rabban Johanan ben Zakkai, since all your days you explained that Job served the Omnipresent only out of fear, as it was said: "A man, artless and straight, fearing God and fleeing from evil[152]"; but behold, Joshua, your student's student[153] deduced that he did it out of love!

152   Job 1:1.
153   It is not clear whose student Joshua ben Hyrkanos was. He probably is not mentioned anywhere else in tannaïtic literature.

(fol. 20c) **הלכה ח**: אָמַר רִבִּי יְהוֹשֻׁעַ מִי יְגַלֶּה עָפָר מֵעֵינֶיךָ רַבָּן יוֹחָנָן בֶּן זַכַּיי כול׳. אֵימָתַי הָיָה אִיוֹב. רִבִּי שִׁמְעוֹן בֶּן לָקִישׁ בְּשֵׁם בַּר קַפָּרָא. בִּימֵי אַבְרָהָם אָבִיבוּ הָיָה. הָדָא הִיא דִכְתִיב אִישׁ הָיָה בְאֶרֶץ עוּץ אִיּוֹב שְׁמוֹ. וּכְתִיב אֶת עוּץ בְּכוֹרוֹ. רִבִּי אַבָּא אָמַר. בִּימֵי אָבִינוּ יַעֲקֹב. וְדִינָה הָיְתָה אִשְׁתּוֹ. הָדָא הִיא דִכְתִיב כְּדַבֵּר אַחַת הַנְּבָלוֹת תְּדַבֵּרִי. וּכְתִיב כִּי נְבָלָה עָשָׂה בְיִשְׂרָאֵל. רִבִּי לֵוִי אָמַר. בִּימֵי הַשְּׁבָטִים הָיָה. הָדָא הִיא דִכְתִיב אֲשֶׁר חֲכָמִים יַגִּידוּ וְלֹא כִחֲדוּ מֵאֲבוֹתָם. רִבִּי יוֹסֵי בֶּן חֲלַפְתָּא אָמַר. בִּירִידָתָן לְמִצְרַיִם הָיָה וּבַעֲלִיָּיתָן מֵת. מָשָׁל לְרוֹעֶה שֶׁבָּא זְאֵב וְנִזְדַּוֵּוג לְצֹאנוֹ. מַה עָשָׂה. הֶעֱמִיד תַּיִשׁ אֶחָד לְנֶגְדּוֹ. הָדָא הוּא דִכְתִיב. יַסְגִּירֵנִי אֵל אֶל עֲוִיל וְעַל יְדֵי רְשָׁעִים יִרְטֵינִי. תַּנֵּי רִבִּי יִשְׁמָעֵאל. אִיּוֹב מֵעַבְדֵי פַרְעֹה הָיָה וּמִגְּדוֹלֵי פַמִילְיָיא שֶׁלּוֹ הָיָה. הָדָא הוּא דִכְתִיב הַיָּרֵא אֶת דְּבַר י"י וגו׳. וּכְתִיב בֵּיהּ אִישׁ תָּם וְיָשָׁר וִירֵא אֱלֹהִים וְסָר מֵרָע. רִבִּי יוֹסֵי בֵּירִבִּי יְהוּדָה אוֹמֵר. בִּימֵי שְׁפוֹט הַשּׁוֹפְטִים הָיָה. הָדָא הוּא דִכְתִיב הֵן אַתֶּם כֻּלְּכֶם חֲזִיתֶם וְלָמָּה זֶה הֶבֶל תֶּהְבָּלוּ. חֲזִיתֶם מַעֲשֵׂה דוֹרִי. שֶׁהָיוּ נוֹטְלִים מַעֲשֵׂר בְּגָרְנוֹת. אָהַבְתָּ אֶתְנָן עַל כָּל־גָּרְנוֹת דָּגָן. רִבִּי שְׁמוּאֵל בַּר נַחְמָן בְּשֵׁם רִבִּי יוֹנָתָן. בִּימֵי מַלְכַּת שְׁבָא הָיָה. וַתִּפּוֹל שְׁבָא וַתִּקָּחֵם. רִבִּי נָתָן אָמַר. בִּימֵי כַּשְׂדִּים הָיָה. שֶׁנֶּאֱמַר כַּשְׂדִּים שָׂמוּ שְׁלֹשָׁה רָאשִׁים. רִבִּי יְהוֹשֻׁעַ בֶּן קָרְחָה אָמַר. בִּימֵי אֲחַשְׁוֵרוֹשׁ הָיָה. שֶׁנֶּאֱמַר יְבַקְשׁוּ לַמֶּלֶךְ נְעָרוֹת בְּתוּלוֹת טוֹבוֹת מַרְאֶה. וּכְתִיב וְלֹא נִמְצָא נָשִׁים כִּבְנוֹת אִיוֹב. רִבִּי יְהוֹשֻׁעַ בֶּן לֵוִי אָמַר. מֵעוֹלֵי גוֹלָה הָיָה. רִבִּי יוֹחָנָן אָמַר. מֵעוֹלֵי גוֹלָה הָיָה וְיִשְׂרָאֵל הָיָה. לְפוּם כֵּן רִבִּי יוֹחָנָן לָמַד מִמֶּנּוּ הִלְכוֹת אָבֵל. וַיָּקָם אִיוֹב וַיִּקְרַע אֶת מְעִילוֹ. רִבִּי יְהוּדָה בֶּן פָּזִי בְּשֵׁם רִבִּי יוֹחָנָן. מִכָּאן שֶׁאָבֵל צָרִיךְ לִקְרוֹעַ מְעוּמָּד. תַּנֵּי רִבִּי חִיָּיא. הָיָה לִי

בְּעוֹלָמִי גּוֹי אֶחָד צַדִּיק וְנָתַתִּי לוֹ שְׂכָרוֹ וּפְטַרְתִּיו מֵעוֹלָמִי. רִבִּי שִׁמְעוֹן בֶּן לָקִישׁ אָמַר. אִיוֹב לֹא הָיָה וְלֹא עָתִיד לִחְיוֹת. מַחְלְפָה שִׁיטָתֵיהּ דְּרִבִּי שִׁמְעוֹן בֶּן לָקִישׁ. תַּמָּן אָמַר רִבִּי שִׁמְעוֹן בֶּן לָקִישׁ בְּשֵׁם בַּר קַפָּרָא. בִּימֵי אַבְרָהָם אָבִיבוּ הָיָה. וְהָכָא אָמַר הָכֵין. אֶלָּא הוּא הָיָה וְיִיסוּרִין לֹא הָיוּ. וְלָמָּה נִכְתְּבוּ עָלָיו. אֶלָּא לוֹמַר שֶׁאִילּוּלֵי בָאוּ עָלָיו הָיָה יָכוֹל לַעֲמוֹד בָּהֶן.

Halakhah 8: "Rebbi Joshua said, who would remove the dust from your eyes, Rabban Johanan ben Zakkai," etc. [154]When was Job? Rebbi Simeon ben Laqish in the name of Bar Qappara: He was in the days of our father Abraham; that is what is written: "[155]A man was in the land of Oz, his name was Job." And it is written, "[156]Oz his firstborn." Rebbi Abba said[157], in the days of our father Jacob and Dinah was his wife; that is what is written: "[158]You speak like one of the impious ones", and it is written: "[159]For an impiety he did in Israel." Rebbi Levi said, he was in the days of the tribes; that is what is written: "[160]What Sages would tell, they did not conceal from their fathers." Rebbi Yose ben Halaphta said, he was born when they descended into Egypt and he died when they left[161]. A parable of a shepherd when a wolf came and attacked his flock. What did he do? He put up a ram against him[162]. That is what is written: "[163]He delivered me to the evil one, he threw me amongst evildoers." Rebbi Ismael stated: Job was one of Pharao's servants, a great one in his government[164,165]. That is what is written: "[166]One who feared the word of the Eternal etc.", and it is written about him, "[155]a man, artless and straight, fearing God and fleeing from evil[152]". Rebbi Yose bar Jehudah[167] says, he was in the days when the Judges judged; that is what is written: "Behold, you all did see, why do you turn all into vapor[168]." You saw what my generation did, that they collect tithes on the threshing floors;

"you loved whore's wages on all grain threshing floors[169]." Rebbi Samuel bar Nahman in the name of Rebbi Jonathan[170]: He was in the days of the queen of Seba, as it is said: "Seba attacked and took them[171]." Rebbi Nathan[172] said, he was in the days of the Chaldeans, as it is said: "The Chaldeans attacked from three sides.[173]" Rebbi Joshua ben Qorha[174] said, he was in the days of Asuerus, as it is said: "One shall look for beautiful virgins for the king[175]." And it is written, "no women were found like Job's daughters[176]." Rebbi Joshua ben Levi said, he was of the returnees of the diaspora. Rebbi Johanan said, He was of the returnees from the diaspora and was a Jew[177]. Therefore Rebbi Johanan learned from him the rules of mourning. "Job got up and tore his coat[178]"; Rebbi Jehudah ben Pazi in the name of Rebbi Johanan: From here [one learns] that a mourner has to tear [his garment] while standing[179]. Rebbi Hiyya[180] stated: In My world I had one just Gentile, I gave him his reward and removed him from My world[181]. Rebbi Simeon ben Laqish[182] said, Job did not exist and will never live. The opinion of Rebbi Simeon ben Laqish is inconsistent: There, Rebbi Simeon ben Laqish said in the name of Bar Qappara: He was in the days of our father Abraham, but here he says so? But he did exist but his suffering did not. Then why is it written about him? To tell you that if it had come upon him, he would have withstood it.

154   The parallel is in Babli, *Baba Batra* 15a/b.
155   *Job* 1:1.
156   *Gen.* 23:21, in the list of Aramean Nahor tribes.
157   In the Babli, this is the opinion of R. Nathan in an alternate version.
158   *Job* 2:10.
159   *Gen.* 34:7.
160   *Job.* 15:18. The previous verse ends: This I have seen, I shall tell it; the verses are interpreted as referring

to Judah and Reuben who confessed their sins; cf. Chapter 1, Note 195.

161 This is an anonymous tannaïtic opinion in the Babli. The traditional duration of the tribes' stay in Egypt is 210 years; cf. the author's *The Scholar's Haggadah*, pp. 283-284. Job lived another 140 years after his tribulations (*Job* 42:16). Since God gave double restitution for everything he had lost, it is concluded that he suffered in his 70th year and lived for 210 years.

162 In the Babli, 14b, this is hinted at by the statement that Job's goats were able to attack wolves, being supernaturally safe from predators.

163 *Job* 16:11.

164 In the later Midrash, *Ex. rabba* 1(12), this is extended to include in Pharao's council Bileam, who voted for killing the Jewish children and was killed, Job who abstained from voting and suffered, and Jethro who voted against Pharao's decree and was rewarded in that his descendants sat in the Synhedrion.

165 *Familia* as a term for government is from the time of the principate when the emperor ran the state by his freedmen and slaves, his *familia*.

166 *Ex.* 9:20.

167 In the Babli, R. Eleazar.

168 *Job* 27:12.

169 *Hos.* 9:1. Since it is in the hand of the farmer to whom to give his tithes; the Levite or Cohen who comes to the threshing floor to collect his tithes is an extortionist (Cf. *Demay* 6:3, Note 69).

170 In the Babli, R. Nathan.

171 *Job* 1:15.

172 In the Babli, the anonymous Sages.

173 *Job* 1:17.

174 Same argument in the Babli.

175 *Esth.* 2:2.

176 *Job* 42:15.

177 In the Babli, R. Johanan and R. Eleazar.

178 *Job* 1:20.

179 In *Mo'ed Qaṭan* 3:7, Babli 20b, the verse is quoted without asking whether Job was Jewish or not.

180 In the Babli this is an anonymous tannaïtic statement.

181 Since Job, in contrast to Jewish saintly persons, received his reward in this world, he seems to be excluded from the World to Come.

182 In the Babli, 14a, this is the opinion of an anonymous author who proves that Scripture in effect contains tales that do not correspond to reality, such as Nathan's tale of the poor man and his sheep.

(20d, line 17) דָּרַשׁ רִבִּי עֲקִיבָה. וַיִּחַר אַף אֱלִיהוּ בֶן בַּרַכְאֵל הַבּוּזִי מִמִּשְׁפַּחַת רָם. אֱלִיהוּ זֶה בִּלְעָם. בֶּן בַּרַכְאֵל. שֶׁבָּא לְקַלֵּל אֶת יִשְׂרָאֵל וּבֵירְכָן. וְלֹא אָבָה יי אֱלֹהֶיךָ לִשְׁמוֹעַ אֶל בִּלְעָם. הַבּוּזִי. שֶׁהָיְתָה נְבוּאָתוֹ בְזוּיָה. נֹפֵל וּגְלוּי עֵינָיִם. מִמִּשְׁפַּחַת רָם. מִן אֲרָם יַנְחֵנִי בָלָק. אָמַר לוֹ רִבִּי אֶלְעָזָר בֶּן עֲזַרְיָה. אִין הוּא הוּא. כְּבָר כִּסָּה עָלָיו הַמָּקוֹם. וְאִין לֵית הוּא הוּא. עָתִיד לְהִתְוַכַּח עִמָּךְ. אֶלָּא אֱלִיהוּ זֶה יִצְחָק. בֶּן בַּרַכְאֵל. בֶּן שֶׁבֵּירְכוֹ הָאֵל. שֶׁנֶּאֱמַר וַיְבָרְכֵהוּ יי. הַבּוּזִי. שֶׁבִּיזָה כָל בָּתֵּי עֲבוֹדָה זָרָה בְשָׁעָה שֶׁנֶּעֱקַד עַל גַּבֵּי הַמִּזְבֵּחַ. מִמִּשְׁפַּחַת רָם. בֶּן אַבְרָם.

Rebbi Aqiba explained: "Elihu Ben Barakhel the Buzite from the family Ram got angry.[183]" Elihu that is Bileam. Ben Barakhel, who came to curse Israel but blessed them. The Buzite[184], whose prophecy was degraded, "who falls down open-eyed[185]." From the family Ram, "from Aram did Balaq lead me[186]." Rebbi Eleazar ben Azariah said to him, if he is he, then the Omnipresent already covered it up. If he is not he, in the future [world] he will argue with you. But Elihu that is Isaac. Ben Barakhel, the son whom God blessed, as it was said: "The Eternal had blessed him[187]". The Buzite[184], who degraded all temples of foreign worship at the moment he was bound on the altar. From the family Ram, the son of Abram.

183 *Job* 32:2.
184 From the root בוז "to insult, to degrade".
185 *Num.* 24:4.
186 *Num.* 23:7.
187 *Gen.* 26:12. In the Babli, *Baba Batra* 15b, the consensus it that Elihu was Jewish; cf. Tosaphot *s. v.* אליהוא Some commentators note that *Gen.* 25:11 would have been a better quote since it mentions Isaac's status as son and uses the term Elohim, contained in the name, and not YHWH, as in *Gen.* 26:12.

מֹשֶׁה כָּתַב חֲמִשָּׁה סִפְרֵי תוֹרָה. וְחָזַר וְכָתַב פָּרָשַׁת בָּלָק וּבִלְעָם.(20d, line 25) וְכָתַב סִפְרוֹ שֶׁל אִיּוֹב.

Moses wrote the five books of the Torah and added the chapters about Balaq and Bileam. He also wrote the book of Job[188].

188 The same statement in the Babli, *Baba Batra* 13b; only that the last eight verses of the Torah are attributed to Joshua. The chapter about Balaq and Bileam is a recitation of facts, ostensibly not needed as part of the Law.

(20d, line 27) אִישׁ תָּם וְיָשָׁר וִירֵא אֱלֹהִים וְסָר מֵרָע. אָמַר רִבִּי תַחְלִיפָא קַיְסָרְיָא. שֶׁהָיָה וַתְּרָן. אָמַר לֵיהּ רִבִּי זְעִירָא. וּמָאן דְּלֵית הוּא וַתְּרָן לֵית הוּא כָשֵׁר. אֶלָּא שֶׁהָיָה מְוַתֵּר עַל קִלְלָתוֹ.

""A man, artless and straight, fearing God and fleeing from evil[152]". Rebbi Taḥlifa from Caesarea said, he was conciliatory. Rebbi Zeʿira said to him, is a person who is not conciliatory not acceptable? But he was conciliatory even if cursed[189].

189 Since it is forbidden to hate one's neighbor in one's heart (*Lev.* 19:17), if the verse attests that he was "fleeing from evil", this proves that even that prohibition he did not fail to honor.

In the Babli, *Baba Batra* 15b, *Megillah* 28a, he is declared to have been conciliatory in money matters.

מי שקינא פרק ששי

(fol. 20d) **משנה א**: מִי שֶׁקִּנֵּא לָהּ וְנִסְתְּרָה אֲפִילוּ שָׁמַע מִן הָעוֹף הַפּוֹרֵחַ יוֹצִיא וְיִתֵּן כְּתוּבָּה דִּבְרֵי רִבִּי אֱלִיעֶזֶר. רִבִּי יְהוֹשֻׁעַ אוֹמֵר מִשֶּׁיִּשָּׂאוּ וְיִתְּנוּ בָהּ מוֹזְרוֹת בַּלְּבָנָה.

Mishnah 1: If somebody declared his jealousy to [his wife] and she went to a secluded place[1], even if he heard about it from a bird flying by[2] he has to divorce her[3] and pay the *ketubah*, the words of Rebbi Eliezer. Rebbi Joshua says, from the moment she is the subject of talk of women spinning by moonlight[4].

1   He declared his jealousy to his wife and he has no witnesses that she went to a rendez-vous with the presumed paramour.

2   A rumor whose source he cannot trace.

3   R. Eliezer stated in Mishnah 1:1 that a husband needs no witnesses to bring his wife to the Temple after he declared his jealousy before two witnesses. If he heard a rumor that would give him a reason to act, his wife becomes forbidden to him until after she drank the water and was found innocent. If he is unwilling or unable to bring her to the Temple, he must divorce his wife and pay the *ketubah* since the divorce is a result of his own action.

4   That means, if her infidelity is the talk of the town. R. Joshua holds in Mishnah 1:1 that the wife can be brought to the Temple only on the testimony of two reliable witnesses. But if her conduct is the talk of the town, the husband would have to assume that the rumor is true and that any sexual relations with her would be potentially sinful.

הלכה א: מִי שֶׁקִּינֵּא לָהּ וְנִסְתְּרָה כול׳. רִבִּי יוֹחָנָן בְּשֵׁם רִבִּי יַנַּיי. כָּל הָהֵן פִּירְקָא מִשֶּׁהִתְרָה בָהּ וְאָמַר לָהּ. אַל תִּיסְתְּרִי עִם אִישׁ פְּלוֹנִי. מַשְׁקִינֵּא לָהּ וְנִסְתְּרָה. רִבִּי שִׁמְעוֹן בֶּן לָקִישׁ אָמַר. אֲפִילוּ לֹא נִסְתְּרָה. אָמַר רִבִּי זְעִירָא קוֹמֵי רִבִּי יָסָא. לֹא דְרִבִּי שִׁמְעוֹן בֶּן לָקִישׁ פְּלִיג. אֶלָּא סָבַר כְּהָהֵן תַּנָּייָה וְהוּא מֵיקַל בְּעֵידֵי סְתִירָה. אֲנָן תַּנִּינָן. מַחֲלוֹקֶת. אִית תַּנָּיֵי תַנֵּי. סְתָם. אָמַר רִבִּי זְעִירָא קוֹמֵי רִבִּי מָנָא. לֹא עַל מַה דְּרִבִּי אֱלִיעֶזֶר אָמַר רִבִּי יְהוֹשֻׁעַ פְּלִיג. אֶלָּא בְגִין דְּתַנִּינָן. רִבִּי יְהוֹשֻׁעַ אוֹמֵר עַד שֶׁיִּשָּׂאוּ וְיִתְּנוּ בָהּ מוֹצְרוֹת בַּלְּבָנָה. רִבִּי אַבָּא מָרִי בָּעֵי. תַּמָּן אָמַר רִבִּי חִזְקִיָּה רִבִּי אַבָּהוּ בְּשֵׁם רִבִּי אֶלְעָזָר. כָּל־מָקוֹם שֶׁשָּׁנָה רִבִּי מַחֲלוֹקֶת וְחָזַר וְשָׁנָה סְתָם הֲלָכָה כִּסְתָם. וְכָא הוּא אָמַר הָכֵין.

"If somebody declared his jealousy and she went to a secluded place," etc. Rebbi Joḥanan in the name of Rebbi Yannai: This entire chapter [deals with the case that] he warned her and said to her, do not be at a secluded place with man X, after he declared his jealousy and she went to a secluded place[5]. Rebbi Simeon ben Laqish said, even if she did not go to a secluded place[6]. Rebbi Ze'ira said before Rebbi Yasa: Not that Rebbi Simeon ben Laqish disagrees, only he is lenient about witnesses to the hiding[7]. We have stated a disagreement. Some state it anonymously[8]. Rebbi Ze'ira said before Rebbi Mana[9]: Rebbi Joshua does not disagree with what Rebbi Eliezer said, only that we have stated: "Rebbi Joshua says, only if[10] she is the subject of talk of women carding by moonlight." Rebbi Abba Mari asked: There[11], Rebbi Ḥizqiah, Rebbi Abbahu said in the name of Rebbi Eleazar, everywhere where Rebbi taught a disagreement and returned to the problem later and taught it anonymously, practice follows the anonymous opinion. And here he says so[12]?

5   That the husband had some information that his wife met the man forbidden to her.

6   If there is not even a single witness against her.

7   There is no difference of interpretation between R. Joḥanan and R. Simeon ben Laqish; the latter only follows the opinion attributed to R. Eliezer in Mishnah 1:1.

8   The opinion attributed to R. Eliezer in Mishnah 6:1.

9   R. Mana I.

10   This is the reading of the Mishnah in the Babli, which can be read as meaning that if the wife is the talk of the town, even a rumor of unknown origin forces the husband to divorce his wife.

11   *'Orlah*, Chapter 2, Note 30.

12   If Mishnah 6:1 is stated anonymously, it would imply that in Mishnah 1:1 practice follows R. Eliezer. However, it is evident not only that general practice follows R. Joshua against R. Eliezer but also that in the case of the suspected wife, two witnesses of her misbehavior are needed to prohibit her to her husband. Therefore, the argument that R. Joshua only makes an anonymous statement precise is invalid.

(20d line 61) אֲנָן תַּנִּינָן. אִית תַּנָּיֵי תַנֵּי. מוֹצְרוֹת. מוֹצְרוֹת. מָאן דָּמַר. מוֹצְרוֹת. מָצְרָן עֲמַר. וּמָאן דָּמַר. מוֹזְרוֹת. שָׁזְרָן כִּיתָּן.

We have stated: carders. Some Tannaïm state: spinners. He who said carders, they card wool. He who said spinners, they spin flax.

מַה נָן קַיָּימִין. אִין בְּהַהוּא[13] דְּשָׁמַע וְלָא יָדַע מִן מָאן שָׁמַע. כְּעוֹף הַפּוֹרֵחַ הוּא. וְאִין בְּהַהוּא[13] דְּשָׁמַע וְיָדַע מִמָּאן שָׁמַע. כְּעֵד מִפִּי עֵד הוּא. אֶלָּא כֵן אֲנָן קַיָּימִין פְּלוֹנִי מִפְּלוֹנִי וּפְלוֹנִי מִפְּלוֹנִי. מִילָּה דְלֵית בָּהּ תֵּימְלִיוֹסִים.

Where do we hold[14]? If about him who heard and did not know from whom he heard, it is like a bird flying by. If about him who heard and knew from whom he heard, it is a witness reporting the words of another witness[15]. But here we deal with the case that X [heard] from Y and Y from Z[16]; a word without foundation[17].

13   Reading of a Geniza fragment. In the Leiden ms., the reading may be either בהן "in the case of" or כהן "as the case".

14   The information discussed by the women working by moonlight.

15   This is hearsay evidence about which in the case of a suspected wife Rabbis Eliezer and Joshua disagree in Chapter 1 (Notes 27, 28).

16   Hearsay of hearsay.

17   Reading of a Geniza fragment: תמילווסיס, which identifies the final letter as *s*. *Arukh* explains as Greek θεμέλιος "of the foundation"; Krauss suggests θεμελίωσις, ἡ, -εως "foundation".

משנה ב: (fol. 20d) אָמַר עֵד אֶחָד אֲנִי רְאִיתִיהָ שֶׁנִּיטְמֵאת לֹא הָיְתָה שׁוֹתָה. וְלֹא עוֹד אֶלָּא אֲפִילוּ עֶבֶד אֲפִילוּ שִׁפְחָה הֲרֵי אֵלּוּ נֶאֱמָנִין אַף לְפָסְלָהּ מִכְּתוּבָּתָהּ. חֲמוֹתָהּ וּבַת חֲמוֹתָהּ וְצָרָתָהּ וִיבִמְתָּהּ וּבַת בַּעֲלָהּ הֲרֵי אֵלּוּ נֶאֱמָנוֹת. לֹא לְפָסְלָהּ מִכְּתוּבָּתָהּ אָמְרוּ אֶלָּא שֶׁלֹּא תִשְׁתֶּה.

Mishnah 2: If a single witness said "I saw her when she became impure", she could not drink[18]. Not only that, but even a slave or a slave-girl are believed to cause her to lose her *ketubah*. Her mother-in-law, the mother-in-law's daughter, her co-wife, her sister-in-law, and her husband's daughter are trustworthy[19]. They said this not to make her lose her *ketubah* but that she could not drink[20].

18   Even though by biblical standards a single witness usually is not considered, here he is accepted by biblical standards as explained in Mishnah 4 to bar the husband from bringing his wife to the Temple. He is not a witness in a criminal case (against the wife and her paramour) but his testimony indirectly forces the husband to divorce his wife and also frees him from payment of the *ketubah* since, as stated at the end of Halakhah 4, his testimony "has feet", i. e., after two witnesses for the declaration of

jealousy and two witnesses that she went to a secluded place, the testimony that he saw them having sex is credible (if his testimony holds up under cross examination).

19   These women are barred from testifying to her husband's death (Mishnah *Yebamot* 15:4, Notes 81,82) because they are presumed to hate her.

20   Then the husband has to divorce her *and* pay the *ketubah*, which is not in the personal interest of these women.

(fol. 20d) **הלכה ב**: אָמַר עֵד אֶחָד אֲנִי רְאִיתִיהָ שֶׁנִּיטְמֵאת כול'. וְעֵד אֵין בָּהּ. אֵין לִי אֶלָּא עֵד. מְנַיִין אֲפִילוּ עֶבֶד אֲפִילוּ שִׁפְחָה. תַּלְמוּד לוֹמַר וְעֵד אֵין בָּהּ מִכָּל־מָקוֹם. וּכְרִבִּי יִשְׁמָעֵאל. דְּרִבִּי יִשְׁמָעֵאל אָמַר. כָּל־מָקוֹם שֶׁנֶּאֱמַר בַּתּוֹרָה עֵד סְתָם הֲרֵי אֵלוּ בִּכְלָל שְׁנֵי עֵדִים עַד שֶׁיְּפָרֵשׁ הַכָּתוּב שֶׁהוּא עֵד אֶחָד. אַשְׁכָּח תַּנֵּי. רִבִּי יִשְׁמָעֵאל אוֹמֵר. שְׁנֵי עֵדִים.

Halakhah 2: "If a single witness said 'I saw her when she became impure',"etc. "And there is no witness against her[21]"; not only a witness [of good standing], from where even a male or female slave? The verse says, "*and* there is no witness against her", any one[22]. And following Rebbi Ismael? As Rebbi Ismael said[23], at any place where the Torah mentions "a witness", in principle that means two witnesses unless the verse makes it clear that he is a single witness. It was found stated: Rebbi Ismael says two witnesses[24].

21   *Num.* 5:13.

22   This follows R. Aqiba, who interprets every "and" as an addition [more explicitly *Num. rabba* 9(6)].

23   In the Babli, 31b and *Sanhedrin* 30a, and *Sifry Num.* 7, this is quoted as everybody's opinion.

24   This seems to be the opinion of the Tanna of *Sifry Num.* 7. The Babli, 31b, explains the problem away by reading the verse "and *two* witnesses are not against her," meaning that one is. If one does not need two witnesses, one does not need quality witnesses.

(21a line 2) מַתְנִיתָא מִשֶׁהוֹדָה רִבִּי עֲקִיבָה לְרִבִּי טַרְפוֹן. דְּתַנֵּי. רִבִּי טַרְפוֹן אוֹמֵר. עֵד אֶחָד נֶאֱמָן לְטַמְאוֹתָהּ וְאֵין עֵד אֶחָד נֶאֱמָן לְהַפְסִידָהּ מִכְּתוּבָּתָהּ. רִבִּי עֲקִיבָה אוֹמֵר. כְּשֵׁם שֶׁעֵד אֶחָד נֶאֱמָן לְטַמוֹתָהּ. כֵּן עֵד אֶחָד נֶאֱמָן לְהַפְסִידָהּ מִכְּתוּבָּתָהּ. אָמַר לוֹ רִבִּי טַרְפוֹן. אֵיכָן מָצִינוּ עֵד אֶחָד בְּמָמוֹן כְּלוּם. אָמַר לוֹ רִבִּי עֲקִיבָה. וְאֵיכָן מָצִינוּ עֵד אֶחָד בְּאֵשֶׁת אִישׁ כְּלוּם. אֶלָּא כְּשֵׁם שֶׁעֵד אֶחָד נֶאֱמָן לְטַמוֹתָהּ. כָּךְ עֵד אֶחָד נֶאֱמָן לְהַפְסִידָהּ מִכְּתוּבָּתָהּ. חָזַר רִבִּי עֲקִיבָה לִהְיוֹת שׁוֹנֶה כְּרִבִּי טַרְפוֹן.

Was our Mishnah [formulated] after Rebbi Aqiba agreed with Rebbi Tarphon[25]? As it was stated: Rebbi Tarphon says, a single witness is believed to declare her impure[26] but not to let her lose her *ketubah*[27]. Rebbi Aqiba says, just as a single witness is believed to declare her impure, so he is believed to let her lose her *ketubah*. Rebbi Tarphon said to him: Where do we find that a single witness proves anything in money matters[28]? Rebbi Aqiba answered him, but where do we find that a single witness proves anything in matrimonial matters[29]? But just as a single witness is believed to declare her impure, so he is believed to let her lose her *ketubah*. Rebbi Aqiba changed his mind and taught following Rebbi Tarphon[30].

25 Since the Mishnah states that the single witness can also deprive the wife of her *ketubah*, the Mishnah follows R. Aqiba before he changed his mind.

26 This follows a general principle formulated in the Babli as: "A single witness is believable in matters of prohibitions." For example, if a single witness shows that some food a person ate was of a forbidden kind, if the eater was unaware of the fact and therefore the sin was unintentional, he is obligated for a purification sacrifice on the testimony of a single witness.

27 Since this needs two witnesses.

28 While a single witness cannot *prove* anything in court (*Deut.* 19:15), the same verse is interpreted to mean that the testimony of a single witness in

support of a claim of one of the parties can obligate a defendant to swear that he owes nothing (*Šebuot* 6:1 fol. 36d; Babli *Ketubot* 87b). In the case here, there is no claim from any of the concerned parties.

29   Since they have implications in criminal law, marriage or divorce are invalid unless executed in front of two witnesses. It is true that a single witness can inform about the dissolution of a marriage by the husband's death, but this does not have the status of testimony (*Yebamot* Chap. 15).

30   The rules of testimony for prohibitions (in cases which cannot lead to criminal prosecution) and money matters are distinct and testimony acceptable for one facet of a case may not be acceptable for the rest.

(21a line 9) רְבִּי בּוּן בַּר חִייָה בָּעֵי. חֲמוֹתָהּ שֶׁאָמְרָה. אֲנִי רְאִיתִיהָ שֶׁנִּיטְמֵאת. [וְאַתְּ אָמַר. לֹא הָיְתָה שׁוֹתָה. וּבָא אַחֵר וְאָמַר אֲנִי רְאִיתִיהָ שֶׁנִּיטְמֵאת.]³¹ מָה [הָיָה]³¹ בָּא לְהָעִיד. אִם לְהַשְׁקוֹתָהּ. כְּבָר נִרְאֵית שֶׁלֹּא לִשְׁתּוֹת. אֶלָּא לֹא בָא [אֶלָּא]³¹ לְהַפְסִידָהּ מִכְּתוּבָּתָהּ. שֶׁאֵין מַפְסִידִין מָמוֹן עַל פִּי עֵד אֶחָד. רְבִּי יוֹסֵי בָּעֵי. שָׁמַע מִן הָעוֹף הַפּוֹרֵחַ. אֲנִי רְאִיתִיהָ שֶׁנִּיטְמֵאת. אַתְּ אָמַר. לֹא הָיְתָה שׁוֹתָה. וּבָא אֶחָד וְאָמַר. אֲנִי רְאִיתִיהָ שֶׁנִּיטְמֵאת. מָה בָא לְהָעִיד. אִם לְהַשְׁקוֹתָהּ. כְּבָר נִרְאֵית שֶׁלֹּא [לִשְׁתּוֹת].³² אֶלָּא לֹא בָא אֶלָּא לְהַפְסִידָהּ מִכְּתוּבָּתָהּ. שֶׁאֵין מַפְסִידִין מָמוֹן עַל פִּי עֵד אֶחָד.

Rebbi Abun bar Ḥiyya asked: If her mother-in-law said "I saw her when she became impure", [you say that she did not drink. If then somebody else came and said, "I saw her when she became impure"], about what does he testify? If to make her drink, it was clear beforehand that she does not drink. He would come only to deny her *ketubah* to her, but one cannot make a person lose money on the testimony of one witness³³!

Rebbi Yose asked: If he heard from a bird flying by: "I saw her when she became impure", you say that she did not drink. If then somebody came and said, "I saw her when she became impure", about what does he testify? If to make her drink, it was clear beforehand that she does not drink. He would come only to deny her *ketubah* to her, but one cannot make a person lose money on the testimony of one witness[33]!

31 Reading of a *Geniza* fragment; missing in Leiden ms. and *editio princeps*.

32 Reading of the Rome ms. and a *Geniza* fragment; missing in Leiden ms. and *editio princeps*.

33 Even if we agree with the Mishnah that a single witness is empowered to forbid the woman to her husband and as a consequence to make her forfeit her *ketubah* (Note 18), this is because the court is biblically empowered to forbid her to her husband on the testimony (Note 24). But if the acceptable testimony is not needed, it is questionable whether its consequence should be enforced.

(21a line 17) מִמַּה דְרִבִּי יוֹסֵי אָמַר. פְּלוֹנִי אָכַל חֵלֶב וְהִתְרוּ בוֹ אֵינוֹ לוֹקֶה. אָמַר לוֹ אֶחָד. חֵלֶב הוּא. וְהִתְרוּ בוֹ שְׁנַיִם. לוֹקֶה. וְעִיקַר עֵידוּתוֹ לֹא בְעֵד אֶחָד הוּא. מִמַּה דְרִבִּי יוּדָה אוֹמֵר. פְּלוֹנִי נָזִיר וְנִיטְמָא. הִתְרֵיתִי בוֹ. אֵינוֹ לוֹקֶה. אָמַר לוֹ אֶחָד. נָזִיר אַתָּה. וְהָיָה נוֹהֵג בִּנְזִירוּת עַל פִּיו. שָׁתָה יַיִן וְנִיטְמָא לַמֵּתִים. הִתְרוּ בוֹ שְׁנַיִם. לוֹקֶה. וְעִיקַר עֵידוּתוֹ לֹא בְעֵד אֶחָד הוּא. מִמַּה דְרִבִּי מָנָא אָמַר. פְּלוֹנִית כּוֹהֶנֶת וְזִינָת. וּבָא עָלֶיהָ בַּעֲלָהּ הַכֹּהֵן[34] וְהִתְרֵיתִי בוֹ. [אֵינוֹ][35] לוֹקֶה. נִסְתְּרָה בִּפְנֵי שְׁנַיִם. אָמַר אֶחָד. אֲנִי רְאִיתִיהָ שֶׁנִּיטְמֵאת. וּבָא עָלֶיהָ בַּעֲלָהּ[36] כֹּהֵן. הִתְרוּ בוֹ שְׁנַיִם. לוֹקֶה. עִיקַר עֵידוּתוֹ לֹא בְעֵד אֶחָד הוּא.

From what Rebbi Yose said, "X ate suet, and they warned him," he is not whipped[37]. If one person said to him, that is suet, and two warned him, he is whipped[38]. Is not the main testimony given by a single witness[39]?

From what Rebbi Jehudah is saying: "X is a *nazir*[40], he became defiled, and I had warned him," he is not whipped. If one person said to him, you are a *nazir*, and based on this testimony he behaved like a *nazir*, when then he drank wine or became impure in the impurity of the dead, if two warned him, he is whipped. Is not the main testimony given by a single witness[41]?

From what Rebbi Mana said, "X is the wife of a Cohen and whored; her husband, a Cohen, then had relations with her[42] but I had warned him;" he is [not] whipped. If she went to a secluded place in the presence of two, and one said, I saw her that she became impure; when her husband, the Cohen, had relations with her but two had warned him, he is whipped. Is not the main testimony given by a single witness[41]?

34 From a *Geniza* ms. Leiden ms. and *editio princeps* ובא עליה בעלה ובעלה כהן "her husband had relations with her and copulated with her as a Cohen".

35 From a *Geniza* ms. Missing in Leiden ms. and *editio princeps*.

36 From a *Geniza* ms. Leiden ms. and *editio princeps* ובא בעלה עליה כהן, an unidiomatic word order.

37 Eating suet from cattle, sheep, or goats, the part of the fat of sacrificial animals which is burned on the altar, is a crime (*Lev.* 7:23,25). If a single witness comes and accuses somebody of having eaten suet criminally, i. e., after having been duly informed by two adults that eating that suet would be a criminal offense, his testimony is nothing since he is a single witness.

The entire paragraph is also in *Nazir* 8:1, fol. 57a

38 If a single witness (after due examination by the court) testifies that a certain piece of meat is suet, that piece legally has the status of suet (Note 26). If then two people warn a third person that eating the meat would be criminal (thereby establishing intent; cf. Chapter 3, Note 121) and two witnesses testify to the act, this is testimony by two witnesses, valid in court, even though the status of the piece of meat as suet was based on the testimony of only one witness.

39 By analogy, on the questions raised in the preceding paragraph, one might argue that the preceding information given either from a person precluded from being a witness in court or from an unsubstantiated rumor does not impair the validity of the later

testimony.

40 *Num.* 6. The witness testified that he heard X declaring a vow of *nazir* (cf. *Berakhot* Chapter 7, Note 79) but that he did not keep it. Again he is a single witness whose word carries no weight in court.

41 The argument is totally parallel to the first one.

42 After she was desecrated, a felony (cf. Chapter 1, Note 123).

(fol. 20d) **משנה ג**: שֶׁהָיָה בַדִּין. וּמָה אִם עֵדוּת הָרִאשׁוֹנָה שֶׁאֵינָהּ אוֹסְרַתָּהּ אִיסּוּר עוֹלָם אֵינָהּ מִתְקַיֶּימֶת בְּפָחוֹת מִשְּׁנַיִם עֵדוּת הָאַחֲרוֹנָה שֶׁאוֹסְרַתָּהּ אִיסּוּר עוֹלָם אֵינוֹ דִין שֶׁלֹּא תִתְקַיֵּים בְּפָחוֹת מִשְּׁנַיִם. תַּלְמוּד לוֹמַר וְעֵד אֵין בָּהּ כָּל־עֵדוּת שֶׁיֵּשׁ בָּהּ.

Mishnah 3: It would have been logical: Since the first testimony,[43] which does not forbid her permanently, is not confirmed if not from two [witnesses], the last testimony,[43] which forbids her permanently, should reasonably only be confirmed by [witnesses]. The verse says: "There is *no* witness about her[44]", any kind of testimony about her.

43 As the Halakhah explains, the first testimony is the testimony about the wife's going to a secluded place, where R. Joshua requires two witnesses of good standing. The last testimony is that of adultery, where the preceding Mishnaiot accept even the proverbial "bird flying by". The confirmation is the acceptance of the testimony by a competent court.

44 *Num.* 5:13.

(fol. 21a) **הלכה ג**: שֶׁהָיָה בַדִּין. וּמָה אִם עֵדוּת הָרִאשׁוֹנָה כול'. עֵדוּת הָרִאשׁוֹנָה זוֹ סְתִירָה. עֵדוּת הָאַחֲרוֹנָה זוֹ טוּמְאָה. מַתְנִיתָא דְּרִבִּי יְהוֹשֻׁעַ. דְּרִבִּי יְהוֹשֻׁעַ אָמַר. מְקַנֵּא מַתְרֶה לָהּ עַל פִּי שְׁנַיִם וּמַשְׁקֶה לָהּ עַל פִּי שְׁנַיִם. אָמַר רִבִּי מָנָא.

וַאֲפִילוּ כָּאהֵן תַּנָּא אֲתָיָיא הִיא. דְּתַנֵּי. רִבִּי יוֹסֵי בֵּירִבִּי יְהוּדָה אוֹמֵר מִשּׁוּם רִבִּי לְעֶזֶר. מְקַנֵּא לָהּ עַל פִּי עֵד אֶחָד אוֹ עַל פִּי עַצְמוֹ. וּמַשְׁקֶה עַל פִּי שְׁנָיִם.

Halakhah 3: "It would have been logical: Since the first testimony," etc. The first testimony is about being in a secluded place; the last testimony is about impurity. The Mishnah follows Rebbi Joshua, since Rebbi Joshua says[45], "he declares his jealousy and warns her by the testimony of two [witnesses], and makes her drink by the testimony of two [witnesses]." Rebbi Mana said, it even follows the Tanna, about whom was stated[46]: "Rebbi Yose ben Rebbi Jehudah says in the name of Rebbi Eliezer: He declares his jealousy before one witness or by himself, but makes her drink by the testimony of two [witnesses]."

---

45   Mishnah 1:1, Note 4.   46   Chapter 1, Note 16.

(fol. 20d) **משנה ד**: קַל וָחוֹמֶר לְעֵדוּת הָרִאשׁוֹנָה מֵעַתָּה. וּמָה עֵדוּת הָאַחֲרוֹנָה שֶׁאוֹסְרַתָּהּ אִיסּוּר עוֹלָם הֲרֵי הִיא מִתְקַייֶמֶת בְּעֵד אֶחָד עֵדוּת הָרִאשׁוֹנָה שֶׁאֵינָהּ אוֹסְרַתָּהּ אִיסּוּר עוֹלָם אֵינוֹ דִין שֶׁתִּתְקַיֵּים בְּעֵד אֶחָד. תַּלְמוּד לוֹמַר כִּי מָצָא בָהּ עֶרְוַת דָּבָר וּלְהַלָּן הוּא אוֹמֵר עַל פִּי שְׁנַיִם עֵדִים יָקוּם דָּבָר. מַה לְהַלָּן עַל פִּי שְׁנַיִם עֵדִים אַף כָּאן עַל פִּי שְׁנַיִם עֵדִים.

Mishnah 4: [47]There would now be an argument *de minore ad majus* for the first testimony! Since the last testimony, which forbids her permanently, is confirmed from a single witness, the first testimony, which does not forbid her permanently, should logically be confirmed from a single witness. The verse says, "for he found out about her a matter of sexual misbehavior,[48]" and further, it says, "by the mouth of two witnesses a matter should be confirmed.[49]"

משנה ה: עֵד אוֹמֵר נִיטְמֵאת וְעֵד אוֹמֵר לֹא נִיטְמֵאת. אִשָּׁה אוֹמֶרֶת נִיטְמֵאת וְאִשָּׁה אוֹמֶרֶת לֹא נִיטְמֵאת הָיְתָה שׁוֹתָה. אֶחָד אוֹמֵר נִיטְמֵאת וְעֵדִים שְׁנַיִם אוֹמְרִים לֹא נִיטְמֵאת הָיְתָה שׁוֹתָה. שְׁנַיִם אוֹמְרִים נִיטְמֵאת וְאֶחָד אוֹמֵר לֹא נִיטְמֵאת לֹא הָיְתָה שׁוֹתָה.

Mishnah 5: If one witness says, she became impure, but another witness says, she did not become impure, or one woman[50] says, she became impure, but another woman says, she did not become impure, she would drink[51]. If one [witness] says, she became impure, but two [witnesses] say, she did not become impure, she did drink[52]. If two [witnesses] say, she became impure, but one [witness] says, she did not become impure, she would not drink.

47 This is the second half of Mishnah 3.

48 *Deut.* 24:1. For the House of Shammai, this is the only reason admitted for a divorce (Mishnah *Giṭṭin* 9:10); for the House of Hillel, this is a reason why there must be a divorce.

49 *Deut.* 19:15. The verse proves that in any judicial proceedings, דבר means a proof by two witnesses. Since the husband cannot make his wife drink unless he presents his case to the Temple court, all judicial rules apply here. But a divorce because of the wife's adultery can be given by the husband on his own (even though to deprive her of her *ketubah* after the divorce he needs the judgment of a court.)

50 This case has to be treated separately since a woman, while she can point out facts, cannot be a formal witness.

51 Mishnah 1 stated that in case of certainty, the woman may not be brought to the Temple. In the case here, two contradicting statements cancel one another; there is uncertainty. In all cases, it is supposed that there are two witnesses who attest that the wife met another man in a secluded place.

52 One witness against two witnesses accounts for nothing.

הלכה ד: (fol. 21a) קַל וָחוֹמֶר לָעֵדוּת הָרִאשׁוֹנָה מֵעַתָּה כול'. גִּידוּל בַּר מִינְיָימִין בְּשֵׁם רַב. כָּל־מָקוֹם שֶׁהִכְשִׁירוּ עֵדוּת אִשָּׁה בָּאִישׁ הָאִישׁ מַכְחִישׁ אֶת הָאִשָּׁה וְהָאִשָּׁה מַכְחֶשֶׁת אֶת הָאִישׁ. נִיתְנֵי. עֵד אֶחָד אוֹמֵר. נִטְמֵית. וְאִשָּׁה אָמְרָה. לֹא נִטְמֵית. אִשָּׁה אָמְרָה. נִטְמֵית. וְעֵד אוֹמֵר. לֹא נִטְמֵת. תַּנֵּיי דְּבֵית רִבִּי כֵן. תַּנֵּי בְּשֵׁם רִבִּי נְחֶמְיָה. הוֹלְכִין אַחַר רוֹב עֵדוּת. הֵיךְ עֲבִידָא. שְׁתֵּי נָשִׁים וְאִשָּׁה אַחַת עָשׂוּ אוֹתָהּ כִּשְׁנֵי עֵדִים וְעֵד אֶחָד. הָדָא דְּתֵימַר בְּאִשָּׁה וְנָשִׁים. אֲבָל אִם הָיוּ מֵאָה נָשִׁים וְעֵד אֶחָד כְּעֵד בְּעֵד אִינּוּן.

Halakhah 4: "There would now be an argument *de minore ad majus* for the first testimony," etc. [53]Gidul bar Miniamin in the name of Rav: Anywhere they accepted the testimony of a woman parallel to that of a man, a man can contradict a woman and a woman can contradict a man. Then one should state: "A witness says that she became impure, and a woman says that she did not become impure; a woman said that she became impure and a witness said that she did not become impure." In the House of Rebbi they stated it this way. It was stated in the name of Rebbi Nehemiah: One follows the majority of the testimonies. How is that? Two women against one woman they considered as if there were two witnesses against one witness. What you say refers to a woman and women. But if there were a hundred women against one [male] witness, they are like one witness.

53 Essentially the same text, only referring to testimony of the husband's death instead of the wife's infidelity, in *Yebamot* Chapter 15, Notes 135-138 and here, Chapter 9, Halakhah 7. .

(21a line 38) רַב אָדָא בַּר אֲחַוָה אָמַר. עֵד אֶחָד נֶאֱמָן לְטַמּוֹתָהּ. אֵין עֵד אֶחָד נֶאֱמָן לְהַפְסִידָהּ מִכְּתוּבָּתָהּ. אָמַר רַב חִסְדָּא. מַה טַּעַם אָמְרוּ. עֵד אֶחָד נֶאֱמָן לְטַמּוֹתָהּ. מִפְּנֵי שֶׁרַגְלַיִם לַדָּבָר.

Rav Ada bar Aḥawah said, a single witness is believed to declare her impure, but a single witness is not believed to make her lose her *ketubah*.[54] Rav Ḥisda said, why did they say that a single witness is believed to declare her impure? Because the thing has feet to stand on[55].

54   He strictly follows the rule that a single witness is acceptable about prohibitions but not in money matters.

55   The single witness is believed to prohibit her to her husband because there are two other witnesses who accuse her of going to a secluded place with another man. Then he can also be believed, by rabbinic rule, that the husband does not have to pay (certainly for those who hold that the *ketubah* is a rabbinic institution.)

(21a line 41) שִׁמְעוֹן בַּר בָּא בְשֵׁם רִבִּי יוֹחָנָן. כָּאן לֹא הָיְתָה שׁוֹתָה וּבְעֶגְלָה עֲרוּפָה הָיוּ עוֹרְפִין. רַב אָמַר. הָיְתָה[56] שׁוֹתָה. מַתְנִיתָא פְּלִיגָא עַל רַב. עֵד אֶחָד אוֹמֵר. נִטְמֵאת. וּשְׁנַיִם אוֹמְרִים. לֹא נִטְמֵאת. הָיְתָה שׁוֹתָה. הָא [עֵד][57] בְּעֵד אֶחָד לֹא הָיְתָה שׁוֹתָה. פָּתַר לָהּ בִּפְסוּלֵי עֵדוּת. וְאֵין בִּפְסוּלֵי עֵדוּת אֱמוֹר סוֹפָהּ. שְׁנַיִם אוֹמְרִים. נִיטְמֵאת. וְעֵד אֶחָד אוֹמֵר. לֹא נִיטְמֵאת. לֹא הָיְתָה שׁוֹתָה. הָא עֵד בְּעֵד לֹא הָיְתָה שׁוֹתָה. וְהֵיךְ רַב אָמַר. הָיְתָה שׁוֹתָה. רִבִּי יוֹחָנָן אָמַר. לֹא הָיְתָה שׁוֹתָה. מַתְנִיתָא פְּלִיגָא עַל רִבִּי יוֹחָנָן. שְׁנַיִם אוֹמְרִים נִיטְמֵאת. וְעֵד אוֹמֵר לֹא נִיטְמֵאת [לֹא הָיְתָה][57] שׁוֹתָה. הָא עֵד בְּעֵד (לֹא)[58] הָיְתָה שׁוֹתָה. פָּתַר לָהּ בִּפְסוּלֵי עֵדוּת. וְאֵין בִּפְסוּלֵי עֵדוּת אֱמוֹר רֹאשָׁהּ. עֵד אוֹמֵר. נִטְמֵאת. וּשְׁנַיִם אוֹמְרִים לֹא נִטְמֵית. הָיְתָה שׁוֹתָה. הָא עֵד בְּעֵד הָיְתָה שׁוֹתָה. הֵיךְ רִבִּי יוֹחָנָן אָמַר. לֹא הָיְתָה שׁוֹתָה. אָמְרוֹן בְּשֵׁם רִבִּי שְׁמוּאֵל. בִּפְסוּלֵי עֵדוּת הִיא מַתְנִיתָא. אָמְרִין בְּשֵׁם רִבִּי שְׁמוּאֵל. בִּסְתִירָה אַחֶרֶת הִיא מַתְנִיתָא. תֵּיבֵי זְעִירָא בְּעָא קוֹמֵי רִבִּי מָנָא. מַהוּ בִּסְתִירָה אַחֶרֶת הִיא מַתְנִיתָא. אָמַר לֵיהּ. כֵּן אָמַר רִבִּי יוֹחָנָן בְּשֵׁם רִבִּי יַנַּאי. כָּל־הָהֵן פִּירְקָא מַשְׁקִינָהּ לָהּ וְנִסְתְּרָה. נִסְתְּרָה בִּפְנֵי שְׁנַיִם. אָמַר אֶחָד. אֲנִי רְאִיתִיהָ שֶׁנִּיטְמֵאת בְּתוֹךְ כְּדֵי סְתִירָה. יֵשׁ כָּאן סְתִירָה וְיֵשׁ כָּאן טוּמְאָה. לְאַחַר כְּדֵי סְתִירָה. יֵשׁ כָּאן סְתִירָה

וְאֵין כָּאן טוּמְאָה. הָיוּ שְׁלֹשָׁה. אֶחָד אוֹמֵר. אֲנִי רְאִיתִיהָ שֶׁנִּיטְמֵאת בְּתוֹךְ כְּדֵי סְתִירָה. יֵשׁ כָּאן סְתִירָה וְאֵין כָּאן טוּמְאָה. לְאַחַר כְּדֵי סְתִירָה. אֵין כָּאן סְתִירָה וְאֵין כָּאן טוּמְאָה. הָיוּ שְׁלֹשָׁה. אֶחָד אוֹמֵר . אֲנִי רְאִיתִיהָ שֶׁלֹּא נִיטְמֵאת בְּתוֹךְ כְּדֵי סְתִירָה. מַה אַתְּ עָבַד לָהּ. כְּעֵדוּת שֶׁבֵּטְלָה מִקְצָתָהּ בֵּטְלָה כּוּלָהּ אוֹ תִּתְקַיֵּים הָעֵדוּת בִּשְׁאָר. אָמַר רִבִּי אַבָּמְרִי. מִכֵּיוָן דְּאַתְּ מַר. בְּעֵדוּת שֶׁבֵּטְלָה מִקְצָתָהּ בֵּטְלָה כּוּלָהּ מוֹדֶה הוּא הָכָא שֶׁתִּתְקַיֵּים הָעֵדוּת בִּשְׁאָר. מִפְּנֵי שֶׁרְגְלַיִם לַדָּבָר.

[59]Simeon bar Abba in the name of Rabbi Johanan: Here[60], she did not drink but in the case of breaking the calf's neck they did break it[61]. Rav said, she did drink. The Mishnah disagrees with Rav[62]: "If one [witness] says, she became impure, but two [witnesses] say, she did not become impure, she would drink." That[63] implies that if one witness was against another single witness, she would not drink. He explains it for those whose testimony is invalid[64]. But if for those whose testimony is invalid, does not the end say: "If two [witnesses] say, she became impure, but one witness says, she did not become impure, she would not drink." That implies that if one witness was against another single witness, she would drink[65]. How could Rav say, she would drink? [59]Rebbi Johanan said, she would not drink. A Mishnah disagrees with Rebbi Johanan. "If two [witnesses] say, she became impure, but one witness says, she did not become impure, she would not drink." That implies that if one witness was against another single witness, she would drink. He explains it for those whose testimony is invalid. But if for those whose testimony is invalid, does not the first statement say: "If one [witness] says, she became impure, but two [witnesses] say, she did not become impure, she would drink." That implies that if one witness was against another single witness,

she would drink. How could Rebbi Joḥanan say, she would not drink[65]? They said in the name of Rebbi Samuel, the Mishnah talks about those whose testimony is invalid[66]. They said in the name of Rebbi Samuel: The Mishnah speaks about another rendez-vous. Rebbi Ze'ira asked before Rebbi Mana: What does it mean, "the Mishnah speaks about another rendez-vous"? He said to him, so says Rebbi Joḥanan in the name of Rebbi Yannai[67]: This entire chapter [deals with the case that] he had declared his jealousy and she went to a secluded place. She went to a secluded place by the testimony of two [witnesses]. If one of them said, I saw her that she became impure while in the secluded place, there [is testimony] about the seclusion and about impurity[68]. After the time of seclusion, there [is testimony] about the seclusion but not about impurity[69]. If there were three [witnesses]. One said, I saw her that she became impure while in the secluded place, there [is testimony] about the seclusion but not about impurity. If there were three [witnesses]. One said, I saw that she did not become impure while in the secluded place, how do you treat this? As a testimony which, if part of the testimony is thrown out, the entire testimony is thrown out, or does one accept the remainder of the testimony[70]? They said in the name of Rebbi Abba Mari: Even he who says, if part of it is thrown out, all is thrown out, here one accepts the remainder of the testimony, since the matter has feet to stand on[71].

56 Reading of the Rome ms. and the Geniza fragment. Leiden ms: הָיָה "he was".

57 Reading of the Rome ms. and the Geniza fragment; missing in Leiden ms.

58 Missing in Rome ms. and Geniza fragment; is in Leiden ms. but makes no sense.

59 In the Yerushalmi text quoted

by Tosaphot, 32b, s. v. הא, the discussion starts: עֵד אֶחָד אוֹמֵר נִטְמֵאת וְעֵד אֶחָד אוֹמֵר לֹא נִטְמֵאת. "A single witness says, she became impure, but another single witness says, she did not become impure, . . ."

60   In the first case treated in Mishnah 5, that there is the word of one witness against the word of another single witness, cf. Note 59. He amends the Mishnah to read: "She does not drink." The reason seems to be the order in which the testimony is described in the Mishnah: The first witness says that she became impure. By rabbinic rules, he is believed. This means that his testimony counts as much as the testimony of two witnesses. In the language of the Babli (*Soṭah* 32b, 47b; *Yebamot* 88b, 117b; *Ketubot* 22b): "In any case where the Torah declared that a single witness can be believed, he has the status of two." If the Yerushalmi would accept such a statement, it would have to accept R. Johanan's statement here. One has to assume that the second witness states that he observed the woman and the other man during the entire time they were together in a secluded place and that nothing untoward happened.

61   *Deut.* 21:1-9. If two witnesses came and one said that he saw the murderer but the other one said that he saw the murder but not the murderer, there is no testimony which has any standing in court. Therefore, the murderer is unknown.

62   Since Rav accepts the text of the Mishnah as is, one attempts to show that that text is self-contradictory.

63   Since the sentence states that in the presence of a witness who states that she became impure one needs at least two witnesses who state that she did not become impure in order to declare the matter one of doubt, it would follow that there is no scenario in which a single witness can invalidate the testimony of another single witness. This contradicts the first sentence of the Mishnah and Rav's statement.

64   A witness who cannot testify in money matters because his integrity is in question (Mishnah *Sanhedrin* 3:3-4), or a woman or a slave. These have no standing against a single believable witness; one needs at least two, following R. Nehemiah in the first paragraph.

In the Babli, 32b, the problem is solved in a first explanation that in the case of the first sentence, the two contradicting witnesses came to court together. Then there never was testimony and the woman is not held to be an adulteress. For the second case, the single witness came first and his testimony was accepted as fact. Then one needs two witnesses to annul the first testimony. The second explanation follows the Yerushalmi.

65 If the Mishnah would state only the second and third cases, it would be a case of the undistributed middle and could be solved by postulating different scenarios for the different cases. But since the first case is stated apodictically, that way (the first explanation of the Babli) seems to be excluded and neither Rav nor R. Joḥanan can have a totally coherent position.

66 In the Babli, an anonymous statement in support of R. Ḥiyya (bar Abba, student of R. Joḥanan).

67 Cf. Note 5.

68 Since the testimony of this witness about the wife going to a secluded place must be accepted, since it is supported by a second witness, his testimony about her infidelity also must be accepted.

69 There is no difference whether one of two witnesses first testifies together with another that the wife went with another man to a secluded place and then he alone testifies that at the occasion of another rendez-vous she committed adultery, or if the second occasion is mentioned by a third witness. In any case, since it is not claimed that the second witness was present at the second occasion, there are distinct testimonies and the statement about adultery does not have the status of validity conferred by two independent testimonies.

70 This is a separate case. The two witnesses agree about time and place when the wife went to a secluded place with another man. The first witness claims to have witnessed the sexual act, the second witness claims to have observed the couple all the time but that nothing untoward happened. Their testimonies about what happened in seclusion must be thrown out. Does this invalidate the testimony that a secluded rendez-vous took place? In criminal proceedings, the entire testimony would have to be thrown out.

71 That there are two witnesses who testify that the husband formally declared his jealousy before them gives all following testimonies a basis which allows for the relaxation of the rules of criminal proceedings.

אילו נאמרין פרק שביעי

(fol. 21a) **משנה א:** אֵילוּ נֶאֱמָרִין בִּלְשׁוֹנָם. פָּרָשַׁת סוֹטָה וּוִידּוּי מַעֲשֵׂר וּקְרָיַת שְׁמַע וּתְפִילָה וּבִרְכַּת הַמָּזוֹן וּשְׁבוּעַת הָעֵדוּת וּשְׁבוּעַת הַפִּיקָדוֹן.

Mishnah 1: The following are recited in the vernacular: The verses of the suspect wife[1], and the declaration of tithes[2], and the recitation of the *Šemaʿ*[3], and prayer[4], and grace[5], and the oath of a witness[6], and the oath about a deposit[7].

1 The verses the Cohen has to read to the wife before she drinks. While the scroll has to be written in Hebrew, the wife has to understand them and, therefore, they have to be translated into her vernacular.

2 *Deut.* 26:12-16.

3 Cf. *Berakhot*, Chapters 1-2.

4 The eighteen (respectively 7 or 9) benedictions of the '*Amidah*; cf. *Berakhot*, Chapters 1-2.

5 After a meal.

6 If somebody puts an oath on a possible witness that he should come and testify for him; *Lev.* 5:1. Testimony itself is given without an oath.

7 *Ex.* 22:6-12.

(fol. 21b) **הלכה א:** אֵילוּ נֶאֱמָרִין כול'. כְּתִיב וְאָמַר הַכֹּהֵן לָאִשָּׁה. בְּכָל־לָשׁוֹן שֶׁהִיא שׁוֹמַעַת. דִּבְרֵי רִבִּי יֹאשִׁיָּה. אָמַר לֵיהּ רִבִּי יוֹנָתָן. וְאִם אֵינָהּ שׁוֹמַעַת וְלָמָּה הִיא עוֹנָה אַחֲרָיו אָמֵן. אֶלָּא שֶׁלֹּא יֹאמַר לָהּ עַל יְדֵי תּוּרְגְּמָן.

Halakhah 1: "The following are recited," etc. It is written[8]: "The Cohen shall tell the woman," in any language she understands, the words of Rebbi Joshia. Rebbi Jonathan said to him, if she does not understand, how could she answer "Amen, Amen"9? But that he should not talk to her through an interpreter.

8   *Num.* 5:21. The argument being that this clause is redundant. The full verse reads: "The Cohen shall make the woman swear by a curse-oath, the Cohen shall tell the woman:...".

9   In *Sifry Num.* 12, the objection is attributed to R. Ismael, R. Joshia's teacher, not to R. Jonathan, R. Joshia's student. R. Ismael's interpretation is that the Cohen has to go into all details of the proceedings. The Babli, 32b, is the only source which accepts R. Joshia's derivation. Then the Babli, without mentioning names, follows R. Ismael's interpretation but treats it as purely rabbinic.

(21b, line 50) רְבִּי יוֹחָנָן בְּשֵׁם רְבִּי לָעְזָר בֵּירְבִּי שִׁמְעוֹן. לֹא מָצִינוּ שֶׁדִּיבֵּר הַמָּקוֹם עִם אִשָּׁה אֶלָּא עִם שָׂרָה בִּלְבַד. וְהָא כְתִיב אֶל הָאִשָּׁה אָמַר הַרְבָּה אַרְבֶּה וגו׳. אָמַר רִבִּי יַעֲקֹב דִּכְפַר חָנִין. עַל יְדֵי הַתּוּרְגְּמָן. וְהָא כְתִיב וַיֹּאמֶר לִ' לָהּ שְׁנֵי גוֹיִם בְּבִטְנֵךְ. אָמַר רִבִּי בָּא בַר כַּהֲנָא. הַדִּיבּוּר נָפְלָה לָהּ. אָמַר רִבִּי בִּירִי. כַּמָּה כִּירְכּוּרֵי כִירְכּוּרִים. הַקָּדוֹשׁ בָּרוּךְ הוּא מִתְאַוֶּה לִשְׁמוֹעַ שִׂיחָתָן שֶׁלַצַּדְקָנִיּוֹת וַיֹּאמֶר לֹא כִּי צָחַקְתְּ.

[10]Rebbi Johanan in the name of Rebbi Eleazar ben Rebbi Simeon: We do not find that the Omnipresent talked to a woman, except only to Sarah. But is there not written[11]: "To the woman He said: I shall increase," etc.? Rebbi Jacob of Kefar Hanin[12] said, through an interpreter[13]. But is there not written[14]: "The Eternal said to her, two peoples are in your womb"? Rebbi Abba bar Cahana said, the Word fell to her[15]. Rebbi Biri said, how many weaver's shuttles! The Holy One, praise to Him, desires to hear the talk of the just women: "He said no, but you laughed.[16]"

10 *Gen. rabba* 20(12), 45(14), 63(8).
11 *Gen.* 3:16.
12 Elsewhere he is called "from Kefar Hanan".

13 Adam is addressed by the Eternal in 3:9, the woman in 3:13, the snake in 3:14.

14 *Gen.* 25:23.

15 A word about her fell to a prophet (in the opinion of *Gen. rabba*, Sem ben Noah.)

16 The only time we find a mention of God addressing a woman directly it is about an unimportant matter.

(21b, line 55) וִידוּי מַעֲשֵׂר. דִּכְתִיב וְעָנִיתָ וְאָמַרְתָּ.

"The declaration of tithes, as it is written[17]: "You should declare and say."

17 There is no such verse. It really should read (*Deut.* 26:13): "You should say before the Eternal, your God," Who understands all languages, in contrast to the declaration of First Fruits (v. 3), where it says "you should say to him (the priest)", who is supposed to speak only Hebrew. The quote contradicts Halakhah 2, Notes 43ff; it is correct in *Sifry Deut.* 303 and in the Babli, 32b, where it is pointed out that "declare and say" always means Hebrew only (as in *Deut.* 27:14).

(21b, line 56) וּקְרִיַת שְׁמַע. דִּכְתִיב וְדִבַּרְתָּ בָּם. רַבִּי אוֹמֵר. אוֹמֵר אֲנִי. קְרִיַת שְׁמַע אֵינָהּ נֶאֶמְרָה אֶלָּא בִּלְשׁוֹן הַקּוֹדֶשׁ. וְהָיוּ הַדְּבָרִים הָאֵלֶּא. מָה טַעְמָא. רַבִּי לֵוִי בַּר חַיָּתָא אֲזַל לְקֵיסָרִין. שְׁמַע קָלוֹן קָרְיָין שְׁמַע אֱלוֹנִיסְתִּין. בְּעָא מְעַכְּבָתוֹן. שְׁמַע רַבִּי יוֹסֵי וְאִקְפַּד. אָמַר. כָּךְ אוֹמֵר אֲנִי. מִי שֶׁאֵינוּ יוֹדֵעַ לִקְרוֹת אֲשׁוּרִית לֹא יִקְרֵינָהּ כָּל־עִיקָּר. אֶלָּא יוֹצֵא בְּכָל־לָשׁוֹן שֶׁהוּא יוֹדֵעַ. הֵשִׁיב רַבִּי בֶּרֶכְיָה. הֲרֵי מְגִילַּת אֶסְתֵּר. הָיָה יוֹדֵעַ לִקְרוֹת אֲשׁוּרִית וְלָעֵז. אֵינוֹ יוֹצֵא בָהּ אֶלָּא אֲשׁוּרִית. אָמַר רַבִּי מָנָא. מְגִילַּת אֶסְתֵּר הָיָה יוֹדֵעַ לִקְרוֹתָהּ אֲשׁוּרִית וְלָעֵז אֵינוֹ יוֹצֵא בָהּ אֶלָּא אֲשׁוּרִית. בְּלַעַז יוֹצֵא בָהּ בְּלַעַז. וְכֵן יוֹצֵא בָהּ בְּכָל־לָשׁוֹן שֶׁהוּא יוֹדֵעַ.

"And the recitation of the *Šemaʿ*." For it is written[18]: "You shall talk about them." Rebbi says, I say that the *Šemaʿ* is recited only in the holy language. What is the reason? "The words shall be[19]". Rebbi Levi bar Haita[20] went[21] to Caesarea. He heard their voices when they were reading the *Šemaʿ* in Hellenistic[22] manner. He wanted to hinder them, but Rebbi Yose heard of it and was offended. He said, do I say that someone who does not know to read Assyrian letters[23] should not recite it at all? But he fulfills his duty in any language he knows. Rebbi Berekhiah objected: But there is the Esther scroll, where somebody who knows to read both Asssyrian script and Greek[24] can fulfill his obligation only from Assyrian script[25]. Rebbi Mana said: About the Esther scroll, somebody who knows to read both Asssyrian script and Greek can fulfill his obligation only from Assyrian script; Greek only, he fulfills his obligation in Greek; and so he can fulfill his obligation in any language he understands.

18   *Deut.* 6:7. Nobody can discuss something he does not understand.

19   *Deut.* 6:7. It is understood that the verb היה "to be" in general describes a permanent state. In our case, this means that the words, *Deut.* 6:1-9, should not be changed. Then they cannot be recited in translation. The Babli, 32b, goes into an extended discussion on the relative merits of the two positions.

20   In the *Arukh, s. v.* אלנסתין, reads בר הזוחא but the reading here seems to be original. A Galilean preacher of the fourth/fifth generation.

21   In the *Arukh,* על "he ascended", to Caesarea Philippi.

22   Greek ἑλληνιστί, adv., "in the Greek language", here probably Judeo-Greek. [The final ן might indicate a nasal pronuciation]. In *Tanḥuma* texts, the word is always written אלנסטי. {While in the commentary to *Gen.* 35:8 [*Tanhuma Buber Wayyišlaḥ* 26 (Note 100)], the word ἄλλον is Greek and is characterized as such in *Gen. rabba* 81(5), the identification of the root in קָטָבְךָ (*Hos.* 13:14) as κατάβα קאטאבא ("go down", imperative, short for κατάβηθι) with a Semitic suffix [*Tanḥuma Buber Ṣaw* 4 (Note 30), *Tanḥuma Ṣaw* 2] can only be described

as Judeo-Greek.)

23 Hebrew Square letters, which replaced the paleo-Hebrew script. Since the latter was retained by the Samaritans, the rabbinic authorities insisted on the exclusive use of the square alphabet. One might wonder whether the text expressly authorizes, e. g., Judeo-Arabic or Judeo-German translations written in "Assyrian" characters.

24 לעז "barbaric", is used in talmudic literature exclusively for Greek, for which approved translations existed.

25 The Babli, *Megillah* 18a, permits the bilingual person to hear the Esther story in Greek but rules that reading from a Hebrew scroll written in square letters is acceptable for everybody, even for those who do not know Hebrew. (In Halakhah 2, there is a discussion whether square letters are "Assyrian" or "rich" script.)

(21b, line 65) וּתְפִילָה. כְּדֵי שֶׁיְּהֵא יוֹדֵעַ לִתְבּוֹעַ צְרָכָיו. וּבִרְכַּת הַמָּזוֹן. כְּדֵי שֶׁיְּהֵא יוֹדֵעַ לְמִי מְבָרֵךְ.

"And prayer," that one should know how to ask according to his needs. "And grace," that one should know to Whom he gives praise.

וּשְׁבוּעַת הָעֵדוּת וּשְׁבוּעַת הַפִּקָּדוֹן. מַשְׁבִּיעִין אוֹתוֹ בִּלְשׁוֹנוֹ. הִשְׁבִּיעָן שֶׁלֹּא בִלְשׁוֹנָן וְאָמְרוּ. אָמֵן. הֲרֵי אִילּוּ פְטוּרִין. כְּהָדָא דְתַנֵּי. שְׁבוּעַת הַדַּיָּינִין כְּתַנְיֵין שֶׁבְּלִבֵּינוּ לֹא כִתְנַיֵּין שֶׁבְּלִבְּכֶם. אָמַר רִבִּי יוּדָן. חֲזָקָה כְּתַנְיֵין שֶׁבְּלִיבּוֹ הוּא מַשְׁבִּיעוֹ. וְלָמָּה הוּא מַתְנֶה עִמּוֹ. מִפְּנֵי הַהֶדְיוֹטוֹת. שֶׁלֹּא יֹאמְרוּ. יֵשׁ תְּנַיִין בַּשְּׁבוּעוֹת. תַּנָּא רִבִּי חֲנַנְיָה קוֹמֵי רִבִּי מָנָא. וְהָא כְתִיב. כִּי אֶת אֲשֶׁר יֶשְׁנוֹ פֹה עִמָּנוּ עוֹמֵד הַיּוֹם. מַה מַשְׁמַע מִינָהּ. אָמַר לֵיהּ. הַדּוֹרוֹת הַבָּאִים אַחֲרֵינוּ אֵין בְּלִיבָּם תְּנָיֵי.

"And the oath of a witness and the oath about a deposit." One makes him swear in his own language. If one made them swear not in their language and they said "Amen", they are not prosecutable[26]. As we have stated[27]: The oath before the judges is according to our understanding, not according to your understanding. Rebbi Yudan said, it is to be assumed that he makes them swear according to his understanding. Why does he have to spell out this condition to him? Because of the uneducated, lest they say that there may be mental reservations for oaths. Rebbi Ḥanania stated before Rebbi Mana: Is there not written[28]: "But with everybody who stands here with us today"? He said to him, the future generations do not have mental reservations[29].

---

26 Nobody is prosecutable for perjury if he was not admonished in his own language by the court before answering the oath read to him. In the Babli, 33a, the rule is derived from verses. The Tosephta, 7:1, has a different version: If the court explained to him five times in any language he understands and he confirms his oath, he is guilty (if he swears falsely).

27 The text is also in *Nedarim* 3:1; a parallel text in Babli *Šebuot* 29a, *Nedarim* 25a.

28 *Deut.* 29:14. The argument is about what is written before and after the fragment quoted: "Not with you alone am I concluding this covenant and this oath. But with everybody who stands here with us today, and with those who are not with us today." How can you have an oath with anybody not involved?

29 Since the unborn cannot have mental reservations, so the mental reservations of the living are invalid.

(fol. 21a) **משנה ב**: וְאֵילוּ נֶאֱמָרִין בִּלְשׁוֹן הַקֹּדֶשׁ. מִקְרָא הַבִּיכּוּרִים וַחֲלִיצָה בְּרָכוֹת וּקְלָלוֹת בִּרְכַּת כֹּהֲנִים וּבִרְכַּת כֹּהֵן גָּדוֹל וּפָרָשַׁת הַמֶּלֶךְ וּפָרָשַׁת עֶגְלָא עֲרוּפָה וּמְשׁוּחַ מִלְחָמָה בְּשָׁעָה שֶׁהוּא מְדַבֵּר אֶל הָעָם. מִקְרָא הַבִּיכּוּרִים כֵּיצַד. וְעָנִיתָ וְאָמַרְתָּ לִפְנֵי יי אֱלֹהֶיךָ וּלְהַלָּן הוּא אוֹמֵר וְעָנוּ הַלְוִיִּם וְאָמְרוּ אֶל כָּל־אִישׁ יִשְׂרָאֵל קוֹל רָם. מָה עֲנִייָה הָאֲמוּרָה לְהַלָּן בִּלְשׁוֹן הַקֹּדֶשׁ אַף כָּאן בִּלְשׁוֹן הַקֹּדֶשׁ.

חֲלִיצָה כֵּיצַד. וְעָנְתָה וְאָמְרָה כָּכָה יֵעָשֶׂה לָאִישׁ וּלְהַלָּן הוּא אוֹמֵר וְעָנוּ הַלְוִיִּם וְאָמְרוּ מָה עֲנִיָּיה הָאֲמוּרָה לְהַלָּן בִּלְשׁוֹן הַקֹּדֶשׁ אַף כָּאן בִּלְשׁוֹן הַקֹּדֶשׁ. רִבִּי יְהוּדָה אוֹמֵר וְעָנְתָה וְאָמְרָה כָּכָה עַד שֶׁתֹּאמַר בַּלָּשׁוֹן הַזֶּה.

Mishnah 2: But the following must be said in the holy language: The recitation for the first fruits[30], ḥaliṣah[31], blessings and curses[32], the priestly blessing[33], the benedictions of the High Priest[34], the portion about the king[35], the portion about the calf whose neck was broken[36], the [priest] anointed for war at the time he speaks to the people[37].

The recitation for the first fruits, how? "You shall begin and say before the Eternal, your God[38]" but further on it says, "the Levites shall begin and say to all the men of Israel in an elevated voice[39]". Since "beginning" further on means in the holy language, so also here in the holy language[40].

Ḥaliṣah how? "She shall begin and say: So shall be done to the man[41]" but further on it says, "the Levites shall begin and say to all the men of Israel in an elevated voice". Since "beginning" further on means in the holy language, so also here in the holy language. Rebbi Jehudah says, "She shall begin and say so," [it is invalid] unless she says exactly that text[42].

30   The declaration in the Temple, Mishnah *Bikkurim* 2:5.

31   The required declarations by the childless widow and brother-in-law in the ceremony which frees her to marry outside the family; cf. *Yebamot* 12:3-4.

32   This is of purely antiquarian character, asserting that the curses detailed in *Deut.* 27:11-26 (each curse prefaced by a corresponding blessing: "Blessed be the man who will not . . .") were pronounced in Hebrew, based on *Jos.* 8:34; cf. Halakhah 4.

33   *Num.* 6:22-26.

34   In the service of the Day of Atonement, Mishnah *Yoma* 7:1; cf. Halakhah 6.

35   The public reading from the Torah at the end of a Sabbatical year, *Deut.* 31:10-13; cf. Halakhot 7-8.

36   The declarations *Deut.* 21:7 (the

Elders), 8 (the priests); cf. Chapter 9.

37 *Deut.* 20:1-9; cf. Chapter 8.

38 *Deut.* 26:5.

39 *Deut.* 27:14. The implication of this verse is explained in the Halakhah.

40 This is an application of the third hermeneutical rule of R. Ismael: The meaning of a word is defined by one paradigm. It does not fit the mold of the second rule, "equal cut", preferred by the commentators.

41 *Deut.* 25:9.

42 He disregards the dividing accent in the sentence and reads: "She shall begin and say so: it will be done to the man who will not build his brother's house" instead of "She shall begin and say: thus will be done . . ." It gives a different twist to a derivation originating with R. Jehudah's father's teacher R. Eliezer in Mishnah *Yebamot* 12:4; cf. Babli 33a/b.

(fol. 21c) **הלכה ב**: תַּנֵי בְשֵׁם רִבִּי יוּדָה. כָּל־מָקוֹם שֶׁנֶּאֱמַר בְּלָשׁוֹן הַזֶּה עֲנִיָּיה וַאֲמִירָה כָּכָה וְכֹה הֲרֵי הוּא בְלָשׁוֹן הַקּוֹדֶשׁ. אָמַר רִבִּי אֶלְעָזָר. בִּנְיָין אַב שֶׁבְּכוּלָּן מֹשֶׁה יְדַבֵּר וְהָאֱלֹהִים יַעֲנֶנּוּ בְקוֹל. הָתִיב רִבִּי חַגַּי. וְהָכְתִיב וַיַּעַן לָבָן וּבְתוּאֵל. אֵין תֵּימַר עַל יְדֵי עֲנִיָּיה. וְהָכְתִיב וַיֹּאמְרוּ. אֵין תֵּימַר עַל יְדֵי אֲמִירָה. וְהָכְתִיב מֵיי יָצָא הַדָּבָר. אֵין תֵּימַר. בְּלָשׁוֹן הַקּוֹדֶשׁ. וְהָכְתִיב וַיִּקְרָא לוֹ לָבָן יְגַר שָׂהֲדוּתָא. וְאֵין תֵּימַר. קוֹדֶם לְמַתַּן תּוֹרָה. הֲרֵי פָּרָשַׁת וִידּוּי מַעֲשֵׂר הֲרֵי הוּא לְאַחַר מַתַּן תּוֹרָה וְהוּא נֶאֱמַר בְּכָל־לָשׁוֹן.

Halakhah 2: It was stated in the name of Rebbi Jehudah: Any place where it was said in any of these expressions: you begin and say, thus, and thus[43], it means in the holy language. Rebbi Eleazar said, the defining paradigm for all is: "Moses would speak and God would answer him by voice[44]." Rebbi Haggai objected, is there not written, "Laban and Bethuel began[45]," if you say because of "beginning" only, is there not written "and said[46]"? If you want to say, by "saying" only, is there not written "from the Eternal came the word[47]"? If you want to say, in the holy language, is there not written "the stone heap of testimony[48]"? If you want to say, before the Torah was given, is there not the text of the declaration of tithes[49] which may be recited in any language[50]?

43 The first and last expressions were mentioned in the Mishnah. כה "thus" is the introduction to the priests' blessing, *Num.* 6:23.

44 *Ex.* 19:19. This is not a reference to the statement of R. Jehudah, but to the argument of the Mishnah. While in that verse, the root ענה does not have the meaning of "to begin to speak" but "to answer", the mention of קול "voice", which was in Hebrew, transfers to the recitation of the Levites, who have to speak בְּקוֹל רָם "in the voice of the High", where High is a Title of God, *Is.* 56:15; cf. below, Note 61.

45 *Gen.* 24:50. As noted later, they spoke Aramaic.

46 That verse contains both roots, ענה and אמר, even if they are separated by the names of the speakers. Therefore, the argument of R. Jehudah is invalid.

47 This is a counter-argument. Since Laban and Bethuel admitted that the betrothal of Rebecca was a word of the Eternal, did they not speak Hebrew at that moment?

48 *Gen.* 31:47. Since Laban had to translate Jacob's גַּלְעֵד into Aramaic, it follows that he did not speak Hebrew.

49 *Deut.* 26:16. However, there only the root אמר is used.

50 Cf. Mishnah 1.

(21c, line 8) רִבִּי שְׁמוּאֵל בַּר נַחְמָן בְּשֵׁם רִבִּי יוֹחָנָן. שֶׁלֹּא יְהֵא לָשׁוֹן סוּרְסִי קַל בְּעֵינֶיךָ. שֶׁבַּתּוֹרָה וּבַנְּבִיאִים וּבַכְּתוּבִים הוּא אָמוּר. בַּתּוֹרָה כְּתִיב וַיִּקְרָא לוֹ לָבָן יְגַר שָׂהֲדוּתָא. בַּנְּבִיאִים כְּתִיב כִּדְנָה תֵּימְרוּן לְהוֹן. בַּכְּתוּבִים כְּתִיב וַיְדַבְּרוּ הַכַּשְׂדִּים לַמֶּלֶךְ אֲרָמִית. אָמַר רִבִּי יוֹנָתָן דְּבֵית גּוּבְרִין. אַרְבָּעָה לְשׁוֹנוֹת נָאִין לְהִשְׁתַּמֵּשׁ בָּהֶן הָעוֹלָם. וְאֵילוּ הֵן. לָעַז לְזֶמֶר. רוֹמִי לִקְרָב. סוּרְסִי לְאֵילִייָא. עִבְרִי לְדִיבּוּר. וְיֵשׁ אוֹמְרִים. אַף אֲשּׁוּרִי לִכְתָב. אֲשּׁוּרִי יֵשׁ בּוֹ כְּתָב וְאֵין בּוֹ לָשׁוֹן. עִבְרִי יֵשׁ בּוֹ לָשׁוֹן וְאֵין בּוֹ כְּתָב. בָּחֲרוּ לָהֶם כְּתָב אֲשּׁוּרִי וְלָשׁוֹן עִבְרִי. וְלָמָּה נִקְרָא שְׁמוֹ אֲשּׁוּרִי. שֶׁהוּא מְאוּשָּׁר בִּכְתָבוֹ. אָמַר רִבִּי לֵוִי עַל שֵׁם שֶׁעָלָה בְּיָדָם מֵאֲשּׁוּר.

Rebbi Samuel bar Naḥman in the name of Rebbi Joḥanan: The Syriac language should not be unimportant in your eyes, for it is mentioned in the Torah, the Prophets, and the Hagiographs. In the Torah, it is written: "Laban called it *the heap of testimony*[48]". In Prophets, it is written: "*So you shall say to them.*[51]" In Hagiographs, it is written: "The Chaldeans spoke to the king in Aramaic.[52]" Rebbi Jonathan from Bet Gubrin said, four languages are good for use: The foreign language[53] for song, Latin for war, Syriac for elegies, Hebrew for speech. Some people say, also Assyrian[54] for writing. Assyrian has a script but no language[55], Hebrew has a language but no script[56]. They chose for them Assyrian script and Hebrew language[57]. Why is its name called אָשּׁוּרִי? Because one is made happy in writing it[58]. Rebbi Levi said, because they brought it with them from Assyria[59].

---

51 *Jer.* 10:11.

52 *Dan.* 2:4.

53 Greek.

54 "Hebrew" square script, which originally is an Aramaic development of paleo-Hebrew.

55 Since it is used for Hebrew, Aramaic, Mandaic etc.

56 Once paleo-Hebrew script was abandoned.

57 This is a shortened version of a Babylonian tradition (by the "Heads of the Diaspora") that Moses wrote the Torah in Hebrew script and language, Ezra wrote the Torah in Aramaic translation and Assyrian script, but the people chose Hebrew text and Assyrian (Aramaic) letters: *Sanhedrin* 21b; also cf. *Megillah* 1:11 (fol. 71b, line 67).

58 The meaning of the sentence is not clear. One could translate: Because its writing is plain.

59 Square script is not found before the return from Mesopotamia, where the exiles lived mostly in the Aramaic-speaking Northern parts.

HALAKHAH 3   273

(21c, line 17) כְּתִיב וְעָנוּ הַלְוִיִּם וְאָמְרוּ אֶל כָּל־אִישׁ יִשְׂרָאֵל קוֹל רָם. בְּקוֹלוֹ שֶׁלָּרָם. מְלַמֵּד שֶׁשִּׁיתֵּף הַקָּדוֹשׁ בָּרוּךְ הוּא קוֹלוֹ עִמָּהֶן. דָּבָר אַחֵר. קוֹל רָם. הַמְעוּלֶּה שֶׁבַּקּוֹלוֹת. אָמַר רִבִּי יִצְחָק. לֹא קָטוֹן וְלֹא גָדוֹל אֶלָּא בֵינוֹנִי.

It is written[60]: "The Levites shall begin and say to all the men of Israel in an elevated voice[61]", this teaches that the Holy One, praise to Him, associated His voice to theirs. Another explanation, "the best of voices". Rebbi Isaac said, not low, not high, but moderate.

60   *Deut.* 27:14.   cf. Note 44.
61   Or, "the voice of the Most High,"

(fol. 21b) **משנה ג**: בְּרָכוֹת וּקְלָלוֹת כֵּיצַד. כֵּיוָן שֶׁעָבְרוּ יִשְׂרָאֵל אֶת הַיַּרְדֵּן וּבָאוּ אֶל הַר גְּרִיזִים וְאֶל הַר עֵיבָל הַר שֶׁבְּשׁוֹמְרוֹן שֶׁבְּצַד שְׁכֶם שֶׁאֵצֶל אֵילוֹנֵי מוֹרֶה שֶׁנֶּאֱמַר הֲלֹא הֵמָּה בְּעֵבֶר הַיַּרְדֵּן וגו' וּלְהַלָּן הוּא אוֹמֵר וַיַּעֲבֹר אַבְרָם בָּאָרֶץ עַד מְקוֹם שְׁכֶם עַד אֵלוֹן מוֹרֶה מָה הָאֵלוֹן מוֹרֶה הָאָמוּר לְהַלָּן שְׁכֶם אַף אֵלוֹנֵי מוֹרֶה הָאָמוּר כָּאן שְׁכֶם.

Mishnah 3: Blessings and curses[32], how? When Israel had crossed the Jordan they came to Mount Gerizim and Mount Ebal in Samaria, next to Sichem which is close to the terebinths of guidance, as it is said[62]: "They are on the other side of the Jordan, etc.", and at another place it says[63]: "Abram traveled through the Land up to the place of Sichem, up to the terebinth of guidance." Since the terebinth of guidance mentioned there is at Sichem so the the terebinths of guidance mentioned here are at Sichem[64].

62 *Deut.* 11:30: "They are on the other side of the Jordan, westward, on the road to sunset, in the Land of the Canaanite who dwells in the prairie, opposite Gilgal, near the terebinths of guidance."

63 *Gen.* 12:6. The terebinth may have been a holy tree (or in the language of *Deut.*, a holy grove) at the crossing on the North-South route (Damascus) - Ir Gannim - Beër Šeba - (Egypt) and the "road towards sundown" from Adam-the-City to the Mediterranean.

64 The lengthy discussion in the Mishnah is a polemic against R. Eleazar in the Halakhah. For all of Halakhot 3-5, cf. *Seder 'Olam*, Chapter 11, in the author's edition pp. 109-119; Tosephta Chapter 8.

(fol. 21c) **הלכה ג**: הֲלֹא הֵמָּה בְּעֵבֶר הַיַּרְדֵּן מִן הַיַּרְדֵּן וּלְהַלָּן. אַחֲרֵי דֶּרֶךְ מְבוֹא הַשֶּׁמֶשׁ. מָקוֹם שֶׁהַחַמָּה זוֹרַחַת. בְּאֶרֶץ הַכְּנַעֲנִי הַיּוֹשֵׁב בָּעֲרָבָה מוּל הַגִּילְגָּל אֵצֶל אֵלוֹנֵי מוֹרֶה. זֶה הַר גְּרִיזִים וְהַר עֵיבָל שֶׁבֵּין הַכּוּתִים. דִּבְרֵי רִבִּי יְהוּדָה. רִבִּי אֶלְעָזָר אוֹמֵר. אֵין זֶה הַר גְּרִיזִים וְהַר עֵיבָל שֶׁלַּכּוּתִים. שֶׁנֶּאֱמַר הֲלֹא הֵמָּה בְּעֵבֶר הַיַּרְדֵּן מִן הַיַּרְדֵּן וְלָכֵן.65 אַחֲרֵי דֶּרֶךְ מְבוֹא הַשֶּׁמֶשׁ. מָקוֹם שֶׁהַחַמָּה שׁוֹקַעַת. בְּאֶרֶץ הַכְּנַעֲנִי. אֵילוּ בֵּין הַחִוִּי. הַיּוֹשֵׁב בָּעֲרָבָה. אֵילוּ בֵּין הֶהָרִים. מוּל הַגִּילְגָּל. אֵין כָּאן גִּלְגָּל. אֵצֶל אֵלוֹנֵי מוֹרֶה. אֵין כָּאן אֵלוֹנֵי מוֹרֶה. מָה מְקַיֵּים רִבִּי אֶלְעָזָר הַר גְּרִיזִים וְהַר עֵיבָל. שְׁתֵּי גְּבָשׁוֹשִׁיּוֹת עָשׂוּ וְקָרְאוּ זֶה הַר גְּרִיזִים וְזֶה הַר עֵיבָל. עַל דַּעַת דְּרִבִּי יְהוּדָה מֵאָה וְעֶשְׂרִים מִיל הָלְכוּ בְּאוֹתוֹ הַיּוֹם. עַל דַּעַת דְּרִבִּי אֶלְעָזָר לֹא זָזוּ מִמְּקוֹמָן.

Halakhah 3: [66]"[62]They are on the other side of the Jordan," away from the Jordan. "Far away[67] from the road towards the sun's coming", the place from where the sun shines. "In the Land of the Canaanite who dwells in the prairie, opposite Gilgal, near the terebinths of guidance." That refers to Mount Gerizim and Mount Ebal among the Samaritans, the words of Rebbi Jehudah. Rebbi Eleazar[68] said, this does not refer to Mount Gerizim and Mount Ebal of the Samaritans. "They are on the other side of the Jordan," by the Jordan. "To the West, on the road to sunset," a place where the sun goes down. "In the Land of the Canaanite," but there is the Hiwwite[69]. "Who dwells in the prairie," but there it is in the mountains. "Opposite Gilgal," Gilgal is nowhere there[70]. "Near the terebinths of guidance." The terebinths of guidance are not there[71]. How does Rebbi Eleazar uphold "Mount Gerizim and Mount Ebal"? They made two elevations and called them Mount Gerizim and Mount Ebal. In the opinion of Rebbi Jehudah, they walked 120 *mil* on that day[72]. In the opinion of Rebbi Eleazar, they did not move at all.

65 Reading of the Rome ms. Leiden text and *editio princeps*: להלך "away from".

66 Parallel texts in Babli 33b, Tosephta Chapter 8, *Sifry Deut.* 56.

67 Rashi, Commentary to *Sota* 33b, attributes this meaning of אחרי to *Gen. rabba*. If one accepts the usual meaning "westward" (adopted by Rashi in his Commentary to *Deut.*), one would have to read "sunset" in the opinion of R. Jehudah and "sunrise" in that of R. Eleazar, as suggested by L. Finkelstein, *Sifry Deut.*, pp. 123-124.

68 Only in *Sifry Deut.* the reading is: R. Eliezer. That reading is very unlikely since R. Ilaï, R. Jehudah's father, was R. Eliezer's student. (The one reading "R. Eleazar" quoted by Finkelstein in his apparatus comes from a secondary source not necessarily dependent upon *Sifry*.)

69 In Sichem, *Gen.* 34:2.

70 East of Jericho, *Jos.* 4:19.

71 Here one speaks of a grove, in the verse referring to Abraham of a single tree.

72 The distance from Jericho to Sichem is estimated at 60 *mil* (in the Babli, 36a, and one Tosephta source, "more than 60 *mil*"). In R. Jehudah's opinion they crossed the Jordan, put up the stones, walked to Sichem, completed the ceremony, and walked back, all in one day. This contradicts *Jos.* 8:30-35.

(21c, line 31) תַּנֵּי רִבִּי אֱלִיעֶזֶר בֶּן יַעֲקֹב אוֹמֵר לֹא [בָא הַכָּתוּב][73] אֶלָּא לְהַשְׁווֹת לָהֶן אֶת הַדֶּרֶךְ וְלוֹמַר. בַּדֶּרֶךְ יֵלְכוּ וְלֹא בַשָּׂדוֹת. בְּיִישׁוּב יֵלְכוּ וְלֹא בַמִּדְבָּר. בָּעֲרָבָה יֵלְכוּ וְלֹא בֶהָרִים.

It was stated[74]: "Rebbi Eliezer ben Jacob says, the verse comes only to prepare the road for them and say that they should walk on the road, not in fields, in inhabited regions, not in the desert, in the valley[75], not in the mountains.

---

73 Illegible in Leiden ms., from *editio princeps* and Rome ms.

74 Babli 33b, *Sifry Deut.* 56.

75 *Sifry Deut.* explains ערבה as מישור "plain".

(21c, line 37) אָמַר רִבִּי אֶלְעָזָר בְּרִבִּי שִׁמְעוֹן. נוֹמֵיתִי לְסוֹפְרֵי כוּתִים. זְיַיפְתֶּם תּוֹרַתְכֶם וְלֹא הוֹעַלְתֶּם לְעַצְמְכֶם כְּלוּם. שֶׁהִכְתַּבְתֶּם בְּתוֹרַתְכֶם אֵצֶל אֵלוֹנֵי מוֹרֶה שְׁכֶם. וַהֲלֹא יָדוּעַ שֶׁהוּא שְׁכֶם. אֶלָּא שֶׁאֵין אַתֶּם דּוֹרְשִׁין לִגְזֵירָה שָׁוָה. וְאָנוּ דּוֹרְשִׁין לִגְזֵירָה שָׁוָה. נֶאֱמַר כָּאן אֵלוֹנֵי מוֹרֶה. וְנֶאֱמַר לְהַלָּן אֵלוֹנֵי מוֹרֶה. מָה אֵילוֹנֵי מוֹרֶה הָאָמוּר לְהַלָּן שְׁכֶם אַף אֵילוֹנֵי מוֹרֶה הָאָמוּר כָּאן שְׁכֶם. וְכִדְרִבִּי יִשְׁמָעֵאל. דְּרִבִּי יִשְׁמָעֵאל אָמַר. כָּל־בִּיאוֹת שֶׁנֶּאֶמְרוּ בַתּוֹרָה לְאַחַר אַרְבַּע עֶשְׂרֵה שָׁנָה נֶאֱמְרוּ. שֶׁבַע שֶׁכִּיבְּשׁוּ וְשֶׁבַע שֶׁחִילְּקוּ. וְדִכְוָותָהּ לֹא נֶאֶמְרוּ בְּרָכוֹת וּקְלָלוֹת אֶלָּא לְאַחַר אַרְבַּע עֶשְׂרֵה שָׁנָה. הָתִיב רִבִּי חֲנַנְיָה קוֹמֵי רִבִּי מָנָא. וְהָכְתִיב וְהָיָה בְּעָבְרְכֶם אֶת הַיַּרְדֵּן תָּקִימוּ אֶת הָאֲבָנִים הָאֵלֶּה. אָמַר לֵיהּ. אֲבָנִים הֵקִימוּ אוֹתָם מִיָּד. בְּרָכוֹת וּקְלָלוֹת לְאַחַר אַרְבַּע עֶשְׂרֵה שָׁנָה נֶאֱמְרוּ.

Rebbi Eleazar ben Rebbi Simeon[76] said: I told the Samaritan scribes: You falsified your Torah and did not gain anything, because you cause to be written in your Torah "near the terebinths of guidance, Sichem[77]". Is it not known that this is Sichem? It is only because you do not explain by "equal cut[78]", but we explain by "equal cut". [79]It is written here, "the terebinths of guidance", and it is said there, "the terebinths of guidance."

Since "the terebinth*s* of guidance" there are at Sichem, also "the terebinth*s* of guidance" here are at Sichem; and following Rebbi Ismael. For Rebbi Ismael said, any "comings" which were said in the Torah refer to after fourteen years, seven during which they conquered and seven during which they distributed[80]. Therefore, blessings and curses were recited only after fourteen years. Rebbi Ḥanania objected before Rebbi Mana: Is it not written[81], "It shall be when you cross the Jordan you shall erect these stones"? He said to him, they erected the stones immediately[82] but blessings and curses were said only after fourteen years.

76 In the other sources (Babli 33b, *Sifry Deut.* 56): R. Eleazar ben R. Yose. This is the Babylonian tradition which attributes the material of *Seder Olam* to the school of R. Yose.

77 An additional word which is not original.

78 The second hermeneutical rule which stipulates that a word in the Torah can have only one meaning; cf. *Berakhot* 1:1, Note 70.

79 See the Mishnah.

80 Any commandment in the Torah which is prefaced by "when you come into the Land" is activated only after each tribe has received their portion of land (*Seder Olam* Chapter 11, pp. 108-109; Babli *Zebaḥim* 118b, *Arakhin* 13a).

81 *Deut.* 27:4. These stones had to be erected on Mount Ebal.

82 In that case, *Jos.* 4:8, 8:30-35, support the interpretation of R. Eleazar.

משנה ד: שִׁשָּׁה שְׁבָטִים עָלוּ לְרֹאשׁ הַר גְּרִיזִים וְשִׁשָּׁה שְׁבָטִים עָלוּ לְרֹאשׁ הַר עֵיבָל וְהַכֹּהֲנִים וְהַלְוִיִּם וְהָאָרוֹן עוֹמְדִין מִלְּמַטָּה בָּאֶמְצַע. הַכֹּהֲנִים מַקִּיפִין אֶת הָאָרוֹן וְהַלְוִיִּם אֶת הַכֹּהֲנִים וְכָל־יִשְׂרָאֵל מִכָּן וּמִכָּן שֶׁנֶּאֱמַר וְכָל־יִשְׂרָאֵל וּזְקֵינָיו וְשׁוֹטְרָיו וְשׁוֹפְטָיו עוֹמְדִים מִזֶּה וּמִזֶּה לָאָרוֹן וגו'. הָפְכוּ (fol. 21b)

פְּנֵיהֶם כְּלַפֵּי הַר גְּרִיזִים וּפָתְחוּ בַּבְּרָכָה. בָּרוּךְ הָאִישׁ אֲשֶׁר לֹא יַעֲשֶׂה פֶסֶל וּמַסֵּכָה תּוֹעֲבַת יי מַעֲשֵׂה יְדֵי חָרָשׁ וְלֹא שָׂם בַּסָּתֶר וְהָיוּ אֵילוּ וָאֵילוּ עוֹנִין וְאוֹמְרִים אָמֵן. הָפְכוּ פְנֵיהֶם כְּלַפֵּי הַר עֵיבָל וּפָתְחוּ בַּקְּלָלָה אָרוּר הָאִישׁ אֲשֶׁר יַעֲשֶׂה פֶסֶל וּמַסֵּכָה תּוֹעֲבַת יי וגו'. וְהָיוּ אֵילוּ וָאֵילוּ עוֹנִין וְאוֹמְרִים אָמֵן עַד שֶׁגּוֹמְרִין בְּרָכוֹת וּקְלָלוֹת.

Mishnah 4: Six tribes climbed to the top of Mount Gerizim and six tribes climbed to the top of Mount Ebal[83] while the Cohanim, the Levites, and the ark were below in the middle. The Cohanim were surrounding the ark, the Levites the Cohanim, and all of Israel [were] on both sides, as it was said[84]: "And all of Israel, its Elders, its policemen, its judges were standing on both sides of the ark . . ." They turned their faces towards Mount Gerizim and opened with the blessing: "Blessed be the man who will not make a hewn or molten [image], the Eternal's abomination, made by an artisan, and will not put it up in secret." These and those did answer and say: Amen. They turned their faces towards Mount Ebal and opened with the curse[85]: "Cursed be the man who would make a hewn or molten [image], the Eternal's abomination, made by an artisan, and would put it up in secret." These and those did answer and say: Amen, until they finished blessings and curses.

83   *Deut.* 27:12-13; *Jos.* 8:33.   85   *Deut.* 27:15.
84   *Jos.* 8:33.

(fol. 21c) **הלכה ד**: תַּנֵּי. רִבִּי אוֹמֵר. אִי אִיפְשָׁר לוֹמַר לֵוִי לְמַעֲלָן שֶׁכְּבָר נֶאֱמַר לֵוִי לְמַטָּן. אִי אִיפְשָׁר לוֹמַר לֵוִי לְמַטָּן שֶׁכְּבָר נֶאֱמַר לֵוִי לְמַעֲלָן. אֱמוֹר מֵעַתָּה. זִקְנֵי כְהוּנָּה וּלְוִייָה לְמַטָּן וּשְׁאָר כָּל־הַשֵּׁבֶט לְמַעֲלָן. רִבִּי שִׁמְעוֹן אוֹמֵר. אִי אִיפְשָׁר לוֹמַר לֵוִי לְמַעֲלָן שֶׁכְּבָר נֶאֱמַר לֵוִי לְמַטָּן. וְאִי אִיפְשָׁר לוֹמַר לֵוִי לְמַטָּן

שֶׁכְּבָר נֶאֱמַר לֵוִי לְמַעְלָן. אֱמוֹר מֵעַתָּה. הָרְאוּיִ לְשָׁרֵת לְמַטָּה וּשְׁאָר כָּל־הַשֵּׁבֶט לְמַעְלָה. רִבִּי שִׁמְעוֹן אוֹמֵר. שִׁמְעוֹן וְלֵוִי. מַה שִּׁמְעוֹן כּוּלּוֹ לְמַעְלָה אַף לֵוִי כּוּלּוֹ לְמַעְלָה. מַה מְקַיְּיָם הָדֵין תַּנָּיָיה נֶגֶד הַכֹּהֲנִים הַלְוִיִּם. כַּיי דְּאָמַר רִבִּי יְהוֹשֻׁעַ בֶּן לֵוִי. בְּעֶשְׂרִים וְאַרְבַּע מְקוֹמוֹת נִקְרְאוּ הַכֹּהֲנִים לְוִיִּם וְזֶה אֶחָד מֵהֶן וְהַכֹּהֲנִים הַלְוִיִּם בְּנֵי צָדוֹק.

Halakhah 4: It was stated: Rebbi says, it is impossible to say that Levi is up[86] because it already was said that Levi is down. It is impossible to say that Levi is down because it already was said that Levi is up. From this you say, the Elders of the Levites and the priests are down and the rest of the tribe are up[87]. Rebbi Simeon says, it is impossible to say that Levi is up because it already was said that Levi is down and it is impossible to say that Levi is down because it already was said that Levi is up. From this you say, anyone able to serve[88] is down and the rest of the tribe is up. Rebbi Simeon says, "Simeon and Levi", since all of Simeon are up, also all of Levi are up. How do I confirm "in face of the Cohanim, the Levites"? [89]As Rebbi Joshua ben Levi said, in 24 places are Cohanim called Levites and this is one of them[90]: "The Cohanim Levites, the descendants of Ṣadoq."

86 *Deut* 27:11-14 seems to be self-contradictory. In v. 12, it is stated that the tribes of Simeon, Levi, Jehudah, etc. have to stand on Mount Gerizim but in v. 14 the Levites are in the middle to recite the curses.

87 In the Tosephta, 8:8, and the Babli, 37a, Rebbi is reported to say that all tribes were standing at the foot of the respective mountains (cf. *Jos.* 8:33). The opinion given here is there ascribed to R. Eliezer ben Jacob.

88 In the Tabernacle, between the ages of 25 and 50 (*Num.* 8:24-25). In Tosephta and Babli, this opinion is ascribed to R. Joshia.

89 *Ma'aśer Šeni* 5:5, Note 90; Babli *Yebamot* 86b, *Ḥulin* 24b.

90 *Ez.* 44:15.

(21c, line 54) יָכוֹל אֵילוּ שֶׁבְּהַר גְּרִיזִים הָיוּ אוֹמְרִים בְּרָכוֹת וְאֵילוּ שֶׁבְּהַר עֵיבָל הָיוּ אוֹמְרִים קְלָלוֹת. תַּלְמוּד לוֹמַר הַבְּרָכוֹת וְהַקְּלָלוֹת. אֵילוּ וָאֵילוּ הָיוּ אוֹמְרִים בְּרָכוֹת וּקְלָלוֹת. יָכוֹל מִשֶּׁהָיוּ אוֹמְרִים הַבְּרָכוֹת הָיוּ אוֹמְרִים הַקְּלָלוֹת. תַּלְמוּד לוֹמַר הַבְּרָכָה וְהַקְּלָלָה. בְּרָכָה אַחַת וּקְלָלָה אַחַת. יָכוֹל אֵילוּ שֶׁבְּהַר גְּרִיזִים הָיוּ עוֹנִין אַחַר הַבְּרָכוֹת אָמֵן. וְאֵילוּ שֶׁבְּהַר עֵיבָל הָיוּ עוֹנִין אַחַר הַקְּלָלוֹת אָמֵן. תַּלְמוּד לוֹמַר וְעָנוּ כָל־הָעָם וְאָמְרִי אָמֵן. אֵילוּ וָאֵילוּ הָיוּ עוֹנִין אַחַר הַבְּרָכוֹת וְאַחַר הַקְּלָלוֹת אָמֵן. הָא כֵיצַד. בְּשָׁעָה שֶׁהָיוּ אוֹמְרִים בְּרָכוֹת הָיוּ הוֹפְכִין פְּנֵיהֶן כְּלַפֵּי הַר גְּרִיזִים. וּבְשָׁעָה שֶׁהָיוּ אוֹמְרִים קְלָלוֹת הָיוּ הוֹפְכִין פְּנֵיהֶן כְּלַפֵּי הַר עֵיבָל.

One could think that those on Mount Gerizim did recite the blessings and those on Mount Ebal did recite the curses, the verse[91] says "the blessings and the curses"; both were saying blessings and curses. One could think that after they had recited the blessings they were reciting the curses, the verse[92] says "the blessing and the curse", one blessing and one curse. One could think that those on Mount Gerizim did answer "Amen" after the blessings and those on Mount Ebal did answer "Amen" after the curses, the verse[93] says "the entire people will answer and say "Amen"; these and those did answer "Amen" after the blessings and after the curses. How is that? When they were reciting the blessings they were turning their faces towards Mount Gerizim; when they were reciting the curses they were turning their faces towards Mount Ebal.

91 There is no such verse; both in *Deut.* 30:1 and *Jos.* 8:34 the singular is used. The plural is used for "blessings" in *Deut.* 28:2, for "curses" in *Deut.* 28:15.
92 *Deut.* 11:26, *Jos.* 8:34. From here on, a similar argument is in *Sifry Deut.* 55; that text is reproduced in the Babli, 37b.
93 *Deut.* 27:15.

(21d, line 64) בָּרוּךְ בִּכְלָל וּבָרוּךְ בִּפְרָט. אָרוּר בִּכְלָל וְאָרוּר בִּפְרָט. שֵׁשׁ עֶשְׂרֵה בְרִיתוֹת עַל כָּל־דָּבָר וְדָבָר. לִלְמוֹד וּלְלַמֵּד לִשְׁמוֹר וְלַעֲשׂוֹת. וְכֵן בְּהַר סִינַי וְכֵן בְּעַרְבוֹת מוֹאָב. רבִּי שִׁמְעוֹן הָיָה מוֹצִיא שֶׁלְּהַר גְּרִיזִים וְשֶׁלְּהַר עֵיבָל וּמֵבִיא שֶׁלְּאוֹהֶל מוֹעֵד תַּחְתֵּיהֶן. וְכֵן הָיָה רַבִּי שִׁמְעוֹן אוֹמֵר. אֵין כָּל־דָּבָר וְדָבָר מִן הַתּוֹרָה שֶׁאֵין כָּרוּת עָלָיו חָמֵשׁ מֵאוֹת וְשִׁבְעִים וְשֵׁשׁ בְּרִיתוֹת. שְׁתֵּים עֶשְׂרֵה בְּבָרוּךְ וּשְׁתֵּים עֶשְׂרֵה בְּאָרוּר. וּשְׁתֵּים עֶשְׂרֵה בִּכְלָל וּשְׁתֵּים עֶשְׂרֵה בִּפְרָט. הֲרֵי אַרְבָּעִים וּשְׁמוֹנֶה בְרִיתוֹת. לִלְמוֹד וּלְלַמֵּד לִשְׁמוֹר וְלַעֲשׂוֹת הֲרֵי מֵאָה וְתִשְׁעִים וּשְׁנַיִם בְּרִיתוֹת. וְכֵן בְּהַר סִינַי וְכֵן בְּעַרְבוֹת מוֹאָב. הֲרֵי חָמֵשׁ מֵאוֹת וְשִׁבְעִים וְשֵׁשׁ בְּרִיתוֹת. רִבִּי שִׁמְעוֹן בֶּן יְהוּדָה אִישׁ כְּפַר אִמּוֹס אוֹמֵר מִשּׁוּם רַבִּי שִׁמְעוֹן. שֵׁשׁ מֵאוֹת אֶלֶף וּשְׁלֹשֶׁת אֲלָפִים וַחֲמֵשׁ מֵאוֹת וַחֲמִשִּׁים. רַבִּי אוֹמֵר. אִם כְּדִבְרֵי רִבִּי שִׁמְעוֹן בֶּן יְהוּדָה אִישׁ כְּפַר אִמּוֹס שֶׁאָמַר מִשּׁוּם רַבִּי שִׁמְעוֹן. אֵין כָּל־דָּבָר וְדָבָר מִן הַתּוֹרָה שֶׁאֵין כָּרוּת עָלָיו אַרְבָּעִים וּשְׁמוֹנֶה פְּעָמִים עַל כָּל־פַּעַם וּפַעַם שֵׁשׁ מֵאוֹת אֶלֶף וּשְׁלֹשֶׁת אֲלָפִים וַחֲמֵשׁ מֵאוֹת וַחֲמִשִּׁים.

[94]Blessed in general and blessed in particular[95]; cursed in general and cursed in particular. Sixteen covenants on every detail, to study, to teach, to keep, and to do[96]; and the same on Sinai[97] and the same in the prairie of Moab[98]. Rebbi Simeon does exclude that of Mount Gerizim and Mount Ebal[99] and instead includes that of the Tent of Meeting[100]. Also Rebbi Simeon[101] did say, there is no single detail in the Torah about which not 576 covenants were concluded. Twelve[102] in blessing, twelve in cursing. Twelve in general, twelve in detail. That makes 48 covenants. To study, to teach, to keep, and to do, that makes 192 covenants. The same on Sinai and the same in the prairie of Moab, that makes 576 covenants. Rebbi Simeon ben Jehudah from the village of Emmaus[103] says in the name of Rebbi Simeon: 603'550[104]. Rebbi says, if one follows the words of Rebbi Simeon ben Jehudah from the village of Emmaus who said in the name of

Rebbi Simeon, then there is no single detail in the Torah about which not 48 times 603'550 covenants were concluded.

94 Babli 37 a/b, Tosephta 8:10-11. The explanation follows Rashi in the Babli.

95 *Deut.* 27:26 is general, referring to "the words of this Torah", but vv. 15-25 refer to particular sins.

96 For each commandment one is obligated to study it (*Deut.* 6:6), to teach it (*Deut.* 6:7, 11:19), to keep and execute it (*Deut.* 4:6,5:1). There are four obligations that bring blessings and four omissions that bring curses, in all 8. Since every commandment is also part of "the words of this Torah", that equals 16 for each single commandment.

97 *Lev.* 26:46.

98 *Deut.* 28:69.

99 Since Joshua executed only a commandment of Moses; he did not conclude a new covenant at that moment, but did so later, cf. *Jos.* 24:25.

100 The Babli, 27b, quotes here a disagreement between R. Aqiba, who holds that the entire Torah was given at Sinai and repeated in the Tent of Meeting, and R. Ismael who holds that the general outline was given at Sinai but the details only in the Tent of Meeting (cf. *Lev.* 1:1).

101 In the Tosephta, R. Simeon is credited with the statement that a total of 3 times 16 covenants were established for every commandment.

102 One for each verse of *Deut.* 27:15-26.

103 In the Babylonian sources, the name of the village is עכו or עיבום, עיכוס but in the Tosephta also once עמוס, cf. S. Lieberman, *Tosefta kiFshutah Nasim* p. 711; A. Liss, ed., *The Babylonian Talmud with variant readings, Sotah,* vol. 2, p. 148, Notes 33,39*.

104 This is the census of the tribes in *Num.* 1:46, excluding the Levites. This means that he counts one individual covenant for each Israelite. This is the explicit statement in the Tosephta. In the Babli: 48 covenants for 603'550, attributed to Rebbi in our text. The statement of Rebbi in the Tosephta is: 13 covenants for 603'550.

(21d, line 1) עַד כְּדוֹן דְּבָרִים שֶׁנִּכְלְלוּ וְנִפְרְטוּ. דְּבָרִים שֶׁנִּכְלְלוּ וְלֹא נִפְרְטוּ. אָמַר לֵיהּ. כֵּן אָמַר רִבִּי יוֹחָנָן מִשּׁוּם רִבִּי שִׁמְעוֹן. כָּל־שֶׁהָיָה בִּכְלָל וְיָצָא מִן

הַכְּלָל לְלַמֵּד. לֹא לְלַמֵּד עַל עַצְמוֹ יָצָא אֶלָּא לְלַמֵּד עַל הַכְּלָל כּוּלוֹ יָצָא. אָמַר לֵיהּ. לֹא בְדָבָר אֶחָד. דִּילְמָא בִשְׁנֵי דְּבָרִים. וְהָכָא בִשְׁנֵי דְבָרִים אֲנָן קַייָמִין. אָמַר רִבִּי תַנְחוּמָא. מִכֵּיוָן דִּכְתִיב בְּסוֹף אָמֵן. כְּמִי שֶׁכּוּלוֹ דָבָר אֶחָד.

So far subjects which were stated in general and in detail[105]. Subjects which were stated in general but not in detail[106]? He said to him: So says Rebbi Joḥanan in the name of Rebbi Simeon[107]. Anything which was in a set and and left the set to teach, not to teach only about itself did it leave but to teach about the entire set[108]. He said to him: Is that not about a single subject? Perhaps for two subjects? And here[109], we deal with two different subjects. Rebbi Tanḥuma said, since at the end is written "Amen", it is as if everything were one subject.

105 Of the twelve blessings and curses (cf. Note 102), one is general and 11 are in detail. The ones in detail are also contained in the last, general, blessing and curse.

106 Any other commandment in the Torah. Are there any covenants that force one to obey those?

107 In all Babli-inspired sources, this is the 9th hermeneutic rule of R. Ismael; *Sifra, Introduction*. In Chapter 9, the authorship is attributed to (tannaitic) rabbis who oppose R. Ismael; Chapter 9, Notes 87-89.

108 The example given in *Sifra* is: It is written in *Lev.* 7:20 that eating from a well-being sacrifice that had become impure is a deadly sin. But well-being sacrifices are only one element of the set of all sacrifices. In the absence of a biblical statement to the contrary, it can be asserted that eating from *any* sacrifice that had become impure is a deadly sin. The set is that of all sacrifices, from which the well-being sacrifice was singled out for a special statement.

109 And in this case there are 11 particular statements and one defining the set as all commandments of the Torah.

(21d, line 6) כְּתִיב אָרוּר אֲשֶׁר לֹא יָקִים אֶת כָּל־דִּבְרֵי הַתּוֹרָה הַזֹּאת. וְכִי יֵשׁ תּוֹרָה נוֹפֶלֶת. שִׁמְעוֹן בֶּן יָקִים אוֹמֵר. זֶה הַחַזָּן שֶׁהוּא עוֹמֵד. רִבִּי שִׁמְעוֹן בֶּן חֲלַפְתָּא אוֹמֵר. זֶה הַבַּיִת שֶׁלְּמַטָּן. דְּאָמַר רַב חוּנָה רַב יְהוּדָה בְּשֵׁם שְׁמוּאֵל. עַל הַדָּבָר הַזֶּה קָרַע יֹאשִׁיָּה וְאָמַר. עָלַי לְהָקִים.

It is written: "Cursed be he who would not raise all the words of this Torah." Can the Torah fall down? Simeon ben Yaqim[110] says, that is the *ḥazzan* who stands[111]. Rebbi Simeon ben Ḥalaphta says, that is the earthly house[112], as Rav Ḥuna, Rav Jehudah said in the name of Samuel: Josia tore [his garments] about this verse[113] and said, I have to raise.

110 Nachmanides (Commentary to *Deut.* 27:26) reads Rebbi Simeon ben Yaqim.

111 Nachmanides does not read the last two words. It would seem that his reading is correct. In Europe, the word חזן always denoted the reader who *stood* before the congregation and led it in prayer. However, in the East, the חזן was always the employee of the congregation who functioned as rabbi, reader, ritual slaughterer, and general organizer of the community (cf. *Berakhot* 3:1, Note 60). At Torah readings, the *ḥazzan* had to see to it that the Torah scroll was lifted and shown to all present.

112 Nachmanides reads זֶה בֵּית דִּין שֶׁלְּמַטָּה "that is the earthly court" (which has to supervise the moral state of the community.)

113 *2K.* 22:11. He asserts that upon hearing the Torah [which by tradition had been forbidden by his father Amon (cf. *Midrash Haggadol Deut.* on *Deut.* 27:26)], Josia tore his garments on hearing *Deut.* 27:26.

(21d, line 10) רִבִּי אָחָא בְּשֵׁם רִבִּי תַנְחוּם בְּרִבִּי חִיָּיה. לָמַד וְלִימֵּד וְשָׁמַר וְעָשָׂה וְהָיְתָה סְפִּיקָה בְּיָדוֹ לְהַחֲזִיק וְלֹא הֶחֱזִיק. הֲרֵי זֶה בִּכְלָל אָרוּר. רִבִּי יִרְמְיָה בְּשֵׁם[114] רִבִּי חִיָּיה בַּר בָּא. לֹא לָמַד וְלֹא לִימֵּד וְלֹא שָׁמַר וְלֹא עָשָׂה וְלֹא הָיְתָה סְפִּיקָה בְּיָדוֹ לְהַחֲזִיק וְהֶחֱזִיק. הֲרֵי זֶה בִּכְלָל בָּרוּךְ. וְאָמַר רִבִּי חָנָה רִבִּי יִרְמְיָה בְּשֵׁם רִבִּי חִיָּיה. עָתִיד הַקָּדוֹשׁ בָּרוּךְ הוּא לַעֲשׂוֹת צֵל לְבַעֲלֵי מִצְוֹת בְּצִילָּהּ

שֶׁלְּבַעֲלֵי תוֹרָה. מַה טַעֲמָא. כִּי בְּצֵל הַחָכְמָה בְּצֵל הַכָּסֶף. וְאוֹמֵר עֵץ חַיִּים הִיא לַמַּחֲזִיקִים בָּהּ.

[115]Rebbi Aha in the name of Rebbi Tanḥum ben Rebbi Ḥiyya. If somebody studied and taught, kept and did, and it was in his power to strengthen[116], but he did not strengthen, that one is in the set of the cursed. Rebbi Jeremiah in the name of Rebbi Ḥiyya bar Abba: If somebody did not study, did not teach, did not keep and did not do, and it was not in his hand to strengthen but he did strengthen[117], that one is in the set of the blessed. And Rebbi Ḥana, Rebbi Jeremiah, said in the name of Rebbi Ḥiyya bar Abba: In the future [world], the Holy One, praise to Him, will make shadow of those who perform commandments[118] in the shadow of those who study Torah. What is the reason? "For in the shadow of Torah, in the shadow of money[119]". And it is said, "it[120] is a tree of life for those who support it.[121]"

114 From the Rome ms. Leiden: בָּעֵי "asked".
115 A fundraiser's sermon.
116 To give financial support to institutions of Torah learning.
117 He gave financial support to institutions of Torah learning even though he was not rich.
118 They give money to charity. A similar statement in the name of R. Joḥanan is in the Babli, *Pesahim* 53b.
119 *Eccl.* 7:12
120 The Torah (taken here as symbol for the institutions of Torah study).
121 *Prov.* 3:18. *Midrash rabba Lev.* 25(1): "It does not say 'is a tree of life for those who study it', but 'who support it'.

(21d, line 17) מַה תַּלְמוּד לוֹמַר וְהֶחָצְיוֹ. אֶלָּא מְלַמֵּד שֶׁמְּעוּטִין בְּהַר גְּרִזִים וּמְרוּבִּים בְּהַר עֵיבָל. לָמָּה. שֶׁאֵין שִׁבְטוֹ שֶׁלְּלֵוִי כּוּלּוֹ שָׁם. שֶׁאִים הָיָה כָל־שֵׁבֶט לֵוִי כּוּלּוֹ שָׁם הָיוּ שָׁוִין. רִבִּי שְׁמוּאֵל בַּר נַחְמָן בְּשֵׁם רִבִּי יוֹנָתָן. אִילוּ הָיָה

כָּל־שִׁבְטוֹ שֶׁלְּלֵוִי שָׁם לֹא הָיוּ שָׁוִין. לָמָּה. שֶׁכְּבָר נָפְלוּ מִשִּׁבְטוֹ שֶׁלְּשִׁמְעוֹן עֶשְׂרִים וְאַרְבָּעָה אֶלֶף בַּשִּׁיטִים. אָמַר רִבִּי יוֹסֵי בֵּירִבִּי בּוּן. אִילּוּ הָיָה כָּל־שִׁבְטוֹ שֶׁלְּלֵוִי שָׁם הָיוּ שָׁוִין. לָמָּה. שֶׁלֹּא בָא מִשֵּׁבֶט רְאוּבֵן וְגָד אֶלָּא אַרְבָּעִים אֶלֶף חֲלוּצֵי צָבָא.

Why does the verse[122] say: "and the half of it"? This teaches that a minority was on Mount Gerizim and a majority on Mount Ebal[123]. Why? Because the tribe of Levi was not completely there. For if the tribe of Levi had been completely there, they would have been equal. Rebbi Samuel bar Naḥman in the name of Rebbi Jonathan: If the tribe of Levi had been completely there, they would not have been equal. Why? Since already 24'000 had fallen at Shiṭṭim from the tribe of Simeon[124]. Rebbi Yose ben Rebbi Abun said, if the tribe of Levi had been completely there, they would have been equal[125]. Why? Because from the tribes of Reuben and Gad only 40'000 front line troops came there.

---

122 In *Jos.* 8:33, those who went to Mount Gerizim are חֲצִיוֹ "half", but those on Mount Ebal are "וְהַחֲצִיוֹ" and *the* half". The appearance of the definite article has to be explained.

123 Based on the figures of *Num.* 26, there would be about 20'000 fewer persons on Mount Gerizim than on Mount Ebal, the Levites not counted. Since the Levites were counted separately, as unfit for war, and they were counted from one month of age, the numbers cannot be compared. Including children from the age of one month, there were only 23'000 Levites.

124 In the count of *Num.* 1, the tribe of Simeon had 59'300 warriors, but in *Num.* 26, that number had shrunk to 22'200. The people who had died at Shiṭṭim were 24'000 (*Num.* 25:9). This is less than the total diminution of the tribe of Simeon.

125 This is difficult to understand. Following *Jos.* 4:13, the Transjordanian tribes together delivered "about 40'000 frontline soldiers". There is no indication that the Transjordanien tribe of Manasse was counted separately. In any case, the data in Scripture are insufficient to express any opinion in the matter.

(21d, line 23) כַּהֲנָא אָמַר. כְּשֵׁם שֶׁהֵן חוֹלְקִין כָּאן הֵן חוֹלְקִין בִּתְחִילַת הַחוּמָשׁ הַשֵּׁינִי. אִית תַּנָּיֵי תַנֵּי. כְּשֵׁם שֶׁהֵן חוֹלְקִין כָּאן הֵן חוֹלְקִין בִּדְגָלִים. בְּנֵי לֵאָה מִיכָּן. וּבְנֵי רָחֵל חַד מִכָּן וְחַד מִכָּן. וּבְנֵי הַשְּׁפָחוֹת בָּאֶמְצַע. אָמַר רִבִּי מַתַּנְיָה. טַעֲמָא דְהָדֵין תַּנְיָיה שְׁמַע אֵלַי יַעֲקֹב עַבְדִּי יִשְׂרָאֵל מְקוֹרָאִי. מַה הַתִּקְרָה הַזוּ עוֹבְיָיהּ דְהֵן גַּבֵּי קוֹטְנָהּ דְּהָהֵן וְעוֹבְיָיהּ דְּהֵן גַּבֵּי קוֹטְנָהּ דְּהָהֵן. אִית תַּנָּיֵי תַנֵּי. כְּשֵׁם שֶׁהֵן חֲלוּקִין כָּאן כָּךְ הֵן חֲלוּקִין בְּאַבְנֵי אֵפוֹד. בְּמִלוּאוֹתָם. כְּדֵי שֶׁיְּהוּ עֶשְׂרִים וַחֲמִשָּׁה מִיכָּן וְעֶשְׂרִים וַחֲמִשָּׁה מִיכָּן. וַהֲלֹא אֵינָן אֶלָּא אַרְבָּעִים וְתִשְׁעָה. אָמַר רִבִּי יוֹחָנָן. בִּנְיָמִן דְּוּתוֹלְדוֹתָם מָלֵא. אָמַר רִבִּי יוּדָה בַּר זְבִידָה. יְהוֹסֵף מָלֵא. עֵדוּת בִּיהוֹסֵף שָׂמוֹ. וַהֲלֹא אֵינָן אֶלָּא עֶשְׂרִים וּשְׁלֹשָׁה מִיכָּן וְעֶשְׂרִים וְשִׁבְעָה מִיכָּן. אָמַר רִבִּי יוֹחָנָן. בִּנְיָמִן הָיָה חָצוּי. בֶּן מִכָּן יָמִין מִכָּן. אָמַר רִבִּי זְבִידָה. וְיָאוּת. מִי כְתִיב שִׁשָּׁה שְׁמוֹתָם. לֹא. אֶלָּא מִשְּׁמוֹתָם. מִשְּׁמוֹתָם וְלֹא כָל־שְׁמוֹתָם. הָרִאשׁוֹנִים נִכְתָּבִין מִימִינוּ שֶׁלַּכֹּהֵן הַגָּדוֹל מִשְּׂמֹאלוֹ שֶׁלַּקּוֹרֵא. וְהָאַחֲרוֹנִים נִכְתָּבִין מִשְּׂמֹאלוֹ שֶׁלַּכֹּהֵן הַגָּדוֹל מִימִינוּ שֶׁלַּקּוֹרֵא. הָרִאשׁוֹנִים אֵינָן נִכְתָּבִין עַל סֵדֶר. שֶׁיְּהוּדָה מֶלֶךְ. הָאַחֲרוֹנִים נִכְתָּבִין עַל סֵדֶר.

Cahana said, just as they divide here, so they divide at the beginning of the second book of the Pentateuch[126]. Some Tannaïm state: Just as they divide here, so they divide in the standards[127]. The sons of Leah on one side, the sons of Rachel one on one side, the other one on the other side, and the sons of the handmaidens in the middle[128]. Rebbi Mattania said, the reason of this Tanna is: "Hear me, Jacob my servant, Israel my roofed in[129]." Just as on the roof the thick part of one [beam] is next to the slim part of the other [beam][130]. Some Tannaïm state: Just as they are split here, so they are split on the stones of the ephod[131]. "In their fulnesses", that there should be 25 on one side and 25 on the other side[132]. But they are only 49[133]! Rebbi Joḥanan said, "Benjamin" of "and their births" is *plene*[134]. Rebbi Judah bar Zabida said, Jehoseph is *plene*, "He put it up as a testimony in Jehoseph.¹³⁵" But they are only 23 on one side and 27 on the other¹³⁶! Rebbi Johanan said, Benjamin was split, Ben on one side, Jamin on the other side¹³⁷. Rebbi Zabida said, this is fine. Does it say "their six names"? No, but, "of their names", not their entire names¹³⁸! The first were written on the right hand side of the High Priest, to the left of the viewer. The last were written on the left hand side of the High Priest, to the right of the viewer. The first ones were not written in order, for Jehudah is king. The last ones were written in order¹³⁹.

126 *Ex.* 1:2-3. There, the order is quite different: First the sons of the wives, then the sons of the handmaidens. In the Babli, 36a/b, the opinion is attributed to R. Ḥanina ben Gamliel.

127 This opinion is not found in the Babli. Cf. *Num.* 2. There the order is: Standard of Judah: Judah, Issachar, Zebulun. Standard of Reuben: Reuben, Simeon, Gad. Standard of Ephraim: Ephraim, Manasse, Benjamin. Standard of Dan: Dan, Asher, Naftali. This also is incompatible with the order given in *Deut.* 27:13-14: Simeon, Levi, Jehudah, Issachar, Joseph, Benjamin - Reuben, Gad, Asher, Zebulun, Dan, Naftali.

128 The verse indicates which tribes were standing on which mountain but does not indicate how they were standing. The opinion here is that on Mount Gerizim the two Rachel tribes, Joseph and Benjamin, were standing at the right and left extremes and the Leah tribes in the middle; on Mount Ebal the two Leah tribes, Reuben and Zebulun were standing at the right and left extremes and the handmaidens' tribes in the middle. (Explanation of *Pene Moshe*). In the Babli, 36b.

129 *Jes.* 48:12. The verse is misquoted; "my servant" is not written. The interpretation of this conceit is based on rabbinic Hebrew קוֹרָא "roof girder"; modern Hebrew קוֹרָה.

130 It seems that their roofs were made from wooden beams of a slightly conical shape so that they could be pressed together to protect against the rains. A similar picture *Ex. rabba* 1(6).

131 *Ex.* 28:9-10. The order in which the names of the tribes were to be engraved on the Shoham stones is indicated only obliquely as כְּתוֹלְדֹתָם "in

the order of their birth"; that would be Reuben, Simeon, Levi, Jehudah, Dan, Naftali; Gad, Asher, Issachar, Zebulun, Joseph, Benjamin. In the Babli, 36a, this is the opinion of Rav Cahana.

132   The word is written not for the Shoham stones of the *ephod* but for the stones representing the tribes on the ḥoshen (*Ex.* 28:20), on which the names of the tribes were engraved (v. 21) and which were set *to fill* the settings prepared for them.

133   As written, the names of the Gerizim tribes add up to 27 letters, those of the Ebal tribes to 22. The same objection in the Babli, 36b.

134   On the stone, the name of Benjamin was written בנימין for a total of 28 letters. This opinion is not quoted in the Babli; it is dismissed in the Yerushalmi.

135   *Ps.* 81:6. In the Babli, 36b, this is the opinion of R. Isaac.

136   This questioner reads זבולון *plene* but בנימן defective and יוסף in its usual form.

137   R. Joḥanan cannot follow his own opinion that Benjamin was spelled *plene* but must follow R. Judah bar Zabida. Then on the right hand side there were 27 + 1 - 3 = 25 letters and on the left hand side 22 + 3 = 25 letters.

138   In *Ex.* 28:10, the group of the first six names is charaterized as מִשְּׁמֹתָם, "of their names", taking the מ, as usual in rabbinic texts, as partitive. The other six names are "the six other names", to be written in full (and, according to the Babli, 36a, in the order of their births.)

139   That means, not in the order in which they are enumerated in *Deut.* 27:14.

משנה ה: וְאַחַר כָּךְ הֵבִיאוּ אֶת הָאֲבָנִים וּבָנוּ אֶת הַמִּזְבֵּחַ וְסָדוּהוּ בַּסִּיד וְכָתְבוּ עָלָיו אֶת כָּל־דִּבְרֵי הַתּוֹרָה הַזֹּאת בְּשִׁבְעִים לָשׁוֹן שֶׁנֶּאֱמַר בַּאֵר הֵיטֵב וְנָטְלוּ אֶת הָאֲבָנִים וּבָאוּ וְלָנוּ בִמְקוֹמָן. (fol. 21b)

Mishnah 5: After that they brought the stones[140], built the altar[141], whitewashed it with lime[141], and wrote on it all the words of this Torah in seventy languages[142], as it is written: "well explained[143]". They took the stones[140], went and stayed in their place overnight[144].

140 Which stones they were is a matter of discussion.
141 On Mount Ebal, *Deut.* 27:4.
142 The standard number of peoples on earth as enumerated in *Ber.* 10.
143 *Deut.* 27:8. In *Jos.* 8:35 this is taken to mean that Joshua had to explain the Torah to men, women, and children.
144 At Gilgal, near Jericho.

(fol. 21c) **הלכה ה**: תַּנֵּי. עַל אַבְנֵי הַמָּלוֹן נִכְתְּבוּ. דִּבְרֵי רִבִּי יוּדָה. רִבִּי יוֹסִי אוֹמֵר. עַל אַבְנֵי הַמִּזְבֵּחַ נִכְתְּבוּ. מָאן דָּמַר. עַל אַבְנֵי הַמָּלוֹן נִכְתְּבוּ. בְּכָל־יוֹם וְיוֹם אוּמּוֹת הָעוֹלָם מְשַׁלְּחִין נוֹטָרֵיהֶן וּמַשִּׂיאִין אֶת הַתּוֹרָה שֶׁהָיְתָה כְתוּבָה בְּשִׁבְעִים לָשׁוֹן. מָאן דָּמַר. עַל אַבְנֵי הַמִּזְבֵּחַ נִכְתְּבוּ. לֹא לְשָׁעָה הָיוּ וְנִגְנְזוּ. עוֹד הוּא מַעֲשֵׂה נִיסִּים. נָתַן הַקָּדוֹשׁ בָּרוּךְ הוּא בִּינָה בְּלֵב כָּל־אוּמָּה וְאוּמָּה וְהִשִּׂיאוּ אֶת הַתּוֹרָה שֶׁהָיְתָה כְתוּבָה בְּשִׁבְעִים לָשׁוֹן. מָאן דָּמַר. עַל אַבְנֵי הַמָּלוֹן נִכְתְּבוּ. נִיחָא וְשַׂדְתָּ אוֹתָם בַּשִּׂיד. מָאן דָּמַר. עַל אַבְנֵי הַמִּזְבֵּחַ נִכְתְּבוּ. מַה מְקַיְּמִים וְשַׂדְתָּ אוֹתָם בַּשִּׂיד. בֵּין כָּל־אֶבֶן וָאֶבֶן. רִבִּי שְׁמוּאֵל בַּר נַחְמָנִי בְּשֵׁם רִבִּי יוֹנָתָן. וְהָיוּ עַמִּים מִשְׂרְפוֹת סִיד. מֵסִיד נָטְלוּ אַיְפּוֹפְסִין שֶׁלָּהֶן מִיתָה. רִבִּי אַבָּא בַּר כַּהֲנָא בְּשֵׁם רִבִּי יוֹחָנָן. וְהַגּוֹיִם חָרוֹב יֶחֱרָבוּ. מֵחוֹרֵב נָטְלוּ אַיְפּוֹפְסִין שֶׁלָּהֶן מִיתָה.

Halakhah 5: It was stated: It was written on the stones of the dwelling place, the words of Rebbi Jehudah[145]; Rebbi Yose says, it was written on the stones of the altar[146]. He who says, it was written on the stones of the dwelling place, every day the peoples of the world were sending their stenographers[147] and they carried away the Torah which had been written in seventy languages[148]. He who says, it was written on the stones of the altar, were they not only for a short time and then were hidden? That was another wonder, that the Holy One, praise to Him, gave insight to every people and they carried away the Torah which had been written in seventy languages. For him who says, it was written on the stones of the dwelling place, it is understandable that "you shall whitewash them with lime." But he who says, it was written on the stones of the altar, how does he uphold ""you shall whitewash them with lime"? Between the stones[149]. Rebbi Samuel bar Naḥmani in the name of Rebbi Jonathan: "The peoples will be lime incinerators[150]", from the lime they took their death sentence[151]. Rebbi Abba bar Cahana in the name of Rebbi Joḥanan: "But the Gentiles will be totally destroyed[152]," from Horeb they took their death sentence.

145 In the interpretation of Rashi, Babli 35b, they took the stones, built with them the altar on Mount Ebal, disassembled the altar, took the stones to Gilgal, inscribed the Torah with 70 translations on the stones and covered everything with whitewash. The text of the Babli is paralleled in the Tosephta, 8:6.

Both in the Babli and in the Tosephta this opinion is that of the anonymous majority.

146 In Babli and Tosephta, this is ascribed to R. Jehudah..

147 Latin *notarius*, "stenographer".

148 They lifted the whitewash from the stone and had the letters stand out, and transported everything back to its place. In the opinion of R. Simeon, the translations were written on the whitewash where they could be copied.

In talmudic theory, Adam was created literate since he had a book (*Gen.* 5:1). If at any time in human history, peoples were found who were illiterate, they must have been degenerate [*Sanhedrin* 38b, *Avodah zarah* 5a; *Gen. rabba* 24(7)]. Adam was also created an inventor and engineer (cf. the author's *The Scholar's Haggadah*, pp. 219-221; *A Jewish Fundamentalist Philosophy of Science and Development*, Association F. Gonseth, Bulletin 63, 1992, pp. 9-20.)

149 This is not mentioned in Babli-Tosephta.
150 *Is.* 33:12. In Babli and Tosephta, this is attributed to R. Simeon.
151 Greek ἀπόφασις "judgment, sentence".
152 *Is.* 60:12. This sermon is not mentioned in the parallel sources. It is based on the identification of חרב I, Akkadic ḫarābu "to dry up" and חרב II, Arabic خرب "to destroy". The basis of this sermon and entire paragraph is the theory, based on *Deut.* 33:2, that before the epiphany on Horeb/Mount Sinai, God had offered the Torah to all the other peoples of the earth, who refused, and only Israel accepted. Therefore, only Israel reaps the rewards in the Future World (cf. *Sifry Deut.* 343, ed. L. Finkelstein; all the other sources are given there in Note 14.)

(21d, line 49) נִמְצֵאתָ אוֹמֵר. שְׁלֹשָׁה מִינֵי אֲבָנִים הֵן. אַבְנֵי הַמָּלוֹן. וַאֲבָנִים שֶׁהִנִּיחַ יְהוֹשֻׁעַ תַּחַת כַּפּוֹת רַגְלֵי הַכֹּהֲנִים. וְאִיסְטְלִיּוֹת שֶׁנָּתַן לָהֶן מֹשֶׁה. אָמַר רִבִּי חֲנִינָן. פָּשִׁיט לוֹן. אַרְבָּעָה מִינֵי אֲבָנִים הֵן. אָמַר רִבִּי סִימוֹן בַּר זְבִיד. וִיאוּת. אִין תֵּימַר. אַבְנֵי הַמָּלוֹן. לְשָׁעָה הָיוּ וְנִגְנְזוּ. אִין תֵּימַר. אֲבָנִים שֶׁהֵקִים יְהוֹשֻׁעַ תַּחַת כַּפּוֹת רַגְלֵי הַכֹּהֲנִים. מְשׁוּקָעוֹת הָיוּ בַמַּיִם. אִין תֵּימַר. אִיסְטְלִיּוֹת שֶׁנָּתַן לָהֶן מֹשֶׁה. כְּבָר נִכְנְסוּ עִמָּהֶן לָאָרֶץ. אֶלָּא כֵן אֲנָן קַיָּימִין בָּאֲבָנִים שֶׁהֵקִים לָהֶן יְהוֹשֻׁעַ עַל גַּב הַיַּרְדֵּן.

You may say that there were three kinds of stones[153]: The stones of the resting place[154], and the stones which Joshua put under the soles of the feet of the Cohanim[155], and the steles[156] that Moses had given them[157]. Rebbi Ḥaninan said, it is obvious to us that there were four kinds of stones[158]. Rebbi Simon ben Zebid said, that is correct. If you would say, they were the stones of the resting place; these were temporary and were hidden[159]. If you would say, the stones which Joshua put under the soles of the feet of the Cohanim; these were submerged in the water. If you would say, the steles that Moses had given them; they already had moved with them into the Land[160]. But we must deal with the stones that Joshua put up for them on the banks of the Jordan.

153 Tosephta 8:6, Babli 35b.

154 *Jos.* 4:3,8,20.

155 *Jos.* 4:9.

156 Greek στήλη. For the use of steles in ancient synagogues, cf., י. בראנד, "איצטלין", לשוננו 32 תשכ״ח-1968 ע' 276.

157 This is explained in the Babli, 35b. In *Deut.* 1:5 it is stated that Moses *explained* the Torah. In 27:8 it is commanded to copy the Torah on the stones, *well explained*. Since in the latter cases, "explained" means "engraved in stone", it follows that in the first case "explained" also must mean engraved in stone.

158 That the stones on which the Torah was written translated into 70 languages were none of the above three kinds. This opinion is not mentioned in Babli/Tosephta.

159 This is difficult to understand since the stones should be there as a permanent memorial, *Jos.* 4:21-24. In any case, the verses make it clear that these stones were not to be used to be written on.

160 Even if they had taken the steles with them, the Torah already was written on them and they could not be those on which the Torah was written anew.

(21d, line 56) תַּנֵּי. רִבִּי יוּדָה בַּר אִילָעִי אוֹמֵר. אַבָּא חֲלַפְתָּא וְרִבִּי אֶלְעָזָר בֶּן מַתְיָה וַחֲנִינָה בֶּן חֲכִינַאי עָמְדוּ עַל אוֹתָן הָאֲבָנִים וְשִׁיעֲרוּם כָּל אַחַת וְאַחַת מַשּׂוֹי אַרְבָּעִים סְאָה. מִיכָּן אַתְּ לָמֵד כַּמָּה הָיָה בָּאֶשְׁכּוֹל. כְּתִיב וְהָרִימוּ לָכֶם אִישׁ אֶבֶן אַחַת עַל שִׁכְמוֹ. לָא דָמִי הַהוּא דִטְעַן מִן אַרְעָא לְכַתְפֵיהּ לְהַהוּא דִטְעַן מֵאַרְעָא לְאַרְכּוּבָתֵיהּ. וּמִן אַרְכּוּבָתֵיהּ לְכַתְפֵיהּ. לָא דָמִי הַהוּא דִטְעַן מֵאַרְעָא לְאַרְכּוּבָתֵיהּ וּמִן אַרְכּוּבָתֵיהּ לְכַתְפֵיהּ לְהַהוּא דְאוֹחֳרָן תְּלִי לֵיהּ. לָא דָמִי דְאוֹחֳרָן תְּלִי לֵיהּ לְהַהוּא דִטְעִין בִּתְרֵין. כְּתִיב אִישׁ אֶחָד לַשָּׁבֶט. [161]עַל דַּעְתֵּיהּ דְּרִבִּי עֲקִיבָה דוּ אָמַר לְשׁוֹנוֹת רְבוּיִים הֵן. (3) שְׁנֵים־עָשָׂר הָיוּ. שְׁמֹנָה בָּאֶשְׁכּוֹל וְאַרְבַּע בַּתְּאֵינִים וְרִמּוֹנִים וּבְנוֹשְׂאֵי כֵלִים. (2) עַל דַּעְתֵּיהּ דְּרִבִּי שִׁמְעוֹן דּוּ אָמַר לְשׁוֹנוֹת כְּפוּלִין הֵן. (1) עֶשְׂרִים וְאַרְבָּעָה הָיוּ. שִׁשָּׁה עָשָׂר בָּאֶשְׁכּוֹל וּשְׁמֹנָה בַּתְּאֵינִים וְרִמּוֹנִים וּבְנוֹשְׂאֵי כֵלִים. (4) עַל דַּעְתֵּיהּ דְּרִבִּי יִשְׁמָעֵאל טוּרְטוֹרִין. עַל דַּעְתֵּיהּ דְּרִבִּי עֲקִיבָה טוּרְטוֹרִין וְטוּרְטוֹרֵי טוּרְטוֹרִין.

It was stated: Rebbi Jehudah bar Ilai says: Abba Halaphta, Rebbi Eleazar ben Mattia, and Hanina bar Hakhinai stood on those stones and estimated that each one on them was a load of 40 *seah*. From here you can estimate how big was the bunch of grapes[162]. It is written[163]: "Each one should lift a stone on his shoulder." One cannot compare one who lifts from the ground to his shoulder to one who lifts first from the ground to his knee and then from his knee to his shoulder. One cannot compare one who lifts first from the ground to his knee and then from his knee to his shoulder to one onto whom others hang [the load]. One cannot compare one onto whom others hang [the load] to [a load] carried by two.

It is written: "One man per tribe.[164]" In the opinion of Rebbi Aqiba who says these are expressions of additions, there were 24, sixteen for the grape bunch and eight for figs, pomegranates, and their belongings[165]. In the opinion of Rebbi Simeon[166], who says there are double expressions, there were twelve, eight for the grape bunch and four for figs, pomegranates, and their belongings. In the opinion of Rebbi Ismael a beam[167]; in the opinion of Rebbi Aqiba a beam and beams of beams.

161 The following sentences, while correct in themselves, seem to be out of proper order. They have been translated in the conjectured correct order indicated by the numerals in the text.

162 Babli 34a, Tosephta 8:6.

163 *Jos.* 4:5.

164 *Deut.* 1:23. This is the wrong quote; intended is *Num.* 13:2: "One man, one man per ancestral tribe you shall send." The problem is the interpretation of the duplication.

165 In the Babli, 34a, the verse *Num.* 13:23: "they carried [the grape bunch] on a pole by two" is interpreted that it was carried by eight people with the grape bunch hanging between two poles. There, one is said to have carried a fig, another a pomegranate;

Joshua and Caleb did not carry anything.

166 This attribution seems to be wrong. R. Simeon is not known to reject R. Aqiba's interpretations. Probably it should read: R. Ismael, who insists that the Torah is written in the vernacular and who is quoted in the next sentence.

167 This is the traditional interpretation; in the absence of a convincing etymology the meaning is not guaranteed.

In the Babli, 34b, the interpretation given here following R. Aqiba is attributed to R. Isaac; the wording is טורטני וטרטני דטורטני. The word טורטני appears in quite a number of other sources (collected in Krauss, *Lehnwörter*) where it is perfectly adequate to see in it Greek τρυτάνη "pair of scales". By the concurrent testimony of Rashi and R. Ḥananel, certainly based on Gaonic material, the interpretation of R. Isaac's statement is that the grape bunch was pictured carried between two poles which at each end were fixed to a cross-beam. Each cross-beam at both extremities had smaller cross beams, giving space for 8 bearers, all marching in the same direction. There is no reason not to accept this interpretation for the Yerushalmi; but for the position of the Yerushalmi following R. Ismael, it seems rather that the image is that of a single pole, with four men preceding the grape bunch and four men following behind it.

It is possible that "scale" here stands for "scale bar". But it is possible that טורטני may be a Babylonian corruption of a Semitic word טוּרְטוּר of *pilpel* type.

(21d, line 69) כְּתִיב וַיַּעַמְדוּ הַמַּיִם הַיּוֹרְדִים מִלְמַעְלָה קָמוּ נֵד אֶחָד הַרְחֵק מְאֹד מֵאָדָם הָעִיר אֲשֶׁר מִצַּד צָרְתָן. אָמַר רִבִּי יוֹחָנָן. אָדָם קִרְיָיה וְצָרְתָן קִרְיָיה. שְׁנֵים עָשָׂר מִיל מִזּוֹ לְזוֹ. מְלַמֵּד שֶׁהָיוּ הַמַּיִם גְּדוּשִׁין וְעוֹלִין כְּמַצַּד צָרְתָן. וְכִי אֵי זֶה קַל. הַמַּיִם אוֹ אָדָם. הַמַּיִם קַלִּין מֵאָדָם. תֵּדַע לָךְ שֶׁהוּא כֵן. אֶלָא מְלַמֵּד שֶׁהָיוּ הַמַּיִם גְּדוּשִׁין וְעוֹלִין כִּיפִין עַל כֵּיפִין. רִבִּי לֵוִי אָמַר. עַד לִבּוֹ שֶׁלָּרָקִיעַ. תַּמָּן אָמְרִין. עַד בָּבֶל. נֶאֱמַר כָּאן הַרְחֵק וְנֶאֱמַר לְהַלָּן מֵאֶרֶץ רְחוֹקָה מְאֹד בָּאוּ אֵלַי מִבָּבֶל. תַּנֵּי. רִבִּי אֱלִיעֶזֶר בֶּן יַעֲקֹב אוֹמֵר. יוֹתֵר מִשְּׁלֹשׁ מֵאוֹת מִיל הָיוּ הַמַּיִם גְּדוּשִׁין וְעוֹלִין כֵּיפִין עַל גַּבֵּי כֵיפִין עַד שֶׁרָאוּ אוֹתָן כָּל־אֻמּוֹת הָעוֹלָם.

הָדָא הִיא דִכְתִיב. וַיְהִי כִשְׁמוֹעַ כָּל־מַלְכֵי הָאֱמוֹרִי אֲשֶׁר בְּעֵבֶר הַיַּרְדֵּן וְכָל־הַכְּנַעֲנִי אֲשֶׁר עַל הַיָּם אֶת אֲשֶׁר הוֹבִישׁ יי אֶת מֵי הַיַּרְדֵּן מִפְּנֵי בְנֵי יִשְׂרָאֵל עַד עָבְרָם וגו'.

[168]It is written[169]: "The waters descending from higher up stood like a dam, very far, from the town of Adam which is besides Ṣāretān. Rebbi Joḥanan said, Adam is a town and Ṣāretān is a town; there are twelve *mil* from one to the other. That teaches that the water was stacked up and rose like the citadel of Ṣāretān. [170]Which one is lighter, water or man? Waters are lighter than man; you know that this is so. This teaches that the waters were stacked and increased, wave upon wave. Rebbi Levi said, up to the sky's heart. There[171], they said, as far as Babylon. It says here[169] "far", and it says there[172] "they came from a very far land, from Babylon." It was stated[173]: Rebbi Eliezer ben Jacob said, the waters were stacked and rose, waves on waves, for more than 300 *mil* until all the peoples of the world saw them. That is what is written[174]: "It happened when all the kings of the Emorite on the other side of the Jordan, and all the Canaanite dwelling on the Sea, heard that the Eternal had dried up the waters of the river Jordan for the children of Israel until they had passed across," etc.

168   Cf. Babli 34a and Tosephta 8:2-3.

169   *Jos.* 4:16.

170   This refers to a tannaïtic discussion quoted in the Babli but not here.

171   In Babylonia. This argument is not in the Babli.

172   *2K.* 20:14; *Is.* 39:3.

173   In the Babli, and the Tosephta 8:3, this is attributed to R. Eleazar bar R. Simeon.

174   *Jos.* 5:1.

(22a, line 5) אָמַר רִבִּי שִׁמְעוֹן בֶּן לָקִישׁ. בַּיַּרְדֵּן קִיבְּלוּ עֲלֵיהֶן אֶת הַנִּסְתָּרוֹת. אָמַר לָהֶן יְהוֹשֻׁעַ. [אִם אֵין אַתֶּם]175 מְקַבְּלִין עֲלֵיכֶם אֶת הַנִּסְתָּרוֹת הַמַּיִם בָּאִין וְשׁוֹטְפִין אֶתְכֶם. אָמַר רִבִּי סִימוֹן בַּר זַבְדָא. וְיָאוּת. תֵּדַע לָךְ שֶׁהוּא כֵן. שֶׁהֲרֵי עָכָן חָטָא וְרוּבָּהּ שֶׁלַּסַּנְהֶדְרִין נָפְלָה בָעַי. אָמַר רִבִּי לֵוִי. בְּיַבְנֶה הוּתְּרָה הָרְצוּעָה. יָצְתָה בַת קוֹל וְאָמְרָה. אֵין לָכֶם עֵסֶק בַּנִּסְתָּרוֹת.

Rebbi Simeon ben Laqish said, in the Jordan they accepted the secret matters[175]. Joshua told them, if you do not accept the secret matters, the waters will come and sweep you away. Rebbi Simon bar Zabida said, that is correct. You should know that this is so, for Akhan sinned and the majority of the Synhedrion fell at Ai[176]. Rebbi Levi said, at Jabneh the rope was untied; there came a disembodied voice and said: You have nothing to do with secret matters[177].

175   That the people as a whole will be punished for secret sins of an individual. Moses had explicitly ruled out responsibility of the public for hidden deeds of the individual, *Deut.* 29:28.

In the Babli, *Sanhedrin* 43b, the position of R. Simon ben Laqish is similar to that of the Tanna R. Jehudah. The responsibility of the public for hidden deeds of the individual is denied by R. Nehemiah.

176   *Jos.* 7:5; Cf. Babli *Sanhedrin* 44a. In the opinion of the Babli, Akhan's sin was not private since his family knew about it.

177   In later rabbinic language, this phrase was used in the sense that mystical sayings should have no standing in matters of religious law or practice.

(fol. 21b) **מִשְׁנָה ו**: בִּרְכַּת כֹּהֲנִים כֵּיצַד. בַּמְּדִינָה אוֹמְרִים אוֹתָהּ שָׁלֹשׁ בְּרָכוֹת וּבַמִּקְדָּשׁ בְּרָכָה אַחַת. בַּמִּקְדָּשׁ אוֹמֵר אֶת הַשֵּׁם כִּכְתָבוֹ וּבַמְּדִינָה בְּכִנּוּיוֹ.

בַּמְּדִינָה כֹּהֲנִים נוֹשְׂאִים אֶת יְדֵיהֶן כְּנֶגֶד כִּתְפוֹתֵיהֶן וּבַמִּקְדָּשׁ עַל גַּבֵּי רָאשֵׁיהֶן חוּץ מִכֹּהֵן גָּדוֹל שֶׁאֵינוֹ מַגְבִּיהַּ אֶת יָדָיו לְמַעְלָה מִן הַצִּיץ. רִבִּי יְהוּדָה אוֹמֵר אַף כֹּהֵן גָּדוֹל מַגְבִּיהַּ אֶת יָדָיו לְמַעְלָה מִן הַצִּיץ שֶׁנֶּאֱמַר וַיִּשָּׂא אַהֲרֹן אֶת יָדָיו אֶל הָעָם וַיְבָרְכֵם. בִּרְכוֹת כֹּהֵן גָּדוֹל כֵּיצַד. חַזַּן הַכְּנֶסֶת נוֹטֵל סֵפֶר הַתּוֹרָה וְנוֹתְנוֹ לְרֹאשׁ הַכְּנֶסֶת וְרֹאשׁ הַכְּנֶסֶת נוֹתְנוֹ לַסְּגָן וְהַסְּגָן נוֹתְנוֹ לַכֹּהֵן הַגָּדוֹל. וְכֹהֵן גָּדוֹל עוֹמֵד וּמְקַבֵּל עוֹמֵד וְקוֹרֵא אַחֲרֵי מוֹת וְאַךְ בֶּעָשׂוֹר. וְגוֹלֵל אֶת הַתּוֹרָה וּמַנִּיחָהּ בְּחֵיקוֹ וְאוֹמֵר יוֹתֵר מִמַּה שֶּׁקָּרִיתִי לִפְנֵיכֶם כָּתוּב כָּאן. וּבֶעָשׂוֹר שֶׁבְּחוּמָשׁ הַפְּקוּדִים קוֹרֵא עַל פֶּה וּמְבָרֵךְ עָלֶיהָ שְׁמוֹנֶה בְּרָכוֹת עַל הַתּוֹרָה וְעַל הָעֲבוֹדָה וְעַל הַהוֹדָיָיה וְעַל מְחִילַת הֶעָוֹן וְעַל הַמִּקְדָּשׁ וְעַל יִשְׂרָאֵל וְעַל הַכֹּהֲנִים וּשְׁאָר הַתְּפִילָה.

Mishnah 6: How is the priestly blessing? In the countryside they recited it as three blessings[178], but in the Temple as one blessing[179]. In the Temple one says the Name as it is written, but in the countryside by its circumlocution[180]. In the countryside the Cohanim lift their hands to the height of their shoulders but in the Temple over their heads except for the High Priest who does not lift his hands over the diadem. Rebbi Jehudah says, the High Priest also lifts his hands over his head, as it is said[181]: "Aaron lifted his hands towards the people and blessed them."

How are the blessings of the High Priest[182]? The organizer of the synagogue[183] takes a Torah scroll and gives it to the president of the synagogue; the president of the synagogue gives it to the Second[184]; the Second gives it to the High Priest. The High priest receives it standing, he stands and reads "after the death[185]" and "but on the tenth[186]"; he rolls the Torah tight, puts it in his bosom and says: More than what I read before you is written here. "And on the tenth" in Numbers[187] he recites by heart, and recites eight benedictions[188]: For the Torah, for the Temple service, for thanksgiving, for forgiveness of sins, for the Temple, for Israel, for the Cohanim, and the remainder of the prayer.

178 Each one of the verses *Num.* 6:24-26 to be answered by "Amen".

179 To be answered by the people at the end by "praised be the Name of the glory of His kingdom forever and ever".

180 "The Lord" אֲדוֹנָי or κύριος.

181 *Lev.* 9:22; since the ritual of blessing with raised hands is derived from this verse, it would be unreasonable to have the Cohanim not conform to Aaron's, the High Priest's, example.

182 On the Day of Atonement; cf. Mishnah *Yoma* 7:1.

183 On the Temple Mount. This is a non-scriptural ceremony, purely pharisaic, but followed, at least since Hasmonean times, even by Sadducee High Priests.

184 The second in command in the Temple after the High Priest; in effect his executive officer.

185 *Lev.* 16:1-34, the description of the Atonement service.

186 *Lev.* 23:26-32. Winding from Chap. 17 to 23 does not take much time.

187 *Num.* 29:7-11.

188 These are detailed in Halakhah 7.

(fol. 22a) **הלכה ו**: אָמַר רַב חִסְדָּא. צַעַר גָּדוֹל הָיָה לָהֶן. בְּכָל־אָתָר אַתְּ אָמַר. הוֹלְכִין אֵצֶל הַתּוֹרָה. וְהָכָא אַתְּ אָמַר. מוֹלִיכִין אֶת הַתּוֹרָה אֶצְלָן. אֶלָּא עַל יְדֵי שֶׁהֵן בְּנֵי אָדָם גְּדוֹלִים הַתּוֹרָה מִתְעַלָּה בָּהֶן. וְהָא תַמָּן מְיַבְּלִין אֶת הַתּוֹרָה גַּבֵּי רֵישׁ גָּלוּתָא. אָמַר רִבִּי יוֹסֵי בֵּירִבִּי בּוּן. עַל יְדֵי שֶׁזַּרְעוֹ שֶׁל דָּוִד מְשׁוּקָּע שָׁם אֵינוּן עָבְדִין לוֹ כְּמִנְהַג אַבְהָתְהוֹן.

Halakhah 6: Rav Ḥisda said, they[189] had great difficulty; [190]elsewhere you say that one goes to the Torah, and here you say, one brings the Torah to him? But because they are important personalities, the Torah is honored by them[191]. Does one not bring the Torah to the Head of the

Diaspora over there[192]? Rebbi Yose ben Rebbi Abun said, since the seed of David is immersed there[193] one treats him in the ancestral way.

189 The scholars in his academy.
190 From here to the end of the Halakhah, the text is also in *Yoma* 7:1.
191 In the Babli, *Yoma* 69a, the ceremony is for the glory of the High Priest.
192 At solemn occasions in Babylonia.
193 The family of the Heads of the Diaspora claimed descent from king Yekhoniah (Yoyakhin); the Head of the Diaspora is treated as King (Mishnah 7).

(22a, line 15) תַּמָּן תַּנִּינָן. מְדַלְגִין בַּנְּבִיא וְאֵין מְדַלְגִין בַּתּוֹרָה. מְדַלְגִין בְּנָבִיא וְאֵין מְדַלְגִין מִנָּבִיא לְנָבִיא. וּבַנְּבִיא שְׁלֹשִׁים עָשָׂר מוּתָּר. וְאֵין מְדַלְגִין בַּתּוֹרָה. רִבִּי יִרְמְיָה בְּשֵׁם רִבִּי שִׁמְעוֹן בֶּן לָקִישׁ. לְפִי שֶׁאֵין גּוֹלְלִין סֵפֶר תּוֹרָה בָּרַבִּים. רִבִּי יוֹסֵי בָּעֵי. הַגַּע עַצְמָךְ שֶׁהָיְתָה פָּרָשָׁה קְטַנָּה. אֶלָּא כְדֵי שֶׁיִּשְׁמְעוּ יִשְׂרָאֵל עַל סֵדֶר. וְהָא תַנִּינָן. וְקוֹרֵא אַחֲרֵי מוֹת וְאַךְ בֶּעָשׂוֹר. שַׁנְיָיא הִיא שֶׁהִיא סִדְרוֹ שֶׁלַּיּוֹם. תֵּדַע לָךְ. דָּמַר רִבִּי שִׁמְעוֹן בֶּן לָקִישׁ. בְּכָל־מָקוֹם אֵינוֹ קוֹרֵא עַל פֶּה וְכָא קוֹרֵא עַל פֶּה. רִבִּי יוֹסֵי מְפַקֵּד לְבַר עוּלָּא חַזָּנָא דִכְנִישְׁתָּא דְבַבְלָאֵי. כְּדֵי חֲזָרָה אוֹרַיְיתוֹ גַּיֵיל לָהּ לַחוֹרֵי פָרוֹכְתָּא. כַּד אִינּוּן תַּרְתֵּי תוּ מְיַיבֵּל חָדָא וּמַיְיתֵי חָדָא.

There[195], we have stated: "One winds in Prophets[196] but one does not wind in the Pentateuch." One winds in one prophet, but not from one prophet to another, but among prophets of the Twelve it is permitted[197]. But one does not wind in the Pentateuch; Rebbi Jeremiah in the name of Rebbi Simeon ben Laqish: Because one does not wind the Torah in public. Rebbi Yose asked, think of it, if it was a small portion[198]? But that Israel should hear it in its order[199]. But did we not state[200]: "He reads 'after the death[185]' and 'but on the tenth[186]'"? It is different here, because that is the order of the day[201]. Know that it is so since Rebbi Simeon ben Laqish said, one does not recite by heart, and here he recites by heart[202]. Rebbi Yose commanded Bar Ulla, the organizer of the congregation of Babylonians: When the Torah has been brought back, wind it behind the curtain[203]. If there are two, return one and bring the other[204].

195 Mishnah *Megillah* 4:5.

196 In the public reading from Prophets after the Sabbath reading from the Torah, it is permissible to piece the reading together from different chapters of one prophet.

197 Since all 12 minor prophets are written together in one scroll, moving from one to the next is like winding in one of the major prophets, each of which is written in his own scroll.

198 In the Palestinian $3^1/_2$ year cycle, it might be that the portion was too small to be read by seven different persons; may some readers read from another place after the allotted portion was already recited?

199 Even if one reads more than the allotted portion on one Sabbath, it must be a continuous text.

200 The Mishnah here.

201 This is a holiday reading, not a Sabbath reading; it has to concentrate on the texts dealing exclusively with that holiday.

202 From the text too far removed to be wound without inconveniencing the public.

203 In *Yoma*, the text reads: כַּד דְּהִיא "חָדָא אוֹרְיָא תְּהֵא גַיֵיל לָהּ לְהֲדֵי פָרוֹכְתָא. When you have only one Torah, wind it by the curtain." The text here is preferable since a good organizer will wind the Torah well before it is used the next time. The editors who mishandled the text, replacing the text here by that from Yoma in modern editions, probably never were Torah readers themselves.

204 This is not the common usage where one takes out both scrolls and reads from them one after the other. This shows that in Babylonia already in Talmudic times one read from two different scrolls at special occasions (in particular, holidays). One has to correct the statement by Elbogen (cf. Note 205, p. 127) that this practice is not recorded before Rav Yehudai Gaon.

(וּמְבָרֵךְ עָלֶיהָ שְׁמוֹנָה בְּרָכוֹת עַל הַתּוֹרָה. הַבּוֹחֵר בַּתּוֹרָה. **עַל** 22a, line 24)
הָעֲבוֹדָה. שְׁאוֹתְךָ לְבַדְּךָ בְיִרְאָה נַעֲבוֹד. עַל הַהוֹדָיָה. הַטּוֹב לְךָ לְהוֹדוֹת. עַל
מְחִילַת עָוֹן. מוֹחֵל עֲוֹנוֹת עַמּוֹ יִשְׂרָאֵל בְּרַחֲמִים. עַל הַמִּקְדָּשׁ. הַבּוֹחֵר בַּמִּקְדָּשׁ.
וְאָמַר רִבִּי אִידִי. הַשּׁוֹכֵן בְּצִיּוֹן. וְעַל יִשְׂרָאֵל. הַבּוֹחֵר בְּיִשְׂרָאֵל. וְעַל הַכֹּהֲנִים.
הַבּוֹחֵר בַּכֹּהֲנִים. וְעַל שְׁאָר הַתְּפִילָה תְּחִינָה וּבַקָּשָׁה. שֶׁעַמְּךָ יִשְׂרָאֵל צְרִיכִין
לְהִוָּשֵׁעַ לְפָנֶיךָ. בָּרוּךְ אַתָּה יי שׁוֹמֵעַ תְּפִילָה.

He recites eight benedictions: For the Torah, "He who chooses the Torah[205]." For the Temple service, "For You alone in fear we worship.[206]" For thanksgiving, "the Good One, You one must thank.[207]" For forgiveness of sins, "He Who forgives the sins of His people Israel in mercy.[208]" For the Temple, "He Who chooses the Temple"; and Rebbi Idi said, "He Who dwells in Zion."[209] For Israel, "He Who chooses Israel."[210] For the Cohanim, "He Who chooses the Cohanim." And the remainder of the prayer, "entreaty and begging, for Your people Israel need to be helped before You; Praise to You, Eternal, Who hears prayer"[211].

205 In the Babli, 41a: "The benediction for the Torah in the formulation one recites in the Synagogue." In the opinion of Ismar Elbogen (התפילה בישראל בהתפתחותה ההיסטורית, תרגם יהושע עמיר, תל־אביב 1972 p. 129), the text given here is the original synagogal text; cf. also *Soferim* 13:8; י. היינמן, התפילה בתקופת התנאים והאמוראים - טיבה ודפוסיה; ירושלים תשל״ו, ע' 105).

206 The Palestinian version of the 16th benediction of the *Amidah*. It is to be assumed that in this and the following benedictions the entire text was recited, not only the final doxology.

207 The 17th benediction of the *Amidah*.

208 The final paragraph of the middle benediction of the *Amidah* of the Day of Atonement.

209 The full text of this benediction is unknown. Since the statement of R. Idi is quoted as a commentary, not a disagreement, one has to assume that it refers to a prayer text of which R. Idi quotes the beginning.

210 In the opinion of Elbogen (*loc. cit.* p.16), this is the benediction preceding the recitation of the Šemaʿ.

211 It seems that this is the only prayer text of the eight benedictions which applies only to the reading of the High Priest.

(fol. 21b) **משנה ז**: פָּרָשַׁת הַמֶּלֶךְ כֵּיצַד. מוֹצָאֵי יוֹם טוֹב הָאַחֲרוֹן שֶׁלְּחָג בַּשְּׁמִינִי מוֹצָאֵי שְׁבִיעִית עוֹשִׂין לוֹ בֵּימָה שֶׁלְּעֵץ בָּעֲזָרָה וְהוּא יוֹשֵׁב עָלֶיהָ שֶׁנֶּאֱמַר מִקֵּץ שֶׁבַע שָׁנִים בְּמוֹעֵד שְׁנַת הַשְּׁמִטָּה בְּחַג הַסֻּכּוֹת בְּבוֹא כָל־יִשְׂרָאֵל לֵרָאוֹת. חַזַּן הַכְּנֶסֶת נוֹטֵל סֵפֶר הַתּוֹרָה וְנוֹתְנוֹ לְרֹאשׁ הַכְּנֶסֶת וְרֹאשׁ הַכְּנֶסֶת נוֹתְנוֹ לַסְּגָן וְהַסְּגָן נוֹתְנוֹ לַכֹּהֵן הַגָּדוֹל וְכֹהֵן גָּדוֹל נוֹתְנוֹ לַמֶּלֶךְ. וְהַמֶּלֶךְ עוֹמֵד וּמְקַבֵּל וְקוֹרֵא וְיוֹשֵׁב. אַגְרִיפַּס הַמֶּלֶךְ עָמַד וְקִיבֵּל וְקָרָא עוֹמֵד וְשִׁיבְּחוּהוּ חֲכָמִים. וּכְשֶׁהִגִּיעַ לְלֹא תוּכַל לָתֵת עָלֶיךָ אִישׁ נָכְרִי אֲשֶׁר לֹא אָחִיךָ הוּא זָלְגוּ עֵינָיו דְּמָעוֹת אָמְרוּ לוֹ אַל תִּתְיָרֵא אַגְרִיפַּס אָחִינוּ אַתָּה אָחִינוּ אַתָּה.

Mishnah 7: How does the reading of the king proceed? At the end of the last[212] day of Tabernacles, on the eighth[213], at the end of the Sabbatical year, one makes a wooden platform[214] for him and he sits on it, as it is said[215]: "At the end of seven years, at the assembly of the Sabbatical years at the festival of Tabernacles, when all of Israel appears." The organizer of the synagogue[183] takes a Torah scroll and gives it to the president of the synagogue; the president of the synagogue gives it to the Second[184]; the Second gives it to the High Priest, the High Priest gives it to the king. The king stands to receive it, he reads sitting down. King Agrippas[216] stood to receive, he read while standing, and the Sages praised him. When he reached "you cannot put over yourselves a strange man who is not your brother[217]", tears flowed from his eyes. They said to him, do not fear Agrippas, you are our brother, you are our brother[218].

212 In the Babli, Mishnah and Talmud text, "the first day".

213 In Yerushalmi texts, the eighth day; in Babli texts, the eighth year. Cf. י. נ. אפשטיין, מבוא לנוסח המשנה,² ירושלים-תל אביב תשכ"ד, ע' 537; A. Liss, ed., *The Babylonian Talmud with Variant Readings*, Sotah vol. 2, Jerusalem 1979, p. 196.

214 Greek βῆμα.

215 *Deut.* 31:10-11.

216 Agrippas I, grandson of the Idumean Herod from his Jewish wife Mariamne, so that he was eligible for every office even according to the most restrictive standards (Mishnah *Qiddušin* 4:7). It seems that the party who objected to an Idumean king (when he was inoffensive as Agrippas was) did base their opposition on Mishnah *Qiddušin* 3:12 which states that in any lawful marriage that is not sinful, the child follows his father's status. Therefore, the child of a convert would be a convert, even if his mother is from Jewish stock. This is the opinion opposed by the authoritative R. Yose in *Qiddušin* 4:7.

217 *Deut.* 17:15.

218 Cf. *Sifry Deut.* 157.

(fol. 22a) **הלכה ז**: לֹא כֵן תַּנֵּי רִבִּי חִיָּיה. לֹא הָיְתָה יְשִׁיבָה בָּעֲזָרָה אֶלָּא לְמַלְכֵי בֵית דָּוִד בִּלְבַד. וְאָמַר רִבִּי אַמִּי בְשֵׁם רִבִּי שִׁמְעוֹן בֶּן לָקִישׁ. אַף לְמַלְכֵי בֵית דָּוִד לֹא הָיְתָה יְשִׁיבָה בָּעֲזָרָה. תִּיפְתָּר שֶׁסְּמַךְ לוֹ בַּכּוֹתֶל וְיָשַׁב לוֹ. וְהָא כְתִיב וַיָּבֹא הַמֶּלֶךְ דָּוִד וַיֵּשֶׁב לִפְנֵי ייי. אָמַר רִבִּי אַיְיבוֹ בַּר נַגְרִיי. יֵישֵׁב עַצְמוֹ בַּתְּפִילָה. תַּמָּן תַּנִּינָן. יָצְאַת כַּת רִאשׁוֹנָה וְיָשְׁבָה לָהּ בְּהַר הַבַּיִת. הַשְּׁנִייָה בַחֵיל. וְהַשְּׁלִישִׁית בִּמְקוֹמָהּ. רִבִּי נַחְמָן בְּשֵׁם רִבִּי מָנָא. מַה תַּנִּינָן. יָשְׁבָה לָהּ בִּמְקוֹמָהּ. עָמְדָה לָהּ בִּמְקוֹמָהּ.

Halakhah 7: Did not Rebbi Hiyya state[219]: Nobody could sit in the Temple courtyard except for kings of the Davidic dynasty, and Rebbi Immi said in the name of Rebbi Simeon ben Laqish, even the kings of the Davidic dynasty could not sit in the Temple courtyard![220] Explain it, that he was leaning on the wall in a kind of sitting. But is it not written[221]: "King David came and sat before the Eternal"? Rebbi Ayvo bar Naggari said, he concentrated on his prayer[222]. There[223], we have stated: The first group left and sat on the Temple Mount, the second in the *Ḥel*[224], and the third at its place[225]! Rebbi Naḥman in the name of Rebbi Mana: Did we state that the third *sat* at its place? It stood at its place!

219 Babli 40b,42b; *Sanhedrin* 101b, *Tamid* 27a, *Qiddušin* 23b,78b, *Yoma* 25a,69b.

220 How could a Maccabean or Herodian king sit in the Temple courtyard?

221 2S. 7:18.

222 In rabbinic Hebrew, "concentration" is יְשׁוּב הַדַּעַת "sitting of the mind".

223 Mishnah *Pesaḥim* 5:10.

224 Inside the fortification of the Temple Mount but outside the Temple precinct.

225 From the formulation of the Mishnah, it seems that the third group of people sacrificing the Passover lamb was sitting down in the Temple court while waiting for sundown.

(22a, line 38) תַּנֵּי. רִבִּי חֲנִינָה בֶּן גַּמְלִיאֵל אוֹמֵר. הַרְבֵּה חֲלָלִים נָפְלוּ בְּאוֹתוֹ הַיּוֹם שֶׁהֶחֱנִיפוּ לוֹ.

It was stated[226]: Rebbi Ḥanina ben Gamliel says, many slain fell on the day they were flattering him.

226 In the Babli, 42b, a similar disapproving statement in the name of R. Nathan.

משנה ח (fol. 21b): וְקוֹרֵא מַתְחִילַת אֶלֶּא הַדְּבָרִים עַד שְׁמַע וּשְׁמַע וְהָיָה אִם שָׁמוֹעַ עַשֵּׂר תְּעַשֵּׂר כִּי תְכַלֶּה לַעַשֵּׂר וּבְרָכוֹת וּקְלָלוֹת [וּפָרָשַׁת הַמֶּלֶךְ][227] עַד שֶׁהוּא גוֹמֵר כָּל־הַפָּרָשָׁה. בְּרָכוֹת שֶׁכֹּהֵן גָּדוֹל מְבָרֵךְ אוֹתָן הַמֶּלֶךְ מְבָרֵךְ אוֹתָן אֶלָּא שֶׁהוּא נוֹתֵן שֶׁלָּרְגָלִים תַּחַת מְחִילַת הֶעָוֹן.

Mishnah 8: And he reads from the beginning of "These are the words[228]" to *Šemaʿ*, *Šemaʿ*[229], "And it shall be if you listen,[230]" "tithing you shall tithe,[231]" "when you will have finished tithing,[232]" blessings and curses[233] [and the paragraph of the king][234], until he finishes the entire paragraph. The benedictions which the High Priest recites, the king recites, except that he substitutes "for the holidays of pilgrimage[235]" instead of "forgiving of sins".

227 Reading of the Rome ms., missing in many Mishnah mss., the Leiden ms., and *editio princeps*. In the Babli, the paragraph of the king is mentioned before "blessings and curses," but that also is irregular since someone reading from the Torah should never scroll backwards. Cf. the variant readings of the Babli (Note 213) p. 198, Notes 98,99.

228 *Deut.* 1,1.

229 *Deut.* 6:4-9.

230 *Deut.* 11:13-21.

231 *Deut.* 14:22-27.

232 *Deut.* 26:12-15.

233 *Deut.* 28.

234 *Deut.* 17:8-20.

235 The last paragraph of the middle benediction of the *Amidah* for holidays.

הלכה ח (fol. 22a): אָמַר רִבִּי אַבָּהוּ. וְלָמָּה קוֹרִין עַשֵּׂר תְּעַשֵּׂר. כִּי תְכַלֶּה לַעַשֵּׂר. עַל יְדֵי שֶׁיָּצְאוּ יִשְׂרָאֵל מִשְּׁבִיעִית לַשְּׁמִינִית. שֶׁלֹּא לְשַׁכֵּחַ אֶת הַמַּעְשְׂרוֹת. רִבִּי חַגַּיי בְּעָא קוֹמֵי רִבִּי יוֹסֵי. וְאֵינוֹ צָרִיךְ לְהַבְדִּיל. אָמַר לֵיהּ. כְּבָר הִבְדִּיל מֵרֹאשׁ הַשָּׁנָה.

Halakhah 8: Rebbi Abbahu said, why does one read ""tithing you shall tithe,[231]", "when you will have finished tithing,[232]"? Because Israel went from the Sabbatical year to the eighth, not to have them forget tithes[236]. Rebbi Ḥaggai asked before Rebbi Yose, does he not to make *havdalah*[237]? He said to him, one already said *havdalah* on New Year's Day.

235 Since no tithes may be given from Sabbatical produce.

236 The required benediction when leaving a sanctified state (such as Sabbath or holidays) to enter into profane status. If such a benediction is required after the Sabbath (cf. *Berakhot* 5:2, Note 62), it should also be required after the Sabbatical year in order to permit agricultural work.

משוח מלחמה פרק שמיני

(fol. 22a) **משנה א:** מְשׁוּחַ מִלְחָמָה בְּשָׁעָה שֶׁהוּא מְדַבֵּר אֶל הָעָם בִּלְשׁוֹן הַקּוֹדֶשׁ הָיָה מְדַבֵּר שֶׁנֶּאֱמַר וְהָיָה כְּקָרְבְכֶם אֶל הַמִּלְחָמָה וְנִגַּשׁ הַכֹּהֵן זֶה כֹּהֵן מְשׁוּחַ מִלְחָמָה. וְדִבֶּר אֶל הָעָם בִּלְשׁוֹן הַקּוֹדֶשׁ. וְאָמַר אֲלֵיהֶם שְׁמַע יִשְׂרָאֵל אַתֶּם קְרֵבִים הַיּוֹם לַמִּלְחָמָה עַל אוֹיְבֵיכֶם. עַל אוֹיְבֵיכֶם וְלֹא עַל אֲחֵיכֶם. לֹא יְהוּדָה עַל שִׁמְעוֹן וְלֹא שִׁמְעוֹן עַל בִּנְיָמָן שֶׁאִם תִּפְּלוּ בְיָדָם יְרַחֲמוּ עֲלֵיכֶם.

Mishnah 1: The priest anointed for war[1] was speaking holy language when he was addressing the people, as it is said[2]: "It shall be when you approach war, the Cohen shall come near", that is the priest anointed for war, "shall speak to the people", in the holy language, "and say to them: Hear, o Israel, you are approching today war against your enemies," against your enemies but not against your brothers, not Jehudah against Simeon and not Simeon against Benjamin, for if you would fall in their hands they would have mercy on you[3].

1 Cf. Mishnah 7:2, Note 37.
2 *Deut.* 20:2-3.
3 It is probably unintended that only tribes of the kingdom of Judea are mentioned since Mishnah 2 speaks of Judahites and Ephraimites.

(fol. 22b) **הלכה א:** מְשׁוּחַ מִלְחָמָה כול'. מְשׁוּחַ מִלְחָמָה לָמָּה. בְּגִין דִּכְתִיב וְדִבֶּר. הֲרֵי קִרְיַת שְׁמַע הֲרֵי כָתוּב בָּהּ וְדִבַּרְתָּ בָּם וְהִיא נֶאֱמֶרֶת בְּכָל־לָשׁוֹן. אֶלָּא בְגִין דִּכְתִיב בָּהּ אֲמִירָה. הֲרֵי פָרָשַׁת וִידּוּי מַעֲשֵׂר הֲרֵי כָתוּב בָּהּ אֲמִירָה וְהִיא נֶאֱמֶרֶת בְּכָל־לָשׁוֹן. אָמַר רִבִּי חַגַּיי. נֶאֱמַר כָּאן נְגִישָׁה. וְנֶאֱמַר לְהַלָּן וְנִגְּשׁוּ הַכֹּהֲנִים בְּנֵי לֵוִי. מַה נְּגִישָׁה שֶׁנֶּאֶמְרָה לְהַלָּן בִּלְשׁוֹן הַקּוֹדֶשׁ אַף כָּאן בִּלְשׁוֹן הַקּוֹדֶשׁ. עַד כְּדוֹן כְּרִבִּי עֲקִיבָה דּוּ אָמַר. לְשׁוֹנוֹת רִבּוּיִין הֵן. כְּרִבִּי

יִשְׁמָעֵאל דּוּ אָמַר. לְשׁוֹנוֹת כְּפוּלִין הֵן. אָמַר רִבִּי חִייָה בַּר אַבָּא. נֶאֱמַר כָּאן נְגִישָׁה. וְנֶאֱמַר לְהַלָּן וְנִגַּשׁ מֹשֶׁה אֶל הָעֲרָפֶל. מַה נְגִישָׁה שֶׁנֶּאֱמְרָה לְהַלָּן בִּלְשׁוֹן הַקּוֹדֶשׁ אַף כָּאן בִּלְשׁוֹן הַקּוֹדֶשׁ.

Halakhah 1: "The priest anointed for war," etc. Why[4] the priest anointed for war? Because it is written "he shall speak[5]"? But about the reading of the *Šemaʿ* it is written: "You shall speak about them," and it may be recited in any language. But because it is written there "saying[6]". But for the declaration of tithes it is written "saying[7]" and it may be recited in any language! Rebbi Ḥaggai said, it says here "to come close[5]" and it says there, "the Levitic Cohanim shall come close[8];" since "coming close" there implies [recitation in] the holy language[9], so also "coming close" here implies [recitation in] the holy language[10]. That follows Rebbi Aqiba who says, these are expressions of additions[11]. Following Rebbi Ismael who says, these are double expressions? Rebbi Ḥiyya bar Abba said, it says here "to come close" and it says there, "Moses shall come close to the mist[12]", since "coming close" there implies [recitation in] the holy language[13], so also "coming close" here implies [recitation in] the holy language.

---

4   Why must he speak in Hebrew only?

5   *Deut.* 20:2.

6   *Deut.* 20:3.

7   *Deut.* 26:13.

8   *Deut.* 21:5.

9   Mishnah 7:2.

10   This is an example of an argument outside the hermeneutic rules, used quite frequently in the Babli but very sparingly in the Yerushalmi. It is *not* an "equal cut" since there is no transfer of meaning involved; it is what is known as הֶקֵּשׁ "tying together". Both in the case of the priest chosen for war and the calf selected to atone for an unsolved murder case, it should be quite clear that the people involved cannot be heard unless they are reasonably close. In both cases, the note that they have to come near is somewhat redundant. Therefore, one

may conclude that the additional expression was used to indicate similar circumstances, which by rabbinic authority is declared to concern the language to be used.

11 This refers to the ceremony for the unsolved murder case, where R. Jehudah in 7:2 states that common use of the roots אמר, ענה implies use of the holy language. That argument is acceptable only following R. Aqiba, not following R. Ismael. For the latter, the argument of R. Haggai does not prove anything.

12 *Ex.* 20:21; the word order is incorrect in the quote.

13 Since Moses was deputized by the people to speak to God Who obviously spoke to them and him in Hebrew. This reference to the holy language is acceptable to R. Ismael.

(22b line 37) לֹא מִסְתַּבְּרָה דְלֹא וּפָקְדוּ שָׂרֵי צְבָאוֹת בְּרֹאשׁ הָעָם. וְאַחַר כָּךְ וְנִגַּשׁ הַכֹּהֵן וְדִבֶּר אֶל הָעָם. מָאן דִּי מַתְקֵן לוֹן הוּא מַשְׁמַע לוֹן. אֵין מִקְרָא אָמוּר עַל סֵדֶר. בִּסְפָר אַתְּ אָמַר. שׁוֹטֵר שׁוֹמֵעַ מִפִּי כֹהֵן פָּרָשָׁה וְאוֹמְרָהּ לָעָם[14] בְּכָל־לָשׁוֹן. אֲבָל בְּעַרְכֵי הַמִּלְחָמָה מְסַפְּקִין מַיִם וּמָזוֹן וּמְתַקְּנִין אֶת הַדְּרָכִים. רִבִּי חַגַּיי בָּעֵי. כְּמָה דְתֵימַר בִּסְפָר. שׁוֹטֵר שׁוֹמֵעַ פָּרָשָׁה מִפִּי כֹהֵן וְאוֹמְרָהּ לָעָם בְּכָל־לָשׁוֹן. וֶאֱמוֹר גַּם בְּעַרְכֵי הַמִּלְחָמָה כֵן. הָתִיב רִבִּי חִייָה בַּר אָדָא. לֹא מִסְתַּבְּרָה דְלֹא וְהָיָה כְּכַלּוֹת הַשּׁוֹטְרִים לְדַבֵּר אֶל הָעָם וְאַחַר כָּךְ וְנִגַּשׁ הַכֹּהֵן וְדִבֶּר אֶל הָעָם. אָמַר לֵיהּ. מִכֵּיוָן דְּאַתְּ אָמַר. אֵין מִקְרָא אָמוּר עַל הַסֵּדֶר. לֵית שְׁמַע מִינָהּ כְּלוּם.

Would it not be reasonable that "the commanders should take charge at the head of the people[15]" and then "the Cohen shall come close[16]"? He who directs them should inform them! The text is not in the correct order[17]. At the border, you say that the policeman hears from the Cohen the text and communicates it to the people in any language. But at the battle order (they provide water and food and repair the roads)[18]. Rebbi Haggai asked, since at the border the policeman hears from the Cohen the text and communicates it to the people in any language, should it not be the same with the battle order? Rebbi Hiyya bar Ada objected, is it reasonable that "when the policemen finished talking to the people," after that "the Cohen shall come close and speak to the people"? He said to him, since you say, the text is not in the correct order, you cannot infer anything.

14 From the Rome ms. The Leiden ms. before correction has לעכב "as a necessary condition", deleted by the corrector. The Rome text is correct as shown by the repetition in the same paragraph.

15 *Deut.* 20:9.

16 *Deut.* 20:2.

17 As the text stands, vv. 2-4 are said by the Cohen when the people are formed in battle order, but vv. 5-9 are said before the army units are formed, before the border is crossed.

18 End of Mishnah 5, speaking of the duties of the men freed from combat duty; a larger text must be missing here in both mss. to the effect that only warriors stood in battle order.

(fol. 22a) **משנה ב**: כְּמָה שֶׁנֶּאֱמַר לְהַלָּן וַיָּקוּמוּ הָאֲנָשִׁים אֲשֶׁר נִקְּבוּ בְשֵׁמוֹת וַיַּחֲזִיקוּ בַשִּׁבְיָה וְכָל־מַעֲרוּמֵיהֶם הִלְבִּישׁוּ מִן הַשָּׁלָל. עַל אוֹיְבֵיכֶם אַתֶּם הוֹלְכִים שֶׁאִם תִּפְּלוּ בְיָדָם אֵין מְרַחֲמִין עֲלֵיכֶם.

Mishnah 2: [19]As it was said further[20]: "The men who were mentioned by name got up, they took charge of the prisoners and all their naked ones they clothed from the booty." You are going against your enemies and if you should fall into their hands they would not have mercy on you.

19 Continuation of Mishnah 1. The separate count of this Mishnah is characteristic of Palestinian texts.

20 *2Chr.* 28:15.

(fol. 22b) **הלכה ב**: כְּמָה שֶׁנֶּאֱמַר לְהַלָּן כול׳. אָמַר רִבִּי יוֹחָנָן. כָּל־שֶׁאֵינוּ כְגוֹן אִילּוּ שֶׁהָיְתָה סְפִיקָה [בְּיָדָם][21] לִמְחוֹת אַל יִמְחֶה. רִבִּי אָחָא בְּשֵׁם רִבִּי יוֹנָתָן. כְּשֵׁם שֶׁמִּצְוָה לוֹמַר עַל דָּבָר שֶׁהוּא נַעֲשָׂה. כָּךְ מִצְוָה שֶׁלֹּא לוֹמַר עַל דָּבָר שֶׁאֵינוּ

נַעֲשָׂה. אָמַר רִבִּי לָעָזָר. כְּשֵׁם שֶׁאָסוּר לְטַהֵר אֶת הַטָּמֵא כָּךְ אָסוּר לְטַמֵּא אֶת הַטָּהוֹר. רִבִּי בָּא בַּר יַעֲקֹב בְּשֵׁם רִבִּי יוֹחָנָן. אִם בָּאת הֲלָכָה תַּחַת יָדֶיךָ וְאֵין אַתְּ יוֹדֵעַ אִם לִשְׂרוֹף אִם לִתְלוֹת. לְעוֹלָם הֱוֵי רָץ אַחַר הַשְּׂרֵיפָה יוֹתֵר מִן הַתְּלִייָה. שֶׁאֵין לָךְ חָבִיב בַּתּוֹרָה מִפָּרִים הַנִּשְׂרָפִין וּשְׂעִירִים הַנִּשְׂרָפִין וְהֵן בִּשְׂרֵיפָה. רִבִּי יוֹסֵי בָּעֵי. לְמֵידִין דָּבָר שֶׁאֵין מִצְוָתוֹ לְכָאן מִדָּבָר שֶׁמִּצְוָתוֹ לְכָאן.

Halakhah 2: "As it was said further," etc. Rebbi Johanan said, anybody who is not in the position of those [men]²² who had the power to object, should not object. ²³Rebbi Aha in the name of Rebbi Jonathan: Just as it is a commandment to speak on things that will be done, so it is a commandment not to talk about things that would not be done²⁴. Rebbi Eleazar said, just as it is forbidden to declare the impure pure, so it is forbidden to declare the pure impure. Rebbi Abba bar Jacob in the name of Rebbi Johanan: If a practical case comes before you and you do not know whether to burn or to suspend²⁵, always prefer burning to suspension since nothing is more beloved in the Torah than burned oxen and burned rams²⁶, and they are burned. Rebbi Yose asked: Does one infer something which is not commanded from something which is commanded²⁷?

21 From the Rome ms. The insertion is necessary since "to have power" always is expressed by ספק ביד.

22 The "heads of Ephraim", "princes and community" who forbade to the Ephraimite army to treat the Judahite prisoners as prisoners of war, *2Chr.* 28:12,14.

23 The same text *Terumot* 5:9, Notes 113-115; *Hagigah* 1:8 (76d, line 50).

24 In the Babli, this is formulated as: "Let them be in error, do not turn them into intentional sinners" (*Beṣah* 30a, *Baba batra* 60b). A formulation similar to the one given here in *Yebamot* 65b in the name of R. Eleazar.

25 Heave that is impure by biblical standards has to be burned, if impure by rabbinical standards it only has to be kept until it rots and is no longer food and therefore pure by all

standards. As a practical matter, it would be preferable to burn heave rabbinically impure in the second degree so that it should not cause third degree disability by inadvertent touching.

26 Animals whose blood was used for a purification rite inside the Temple building (*Lev.* 4:12,21; 8:17; 16:27).

27 R. Johanan's argument does not prove anything for rabbinic decisions.

(fol. 22a) **משנה ג**: אַל יֵרַךְ לְבַבְכֶם אַל תִּירְאוּ וְאַל תַּחְפְּזוּ וְאַל תַּעַרְצוּ מִפְּנֵיהֶם. אַל יֵרַךְ לְבַבְכֶם מִפְּנֵי צָהֲלַת סוּסִים וְצִיחֻצוּחַ חֲרָבוֹת. אַל תִּירְאוּ מִפְּנֵי הֲנָפַת הַתְּרִיסִין וְשִׁפְעַת הַקַּלְגַּסִּים. אַל תַּחְפְּזוּ מִקּוֹל קְרָנוֹת אַל תַּעַרְצוּ מִפְּנֵי קוֹל צְוָחוֹת. כִּי יי אֱלֹהֵיכֶם הַהֹלֵךְ עִמָּכֶם לְהִלָּחֵם לָכֶם עִם אוֹיְבֵיכֶם לְהוֹשִׁיעַ אֶתְכֶם. הֵן בָּאִין בְּנִצְחַת בָּשָׂר וְדָם וְאַתֶּם בָּאִין בְּנִצְחוֹנוּ שֶׁל הַמָּקוֹם. פְּלִשְׁתִּים בָּאוּ בְּנִצְחוֹנוּ שֶׁל גָּלְיַת מֶה הָיָה בְּסוֹפוֹ. לַסּוֹף נָפַל בַּחֶרֶב וְהֵם נָפְלוּ עִמּוֹ. אֲבָל אַתֶּם אֵין אַתֶּם כֵּן אֶלָּא כִּי יי אֱלֹהֵיכֶם הַהֹלֵךְ עִמָּכֶם לְהִלָּחֵם לָכֶם וגו' זֶה מַחֲנֵה הָאָרוֹן.

Mishnah 3: "Your heart should not soften, do not fear, nor become impulsive, do not become impressed before them.[28]" Your heart should not soften because of the neighing of horses or the gleam of swords. Do not fear, because of the shaking of shields[29] and the stomping of military boots[30]. Do not become impulsive because of the sound of horns, nor be impressed because of the sound of cries. "For the Eternal, your God, is He Who goes with you to make war on your enemies to save you." They come with victories of flesh and blood, but you come with the victory of the Omnipresent. The Philistines came with the victory of Goliath; how did he end? In the end, he fell by the sword and they fell with him. But you, you are not so but "for the Eternal, your God, is He Who goes with you to make war on your enemies to save you," that is the camp of the Ark.

28 *Deut.* 20:3. This is the speech of the priest appointed for the war.
29 Greek θυρεός, ὁ; "oblong shield"; shutter, stone put against a door", from where modern Hebrew "shutter".
30 Latin *caliga, -ae*, f., "military boot; military service."

(fol. 22b) **הלכה ג:** אַל יֵרַךְ לְבַבְכֶם כול'. כְּתִיב מְנוּגַהּ נֶגְדּוֹ עָבָיו עָבְרוּ. כְּנֶגֶד טוּמְיוֹת שֶׁלָּהֶן. עָבְרוּ. כְּנֶגֶד הַכִּיתִּים שֶׁלָּהֶן. בָּרָד. כְּנֶגֶד בַּלִּיצְטִירָא שֶׁלָּהֶן. וְגַחֲלֵי כְּנֶגֶד טַרְמְנְטוֹ שֶׁלָּהֶן. אֵשׁ כְּנֶגֶד הַנַּפְטְ שֶׁלָּהֶן. וַיַּרְעֵם מִשָּׁמַיִם. כְּנֶגֶד הַלַּפִּידִים שֶׁלָּהֶן. וְעֶלְיוֹן יִתֵּן קוֹלוֹ. כְּנֶגֶד קוֹל הַקְּרָנוֹת שֶׁלָּהֶן. וַיִּשְׁלַח חִצָּיו. כְּנֶגֶד הַחִיצִים שֶׁלָּהֶן. וַיְפִיצֵם. מְלַמֵּד שֶׁהָיוּ מְפַזְּרִין אוֹתָן. אָמַר רִבִּי בָּא בַּר כַּהֲנָא. מְלַמֵּד שֶׁהָיוּ עֲשׂוּיִין תֵּיבוֹת וְהָיוּ הַחִיצִים מְפַזְּרִין אוֹתָן וְהַבְּרָקִים מַכְנִיסִין אוֹתָן. בְּרָקִים. כְּנֶגֶד הַחֲרָבוֹת שֶׁלָּהֶן. וַיְהוּמֵּם. הָמָם וְעִירְבְּבָם וְהִפִּיל סִיגְנָם שֶׁלָּהֶן. רִבִּי אוֹמֵר. אֵין לָשׁוֹן הַזֶּה וַיְהוּמֵּם אֶלָּא לָשׁוֹן מַגֵּיפָה. כְּמָה דְּאַתְּ אֲמַר וְהָמָם מְהוּמָה גְדוֹלָה עַד הִשָּׁמְדָם.

Halakhah 3: "Your heart should not soften," etc. It is written[31]: "From the radiation that surrounds Him, His clouds," against their cavalry squads[32], "passed," against their cohorts. "Hailstorm," against their missile throwers[33]. "And embers," against their throwing machines[34]. "Of fire," against their naphta. "He thundered from Heaven[35]," against their torches[36]. "The Most High made His voice heard," against the sound of their horns. "He sent His arrows," against their arrows. "And dispersed them,", this teaches that they were dispersing them. Rebbi Abba bar Cahana said, this teaches that they were in rectangular formations, that the arrows dispersed them but the lightnings were bringing them together. "Lightnings," against their swords. "And confused them," He confused them, made them disoriented, and felled their standard[37]. Rebbi said,[38] the expression "and confounded them" means only pestilence, as it is written[39]: "He will confuse them in a great confusion until He destroyed them."

31 *Ps.* 18:13-15.

32 Latin *turma* "squadron". In similar stories in *Yalqut Šim'oni* 230, 232: טורמיות.

33 Latin *ballista, ballistra* "military machine, stone-throwing machine". In a Genizah fragment, the word is spelled בליצרה

34 Latin *tormentum*, "missile throwing machine".

35 In the verse, "He thundered *in* Heaven".

36 In a Genizah fragment, כנגד

סלפידס שלהן. One might read סַלְפִּידָס for Greek σάλπιγξ "heavenly trumpet, thunder". This fits much better to "thunder" than the "torches" of both mss.

37 Latin *signum*, "standard". In a similar version, *Tanḥuma Bešallaḥ* 23, "He felled their standard and so made them disoriented." In a Genizah fragment, the word is vocalized הַסִיגְנַס.

38 In a Genizah fragment: דָּבָר אַחֵר "another explanation".

39 *Deut.* 7:23.

(22b line 65) לְהוֹשִׁיעַ אֶתְכֶם. זֶה מַחֲנֵה הָאָרוֹן. וְיֵשׁ אוֹמְרִים זֶה הַשֵּׁם שֶׁהָיָה נָתוּן בָּאָרוֹן. דְּתַנֵּי. רִבִּי יוּדָה בֶּן לָקִישׁ אוֹמֵר. שְׁנֵי אֲרוֹנוֹת הָיוּ מְהַלְּכִין עִם יִשְׂרָאֵל בַּמִּדְבָּר. אֶחָד שֶׁהָיְתָה הַתּוֹרָה נְתוּנָה בּוֹ וְאֶחָד שֶׁהָיוּ שִׁבְרֵי הַלּוּחוֹת מוּנָחִין בְּתוֹכוֹ. זֶה שֶׁהָיְתָה הַתּוֹרָה נְתוּנָה בְּתוֹכוֹ הָיָה נָתוּן בְּאֹהֶל מוֹעֵד. הָדָא הִיא דִכְתִיב וַאֲרוֹן בְּרִית יי וּמֹשֶׁה לֹא מָשׁוּ מִקֶּרֶב הַמַּחֲנֶה. וְזֶה שֶׁהָיוּ שִׁבְרֵי הַלּוּחוֹת נְתוּנִין בְּתוֹכוֹ הָיָה נִכְנָס וְיוֹצֵא עִמָּהֶן.[40] וְרַבָּנָן אֲמְרִי. אֶחָד הָיָה. וּפַעַם אַחַת יָצָא וּבִימֵי עֵלִי נִשְׁבָּה. קִרְיָיא מְסַיֵּיעַ לְהֶן לְרַבָּנִין. אוֹי לָנוּ מִי יַצִּילֵנוּ מִיַּד הָאֱלֹהִים [הָאַדִּירִים] הָאֵלֶּה. מִילָא דְּלָא חָמוֹן מִן יוֹמֵיהוֹן. קִרְיָיא מְסַיֵּיעַ לְרִבִּי יוּדָה בֶּן לָקִישׁ. וַיֹּאמֶר שָׁאוּל לַאֲחִיָּה הַגִּישָׁה אֲרוֹן הָאֱלֹהִים. וַהֲלֹא אָרוֹן בְּקִרְיַת יְעָרִים הָיָה. מַאי עָבְדִין לֵיהּ רַבָּנִין. הַגִּישָׁה אֵלַי הָאֵפוֹד. וּקְרָא מְסַיֵּיעַ לְרִבִּי יוּדָה בֶּן לָקִישׁ. הָאָרוֹן וְיִשְׂרָאֵל וִיהוּדָה יוֹשְׁבִים בַּסֻּכּוֹת. וַהֲלֹא אָרוֹן בְּצִיּוֹן הָיָה. מֶה עָבְדִין לֵיהּ רַבָּנִין. סְכָךְ שֶׁהָיָה בְּקִירוּיֵי.[41] שֶׁעֲדַיִין לֹא נִבְנָה בֵית הַבְּחִירָה.

"'To save you', that is the camp of the Ark." But some say, that is the Name which was given in the Ark[42], as it was stated[43,44]: "Rebbi Jehudah ben Laqish says, two arks were travelling with Israel in the desert; one in which the Torah was deposited and one in which the broken pieces of the tablets were deposited[45]. The one in which the Torah was deposited was put into the Tent of Meeting; that is what is written[46]: "Moses and the Ark of the Eternal's covenant did not move from the camp." The one in which the broken pieces of the tablets were deposited was going out and coming in with them. But the Rabbis say, it was only one[47], and once it went out in the days of Eli and was taken prisoner. A verse supports the Rabbis: [48]"Woe to us, who will save us from this mighty god?" A word [which shows that] they never had seen it before. A verse supports Rebbi Jehudah ben Laqish. "Saul said to Aḥiya: present God's Ark[49]". But was the Ark not at Qiryat Ye'arim[50]? What do the rabbis with it? 'Present to me the High Priest's diadem.' Another verse supports Rebbi Jehudah ben Laqish: "The Ark, Israel, and Jehudah, dwell in huts.[51]". Was the Ark not in Zion? What do the rabbis with it? The straw roof cover[52] that was in the walls[41], since the Temple was not yet built.

40   The Genizah text adds: וּפְעָמִים הָיָה מַתְרֵי עִימָהֶם "and sometimes it was encamped with them."

41   In the Genizah fragment: כַּקִירוּי "acted as roof". This is the better reading.

42   Similarly, the Babli (Soṭah 42b/43a, Baba batra 14b) notes that "The Name and all its replacements are deposited in the Ark" (in one of Rashi's versions, "standing in the Ark"). In the Tosephta (7:17): "For the Eternal, your God, is He Who goes with you," that is the Name deposited in the Ark". Midrash Num. rabba 4(20) refers to 1Chr. 13:6 which calls the ark Name: "God's ark, the Eternal, Who resides above the Cherubim, which is called Name."

43   From here to the end of the Halakhah the text is in Šeqalim 7:1, (49c, line 26 ff.)

44	Tosephta 7:18; Baraita Melekhet Hamishkan 6.	49	1Sam. 14:18.
		50	1Sam. 7:1-2.
45	The ark mentioned in Deut. 10:1.	51	2Sam. 11:11.
46	Num. 14:44; the exact description of the ark implies that another ark went out with the people.	52	The legal definition of a "hut" to be used on Tabernacles is any dwelling place whose roof is made from vegetable matter immune to impurity, called סְכָךְ. The construction of the walls is immaterial.
47	Babli Berakhot 8b, Baba batra 14b, Menaḥot 99a.		
48	1Sam. 4:8.		

(22c line 8) מִשֶּׁנִּגְנַז הָאָרוֹן נִגְנַז עִמּוֹ צִנְצֶנֶת הַמָּן וְצְלוֹחִית שֶׁמֶן הַמִּשְׁחָה וּמַקְלוֹ שֶׁלְאַהֲרֹן וּפְרָחָיו וּשְׁקֵידָיו וְאַרְגַּז שֶׁהֵשִׁיבוּ פְלִשְׁתִּים אָשָׁם לֵאלֹהֵי יִשְׂרָאֵל. וּמִי גְנָזוֹ. יוֹשִׁיָּהוּ. וְכֵיוָן שֶׁרָאָה⁵³ שֶׁכָּתוּב יוֹלֵךְ יְיָ אוֹתְךָ וְאֶת מַלְכְּךָ [אֲשֶׁר תָּקִים עָלֶיךָ אֶל גּוֹי אֲשֶׁר לֹא יָדַעְתָּ אַתָּה וַאֲבוֹתֶיךָ עָמַד וּגְנָזוֹ.]⁵⁴ הָדָא הִיא דִכְתִיב וַיֹּאמֶר לַלְוִיִּם הַמְבִינִים לְכָל־יִשְׂרָאֵל הַקְּדוֹשִׁים לַיְיָ תְּנוּ אֶת אֲרוֹן הַקֹּדֶשׁ בַּבַּיִת אֲשֶׁר בָּנָה שְׁלֹמֹה בֶן דָּוִד מֶלֶךְ יִשְׂרָאֵל אֵין לָכֶם מַשָּׂא בַּכָּתֵף. אָמַר⁵⁵ אִם גוֹלָה הוּא עִמָּכֶם לְבָבֶל [עוֹד]⁵⁶ אֵין אַתֶּם מַחֲזִירִין אוֹתוֹ לִמְקוֹמוֹ. אֶלָּא עַתָּה עִבְדוּ אֶת יְיָ אֱלֹהֵיכֶם וְאֶת עַמּוֹ יִשְׂרָאֵל.

⁵⁷When the ark was hidden, there were hidden with it the flask of Manna⁵⁸, the bottle of anointing oil⁵⁹, Aaron's staff with its flowers and almonds⁶⁰, and the chest which the Philistines returned as a reparation sacrifice for Israel's God⁶¹. Who hid it? Josiah! When he saw that it was written⁶²: "The Eternal will lead you and your king whom you will have put above you, to a people whom neither you nor your fathers had known," he started and hid it. That is what is written⁶³: "He said to the Levites, who instruct all of Israel, the ones holy to the Eternal, put the Ark into the House that Salomon, son of David, king of Israel, built; you do not have to carry it on your shoulder." He said, if it is exiled with you to Babylonia, you will never return it to its place. But "⁶³now, serve the Eternal, your God, and his people Israel."

53 In *editio princeps* and the Genizah fragment, not in the Leiden ms.	*Soṭah* 13:1; *Seder 'Olam* 24; *Abot dR. Nathan A* 31. In the Babli and the sources depending on it, some Tannaïm hold that the Ark was brought to Babylon.
54 From the Genizah fragment, not in the Leiden ms. or *editio princeps*.	
55 In the Genizah fragment: אָמַר לָהֶן "he said to them" (to the Levites)	58 *Ex.* 16:33-34.
	59 *Ex.* 30:22-33.
56 From the Genizah fragment, not in the Leiden ms. or *editio princeps*. The word seems to be required by the context.	60 *Num.* 17:25.
	61 *1Sam.* 6.
	62 *Deut.* 28:36.
57 Babli *Yoma* 52b, *Horaiot* 12a, *Keritut* 5b; Tosephta *Kippurim* 2:15,	63 *2Chr.* 35:3. The Levites had not carried the Ark since the time of Samuel.

(22c line 14) **פיטום** שֶׁמֶן הַמִּשְׁחָה. וְאַתָּה קַח לְךָ בְּשָׂמִים רֹאשׁ מָר דְּרוֹר חֲמֵשׁ מֵאוֹת וגו'. וְקִדָּה חֲמֵשׁ מֵאוֹת בְּשֶׁקֶל הַקּוֹדֶשׁ. שֶׁהֵן אֶלֶף וַחֲמֵשׁ מֵאוֹת מָנִים. וְשֶׁמֶן זַיִת הִין. שֶׁהֵן שְׁנֵים עָשָׂר לוֹג. שֶׁבּוֹ הָיָה שׁוֹלֵק אֶת הָעִיקָּרִין. דִּבְרֵי רַבִּי מֵאִיר. רַבִּי יְהוּדָה אוֹמֵר. שׁוֹלְקִין הָיוּ בַּמַּיִם וְנוֹתֵן שֶׁמֶן עַל גַּבֵּיהֶן. וְכֵיוָן שֶׁהָיָה קוֹלֵט אֶת הָרֵיחַ הָיָה מַעֲבִירוֹ כְּדֶרֶךְ שֶׁהַפַּטָּמִין עוֹשִׂין. הָדָא הוּא דִכְתִיב וְעָשִׂיתָ אוֹתוֹ שֶׁמֶן מִשְׁחַת קֹדֶשׁ יִהְיֶה זֶה לִי לְדֹרֹתֵיכֶם. תַּנֵּי. רַבִּי יְהוּדָה בֵּירְבִּי אִילָעִי אוֹמֵר. שֶׁמֶן מִשְׁחָה שֶׁעָשָׂה מֹשֶׁה בַּמִּדְבָּר מַעֲשֵׂה נִסִּים נַעֲשָׂה בּוֹ מִתְּחִילָּה וְעַד סוֹף. שֶׁמִּתְּחִילָּה לֹא הָיָה בּוֹ אֶלָּא שְׁנֵים עָשָׂר לוֹג. שֶׁנֶּאֱמַר וְשֶׁמֶן זַיִת הִין. אִם לָסוּךְ בּוֹ אֶת הָעֵצִים לֹא הָיָה מַסְפִּיק. עַל אַחַת כַּמָּה וְכַמָּה שֶׁהָאוֹר בּוֹלֵעַ וְהָעֵצִים בּוֹלְעִין וְהַיּוֹרָה בּוֹלַעַת. וּמִמֶּנּוּ נִמְשְׁחוּ הַמִּשְׁכָּן וְכָל־כֵּילָיו. הַשּׁוּלְחָן וְכָל־כֵּילָיו. הַמְּנוֹרָה וְכָל־כֵּלֶיהָ. מִמֶּנּוּ נִמְשַׁח אַהֲרֹן וּבָנָיו כָּל־שִׁבְעַת יְמֵי הַמִּלּוּאִים. מִמֶּנּוּ נִמְשְׁחוּ כֹּהֲנִים גְּדוֹלִים וּמְלָכִים. מֶלֶךְ בַּתְּחִילָּה טָעוּן מְשִׁיחָה. מֶלֶךְ בֶּן מֶלֶךְ אֵינוֹ טָעוּן מְשִׁיחָה. שֶׁנֶּאֱמַר קוּם מְשָׁחֵהוּ כִּי זֶה הוּא. זֶה טָעוּן מְשִׁיחָה. אֵין בְּנוֹ טָעוּן מְשִׁיחָה. אֲבָל כֹּהֵן גָּדוֹל בֶּן כֹּהֵן גָּדוֹל אֲפִילוּ עַד עֲשָׂרָה דוֹרוֹת טְעוּנִין מְשִׁיחָה. וְכוּלּוֹ קַיָּים לֶעָתִיד לָבוֹא. שֶׁנֶּאֱמַר שֶׁמֶן מִשְׁחַת קֹדֶשׁ יִהְיֶה זֶה לִי לְדֹרֹתֵיכֶם.

[64]The preparation of the anointing oil. "Take for yourself select spices: Flowing myrrh 500, etc., and casia 500 in Temple sheqel, altogether 1500 parts[65]. "And olive oil one *hin*," that is twelve *log*[66], in which the roots were cooked, the words of Rebbi Meïr. Rebbi Jehudah says, they cooked in water, then poured the oil on them, and when it had absorbed the fragrance one removed it, just as the perfumers do. That is what is written: "Make it into holy anointing oil.[67]" "That will be for Me for your generations.[68]" It was stated, [69]Rebbi Jehudah bar Ilaï says: The anointing oil made by Moses in the desert was from the start to the end a work of wonders, since there were only twelve *log* to start with, as it was said, "and olive oil one *hin*[70]". It would not have been enough to rub the wooden planks with it; so much more since the fire swallows, wood absorbs, and the kettle absorbs! From it the Tabernacles and all its vessels were anointed, the table and its vessels, the candelabra and all its vessels. From it Aaron and his sons were anointed all of the seven days of induction, from it all high priests and kings were anointed. A king who is first needs anointing, a king who is a king's son does not need anointing, for it is said[71]: "Do anoint him, for this one is it," this one needs anointing but his son does not need anointing. But a High Priest who is the son of a High Priest needs anointing, even for ten generations[72]. Nevertheless, it is all there for the future, as it was said, "a holy anointing oil will this[73] be for Me, for all your generations.[68]"

64 Babli *Keritut* 5a.
65 *Ex.* 30:23-24. The amounts given there are myrrh 500, cinnamon half the weight, 250, spice sticks 250, casia 500 in the holy šeqel weight, together 1500 (šeqel). The Babli notes that the verse could be translated: "myrrh 500, the half of the cinnamon weight 250, spice sticks 250; casia 500 in the holy šeqel weight," for a total of either 2000 or 1750. The *baraita* shows that the traditional inter-

pretation is as given first. A similar argument must be understood in the Yerushalmi.

It is impossible to translate מנה as "mina" since the holy šeqel by archeological evidence was between 13.77 and 14.28 g (Y. Meshorer, *Ancient Means of Exchange, Weights and Coins*, Haifa 1998), practically equal to the official weight of a tetradrachma. In the tradition of the Babli, the holy šeqel was twice the weight of the common šeqel; in Babylonian weight this would make it about 18 g. (In any case, spices in the weight of at least 21 kg are a large quantity for only 6.4 liters of oil.) But a mina is defined in the Talmudim as 100 tetradrachmas. This is out of line with the small amount of oil used. It may be that the word "mina", which is missing in the parallel Babli text, is an intrusion from the *baraita* on the preparation of the holy incense of which 365 portions were prepared for an entire year at once and where all weights, missing in the biblical text, are indicated in minas [*Yoma* 4:5 (41d line 27), Babli *Keritut* 6a].

66   The *log* is the Roman *sextarius*, cf. *Berakhot* 3:4, Note 164. 12 *log* are three quarters of a *modius* or about 6.4 liter.

67   *Ex.* 30:25.

68   *Ex.* 30:31.

69   Babli *Keritut* 5a/b.

70   *Ex.* 30:24.

71   *1Sam.* 16:12.

72   *Lev.* 6:13, 21:10. The same statement in Babli *Keritut* 5a, *Horaiot* 11b.

73   In the Babli, an amoraic gloss in this *baraita* of R. Jehudah notes that the numerical value of זה "this" is 12, implying that all 12 *log* remain for the Lord.

(22c line 31) אֵין מוֹשְׁחִין אֶת הַמְּלָכִים אֶלָּא עַל גַּבֵּי הַמַּעְיָין. שֶׁנֶּאֱמַר וְהִרְכַּבְתֶּם אֶת שְׁלֹמֹה בְנִי עַל הַפִּרְדָּה אֲשֶׁר לִי וְהוֹרַדְתֶּם אוֹתוֹ אֶל גִּיחוֹן וּמָשַׁח אוֹתוֹ שָׁם צָדוֹק הַכֹּהֵן וְנָתָן הַנָּבִיא וגו'. אֵין מוֹשְׁחִין מְלָכִים אֶלָּא מִפְּנֵי הַמַּחֲלוֹקֶת. מִפְּנֵי מַה נִּמְשַׁח שְׁלֹמֹה. מִפְּנֵי מַחֲלוֹקְתוֹ שֶׁלַּאֲדוֹנִיָּהוּ. יוֹאָשׁ. מִפְּנֵי עֲתַלְיָה. יֵהוּא מִפְּנֵי יוֹרָם.[74] לֹא כֵן כָּתוּב קוּם מְשָׁחֵהוּ כִּי זֶה הוּא. זֶה טָעוּן מְשִׁיחָה וְאֵין מַלְכֵי יִשְׂרָאֵל טְעוּנִין מְשִׁיחָה. [אֶלָּא][75] יְהוֹאָחָז מִפְּנֵי יְהוֹיָקִים אָחִיו שֶׁהָיָה גָדוֹל מִמֶּנּוּ שְׁתֵּי שָׁנִים. וְלֹא יֹאשִׁיָּהוּ גְנָזוֹ. הָדָא אָמְרָה. בַּאֲפַרְסְמוֹן מָשְׁחוּ. אֵין מוֹשְׁחִין אֶת הַמְּלָכִים אֶלָּא מִן הַקֶּרֶן. שָׁאוּל וְיֵהוּא נִמְשְׁחוּ מִן הַפַּךְ. שֶׁהָיְתָה

מַלְכוּתָן מַלְכוּת עוֹבֶרֶת. דָּוִד וּשְׁלֹמֹה נִמְשְׁחוּ מִן הַקֶּרֶן. שֶׁהָיְתָה מַלְכוּתָם מַלְכוּת קַיֶּימֶת. אֵין מוֹשְׁכִין מְלָכִים כֹּהֲנִים. אָמַר רִבִּי יוּדָן עַנְתּוֹדְרוּיָה.[76] עַל שֵׁם לֹא יָסוּר שֵׁבֶט מִיהוּדָה. אָמַר רִבִּי חִייָה בַּר אָדָא. עַל שֵׁם לְמַעַן יַאֲרִיךְ יָמִים עַל מַמְלַכְתּוֹ הוּא וּבָנָיו בְּקֶרֶב יִשְׂרָאֵל. מַה כְּתִיב בַּתְרֵיהּ. לֹא יִהְיֶה לַכֹּהֲנִים הַלְוִיִּם.

[77]One anoints kings only at a spring, as it was said[78]: "Let Solomon, my son, ride on my mule and take him down to the Giḥon; there Ṣadoq the priest and Nathan the prophet shall anoint him, etc." One anoints kings only because of disputes. Why was Solomon anointed? Because of the dispute of Adoniahu; Joash because of Athaliah, Jehu because of Joram. Is it not written[71]: "Do anoint him, for this one is it," this one needs anointing, but the kings of Israel do not need anointing[79]! But Joaḥaz because of his brother Joakim who was two years his elder[80]. But did not Josiahu hide it[81]? That means, they anointed with balsamum. One anoints kings only from a horn. Saul and Jehu were anointed from a can because their kingdom was temporary; David and Solomon were anointed from a horn because their kingdom was permanent[82]. One does not anoint priests as kings[83]. Rebbi Yudan Antordiyya said, because of "the scepter shall not be removed from Jehudah[84]". Rebbi Ḥiyya bar Ada said, because "he shall have many days of his kingdom, he and his sons in the midst of Israel[85]." What is written after that? "The levitic Cohanim should not.[86]"

74   Reading of the Geniza ms. Leiden and *editio princeps*: יורם מפני יהוא "Joram because of Jehu." Cf. Babli *Horaiot* 11b.

75   Insert from the Genizah ms., missing in Leiden ms. and *editio princeps* here but found in the parallel in *Šeqalim*.

76   Reading of the Geniza ms. Leiden and *editio princeps* here and in *Šeqalim*: ענתונדריה.

77   A parallel to the entire paragraph is in the Babli, *Keritut* 5b.

78   *1K*. 1:33-34.

79   There is no indication that Yehu was anointed with the oil deposited in Jerusalem.

80   In *2K*. 23:31,36 and *2Chr*. 36:2,5

it is noted that Joaḥaz was 23 years old in the same year in which Joakim was 25. Cf. *Seder 'Olam*, Chapter 24 (in the author's edition, pp. 213-215); Babli *Arakhin* 12a.

81   As indicated in the previous paragraph. Then Josiah's son could not have been anointed with the oil made by Moses. The explanation given here is in the Babli, *Horaiot* 11b, in the name of the later Amora Rav Papa.

82   Quoted in Babli, *Megillah* 14a, *Keritut* 6a.

83   The Maccabean kings were anointed as High Priests, not as kings.

84   Gen. 49:10.

85   *Deut.* 7:20, last verse in the chapter.

86   *Deut.* 8:1.

(22c line 45) אָמַר רִבִּי יוֹחָנָן. הוּא יוֹחָנָן הוּא יְהוֹאָחָז. וְהָא כְתִיב הַבְּכוֹר יוֹחָנָן. בְּכוֹר לַמַּלְכוּת. אָמַר רִבִּי יוֹחָנָן. הוּא שַׁלּוּם הוּא צִדְקִיָּהוּ. וְהָכְתִיב הַשְּׁלִישִׁי צִדְקִיָּהוּ וְהָרְבִיעִי שַׁלּוּם. שְׁלִישִׁי לְתוֹלָדוֹת וּרְבִיעִי לַמַּלְכוּת. צִדְקִיָּהוּ שֶׁצִּידֵק עָלָיו אֶת הַדִּין. שָׁלוֹם שֶׁבְּיָמָיו שָׁלְמָה מַלְכוּת בֵּית דָּוִד. לֹא שָׁלוֹם הֲוָה שְׁמֵיהּ וְלֹא צִדְקִיָּהוּ הֲוָה שְׁמֵהּ אֶלָּא מַתַּנְיָה. הָדָא הִיא דִכְתִיב וַיַּמְלֵךְ מֶלֶךְ בָּבֶל אֶת מַתַּנְיָה דֹדוֹ תַּחְתָּיו וַיַּסֵּב אֶת שְׁמוֹ צִדְקִיָּהוּ.

[87]Rebbi Joḥanan said, Joḥanan is Joaḥaz. But is it not written[88]: "The first born Joḥanan"? The first in kingdom. Rebbi Joḥanan said, Shallum is Sedekia. But is not written[88]: "The third Sedekiah, the fourth Shallum"? The third to be born, the fourth in kingdom[89]. "Sedekiah" because he accepted the judgment on himself[90]. "Shallum" because in his days the dynasty of David was completed[91]. His name was neither Shallum nor Sedekiah but Mattaniah. That is what is written[92]: "The king of Babylon made his uncle Mattaniah king in his stead and changed the latter's name to Sedekiah."

87   The entire paragraph is paralleled in *Horaiot* (3:3; 47c, line 35 ff.), Babli *Horaiot* 11b, *Keritut* 5b.

88   *1Chr.* 3:15. Joaḥaz does not appear in the list.

89   Since Sedekiah was 21 when he became king, 11 or 12 years after his brother Joakim, he was 15 years

90 From the root צדק "equity, justice".	91 From the root שלם "complete; perfect; paid-up".
	92 *1K* 24:17.

(22c line 51) אָמַר רִבִּי יוֹחָנָן. בְּאַמָּה שֶׁלְּשִׁשָּׁה טְפָחִים הָיָה הָאָרוֹן עָשׂוּי. מָאן תַּנָּא. אַמָּה שֶׁלְּשִׁשָּׁה טְפָחִים. רִבִּי מֵאִיר הִיא. דִּתְנָן⁹³ רִבִּי מֵאִיר אוֹמֵר. כָּל־הָאַמּוֹת הָיוּ בְּבֵינוֹנִיּוֹת. עַל דַּעְתֵּיהּ דְּרִבִּי מֵאִיר דְּאָמַר. בְּאַמָּה שֶׁלְּשִׁשָּׁה טְפָחִים הָיָה הָאָרוֹן עָשׂוּי. אָרְכּוֹ שֶׁלָּאָרוֹן חֲמִשָּׁה עָשָׂר. דִּכְתִיב אַמָּתַיִם וָחֵצִי אָרְכּוֹ. אַמָּה אֶשְׁתָּה וְאַמָּה אֶשְׁתָּה וּפַלְגּוּת אַמְתָא תְלָתָא. וְאַרְבָּעָה לוּחוֹת הָיוּ בוֹ. שְׁנַיִם שְׁבוּרִים וּשְׁנַיִם שְׁלֵמִים. דִּכְתִיב אֲשֶׁר שִׁבַּרְתָּ וְשַׂמְתָּם בָּאָרוֹן. וְהַלּוּחוֹת הָיוּ כָּל־אֶחָד וְאֶחָד אָרְכָּן שִׁשָּׁה טְפָחִים וְרָחְבָּן שְׁלֹשָׁה. תֵּן רָחְבָּן⁹⁴ שֶׁלַּלּוּחוֹת לְאָרְכּוֹ שֶׁלָּאָרוֹן נִשְׁתַּיְּירוּ שָׁם שְׁלֹשָׁה טְפָחִים. תְּנָם לָאִיסְטְוָה⁹⁵. וְרָחְבּוֹ שֶׁלָּאָרוֹן תִּשְׁעָה טְפָחִים דִּכְתִיב אַמָּה וָחֵצִי רָחְבּוֹ. אַמָּה אֶישְׁתָּה וּפַלְגּוּת אַמְתָא תְלָתָא. וְאַרְבָּעָה לוּחוֹת הָיוּ בוֹ. שְׁנַיִם שְׁבוּרִים וּשְׁנַיִם שְׁלֵמִין. דִּכְתִיב אֲשֶׁר שִׁבַּרְתָּ וְשַׂמְתָּם בָּאָרוֹן. וְהַלּוּחוֹת הָיוּ כָּל־אֶחָד וְאֶחָד אָרְכָּן שִׁשָּׁה טְפָחִים⁹⁶. וְתֵן רָחְבָּן שֶׁלַּלּוּחוֹת לְאָרְכּוֹ שֶׁלָּאָרוֹן.⁹⁷ נִשְׁתַּיֵּיר שָׁם שְׁלֹשָׁה טְפָחִים. חֲצִי טֶפַח מִכָּאן וַחֲצִי טֶפַח מִכָּאן לְשִׁילוּט. וּמָקוֹם שֶׁמַּנִּיחִין בּוֹ סֵפֶר תּוֹרָה טְפָחַיִם.

Rebbi Joḥanan said, the Ark was made with a cubit of six handbreadths. Who stated "a cubit of six handbreadths"? This is Rebbi Meïr. As we have stated[98]: "Rebbi Meïr says, all cubits were average[99]." According to Rebbi Meïr who says that the Ark was made with a a cubit of six handbreadths, the length of the Ark was fifteen cubits, as it is written[100]: "Its length two cubits and a half." Each cubit was six and half a cubit three[101]. Four tablets were in it, two broken ones and two whole ones[102], as it is written[103]: "Which you broke and put into the Ark." Each of the tablets was six handbreadths in length and three in width[104]. If the widths of the tablets were in the length of the Ark, there were three handbreadths left[105]. Apply them to the cylinder[106]. The width of the

Ark was nine handbreadths, as it is written: "A cubit and half a cubit." A cubit six and half a cubit three. Four tablets were in it, two broken ones and two whole ones. Each of the tablets was six handbreadths in length and three in width. If the lengths of the tablets were in the length of the Ark[97], there were three handbreadths left[107]. On each side half a handbreadth to have a handle, and two handbreadths as place to put there the Torah scroll[108].

93 A Babylonism, found also in *Šeqalim* 6:2.

94 In *Šeqalim* אוֹרְכָּן "their length". But then the original scribe had "the width of the Ark", corrected (probably wrongly) into "the length of the Ark."

95 This text was also the original scribe's in *Šeqalim*, corrected into: תֵּן מֵהֶם חֲצִי טֶפַח לְכָל־כּוֹתֶל נִשְׁתַּיֵּיר שְׁנֵי טְפָחִים לְסֵפֶר תּוֹרָה. "Take half a handbreadth for each wall, there were two handbreadths left for the Torah scroll."

96 The text in *Šeqalim* adds: וְרָחְבָּן שִׁשָּׁה "and their width six handbreadths"; the original scribe had שְׁלֹשָׁה "three". The correction, as also an earlier one (Note 94) is based on the Babli and must be rejected since the uncorrected reading is confirmed as Yerushalmi reading by Tosaphot *Menaḥot* 99a, s. v. מלמד.

97 In *Šeqalim*: תֵּן אָרְכָּן שֶׁלַּלּוּחוֹת לְאָרְכּוֹ שֶׁלָּאָרוֹן "If the lengths of the tablets were in the length of the Ark". This text is the correct one since in the text here the second case is identical with the first.

98 Mishnah *Kelim* 17:10.

99 There was also a small cubit of 5 handbreadths and a large one of 7.

100 *Ex.* 25:10.

101 This Aramaic insert of elementary counting seems to be a gloss.

102 In the Babli (*Baba batra* 14b, *Menaḥot* 99a) attributed to the fourth generation Amora Rav Joseph.

103 *Deut.* 10:2. This explanation of the verse requires the removal of the masoretic dividing accent. and a revocalization וַשַׂמְתָּם with *waw conversive*.

104 In the Babli (*Baba batra* 14a, *Nedarim* 38a, *Menaḥot* 99a), the tablets are said to have been six by six handbreadths with a height of three, lying one after the other in the Ark for a total length of 12 and width 6.

105 Four tablets lying side by side with their long sides touching one

another fill an area of 12 by 6 handbreadths.

106 Probably the Torah scroll, cf. Note 95. The Torah scroll should have been "next to the Ark", *Deut.* 31:26.

107 If the tablets were put into the Ark lengthwise in pairs, they fill a rectangle of length 12 and width 6.

108 The first hand in *Šeqalim* here also has "for the cylinder" (الـسطرنة), proving the equivalence of "cylinder" and "Torah scroll"; cf. Note 121.

(22c line 66) רִבִּי שִׁמְעוֹן בֶּן לָקִישׁ אָמַר. בְּאַמָּה שֶׁלַּחֲמִשָּׁה טְפָחִים הָיָה הָאָרוֹן עָשׂוּי. מָאן תַּנָּא. אַמָּה שֶׁלַּחֲמִשָּׁה טְפָחִים. רִבִּי יְהוּדָה. דְּתַנִינָן תַּמָּן. רִבִּי יְהוּדָה אוֹמֵר. אַמַּת הַבִּנְיָין שִׁשָּׁה טְפָחִים וְשֶׁלַכֵּלִים חֲמִשָּׁה. וְהֵן אָרוֹן כְּלִי הוּא. עַל דַּעְתֵּיהּ דְּרִבִּי יוּדָה דְּאָמַר. שֶׁלַּחֲמִשָּׁה טְפָחִים הָיָה הָאָרוֹן עָשׂוּי. אָרְכּוֹ שֶׁלָּאָרוֹן שְׁנֵים עָשָׂר טְפָחִים וּמֶחֱצָה. דִּכְתִיב אַמָּתַיִם וָחֵצִי אָרְכּוֹ. אַמָּתָא חֲמִשָּׁה וְאַמָּתָא חֲמִשָּׁה וּפַלְגּוּת אַמָּתָא תְּרֵין וּפְלָג. וְאַרְבָּעָה לוּחוֹת הָיוּ בּוֹ. שְׁנַיִם שְׁלֵמִין וּשְׁנַיִם שְׁבוּרִין. דִּכְתִיב אֲשֶׁר שִׁבַּרְתָּ וְשַׂמְתָּם בָּאָרוֹן. וְהַלּוּחוֹת הָיוּ כָּל־אֶחָד וְאֶחָד אָרְכָּן שִׁשָּׁה טְפָחִים וְרָחְבָּן שְׁלֹשָׁה. תֵּן רָחְבָּן שֶׁלְּלוּחוֹת לְאָרְכּוֹ שֶׁלָּאָרוֹן. נִשְׁתַּיֵּיר שָׁם חֲצִי טֶפַח. אֶצְבַּע לִכְתָלִים מִכָּן וְאֶצְבַּע לִכְתָלִים מִכָּן. וְרָחְבּוֹ שֶׁלָּאָרוֹן שִׁבְעָה טְפָחִים וּמֶחֱצָה. דִּכְתִיב וְאַמָּה וָחֵצִי רָחְבּוֹ. אַמָּתָא חֲמִשָּׁה טְפָחִים וּפַלְגּוּת אַמָּתָא תְּרֵין וּפְלָג. וְאַרְבָּעָה לוּחוֹת הָיוּ בּוֹ. שְׁנַיִם שְׁלֵמִין וּשְׁנַיִם שְׁבוּרִין. דִּכְתִיב אֲשֶׁר שִׁבַּרְתָּ וְשַׂמְתָּם בָּאָרוֹן. וְהַלּוּחוֹת הָיוּ כָּל־אֶחָד וְאֶחָד אָרְכָּן שִׁשָּׁה טְפָחִים וְרָחְבָּן שְׁלֹשָׁה. תֵּן אָרְכָּן שֶׁלְּלוּחוֹת לְרָחְבּוֹ שֶׁלָּאָרוֹן. נִשְׁתַּיֵּיר שָׁם טֶפַח וּמֶחֱצָה. אֶצְבַּע לִכְתָלִים מִכָּן וְאֶצְבַּע לִכְתָלִים מִכָּן. וַחֲצִי טֶפַח מִיכָּן וַחֲצִי טֶפַח מִיכָּן לְשִׁילוּט.

Rebbi Simeon ben Laqish said, the Ark was made using a cubit of five handbreadths. Who stated "a cubit of five handbreadths"? This is Rebbi Jehudah. As we have stated there[98]: "Rebbi Jehudah says, the builders' cubit was of six handbreadths, but that of vessels five handbeadths." And the Ark is a vessel. According to Rebbi Jehudah who says that the Ark was made with a cubit of five handbreadths, the length of the Ark was twelve and one half cubits, as it is written[100]: "Its length two cubits and a half." Each cubit was five and half a cubit two and one half[101]. Four tablets were in it, two whole ones and two broken ones[102], as it is written[103]: "Which you broke and put into the Ark." Each of the tablets was six handbreadths in length and three in width[104]. If the widths of the tablets were in the length of the Ark, there was half a handbreadth left[109]. One finger's thickness for the wall on either side. The width of the Ark was seven and one half handbreadths, as it is written[100]: "A cubit and half a cubit." A cubit five and half a cubit two and one half. Four tablets were in it, two whole ones and two broken ones, as it is written[103]: "Which you broke and put into the Ark.". Each of the tablets was six handbreadths in length and three in width. If the lengths of the tablets were in the width of the Ark, there were one and a half handbreadths left[110]. One finger's thickness for the wall on either side, and on each side half a handbreadth to have a handle[111].

109   12.5 - 4·3 = 0.5.   by necessity was outside the Ark; cf.
110   7.5 - 6 = 1.5.   Note 106.
111   In this opinion, the Torah scroll

(22d line 6) כֵּיצַד עָשָׂה בְּצַלְאֵל אֶת הָאָרוֹן. רִבִּי חֲנִינָה אָמַר. שָׁלֹשׁ תֵּיבוֹת עֲשָׂאָן. שְׁתַּיִם שֶׁלְּזָהָב וְאַחַת שֶׁלְּעֵץ. וְנָתַן שֶׁלְּזָהָב בְּשֶׁלְּעֵץ וְשֶׁלְּעֵץ בְּשֶׁלְּזָהָב וְצִיפָהוּ. הָדָא הִיא דִכְתִיב וְצִפִּיתָ אוֹתוֹ זָהָב טָהוֹר מִבַּיִת וּמִחוּץ. מַה תַּלְמוּד לוֹמַר תְּצַפֶּנּוּ. לְהָבִיא שְׂפָתוֹ הָעֶלְיוֹנָה. רִבִּי שִׁמְעוֹן בֶּן לָקִישׁ אָמַר. תֵּיבָה אַחַת עֲשָׂאוֹ וְצִיפָהוּ. הָדָא הִיא דִכְתִיב וְצִפִּיתָ אוֹתוֹ זָהָב טָהוֹר מִבַּיִת וּמִחוּץ. מַה תַּלְמוּד לוֹמַר תְּצַפֶּנּוּ. אָמַר רִבִּי פִינְחָס. לְהָבִיא בֵּין נֶסֶר לַנֶּסֶר.

How did Beṣalel make the Ark? Rebbi Ḥanina said[112], he made three boxes, two of gold and one of wood. He put one of gold inside the one of wood, and the one of wood inside the other one of gold. That is what is written[113]: "You shall cover it inside and out with pure gold inside and out." Why does the verse say, "you shall cover it"? To include the upper rim[114]. Rebbi Simeon ben Laqish said, he made one box and gilded it. That is what is written: "You shall cover it inside and out with pure gold inside and out." Why does the verse say, "you shall cover it"? Rebbi Phineas said, also between the planks.

112   In the Babli, *Yoma* 72b, this is the opinion of Rav Jehudah, contemporary of R. Ḥanina. The other opinion is not mentioned there.

113   *Ex.* 25:11: "You shall cover it with pure gold, inside and out you shall cover it".

114   Which was covered by the gold cover separate from the Ark (*Ex.* 25:17-21.)

(22d line 12) כֵּיצַד הָיוּ הַלּוּחוֹת כְּתוּבִים. רִבִּי חֲנַנְיָה בֶּן גַּמְלִיאֵל אוֹמֵר. חֲמִשָּׁה עַל לוּחַ זֶה וַחֲמִשָּׁה עַל לוּחַ זֶה. וְרַבָּנִין אָמְרִין. עֲשָׂרָה עַל לוּחַ זֶה וַעֲשָׂרָה עַל לוּחַ זֶה. דִּכְתִיב וַיַּגֵּד לָכֶם אֶת בְּרִיתוֹ אֲשֶׁר צִוָּה אֶתְכֶם לַעֲשׂוֹת עֲשֶׂרֶת הַדְּבָרִים. עֲשָׂרָה עַל לוּחַ זֶה וַעֲשָׂרָה עַל לוּחַ זֶה. רִבִּי שִׁמְעוֹן בֶּן יוֹחַי אוֹמֵר. עֶשְׂרִים עַל לוּחַ זֶה וְעֶשְׂרִים עַל לוּחַ זֶה. דִּכְתִיב וַיַּגֵּד לָכֶם אֶת בְּרִיתוֹ אֲשֶׁר צִוָּה אֶתְכֶם לַעֲשׂוֹת עֲשֶׂרֶת הַדְּבָרִים. עֶשְׂרִים עַל לוּחַ זֶה וְעֶשְׂרִים עַל לוּחַ זֶה. רִבִּי סִימַאי אוֹמֵר. אַרְבָּעִים עַל לוּחַ זֶה וְאַרְבָּעִים עַל לוּחַ זֶה. מִזֶּה וּמִזֶּה הֵם כְּתוּבִים. טְטְרַגּוֹנָה. חֲנַנְיָה בֶּן אֲחִי רִבִּי יְהוֹשֻׁעַ אוֹמֵר. בֵּין כָּל־דִּיבּוּר וְדִבּוּר דִּיקְדּוּקֶיהָ וְאוֹתִיוֹתֶיהָ [שֶׁל תּוֹרָה].[115] מְמוּלָּאִים בַּתַּרְשִׁישׁ. כְּיַמָּא רַבָּא. רִבִּי שִׁמְעוֹן בֶּן לָקִישׁ כַּד הֲוָה מָטֵי לְהָדֵין קִרְיָיא הֲוָה אָמַר. יָפָה לִימְּדָנִי חֲנַנְיָה בֶּן אֲחִי רִבִּי יְהוֹשֻׁעַ. מַה הַיָּם הַזֶּה בֵּין גַּל גָּדוֹל לְגַל גָּדוֹל גַּלִּים קְטַנִּים. כָּךְ בֵּין כָּל דָּבָר וְדָבָר דִּיקְדּוּקֶיהָ וְאוֹתִיוֹתֶיהָ שֶׁלַּתּוֹרָה.

How were the tablets written[116]? Rebbi Ḥanania ben Gamliel says, five on one tablet each. But the rabbis say, ten on each tablet, as it is written[117]: "He informed you of His covenant which He had commanded you to do, the ten words", ten on each tablet. Rebbi Simeon ben Iohai said, twenty on each tablet, as it is written[118]: "He informed you of His covenant which He had commanded you to do, the ten words", twenty on each tablet. Rebbi Simai says, forty on each tablet, as it is written, "on each side they were written," a square[119] Hananiah, the son of Rebbi Joshua's brother[120], says: Between every two commandments, the details and the letters [of the Torah] were written. "Filled with *taršiš*[121]", like the Great Sea. When Rebbi Simeon ben Laqish had occasion to discuss this verse, he said, Hananiah, the son of Rebbi Joshua's brother, did teach us correctly. Just as in the sea there are small waves between a large wave and the next, so between any two commandments there are the details and the letters of the Torah[122].

115 From the Rome ms., confirmed by the end of the paragraph.

116 In *Ex. rabba* 47(10) (a somewhat suspect source), the opinions are attributed to R. Jehudah and R. Nehemiah. In Mekhilta dR. Ismael (*Yitro Masekhta dibeḥodeš* 8), *Cant. rabba* on 5:14, *Tanḥuma Eqeb* 9, *Tanḥuma Buber Ki Tissa* 20, *Pesiqta rabbati* 21(7), the first two opinions given here.

117 *Deut.* 4:13. The verse ends: "He wrote them on two stone tablets." The emphasis on *two* tablets is taken to mean that the Ten Commandments were written twice, once on each of the tablets.

118 It is difficult to see what this quote means. A more appropriate quote would have been *Ex.* 32:15: "The tablets were written on both sides, on each side they were written."

119 Greek τετράγωνον "a square". He seems to think that the tablets were cubes, an opinion not found elsewhere.

120 His name was Hananiah ben Hananiah, which shows that he was a posthumous child. Names indicating this kind of bad luck are usually replaced by circumlocutions; cf. E. und H. Guggenheimer, *Etymologisches Lexikon der jüdischen Familiennamen*, München 1996, p. xviii; *Jewish Family Names and Their Origins*, Hoboken 1992, p. xviii.

121 *Cant.* 5:14. "His hands are golden cylinders, inlaid with *taršiš*," the cylinders being Torah scrolls (*Cant. rabba* 5:12), cf. Note 108. The Palestinian Targum to *Ex.* 28:20, 39:13 translates *taršiš* by כְּרוֹם יַמָּא רַבָּא "the color of the Great Sea.". One may

assume that the scribe of the Yerushalmi did not understand the Greek כרום χρῶμα "color" and shortened it to בְּ. The Targum to *Cant.* translates חרשיש by the Syriac/Pahlevi word פֵּירוֹזַג (Farsi نیروزه) "turquoise".

122 In *Cant. rabba* 5(12), this is a commentary of R. Joḥanan.

(22d line 22) אָמַר רִבִּי תַּנְחוּמָא. אִיתְקַשְׁשִׁיַת קוֹמֵי רִבִּי פִינְחָס. אָתְיָיא כְרִבִּי יוּדָה וְלָא אַתְיָיא כְרִבִּי מֵאִיר. מַה טַעֲמָא דְרִבִּי יוּדָה. לָקוֹחַ אֶת סֵפֶר הַתּוֹרָה הַזֶּה. עַל דַּעְתֵּיהּ דְּרִבִּי יוּדָה דּוּ אָמַר. אֵיכָן סֵפֶר תּוֹרָה הָיָה נָתוּן. כְּמִין גְּלוֹסְקוֹס עָשׂוּ לוֹ מִבַּחוּץ וְהָיָה סֵפֶר תּוֹרָה נָתוּן בְּתוֹכוֹ. מַה טַעֲמָא דְרִבִּי מֵאִיר. וְנָתַתָּ אֶת הַכַּפּוֹרֶת עַל הָאָרוֹן מִלְמָעְלָה. עַל דַּעְתֵּיהּ דְּרִבִּי מֵאִיר דּוּ אָמַר. אֵין מוּקְדָּם וּמְאוּחָר בַּתּוֹרָה. וְאֶל הָאָרוֹן תִּתֵּן אֶת הָעֵדוּת אֲשֶׁר אֶתֵּן אֵלֶיךָ. וְאַחַר כָּךְ וְנָתַתָּ אֶת הַכַּפּוֹרֶת עַל הָאָרוֹן מִלְמָעְלָה. רִבִּי פִינְחָס בְּשֵׁם רִבִּי שִׁמְעוֹן בֶּן לָקִישׁ. תּוֹרָה שֶׁנָּתַן הַקָּדוֹשׁ בָּרוּךְ הוּא עוֹרָהּ אֵשׁ לְבָנָה חָרוּתָהּ אֵשׁ שְׁחוֹרָה. הִיא אֵשׁ וּמְבוֹלֶלֶת בָּאֵשׁ. חֲצוּבָה מֵאֵשׁ. נְתוּנָה מֵאֵשׁ. מִימִינוֹ אֵשׁ דָּת לָמוֹ.

Rebbi Tanḥuma said, I asked before Rebbi Phineas: It is acceptable following Rebbi Jehudah, it is not acceptable following Rebbi Meïr[123]. What is the reason of Rebbi Jehudah? "To take this Torah scroll[124]". In the opinion of Rebbi Jehudah, who said, where the Torah scroll was put? They made for it a kind of case[125] outside and the Torah scroll was put into it. What is the reason of Rebbi Meïr? "You should put the cover on top of the Ark.[126]" In the opinion of Rebbi Meïr who says that there is no earlier and later in the Torah[127], "in the Ark you shall put the testimony that I shall give to you,[128]" and after that, "you should put the cover on top of the Ark." Rebbi Phineas in the name of Rebbi Simeon ben Laqish[129]: The Torah which the Holy One, Praise to Him, gave, its leather was white fire, its inscription was black fire, it was fire mixed with fire; hewn from fire, given from fire: "From His right hand, the fiery law to them.[130]"

123 The verses seem to imply that the Torah scroll was not in the ark.
124 *Deut.* 31:26, "and put it *beside* the Ark", cf. Note 106.
125 Read גלוסקוס for גלוסקום, Greek γλωσσόκομον "case, covering, chest".
126 *Ex.* 25:21.
127 The order of verses in the Torah does not imply either logical or temporal dependency. Accepted in the Babli, *Pesaḥim* 6b; *Num. rabba* 9(44).
128 *Ex.* 25:16, five verses earlier.
129 Cf. *Tanḥuma Berešit* 1, *Cant. rabba* 5(12).
130 *Deut.* 33:2.

משנה ד: וְדִבְּרוּ הַשּׁוֹטְרִים אֶל הָעָם לֵאמוֹר מִי הָאִישׁ אֲשֶׁר בָּנָה בַיִת (fol. 22a) חָדָשׁ וְלֹא חֲנָכוֹ יֵלֵךְ וְיָשׁוֹב לְבֵיתוֹ וְגוֹמֵר. אֶחָד הַבּוֹנֶה בַיִת חָדָשׁ וְאֶחָד הַבּוֹנֶה בֵּית הַתֶּבֶן בֵּית הַבָּקָר בֵּית הָעֵצִים בֵּית הָאוֹצָרוֹת. אֶחָד הַבּוֹנֶה וְאֶחָד הַלּוֹקֵחַ וְאֶחָד הַיּוֹרֵשׁ וְאֶחָד שֶׁנִּיתַּן לוֹ בְמַתָּנָה.

Mishnah 4: "The policemen shall speak to the people, saying: Who is the man who built a new house and did not inaugurate it; he should go and return to his house,[131]" etc. Not only he who builds a house, but also one who builds a barn, a cow-shed, a wood-shed, a storage facility. Not only he who builds, but also one who buys, or inherits, or who received as a gift.

131 *Deut.* 20:5. "Lest he should die in the war and another would inaugurate it." He is recruited for auxiliary services (Mishnah 7). The policemen speak after the Cohen whose words were treated in the preceding Mishnaiot. It is not necessary that the original builder inaugurate his house; anybody in legal possession of a not inaugurated house is included.

הלכה ד: אֲשֶׁר בָּנָה בַיִת. אֵין לִי אֶלָּא אֲשֶׁר בָּנָה. לָקַח יָרַשׁ נִיתַּן לוֹ (fol. 22d) בְמַתָּנָה מְנַיִין. תַּלְמוּד לוֹמַר הָאִישׁ מִי הָאִישׁ. מְנַיִין הַבּוֹנֶה בֵית הַתֶּבֶן בֵּית

הַבָּקָר בֵּית הָעֵצִים בֵּית הָאוֹצָרוֹת בֵּית הָאוֹצָרוֹת מְנַיִין. תַּלְמוּד לוֹמַר אֲשֶׁר בָּנָה. מִכָּל־מָקוֹם. יָכוֹל הַבּוֹנֶה בֵּית שַׁעַר וְאַכְסַדְרָה וּמִרְפֶּסֶת יְהֵא חוֹזֵר. תַּלְמוּד לוֹמַר בַּיִת. מַה בַּיִת מְיוּחָד שֶׁהוּא בֵית דִּירָה. יָצְאוּ אִילוּ שֶׁאֵינָן בֵּית דִּירָה. יָצָא בַיִת שֶׁאֵין בּוֹ אַרְבַּע אַמּוֹת עַל אַרְבַּע אַמּוֹת. דְּתַנֵּי. בַּיִת שֶׁאֵין בּוֹ אַרְבַּע אַמּוֹת עַל אַרְבַּע אַמּוֹת פָּטוּר מִן הַמַּעֲקֶה וּמִן הַמְזוּזָה וּמִן הָעֵירוּב. וְאֵינוֹ טוֹבֵל לְמַעְשְׂרוֹת. וְאֵין נוֹתְנִין לוֹ אַרְבַּע אַמּוֹת לִפְנֵי פִּתְחוֹ. וְאֵין עוֹשִׂין אוֹתוֹ חִיבּוּר לָעִיר. וְהַנּוֹדֵר מִן הַבַּיִת מוּתָּר לֵישֵׁב בּוֹ. וְאֵינוֹ צָמִית בַּיּוֹבֵל. וְאֵינוֹ מִיטַּמֵּא בִנְגָעִים. וְאֵין הַבְּעָלִים חוֹזְרִין לוֹ בַּמִּלְחָמָה.

Halakhah 4: [132]"Who built a house", not only who built; if he bought, inherited, or it was given to him as a gift, from where? The verse says, "the man," "who is the man"[133]. From where he who builds a barn, a cowshed, a wood-shed, a storage facility, from where? The verse says, "who builds". I could think that one who builds a portico[134], a covered walkway[135], and a verandah would return; the verse says "house"; the house is distinguished by the fact that it can be used as a dwelling[136]. This excludes those items which cannot be dwellings. It also excludes a house which does not enclose four by four cubits. As it was stated[137]: A house which does not enclose four by four cubits is free from the obligation of a parapet[138], or a *mezuzah*[139], or an *erub*[140]. It also does not induce *ṭevel* for tithes[141] and one does not give it four cubits in front of its door[142], and it is not counted as a connection to the town[143], and one who forswears any use of a house is permitted to sit in it[144], and it does not remain with the buyer in the Jubilee year[145], and it cannot become impure by disease[146], and its owner does not become exempt from the war because of it.

132 Partial parallels are in the Babli, 43a; *Sifry Deut.* 194; Tosephta

7:17.

133 In the interpretation of Rashi,

this means that the verse would have been intelligible if the word הָאִישׁ were missing: מִי אֲשֶׁר בָּנָה "Who built . . . ". Therefore, the additional word must imply an extension of the circle of those who have to go and start using their new property.

134 A formal structure at the entrance to a courtyard common to several houses. It has no walls and confers no privacy.

135 Greek ἐξέδρα, cf. *Ma'serot* 3:6, Note 101.

136 Even if it is used as agricultural facility, a barn etc. could be used as a dwelling, having walls on all sides.

137 *Ma'serot* 3:7, Notes 114-122. Babli *Sukkah* 3a/b.

138 *Deut.* 22:8.

139 *Deut.* 6:9, 11:20.

140 If a courtyard belongs to a single owner except that a hut enclosing an area less that four cubits square belongs to another person, that courtyard may be used on the Sabbath by the majority owner without an *eruv* (cf. *Demay* 1, Notes 192-193).

141 Freshly harvested produce may be eaten untithed. Once the harvest has been removed to a storage area, it is forbidden as food until heave and tithes were given; cf. *Ma'serot* 3:5-8. A small shed does not qualify as a storage area.

142 In a courtyard belonging to several owners, the four cubits in front of the entrance to each house are the private domain of this house, to be used to load and unload, and is out of bounds for the other owners. This does not apply to a small hut.

143 On the Sabbath, one may not go outside one's town more than 2000 cubits (cf. *Peah* 8, Note 56). Any house which is within 70 cubits of a house or the city wall of the town is also counted as part of the town; the count of 2000 cubits starts only at the outermost house. A small building does not count as a house.

144 In popular language, a small shelter is not called a house. Therefore, a person vowing not to sit in a house may sit in a small shelter.

145 It is agricultural property, not a city dwelling; *Lev.* 25:30.

146 *Lev.* 14:34 ff. The rules of diseased structures are explicitly restricted to "a *house* of the Land of your inheritance".

(22d line 44) מַה תַּלְמוּד לוֹמַר אֲשֶׁר בָּנָה. פְּרָט לְשֶׁנָּפַל בֵּיתוֹ וּבְנָאוֹ. אָמַר רִבִּי יוֹסֵי. זֹאת אוֹמֶרֶת. הַמַּחֲזִיר אֶת גְּרוּשָׁתוֹ לֹא הָיָה חוֹזֵר. יָכוֹל הַבּוֹנֶה בַיִת בְּחוּצָה לָאָרֶץ יְהֵא חוֹזֵר. תַּלְמוּד לוֹמַר וְלֹא חֲנָכוֹ. אֶת שֶׁמִּצְוָה לַחֲנָכוֹ. יָצָא זֶה

שֶׁאֵינוֹ מִצְוָה לְחַנְּכוֹ. הִקְדִּים לוֹ שְׂכָרוֹ. כְּמִי שֶׁחֲנָכוֹ. נָתַן לוֹ שְׂכָרוֹ לְאַחַר שְׁנֵים עָשָׂר חוֹדֶשׁ. כְּמִי שֶׁלֹּא חֲנָכוֹ. נָעֲלוֹ. אִם הָיָה בְתוֹכוֹ חֲפָצִים. אֶת שֶׁדַּרְכּוֹ לִיבָּטֵל עָלֶיהָ. כְּמִי שֶׁחֲנָכוֹ. וְאִם לָאו. כְּמִי שֶׁלֹּא חֲנָכוֹ.

Why does the verse say, "who built"[147]? This excludes him whose house collapsed and he rebuilt it. (Rebbi Yose said, this implies that one who remarries his divorcee does not return.)[148] One could think that somebody who builds a house outside the Land would return; the verse said, "and he did not inaugurate it," meaning where there is an obligation of inauguration; this excludes cases where there is no obligation of inauguration[149]. If he received prepaid rent, it is as if he inaugurated it[150]; if [the rent is payable] only after twelve months, it is as if he had not inaugurated it. If he locked it, if it contains valuables for which one usually stops working[151], it is as if he inaugurated it; otherwise, it is as if he had not inaugurated it.

147 *Deut.* 20:5. The quote is only to indicate the verse, not the reason for that deduction. The emphasis is on "who built a *new* house". Cf. also Halakhah 7.

148 This sentence is paralleled by a tannaïtic statement in Halakhah 6, Note 186. The person who had married a woman in preliminary marriage (cf. *Demay* 4:2, Note 19; *Peah* 6:2, Note 46; *Yebamot* 1:1, Note 63) but had not lived with her returns from the war if she is a *new* wife; i. e., not one previously married to him.

149 It is inferred from here that a formal inauguration of a newly built house is a religious commandment in the Land.

150 If the house was built not for the family of the builder but for rental purposes, receipt of the first rental payment is the inauguration, but only if the payment is made not later than the end of the usual rental period of 12 months.

151 If the value of the things stored is so high that either the owner has to be present to guard against thieves or he has to pay a watchman; that is use equivalent to living in the building.

(fol. 22a) **משנה ה**: וּמִי הָאִישׁ אֲשֶׁר נָטַע כֶּרֶם וְלֹא חִילְלוֹ וגו' אֶחָד הַנּוֹטֵעַ אֶת הַכֶּרֶם וְאֶחָד הַנּוֹטֵעַ חֲמִשָּׁה אִילָנֵי מַאֲכָל אֲפִילוּ מֵחֲמֵשֶׁת הַמִּינִין. אֶחָד הַנּוֹטֵעַ וְאֶחָד הַמַּבְרִיךְ וְאֶחָד הַמַּרְכִּיב וְאֶחָד הַלּוֹקֵחַ וְאֶחָד הַיּוֹרֵשׁ וְאֶחָד שֶׁנִּיתַּן לוֹ בְּמַתָּנָה.

Mishnah 5: "And who is the man who planted a vineyard and did not redeem it,[152]" etc. Not only one who planted a vineyard but also one who planted five fruit trees[153], even from five different kinds. Not only one who planted but also one who sank[154] or grafted, also one who buys, or inherits, or who received as a gift.

152 Deut. 20:6. The fruit of a newly planted vineyard or orchard cannot be used unless it was redeemed in his fourth year, Lev. 19:23-24.

153 An orchard, whose rules of redemption are identical to those of a vineyard; cf. *Ma'aser Šeni* 5:4.

154 He produces a new tree by covering a branch of an existing tree with earth; cf. *Kilaim* 7:1, Note 1.

(fol. 22d) **הלכה ה**: אֲשֶׁר נָטַע. אֵין לִי אֶלָּא אֲשֶׁר נָטַע. לָקַח יָרַשׁ נִיתַּן לוֹ בְּמַתָּנָה מְנַיִּין. תַּלְמוּד לוֹמַר הָאִישׁ מִי הָאִישׁ. מְנַיִּין הַנּוֹטֵעַ חֲמִשָּׁה אִילָנֵי מַאֲכָל אֲפִילוּ מֵחֲמֵשֶׁת הַמִּינִין. תַּלְמוּד לוֹמַר אֲשֶׁר נָטַע. מִכָּל־מָקוֹם. יָכוֹל הַנּוֹטֵעַ אַרְבָּעָה אִילָנֵי מַאֲכָל אוֹ חֲמִשָּׁה אִילָנֵי סְרָק יְהֵא חוֹזֵר. תַּלְמוּד לוֹמַר כֶּרֶם. מַה כֶּרֶם מְיוּחָד שֶׁהוּא שֶׁלְּחָמֵשׁ גְּפָנִים. יָצָא זֶה שֶׁאֵינוֹ שֶׁלְּחָמֵשׁ גְּפָנִים.

Halakhah 5: "Who planted". Not only who planted; if he bought, inherited, or it was given to him as a gift, from where? The verse says, "the man," "who is the man"[155]. From where about him who planted a vineyard but also who planted five fruit trees[153], even from five different kinds? The verse says, "who planted", in any circumstance. I could think that one who planted four fruit trees or five futile trees[156] may return? The verse says, "a vineyard." Since a vineyard is special in that it is composed of five vines[157], this excludes the case where there are not five vines[158].

155 The same argument as in Note 133, applied to v. 6, not v. 5. Parallels in Babli 43b; *Sifry Deut.* 195.	157 The minimal size of a legal vineyard, cf. *Kilaim* 4:3, Note 38. The vineyard must be planted in orderly rows; in an orchard, the trees must grow at least four and at most √250 (= 15.8) cubits apart; cf. *Ševi'it* 1:2, Notes 18,22.
156 The definition of a futile tree is in dispute (Mishnah *Kilaim* 6:6); the majority opinion holds that a tree is futile if and only if its fruits are not edible.	
	158 Or fruit trees.

(22d line 55) שֶׁהַיַּיִן מַגִּיתוֹ. שֶׁהַיַּיִן קוֹסֵס. [דְּתַנֵּי. יַיִן קוֹסֵס].¹⁵⁹ מְעָרְבִין בּוֹ וּמִשְׁתַּתְּפִין בּוֹ וּמְבָרְכִין עָלָיו וּמְקַדְּשִׁין בּוֹ אֶת הַכַּלָּה וּמְנַחֲמִין בּוֹ אֶת הָאָבֵל וְנִמְכָּר בְּחָנוּת לְשֵׁם יַיִן. וְהַמּוֹכֵר לַחֲבֵירוֹ יַיִן סְתָם לֹא מָכַר לוֹ יַיִן קוֹסֵס. וְאָסוּר בְּהוֹרָיָיה וּבְהֶיתֵּר נְדָרִים. וְעַל בִּיאַת מִקְדָּשׁ. לֵית לָךְ אֶלָּא שֶׁהוּא אָסוּר עַל גַּבֵּי הַמִּזְבֵּחַ. וְהֵן בֶּן סוֹרֵר וּמוֹרֶה צְרִיכָה.

If the wine[160] is freshly pressed, if the wine[160] is sour[161]? As it was stated: Sour wine may be used to make an *eruv*[162] and participating, one makes a benediction for it[163], and one may use it for the preliminary marriage of a bride[164], for consoling the mourner[165], and it may be sold in a store as wine. If somebody made an unqualified contract for wine, he did not sell sour wine[166]. One is prohibited from delivering a decision, or to dissolve a vow, or to enter the Temple[167]. Only it is forbidden on the altar[168]. And about the rebellious son it is problematic[169].

159 From the Rome ms., missing in Leiden ms. and *editio princeps*.	matter of opinion whether it is sour wine or sweet vinegar. It still must contain some alcohol. The first hand of the Leiden ms. wrote יַיִן חוֹסֵס "wine fermenting". This may be an intrusion from a similar Babylonian *baraita*, *Sanhedrin* 70a.
160 In the Rome ms. שְׁתָיוֹ "if he drank it as . . ." Since this paragraph is not connected with the preceding or the following ones, it is difficult to decide between the readings.	
161 This is wine for which it is a	162 If several houses share a

common courtyard, the latter can be turned into common property to be available to all dwellers for use on the Sabbath by everyone donating food for a common meal, This is called *eruv*, "mixing". If the inhabitants of a dead-end stret decide to turn their street into common property for Sabbath purposes, they have to install a symbolic door at the entrance to the street and prepare common food by "participating". Cf. *Demay* 1:4, Notes 192, 193.

163 Before one drinks sour wine, one has to recite the benediction for wine, not vinegar (Mishnaiot *Berakhot* 6:1,3).

164 Cf. *Demay* 4:2, Note 19; *Peah* 6:2, Note 46; *Yebamot* 1:1, Note 63.

165 The first meal of a mourner after the burial of a close relative must be given to him by others and it includes wine; cf. *Berakhot* 3:1, Notes 48,49,54; Babli *Ketubot* 8b, *Sanhedrin* 90a.

166 On the wholesale level, sour wine has to be labelled as such. However, if an entire inventory was sold, the buyer must expect 10% of the barrels to contain sour wine (Mishnah *Baba batra* 6:1).

167 *Lev.* 10:8-11 forbids entering the Temple, officiating, and delivering any religious instruction to anybody who is still under the influence of any alcoholic beverage. Since sour wine contains alcohol, it disables as wine.

168 *Mal.* 1:8 declares sinful any offering on the altar which would not be received by the Pasha as a bribe.

169 The rebellious son (*Deut.* 21:18-21) is not guilty unless he eats and drinks immoderately, including half a *log* of wine (2.7 dl) in one sip. It is undecided whether drinking almost-vinegar is drinking wine in this case. The Babli (*Baba batra* 96a) discusses whether smell or taste decide between wine and vinegar. It is obvious (*Sanhedrin* 70a) that grape juice does not qualify as wine in this respect.

(22d line 60) יָכוֹל הַנּוֹטֵעַ כֶּרֶם בְּחוּצָה לָאָרֶץ יְהֵא חוֹזֵר. תַּלְמוּד לוֹמַר וְלֹא חִלְּלוֹ. אֶת שֶׁמִּצְוָה לְחַלְּלוֹ. יָצָא זֶה שֶׁאֵין מִצְוָה לְחַלְּלוֹ. תַּנֵּי. רִבִּי אֱלִיעֶזֶר בֶּן יַעֲקֹב אוֹמֵר. אֵין מַשְׁמַע אֶלָּא כֶרֶם. וְדִכְוָתָהּ. אֵין מַשְׁמַע אֶלָּא נָטַע. תַּנֵּי. וְלֹא חִלְּלוֹ. פְּרָט לַמַּבְרִיךְ וְלַמַּרְכִּיב. אָמַר רִבִּי יוֹחָנָן. דְּרִבִּי אֱלִיעֶזֶר בֶּן יַעֲקֹב הִיא. אָמַר רַב חִסְדָּא. דִּבְרֵי הַכֹּל הִיא. כְּשֶׁהִרְכִּיב פֵּירוֹת עֲבֵירָה. מָה אָנוּ קַיָּימִין. אִם בְּשֶׁהִרְכִּיב אִילָן מַאֲכָל עַל גַּבֵּי אִילָן מַאֲכָל. מִין בְּשֶׁאֵינוֹ מִינוֹ. פֵּירוֹת עֲבֵירָה הֵן. וְאִם בְּשֶׁהִרְכִּיב אִילָן מַאֲכָל עַל גַּבֵּי אִילָן סְרָק. מִין בְּמִינוֹ.

HALAKHAH 5

נוֹטֵעַ כְּבַתְּחִילָּה הֵן. אֶלָּא כֵן אֲנָן קַיָּימִין. בְּשֶׁהִרְכִּיב תְּאֵינָה שְׁחוֹרָה עַל גַּבֵּי תְּאֵינָה לְבָנָה.

I could think that somebody who redeems a vineyard outside the Land would return, the verse says[170]: "And he did not redeem it". In case one is commanded to redeem it[171]; this excludes where there is no commandment to redeem. It was stated[172]: Rebbi Eliezer ben Jacob says, one only understands "vineyard". And similarly, one only understands "planted". It was stated: "And he did not redeem it[170]", that excludes him who sinks or grafts. Rebbi Joḥanan said, this follows Rebbi Eliezer ben Jacob. Rav Ḥisda said, this is everybody's opinion if he grafted fruits of sin[173]. Where do we hold?[174] If he grafted a fruit tree on another fruit tree of a different kind; these are fruits of sin[175]. But if he grafted a fruit tree on a futile tree, as if it were its own kind, he is planting anew[176]. But we hold if he grafted a black fig tree on a white one[177].

---

170 *Deut.* 20:6.

171 In *Lev.* 19:23, the duty of redemption is clearly restricted to the Promised Land.

172 Also quoted in the Babli, 43b. R. Eliezer ben Jacob rejects the extension of the exemption from combat duty given in the Mishnah.

173 Since reciting a benediction over any forbidden fruit is blasphemy (*Hallah* 1:9, 58a line 53; Babli *Baba qama* 94a), it is obvious that since an orchard of *kilaim* cannot be redeemed, the person who planted it cannot be exempted.

174 What kind of grafting entitles a man to leave the war zone following the Mishnah but not R. Eliezer ben Jacob?

175 These are unquestionably forbidden *kilaim*.

176 The stump of the futile tree is simply considered as earth; according to everybody grafting on such a stem is the same as planting in the earth.

177 This is permitted; the owner returns following the Mishnah but not R. Eliezer ben Jacob. A "black" fig is a purple one; a "white" fig is green.

(22d line 69) אֵימָתַי הוּא מְחַלְלוֹ. בָּרְבִיעִית וּבַחֲמִישִׁית. מִסְתַּבְּרָה בַחֲמִישִׁית. אֲבָל בָּרְבִיעִית דָּמִים הוּא חַיָּיב לוֹ. וְרַבָּנִין דְּקַיְסָרִין אָמְרִין. לֹא מִסְתַּבְּרָה אֶלָּא בָרְבִיעִית. דִּכְתִיב וּבַשָּׁנָה הָרְבִיעִית יִהְיֶה כָּל־פִּרְיוֹ קוֹדֶשׁ הִילּוּלִים לַיי.

When does he redeem it[178]? In the fourth or the fifth [year]? It seems reasonable in the fifth, since in the fourth it costs him money. But the rabbis of Caesarea say, it is only reasonable in the fourth, since it is written[179]: "And in the fourth year, all its fruit shall be holy for praise to the Eternal."

178 In *Lev.* 19, v. 24 states that in the fourth year after planting, "all fruit shall be holy" as quoted in this paragraph. This is considered a burden rather than a joy. V. 25 permits the fruits of the fifth and later years without any restriction.

179 *Lev.* 19:24. Because of the disappearence of gutturals, the word הילולים is interpreted as חילולים, cf. *Peah* 7:6, Notes 112-113; Babli *Berakhot* 35a.

(fol. 22a) **משנה ו:** וּמִי הָאִישׁ אֲשֶׁר אֵירַשׂ אִשָּׁה וְלֹא לְקָחָהּ וְגוֹמֵר. אֶחָד הַמְאָרֵשׂ בְּתוּלָה וְאֶחָד הַמְאָרֵשׂ אֶת הָאַלְמָנָה אֲפִילוּ שׁוֹמֶרֶת יָבָם וַאֲפִילוּ שָׁמַע שֶׁמֵּת אָחִיו בַּמִּלְחָמָה חוֹזֵר וּבָא לוֹ. כָּל־אֵילוּ שׁוֹמְעִין דִּבְרֵי כֹהֵן מֵעַרְכֵי מִלְחָמָה וְחוֹזְרִין וּמְסַפְּקִין מַיִם וּמָזוֹן וּמְתַקְּנִין אֶת הַדְּרָכִים.

Mishnah 6: "[180]Who is the man who became betrothed[181] to a woman and did not take her," etc. Not only one betrothed to a virgin, even one betrothed to a widow, even to one who waits for her brother-in-law[182]. Even if he heard that his brother had died in the war he then returns and leaves. All those who listen to the Cohen in the front lines return and provide food and water and improve the roads[183].

180 *Deut.* 20:7.

181 He married her in the preliminary ceremony (Note 146) but did not take her into his house..

182 The widow of his childless brother. The surviving brother can marry her based on the dead brother's preliminary marriage; but rabbinically one requires a new preliminary "bespeaking", cf. *Yebamot* 2:1, Note 6. The next sentence shows that the Mishnah does not refer to this rabbinic ceremony.

183 They serve the army in the rear.

הלכה ו: (fol. 22d) אֲשֶׁר אֵרַשׂ אִשָּׁה. אֵין לִי אֶלָּא רוֹבֶה שֶׁנָּשָׂא רִיבָה.¹⁸⁴ מְנַיִין רוֹבֶה שֶׁנָּשָׂא אַלְמָנָה. אַלְמוֹן שֶׁנָּשָׂא רִיבָה. [אַלְמוֹן שֶׁנָּשָׂא אַלְמָנָה]¹⁸⁵ מְנַיִין. תַּלְמוּד לוֹמַר אִשָּׁה. מִכָּל־מָקוֹם. מַה תַּלְמוּד לוֹמַר חֲדָשָׁה. פְּרָט לַמַּחֲזִיר אֶת גְּרוּשָׁתוֹ. אָמַר רִבִּי יוֹסֵי. זֹאת אוֹמְרָת הַנּוֹשֵׂא אֶת הָאַיְילוֹנִית הוֹאִיל וְאֵין מִצְוָה לֵישֵׁב עִמָּהּ אֵינוֹ חוֹזֵר.

Halakhah 6: "Who became betrothed". Not only a young man who married a young woman. From where even a young man who married a widow, a widower who married a young woman, a widower who married a widow? From where? The verse says, "a woman", of any kind. Why does the verse say, "new"? That excludes him who remarries his divorcee¹⁸⁶. Rebbi Yose said, this implies that one who marries a she-ram¹⁸⁷ does not return since he has no religious obligation to live with her.

184 The vocalization is from the Leiden ms. In the Genizah ms., one reads רובא, probably רוֹבָא. The usual rabbinic pronunciation is רִיבָה.

185 From the Genizah fragment; missing in ms. Leiden, *editio princeps*, *Sifry Deut.* 196 and the Babli, 44a.

186 Babli, 44a.

187 A woman without secondary female sex characteristics who is considered sterile; cf. *Yebamot* 1:1, Note 65. Her marriage has rabbinic status only.

(23a line 2) אֲפִילוּ שׁוֹמֶרֶת יָבָם לַחֲמִשָּׁה אַחִים. וְדִכְוָותָהּ אֲפִילוּ בַּיִת אֶחָד לַחֲמִשָּׁה אַחִים. תַּמָּן אֵין כָּל־אֶחָד וְאֶחָד רָאוּי לֵישֵׁב בּוֹ. בְּרַם הָכָא כָּל־אֶחָד וְאֶחָד רָאוּי לְיַיבֵּם. מַה דָּמֵי לָהּ. קִידֵּשׁ אִשָּׁה מֵעַכְשָׁיו לְאַחַר שְׁנֵים עָשָׂר חוֹדֶשׁ וְשָׁלֵם הַזְּמָן בַּמִּלְחָמָה חוֹזֵר וּבָא לוֹ.

Even one who waits for her brother-in-law with five brothers[188]. Similarly, even one house for five brothers[189]? There not one of them would be able to live in it[190]. But here, each one of them is able to marry in levirate[191]. What would be like it? Somebody who preliminarily married a woman from now on in twelve months[192] and the time is up while he is in the war; he returns and goes.

188 This refers to the statement that a man who hears that his childless brother has died, returns from the army to marry his sister-in-law. This implies that *every* brother returns in this case. The Babli agrees, 43b.

189 Why does Mishnah 4 not make a proviso that every man who built a house together with his brothers does return?

190 In the language of the Mishnah, בית always means a one-room house, in which only a single family can live.

191 While only one man can marry the widow, each one could be the one taking her away from the others.

192 The prospective groom delivers an object of value to his bride and stipulates that what she receives and acknowledges at that time shall be valid for preliminary marriage in 12 months' time. This is a valid contract and after 12 months he is preliminarily married and obligated to marry in final form. (If she sleeps with another man during the 12 months it would be criminal if and only if the preliminary husband is alive at the end of the 12 months' period and the contract is activated.)

(fol. 22a) **מִשְׁנָה ז:** וְאֵילּוּ שֶׁאֵינָן חוֹזְרִין. הַבּוֹנֶה בֵּית שַׁעַר אֲכְסַדְרָה מִרְפֶּסֶת הַנּוֹטֵעַ אַרְבָּעָה אִילָנֵי מַאֲכָל וַחֲמִשָּׁה אִילָנֵי סְרָק הַמַּחֲזִיר אֶת גְּרוּשָׁתוֹ אַלְמָנָה

לְכֹהֵן גָּדוֹל גְּרוּשָׁה וַחֲלוּצָה לְכֹהֵן הֶדְיוֹט מַמְזֶרֶת וּנְתִינָה לְיִשְׂרָאֵל בַּת יִשְׂרָאֵל לְמַמְזֵר וּלְנָתִין לֹא הָיָה חוֹזֵר. רִבִּי יְהוּדָה אוֹמֵר אַף הַבּוֹנֶה בַיִת עַל מְכוֹנוֹ לֹא הָיָה חוֹזֵר. רִבִּי לֶעְזָר אוֹמֵר אַף הַבּוֹנֶה בֵית לְבֵינִים בַּשָּׁרוֹן לֹא הָיָה חוֹזֵר.

Mishnah 7: The following do not return: If somebody builds a portico[134], a covered walkway[135], or a verandah, or planted four fruit trees or five futile[156] trees, or remarried his divorcee. [In the case of] a widow for the High Priest, a divorcee or one having received *ḥaliṣah* for an ordinary Cohen, a bastard or Gibeonite girl for an Israel, a Jewish girl for a bastard or a Gibeonite[193], he would not be returning. Rebbi Jehudah says, also he who rebuilt his house on its foundations[194] would not be returning. Rebbi Eleazar said, also one who built a brick house[195] in the Sharon would not return.

193 These unions are all forbidden, cf. *Yebamot*, Mishnah 2:4, Notes 68-73.
194 Rebuilding a collapsed house on the remaining foundations is not the same as building a new house.

195 An adobe house, built from unfired clay bricks, which needs thorough repair before each rainy season.

הלכה ז: תַּנֵּי. רִבִּי יוּדָה אוֹמֵר. אִם חִידֵּשׁ בּוֹ דָּבָר חוֹזֵר. וְאִם לָאו לֹא הָיָה חוֹזֵר. סָדוֹ בָסִיד וּפָתַח בּוֹ חֲלוֹנוֹת לֹא הָיָה חוֹזֵר. הָיָה גָּדוֹל וְעָשָׂאוֹ קָטָן חוֹזֵר. וְאֶחָד וְעָשָׂאוֹ שְׁנַיִם.[196] (fol. 23a)

Halakhah 7: It was stated: Rebbi Jehudah said, if he changed anything, he would be returning. If he whitewashed it or added windows[197], he would not return, if it had been great and he made it small he returns, or one room and he made it two.

196 Reading of the Genizah fragment: הָיָה גָּדוֹל וְעָשָׂאוֹ קָטָן אֶחָד וְעָשָׂאוֹ שְׁתַּיִים.

197 While the original room was not whitewashed or had fewer windows.

(23a line 8) תָּנֵי רְבִּי אֶלְעָזָר אוֹמֵר. אַף אַנְשֵׁי הַשָּׁרוֹן לֹא הָיוּ חוֹזְרִין. שֶׁהֵן מִתְחַדְּשִׁין פַּעֲמַיִם בַּשָּׁבוּעַ. אַף כֹּהֵן גָּדוֹל הָיָה מִתְפַּלֵּל עֲלֵיהֶן בְּיוֹם הַכִּיפּוּרִים שֶׁלֹּא יֵעָשׂוּ בָתֵּיהֶן קִבְרֵיהֶן.

It was stated[198]: Rebbi Eleazar[199] said, also the people from the Sharon did not return since they have to rebuild two times in a Sabbatical period. Also the High Priest was praying for them[200] on the Day of Atonement that their houses should not become their graves.

198 Tosephta 7:19.
199 In the Babli in all cases: R. Eliezer. This reading also in the Tosephta, except the Erfurt ms. The reading of the Yerushalmi is superior since R. Eliezer would have to precede R. Jehudah, his student's son.
200 In the Holiest of Holies. This prayer is mentioned in all liturgical compositions for the *musaf* prayer of the Day of Atonement.

(fol. 22b) **משנה ח:** וְאֵילוּ שֶׁאֵינָן זָזִין מִמְּקוֹמָן. בָּנָה בַיִת וַחֲנָכוֹ נָטַע כֶּרֶם וְחִילְּלוֹ וְהַנּוֹשֵׂא אֶת אֲרוּסָתוֹ הַכּוֹנֵס אֶת יְבִמְתּוֹ שֶׁנֶּאֱמַר נָקִי יִהְיֶה לְבֵיתוֹ. לְבֵיתוֹ זֶה בֵיתוֹ. יִהְיֶה זֶה כַּרְמוֹ. וְשִׂמַּח אֶת אִשְׁתּוֹ זוֹ אִשְׁתּוֹ. אֲשֶׁר לָקַח לְהָבִיא אֶת יְבִמְתּוֹ. וְאֵינָם מְסַפְּקִין מַיִם וּמָזוֹן וְאֵינָן מְתַקְּנִין אֶת הַדְּרָכִים.

Mishnah 8: But the following do not leave at all[201]: If he built a house and inaugurated it, planted a vineyard and redeemed it, he who married his preliminarily married spouse, he who took in his sister-in-law, for it is said[202]: "Free he shall be for his house for one year". "His house", that is his house; "shall be", that is his vineyard; "and give pleasure to his wife", that is his wife; "whom he took", to include his sister-in-law[203]. These do not provide food and water and do not improve the roads.

201 They do not join the army even to the border, even though the verse mentions only the newly-wed.

202 *Deut.* 24:5: If a man take a new wife, he shall not go out with the army, nor should anything be imposed on him; free for his house he shall be for one year and give pleasure to his wife whom he took.

203 The same text in *Sifry Deut.* 271.

(fol. 23a) **הלכה ח**: בָּנָה בַיִת וַחֲנָכוֹ וְלֹא שָׁהָא בְּתוֹכוֹ שְׁנֵים עָשָׂר חוֹדֶשׁ. נָטַע כֶּרֶם וְחִילְּלוֹ וְלֹא שָׁהָא בְּתוֹכוֹ שְׁנֵים עָשָׂר חוֹדֶשׁ. וְכוּלְּהוֹן לְמֵידִין מִן הָאִשָּׁה. מַה אִשָּׁה צְרִיכָה שְׁנֵים עָשָׂר חוֹדֶשׁ אַף כּוּלְּהוֹן צְרִיכִין שְׁנֵים עָשָׂר חוֹדֶשׁ. תַּנֵּי. כָּל־אֵילוּ שֶׁהָיוּ אוֹמְרִין יוֹשְׁבִין בְּטֵילִין בְּתוֹךְ הָעִיר [וְאֵינָן נוֹתְנִין פִּיסֵי הָעִיר][204] וְאֵינָן מְסַפְּקִין מַיִם וּמָזוֹן וְאֵינָן מְתַקְּנִין אֶת הַדְּרָכִים. שֶׁנֶּאֱמַר וְלֹא יַעֲבוֹר עָלָיו לְכָל־דָּבָר. עָלָיו אֵינוֹ עוֹבֵר. אֲבָל עוֹבֵר הוּא עַל אֲחֵרִים.

Halakhah 8: "If he built a house and inaugurated it," but did not use it for twelve months. "If he planted a vineyard and redeemed it," but did not use it for twelve months. And all are derived from the wife: Since the wife needs twelve months, also all of them need twelve months. It was stated: All those mentioned remain unoccupied in town, [do not pay city taxes], and do not provide food and water nor improve the roads, as it is said[202]: "nor should anything be imposed on him," but it may be imposed on others[205].

204 Added from the Genizah fragment. If פיסים are commercial taxes, following Levy's interpretation in his Dictionary, then the statement implies that the exemption from military duty applies only to a person not gainfully employed for a year. Therefore, one should hesitate to declare the absence of this text in the Leiden and Rome mss. an omission. In a Babli source, *Tosephta* 7:24 (Erfurt 23), it is stated that those who return from the front do pay taxes.

203 In the opinon of the Babli, 44a, and *Sifry Deut.* 271, people preliminarily but not finally married, etc. Following the Genizah fragment, this would include people gainfully employed in the first year of their marriage, etc.

(fol. 22b) **משנה ט:** וְיָסְפוּ הַשּׁוֹטְרִים לְדַבֵּר אֶל הָעָם וְאָמְרוּ מִי הָאִישׁ הַיָּרֵא וְרַךְ הַלֵּבָב יֵלֵךְ וְיָשׁוּב לְבֵיתוֹ. רִבִּי עֲקִיבָה אוֹמֵר הַיָּרֵא וְרַךְ הַלֵּבָב כִּשְׁמוּעוֹ שֶׁאֵינוֹ יָכוֹל לַעֲמוֹד בְּקִישְׁרֵי[206] הַמִּלְחָמָה וְלִרְאוֹת חֶרֶב שְׁלוּפָה. רִבִּי יוֹסֵי הַגְּלִילִי אוֹמֵר הַיָּרֵא וְרַךְ הַלֵּבָב זֶה שֶׁהוּא מִתְיָרֵא מִן הָעֲבֵירוֹת שֶׁבְּיָדוֹ לְפִיכָךְ תָּלַת לוֹ הַתּוֹרָה אֶת כָּל־אֵילוּ שֶׁיַּחֲזוֹר בִּגְלָלָן. רִבִּי יוֹסֵי אוֹמֵר אַלְמָנָה לְכֹהֵן גָּדוֹל גְּרוּשָׁה וַחֲלוּצָה לְכֹהֵן הֶדְיוֹט מַמְזֶרֶת וּנְתִינָה לְיִשְׂרָאֵל בַּת יִשְׂרָאֵל לְמַמְזֵר וּלְנָתִין הֲרֵי הוּא הַיָּרֵא וְרַךְ הַלֵּבָב.

Mishnah 9: "The policemen shall add and say to the people: 'Who is the man fearful and faint-hearted, let him go and return to his house. Rebbi Aqiba says, "fearful and faint-hearted" in its simple meaning, that he cannot stand in military engagements and see a drawn sword. Rebbi Yose the Galilean says, "fearful and faint-hearted" is one who is fearful because of his sins; therefore the Torah appended him to all of these[207] that he should return because of them[208]. Rebbi Yose said, a widow for the High Priest, a divorcee or one having received *halîṣah* for an ordinary Cohen, a bastard or Gibeonite girl for an Israel, a Jewish girl for a bastard or a Gibeonite[193], that is the "fearful and faint-hearted"[209].

206 Reading of the Rome ms., with all Mishnah mss. Leiden ms. and *editio princeps*: קישוי "the difficulty (of war)"; but in the Halakhah the text agrees with the Mishnah mss.

207 The person betrothed or who had built, etc.

208 That only his officer but not the public would know that he returns as a coward but not as one of the legitimate cases.

In *Sifry Deut.* 197, R. Yose is quoted to exclude anyone over 40 years old. But in Tosephta 7:22, and *Midrash Tannaïm Deut.* 20:8, the reading is similar to the Mishnah.

209 The Babli considers the cases quoted by R. Yose the Tanna as examples of biblical prohibitions and, therefore, holds that R. Yose the Galilean also recognizes the right of return for one who has overstepped rabbinic decrees. There is no hint in the Yerushalmi that R. Yose includes anything except forbidden but valid marriages.

(fol. 23a) **הלכה ט**: כְּתִיב וְיָסְפוּ הַשּׁוֹטְרִים. אֵין לָשׁוֹן זֶה וְיָסְפוּ אֶלָּא לָשׁוֹן תּוֹסֶפֶת. כְּאֵינַשׁ דְּאָמַר. מוֹסִיף אֲנִי עַל דִּבְרֵי רַבִּי. תַּנֵּי. הָאַחֲרוֹנִים מִן הַתּוֹסֶפֶת. אָמַר רִבִּי יוֹסֵי. תְּרֵין תַּנָּיִין אִינּוּן. מָאן דְּאָמַר. מוֹסִיף אֲנִי עַל דִּבְרֵי רַבִּי. אֶחָד הָרִאשׁוֹנִים וְאֶחָד הָאַחֲרוֹנִים אֲמָרָן הוּא אֲמָרָן רַבּוֹ. מָאן דְּאָמַר. הָאַחֲרוֹנִים מִן הַתּוֹסֶפֶת. הָרִאשׁוֹנִים אֲמָרוֹ הוּא אֲמָרוֹ רַבּוֹ. וְהָאַחֲרוֹנִים אֲמָרוֹ הוּא וְלֹא אֲמָרוֹ רַבּוֹ. אָמַר רִבִּי מָנָא. חַד תַּנָּיֵי הוּא. רָאשׁוֹנִים אֲמָרָן הוּא אֲמָרָן רַבּוֹ. הָאַחֲרוֹנִים אֲמָרָן הוּא לֹא אֲמָרָן רַבּוֹ. מַתְנִיתָא פְּלִיגָא עַל רִבִּי יוֹסֵי. שׁוֹמֵעַ פָּרָשָׁה מִפִּי כֹהֵן וְאוֹמְרָהּ לָעָם בְּכָל־לָשׁוֹן. וְסוֹפָא פְּלִיגָא עַל רִבִּי מָנָא. עוֹד דָּבָר אֶחָד הָיָה מוֹסִיף. מְשָׁלוֹ. אֵין תֵּימַר כֵּן. אֲפִילוּ עַל דְּרִבִּי יוֹסֵי לֵית הוּא פְּלִיגָא. דְּתַנֵּי. הָרִאשׁוֹנִים אֲמָרָן הוּא אֲמָרָן רַבּוֹ. הָאַחֲרוֹנִים אֲמָרָן הוּא לֹא אֲמָרָן רַבּוֹ.

Halakhah 9: It is written: "The policemen shall add." This expression "shall add" only means an addition[210]. Like a man who says, I am adding to the words of my teacher. It was stated: The latter [words] are additions. Rebbi Yose said, there are two Tannaïm[211]. He who said, "I am adding to the words of my teacher," both the first[212] and the later declarations both he and his teacher said[213]. He who said, the later ones are additions, the first [declarations] both he and his teacher said, but the later ones he said but not his teacher. Rebbi Mana said, there is only one Tanna. The first [declarations] both he and his teacher said, but the later ones he said but not his teacher. A *baraita* disagrees with Rebbi Yose: He hears a sentence from the Cohen and tells it to the people in all languages[214]. But its end disagrees with Rebbi Mana: He adds a final word of his own[215]. If you say so, it does not disagree at all with Rebbi Yose, as it was stated: The first [declarations] both he and his teacher said, but the later ones he said but not his teacher[216].

210 The last declarations are not said on the authority of the Cohen.

211 The statement explained in Note 210 is also a *baraita*, different from the one quoted last.

212 The first declarations are those attributed to the Cohen, the later ones those put in the mouth of the policemen.

213 The addition is the policemen's explanation in the vernacular.

214 This follows only the first Tanna recognized by R. Yose (the Amora, colleague of R. Mana II).

215 But any text reported in the verses was first spoken by the Cohen.

216 One is free to interpret "the later ones" either as the declaration of the policemen spelled out in the verse or as the additions after the official text.

(23a line 27) וְתַנֵּי. כּוּלְּהוֹן צְרִיכִין לְהָבִיא רְאָיָה לְדִבְרֵיהֶן חוּץ מִזֶּה שֶׁעֵדָיו עִמּוֹ. וְאָתְיָיא כְּמָאן דְּאָמַר. שֶׁאֵינוֹ יָכוֹל לַעֲמוֹד בְּקִישְׁרֵי הַמִּלְחָמוֹת [וְלִרְאוֹת]²¹⁷ (וְ)חֶרֶב שְׁלוּפָה. בְּרַם כְּמָאן דָּמַר. שֶׁהוּא מִתְיָירֵא מִן הָעֲבֵירוֹת שֶׁבְּיָדוֹ עוֹד הוּא צָרִיךְ לְהָבִיא רְאָיָיה. לְפִיכָךְ תָּלַת לוֹ הַתּוֹרָה אֶת כָּל־אֵילּוּ שֶׁיַּחֲזוֹר בִּגְלָלָן. שֶׁלֹּא לְפַרְסֵם אֶת הַחַטָּאִים. וְאָתְיָיא כַּיי דָּמַר רִבִּי לֵוִי בְּשֵׁם רִבִּי שִׁמְעוֹן בֶּן לָקִישׁ. בִּמְקוֹם אֲשֶׁר תִּשָּׁחֵט הָעוֹלָה תִּשָּׁחֵט הַחַטָּאת לִפְנֵי יי. שֶׁלֹּא לְפַרְסֵם אֶת הַחַטָּאִים.

Also, it was stated²¹⁸: They all have to bring proof except from this one whose witnesses are with him²¹⁹. This follows him who said that he cannot stand in military engagements and see a drawn sword. But following him who says that he is one who is fearful because of his sins, he has to bring proof. Therefore the Torah appended him to all of these²⁰⁷ that he should return because of them²⁰⁸, not to publicize the sinners. This comes as Rebbi Levi said in the name of Rebbi Simeon ben Laqish²²⁰: ²²¹"At the place where the elevation offering is being slaughtered, the purification offering is being slaughtered before the Eternal," not to publicize the sinners²²².

217 ולראות חרב שלופה reading of the Rome and Genizah mss. The Leiden ms. reads וחרב שלופה.	statement by R. Johanan in the name of R. Simeon ben Iohai. Cf. *Yebamot* 8:3, Note 198.
218 *Sifry Deut.* 192.	221 Lev. 6:18.
219 The military instructors realize that they are better off without the coward. But all others have to prove their case.	222 Even though elevation offerings are male and purification offerings female, the difference can be seen only by close inspection, so also the sinner could be detected only by inquiry.
220 In the Babli, 32b, a similar	

(fol. 22b) **משנה י:** וְהָיָה כְּכַלּוֹת הַשּׁוֹטְרִים לְדַבֵּר אֶל הָעָם וּפָקְדוּ שָׂרֵי צְבָאוֹת בְּרֹאשׁ הָעָם. בַּעֲקֵיבוֹ שֶׁלָּעָם מַעֲמִידִין זְקִיפִים לִפְנֵיהֶם וַאֲחֵרִים מֵאֲחוֹרֵיהֶם וְכַשִּׁילִים שֶׁלְבַּרְזֶל בִּידֵיהֶן וְכָל־הַמְבַקֵּשׁ לַחֲזוֹר הָרְשׁוּת בִּידֵיהֶן לְקַפֵּחַ אֶת שׁוֹקָיו שֶׁתְּחִילַת נְפִילָה נִיסָה שֶׁנֶּאֱמַר נָס יִשְׂרָאֵל לִפְנֵי פְלִשְׁתִּים וְגַם מַגֵּיפָה גְדוֹלָה הָיְתָה בָעָם. וּלְהַלָּן הוּא אוֹמֵר וַיָּנוּסוּ אַנְשֵׁי יִשְׂרָאֵל לִפְנֵי פְלִשְׁתִּים וַיִּפְּלוּ חֲלָלִים בְּהַר הַגִּלְבּוֹעַ. בַּמֶּה דְבָרִים אֲמוּרִים בְּמִלְחֶמֶת הָרְשׁוּת אֲבָל בְּמִלְחֶמֶת מִצְוָה הַכֹּל יוֹצְאִין אֲפִילוּ חָתָן מֵחֶדְרוֹ וְכַלָּה מֵחוּפָּתָהּ. אָמַר רִבִּי יְהוּדָה בַּמֶּה דְבָרִים אֲמוּרִים בְּמִלְחֶמֶת מִצְוָה אֲבָל בְּמִלְחֶמֶת חוֹבָה הַכֹּל יוֹצְאִין אֲפִילוּ חָתָן מֵחֶדְרוֹ וְכַלָּה מֵחוּפָּתָהּ.

Mishnah 10: "When the policemen finish to speak to the people, the officers will have taken up position at the head of the people.[223]" Behind the people one puts up people with backups armed with iron axes and they have permission to break the legs of anyone who desires to abandon his post since flight is the start of falling, as it is said[224]: "Israel fled from before the Philistines and a great plague was among the people." Further on it says[225], "the men of Israel fled from before the Philistines and slain fell on Mount Gilboa." About what have these things be said[226]? About a war of choice, but in a war of obligation[227] everybody goes out, even a groom from his room and a bride from her bridal chamber[228]. Rebbi Jehudah said, about what have these things been said? About a war of obligation, but in a war of duty everybody goes out, even a groom from his room and a bride from her bridal chamber.

223 *Deut.* 20:9.
224 *1S.* 4:17.
225 *1S.* 31:1.
226 The preceding Mishnaiot which gave permission to a number of people to be excused from military service.

227 The definitions are a matter of discussion in the Halakhah.
228 One might assume that the groom's room is the bride's bridal chamber. The expression is from *Joel* 2:16.

הלכה י: (fol. 23a) כְּתִיב וְהָיָה כְּכַלּוֹת הַשּׁוֹטְרִים לְדַבֵּר אֶל הָעָם וּפָקְדוּ שָׂרֵי צְבָאוֹת בְּרֹאשׁ הָעָם. אֵין לִי אֶלָּא בְּרֹאשׁ הָעָם. בְּסוֹף הָעָם מְנַיִין. תַּלְמוּד לוֹמַר פָּקְדוּ וּפָקְדוּ. עַד כְּדוֹן כְּרִבִּי עֲקִיבָה. כְּרִבִּי יִשְׁמָעֵאל. רִבִּי יִשְׁמָעֵאל כְּרִבִּי מֵאִיר. דְּרִבִּי מֵאִיר צָוַח לְסוֹפֵי דְחַבְלָא רֵישֵׁיהּ.

It is written: "When the policemen finish to speak to the people, the officers will have taken up position at the head of the people." Not only in front of the people, from where also behind the people? The verse says, "take up position", "*and* take up position"[229]. That follows Rebbi Aqiba. Following Rebbi Ismael? Rebbi Ismael follows Rebbi Meïr, since Rebbi Meïr used to call the end of a rope its head.

229 R. Aqiba considers every *vaw* at the beginning of a word as indication of an addition, even in a case of a *vaw* *conversive* when an imperative would need the same number of letters.

(23a line 38) אָמַר רִבִּי מֵאִיר. כְּתִיב הֶחָכָם עֵינָיו בְּרֹאשׁוֹ. הַכְּסִיל בַּמֶּה. בְּרַגְלָיו. אָמַר רִבִּי אַבָּא מָרִי. הֶחָכָם עַד שֶׁהוּא בְּרֹאשׁוֹ שֶׁלְּדָבָר הוּא יוֹדֵעַ מַה שֶּׁבְּסוֹפוֹ. נַד גְּדוּד יְגוּדֶנּוּ. גַּיְיסָא אָתֵי מְנַיְיסַתֵּיהּ וְהוּא מְנַיֵּיס לֵיהּ.

Rebbi Meïr said: It is written[230], "the wise man's eyes are in his head." The stupid one's are where? In his legs[231]. Rebbi Abba Mari said, the wise man knows what will be the final outcome when he starts something. "Gad, a troop will gang up on him[232]." A troop comes to rob him, and he robs them.

230 *Eccl.* 2:14.

231 This parallels the German saying that one must have in one's legs what he does not have in his head.

232 *Gen.* 49:19. The reference naturally is to the entire verse, "Gad, a troop will gang up on him but he will catch their heel."

(23a line 41) כֵּינֵי מַתְנִיתָא. שֶׁתְּחִילַת נְפִילָה נִיסָה.

So is the Mishnah: "Since flight is the start of falling[233]".

233 This is the text of the Mishnah in the Leiden ms., but not in the Rome ms. nor in the Babli or the overwhelming majority of Mishnah mss. The original text reads שֶׁתְּחִילַת נִיסָה נְפִילָה "since falling is the start of flight." In the Babli, 44b, the text is corrected as it is here.

(23a line 41) אָמַר רִבִּי יוֹחָנָן מַשְׁמָעוּת בֵּינֵיהֶן. רִבִּי יְהוּדָה הָיָה קוֹרֵא לְמִלְחֶמֶת הָרְשׁוּת מִלְחֶמֶת מִצְוָה. אֲבָל בְּמִלְחֶמֶת חוֹבָה הַכֹּל יוֹצֵא אֲפִילוּ חָתָן מֵחֶדְרוֹ וְכַלָּה מֵחוּפָּתָהּ. אָמַר רַב חִסְדָּא. מַחֲלוֹקֶת בֵּינֵיהוֹן. רַבָּנִין אָמְרִין. מִלְחֶמֶת מִצְוָה זוֹ מִלְחֶמֶת דָּוִד. מִלְחֶמֶת חוֹבָה זוֹ מִלְחֶמֶת יְהוֹשֻׁעַ. רִבִּי יְהוּדָה הָיָה קוֹרֵא מִלְחֶמֶת [מִצְוָה][234] כְּגוֹן אֲנָן דְּאָזְלִין עֲלֵיהוֹן. מִלְחֶמֶת חוֹבָה כְּגוֹן דְּאָתְיָין אִינּוּן עֲלֵינָן. כְּתִיב וְהַמֶּלֶךְ אָסָא הִשְׁמִיעַ אֶת כָּל־יְהוּדָה אֵין נָקִי. מַהוּ אֵין נָקִי. רִבִּי סִימוֹן וְרַבָּנִין. רִבִּי סִימוֹן אָמַר. אֵין נָקִי לְבֵיתוֹ שָׁעָה אַחַת. וְרַבָּנִין אָמְרִין. לֵית רַבִּי בְּיַרְבִּי.

Rebbi Joḥanan said, usage is between them; Rebbi Jehudah called a war of choice a war of obligation. "But in a war of duty everybody goes out, even a groom from his room and a bride from her bridal chamber." Rav

Hisda said[235], they disagree. The rabbis say, a war of obligation was the war of David. A war of duty was the war of Joshua. Rebbi Jehudah called it a war of obligation if we went out against them[236]; a war of duty if they attacked us. It is written: "King Asa proclaimed in all of Jehudah, nobody is free[237]". What means "nobody is free"? Rebbi Simon and the rabbis. Rebbi Simon said, nobody is free to return home even for one hour[238]. But the rabbis say, there is no exemption for a scholar, son of a scholar[239].

234 From the Rome and Geniza mss., missing in the Leiden ms.
235 In the Babli, 44b, this is the opinion of Rav Hisda's son-in-law Rava.
236 In the Babli, this is restricted to a preventive attack.
237 *1K.* 15:22.
238 He abolished the exemption of the newlywed, *Deut.* 24:5.
239 Who claim a general exemption from public works. In the opinion of the Babli, 10a, he abolished the exemptions both of the newlywed and of the scholar.

עגלה ערופה פרק תשיעי

(fol. 23a) **משנה א:** עֶגְלָה עֲרוּפָה בִּלְשׁוֹן הַקּוֹדֶשׁ. שֶׁנֶּאֱמַר כִּי יִמָּצֵא חָלָל בָּאֲדָמָה וְגוֹ׳. וְיָצְאוּ זְקֵנֶיךָ וְשׁוֹפְטֶיךָ. שְׁלֹשָׁה מִבֵּית דִּין הַגָּדוֹל שֶׁבִּירוּשָׁלֵם הָיוּ יוֹצְאִין. רִבִּי יְהוּדָה אוֹמֵר חֲמִשָּׁה שֶׁנֶּאֱמַר זְקֵנֶיךָ שְׁנַיִם וְשׁוֹפְטֶיךָ שְׁנַיִם וְאֵין בֵּית דִּין שָׁקוּל מוֹסִיפִין עֲלֵיהֶן עוֹד אֶחָד.

Mishnah 1: [The portion of] the calf whose neck was broken[1], in the holy language. For it is said[2]: "If a murder victim be found on the land, etc. [3]Then your Elders and judges should go out." Three from the High Court in Jerusalem had to go out[4]. Rebbi Jehudah says five, since it is written "your Elders", two, "and your judges", two[5]. Since no court may have an even number of members[6], one adds another one.

1 To atone for an unsolved murder; cf. Chapter 7:2, Note 36.

2 *Deut.* 21:1.

3 *Deut.* 21:2.

4 In Mishnah *Sanhedrin* 1:3 and *Sifry Deut*, 205, this opinion is ascribed to R. Simeon.

5 Since a plural means at least two, an unspecified plural always means 2. (Cf. H. Guggenheimer, *Logical Problems in Jewish Tradition*, in: Confrontations with Judaism, P. Longworth, ed., London 1966; pp. 174-175).

6 So that an immediate verdict can be rendered in all cases that come before the court.

(fol. 23b) **הלכה א:** עֶגְלָה עֲרוּפָה כול׳. לֹא מִסְתַּבְּרָא דְלָא וְעָנוּ וְאָמְרוּ בָּא לְהַתְחִיל מִתְּחִילַת הַפָּרָשָׁה. כִּי יִמָּצֵא. לֹא בְשָׁעָה שֶׁהֵן מְצוּיִין. כִּי יִמָּצֵא. לֹא שֶׁתְּהֵא חוֹזֵר וּמְצוּתֵת עָלָיו. כִּי יִמָּצֵא. אֵין מְצִיאָה בְּכָל־מָקוֹם אֶלָּא בְעֵדִים.

לֹא נוֹדַע מִי הִכָּהוּ. הָא אִם נוֹדַע מִי הִכָּהוּ אֲפִילוּ עֶבֶד אֲפִילוּ שִׁפְחָה לֹא הָיוּ עוֹרְפִין. [תַּמָּן אַתְּ אָמַר. אֲפִילוּ עֶבֶד אֲפִילוּ שִׁפְחָה לֹא הָיוּ עוֹרְפִין][7] וָכָא אַתְּ אָמַר אָכֵין. כָּאן לָהוֹרֵג כָּאן לַנֶּהֱרָג. וְדָא דְאַתְּ אָמַר אֲפִילוּ עֶבֶד אֲפִילוּ שִׁפְחָה לֹא הָיוּ עוֹרְפִין. בְּאוֹתָן שֶׁאָמְרוּ. אִם רוֹאִין אָנוּ אוֹתוֹ מַכִּירִין אָנוּ אוֹתוֹ. אֲבָל בְּאוֹתָן שֶׁאָמְרוּ. אִם רוֹאִין אָנוּ אוֹתוֹ אֵין אָנוּ מַכִּירִין אוֹתוֹ. [לֹא][8] הָיוּ עוֹרְפִין. דִּכְתִיב וְעֵינֵינוּ לֹא רָאוּ. וַהֲרֵי רָאוּ. [9]מִכָּל־מָקוֹם.

Halakhah 1: "The calf whose neck was broken," etc. It is reasonable only from "they begin and say"[10]. He starts from the beginning of the paragraph[11]. "If there be found,[2]" not in a time when they are frequent[12]. "If there be found," not that you have to search[13]. "If there be found," finding anywhere is only by witnesses[14]. "It is not known who killed him", therefore if it was known, even by a male or female slave, one did not break the neck[15]. There, you say, if it was known, even by a male or female slave, one did not break the neck, and here, you say so? One for the killer, one for the victim[16]. [17]And that which you say that if it was known, even by a male or female slave, one did not break the neck, [is it only] if they say that if we see him we will be able to identify him. Even those who say, if we see him we will not be able to identify him, one did not break the neck since it is written: "Our eyes did not see." But somebody did see!

7 From the Rome and Genizah mss., missing in Leiden ms. and *editio princeps*.

8 From the Genizah ms., missing in Rome and Leiden mss. and *editio princeps*.

9 Reading of the Genizah ms., in Rome and Leiden mss. here בכל מקום but correctly in the parallel *Roš Haššanah* 3:1.

10 This refers to the discussion which shows that the Levites and the Elders have to recite the verses as written, Chapter 7:2, Notes 43 ff.

11   The Tanna of the Mishnah quotes from v. 1 when the recitation starts only at v. 9, to explain that the rules of the ceremony have to be deduced from the earlier verses.

12   Cf. Mishnah 9. The same statement in *Sifry Deut.* 205.

13   If the body of a missing person is found after a search, this does not qualify for the ceremony.

14   The High Court in Jerusalem will be involved only if two witnesses of good character testify that the corpse was found.

15   To avoid the ceremony, even a single witness of questionable character is sufficient whose testimony could not lead to a conviction.

16   As explained before, to aid the hunt for the killer, one witness is enough. To involve the High Court for the victim, two witnesses are needed.

17   This and the next paragraph are also in *Roš Haššanah* 3:1 (58c l. 73), partially in *Sanhedrin* 1:2 (18c l. 17).

(23b, line 66) בֵּית דִּין [שֶׁרָאוּ] אֶת הַהוֹרֵג. אִית תַּנָּיֵי תַנֵּי. יַעַמְדוּ שְׁנַיִם וְיָעִידוּ לִפְנֵיהֶם. אִית תַּנָּיֵי תַנֵּי. יַעַמְדוּ כוּלָּן וְיָעִידוּ בְּמָקוֹם אֶחָד. רִבִּי יְהוּדָה בֶּן פָּזִי בְּשֵׁם רִבִּי זְעִירָא. כְּשֵׁם שֶׁהֵן חֲלוּקִין כָּאן כָּךְ הֵן חֲלוּקִים בְּעֵדוּת הַחוֹדֶשׁ.

If the court saw the killer. Some Tannaïm state, two of them should stand up and testify before them. There are Tannaïm who state that they all should go and testify at another place[18]. Rebbi Jehudah ben Pazi in the name of Rebbi Ze'ira: As they differ here, so they differ about testimony for the New Moon[19].

18   The Babli, *Roš Haššanah* 25b, *Baba qama* 90b, makes it clear that a judge who is an accidental witness is by that fact disqualified as judge in the case. There, the *baraitot* are interpreted to mean that R. Tarphon holds that a judge can appear as witness before his colleagues, but R. Aqiba states that a judge as witness has to appear before a different court.

19   And in effect in all court proceedings based on biblical standards. The Babli, Ketubot 21b, relaxes these standards in rabbinic cases involving money; accepting that a judge from his own knowledge may recognize a signature on a contract.

(23b, line 66) רִבִּי יוּדָה בַּר פָּזִי בְשֵׁם רִבִּי זְעִירָא. [חָלָל וְלֹא מְפַרְפֵּר.]²⁰ חָלָל וְלֹא מְפַרְכֵּס. רָאוּהוּ מְפַרְפֵּר כָּן וּבָא לְאַחַר זְמָן וְלֹא מְצָאוֹ. אֲנִי אוֹמֵר. נַעֲשׂוּ לוֹ נִיסִים [וְחָיָיה].²¹ רָאוּהוּ מְפַרְכֵּס כָּן וּבָא לְאַחַר זְמָן וּמְצָאוֹ מֵת בְּמָקוֹם אַחֵר. מוֹדְדִין מִמָּקוֹם שֶׁנִּמְצָא. אֲשֶׁר יי אֱלֹהֶיךָ נוֹתֵן לָךְ. פְּרָט לְחוּצָה לָאָרֶץ. לְרִשְׁתָּהּ. פְּרָט לִירוּשָׁלֵם שֶׁהִיא לְכָל־הַשְּׁבָטִים. וּכְרִבִּי יִשְׁמָעֵאל. דְּרִבִּי יִשְׁמָעֵאל אָמַר. כָּל־בִּיאוֹת שֶׁנֶּאֱמְרוּ בַּתּוֹרָה לְאַחַר אַרְבַּע עֶשְׂרֵה שָׁנָה נֶאֱמְרוּ. שֶׁבַע שֶׁכִּיבְּשׁוּ וְשֶׁבַע שֶׁחִילְּקוּ. אָמַר רִבִּי פִינְחָס בְּירִבִּי בּוּן.²² נֹאמַר כָּל־אוֹתָן אַרְבַּע עֶשְׂרֵה שָׁנָה [לֹא הָיוּ עוֹרְפִים. דִּכְתִיב כִּי יִמָּצֵא. וְלֹא בְשָׁעָה שֶׁהֵן מְצוּיִין. וְכָל־אוֹתָן אַרְבַּע עֶשְׂרֵה שָׁנָה מְצוּיִים]²³ הָיוּ.

Rebbi Jehudah bar Pazi in the name of Rebbi Ze'ira: "A slain one", not one in convulsions; "a slain one", not one in death-throes[24]. If one saw him in convulsions and after some time he came back and did not find him, I say that a miracle occurred and he survived. If one saw him in death-throes here and then found him at another place, one measures from the place where he was found. "Which the Eternal, your God, is giving to you," this excludes places outside the Land. "To inherit it," this excludes Jerusalem[25] which belongs to all tribes, and following Rebbi Ismael. For Rebbi Ismael said, any "comings" which were said in the Torah mean after fourteen years, seven during which they conquered and seven during which they distributed[26]. Rebbi Phineas ben Rebbi Abun said, we may say that all these fourteen years they were not breaking the neck, for it is written "if there be found,[2]" not in a time when they are frequent[12]. And all these fourteen years they were frequent[23].

20 From the Genizah ms., missing in the other two mss.

21 From the Genizah ms. and *editio princeps*. In Leiden ms. והיה, an easily corrected mistake.

22 In the Genizah ms.: בירבי סימון It

is difficult to decide between the readings since neither name appears a second time.

23 From the Genizah ms. In the Leiden ms. and *editio princeps*: נאמר כָּל־אוֹתָן אַרְבַּע עֶשְׂרֵה שָׁנָה מְצוּיָינִים הָיוּ "we may say, all these fourteen years they were identified" (the case simply never happened). There are no conclusive arguments for or against either reading.

24 These are tannaïtic statements in the Babli, 45b, and *Sifry Deut*. 205.

25 The same argument in the Babli, 45b, where however one accepts the possibility of an opposing opinion. For the details of the argument for the exclusion of Jerusalem from the rules of inheritance, cf. *Orlah* 1:2, Note 64.

26 Cf. Chapter 7, Note 80; in detail *Orlah* 1:2, Note 56 and the sources mentioned there; Babli *Qiddušin* 37a-38a; *Seder 'Olam* Chapter 11.

תַּנֵּי. כֵּיצַד הָיוּ עוֹשִׂין. שְׁלוּחֵי בֵית דִּין יוֹצְאִין וּמְלַקְּטִין אֶת סִימָנָיו (23c, line 7) וְקוֹבְרִים‎[27] אוֹתוֹ. וּמְצַיְּינִין עַל קִבְרוֹ כְּדֵי שֶׁיֵּצְאוּ בֵית דִּין מִלִּשְׁכַּת הַגָּזִית וְיָמוֹדוּ.

It was stated: How is it done? The emissaries of the court[28] come out, collect all his signs and bury him. They put up a marker on his grave so that the court who come from the stone hall[29] may measure.

27 From the Genizah ms. Leiden: ומובריו "they move him"; a reading which seems quite impossible since an unknown corpse has to be buried at the place it was found. In the Tosephta, 9:1(both versions), וחופרין וקוברין "they dig and bury". *Editio princeps* (from the first hand of the Leiden ms): ומוכרין "and they sell", certainly an impossible reading.

28 The local court which has to conduct the burial of persons without local relatives.

29 The place of residence of the High Court in Jerusalem.

מְנַיִין לְצִיּוּן. רִבִּי בְּרֶכְיָה וְרִבִּי יַעֲקֹב בַּר בַּת יַעֲקֹב בְּשֵׁם רִבִּי חוֹנְיָיא (23c, line 9) דִּבְרַת חַוְורָן. רִבִּי יוֹסֵי אָמַר לָהּ רִבִּי יַעֲקֹב בַּר אָחָא בְּשֵׁם רִבִּי חוֹנְיָא דִּבְרַת חַוְורָן. רִבִּי חִזְקִיָּה רִבִּי עוּזִיאֵל בְּרֵיהּ דְּרִבִּי חוֹנְיָה דִּבְרַת חַוְורָן בְּשֵׁם רִבִּי

חוֹנְיָיא דְּבָרַת־חַוְרָן וְטָמֵא טָמֵא יִקְרָא. כְּדֵי שֶׁתְּהֵא טוּמְאָה קוֹרָא לָךְ בְּפִיהָ וְהִיא אוֹמֶרֶת לָךְ. פְּרוֹשׁ. רִבִּי אִילָא בְּשֵׁם רִבִּי שְׁמוּאֵל בַּר נַחְמָן. וְעָבְרוּ הָעוֹבְרִים בָּאָרֶץ וְרָאָה עֶצֶם. מִכָּן שֶׁמְּצַיְּינִין עַל הָעֲצָמוֹת. אָדָם מִכָּן שֶׁמְּצַיְּינִין עַל הַשִּׁיזְרָה וְעַל הַגּוּלְגּוֹלֶת. וּבָנָה. מִכָּן שֶׁמְּצַיְּינִים עַל אֶבֶן קְבוּעָה. אִם אוֹמֵר אַתְּ עַל גַּבֵּי אֶבֶן תְּלוּשָׁה. אַף הִיא הוֹלֶכֶת וּמְטַמָּא בְּמָקוֹם אַחֵר. אֶצְלוֹ. בְּמָקוֹם טָהֳרָה. צִיּוּן. מִכָּן לְצִיּוּן.

[30] From where about marks? Rebbi Berekhiah, Rebbi Jacob the son of the daughter of Jacob, in the name of Rebbi Onias from Hauran. Rebbi Yose said it in the name of Rebbi Jacob bar Aḥa in the name of Rebbi Onias from Hauran. Rebbi Ḥizqiah, Rebbi Uziel the son of Rebbi Onias from Hauran in the name of Rebbi Onias from Hauran (*Lev.* 13:45): "impure, impure, he shall call out;" the impurity itself has to call out and say to you: go away! Rebbi Hila in the name of Rebbi Samuel bar Naḥman (*Ez.* 39:15): "The emissaries shall crisscross the land; if one sees a bone", from here that one makes markers for bones. *A human*, from here that one makes markers for spine and skull. *He builds*, from here that one makes markers on fixed stones. If you say on loose stones, it would move and make other places impure. *Near it*, on a place of purity. *A marker*, from here the marks.

(23c, line 18) מָצָא אֶבֶן אַחַת מְצוּיֶּינֶת. אַף עַל פִּי שֶׁאֵין מְקַיְּימִין כֵּן. הַמַּאֲהִיל עָלֶיהָ טָמֵא. אֲנִי אוֹמֵר מֵת קַמְצוּץ הָיָה נָתוּן תַּחְתֶּיהָ. הָיוּ שְׁתַּיִם. הַמַּאֲהִיל עֲלֵיהֶן טָהוֹר. בֵּינֵיהֶן טָמֵא. הָיָה חָרוּשׁ בֵּנְתַיִם. הֲרֵי הֵן כִּיחִידִיּוֹת. בֵּינֵיהֶן טָהוֹר. וּסְבִיבוֹתֵיהֶן טָמֵא.

[31] If one found a single marked stone, even though one should not keep it so, if somebody forms a tent over it he is impure; I say a compressed corpse was under it. If there were two, he who forms a tent over any one

of them is pure; between them he is impure. If between them was a ploughed strip they are single stones, between them the area is pure and around them impure.

(23c, line 21) תַּנֵּי. אֵין מְצַיְינִין עַל הַבָּשָׂר שֶׁמָּא נִיתְאַכֵּל הַבָּשָׂר. רִבִּי יוּסְטָא בַּר שׁוּנֵם בְּעָא קוֹמֵי רִבִּי מָנָא. וְלֹא נִמְצָא מְטַמֵּא טַהֲרוֹת לְמַפְרֵעַ. אָמַר לֵיהּ. מוּטָב שֶׁיִּתְקַלְקְלוּ בּוֹ לְשָׁעָה וְלֹא יִתְקַלְקְלוּ בּוֹ לְעוֹלָם.

It was stated[31]: One does not mark flesh, for perhaps it will decompose. Rebbi Justus bar Shunem asked before Rebbi Mana: Will that not cause pure foods to be retroactively made impure? He said to him, it is better that these should become unusable for a limited time than that [the earth] become unusable forever.

30 This and the following two paragraphs are also in *Ma'aser Šeni* 5:1, explained there in Notes 14-25; *Šeqalim* 1:1, fol. 46a; *Mo'ed Qaṭan* 1:1, fol. 80b/c. Similar arguments, in the name of different authorities, in Babli *Mo'ed Qaṭan* 5a.

31 Tosephta *Šeqalim* 1:5. The Tosephta follows the other Yerushalmi sources which read "pure" in the first sentence, against the mss. here and the Babli, *Moëd Qaṭan* 6a, which read "impure".

(23c, line 24) תַּמָּן תַּנִּינָן. סְמִיכַת זְקֵנִים וַעֲרִיפַת הָעֶגְלָה בִּשְׁלֹשָׁה. דִּבְרֵי רִבִּי שִׁמְעוֹן. רִבִּי יְהוּדָה אוֹמֵר. בַּחֲמִשָּׁה. מַה טַעֲמָא דְּרִבִּי שִׁמְעוֹן. וְסָמְכוּ [זִקְנֵי][32] שְׁנַיִם. אֵין בֵּית דִּין שָׁקוּל. מוֹסִיפִין עֲלֵיהֶן עוֹד אֶחָד. הֲרֵי שְׁלֹשָׁה. מַה טַעֲמָא דְּרִבִּי יְהוּדָה. וְסָמְכוּ שְׁנַיִם. זִקְנֵי שְׁנַיִם. אֵין בֵּית דִּין שָׁקוּל. מוֹסִיפִין עֲלֵיהֶן עוֹד אֶחָד. הֲרֵי חֲמִשָּׁה. וּבְעֶגְלָה עֲרוּפָה [מַה טַעֲמָא דְּרִבִּי שִׁמְעוֹן. זְקֵנֶיךָ שׁוֹפְטֶיךָ שְׁנַיִם אֵין בֵּית דִּין שָׁקוּל. מוֹסִיפִין עֲלֵיהֶן עוֹד אֶחָד. הֲרֵי שְׁלֹשָׁה. מַה טַעֲמָא][33] דְּרִבִּי יוּדָה. וְיָצְאוּ זְקֵנֶיךָ שְׁנַיִם. וְשׁוֹפְטֶיךָ שְׁנַיִם. אֵין בֵּית דִּין שָׁקוּל. מוֹסִיפִין עֲלֵיהֶן. הֲרֵי כָאן חֲמִשָּׁה. אָמַר רִבִּי. נִרְאִין דִּבְרֵי רִבִּי שִׁמְעוֹן

בִּסְמִיכָה וְדִבְרֵי רִבִּי יְהוּדָה בָּעֲרִיפָה. נִרְאִין דִּבְרֵי רִבִּי שִׁמְעוֹן בִּסְמִיכָה. דְּלֹא דָרַשׁ וְסָמְכוּ. וְדִבְרֵי רִבִּי יְהוּדָה בָּעֲרִיפָה. דְּלֹא דָרַשׁ וְיָצְאוּ. אִין תֵּימַר. נִרְאִין דִּבְרֵי רִבִּי יְהוּדָה בְּעֶגְלָה עֲרוּפָה. דְּדָרַשׁ וְסָמְכוּ וְדָרַשׁ וְיָצְאוּ. אַשְׁכָּחַת אַתְּ אָמַר. וְיָצְאוּ. שְׁנַיִם. זְקֵינֶיךָ. שְׁנַיִם. וְשׁוֹפְטֶיךָ. שְׁנַיִם. אֵין בֵּית דִּין שָׁקוּל. מוֹסִיפִין עֲלֵיהֶן עוֹד אֶחָד. הֲרֵי כָּאן שִׁבְעָה. מַה מְקַיְימִין רַבָּנִין זְקֵינֶיךָ וְשׁוֹפְטֶיךָ. זְקֵינֶיךָ שֶׁהֵן שׁוֹפְטֶיךָ. תַּנֵּי רִבִּי אֱלִיעֶזֶר בֶּן יַעֲקֹב אוֹמֵר. זְקֵינֶיךָ. זֶה בֵּית דִּין הַגָּדוֹל. וְשׁוֹפְטֶיךָ. זֶה מֶלֶךְ וְכֹהֵן גָּדוֹל.

[34]There[35], we have stated: The leaning of the hands of the Elders[36] and the breaking of the neck of the calf is done by three [judges]; Rebbi Jehudah says, by five. What is the reason of Rebbi Simeon? "The Elders shall lean[37]," two. No court has an even number of members; one adds another one, that makes three. What is the reason of Rebbi Jehudah? "They shall lean," two; "the Elders," two. No court has an even number of members; one adds another one, that makes five. And for the calf whose neck is broken, what is the reason of Rebbi Simeon? "Your Elders, your judges,[38]" two. No court has an even number of members; one adds another one, that makes three. What is the reason of Rebbi Jehudah? "Your Elders shall go out," two, "and your judges," two. No court has an even number of members; one adds, that makes five. Rebbi said, the words of Rebbi Simeon are reasonable for the leaning of the hands and those of Rebbi Jehudah for the breaking of the neck. The words of Rebbi Simeon are reasonable for the leaning of the hands, for he does not refer to "they shall lean"[39]. And those of Rebbi Jehudah for the breaking of the neck, for he does not refer to "they shall go out.[40]" If you would say that the words of Rebbi Jehudah are reasonable for the calf whose neck is broken because he refers to both to "they shall lean" and "they shall go

out," it turns out that you have to say "there shall go out" two, "your Elders" two, "and your judges," two. No court has an even number of members; one adds another one, that makes seven[41]. How do the rabbis[43] explain "your Elders and your judges"? Your Elders who are your judges[43]. It was stated[44]: Rebbi Eliezer ben Jacob says "your Elders," that is the High Court; "and your judges" these are king and High Priest[45].

32 Added from the Genizah text. While the defective Leiden text is also reproduced in *Sanhedrin*, the Genizah text is confirmed by Rebbi's argument at the end of this paragraph and *Sifra Wayyiqra Pereq* 6(2).

33 Text of the Genizah. The Leiden text is fragmentary here. In the parallel *Sanhedrin* 1:3, the arguments of R. Simeon and R. Jehudah are switched.

34 The parallel text is in *Sanhedrin* 1:3.

35 Mishnah *Sanhedrin* 1:3.

36 *Lev.* 4:15. If the entire community (or their representative, the High Court) have erred, the purification offering requires that the Elders shall lean their hands on the head of the bull.

37 *Lev.* 4:15; Babli 44b. The quote of the verb is unnecessary. The plural "Elders" means "at least two Elders,", cf. Note 5.

38 *Deut.* 21:2; *Sifry Deut.* 205.

39 Since the number of the verb is in general determined by the number of the subject, this number cannot be considered independent information.

40 This argument is less clear since R. Simeon likewise does not refer to the verb. The difference between R. Simeon and R. Jehudah is that for R. Jehudah "Elders, judges" represent independent plurals but for R. Simeon one is restricted to "judges who are Elders" (the Babli concurs in this, 34b).

41 Since this number is never mentioned, no author considers the plural form of the verb as information.

42 This is the Leiden/*editio princeps* text here. But in the Genizah ms. and in the Leiden text in *Sanhedrin* the reading is: R. Simeon. The Leiden ms. reading can be supported since the position of R. Simeon is that of the anonymous majority in the Mishnah.

43 In the Babli, "the select of your

judges", i. e., one disqualifies any judges who are not members of the High Court.

44 Babli 45a, *Sanhedrin* 14b.

45 He requires the entire High Court to appear (Rashi in Babli 45a). The king (or, in a tribal society, the head of the tribe) is involved since he represents the police powers who alone can determine whether the murderer is unknown. The High Priest is involved since he has to send the priests to conduct the ceremony.

(fol. 23a) **משנה ב:** נִמְצָא טָמוּן בַּגַּל אוֹ תָּלוּי בָּאִילָן אוֹ צָף עַל פְּנֵי הַמַּיִם לֹא הָיוּ עוֹרְפִין. שֶׁנֶּאֱמַר בָּאֲדָמָה וְלֹא טָמוּן בַּגַּל. נוֹפֵל וְלֹא תָלוּי בָּאִילָן. בַּשָּׂדֶה וְלֹא צָף עַל פְּנֵי הַמַּיִם. נִמְצָא סָמוּךְ לַסְּפָר. לְעִיר שֶׁיֵּשׁ בָּהּ גּוֹיִם אוֹ לְעִיר שֶׁאֵין בָּהּ בֵּית דִּין לֹא הָיוּ מוֹדְדִין אֶלָּא מֵעִיר שֶׁיֵּשׁ בָּהּ בֵּית דִּין. נִמְצָא מְכוּוָּן בֵּין שְׁתֵּי עֲיָירוֹת שְׁתֵּיהֶן מְבִיאוֹת שְׁתֵּי עֲגָלוֹת דִּבְרֵי רִבִּי אֱלִיעֶזֶר. וַחֲכָמִים אוֹמְרִים עִיר אַחַת מְבִיאָה עֶגְלָה עֲרוּפָה. וְאֵין שְׁתֵּי עֲיָירוֹת מְבִיאוֹת שְׁתֵּי עֲגָלוֹת. וְאֵין יְרוּשָׁלֵם מְבִיאָה עֶגְלָה עֲרוּפָה.

Mishnah 2: If [the corpse] was found hidden in a heap[46], or hanging from a tree, or floating on the water, one did not break the neck as it is written[47] "on the earth" but not hidden in a heap, "fallen" but not hanging from a tree, "on the field" but not floating on the water. If he was found close to the border, a town in which Gentiles live, or a town without a court[48], one did measure only from a town with a court[49]. If he was found exactly in the middle between two towns, both bring a total of two calves, the words of Rebbi Eliezer; [50]but the Sages say that one town brings one calf whose neck is broken but two towns do not bring two calves, and Jerusalem does not bring a calf whose neck is broken[51].

46 Of earth or debris.

47 *Deut.* 21:1. If there only had been written "if one finds a corpse and the murderer is unknown", one would have had to bring a calf in any case. The added details should be interpreted as necessary conditions in whose absence the rules do not apply.

48 Without a permanent court with authority over the local police. In Mishnaic Hebrew, עיר denotes any cluster of human dwellings, from hamlet to village to town; occasionally it may refer even to a walled city.

49 This is the reading in most mss., including independent Mishnah mss. and those of the Babli. A few mss. and *Sifry Deut.* 205 show that the clause "one did not measure" does double duty and the meaning of the sentence is: "If it was found close to the border, a town in which Gentiles live, or a town without a court, one did not measure; one did measure only from a town with a court."

50 This sentence is found only in the Leiden ms., a single Mishnah ms., and *Sifry Deut.* 206; not in the Rome ms. nor in the Babli. Since the Yerushalmi discusses the position of the Sages but the Babli does not, it is clear that the omission in the Babylonian Mishnah is original.

51 Since Jerusalem was not divided as tribal property, cf. Note 24.

(fol. 23c) **הלכה ב:** תַּנֵּי. רִבִּי אֱלִיעֶזֶר אוֹמֵר. נִמְצָא חָנוּק וְתָלוּי בָּאִילָן לֹא הָיוּ עוֹרְפִין. אָמַר רִבִּי יוֹסֵי בַּר יוּדָה. אֵין צָרִיךְ לוֹמַר חָנוּק וְתָלוּי בָּאִילָן. מְנַיְין אֲפִילוּ מוּשְׁלָךְ. תַּלְמוּד לוֹמַר נוֹפֵל. מַה תַּלְמוּד לוֹמַר חָלָל. אֶלָּא אֲפִילוּ חָנוּק וְתָלוּי בָּאִילָן לֹא הָיוּ עוֹרְפִין.

Halakhah 2: It was stated: Rebbi Eliezer[52] says, if he was found strangled and hanging from a tree they did not break its neck. Rebbi Yose ben Rebbi Jehudah said, one does not have to say strangled *and* hanging from a tree, from where even if he was found cast away? The verse[47] says "fallen", why does the verse say "slain"? But even if he was found strangled *or* hanging from a tree they did not break its neck.

52 In the Genizah ms., the Tosephta (9:1), *Sifry Deut.* 205, and the Babli (45b) except for Ashkenazic mss.: R. Eleazar.

(23c, line 40) תַּנֵּי רִבִּי יוֹסֵי בֵּירִבִּי בּוּן בְּשֵׁם רִבִּי יוֹחָנָן. נִמְצָא עוֹמֵד עַל מִיטָתוֹ וְהַסַּכִּין תְּקוּעָה בְלִיבּוֹ אֵין עוֹרְפִין. תַּנֵּי רִבִּי שִׁמְעוֹן בֶּן יוֹחַי. הָיוּ עוֹרְפִין. דְּהָדָא דְרִבִּי שִׁמְעוֹן בֶּן יוֹחַי מִן אִילֵּין דְּהָכִין הָכִין. דְּאָמַר רִבִּי יוֹחָנָן. כָּל־אִילֵּין דְּרִבִּי שִׁמְעוֹן בֶּן יוֹחַי מִן אִילֵּין דְּהָכִין הָכִין יְחִידִין אִינּוּן וְלֹא סֶמְכִין עֲלֵיהוֹן.

Rebbi Yose ben Rebbi Abun stated[53] in the name of Rebbi Johanan: "If he was found standing on his bed and the knife was sticking in his heart, one did not break its neck. Rebbi Simeon ben Iohai stated, one did break its neck." But that of Rebbi Simeon ben Iohai is of those which are so-and-so[54]. As Rebbi Johanan said, all those [statements] of Rebbi Simeon ben Iohai which are so-and-so are isolated opinions and one cannot rely on them.

53 The word is missing in the Genizah ms. It can be justified in that R. Yose b. Abun recited a *baraita* on the authority of R. Johanan. In the version of the Genizah, this is an amoraic statement intended to brand a contradicting tannaitic one as unreliable.

54 The statement is not from a recognized *baraita* collection, nor does it contain a name of a tradent which would vouchsafe the text for the 100 years between R. Simeon and R. Johanan.

(23c, line 44) נִמְצָא בְּעָלִיל לָעִיר הָיוּ עוֹרְפִין כְּדֵי לְקַיְּימֵם בּוֹ מִצְוַת עִיסּוּק מְדִידָה.

If he was found at the entrance of the city one did break its neck[55] in order to perform the commanded measurement.

55 In the Babli sources (45a, Tosephta 9:1): "one did measure". In all cases one has to measure the distanec of the corpse from the nearest city even if it is obvious which city is the nearest one.

(23c, line 45) רַב נְחַת לְתַמָּן אָמַר אֲנָא הוּא בֶּן עַזַּאי דְּהָכָא. אָתָא חַד סָב שְׁאַל לֵיהּ שְׁנֵי הֲרוּגִים זֶה עַל גַּב זֶה. סְבַר שֶׁהֵן עוֹרְפִין. אָמַר לֵיהּ אֵין עוֹרְפִין. אָמַר לֵיהּ. לָמָה. אָמַר לֵיהּ. הַתַּחְתּוֹן מִשּׁוּם טָמוּן וְהָעֶלְיוֹן מִשּׁוּם צָף. כַּד סָלַק לְהָכָא אָתָא לְקַמֵּיהּ דְּרִבִּי. אָמַר לֵיהּ. יָאוּת אָמַר לָךְ. כִּי יִמָּצֵא. וְלֹא כִי יִמָּצְאוּ. לֹא מִסְתַּבְּרָא דְּלָאו בְּאַדְמָה. לֹא צָף עַל פְּנֵי הַמַּיִם. בַּשָּׂדֶה. לֹא טָמוּן בַּגַּל. וְתַנֵּיי דְבֵית רִבִּי כֵן.

⁵⁶When Rav descended there⁵⁷, he declared: I am this place's Ben Azai⁵⁸. There came an old man and asked him, two slain people, one on top of the other? Rav was of the opinion that one breaks its neck. He told him, one does not break its neck. He asked him, why? He said to him, not the lower one for he is hidden⁵⁹, not the upper one because he floats. When he ascended here, he came to Rebbi, who told him: He told you correctly, "if he is found," and not "if they are found." It is reasonable to say "on the land," not floating on the water, "on a field", not hidden in a heap. That is how it was stated in the House of Rebbi⁶⁰.

56   *Peah* 6:3, Notes 78-80.

57   "There" always means Babylonia; going to Babylonia is "descending," going to the Land of Israel is "ascending." The story appears in the same context in the Babli 45a, the actor being Abbaie, three generations after Rav.

58   Ben Azai, one of the most outstanding students of Rebbi Aqiba, was a walking encyclopedia and used to stroll through the markets of Tiberias, ready to immediately answer any question of Jewish learning. He died during mystical studies before he could marry R. Aqiba's daughter. In the Talmudim, several Sages are reported to have tried to imitate Ben Azai but all of them were quickly confronted with a question for which they gave the wrong answer or did not know any answer at all. The story is inserted in *Peah* because a few paragraphs down hidden sheaves will be discussed.

59   The lower body is not "found";

he is only discovered when the body on top is removed. The upper body is not found *on the land*.

60 However, our parallel sources follow the Mishnah.

(23c, line 50) מִחְלְפָה שִׁיטָתוֹן דְּרַבָּנִין. תַּמָּן אִינּוּן אָמְרִין. [לְרַבּוֹת אֶת הַטָּמוּן].⁶¹ וְכָא אִינּוּן אָמְרִין [פְּרָט לְטָמוּן].⁶¹ תַּמָּן שָׂדְךָ בְּגָלוּי. פְּרָט לְטָמוּן. וּקְצִירְךָ בְּגָלוּי. פְּרָט לְטָמוּן. מִיעוּט אַחַר מִיעוּט. לְרַבּוֹת אֶת הַטָּמוּן. בְּרַם הָכָא בָּאֲדָמָה. לֹא צָף עַל פְּנֵי הַמַּיִם.

The argument of the rabbis seems inverted; there they say to exclude the hidden things⁶², but here they say to include the hidden things. There, "your field," in the open, to exclude that which is hidden; "your harvest," in the open, to exclude that which is hidden. It is a restriction after a restriction⁶³ to add the hidden things. But here, "on the land," not floating on the water.

61 Reading of the Genizah ms. The Leiden ms. switches the two expressions. The entire argument is modelled after one in *Peah* 6:9, Notes 151-154; it is possible that the Leiden text refers to *Peah* as "here" and *Soṭah* as "there".

62 This refers to Mishnah *Peah* 6:9, *Sifry Deut.* 283, interpreting *Deut.* 24:19: If you cut *your harvest* on *your field* and you forget a sheaf on *the field*, you may not return to take it. R. Jehudah says, this excludes anything hidden, the Sages say this includes everything hidden. But in *Deut.* 21:1, on *your field* is interpreted as "not hidden in a heap," excluding any hidden corpse.

63 The principle that a restriction after a restriction is an extension is universally accepted in both Talmudim; in *Horaiot* 1:1 it is generalized to the statement that any sequence of restrictions of an even number of elements is an extension; for an odd number of elements it is a restriction.

HALAKHAH 2   365

(23c, line 54) נִמְצָא סָמוּךְ לכפר.[64] אֲנִי אוֹמֵר סַרְקִיִּים הֲרָגוּהוּ. לְעִיר שֶׁיֵּשׁ בָּהּ גּוֹיִם. אֲנִי אוֹמֵר. גּוֹיִם הֲרָגוּהוּ. אוֹ לְעִיר שֶׁאֵין בָּהּ בֵּית דִּין. לֹא הָיוּ מוֹדְדִין אֶלָּא מֵעִיר שֶׁיֵּשׁ בָּהּ בֵּית דִּין. דִּכְתִיב יָדֵינוּ לֹא שָׁפְכוּ אֶת הַדָּם הַזֶּה וגו'.

"If he was found close to the border," I say that Saracens killed him. "To a town in which Gentiles live," I say that Gentiles killed him. "Or a town without a court, one did measure only from a town with a court," as it is written[65]: "Our hands did not spill this blood."

64   A clear misspelling, faithfully copied in *editio princeps* and some medieval authors. Unfortunately, only the letters פר. are readable in the Genizah ms. The translation presupposes the reading לִסְפָר.

65   *Deut.* 21:7. Since the members of the local court have to recite the declaration which acknowledges that the crime was perpetrated within the domain of their authority, it is clear that they must come from the seat of the court.

(23c, line 57) מַה טַעֲמוֹן דְּרַבָּנִין. דִּכְתִיב וְהָיְתָה הָעִיר הַקְּרוֹבָה אֶל הֶחָלָל. מַה טַעֲמָא דְּרִבִּי אֶלְעָזָר. דִּכְתִיב וּמָדְדוּ אֶל הֶעָרִים אֲשֶׁר סְבִיבֹת הֶחָלָל.

What is the reason of the rabbis? As it is written[66]: "It shall be *the town* close to the slain." What is the reason of Rebbi Eliezer? As it is written[67]: "They shall measure to *the towns* which surround the slain."

66   *Deut.* 21:3.
67   *Deut.* 21:2. The Babli, *Bekhorot* 16b, which never quotes the Sages, disagrees, and holds that for R. Eliezer it is possible to determine lengths with the utmost precision because if it were possible to measure only with limited precision, the two towns together could bring one calf and stipulate that it should count for that town which really is closest if unlimited precision were possible.

(23c, line 59) עָרֵי מִקְלָט מַה הֵן. אִין תֵּימַר. לְמַחֲלוֹקֶת נִיתְּנוּ. מְבִיאוֹת עֶגְלָה עֲרוּפָה. אִין תֵּימַר. לְבֵית דִּירָה נִיתְּנוּ. אֵינָן מְבִיאוֹת עֶגְלָה עֲרוּפָה.

What is the status of cities of refuge[68]? If you say, they were given as distribution, they bring a calf whose neck is broken. If you say, they were given as living quarters, they do not bring a calf whose neck is broken.

68 The levitic cities which served as refuges for the homicide. These cities certainly have a court which has to supervise the trial of the homicide. The problem alluded to here is not mentioned in the Babli; the main reference in the Yerushalmi is *Makkot* 2:7 (fol. 32a); the statement is alluded to in *Ma'aser Šeni* 5:8 (fol. 56d, Note 165). If the Levitical cities and the cities of refuge were parcelled out to their inhabitants, they would own land given by God and would be under the obligation of the calf, *Deut.* 21:1. But if the cities were tribal property and the houses given to the inhabitants as living quarters by the tribal council, not as property, then individual Levites and Cohanim never obtained land and their court cannot participate in the ceremony.

(fol. 23a) **משנה ג:** מֵאַיִן הָיוּ מוֹדְדִין. רִבִּי אֱלִיעֶזֶר אוֹמֵר מִטִּיבּוּרוֹ. רִבִּי עֲקִיבָה אוֹמֵר מֵחוֹטְמוֹ. רִבִּי אֱלִיעֶזֶר בֶּן יַעֲקֹב אוֹמֵר מִמָּקוֹם שֶׁנַּעֲשָׂה חָלָל מִצַּוָּארוֹ.

Mishnah 3: From where did they measure? Rebbi Eliezer says, from his navel. Rebbi Aqiba says, from his nose. Rebbi Eliezer ben Jacob said, from the place which makes him slain, from his neck.

(fol. 23c) **הלכה ג:** וּמֵאַיִן הָיוּ מוֹדְדִין. רִבִּי אֱלִיעֶזֶר אוֹמֵר מִטִּיבּוּרוֹ. מִמְּקוֹם שֶׁהַוָּלָד נוֹצָר. רַבִּי עֲקִיבָה אוֹמֵר מֵחוֹטְמוֹ. מִמְּקוֹם הַכָּרַת פָּנִים. וְאָתְיָא כַיי

דָּמַר רַב יְהוּדָה בְּשֵׁם רַב. הַכָּרַת פְּנֵיהֶם עָנְתָה בָם. זֶה הַחוֹטֶם. אָמַר רִבִּי חִייָא בַּר בָּא. מָאן דְּבָעֵי דְלָא מִתְחַכְּמָא יְהַב סִיפְלָנֵי עַל נְחִירֵיהּ וְלָא מִתְחַכֵּם. כְּהָדָה בְּיוֹמֵי דְאַרְסְקִינַס מַלְכָּא הַוְיָין צִיפּוֹרָאֵי מִתְבָּעִיָין. וַהֲווֹן יָהֲבִין סִיפְלָנֵי עַל נְחִירֵיהוֹן וְאִינּוּן לָא מִתְחַכְּמִין. וּבְסוֹפָא אִיתְמַר עֲלֵיהוֹן לִישָׁן בִּישׁ. וְאִיתְצָיְידוּן כּוּלְּהוֹן מִן בִּידָא.

Halakah 3: "From where did they measure? Rebbi Eliezer says, from his navel", from the place the child is formed. "Rebbi Aqiba says, from his nose," from the place from which one is identified[69]. [70]This follows what Rav Jehudah[71] said in the name of Rav: "The recognition of their faces testified about them[72]," that is the nose. Rebbi Ḥiyya bar Abba said, if somebody does not want to be recognized, he should put a patch on his nostrils, then he will not be recognized. As in the following: In the times of king Ursicinus, some people from Sepphoris were under arrest warrants. They put patches on their nostrils and were not recognized. Finally they were denunciated and all were caught because of lies.

69   The Babli, 45b, agrees for the reason of R. Eliezer and disagrees for R. Aqiba.

70   The rest of the paragraph is from *Yebamot* 16:3, Notes 39-44.

71   In *Yebamot*: R. Jeremiah.

72   *Is.* 3:9.

(23c, line 68) רִבִּי אֱלִיעֶזֶר בֶּן יַעֲקֹב אוֹמֵר מִמְּקוֹם שֶׁנַּעֲשֶׂה חָלָל מְצַוָּארוֹ. מַה טַעֲמָא. רִבִּי סִימוֹן בְּשֵׁם רִבִּי יְהוֹשֻׁעַ [בֶּן לֵוִי].[73] לָתֵת אוֹתָהּ עַל צַוְּארֵי חַלְלֵי רְשָׁעִים.

"Rebbi Eliezer ben Jacob said, from the place which makes him slain, from his neck." What is the reason? Rebbi Simon in the name of Rebbi Joshua ben Levi: "To put you[74] on the throats of the corpses of sinners."

73 From the Genizah ms., required by the historical context, missing in the other sources.

74 The sword, mentioned in the preceding verse; *Ez.* 21:34. The implication is that חלל means "slain by the sword" and that most victims of the sword have their throats cut. The Babli agrees, 45b.

משנה ד: נִמְצָא ראשׁוֹ בְּמָקוֹם אֶחָד וְגוּפוֹ בְּמָקוֹם אַחֵר מוֹלִיכִין הָראשׁ אֵצֶל הַגּוּף דִּבְרֵי רִבִּי אֱלִיעֶזֶר. רִבִּי עֲקִיבָה אוֹמֵר הַגּוּף אֵצֶל הָראשׁ. (fol. 23a)

Mishnah 4: If his head is found at another place than his body, one brings[75] his head to his body, the words of Rebbi Eliezer; Rebbi Aqiba says, the body to his head.

75 For burial since an unknown slain person must be buried at the place he was found. In the Babli, 45b, and most Mishnah mss., the positions of Mishnaiot 3 and 4 are switched.

הלכה ד: אָמַר רִבִּי לָעְזָר. לִקְבוּרָה נֶחְלְקוּ. רִבִּי שְׁמוּאֵל [בַּר נַחְמָן][76] בְּשֵׁם רִבִּי יוֹנָתָן. מַה פְּלִיגִין. כְּשֶׁהָיָה הָראשׁ מִלְּמַעֲלָן וְהַגּוּף מִלְּמַטָּן. אֲבָל אִם הָיָה הָראשׁ מִלְּמַטָּן וְהַגּוּף מִלְּמַעֲלָן כָּל־עַמָּא מוֹדֵיי שֶׁמּוֹלִיכִין אֶת הָראשׁ אֵצֶל הַגּוּף. הָיָה מוּנְדְּרָן מִיכָּן וּמִיכָּן. אֲנָא אָמַר. רֵישָׁהּ אֲזַל לְחַד אֲתָר וְגוּפָא אֲזַל לְחַד אֲתָר. אוֹ הָראשׁ הַזֶּה אֵין לוֹ גוּף אוֹ הַגּוּף הַזֶּה אֵין לוֹ ראשׁ. הָיָה שָׁוֶה. כָּל־מָקוֹם שֶׁדַּרְכּוֹ לִיתּוֹז גּוּף אֶחָד הוּא. וְאִם לָאו. הָראשׁ הַזֶּה אֵין לוֹ גוּף וְהַגּוּף הַזֶּה אֵין לוֹ ראשׁ. (fol. 23c)

Halakhah 4: Rebbi Eleazar said, they disagree about burial[77]. Rebbi Samuel bar Naḥman in the name of Rebbi Jonathan: When do they disagree? If the head was higher but the body lower. But if the head was lower and the body higher everybody agrees that one brings the head to the body[78]. If there was an incline[79] on both sides, do I say that the head fell to one side and the body to the other[80] or does this head have no body and that body no head? If it was level, any distance it is usual to chop it off[81] is one body; otherwise, the head has no body and the body no head[82].

76 Reading of the Rome and Genizah mss., missing in the Leiden ms. {The student of R. Jonathan was R. Samuel bar Naḥman; the Amora R. Samuel, student of rabbis Abbahu and Zeʿira, lived two generations later.}

77 In the Babli, 45b, R. Isaac based on tannaitic sources.

78 Because the body fell where he was killed but the head rolled down the incline.

79 The corresponding Babli word is מדרון.

80 If head and body are found at two different sides of a mountain ridge.

81 It is reasonable to assume that a chopped-off head would fall so far away from the body which fell at the place he was killed.

82 And they must be buried separately.

משנה ה: נִפְטְרוּ זִקְנֵי יְרוּשָׁלֵם וְהָלְכוּ לָהֶן. זִקְנֵי אוֹתָהּ הָעִיר מְבִיאִין (fol. 23a) עֶגְלַת בָּקָר אֲשֶׁר לֹא עוּבַּד בָּהּ אֲשֶׁר לֹא מָשְׁכָה בְעוֹל. וְאֵין הַמּוּם פּוֹסֵל בָּהּ. וּמוֹרִידִין אוֹתָהּ לְנַחַל אֵיתָן וְאֵיתָן כְּמַשְׁמָעוֹ קָשֶׁה. אַף עַל פִּי שֶׁאֵין אֵיתָן כָּשֵׁר. עוֹרְפִין אוֹתָהּ בְּקוֹפִיץ מֵאֲחוֹרֶיהָ. וּמְקוֹמָהּ אָסוּר מִלִּזְרוֹעַ וּמִלַּעֲבוֹד וּמוּתָּר לִסְרוֹק שָׁם פִּשְׁתָּן וּלְנַקֵּר שָׁם אֲבָנִים.

Mishnah 5: When the Elders of Jerusalem had completed their work[83] and left, the Elders of that town bring "a cattle calf, one which never had been used for work, which never had drawn under a yoke.[84]" Bodily defects do not disqualify it. One brings it down to an *etan* valley; the meaning of *etan* is "hard"[85]. Even if it is not hard it is qualified. One breaks its neck with a stiletto from behind. Its place is forbidden to be used for sowing or agricultural works; it may be used to card flax or to hew stones.

83   To determine which town is responsible for bringing the calf.

84   *Deut.* 21:3.

85   Not ploughable.

(fol. 23d) **הלכה ה:** אֲשֶׁר לֹא עוּבַּד בָּהּ. לְדַעַת. אֲשֶׁר לֹא מָשְׁכָה בְעוֹל. בֵּין לְדַעַת בֵּין שֶׁלֹּא לְדַעַת. רְבִּי יוֹנָה פָּתַר מַתְנִיתָא. אֲשֶׁר לֹא עוּבַּד בָּהּ. לְדַעַת. אֲשֶׁר לֹא מָשְׁכָה בְעוֹל. בֵּין לְדַעַת בֵּין שֶׁלֹּא לְדַעַת. וְהוּא שֶׁיִּמְשׁוֹךְ. רְבִּי יוֹסֵי פָּתַר מַתְנִיתָא. לְדַעַת. אֲפִילוּ לֹא מָשַׁךְ. וְשֶׁלֹּא לְדַעַת. וְהוּא שֶׁיִּמְשׁוֹךְ. וְאַתְיָיא דְּרִבִּי יוֹנָה כְּרִבִּי יִשְׁמָעֵאל וּדְרִבִּי יוֹסֵי כְּרַבָּנָן. דְּרִבִּי יוֹנָה כְּרִבִּי יִשְׁמָעֵאל. דְּרִבִּי יִשְׁמָעֵאל אָמַר. כָּל־דָּבָר שֶׁהָיָה בִּכְלָל וְיָצָא מִן הַכְּלָל לְלַמֵּד נֶעֱקַר מִכְּלָלוֹ וַהֲרֵי הוּא בְחִידוּשׁוֹ. לְפוּם כֵּן צָרֵךְ מֵימַר. אֲשֶׁר לֹא עוּבַּד בָּהּ. לְדַעַת. אֲשֶׁר לֹא מָשְׁכָה בְעוֹל. בֵּין לְדַעַת בֵּין שֶׁלֹּא לְדַעַת. וְהוּא שֶׁיִּמְשׁוֹךְ. וּדְרִבִּי יוֹסֵי כְּרַבָּנָן. דְּרַבָּנִין אָמְרִין. הֲרֵי הוּא בִּכְלָלוֹ וַהֲרֵי הוּא בְחִידוּשׁוֹ. לְפוּם כֵּן צָרֵךְ מֵימַר. לְדַעַת. אֲפִילוּ לֹא מָשַׁךְ. וְשֶׁלֹּא לְדַעַת. וְהוּא שֶׁיִּמְשׁוֹךְ.

Halakhah 5: "One which never had been used for work," intentionally, "which never had drawn under a yoke," intentionally or unintentionally[86]. Rebbi Jonah explains the Mishnah: "One which never had been used for work," intentionally, "which never had drawn under a yoke," intentionally or unintentionally, if it actually had drawn[87]. Rebbi Yose explained the Mishnah: Intentionally even if it had not drawn[88], unintentionally if it actually had drawn. It turns out that Rebbi Jonah follows Rebbi Ismael and Rebbi Yose the rabbis. Rebbi Jonah follows Rebbi Ismael, since Rebbi

Ismael says, anything which was in a set and left the set to teach leaves its set and stands in its new meaning[89]. Therefore, he has to spell out "one which never had been used for work," intentionally, "which never had drawn under a yoke," intentionally or unintentionally, if it actually had drawn[90]. Rebbi Yose follows the rabbis, since the rabbis say, anything which was in a set and left the set to teach remains in its set and in its new meaning[91]. Therefore, he has to spell out: intentionally even if it had not drawn, unintentionally if it actually had drawn.

86   The problem discussed in this paragraph is that if no work ever had been done with the calf, it should be obvious that it never was harnessed under a yoke to draw anything. Therefore the mention of the yoke must give harnessing the animal a status different from any other agricultural work. For the Babli, 46a, imposing a yoke disables the calf whether it was used for work or not, while other agricultural work disables only if it was actually used. This avoids the problem discussed here.

The intention here is that of the farmer who has to decide to use his calf for work. The Babli, *Pesaḥim* 26a/b, gives as example that if the farmer lets the calf accompany its mother while she is threshing and by this helps in threshing, it remains acceptable but if the farmer intends that the calf should suckle and thereby help in threshing, it becomes disqualified.

87   Imposing the yoke does not disqualify the calf, only actually drawing (a cart or a plow) does.

88   In that case, imposing the yoke on the calf disqualifies it.

89   This is a version of the hermeneutical rules not found in the Babli or the *Sifra*; cf. Chapter 7, Note 108. Drawing ploughs or carts was part of the set of works for which cattle are used. If drawing is singled out for separate attention, in this opinion the general rules valid for agricultural works, that the animal has to be made to work, indicated by the passive, are no longer valid. The active mode seems to imply that if the calf drew something on its own initiative, it still will be disabled.

This rule is not to be identified with the 12th rule (*Sifra* Introduction, Babli *Temurah* 13b, *Šebuot* 25b): "Anything which was in a set and was taken out to be judged by different rules you cannot restore into the set unless the verse does this explicitly." Once an animal was dedicated as sacrifice, it is forbidden to exchange it (*Lev.* 27:10). The same is true for animal tithes (*Lev.* 27:33), which are sacrifices. The fact that the rules are spelled out again for tithes (whose status of sanctity is automatic) shows that the differences in the rules are intended; one cannot infer from the rules of one for those of the other.

90   Since the verse puts the emphasis on drawing, not on carrying the yoke.

91   This is close to the formulation of rule 9 (*Sifra*, Introduction): "Anything which was in a set and left the set to teach did not leave to teach about itself alone but to teach about the entire set." The new teaching is that active drawing automatically disables even if not desired by the farmer. This implies that drawing is only an example; the same rule will be valid for any agricultural work.

(23d, line 11) כַּמָּה יִמְשׁוֹךְ. רִבִּי אוֹמֵר כִּמְלוֹאוֹ. רִבִּי יוֹסֵי בֵּירִבִּי יוּדָה אוֹמֵר. שָׁלֹשׁ אֶצְבָּעוֹת. רִבִּי סִימוֹן בְּשֵׁם רִבִּי יוֹסֵי בֶּן נְהוֹרַאי. מְלוֹא הָעוֹל לְרָחְבּוֹ.

How far would it have to draw[92]? Rebbi said, its[93] width. Rebbi Yose ben Rebbi Jehudah said, three finger breadths. Rebbi Simon in the name of Rebbi Yose ben Nehorai said, the entire length of the yoke in its width[94].

92   To become disqualified.

93   The yoke's width. In the Babli, 46a, this is defined as one handbreadth (4 thumbbreadths). Rebbi's opinion is quoted as R. Johanan's in the Babli.

94   The length of the yoke is measured by the breadth of the animal. This opinion is mentioned as a possibility in the Babli only to be immediately dismissed.

HALAKHAH 5

(23d, line 13) רִבִּי בּוּן בַּר חִייָה בְּעָא קוֹמֵי רִבִּי זְעִירָא. אֲשֶׁר לֹא עוּבַּד בָּהּ. כְּלָל. אֲשֶׁר לֹא מֶשְׁכָה בְעוֹל. פְּרָט. כְּלָל וּפְרָט אֵין בִּכְלָל אֶלָּא מַה שֶּׁבִּפְרָט. אָמַר לֵיהּ. אִילּוּ הֲוָה כְּתִיב אֲשֶׁר לֹא עוּבְּדָה וַאֲשֶׁר לֹא מֶשְׁכָה. יָאוּת. לֵית כְּתִיב אֶלָּא אֲשֶׁר לֹא עוּבַּד בָּהּ. אֵין כָּאן כְּלָל וּפְרָט אֶלָּא רִיבּוּיִין עוֹל עוֹל לִגְזֵירָה שָׁוָה. מַה עוֹל הָאָמוּר בָּעֶגְלָה עָשָׂה בָהּ שְׁאָר כָּל־הָעֲבוֹדוֹת כְּעוֹל. אַף עוֹל הָאָמוּר בַּפָּרָה נַעֲשָׂה בָהּ שְׁאָר כָּל־הָעֲבוֹדוֹת כְּעוֹל. מַה עוֹל הָאָמוּר בָּעֶגְלָה עֲבוֹדָה פּוֹסֶלֶת בָּהּ בֵּין לְדַעַת בֵּין שֶׁלֹּא לְדַעַת. אַף עוֹל הָאָמוּר בַּפָּרָה עֲבוֹדָה פּוֹסֶלֶת בָּהּ בֵּין לְדַעַת בֵּין שֶׁלֹּא לְדַעַת. מַה עוֹל הָאָמוּר בַּפָּרָה הָעוֹל פּוֹסֵל בָּהּ. אַף עוֹל הָאָמוּר בָּעֶגְלָה הָעוֹל פּוֹסֵל בָּהּ. אִי מַה עוֹל הָאָמוּר בַּפָּרָה הַמּוּמִין פּוֹסְלִין בָּהּ. אַף עוֹל הָאָמוּר בָּעֶגְלָה הַמּוּמִין פּוֹסְלִין בָּהּ. תַּלְמוּד לוֹמַר אֲשֶׁר אֵין בָּהּ מוּם. הַמּוּמִין פּוֹסְלִין בַּפָּרָה. אֵין הַמּוּמִין פּוֹסְלִין בָּעֶגְלָה. וְאָמַר אֲשֶׁר לֹא עוּבַּד בָּהּ. בָּהּ עֲבוֹדָה פּוֹסֶלֶת אֵין עֲבוֹדָה פּוֹסֶלֶת בַּפָּרָה. הָכָא אֲשֶׁר לֹא עוּבַּד בָּהּ. בָּהּ עֲבוֹדָה פּוֹסֶלֶת אֵין עֲבוֹדָה פּוֹסֶלֶת בַּפָּרָה. אִית לָךְ מֵימַר תַּמָּן. אֲשֶׁר אֵין בָּהּ מוּם. בָּהּ הַמּוּמִין פּוֹסְלִין אֵין הַמּוּמִין פּוֹסְלִין בַּמּוּקְדָּשִׁין.

Rebbi Abun bar Ḥiyya asked before Rebbi Ze'ira: "One which never had been used for work," a general statement, "which never had drawn under a yoke," a detailed statement. If a general statement is followed by a detail, the general does not contain more than the detail[95]. He said to him, if it were written "which never had worked, which never had drawn," you would be justified; but it is written "one which never had been used for work." This does not describe general and detail, but the additional reference to "yoke" for an equal cut[96]. Since relative to "yoke" said for the calf He treated all work as a yoke[97], so for the "yoke" said for the cow[98] we have to treat all work as a yoke[99]. Since relative to "yoke" said for the calf work disables whether intentional or unintentional[100], so for the "yoke" said for the cow work disables whether intentional or unintentional. Since relative to "yoke" said for the cow, the yoke disables[101], also for the "yoke" said for the calf the yoke disables. Then since for the "yoke" said for the cow blemishes disable, so also for the "yoke" said for the calf blemishes disable[102]? The verse[103] says, "where *this one* has no blemish." Blemishes disable the cow, blemishes do not disable the calf[104]. Then it also says[105] "*one* which never had been used for work," for this one work disables, does for the cow work not disable? Can you say there, "where *this one* has no blemish," this one is disabled by blemishes, sacrifices are not disabled by blemishes?[106]

95 The fifth hermeneutical rule. Since the detail is logically contained in the general, its mention serves as definition for the general statement. The same objection is noted in the Babli, 46a; the short answer given in the Babli is intelligible only in the light of the Yerushalmi.

96 The second hermeneutical rule used in an extended sense, not only that a word has identical meaning in all its occurrences in the Pentateuch but also that all rules connected with it are identical in the two cases being compared. This extended rule requires that the word be *free*, i. e., not needed to derive other rules. It is difficult to construct the word "yoke" as free in the case of the red cow.

97 The *gezerah šawah* invoked by R. Ze'ira strictly follows the interpretation of (the later) R. Yose. The interpretation of R. Jonah therefore is rejected implicitly.

98 The red cow whose ashes are used for purification from the impurity of the dead, *Num.* 19. Verse 19:2 states that the cow (1) must be unblemished and (2) cannot have borne a yoke. Condition (1) is not mentioned for the calf and is explicitly excluded by the Mishnah. (2) implies that the cow is disabled even if no work was ever done or intended. In rabbinic interpretation, the cow had "borne a yoke" if she was mounted by a male.

99 Work is not mentioned in *Num.* 19:2; its prohibition is inferred from the case of the calf.

100 Following R. Yose, the yoke disables irrespective of intention (with some qualifications). Since R. Yose

extends the rules of the yoke to all work, he will do the same for the red cow.

101 For the cow, Num. 19:2 makes it clear that even if a yoke accidentally fell on the cow, it disables permanently.

102 This would contradict the Mishnah.

103 Num. 19:2.

104 The same argument Babli 46a, in an expanded version Sifry Num. 123.

105 Deut. 21:3.

106 This is blatantly false, Lev. 22:17-25. Therefore, the only case which the emphatic *this one* excludes is that of the calf. In Sifry Num. 123, it is concluded that the cow must be unblemished but not the Cohen who burns it in a ceremony outside the sanctuary.

(23d, line 29) מְהוּסְרֵי אֵיבָרִין מַהוּ שֶׁיִּפְסְלוּ בָהּ. אֲפִילוּ כְקָרְבְּנוֹת בְּנֵי נֹחַ אֵינָם. לֹא כֵן אָמַר רִבִּי יָסָא. פָּשַׁט רִבִּי לְעָזָר לַחֲבֵרַיָּא. וּמִכָּל־הַחַי מִכָּל־בָּשָׂר [שֶׁיִּהוּ]107 שְׁלֵימִין בְּאֵיבָרֵיהֶן. תַּמָּן. יֵשׁ מֵהֶן לַמִּזְבֵּחַ. בְּרַם הָכָא. אֵין מֵהֶן לַמִּזְבֵּחַ. רִבִּי חוּנָה בְּשֵׁם רִבִּי יִרְמְיָה. מִכֵּיוָן דְּאַתְּ אָמַר. כַּפָּרָה כְּתִיב בָּהּ כְּקֳדָשִׁים. כְּמִי שֶׁיֵּשׁ מֵהֶן לַמִּזְבֵּחַ. טְרֵיפָה מַהוּ שֶׁתִּיפָּסֵל בָּהּ. מִכֵּוָן דְּאַתְּ אָמַר. יֵשׁ מֵהֶן לַמִּזְבֵּחַ. טְרֵיפָה פּוֹסֶלֶת בָּהּ. בְּהַי פְּשִׁיטָא לָךְ שֶׁהַטְּרֵיפָה פּוֹסֶלֶת בָּהּ. הָיְתָה רַגְלָהּ קְלוּטָה כְּשֶׁלַּחֲמוֹר מַה אַתְּ עָבַד לָהּ. כִּמְחוּסֶּרֶת אֵבֶר אוֹ כְבַעֲלַת מוּם. אֵין תַּעֲבְדִינָהּ כִּמְחוּסֶּרֶת אֵבֶר. כְּשֵׁירָה. אֵין תַּעֲבְדִינָהּ כְּבַעֲלַת מוּם. פְּסוּלָה. דָּמָהּ מַהוּ שֶׁיַּכְשִׁיר. מִן מַה דְּתַנֵּי רִבִּי חִייָה. דָּמָהּ טָמֵא. דָּמָהּ מַכְשִׁיר.

Would missing limbs disable it? That would not be even like sacrifices of the descendants of Noah[108]! Did not Rebbi Yasa say that Rebbi Eleazar explained to the colleagues: "From all living, from all flesh[109]," that they should be complete in their limbs? There, some were for the altar[110], but here[111], the altar has no part. Rebbi Huna in the name of Rebbi Jeremiah: Since you say, purgation is written there as for sacrifices[112], it is as if some of it were for the altar. Does *terefa*[113] disable it? Since you say, it is as if some of it were for the altar, in that it should be clear to you that *terefa* disables it. If its foot was undeveloped, as a donkey's foot[114], how do you treat that? If you treat it as if missing a limb, can it be enabled[115]? If you treat it as a bodily defect, can it be disabled[116]? Does its blood prepare[117]? Since Rebbi Hiyya stated that its blood is impure[118], its blood prepares.

107 From the Rome ms. Missing in the Leiden ms. and *editio princeps*. The addition is good style but not absolutely necessary.

108 All of mankind, who have to follow the "natural law" given to Noah. It is accepted both in the Yerushalmi (also *Pesaḥim* 9:4 36d line 71, *Megillah* 1:13 72b line 39) and in the Babli (*Avodah zarah* 5b, 51a, *Zebaḥim* 116a, *Temurah* 7a) that a Gentile's sacrifice on his own altar is accepted by Heaven if only the animal is of the pure kinds and not missing anything observable from the outside. Only in the Temple are Gentile sacrifices subject to the rules of *Lev.* 21:21-25. The same verse is quoted in the Babli as in the Yerushalmi.

109 *Gen.* 6:19. The interpretation of the verse is: From all living creatures, each one with his entire flesh, i. e., a whole body.

110 Since Noah used some of the animals for elevation sacrifices (*Gen.* 8:20) it is inferred that all pure animals entering his ark were acceptable sacrifices.

111 The calf is buried at the place it is killed.

112 *Deut.* 21:8; the purpoise of the entire ceremony is to purge the Land from the guilt of innocent blood. The goal of purgation is spelled out for all purification and reparation offerings in *Lev.* 4 ff.

113 Here, the word is used in its original meaning (*Ex.* 22:30) "Flesh torn on the field you shall not eat," meaning that a carcass torn by a predator is forbidden as food. From this root, the technical term *ṭerefa* means that any life-threatening injury forbids the afflicted animal as food. There is no difference whether the injury is caused by outside action or sickness. For example, tuberculous lesions of the lung are a main source of *ṭerefa*. Obviously there are two kinds of *ṭerefa*: those that can be observed by outward inspection and those which can only be noted when the animal is

cut up after slaughter. Since all animals offered on the altar (except birds) must be offered in pieces, it is clear that all kinds of *terefa* are forbidden for the altar. But in the case of the calf, only what is verifiable on the living animal is intended. The position of the Babli, *Ḥulin* 11a, is that most animals do not have life-threatening internal injuries and, therefore, one may assume that a healthy-looking calf is healthy. (The list of what is considered life-threatening is in Mishnah *Ḥulin* 3:1,3).

114 The calf does not have split hooves.

115 It would seem natural to emend the text by switching the places of "enabled" and "disabled" and consider the text as declarative sentences. That is what all commentators and editors do but it is unacceptable since even the Genizah ms., which derives from an archetype different from the Leiden and Rome mss., does have "enabled" and "disabled" in the positions indicated. It seems necessary to treat the sentences as rhetorical questions.

116 Since it was stated in the Mishnah that bodily defects do not disable.

117 If some of the killed calf's blood comes in touch with fresh food, does it make that food susceptible to ritual impurity. For preparation for impurity, cf. *Demay* 2, Note 141, *Terumot* 1, Note 9, Mishnah *Makhširin* 6:4.

118 Since any impure fluid is impure at least in the first degree, it transmits its impurity and, therefore, does prepare for impurity.

(23d, line 39) חַד סַב שְׁאַל לְרַבָּנָן דְּקַיְסָרִין. עֲרִיפָתָהּ מַהוּ שֶׁתְּטַהֵר טְרֵיפָתָהּ מִטּוּמְאָתָהּ. אָמְרִין לֵיהּ. וְלָאו מַתְנִיתָא הִיא. הַשּׁוֹחֵט וְנִמְצָא טְרֵיפָה. אָמַר לוֹן. מָה אֲנָן בְּעַיָין עֲרִיפָה[119] וְאַתּוּן מַיְיתֵי לֵיהּ שְׁחוּטָה. אָמְרוֹן לֵיהּ. לֹא כֵן אָמַר רִבִּי יַנַּאי. דִּבְרֵי רִבִּי מֵאִיר. אֲפִילוּ טְרֵיפָה חַיָּיב. וְאָמַר לוֹן. וּמִן הָדָא דְּרִבִּי יַנַּאי אַתּוּן מְגִיבִין לִי.

An old man asked the rabbis of Caesarea: Does the breaking of its neck clear its *terefa* from its impurity[120]? They said to him, is that not a Mishnah: "He who cuts the throat and it turns out to be *terefa*.[121]" He said to them, but I asked about breaking the neck and you answer me cutting the throat! They said to him, but did not Rebbi Yannai say[122], the words of Rebbi Meïr, even if it was *terefa* he is guilty? He said to them, you answer me from that of Rebbi Yannai[123]?

119 Reading of the Rome ms. Leiden and *editio princeps*: טריפה.

120 In all cases of ritual slaughter except for the calf, cutting the throat שחיטה is required. The same is prescribed for profane slaughter of animals intended as food (*Deut.* 12:21). Any animal which is killed in any other way becomes a carcass whose impurity is original and severe (*Lev.* 11:39-40). The question arises naturally whether the carcass of the calf is severely impure, not having been slaughtered in the required form, or maybe is pure since its neck was broken by divine decree.

121 Mishnah *Ḥulin* 6:2. This refers to the obligation to cover a wild animal's blood with earth if it was slaughtered for food (*Lev.* 17:13). R. Meïr holds that the intent is all that counts, even if it should turn out in the end that the animal could not be used as food. The argument here is that the animal was slaughtered in the way prescribed and the fact that it is forbidden for consumption (or for any use) should be irrelevant.

122 This is quoted in full in Halakhah 6. The statement refers to *Lev.* 22:28: "Cattle or sheep, you should not cut their and their calves throats on the same day". There is one opinion which holds that guilt is incurred only if both animals are validly slaughtered as food on the name day. It is generally acknowledged in both Talmudim that R. Meïr considers even ineffective cutting the throat as falling under all rules of "cutting the throat." In Halakhah 6, the reading of the mss. is אפילו עריפה חייב "even for breaking its neck he is guilty." It seems that this should be the reading here also, but unfortunately the Genizah fragment is illegible at this spot. Since the reading as written is not impossible, it is better not to disturb the text.

123 In Halakhah 6, R. Simeon ben Laqish disagrees with R. Yannai. Therefore, there is no proof along these lines.

The Babli, *Zebaḥim* 70b, argues that the dead calf must be pure since "purification is written there as for sacrifices" (Note 110).

(23d, line 44) אֵיתָן כְּשמועוֹ קָשֶה. אֵיתָן מוֹשָׁבֶיךָ וְשִׂים בַּסֶּלַע קִנֶּךָ. אַף עַל פִּי שֶׁאֵין אֵיתָן כָּשֵׁר. וְדִכְוָותָהּ. אַף עַל פִּי שֶׁאֵין הַנַּחַל כָּשֵׁר. תַּנֵּי רִבִּי שִׁמְעוֹן בֶּן יוֹחַי. הוֹרִידוּ וְהוֹרִידוּ. אַף עַל פִּי שֶׁאֵין נַחַל. דְּהָדָא רִבִּי שִׁמְעוֹן בֶּן יוֹחַי מִן אִילֵּין דְּהָכָא הָכֵן.[124] דְּאָמַר רִבִּי יוֹחָנָן. כָּל־אִילֵּין דְּרִבִּי שִׁמְעוֹן בֶּן יוֹחַי מִן אִילֵּין דְּהָכְן אָכֵן יְחִידִין אִינוּן וְלֹא סָמְכִין עֲלֵיהוֹן.

"The meaning of *etan* is "hard", "Hard is your seat, make your nest in the rock[125]." "Even if it is not hard it is qualified." Similarly, if there is no brook? Rebbi Simeon ben Iohai stated, "they shall bring down, and they shall bring down," even if there is no brook[126]. But that of Rebbi Simeon ben Iohai is of those which are so-and-so[54]. As Rebbi Johanan said, all those [statements] of Rebbi Simeon ben Iohai which are so-and-so are isolated opinions and one cannot rely on them.

124 Reading of the Genizah ms. The other mss. and *editio princeps* read תמן.
125 Num. 24:21. The same quote in the Babli, 46a/b.
126 Deut. 21:4. While the *vaw* starting the sentence is quite necessary as *vaw consecutive*, R. Simeon wants to construe it as unnecessary addition which enlarges the domain in which the calf could have its neck broken. There are no parallels to this opinion.

(23d, line 48) וְצָרִיךְ לַעֲרוֹף בָּהּ שְׁנַיִם אוֹ רוֹב שְׁנַיִם. נִישְׁמְעִינָהּ מִן הָדָא. דְּאָמַר רִבִּי זְעִירָא רַב יְהוּדָה בְּשֵׁם שְׁמוּאֵל. עַד מָקוֹם שֶׁהַצַּנָּאר כָּשֵׁר לִשְׁחִיטָה כְּנֶגְדּוֹ הָעוֹרֶף כָּשֵׁר לִמְלִיקָה. וְכָן הוּא אָמַר אָכֵן.

Does he break its neck until he has cut two blood arteries[127] or most of them? Let us hear from the following, that Rebbi Ze'ira said, Rav Jehudah in the name of Samuel: Any place the bottom of the neck is acceptable for slaughtering, the back of the neck is acceptable for breaking[128]; here he would say the same.

127 The carotid arteries leading to the brain and the windpipe which must be cut in ritual slaughter.

128 This breaking, מְלִיקָה, is done by the finger nail on the neck of a pidgeon used as a purification offering. Since it says "he may not separate (the head from the body)" (*Lev.* 5:8), it is clear that the Cohen has to cut the arteries and the windpipe. In the absence of an indication to the contrary, this requirement may be transferred to the breaking of the calf's neck.

(23d, line 51) תַּמָּן תַּנִּינָן. יֵשׁ חוֹרֵשׁ תֶּלֶם אֶחָד וְחַיָּיב עָלָיו מִשּׁוּם שְׁמוֹנֶה לָאוִין. רִבִּי הוֹשַׁעְיָה בָּעֵי. נִיתְנֵי הַחוֹרֵשׁ מְקוֹם עֲרִיפָתָהּ שֶׁלָּעֶגְלָה הֲרֵי תִשְׁעָה. אָמְרִין חֲבֵרַיָּיא קוֹמֵי רִבִּי יוֹסֵי. תִּיפְתָּר לְשֶׁעָבַר. אָמַר לוֹן. מַה דְאִית לָהּ לְשֶׁעָבַר כָּל־שֶׁכֵּן לָבֹא.

There[129], we have stated: "One might plough one furrow and infringe thereby on eight prohibitions." Rebbi Hoshaia asked: Could one not state "one who ploughs the place where the calf's neck was broken," for a total of nine[130]? The colleagues said before Rebbi Yose: Explain it by the past[131]. He said to them, since it was for the past, so certainly for the future[132].

129 Mishnah *Makkot* 3:9. A person who is both a Cohen and a Nazir ploughing in a graveyard in which both vines and grain grow, on a holiday of a Sabbatical year, with an ox and a donkey together which both were dedicated to the Temple.

130 The same questions in the Babli, *Makkot* 22a. The obvious answer is that this could not be a graveyard in which both vines and grain grow.

131 Since verse 21:4 says of the hard valley: "which would not be worked on and would not be sown". The imperfect may be interpreted as a past.

132 The primary meaning of the imperfect is as a future.

HALAKHAH 5

(23d, line 54) מְקוֹם גִּיסָתָהּ וּתְפִיסָתָהּ הֲרֵי אֵילוּ אֲסוּרִין. וְכַמָּה הִיא תְפִיסָתָהּ. אַרְבַּע אַמּוֹת. רִבִּי אוֹמֵר. אוֹמֵר אֲנִי שֶׁתְּפִיסָתָהּ חֲמִשִּׁים אַמָּה. רִבִּי שְׁמוּאֵל בְּרֵיהּ דְּרִבִּי יוֹסֵי בֵּירִבִּי בּוּן. אֲשֶׁר לֹא יֵעָבֵד בּוֹ כְּלָל. וְלֹא יִזָּרֵעַ. פְּרָט. כְּלָל וּפְרָט אֵין בִּכְלָל אֶלָּא מַה שֶּׁבִּפְרָט. אָמַר לֵיהּ. אִילוּ הָיָה כְּתִיב. אֲשֶׁר לֹא יֵעָבֵד בּוֹ אֲשֶׁר לֹא יִזָּרֵעַ יָאוּת. לֵית כְּתִיב אֶלָּא אֲשֶׁר לֹא יֵעָבֵד בּוֹ. כִּי הָא דָמַר רִבִּי זְעִירָא. אֵין כָּן כְּלָל וּפְרָט אֶלָּא רִבּוּיִין.

The place where it[132] falls down and its surroundings are forbidden. How much are its surroundings? Four cubits[133]. Rebbi says, I am saying that its surroundings are fifty cubits[134]. Rebbi Samuel the son of Rebbi Yose ben Rebbi Abun: "which would not be worked on," a general statement. "And would not be sown," a detail. If a general statement is followed by a detail, the general does not contain more than the detail[95]. He said to him, if it were written "which would not be worked on, which would not be sown," you would be justified; but it is written "which would not be worked on." This does not describe general statement and detail, but an additional reference[136].

133 Where the calf falls down. The *hapax* גיסה in the opinion of S. Lieberman may be Syriac. In the two Tosephta mss. (9:1) the readings are גיחה, גיזחה

134 In the Tosephta: 40 cubits. Since no reason is given for that number and it does not appear in other agricultural contexts, the reading of the Yerushalmi is preferable. The Genizah ms. is not available at this point. The notion that a strip 4 cubits wide is attached to a given domain appears in several contexts, agricultural (as boundary strip between fields) and not agricultural (as private domain on the Sabbath, as reserved domain in front of a house in a multi-family courtyard).

135 Probably one should not read this as forbidding a circle of radius 50 around the burial place of the calf but as the side length of a standard field (*bet se'ah*) of 50 by 50 cubits centered at the burial place and oriented NS,

EW (cf. *Kilaim* Chapter 1, Note 195). This agrees with standard rabbinic metrology.

136 That "work" means agricultural use, but that industrial use of the place is permitted.

(fol. 23a) **משנה ה:** זִקְנֵי אוֹתָהּ הָעִיר רוֹחֲצִים יְדֵיהֶם בַּמַּיִם בִּמְקוֹם עֲרִיפָתָהּ שֶׁלָעֶגְלָה וְאוֹמְרִים יָדֵינוּ לֹא שָׁפְכוּ אֶת הַדָּם הַזֶּה וגו'. וְכִי עָלָה עַל לִבֵּינוּ שֶׁבֵּית דִּין שׁוֹפְכֵי דָמִים הֵן. אֶלָּא שֶׁלֹּא בָא לְיָדֵינוּ וּפְטַרְנוּהוּ וְלֹא רְאִינוּהוּ וְהִנַּחְנוּהוּ.

Mishnah 5: The Elders of that town wash their hands with water at the place where the calf's neck was broken and say[137]: "Our hands did not spill this blood," etc. Did we ever think that the court was spilling blood? But, that he did not come to our attention and we sent him away, or that we did not see him and left him[138].

137 *Deut.* 21:7. The Yerushalmi version of this Mishnah is rather shorter than the Babli one. The Yerushalmi version is that of *Sifry Deut.*, 210.

138 The court can perform the ceremony only if it did not tolerate a breakdown of social services.

(fol. 23d) **הלכה ה:** רַבָּנִין דְּהָכָא פֵּתְרִין קְרִייָא בָּהוֹרֵג. וְרַבָּנִין דְּתַמָּן פֵּתְרִין קְרִייָא בַּנֶּהֱרָג. רַבָּנִין דְּהָכָא פֵּתְרִין קְרִייָא בָּהוֹרֵג. שֶׁלֹּא בָא עַל יָדֵינוּ וּפְטַרְנוּהוּ. וְלֹא הֲרָגְנוּהוּ. וְלֹא רְאִינוּהוּ וְהִנַּחְנוּהוּ. וְעִימְעַמְנוּ עַל דִּינוֹ. וְרַבָּנִין דְּתַמָּן פֵּתְרִין קְרִייָא בַּנֶּהֱרָג. לֹא בָא עַל יָדֵינוּ וּפְטַרְנוּהוּ. בְּלֹא הַלְוָיָיה. וְלֹא רְאִינוּהוּ וְהִנַּחְנוּהוּ. בְּלֹא פַרְנָסָה.

Halakhah 5: The rabbis here explain the verse[139] about the murderer, the rabbis there explain the verse about the murder victim. The rabbis here explain the verse about the murderer, "he did not come to our attention and we sent him away," and did not execute him; "or that we did not see him and left him," and muddled his trial. But the rabbis there[140] explain the verse about the murder victim, "he did not come to our attention and we sent him away," without company; "or that we did not see him and left him," without provisions.

139 In all occurrences, the Genizah ms. reads "the Mishnah", which is the more accurate text.

140 Babli 46b; an extended version by R. Joshua ben Levi, insisting that unsolved murder cases exist only if social services are insufficient, Babli 38b.

(fol. 23b) **משנה ו:** הַכֹּהֲנִים אוֹמְרִים כַּפֵּר לְעַמְּךָ יִשְׂרָאֵל אֲשֶׁר פָּדִיתָ יי וְלֹא הָיוּ צְרִיכִין לוֹמַר וְנִכַּפֵּר לָהֶם הַדָּם אֶלָּא רוּחַ הַקּוֹדֶשׁ מְבַשְׂרָתָן אֵימָתַי שֶׁתַּעֲשׂוּ כָּכָה הַדָּם מִתְכַּפֵּר לָכֶם. נִמְצָא הַהוֹרֵג עַד שֶׁלֹּא תִיעָרֵף הָעֶגְלָה תֵּצֵא וְתִרְאֶה בָעֵדֶר. מִשֶּׁנֶּעֶרְפָה הָעֶגְלָה תִּיקָּבֵר בִּמְקוֹמָהּ שֶׁעַל סָפֵק בָּאָה מִתְּחִילָתָהּ כִּיפְּרָה סְפֵיקָהּ וְהָלְכָה לָהּ. נֶעֶרְפָה הָעֶגְלָה וְאַחַר כָּךְ נִמְצָא הַהוֹרֵג הֲרֵי זֶה יֵיהָרֵג.

Mishnah 6: The priests say[141]: "Purge for Your people Israel which You did redeem, o Eternal." They did not have to say that[141] "the blood was purged for them," but the Holy Spirit announces to them that when they follow this procedure the blood will be purged for them. If the killer was found before the calf should have its neck broken, it should leave[142] and graze in the flock. If after the calf's neck was broken it should be buried at its place because if came from the start in a doubtful case; it purged its doubt and left. If the killer was found after the calf's neck was broken, he should be executed[143].

| 141 | *Deut.* 21:8. | 143 | The calf atones for the community, not the murderer. |
| 142 | It becomes totally profane. | | |

הלכה ו: (fol. 23d) וְהַזְּקֵנִים רוֹחֲצִין אֶת יְדֵיהֶן בַּמַּיִם עַל מְקוֹם עֲרִיפָתָהּ שֶׁלָּעֶגְלָה. וְאוֹמְרִים יָדֵינוּ לֹא שָׁפְכוּ אֶת הַדָּם הַזֶּה וגו'. וְהַכֹּהֲנִים אוֹמְרִים כַּפֵּר לְעַמְּךָ יִשְׂרָאֵל. וְרוּחַ הַקּוֹדֶשׁ אוֹמֶרֶת וְנִכַּפֵּר לָהֶם הַדָּם. שְׁלֹשָׁה מִקְרִיּוֹת נֶאֱמְרוּ בְעִנְיָין אֶחָד. מַה שֶּׁאָמַר זֶה לֹא אָמַר זֶה וּמַה שֶּׁאָמַר זֶה לֹא אָמַר זֶה. כַּיּוֹצֵא בַדָּבָר אַתָּה אוֹמֵר. וַתֹּאמֶר הַכֶּר נָא לְמִי הַחוֹתֶמֶת וְהַפְּתִילִים וְהַמַּטֶּה הָאֵלֶּה. עַד כָּאן אָמְרָה תָמָר. וַיַּכֵּר יְהוּדָה וַיֹּאמֶר צָדְקָה מִמֶּנִּי כִּי עַל כֵּן לֹא נְתַתִּיהָ לְשֵׁלָה בְנִי. עַד כָּאן אָמַר יְהוּדָה. וְרוּחַ הַקּוֹדֶשׁ אָמְרָה. וְלֹא יָסַף עוֹד לְדַעְתָּהּ. שְׁלֹשָׁה מִקְרִיּוֹת נֶאֱמְרוּ בְעִנְיָין אֶחָד. מַה שֶּׁאָמַר זֶה לֹא אָמַר זֶה [וּמַה שֶּׁאָמַר זֶה לֹא אָמַר זֶה]. כַּיּוֹצֵא בַדָּבָר אַתָּה אוֹמֵר. וַיְסַפְּרוּ לוֹ וַיֹּאמְרוּ בָּאנוּ אֶל הָאָרֶץ אֲשֶׁר שְׁלַחְתָּנוּ וְגַם זָבַת חָלָב וּדְבַשׁ הִיא וְזֶה פִּרְיָיהּ. עַד כָּאן אָמַר יְהוֹשֻׁעַ. אֶפֶס כִּי עַז הָעָם הַיּוֹשֵׁב בָּאָרֶץ וְהֶעָרִים בְּצוּרוֹת גְּדוֹלוֹת מְאֹד וְגַם יְלִידֵי הָעֲנָק רָאִינוּ שָׁם. עַד כָּאן אָמְרוּ הַמְרַגְּלִים. וַיַּהַס כָּלֵב אֶת הָעָם אֶל מֹשֶׁה וַיֹּאמֶר עָלֹה נַעֲלֶה וְיָרַשְׁנוּ אוֹתָהּ כִּי יָכוֹל נוּכַל לָהּ. עַד כָּאן אָמַר כָּלֵב. שָׁלֹשׁ מִקְרִיּוֹת נֶאֱמְרוּ בְעִנְיָין אֶחָד. מַה שֶּׁאָמַר זֶה לֹא אָמַר זֶה וּמַה שֶּׁאָמַר זֶה לֹא אָמַר זֶה. כַּיּוֹצֵא בַדָּבָר אַתָּה אוֹמֵר. בְּעַד הַחַלּוֹן נִשְׁקְפָה וַתְּיַבֵּב אֵם סִיסְרָא וגו'. עַד כָּאן אָמְרָה אִמּוֹ שֶׁלְּסִיסְרָא. חַכְמוֹת שָׂרוֹתֶיהָ תַּעֲנֶינָה. הֲלֹא יִמְצְאוּ יְחַלְּקוּ שָׁלָל. [עַד כָּאן] אָמְרוּ כַלּוֹתֶיהָ. וְרוּחַ הַקּוֹדֶשׁ אוֹמֶרֶת. כֵּן יֹאבְדוּ כָל־אוֹיְבֶיךָ יי.

Halakhah 6: The Elders wash their hands with water at the place where the calf's neck was broken and say[138]: "Our hands did not spill this blood," etc. The priests say[141]: "Purge for Your people Israel." The Holy Spirit says, "the blood was purged for them." Three verses were said on one topic, what this one said the other did not say, and vice-versa. Similarly, you say[144]: "She said, please recognize this seal, strings, and staff," so far Tamar spoke. "Jehudah recognized and said, she is more just than I am because I did not give her to my son Shelah," so far Jehudah spoke. The Holy Spirit said, "he never knew her again.[145]" Three verses were said on one topic, what this one said the other did not say, and vice-versa. Similarly, you say[146]: "They told him and said, we came to the land you sent us to; it really is flowing of milk and honey and that is its fruit;" so far Joshua spoke. "But the people are strong who dwell in the land, the cities are very highly fortified, and also the young giants we saw there;" so far said the spies. "Caleb silenced the people to Moses and said, we certainly can mount and inherit it, for certainly we can do it;" so far Caleb spoke. Three verses were said on one topic, what this one said the other did not say, and vice-versa. Similarly, you say[147]: "Sisera's mother looked out and whimpered, etc.;" so far Sisera's mother spoke. "Her wise princesses answered her, . . ., will they not find and distribute booty;" so far said her daughters-in-law. And the Holy Spirit says, "so all enemies of the Eternal will be lost."

144 *Gen.* 38:25-26. A different version in the Babli, *Makkot* 23b.
145 On could also translate: He never stopped knowing her.
146 *Num.* 13:27-30. The interpretation saves Joshua's reputation, who is silent in the biblical narrative.
147 *Jud.* 5:28-31.

(24a line 8) אָמַר רִבִּי פִּינְחָס. כְּדַיי הוּא שֶׁתְּכַפֵּר עַד יְצִיאַת מִצְרַיִם.

Rebbi Phineas said, it is worthy to provide purification all the time back to the Exodus[148].

148 In *Sifry Deut.* 210, this is an anonymous tannaitic statement. A comment which there entered the text from the margin explains: "This (the response of the Holy Spirit to the priest's prayer) teaches that the

homicide sins against the Jewish people who left Egypt."
in all generations going back to those

(24a, line 9) אָמַר רִבִּי יַנַּאי. דִּבְרֵי רִבִּי מֵאִיר. אֲפִילוּ עָרְפָה חַייָב. רִבִּי יַעֲקֹב בַּר אָחָא רִבִּי אִמִּי בְשֵׁם רִבִּי שִׁמְעוֹן בֶּן לָקִישׁ. דִּבְרֵי רִבִּי מֵאִיר. אֲפִילוּ עָרְפָה [חַייָב. דִּבְרֵי רִבִּי שִׁמְעוֹן. אֲפִילוּ שְׁחָטָהּ]¹⁴⁹ פָּטוּר. אָמַר רִבִּי יַנַּאי. שָׁמַעְתִּי לָהּ גְּבוּל מֵאֵימָתַי הִיא נֶאֱסֶרֶת. וְהוֹרִידוּ. מִשְׁעַת הוֹרָדָהּ. אָמַר רִבִּי אִילָא. לְפוֹטְרָהּ מִשּׁוּם אוֹתוֹ וְאֶת בְּנוֹ כְּרִבִּי שִׁמְעוֹן.

Rebbi Yannai said, the words of Rebbi Meïr: Even if one broke its neck he is guilty[150]. Rebbi Jacob bar Aḥa, Rebbi Immi, in the name of Rebbi Simeon ben Laqish: The words of Rebbi Meïr: Even if one broke its neck he is guilty. The words of Rebbi Simeon: Even if he cut its throat, he is not punishable[151]. Rebbi Yannai said, I heard about a boundary, from when it is forbidden: "They shall bring it down," from the time of bringing down[152]. Rebbi Ila said, to free it from "it and its young" following Rebbi Simeon[153].

(24a, line 13) אָמַר רִבִּי שְׁמוּאֵל בַּר רַב יִצְחָק. עַד שֶׁהִיא בַחַיִּים הִיא קְדוֹשָׁה. מַתְנִיתָא אָמְרָה כֵן. תֵּצֵא וְתִרְעֶה בָעֵדֶר. מַהוּ תֵצֵא. תֵּצֵא מִקְדוּשָׁתָהּ.

Rebbi Samuel bar Rav Isaac said, it is holy while still alive. The Mishnah said so: "it should leave and graze in the flock." What shall it leave? It shall leave its holiness.

(24, line 15) אָמַר רִבִּי מַתַּנְיָא. יֵאוֹת. מַה כְתִיב וְנִכַּפֵּר לָהֶם הַדָּם וְשָׁתָק. אֶלָּא אֲפִילוּ כֵן וְאַתָּה תְּבָעֵר הַדָּם הַנָּקִי מִקִּרְבֶּךָ.

Rebbi Mattania said, this is correct[154]. What is written? "The blood shall be purged *for them*[155];" then it is silent. Nevertheless, "but you shall eliminate innocent blood from your midst"[156].

149 Text from the Genizah, missing in the other two mss. and *editio princeps*. The text from the Genizah is required since (1) R. Simeon ben Laqish cannot differ with a Tanna without tannaitic support and (2) R. Ila's statement makes no sense without it.

150 If a calf has its neck broken the same day its mother was slaughtered for food, cf. Note 120.

151 R. Simeon holds that any use of the verb שחט in the Pentateuch refers to slaughter either for the altar or human consumption (*Hulin* 82a). Since the verse which forbids slaughtering mother and young on the same day uses the word תשחטו, it follows that for him only the provision of food either for the altar or humans is forbidden; nothing done with an atoning calf falls under that law.

152 In the Babli, *Hulin* 82a, R. Yannai stated only that he heard that there is a well defined moment in which the calf becomes sanctified and loses its quality as potential food; the members of his Academy determined that moment to be when the calf enters the unworkable area of the valley.

153 This qualifies the statement of R. Simeon ben Laqish in the name of R. Simeon (ben Iohai). If the mother was slaughtered while her calf was still potential profane food, the calf cannot be slaughtered on the same day. If the mother was slaughtered after the calf had lost its status as potential food, even if the calf was wrongly slaughtered by cutting its throat instead of breaking its neck, the prohibition was not infringed upon. The Babli does not follow this argument.

154 This refers to the statement that if the calf was killed before the murderer was found, the murderer still can be executed.

155 The community, not the murderer.

156 *Deut.* 21:9. Babylonian sources (*Sotah* 47b, *Ketubot* 37b, *Tosephta Keritut* 4:3) quote an unrelated verse, *Num.* 35:33.

(fol. 23b) **משנה ז:** עַד אֶחָד אוֹמֵר רָאִיתִי אֶת הַהוֹרֵג וְעַד אֶחָד אוֹמֵר לֹא רָאִיתִי אִשָּׁה אוֹמֶרֶת רָאִיתִי וְאִשָּׁה אוֹמֶרֶת לֹא רָאִיתִי הָיוּ עוֹרְפִין. עַד אֶחָד

אוֹמֵר רָאִיתִי וּשְׁנַיִם אוֹמְרִים לֹא רָאִינוּ הָיוּ עוֹרְפִין. שְׁנַיִם אוֹמְרִים רָאִינוּ וְאֶחָד אוֹמֵר לָהֶן לֹא רְאִיתֶם לֹא הָיוּ עוֹרְפִין.

Mishnah 7: If one witness says, I saw the murderer[157], and one witness says, I did not see him[158]; or a woman[159] said, I saw, but another woman said, I did not see, they did break the neck. If one witness said I saw, but two said, we did not see, they did break the neck. I two said, we saw, but one said to them, you did not see[160], they did not break the neck.

157 He could identify the murderer if he was caught.

158 He saw the murder being committed but did not see the murderer and could not identify him in court. Then the murderer cannot be prosecuted under biblical law. (This means that when caught he could not be executed. It does not exclude that under the king's police powers he could be punished.)

159 Or any other witness who can testify to facts but not in law. (For example, the testimony of gamblers, criminals, women, or slaves cannot be used to impose the death penalty or to notarize documents.)

160 He was with them and testifies that from their position it was impossible to see the murderer. Since he is one against two, his testimony is disregarded.

(fol. 24a) **הלכה ז**: גִּידֵל בַּר בִּנְיָימִין בְּשֵׁם רַב. בְּכָל־מָקוֹם שֶׁהִכְשִׁירוּ עֵדוּת הָאִשָּׁה בָּאִישׁ. הָאִישׁ מַכְחִישׁ אֶת הָאִשָּׁה וְהָאִשָּׁה מַכְחֶשֶׁת אֶת הָאִישׁ. נִיתְנֵי[161]. עֵד אוֹמֵר. רָאִיתִי אֶת הַהוֹרֵג. אִשָּׁה אָמְרָה. לֹא רָאִיתִי. אִשָּׁה אָמְרָה רָאִיתִי. וְעֵד אוֹמֵר. לֹא רָאִיתִי. כִּדְתַנֵּי בְּשֵׁם רִבִּי נְחֶמְיָה. הוֹלְכִין אַחַר רוֹב הַדֵּיעוֹת. הֵיךְ עֲבִידָה. שְׁתַּיִם נָשִׁים וְאִישׁ אֶחָד עָשׂוּ אוֹתָן כִּשְׁנֵי עֵדִים וְעֵד אֶחָד. הָדָא אַתְּ אָמַר בְּאִשָּׁה וְנָשִׁים. אֲבָל אִם הָיוּ מֵאָה נָשִׁים וְעֵד אֶחָד כְּעֵד בְּעֵד אִינּוּן.

Halakhah 7: [162]Gidul bar Benjamin in the name of Rav: Anywhere they accepted the testimony of a woman parallel to that of a man, a man can contradict a woman and a woman can contradict a man. One should state: "A witness says that he saw the murderer, and a woman says that she did not see; a woman said that he saw and a witness said that he did not see," as it was stated in the name of Rebbi Neḥemiah: One follows the majority of the testimonies. How is that? Two women against one woman they considered as if there were two witnesses against one witness. What you say refers to a woman and women. But if there were a hundred women against one [male] witness, they are like one witness.

161 Reading of the Rome ms. Leiden ms: 'מתני' "the Mishnah". The Genizah ms. has here only a reference to the other occurrences of this text.

162 See the parallel texts *Yebamot* 15, Notes 135-138; *Soṭah* 6:4; *Babli* 47b.

משנה ח: מִשֶּׁרַבּוּ הָרוֹצְחָנִין בָּטְלָה עֶגְלָה עֲרוּפָה. מִשֶּׁבָּא אֶלְעָזָר בֶּן דִּינַאי וּתְחִינָה בֶּן פְּרִישָׁה הָיָה נִקְרָא. חָזְרוּ לִקְרוֹתוֹ בֶּן הָרַצְחָן. (fol. 23b)

Mishnah 8: When professional murderers prevailed, breaking of the calf's neck became obsolete, when Eleazar ben Dinai came[163] who was called Teḥina ben Perisha. They turned to call him murderous son.

הלכה ח: בֶּן הָרַצְחָן.[164] בְּרָא קְטוֹלָא (fol. 24a)

Halakhah 8: "Murderous son," son, professional murderer[165].

163 Josephus, *Antiquities* XX, 6,1; *Jewish War* II, 12,4; 13,6; VII, 8,1.
164 In the Genizah ms: הרוצחן.
165 This shows that professional names of the pattern *pĕ'ôlā* were felt to be Aramaic, not Hebrew.

משנה ט: מִשֶּׁרַבּוּ הַמְנָאֲפִים פָּסְקוּ הַמַּיִם הַמְאָרְרִין וְרַבָּן יוֹחָנָן בֶּן זַכַּיי (fol. 23b)
הִפְסִיקָן שֶׁנֶּאֱמַר לֹא אֶפְקוֹד עַל בְּנוֹתֵיכֶם כִּי תִזְנֶינָה וגו'.

Mishnah 9: When the adulterers prevailed, the spell-inducing water stopped and Rabban Joḥanan ben Zakkai[166] abolished it, as it is said[167]: "I shall not care if your daughters are whoring," etc.

166 It is unclear when he abolished the ritual of the suspected wife and whether this was part of his program to divorce Judaism from Temple rituals.
167 *Hos.* 4:14.

(fol. 24a) **הלכה ט**: דִּכְתִיב כִּי הֵם עִם הַזּוֹנוֹת יְפָרֵדוּ. וּכְתִיב וְהָיְתָה הָאִשָּׁה לְאָלָה בְּקֶרֶב עַמָּהּ. בִּזְמַן שֶׁעַמָּהּ שָׁלוֹם. לֹא בִּזְמַן שֶׁעַמָּהּ פְּרוּצִים. וְנִקָּה הָאִישׁ מֵעָווֹן. אֵימָתַי הָאִשָּׁה נוֹשְׂאָה אֶת עֲווֹנָהּ. בִּזְמַן שֶׁהָאִישׁ נָקִי מֵעָווֹן.

Halakhah 9: For it is written[167], "for they behave like donkeys with the prostitutes," and it is written[168]: "The woman will be a swearword among her people." In times when her people are peaceful, not in times when her people are dissolute. "The man shall be free from sin.[169]" When does the woman carry her iniquity? If the man is free from sin[170].

168 *Num.* 5:27.
169 *Num.* 5:31. In the Genizah ms., the entire verse is copied, as required by the following homily: "The man shall be free from sin, then this woman will bear her iniquity."
170 A more extended treatment in the Babli, 47b; *Num. rabba* 9(53); *Sifry Num.* 21. An opposing opinion *Sifry zuṭa Naśo* 31.

משנה י: מִשֶּׁמֵּת יוֹסֵי בֶּן יוֹעֶזֶר אִישׁ צְרֵדָה וְיוֹסֵי בֶּן יוֹחָנָן אִישׁ יְרוּשָׁלֵם (fol. 23b)
בָּטְלוּ הָאֶשְׁכּוֹלוֹת שֶׁנֶּאֱמַר אֵין אֶשְׁכּוֹל לֶאֱכוֹל בִּיכּוּרָה עִוְּתָה נַפְשִׁי.

When Yose ben Yo'ezer from Sereda and Yose ben Johanan from Jerusalem died[171], the grape bunches[172] disappeared, as it was said[173]: "There is no bunch to eat, no early ripe fig that my soul desires."

171 The first couple of leaders mentioned in *Abot* (1:4).
172 People who united in their personalities knowledge, exemplary behavior, and leadership.

173 *Micah* 7:1. The reference is to v. 2: "The devout man has perished from the earth, there is no upright person among humankind."

הלכה י: וְלֹא עָמַד אֶשְׁכּוֹל עַד שֶׁעָמַד רִבִּי עֲקִיבָה. וְכָל־הַזּוּגוֹת לֹא הָיוּ אֶשְׁכּוֹלוֹת. אֶלָּא אֵילּוּ שִׁמְּשׁוּ פַרְנָסוּת. וְאֵילוּ לֹא שִׁמְּשׁוּ פַרְנָסוּת. (fol. 24a)

Halakhah 10: There did not arise another grape bunch until Rebbi Aqiba rose. Were the other couples[174] not also grape bunches? But these served in a position of leadership[175]; the others did not serve in a position of leadership.

174 Those mentioned in the first Chapter of Mishnah *Abot* after the two Yose.
175 They served just before the Maccabean revolt; Yose ben Yo'ezer was killed as an opponent of the Seleucids. It seems that the two were the heads of the ruling council of the province of Judea. After the revolt, the political power was totally divorced from the spiritual leadership and the later couples could not attain the political role played by the first or by R. Aqiba in the Bar Kokhba years.

(24a, line 29) תַּנֵּי. כָּל־הַזּוּגוֹת שֶׁעָמְדוּ מִשֶּׁמֵת מֹשֶׁה עַד שֶׁעָמַד יוֹסֵי בֶּן יוֹעֶזֶר אִישׁ צְרֵדָה וְיוֹסֵף בֶּן יוֹחָנָן אִישׁ יְרוּשָׁלֵם אֶיפְשַׁר לִיתֵּן בָּהֶן דּוֹפִי. [מִשֶּׁמֵת יוֹסֵי בֶּן יוֹעֶזֶר אִישׁ צְרֵדָה וְיוֹסֵף בֶּן יוֹחָנָן אִישׁ יְרוּשָׁלֵם][176] עַד שֶׁעָמַד רִבִּי יְהוּדָה בֶּן בָּבָא אֶיפְשַׁר לִיתֵּן בָּהֶן דּוֹפִי. אָמְרוּ עַל רִבִּי יְהוּדָה בֶּן בָּבָא שֶׁהָיוּ כָּל־מַעֲשָׂיו לְשׁוּם שָׁמַיִם אֶלָּא שֶׁגִּידֵּל בְּהֵמָה דַקָּה. וְכָךְ הָיָה מַעֲשֶׂה. פַּעַם אַחַת חָלָה וְנִכְנְסוּ

הָרוֹפְאִים אֶצְלוֹ לְבַקְּרוֹ. אָמְרוּ לוֹ. אֵין לָךְ רְפוּאָה אֶלָּא חָלָב רוֹתֵחַ. שֶׁהָיָה גּוֹנֵחַ. מֶה עָשָׂה. לָקַח עֵז וּקְשָׁרָהּ לְכַרְעֵי מִיטָּתוֹ וְהָיָה יוֹנֵק מִמֶּנָּה חָלָב רוֹתֵחַ בְּשָׁעָה שֶׁהָיָה גוֹנֵחַ. וּכְשֶׁבִּקְּשׁוּ חֲכָמִים לְהִיכָּנֵס אֶצְלוֹ אָמְרוּ. הֵיאַךְ אָנוּ יְכוֹלִין לְהִיכָּנֵס וְהַלֵיסְטִיס עִמּוֹ בַּבַּיִת. וּבִשְׁעַת מִיתָתוֹ אָמַר. אֵין בְּיָדִי עָוֹן אֶלָּא אֶלָּא זֶה שֶׁעָבַרְתִּי עַל דִּבְרֵי חֲבֵרָיי. וּכְשֶׁמֵת דִּיקְדְּקוּ חֲכָמִים עַל כָּל־מַעֲשָׂיו. וְלֹא מָצְאוּ בְיָדוֹ עָוֹן אֶלָּא אוֹתָהּ הָעֵז בִּלְבָד.

It was stated: It is possible to raise questions about all couples[177] from the time that Moses died until Yose ben Yoezer from Ṣereda and Joseph ben Joḥanan from Jerusalem. It is possible to raise questions about all couples from the time that Yose ben Yoezer from Ṣereda and Joseph ben Joḥanan from Jerusalem died until Rebbi Jehudah ben Baba arose. They said about Rebbi Jehudah ben Baba that all he did was in the name of Heaven except that he raised an animal of the flock[178]. This happened the following way. Once he fell sick and the medical men went to visit him. They told him: there is no healing for you except freshly warm milk, because he had *angina pectoris*. What did he do? He bought a goat and bound it to the legs of his bed[179] and when he had an attack of angina he sucked from it freshly warm milk. But when the Sages wanted to visit him, they said how could we enter when the robber[180] dwells with him in the house? When he died, he said: I did never sin except that in this case I disregarded the words of my colleagues. After his death they checked all he had done and did not find any sin except that goat alone[181].

176 Text from the Genizah ms., missing in the other mss. and *editio princeps*.

177 The president (נָשִׂיא) and executive officer (אַב בֵּית דִּין) of the high court of the nation at any given moment.

The text here is the opposite of the tradition of the Babli (*Temurah* 15b) which states that the couples who held office between Moses and the two Yoses either taught Torah as well as Moses did or that it was impossible to find anything questionable about them.

178 There exists a rabbinic rule (Babli *Temurah* 15b, *Baba qama* 80a) which forbids raising sheep and goats in agricultural lands because their destructive feeding habits.

179 That it could not roam and damage plants.

180 Greek λῃστής, "robber".

181 The Babli, *Temurah* 15b, tells this story about "a pious man" and doubts whether it is about R. Jehudah ben Baba, who was executed by the Roman government in the aftermath of the war of Bar Kokhba, or R. Jehudah bar Ilai, known simply as R. Jehudah.

(24a, line 40) אָמַר רִבִּי שִׁמְעוֹן שְׁזוּרִי. שֶׁלְּבֵית אַבָּא הָיוּ בַעֲלֵי בָתִּים בַּגָּלִיל. וְלָמָּה חָרְבוּ. שֶׁהָיוּ דָנִין דִּינֵי מָמוֹנוֹת בְּאֶחָד וּמְגַדְּלִין בְּהֵמָה דַקָּה. וְכָךְ הָיָה. חוֹרֶשׁ אֶחָד הָיָה לָנוּ סָמוּךְ לָעִיר וְהָיְתָה הַשָּׂדֶה בֵּינֵינוּ וּבֵינָהּ. וְהָיְתָה הַצֹּאן לִכְנֶסֶת וְיוֹצְאָה וְהַדֶּרֶךְ עָלֶיהָ.

Rebbi Simeon from Shezur said, my father's family were landowners in Galilee. Why were they ruined? Because they judged civil matters alone[182] and were raising animals of the flock. And this was so. We had a copse close to the village but a field was between it and us, and the flock entered it going and coming there[183].

182 While a competent judge may sit alone in judgment, it is bad behavior since only God judges alone (Mishnah *Sanhedrin* 1:1).

183 The goats did damage to agriculture while being driven to the woods. He denies that R. Jehudah ben Baba did anything wrong since he was careful to keep his goat from doing damage and holds him a blameless pious man.

משנה יא: יוֹחָנָן כֹּהֵן גָּדוֹל הֶעֱבִיר הוֹדָיַת הַמַּעֲשֵׂר. אַף הוּא בִּיטֵל אֶת (fol. 23b) הַמְּעוֹרְרִים וְאֶת הַנּוֹקְפִים עַד יָמָיו הָיָה פַּטִּישׁ מַכֶּה בִּירוּשָׁלֵם וּבְיָמָיו אֵין אָדָם צָרִיךְ לִשְׁאוֹל עַל הַדְּמַיי.

Mishnah 11: [184]The High Priest Johanan disestablished the declaration of tithes. He also eliminated the arousers and the hitters. Up to his days the hammer was hitting in Jerusalem and in his days nobody had to ask about *demay*.

184 This Mishnah and its Halakhah are from *Ma'aser Šeni* 5, Mishnah 13, explained there in Notes 171ff. to the end of that Tractate.

(fol. 24a) **הלכה יא**: רִבִּי יִרְמְיָה רִבִּי חִייָה בְּשֵׁם רִבִּי שִׁמְעוֹן בֶּן לָקִישׁ. מַתְנִיתָא מִשֶּׁנֶּחְשְׁדוּ לִהְיוֹת נוֹתְנִין מַעֲשֵׂר לִכְהוּנָה. הָדָא מְסַייְעָא לֵיהּ לְרִבִּי יוֹחָנָן בַּחֲדָא וּפְלִיגָא עָלֵיהּ בַּחֲדָא. [פְּלִיגָא עֲלוֹי][185] דְּתַנִּינָן תַּמָּן וּבַת כֹּהֵן לְלֵוִי לֹא תֹאכַל[186] לֹא יֹאכְלוּ בִתְרוּמָה וְלֹא בְמַעֲשֵׂר. נִיחָא בִתְרוּמָה לֹא תֹאכֵל. בְּמַעֲשֵׂר מַה נַפְשָׁךְ כֹּהֶנֶת הִיא תֹאכַל לְוִייָה הִיא תֹאכַל. רִבִּי אִילָא בְּשֵׁם רִבִּי יוֹחָנָן כְּמָאן דְּאָמַר אֵין נוֹתְנִין מַעֲשֵׂר לִכְהוּנָה. הֲוֵי דּוּ אָמַר נוֹתְנִין מַעֲשֵׂר לִכְהוּנָה.

Halakhah 9: Rebbi Jeremiah, Rebbi Hiyya in the name of Rebbi Simeon ben Laqish: Our Mishnah after the people were suspected of giving tithe to Cohanim. There is support for Rebbi Johanan in one and disagreement with him in one. Disagreement with him as we have stated there: "Similarly, the daughter of a Cohen [married] to a Levite should eat neither heave nor tithe." We understand that she should not eat heave. But tithe any way you take it, if she is a Cohen's daughter she should eat, if she is a Levite's wife she should eat. Rebbi Hila in the name of Rebbi Johanan: [It follows] him who says one does not give tithe to Cohanim. That means, he himself says one gives heave to Cohanim.

(24a, line 50) מְסַיְּיעָא לֵיהּ דּוּ אָמַר. כּוּלָן לְשָׁבַח. דְּאָמַר רִבִּי יוֹחָנָן. יוֹחָנָן כֹּהֵן גָּדוֹל שָׁלַח וּבָדַק בְּכָל־עָרֵי יִשְׂרָאֵל וּמְצָאָן שֶׁלֹּא הָיוּ מַפְרִישִׁין אֶלָּא תְרוּמָה גְדוֹלָה בִּלְבַד. אֲבָל מַעֲשֵׂר רִאשׁוֹן וּמַעֲשֵׂר שֵׁינִי מֵהֶן הָיוּ מַפְרִישִׁין וּמֵהֶן לֹא הָיוּ מַפְרִישִׁין. אָמַר הוֹאִיל וּמַעֲשֵׂר רִאשׁוֹן בַּעֲוֹן מִיתָה. וּמַעֲשֵׂר שֵׁינִי בַּעֲוֹן טֶבֶל יְהֵא אָדָם קוֹרֵא שֵׁם לִתְרוּמָה וְלִתְרוּמַת מַעֲשֵׂר וְנוֹתְנוֹ לְכֹהֵן. וּמַעֲשֵׂר שֵׁינִי מְחַלְּלוֹ עַל הַמָּעוֹת וְהַשְּׁאָר מַעֲשַׂר עָנִי[187] הַמּוֹצִיא מֵחֲבֵירוֹ עָלָיו הָרְאָיָיה.

It supports him because he says it is all praise, as Rebbi Johanan said, Johanan the High Priest sent and checked in all localities of Israel and found that they separated only Great Heave. But First and Second Tithes some were separating and some did not. He said, since [omitting] First Tithe is a deadly sin and [omitting] Second Tithe [implies] the sin of *tevel*, a person should give a name to heave and heave of the tithe and give them to the Cohen; Second Tithe he exchanges for coins. About the remaining tithe of the poor, he who has a claim on another person must bring proof.

(24a, line 56) וְיִתְוַדֶּה. אָמַר רִבִּי הִילָא כַּעַס הוּא לִפְנֵי הַמָּקוֹם מִי שֶׁהוּא אוֹמֵר עָשִׂיתִי וְהוּא לֹא עָשָׂה. מֵעַתָּה מִי שֶׁהוּא מַפְרִישׁ יִתְוַדֶּה. וּמִי שֶׁאֵינוֹ מַפְרִישׁ לֹא יִתְוַדֶּה. כְּהָדָא דְתַנֵּי. עַד הַשְׁקִיפָה הָיוּ אוֹמְרִים קוֹל נָמוּךְ. מִיכָּן וְהֵילָךְ הָיוּ אוֹמְרִים קוֹל גָּבוֹהַּ.

Why should he not make the declaration? Rebbi Hila said, he causes anger before the Omnipresent by saying "I did" when he did not. If it is so, he who separated should make the declaration, he who did not separate should not make the declaration, as we have stated: "Up to 'Look down' they were saying it in an undertone, from 'Look down' onwards in a high voice."

(24a, line 59) אֶת הַמְּעוֹרְרִין. אוֹתָן שֶׁהָיוּ אוֹמְרִים עוּרָה לָמָה תִישַׁן יְיָ וגו'. וְכִי יֵשׁ שֵׁינָה לִפְנֵי הַמָּקוֹם. וַהֲלֹא כְּבָר נֶאֱמַר הִנֵּה לֹא יָנוּם וְלֹא יִישָׁן שׁוֹמֵר יִשְׂרָאֵל. וּמַה תַּלְמוּד לוֹמַר וַיִּקַץ כְּיָשֵׁן יְיָ. אֶלָּא כִּבְיָכוֹל כְּאִלּוּ לְפָנָיו שֵׁינָה בְּשָׁעָה שֶׁיִּשְׂרָאֵל בְּצָרָה וְאוּמוֹת הָעוֹלָם בִּרְוָחָה. וְכֵן הוּא אוֹמֵר וּבְהַמְרוֹתָם תָּלַן עֵינִי.

"The arousers." Those who were saying (*Ps.* 44:24): "Be roused, why do You sleep, o Eternal, etc." Does there exist sleep before the Omnipresent? Has it not already been said (*Ps.* 121:4): "Lo, He will not slumber nor sleep, the Guardian of Israel!" Why does the verse say (*Ps.* 78:65): "Like a sleeper awoke the Eternal, like a hero exhilarated by wine." But in a symbolic way it is as if sleep were before Him when Israel is in trouble and the other peoples are at ease. So it says (*Job* 17:2): "When they apostasize, My Eye will rest."

(24a, line 63) אֶת הַנּוֹקְפִים. אוֹתָן שֶׁהָיוּ מַכִּין עַל גַּבֵּי הָעֵגֶל בֵּין קַרְנָיו. אָמַר לָהֶם יוֹחָנָן כֹּהֵן גָּדוֹל עַד מָתַי אַתֶּם מַאֲכִילִין אֶת הַמִּזְבֵּחַ נְבֵילוֹת. וְעָמַד וְעָשָׂה לָהֶן טַבָּעוֹת. רִבִּי בָּא בְּשֵׁם רִבִּי יְהוּדָה טַבָּעוֹת עָשָׂה לָהֶן. רְחָבוֹת מִלְּמַטָּן וְצָרוֹת מִלְמַעְלָן.

"The hitters." Those who were hitting the calf between its horns. Johanan the High Priest said to them, how long will you feed torn animals to the altar? He went and made them rings. Rebbi Abba in the name of Rebbi Jehudah: He made rings for them, wide below and narrow at the top.

(24a, line 66) עַד יָמָיו הָיָה פַּטִּישׁ מַכֶּה בִירוּשָׁלֶם עַד תְּחִילַּת יָמָיו. וּבְיָמָיו אֵין אָדָם צָרִיךְ לִשְׁאוֹל עַל הַדְּמַאי שֶׁהֶעֱמִיד זוּגוֹת.

"Up to his days the hammer was hitting in Jerusalem," up to his early days. "And in his days nobody had to ask about *demay*" because he sent out teams

(24a, line 68) מִילְתֵיהּ דְּרְבִּי יְהוֹשֻׁעַ בֶּן לֵוִי אָמְרָה מֵהֶן לִגְנַאי וּמֵהֶן לְשֶׁבַח. דְּאָמַר רַבִּי יוֹסֵי בְּשֵׁם רַבִּי תַּנְחוּם רַבִּי חִיָּיה בְּשֵׁם רַבִּי יְהוֹשֻׁעַ בֶּן לֵוִי. בָּרִאשׁוֹנָה הָיָה מַעֲשֵׂר נַעֲשֶׂה לִשְׁלֹשָׁה חֲלָקִים. שְׁלִישׁ לְמַכָּרֵי כְהוּנָה וּלְוָיָה. וּשְׁלִישׁ לָאוֹצָר. וּשְׁלִישׁ לָעֲנִיִּים וְלַחֲבֵרִים שֶׁהָיוּ בִירוּשָׁלֵם. אָמַר רַבִּי יוֹסֵי בֵּירְבִּי בּוּן. מָאן דַּהֲוָה סָלִיק לְמִדִין בִּירוּשָׁלֵם עַד דְּתִלְתָּא אִיגְרִין הֲנָה יָהֵב מִדִּילֵיהּ. מִכָּן וְאֵילָךְ מִשֶּׁלָּאוֹצָר. מִשֶּׁבָּא אֶלְעָזָר בֶּן פְּחוֹרָה וִיהוּדָה בֶּן פְּכוֹרָה הָיוּ נוֹטְלִין אוֹתָן בִּזְרוֹעַ. וְהָיָה סִפֵּיקָן בְּיָדוֹ לִמְחוֹת וְלֹא מִיחָה. וְהֶעֱבִיר הוֹדָיַית הַמַּעֲשֵׂר. וְזוֹ לִגְנַאי. אֶת הַמְעוֹרְרִין לְשֶׁבַח. וְאֶת הַנּוֹקְפִין לְשֶׁבַח.

The word of Rebbi Joshua ben Levi implies some are censure and some praise. Since Rebbi Yose said in the name of Rebbi Tanhum bar Hiyya, Rebbi Hizqiah, Rebbi Eleazar ben Rebbi Yose, Rebbi Tanhum, Rebbi Hiyya in the name of Rebbi Joshua ben Levi, originally tithe was split into three parts. One third to his acquaintances among Cohanim and Levites, one third to the public treasury, one third to the poor and the fellows in Jerusalem. Rebbi Yose ben Rebbi Abun said, a person who went to court in Jerusalem, up to three letters he paid for himself, from there on from the public treasury. When Eleazar ben Pahora and Judah ben Pakora came, they took it by force and it would have been in his hand to stop this but he did not but disestablished the declaration of tithes, and this is for censure. But the arousers for praise and the hitters for praise.

(24a, line 76) עַד יָמָיו הָיָה פַּטִּישׁ מַכֶּה בִירוּשָׁלֵם עַד תְּחִילַת יָמָיו. רַבִּי חֲסִידָא שָׁאַל לְרַבִּי חִזְקִיָה לֹא מִסְתַּבְּרָא עַד סוֹף יָמָיו. אָמַר לֵיהּ אוּף אֲנָא סָבַר כֵּן.

"Up to his days the hammer was hitting in Jerusalem," up to his early days. Rebbi Ḥasida asked Rebbi Ḥizqiah, is it not reasonable to the end of his days. He said, I also am of that opinion.

(24b, line 2) דְּמַאי רִבִּי יוֹסֵי בְשֵׁם רִבִּי אַבָּהוּ רִבִּי חִזְקִיָּה בְשֵׁם רבי יוּדָה בֶּן פָּזִי דְּמַאי דָּמִי תִיקֵן. דָּמִי[188] לא תִיקֵן.

[What means] *demay*? Rebbi Yose in the name of Rebbi Abbahu, Rebbi Ḥizqiah in the name of Rebbi Jehudah ben Pazi: Maybe he put in order, maybe he did not put in order.

185 Missing in the Leiden ms. here; exists in the other mss. and the text in *Ma'aser Šeni*.

186 Redundant text, not in *Ma'aser Šeni*.

187 In the Leiden ms.: שיני. The text follows the other two mss. here and all sources in *Ma'aser Šeni*.

188 In the Leiden ms.: ומי. The text follows the other two mss. here and all sources in *Ma'aser Šeni*.

(fol. 23b) **משנה יב:** מִשֶּׁבָּטְלָה סַנְהֶדְרִין בָּטַל הַשִּׁיר מִבֵּית הַמִּשְׁתָּאוֹת שֶׁנֶּאֱמַר בַּשִּׁיר לֹא יִשְׁתּוּ יָיִן.

Mishnah 12: When the Synhedrion was disestablished[189], the epithalamium stopped at wedding feasts as it was said[190]: "They shall not drink wine in song."

189 Not really disestablished but when criminal jurisdiction was taken away from Jewish courts, transferred to the Roman administration, and only strictly religious matters were left to the High Court which was generally regarded as Synhedrion.

190 *Is.* 24:9.

HALAKHAH 12

(fol. 24a) **הלכה יב**: אַבָּא בַּר רַב יִרְמְיָה אָמַר. זְקֵינִים מִשַּׁעַר שָׁבָתוּ וגו'.

Halakhah 12: Abba bar Rav Jeremiah said: "The Elders are no longer at the gate[191]" etc.

(24b, line 4) אָמַר רַב חִסְדָּא. בָּרִאשׁוֹנָה הָיְתָה אֵימַת סַנְהֶדְרִין עֲלֵיהֶן וְלֹא הָיוּ אוֹמְרִים דִּבְרֵי נְבָלָה בְּשִׁיר. אֲבָל אַכְשָׁיו שֶׁאֵין אֵימַת סַנְהֶדְרִין עֲלֵיהֶן הֵן אוֹמְרִים דִּבְרֵי נְבָלָה בְּשִׁיר.

Rav Hisda said, in earlier times the fear of the court was on them and they did not include lewd language in song. But now when the fear of the court is no longer on them they include lewd language in song[192].

(24b, line 6) בָּרִאשׁוֹנָה לֹא הָיוּ נִפְרָעִין אֶלָּא מֵאוֹתוֹ הָאִישׁ בִּלְבַד. אֲבָל אַכְשָׁיו נִפְרָעִין מִמֶּנּוּ וּמִמִּשְׁפַּחְתּוֹ. אָמַר רִבִּי יוֹסֵי בֵּירִבִּי בּוּן בְּשֵׁם רַב חוּנָה. בָּרִאשׁוֹנָה כָּל־צָרָה שֶׁהָיְתָה בָּאָה עַל הַצִּבּוּר הָיוּ פּוֹסְקִין שִׂמְחָה כְּנֶגְדָּהּ. וּמִשֶּׁבָּטְלָה סַנְהֶדְרִין בָּטַל הַשִּׁיר מִבֵּית הַמִּשְׁתָּיוֹת. מִשֶּׁבָּטְלוּ אֵילוּ וָאֵילוּ שָׁבַת מְשׂוֹשׂ לִבֵּנוּ נֶהְפַּךְ לְאֵבֶל מְחוֹלֵינוּ. וְכִי מַה הָיְתָה סַנְהֶדְרִין גְּדוֹלָה מוֹעֶלֶת. אֶלָּא לְפִי שֶׁנֶּאֱמַר וְאִם הַעְלֵם יַעְלִימוּ עַם הָאָרֶץ אֶת עֵינֵיהֶם מִן הָאִישׁ הַהוּא בְּתִתּוֹ מִזַּרְעוֹ לַמֹּלֶךְ לְבִלְתִּי הָמִית אוֹתוֹ. בְּכָל־מִיתָה שֶׁיִּרְצוּ. מָשְׁלוּ מָשָׁל. לְמָה הַדָּבָר דּוֹמֶה. לְאֶחָד שֶׁקִּילְקֵל בָּעִיר. מָסְרוּ לְבַעַל הָאַגְמוֹן וַחֲבָשׁוֹ. וְהָיָה קָשֶׁה מִבַּעַל הָאַגְמוֹן. מָסְרוּ לְבַעַל הַזְּמוֹרָה וַחֲבָשׁוֹ.[193] וְהָיָה קָשֶׁה מִבַּעַל הַזְּמוֹרָה. מָסְרוּ לְבַעַל הָרְצוּעָה וּסְטָרוֹ. וְהָיָה קָשֶׁה מִבַּעַל הַזְּמוֹרָה. מָסְרוּ לְשִׁלְטוֹן וְהִטִּילוֹ[194] לְקָמִין. כָּךְ צָרוֹת הָאַחֲרוֹנוֹת מְשַׁכְּחוֹת אֶת הָרִאשׁוֹנוֹת.

In earlier times they required payment only from a person alone. But now they require payment from him and his family[195]. Rebbi Yose ben Rebbi Abun said in the name of Rav Huna: In earlier times, for every trouble that came over the community they have a joyous occasion to make up for it[196]. But after the Synhedrion was abolished, song disappeared from wedding feasts. After both disappeared, [197]"our heart's joy stopped, our dance turned into mourning." But what was the high court good for[198]? But because it was said[199] "if the people of the Land consistently turn away their eyes from that man when he is giving of his seed to the Moloch, not to kill him," in any death they would choose[200]. They gave a parable, to what can this be compared? To one who was a criminal in a town. They delivered him to the one wielding reeds, who jailed him, but he turned out to be stronger than the one wielding reeds. They delivered him to the one wielding sticks who hit him, but he turned out to be stronger than the one wielding sticks[201]. They delivered him to the wielder of leather straps who whipped him, but he turned out to be stronger than the wielder of leather straps. They delivered him to the ruler who hung him in the kiln[202]. So the later troubles cause the earlier ones to be forgotten.

191 In the Tosephta, חבטו "he hit him". This is more fitting for the lictor and this version is used for the translation. (There is no Genizah source any more at this point).

192 From the Rome ms. Leiden and *editio princeps* והחזירו "who returned him."

193 *Thr.* 5:14: "The Elders are no longer at the gate, [therefore not] the young men at their songs." The same in the Babli, 48a, in the name of Rav Huna ben Rav Joshua, 2 generations after Abba bar Rav Jeremiah.

194 Lewd language being a regular feature of the Greek epithalamium.

195 In the Tosephta, 15:7, this is combined with the verse *Lev.* 20:5, alluded to later. A court punishes only the criminal but God's justice is against "that man (who sacrifices his children to the Moloch) and his family." This proves that if the courts can no longer enforce biblical law, the Heavenly Court will enforce it in a much harsher way.

196 The delivery from trouble was a festive occasion documented in *Megillat Ta'anit*, the catalogue of days when fasting was forbidden. But now,

in the words of the Tosephta (15:6): Rabban Simeon ben Gamliel says, for every trouble that comes over the community, the court disestablishes another joyous occasion.

197 Thr. 5:15.

198 What is the connection between the disestablishment of Jewish criminal jurisdiction and the disappearance of the epithalamium from Jewish weddings? The rest of the paragraph has a close parallel in Tosephta 15:7.

199 Lev. 20:4. It is implied that the real reason is the following v. 5.

200 This gives the high court emergency powers to act as a secret, Vehmic, court in case the criminal is too powerful.

201 He might be the Roman lictor since the ruler mentioned is a Roman proconsul.

202 Greek κάμινος, ή, "oven, furnace, kiln."

(fol. 23b) **משנה יג**: מִשֶּׁמֵּתוּ נְבִיאִים הָרִאשׁוֹנִים בָּטְלוּ אוּרִים וְתוּמִּים. מִשֶּׁחָרַב בֵּית הַמִּקְדָּשׁ בָּטַל הַשָּׁמִיר וְנוֹפֶת צוּפִים וּפָסְקוּ אַנְשֵׁי אֲמָנָה שֶׁנֶּאֱמַר הוֹשִׁיעָה י׳ כִּי גָמַר חָסִיד כִּי פַסּוּ אֱמוּנִים מִבְּנֵי אָדָם.

Mishnah 13: After the earlier prophets died, Urim and Tummim[203] stopped. When the Temple was destroyed, the *shamir* and flowing bee's honey stopped and trusting men disappeared, as it was said[204]: "Help, o Eternal, for the pious man is finished, for the trusting have vanished from mankind."

203 The oracle carried by the High Priest.

204 Ps. 12:2.

(fol. 24a) **הלכה יג/יד**: מִשֶּׁמֵּתוּ נְבִיאִים הָרִאשׁוֹנִים פָּסְקוּ אוּרִים וְתוּמִּים. רִבִּי שְׁמוּאֵל בַּר נַחְמָן בְּשֵׁם רִבִּי יוֹנָתָן. זֶה שְׁמוּאֵל וְדָוִד. רִבִּי בָּא בַּר כָּהֲנָא בְּשֵׁם רַב.

זֶה גַּד וְנָתָן. רִבִּי יִרְמְיָה רִבִּי שְׁמוּאֵל בַּר יִצְחָק בְּשֵׁם רַב. זֶה יִרְמְיָה וּבָרוּךְ. מִילְתֵיהּ דְּרִבִּי יְהוֹשֻׁעַ בֶּן לֵוִי אֲמָרָה. זֶה יִרְמְיָה וּבָרוּךְ. דְּאָמַר רִבִּי יְהוֹשֻׁעַ בֶּן לֵוִי וַיְהִי לִדְרוֹשׁ אֱלֹהִים בִּימֵי זְכַרְיָהוּ הַמֵּבִין בִּרְאוֹת אֱלֹהִים. מָאן קָם מִבַּתְרֵיהּ. יִרְמְיָה וּבָרוּךְ.

Halakhah 13: "After the earlier prophets died, Urim and Tummim stopped." Rebbi Samuel bar Nahman in the name of Rebbi Jonathan: These are Samuel and David[205]. Rebbi Abba bar Cahana in the name of Rav: These are Gad and Nathan[206]. Rebbi Jeremiah, Rebbi Samuel bar Isaac in the name of Rav: These are Jeremiah and Barukh. The word of Rebbi Joshua ben Levi implies that these are Jeremiah and Barukh. For Rebbi Joshua ben Levi said[207], "it was when he asked God in the days of Zacariah who understood God's visions."

205 Since there is no explicit reference in Scripture about priestly oracles in books later than *Samuel*. In the Babli, 48b, this is the opinion of Rav Huna, the most prominent of Rav's students.

206 David's court prophets.

207 2Chr. 26:5. The quote proves that oracles were used by kings after David (even though Zacariah is not mentioned in the list of high priests in *Ezra* 7 and Urim and Tummim were high-priestly oracles), as pointed out in the Babli by Rabba bar Samuel, a slightly younger contemporary of R. Joshua ben Levi. The Tosephta, 13:3, states that the oracle disappeared only with the destruction of the first Temple. In many quotes in Babli and Yerushalmi (e. g., *Ta'aniot* 2:1 65a line 64, Yoma 21b) the oracle is mentioned in the list of five things missing in the second Temple.

(24b, line 6) מִשֶּׁמֵּתוּ נְבִיאִים הָאַחֲרוֹנִים חַגַּי זְכַרְיָה וּמַלְאָכִי פָּסְקָה מֵהֶן רוּחַ הַקּוֹדֶשׁ. אַף עַל פִּי כֵן הָיוּ מִשְׁתַּמְּשִׁין בְּבַת קוֹל. מַעֲשֶׂה שֶׁשָּׁמַע שִׁמְעוֹן הַצַּדִּיק בַּת קוֹל ()[208] יוֹצֵא מִבֵּית קוֹדֶשׁ הַקֳּדָשִׁים וְאָמַר. נֶהֱרַג גַּייֵס גּוֹלִיקַס וּבָטְלוּ גְזֵירוֹתָיו. מַעֲשֶׂה שֶׁיָּצְאוּ נְעָרִים לְהִלָּחֵם בְּאַנְטוֹכִיָא וְשָׁמַע יוֹחָנָן כֹּהֵן גָּדוֹל בַּת

קוֹל יוֹצֵא מִבֵּית קוֹדֶשׁ הַקֳּדָשִׁים וְאוֹמֶרֶת. נִצְחוּ טַלַיָּיא דְּאַגְחוּ קְרָבָא בְּאַנְטוֹכִיָא. וְכָתְבוּ אוֹתָהּ הָעֵת וְנָתְנוּ בוֹ זְמָן וְכִוְונוּ שֶׁבְּאוֹתָהּ שָׁעָה הָיְתָה.

After the last prophets, Haggai, Zacariah, and Malachi, died, the Holy Ghost stopped from them, but nevertheless they were using the disembodied voice[209]. If happened that Simeon the Just heard a disembodied voice coming out of the holiest-of-holies saying: Gaius Caligula was killed and his decisions became void.[210] It happened that young men went to fight at Antiochia when Joḥanan the High Priest heard a disembodied voice coming out of the holiest-of-holies saying: The young people are victorious who fought at Antiochia. At that time they wrote down the exact time and found that it happened exactly at that hour[211].

208 In the Leiden ms. (not in *editio princeps* or the Rome ms.) one finds here an insert, a commentary that entered the text from the margin: פירוש הוא זה תרגומא הברה. הברה בלשון מקרא בת. בת הברה היא. שלא הקול ממש היו שומעים אלא הברת קול "This is a commentary: the translation is *echo*. An echo in biblical language is called *bat*. *Bat* is an echo. For they did not really hear a voice but the echo of a voice."

209 Tosephta 13:3; Babli 48b. In the Tosephta: "nevertheless they (the Heavenly Court) were communicating the disembodied voice."

210 Tosephta 13:6, Babli 33a. At least one of the names mentioned here cannot be correct.

211 Tosephta 13:5, Babli 33a. It was remarked that the voice spoke Aramaic which is not understood by angels.

(24b, line 29) מַעֲשֶׂה שֶׁנִּכְנְסוּ זְקֵנִים אֵצֶל גַּדְיָא בִּירִיחוֹ. וְיָצְתָה בַּת קוֹל וְאָמְרָה לָהֶן. יֵשׁ בֵּינֵיכֶם אָדָם אֶחָד רָאוּי לְרוּחַ הַקּוֹדֶשׁ אֶלָּא שֶׁאֵין הַדּוֹר כְּדַיי. וְנָתְנוּ עֵינֵיהֶן בְּהִלֵּל הַזָּקֵן. וּכְשֶׁמֵּת הָיוּ אוֹמְרִים עָלָיו. הוֹי עָנָיו חָסִיד תַּלְמִידוֹ שֶׁל עֶזְרָא. וְשׁוּב נִכְנְסוּ זְקֵנִים לַעֲלִיָּיה בְּיַבְנֶה וְיָצְאַת בַּת קוֹל וְאָמְרָה לָהֶן. יֵשׁ

בֵּינֵיכֶם אֶחָד רָאוּי לְרוּחַ הַקּוֹדֶשׁ אֶלָּא שֶׁאֵין הַדּוֹר כְּדָיי. וְנָתְנוּ עֵינֵיהֶם בִּשְׁמוּאֵל הַקָּטָן. וְלָמָּה נִקְרָא שְׁמוֹ קָטָן. לְפִי שֶׁהוּא מַקְטִין עַצְמוֹ. וְיֵשׁ אוֹמְרִים. לְפִי שֶׁמְּעַט הָיָה קָטָן מִשְּׁמוּאֵל הָרָמָתִי. וּכְשֶׁמֵּת הָיוּ אוֹמְרִים עָלָיו. הוֹי עָנָיו חָסִיד תַּלְמִידוֹ שֶׁל הִלֵּל הַזָּקֵן. וּבִשְׁעַת מִיתָתוֹ אָמַר. שִׁמְעוֹן וְיִשְׁמָעֵאל לְחַרְבָּא. וּשְׁאָר כָּל־עַמָּא לְבִיזָּה. וַעֲקָן סַגִּיאִין יְהַוְיָן. וּבְלִשּׁוֹן אֲרַמִּית אֲמָרָן. וְלֹא יָדְעוּ מָה אָמַר. וְעַל רִבִּי יְהוּדָה בֶּן בָּבָא הִתְקִינוּ שֶׁיְּהוּ אוֹמְרִים. הוֹי עָנָיו חָסִיד. אֶלָּא שֶׁנִּטְרְפָה הַשָּׁעָה.

[212]It happened that Elders came together in the house Gadia[213] in Jericho, when a disembodied voice came and said to them: There is among you one man who would be worthy that the Holy Spirit should rest on him[214], only the generation is not worthy. They all looked at Hillel the Elder. When he died, they said about him, o meek, pious student of Ezra. Again it happened that Elders came together in a second floor at Jabne, when a disembodied voice came and said to them: There is among you one man who would be worthy that the Holy Spirit should rest on him, only the generation is not worthy. They all looked at Samuel Minor. Why was he called Minor? Because he effaced himself. Some say, because he was slightly below Samuel from Ramah[215]. When he died, they said about him o meek, pious student of Hillel the Elder. When he was dying he said[216]: Simeon and Ismael[217] to the word, the rest of the people to plunder, immense troubles will be. He said that in Aramaic and they did not understand what he was saying. For Rebbi Jehudah ben Baba they intended to say o meek, pious, but the time was torn[218].

212   Tosephta 13:3-4; Babli 48b, *Sanhedrin* 11a, *Berakhot* 57a; Yerushalmi *Avodah zarah* 3:1 (42c l. 32), *Horaiot* 3:7 (48c l. 41).
213   In both Babli sources: Guriah.
214   That he should be a prophet.

215 The biblical prophet.

216 It is clear that Samuel Minor lived in the time of Gamliel I, Hillel's grandson, and that there already was an academy at Jabneh at that time.

217 Simeon ben Gamliel, president of the revolutionary government in the war of 68-70, and Ismael, the High Priest during the revolt; both executed after Titus's triumph in Rome. (Late and secondary transformation of this source: *Mekhilta dR. Ismael Mišpaṭim* 18, *Šemaḥot* 8).

218 He was executed in the aftermath of the war of Bar Kokhba.

(24b, line 40) תַּנֵּי. אָמַר רִבִּי יוּדָה. מַה טִיבוֹ שֶׁלַּשָּׁמִיר הַזֶּה. בִּירִיָּיה הִיא מִשֵּׁשֶׁת יְמֵי בְרֵאשִׁית. וְכֵיוָן שֶׁהָיוּ מַרְאִין אוֹתוֹ לָאֲבָנִים הָיוּ מִתְפַּתְּחוֹת לְפָנָיו כִּלְוָחִין שֶׁלַּפִּינָקָס. וּבוֹ בָּנָה שְׁלֹמֹה בֵּית הָעוֹלָמִים. הָדָא הִיא דִכְתִיב וְהַבַּיִת בְּהִבָּנוֹתוֹ אֶבֶן שְׁלֵמָה מַסָּע נִבְנָה וּמַקָּבוֹת וְהַגַּרְזֶן וְכָל־כְּלִי בַרְזֶל לֹא נִשְׁמַע בַּבַּיִת בְּהִבָּנוֹתוֹ. רִבִּי נְחֶמְיָה אוֹמֵר. מְגוּרָרוֹת הָיוּ. הָדָא הִיא דִכְתִיב כָּל־אֵלֶּה אֲבָנִים יְקָרוֹת כְּמִידוֹת גָּזִית מְגוּרָרָה בַּמְּגֵירָה מִבַּיִת וּמִחוּץ. אָמוֹר מֵעַתָּה. מִפְּנִים לֹא הָיָה עוֹשֶׂה לָהֶן כְּלוּם. אֶלָּא מְתַקֵּן מִבַּחוּץ וּמַכְנִיס לִפְנִים. רִבִּי אוֹמֵר. נִרְאִין דִּבְרֵי רִבִּי יוּדָה בְּאַבְנֵי בֵית הַמִּקְדָּשׁ. וְדִבְרֵי רִבִּי נְחֶמְיָה בְּאַבְנֵי בֵיתוֹ שֶׁלִּשְׁלֹמֹה. וְאֵין כָּל־דָּבָר יָכוֹל לַעֲמוֹד בּוֹ. אֲפִילוּ נָתוּן עַל גַּבֵּי הָאֶבֶן אוֹ לְתוֹךְ טַס שֶׁלַּמַּתֶּכֶת מִיָּד הָיָה בוֹקֵעַ וְיוֹרֵד. מַה הָיוּ עוֹשִׂין לוֹ לְהַעֲמִידוֹ. הָיוּ כּוֹרְכִין אוֹתוֹ מוּכִין שֶׁלַּצֶּמֶר וְנוֹתְנִין אוֹתוֹ לְתוֹךְ טַנֵּי שֶׁלָּאֶבֶר מָלֵא סוּבִּין שֶׁלַּשְּׂעוֹרִין. הָדָא הוּא דִכְתִיב הַמַּבְלִיג שׁוֹד עַל עָז.

It was stated[219]: Rebbi Jehudah said, what was this *shamir*? It is a creature that existed from the creation of the world and if one shows it stones those would open themselves like the two boards of a *pinax*[220], and Solomon built the Temple with it. That is what is written[221]: "During the building of the House, it was built from whole carried stones, and hammers or axe or any iron implement was not heard in the House when it was built." Rebbi Nehemiah says, they were sawed. That is what is written[222]: "All these were expensive stones, in the measure of ashlars, sawed with a saw inside and out." Say now, at the building site they were not treated at all but they were finished outside and then brought inside[223]. Rebbi says, the words of Rebbi Jehudah are convincing for the stones of the Temple and those of Rebbi Nehemiah for the stones of Solomon's palace. But since nothing can withstand it, and even when it was put on a stone or a box sheet it would split it and fall down, what did they do to restrain it? One was binding it with wool fibers and put it into a lead cylinder filled with barley bran. That is what is written[224]: "He enjoys robbing the strong."

219 Tosephta 15:1 the entire paragraph. The Babli, 48b, quotes only the part referring to R. Jehudah's statement, and that anonymously.

In many places, the *shamir* is listed as a creature whose existence was part of the plan of Creation but which came into being only at its appointed time (the expression being: it was created Friday evening at dusk): Mishnah *Abot* 5:6, Babli *Pesaḥim* 54a, *Sifry Deut.* 355, *Mekhilta Bešallaḥ Wayyissaʿ* 5, *Abot dR. Nathan B* 37, *Pirqe R. Eliezer* 19,31, *Tanḥuma Wayyera* 23, *Pseudo-Jonathan Num.* 22:28, *Midraš Maʿaśeh Torah* (Jellinek vol. 2, p. 100). Cf. also the story of Solomon and the shamir in Babli *Giṭṭin* 68b.

220 A writing tablet of two smooth wooden plates hinged together and covered with wax. Greek πίναξ, -ακος, ὁ, "board, plank, anything made of wood; writing tablet, catalogs, etc."

221 *1K.* 6:7.

222 *1K.* 7:9.

223 Since iron may not be used in the building of the Temple, *Ex.* 20:25.

224 *Am.* 5:9; this is taken as referring to the *shamir*.

(24b, line 53) וְנוֹפֶת צוּפִים. אָמַר רִבִּי לָעְזָר. דְּבַשׁ הַבָּא בִּצְפִיָּיה. אָמַר רִבִּי יוֹסֵי בֵּירִבִּי חֲנִינָה. סוֹלֶת צָפָה עַל גַּבֵּי נָפָה לוּשָׁה בִדְבַשׁ וְחֶמְאָה. אָמַר רִבִּי יוֹחָנָן יָפֶה סִיפְסוּף שֶׁאָכַלְנוּ בְּיַלְדוּתֵינוּ מִפְּנְקְרִיסִין שֶׁאָכַלְנוּ בְּזִקְנוֹתֵינוּ. דִּי בְיוֹמוֹי

אִישְׁתַּנֵּי עָלְמָא. אָמַר רִבִּי חִייָא בַּר בָּא. בְּרֵאשׁוֹנָה הָיְתָה סְאָה אַרְבֵּלִית מוֹצִיאָה סְאָה סוֹלֶת סְאָה קֶמַח סְאָה קֵיבָר סְאָה סוּבִּין סְאָה מוּרְסָן. וּכְדוֹן אֲפִילוּ חָדָא בְחָדָא לָא קַייְמָא.

"And flowing bee's honey". Rebbi Eleazar said, honey that comes with floaters. Rebbi Yose ben Rebbi Ḥanina said, farina which floats on the sieve kneaded with honey and butter[225]. [226]Rebbi Joḥanan said, the second quality fruit we ate in our youth tasted better that the peaches we ate in our old age, because during his lifetime the world changed. Rebbi Ḥiyya bar Abba said, one *seah* of Arbel grain did yield one *seah* of fine flour, one *seah* of white flour, one *seah* of dark flour, one *seah* of bran, one *seah* of coarse bran. But today, we do not even get one for one.

225 He explains the recipe R. Eleazar had in mind, as a delicacy which lost its taste with the destruction of the first Temple. Babli 48b, in the name of Rav.

226 This is from Chapter 1, Note 298; explained in *Peah* Chapter 7, Notes 71-75.

(24b, line 58) וּפָסְקוּ אַנְשֵׁי אֲמָנָה. אָמַר רִבִּי זְעִירָא. אַנְשֵׁי אֲמָנָה תוֹרָה. כְּהָדָא חַד רִבִּי הֲוָה קְרִי לֵיהּ לְאַחְוָה וַהֲווֹן צְוָחִין בִּפְרַגְמַטְיָא וָהֲוָה אֲמַר. לֵית אֲנָא מְבַטְּלָה עָנְתִי. אִין חֲמִי לְמֵיתֵי. מֵיתֵי הוּא.

"Trusting men disappeared." Rebbi Ze'ira said, men who trusted in Torah, as one teacher who was teaching Bible to his brother in Tyre when they were calling on him for a business deal[227]. He said, I do not push aside my set time[228]. If it is destined to come to me, it will come to me[229].

227 Greek πραγματεία, ἡ, "occupation, business, diligent study, prosecution of business".

228 Time set aside for study every

day at the same hour.

229 This essentially disproves the Mishnah that there are no longer people trusting in God.

(fol. 23b) **משנה יד**: רַבָּן שִׁמְעוֹן בֶּן גַּמְלִיאֵל אוֹמֵר מִשּׁוּם רְבִּי יְהוֹשֻׁעַ מִיּוֹם שֶׁחָרַב בֵּית הַמִּקְדָּשׁ אֵין יוֹם שֶׁאֵין בּוֹ קְלָלָה וְלֹא יָרַד הַטַּל לִבְרָכָה וְנִיטַּל טַעַם הַפֵּירוֹת. רְבִּי יוֹסֵי אוֹמֵר אַף נִיטַּל שׁוֹמֶן הַפֵּירוֹת.

Mishnah 14: Rabban Simeon ben Gamliel says in the name of Rebbi Joshua: Since the day the Temple was destroyed there is no day without a curse, and the dew did not descend for a blessing; and the taste of fruits disappeared. Rebbi Yose says, also the fat of fruits disappeared.

(fol. 23b) **משנה טו**: רְבִּי שִׁמְעוֹן בֶּן אֶלְעָזָר אוֹמֵר הַטַּהֲרָה נָטְלָה אֶת הָרֵיחַ הַמַּעְשְׂרוֹת נָטְלוּ אֶת שׁוֹמֶן הַדָּגָן הַזְּנוּת וְהַכְּשָׁפִים כִּלּוּ אֶת הַכֹּל.

Mishnah 15: Rebbi Simeon ben Eleazar says, purity[230] took away taste, tithes[231] took away the fat of grain, immorality and sorcery killed everything[232].

230 Meaning: lack of purity, the fact that people eat their profane food not under the rules of ritual purity applying to sanctified food, the original distinguishing feature of the old pharisaic sect.

231 The fact that people did not tithe but mostly only gave heave; cf. Tractate *Demay*.

232 Moral, not ritual, defects account for all other troubles. The Babylonian Mishnah essentially is the Tosephta, cf. Note 236.

(fol. 24b) **הלכה טו**: כְּתִיב וְאֵל זוֹעֵם בְּכָל־יוֹם. אָמַר רְבִּי זְעִירָא. רִאשׁוֹנָה רִאשׁוֹנָה מִתְקַיֶּימֶת. מִי מְבַטֵּל. רְבִּי אָבִין בְּשֵׁם רְבִּי אָחָא. בִּרְכַּת כֹּהֲנִים

מְבַטֶּלֶת. אָמַר רַבָּן שִׁמְעוֹן בֶּן גַּמְלִיאֵל תֵּדַע לָךְ שֶׁנִּתְאָרְרוּ הַטְלָלִים. בָּרִאשׁוֹנָה עִיר שֶׁטְלָלֶיהָ מְרוּבִּין פֵּירוֹתֶיהָ מְרוּבִּין. אֲבָל עַכְשָׁיו עִיר שֶׁטְלָלֶיהָ מְרוּבִּין פֵּירוֹתֶהָ מוּעָטִין. בָּרִאשׁוֹנָה הָיָה הַטַּל יוֹרֵד עַל הַקַּשׁ וְעַל הַתֶּבֶן וְהֵן מַלְבִּינִין. אֲבָל עַכְשָׁיו יוֹרֵד עַל הַקַּשׁ וְעַל הַתֶּבֶן וְהֵן מַשְׁחִירִין.

It is written[233]: "But God is angry every day." Rebbi Ze'ira said, the earlier ones[234] all continue. What can do away with them[235]? Rebbi Abin in the name of Rebbi Aḥa: The priestly blessing does away with them. [236]Rabban Simeon ben Gamliel said, you can observe that dew has become cursed. In earlier times, a village abundant in dew was abundant in produce but today, a village abundant in dew is poor in produce[237]! In earlier times, dew descended on chaff and straw and whitened it[238], but today it descends on chaff and straw and blackens it.

233 *Ps.* 7:12.
234 The troubles are cumulative; the new troubles do not eliminate the old ones.
235 The earlier troubles?
236 Tosephta 15:2; there the text of the Mishnah also is repeated.
237 Cf. *Peah* 7:4, Notes 66 ff.
238 In the Tosephta, his proof is from the manna which was made shiny by the dew on it.

(24b, line 67) תַּנֵּי. רַבִּי שִׁמְעוֹן בֶּן אֶלְעָזָר אוֹמֵר הַטַּהֲרָה נָטְלָה אֶת הַטַּעַם וְאֶת הָרֵיחַ. מַעְשְׂרוֹת נָטְלוּ אֶת שׁוֹמֶן הַדָּגָן. וּמִמִּי נִיטַל יוֹתֵר. אָמַר רִבִּי לֵוִי בַּר חַיְתָה. נִישְׁמְעִינָהּ מִן הָדָא. מֵהֱיוֹתָם בָּא אֶל עֲרֵמַת עֶשְׂרִים וְהָיְתָה עֲשָׂרָה. בָּא אֶל הַיֶּקֶב לַחְשֹׂף חֲמִשִּׁים פּוּרָה. וְהָיְתָה עֶשְׂרִים וַחֲמִשָּׁה אֵין כְּתִיב כָּאן אֶלָּא וְהָיְתָה עֶשְׂרִים. וַחֲכָמִים אוֹמְרִים הַזְּנוּת וְהַכְּשָׁפִים כִּלּוּ אֶת הַכֹּל.

It was stated[239]: "Rebbi Simeon ben Eleazar says, purity[230] took away taste and smell, tithes[231] took away the fat of grain." From what was taken most? Rebbi Levi ben Ḥaita said, let us hear from the following[240]:

"One thought to come to a heap of twenty and it was ten. He came to the winepress to draw 50 pitchers," it does not say 'and there were 25' but "and there were 20." "²⁴¹But the Sages say, immorality and sorcery killed everything²³²."

239 Text of the Babylonian Mishnah. In Tosephta 15:2: "tithes took away oils and grain."

240 *Ḥag.* 2:16. Grain shrank from 1 to .5 but wine from 1 to .4, which is 20% less.

241 This is the version of the Babylonian Mishnah.

(fol. 23b) **משנה יו:** בְּפוֹלְמוֹס שֶׁלְאֶסְפַּסְיָנוּס גָּזְרוּ עַל עַטְרוֹת חֲתָנִים וְעַל הָאֵרוּס. בְּפוֹלְמוֹס שֶׁלְטִיטוּס גָּזְרוּ עַל עַטְרוֹת כַּלּוֹת וְשֶׁלֹּא יְלַמֵּד אָדָם אֶת בְּנוֹ יְוָנִית. בְּפוֹלְמוֹס הָאַחֲרוֹן גָּזְרוּ שֶׁלֹּא תֵצֵא כַלָּה בָּאַפִּרְיוֹן בְּתוֹךְ הָעִיר. וְרַבּוֹתֵינוּ הִיתִּירוּ שֶׁתֵּצֵא כַלָּה בָּאַפִּרְיוֹן בְּתוֹךְ הָעִיר.

Mishnah 16: During Vespasian's war²⁴² they decided about²⁴³ grooms' crowns and the *erus*²⁴⁴. During Quietus's²⁴⁵ war they decided about brides' crowns and that nobody should teach Greek to his son²⁴⁶. During the last war they decided that a bride should not be carried in a litter through the city; our teachers²⁴⁷ permitted that a bride should be carried in a litter through the city.

242 The Jewish war which resulted in the destruction of the Temple.

243 The rabbinic High Court, reconstituted at Jabneh under Vespasian's protection by the anti-war leader Joḥanan ben Zakkai forbade grooms to wear crowns as a sign of national mourning.

244 In the Babli, this is defined as "one-sided percussion instrument;" in the interpretation of the Gaonim and *Arukh* a tymbal or tambourine. The

Yerushalmi explanation is unintelligible.

245 The Jewish revolt against Trajan, outside the Land of Israel. קיטוס instead of טיטוס is the reading of the Geniza mss. of the Mishnah, of the Palestinian Mishnah (Cambridge ms.), and the Kaufman ms., of important mss. of *Seder 'Olam* (cf. the author's edition, Northvale NJ 1998, p. 260 ff.), and of a Gaonic responsum (*Ginze Schechter* 2, No. 17, p. 244, 249). That reading has been chosen for the translation. Cf. H. Graetz, *Geschichte der Juden*[3], vol. 4, Note 14.

246 The Babli, 49b, dates the prohibition of Greek to the time of Pompey.

247 In general, "our teachers" refers either to Rebbi, R. Jehudah I the Prince, or his grandson, R. Jehudah II the Prince. In any case, the last sentence is a post-Mishnaic correction of the Mishnah.

(fol. 24b) **הלכה יו**: נָפְלָה עֲטֶרֶת רֹאשֵׁנוּ. אֵילוּ הֵן עַטְרוֹת חֲתָנִים. זוֹ זְהוֹרִית מוּזְהֶבֶת. רִבִּי בָּא בְשֵׁם רַב. שֶׁלְּמֶלַח וְשֶׁלְגָפְרִית. רַב יִרְמְיָה בְשֵׁם רַב. שֶׁלְּמֶלַח וְשֶׁלְזַיִת. רַב נַחְמָן בַּר יַעֲקֹב אָמַר. אֲפִילוּ דְחִילְפֵי. רַב יִרְמְיָה שִׁיבְשֵׁב וְלָבַשׁ[248] עֲטָרָה שֶׁלְזַיִת. שָׁמַע שְׁמוּאֵל וְאָמַר. נַיַּח לֵיהּ אֵילוּ אִיתְרִים רֵישֵׁיהּ וְלָא עֲבַד כֵּן. וַהֲוָת כֵּן. כִּשְׁגָגָה שֶׁיָּצָא לִפְנֵי הַשַּׁלִּיט.

Halakhah 16: "Our head's crown fell"; these are the grooms' crowns, that is gilded woolen strips. Rebbi Abba in the name of Rav: Of salt and sulfur[249]. Rav Jeremiah in the name of Rav: Of salt and olives. Rav Naḥman bar Jacob said, even of willows[250]. Rav Jeremiah of Šibšeb wore a crown of olive branches. Samuel heard this and said, it would have been better for him it he had been beheaded but not done this thing. That happened to him, as "an error coming from before the ruler.[251]"

248 In the parallel *Thren. rabba* 5, the ו is missing. That seems to be correct since the Rav Jeremiah here needs a qualifyer to his name. He is not Rav Jeremiah, the elder authority in Rav's academy.

249 In the Babli, 49b, Rav holds that crowns of myrrh and roses are

permitted, but of salt and sulfur prohibited. This is the tannaitic position in Tosephta 15:8. Rashi explains that one makes a crown out of a solid rock of salt and uses sulfur to paint ornaments in gold color on the crown.

250 In the Babli, Samuel holds that crowns of salt rock are forbidden, of reeds or willows permitted, but Levi holds that even reeds and willows are forbidden.

251 *Eccl.* 10:5.

(24c, line 2) אֵילוּ הֵן חוּפּוֹת חֲתָנִים. סָדִינִים מְצוּיָּירִין וְסָהֲרוֹנֵי זָהָב תְּלוּיִין בָּהֶם. תַּנֵּי. אֲבָל עוֹשֶׂה הוּא אפיפיירוֹת וְתוֹלֶה בָהֶן כָּל־מִין שֶׁיִּרְצֶה.

The following are grooms' chambers[252]: Ornamented sheets on which hang golden halfmoons[253]. It was stated: But he makes papyrus[254] ropes and hangs on them anything he wants.

252 Here is missing a statement similar to Tosephta 15:9, hinted at in Babli 49b: During the last war, they decided on grooms' chambers (to forbid extravagant decorations of the bridal chamber.)

253 In the Tosephta: golden chambers. In the Babli: golden sheets.

254 The word אפיפיירות is discussed at length in *Kilaim* 6:3, Note 38.

(24c, line 4) מַתְנִיתָא. וְעַל הָאִירוּס. רְסִיסָה.

Mishnah: "And the *erus.*" *resisa*[255].

255 In biblical Hebrew, this would mean "splinters". Levy in his Dictionary conjectures that it refers to a musical instrument full of holes. Kohout proposes to amend to רביכה, a rebeq, a music instrument. It seems futile to try to explain the Yerushalmi in the light of the Babli. The word *erus* might be Accadic *erēšum* "smell, perfume" and רסיסה good Hebrew ריסוס "spraying (with perfume *erēšum ṭābum*)".

(24c, line 4) אֵילוּ הֵן עֲטָרוֹת כַּלּוֹת. זוֹ עִיר שֶׁלְּזָהָב. רִבִּי עֲקִיבָה עָשָׂה לְאִשְׁתּוֹ עִיר שֶׁלְּזָהָב. וְקִנְיאַת בָּהּ אִיתְּתֵיהּ דְּרַבָּן גַּמְלִיאֵל. אָמַר לָהּ. מַה הֲוֵית עַבְדַת

הֵיךְ מַה דַּהֲוָת עָבְדָה. דַּהֲוָת מְזַבְּנָה קְלִיעָתָא דְשַׂעֲרָהּ וְיָהֲבָה לֵיהּ וְהוּא לָעֵי בְּאוֹרַיְתָא.

The following are brides' crowns, that is a city of gold[256]. Rebbi Aqiba made for his wife a city of gold[257], which made Rabban Gamliel's wife jealous. He said to her, did you ever do what she did? She sold her braided hair, gave the money to him so he could study Torah[258].

256 A golden diadem in the shape of a city wall. The same explanation in the Babli, 49b. In the Tosephta, "a golden headband".

257 Reported also in the Babli, *Šabbat* 86a.

258 In the tradition of the Babli, she was a daughter from a very rich house who was disinherited for marrying an ignorant nobody. She had married him on condition that he would study to become a famous Sage.

(24c, line 8) שָׁאֲלוּ אֶת רִבִּי יְהוֹשֻׁעַ. מַהוּ שֶׁיְּלַמֵּד אָדָם אֶת בְּנוֹ יְוָונִית. אָמַר לָהֶן. יְלַמְּדֵינוּ בְּשָׁעָה שֶׁאֵינָהּ לֹא יוֹם וְלֹא לַיְלָה. דִּכְתִיב וְהָגִיתָ בּוֹ יוֹמָם וָלַיְלָה. מֵעַתָּה אָסוּר לְאָדָם לְלַמֵּד אֶת בְּנוֹ אוּמָנוּת. בְּגִין דִּכְתִיב וְהָגִיתָ בּוֹ יוֹמָם וָלַיְלָה. וְהָתַנֵּי רִבִּי יִשְׁמָעֵאל וּבָחַרְתָּ בַּחַיִּים. זוֹ אוּמָנוּת. רִבִּי בָּא בְּרֵיהּ דְּרִבִּי חִיָּיה בַּר בָּא בְּשֵׁם רִבִּי יוֹחָנָן. מִפְּנֵי הַמְּסוֹרוֹת. רִבִּי אַבָּהוּ בְּשֵׁם רִבִּי יוֹחָנָן. מוּתָּר לְאָדָם לְלַמֵּד אֶת בִּתּוֹ יְוָונִית מִפְּנֵי שֶׁהִיא תַכְשִׁיט לָהּ. שָׁמַע שִׁמְעוֹן בַּר בָּא וְאָמַר. בְּגִין דְּרִבִּי אַבָּהוּ בָּעֵי מֵילַף בְּרַתֵּיהּ הוּא תָלֵי לָהּ בְּרִבִּי יוֹחָנָן. יָבוֹא עָלַי אִם לֹא[259] שְׁמַעְתִּיהָ מֵרִבִּי יוֹחָנָן.

[260]They asked Rebbi Joshua: May a person teach Greek to his son? He said to them, he may teach him at an hour that is neither day nor night as it is written (*Jos.* 1:8): "You shall meditate about it day and night." If it is so, a man would be forbidden to teach a profession to his son since it is written: "You shall meditate about it day and night." But Rebbi Ismael stated (*Deut.* 30:19): "Choose life!" That refers to a profession. Rebbi

Abba, son of Rebbi Ḥiyya bar Abba, Rebbi Ḥiyya in the name of Rebbi Joḥanan: Because of informants. Rebbi Abbahu in the name of Rebbi Joḥanan: A person may teach Greek to his daughter since it is an ornament for her. Simeon bar Abba heard that and said: Because he wants to teach his daughters, he attaches it to Rebbi Joḥanan. It should come over me that I never heard it from Rebbi Joḥanan.

259 This word is not in the parallel in *Peah*. But since this an oath formula, it is not necessary to delete the word.

260 This is from *Peah* 1:1, Notes 94-97. Cf. Babli *Menaḥot* 99b.

(24c, line 16) מִי שֶׁהוּא מַתִּיר אֶת הָרִאשׁוֹנוֹת. אָמַר רִבִּי יוֹסֵי בֵּי רִבִּי בּוּן. מִי שֶׁהוּא מַתִּיר אֶת אִילּוּ הוּא מַתִּיר אֶת אִילּוּ. כְּהָדָא רֵישׁ גָּלוּתָא שָׁלַח שָׁאַל לְרַב חִסְדַּאי. מָהוּ הָדֵין דִּכְתִיב כֹּה אָמַר יְ"י הָסִיר הַמִּצְנֶפֶת וְהָרִים הָעֲטָרָה. אָמַר לֵיהּ. הוּסְרָה הַמִּצְנֶפֶת הוּרְמָה הָעֲטָרָה. שָׁמַע רִבִּי יוֹחָנָן וְאָמַר. הוּא חֶסֶר²⁶¹ וּמִילוֹי חֶסֶר.²⁶¹

Who permits the earlier ones²⁶²? Rebbi Yose ben Rebbi Bun said, the one who permitted these permitted those²⁶³. As the following: The Head of the Diaspora sent and asked Rav Ḥisdai: what is the meaning of "taking away the head cover, removing the crown"²⁶⁴? He said to him, when the head cover was taken away, the crown was removed²⁶⁵. Rebbi Joḥanan heard this and said, he is grace and his words are gracious²⁶⁶.

261 Read חֶסֶד both times.
262 We find that "our teachers" permitted a prohibition dating from the war of Bar Kokhba. What is the status of the earlier decrees mentioned in the Mishnah.
263 He holds that "our teachers" abolished the entire Mishnah.
264 *Ez.* 21:31.
265 When the Temple was destroyed and the head cover of the High Priest (*Ex.* 28:37) was taken away,

then the grooms' crowns should be removed. He found a biblical reason for the rabbinic decision.

266   A parallel in the Babli, *Giṭṭin* 7a, based on the same etymological pun. A totally different interpretation of the verse, also endorsed by R. Joḥanan, in *Ruth rabba* 3(1).

(fol. 23b) **משנה יז:** מִשֶּׁמֵּת רַבָּן יוֹחָנָן בֶּן זַכַּיי בָּטַל זִיו הַחָכְמָה. מִשֶּׁמֵּת רַבָּן גַּמְלִיאֵל הַזָּקֵן בָּטַל כְּבוֹד הַתּוֹרָה וּמֵתָה טָהֳרָה וּפְרִישׁוּת. מִשֶּׁמֵּת יִשְׁמָעֵאל בֶּן פִּיאָבִי בָּטַל זִיו הַכְּהוּנָה. מִשֶּׁמֵּת רַבִּי בְּטֵלָה עֲנָוָה וְיִרְאַת חֵטְא. מִשֶּׁמֵּת רַבִּי מֵאִיר בָּטְלוּ מוֹשְׁלֵי מְשָׁלִים. מִשֶּׁמֵּת רַבִּי עֲקִיבָה בָּטְלוּ הַדַּרְשָׁנִים. מִשֶּׁמֵּת בֶּן עַזַּאי בָּטְלוּ הַשַּׁקְדָּנִים. מִשֶּׁמֵּת בֶּן זוֹמָא בָּטְלוּ הַתַּלְמִידִים. מִשֶּׁמֵּת רַבִּי יְהוֹשֻׁעַ פָּסְקָה טוֹבָה מִן הָעוֹלָם. מִשֶּׁמֵּת רַבִּי אֶלְעָזָר בֶּן עֲזַרְיָה פָּסַק הָעוֹשֶׁר מִן הַחֲכָמִים. מִשֶּׁמֵּת רַבָּן גַּמְלִיאֵל בָּא גוֹבַּיי וְרָבוּ צָרוֹת. מִשֶּׁמֵּת רַבִּי חֲנִינָה בֶּן דּוֹסָא וְרַבִּי יוֹסֵי קִיטוֹנְתָא פָּסְקָה הַחֲסִידוּת וְלָמָּא נִקְרָא שְׁמוֹ בֶּן קִיטוֹנְתָא שֶׁהָיָה תַּמְצִיתָן שֶׁלַּחֲסִידִים. רַבִּי פִּינְחָס בֶּן יָאִיר אוֹמֵר מִשֶּׁחָרַב בֵּית הַמִּקְדָּשׁ בּוֹשׁוּ חֲבֵרִים וּבְנֵי חוֹרִין וְחָפוּ רֹאשָׁם וְנִדַּלְדְּלוּ אַנְשֵׁי מַעֲשֶׂה וְגָבְרוּ בַּעֲלֵי זְרוֹעַ וּבַעֲלֵי לָשׁוֹן וְאֵין דּוֹרֵשׁ וְאֵין מְבַקֵּשׁ וְאֵין שׁוֹאֵל. עַל מִי לָנוּ לְהִשָּׁעֵן עַל אָבִינוּ שֶׁבַּשָּׁמַיִם. רַבִּי אֱלִיעֶזֶר הַגָּדוֹל אוֹמֵר מִיּוֹם שֶׁחָרַב בֵּית הַמִּקְדָּשׁ שָׁרוּ חֲכִימַיָּא לְמֶהֱוֵי כְּסָפְרַיָּא וְסָפְרַיָּא כְּחַזָּנָא וְחַזָּנָא כְּעַמָּא דְאַרְעָא וְעַמָּא דְאַרְעָא אָזְלָה וְדַלְדְּלָה וְאֵין שׁוֹאֵל וְאֵין מְבַקֵּשׁ. עַל מִי יֵשׁ לְהִשָּׁעֵן עַל אָבִינוּ שֶׁבַּשָּׁמַיִם. בְּעִקְּבוֹת מְשִׁיחָה חוּצְפָּא יִסְגָּא וְיוֹקֶר יַאֲמִיר הַגֶּפֶן תִּתֵּן פִּרְיָהּ וְהַיַּיִן בְּיוֹקֶר וְהַמַּלְכוּת תֵּהָפֵךְ לְמִינוּת וְאֵין תּוֹכַחַת בֵּית וַעַד יִהְיֶה לִזְנוּת וְהַגָּלִיל יֶחֱרַב וְהַגַּבְלָן יִישׁוֹם וְאַנְשֵׁי הַגְּבוּל יְסוֹבְבוּ מֵעִיר לְעִיר וְלֹא יְחוֹנָנוּ וְחָכְמַת סוֹפְרִים תִּסְרַח וְיִרְאֵי חֵטְא יִמָּאֵסוּ וְהָאֱמֶת תְּהֵא נֶעֱדֶרֶת נְעָרִים פְּנֵי זְקֵנִים יַלְבִּינוּ זְקֵנִים יַעַמְדוּ מִפְּנֵי קְטַנִּים בֵּן מְנַוֵּול אָב בַּת קָמָה בְאִמָּהּ כַּלָּה בַּחֲמוֹתָהּ אוֹיְבֵי אִישׁ אַנְשֵׁי בֵיתוֹ. פְּנֵי הַדּוֹר כִּפְנֵי הַכֶּלֶב הַבֵּן אֵינוֹ מִתְבַּיֵּישׁ מֵאָבִיו. וְעַל מָה יֵשׁ לְהִשָּׁעֵן עַל אָבִינוּ שֶׁבַּשָּׁמַיִם.

Mishnah 17: [267]When Rabban Joḥanan ben Zakkai died, the splendor of wisdom disappeared. When the elder Rabban Gamliel[268] died, the honor of Torah disappeared, purity and self-discipline died. When Ismael ben Phiabi[269] died, the splendor of priesthood died. When Rebbi died, meekness and fear of sin died. When Rebbi Meïr died, the inventors of parables disappeared. When Rebbi Aqiba died, the preachers[270] disappeared. When Ben Azai died, the perseverers[271] disappeared. When Ben Zoma died, the students[272] disappeared. When Rebbi Joshua died, good disappeared from the world[273] When Rebbi Eleazar ben Azariah died, wealth disappeared from the Sages. When Rabban Gamliel died[274], locusts came and troubles increased. When Rebbi Ḥanina ben Dosa and Yose the small[275] died, piety disappeared. Why was he called Yose of the small room? For he was the concentrate of pious men.

Rebbi Phineas ben Yaïr says, after the Temple was destroyed, fellows and freeborn were ashamed and covered their heads, people of [good] deeds shrivelled, strong-armed people and informers became dominant, nobody explains, nobody desires and nobody asks. On whom can we rely? On our Father in Heaven.

The great Rebbi Eliezer[276] says, from the day the Temple was destroyed, the Sages were diminished to be like scribes, the scribes like community servants, the community servants like common people; the common people go and degenerate, nobody desires and nobody asks. On whom can we rely? On our Father in Heaven.

On the heels of the Messiah impertinence will grow, inflation will lead, the vine will give its fruit but the wine will be expensive, the government will turn heretic[277], nobody rebukes, the assembly hall will be a brothel,

Galilee will be destroyed and Gaulanitis[278] become deserted, frontier dwellers will move from city to city and nobody will have mercy on them, the wisdom of scholars will be defective, those who fear sin will be despised, truth will be absent, young men will insult Elders, Elders will stand before the young, "a son will abuse his father, a daughter rebel against her mother and a daughter-in-law against her mother-in-law, the enemies of a person are his family"[279], the generation is dog-faced, a son is not ashamed before his father. What do we have to rely on? Our Father in Heaven.

267 The Mishnah in the Babli is quite different in this first paragraph; it is close to the *baraita*/Tosephta quoted in the Halakhah as alternative version. The mention of Rebbi and R. Phineas ben Yaïr characterizes the entire Mishnah as a late addition.

268 Hillel's grandson, whom the Apostle Paul claimed as his teacher.

269 The last High Priest of good character.

270 It may be that "interpreters of biblical verses" is meant. R. Aqiba is the last authority who systematically derived laws directly from an interpretation of verses.

271 Who study day and night.

272 It is difficult to know what this means. In the Babli, "the preachers disappeared". Ben Zoma is known for his gnostic studies.

273 Had he lived, he probably could have averted the uprising of Bar Kochba.

274 In many independent Mishnah mss. (and the following Tosephta) "Rabban Simeon ben Gamliel"; missing in the Babli. The Yerushalmi reading is preferable since Rabban Gamliel died just before the Bar Kochba revolt but his son died at the beginning of the Severan dynasty which was a good time for the Jewish population of Palestine.

275 קיטונתה is usually derived from Greek κοιτών "bedroom", Syriac קיטונא "room". In Babli and independent Mishnah he is called קטנתא "the little one", because, according to some mss., he was the most insignificant of the pious. It is more than likely that the Yerushalmi קיטונתה is identical with קטונתא except for the addition of a

stray ‏׳‎. This is accepted in the translation. Other Babli mss. and early medieval authors also call him "the concentrate of piety".

276 R. Eliezer ben Hyrkanos.

277 This Mishnah expected the Messiah to appear when the Roman state turned Christian.

278 Which was densely settled by Jews in talmudic times, cf. *Ševi'it* 6:1, Notes 31-51.

279 *Micah* 7:6.

(fol. 24b) **הלכה יז**: מִשֶּׁמֵּת רִבִּי אֱלִיעֶזֶר נִגְנַז סֵפֶר הַחָכְמָה. מִשֶּׁמֵּת רִבִּי יְהוֹשֻׁעַ פָּסְקוּ עֵצוֹת טוֹבוֹת וּמַחֲשָׁבוֹת טוֹבוֹת מִיִּשְׂרָאֵל. מִשֶּׁמֵּת רִבִּי עֲקִיבָה פָּסְקוּ מַעְיָינוֹת הַחָכְמָה. מִשֶּׁמֵּת רִבִּי אֶלְעָזָר בֶּן עֲזַרְיָה פָּסַק הָעוֹשֶׁר מִן הַחֲכָמִים. מִשֶּׁמֵּת רִבִּי יוֹסֵי פָּסְקָה הַבִּינָה. מִשֶּׁמֵּת בֶּן עַזַּאי פָּסְקוּ הַשְּׁקְדָנִים. מִשֶּׁמֵּת בֶּן זוֹמָא פָּסְקוּ הַדַּרְשָׁנִים. מִשֶּׁמֵּת רִבִּי חֲנִינָה בֶן דּוֹסָא פָּסְקוּ אַנְשֵׁי הַמַּעֲשֶׂה. מִשֶּׁמֵּת רִבִּי יוֹסֵי חֲסִידָא וְרִבִּי יוֹסֵי קָטוֹנְתָא פָּסְקוּ אַנְשֵׁי חֲסִידוּת. וְלָמָּה נִקְרָא קִיטוֹנְתָא שֶׁהָיָה תַּמְצִיתָן שֶׁלַּצַּדִּיקִים וְשֶׁלַּחֲסִידִים. מִשֶּׁמֵּת רַבָּן שִׁמְעוֹן בֶּן גַּמְלִיאֵל בָּא גוּבַּיי וְרַבּוּ צָרוֹת. מִשֶּׁמֵּת רִבִּי הוּכְפְּלוּ הַצָּרוֹת.

Halakhah 17: [280]"When Rebbi Eliezer died, the book of wisdom was hidden[281]. When Rebbi Joshua died, good counsel and good deeds disappeared from Israel. When Rebbi Aqiba died, the souces of wisdom disappeared. When Rebbi Eleazar ben Azariah died, wealth disappeared from the Sages. When Rebbi Yose died, insight disappeared. When Ben Azai died, the perseverers disappeared. When Ben Zoma died, the preachers disappeared. When Rebbi Joshua died, good disappeared from the world. When Rebbi Hanina ben Dosa died, the workers [of wonders] disappeared. When Rebbi Yose the pious and Rebbi[282] Yose the minor died, pious men disappeared. Why is he called minor? For he was the concentrate of the just and the pious. When Rabban Simeon ben Gamliel died, locusts came and troubles increased. When Rebbi died, troubles were doubled."

280 A similar version in Tosephta 15:3-5; Babli 49b.

281 In Tosephta and Babli: The Torah scroll was hidden.

282 In the Tosephta sources, in the Babylonian *baraita*, and in a few Mishnah mss., he is called Abba Yose, placing him before the destruction of the Temple. In *Baba qama* 3:7 (3d, l. 37) he is called Yose the Babylonian or Yose ben Jehudah, without title.

(24c, line 29) רִבִּי יַעֲקֹב בַּר אִידִי בְשֵׁם רִבִּי יְהוֹשֻׁעַ בֶּן לֵוִי. רַבָּן יוֹחָנָן בֶּן זַכַּאי מִי דְמִיךְ פְּקִיד וַאֲמַר. פַּנּוּ חָצֵר מִפְּנֵי הַטּוּמְאָה וְהַתְקִינוּ כִסֵּא לְחִזְקִיָּה מֶלֶךְ יְהוּדָה. רִבִּי לִיעֶזֶר תַּלְמִידֵיהּ מִי דְמִיךְ פְּקִיד וַאֲמַר. פַּנּוּ חָצֵר מִפְּנֵי הַטּוּמְאָה וְהַתְקִינוּ כִסֵּא לְרַבָּן יוֹחָנָן בֶּן זַכַּאי. וְאִית דְּאָמְרִין. מָן דְּחָמָא רַבֵּיהּ חָמָא. חַד מִן אִילֵּין דְּבֵית פָּזִי הֲוֹון בָּעֵי מְחַתְּנִנְתֵּיהּ לִנְסִיוּתֵיהּ וְלָא הֲוָה מְקַבֵּל. אָמַר. דְּלָא יְהוֹן בָּהַתּוֹן. מִי דְמִיךְ פְּקִיד וַאֲמַר. פַּנּוּ חָצֵר מִפְּנֵי הַטּוּמְאָה וְהַתְקִינוּ כִסֵּא לִיהוֹשָׁפָט מֶלֶךְ יְהוּדָה. אָמְרוּ. יָבוֹא זֶה שֶׁרָץ אַחַר כָּבוֹד אַחַר זֶה שֶׁבָּרַח מִן הַכָּבוֹד.

283Rebbi Jacob bar Idi in the name of Rebbi Joshua ben Levi: When Rabban Joḥanan ben Zakkai died, he commanded and said, clear the courtyard because of the impurity and prepare a chair for Hezekiah, the king of Judah. When his student Rebbi Eliezer died, he commanded and said, clear the courtyard because of the impurity and prepare a chair for Rabban Joḥanan ben Zakkai. But some say, what his teacher saw, he saw. They proposed marriage into the family of the Patriarch to one of the family Pazi, but he did not accept and said that they should not be ashamed. When he was dying, he commanded and said, clear the courtyard because of the impurity and prepare a chair for Josaphat, the king of Judah. They said, the one who ran after honor284 should come for him who fled before honor.

283 The entire paragraph is in *Avodah zarah* 3:1 (42c, l. 42). The first sentence is also in the Babli, *Berakhot* 28b.

284 While all other Davidic kings married local women, he married a princess from the House of Omri.

(24c, line 37) רִבִּי יַעֲקֹב בַּר אִידִי בְּשֵׁם רִבִּי יְהוֹשֻׁעַ בֶּן לֵוִי. מַעֲשֶׂה שֶׁנִּכְנְסוּ זְקֵינִים לַעֲלִיַּת בֵּית גַּדְיָא בִּירִיחוֹ. וְיָצָאת בַּת קוֹל וְאָמְרָה לָהֶן. יֵשׁ בֵּינֵיכֶם שְׁנַיִם רְאוּיִין לְרוּחַ הַקּוֹדֶשׁ וְהִלֵּל הַזָּקֵן אֶחָד מֵהֶן. וְנָתְנוּ עֵינֵיהֶן בִּשְׁמוּאֵל הַקָּטָן. וְשׁוּב נִכְנְסוּ זְקֵינִים לָעֲלִיָּיה בְּיַבְנֶה וְיָצָאת בַּת קוֹל וְאָמְרָה לָהֶן. יֵשׁ בֵּינֵיכֶם שְׁנַיִם רְאוּיִין לְרוּחַ הַקּוֹדֶשׁ וּשְׁמוּאֵל הַקָּטָן אֶחָד מֵהֶן. וְנָתְנוּ עֵינֵיהֶן בְּרִבִּי אֱלִיעֶזֶר בֶּן הוּרְקָנוֹס. וְהָיוּ שְׂמֵיחִין שֶׁהִסְכִּימָה דַעְתָּן לְדַעַת הַמָּקוֹם.

[285]Rebbi Jacob bar Idi in the name of Rebbi Joshua ben Levi: It happened that Elders came together in the upper floor of the house Gadia in Jericho, when a disembodied voice came and said to them: There are among you two who would be worthy that the Holy Spirit should rest on them, and one of them is Hillel the Elder. They all looked at Samuel Minor. Again it happened that Elders came together in a second floor at Jabne, when a disembodied voice came and said to them: There are among you two who would be worthy that the Holy Spirit should rest on them, and one of them is Samuel Minor. They all looked at Rebbi Eliezer ben Hyrkanos and were happy that their opinion[286] coincided with that of the Omnipresent.

285 Cf. Notes 209 ff.

286 About Samuel Minor.

Introduction to Tractate Nedarim

Tractate Nedarim, "vows", is a commentary on *Num.* 30. That chapter speaks of "a vow or an oath to forbid something to oneself" (v. 3) or also "any vow or oath of prohibition for the purpose of mortification" (v. 14). There are other vows, not covered by the rules of that chapter, such as vowing money or valuables to Heaven, and vows by which a person undertakes an obligation toward third persons (including vows imposed by a court or a public authority.) Vows to Heaven constitute irrevocable debts since "accepting an obligation toward Heaven by word of mouth is transfer of property, legally equivalent to handing an object over to a buyer"[1]. Obligations toward other persons cannot be abrogated without the consent of the other, since vows cannot be used to abrogate any obligation, as emphasized several times in the Tractate.

The Tractate essentially treats three topics: The definition of "vow", the rules of a possible annulment of a vow by a religious authority, and the dissolution of the vow of a girl by her father and of a wife by her husband. Only the third topic is treated at length in the biblical source. The essential paradigm for a vow is a sacrifice, since a profane animal becomes a sacrifice only by being vowed as a gift to Heaven[2]. Upon dedication, the sacrifice becomes the property of Heaven and no human

---

1 Mishnah *Qiddušin* 1:6.
2 *Lev.* 7:16, 22:23, 27:9.

may derive any benefit from it. Since a sacrifice is material, is it concluded that in contrast to an oath, a vow always must refer to something material. The usual formula for a "vow of prohibition" is: Something should have the status of sacrifice for me; cf. *Math.* 15:5[3]. Since the Hebrew word for "sacrifice", *qorbān*, was used for sacral purposes, in most cases people substituted other words for profane use, such as the corresponding Phoenician *qônām*, a similar sounding artificial word, or words with similar connotations.

Num. 30:2 is interpreted to mean that Moses handed the right to adjudicate matters of vows to the Elders of the tribes, and through them to the Elders of all generations. V. 3 is read to mean that a person himself cannot abrogate his own vow but, by inference, that the Elder can do so[4]. While the verse speaks of both vows and oaths of prohibition, the detailed laws about dissolution of women's vows speak only of vows. Therefore, the Yerushalmi holds that in practice only vows can be annulled, not oaths. In general, making vows is frowned upon (*Deut.* 23:23); in Mishnah 1:1 a "vow of evildoers" is a vow, a "vow of the just" is non-existent. The culture of vowing apparent in this Tractate, a popular subject in the fourth Century, was an embarassment to the Babylonian scholars of the tenth

---

3   Cf. Chapter 1, Note 2.

4   It is difficult to know what the Sadducee position is in this case. While the Damascus Document (CD XVI 7-8) seems to exclude any possibility of abrogation of a vow, that interpretation is not the only one possible, cf. Chapter 3, Note 8. Karaites vehemently deny the possibility of any abrogation of vows. I. Elbogen suggests that the *kol nidre* formula, a disclaimer of vows, recited at the start of the Day of Atonement, is an anti-Karaite demonstration. But Amram Gaon in his *Siddur* disapproves of the formula, Saadya Gaon does not mention it, and Hai Gaon declares it to be the practice of foreign illiterates.

Century, at the height of the intellectual conflict with Karaism, when the Gaon R. Yehudai declared that the Tractate was not studied in his academy and vows not dissolved[5].

Chapter One describes all the oblique ways in which a vow can be formulated; Chapter Two lists similar expressions which nevertheless do not define vows. Chapter Three starts with a discussion of borderline cases which by rabbinic ruling are not considered to be vows and then turns to the next subject, an analysis of the meaning of certain terms of human relations of Mishnaic Hebrew, used in vows. This analysis is taken up again in Chapters Six and Seven, referring to names of things, and in Chapter Eight, applied to notions of time. In between, Chapters Four and Five deal with the rules of vows in which a person forbids to himself any benefit from another, or forbids his property to another person[6]. Chapter Nine deals with the rabbinic powers to abolish vows; the last two Chapters treat the biblical rules of dissolution of vows of underage or married women.

---

5 *Oẓar Hageonim* vol. 11, pp. 20, 23.
6 A non-Jewish example of the renunciation of mutual benefits and the complications arising therefrom appears in Gottfried Keller's "Fähnlein der Sieben Aufrechten" (E. G.).

כל כינויי נדרים פרק ראשון

(fol. 36c) **משנה א**: כָּל־כִּינּוּיֵי נְדָרִים כַּנְּדָרִים וַחֲרָמִים כַּחֲרָמִים וּשְׁבוּעוֹת כַּשְּׁבוּעוֹת וּנְזִירוּת כַּנְּזִירוּת. הָאוֹמֵר לַחֲבֵירוֹ מוּדָּר אֲנִי מִמָּךְ מוּפְרָשׁ אֲנִי מִמָּךְ מְרוּחָק אֲנִי מִמָּךְ. שֶׁאֵינִי אוֹכֵל לָךְ שֶׁאֵינִי טוֹעֵם לָךְ אָסוּר. מְנוּדֶּה אֲנִי לָךְ. רְבִּי עֲקִיבָה הָיָה חוֹכֵךְ בָּזֶה לְהַחֲמִיר. כְּנִדְרֵי רְשָׁעִים נָדַר בְּנָזִיר וּבְקָרְבָּן וּבִשְׁבוּעָה. כְּנִדְרֵי כְשֵׁירִים לֹא אָמַר כְּלוּם. כְּנִדְבוֹתָם נָדַר בְּנָזִיר וּבְקָרְבָּן.

Mishnah 1: All substitute names[1] of vows[2] are like vows, of bans[3] like bans, of oaths[4] like oaths, of *nazir* vows[5] like *nazir* vows. If one says to another, I am vowed away from you[6], I am separated from you, I am distanced from you, that I will not eat from yours, that I will not taste from yours, he is forbidden[7]. I am excommunicated from you, Rabbi Aqiba was stringent in that because of a doubt[8]. As vows of the wicked, he vowed as *nazir*, a sacrifice, and an oath[9]. As vows of the good ones, he did not say anything[10]. As their freewill gifts[11], he made a vow of *nazir* and sacrifice.

1   Since vows and oaths are sacral acts, the invocation of vow or oath is automatically the invocation of God's Name. Just as God's Name should not be invoked in vain, the people shied away from using the expressions "vow, making a vow" or "oath, swearing". As explained in the next Note, one of the oblique references to a vow was the word *qorbān* and its substitute, as given in Mishnah 2.

2   Making a vow is taking on an obligation. There are three kinds of vows found in talmudic literature.

A person may vow to bring a sacrifice or to give a certain sum to the

Temple. This is a relatively simple matter since (Mishnah *Qiddušin* 1:6) "speaking to Higher Powers is like delivering to a human"; i. e., a promise to God is as final as delivering the merchandise in a commercial transaction. Therefore, these vows are only a minor topic in the present tractate.

A person may make a vow to become a *nazir* for a certain time; then he is required to abstain from grapes and grape products as well as from becoming impure by the impurity of the dead, and he must let his hair grow. This kind of vow is discussed in Tractate *Nazir*.

The main topic of Tractate *Nedarim* is "any vow or oath of prohibition to deprive oneself" (*Num.* 30:14), i. e., a vow in which a person for any reason prohibits to himself things which otherwise are permitted. One may also make a vow to forbid certain actions to oneself but the actions must be forbidden as things are forbidden. (Self-flagellation is forbidden in Judaism since inflicting any wound on oneself is forbidden except for medical purposes, Mishnah *Baba qama* 8:5.) Since an animal which was dedicated as a sacrifice is forbidden for any profane use, it became general practice to say about anything of which one wanted to prohibit all use for himself "this is *qorbān* for me", or simply *qorbān* "sacrifice". Therefore, if in *Math.* 15:5 it is noted that a son can say to his parents that all he possesses should be *qorbān* for them; on the surface it is the height of mistreatment of the parents if the son prohibits them any use whatsoever of his property and even prohibits himself to help his parents in any way. The rabbinic answer would be that if the son goes off to fight as a guerilla against the Romans, or the Herodian government, cutting off all ties might save his parents' property from confiscation. (Cf. *Peah* 1:1, Note 113, about the unpredictability of the duty to honor father and mother: "Somebody might serve his father fattened meat and go to hell; another might bind his father to the grindstone and go to paradise.") The vow could also be in error, cf. Mishnah 3:2. Chapter 4 shows that a person forbidding his property to another can nevertheless take care of that other person. Cf. also Chapter 9, Note 38.

[In *Math.* 15:5, Jesus complains that Pharisees declare a person free from prosecution (פָּטוּר) if he violates the commandment to honor and fear father and mother by maliciously forbidding his property to them. The pharisaic rule in question is that "a prohibition violated without an action is not prosecutable" (Babli *Sanhedrin* 63a/b). Speech is not counted as an action in this respect. The rule is opposed by R. Jehudah who in many cases represents older traditions (from his father's teacher R. Eliezer.) The testimony of *Math.* shows that in this case, the majority opinion is the historic position. R. Jehudah's position is that of the Qumran community in the Manual of Discipline and the Damascus Document.)

3   "Ban" is the irrevocable gift of property to the Temple, *Lev.* 27:28.

4   An oath is subject-related, in contrast to a vow which is object-related. If a person prohibits himself to eat any bread, that is an oath of deprivation. If he prohibits the use of a specified loaf, or even any loaf, on himself, that is a vow of deprivation.

5   While this is also a vow of deprivation it follows its own rules, *Num.* 6:1-21.

6   Here starts the detailed explanation of what substitute names are. All expressions in this sentence are examples of נדר הנאה "a vow [to forbid] usufruct", in which A tells B that all of B's property is forbidden to A as if it were a sacrifice or sacred property and A's property to B..

7   All of B's property, not only his food.

8   R. Aqiba decided that, while the exact meaning of "excommunicated" in this context is unknown since the use of a judicial term by a private person is inappropriate, the most extensive interpretation must be adopted.

9   This sentence is very elliptic. Since the *nazir* prohibits vines and all their products for himself and he needs atonement for his status (*Num.* 6:11) one concludes (*Nedarim* 1:1, 36d 1. 50; Babli 10a) that it is essentially sinful to deprive oneself from permitted enjoyments. It follows that just people do not make vows of deprivation or *nezirut*. They also do not make vows of sacrifices since such a vow implies that the person will be financially responsible until a correct sacrifice has been presented in the Temple. Responsible people offer free-will gifts in which they designate an animal as sacrifice; if anything should happen to that animal before it is sacrificed he is not obligated to offer a replacement.

Since the wicked do make vows and swear, any expression of vow or oath declared to be in the form used by the wicked has to be interpreted to imply a maximum obligation. Still, somebody who simply says that he makes a vow of the wicked is not obligated for anything unless some object on which the vow could fall was before him at that moment. For example, if a loaf of bread was before him and he said, this loaf is for me as a vow of the wicked, he is forbidden to eat that loaf. If a long-haired *nazir* was passing before him and he said, that is for me as a vow of the wicked, he is a *nazir* for the standard period of 30 days.

10 Since good people do not make vows nor do they swear.

11 If somebody said, this loaf of bread is to me as a free-will gift of a just person, he means that for him it is *qorbān* and therefore forbidden for all usufruct. Similarly, if a long-haired *nazir* was passing before him and he said, that is for me as a free-will gift of the just, he is a *nazir* for the standard period of 30 days.

(36c, line 19) **הלכה א:** כָּל־כִּינּוּיֵי נְדָרִים כַּנְּדָרִים כול'. כְּתִיב אִישׁ כִּי יִדּוֹר. מַה תַּלְמוּד לוֹמַר נֶדֶר. אֶלָּא מִיכָּן שֶׁכִּינּוּיֵי נְדָרִים כַּנְּדָרִים. אוֹ הַשָּׁבַע מַה תַּלְמוּד לוֹמַר שְׁבוּעָה. אֶלָּא מִיכָּן שֶׁכִּינּוּיֵי שְׁבוּעוֹת כַּשְּׁבוּעוֹת. אַךְ כָּל־חֵרֶם. מַה תַּלְמוּד לוֹמַר יַחֲרִים. אֶלָּא מִיכָּן שֶׁכִּינּוּיֵי חֲרָמִים כַּחֲרָמִים. נֶדֶר נָזִיר. מַה תַּלְמוּד לוֹמַר לְהַזִּיר. אֶלָּא מִיכָּן שֶׁכִּינּוּיֵי נְזִירוּת כַּנְּזִירוּת. עַד כְּדוֹן כְּרִבִּי עֲקִיבָה דְּאָמַר. לְשׁוֹנוֹת רִבּוּיִין הֵן. כְּרִבִּי יִשְׁמָעֵאל דְּאָמַר. לְשׁוֹנוֹת כְּפוּלִין הֵן וְהַתּוֹרָה דִיבְּרָה כְדַרְכָּהּ. הָלוֹךְ הָלַכְתָּ. נִכְסוֹף נִכְסַפְתָּ. גָּנֹב גּוּנַּבְתִּי. מְנָלָן. אִישׁ כִּי יִדּוֹר נֶדֶר לַי"י אוֹ הַשָּׁבַע שְׁבוּעָה לֶאְסוֹר אִסָּר עַל נַפְשׁוֹ לֹא יַחֵל דְּבָרוֹ. מַה תַּלְמוּד לוֹמַר כְּכָל־הַיּוֹצֵא מִפִּיו יַעֲשֶׂה. אֶלָּא מִיכָּן שֶׁכִּינּוּיֵי נְדָרִים כַּנְּדָרִים וְכִינּוּיֵי שְׁבוּעוֹת כַּשְּׁבוּעוֹת. וּמִנַּיִן שֶׁכִּינּוּיֵי חֲרָמִים כַּחֲרָמִים. נֶדֶר נֶדֶר. מַה נֶּדֶר שֶׁנֶּאֱמַר לְהַלָּן כִּינּוּי נְדָרִים כַּנְּדָרִים וְכִינּוּי שְׁבוּעָה כַּשְּׁבוּעָה. אַף נֶדֶר שֶׁנֶּאֱמַר כָּאן כִּינּוּי חֲרָמִין כַּחֲרָמִין. וּמִנַּיִן שֶׁכִּינּוּיֵי נְזִירוּת כַּנְּזִירוּת. נֶדֶר נֶדֶר. מַה נֶּדֶר שֶׁנֶּאֱמַר לְהַלָּן כִּינּוּי שְׁבוּעָה כַּשְּׁבוּעָה אַף נֶדֶר שֶׁנֶּאֱמַר כָּאן כִּינּוּי נְזִירוּת כַּנְּזִירוּת.

"All substitute names of vows are like vows," etc. It is written[12] "Any person who vows," why does the verse say "a vow"? From here that substitute names of vows are like vows. "Or he swears," why does the verse say "an oath"? From here that substitute names of oaths are like oaths. "But any ban,[13]" why does the verse say "which he bans"? From here that substitute names of bans are like bans. "A vow of *nazir*[14]", why does the verse say "to be a *nazir*"? From here that substitute names of *nazir* vows are like *nazir* vows. So far for Rebbi Aqiba who says that these are expressions of additions. [15]For Rebbi Ismael who said, these are double expressions in the normal style of the Torah, "going you went, desiring you desired, by stealing I was stolen", from where? "[12]Any person who vows a vow to the Eternal or swears an oath to forbid a prohibition on himself shall not profane his word," why does the verse say "he must fulfill anything coming out of his mouth"? From here that substitute names of vows are like vows and substitute names of oaths are like oaths[16]. And from where that substitute names of bans are like bans? "A vow, a vow"[17]. Since "a vow" at one place means that substitute names of vows are like vows and substitute names of oaths are like oaths, "a vow" at the other place means that substitute names of bans are like bans. And from where that substitute names of being a *nazir* are like being a *nazir*? "A vow, a vow"[18]. Since "a vow" at one place means that substitute names of oaths are like oaths[19], "a vow" at the other place means that substitute names of being a *nazir* are like being a *nazir*.

12   *Num.* 30:3.
13   *Lev.* 27:28.
14   *Num.* 6:2.
15   Cf. *Yebamot* 8:1, Note 72, Babli *Avodah zarah* 27a (and another 18 times without attribution). The quotes are from speeches of Laban and Joseph in *Gen.* which have no legal implications. This proves that the repetitions are a matter of style.
16   The second half of the verse is clearly written for emphasis. It implies

(a) that a vow is valid only if pronounced, not if only thought of and (b) that any speech which can be interpreted as a vow is a vow.

The Babli, 3a/b, quotes both the argument in the style of R. Aqiba and that of R. Ismael without mentioning any names.

17 This is an application of the second hermeneutical rule of *gezerah šawah* "equal cut". If it was established in *Num*. 30:3 that "vow" means "anything that implies a vow" and in *Lev*. 27:2 any dedication to the Temple, including bans, is classified as "vow", it follows that anything which implies a ban is a ban.

18 Again this is an application of *gezerah šawah*, but this time the reference quote is *Num*. 6:2, cf. Note 14.

19 This reference is odd since the argument is about vows, not oaths. One has to assume that the scribe left out the relevant portion of the sentence which should be identical to the one used in the preceding case.

(36c, line 19) מַה מְקַיֵּים רִבִּי עֲקִיבָה כְּכָל־הַיּוֹצֵא מִפִּיו יַעֲשֶׂה. מִיכָּן לְנֶדֶר שֶׁבָּטֵל מִקְצָתוֹ בָּטַל כּוּלוֹ. וְלֵית לֵיהּ לְרִבִּי יִשְׁמָעֵאל כֵּן. כּוּלָהּ מִן תַּמָּן. אִית לֵיהּ מִיכָּן שֶׁכִּינּוּיֵי נְדָרִים כַּנְּדָרִים וְכִינּוּיֵי שְׁבוּעוֹת כַּשְּׁבוּעוֹת. אִית לֵיהּ מִיכָּן לְנֶדֶר שֶׁבָּטֵל מִקְצָתוֹ בָּטַל כּוּלוֹ. מַה מְקַיֵּים רִבִּי יִשְׁמָעֵאל נֶדֶר נָזִיר לְהַזִּיר. מִיכָּן שֶׁאָדָם קוֹבֵעַ עָלָיו נְזִירוּת בְּתוֹךְ נְזִירוּתוֹ. וְלֵית לֵיהּ לְרִבִּי עֲקִיבָה כֵּן. אִית לֵיהּ כּוּלָהּ מִתַּמָּן. אִית לֵיהּ מִיכָּן שֶׁאָדָם קוֹבֵעַ עָלָיו נְזִירוּת בְּתוֹךְ נְזִירוּתוֹ.

How does Rebbi Aqiba explain "he must fulfill anything coming out of his mouth"[20]? From here that if part of a vow is invalid, all of it is invalid. Does Rebbi Ismael not agree with this? Everything derives from there. It follows from there that substitute names of vows are like vows and substitute names of oaths[21] are like oaths and it follows from there that if part of a vow is invalid, all of it is invalid. How does Rebbi Ismael explain "any person who vows a vow of *nazir*[14]"? From there that a person can obligate himself as *nazir* while he currently is a *nazir*[22]. Does

Rebbi Aqiba not agree with this? He agrees and everything derives from there[23]. He agrees that from there a person can obligate himself as *nazir* while he currently is a *nazir*.

20   If a vow cannot be fulfilled completely, it is not a vow.

21   That conclusion could have been drawn even if the word כל "all, anything" were not written. Therefore, the clause admits two conclusions independent of one another.

22   The pentateuchal state of *nazir* is always limited in time (when a Temple is in existence. Since a *nazir* is only permitted to drink wine after he has absolved the required Temple ritual, a person vowing to be a *nazir* today must remain in that state until the Temple is rebuilt and officiating Cohanim are found who have complete documentary proof of their priestly status going back to the priests officiating in the second Temple.) The prophetic state of *nazir*, as exemplified by Simson and Samuel, is unlimited but does not include a prohibition of the impurity of the dead. It is noted here that while a person is in the state of a *nazir* for a fixed period, he can undertake to be a *nazir* for an additional period, to begin after the Temple procedure for the current *nezirut* was performed. This statement is needed since the vow of *nazir* of an unincumbered person makes that person a *nazir* immediately upon pronouncing his vow.

23   The same verse.

(36c, line 39) וַהֲלֹא הָעֲרָכִין וְהַחֲרָמִים וְהַתְּמוּרוֹת וְהַהֶקְדֵּישׁוֹת בַּפָּרָשָׁה הָיוּ. וְלֹא תַנִּינָן. כִּינּוּיֵי עֲרָכִין וְכִינּוּיֵי תְמוּרוֹת וְהֶקְדֵּישׁוֹת. וְאִילּוּ תַנִּינָן מַה הֲוֵינָן מִיתְנֵי. עֲרָפִין עֲרָצִין עֲרָקִין. תְּמוּפָה תְּמָרְנָה[24] תְּמוּקָה. הֶגְדֵּר הֶגְזֵר הֶגְרֵם. נִיחָא כְּמַאן דְּאָמַר סְתָם חֲרָמִים לְבֶדֶק הַבַּיִת. בְּרַם כְּמַאן דְּאָמַר. סְתָם חֲרָמִים לַכֹּהֲנִים. וְלָמָּה לֹא תַנִּינָן כִּינּוּיֵי תְרוּמָה. וְאִילּוּ[25] תַנִּינָן מַה הֲוֵינָן מִיתְנֵי. תְּרוּפָה תְּרוּצָה תְּרוּקָה.

Now estimates[26], bans, exchanges[27], and dedications[28] were in the same paragraph[29], but we did not state 'substitute names of estimates, substitute names of exchanges and dedications.' But if these were stated, what would we state[30]? *'Araphin, 'araṣin, 'araqin*[31]? *Temupha, temuna*[32], *temuqa*? *Hegder, hegzer, hegres*[33]. It is understandable following him who says, unspecified bans are for the support of the Temple[34]. But according to him who says, unspecified bans are for the priests? Why did we not state 'substitute names for heave'? But if it were stated, what would we state[30]? *Terupha*[35], *teruṣa, teruqa*?

24 This looks like a slip of the pen for תְּמוּנָה, which is indicated thus in the translation.

25 This looks like a slip of the pen for אִילוּ, which is indicated thus in the translation.

26 A person who offers to pay to the Temple the monetary value of his person, *Lev.* 27:1-8, which in general is a fixed sum but becomes an estimate for poor persons.

27 Exchanging a dedicated animal for another, *Lev.* 27:9-10.

28 Giving non-sacrificial animals or any other valuables to the Temple to cover its expenses, *Lev.* 27:11-25.

29 *Lev.* 27, where bans are treated in v. 28. Why should bans be treated differently from all other categories of gifts?

30 Recognized substitutes for vows, bans, *nazir* vows, and oaths are listed in Mishnah 2. The other dedications do not have recognized substitute names. The hypothetical names quoted in the sequel are built on the linguistic pattern of the accepted ones but either they make no sense or they have a sense very far from the intended one. Since they are not part of the current vocabulary as substitute names, they cannot be used.

31 "Disappearances".

32 "Picture".

33 The substitution of ג for ק in this series shows that the pronunciation of *q* was close to that of Arabic ج.

34 If bans are gifts to the Temple they are gifts to God and, as stated in Note 2, they become absolute the moment the intention to give is declared. Therefore, substitute names which are in common use are as effective as the explicit mention of the word "ban". But if an unspecified ban is intended for Cohanim (the majority

opinion in Mishnah *Arakhin* 8:6), the collection of the gift is a money transaction between Cohanim and the giver, subject to the rule that "the proof is on the claimant" (*Sanhedrin* 3:9, 21b l. 70; Babli *Baba qama* 46b). The Cohanim would have to prove that the putative giver in his use of the substitute words really did intend to refer to bans. This proof seems almost impossible. Therefore, substitute bans could not be like bans and the Mishnah here must be interpreted as supporting the opinion that unspecified bans are for the Temple.

35 "Medicine".

(36c, line 44) רִבִּי יַעֲקֹב בַּר אָחָא אָמַר. אִיתְפַּלְּגוּן רִבִּי יוֹחָנָן וְרִבִּי אֶלְעָזָר. דְּרִבִּי יוֹחָנָן אָמַר. לוֹקִין עַל הָאִיסָּרוֹת. וְרִבִּי אֶלְעָזָר אָמַר. אֵין לוֹקִין. אָמַר רִבִּי יַעֲקֹב בַּר אָחָא. כָּךְ מֵשִׁיב רִבִּי יוֹחָנָן אֶת רִבִּי אֶלְעָזָר. עַל דַּעְתָּךְ דְּאַתְּ אָמַר. אֵין לוֹקִין עַל הָאִיסָּרוֹת. וְהָא תַּנִּינָן. הַמּוּדָּר הֲנָייָה מֵחֲבֵירוֹ וְנִכְנַס לְבַקְּרוֹ. לֹא יִכָּנֵס. אָמַר רִבִּי יִרְמְיָה. שַׁנְיָיה הִיא תַּמָּן מִפְּנֵי דַרְכֵי שָׁלוֹם. רִבִּי יוֹסֵי בָּעֵי. אִם מִפְּנֵי דַרְכֵי שָׁלוֹם אֲפִילוּ בִשְׁבוּעוֹת יְהֵא מוּתָּר. וְתַנִּינָן. נְדָרִים אָסוּר וּשְׁבוּעוֹת מוּתָּר.

Rebbi Jacob bar Aḥa said, Rebbi Joḥanan and Rebbi Eleazar disagree, for Rebbi Joḥanan said, one whips for prohibitions[36] and Rebbi Eleazar said, one does not whip[36]. Rebbi Jacob bar Aḥa said, so did Rebbi Joḥanan answer Rebbi Eleazar: According to you, who says one does not whip on prohibitions, did we not state[37]: "If somebody has vowed not to have any usufruct from another and he goes to visit him," let him not enter[38]! Rebbi Jeremiah said, there is a difference there because of the ways of peace[39]. Rebbi Yose asked: If it is because of the ways of peace, should he not also be permitted in case of an oath? But we have stated[40]: "Vows are forbidden, oaths permitted."

36 Somebody forbade something for himself without using the language either of vows or of oaths or any of the recognized substitute expressions. If he

then breaks his own prohibition this falls under the biblical prohibition of "he shall not profane his word" (*Num.* 30:3). The question is whether this is a sin or a prosecutable offense. In *Nazir* 1:1 (51a l. 34), R. Joḥanan is quoted as holding that it is not a prosecutable offense. Accordingly, one has to read here "one does not whip", and in the opinion of R. Eleazar "one does whip" since this is also required by the argument quoted later by R. Jacob bar Aḥa. (Alternatively one would have to switch names in that argument, but then the quote in *Nazir* would remain unexplained.)

37 Mishnah 4:4: "If somebody has vowed not to have any usufruct from another and he goes to visit him (when he is sick), he may stand but not sit down and heal him (but not his animals)." He cannot sit down because he would derive usufruct from the other's possessions. The question makes sense only if R. Eleazar holds that transgressing the prohibition is prosecutable.

38 If transgressing a private prohibition is not prosecutable, one can explain the Mishnah as referring to a prohibition of usufruct, not a formal vow or oath. But if it is prosecutable as a formal vow, why permit to enter since the person entering will find shelter there from the sun in summer and the rain in winter?

39 "Ways of peace" are the obligations of interpersonal relationships necessary in a civilized society; in this case, visiting the sick.

40 Mishnah 2:2: "A vow that I shall not build a tabernacle, that I shall not take a *lulab*, that I will not wear phylacteries: vows are forbidden, oaths permitted, for one cannot swear to break religious obligations." If somebody makes a vow that religious objects should be forbidden to him (as if they were dedicated sacrifices), he commits a twofold sin in making a frivolous vow and breaking biblical commandments, but what he did is done. But if he swears that he will not fulfill his religious obligations, the oath is invalid since, in the language of the Babli, "he already is under oath from Mount Sinai", and a valid oath cannot be superseded by another oath. Since visiting the sick is a religious obligation, if the prohibition of usufruct is interpreted as an oath it should be nonexistent in the case of a visit to a sick person. No answer is given since practice follows R. Joḥanan.

HALAKHAH 1   435

(36c, line 51) אֵי זֶהוּ אִיסָר. כְּכָר זֶה עָלַי כַּיּוֹם שֶׁמֵּת בּוֹ אַבָּא. כַּיּוֹם שֶׁנֶּהֱרַג בּוֹ פְלוֹנִי. כַּיּוֹם שֶׁרָאִיתִי יְרוּשָׁלֵם חֲרֵיבָה. זֶהוּ אִיסָר שֶׁאָמְרָה הַתּוֹרָה. רִבִּי בָּא בְשֵׁם רִבִּי יוֹחָנָן וְרַב. תְּרֵיהוֹן אָמְרִין. וְהוּא שֶׁיְּהֵא נָדוּר בְּאוֹתוֹ הַיּוֹם. רִבִּי יוֹסֵי בָּעֵי. אִם בִּשְׁיְּהֵא נָדוּר בְּאוֹתוֹ הַיּוֹם לָמָּה לִי אִיסָר. וְיֹאמַר. בְּאוֹתוֹ הַיּוֹם.

[41]"What is a prohibition? This loaf is for me as the day of my father's death[42], as the day X was killed[43], as the day I saw Jerusalem in ruins; that is the prohibition the Torah spoke of[44]." Rebbi Abba in the name of Rebbi Johanan and Rav: Both say, only if he had made a vow about that day[45]. Rebbi Yose asked: If only he had made a vow about that day, why a separate prohibition? He should say on that day[46]!

41 A similar text in Tosephta 1:4, quoted in Babli 12a, 14a; Šebuot 20a.

42 If he keeps the anniversary of his father's death as a private fast day. In the Babli sources (including the Tosephta) the reference is not to a loaf but to meat and wine, assuming the person had vowed not to eat meat and drink wine at the anniversary of his father's death.

43 In the Babli: As the day Gedaliah ben Ahiqam was killed (2K. 25:25, Jer. 41:2), which is a fast day by tradition, not by law, and which therefore needs a declaration to be a binding obligation. (In practice, fasting three consecutive years on a particular date creates the equivalent of a vow to fast.)

44 "A person who vows a vow to the Eternal or swears an oath to forbid a prohibition to deprive oneself" (Num. 30:3). "If in her husband's house she vowed, or forbade a prohibition on herself by an oath." (Num. 30:11). Since the prohibition can refer both to a vow (tied to a material object that can be vowed to sacrificial use) and an oath (not tied to any object), it creates a category by itself.

45 If the person did not *earlier* make a vow that food on the anniversary of his father's death should be forbidden to him like a dedicated sacrifice or had sworn to the same effect, the reference to that day has no effect. In the Babli, the person quoted is Samuel.

46 Since the status of a prohibition is in doubt as to whether it is a vow or

an oath (Note 44), the reference given will determine its status. If the person fasts in consequence of a vow, the additional prohibition is a vow; if it refers to an oath, it is an oath. In no case is a separate category created. The only case in which one could speak of a separate category is if the additional prohibition is made together with the original one while the status is still undefined.

(36c, line 55) אִיסָר זוֹ שְׁבוּעָה. מִבְטָא זוֹ שְׁבוּעָה. אִם אוֹמֵר אַתְּ. אִיסָר זוֹ שְׁבוּעָה. חַיָּיב עַל כָּל־אִיסָר וְאִיסָר וְעַל כָּל־שְׁבוּעָה וּשְׁבוּעָה. אִם אוֹמֵר אַתְּ. אִסָּר מִין שְׁבוּעָה. חַיָּיב עַל זֶה בִּפְנֵי עַצְמוֹ וְעַל זֶה בִּפְנֵי עַצְמוֹ. אָסַר זוֹ שְׁבוּעָה. וְתֹאמַר. אִם אוֹמֵר אַתְּ כֵּן. אָמַר רִבִּי אֶלְעָזָר. תְּרֵין תַּנָּיִין אִינּוּן. אָמַר רִבִּי יִרְמְיָה. חַד תַּנַּיי הוּא. אָמְרוֹ בִּלְשׁוֹן נֶדֶר אַתְּ תּוֹפְסוֹ בִּלְשׁוֹן נֶדֶר. אָמְרוֹ בִּלְשׁוֹן שְׁבוּעָה אַתְּ תּוֹפְסוֹ בִּלְשׁוֹן שְׁבוּעָה. אָסַר הֲרֵי הוּא עַל יָדִי. אִם[47] תּוֹפְסוֹ בִּלְשׁוֹן נֶדֶר. אָסַר וְאֵינִי טוֹעֲמוֹ. אִם תּוֹפְסוֹ בִּמְקוֹם שְׁבוּעָה. אִם אוֹמֵר אַתְּ. אִסָּר מִין שְׁבוּעָה. חַיָּיב עַל כָּל־אִיסָר וְאִיסָר וְעַל כָּל־שְׁבוּעָה וּשְׁבוּעָה. אָמַר רִבִּי יוֹסֵי. לָא אַתְיָיא אֶלָּא בַחֲמִשָּׁה כִּכָּרִין. אֲבָל בְּכִכָּר אֶחָד מִכֵּיוָן שֶׁהִזְכִּיר עָלָיו שְׁבוּעָה עֲשָׂאוֹ כִּנְבִילָה. מִיכָּן וָאֵילַךְ בִּמְיַיחֵל שְׁבוּעוֹת עַל הָאִיסָּרִין וְאֵין שְׁבוּעוֹת חָלוֹת עַל הָאִיסָּרִין. אָמַר רִבִּי חֲנַנְיָה. אֲפִילוּ בְּכִכָּר אֶחָד אַתְיָיא הִיא. כְּהָדָא דְתַנֵּי. זֶה חוֹמֶר לְשֶׁעָבַר מִלָּבֹא. שֶׁאִם אָמַר. לֹא אָכַלְתִּי לֹא אָכַלְתִּי. חָב עַל כָּל־אֶחָד וְאֶחָד. לֹא אוֹכַל לֹא אוֹכֵל. אֵינוֹ חָב אֶלָּא אַחַת. אִם אוֹמֵר אַתְּ. אֵין אִסָּר מִין שְׁבוּעָה. חָב עַל זֶה בִּפְנֵי עַצְמוֹ וְעַל זֶה בִּפְנֵי עַצְמוֹ. אָמַר רִבִּי יוּדָן. וְהוּא שֶׁהִזְכִּיר נֶדֶר וְאַחַר כָּךְ הִזְכִּיר שְׁבוּעָה. אֲבָל אִם הִזְכִּיר שְׁבוּעָה וְאַחַר כָּךְ הִזְכִּיר נֶדֶר נְדָרִין חָלִין עַל הָאִסָּרִין וְאֵין שְׁבוּעוֹת חָלוֹת עַל הָאִסָּרִין.

[48]"'Prohibition', is an oath. 'Expression'[49], is an oath. If you say prohibition is an oath, he is guilty for every single prohibition and for every single oath. If you say prohibition is[50] a kind of oath, he is guilty for this separately and that separately." "Prohibition is an oath", and you say "if you say so"?[51] Rebbi Eleazar said, these are two Tannaïm[52]. Rebbi

Jeremiah said, it is from one Tanna[53]. If he said it in the language of a vow[54] you catch him in the language of a vow. If he said it in the language of an oath[55] you catch him in the language of an oath. If you say, prohibition is a kind of oath, he is guilty for every single prohibition and for every single oath[56]. Rebbi Yose said, this comes only for five loaves[57]. But for a single loaf, from the moment he mentioned "oath" for it, he made it a cadaver[58]. Furthermore, he may want to have oaths apply to prohibited items, but oaths cannot apply to prohibitited items[40]. Rebbi Hananiah said, it applies even to a single loaf. As we have stated[59], "in that the past is more stringent than the future, if he said I did not eat, I did not eat, he is guilty for every statement[60]; I shall not eat, I shall not eat, he is guilty only once[61]." Rebbi Yudan said[62], only if he first mentioned "vow" and then mentioned "oath". But if he mentioned oath and then vow, vows can apply to prohibitions but oaths cannot apply to prohibitions[63].

47 It seems that one should read את instead of אם, as suggested by the later discussion. The translation uses אַתְּ "you".

48 A *baraita* similar to this one is quoted and explained in the Babli *Šebuot* 20a.

49 *Num.* 30:4: "If she be married to a man and her vows are on her or the expression of her lips which she forbade on herself." Since "expression" is opposed to "vows", it must refer to oaths. Similarly, "to express with one's lips" is used for "to swear an oath" in *Lev.* 5:4; cf. *Šebuot* 20a.

50 It seems that "not" has fallen out here. The two cases will be explained below.

51 First one states that 'prohibition' is an expression of an oath. Then one argues 'if it is an oath', 'if it is not an oath'. This contradicts the first statement.

52 The first two sentences have one author, the last two a different one.

53 The *baraita*, as one would

reasonably expect, is from one author. But the implicit verb in the first two sentences should not be read as "is" but as "may be".

54 That he forbids the object for himself.

55 That he forbids himself the use of the object. Since "prohibition" is applied to both vows and oaths, the meaning of the word is determined by the syntax of the sentence in which it is used; cf. Note 4.

56 Violating a vow is a prohibition which, if proved in court by two witnesses, might subject the perpetrator to punishment by whipping. Even if the violation was inadvertent, there never is a possibility of a sacrifice. But inadvertently violating an oath imposes on the perpetrator the duty to offer a reparation or a purification offering in the Temple, *Lev.* 5:1-13.

57 Multiple guilt (multiple sacrifices) are possible only for multiple objects of prohibitions, not for repeated prohibitions of the same object.

58 If somebody made an oath to the effect that he would not eat a certain food, that food is forbidden to him as if it were cadaver meat, forbidden to any Jew.

59 Tosephta *Šebuot* 2:4, referred to in Babli *Šebuot* 28b.

60 If he swore falsely that he had not eaten, he committed the sin of a false oath. Since that oath does not forbid anything, each statement stands on its own and subjects him to the punishment for swearing falsely.

61 The first oath established the prohibition; the following oaths are futile, forbidden in the Third Commandment, but not triggering any obligation of sacrifice.

62 He explains the prior statement "If you say prohibition is *not* a kind of oath, he is guilty for this separately and that separately."

63 Since vows are subject related, if he forbade himself the use of a loaf, he may later declare the loaf to have the status of *qorbān*, to add the prohibition of sacrilege to the prohibition of eating. But if he first declared the loaf to be *qorbān*, it is automatically forbidden to him and no oath can increase the degree of prohibition. Therefore, the oath following the vow is a futile oath.

HALAKHAH 1

(36d, line 10) רִבִּי יוֹסֵי פָּתַר לֶאְסוֹר. הֲרֵי הוּא עָלַי. אָסוּר. הֲרֵי עָלָיו אִסָּר. אָסוּר. שְׁבוּעָה הֲרֵי הוּא עָלַי. אָסוּר. הֲרֵי עָלָיו בִּשְׁבוּעָה. אָסוּר. אָמַר רִבִּי יוּדָן. בִּנְדָרִים אָסוּר וּבִשְׁבוּעוֹת מוּתָּר. אִסָּר הֲרֵי עָלַי. אָסוּר. הֲרֵי עָלָיו אִסָּר. אָסוּר. שְׁבוּעָה הֲרֵי עָלַי. אָסוּר. הֲרֵי שְׁבוּעָה עָלַי. מוּתָּר.

Rebbi Yose explained "to forbid"[64]: That should be forbidden to me[65]; there should be a prohibition on it, it is forbidden[66]. An oath is on me, it is forbidden, there should be an oath on it, it is forbidden[67]. Rebbi Yudan said, in vows it is forbidden, in oaths it is permitted[68]. There is a prohibition on me, it is forbidden. There is a prohibition on it, it is forbidden. An oath is there on me, it is forbidden. There is an oath on (me) [it][69] is permitted[70].

64 *Num.* 30:3, "to forbid a prohibition to himself", which can be either a vow or an oath.

65 Even though no oath formula was mentioned, this is an oath since it is person-related.

66 Even though no vow was mentioned, this is a vow since it is object-related.

67 The only problem is in the last statement, since an oath cannot be binding on a thing. R. Yose holds that an oath formula, used when a vow formula would have been appropriate, induces a vow since it cannot induce a valid oath. In the language of the Talmudim, the oath formula is a *handle* to introduce the vow.

68 He holds that an oath formula applied to a thing is ineffective; it is as if it had not been said. This paragraph is discussed at length in the Commentary of R. Nissim Gerondi on the Babli, 2b.

69 It seems that it must be read עליו instead of עלי in order to make sense.

70 An oath directed to a thing is void and has no consequences.

(36d, line 13) מוּדָּר אֲנִי מִמָּךְ. רִבִּי יוֹסֵי בֶּן חֲנִינָה אָמַר. שְׁנֵיהֶן אֲסוּרִין זֶה בָּזֶה. כְּמָאן דְּאָמַר. וַאֲנָא מִינָךְ. אָמַר. הַכִּכָּר הַזֶּה נָדוּר מִמֶּנִּי וַאֲנִי מִינָּהּ. הֲרֵינִי נָדוּר מִכִּכָּר זֶה וְהוּא מִמֶּנִּי. הִיא הֵימָךְ הִיא מִמָּךְ. אָמַר. הִיא הֲרֵי אֲנִי לָךְ הִיא

הֲרֵי אֲנִי עָלַיִךְ. הִיא הֲרֵי אַתְּ לִי הִיא הֲרֵי אַתְּ עָלַי. תַּנֵּי. כָּלוּי אֲנִי מִמָּךְ. פָּרוּשׁ אֲנִי מִמָּךְ. רִבִּי יִרְמְיָה בָּעֵי. וְלָמָּה לֹא תַּנִּינָן נָטוּל. אָמַר רִבִּי יוֹסֵי. וְתַנִּיתָהּ בְּסוֹפָהּ וּנְטוּלָה אֲנִי מִן הַיְּהוּדִים.

"I am vowed away from you". Rebbi Yose ben Ḥanina said, both of them are mutually forbidden[6]; as if [the other person] had said: and I from you[71]. If he said, this loaf is vowed away from me and I from it, or I am vowed away from this loaf and it from me[72]. It does not make any difference whether he said "from me" in Aramaic (מינך) or in Hebrew (מימך), or he said "I am to you [forbidden]" or "I am on you [forbidden]", "you are to me [forbidden]" or "you are on me [forbidden]."[73] [74]It was stated: "I am jailed away from you, I am separated away from you". Rebbi Jeremiah asked, why did one not state "taken away from"? Rebbi Yose said, that was stated at the end, "I am taken away from the Jews."

71 In the absence of a specific restriction. For example, if A would say to B: I am separated from you, I shall not eat at your place, then the vow falls only on the specific activity indicated. But in absence of such a qualification, a vow of separation is understood to go both ways as indicated in Note 6. The statement of R. Yose ben Ḥanina is quoted in the Babli, 5a.

72 While an inanimate object cannot be told anything, as long as the vow is object directed it is a valid vow, irrespective of the language.

73 The Babli disagrees in principle, 5a.

74 This is from Halakhah 11:13. The Mishnah, quoted by R. Yose, speaks of a woman who wants to force a divorce by making a vow that sexual relations with any Jew shall be forbidden to her by saying "I am taken away from the Jews." The other expressions mentioned are equivalents of that statement.

(36d, line 19) שֶׁאֵינִי אוֹכֵל לָךְ שֶׁאֵינִי טוֹעֵם לָךְ. רִבִּי לָעֶזֶר בְּשֵׁם רִבִּי הוֹשַׁעְיָה. תּוֹפְשִׂין אוֹתוֹ מִשֵּׁם יַד לְקָרְבָּן. רִבִּי בּוּן בַּר חִייָה בָּעֵי. אִם אָמַר. לֹא אוֹכַל לָךְ. תּוֹפְסִין אוֹתוֹ מִשֵּׁם יַד לִשְׁבוּעָה. אָמַר רִבִּי יוֹסֵה. אוֹרְחֵיהּ דְּבַר נַשׁ מֵימַר. קַנְתָּהּ דְּכוּלְכָּה. דִּילְמָא כּוּלְכָּה דְּקַנְתָּהּ.

"That I will not eat from yours, that I will not taste from yours." Rebbi Eleazar in the name of Rebbi Hoshaiah. One catches him because of a handle for *qorbān*[75]. Rebbi Abun bar Ḥiyya asked, if he said, I shall not eat from you, does one catch him because of a handle of an oath[76]? Rebbi Yose said, people usually say "handle of an axe", do they ever say "axe of a handle"[77]?

75 Even if he did not spell out: *qorbān* that I shall not eat from yours. Since he used the language of vows, referring to the other person's food instead of his person, he made it clear that he intended a vow.

76 The answer is negative.

77 In the parallel, *Nazir* 1:2 (51b l. 28), R. Yose notes that common usage requires the word "oath" to be at the beginning of the sentence, not at the end, to which R. Mattaniah adds the example of the handle of the axe to show that (in rabbinic Hebrew) word order counts. The translation of כולכה (in the parallel כולבא) as "axe" follows J. Levy's Dictionary.

(36d, line 23) מְנוּדֶּה אֲנִי לָךְ. רִבִּי עֲקִיבָה הָיָה חוֹכֵךְ בָּזֶה לְהַחֲמִיר. לוֹסֵר אֶת כָּל־נְכָסָיו. כְּמָה דְאַתְּ מַר יָחֳרַם כָּל־רְכוּשׁוֹ וְהוּא יִבָּדֵל מִקְּהַל הַגּוֹלָה. מַה עָבְדִין לָהּ רַבָּנָן. חוֹמֶר הוּא בְנִידּוּי בֵּית דִּין.

"I am excommunicated from you, Rabbi Aqiba was stringent in that because of a doubt." To forbid all his possessions[8]. As you say[78], "all his property should be banned and he should be separated from the community of the diaspora." What do the rabbis do with this? An excommunication by the court is weightier.

78   *Ezra* 10:8.

(36d, line 26)   כְּנִדְרֵי רְשָׁעִים נָדַר בְּנָזִיר וּבְקָרְבָּן וּבִשְׁבוּעָה. שְׁמוּאֵל אָמַר. לִצְדָדִין הִיא מַתְנִיתָא. אוֹ בְנָזִיר אוֹ בְקָרְבָּן אוֹ בִשְׁבוּעָה. רִבִּי זְעִירָה אָמַר. נָזִיר בִּשְׁלָשְׁתָּן. אָמַר רִבִּי אָבִין. מָאן דְּבָעֵי מִיפְתּוֹר הָדָא דְּרִבִּי זְעִירָא כֵּינִי. הָיָה לְפָנָיו אֶשְׁכּוֹל אֶחָד וּבָא אַחֵר וְאָמַר. הֲרֵי עָלַי שְׁבוּעָה. הֲרֵי עָלָיו שְׁבוּעָה. וּבָא אַחֵר וְאָמַר. הֲרֵי עָלַי קָרְבָּן. הֲרֵי עָלָיו קָרְבָּן. וּבָא אַחֵר וְאָמַר. הֲרֵי עָלַי שְׁבוּעָה. הֲרֵי עָלָיו שְׁבוּעָה. וּבָא אַחֵר וְאָמַר. מַה שֶּׁאָמְרוּ שְׁלָשְׁתָּן עָלַי. לֹא נִמְצָא זֶה נוֹדֵר וּבְקָרְבָּן וּבִשְׁבוּעָה.

"As vows of the wicked, he vowed as *nazir*, a sacrifice, and an oath." [79]Samuel said, the Mishnah speaks about several cases, either as *nazir*, or a sacrifice, or an oath. Rebbi Ze'ira said, he is a *nazir* in all three of them. Rebbi Abin said, if somebody wants to explain that of Rebbi Ze'ira, it is such: There was before him a bunch of grapes and another person came and said, there is an oath on me, then there is an oath on him. Another person came and said, that is *qorbān* for me, it is *qorbān* for him. Another person came and said, there is an oath on me, then there is an oath on him. Another person came and said, what these three said is on me, does it not turn out that this one is obligated for *qorbān* and oath?

79   This text is obviously corrupt. A consistent text is quoted by Rashba [R. Shelomo ibn Adrat, Barcelona (d. 1310)] in his Novellae to the Babli, 9a, *s. v.* Mishnah. However, one should be reluctant to consider this the original text; it might well be Rashba's reconstruction (it replaces Yerushalmi או by Babli אי and is elliptic elsewhere). But since the text certainly captures the intent of the Yerushalmi, it is presented here with commentary (from edition Brno 1798, reprint New York 1961):

שְׁמוּאֵל אָמַר. לִצְדָדִין הִיא מַתְנִיא. אִי בְנָזִיר אִי בְקָרְבָּן אִי בִשְׁבוּעָה. רִבִּי זְעִירָה אָמַר. נָדַר בִּשְׁלָשְׁתָּן. אָמַר רִבִּי אָבִין. מָאן דְּבָעֵי מִיפְתַּר הָדָא רִבִּי זְעִירָא בְּמִי שֶׁהָיָה לְפָנָיו אֶשְׁכּוֹל אֶחָד וּבָא אֶחָד וְאָמַר. הֲרֵינִי נָזִיר מִמֶּנּוּ. הֲרֵי זֶה נָזִיר. בָּא אַחֵר וְאָמַר. הֲרֵי עָלַי כְּקָרְבָּן. וּבָא אַחֵר וְאָמַר. הֲרֵי עָלַי כְּנִדְרֵי רְשָׁעִים. בָּא אַחֵר וְאָמַר. מַה שֶׁאָמְרוּ שְׁלָשְׁתָּן עָלַי. נִמְצָא זֶה נָדוּר בְּנָזִיר וּבְקָרְבָּן וּבִשְׁבוּעָה.

Samuel said, it is taught about several cases, either about the *nazir*, or a sacrifice, or an oath. Rebbi Ze'ira said, he made a vow in all three of them. Rebbi Abin said, one wants to explain that of Rebbi Ze'ira about a person who has before him a bunch of grapes. A person came and said, I will be a *nazir* from these[80], he is a *nazir*. Another person came and said, these are for me *qorbān*[81]; another person came and said, they are for me like vows of the wicked[82]. Another person came and said, what these three said is on me; it turned out that this one vowed for *nazir*, *qorbān*, and oath.

80 He makes a vow by referring to the bunch of grapes which will be forbidden to him. But since the status of *nazir* cannot be split, he is a *nazir* in all its aspects.

81 That bunch of grapes is forbidden to him as if it were a dedicated sacrifice.

82 As the Mishnah said, since the "wicked" are impulsive people who swear on every occasion, he is considered not only to have vowed but also to have sworn that he will not eat the grapes.

(36d, line 33) תַּנֵּי. וּכְנִדְבוֹתָם. לֹא אָמַר כְּלוּם. הָדָא אָמְרָה שֶׁהָרְשָׁעִים מִתְנַדְּבִים. מִכֵּיוָן שֶׁהִתְנַדֵּב אֵין זֶה רָשָׁע. מַתְנִיתָא דְּרִבִּי יוּדָן. דְּתַנֵּי בְּשֵׁם רִבִּי יוּדָן. טוֹב אֲשֶׁר לֹא תִדּוֹר מִשֶּׁתִּדּוֹר וְלֹא תְשַׁלֵּם. טוֹב מִזֶּה וּמִזֶּה שֶׁלֹּא תִדּוֹר. רִבִּי מֵאִיר אוֹמֵר. טוֹב אֲשֶׁר לֹא תִדּוֹר מִשֶּׁתִּדּוֹר וְלֹא תְשַׁלֵּם. טוֹב מִזֶּה וּמִזֶּה נוֹדֵר וּמְשַׁלֵּם. וְכֵן הוּא אוֹמֵר נִדְרוּ וְשַׁלְּמוּ לַאלֹהֵיכֶם. כֵּיצַד הוּא עוֹשֶׂה עַל נְדָבָה. מֵבִיא כִשְׂבָּתוֹ לָעֲזָרָה וְאוֹמֵר. הֲרֵי זֶה עוֹלָה. רִבִּי אָבִין אָמַר. רִבִּי יְהוּדָה פָּתַח. אִילּוּ הָיִיתָ יוֹדֵעַ שֶׁהַנּוֹדֵר נִקְרָא רָשָׁע נוֹדֵר הָיִיתָ. אָמַר רִבִּי יַנַּאי. מוֹקֵשׁ אָדָם יָלַע קוֹדֶשׁ וְאַחַר נְדָרִים לְבַקֵּר. הִתְחִיל לִנְדּוֹר פִּינַקְסָתוֹ נִפְתַּחַת. דָּבָר אַחֵר. מוֹקֵשׁ אָדָם יָלַע קוֹדֶשׁ וְאַחַר נְדָרִים לְבַקֵּר. אִיחוּר נְדָרִים. אִיחֵר

אָדָם אֶת נְדָרוֹ פִּינְקְסָתוֹ נִפְתַּחַת. מַעֲשֶׂה בְּאֶחָד שֶׁאָמַר. הֲרֵי עָלַי עוֹלָה. וְשָׁהָא לַהֲבִיאָהּ וְשָׁקְעָה סְפִינָתוֹ בַיָּם.

It was stated[82]: "As to their free-will offerings, he did not say anything." Does that mean that the wicked give free-will offerings[83]? Since he gave a free-will offering, he is not wicked. The Mishnah follows Rebbi Jehudah, since it was stated in the name of Rebbi Jehudah[84]: "It is better that you should not make a vow than that you make a vow but do not pay," better in any case is that you should not make a vow at all. Rebbi Meïr says, "it is better that you should not make a vow than that you make a vow but do not pay," better in any case is that you should make a vow and pay. And so it says[85], "make vows and pay to your God." How does one handle a free-will offering? He brings his sheep to the Temple courtyard and says, that one is an elevation offering[86]. Rebbi Abin said, Rebbi Jehudah[87] used to open a door[88]: If you had known that one who makes a vow is called wicked, would you have vowed? Rebbi Yannai said, "it is a trap for a human to call 'sanctified' and afterwards to check out the vows,[89]" if one started to make vows, his account book[90] is opened. Another explanation: "it is a trap for a human to call 'sanctified' and to be late to check out the vows," if a person is in arrears with his vows, his account book is opened. It happened to one who said, I undertake to bring an elevation offering and he tarried to bring it. His ship sank at sea[91].

82 Tosephta 1:1: "Like free-will gifts of the wicked, he said nothing since the wicked do not make free-will gifts."

83 The formulation seems to imply that free-will offerings of the wicked do exist; otherwise how could one speak about them?

84 *Eccl.* 5:4. In all parallel sources, the attributions are switched between

R. Jehudah and R. Meïr [*Eccl. rabba* 5(2) a Yerushalmi source; Babli *Nedarim* 9a, *Ḥulin* 2a, Tosephta *Ḥulin* 2:17]. *Eccl. rabba* 5(2) is a shortened parallel to the entire paragraph. There, and in *Lev. rabba* 16(5), the next verse, "do not let your mouth make your flesh sin" is referred to people who pledge money for charity but do not redeem their pledges.

85   *Ps.* 76:12.

86   In this way he is sure to have taken on an open-ended financial obligation.

87   In the Babli, 22a, this is attributed to R. Yannai, in connection with his interpretation of *Prov.* 20:25, and is rejected in practice.

88   This refers to the topic of Chapter Nine. While it is written that the maker of a vow shall not profane his word, it is rabbinic tradition (contested by Samaritans, Karaites, and probably Sadducees) that while he cannot profane his word, the "heads of the tribes" addressed in *Num.* 30, and in their stead one ordained rabbi or a court of three lay people, can free a person from the obligations of his vow. But such a ruling depends on the person making the vow repenting it. An argument which induces such repentance is called "door of regret", פֶּתַח חֲרָטָה, or simply "door".

89   *Prov.* 20:25.

90   Greek πίναξ, cf. *Soṭah* Chapter 9, Note 220.

91   In *Eccl. rabba* 5(2), the man perished in his ship.

(36d, line 44) כִּנְדְרֵי כְשֵׁרִים לֹא אָמַר כְּלוּם. הָדָא אָמְרָה שֶׁהַכְּשֵׁרִים נוֹדְרִין. וּמִכֵּיוָן שֶׁנָּדַר אֵין זֶה כָשֵׁר. מַתְנִיתָא דְרִבִּי יוּדָה. דְּתַנֵּי בְשֵׁם רִבִּי יוּדָה. חֲסִידִים הָרִאשׁוֹנִים מִתְאַוִּין לְהָבִיא קָרְבַּן חַטָּאת. לֹא הָיָה הַמָּקוֹם מַסְפִּיק בְּיָדָם חֵטְ וְהָיוּ נוֹדְרִים בְּנָזִיר בִּשְׁבִיל לְהָבִיא קָרְבַּן חַטָּאת. רִבִּי שִׁמְעוֹן אוֹמֵר. חוֹטְאִים הָיוּ שֶׁהָיוּ נוֹדְרִים בְּנָזִיר. שֶׁנֶּאֱמַר וְכִפֶּר עָלָיו מֵאֲשֶׁר חָטָא עַל הַנָּפֶשׁ. חָטָא זֶה עַל נַפְשׁוֹ שֶׁמָּנַע עַצְמוֹ מִן הַיַּיִן. וְאַתְיָא דְשִׁמְעוֹן הַצַּדִּיק כְּרִבִּי שִׁמְעוֹן. דְּתַנֵּי. אָמַר שִׁמְעוֹן הַצַּדִּיק. מִיָּמַי לֹא אָכַלְתִּי אֲשַׁם נָזִיר אֶלָּא אֶחָד. פַּעַם אַחַת עָלָה אֵלַי אָדָם אֶחָד מִדָּרוֹם. וּרְאִיתִיו אַדְמוֹנִי עִם יְפֵא עֵינַיִם וְטוֹב רוֹאִי וּקְווּצוֹתָיו מְסוּדָּרוֹת תִּלִּים תִּלִּים. וְאָמַרְתִּי לוֹ. בְּנִי. מַה רָאִיתָ לְהַשְׁחִית אֶת הַשֵּׂיעָר

הַנָּאֶה הַזֶּה. וְנָם לִי. רַבִּי. רוֹאֶה הָיִיתִי בְעִירִי וְהָלַכְתִּי לְמַלְאוֹת אֶת הַשְּׁאוּב מַיִם. וְרָאִיתִי אֶת הַבּוּבִיָּה שֶׁלִּי בְּתוֹךְ הַמַּיִם וּפָחַז יִצְרִי עָלַי וּבִיקֵּשׁ לְאַבְּדֵינִי מִן הָעוֹלָם. אָמַרְתִּי לוֹ. רָשָׁע. אַתָּה מִפְחֵז בַּדָּבָר שֶׁאֵינוֹ שֶׁלָּךְ. עָלַי לְהַקְדִּישָׁךְ לַשָּׁמַיִם. וְהִרְכַּנְתִּיו בְּרֹאשִׁי וְאָמַרְתִּי לוֹ. בְּנִי. כְּמוֹתָךְ יִרְבּוּ עוֹשֵׂי רְצוֹן הַמָּקוֹם בְּיִשְׂרָאֵל. עָלֶיךָ הַכָּתוּב אוֹמֵר אִישׁ אוֹ אִשָּׁה כִּי יַפְלִיא לִנְדּוֹר נֶדֶר נָזִיר לְהַזִּיר לַיי'. רִבִּי מָנָא בָעֵי. לָמָּה לִי כְשִׁמְעוֹן הַצַּדִּיק אֲפִילוּ כְרִבִּי שִׁמְעוֹן. לֹא אָכַל שִׁמְעוֹן הַצַּדִּיק חַטָּאת חֵלֶב מִיָּמָיו. לֹא אָכַל שִׁמְעוֹן הַצַּדִּיק חַטָּאת דָּם מִיָּמָיו. סָבַר שִׁמְעוֹן הַצַּדִּיק. בְּנֵי אָדָם מִתּוֹךְ הַקְפָּדָה הֵן נוֹדְרִין. מִכֵּיוָן שֶׁנּוֹדְרִין מִתּוֹךְ הַקְפָּדָה סוֹפוֹ לִתְהוֹת. מִכֵּיוָן שֶׁהוּא תּוֹהֶא נַעֲשׂוּ קָרְבְּנוֹתָיו כְּשׁוֹחֵט חוּלִּין בָּעֲזָרָה. וְזֶה מִתּוֹךְ יִישׁוּב נָדַר וּפִיו וְלִבּוֹ שָׁוִין.

"Like vows of the good ones, he did not say anything." Does this mean that good people make vows[83]? Since that one made a vow, he is not a good one. [92]The Mishnah follows Rebbi Jehudah since it was stated in the name of Rebbi Jehudah, the ancient pious ones desired to bring a purification offering[93], but the Omnipresent did not let a sin happen to them; so they made a vow of *nazir* in order to be able to bring a purification offering[94]. Rebbi Simeon says, they became sinners because they made a vow of *nazir*, for it was said: "He shall atone for him for what he sinned about the person[95]," that one sinned against his own person because he barred himself from [drinking] wine. It turns out that that of Simeon the Just parallels Rebbi Simeon. As it was stated[96]: Simeon the Just said, I never ate the reparation offering of a *nazir* except once. Once a man came to me from the South, I saw that he was reddish, with beautiful eyes and good looks, and his hair in nice rows of waves[97]. I said to him, my son, what induced you to cut off that beautiful hair? He said to me: Great man, I was a shephard in my village and I went to fill the water vessel with water when I saw my mirror image in the water and my instinct rushed over me and tried to lose me from the World[98]. I said to it, wicked! You are rushing me to something which is not yours; it is upon me to sanctify you to Heaven! I bent my head to him and said, my son, there should be many more in Israel who fulfill the Omnipresent's will like you. About you the verse says[14], "man or woman, if he clearly articulates vowing a vow of *nazir,* to be a *nazir* for the Eternal." Rebbi Mana asked[99]: Why following Simeon the Just, even following Rebbi Simeon? Did Simeon the Just never eat a purification offering for suet[100]? Did Simeon the Just never eat a purification offering for blood? Simeon the Just holds that people make a vow while they are upset. Since they make the vow while they are upset, in the end, they wonder[101]. But if he wonders, his sacrifices become similar to one of those who slaughtered profane animals in the Temple courtyard. But this one made a well thought-out dedication, when his mouth and his thoughts were in unison[102].

92 Purification offerings cannot be voluntary; they are required either for an inadvertent sin or for purification from a state of impurity. A male who does not sin inadvertently and who does not suffer from an impure sickness has no way to fulfill the commandments relative to the purification offerings. A woman can always bring a purification offering after childbirth.

93 From here to the end of the paragraph, the text is also in *Nazir* 1:6, 51c l. 36.

94 One of the 3 prescribed animal sacrifices at the end of the *nazir* period; *Num.* 6:14.

95 *Num.* 6:11. In *Sifry Num.* 30, R. Ismael points out that this verse is written about the *nazir* who became inadvertently impure in the impurity of the dead, who is in effect a sinner in respect to the dead person. The Babli, 10a, accepts the argument of R. Simeon,

96   Babli 9b, *Nazir* Yerushalmi 1:6, Babli 4b, *Sifry Num.* 22, *Num. rabba* 10(20).

97   A combination of images referring to David (*1S.* 17:42) and the friend in the Song of Songs (5:11).

98   He realized how much money he could make as a male prostitute in a hellenized city but that he would lose the World to Come.

99   Babli 9b.

100   The standard purification offering is for the purification from an inadvertent sin which at least carries a penalty of extirpation by Divine decree, e. g., if somebody ate suet or blood inadvertently. In order to effect the purification, the Cohanim have to eat the sacrificial meat (*Lev.* 6:19). How can somebody called "the Just" refuse to purify people?

101   They feel that they should not have made the vow. This becomes acute in particular in the case of the reparation offering, which is brought only in case of impurity of the *nazir*, who has to restart his entire time as *nazir* after his impurity has been repaired. Since the verse repeatedly requires that offerings in the Temple must be brought willingly (*Lev.* 1:3, 22:29), an offering brought unwillingly is of questionable validity.

102   Which alone makes the vow unquestionably valid.

משנה ב: הָאוֹמֵר קוֹנָם קוֹנָח קוֹנָס הֲרֵי אֵילוּ כִּנוּיִין לְקָרְבָּן. חֶרֶק חֶרֶךְ חֶרֶף הֲרֵי אֵילוּ כִּנוּיִין לְחֵרֶם. נָזִיק נָזִיחַ פָּזִיחַ הֲרֵי אֵילוּ כִּנוּיִים לִנְזִירוּת. שְׁבוּתָה שְׁקוּקָה נָדַר בְּמוֹהִי הֲרֵי אֵילוּ כִּנוּיִים לִשְׁבוּעָה. (fol. 36c)

Mishnah 2: If somebody says *qônām*[103], or *qônāḥ*, or *qônās*, these are substitute names for *qorbān*. *Ḥēreq, ḥerek, ḥereph*, these are substitute names for ban. *Nāzîq, nāziaḥ, pāziaḥ*, these are substitute names for *nazir*. *Šĕbûtâ, šĕqûqâ*, or he made a vow of *Moy*[104], these are substitute names for an oath.

103 "Sacrifice" in Phoenician. The other words have not been identified in any language. Cf. Note 1.

104 The first half of the name *Moyses* (Moses). The connection between Moses and oaths is given later, Note 122. While the difference between vow and oath is important in rabbinic law, people in everyday speech do not make these fine distinctions. If the verb is an expression of making a vow but the noun is "oath", the entire sentence has to be interpreted as being an oath.

הלכה ב: הָאוֹמֵר קוֹנָם קוֹנָח כּוֹל׳. עַד כְּדוֹן עַצְמוֹ. מַהוּ שֶׁיַּקְדִּישׁ (36d, line 66) לַשָּׁמַיִם בִּלְשׁוֹן קוֹנָם. נִשְׁמְעִינָהּ מִן הָדָא. הַשְׁאִילֵינִי קַרְדּוֹמָךְ. אָמַר קוֹנָם קוֹרְדּוֹם יֵשׁ לִי. קוֹנָם נְכָסַיי עָלַי. וְיֵשׁ לוֹ קוֹרְדּוֹם. נְכָסָיו אֲסוּרִין שֶׁאֵין לַזֶּה קוֹרְדּוֹם. אָמַר רְבִּי תַחְלִיפָא קַיסָרַיָּיא. שַׁנְיָיא הִיא. שֶׁבּוֹ בִּלְשׁוֹן שֶׁהִתְפִּיס אֶת הַקַּרְדּוֹם בּוֹ בִּלְשׁוֹן הִתְפִּיס אֶת הַנְּכָסִים. מַה נַּפְשָׁךְ. קָדַשׁ קוֹרְדּוֹם קָדְשׁוּ נְכָסִים. לֹא קָדַשׁ קוֹרְדּוֹם אֲפִילוּ הַנְּכָסִים לֹא קָדְשׁוּ. אִילוּ אָמַר. קוֹנָם קוֹרְדּוֹם יֵשׁ לִי. וְחָזַר וְאָמַר. קוֹנָם נְכָסַיי עָלַי. וְיֵשׁ לוֹ קוֹרְדּוֹם. נְכָסָיו אֲסוּרִין יָאוּת. אָמַר רְבִּי יֹושֻׁעַ בֶּן חֲנַנְיָה. נְכָסַיי מוּתָּרִין. וְקָם לֵיהּ. יָאוּת. לֹא אָמַר אֶלָּא שֶׁאֵין לַזֶּה קוֹרְדּוֹם. הָא אִם יֵשׁ לוֹ קוֹרְדּוֹם נְכָסָיו אֲסוּרִין. הָדָא אָמְרָה שֶׁקָּדַשׁ קוֹרְדּוֹם. הָדָא אָמְרָה שֶׁקָּדְשׁוּ נְכָסִים. הָדָא אָמְרָה שֶׁאָדָם מַקְדִּישׁ לַשָּׁמַיִם בִּלְשׁוֹן קוֹנָם.

Halakhah 2: "If somebody says *qônām*, or *qônāḥ*," etc. So far for himself. Can one dedicate to Heaven by saying *qônām*[105]? Let us hear from the following[106]: One said to another, lend me your spade[107]. He said, *qônām* the spade if I have it, *qônām* my property on me. If he has a spade, his property would be forbidden for this one "has no spade"[108]. Rebbi Taḥlifa from Caesarea said, there is a difference, for he used the same expression to attach the spade and to attach his property[109]. As you look at it, if the spade is sanctified, so is his property. If the spade is not sanctified, neither is his property. If he said, *qônām* the spade if I have it, and added *qônām* my property on me, if he owns a spade, his property is forbidden[110]. That is correct. Rebbi Joshua ben Hananiah said, if he had said "my property"[111], it would be permitted for he stopped. That is correct. He only asserted that the person had no spade. Therefore, if he has a spade, his property is forbidden. That means that the spade was sanctified. That means that the property was sanctified[112]. This means that a person may dedicate to Heaven using the expression *qônām*.

105 Can one dedicate property to the Temple using the expression *qônām* or any other of the recognized substitutes for *qorbān*?

106 There exists a Babylonian version of this *baraita*, Babli 35a and in abbreviated form Tosephta 4:6. The Babylonian version differs from the Yerushalmi in that the lender asserts that he has only one spade which he needs for himself and only asserts that he has no spare and, most importantly, that the lying lender's property is only forbidden to him during his lifetime but becomes the property of his heir while in the Yerushalmi the property becomes the Temple's. Therefore, the position of the Babli is opposed to that of the Yerushalmi and every attempt to emend and explain the Yerushalmi in the light of the Babli falsifies the text.

107 In modern Hebrew, קרדום is an axe. But in Mishnaic Hebrew it means "spade" as shown by the formulaic expression קרדום לחפור בו "a *qardom* used for digging."

108 He made a conditional vow. The vow must refer to an object. If he has no spade, there is nothing the vow refers to, and the vow is nonexistent. But should he have a spade, the vow refers to an object and is valid.

109 As described in detail now, the two vows are one and both refer to the spade.

110 To himself, but not to any other person in the world.

111 Without repeating the word *qônām*, or any equivalent expression, there is no vow.

112 R. Joshua ben Hanania holds that the property is permanently forbidden to everyone, including the heirs, and must be surrendered to the Temple administrator. This proves that *qônām* is as valid for dedications as *qorbān*.

(37a, line 1) רִבִּי יִרְמְיָה בָּעֵי. דָּבָר שֶׁהוּא מְשַׁמֵּשׁ לְשֵׁם חוּלִּין וּלְשֵׁם קָרְבָּן מַהוּ לוֹסַר עַצְמוֹ בוֹ. וְהָא תַנִּינָן. קוֹנָס. קוֹנָסָא שְׁמָהּ. וְהָא תַנִּינָן שְׁבוּתָהּ. שְׁפוּתָה שְׁמָהּ. וְהָא תַּנֵּי בַּר קַפָּרָא. חֶרֶס. לֹא חַסְפָּא הִיא. אָמַר רִבִּי זְעִירָא. לְשׁוֹן גָּבוֹהַּ הוּא. הָאוֹמֵר לַחֶרֶס וְלֹא יִזְרָח. רִבִּי שִׁמְעוֹן בֶּן לָקִישׁ אָמַר. לְשׁוֹן אוּמוֹת הוּא. כְּגוֹן אִילֵּין גִּיוָתָאֵי דִּינּוּן קַרְיָין לְחַסְפָּא כַסְפָּא. אָמַר רִבִּי יוֹסֵי. נִרְאִין הַדְּבָרִים בִּמְקוֹמוֹת אֲחֵרִים. אֲבָל בְּמָקוֹם שֶׁקּוֹרְאִין לְנָזִיר נָזִיק כֵּן אֲנִי אוֹמֵר. נְזִיר פְּסִילִים לֹא יְהֵא נָזִיר.

Rebbi Jeremiah asked: May a person bind himself by a word which has both a profane and a sacral meaning? Did we not state קוֹנָס? Its name is קונסה[113]. Did we not state שְׁבוּתָה? Its name is שְׁפוּתָה[114]. [115]But did not Bar Qappara state *ḥeres*[116]? Rebbi Ze'ira said, that is a name relating to the High One: [117]"If He commands the sun: would it not shine?". Rebbi Simeon ben Laqish said, these are Gentile words[118], like those Nabateans who say *khaspa* for *ḥaspa*[119]. Rebbi Yose said, it is reasonable in other places, but in a place where the *nazir* is called *naziq*[120], do I say that a *nazir* of people with speech defects should not be a *nazir*?

113   Which word is intended is not quite clear. The early commentators vote for קְנָס "a fine"; then קוּנְסָה could be a stand-in for קְנָסָא. Another possibility would be קֵינָסָא "a chip". There is no problem in asserting that קוֹנָס is used only for vows. Note Arabic ﻗﻮﻧﺲ "point of the helmet".

114   "Cooking". It also could be a word שפתא [*Tanḥuma Re'e* (5) "a bench".] This is another example to show that in Galilee, under the influence of Greek, β was /v/ and /v/ close to /f/.

115   From here to the end of the paragraph, the text is also in *Nazir* 1:1, 51a l. 52.

116   In Mishnaic Hebrew the word usually means "potsherd", which certainly is not coming close to the meaning "ban" for which it may be substituted according to Bar Qappara. In Biblical Hebrew, it may be "sun" or "scabies".

117 *Job* 9:7.

118 The Yerushalmi is inconsistent in its attribution. In *Nazir* 1:1 (and the Babli 10a), R. Joḥanan is reported to hold that the substitutes are words from foreign languages whereas R. Simeon ben Laqish holds that they are artificial words created by the Sages to avoid using Hebrew sacral words. In the latter case it would be obvious that only officially sanctioned words may be used.

119 They cannot distinguish between ح and خ.

120 Where ר is not a dental sound but close to a French /r/, which may be confounded with ج or غ. If the locals hear the equivalent of *nazir*, that is enough to establish the vow.

(37a, line 8) מִיתְנֵי. שְׁבוּתָהּ שְׁקוּקָה. תַּנֵּי רַבִּי חִיָּיא. שְׁבוּקָה שְׁקוּעָה שְׁקוּרָה. נֶדֶר. דְּנָדַר בְּמוֹהִי דְּנָדַר מֹשֶׁה וַיּוֹאֶל מֹשֶׁה. רַבִּי יוֹנָה בָּעֵי. וְלָמָּה לֵינָן אָמְרִין בְּמוֹמֵי דְּנָדַר שָׁאוּל וַיּוֹאֶל שָׁאוּל. יְמִינָא הֲרֵי זוֹ שְׁבוּעָה. שְׂמֹאלָא הֲרֵי זוֹ שְׁבוּעָה. אָמַר רִבִּי מַתַּנְיָה. דִּכְתִיב וַיָּרֶם יְמִינוֹ וּשְׂמֹאלוֹ לַשָּׁמַיִם וַיִּשָּׁבַע בְּחֵי הָעוֹלָם.

It was stated[121]: *šĕbutâ, šĕquqâ*; Rebbi Ḥiyya stated: *šĕbuqâ, šĕquʻâ, šĕqurâ*. "A vow", when he made a vow by Moy, by the oath which Moses vowed, "and Moses accepted the curse.[122]" Rebbi Jonah asked, why do we not say, by the oath which Saul vowed, "Saul menaced the people with a curse[123]"? By my right hand, that is a vow, by my left hand, that is a vow[124]. Rebbi Mattaniah said, for it is written[125]: "He lifted his right hand and his left hand to the Heavens and swore by the Eternally Living."

121 The Babli, 10b, has a different collection of substitutes for "oath".

122 *Ex.* 2:21. "Moses swore to stay by the man," not "Moses agreed to stay with the man," cf. the Targumim.

123 *1S.* 14:24. Why is the invocation of Saul's name not a form of oath. In the verse quoted, the meaning of "imposing a curse by an oath" is clear and undisputed. There is no answer, probably because religious fear was never connected with the name of Saul.

It is noteworthy that all through proto-Mishnaic, Mishnaic, and Talmudic periods the name Moses is not used for living persons; there are a few appearances of a substitute name such as Maishe.

124 In the Babli, 10b, only "right hand" is accepted.

125 *Dan.* 12:7.

(fol. 36c) **משנה ג:** לֹא חוּלִים לֹא אוֹכַל לָךְ לֹא כָשֵׁר לֹא דְכִי טָהוֹר וְטָמֵא נוֹתָר וּפִיגּוּל אָסוּר. כְּאִמְרָא כַּדִּירַיִים כָּעֵצִים כָּאִישִּׁים כַּמִּזְבֵּחַ כַּהֵיכָל כִּירוּשָׁלֵם נָדַר בְּאֶחָד מִכָּל מְשַׁמְּשֵׁי הַמִּזְבֵּחַ אַף עַל פִּי שֶׁלֹּא הִזְכִּיר קָרְבָּן הֲרֵי זֶה נָדַר בְּקָרְבָּנוֹ. רִבִּי יְהוּדָה אוֹמֵר הָאוֹמֵר יְרוּשָׁלֵם לֹא אָמַר כְּלוּם.

Mishnah 3: Not profane I shall not eat from yours, not usable, not pure, pure, or impure, leftover, or mushy, is forbidden. Like a sheep, like the storage places, like wood, like altar gifts, like the altar, like the Temple, like Jerusalem. If one made a vow by one of the serving pieces of the altar even though he did not mention "sacrifice", it is as if he made a vow by the sacrifice. Rebbi Jehudah says, he who says "Jerusalem" did not say anything[126].

126 The Mishnah enumerates substitute terms for *qorbān* in making an oath which forbids the use of certain things to the maker of the vow. Most details are explained in the Halakhah. "Leftover" are the leftovers of a valid sacrifice after the time allotted for its consumption; this is forbidden both as a sacrifice and as leftover. "Mushy" is the biblical term for a sacrifice which was brought from the start with the idea that it should be eaten out of its time and/or its place. This also is doubly forbidden.

An extended list of substitute expressions is in the Tosephta, 1:3 (partially quoted in the Babli, 13a).

(37a, line 13) **הלכה ג:** לֹא חוּלִין לֹא אוֹכַל לָךְ כול'. הָא מַה דָּנָא אֲכִיל מִן דִּידָךְ לָא יְהוּ חוּלִין אֶלָּא קָרְבָּן.

לֹא כָשֵׁר לִי אֶלָּא לַמִּזְבֵּחַ.

לֹא דְכִי לִי אֶלָּא לַמִּזְבֵּחַ.

טָהוֹר לַמִּזְבֵּחַ וְלֹא לִי.

טָמֵא לִי וְלֹא לַמִּזְבֵּחַ. כָּשֵׁר וְדָכִי מִטָהוֹר וְטָמֵא. לֹא כָשֵׁר לֹא דְכִי מִלְּטָהֵר וְטָמֵא.

פִּיגּוּל. לֹא שַׁנְיָיא. הִיא פִּיגּוּל שֶׁלָּעוֹלָה הִיא פִּיגּוּל שֶׁלִּשְׁלָמִים. נוֹתָר שֶׁלָּעוֹלָה הָיָה לוֹ שְׁעַת כּוֹשֶׁר. נוֹתָר שֶׁלִּשְׁלָמִים לֹא הָיָה לוֹ שְׁעַת כּוֹשֶׁר. אָמַר הֲרֵי עָלַי כַּנּוֹתָר שֶׁלִּשְׁלָמִים מָהוּ.

Halakhah 3: "Not profane I shall not eat from yours," etc. That which I would eat from you shall not be profane but a sacrifice[127].

"Not usable" for me but it is for the altar.

"Not pure," for me but it is for the altar.

"Pure," for the altar but not for me.

"Impure," for me but [pure] for the altar.

"Mushy". There is no difference whether mushy for an elevation offering or mushy for a well-being offering[128]. The leftover of an elevation offering [never][129] had a time when it was usable, the leftover of an elevation offering (never) had a time when it was usable[130]. If he said, this is for me as a leftover of a well-being offering, what is it?

127 The same explanation in the Babli, 11a.

128 The elevation offering is totally burned on the altar; no part of it is eaten. Nevertheless, there is a time limit on the sacrifice; it must be burned on the altar during the day it was slaughtered and the following night. If the blood was received by the officiating Cohen with the idea of burning the sacrifice the next day, the sacrifice itself becomes forbidden as

mushy. The well-being offering can be eaten for two days and the intervening night or, for a thanksgiving offering, the day and the following night; but if its blood is brought to the altar with the idea of eating from the sacrifice when mushy, immediately it is permanently forbidden.

129   It seems that the scribe switched "had" and "did not have" between elevation and well-being offerings. Since the elevation offering never was permitted to anybody, it was forbidden to use it while it was a sacrifice and it remained forbidden as leftover after its time had expired. Therefore, "leftover from an elevation sacrifice" is a thing which is permanently forbidden. Used in a vow formula it implies permanent prohibition.

130   Since a well-being offering can be eaten for some time by the offerer and his family and the prohibition of "leftover" is one after the fact, if somebody refers to food as "leftover from a well-being offering" it is unclear whether one refers to the time it was permitted or when it was forbidden. The Babli (12a) takes it for granted that "leftover" as object of a vow can only refer to leftover from an elevation offering, implicitly answering the open question of the Yerushalmi.

(37a, line 19) כְּאִימְרָא. רְבִּי יוֹחָנָן אָמַר. כְּאִימָּר תְּמִידָא. תַּמָּן אָמְרִין. כְּווֹלַד חַטָּאת. רְבִּי שִׁמְעוֹן בֶּן לָקִישׁ אָמַר. כְּאֵילוֹ שֶׁלְאַבְרָהָם אָבִינוּ. תַּנֵּי רְבִּי חִייָה מְסַייֵעַ לְרְבִּי שִׁמְעוֹן בֶּן לָקִישׁ. כְּאִימְרָא דְלָא יָנַק מִן יוֹמוֹהִי. עַל דַּעְתִּין דְּרַבָּנִין דְּתַמָּן נִיתְנֵי. כָּעֲזָרָה. אָמַר רִבִּי אָבִין. עַל דַּעְתֵּיהּ דְּרִבִּי שִׁמְעוֹן בֶּן לָקִישׁ נִיתְנֵי. כְּקָרְבָּנוֹת הַמִזְבֵּחַ. אָמַר רִבִּי יוֹסֵי בֵּירִבִּי בּוּן. עַל דַּעְתֵּיהּ דְּרִבִּי יוֹחָנָן נִיתְנֵי. כְּדִישׁוֹן מִזְבֵּחַ הַפְּנִימִי וְהַמְּנוֹרָה.

"Like a sheep." Rebbi Johanan said, like the sheep of the daily offering[131]. There, they say, like the young of a purification offering[132]. Rebbi Simeon ben Laqish said, like our father Abraham's ram[133]. What Rebbi Hiyya[134] stated supports Rebbi Simeon ben Laqish: Like a sheep which never suckled. Following the opinions of the rabbis there, one could state: Like the Temple courtyard[135]. Rebbi Abin said, following the opinion of Rebbi Simeon ben Laqish one could state: Like the sacrifices on the altar[136]. Rebbi Yose ben Abun said, following Rebbi Joḥanan one could state: Like the cleansing of the inner altar and the candelabra[137].

131 The most common sacrifice, a natural substitute for *qorbān*. In that case, one should read כְּאִימְרָא. The statements are quoted in *Gen. rabba* 56(14).

132 The purification offering of a common person is a female animal. If she gives birth after dedication, the lamb is totally forbidden; it cannot be used for anything and nothing can be done for it. What the rabbis there (Babylonia) assert is that a substitute for *qorbān* can be something which is forbidden even to the altar (and so could be considered as the opposite of *qorbān*). This opinion is not mentioned in the Babli.

133 *Ber.* 22:13. This was a sacrifice on an altar; one reads כְּאִימְרָא.

134 In *Gen. rabba*, this is attributed to Bar Qappara. In one opinion, the ram was created at the end of the Sixth Day of Creation [Mishnah *Abot* 5(9)].

135 This also is forbidden for profane use and is not a sacrifice.

136 See next paragraph.

137 This really refers to the statement that one may make a vow by referring to the serving pieces of the altar. R. Joḥanan prefers that one make the vow by something which is served daily.

(37a, line 25) כַּדִירִיים. כְּדִירִים שֶׁלָעֵצִים. כְּדִירִיים שֶׁלַקָּרְבָּנוֹת. כָּעֵצִים. כִּשְׁנֵי גִיזְרֵי עֵצִים. כָּאִישִׁים. כְּשַׁלְהָבוֹת שֶׁלָאֵשׁ. כַּמִּזְבֵּחַ. כְּקָרְבָּנוֹת הַמִּזְבֵּחַ. כַּהֵיכָל. כְּקָרְבָּנוֹת הַהֵיכָל. כִּירוּשָׁלֵם. כְּקָרְבָּנוֹת יְרוּשָׁלֵם.

"Like the storage places," like the storage places of wood, like the storage places of sacrificial animals[138]. "Like wood," like the two logs[139]. "Like altar gifts," like the flame of the fire[140]. "Like the altar," like the sacrifices on the altar. "Like the Temple hall," like the sacrifices in the Temple hall[141]. Like Jerusalem," like the sacrifices in Jerusalem.

138 The storage place for altar wood was in the Temple courtyard, where wood was checked for worms (Mishnah *Middot* 2:5). The holding area for the animals was outside the Temple on the Temple Mount, where animals were checked for blemishes.

139 The logs needed to burn on them the daily sacrifice, Mishnah *Yoma* 2:5.

140 Everywhere in talmudic literature, אִשֶּׁה is derived from the root אֵשׁ "fire". But fire is not anything a vow can fall on. The same problem arises with the last three terms which cannot represent *qorbān*, but only the place of the *qorbān*.

141 The daily incense and the blood of those special sacrifices whose blood has to be sprinkled on the incense altar.

(37a, line 27) נָדַר בְּאֶחָד מִכָּל מְשַׁמְּשֵׁי הַמִּזְבֵּחַ. כְּגוֹן כַּף וּמַחְתָּה וּמִזְרָק.

"If one made a vow by one of the serving pieces of the altar," e. g., cup[142], shovel[143], and pouring cup.

142 To catch the blood at the moment of slaughter.

143 For incense.

(37a, line 28) רִבִּי יְהוּדָה אוֹמֵר. הָאוֹמֵר כִּירוּשָׁלֵם לֹא אָמַר כְּלוּם. שֶׁלֹּא נִתְכַּוֵּון אֶלָּא לָעֵצִים וְלָאֲבָנִים שֶׁבָּהּ. כַּתּוֹרָה. הֲרֵי זֶה מוּתָּר. כִּקְדוּשַׁת תּוֹרָה כַּכָּתוּב בָּהּ. הֲרֵי זֶה אָסוּר כַּקָּרְבָּנוֹת הַכְּתוּבִין שֶׁבָּהּ. אִית תַּנָּיֵי תַנֵּי. כַּתּוֹרָה וְכַכָּתוּב בָּהּ. הֲרֵי זֶה מוּתָּר. רִבִּי אָבִין בַּר כַּהֲנָא אָמַר. דְּרִבִּי שִׁמְעוֹן הִיא. אָמַר רִבִּי יוֹחָנָן. דִּבְרֵי רִבִּי שִׁמְעוֹן נִמְצָא שֶׁאֵין בְּיָדוֹ חִטִּין וּפָטוּר עַל הַשְּׁאָר. אָמַר רִבִּי יוֹסֵי. דִּבְרֵי הַכֹּל הִיא. כַּתּוֹרָה. כִּקְדוּשַׁת תּוֹרָה. כַּכָּתוּב בָּהּ. כִּקְדוּשַׁת כְּתוּבַיָּא.

"Rebbi Jehudah says, he who says 'like Jerusalem'[144] did not say anything," since this one intended to refer only to its wood and stones[145]. "Like the Torah," that is permitted[146]. "Like the sanctity of the Torah, like what is written in it," that is forbidden[146] like the sacrifices written in it. There are Tannaïm who state, "like the Torah and what is written in it," is permitted. Rebbi Abin bar Cahana said, that is Rebbi Simeon's, as Rebbi Joḥanan said, by the words of Rebbi Simeon, if it turns out that he had no wheat, he is free also for the rest[147]. Rebbi Yose said, it is everybody's opinion. "Like the Torah", like the sanctity of the Torah. "Like what is written in it," like the sanctity of the verses[148].

144 This is a reformulation of the Mishnah. According to the Babli, 11a, according to the Tanna of the Mishnah, R. Jehudah would accept "like Jerusalem" as a *qorbān* formula. There is no hint of this in the Yerushalmi.

145 Which are permitted.

146 Tosephta 1:4, Babli 14b.

147 This refers to the discussion in *Šebuot* 5:4. A (who has no witnesses and no documents to prove his case) says to B, give me the wheat, barley, and spelt which you hold for me. B says, I have nothing of yours. A says to B, swear that you have no wheat, barley, and spelt of mine, and B says Amen. If it turns out that he swore falsely, he is guilty of one crime. R. Simeon says, if he swore correctly about the wheat, he cannot be prosecuted for swearing falsely about barley and spelt since an oath (and a vow) which is partially voided is totally voided.

148 Since the second opinion is treated second and at length, it is the opinion accepted in the Yerushalmi, in contrast to the Babli.

(fol. 36c) **משנה ד:** הָאוֹמֵר קָרְבָּן עוֹלָה וּמִנְחָה חַטָּאת תּוֹדָה וּשְׁלָמִים שֶׁאֵינִי אוֹכֵל לָךְ אָסוּר וְרִבִּי יְהוּדָה מַתִּיר. הַקָּרְבָּן כַּקָּרְבָּן קָרְבָּן שֶׁאוֹכַל לָךְ אָסוּר. לַקָּרְבָּן לֹא אוֹכַל לָךְ רִבִּי מֵאִיר אוֹסֵר. הָאוֹמֵר לַחֲבֵירוֹ קוֹנָם פִּי הַמְדַבֵּר עִמָּךְ וְיָדִי עוֹשָׂה עִמָּךְ וְרַגְלִי מְהַלֶּכֶת עִמָּךְ אָסוּר.

Mishnah 5: If somebody says sacrifice, elevation offering, or flour offering, purification offering, or well-being offering, that I will not eat with you, he is forbidden; Rebbi Jehudah permits[149]. The sacrifice, like a sacrifice, sacrifice if I would eat with you, he is forbidden[150]. It is for sacrifice what I will not eat with you, Rebbi Meïr forbids. If somebody says to another person, a *qônām* that my mouth speaks with you, that my hand works with you, that my foot goes with you, he is forbidden[151].

149 R. Jehudah requires that the object to which the vow refers be mentioned. Therefore, if he had said "like a sacrifice, like an offering" it would be a valid vow (Tosephta 1:2).

150 Since in this case one might read the sentence as: Any food I would eat from you should be a (the, like a) sacrifice.

151 At first glance it seems that these vows are not object-oriented since speech, working, and walking are no concrete objects. But since mouth, hand, and foot are concrete objects, the vow can refer to them and then this person's mouth, hands, and feet are forbidden any contact with the other person, which can be realized only if the person swearing the oath refrains from doing anything for the person intended by the vow.

(37a, line 13) **הלכה ה:** הָאוֹמֵר קָרְבָּן עוֹלָה וּמִנְחָה. כּוּל׳. כָּל־עַמָּא מוֹדֵיי. הָקָרְבָּן מוּתָּר. כַּקָרְבָּן אָסוּר. מַה פְּלִיגִין. קָרְבָּן. רִבִּי יְהוּדָה אוֹמֵר. הָאוֹמֵר קָרְבָּן כְּאוֹמֵר הָקָרְבָּן וְהוּא מוּתָּר. וְרַבָּנִין אֲמָרִין. קָרְבָּן כְּאוֹמֵר כַּקָרְבָּן וְהוּא אָסוּר. אָמַר לָהֶן רִבִּי יְהוּדָה. אֵין אַתֶּם מוֹדִין לִי בָּאוֹמֵר שְׁבוּעָה כְּאוֹמֵר הַשְּׁבוּעָה וְהוּא אָסוּר. וְכָא הָאוֹמֵר קָרְבָּן כְּאוֹמֵר כַּקָרְבָּן[152] וְהוּא מוּתָּר. וְרַבָּנִין מַטִּילִין אוֹתוֹ לַחוּמְרִין. הָאוֹמֵר שְׁבוּעָה כְּאוֹמֵר הַשְּׁבוּעָה וְהוּא אָסוּר. וְכָא הָאוֹמֵר קָרְבָּן כְּאוֹמֵר הָקָרְבָּן וְהוּא אָסוּר.

Halakhah 5: "If somebody says sacrifice, elevation offering, or flour offering," etc. Everybody agrees *this* sacrifice[153] is permitted, *like a* sacrifice is forbidden. Where do they disagree? Sacrifice. Rebbi Jehudah says, he who says 'sacrifice' is as if he said '*this* sacrifice' and is permitted;

but the rabbis say, he who says 'sacrifice' is as if he said *'like a* sacrifice' and is forbidden. Rebbi Jehudah said to them: Do you not agree that one who said "oath" is like one who said "this oath" and is forbidden[154]? And here he who says 'sacrifice' is as if he said *'this* sacrifice' and is permitted! But the rabbis throw restrictions on it[155]. One who said "oath" is like one who said "this oath" and is forbidden. But here, he who says 'sacrifice' is as if he said *'like a* sacrifice' and is forbidden.

152   This seems to be an error for הָקָרְבָּן and is translated as such.

153   הָא קָרְבָּן "this is a sacrifice" is not an expression of referral.

154   If he would say "like an oath" it would be a denial of oath and would be invalid, but "like a sacrifice" is the essential formula of a vow.

155   In matters of vows and oaths, the translation of the vernacular into the formal language of the law always must follow the restrictive interpretation (Mishnah 2:4).

(37a, line 42) חָלִיל הֶחָלִיל בֶּחָלִיל. בֵּין שֶׁאוֹכַל לָךְ בֵּין שֶׁלֹּא אוֹכַל לָךְ. מוּתָּר. לָחוּלִין שֶׁאוֹכַל לָךְ. אָסוּר. חוּלִין שֶׁאוֹכַל לָךְ. מוּתָּר.

Fife, the fife, with a fife, either 'that I shall eat with you' or 'that I shall not eat with you', is permitted[156]. No profane food[157] that I would eat with you, forbidden. Profane food I would eat with you, permitted.

156   *Ḥalîl* "fife" is derived from the root חלל II, Arabic خَلَّ "to pierce, make a hole" (among other meanings). Nobody takes this as close to *ḥulîn* "profane", derived from חלל I, Arabic حَلَّ "being permitted, not holy" (among other meanings) or חֲלִילָה "desecration, God forbid!". The expression cannot be interpreted as a vow.

157   Read לָא חוּלִין.

(37a, line 44) רִבִּי יָסָא בְּשֵׁם רִבִּי יוֹחָנָן. דִּבְרֵי רִבִּי מֵאִיר מִמַּשְׁמַע לָאו אַתְּ שׁוֹמֵעַ הֵין. לֹא קָרְבָּן מִזֶּה. דְּלָא נָא אָכִיל מִן דִּילָךְ. הָא מַה דָּנָא אָכִיל מִן דִּידָךְ חוּלִין הוּא. לֵית הוּא קָרְבָּן.

Rebbi Yasa in the name of Rebbi Joḥanan: Are there words of Rebbi Meïr that from a negative one understands a positive? There is no sacrifice from this. What I shall not eat from you. Therefore, what I shall eat from you is profane, it is not *qorbān*[158].

158   The Mishnah about לָא קָרְבָּן mentions only R. Meïr but does not mention the anonymous majority which must hold that no vow is intended. It is generally accepted that R. Meïr does not accept to derive a positive statement from the inversion of a negative (Babli 11a, 13b; *Šebuot* 36a, *Soṭah* 17a; Yerushalmi *Erubin* 3, 21b l. 24, *Qiddušin* 1:3 64a l. 16, *Šebuot* 4:14 35d l. 66, 7:1 37c l. 45). It is obvious that the first sentence is a rhetorical question.

(37a, line 46) הִילוּכִי עָלֶיךָ. דִּיבּוּרִי עָלֶיךָ. לֹא אָמַר כְּלוּם. לָמָּה. שֶׁמַּתְפִּיס אֶת הַנֶּדֶר בְּדָבָר שֶׁאֵין בּוֹ מַמָּשׁ. נֶדֶר נֶדֶר. מַה נֶּדֶר שֶׁנֶּאֱמַר לְהַלָּן דָּבָר שֶׁאֵין בּוֹ מַמָּשׁ. אַף נֶדֶר שֶׁנֶּאֱמַר כָּאן דָּבָר שֶׁאֵין בּוֹ מַמָּשׁ. עֵינִי רוֹאָה לָךְ. אָזְנִי שׁוֹמַעַת לָךְ. אָסוּר. אַתְּ אוֹמֵר. יָדַי עוֹשָׂה עִמָּךְ. אָסוּר. חָרַשׁ עִמּוֹ בַּקַּרְקַע עַד כַּמָּה הוּא אָסוּר. עִמּוֹ כְּדֵי שְׂכָרוֹ אוֹ עַד כְּדֵי הֲנָיַית קַרְקַע. גָּדַר עִמּוֹ בַּתַּנּוּר עַד כַּמָּה הוּא אָסוּר. עַד כְּדֵי שְׂכָרוֹ אוֹ עַד כְּדֵי הֲנָיַית תַּנּוּר.

'My going [is forbidden] to you, my speech [is forbidden] to you,' he said nothing. Why? Because he referred the vow to something immaterial. "Vow, vow"[159]. Just as "vow" which was said there refers to something (im-)material[160], so "vow" said here refers to something (im-)material. 'My eye [is forbidden] to see for you, my ear [is forbidden] to hear you,' he is forbidden[161]. You say, 'my hand [is forbidden] to work with you,' he is forbidden. If he ploughed with him[162] on the ground, what is forbidden to him? Up to the amount of his wages or any improvement of the ground? If he fenced in[163] an oven with him, what is forbidden to him? Up to the amount of his wages or any improvement of the oven?

159 This is an application of the second hermeneutical rule *gezerah šawah* (cf. *Berakhot* Chapter 1, Note 70) that in legal texts, a word has only one definite meaning. The word "vow" is used in *Lev.* 27:2 to describe the pledge of a predetermined sum of money, which is material. Therefore in *Num.* 30:3, the word "vow" also must refer to something material.

160 The context requires that both times the expression שֶׁאֵין בּוֹ מַמָּשׁ "immaterial" must be emended to שֶׁיֵּשׁ בּוֹ מַמָּשׁ "material". Unfortunately, there are no parallels to this argument in talmudic literature.

161 Since now the vow is referred to something material.

162 If the worker makes a vow not to enjoy anything from his employer, can he work for him since the transaction is a simple exchange of work for money, or is he forbidden to work in case his work causes a permanent improvement of the employer's property? The question is not answered.

163 Some commentators and editors want to emend here either to גרר "to grate", or גדד "to cut". There seems to be no reason for emendation.

אלו נדרים פרק שני

(fol. 37a) **משנה א**: אֵילוּ נְדָרִים מוּתָּרִין חוּלִין שֶׁאוֹכַל לָךְ כַּבָּשָׂר חֲזִיר כַּעֲבוֹדָה זָרָה כַּנְּבִילוֹת כַּטְּרֵיפוֹת כַּשְּׁקָצִים כָּרְמָשִׂים כְּחַלַּת אַהֲרֹן וְכִתְרוּמָתוֹ מוּתָּר. הָאוֹמֵר לְאִשְׁתּוֹ הֲרֵי אַתְּ עָלַי כְּאִימָּא פּוֹתְחִין לוֹ פֶּתַח מִמָּקוֹם אַחֵר שֶׁלֹּא יָקֵל רֹאשׁוֹ לְכָךְ. קוֹנָם שֶׁאֵינִי יָשֵׁן שֶׁאֵינִי מְדַבֵּר שֶׁאֵינִי מְהַלֵּךְ הָאוֹמֵר לְאִשְׁתּוֹ קוֹנָם שֶׁאֵינִי מְשַׁמְּשֵׁךְ הֲרֵי זֶה בְּלֹא יַחֵל דְּבָרוֹ. שְׁבוּעָה שֶׁאֵינִי יָשֵׁן שֶׁאֵינִי מְדַבֵּר שֶׁאֵינִי מְהַלֵּךְ אָסוּר.

Mishnah 1: The following vows are permitted[1]: Profane I would eat with you[2]; like pork[3], like idolatry, like carcasses[4], like meat from a torn animal[5], like abominations[6], like crawling things[7], like Aaron's *ḥallah* and his heave[8], are permitted. One who says to his wife, you are for me like my mother[9], one finds for him an opening from another place that he should not be flippant about this. A *qônām* that I shall not sleep, that I shall not speak, that I shall not walk, or one who says to his wife, a *qônām* that I shall not sleep with you, he is under the obligation[10] "he shall not profanate his word." An oath that I shall not sleep, that I shall not speak, that I shall not walk, he is forbidden[11].

1 Even though they sound like vows, they are not vows.

2 Since he vows to eat what is permitted, there is nothing to it.

3 As the Halakhah explains, a vow must refer to something which can be a sacrifice. Since swine cannot be sacrificial animals, if he says "what I would eat from you is like pork", there is no vow and no legal consequence. If he would say, a *qônām* that what I would eat from you is like pork, he

would be forbidden since he referred to the sacrifice.

4   Forbidden food, *Deut.* 14:21.
5   Forbidden food, *Ex.* 22:30.
6   Forbidden food, *Lev.* 11:29 ff.
7   Forbidden food, anything not on the list of permitted animals. These are explicitly permitted to Gentiles, *Gen.* 9:3.
8   Heave and *ḥallah*, the heave from dough, are holy. Sacrifices can only be brought from sources that are profane before dedication. Therefore, heave and *ḥallah* cannot become sacrifices. As long as the person making the vow does not mention *qorbān* or any of its substitutes, there is no vow.
9   He says that sexual relations with his wife should be forbidden as they are with his mother. Since his mother cannot be a sacrifice, there is no vow but the rabbi is not permitted to tell him this but must find another reason (e. g., do you realize how much money a divorce would cost you?) to find a cause to annul the vow because people should be made uncomfortable vowing. If the vow is not dissolved within one week, the wife can ask the court to force a divorce; the husband being the guilty party (Mishnah *Ketubot* 5:6). (Cf. Qor'an 58:2.)
10   *Num.* 30:3. As long as *qorbān* or one of its substitutes is not mentioned, sleeping, speaking, and walking are all immaterial and there really is no vow. But since there was intent to make a vow, the verse may be applied (at least by rabbinic standards).
11   Since an oath does not depend on any material substrate (Chapter 1, Note 4).

(37b, line 13) **הלכה א:** אֵילוּ נְדָרִים מוּתָּרִין כול׳. לֹ״י. אֵין אָדָם אוֹסֵר עָלָיו דָּבָר אֶלָּא שֶׁהוּא לֹ״י. תַּנֵּי דְּבֵית רַב פְּלִיג. מְנַיִין לִנְדָרִים שֶׁהֵן מוּתָּרִין לָךְ מִן הַשָּׁמַיִם וּבְנֵי אָדָם נוֹהֲגִין בָּהֶן בְּאִיסוּר שֶׁלֹּא תְהֵא נוֹדֵר וּמְבַטֵּל. תַּלְמוּד לוֹמַר לֹא יַחֵל דְּבָרוֹ. שֶׁלֹּא יַעֲשֶׂה דְּבָרָיו חוּלִין. הֲוֹון בָּעֵי מֵימַר. כְּגוֹן הַקָּרְבָּן בִּשְׁבוּעָה. הָא בִּשְׁאָר כָּל־הַדְּבָרִים לֹא. אָתָא מֵימַר לָהּ. אֲפִילוּ בִשְׁאָר כָּל־הַדְּבָרִים. לֶאֱסוֹר אִסָּר עַל נַפְשׁוֹ. אִית תַּנָּיֵי תַּנֵּי. עַל נַפְשׁוֹ לֹא עַל אֲחֵרִים. אִית תַּנָּיֵי תַּנֵּי. אֲפִילוּ עַל אֲחֵרִים. הֲוֹון בָּעֵי מֵימַר. מַאן דָּמַר. עַל נַפְשׁוֹ לֹא עַל

HALAKHAH 1 465

אֲחֵרִים. לוֹסַר נְכָסָיו שֶׁל אֲחֵרִים. וּמָאן דָּמַר. אֲפִילוּ עַל אֲחֵרִים. לוֹסַר נְכָסָיו עַל אֲחֵרִים. הָא נִיכְסֵי אֲחֵרִים עָלָיו לוֹ.

"The following vows are permitted," etc. "To the Eternal[12]", nobody can forbid anything on himself unless it could be given to the Eternal[13]. What is stated in the House of Rav disagrees: "From where that one may not make and dissolve vows which are dissolved for you from Heaven but people consider them as binding? The verse says[12], 'he shall not profanate his word.' He should not make his words profane." They wanted to say, for example using "*qorbān*" or "oath"; but in all other respects it would be permitted. It comes to tell you, also all other respects[14]. "To prohibit a prohibition on himself[12]". There are Tannaïm who state: on himself, not on others. There are Tannaïm who state: even on others. They wanted to say that he who says on himself, not on others, to forbid others' property[15], but he who says even on others, to forbid his own property for others, but not the property of others for himself.

12 *Num.* 30:3.

13 The comparison used in a vow must refer either to a sacrifice or to something that could be a sacrifice or a *ḥerem*. In the language of the Babli, 14a, "there is no vow unless it relates to something that can be vowed." A lenghty paraphrase in *Sifry Num.* 153.

14 The opinion of R.Yose, Chapter 1, Notes 64 ff.

15 This sentence has been badly distorted by editors and commentators of recent editions of the Yerushalmi. The original scribe of the ms. wrote in both cases על אחרים. The corrector changed the first occurence into של אחרים. It seems that the correct version is על של אחרים "[to forbid his own property] to others." It is clear that in both opinions, a person may forbid his own property (permanently) on another (in the Babli, 47a, compared to the power of a father to disinherit a son), but only according to the second opinion one may not forbid the property of others, over which he has

no control, to himself. The second opinion has no parallel in either Talmud.

In *Sifry Num.* 153 one reads: "'To prohibit a prohibition on himself', he prohibits for himself but not for others." This is opposed to both Talmudim.

(37b, line 22) הָאוֹמֵר לְאִשְׁתּוֹ הֲרֵי אַתְּ עָלַי כְּאִימָּא. בִּיאָתֵךְ עָלַי כְּבִיאַת אִימָּא. כִּבְשַׂר אִימָּא. לֹא אָמַר כְּלוּם. אָמַר הַכִּכָּר הַזֶּה עָלַי כְּבִיאַת אִימָּא. מָהוּ. נִשְׁמְעִינָהּ מִן הָדָא. הָאוֹמֵר לְאִשְׁתּוֹ. קוֹנָם אֵינִי מְשַׁמְּשֵׁךְ. רַב אָמַר. אָסוּר. וּשְׁמוּאֵל אָמַר. מוּתָּר. מַה מְקַיֵּים שְׁמוּאֵל בְּלֹא יַחֵל דְּבָרוֹ. כְּאִילּוּ בַּל יַחֵל דְּבָרוֹ. רַב כְּדַעְתֵּיהּ. תַּנָּיֵי דְּבֵית רַב פְּלִיג. מִנַּיִין לִנְדָרִים שֶׁהֵן מוּתָּרִין לָךְ מִן הַשָּׁמַיִם וּבְנֵי אָדָם נוֹהֲגִין בָּהֶן בְּאִיסּוּר כְּדֵי שֶׁלֹּא תְהֵא נוֹדֵר וּמְבַטֵּל. תַּלְמוּד לוֹמַר לֹא יַחֵל דְּבָרוֹ. שֶׁלֹּא יַעֲשֶׂה דְּבָרָיו חוּלִּין.

"One who says to his wife, you are for me like my mother". Your cohabitation is for me like cohabitation with my mother, like my mother's flesh; he did not say anything[16]. If he said, this loaf is for me like cohabitation with my mother, what[17]? Let us hear from the following: A *qônām* that I shall not sleep with you, Rav says, he is forbidden, Samuel says he is permitted. How does Samuel uphold "he shall not profanate his word"? As if he shall not profanate his word[18]. Rav sticks with his opinion[19]: The Tannaïm in the House of Rav disagree: "From where that one may not make and dissolve vows which are dissolved for you from Heaven but people consider them as binding? The verse says[12], 'he shall not profanate his word.' He should not make his words profane."

16 The translation and interpretation of these sentences are uncertain. Another approach to the text, based on a different reading of the meaning of the periods, would be: "One who says to his wife, you are for me like my mother, your cohabitation is for me like cohabitation with my mother. Like my mother's flesh, he did not say anything." In that case, the first

example is an explanation of the Mishnah, the second is a separate statement which might not conflict with the Mishnah. This is the approach of the Babli, 14a. If the translation in the text is chosen, the requirement that a formal annulment of the vow is required, is restricted to the wording in the Mishnah, where it is not so clear even to the unlearned that the vow is null and void.

17 What are the rules?

18 The statement of the Mishnah is purely rabbinical; it cannot possibly have a biblical basis.

19 From the previous paragraph.

(37b, line 29) שְׁבוּעָה שֶׁלֹּא אִישָׁן שְׁלֹשָׁה יָמִים. מַלְקִין אוֹתוֹ וְיָשֵׁן מִיָּד. שְׁבוּעָה שֶׁלֹּא אוֹכַל שְׁלֹשָׁה יָמִים. מַמְתִּינִין אוֹתוֹ עַד שֶׁיֹּאכַל וּמַלְקִין אוֹתוֹ.

"An oath that I shall not sleep for three days," one whips him and he can sleep immediately[20]. "An oath that I shall not eat for three days," one waits until he eats and then whips him[21].

20 Since nobody can go without sleep for three days, this is a vain oath forbidden by the Third Commandment. For the transgression he is sentenced to whipping; the oath itself is void. A similar statement, attributed to R. Joḥanan, appears in the Babli, 15a.

21 Since people can live for three days without food, the oath is not in vain and he can be punished only if he transgresses his oath.

(fol. 37a) **משנה ב:** קָרְבָּן לֹא אוֹכַל לָךְ וְקָרְבָּן שֶׁאוֹכַל לָךְ לֹא קָרְבָּן לֹא אוֹכַל לָךְ מוּתָּר. שְׁבוּעָה לֹא אוֹכַל לָךְ שְׁבוּעָה שֶׁאוֹכַל לָךְ לֹא שְׁבוּעָה לֹא אוֹכַל לָךְ אָסוּר. זֶה חוֹמֶר בַּשְּׁבוּעוֹת מִבַּנְּדָרִים. וְחוֹמֶר בַּנְּדָרִים מִבַּשְּׁבוּעוֹת. כֵּיצַד אָמַר קוֹנָם סוּכָּה שֶׁאֵינִי עוֹשֶׂה לוּלָב שֶׁאֵינִי נוֹטֵל. תְּפִילִין שֶׁאֵינִי נוֹתֵן בַּנְּדָרִים אָסוּר בַּשְּׁבוּעוֹת מוּתָּר. שֶׁאֵין נִשְׁבָּעִין לַעֲבוֹר עַל הַמִּצְוֹת.

Mishnah 2: *Qorbān* [shall be] what I shall not eat at your place[22], or *qorbān* [shall be] what I shall eat from you[23], no *qorbān* [shall be] what I shall not eat from you[24]; he is permitted. An oath that I shall not eat at your place, an oath that I shall eat from you, no oath that I shall not eat from you[25]; he is forbidden[26]. That is more restrictive for oaths than for vows. What is more restrictive for vows than for oaths? If he said *qônām* that I shall not make a *sukkah*[27], that I shall not take a *lulab*[28], that I shall not put on phylacteries[29], as a vow he is forbidden, as an oath he is permitted since one cannot swear to transgress commandments[30].

22 Since he forbids only what he did not eat but nobody can forbid another person's property for other people, he did not say anything.

23 This clause is extremely difficult to explain since it is formulated exactly the standard way in which a person can prohibit another's food for himself. The Babli reads הַקָרְבָּן, an expression which had been determined not to be an oath (Chapter 1, Note 153). It is clear in all three cases that the same vow declared as *qônām* or any other substitute would be valid and the person making the vow would be forbidden to eat from the other person since then the intent would be clear. It is only the use of the word which refers directly to sacrifice which makes the vow invalid.

24 This clearly is idle talk.

25 For a person who holds that a double negation is a positive this is an oath that he will eat; this excludes R. Meïr who does not accept that argument, cf. Chapter 1, Note 158.

26 He is bound by his oath for negative or positive.

27 *Lev.* 23:42. The hut must at least get a new roof each year, Mishnah *Sukkah* 1:1.

28 *Lev.* 23:40, the palm branch of the "4 kinds".

29 *Ex.* 13:9, 16.

30 This is a principle accepted by all Jewish groups: *Philo, The Special Laws* II, 12-15; *Damascus Document CD* XIV 9.

HALAKHAH 2

הלכה ב: קָרְבָּן לֹא אוֹכַל לָךְ כול׳. וְלָמָּה לֹא תַּנִּינָן. שְׁבוּעָה שֶׁלֹּא (37b, line 31) אוֹכַל לָךְ. מוּתָּר. אֶלָּא בְגִין דְּתַנִינָן. חוֹמֶר בַּשְּׁבוּעוֹת מִבַּנְּדָרִים. וְסָבְרִינָן מֵימַר. שְׁבוּעָה לֹא אוֹכַל לָךְ. דִּבְרֵי חֲכָמִים אָסוּר. לְפוּם כֵּן לֹא תַּנִּינָן.

"*Qorbān* [shall be] what I shall not eat at your place," etc. Why did we not state: An oath that I shall eat from you, he is permitted[31]? Only because we stated: "That is more restrictive for oaths than for vows." We wanted to say about "an oath that I shall not eat of yours," that the words of the Sages are: he is forbidden. Therefore it was not stated.

31 He not only is permitted, he is obligated to eat at the other person's place, whereas in the case of a vow he would be free to eat or not to eat.

(37b, line 34) הֲרֵי הוּא קָרְבָּן. הֲרֵי הוּא לַקָּרְבָּן. הֲרֵי הוּא כְקָרְבָּן. מוּתָּר. הֲרֵי הוּא שְׁבוּעָה. הֲרֵי הוּא לַשְּׁבוּעָה. הֲרֵי הוּא כִשְׁבוּעָה. אָסוּר.

"That is a sacrifice, that is for a sacrifice, that is like a sacrifice," is permitted. "That is an oath, that is for an oath, that is like an oath," is forbidden[32].

32 In all cases quoted in the Mishnah, it makes no difference whether *qorbān* is stated alone or modified by one of the inseparable prepositions. In the Babli, 15a, it is held that R. Meïr would not accept this statement since he holds that לַקָּרְבָּן might be understood as a negation לָא קָרְבָּן = לַקָּרְבָּן.

(37b, line 36) זֶה חוֹמֶר בַּשְּׁבוּעוֹת מִבַּנְּדָרִים. וְחוֹמֶר בַּנְּדָרִים מִבַּשְּׁבוּעוֹת. כֵּיצַד. אוֹ נֶפֶשׁ כִּי תִשָּׁבַע לְבַטֵּא בִשְׂפָתַיִם לְהָרַע אוֹ לְהֵיטִיב. מַה הַטָּבָה רְשׁוּת אַף הֲרָעָה רְשׁוּת. יָצָא דָבָר שֶׁלְּאִיסוּר בְּדָבָר שֶׁל מִצְוָה. הֲווֹן בָּעֵיי מֵימַר. שׁוֹגֵג. הָא מֵזִיד לֹא. אַשְׁכָּח תַּנֵּי. רִבִּי יִשְׁמָעֵאל אוֹמֵר. כְּכָל־הַיּוֹצֵא מִפִּיו יַעֲשֶׂה. לֹא הַיּוֹצֵא מִפִּי שָׁמַיִם. וָמַר. אַף בְּהֶקְדֵּשׁ כֵּן. רִבִּי יוֹסֵי בְּשֵׁם רִבִּי הִילָא. שֶׁכֵּן אָדָם מַקְדִּישׁ סוּכָּתוֹ לַשָּׁמַיִם.

"That is more restrictive for oaths than for vows. What is more restrictive for vows than for oaths?" "Or a person who swears to lightly express with his lips for bad or for good[33]." Just as doing good is a matter of choice, so doing bad is a matter of choice; that excludes any prohibition which is a commandment[34]. They wanted to say, inadvertently, but not intentionally. It was found stated: Rebbi Ismael says, "*anything* that comes out of *his* mouth he shall do,[35]" not what comes out of Heaven's mouth. Should we say that this is the same for vows of sanctification? Rebbi Yose in the name of Rebbi Hila: For a man may vow his *sukkah* to Heaven[36].

---

33 *Lev.* 5:4.

34 In the Babli, 16b/17a, this verse, dealing with the obligation of a sacrifice for an oath inadvertently not kept, only frees the maker of an oath to violate some commandment from the obligation to bring a sacrifice.

35 *Num.* 30:3. In the Babli, this verse frees him from the sin of not keeping his vow. In the Yerushalmi, it extends the rule to *any* oath, including an intentional one.

36 Mishnah *Temurah* 7:2: Anything whatsoever can be vowed to support the Temple.

(fol. 37a) **משנה ג**: יֵשׁ נֶדֶר בְּתוֹךְ נֶדֶר וְאֵין שְׁבוּעָה בְּתוֹךְ שְׁבוּעָה. כֵּיצַד אָמַר הֲרֵינִי נָזִיר אִם אוֹכַל הֲרֵינִי נָזִיר אִם אוֹכַל וְאָכַל חַיָּיב עַל כָּל־אַחַת וְאַחַת. שְׁבוּעָה שֶׁלֹּא אוֹכַל שְׁבוּעָה שֶׁלֹּא אוֹכַל וְאָכַל אֵינוֹ חַיָּיב אֶלָּא אַחַת.

Mishnah 3: A vow inside a vow is possible, an oath inside an oath is impossible. For example, if one said, I shall be a *nazir* if I would eat, I shall be a *nazir* if I would eat, if he eats he is obligated for each pronouncement separately[37]. An oath that I will not eat, an oath that I will not eat, if he eats he is guilty only once[38].

37 If he drinks wine after eating, he can be sentenced to two whippings. If he keeps his vow, he has to observe two 30-day periods of *nezirut* and bring two sets of sacrifices.

38 If he breaks his oath, he can be punished only once.

(37b, line 42) **הלכה ג:** יֵשׁ נֶדֶר בְּתוֹךְ נֶדֶר כול'. רִבִּי יוֹסֵי בָּעֵי. שְׁבוּעָה שְׁבוּעָה שֶׁלֹּא אוֹכַל. וְאָכַל. אָמַר רִבִּי יוֹסֵי בֵּי רִבִּי בּוּן. נִישְׁמְעִינָהּ מִן הָדָא. שְׁבוּעָה שֶׁלֹּא אוֹכַל כִּכָּר זֶה. שְׁבוּעָה שֶׁלֹּא אוֹכַל. שְׁבוּעָה שֶׁלֹּא אוֹכַל. וְאָכַל. אֵינוֹ חַיָּיב אֶלָּא אַחַת. מִפְּנֵי שֶׁאָמַר זוֹ. הָא אִם לֹא אָמַר זוֹ חַיָּיב עַל כָּל־אַחַת וְאַחַת. אֲבִימִי אַחוֵי דְחֵיפָה אָמַר שַׁמָּשִׁית בִּנְדָרִים שַׁמָּשִׁית בִּשְׁבוּעוֹת. בָּעֵי חֵיפָה מִבְּדָקוֹנֶיהּ. הָיוּ לְפָנָיו חֲמִשָּׁה כִּכָּרִים וְאָמַר. שְׁבוּעָה שֶׁאוֹכַל כִּכָּר זוֹ. וְחָזַר וְאָמַר. שְׁנַיִם אֵילוּ. וְחָזַר וְאָמַר. שְׁלֹשָׁה אֵילוּ. וְחָזַר וְאָמַר. אַרְבָּעָה אֵילוּ. וְחָזַר וְאָמַר. חֲמִשָּׁה אֵילוּ. וְאָכַל אֶת הָרִאשׁוֹן מָהוּ. אָמַר לֵיהּ. חַיָּיב עַל כָּל־אַחַת וְאַחַת. אָמַר לֵיהּ. אֵינוֹ חַיָּיב אֶלָּא אַחַת. מִכֵּיוָן שֶׁהִזְכִּיר עָלָיו שְׁבוּעָה עֲשָׂאוֹ כִּנְבֵילָה. מִיכָּן וְאֵילַךְ כְּמִיחַל שְׁבוּעוֹת עַל הָאִיסּוּרִין. וְאֵין שְׁבוּעוֹת חָלוֹת עַל הָאִיסּוּרִין. חָזַר וּבְדָקֵיהּ. הָיוּ חֲמִשָּׁה כִּכָּרִים וְאָמַר. שְׁבוּעָה חֲמִשָּׁה כִּכָּרִים הָאֵילוּ. וְחָזַר וְאָמַר. אַרְבָּעָה אֵילוּ. וְחָזַר וְאָמַר. שְׁלֹשָׁה אֵילוּ. וְחָזַר וְאָמַר. שְׁנַיִם אֵילוּ. וְחָזַר וְאָמַר. אֶחָד זֶה. וְאָכַל אֶת כּוּלָּן. אָמַר לֵיהּ. אֵינוֹ חַיָּיב אֶלָּא אַחַת. אָמַר לֵיהּ. חַיָּיב עַל כָּל־אַחַת וְאַחַת. אִילּוּ מִי שֶׁאָמַר. שְׁבוּעָה שֶׁאוֹכַל חֲמִשָּׁה. וְאָכַל אַרְבָּעָה. שֶׁמָּא אֵינוֹ פָטוּר. אָמַר רִבִּי יוֹסֵי. מִסְתַּבְּרָא כְּאַחוֵי דְחֵיפָה בָּאַחֲרִיתָא. וּדְחֵיפָה בְּקַדְמִיתָא.

"A vow inside a vow is possible," etc. [39]Rebbi Yose asked: An oath, an oath, an oath that I shall not eat, but he ate? Rebbi Yose ben Rebbi Abun said, let us hear from the following[40]: "An oath that I shall not eat this loaf, an oath that I shall not eat, an oath that I shall not eat. If he ate, he is guilty only once." Because he said *this*. Therefore, if he had not said *this*, he would be guilty for each of the oaths[41].

[42]Avime the brother of Hefa[43] said, I studied vows, I studied oaths. Hefa wanted to examine him: There were five loaves before him and he said, an oath that I shall not eat this loaf. Then he said, these two loaves. Then he said, these three loaves. Then he said, these four loaves. Then he said, these five loaves. Then he ate the first, what are the rules? He said to him, he is guilty for each [oath] separately[44]. He said to him, he is guilty only once. From the moment he mentioned "oath" about it, he made it like carcass meat[4]. From there on he is as if he wanted to apply oaths to prohibitions, but no oath can be applied to prohibitions.

He examined him a second time. There were five loaves and he said, an oath about these five loaves. Then he said, these four. Then he said, these three. Then he said, these two. Then he said, this single one. Then he ate all of them? He said to him, he is guilty only once. He said to him, he is guilty for each [oath] separately. If somebody had said, an oath that I shall not eat five, and he ate four, would he be free from punishment[45]?

Rebbi Yose said, it is reasonable following Hefa's brother in the last case, following Hefa in the first[46].

---

39 The entire Halakhah is also in *Šebuot* 3:8.
40 Mishnah *Šebuot* 3:8.
41 This paragraph admits of two quite different interpretations. The first, by R. David Fraenckel, notes that in the question, the three oaths are mentioned before the object of the oath is specified, but in the Mishnah the object is specified before the second oath is pronounced. In the Mishnah, the second and third oaths are void since the loaf is already forbidden. But in R. Yose's question,

nothing is forbidden when the second and third oaths are pronounced; therefore, they all are valid and with one act the person who then eats the loaf commits three sins in one act.

The second, not very likely, explanation, by R. Moses Margalit, assumes that many loaves are before the person when he makes the multiple oath and one may assume that each single oath refers to a different loaf. Therefore, if he eats all of them he is guilty for each loaf separately since the Mishnah states only that if he expressly refers to the same loaf each time he swears, he is guilty only once.

42 There is a parallel in the Babli, Šebuot 28b/29a.

43 In the Babli, he is called 'Epha. In the Babli, where Avime is called "his brother", Avime is the superior scholar. In the Munich ms., the notation "his brother" is missing.

44 Assuming that the first loaf was included in every subsequent oath.

45 Since he did not keep his oath. But in Avime's opinion, the first oath voids all the subsequent ones.

46 In no case can an oath be added to an oath.

(fol. 37a) **משנה ד:** סְתָם נְדָרִים לְהַחֲמִיר וּפֵירוּשָׁם לְהָקֵל. כֵּיצַד אָמַר הֲרֵי עָלַי כְּבָשָׂר מָלִיחַ כְּיֵין נֶסֶךְ אִם שֶׁלַּשָּׁמַיִם נָדַר אָסוּר אִם שֶׁלַעֲבוֹדָה זָרָה נָדַר מוּתָּר. וְאִם סְתָם אָסוּר. הֲרֵי עָלַי כְּחֵרֶם אִם כְּחֵרֶם שֶׁלַּשָּׁמַיִם אָסוּר וְאִם שֶׁלַּכֹּהֲנִים מוּתָּר וְאִם סְתָם אָסוּר. הֲרֵי עָלַי כַּמַּעֲשֵׂר אִם בְּמַעֲשַׂר בְּהֵמָה נָדַר אָסוּר וְאִם שֶׁלַּדָּגָן מוּתָּר וְאִם סְתָם אָסוּר. הֲרֵי עָלַי כַּתְּרוּמָה אִם כִּתְרוּמַת הַלִּשְׁכָּה נָדַר אָסוּר וְאִם שֶׁלַּגּוֹרֶן מוּתָּר וְאִם סְתָם אָסוּר דִּבְרֵי רַבִּי מֵאִיר. וַחֲכָמִים אוֹמְרִים סְתָם תְּרוּמָה בִּיהוּדָה אֲסוּרָה בַּגָּלִיל מוּתֶּרֶת שֶׁאֵין אַנְשֵׁי הַגָּלִיל מַכִּירִין אֶת תְּרוּמַת הַלִּשְׁכָּה. סְתָם חֲרָמִים בִּיהוּדָה מוּתָּרִין וּבַגָּלִיל אֲסוּרִין שֶׁאֵין אַנְשֵׁי הַגָּלִיל מַכִּירִין אֶת חֶרְמֵי הַכֹּהֲנִים.

Mishnah 4: Indeterminate oaths are interpreted restrictively and explicit ones liberally. How is this? If one said, this is for me like salted meat⁴⁷, like libation wine⁴⁸, if his intent was for Heaven, he is forbidden, if for idolatry, he is permitted⁴⁹, if indeterminate⁵⁰ he is forbidden. This is for me like a ban, if by a ban for Heaven⁵¹, he is forbidden, if priest's⁵², he is permitted, if indeterminate he is forbidden. This is for me like tithe, if animal tithe, he is forbidden⁵³, if from grain, he is permitted⁵⁴, if indeterminate he is forbidden. This is for me like heave, if Temple heave⁵⁵, he is forbidden, if heave from the threshing floor, he is permitted⁵⁶, if indeterminate he is forbidden, the words of Rebbi Meïr. But the Sages say, indeterminate heave in Judea is prohibited, in Galilee permitted, since Galileans do not know of Temple heave⁵⁷. Indeterminate bans in Judea are permitted, in Galilee prohibited, since Galileans do not know of priest's bans⁵⁸.

47 I. e., a sacrifice (*Lev.* 2:13).

48 *Num.* 15:1-13.

49 Since everything destined for idolatrous worship is forbidden for any use, it cannot become *qorbān*.

50 If the person making the vow had nothing special in mind, his words have to be interpreted as referring to an instance which makes his vow valid.

51 A gift to the Temple which is forbidden for any use until redeemed from the Temple treasury.

52 Bans given to priests become their fully profane private property, not restricted in any way. A referral to such bans cannot prohibit.

53 Animal tithe is automatically a sacrifice which does not need dedication (*Lev.* 27:32); it is *qorbān*.

54 Tithe from which its heave was separated is totally profane in the Levite's hand.

55 The half-šeqel yearly Temple tax which was used to buy public sacrifices; cf. Mishnah *Šeqalim* 3:1.

56 Since heave is private property of the receiving Cohen; cf. Note 8.

57 The Temple tax there was never known as "Temple heave" but as "half-šeqel."

58 They know bans only as expression of total prohibitions for everybody.

(37b, line 58) **הלכה ד:** סְתָם נְדָרִים לְהַחֲמִיר כול'. הֲוֹון בָּעֵי מֵימַר. מָלוּחַ לְעוֹלָם. הָא לְשָׁעָה לֹא. אָמַר רִבִּי יוּדָן. מִן מָה דְּתַנִּינָן הֲרֵי עָלַי כִּבְשַׂר מָלִיחַ כְּיֵין נֶסֶךְ. הָדָא אֲמְרָה מָלוּחַ לְשָׁעָה מָלוּחַ הוּא. אֵי זֶהוּ מָלוּחַ לְשָׁעָה. כָּיֵי דְּתַנֵּי. כֵּיצַד הוּא עוֹשֶׂה. נוֹתֵן אֶת הָאֵיבָרִים עַל גַּבֵּי הַמֶּלַח וְהוֹפְכָן. אָמַר רִבִּי אַבָּא מָרִי. שַׁנְיָיא הִיא. שָׂאִים מַשְׁהֵא הוּא אוֹתָן שֶׁהֵן נִמְלָחִין. וְיֵידָא אֲמְרָה דָא. דָּאֲמַר רִבִּי חִייָה בַּר אַבָּא הַנּוֹטֵל זֵיתִים מִן הַמַּעֲטָן טוֹבֵל אֶחָד אֶחָד בַּמֶּלַח וְאוֹכֵל. הָדָא אֲמְרָה. מָלוּחַ לְשָׁעָה מָלוּחַ הוּא.

"Indeterminate oaths are interpreted restrictively," etc. [59]They wanted to say, salted for preservation[60], not short-term salted. Rebbi Yudan said, since we have stated: "this is for me like salted meat[61], like libation wine," this implies that short-term salted is called "salted". What is short-term salted? As it was stated: "He puts the limbs on the salt and turns them over." Rebbi Abba Mari said, there is a difference, for if he leaves them there, they become salted meat[62]. But which text says it? As Rebbi Ḥiyya bar Abba said, "one who takes olives from the vat dips each single one in salt and eats it[63]." That implies that short-term salted is called "salted".

59 This paragraph is a copy of the parallel in Halakhah 6:3, where the question is what a person forbids to himself if he vows not to eat salted meat.

60 Salted meat than can be stored a long time (without refrigeration).

61 As explained in the *baraita*, that is meat dipped twice in salt.

62 Taking a piece of meat, putting it into a large vessel full of salt, turning it over there, and not washing the salt off, makes the meat much more salty than salting for immediate consumption. In the parallel in the Babli, *Menaḥot* 21a: "He puts salt on the limb, turns it over, and puts salt on the other side".

63 Mishnah *Ma'serot* 4:3 (Notes 50,51) speaking about the agricultural worker who may eat untithed olives during the harvest.

(37b, line 66) הֲרֵי עָלַי כַּתְּרוּמָה. אִם כִּתְרוּמַת הַלִּשְׁכָּה נָדַר אָסוּר. הָא בִתְרוּמַת תּוֹרָה[64] מוּתָּר. וְאִם שֶׁלַּגּוֹרֶן מוּתָּר. הָא בִתְרוּמַת תּוֹרָה אָסוּר. הָכָא אַתְּ אָמַר. אָסוּר. וְהָכָא אַתְּ אָמַר. מוּתָּר. נִישְׁמְעִינָהּ מִן הָדָא. כְּחַלַּת אַהֲרֹן וְכִתְרוּמָתוֹ מוּתָּר. הָא כִתְרוּמַת תּוֹרָה אָסוּר.

"This is for me like heave, if Temple heave, he is forbidden," therefore 'heave of thanksgiving' is permitted. "If heave from the threshing floor, he is permitted," therefore 'heave of thanksgiving' is forbidden. Here you say, forbidden; there, you say, permitted. Let us hear from the following: "Like Aaron's *ḥallah* and his heave" is permitted, therefore 'heave of thanksgiving' is forbidden[65].

64 This is the text in the ms. and *editio princeps* all three times in this paragraph. It seems that one has to read תּוֹדָה all three times; the translation assumes that reading.

65 A thanksgiving sacrifice (*Lev.* 7:11-14) needs a concurrent gift of 40 loaves, of which 4 are given to the officiating priest as heave (v. 14). This is a heave not mentioned in the Mishnah. Since Mishnah 1 notes only agricultural heave as not subject to vows, it follows that any accessory to a sacrifice must be vowed together with the sacrifice and, therefore, can represent a vow. The Babli, 12a/b, comes to the same conclusion by a very involved argument.

(37b, line 69) וַחֲכָמִים אוֹמְרִים סְתָם תְּרוּמָה בִּיהוּדָה אֲסוּרָה בַּגָּלִיל מוּתֶּרֶת. שֶׁאֵין אַנְשֵׁי הַגָּלִיל מַכִּירִין אֶת תְּרוּמַת הַלִּשְׁכָּה. אֲבָל אִם הָיוּ מַכִּירִין סְתָם אָסוּר. סְתָם חֲרָמִים בִּיהוּדָה מוּתָּרִין וּבַגָּלִיל אֲסוּרִין. שֶׁאֵין אַנְשֵׁי הַגָּלִיל מַכִּירִין חֶרְמֵי הַכֹּהֲנִים. אֲבָל אִם הָיוּ מַכִּירִין סְתָמָן מוּתָּר. הָכָא אַתְּ אָמַר. מוּתָּר. וְכָא אַתְּ אָמַר. אָסוּר. אָמַר רִבִּי לְעָזָר. תְּרֵין תַּנָּיִין אִינּוּן. אָמַר רִבִּי יִרְמְיָה. חַד תַּנָּיֵי הוּא. כְּמַאן דָּמַר סְתָם חֲרָמִים לְבֶדֶק הַבַּיִת. בְּרַם כְּמָאן דָּמַר סְתָם חֲרָמִים לַכֹּהֲנִים. אֲפִילוּ בַגָּלִיל יְהֵא מוּתָּר. רִבִּי יוֹסֵי בְּשֵׁם רִבִּי הִילָא. בַּגָּלִיל עַל יְדֵי שֶׁרְגִילִין בְּחֵרֶם עָכָן אַתְּ אָמַר. אָסוּר. וּבִיהוּדָה עַל שֶׁאֵינָן רְגִילִין בְּחֵרֶם עָכָן אַתְּ אוֹמֵר. מוּתָּר.

"But the Sages say, indeterminate heave in Judea is prohibited, in Galilee permitted, since Galileans do not know of Temple heave." But if they did know it, the indeterminate would be forbidden[66]. "Indeterminate bans in Judea are permitted, in Galilee prohibited, since Galileans do not know of priest's bans." But if they did know it, the indeterminate would be permitted. Here you say permitted, but there you say forbidden[67]. Rebbi Eleazar says, these are statements of two Tannaïm[68]. Rebbi Jeremiah said, all is from one Tanna, following the one who said[69]: "indeterminate bans are for the upkeep of the Temple." But for the one who said[70], "indeterminate bans are for priests," even in Galilee they would be permitted. In Galilee where they are used to invoke Akhan's ban[71], you have to say forbidden; in Judea where they are not used to invoke Akhan's ban, you have to say permitted.

66 The meaning of vows has to be determined by popular usage. Since learned people are not supposed to make vows, it is clear that the interpretation of vows depends on the meaning of the words in the vernacular, independent of the place where the vow was made.

67 This is an attempt to explain the rules in legal terminology, without appeal to the vernacular. The indeterminate vow would be a case of doubt; in one case one rules that doubt removes the vow, in the other that it confirms the vow. This is the attitude of the Babli, 19b.

68 This is the solution of the Babli and Tosephta 1:6 which ascribe the statement on bans to R. Eleazar ben R. Sadoq. This solution is appropriate for the Yerushalmi, the Munich and Cambridge mss. of the Babli, and the quotes in many Medieval authors, which ascribe both statements to "the Sages" who would be free to rule in one case with R. Jehudah and in the other with R. Eleazar ben R. Sadoq. But in the printed Babli which, together with most independent Mishnah mss., attributes the statement of the Sages to R. Jehudah, the two-Tanna solution, rejected in the

Yerushalmi but given in the Babli in the name of the Fourth Century Amora Abbai, is rather forced.

69 Mishnah *Arakhin* 8:6, opinion of R. Jehudah ben Bathyra.

70 The anonymous Sages. The Babli, *Arakhin* 29a, states that in the absence of a Temple, bans for the upkeep of the Temple can be redeemed by pennies.

71 *Jos.* 7:25-26, the expression of an absolute and irredeemable prohibition of all use.

(fol. 37b) **משנה ה:** נָדַר בַּחֵרֶם וְאָמַר לֹא נָדַרְתִּי אֶלָּא בְחֶרְמוֹ שֶׁלַיָּם. נָדַר בַּקָּרְבָּן וְאָמַר לֹא נָדַרְתִּי אֶלָּא בְקָרְבְּנוֹת מְלָכִים. הֲרֵי עַצְמִי קָרְבָּן וְאָמַר לֹא נָדַרְתִּי אֶלָּא בְעֶצֶם שֶׁהִינַּחְתִּי לִי לִהְיוֹת נוֹדֵר בּוֹ. קוֹנָם אִשְׁתִּי נֶהֱנִית לִי וְאָמַר לֹא נָדַרְתִּי אֶלָּא בְאִשְׁתִּי רִאשׁוֹנָה שֶׁגֵּרַשְׁתִּי עַל כּוּלָּן אֵין נִשְׁאָלִין עֲלֵיהֶן. וְאִם נִשְׁאֲלוּ עוֹנְשִׁין וּמַחְמִירִין עֲלֵיהֶן דִּבְרֵי רִבִּי מֵאִיר. וַחֲכָמִים אוֹמְרִים פּוֹתְחִין לָהֶם פֶּתַח מִמָּקוֹם אַחֵר וּמְלַמְּדִין אוֹתָן כְּדֵי שֶׁלֹּא יִנְהֲגוּ קַלּוּת רֹאשׁ בַּנְּדָרִים.

Mishnah 5: If somebody made a vow of *ḥerem* and said, I referred the vow only to mariner's nets[72], or made a vow of *qorbān* and said, I referred the vow only to the gifts for kings[73], or said, my bone[74] is *qorbān* and said, I referred the vow only to the bone that I keep in my house for purposes of vows, [or said] a *qônām* that my wife may not have any use from me and said, I referred the vow only to my first wife whom I divorced, all these do not need a question[75]. If they do question[76], one punishes them and makes it difficult for them, the words of Rebbi Meïr, but the Sages say, one finds for them an opening from another place[77] and teaches them that they should not be flippant about vows.

72 A homonym of חרם "ban", derived from חרם II, Arabic خرم "to break, to make holes", as a net is composed of holes. "Ban" is from חרם I, Arabic حرم "prohibit, excommunicate".

73 Crown money, the "voluntary" tax exacted at the accession of an emperor.

74 "My bone" means "myself" in biblical and rabbinic Hebrew.

75 Obviously these are no vows and they are invalid in themselves.

76 If an uneducated person has qualms about such a vow it shows that he considers it as a vow and, therefore, it must be considered a vow even if the language does not qualify it as such.

77 One finds a reason that he should repent having made the vow and permits it; cf. Note 9 and Halakhah 3:1.

(37c, line 8) **הלכה ה:** נָדַר בַּחֵרֶם כול'. חַד בַּר נַשׁ נָדַר בְּאִילֵּין מִילַּיָּיא. אֲתָא לְגַבֵּי רִבִּי מֵאִיר וּשְׁלָחֵיהּ גַּבֵּי רִבִּי יְהוּדָה. אָמַר לֵיהּ. אוֹדְעֵיהּ דְּאָתִית לְגַבַּיי וּשְׁלַחְתִּיךְ לְגַבֵּיהּ. אֲתָא לְגַבֵּי רִבִּי יְהוּדָה וּשְׁלָחֵיהּ גַּבֵּי רִבִּי יוֹסֵי. אָמַר לֵיהּ. אוֹדְעֵיהּ דִּשְׁלָחָהּ רִבִּי מֵאִיר לְגַבַּיי וּשְׁלַחְתִּיהּ לְגַבֵּיהּ. אֲתָא לְגַבֵּי רִבִּי יוֹסֵי. אָמַר לֵיהּ. אִין לֵית קַדְמָאָה מַשְׁרֵי לָךְ לֵית חוֹרָן מַשְׁרֵי לָךְ. דְּאִית לֵיהּ אִם נִשְׁאֲלוּ עוֹנְשִׁין אוֹתָן וּמַחְמִירִין עֲלֵיהֶן. חָזַר וְאָתָא קוֹמֵי רִבִּי מֵאִיר. אָמַר לֵיהּ. הֲוֵיתָהּ יָדַע כֵּן לָמָּה לֹא אֲמַרְתְּ לִי בְּקַדְמִיתָא. אָמַר לֵיהּ. חֲמִיתָךְ מֵיקַל וַחֲמָרִית עֲלָךְ.

Halakhah 5: "If somebody made a vow of *ḥerem*," etc. A person made a vow by one of these expressions. He came before Rebbi Meïr who sent him to Rebbi Jehudah and told him, inform him that you came to me and I sent you to him. He came before Rebbi Jehudah who sent him to Rebbi Yose and told him, inform him that you came to Rebbi Meïr who sent you to me and I sent you to him. He came to Rebbi Yose, who told him, if the first one does not permit it, nobody else can permit it to you, for he holds that "if they do question, one punishes them and makes it difficult for them." He returned before Rebbi Meïr and said to him, since you knew that, why did you not tell me from the start? He said to him, I saw you flippant and made it difficult for you.

ארבעה נדרים פרק שלישי

(fol. 37c) **משנה א**: אַרְבָּעָה נְדָרִים הִתִּירוּ חֲכָמִים נִדְרֵי זֵרוּזִין וְנִידְרֵי הֲבַאי וְנִידְרֵי שְׁגָגוֹת וְנִידְרֵי אוֹנָסִין. נִדְרֵי זֵרוּזִין כֵּיצַד הָיָה מוֹכֵר חֵפֶץ וְאָמַר קוֹנָם שֶׁאֵינִי פּוֹחֵת לָךְ מִן הַסֶּלַע. וְהַלָּה אָמַר קוֹנָם שֶׁאֵינִי מוֹסִיף לָךְ עַל הַשֶּׁקֶל שְׁנֵיהֶן רוֹצִין בִּשְׁלֹשָׁה דִינָרִין. רִבִּי אֱלִיעֶזֶר בֶּן יַעֲקֹב אוֹמֵר אַף הָרוֹצֶה לְהַדִּיר אֶת חֲבֵירוֹ שֶׁיֹּאכַל אֶצְלוֹ וְאָמַר לוֹ כָּל־נֶדֶר שֶׁאֲנִי עָתִיד לִידוֹר הוּא בָטֵל וּבִלְבָד שֶׁיְּהֵא זָכוּר בִּשְׁעַת הַנֶּדֶר.

Mishnah 1: Four kinds of vows did the Sages dissolve: Speeding-up vows, exaggeration vows, vows in error, and vows about acts of God[1]. What are speeding-up vows? One who has something to sell says, a *qônām*[2] that I shall not reduce the price below a tetradrachma, and the other one says, a *qônām* that I shall not increase my bid to more than a sheqel; both of them intend three denarii[3]. Rebbi Eliezer ben Jacob says, also one who wants by a vow to get his neighbor to eat at his place. If he says to himself[4]: any vow which I make in the future shall be void, [it is void] if he remembers at the moment he makes the vow.

1 These will all be explained in the Mishnah.

2 In this form, the vow is void and does not have to be dissolved since it is not indicated to what it refers. One has to assume that the vendor says the money received for the sale shall be *qônām* if I sell for less.

3 A tetradrachma is 4 denarii, a sheqel 2. They split the difference.

4 The Mishnah in the Babli יאמר instead of ואמר This requires a reformulation of what R. Eliezer ben Jacob said, 23b. The second statement

of R. Eliezer ben Jacob is not connected to the first which simply extends the definition of speeding-up vows.

(37d, line 7) **הלכה א:** אַרְבָּעָה נְדָרִים הִתִּירוּ חֲכָמִים כול׳. וְכָל־הַנְּדָרִים לָאו חֲכָמִים הֵן שֶׁהֵן מַתִּירִין. כְּתִיב וַיְדַבֵּר מֹשֶׁה אֶל רָאשֵׁי הַמַּטּוֹת. תָּלָה[5] הַפָּרָשָׁה בְּרָאשֵׁי הַמַּטּוֹת שֶׁיִּהוּ מַתִּירִין נִדְרֵי הָעָם. רַב יְהוּדָה בְשֵׁם שְׁמוּאֵל. לֹא יַחֵל דְּבָרוֹ. הוּא אֵינוֹ מוֹחֵל דְּבָרוֹ. הָא אַחֵר עוֹשֶׂה דְּבָרָיו חוּלִין. וְאֵי זֶה זֶה. זֶה חָכָם שֶׁמַּתִּיר נִדְרוֹ. חֲנַנְיָה בֶן אֲחִי רִבִּי יְהוֹשֻׁעַ אוֹמֵר. נִשְׁבַּעְתִּי וַאֲקַיְּיֵמָה. פְּעָמִים שֶׁאֲנִי מְקַיֵּים. רִבִּי יְהוֹשֻׁעַ אוֹמֵר. אֲשֶׁר נִשְׁבַּעְתִּי בְאַפִּי. בְּאַפִּי נִשְׁבַּעְתִּי. חוֹזֵר אֲנִי בִי.

"Four kinds of vows did the Sages dissolve," etc. Do not the Sages permit all kinds of vows? It is written[6]: "Moses spoke to the heads of the tribes." He referred the paragraph to the heads of the tribes that they should dissolve the people's vows. Rav Jehudah in the name of Samuel[7]: "*He shall not profane his word.*" *He* cannot profane his word; this implies that others can profane his words. Who is that? That is the Sage who dissolves the vow. Ḥananiah the nephew of Rebbi Joshua said[8], "I swore and I shall keep it." Sometimes I keep it. Rebbi Joshua said[9], "What I swore in my rage:" In my rage I swore; I change my mind.

5   Reading of the Parallel 9:1. The text here reads חלה "it fell" or "it fell sick".

6   *Num.* 30:2.

7   *Num.* 30:3. The same argument in the Babli, *Ḥagigah* 10a, in response to Mishnah 1:8: Dissolutions of vows "hang in the air" (have no biblical basis). This is the only argument accepted in the Babli.

8   *Ps.* 119:106. Also in the Babli, *Ḥagigah* 10a. In *Nedarim* 8a, the verse is interpreted to authorize vows to keep commandments of the Torah. In Sadducee theory (Damascus Document CD XVI 7-8), the consequence of such a vow is that the corresponding commandment cannot be broken even

under extreme pain, which in pharisaic theory applies only to idolatry, incest and adultery, and murder.

9 *Ps.* 95:11. Also in the Babli, Ḥagigah 10a.

(37d, line 13) וְכָל־הַנְּדָרִים חֲכָמִים הֵם שֶׁהֵם מַתִּירִין. וְתַנִּינָן. אַרְבָּעָה נְדָרִים הִתִּירוּ חֲכָמִים. רִבִּי לָעֶזֶר בְּשֵׁם רִבִּי חִייָה רוֹבָה. אִילּוּ אֵינָן צְרִיכִין הֵיתֵר חָכָם. רַב וּשְׁמוּאֵל תְּרֵיהוֹן אָמְרִין. אִילּוּ הֵן צְרִיכִין הֵיתֵר חָכָם. הָתִיב אִיסִי. וַהֲרֵי לֹא מָצִינוּ פֶּתַח לִנְדָרִים אֶלָּא מִכָּן. אָמַר לֵיהּ שְׁמוּאֵל. חֲגַר עֲלֵיהּ מוּתְנָא. מַתְנִיתָא פְלִיגָא עַל אִיסִי. אַף זֶה יָכוֹל לְהָפֵר נִדְרוֹ שֶׁלֹא עַל פִּי חָכָם. פָּתַר לָהּ. כָּל־הַנְּדָרִים צְרִיכִין פֶּתַח מִמָּקוֹם אַחֵר וְאִילּוּ פִתְחָן בְּצִידָן. אָמַר רִבִּי זְעִירָא. הָדָא דְאַתְּ אָמַר בְּשֶׁאֵינָן מַעֲמִידִים. אֲבָל אִם הָיוּ מַעֲמִידִין צְרִיכִין הֵיתֵר חָכָם. הֲרֵי זֶה מַעֲמִיד וְזֶה אֵינוֹ מַעֲמִיד. מֵאַחַר שֶׁבָּטֵל אֵצֶל זֶה יַבָּטֵל זֶה. תַּלְמִידוֹי דְרִבִּי חִייָה בַר לוּלְיָינִי אָמַר רִבִּי יוּדָן. שֶׁאִילּוּ הָיָה אוֹמֵר זֶה בְּסֶלַע. וְזֶה אוֹמֵר לִיתֵּן לוֹ בְשָׁל'ש. וְזֶה אוֹמֵר בְּשֶׁקֶל. מַעֲמִיד. מֵאַחַר שֶׁבִּיטֵּל דִּינָר זֶה עַל זֶה יְבַטֵּל עוֹד דִּינָר אַחֵר אֶצְלוֹ וְיִתְּנוּ לוֹ בִשְׁנַיִם.

Do the Sages permit all kinds of vows? "Four kinds of vows did the Sages dissolve"! Rebbi Eleazar in the name of the elder Rebbi Ḥiyya: Those do not need the permission of a Sage[10,11] Rav and Samuel both say that these need the permission of a Sage[12]. Issy objected: Did we not find an opening for vows from there only[13]? Samuel said to him, bind a rope on it[14]. A Mishnah disagrees with Issy[15]: "This one also can dissolve his vow without asking a Sage." He explains it, that all vows need an opening from another place but these have their openings in themselves[16]. Rebbi Ze'ira said, that is, if they do not insist[17]. But if they did insist they need the permission of a Sage. If one did insist but the other did not insist, since this one's is invalid, the other one's also should be invalid[18]. A student of Rebbi Ḥiyya bar Julianus said [after] Rebbi Yudan: If one asked a tetradrachma, one was ready to give him three[19], and another one said a sheqel. (Does he insist?)[20] Since he renounces one denar for this one he may renounce another one for the other one and give it to him for two[21].

10 In the Babli, this is the authoritative opinion of Samuel, 21b.

11 Rosh (R. Asher ben Ieḥiel (~ 1250 Germany - 1327 Toledo) quotes (3,1) a different text: רִבִּי שִׁמְעוֹן בַּר רַבָּא בְשֵׁם רִבִּי יוֹחָנָן אִילוּ אֵין צְרִיכִין הֶתֵר חָכָם. רַב וּשְׁמוּאֵל דְּאָמְרֵי תְּרַוַויְיהוּ. אֵין צְרִיכִין הֶיתֵר חָכָם. "Rebbi Simeon ben Rebbi Abba in the name of Rebbi Joḥanan: *these* need the permission of a Sage. Rav and Samuel both say: they do not need the permission of a Sage." It is obvious that this cannot be the Yerushalmi text since דְּאָמְרֵי תְּרַוַויְיהוּ is pure Babylonian Aramaic.

12 In the Babli, this is the rejected opinion of Rav Assi (Issy).

13 This is confirmed in the Babli, 21a, where Rav Assi holds that a vow can be dissolved by a Sage (an ordained rabbi) only if its invalidity is obvious, not because the person making the vow repents his action.

14 It is not quite clear what this expression means. It might be that this kind of obviously void vow is the "rope with which one lifts other kinds of vows" to dissolution.

15 Mishnah 8:7, speaking of a person who threatens to forbid to himself all intercourse with another if the other refuses to take gifts from him.

16 It still needs to be dissolved by a Sage but the dissolution is granted automatically.

17 If the person never had intended that the offered price should be the final price. R. Nissim Gerondi ("Ran"), in quoting this Yerushalmi (Commentary to the Babli, 21a), holds that the three sheqels quoted in the Mishnah are only an example and that any price between 2 and 4 denarii is acceptable but that the seller may not sell for 4 and the buyer not buy for 2 denarii without confirming their vows as real and requiring the counsel of a Sage.

18 If, e. g., the seller makes the same vow for two customers and he intends to insist on the full price for one but not for the other, his vow for the first is void since it is void for the

second. (Concurrent explanation of Ran and Rashba.)

19 Denarii.

20 This is missing in the text quoted by Rashba (Novellae, Chapter 3, 20b), probably correctly. (This text not quoted by Ran.)

21 It would be incorrect to read the Mishnah as not permitting the seller to lower the price more than half the original difference. (Cf. Note 17.)

(37d, line 25) אָמַר רִבִּי אִמִּי. מָאן תַּנָּא נִידְרֵי זְרוּזִין. רִבִּי טַרְפוֹן. דּוּ פָתַר לָהּ בִּמְעָמִידִין. אָמַר רִבִּי בָּא. תִּיפְתָּר דִּבְרֵי הַכֹּל שֶׁאֵין מַעֲמִידִין. אִין תֵּימַר בִּמְעָמִידִין. נִיתְנֵי. רִבִּי אֱלִיעֶזֶר בֶּן יַעֲקֹב וְרִבִּי טַרְפוֹן שְׁנֵיהֶן אָמְרוּ דָבָר אֶחָד. אִית תַּנָּיֵי תַנֵּי. הָרוֹצֶה. אִית תַּנָּיֵי תַנֵּי. אַף הָרוֹצֶה. מָאן דָּמַר. הָרוֹצֶה. מְסַיֵּעַ לְרִבִּי בָא. מָאן דָּמַר. אַף הָרוֹצֶה. מְסַיֵּעַ לְרִבִּי אִמִּי. רִבִּי פְּדָת בְּשֵׁם רִבִּי יוֹחָנָן. מָאן תַּנָּא נִידְרֵי זְרוּזִין. רִבִּי טַרְפוֹן.

Rebbi Immi said, who is the Tanna of speeding-up vows? Rebbi Tarphon[22]! For he explains it for those who insist. Rebbi Abba said, explain it according to everybody for those who do not insist[23]. If you say for those who insist, one should have stated that Rebbi Eliezer ben Jacob[24] and Rebbi Tarphon say the same thing. Some Tannaïm say, "one who wants"; some Tannaïm say, "also one who wants"[25]. He who says "one who wants" supports Rebbi Abba[26]; he who says "also one who wants", supports Rebbi Immi. Rebbi Pedat in the name of Rebbi Joḥanan: who is the Tanna of speeding-up vows? Rebbi Tarphon[27]!

22 He says in Mishnah and Halakhah *Nazir* 5:5, and in Tosephta *Nazir* 3:19 R. Jehudah in his name (Mishnah *Tahorot* 4:12 in his own name), that a vow of *nezirut* is only valid if it is unquestionable. One then assumes that all other vows follow the same rule. (The Tosephta is quoted another 6 times in the Babli.)

In the Babli, 21a, this is quoted by R. Ammi in the name of R. Jehudah Neśia.

23 As explained in the preceding

paragraph.

24 Who in the Mishnah permits self help in the dissolution of vows.

25 In the Mishnah. In the first version, R. Eliezer ben Jacob's statement is not a continuation of the first part of the Mishnah and does not necessarily deal with the same situation. In the second version, the one of our Mishnah, R. Eliezer ben Jacob's first statement continues the Mishnah and, if the first part follows R. Tarphon, he does the same.

26 The first part refers to people who intend to change their mind but it implies nothing for R. Eliezer ben Jacob.

27 R. Pedat disputes the originality of R. Immi's statement and claims priority for the latter's teacher.

(37d, line 31) כֵּינִי מַתְנִיתָא. כָּל־נֶדֶר שֶׁאֲנִי עָתִיד לִידוֹר הֲרֵי הוּא בָּטֵל וּבִלְבַד שֶׁיְּהֵא זָכוּר בְּשָׁעַת הַנֶּדֶר. בְּשֶׁלֹּא הִתְנָה. אֲבָל אִם הִתְנָה אַף עַל פִּי שֶׁאֵינוֹ זָכוּר. בִּנְדָרִים. אֲבָל בַּשְּׁבוּעוֹת תְּנַיֵי בִּנְדָרִים וְאֵין תְּנַיֵי בַּשְּׁבוּעוֹת. כְּהָדָא דְתַנֵּי. שְׁבוּעַת הַדַּיָּינִין כְּתַנְיָין שֶׁבְּלִיבֵּינוּ לֹא כִתְנָיִין שֶׁבְּלִבְבְכֶם. אָמַר רִבִּי יוּדָה. כְּתַנְיָין שֶׁבְּלִיבּוֹ הוּא מַשְׁבִּיעוֹ. וְלָמָּה הוּא מַתְנֶה עִמּוֹ. מִפְּנֵי הַהֶדְיוֹטוֹת שֶׁלֹּא יֹאמְרוּ. יֵשׁ תְּנַיֵין בַּשְּׁבוּעוֹת. תַּנֵּי רִבִּי חֲנַנְיָה קוֹמֵי רִבִּי מָנָא. וְהָא כְּתִיב כִּי אֶת אֲשֶׁר יֶשְׁנוֹ פֹה. מָה אַתְּ שְׁמַע מִינָהּ. אָמַר לֵיהּ. מָה דּוֹרוֹת הַבָּאִים אַחֲרֵינוּ אֵין בְּלִיבָּן תְּנַיֵי אַף אָנוּ אֵין בְּלִיבֵּינוּ תְּנַיֵי

So is the Mishnah[28]: "Any vow which I make in the future shall be void, [it is void] if he remembers at the moment he makes the vow," if he did not stipulate a reservation[29]. But if he stipulated a reservation, then even if he does not remember. That is for vows; but for oaths? There are reservations for vows, there are no reservations for oaths, as it was stated about oaths imposed by judges[30]: "According to our understanding, not according to your understanding." Rebbi Jehudah said, he makes him swear according to his understanding. Why does he stipulate with him?

Because of the uneducated, lest they say that there may be mental reservations for oaths.

28 This language is somewhat unexpected since it usually introduces an emendation of the Mishnah.

29 If a person stipulates expressly that his vows shall be void even if he does not remember that stipulation at the moment of the vow, the stipulation is valid and active.

30 Text from *Soṭah* 7:1, Note 27.

(fol. 37c) **משנה ב**: נִדְרֵי הֲבַאי אָמַר אִם לֹא רָאִיתִי בַּדֶּרֶךְ הַזּוֹ כְּעוֹלֵי מִצְרַיִם. אִם לֹא רָאִיתִי נָחָשׁ כְּקוֹרַת בֵּית הַבַּד. נִדְרֵי שְׁגָגוֹת כֵּיצַד אָמַר אִם אָכַלְתִּי וְאִם שָׁתִיתִי וְנִזְכַּר שֶׁאָכַל וְשֶׁשָּׁתָה שֶׁאֵינִי אוֹכֵל וְשֶׁאֵינִי שׁוֹתֶה וְשָׁכַח וְאָכַל וְשָׁתָה. אָמַר קוֹנָם אִשְׁתִּי נֶהֱנֵית לִי שֶׁגָּנְבָה אֶת כִּיסִי וְשֶׁהִכָּתָה אֶת בְּנִי וְנוֹדַע שֶׁלֹּא הִכַּתּוּ וְנוֹדַע שֶׁלֹּא גָנְבָה. רָאָה אוֹתָן אוֹכְלִין תְּאֵנִים וְאָמַר לָהֶן הֲרֵי הֵן עֲלֵיכֶם כְּקָרְבָּן וְנִמְצְאוּ אָבִיו וְאֶחָיו וְהָיוּ עִמָּהֶן אֲחֵרִים. בֵּית שַׁמַּאי אוֹמְרִים הֵן מוּתָּרִין וּמַה שֶׁעִמָּהֶן אֲסוּרִין. וּבֵית הִלֵּל אוֹמְרִים אֵילוּ וָאֵילוּ מוּתָּרִין.

Mishnah 2: Exaggeration vows: If he said[31], if I did not see on this road [crowds] like those who left Egypt[32]; if I did not see a snake [as thick] as the beam of the olive press. Vows in error how? If he said, if I ate or drank, and he remembers[33] that he had eaten or drunk, that I shall not eat or shall not drink, and he forgot and ate or drank. If he said, a *qônām* that my wife cannot enjoy anything from me because she stole my wallet or hit my son[34], and it turns out that she did not hit him or became known that she did not steal. If he saw people eating [his] figs and said to them, these are for you as *qorbān*[35], but the persons turned out to be his father or brothers with others. The House of Shammai say, these are permitted, those with them forbidden. But the House of Hillel say, these and those are permitted[36].

31 In all these cases, it is understood that he says such and such should be *qônām* for me if . . .	34 From another wife.
32 About 600'000 men; *Ex.* 12:37.	35 It is to be assumed that people were not afraid to steal but would never break a vow.
33 He remembers later but at the moment of his vow he was oblivious of the fact.	36 Since a vow which is partially voided is completely voided; Mishnah 9:6.

(37d, line 39) **הלכה ב:** נִדְרֵי הֲבַאי וכו'. אֵיפְשָׁר שֶׁלֹא עָבַר בָּהּ כְּעוֹלֵי מִצְרַיִם. אֶלָּא כֵן אָנַן קַיָּימִין בִּרְאִיָּיה אַחַת. וְהָא לוּלְיָינוּס מַלְכָּא כַּד נְחַת לְתַמָּן נְחוֹת עִימֵּיהּ מֵאָה עֶשְׂרִים רִיבְוָון. אֶלָּא אָכֵן אָנַן קַיָּימִין בִּרְאִיָּיה אַחַת.

Halakhah 2: "Vows of exaggeration," etc. [37]Is it impossible that crowds like those who left Egypt went by? But we are dealing with one look. Was it not the case that when Emperor Julianus went there[38], 1'200'000 [men] went with him? But we must be dealing with one look.

37 From here on, most of the Halakhah is also in *Šebuot* 3:9-11.	38 The Babylonian campaign against Sapor II in the year 383 C. E..

(37d, line 42) וְהָא חִיוְיָה דְשָׁבוּר מַלְכָּא בָּלַע גְּמַלִּין בְּלַע קָרוֹנִין. [39] כַּד בָּעוּ מִקְטְלוֹנֵיהּ מְלוֹן פְּחָלִין שֶׁלַּגְמַלִּין תֶּבֶן וִיהָבוֹן בּוֹן גּוּמְרִין וּבְלָעוֹן וָמֵית. אָמַר רִבִּי יְהוּדָה בַּר פָּזִי. אֲנָא חָמִית מְשַׁךְ דְּחִיוִי עֲבַד אוֹרֵי עַל עוֹמְנֵי מִסְטוֹלֵי.[40] אָמַר רִבִּי שְׁמוּאֵל בַּר יַעֲקֹב. אֲנָא חָמִית מְשַׁךְ דְּחִיוִי סָלִיק בְּדִיוְיָין[41] דְּמַלְכוּתָא. שְׁמוּאֵל אָמַר. בִּמְרוּבָּע. אִין תֵּימַר בְּשֶׁאֵינוֹ מְרוּבָּע.[42] לָמָּה לִי גָדוֹל. אֲפִילוּ קָטוֹן. אָמַר רִבִּי מַתַּנְיָה. לֵית אוֹרְחֵיהּ דְּהָדֵין תַּנָּיָה מַתְפִּיס אֶלָּא מִילָּה רוּבָא. תֵּדַע לָךְ שֶׁהוּא כֵן. דְּתַנִּינָן גָּמָל פּוֹרֵחַ בָּאֲוֵיר. נִיתְנֵי עַכְבָּר פּוֹרֵחַ בָּאֲוֵיר.

Did not the snake of king Sapor swallow camels and carts[43]? When they wanted to kill it, they filled camel bags[44] with straw and put glowing coals inside; it swallowed them and died. Rebbi Jehudah bar Pazi said, I saw a snake skin which filled[45] the space between two columns. Rebbi Samuel bar Jacob said, I saw a snake skin which covered the genii[46] of government. Samuel said, square[47]. Could you say it was not square[42], why must it be large? Even if it was small! Rebbi Mattaniah said, it is the way of this Tanna to speak only about large things. You should know that it is so, for we have stated[48]: "A flying camel". Could he not have stated "a flying rat"?

39 This is the reading of the text in *Šebuot*. Here, the reading is קַבָּרִין "grave diggers" which might be a misreading for קָרוּכִין Latin *carrucha, -ae, f.* "four-wheeled travelling and state coach".

40 In *Šebuot* תְּמַנְיָא מְסוֹסְטְלָא "eight spaces between pillars". The underlying Greek is μεσοστύλιον, τό, "space between columns."

41 In *Šebuot* קָרוּכִין דְּמַלְכוּתָא "a state coach", cf. Note 39.

42 In *Šebuot* וְאִם בִּמְרוּבַּע "if square, why must it be large?"

43 A toned down version of King Sapor's snake is in the Babli, 25a and *Šebuot* 29a. There, the story of the snake is discussed by Samuel, which shows that the reference is to Sapor I.

44 In Mishnah *Kelim* 24:9 חֲחָלָץ.

45 Reading עומני from Arabic عمن "to stay". Cf. also Note 40.

46 Possibly statues of emperors who after death became *divi*. But cf. Note 41.

47 The snake was perhaps not particularly large but it had the form of a beam with square cross-section.

48 Mishnah *Šebuot* 3:8, example of something impossible.

(37d, line 49) תַּנֵּי. רַבָּן שִׁמְעוֹן בֶּן גַּמְלִיאֵל אוֹמֵר. אֵין מְרוּבָּע מִשֵּׁשֶׁת יְמֵי בְּרֵאשִׁית. הָתִיב רִבִּי בְּרֶכְיָה. וְהָתַנִּינָן. גּוּפָהּ שֶׁלַּבַּהֶרֶת כִּגְרִיס הָאִיטַלְקִי מְרוּבָּע. אָמַר רִבִּי בִּיסְנָה. כָּל־גַּרְמָא דָא דְלֵית הוּא מְרוּבָּע. וְלָמָה תַּנִּינָן

מְרוּבָּע. יְרבְעָנָה הוּא. וְהוּא כְנָעָה. מָלֵי קְטָרִין. וְהָא אַרְכּוּבָה דַעֲיָלָה. עָגִיל הוּא מִלְמַטָּה. לֹא אָמַר רַבָּן שִׁמְעוֹן בֶּן גַּמְלִיאֵל אֶלָּא בַּבְּרִיוֹת. וְתַנִּי כֵן. מְרוּבָּע בָּאוֹכְלִין. אֵין מְרוּבָּע בַּבְּרִיוֹת.

[49]It was stated: "Rabban Gamliel says, there is nothing square from the six days of Creation." Rebbi Berekhiah objected: Did we not state: "The body of *baheret* is like a square Italian grit." Rebbi Bisna said, that in itself says that there is no square. Why did we state that? That he should square it. But there are lice! They are full of knots. But there is the knee of a mountain goat! It is round below. Rabban Simeon ben Gamliel spoke only about animals. It was stated so: There is square in foods, there is no square in animals.

49 This text is from *Ma'serot* 5:7, fol. 52a, with variants and commentary in Notes 122-129. The text is also in *Šebuot* 3:9 (fol. 34d).

(37d, line 55) שָׁוְא וְשֶׁקֶר שְׁנֵיהֶם נֶאֶמְרוּ בְדִיבּוּר אֶחָד. מַה שֶׁאֵי אֶיפְשָׁר לַפֶּה לוֹמַר וְלֹא לָאוֹזֶן לִשְׁמוֹעַ. זָכוֹר וְשָׁמוֹר שְׁנֵיהֶם בְּדִיבּוּר אֶחָד נֶאֶמְרוּ. מַה שֶׁאֵי אֶיפְשָׁר לַפֶּה לוֹמַר וְלֹא לָאוֹזֶן לִשְׁמוֹעַ. מְחַלְלֶיהָ מוֹת יוּמָת וּשְׁנֵי כְבָשִׁים בְּנֵי שָׁנָה תְמִימִים נֶאֶמְרוּ בְדִיבּוּר אֶחָד. מַה שֶׁאֵי אֶיפְשָׁר לַפֶּה לוֹמַר וְלֹא לָאוֹזֶן לִשְׁמוֹעַ. עֶרְוַת אֵשֶׁת אָחִיךָ לֹא תְגַלֵּה יְבָמָה יָבֹא עָלֶיהָ שְׁנֵיהֶן נֶאֶמְרוּ בְדִיבּוּר אֶחָד. וְלֹא תִסּוֹב נַחֲלָה לִבְנֵי יִשְׂרָאֵל מִמַּטֶּה לְמַטֶּה אַחֵר וְכָל־בַּת יוֹרֶשֶׁת נַחֲלָה שְׁנֵיהֶן בְּדִיבּוּר אֶחָד. גְּדִילִים תַּעֲשֶׂה לָךְ לֹא תִלְבַּשׁ שַׁעַטְנֵז שְׁנֵיהֶן בְּדִיבּוּר אֶחָד נֶאֶמְרוּ. וְכֵן הוּא אוֹמֵר אַחַת דִּיבֶּר אֱלֹהִים שְׁתַּיִם זוּ שָׁמַעְתִּי. וּכְתִיב הֲלֹא כֹה דְבָרִי כָּאֵשׁ נְאוּם יי וּכְפַטִּישׁ יְפוֹצֵץ סָלַע.

"Vain" and "untruth" both were said together, which is impossible for the mouth to say and the ear to hear[50]. "Remember" and "keep"[51] both were said together, which is impossible for the mouth to say and the ear to hear. "Its desecrator shall be put to death" and "two unblemished one year old sheep[52]" both were said together[53], which is impossible for the mouth to say and the ear to hear. "The nakedness of your brother's wife you shall not uncover[54]", "her brother-in-law shall come to her[55]", both were said together. "You shall not move real property from one tribe to another," "any daughter inheriting real property," both together[56]. "Fringes you shall make for yourself," "do not wear *sha'tnez*", both were said together[57]. And so it says[58], "God spoke once, two I heard from this." And it is written: "Is not my word like fire, says the Eternal, and like a hammer which shatters a rock."

50 The two versions of the Ninth Commandment, *Ex.* 20:16 and *Deut.* 5:17, both are Sinaitic versions which had been said in parallel and were written serially.

51 The two versions of the Fourth Commandment, *Ex.* 20:8 and *Deut.* 5:12. The first two examples are also in the Babli, *Šebuot* 20b, this example only in Babli *Roš Haššanah* 27a, *Mekhilta dR. Simeon ben Iohai* 20:5 (p. 148). A parallel text from here to the end of the Halakhah is *Sifry Deut.* 233; *Midrash Tannaïm* p. 138 (*Midrash Haggadol Deut.* 22:11), *Mekhilta dR. Ismael Yitro* Chap. 7.

52 From here to the end of the paragraph one speaks of laws that contradict one another, not different parallel texts. Another approach to the problem of contradiction in pentateuchal legislation is in *Sifry Num.* 3; a radically different one in Babli *Ḥulin* 109b, where Yalta, Rav Naḥman's wife, holds that all of Sinaitic legislation has exceptions (in contrast to the commandments given to Noah which represent Natural Law and are without exceptions).

53 The first verse is *Ex.* 31:14 on the observation of the Sabbath, the second is *Num.* 28:9 on the Sabbath sacrifice which requires many actions which if performed outside the Temple on a Sabbath would be capital crimes.

54 *Lev.* 18:16.

55 *Deut.* 25:5; cf. Introduction to Tractate *Yebamot*.

56 On the face of it, both verses, *Num.* 36:8-9, say the same, viz., that an

heiress may marry only a man of her own tribe. The explanation is given in Babli *Baba batra* 111b, where it is shown that the entire chapter 36 only refers to the daughters of Ṣelofḥad; for all others only the rules of *Num.* 27:7-11 are applicable without restrictions. In this case, *Num.* 36:8-9 is the exception from *Num.* 27:8.

57   In *Deut.* 22:11, wearing wool and linen together is forbidden. In v. 12, *any* garment, including linen ones, is required to have fringes, which according to *Num.* 15:38 must contain a dark blue woolen thread.

58   *Ps.* 62:12.

59   *Jer.* 23:29. Both verses express the idea that no word of God has only one meaning.

(37d, line 65) שְׁבוּעַת שָׁוְא. בְּנִשְׁבָּע לְשַׁנּוֹת אֶת הַיָּדוּעַ לָאָדָם. שְׁבוּעַת שֶׁקֶר. בְּשֶׁנִּשְׁבַּע וּמַחֲלִיף. אֵי זֶהוּ שָׁוְא וְאֵי זֶהוּ שֶׁקֶר. רִבִּי יַעֲקֹב בַּר אָחָא בְּשֵׁם רִבִּי יוֹחָנָן. יָדוּעַ לִשְׁנַיִם זֶהוּ שְׁבוּעַת שֶׁקֶר. לִשְׁלֹשָׁה זֶהוּ שְׁבוּעַת שָׁוְא. רִבִּי הִילָא בְּשֵׁם רִבִּי אֶלְעָזָר. אֲפִילוּ יָדוּעַ לִשְׁנַיִם וְאֶחָד בְּסוֹף הָעוֹלָם מַכִּירוֹ שְׁבוּעַת שָׁוְא הִיא. מַה נְפַק מִבֵּינֵיהוֹן. שִׁינָּה בָהּ בִּפְנֵי שְׁנַיִם וְהִשְׁלִיכוֹ לַיָּם וְהִתְרוּ בּוֹ מִשּׁוּם שְׁבוּעַת שָׁוְא. עַל דַּעְתֵּיהּ דְּרִבִּי יוֹחָנָן אֵינוֹ לוֹקֶה. עַל דַּעְתֵּיהּ דְּרִבִּי לָעְזָר לוֹקֶה. הִתְרוּ בּוֹ מִשּׁוּם שְׁבוּעַת שֶׁקֶר. עַל דַּעְתֵּיהּ דְּרִבִּי יוֹחָנָן לוֹקֶה. עַל דַּעְתֵּיהּ דְּרִבִּי לָעְזָר אֵינוֹ לוֹקֶה. רִבִּי בָּא בְּשֵׁם רַב יְהוּדָה. אֲפִילוּ בֵּיעָה וּמַרְגָּלִיתָא. וְהֵן אֲפִילוּ. אֶלָּא כְּגוֹן בֵּיעָה וּמַרְגָּלִיתָא.

A vain oath, if one swears to change what is known to men; a false oath if he swears and changes[60]. What is vain and what is false? Rebbi Jacob bar Aḥa in the name of Rebbi Joḥanan: If it is known to two persons, that is a false oath, to three, it is vain. Rebbi Hila in the name of Rebbi Eleazar: If it is known to two persons and another one at the end of the earth knows about it, that is a vain oath[61]. What is the difference between them? If he was untrue before two [persons], threw it[62] into the sea, and they had warned him because of a vain oath[63], in the opinion of

Rebbi Johanan he is not whipped, in the opinion of Rebbi Eleazar he is whipped[64]. If they had warned him because of a false oath, in the opinion of Rebbi Johanan he is whipped, in the opinion of Rebbi Eleazar he is not whipped. Rebbi Abba in the name of Rav Jehudah: Even an egg and a pearl[65]. What means *even*? But, *for example* an egg and a pearl.

60   He changes what is true. This and the following paragraphs refer to Mishnah *Šebuot* 3:8.

61   Since according to R. Eleazar the three people who know the truth do not have to be at the same place, it follows that for R. Johanan they have to be at the same place. In the Babli, *Šebuot* 29a, Ulla (= R. Hila) simply states that 3 people have to know to make an oath vain, without discussion whether they have to be together or not.

62   The object about which he swore, e. g., (Mishnah *Šebuot* 3:8) of a stone that it was gold.

63   To establish criminal intent, essential for criminal conviction; cf. *Kilaim* 8:1, Note 9.

64   Since certainly some other person at another place knew the truth.

65   If he swears about an egg that it is a pearl (R. David Fraenckel) or that he had seen a pearl the size of an egg (R. Moshe Margalit). In connection with Mishnah *Šebuot* 3:8, the first explanation is more likely to be the correct one.

(38a, line 3) תַּנֵּי. כְּשֵׁם שֶׁנִּדְרֵי הֲבַאי מוּתָּרִין כָּךְ שְׁבוּעוֹת הֲבַאי מוּתָּרוֹת. וְהָתַנֵּי. שְׁבוּעוֹת הֲבַאי אֲסוּרוֹת. רִבִּי יִרְמְיָה בְּשֵׁם רִבִּי פְּדָת. כָּאן בְּמַעֲמִידִין וְכָאן בְּשֶׁאֵינָן מַעֲמִידִין. אָמַר רִבִּי בָּא. אֲפִילוּ תֵּימָא. כָּאן וְכָאן בְּמַעֲמִידִין כָּאן וְכָאן בְּשֶׁאֵין מַעֲמִידִין. כָּאן בְּמֵיחַל שְׁבוּעָה עַל נְכָסָיו. שְׁבוּעַת נְכָסַיי עָלַי. נְכָסָיו אֲסוּרִין. הָא לִלְקוֹת אֵינוֹ לוֹקֶה. כְּשֵׁם שֶׁנִּדְרֵי זֵירוּזִין מוּתָּרִין כָּךְ שְׁבוּעוֹת זֵירוּזִין מוּתָּרוֹת. עוֹד הוּא כְּמֵיחַל שְׁבוּעָה עַל נְכָסָיו. שְׁבוּעַת נְכָסַיי עָלַיי. נְכָסָיו אֲסוּרִין. הָא לִלְקוֹת אֵינוֹ לוֹקֶה.

It was stated[66]: "Just as vows of exaggeration are permitted so oaths of exaggeration are permitted." But was it not stated: Vows of exaggeration are forbidden⁶⁷? Rebbi Jeremiah in the name of Rebbi Pedat: Here about those who insist⁶⁸, there about those who do not insist. Rebbi Abba said, you may even say in either case if they insist or if they do not insist; here about one who intends that his oath should fall on his property, "an oath that my property [should be forbidden] to me." Then his property is forbidden [to him]. But in the matter of whipping, he cannot be whipped⁶⁹. Just as speeding-up vows are permitted so speeding-up oaths are permitted. It is the same case; if he intends that his oath should fall on his property then his property is forbidden [to him]. But concerning the matter of whipping, he cannot be whipped.

66 Tosephta 2:1.
67 Babli 24b.
68 They show that their oaths should not be considered as exaggerations. Then they are bound by them.
69 Both Tosephta and *baraita* deal with the same case; "permitted" means that the maker of such a vow, even if he uttered it after due warning, cannot be prosecuted; but what he forbade on himself remains forbidden. As noted by Rashba (*Novellae* to 24b), this contradicts the position of the Babli in the reading of most mss.

(38a, line 3) חִזְקִיָּה אָמַר. הָהֵן דְּמִישְׁתַּבַּע עַל תְּרֵיי דִּינוּן תְּרֵיי לוֹקֶה מִשּׁוּם שְׁבוּעַת שָׁוְא. רִבִּי חַגַּיי בְּשֵׁם רִבִּי שִׁמְעוֹן בֶּן לָקִישׁ. הָהֵין דְּחָמָא מִיטְרָא נְחֵית וָמַר. בְּלִי קוֹרֵי בְרִיקְשׁוֹן.⁷⁰ לוֹקֶה מִשּׁוּם שְׁבוּעַת שָׁוְא. רִבִּי חוֹנְיָא רִבִּי יַעֲקֹב בַּר אָבוּן בְּשֵׁם רִבִּי שְׁמוּאֵל בַּר נַחְמָן. עֶשְׂרִים וְאַרְבַּע בּוּלַיּוֹת הָיוּ בִיהוּדָה וְכוּלָּן חָרְבוּ מִשּׁוּם שְׁבוּעַת שָׁוְא שֶׁהִיא שֶׁלֱּאֱמֶת. דִּכְתִיב לַשָּׁוְא הִכֵּיתִי אֶת בְּנֵיכֶם.

⁷¹Hizqiah said, he who swears that two are two is whipped for a vain oath. Rebbi Ḥaggai in the name of Rebbi Simeon ben Laqish: One who saw rain falling and said: "O Lord, inundate with much water⁷⁰", is

whipped for a vain oath. Rebbi Onias, Rebbi Jacob bar Abun in the name of Rebbi Samuel bar Naḥman: 24 city councils[72] were in Judea and they all were destroyed because of true vain oaths, as it is written[73]: "For the vain did I hit your sons."

70 In *Šebuot*, the reading is קוּרִי פָּלֵי בְּרִיכְסוֹן which N. Brüll (Jahrbuch für jüdische Geschichte und Literatur 1, p. 130) reads as κύριε πολὺ βρέξον "o Lord, give abundant water", as first verse of a prayer for rain. S. Lieberman, in a full discussion of this text (יוונית ויוונות בארץ ישראל, Jerusalem 1962, pp. 25-27), points out that the invocation of God's name in a vain prayer is forbidden by the Third Commandment and that the characterization as "vow" is only a reference to that Commandment.

71 A somewhat different text is in *Pesiqta rabbati* 22 (ed. M. Friedmann p. 113a).

72 Greek βουλή.

73 *Jer.* 2:30. Another version in *Tanḥuma Maṭṭot* 1, *Vayiqra* 7.

(38a, line 15) תַּמָּן תַּנִּינָן. שְׁבוּעָה שֶׁלֹּא אוֹכַל כִּכָּר זֶה. דָּבָר שֶׁאִילוּ בִנְדָרִין אָסוּר וּבִשְׁבוּעוֹת מוּתָּר. לֹא הָדָא אָמְרָת אֶלָּא עַל הָדָא. אֶחָד דְּבָרִים שֶׁלְּעַצְמָן וְאֶחָד דְּבָרִים שֶׁלַּאֲחֵרִים. אָמַר רִבִּי בָּא בְּשֵׁם שְׁמוּאֵל. שְׁבוּעָה שֶׁנָּתַן פְּלוֹנִי לִפְלוֹנִי מָנֶה. וְנִמְצָא שֶׁלֹּא נָתַן. מֵאַחַר שֶׁאֵין בְּיָדוֹ לָבֹא אֵין בְּיָדוֹ לְשֶׁעָבַר.

[74]There, we have stated[75]: "An oath that I shall not eat this loaf." Something which would be forbidden for vows and is permitted for oaths[76]. Not on that it was said but on the following[77]: "Whether it was for himself or for others." Rebbi Abba said in Samuel's name: An oath that X gave a mina to Y. If it turns out that he had not given [a mina], since it is not in his hand for the future, it is not in his hand for the past[78].

74 The first part of this paragraph has a parallel in *Šebuot* 3:11 but it is not a copy.

75 This Mishnah, *Šebuot* 3:7, reads: "An oath that I shall not eat this loaf, an oath that I shall not eat it, an oath

that I shall not eat it, he is guilty only once" if he ate the loaf. This parallels Mishnah *Nedarim* 2:3 which explains that repeated vows are separate vows but repeated oaths are one and the same oath.

76 Repeated oaths are not permitted but they do not add prohibitions to a simple oath.

77 Mishnah, *Šebuot* 3:5. An oath can refer to others; e. g., he swears to give a certain sum to another person.

78 Since X cannot swear that Y will give a mina to Z, having no power over Y's actions, if he swears that Y gave to Z it is an invalid oath, neither vain not false.

(38a, line 20) אַשְׁכָּח תַּנֵּי עַל תַּרְתֵּיהוֹן. זֶה חוֹמֶר בַּשְׁבוּעוֹת מִבַּנְּדָרִים. שֶׁשִּׁגְגַת שְׁבוּעוֹת אֲסוּרָה וְשִׁגְגַת נְדָרִים מוּתֶּרֶת. רִבִּי שִׁמְעוֹן בֶּן לָקִיש בְּעָא קוֹמֵי רִבִּי בָּא רִבִּי עֲקִיבָה לְהוֹסִיף עַל דִּבְרֵי בֵית הִלֵּל. כַּיֵּי דְתַנִּינָן תַּמָּן. עַד שֶׁבָּא רִבִּי עֲקִיבָה וְלִימֵּד שֶׁנֶּדֶר שֶׁהוּתָּר מִכְּלָלוֹ הוּתָּר כּוּלּוֹ. אָמַר לֵיהּ. מַה אִם תַּמָּן נֶדֶר שֶׁהוּא צָרִיךְ חֲקִירַת חָכָם אַתְּ אָמַר. נֶדֶר שֶׁבָּטַל מִקְצָתוֹ בָּטַל כּוּלּוֹ. כָּאן שֶׁאֵינוֹ צָרִיךְ חֲקִירַת חָכָם לֹא כָּל־שֶׁכֵּן. רִבִּי יוֹסֵי בְשֵׁם רִבִּי הִילָא. מִשּׁוּם נֶדֶר טָעוּת. שְׁאִילוּ הָיִיתִי יוֹדֵעַ שֶׁאַבָּא וַאֲחַי שָׁם לֹא הָיִיתִי נוֹדֵר.

[79]It was found stated about both cases[80]: It is more restrictive for oaths than for vows that an erroneous oath is forbidden but an erroneous vow is permitted[81]. Rebbi Simeon ben Laqish asked before Rebbi [ ][82], does Rebbi Aqiba add to the words of the House of Hillel? As we have stated there[83], "until Rebbi Aqiba came and taught that a vow of which any part was permitted is totally permitted.[84]" He said to him, if you say that there, in the case of a vow which has to be investigated by a Sage, you say that a vow of which any part was invalidated is totally invalidated, here, where it does not need investigation by a Sage, so much more[85]! Rebbi Yose in the name of Rebbi Hila: Because of an erroneous vow; if I had known that my father and my brothers were there I would not have made the vow[86].

79 Here the text in Šebuot is no longer a parallel.

80 About vows and oaths.

81 The Babli, 25b and Šebuot 28b, states the opposite: Both erroneous vows and oaths are permitted.

82 It is clear that something must be missing since R. Simeon ben Laqish could have asked Rebbi only as a very little boy but this is improbable since he was a wild youth not interested in studies. The commentaries all assume that the original text was בְּעָא קוֹמֵי רִבִּי [מַה בָּא רִבִּי עֲקִיבָה] and the copyist mistook the name בָּא for the verb בָּא "Rebbi Simeon ben Laqish asked before Rebbi Abba, what does Rebbi Aqiba add to the words of the House of Hillel?" However this is not more than a weak conjecture since R. Abba I belongs to the generation of the students of R. Joḥanan. Probably the question was asked before R. Yannai, as most of R. Simeon ben Laqish's other questions.

83 Mishnah 9:6.

84 R. Aqiba adds much in that Mishnah, that a vow which is voided because the maker of the vow did not consider that it would deprive him of the enjoyment of sabbaths or holidays. Before him, the vow was lifted only for sabbaths or holidays. But in the Mishnah here, the House of Hillel lifts the vow for all people who were eating the figs when his vow was lifted as an erroneous vow only for his father and brothers. So why is the teaching of Mishnah 9:6 not credited to the House of Hillel, who are not mentioned in the Mishnah?

85 From 9:6 one can infer the last statement of 3:2 but not vice-versa; the House of Hillel held that the principle does not apply to vows which have to be investigated by a Sage.

86 R. Hila holds that in Mishnah 3:2 the vow is not partially but totally in error; the farmer would not have made the vow at all had he known that his father was there, and did not object to the presence of others. One has no information about the views of the House of Hillel in the matter of partially voided vows.

(fol. 37c) **משנה ג:** נִדְרֵי אוֹנָסִין הִדִּירוֹ חֲבֵירוֹ שֶׁיֹּאכַל אֶצְלוֹ וְחָלָה הוּא אוֹ שֶׁחָלָה בְּנוֹ אוֹ שֶׁאִיכְּבוֹ נָהָר הֲרֵי אֵילוּ נִדְרֵי אוֹנָסִין.

Mishnah 3: Vows in connection with acts of God: His friend made him vow that he would eat with him but he or his child fell sick[87] or a river prevented him[88]; these are vows in connection with acts of God[89].

87 And he has to stay home to treat him.
88 By a flood.
89 Since none of the parties had intended that the vow should include the case that the invited party was prevented by an act of God.

(38a, line 27) **הלכה ב:** נִדְרֵי אוֹנָסִין. הִדִּירוֹ חֲבֵירוֹ כול'. מִפְּנֵי שֶׁחָלָה. הָא אִם לֹא חָלָה לֹא. אָמַר רִבִּי יִרְמְיָה. דְּרִבִּי מֵאִיר הִיא. דְּרִבִּי מֵאִיר אָמַר. אָסוּר עַד שֶׁיִּתֵּן. אָמַר רִבִּי יוֹסֵה. וְלָמָּה לֵית אֲנָן פֵּתְרִין לָהּ דִּבְרֵי הַכֹּל. כַּיי דָּמַר רִבִּי. בִּסְתָּם חֲלוּקִין. מָה אֲנָן קַיָּימִין. אִם בְּזֶה אוֹמֵר. מִפְּנֵי כְבוֹדִי. וְזֶה אוֹמֵר. מִפְּנֵי כְבוֹדִי. דִּבְרֵי הַכֹּל אָסוּר. אִם בְּזֶה אוֹמֵר. מִפְּנֵי כְבוֹדִי. וְזֶה אוֹמֵר. מִפְּנֵי כְבוֹדָךְ אָמַרְתִּי. דִּבְרֵי הַכֹּל מוּתָּר. אָמַר רִבִּי הִילָא. כֵּן אוֹרְחֵיהּ דְּבַר נָשָׁה מֵימוֹר לְחַבְרֵיהּ. בּוֹרוּסְתִּי בַּיָּיהּ.

Halakhah 3: "Vows in connection with acts of God: His friend made him vow," etc. because he fell ill. Therefore, if he did not fall ill, no[90]. Rebbi Jeremiah said, this is Rebbi Meïr's, since Rebbi Meïr said, "he is forbidden until he gives[91]." Rebbi Yose said, why do we not explain it according to everybody[92]? As my teacher said[93], they disagree when it was indeterminate. Where do we hold? If each one of them said, because of my honor, everybody agrees that he is forbidden[94]. If one of them said, because of my honor, and the other said, I said it in your honor, everybody agrees he is permitted[95]. Rebbi Hila said, is it the way of people to say χαρίζεσθαι βίᾳ[96]?

90 It is a valid vow which must be kept.

91 Mishnah 8:11: "If somebody says to his friend, a *qônām* that I shall not have anything from you unless you come and take so and so much grain and wine for your son, he can annul his vow alone by saying, I said that only for my honor and that is my honor. But one who says, a *qônām* that you will not have anything from me unless you give so and so much grain and wine to my son, *R. Meïr says he is forbidden until he gives*. But the Sages say, this one also can annul his vow alone by saying, it is as if I received it."

92 Since the entire vow falls under the category of speeding-up vows. But in the case of 8:11 there is another principle involved.

93 R. Ze'ira, in Halakhah 8:11, explaining the difference between R. Meïr and the Sages.

94 Both parties agree that they meant the vow to mean what it said; the vow is valid.

95 Since the vow never was accepted by the other party.

96 An interpretation by N. Brüll (cf. Note 70, p. 138), erroneously ascribed to Jastrow by S. Lieberman (p. 34). Lieberman reads כורזסתי instead of בורוסתי of the Leiden ms., כורוסתי of the *editio princeps*.

As Lieberman explains, in Egyptian legal papyri one frequently finds the formula ὁμολογῶ χαρίζεσθαί σοι "I agree that I gave you". R. Hila asked, would anybody say ὁμολογῶ χαρίζεσθαί σοι βίᾳ "I agree that I gave you by force?" A gift can be given only with the consent of the recipient; in the case of Mishnah 8:11, a vow involving a gift can be valid only with the agreement of both parties.

משנה ד: נוֹדְרִין לְהָרָגִים וְלַחֲרָמִים וְלַמּוֹכְסִין שֶׁהִיא תְרוּמָה אַף עַל (fol. 37c) פִּי שֶׁאֵינָהּ תְּרוּמָה שֶׁהֵן שֶׁלְּבֵית הַמֶּלֶךְ אַף עַל פִּי שֶׁאֵינָן שֶׁלָּהֶן. בֵּית שַׁמַּאי אוֹמְרִים בַּכֹּל נוֹדְרִין חוּץ מִבִּשְׁבוּעָה וּבֵית הִלֵּל אוֹמְרִים אַף בִּשְׁבוּעָה. בֵּית שַׁמַּאי אוֹמְרִים לֹא יִפְתַּח לוֹ בְנֶדֶר. וּבֵית הִלֵּל אוֹמְרִים אַף יִפְתַּח לוֹ. בֵּית שַׁמַּאי אוֹמְרִים בַּמֶּה שֶׁהוּא מַדִּירוֹ. וּבֵית הִלֵּל אוֹמְרִים אַף בַּמֶּה שֶׁאֵינוֹ מַדִּירוֹ.

Mishnah 4: One makes a vow to tax assessors[97] and to people who condemn property[98] and to toll collectors[99] that it is heave even though it is not heave[100], that it is king's family's property even though it is not theirs[101]. The House of Shammai say, one vows anything except an oath, but the House of Hillel say, even an oath. The House of Shammai say, one may not offer a vow[102], but the House of Hillel say, one may offer. The House of Shammai say, only what he prescribes as vow, but the House of Hillel say, even what he does not prescribe.

משנה ה: כֵּיצַד אָמְרוּ לוֹ קוֹנָם אִשְׁתִּי נֶהֱנֵית לִי וְאָמַר קוֹנָם אִשְׁתִּי וּבָנַי נֶהֱנִין לִי בֵּית שַׁמַּאי אוֹמְרִים אִשְׁתּוֹ מוּתֶּרֶת וּבָנָיו אֲסוּרִין. וּבֵית הִלֵּל אוֹמְרִים אֵילוּ וְאֵילוּ מוּתָּרִין.

Mishnah 5: How is this? They said to him, say: a *qônām* that my wife cannot have any use from me[103], and he said: a *qônām* that my wife and my children cannot have any use from me; the House of Shammai say, his wife is permitted but his children are forbidden[104]; but the House of Hillel say, both are permitted.

97   Reading with the Vienna ms. of Tosephta 2:2 edited by S. Lieberman: חָרָג, "fiscal agent" [Y. Kutscher, לשוננו 27 (1963), p.35], as in Arabic خراج "real estate tax, revenue." This refers to the periodical assessment of wealth by the Roman government known as *indiction* (Roman 15 year periods, Byzantine 5 year periods). This reading is confirmed as that of the Babylonian Mishnah by Ravad (R. Abraham ben David of Posquières, *Temim De'im* No. 59). Earlier commentators explain הרגים as criminal gangs who kill people unless they deliver to them all their money and/or valuables.

98   Government fiscal agents acting on an arbitrary decree (in the way it was Roman practice, introduced by Augustus, to condemn any inherited property if the emperor was not named principal heir for a third of the property, with the real heirs being reduced to the status of co-heirs to the

emperor.)

99 Since tolls were always farmed out, the tax farmer had to try to collect more than the legal rate in order to make money on the transaction, and the toll collector may be presumed to have asked for more than he would deliver to the tax farmer. These practices are classified as robbery; cf. Mishnah *Baba qama* 10:1-2, where toll collectors are classified with robbers.

100 A Jewish killer, robber, or toll collector would be much too superstitious to touch heave.

101 Property of a member of the emperor's *familia*, his slaves and freedmen, whom he uses to administer the empire. Their property would be exempt of taxes and shielded from confiscation. This vow would be valuable also against Gentile claimants.

102 One may make such a false vow only if required to do so by the extortionist who does not believe his victim's assertions.

103 That the *qônām* be valid if anything he said was untrue.

104 Since that part of the vow was not imposed on him.

(38a, line 34) **הלכה ד-ה:** נוֹדְרִין לְהָרָגִים וְלַחָרְמִים כול׳. לְהָרָגִים בְּהָרָגָה. לְחָרְמִים בִּשְׁעַת הַחֵרֶם. תַּנֵּי רִבִּי יוּדָה בֶּן פָּזִי בְּשֵׁם רִבִּי יוֹחָנָן. אִם הָיָה דָבָר שֶׁלַּסַּכָּנָה מוּתָר. רִבִּי אָחָא רִבִּי חִינְנָא בְּשֵׁם רִבִּי יוֹחָנָן. אִם הָיָה דָבָר שֶׁל יִישּׁוּב אָסוּר. תַּנֵּי. תּוֹלִים בַּגּוֹיִים וּבַמַּלְכוּת אֲבָל לֹא בְיִשְׂרָאֵל. שֶׁבַּעֲלֵי זְרוֹעַ מְצוּיִין לִיפּוֹל. וְלָא יַפֵּל וְיִנַּלְגֵּל עֲלוֹהִי קַדְמִיתָא.

"One makes a vow to assessors and to people who condemn property," etc. To assessors in time of *indiction*[97]; to condemners in times of expropriations. Rebbi Jehudah ben Pazi stated in the name of Rebbi Johanan: If it was a dangerous situation, it is permitted. Rebbi Aha, Rebbi Hinena in the name of Rebbi Johanan: If it was civilized, it is forbidden[105]. It was stated: One hangs on Gentiles and government but not on Jews[106], because the strong-armed will fall and he should not risk that the prior [obligations] fall on him.

105 If the tolls were collected according to a published tariff, or a condemnation was collected pursuant to a court judgment. In the Babli, 28a, the Babylonian opinion is quoted that one may lie to the toll collector if he does not work following an official tariff, and the Galilean that one may not lie to a toll collector appointed by the government.

106 If a person frees himself from paying tolls, he may claim that certain of his properties belong to other people. But he should not claim that they were another Jew's property since the other Jew may sue him for damages once the rule of law has been re-established.

(38a, line 38) עָבַר וּפָתַח. עַל דְּבֵית שַׁמַּי מָהוּ. נִשְׁמְעִינָהּ מִן הָדָא. בֵּית שַׁמַּאי אוֹמְרִים אִשְׁתּוֹ מוּתֶּרֶת וּבָנָיו אֲסוּרִין. הָדָא אָמְרָה. עָבַר וּפָתַח עַל דְּבֵית שַׁמַּי מוּתָּר. הֲוֹון בָּעֵי מֵימַר. בִּנְדָרִים. הָא בִשְׁבוּעוֹת לֹא. אַשְׁכָּח תַּנֵּי. רִבִּי יִשְׁמָעֵאל אוֹמֵר. לֹא תִשָּׁבְעוּ בִשְׁמִי לַשָּׁקֶר. נִשְׁבַּע אַתְּ לֶהָרָגִין וְלֶחָרָמִין וּלְמוֹכְסִין.

If he transgressed and offered [a vow], how is that in the opinion of the House of Shammai? Let us hear from the following: "The House of Shammai say, his wife is permitted but his children are forbidden." That means, if he transgressed and offered [a vow], in the opinion of the House of Shammai he is permitted[107]. They wanted to say, vows but not oaths. It was found stated: Rebbi Ismael says, "[108]do not swear falsely in My Name," you may swear to assessors and to people who condemn property and to toll collectors.

107 It seems that since his wife is permitted even following his voluntary addition of his children, that this addition has no influence on the rest of the vow. (R. David Fraenckel emends the text from "permitted" to "prohibited".)

109 Lev. 19:12. It seems that the argument is based on the second half of the verse, not quoted in the text: "for you would desecrate your God's Name, I am the Eternal". It is general rabbinic doctrine that the note "I am the Eternal" at the end of a verse

indicates that a transgression depends on the intention, that God will judge whether a person intended evil or not (*Sifra Qedošim Parašah* 2(14)). This means that when clearly no desecration of the Name is intended, the oath cannot be forbidden.

(fol. 37c) **משנה ו:** הֲרֵי נְטִיעוֹת הָאֵילוּ קָרְבָּן אִם אֵינָן נִקְצָצוֹת טַלִּית זוֹ קָרְבָּן אִם אֵינָהּ נִשְׂרֶפֶת יֵשׁ לָהֶן פִּדְיוֹן. הֲרֵי נְטִיעוֹת הָאֵילוּ קָרְבָּן עַד שֶׁיִּקָּצְצוּ טַלִּית זוֹ קָרְבָּן עַד שֶׁתִּישָׂרֵף אֵין לָהֶן פִּדְיוֹן.

Mishnah 6: These orchard trees shall be *qorbān* if they are not cut, this garment be *qorbān* if it is not burned; these have redemption[110]. These orchard trees shall be *qorbān* until they are cut, this garment be *qorbān* until it is burned; these have no redemption[111].

110 The circumstances of the vow are explained in the Halakhah. Since neither trees nor garments can be sacrifices, by dedication they become Temple property and can be bought back from the Temple, i.e., redeemed.

111 All Temple property other than sacrificial animals can be bought back from the Temple administration. But in this case, buying the property back would have no effect; immediately it would be rededicated if the trees were not cut or the garment burned.

(38a, line 43) **הלכה ו:** הֲרֵי נְטִיעוֹת הָאֵילוּ קָרְבָּן כול׳. רָאָה קְצִיעוֹת הַמֶּלֶךְ מְמַשְׁמְשִׁין וּבָאִין. רָאָה דְלֵיקָה מְמַשְׁמֶשֶׁת וּבָאָה וְאָמַר. הֲרֵי נְטִיעוֹת הָאֵילוּ קָרְבָּן אִם אֵינָן מְקֻצָּצוֹת. טַלִּית זוֹ קָרְבָּן אִם אֵינָהּ נִשְׂרֶפֶת וְנִקְרָעָה. לְמַפְרִיעָן קָדְשׁוּ אוֹ מִיכָּן וְלָבָא. מַה נְפִיק מִבֵּינֵיהוֹן. נֶהֱנָה מֵהֶן. אִין תֵּימַר. לְמַפְרִיעָן קָדְשׁוּ. מָעַל. אִין תֵּימַר. מִיכָּן וְלָבָא. לֹא מָעַל.

Halakhah 6: "These orchard trees shall be *qorbān*," etc. If he saw the king's cutting crew coming near[112], if he saw fire coming near, and he said: These orchard trees shall be *qorbān* if they are not cut, this garment shall be *qorbān* if it is not burned or torn. Were they sanctified retroactively or only for the future[113]? What is the difference? If he used them. If you say that they are sanctified retroactively, he committed larceny. If you say for the future, he did not commit larceny.

112 They will cut trees for public works without paying for them. The owner promises money to Heaven if he will be protected.

113 If it turns out that his property was saved, what is the exact moment when his vow becomes active. If one says from the moment he made the vow, that point in time is well defined. If one says, from the moment it is clear that his property will be spared, that moment is difficult to pin down. The question is not answered.

(38a, line 48) חִזְקִיָה אָמַר. פְּדָיָין חָזְרוּ לִקְדוּשָׁתָן. רִבִּי יוֹחָנָן אָמַר. פְּדָיָין פְּדוּיִין. מַתְנִיתָא פְּלִיגָא עַל רִבִּי יוֹחָנָן. אֵין לָה פִּדְיוֹן. פָּתַר לָהּ. לִכְשֶׁיִקָצְצוּ אֵין לָהֶן פִּדְיוֹן. אָמַר רִבִּי יוֹסֵי. מַה דְּאָמַר חִזְקִיָה בְּשֶׁפְּדָיָין הוּא. אֲבָל אִם פְּדָיָין אַחֵר פָּקְעָה מִמֶּנּוּ קְדוּשָׁתָן. מַחְלְפָה שִׁיטָתֵיהּ דְּרִבִּי יוֹסֵי. תַּמָּן הוּא אָמַר. פְּדָיָין פָּקְעָה מֵהֶן קְדוּשָׁתָן. וְכָא הוּא אָמַר. נִישֵּׂאת לְאַחֵר לֹא פָקְעוּ מִמֶּנָּה קִידּוּשִׁין. לֹא צוֹרְכָה דְלֹא בְּשֶׁנָּתַן לָהּ שְׁתֵּי פְרוּטוֹת אַחַת מִכְּבָר וְאַחַת לִכְשֶׁיְגָרְשֶׁנָּה מָהוּ.

[114]Hizqiah said, if he redeemed them they revert to their sanctity[115]. Rebbi Johanan said, if he redeemed them they are redeemed[116]. The Mishnah disagrees with Rebbi Johanan: "These have no redemption." He explains thus: After they have been cut they do not need redemption[117]. Rebbi Yose said, what Hizqiah said refers to the case that he himself redeemed them[118]. But if another person redeemed them, the sanctity is

removed from them[119]. The argument of Rebbi Yose is switched: There, he says that if [another] redeemed them, the sanctity is removed from them, but here[120], he says that if she was married to another man the *qiddušin* [of the first] were not removed! All that is questionable for him is if he gave her two *peruṭot*, one for the moment and one for after he has divorced her, what is the situation[121]?

114 This paragraph is copied from *Qiddušin* 3:5 (64a, 1. 72). Therefore "there" means here and "here" the text in *Qiddušin*.

115 This refers to the second part of the Mishnah, where the orchard was vowed for the time before it was cut. The opinion of Ḥizqiah is that described in Note 111. In the Babli, 28b, the opinion is ascribed to bar Pada, a contemporary of Ḥizqiah.

116 In the Babli, 28b, this is the opinion of Ulla (R. Hila).

117 In general, we say that anything sanctified cannot become profane without some form of redemption. But in this case, the cutting of the trees or the burning of the garment is the act of profanation.

118 Because he himself stated that his orchard be holy until cut down. In the Babli, 130a, this is the opinion of R. Johanan.

119 For a third party the orchard is Temple property and becomes profane by payment of the redemption price.

120 In *Qiddušin* 3:5, where the question was raised, what is the status of a woman whose husband gives her some valuables and says that these should serve as *qiddušin* (preliminary marriage, cf. *Yebamot* 1:1, Note 63) after he will have divorced her. It is obvious that if another man gives *qiddušin* to a married woman to be valid once she will be divorced, those *qiddušin* are invalid (Mishnah *Qiddušin* 3:5) since the divorce depends on a third party (the husband). R. Yose holds that the husband himself can give *qiddušin* for after a divorce since no third party is involved. Therefore, there is no contradiction in R. Yose's position here and there.

121 In the Babli, 30a, this is a question of R. Hoshaia.

משנה ז: (fol. 37c) הַנּוֹדֵר מִיּוֹרְדֵי הַיָּם מוּתָּר בְּיוֹשְׁבֵי הַיַּבָּשָׁה מְיוֹשְׁבֵי הַיַּבָּשָׁה אָסוּר בְּיוֹרְדֵי הַיָּם. שֶׁיּוֹרְדֵי הַיָּם בִּכְלָל יוֹשְׁבֵי הַיַּבָּשָׁה. לֹא כְּאִילּוּ שֶׁהוֹלְכִין מֵעַכּוֹ לְיָפוֹ אֶלָא מִי שֶׁדַּרְכּוֹ לְפָרֵשׁ.

Mishnah 7: One who makes a vow[122] away from the seafaring men is permitted the dwellers on dry land; from the dwellers on dry land he is forbidden the seafaring men[123] because the seafaring men are part of the dwellers on dry land. [One speaks] not of those who go from Acco to Jaffa but those who frequently take to the sea.

משנה ח: הַנּוֹדֵר מֵרוֹאֵי הַחַמָּה אָסוּר אַף בְּסוּמִין שֶׁלֹּא נִתְכַּוֵּון זֶה אֶלָּא לְמִי שֶׁהַחַמָּה רוֹאָה אוֹתוֹ.

Mishnah 8: One who makes a vow away from those who see the sun is also forbidden the blind since he intended only that seen by the sun[124].

משנה ח: הַנּוֹדֵר מִשְּׁחוֹרֵי הָרֹאשׁ אָסוּר בַּקֵּרְחִין וּבְבַעֲלֵי שֵׂיבוֹת וּמוּתָּר בַּנָּשִׁים וּבַקְּטַנִּים שֶׁאֵין נִקְרָאִין שְׁחוֹרֵי רֹאשׁ אֶלָּא אֲנָשִׁים.

Mishnah 9: One who makes a vow away from the black-haired is forbidden bald and white-haired men[125] and is permitted women and minors since only men are called "black haired".

122 A "vow away from X" is always a vow that all of X's property should be considered *qorbān* by the maker of the vow, who then is forbidden any use of X's property and may not receive any favors from him.

123 I. e., also the seafaring men.

124 Cf. *Eccl.* 7:11.

125 If a young man for some reason is white-haired, he still is a young male and such persons are called "black-haired" or תִּשְׁחוֹרֶת, cf. Mishnah *Abot* 3:12.

הלכה ז: (38a line 54) הַנּוֹדֵר מִיּוֹרְדֵי הַיָּם כול׳. שֶׁלֹּא תֹאמַר. אֵילּוּ הַהוֹלְכִין מֵעַכּוֹ לְיָפוֹ אֶלָא בְּמִי[126] שֶׁדַּרְכּוֹ לְפָרֵשׁ. מְיוֹשְׁבֵי הַיַּבָּשָׁה אָסוּר בְּיוֹרְדֵי הַיָּם.

HALAKHAH 7   507

וְלֹא סוֹף דָּבָר אֶלָּא כְּגוֹן אֵילוּ הַהוֹלְכִין מֵעַכּוֹ לְיָפוֹ אֶלָּא בְּמִי שֶׁדַּרְכּוֹ לְפָרֵשׁ. וְלֹא מִיּוֹשְׁבֵי הַיַּבָּשָׁה נָדַר. הֲדָא אֲמָרָה שֶׁיּוֹרְדֵי הַיָּם בִּכְלָל יוֹשְׁבֵי הַיַּבָּשָׁה. נָדַר מִיּוֹרְדֵי הַיָּם. לְאַחַר שְׁלֹשִׁים יוֹם נַעֲשׂוּ בְּנֵי יַבֶּשֶׁת. תַּפְלוּגְתָּא דְּרִבִּי יִשְׁמָעֵאל וְרִבִּי עֲקִיבָה. דְּרִבִּי יִשְׁמָעֵאל אָמַר. אַחַר הַנֶּדֶר. וְרִבִּי עֲקִיבָה אוֹמֵר. אַחַר הָאִיסּוּר. וּבְאִילֵין טַלְיָיתָא צְרִיכָה.

Halakhah 7: "One who makes a vow away from the seafaring men," etc. That you should not say, not from those who go from Acco to Jaffa but those who frequently take to the sea. "From the dwellers on dry land he is forbidden the seafaring men," not only those who go from Acco to Jaffa but even those who frequently take to the sea. But did he not make a vow regarding the dwellers on dry land? This implies that the seafaring men are part of the dwellers on dry land[127]. If he made a vow away from the seafaring men after thirty days but [a certain mariner] became a land dweller, there is a dispute between Rebbi Ismael and Rebbi Aqiba[128]. For Rebbi Ismael says, after the vow, and Rebbi Aqiba says, after the prohibition. And about children it is a problem[129].

126   This is the reading of the Mishnah in the Babli.

127   In the words of the Babli, 30b, "every seafaring man will eventually reach land."

128   The problem is compared to that of Halakhah 11:9 (Babli 89a) dealing with a widow who vowed to be a *nezirah* after 30 days and before the 30 days elapsed she married. R. Ismael holds that the time of the vow is determining, and since she made the vow while on her own, the husband cannot dissolve her vow even though it will start to become active only during marriage. He will hold that any mariner who became a land dweller within 30 days of the vow is forbidden since he was a mariner at the moment the vow was made. R. Aqiba holds that the moment the vow becomes active is determining. Therefore, he holds that the husband can dissolve his wife's vow and in the case of a vow against

mariners, the person who became a dweller on dry land before the vow was activated is permitted.

129 All commentators identify טלייתא with חלייתא "people going on pleasure trips." This procedure has no basis. טליא only means "boy, young man". Since minors are subject to their parents' will, is a boy who is taken on a sea trip automatically a mariner or becomes a mariner in *halakhic* sense only when he enters a seagoing vessel of his own will?

(fol. 37c) **משנה י**: הַנּוֹדֵר מִן הַיִּלּוֹדִים מוּתָּר בַּנּוֹלָדִים. מִן הַנּוֹלָדִים רִבִּי מֵאִיר מַתִּיר אַף בַּיִּלּוֹדִים. וַחֲכָמִים אוֹמְרִים לֹא נִתְכַּוֵּון זֶה אֶלָּא בְמִי שֶׁדַּרְכּוֹ לְהִוָּלֵד.

Mishnah 10: One who makes a vow away from those who will be born[139] is permitted those who are already born. From those who are born, Rebbi Meïr permits even those who will be born, but the Sages say, he intended only those in whose nature it is to be born.

משנה יא: הַנּוֹדֵר מְשׁוֹבְתֵי שַׁבָּת אָסוּר בְּיִשְׂרָאֵל וְאָסוּר בַּכּוּתִים. מֵאוֹכְלֵי שׁוּם אָסוּר בְּיִשְׂרָאֵל וְאָסוּר בַּכּוּתִים. מֵעוֹלֵי יְרוּשָׁלַיִם אָסוּר בְּיִשְׂרָאֵל וּמוּתָּר בַּכּוּתִים.

Mishnah 11: One who makes a vow away from those who keep the Sabbath is forbidden Jews and Samaritans[140], from garlic eaters[141] is forbidden Jews and Samaritans, from those who make pilgrimage to Jerusalem is forbidden Jews but permitted Samaritans[142].

139 The Babli, 30b, switches the meanings between ילודים and נולדים. However, the Halakhah here confirms the translation as given; which is also confirmed by biblical usage; in *Ex*. 1:22 יִלּוֹד clearly means "will be born".

140 But Sabbatist Christians who do not accept the obligation to keep all laws of the Pentateuch are not included in the prohibition.

141 In general use as fertility medication.

142 For their pilgrimages are to Mount Gerizim.

(38a line 61) **הלכה י:** הַנּוֹדֵר מִן הַיִּלּוֹדִים כול׳. מַאי טַעֲמָא דְּרִבִּי מֵאִיר. וְעַתָּה שְׁנֵי בָנֶיךָ הַנּוֹלָדִים לְךָ. וּכְבָר נוֹלְדוּ. מַאי טַעֲמָא דְּרַבָּנִין. הִנֵּה בֵן נוֹלָד לְבֵית דָּוִד יֹאשִׁיָּהוּ שְׁמוֹ. וְעֲדַיִין לֹא נוֹלַד.

Halakhah 10: "One who makes a vow away from those who will be born," etc. What is Rebbi Meïr's reason? "And now your two sons born to you[143]", and they already were born. What is the Sages' reason? "Lo, a son is born to the House of David, Josiah his name,[144]" and he was not yet born.

143 *Gen.* 48:5.

144 *1K.* 13:2.

(fol. 3/c) **משנה יב:** קוֹנָם שֶׁאֵינִי נֶהֱנֶה לִבְנֵי נֹחַ מוּתָּר בְּיִשְׂרָאֵל וְאָסוּר בָּאוּמוֹת. שֶׁאֵינִי נֶהֱנֶה לִבְנֵי אַבְרָהָם אָסוּר בְּיִשְׂרָאֵל וּמוּתָּר בָּאוּמוֹת. שֶׁאֵינִי נֶהֱנֶה לְיִשְׂרָאֵל לוֹקֵחַ בְּיֶתֶר וּמוֹכֵר בְּפָחוֹת. שֶׁיִּשְׂרָאֵל נֶהֱנִין לִי לוֹקֵחַ בְּפָחוֹת וּמוֹכֵר בְּיֶתֶר אֵין שׁוֹמְעִים לוֹ. שֶׁאֵינִי נֶהֱנֶה לָהֶם וְהֵם לִי יַהֲנֶה לָאוּמוֹת.

Mishnah 12: A *qônām* that I shall not enjoy from the descendants of Noah; he is permitted Jews and forbidden Gentiles[145]. That I shall not enjoy from the descendants of Abraham; he is forbidden Jews and permitted Gentiles[146]. That I shall not enjoy from Jews; he buys higher and sells lower[147]. That Jews shall not enjoy from me; he buys lower and sells higher, if they agree[148]. That I shall not enjoy from them nor they from me; he should deal with Gentiles.

משנה יג: קוֹנָם שֶׁאֵינִי נֶהֱנֶה לָעֲרֵלִים מוּתָּר בְּעַרְלֵי יִשְׂרָאֵל וְאָסוּר בְּמוּלֵי אוּמוֹת הָעוֹלָם. קוֹנָם שֶׁאֵינִי נֶהֱנֶה לַמּוּלִים אָסוּר בְּעַרְלֵי יִשְׂרָאֵל וּמוּתָּר בְּמוּלֵי אוּמוֹת הָאוֹלָם. שֶׁאֵין הָעָרְלָה קְרוּיָה אֶלָּא לְשֵׁם הַגּוֹיִם שֶׁנֶּאֱמַר כִּי כָל־הַגּוֹיִם עֲרֵלִים וְכָל־בֵּית יִשְׂרָאֵל עַרְלֵי לֵב.

Mishnah 13: A *qônām* that I shall not enjoy from the uncircumcized, he is permitted uncircumcized Jews and forbidden circumcized peoples of the world. That I shall not enjoy from the circumcized, he is forbidden uncircumcized Jews and permitted circumcized peoples of the world, since the prepuce is simply a name for Gentiles as it was said[149]: "For all Gentiles are uncircumcized and all the House of Israel are uncircumcised of heart."

145 Even though Jews also are descendants of Noah, the technical term "descendants of Noah" applies only to those outside the Sinaitic covenant, who are only bound by the natural law given to Adam and Noah.

146 Including the descendants of Hagar and Qeturah since only Isaac is called "Abraham's descendant" (*Gen.* 21:12).

147 Than the going market rate. In that case, he is guaranteed a loss in any commercial transaction; he may trade without violating his vow.

148 He would have to tell his customers that he was overcharging them.

149 *Jer.* 9:25.

(38a line 64) **הלכה יב:** קוֹנָם שֶׁאֵינִי נֶהֱנֶה לִבְנֵי נֹחַ. מוּתָּר בְּיִשְׂרָאֵל וְאָסוּר בָּאוּמוֹת. שֶׁאֵינִי נֶהֱנֶה לְזֶרַע אַבְרָהָם. אָסוּר בְּיִשְׂרָאֵל וּמוּתָּר בָּאוּמוֹת כּוֹל'. וְאֵין יִשְׁמָעֵאל בִּכְלַל זַרְעוֹ שֶׁלְּאַבְרָהָם. כִּי בְיִצְחָק יִקָּרֵא לְךָ זָרַע. וְאֵין עֵשָׂיו בִּכְלַל זֶרַע יִצְחָק. אָמַר רִבִּי יוּדָן בַּר שָׁלוֹם. בְּיִצְחָק. בְּמִקְצָת יִצְחָק. רִבִּי הוּנָא אָמַר. בֵּית תְּרֵי. בֶּן שֶׁהוּא עָתִיד לִנְחוֹל שְׁנֵי עוֹלָמוֹת. הָעוֹלָם הַזֶּה וְהָעוֹלָם הַבָּא. רִבִּי גֵּרְשׁוֹם בְּשֵׁם רִבִּי אָחָא. דָּרַךְ כּוֹכָב מִיַּעֲקֹב. מִמִּי דֶּרֶךְ כּוֹכָב וְעָתִיד לַעֲמוֹד. מִיַּעֲקֹב. רִבִּי אָחָא בְשֵׁם רִבִּי חוּנָא. עָתִיד עֵשָׂיו הָרָשָׁע לַעֲטוֹף טַלִּיתוֹ

וְלֵישֵׁב עִם הַצַּדִּיקִים בְּגַן עֵדֶן לֶעָתִיד לָבוֹא. וְהַקָּדוֹשׁ בָּרוּךְ הוּא גּוֹרְרוֹ וּמוֹצִיאוֹ מִשָּׁם. מָה טַעֲמָא. אִם תַּגְבִּיהַּ כַּנֶּשֶׁר וְאִם בֵּין כּוֹכָבִים שִׂים קִנֶּךָ מִשָּׁם אוֹרִידְךָ נְאֻם יי׳. וְאֵין כּוֹכָבִים אֶלָּא צַדִיקִים. כְּמָה דְאַתְּ אָמַר וּמַצְדִּיקֵי הָרַבִּים כַּכּוֹכָבִים לְעוֹלָם וָעֶד.

Halakha 12: "A *qônām* that I shall not enjoy from the descendants of Noah; he is permitted Jews and forbidden Gentiles[145]. That I shall not enjoy from the descendants of Abraham; he is forbidden Jews and permitted Gentiles," etc. Is Ismael not part of Abraham's seed? "[150]For in Isaac will be called your seed." And is not Esaw part of Isaac's seed? Rebbi Yudan bar Shalom said, "in Isaac," in part of Isaac. Rebbi Huna said, "ב" are two[151], the son who will be inheriting two worlds, this world and the world to come. Rebbi Gershom in the name of Rebbi Aha, "[152]a star did step out from Jacob," from whom did a star step out and will appear in the future? From Jacob! Rebbi Aha in the name of Rebbi Huna: In the future world, evil Esaw will put on his prayer shawl and sit with the Just in Paradise, but the Holy One, Praise to Him, draws him away. Why? "[153]If you climb as high as an eagle or if you would make your nest between stars, from there I would take you down, says the Lord." But "stars" are only the Just. As you say[154], "those who justify the many are like stars, eternally."

150 *Gen.* 21:12. The same in the Babli 31a, *Sanhedrin* 59b..
151 Following the Alexandrian practice to denote numbers by letters.
152 *Num.* 24:17.
153 *Ob.* 1:4.
154 *Dan.* 12:3.

(fol. 37c) **משנה יד**: רִבִּי יִשְׁמָעֵאל אוֹמֵר גְּדוֹלָה מִילָה שֶׁשָּׁלֹשׁ עֶשְׂרֵה בְּרִיתוֹת נִכְרְתוּ עָלֶיהָ. רִבִּי יוֹסֵי אוֹמֵר גְּדוֹלָה מִילָה שֶׁהִיא דּוֹחָה שַׁבָּת הַחֲמוּרָה. רִבִּי יְהוֹשֻׁעַ בֶּן קָרְחָה אוֹמֵר גְּדוֹלָה מִילָה שֶׁלֹּא נִתְלָה לוֹ לְמֹשֶׁה הַצַּדִּיק עָלֶיהָ מְלֹא שָׁעָה. רִבִּי נְחֶמְיָה אוֹמֵר גְּדוֹלָה מִילָה שֶׁהִיא דּוֹחָה אֶת הַנְּגָעִים.

Mishnah 14: Rebbi Ismael says, circumcision is great, for its covenant was concluded thirteenfold. Rebbi Yose says, circumcision is great, for it pushes aside the stringencies of the Sabbath. Rebbi Joshua ben Qorḥa says, circumcision is great, for it was not suspended even one hour for Moses the Just. Rebbi Nehemiah says, Rebbi Yose says, circumcision is great, for it pushes aside skin disease[155].

משנה טו: רִבִּי אוֹמֵר גְּדוֹלָה מִילָה שֶׁכָּל־הַמִּצְווֹת שֶׁעָשָׂה אַבְרָהָם אָבִינוּ לֹא נִקְרָא שָׁלֵם עַד שֶׁמָּל שֶׁנֶּאֱמַר הִתְהַלֵּךְ לְפָנַי וֶהְיֵה תָמִים.

Mishnah 15: Rebbi says, circumcision is great, for with all the commandments which Abraham fulfilled he was not called whole until he circumcized himself as it is written[156]: "Walk before me and be perfect."

משנה טז: דָּבָר אַחֵר גְּדוֹלָה מִילָה שֶׁאִלְמָלֵא הִיא לֹא בָרָא הַקָּדוֹשׁ בָּרוּךְ הוּא אֶת עוֹלָמוֹ שֶׁנֶּאֱמַר כֹּה אָמַר יי אִם לֹא בְרִיתִי יוֹמָם וָלַיְלָה חֻקּוֹת שָׁמַיִם וָאָרֶץ לֹא שָׂמְתִּי. דָּבָר אַחֵר גְּדוֹלָה הַמִּילָה שֶׁהִיא שְׁקוּלָה כְּנֶגֶד כָּל־הַמִּצְוֹת שֶׁבַּתּוֹרָה שֶׁנֶּאֱמַר הִנֵּה דַם הַבְּרִית אֲשֶׁר כָּרַת יי עִמְּכֶם עַל כָּל־הַדְּבָרִים הָאֵלֶּה.

Mishnah 16: Another word: Circumcision is great, for without it the Holy One, praise to Him, would not have created his world as it is said[157]: "So says the Eternal, if it were not for my covenant day and night, I would not have put in place the laws of heaven and earth." [158]Another word: Circumcision is great, for it is weighty corresponding to all other commandments of the Torah, as it is said[159]: "Behold the blood of the covenant which the Eternal concluded with you about *all* these words."

155 The Halakhah will explain the Mishnah.
156 *Gen.* 17:1.
157 *Jer.* 33:25. In the Babli, this is mostly explained as referring to the Torah (which has to be studied day and night, *Jos.* 1:8) as blueprint for the world; 32a, *Pesaḥim* 68b; *Avodah zarah* 3a. A similar text is in Tosephta 2:7.

158 This addition is not in the Babylonian Mishnah; it is in Tosephta 2:6.
159 *Ex.* 24:8. This verse speaks about the Sinaitic covenant; it is used here because in rabbinic and modern Hebrew the word בְּרִית "covenant" is synonymous with "circumcision".

(38a line 75) **הלכה יד:** אָמַר רִבִּי יוֹחָנָן בַּר מַרְיָיה. כְּתִיב בַּיּוֹם הַהוּא כָּרַת יְיָ בְּרִית אֶת אַבְרָם לֵאמוֹר וגו' עַד וְאֶת בְּרִיתִי אָקִים אֶת יִצְחָק וגו' שְׁלֹשׁ עֶשְׂרֵה בְּרִיתוֹת.

Halakhah 14: Rebbi Yoḥanan bar Marya said, it is written: "On that day, the Eternal concluded a covenant with Abram as follows," etc., up to "but my covenant I shall affirm with Isaac," etc., thirteen covenants[160].

160 In *Gen.* 17:2-21 the word "covenant" appears 12 times. Therefore, *Gen.* 15:18 is added to reach the lucky number 13, the number of God's attributes of mercy (*Ex.* 34:6-7) even though it speaks of a prior covenant; cf. the preceding Note.

(38b, line 2) בַּיּוֹם הַשְּׁמִינִי יִמּוֹל. אֲפִילוּ בְשַׁבָּת. מָה אֲנִי מְקַיֵּים מְחַלְלֶיהָ מוֹת יוּמָת. אַף בְּמִילָה. מָה אֲנִי מְקַיֵּים בַּשְּׁמִינִי יִמּוֹל. חוּץ מִן הַשַּׁבָּת. תַּלְמוּד לוֹמַר וּבַיּוֹם. אֲפִילוּ בְשַׁבָּת. בַּתּוֹרָה וּבַנְּבִיאִים וּבַכְּתוּבִים מָצִינוּ שֶׁהַשַּׁבָּת שְׁקוּלָה כְּנֶגֶד כָּל־הַמִּצְוֹת שֶׁבַּתּוֹרָה. בַּתּוֹרָה. דִּכְתִיב עַד אָנָה מֵאַנְתֶּם לִשְׁמוֹר מִצְוֹתַי וְתוֹרוֹתָיי. וּכְתִיב רְאוּ כִּי יְיָ נָתַן לָכֶם אֶת הַשַּׁבָּת. בַּנְּבִיאִים. דִּכְתִיב וַיַּמְרוּ בִי הַבָּנִים בְּחוּקוֹתַי לֹא הָלָכוּ וגו'. וּכְתִיב וְאֶת שַׁבְּתוֹתַי חִילְּלוּ מְאֹד. בַּכְּתוּבִים. דִּכְתִיב וְעַל הַר סִינַי יָרַדְתָּ וּכְתִיב וְאֶת שַׁבַּת קָדְשְׁךָ הוֹדַעְתָּ לָהֶם וגו'. אָמַר רִבִּי אֶלְעָזָר בֵּירִבִּי אֲבוּנָא. מִצְווֹת שַׁבָּת מָלֵא. לְהוֹדִיעָךְ שֶׁהִיא שְׁקוּלָה כְּנֶגֶד

כָּל־מִצְוֹותֶיהָ שֶׁלַּתּוֹרָה וְהַמִּילָה דוֹחָה אוֹתָהּ. מָשָׁל לִשְׁנֵי מַטְרוֹנִיּוֹת שֶׁהָיוּ בָאוֹת זוֹ עַל גַּב זוֹ וְאֵין אַתְּ יוֹדֵעַ אֵי זוֹ גְדוֹלָה מֵחֲבֵירָתָהּ. זוֹ שֶׁהִיא יוֹרֶדֶת מִפְּנֵי חֲבֵירָתָהּ אַתְּ יוֹדֵעַ שֶׁחֲבֵירָתָהּ גְדוֹלָה מִמֶּנָּה.

"On the eighth day one shall circumcize[161]," even on the Sabbath. How can I confirm "its desecrator shall certainly die[162]?" Even for circumcision? How can I confirm "on the eighth day one shall circumcize"? Even on the Sabbath? The verse says "[161]*But* on the eighth day one shall circumcize," even on the Sabbath[163]. In Torah, Prophets, and Hagiographs we find that the Sabbath is as weighty as all other commandments of the Torah[164] [taken together]. In the Torah, "until when will you refuse to keep My Commandments and Teachings[165]," and it is written: "See that the Eternal gave you the Sabbath[166]." In Prophets, as is written[167]: "But the sons rebelled against Me; My Laws they did not follow" etc., and it is written[168]: "My Sabbaths they much desecrated." In Hagiographs, as it is written: "On Mount Sinai You descended[169]," and it is written: "And about Your holy Sabbath You informed them[170]," etc. Rebbi Eleazar ben Rebbi Abuna said, *commandment* of Sabbath is written *plene*[171], to inform you that it is as weighty as all other commandments of the Torah. A parable of two ladies who meet and you do not know which one is of higher standing. If one makes room for the other, you know that the other is of higher standing.

161 *Lev.* 12:2.
162 *Ex.* 31:14.
163 In the Babylonian versions [*Šabbat* 132a, *Sifra Tazria' Pereq* 1(4)] the argument for performing circumcision on the Sabbath is based on the expression "on the Sabbath day" and not simply "on the Sabbath".
164 Cf. *Berakhot* 1:8, Note 207. The text is copied in *Ex. rabba* 25(16).
165 *Ex.* 15:28.
166 *Ex.* 15:29. The Sabbath is called

"commandments and teachings" when no other prohibitions were yet given to the Israelites.
167   Ez. 20:21.
168   Ez. 20:13. In *Ex. rabba* the quote is instead from *Ez.* 20:21, where the Sabbath is the only commandment singled out of all "laws and rules". The word מאד "much" probably should be deleted.
169   *Neh.* 9:13.
170   *Neh.* 9:14; again the Sabbath is the only commandment singled out of all "commandments and laws".
171   In all other occurrences in the Hebrew Bible the spelling is מִצְוֹת, only at this place it is מִצְווֹת.

(38b, line 13) עֲבוֹדָה זָרָה קָשָׁה מִכּוּלָם. וְכִי תִשְׁגּוּ וְלֹא תַעֲשׂוּ אֶת כָּל־הַמִּצְוֹת הָאֵלֶּה. אָמַר רִבִּי יוּדָה בַּר פָּזִי. חִילוּל הַשֵּׁם קָשֶׁה מִכּוּלָן. הָדָא הוּא דִכְתִיב וְאַתֶּם בֵּית יִשְׂרָאֵל כֹּה אָמַר יי אֱלֹהֵי יִשְׂרָאֵל אִישׁ גִּילוּלָיו לְכוּ עֲבוֹדוּ וְאֶת שֵׁם קָדְשִׁי לֹא תְחַלְּלוּ וגו'.

Idolatry is worse than all others: "But if you should err and not fulfill all these commandments.[172]" Rebbi Judah bar Pazi said, the desecration of the Name is worse than all others. That is what is written[173]: "But to you, the House of Israel, so says the Eternal, Israel's God, go and worship everybody his abominations but My holy Name do not desecrate, etc.

172   *Num.* 15:22. The rules for purification offerings are given in *Lev.* 4-5. The appearance of another set of purification offerings in *Num.* 15:22-28 is explained by the rule that these offerings are only for expiation of inadvertent idolatry (*Sifry Num.* 111). The Babli, *Erubin* 69b, equates desecration of the Sabbath and idolatry in severity.
173   Truncated from *Ez.* 20:39.

(38b, line 17) וְעַל יְדֵי שֶׁנִּתְעַצֵּל מֹשֶׁה בְּמִילָה בִּיקֵשׁ הַמַּלְאָךְ לְהוֹרְגוֹ. הָהוּא דִכְתִיב וַיִּפְגְּשֵׁהוּ יי וַיְבַקֵּשׁ הֲמִיתוֹ. אָמַר רִבִּי יוֹסֵי. חַס וְשָׁלוֹם לֹא נִתְעַצֵּל מֹשֶׁה בְּמִילָה אֶלָּא שֶׁהָיָה דָן בְּעַצְמוֹ וְאוֹמֵר. אִם לָמוּל וְלָצֵאת סַכָּנָה הִיא. וְאִם

לִשָׁהוֹת הַקָּדוֹשׁ בָּרוּךְ הוּא אָמַר לוֹ. לֵךְ שׁוּב מִצְרָיְמָה. אֶלָּא עַל יְדֵי שֶׁנִּתְעַצֵּל בְּלִינָה קוֹדֶם הַמִּילָה. הֲהוּא דִכְתִיב וַיְהִי בַדֶּרֶךְ בַּמָּלוֹן. אָמַר רַבָּן שִׁמְעוֹן בֶּן גַּמְלִיאֵל. חַס וְשָׁלוֹם. לֹא בִיקֵּשׁ הַמַּלְאָךְ לַהֲרוֹג לְמֹשֶׁה אֶלָּא לְתִינוֹק. בּוֹא וּרְאֵה. מִי קָרוּי חָתָן. מֹשֶׁה אוֹ הַתִּינוֹק. אִית תַּנָּיֵי תַנֵּי. מֹשֶׁה קָרוּי חָתָן. וְאִית תַּנָּיֵי תַנֵּי. הַתִּינוֹק קָרוּי חָתָן. מָאן דָּמַר. מֹשֶׁה קָרוּי חָתָן. חָתָן. דָּמִים מִתְבַּקֵּשׁ מִיָּדָךְ. וּמָאן דָּמַר. הַתִּינוֹק קָרוּי חָתָן. חָתָן. בְּדָמִים אַתְּ עוֹמֵד לִי. וַתִּקַּח צִפּוֹרָה צֹר וַתִּכְרוֹת אֶת עָרְלַת בְּנָהּ וַתַּגַּע לְרַגְלָיו וגו'. רִבִּי יְהוּדָה וְרִבִּי נְחֶמְיָה וְרַבָּנִין. חַד אָמַר. לְרַגְלָיו שֶׁלְּמֹשֶׁה. וְחָרָנָה אָמַר. לְרַגְלָיו שֶׁלְּמַלְאָךְ. וְחָרָנָה אָמַר. לְרַגְלָיו שֶׁלַתִּינוֹק. מָן דָּמַר. לְרַגְלָיו שֶׁלְּמֹשֶׁה. הֵילָךְ גְּזִי חוֹבָךְ. מָן דָּמַר. לְרַגְלָיו שֶׁלְּמַלְאָךְ. הֵילָךְ עֲבַד שְׁלִיחֻתֶּךְ. מָן דָּמַר. לְרַגְלָיו שֶׁלַתִּינוֹק. נָגְעָה בְגוּף הַתִּינוֹק. וַיֶּרֶף מִמֶּנּוּ אָז אָמְרָה חֲתַן דָּמִים לַמּוּלוֹת. מִיכָּן לִשְׁתֵּי מִילוֹת. אַחַת לִפְרִיעָה וְאַחַת לְצִיצִין.

Because Moses was lazy for circumcision, the angel tried to kill kim. That is what is written[174]: "The Eternal met him and wanted to kill him." Rebbi Yose said, far be the thought that Moses was lazy for circumcision but he argued on his own: To perform circumcision and leave would be dangerous[175]. To wait[176], the Holy One, praise to Him, told him: "Go, return to Egypt." But because he was lazy in preparing for the overnight stay before circumcision; that is what is written[174]: "It was on the way, at the overnight stay." Rabban Simeon ben Gamliel said, far be the thought that the angel wanted to kill Moses; it was the baby. Come and see, who is called *ḥātān*[177]? Moses or the baby? There are Tannaïm who state that Moses is called *ḥātān*. There are Tannaïm who state that the baby is called *ḥātān*. He who said that Moses is called *ḥātān*: *Ḥātān*, blood is required from you[178]. And he said that the baby is called *ḥātān*: *Ḥātān*, in blood you are preserved for me. "Ṣippora took a flintstone and cut her son's prepuce and touched his feet.[179]" Rebbi Jehudah, Rebbi Nehemiah, and the rabbis. One said, Moses's feet. Another said, the angel's feet. Another said, the baby's feet. He who said Moses's feet: Here I cut your obligation for you. He who said, the angel's feet: Here your mission was accomplished. He who said the baby's feet, she touched the baby's body. "He left off from him; then she said, a blood *ḥātān* for circumcisions[180]." From here that there are two circumcisions; one for baring the gland and one for the fibers[181].

174 *Ex.* 4:24.

175 Acute danger to a person's life suspends all commandments and prohibitions (except those of murder, incest and adultery, and idolatry). In practice, this means that it is forbidden to circumcize a sick baby.

176 To wait in Midyan until the baby had recovered. In the Babli, 31b, this argument is attributed to Rebbi. The argument of Rabban Simeon ben Gamliel is quoted in his name, 32a.

177 Since Ṣippora, being a Midyanite Arab, spoke Arabic, the root ختن can mean either to circumcize or to become a relative through one's wife. Therefore, the word is appropriate both for the boy and his father.

178 Explanations of the expression חתן דמים.

179 *Ex.* 4:25.

180 *Ex.* 4:26.

181 A circumcision is not valid unless the gland is exposed and the wound is smooth; cf. Babli *Yebamot* 71b.

(38b, line 17) יִמּוֹל בְּשַׂר עָרְלָתוֹ. אַף עַל פִּי שֶׁיֵּשׁ שָׁם בַּהֶרֶת. מָה אֲנִי מְקַיֵּים הִשָּׁמֶר בְּנֶגַע הַצָּרַעַת לִשְׁמוֹר מְאֹד וְלַעֲשׂוֹת וְגוֹ׳. אַף בְּמִילָה. מָה אֲנִי מְקַיֵּים יִמּוֹל בְּשַׂר עָרְלָתוֹ. בִּזְמַן שֶׁאֵין שָׁם בַּהֶרֶת. תַּלְמוּד לוֹמַר. בָּשָׂר. אַף עַל פִּי שֶׁיֵּשׁ שָׁם בַּהֶרֶת. עַל דַּעְתֵּיהּ דְּרִבִּי יוֹנָה דְּאָמַר. מִצְוַת עֲשֵׂה דּוֹחָה אֶת מִצְוַת לֹא תַעֲשֶׂה אַף עַל פִּי שֶׁאֵינָהּ כְּתוּבָה בְּצִידָהּ. נִיחָא. עַל דַּעְתֵּיהּ דְּרִבִּי יוֹסֵי דְּאָמַר.

אֵין מִצְוַת עֲשֵׂה דּוֹחָה אֶת מִצְוַת לֹא תַעֲשֶׂה אֶלָּא אִם כֵּן הָיְתָה כְתוּבָה בְּצִידָּהּ. מִכֵּיוָן דִּכְתִיב בְּשַׂר עָרְלָתוֹ כְּמִי שֶׁהִיא כְתוּבָה בְּצִידָּהּ.

[182]"The flesh of his prepuce should be circumcized.[183]" Even if it has white skin disease[184]. How can I confirm: "Beware of skin disease to watch it carefully and to do . . .[185]"? Also at a circumcision. Then how can I confirm: "The flesh of his prepuce should be circumcized"? If there is no white skin disease? The verse says, "the flesh[186]", even if it has white skin disease.

[187]This is simple in the opinion of Rebbi Jonah, who says that a positive commandment supersedes a prohibition even if they are not written together. But in the opinion of Rebbi Yose, who says that a positive commandment supersedes a prohibition only if they are written together? Since it is written "the flesh of his prepuce," it is as if it were written together[188].

---

182 This paragraph is in *Sifra Tazria' Pereq* 1(4), Babli *Šabbat* 132b.

183 *Lev.* 12:3.

184 *Lev.* 13:2-28.

185 *Deut.* 24:8. The injunction to follow all instructions of the priests in matters of impure skin disease is interpreted to mean that it is forbidden to cut out the diseased part of the skin. Then if a baby is born with diseased prepuce, how could it be circumcised?

186 Since the intent is to cut the flesh, cutting the skin is only incidental and is not in the mind of the person who does the circumcision.

187 The disagreement between rabbis Jonah and Yose is discussed in *Ḥallah* 2:1, Notes 9,10.

188 The prohibition is irrelevant, cf. Note 186.

אין בין המודר פרק רביעי

(fol. 38b) **משנה א**: אֵין בֵּין הַמּוּדָּר הֲנָיָה מֵחֲבֵירוֹ לַמּוּדָּר הֵימֶנּוּ מַאֲכָל אֶלָּא דְּרִיסַת הָרֶגֶל וְכֵלִים שֶׁאֵין עוֹשִׂין בָּהֶן אוֹכֶל נֶפֶשׁ. הַמּוּדָּר הֲנָיַת מַאֲכָל מֵחֲבֵירוֹ לֹא יַשְׁאִילֶנּוּ נָפָה וּכְבָרָה וְרֵחַיִם וְתַנּוּר. אֲבָל מַשְׁאִיל לוֹ חָלוּק וְטַלִּית נְזָמִים וְטַבָּעוֹת וְכָל־דָּבָר שֶׁאֵין עוֹשִׂין בּוֹ אוֹכֶל נֶפֶשׁ. מָקוֹם שֶׁמַּשְׂכִּירִין כַּיּוֹצֵא בָהֶן אָסוּר.

Mishnah 1: The only difference between one who is under a vow [not to have] usufruct from another[1] and one who is under a vow about use of food is passing through his real estate[2] and vessels that cannot be used to prepare food. One who is under a vow about use[3] of food should not borrow from him a fine or coarse sieve, a grindstone, or an oven. But he may borrow from him a robe or a stole, nose rings and finger rings, and anything that is not used to prepare food. At a place where one rents out any of these it is forbidden[4].

1 B made a vow that A may have no usufruct from him.. If A makes a vow that B shall have no usufruct from him, the expression is in the active mode, הַמּוֹדֵר בְּ.

2 Setting his foot on the other's property.

3 The word הניית is not in the Babli and most independent Mishnah mss. From the Halakhah it will be seen that it was not in the original version of the Mishnah.

4 Since he could buy food for the money saved by not renting; this is counted as usufruct used for food.

(**הלכה א:** אֵין בֵּין הַמּוּדָּר הֲנָיָיה מֵחֲבֵירוֹ כול'. הָא דָּבָר שֶׁעוֹשִׂין (38c, line 11
בּוֹ אוֹכֶל נֶפֶשׁ אָסוּר. וְלֹא מִמַּאֲכָל נָדַר. אָמַר רִבִּי שִׁמְעוֹן בֶּן לָקִישׁ. כֵּינִי
מַתְנִיתָא. אֵין בֵּין מוּדָּר הֲנָיָיה מֵחֲבֵירוֹ לַמּוּדָר הֲנָיַת מַאֲכָל מֵחֲבֵירוֹ. תַּנֵּי
דְּבֵית רִבִּי כֵן. הַמּוּדָּר הֲנָיַת מַאֲכָל מֵחֲבֵירוֹ לֹא יַשְׁאִילֶנּוּ נָפָה וּכְבָרָה רֵיחַיִם
וְתַנּוּר. תַּנֵּי. אֲבָל מַשְׁאִילוֹ כּוֹסוֹת וּקְעָרוֹת וְתַמְחוּיִין. שֶׁאֵינָן מֵהַנִּין אֶת הָאוֹכֵל
אֲבָל מַכְנִיסִין אֶת הָאוֹכֶל. לָפָסִים וּקְדֵירוֹת אָסוּר. לִטְחוֹן וְלִדְרוֹךְ אָסוּר.
לִקְצוֹר צְרִיכָה וְלִבְצוֹר צְרִיכָה. הֲנָיַית⁵ מָהוּ. תַּנֵּי אֲבָל מַשְׁאִילוּ קוֹרְדּוֹם. הֲוֵינָן
סָבְרִין מֵימַר. בְּקוֹרְדּוֹם שֶׁלַּבַּקָּעִי. תִּיפְתָּר בְּקוֹרְדּוֹם שֶׁלַּמַּכּוֹשׁ. וְלֵית שְׁמַע מִינָּהּ
כְּלוּם. רִבִּי אֲבוּנָא אָמַר. רִבִּי יִרְמְיָה בָּעֵי אָהֶן יוסטא⁶ מִכֵּיוָן דִּי מְרָחֵק וַחֲשַׁר
בָּהּ קִמְחָא אֲסִיר מִישְׁאַל לֵיהּ.

[7]"The only difference between one who is under a vow [not to have] usufruct from another," etc. This means that vessels used to prepare food are forbidden. But did he not make the vow about food? Rebbi Simeon ben Laqish, so is the Mishnah: The only difference between one who is under a vow [not to have] usufruct from another and one who is under a vow about use for food. In the House of Rebbi it was stated thus: "One who is under a vow about use[3] of food should not borrow from him a fine or coarse sieve, a grindstone, or an oven[8]." It was stated: But he may borrow from him cups and bowls and fruit bowls, since these are not used to prepare food, only to serve food. Pans[9] and pots are forbidden. To mill and to press is forbidden[10]. Cutting is a problem, harvesting[11] is a problem. What kind of usufruct? It was stated: But he may borrow a spade from him. We wanted to say, a spade of a digger. Explain it by a spade for weeding, and you cannot infer anything. Rebbi Abuna said, that *yst'*[12], since one removes and separates the bran from flour with it, it is forbidden to borrow from him.

5   In the parallel in *Megillah*, הֲנָיַיה מַאֲכָל "use of food".

.6 In the parallel in *Megillah*, זוטטא.

7   The entire paragraph is in *Megillah* 1:9, 71a l. 73.

8   This is the language of the Yerushalmi Mishnah. This and the explanation of R. Simeon ben Laqish shows that the Mishnah text was that of the Babli and most independent Mishnah mss: הַמּוֹדָר מַאֲכָל מֵחֲבֵירוֹ and that the Yerushalmi text is the corrected one. Question and answer are also in the Babli, 33a.

9   Greek; cf. *Peah* 7:4, Note 69.

10 Milling grain and pressing grapes.

11 Cutting grains and harvesting grapes.

12 In *Megillah* זוּסְטָא. Mussaphia sees Greek ζωστήρ -ῆρος, ὁ "belt" in the *Megillah* form; but is is difficult to separate coarse from fine flour by using a belt. {Cf. Latin *haustrum* (also *austrum*) from *haurire* "to draw (water), to pluck, take, etc.," and gloss *hauritorium* (Greek ἀντλητήριος, adj., "for drawing up"), "a bucket" (Lewis and Short) (E. G.).}

(38c, line 11) רִבִּי בָּא בְשֵׁם רִבִּי זְעִירָא. שֶׁהוּא כְנוֹתֵן לוֹ מָעוֹת לִיקַח בָּהֶן כִּכָּר. רִבִּי בּוּן בַּר חִייָה בָּעֵי. מֵעַתָּה אָסוּר לְהַשְׁאִיל לוֹ מָעוֹת. שֶׁהוּא כְנוֹתֵן לוֹ מָעוֹת לִיקַח בּוֹ כִּכָּר. רִבִּי אֲבִינָא אָמַר. רִבִּי יִרְמְיָה בָּעֵי. אִילֵּין קוֹזְמִידַיָּיה דְּאִית עֲלֵיהוֹן אָסִיר מִישְׁאַל לוֹן.

Rebbi Abba in the name of Rebbi Ze'ira: Because it is as if he gave him money to buy a loaf with[4]. Rebbi Abun bar Ḥiyya asked: Then is it forbidden to borrow money from him, for it is as if he gave him money to buy a loaf with? Rebbi Abina said, Rebbi Ze'ira asked: That jewellery[13] on them, is it forbidden to lend to them?

13 J. Levy in his Dictionary refers to κοσμίδιον (κόσμιον) "jewellery" in Du Cange's Greek glossary. S. Lieberman (הירושלמי כפשוטו[2], New York-Jerusalem 1995, p. ח) thinks that this refers to professional dancers at weddings.

(fol. 38b) **משנה ב:** הַמּוּדָּר הֲנָיָיה מֵחֲבֵירוֹ שׁוֹקֵל לוֹ אֶת שִׁקְלוֹ וּפוֹרֵעַ לוֹ אֶת חוֹבוֹ וּמַחֲזִיר לוֹ אֲבֵידָתוֹ. מְקוֹם שֶׁנּוֹטְלִין עָלֶיהָ שָׂכָר תִּיפּוֹל הֲנָיָיה לְהֶקְדֵּשׁ.

Mishnah 2: If one is under a vow [not to have] usufruct from another, [the other] may give his *šeqel*[14], pay his debt[15] and return what he has lost[16]. At a place where one takes a fee for this, the gain should be given to the sacred fund[17].

14   If A has vowed that B should have nothing from him, A may pay B's Temple tax of half a *šeqel* due every year. Since the money is paid to the Temple, B does not receive anything.

15   As long as the debt is not due, A simply restrains the creditor from asking money from B.

16   Since he returns B's own property, B receives nothing from A.

17   The Temple, or in its absence the communal welfare fund.

(38c, line 24) **הלכה ב:** הַמּוּדָּר הֲנָיָיה מֵחֲבֵירוֹ כול'. רִבִּי בָּא בַּר מָמָל בָּעֵי. הַפּוֹרֵעַ שְׁטַר חוֹבוֹ שֶׁלַּחֲבֵירוֹ שֶׁלֹּא מִדַּעְתּוֹ. תַּפְלוּגְתָּא דְחָנָן וּבְנֵי כֹהֲנִים גְּדוֹלִים. אָמַר רִבִּי יוֹסֵי. טַעֲמָא דִּבְנֵי כֹהֲנִים גְּדוֹלִים. תַּמָּן לֹא עָלַת עַל דַּעְתָּן שֶׁתָּמוּת אִשְׁתּוֹ[18] בְּרָעָב. בְּרַם הָכָא מְפַייֵס הֲוֵינָא לֵיהּ וְהוּא מוֹחֵל לִי. הַגַּע עַצְמָךְ דַּהֲוָה נְבֵיהּ מַשְׁכּוֹן. מְפַייֵס הֲוֵינָא לֵיהּ וְהוּא יָהֵב לִי מַשְׁכּוֹנִי. עַד כְּדוֹן בְּבַעַל חוֹב שֶׁאֵינוֹ דוֹחֵק. וַאֲפִילּוּ בְּבַעַל חוֹב שֶׁדּוֹחֵק. נִשְׁמְעִינָהּ מִן הָדָא. [וְשׁוֹקֵל אֶת שִׁקְלוֹ. וְלֹא שֶׁקַל אֵין מְמַשְׁכְּנִין אוֹתוֹ.][19] תֵּדַע לָךְ שֶׁהוּא כֵן. דְּתַנִּינָן. וּמַקְרִיב עָלָיו קִינֵּי זָבִין קִינֵּי זָבוֹת קִינֵּי יוֹלְדוֹת חַטָּאוֹת וַאֲשָׁמוֹת. בְּשֶׁלֹּא נִכְנַס לְתוֹךְ יָדָיו כְּלוּם. וְכָא בְּשֶׁלֹּא יַכְנֵס לְתוֹךְ יָדָיו כְּלוּם.

Halakhah 2: "If one is under a vow [not to have] usufruct from another," etc. [20]Rebbi Abba bar Mamal asked: If somebody pays off somebody else's debt without the latter's knowledge, is that the disagreement of Ḥanan and the High Priests' sons[21]? Rebbi Yose said, there the reason of the High Priest's sons is that nobody expects his wife to die from hunger. But here, [the debtor could say:] "I could negotiate with him and he would forgive some." Think of it, if [the loan] was on a pledge! "I could negotiate with him and he would return my pledge." So far about a creditor who does not push [for repayment]. Even for a creditor who pushes, we can hear from the following: "He may give his *šeqel*[14]. If somebody does not pay his *šeqel*, does one not take a pledge from him? This says, even for a creditor who pushes. You should know that this is so, as we have stated[22]: "He can bring for him nests for males or females suffering from genital discharges[23], nests for childbirth[24], purification and reparation offerings[25]" since nothing of these comes to [the other person's] hand. And here[26] also, that nothing should come into his hand.

18 Text from the parallel in *Ketubot*. Here: שְׁיָמוּת עַבְדּוֹ "that his slave should die", which has no connection to the text referred to.

19 Text from the parallel in *Ketubot*, missing here.

20 The entire Halakhah is found also in *Ketubot* 13:2 (35d line 30 ff.)

21 *Ketubot* Mishnah 13:2: "If somebody went overseas and another person paid for the upkeep of his wife (without a court order or a contract with the wife), Hanan said, that person lost his money. The High Priest's sons disagreed with him and said, he shall swear how much he spent and collect it."

22 Mishnah 3, a continuation of Mishnah 2 about the person to whom usufruct from another was forbidden.

23 "Nest" is the technical term for a couple of birds from the pigeon family, prescribed sacrifice for the person healed from genital discharge *before* he could enter the Temple. For a male, *Lev.* 15:14. For a female, *Lev.* 15:29.

24 Due before the mother could enter the Temple, *Lev.* 12:8, for the wife of a man who could not afford a sheep, *Lev.* 12:6.

25 *Lev.* 4:27-5:26. These sacrifices are in part burned on the altar, in part eaten by the priests; nothing is given to

the offerer and his family, in contrast to well-being offerings.

26 In the case of a debt paid by the third party, the deal has to be structured so that nothing ever comes into the possession of the debtor.

(38c, line 33) רִבִּי יְהוֹשֻׁעַ בֶּן לֵוִי אוֹמֵר. אֵין לָךְ נִתְפַּס עַל חֲבֵירוֹ וְחַיָּיב לִיתֵּן לוֹ אֶלָּא בְּאַרְנוֹן וּבְגוּלְגּוֹלֶת. רַב אָמַר. כָּל־הַנִּתְפַּשׂ עַל חֲבֵירוֹ חַיָּיב לוֹ. חֵיילֵיהּ דְּרַב מִן הָדָא. הַגּוֹזֵל שָׂדֶה וּנְטָלוּהָ מְסִיקִין. לֹא שָׁמַע דְּאָמַר רִבִּי יוֹחָנָן. קְנָס קָנְסוּ בְּגַזְלָן. רִבִּי אָבִין בָּעֵי דַהֲוָה רַבֵּיהּ²⁷ רִבִּי יוֹסֵי בֵּירִבִּי בּוּן וְרִבִּי חִייָה בַּר לוּלְיָינִי תְּרֵיהוֹן בְּשֵׁם רִבִּי שְׁמוּאֵל. חַד אָמַר. בְּאַרְנוֹן וּבְגוּלְגּוֹלֶת. [וְחָרָנָה אָמַר. אֵינָהּ כְּאַרְנוֹן וּכְגוּלְגּוֹלֶת.]²⁸

Rebbi Joshua ben Levi says, nobody is held responsible for his neighbor except for *annona*²⁹ and head-tax. Rav said, anything for which one is held responsible for one's neighbor has to be repaid. The strength of Rav is from the following³⁰: "He who appropriated a field and oppressors took it." He did not hear that Rebbi Johanan said³¹, they exacted a fine from a robber. Rebbi Abin³² asked, (who was the father of) Rebbi Yose ben Rebbi Abun, and Rebbi Hiyya ben Julianus both said in the name of Samuel; one said, it is like *annona* and head-tax³³; the other one said, it is not like *annona* and head-tax.

27 Text in *Šebuot* וְהֵן דַּהֲוָה רַבָּהּ "which one is better?"

28 Text from *Šebuot*. Missing in the text here.

29 The requisition for the Roman army, the amounts being determined in advance every year. It seems from this statement that both *annona* and the head-tax were imposed as communal obligations. Cf. *Demay* 2, Note 12.

30 Mishnah *Baba Qama* 10:6: "He who appropriated a field and oppressors took it, if the entire country is hit, he may say to him: Here is yours before you. But if it was because of the robber, he is obligated to give him another field. If a river washed it away, he may say to him: Here is yours

before you."

Somebody took real estate from another by threats and/or force. In general, we say that "real estate cannot be stolen" since the original owner can prove his claim in court once anarchy has been suppressed. But here we deal with the case that something happened before the original owner could sue the robber and the field is no longer available. If the field was taken by an "oppressor", a Roman official against whom there is no recourse in the courts then, if everybody's field was taken, the original owner has no claim since the field would have been taken even if it had not been stolen. But if the field was taken because the robber had a run-in with the law, the robber must pay for a replacement even though legally the field was still the original owner's property when it was taken.

The Yerushalmi (*Neziqin*, 7c, line 20) notes that even if the oppressors took the field from the robber because of the robbed, the robbed could claim replacement from the robber since he might say: Give me what is mine and let any other person deal with me. On this, R. Joshua ben Levi and Rav disagree there as they disagree here.

31   *Baba Qama* 10:6. In the Babli, *Baba Qama* 116b/117a, it remains a question whether the rule represents a fine or a generally valid legal principle.

32   R. Abin II.

33   If a Roman official took the field illegally it nevertheless has the status of *annona* or head-tax. This supports R. Johanan that the rule represents a fine. The opposite opinion supports Rav against R. Johanan.

(38c, line 33) תַּמָּן תַּנִּינָן. מְרַפְּאֵהוּ רְפוּאַת נֶפֶשׁ אֲבָל לֹא רְפוּאַת מָמוֹן. רִבִּי יוּדָה וְרִבִּי יוֹסֵי. חַד אָמַר. כָּאן בִּמְדִירָה מְגוּפוֹ וְכָאן בִּמְדִירָה מִנְּכָסָיו. וְחָרָנָה אָמַר. כָּאן בְּשֶׁיֵּשׁ לוֹ מִי שֶׁיְּרַפְּאֶנּוּ וְכָאן בְּשֶׁאֵין לוֹ מִי שֶׁיְּרַפְּאֶנּוּ. אִם בְּשֶׁיֵּשׁ לוֹ מִי שֶׁיְּרַפְּאֶנּוּ אֲפִילוּ רְפוּאַת נֶפֶשׁ לֹא יְרַפְּאֶנּוּ. לֹא מִכָּל־אָדָם זוֹכֶה לְהִתְרַפּוֹת.

There, we have stated[34]: "He heals him in the sense of personal healing but not in the sense of financial healing." Rebbi Judan and Rebbi Yose. One of them said, here if the vow refers to his body, there if the vow refers to his property[35]. But the other one said, here if he has somebody else who can heal him, there if there is nobody else who can heal him. If he has somebody else who can heal him, he should not be able to heal him personally! Not by everybody is a person successfully healed[36].

34 Mishnah 4. Personal healing is healing a human, which is a biblical commandment (*Deut.* 22:2) and cannot be abolished by a vow. Financial healing is veterinary medicine. The question is, if he is required to return what the other one had lost as required in Mishnah 2, why can he not heal his cow which is lost without medical help?

35 Mishnah 2 refers to a vow that B cannot personally have any gain from A; therefore A may return what B lost. Mishnah 3 deals with the case that B cannot have any material advantage from A; therefore A cannot heal B's animal.

36 The personal skills of a medical man are not transferable.

(38c, line 42) וְלֹא נִיכְסֵי הַמַּחֲזִיר הֵן שֶׁהֵן אֲסוּרִין לְבַעַל הַפָּרָה. עוּלָּא בַּר יִשְׁמָעֵאל בְּשֵׁם רִבִּי יִצְחָק. כְּשֶׁהָיוּ נִיכְסֵי זֶה אֲסוּרִין עַל זֶה וְנִיכְסֵי זֶה אֲסוּרִין עַל זֶה.

Is not the property of the finder forbidden to the owner of the cow[37]? Ulla bar Ismael in the name of Rebbi Isaac: If each man's property was forbidden to the other.

37 If A's property was forbidden to B and A returned a stray cow to B, why should the finder's fee go to charity and not to A? It must be that B's property was forbidden to A.

(38c, line 44) מָאן תַּנָּא תִּפּוֹל הֲנָייָה לְהֶקְדֵּשׁ. רִבִּי מֵאִיר. דְּרִבִּי מֵאִיר אוֹמֵר. מוֹעֲלִין בְּאִיסָּרוֹת. רִבִּי בּוּן בַּר חִייָה בָּעֵי. נָדַר מִן כִּיכָּר מָהוּ לְחַמֵּם בּוֹ אֶת יָדָיו. נִישְׁמְעִינָהּ מִן הָדָא. אָמַר. כִּכָּר זֶה הֶקְדֵּשׁ. אֲכָלוֹ בֵּין הוּא בֵּין אַחֵר מָעַל. לְפִיכָךְ יֵשׁ לוֹ פִדְיוֹן. אִם אָמַר. הֲרֵי הוּא עָלַי. אֲכָלוֹ מָעַל בּוֹ בְּטוֹבַת הֲנָייָה.

דִּבְרֵי רבִּי מֵאִיר. אֲחֵרִים לֹא מָעֲלוּ. לְפִיכָךְ אֵין לוֹ פִּדְיוֹן. לֹא אָמַר אֶלָּא אֲכָלוֹ. הָא לְחַמֵּם בּוֹ אֶת יָדָיו מוּתָּר. תַּלְמִידוֹהִי דְּרִבִּי יוֹנָה בְּשֵׁם רִבִּי בּוּן בַּר חִייָה. כֵּינִי בָּאוֹמֵר. לֹא אוֹכְלֶינָּהּ וְלֹא אַטְעַמֶנָּהּ. לֹא אָסְרוֹ עָלָיו אֶלָּא לַאֲכִילָה. עַד כְּדוֹן צְרִיכָה נָדַר מִן כִּיכָּר מָהוּ לְחַמֵּם בּוֹ אֶת יָדָיו.

Who is the Tanna of "the gain should be given to the sacred fund"? Rebbi Meïr! For Rebbi Meïr said, one commits sacrilege with prohibitions[38]. Rebbi Abun bar Ḥiyya asked: If somebody made a vow [to forbid] a loaf to himself, can he use it to warm his hands[39]? Let us hear from the following[40]: "If he said, this loaf shall be dedicated, if he or another person ate it, they committed sacrilege[41]; therefore, it can be redeemed. But if he said, it is for me [as if dedicated], if he ate it he committed sacrilege on goodwill[42] but others would not commit sacrilege." He said only, if he ate it. Therefore, to warm his hands is permitted[43]. The students of Rebbi Jonah in the name of Rebbi Abun bar Ḥiyya: That is if he said I shall not eat it nor taste it; if he forbade only eating to himself. But the question was, if somebody made a vow [to forbid] a loaf to himself, can he use it to warm his hands[44]?

38 If somebody forbids something for himself by the language of *qorbān* or any of its equivalents, the rules of sacrifices apply and any unauthorized use is sacrilege subject to the penalties described in *Lev.* 5:14-16: A sacrifice in the value of one Temple *šeqel* and restitution of 125% of the value taken.

39 If the loaf is fresh from the oven.

40 Tosephta 2:9, Babli 35a, *Šebuot* 22a/23b, in the name of R. Meïr. In all Babli sources, R. Simeon dissents.

41 It follows all the rules of a sacrifice since it is called *qorbān*. But since a loaf of bread cannot be a sacrifice, it can be redeemed (*Lev.* 27:11-14.)

42 Since he cannot eat the loaf or use it commercially, the only use open to him is to donate the loaf to somebody. The monetary value of the

goodwill acquired in this act is the basis for computing the restitution (Note 38).

43   Even for R. Meïr.

44   For an unspecified vow and use which cannot be quantified in monetary terms. The question remains open.

(fol. 38b) **משנה ג:** וְתוֹרֵם אֶת תְּרוּמָתוֹ וּמַעְשְׂרוֹתָיו לְדַעְתּוֹ. וּמַקְרִיב עָלָיו קִינֵּי זָבִין קִינֵּי זָבוֹת קִינֵּי יוֹלְדוֹת חַטָּאוֹת וַאֲשָׁמוֹת וּמְלַמְּדוֹ מִדְרָשׁ הֲלָכוֹת וְאַגָּדוֹת וְלֹא יְלַמְּדֶנּוּ מִקְרָא אֲבָל מְלַמֵּד הוּא אֶת בָּנָיו וְאֶת בְּנוֹתָיו מִקְרָא. וְזָן אֶת אִשְׁתּוֹ וְאֶת בָּנָיו אַף עַל פִּי שֶׁהוּא חַיָּיב בִּמְזוֹנוֹתָן. וְלֹא יָזוּן אֶת בְּהֶמְתּוֹ בֵּין טְמֵיאָה וּבֵין טְהוֹרָה. רִבִּי אֱלִיעֶזֶר אוֹמֵר זָן אֶת הַטְּמֵיאָה וְאֵינוֹ זָן אֶת הַטְּהוֹרָה. אָמְרוּ לוֹ מַה בֵּין טְמֵיאָה לַטְּהוֹרָה. אָמַר לָהֶן שֶׁהַטְּהוֹרָה נַפְשָׁהּ לַשָּׁמַיִם וְגוּפָהּ שֶׁלּוֹ וְהַטְּמֵיאָה נַפְשָׁהּ וְגוּפָהּ לַשָּׁמַיִם. אָמְרוּ לוֹ אַף הַטְּמֵיאָה נַפְשָׁהּ לַשָּׁמַיִם וְגוּפָהּ שֶׁלּוֹ שֶׁאִם יִרְצֶה הֲרֵי מוֹכְרָהּ לַגּוֹיִם אוֹ מַאֲכִילָהּ לַכְּלָבִים.

Mishnah 3: Also he[45] can separate his heave and tithes with the other's knowledge, and can bring for him nests for males or females suffering from genital discharges[23], nests for childbirth[24], purification and reparation offerings[25] and teach him interpretations[46], religious rules, and sermons[47]; but he may not teach him Bible; he may teach Bible to his sons and daughters[48]. Also, he can feed his wife and children[49] even though the other is obligated for their upkeep. But he cannot feed his animals[50], whether pure or impure; Rebbi Eliezer says, he may feed his impure[51] animals but not the pure ones. They asked him, what is the difference between pure and impure animals? He said to them, the pure animal's soul is Heaven's but its body is his[52], but the impure's soul and body is Heaven's. They said to him, also the impure animal's soul is Heaven's but its body is his, since he could sell it to Gentiles[53] or feed it to the dogs.

45 The person who made a vow that the other shall have no profit from him. Heave and tithes diminish the farmer's wealth; they do not increase it.

46 Rabbinic interpretations of biblical verses, of the kind preserved in the *Mekhiltot, Sifra,* and *Sifry.*

47 As the Halakhah explains, in imitation of Moses who taught the Children of Israel without taking money, one may not take money for teaching the Oral Law. (In rabbinic practice, one may take money for teaching during regular business hours to make up for the loss incurred by not being in business at that time.)

48 Since Moses wrote the Torah only at the end of his life, he never taught it. Therefore, one may take money to teach to read, sing, and understand the biblical text. This anonymous Mishnah proves that practice should not follow R. Eliezer in Mishnah *Soṭah* 3:4, Note 85.

49 If they are needy, since charity is a universal obligation.

50 Since this would increase the animal's worth; i. e., the other man's property.

51 Those which cannot be eaten.

52 As food.

53 Who may eat any kind of animal; Gen. 9:3.

(38c, line 53) **הלכה ג**: וְתוֹרֵם אֶת תְּרוּמָתוֹ כול׳. הַמְתַקֵּן פֵּירוֹתָיו שֶׁלַּחֲבֵירוֹ שֶׁלֹּא מִדַּעְתּוֹ טוֹבַת הֲנָיַית מַעְשְׂרוֹתָיו שֶׁל מִי. רְבִּי אַבָּהוּ אוֹמֵר. שֶׁלַּמְתַקְּן. רְבִּי זְעִירָא אָמַר שֶׁלַּבַּעַל הַפֵּירוֹת. רְבִּי זְעִירָא כְדַעְתֵּיהּ. דְּאָמַר רְבִּי זְעִירָא בְשֵׁם רְבִּי שִׁמְעוֹן בֶּן לָקִישׁ. הִפְרִישׁ קָרְבַּן נָזִיר וְקָרְבַּן מְצוֹרָע שֶׁל חֲבֵירוֹ הַמִּתְכַּפֵּר הוּא שֶׁעוֹשֶׂה (תְרוּמָה). מַתְנִיתָא פְלִיגָא עַל רְבִּי שִׁמְעוֹן בֶּן לָקִישׁ. וְתוֹרֵם תְּרוּמָתוֹ וּמַעְשְׂרוֹתָיו שֶׁלַּחֲבֵירוֹתָיו לְדַעְתּוֹ. פָּתַר לָהּ בְּשֶׁלֹּא יְהֵא לוֹ טוֹבַת הֲנָייָה בָּהֶן.

Halakhah 3: "Also he can separate his heave" etc. If somebody fixes the harvest of another person without the latter's knowledge, who receives the goodwill[54] from the tithes? Rebbi Abbahu says, the one who does the fixing[55]. Rebbi Ze'ira says, the owner of the produce. Rebbi Ze'ira is consistent since Rebbi Ze'ira said in the name of Rebbi Simeon ben Laqish[56], if somebody gave the sacrifice of a *nazir*[57] or of a [healed] person afflicted with skin disease[58], the person purged makes (heave)[59]. The Mishnah disagrees with Rebbi Simeon ben Laqish: "Also he can separate his heave and tithes with his knowledge.[60]" Explain it, that [it was stipulated] that the other should not get the goodwill[61].

54 That value is estimated by what a third party Israel would be willing to pay to the farmer to have the latter give his heave to his grandson, the son of his daughter and his Cohen son-in-law, or the tithes to a levitic grandson. "To fix" means to separate heave and tithes, to prepare the harvest for use and sale.

55 Since he uses his own produce to make the other person's produce permitted for profane use.

56 In the Babli, 36b (and also *Yoma* 50b, *Zebaḥim* 6a, *Temurah* 2b, 10b), a statement of R. Abbahu in the name of R. Joḥanan states that the person purged only can make the exchange but the goodwill belongs to the person who gives the produce. The Babli also quotes R. Ze'ira in the same sense as the Yerushalmi but clearly prefers R. Abbahu over R. Ze'ira against the Yerushalmi.

57 *Num.* 6:14-15.

58 *Lev.* 14:10.

59 This word, found in the ms. and the *editio princeps*, makes no sense since the sacrifices are given to the Cohen who alone directs the purging ceremony. With all commentaries one has to read תְמוּרָה "substitution" instead of תְרוּמָה "heave", a simple metathesis. It is asserted that if somebody dedicates an animal as somebody else's obligatory sacrifice, then only the person for whom the sacrifice is destined may substitute another animal (which action is sinful, *Lev.* 27:9-10). If the donor would substitute another animal after dedication, the action would be invalid and the substitute profane as before. In analogy, R. Simeon ben Laqish must hold that sanctified food can be disposed of only by the person whose obligation is satisfied by the sanctification.

60 In that case, A would make a donation of the value of the goodwill to B while B is forbidden to receive any gain from A!

61 This stipulation overrides any general rule and makes the transaction legal.

HALAKHAH 3   531

(38c, line 59) כְּתִיב רְאֵה לִמַּדְתִּי אֶתְכֶם חֻקִּים וּמִשְׁפָּטִים. מָה אֲנִי בְחִנָּם אַף אַתֶּם בְּחִנָּם. יָכוֹל מִקְרָא וְתַרְגּוּם כֵּן. תַּלְמוּד לוֹמַר חֻקִּים וּמִשְׁפָּטִים. חֻקִּים וּמִשְׁפָּטִים אַתֶּם מְלַמְּדִים בְּחִנָּם. וְאִי אַתֶּם מְלַמְּדִין בְּחִנָּם מִקְרָא וְתַרְגּוּם. וְכֵן חָמֵיי מַתְנִיָּיתָא נָסְבִין אַגְרֵיהוֹן. אָמַר רבי יוּדָן בֵּירִבִּי יִשְׁמָעֵאל. שָׂכָר בְּטֵילָן הֵן נוֹטְלִין.

It is written[62]: "Behold, I taught you laws and rules." Just as I did it for free, so you have to do it for free. One could think the same is true for Bible and translations? The verse says laws and rules. You have to teach laws and rules[63] for free; you do not have to teach Bible and translations for free[64]. But do we not see that the *baraita* teachers take their fees? Rebbi Yudan, the son of Rebbi Ismael, said: They take payment for lost time.

62   *Deut.* 4:5. The same argument in the Babli, 37a.
63   In their practical rabbinic form.
64   Elementary school teachers have to be paid well. The text is quoted by Ran, commentary to 37a.

(38c, line 63) אָמַר רבי זְעוּרָא. מִדִּבְרֵיהֶן זָן אֶת עֲבָדָיו וְאֵינוֹ זָן אֶת עַבְדּוֹ. הֲווֹן בָּעֵיי מֵימַר. מָאן דָּמַר. הַטְּהוֹרָה נַפְשָׁהּ לַשָּׁמַיִם וְגוּפָהּ שֶׁלּוֹ. וְזוֹ הוֹאִיל וְגוּפָהּ וְנַפְשָׁהּ לַשָּׁמַיִם זָן אֶת עַבְדּוֹ. מָאן דָּמַר. שֶׁאִם יִרְצֶה הֲרֵי מוֹכְרָהּ לַגּוֹיִם אוֹ מַאֲכִילָהּ לַכְּלָבִים. וְזוֹ הוֹאִיל וְגוּפָהּ שֶׁלּוֹ וְאֵינוֹ מוֹכְרָהּ לַגּוֹיִם וְאֵינָהּ מַאֲכִילָהּ לַכְּלָבִים זָן אֶת עַבְדּוֹ. אַשְׁכָּח תַּנֵּי. זָן אֶת עַבְדּוֹ.

Rebbi Ze'ira said, from their words [we can deduce] whether he[65] may feed his slaves or may not feed his[66] slave[67]. They wanted to say that he who says[68] "the pure animal's soul is Heaven's but its body is his," and this one, because her[67] body and soul is Heaven's, he[65] may feed his[66] slave. And he who says[69], since he could sell it to Gentiles or feed it to the dogs, since this one's body is his[66] but he cannot sell her to Gentiles[70] nor feed her to the dogs, he may feed his slave. It was found stated: He may feed his slave[71].

65 A, the maker of the vow.
66 B, the person forbidden profit from A.
67 The inconsistencies in number and gender are in the text.
68 R. Eliezer.
69 The Sages.
70 Since a circumcized slave cannot be sold to Gentiles and an uncircumcized slave cannot be kept in the household.
71 In the Babli, 38b, a named *baraita*. The reason is given that slaves are not bought for fattening.

(fol. 38b) **משנה ד:** הַמּוּדָּר הֲנָיָיה מֵחֲבֵירוֹ וְנִכְנָס לְבַקְּרוֹ עוֹמֵד אֲבָל לֹא יוֹשֵׁב. וּמְרַפְּאֵהוּ רְפוּאַת נֶפֶשׁ אֲבָל לֹא רְפוּאַת מָמוֹן. וְרוֹחֵץ עִמּוֹ בְּאַמְבָּטִי גְדוֹלָה אֲבָל לֹא בִקְטַנָּה. וְיָשֵׁן עִמּוֹ בַּמִּטָּה. רִבִּי יְהוּדָה אוֹמֵר בִּימוֹת הַחַמָּה אֲבָל לֹא בִימוֹת הַגְּשָׁמִים מִפְּנֵי שֶׁהוּא מְהַנֵּהוּ. וּמֵסִיב עִמּוֹ עַל הַמִּטָּה וְאוֹכֵל עִמּוֹ עַל הַשּׁוּלְחָן אֲבָל לֹא מִן הַתַּמְחוּי. אֲבָל אוֹכֵל הוּא עִמּוֹ מִן הַתַּמְחוּי הַחוֹזֵר.

Mishnah 4: If somebody is forbidden by a vow any profit from another person and that one comes to make a visit, he may stand but not sit down[72]. He heals him in the sense of personal healing but not in the sense of financial healing[34], and may bathe with him in a large pool but not in a small one[73], and he may sleep with him on the same couch. Rebbi Jehudah says, in summer but not in the rainy season because he would profit. He can lie with him [at a dinner] on the same couch and eat with him at one table but not from the same pot[74]. But he may eat with him from a returning pot[75].

72 If B is forbidden any profit from A it is obvious that B cannot sit on any of A's chairs. But here it is stated that A cannot sit in B's chair even if he makes a medical visit.

73 If the pool is so small that one additional person visibly raises the water level, this would be a profit and is forbidden. (In modern Hebrew, the word means "bathtub". The root بط means "hollow").

74 One is afraid that he purposely would take less food so the other man would have more.

75 As explained in the Halakhah, a pot so full that in any case it will not be emptied by the guests.

(38c, line 68) **הלכה ד**: הַמּוּדָּר הֲנָיָיה מֵחֲבִירוֹ כּוֹל׳. רִבִּי שִׁמְעוֹן בֶּן יָקִים אָמַר. שֶׁלֹּא יִשְׁהֶה.

Halakhah 4: "If somebody is forbidden by a vow any profit from another person," etc. Rebbi Simeon ben Yaqim said, that he should not stay long[76].

76 There is no intrinsic reason why A cannot sit in B's chair (Note 72). The rule is simply a precaution that A should not come to violate his own vow. The same tradition is mentioned in the Babli, 39a, in the name of R. Simeon ben Elyaqim.

(38c, line 69) מַתְנִיתָא בְּשֶׁאָסַר הָרוֹפֵא נְכָסָיו עָלָיו. אֲבָל אִם אָסַר הַחוֹלֶה נְכָסָיו עָלָיו שֶׁלָּרוֹפֵא הוּא חָטָא עַל נַפְשֵׁיהּ.

The Mishnah [deals with the case] that the healer forbade his property on the sick person[77]. But if the sick person forbade his property on the healer he sinned against himself[78].

77 We did not say that the knowledge of the healer is his capital and he is forbidden to heal the sick.

78 The healer is forbidden to treat the sick person since the sick forbade to himself to pay the healer or to show any recognition for the services received.

(38c, line 71) אֲבָל לֹא בְּאַמְבָּטִי קְטַנָּה. דְּהוּא מְרַתְּחַ[79] לֵיהּ. תַּנֵּי רוֹחֵץ עִמּוֹ בְּמֶרְחָץ קְטַנָּה. דִּי נָסַב אִישָׁתָהּ.[80]

"But not in a small pool," for he heats it. It was stated: He bathes with him in a small bathhouse, for he takes away heat.

79 Reading of the corrector. Reading of the scribe and *editio princeps*: מַפְחָת "diminishes".

80 Reading of the corrector. Reading of the scribe and *editio princeps*: אֲשׁוּנָה "the glow". The vocalization of the text is from the ms. In the Tosephta (2:7): He sweats with him in a small sauna.

(38d, line 1) תַּנֵּי. מִן הַתַּמְחוּי הַחוֹזֵר. מַהוּ תַמְחוּי הַחוֹזֵר. תַּמָּן אָמְרִין. פִּיסְגָּתָא. רַבָּנִין דְּהָכָא אָמְרִין. תַּמְחוּי שֶׁיֵּשׁ בּוֹ לֶאֱכוֹל וְלִשְׂבּוֹעַ וּלְהוֹתִיר. תַּנֵּי. מִן הַכּוֹס הַחוֹזֵר. אֵי זֶהוּ כּוֹס הַחוֹזֵר. תַּמָּן אָמְרִין קוֹנְדִיטוֹן. רַבָּנִין דְּהָכָא אָמְרִין. מָלֵיי מִי סוּרס[81] וְקָרְחִין[82] וְשָׁתְיָן וּמַחֲזִירִין.

It was stated: From the returning pot. What is a returning pot? There, they say, portions[83]. The rabbis here say, a pot which contains [enough food] to eat, to be full, and to leave leftovers. It was stated: From the returning cup. What is a returning cup? The rabbis there say, spiced wine[84]. The rabbis here say, one fills a מיסורס, they draw, drink, and return[85].

81 Rashba (*Novellae ad* 41b) reads מי סויכוס, Ravad (Note to Maimonides, *Hilkhot Nedarim* 6:9) reads מיכירוס. There is no traditional explanation for the words. Lieberman (*Tosephta kiFshutah Šabbat* p. 284) reads one word: *missorium*. {Perhaps *mistarius*, -*ii, m.*, from *misceo* "to mix", "vessel in which wine was mixed with water" (E. G.).}

82 Rashba (cf. Note 81) and Ravad (cf. Note 81) read קָדְחִין "one draws". This has been taken as basis for the translation.

83 The pot contains equal portions for everybody; there is no possibility

that one guest would take less so the other could have more. In the Babli, 41b, the explanation of the rabbis "here" (in Galilee) is accepted.

84 Latin *conditum vinum* (cf. *Berakhot* 6:5, Note 157). This is drunk only in small portions.

85 The vessel is newly filled for each guest; there is no fear of interference.

(fol. 38b) **משנה ה:** לֹא יֹאכַל עִמּוֹ מִן הָאֵבוּס שֶׁלִּפְנֵי הַפּוֹעֲלִים וְלֹא יַעֲשֶׂה עִמּוֹ בְּאוֹמֶן דִּבְרֵי רִבִּי מֵאִיר. וַחֲכָמִים אוֹמְרִים עוֹשֶׂה הוּא בְּרָחוֹק מִמֶּנּוּ.

Mishnah 5: He should not eat with him from the common pot set before the workers[86] nor work with him in a profession[87], the words of Rebbi Meïr. But the Sages say, he can work at a distance from him.

86 It belongs to the standard contract of day laborers that the employer has to feed them. This he usually does by preparing a pot from which everybody takes (literally "a trough"). This is then the same as a non-returning *tamḥui*.

87 This is the interpretation of the Yarushalmi. The Babli, 41b, takes אומן to be a synonym of ניר "a furrow" and holds that both cannot work on the same field at the same time.

(38d, line 5) **הלכה ה:** לֹא יֹאכַל כו'. עַל דַּעְתֵּיהּ דְּרִבִּי מֵאִיר אָסוּר לְלַמְּדוֹ אוּמָנוּת. עַל דַּעְתֵּיהּ דְּרִבִּי מֵאִיר אָסוּר לְלַמֵּד עָלָיו זְכוּת.

Halakhah 5: "He should not eat," etc. In the opinion of Rebbi Meïr he is forbidden to teach him a trade. In the opinion of Rebbi Meïr he is forbidden to act in his defense.

משנה ו: (fol. 38b) הַמּוּדָּר הֲנָיָה מֵחֲבֵירוֹ לִפְנֵי שְׁבִיעִית לֹא יוֹרֵד לְתוֹךְ שָׂדֵהוּ וְאֵינוֹ אוֹכֵל מִן הַנּוֹטוֹת. וּבַשְּׁבִיעִית לֹא יוֹרֵד לְתוֹךְ שָׂדֵהוּ אֲבָל אוֹכֵל הוּא מִן הַנּוֹטוֹת. נָדַר הֵימֶינּוּ מַאֲכָל לִפְנֵי שְׁבִיעִית יוֹרֵד בְּתוֹךְ שָׂדֵהוּ וְאֵינוֹ אוֹכֵל מִן הַפֵּירוֹת. וּבַשְּׁבִיעִית יוֹרֵד וְאוֹכֵל.

Mishnah 6: If somebody is forbidden any profit from another person by a vow made before the Sabbatical year, he cannot enter that person's field nor can he eat from the overhang[88]. In the Sabbatical year, he cannot enter his field[89] but he can eat from the overhang. If he vowed not to eat from the other before the Sabbatical year, he can enter[90] his field but he cannot eat of its fruits. During the Sabbatical year he enters and eats.

88   Fruits of trees that hang over a public road, which do not belong to the tree's owner but are ownerless.

89   As the Halakhah points out, if by biblical decree everybody is permitted to eat from the yield of the Sabbatical, it must be permitted to enter all agricultural property for the purpose of harvesting. But in our case, if the maker of the vow would stay one moment too long, he would be sinning.

90   Since he did not forbid that for himself.

הלכה ו: (38d, line 7) הַמּוּדָּר הֲנָיָה מֵחֲבֵירוֹ לִפְנֵי שְׁבִיעִית כול׳. וְיֵרֵד. כִּדְאָמַר רִבִּי שִׁמְעוֹן בֶּן יָקִים. שֶׁלֹּא יִשְׁהֶה.

Halakhah 6: "If somebody is forbidden any profit from another person by a vow made before the Sabbatical year," etc. Why can he not enter[89]? As Rebbi Simeon ben Yaqim said, that he should not stay long[91].

91   The same in the Babli, 42b.

(38d, line 8) רִבִּי יוֹחָנָן פָּתַר מַתְנִיתָא. הַמּוּדָּר הֲנָאָה⁹² מֵחֲבֵירוֹ לִפְנֵי שְׁבִיעִית אֵינוֹ יוֹרֵד לְתוֹךְ שָׂדֵהוּ וְאֵינוֹ אוֹכֵל מִן הַנּוֹטוֹת. וּבַשְּׁבִיעִית יוֹרֵד לְתוֹךְ שָׂדֵהוּ וְאוֹכֵל מִן הַפֵּירוֹת. וְאִם נָדַר בַּשְּׁבִיעִית יוֹרֵד וְאוֹכֵל. רִבִּי שִׁמְעוֹן בֶּן לָקִישׁ פָּתַר מַתְנִיתָא. הַמּוּדָּר הֲנָייָה מֵחֲבֵירוֹ לִפְנֵי שְׁבִיעִית לֹא יוֹרֵד לְתוֹךְ שָׂדֵהוּ וְאֵינוֹ אוֹכֵל מִן הַפֵּירוֹת. וְאִם נָדַר בַּשְּׁבִיעִית לֹא יוֹרֵד בְּתוֹךְ שָׂדֵהוּ אֲבָל אוֹכֵל מִן הַפֵּירוֹת. נָדַר מִמֶּנּוּ מַאֲכָל לִפְנֵי שְׁבִיעִית יוֹרֵד לְתוֹךְ שָׂדֵהוּ וְאֵינוֹ אוֹכֵל מִן הַפֵּירוֹת. וְאִם נָדַר בַּשְּׁבִיעִית יוֹרֵד וְאוֹכֵל. וַתְיָיא דְּרִבִּי שִׁמְעוֹן בֶּן לָקִישׁ כְּרִבִּי יוֹסֵי. דּוּ רִבִּי יוֹסֵי אוֹמֵר. מִפְּנֵי שֶׁקָּדַם נִדְרוֹ לְהֶפְקֵירוֹ.⁹² כֵּן רִבִּי שִׁמְעוֹן בֶּן לָקִישׁ אוֹמֵר. שֶׁקָּדַם נִדְרוֹ לְהֶבְקֵירוֹ הֶבְקֵירוֹ לְנִדְרוֹ. רִבִּי יוֹנָה רִבִּי בָּא בַּר חִייָה בְּשֵׁם רִבִּי יוֹחָנָן. מוֹדֶה רִבִּי יוֹסֵי בְּהֶבְקֵר תּוֹרָה שֶׁהוּא מוּתָּר.

Rebbi Johanan explained the Mishnah: If somebody is forbidden any profit from another person by a vow made before the Sabbatical year, he cannot enter that person's field nor can he eat from the overhang[93]. In the Sabbatical year, he can enter his field and eat of the fruits[94]. If he vowed during the Sabbatical year, he enters and eats[95]. Rebbi Simeon ben Laqish explains the Mishnah: If somebody is forbidden any profit from another person by a vow made before the Sabbatical year, he cannot enter that person's field nor can he eat of its fruits[96]. If he made the vow in the Sabbatical year, he cannot enter his field but he can eat of the fruits[94]. If he vowed not to eat from the other before the Sabbatical year, he can enter his field but he cannot eat of its fruits. If he made the vow during the Sabbatical year he enters and eats[95]. That statement of Rebbi Simeon ben Laqish follows Rebbi Yose, for Rebbi Yose said, for his vow preceded his abandoning, his abandoning his vow[97]. Rebbi Jonah, Rebbi Abba bar Hiyya, in the name of Rebbi Johanan: Rebbi Yose agrees that he is permitted in the case of biblical abandoning[98].

92   An intrusion of Babylonian spelling.

93   While the fruits overhanging the public domain are ownerless, the tree belongs to the person he forbade to himself.

94   The reading here is uncertain. The text given is that of the first hand of the ms. The corrected version reads וּבַשְּׁבִיעִית יוֹרֵד לְתוֹךְ שָׂדֵהוּ וְאֵינוּ אוֹכֵל מִן הַפֵּירוֹת "In the Sabbatical year, he can enter his field but *not* eat of the fruits." This makes no sense. It seems that the text should be corrected to וּבַשְּׁבִיעִית אֵינוּ יוֹרֵד לְתוֹךְ שָׂדֵהוּ וְאוֹכֵל מִן הַפֵּירוֹת "In the Sabbatical year, he can*not* enter his field but eat of the fruits" where the fruits are either the overhang or harvested by others on the field. This version is quoted in the Babli, 42a, as concurrent opinion of R. Joḥanan and R. Simeon ben Laqish. A similar statement in Tosephta 2:8.

95   This last clause of the Mishnah applies to both cases; there is no difference whether the vow refers to all property or only to food.

96   Including the overhang.

97   These two words are probably superfluous; they are missing in the parallel in Halakhah 10. It is stated in Mishnah 10 that if A and B walk together and B has no food, then A may put some food on a rock and declare it ownerless, whereupon B can take it. R. Yose objects since A's food remains forbidden to B if nobody else acquired it before it came to A. R. Yose [*Peah* 6:1 (fol. 19b), *Demay* 3:2 (fol. 23b), *Nedarim* 4:10] rejects the concept of ownerless property and holds that the owner has full responsibility for his abandoned property until it is taken up and acquired by another person.

98   Sabbatical produce is available for everybody by biblical decree, not by human action. Therefore, there is no comparison between Mishnaiot 6 and 10.

משנה ז: הַמּוּדָּר הֲנָיָיה מֵחֲבֵירוֹ לֹא יַשְׁאִילֶנּוּ וְלֹא יִשְׁאַל מִמֶּנּוּ לֹא יַלְוִינּוּ וְלֹא יִלְוֶה מִמֶּנּוּ וְלֹא יִמְכּוֹר לוֹ וְלֹא יִקַּח מִמֶּנּוּ. אָמַר לוֹ הַשְׁאִילֵנִי פָרָתָךְ (fol. 38b)

אָמַר לוֹ אֵינָהּ פְּנוּיָה. אָמַר קוֹנָם שֶׁאֲנִי חוֹרֵשׁ בָּהּ לְעוֹלָם אִם הָיָה דַרְכּוֹ לַחֲרוֹשׁ הוּא אָסוּר וְכָל־אָדָם מוּתָּרִין. אִם אֵין דַּרְכּוֹ לַחֲרוֹשׁ הוּא וְכָל־אָדָם אֲסוּרִין.

If somebody is forbidden any profit from another person by a vow, he should not borrow from him nor ask him for anything[99], should not give him a loan nor take a loan for him, should not sell to him nor buy from him. If he said, lend me your cow, he says: she is not available. If he said, a *qônam* that I shall never plough with her, if he usually ploughs, he is forbidden, the rest of the world is permitted[100]. If he does not usually plough, he and the rest of the world are forbidden.

99   Tools or animals.
100 His agricultural workers may still use that cow to plough his field.

(38d, line 19) **הלכה ז**: הַמּוּדָּר הֲנָיָיה מֵחֲבֵירוֹ לֹא יַשְׁאִילֶנּוּ כול'. בְּאוֹמֵר. קוֹנָם שָׂדִי שֶׁאֵינִי חוֹרֵשׁ לְעוֹלָם. כְּאוֹמֵר. קוֹנָם שָׂדִי נֶחֱרֶשֶׁת לְעוֹלָם.

Halakhah 7: "If somebody is forbidden any profit from another person by a vow, he should not lend him," etc. If somebody says, a *qônām* that I shall never plough, it is the same as if he said, a *qônām* that my field should never be ploughed[101].

100 Therefore, his vow also forbids his agricultural workers who were not mentioned in the text of the vow.

(fol. 38b) **משנה ח**: הַמּוּדָּר הֲנָיָיה מֵחֲבֵירוֹ וְאֵין לוֹ מַה יֹּאכַל הוֹלֵךְ אֵצֶל הַחֶנְוָונִי וְאוֹמֵר אִישׁ פְּלוֹנִי מוּדָּר מִמֶּנּוּ הֲנָיָיה וְאֵינִי יוֹדֵעַ מַה אֶעֱשֶׂה. וְהוּא נוֹתֵן לוֹ וּבָא וְנוֹטֵל מִמֶּנּוּ.

Mishnah 8: If somebody is forbidden any profit from another person by a vow and he has nothing to eat, the other person goes to the grocer and tells him, X is forbidden any profit from me by a vow and I do not know what to do[101]. Then he pays him and X comes and takes from him.

[101] The grocer understands that he has to acquire the money before he gives anything to X in order not to infringe on the vow.

(38d, line 21) **הלכה ח**: הַמּוּדָּר הֲנָיָיה מֵחֲבֵירוֹ וְאֵין לוֹ מַה יֹאכַל כול׳. שֶׁאֵינוֹ יָכוֹל לְהוֹצִיא מִמֶּנּוּ בַּדִּין.

Halakhah 8: "If somebody is forbidden any profit from another person by a vow and he has nothing to eat," etc. For he cannot recover from him in a court of law[102].

[102] Neither the donor nor the recipient can go to court if the grocer takes the money and does not deliver since the donor cannot be more explicit if he does not want to violate his vow. Therefore, the money really becomes the grocer's and this method is not circumventing the law.

(fol. 38c) **משנה ט**: הָיָה בֵיתוֹ לִבְנוֹת גְּדֵירוֹ לִגְדּוֹר שָׂדֵהוּ לִקְצוֹר הוֹלֵךְ אֵצֶל הַפּוֹעֲלִים וְאוֹמֵר אִישׁ פְּלוֹנִי מוּדָּר מִמֶּנּוּ הֲנָיָיה וְאֵינִי יוֹדֵעַ מַה אֶעֱשֶׂה. הֵן עוֹשִׂין עִמּוֹ וּבָאִין וְנוֹטְלִין שָׂכָר מִזֶּה.

Mishnah 9: If he had his house to build, his fence to repair, his field to harvest, the other person goes to the journeymen and tells them, X is forbidden any profit from me by a vow and I do not know what to do. They work with him and come and take their wages from the other person.

(38d, line 22) **הלכה ט**: הָיָה בֵיתוֹ לִבְנוֹת גְּדֵירוֹ לִגְדּוֹר כול'. מַהוּ דְיֵימַר. מָאן דַעֲבַד לָא מַפְסִיד. נִשְׁמְעִינָהּ מַן הָדָא. בְּיוֹמוֹי דְרִבִּי אִמִּי נָפְלָה דְלֵיקָה בַּכְּפָר. וְאַפִּיק רִבִּי אִמִּי כְּרוּז בְּשׁוּקָאֵי דַאֲרָמָאֵי וְאָמַר. כָּל־דַעֲבַד לָא מַפְסִיד. אָמַר רִבִּי אֶלְעָזָר בֵּי רִבִּי יוֹסֵי קוֹמֵי רִבִּי יוֹסֵי. סַכָּנָה הֲוֵית. וְאִי סַכָּנָה הֲוֵית אֲפִילוּ רִבִּי אִימִּי יִטְפֵּי. לֹא תַנֵּי. כָּל־דָּבָר סַכָּנָה אֵין אוֹמְרִים. יֵיעָשׂוּ בַגּוֹיִים וּבַקְּטַנִּים. אֶלָּא אֲפִילוּ בִּגְדוֹלִים וַאֲפִילוּ בְיִשְׂרָאֵל. מַעֲשֶׂה שֶׁנָּפְלָה דְלֵיקָה בַּחֲצַר יוֹסֵי בֶן סִימַאי בְשִׁיחִין. וְיָרְדוּ בְנֵי קַצְרָה שֶׁלְצִיפּוֹרִין לְכַבּוֹתוֹ וְלֹא הִנִּיחַ לָהֶן לְכַבּוֹת. אָמַר לָהֶן. הַנִּיחוּ לַגַּבַּאי שֶׁיִּגְבֶּה אֶת חוֹבוֹ. מִיַּד קָשַׁר עָלָיו הֶעָנָן וְיָרְדוּ גְשָׁמִים וְכִיבּוּהוּ. בְּמוֹצָאֵי שַׁבָּת שָׁלַח לְכָל אֶחָד וְאֶחָד מֵהֶן סֶלַע. וּלְאַפַרְכוֹס שֶׁלָּהֶן חֲמִשִּׁים דִּינָר. אָמַר רִבִּי חֲנִינָה. לֹא הֲוָה צָרִיךְ לַעֲשׂוֹת כֵּן. חַד כּוּתַיי הֲוָה מְגִירֵיהּ דְּרִבִּי יוֹנָה. נָפְלָה דְלֵיקָה בִּמְגִירוּתֵיהּ דְּרִבִּי יוֹנָה. אֲזַל הַהוּא כּוּתָאָה בָּעֵי מִיטַפְיֵיהּ וְלָא שָׁבְקֵיהּ רִבִּי יוֹנָה. אֲמַר לֵיהּ בְּגִין מִדְלִי. אֲמַר לֵיהּ. אִין. וְאִישְׁתֵּיזִיב כּוּלָהּ. רִבִּי יוֹנָה דִכְפַר אִימִּי פָּרַס גּוּלְתֵיהּ עַל גָּדִישָׁה וְנוּרָא עָרְקַת מִינָהּ.

Halakhah 9: "If he had his house to build, his fence to repair," etc. May he say, he who works will not lose[103]? Let us hear from the following. [104]In the days of Rebbi Immi there was a fire in the village. Rebbi Immi sent a crier to the markets of the Gentiles saying: "He who works will not lose.[105]" Rebbi Eleazar ben Rebbi Yose said, that was danger to life. But if there was danger to life, Rebbi Immi himself should have fought the fire! Did we not state[106], in any case of danger to life one does not say that [the necessary work] be done by Gentiles or minors, but [it should be done] even by important Jewish persons. It happened that there was a fire in the courtyard of Yose ben Simai in Šiḥin, and the garrison of the barracks[107] of Sepphoris came to fight it but he did not let them fight it; he said, let the collector collect his due[108]. [Immediately there formed a cloud, there was rain which extinguished it[109]. After the Sabbath he sent to each of them a tetradrachma and to their commander[110] 50 denarii. Rebbi Ḥanina said, there was no need for him to do that[111] A Samaritan was a neighbor of Rebbi Jonah. There was a fire in Rebbi Jonah's neighborhood; he wanted to fight it but Rebbi Jonah did not let him[112]. He said to him, because of my property! He said, yes[113]. And everything was saved. Rebbi Jonah from Kefar-Immi spread his garment over the grain stack and the fire retreated from it.

103 While clearly A cannot contract with the workers that they should work with X on his account, can he tell them that he will pay (in a way which would not be enforceable in court if they were not journeymen under special protection by biblical law and custom.)

104 From here to the end of the paragraph, the text is also in Šabbat 16, fol. 15c l. 35. It refers to Mishnah Šabbat 15:7: "If a Gentile comes to extinguish a fire, one does not tell him to extinguish or not extinguish since one is not responsible for his rest." All fires mentioned here happened on a Sabbath.

105 Therefore, in the case here one also is permitted to assure people of their wages. In the Babli, Šabbat 121a, R. Ammi (= Immi) says directly that suggesting payment is permitted in the case of a fire on the Sabbath.

106 Also in the Babli, Yoma 84b.

107 Latin castra, -orum, n. "military camp, barracks, fortress."

108 Since the fire was on a Sabbath, he took it as divine punishment.

109 As reward for his piety.

110 Greek ἔπαρχος, equivalent of Latin praefectus (castrorum).

111 In the Babli, Šabbat 121a, this is the opinion of the Sages, based on the Mishnah (Note 104), while Yose ben Simai wanted to encourage them to fight Sabbath fires at Sepphoris.

112 Since as a Samaritan he has to keep the Sabbath and, therefore, might fight fires only if there is a danger to life, rather than to property.

113 R. Jonah agreed to be responsible for the Samaritan's loss if the fire reached his property.

(fol. 38d) **משנה י**: הָיוּ מְהַלְּכִין בַּדֶּרֶךְ וְאֵין לוֹ מַה יֹּאכַל נוֹתֵן לְאַחֵר לְשֵׁם מַתָּנָה וְהַלָּה מוּתָּר בָּהּ. אִם אֵין עִמָּהֶן אַחֵר מַנִּיחַ עַל הַסֶּלַע אוֹ עַל הַגָּדֵר וְאוֹמֵר הֲרֵי הֵן מוּבְקָרִים לְכָל־מִי שֶׁיַּחְפּוֹץ וְהַלָּה נוֹטֵל וְאוֹכֵל וְרִבִּי יוֹסֵי אוֹסֵר.

Mishnah 10: If they were walking on the road and he had nothing to eat, the other gives something to a third person as a gift, and this one is permitted it. If nobody is with them, he puts it on a rock or a fence and says, this is ownerless for everyone to take and this one can come and eat, but Rebbi Yose forbids[97].

(38d, line 36) **הלכה י**: הָיוּ מְהַלְּכִין בַּדֶּרֶךְ וְאֵין לוֹ מַה יֹּאכַל כול'. תַּנֵּי רִבִּי מֵאִיר אוֹמֵר. כֵּיוָן שֶׁאָדָם מַבְקִיר יָצָא דָּבָר מֵרְשׁוּתוֹ. רִבִּי יוֹסֵי אוֹמֵר אֵין הֶבְקֵר יוֹצֵא מִתַּחַת יְדֵי הַבְּעָלִים אֶלָּא בִּזְכִייָה.[114] רִבִּי יִרְמְיָה רִבִּי בָּא בַּר חִייָה תְּרֵיהוֹן אָמְרִין רִבִּי יוֹחָנָן בְּשֵׁם רִבִּי יַנַּאי. דִּבְרֵי רִב יוֹסֵי בְּנוֹתֵן מַתָּנָה לַעֲשָׂרָה וְזֶה אֶחָד מֵהֶן. הִבְקִיר שָׂדֵהוּ. אִית תַּנָּיֵי תַּנֵּי. חוֹזֵר בּוֹ. וְאִית תַּנָּיֵי תַּנֵּי. אֵינוֹ חוֹזֵר בּוֹ. רִבִּי חִזְקִיָּה רִבִּי אַבָּהוּ בְּשֵׁם רִבִּי שִׁמְעוֹן בֶּן לָקִישׁ. מָאן דָּמַר. חוֹזֵר. כְּרִבִּי יוֹסֵי. וּמָאן דָּמַר. אֵינוֹ חוֹזֵר. כְּרִבִּי מֵאִיר. הָדָא אָמְרָה. הֶבְקֵר כְּרִבִּי יוֹסֵי וְחַיָּיב בְּמַעְשְׂרוֹת. מָה אָמַר. הֶבְקֵר. לֹא מַתָּנָה. אָתָא רִבִּי יַעֲקֹב בַּר אָחָא בְּשֵׁם רִבִּי שִׁמְעוֹן בֶּן לָקִישׁ. הֶבְקֵר כְּרִבִּי יוֹסֵי וְחַיָּיב בְּמַעְשְׂרוֹת. תַּמָּן אָמְרִין. הֶבְקֵר כְּרִבִּי יוֹסֵי וְאֵינוֹ חַיָּיב בְּמַעְשְׂרוֹת. דְּאָמַר רִבִּי יוֹחָנָן בְּשֵׁם רִבִּי יַנַּאי. וּבָא הַלֵּוִי כִּי אֵין לוֹ וגו'. מִמַּה שֶׁיֵּשׁ לָךְ וְאֵין לוֹ חַיָּיב אַתָּה לִיתֵּן לוֹ. יָצָא הֶבְקֵר שֶׁיָּדְךָ וְיָדוֹ שָׁוִין בָּהּ. הִיא לֶקֶט הִיא שִׁכְחָה הִיא פֵּיאָה הִיא הֶבְקֵר.

It was stated: Rebbi Meïr says that as soon as a person abandons anything from his property, it is no longer in his possession. Rebbi Yose says, nothing may leave the hands of its owners except if it is taken up by another person[115]. Rebbi Jeremiah, Rebbi Abba bar Ḥiyya, both say, Rebbi Joḥanan in the name of Rebbi Yannai: The words of Rebbi Yose [deal with the case] that a person gave a gift to ten people and this one was one of them[116]. If somebody abandoned his field, some Tannaïm say, he can retract[117], but some Tannaïm say, he cannot retract. Rebbi Ḥizqiah, Rebbi Abbahu in the name of Rebbi Simeon ben Laqish: The one who says that he can retract follows Rebbi Yose[118]. But the one who says that he cannot retract follows Rebbi Meïr. Does this mean that abandoned property in the sense of Rebbi Yose is subject to tithes[119]? What did he say? Abandoned property, not gift[120]! Rebbi Jacob bar Aḥa came in the name of Rebbi Simeon ben Laqish: Abandoned property in the sense of Rebbi Yose is subject to tithes. There[121], they say that abandoned property in the sense of Rebbi Yose is not subject to tithes, [122]since Rebbi Joḥanan said in the name of Rebbi Yannai: [123]"The Levite shall come," etc. You are obliged to give him from what you have but he has not. This excludes abandoned property for which your and his hands are equal. Gleanings, forgotten sheaves, *peah*, and abandoned property are all equal.

114 Reading of the text in *Peah* 6:1 (Note 17). Text here: בדמיה "by its value".

115 E. g., if somebody is injured on abandoned property which had not been taken up by another person, the original owner has to pay according to R. Yose but not according to R. Meïr.

116 R. Yose compares abandoning property to giving something to a group of people without specifying who gets what. In that case, the transfer of ownership rights certainly depends on the new owner taking possession. This is also R. Joḥanan's position in the Babli, 43a.

117 If nobody took the property in the meantime.

118 Since the property still is his to do with as he pleases.

119 Since a gift does not remove the obligation of heave and tithes; cf. *Ma'serot* 1:1, Notes 18-23.

120 Since the statement of R. Yose is about abandoned property; it cannot follow all the rules of gifts.

| 121 | In Babylonia. | 1:1, Note 20. |
| 122 | From here to the end of the paragraph, the text is from *Ma'serot* | 123 Deut. 14:29. |

(38d, line 49) עַד כְּדוֹן בְּשֶׁהִבְקִירָהּ לִזְמָן מְרוּבָּה. אֲבָל הִבְקִירָהּ לִזְמָן מְמוּעָט. נִישְׁמְעִינָהּ מִן הָדָא. הַמַּבְקִיר אֶת שָׂדֵהוּ שְׁלֹשָׁה יָמִים חוֹזֵר. אָמַר רִבִּי זְעִירָא. לֹא אָמַר אֶלָּא שְׁלֹשָׁה. הָא לְאַחַר שְׁלֹשָׁה אֵינוֹ חוֹזֵר בּוֹ. תַּנֵּי רִבִּי שִׁמְעוֹן דַּיָּינָא קוֹמֵי רִבִּי זְעִירָא. אֲפִילוּ לְאַחַר שְׁלֹשָׁה חוֹזֵר בּוֹ. אָמַר לֵיהּ. מִכֵּיוָן דְּאַתְּ אָמַר. לְאַחַר שְׁלֹשָׁה חוֹזֵר בּוֹ. הִיא לְאַחַר שְׁלֹשָׁה הִיא לְאַחַר כַּמָּה יָמִים. מַתְנִיתָא מְסַיְּיעָה לְרִבִּי זְעִירָה. בַּמֶּה דְּבָרִים אֲמוּרִים. בְּשֶׁהִבְקִיר סְתָם. אֲבָל אִם אָמַר. שָׂדִי מוּבְקֶרֶת יוֹם אֶחָד שַׁבָּת אַחַת חֹדֶשׁ אֶחָד שָׁנָה אַחַת שָׁבוּעַ אֶחָד. עַד שֶׁלֹּא זָכָה בֵּין הוּא בֵּין אַחֵר יָכוֹל לַחֲזוֹר בּוֹ. מִשֶּׁזָּכָה בֵּין הוּא בֵּין אַחֵר אֵינוֹ יָכוֹל לַחֲזוֹר בּוֹ. הָדָא אֲמָרָה הוּא זְמָן מְרוּבָּה הוּא זְמָן מְמוּעָט. הָדָא אֲמָרָה שֶׁלֹּא חָשׁוּ לְהַעֲרָמָה. הָדָא אֲמָרָה שֶׁאָדָם מַבְקִיר וְחוֹזֵר וְזוֹכֶה. הָדָא פְּשִׁיטָא שְׁאֵלַת דְּרִבִּי זְעִירָא. דְּרִבִּי זְעִירָא אָמַר. הוּא זְמָן מוּעָט הוּא זְמָן מְרוּבָּה.

[124]So far, if he abandoned it for a longer period of time. But if he abandoned only for a short time? Let us hear from the following: "If he abandoned his field, he may cancel his action during three days." Rebbi Ze'ira said, it says only "three days". Therefore, after three days he may not cancel his action. Rebbi Simeon Dayana stated before Rebbi Ze'ira: Even after three he may cancel his action. He said to him, since you say after three days, is it the same after three or after many? A *baraita* supports Rebbi Ze'ira[125]: "About when is this said? If he abandoned in an unspecified way. But if he said: My field shall be abandoned one day, one week, one month, one year, a sabbatical period, as long as nobody took it over, either he or another person, he may cancel. But after somebody acquired it, either he or somebody else, he cannot cancel." This means

that short or long periods are the same. It also means that they were not worried about dishonesty. This means that a person may abandon and reacquire. That obviously answers Rebbi Zeïra's question, since Rebbi Zeira had said, are short and long times the same?

124 The entire paragraph is also in   27.
Peah 6:1, explained there in Notes 23-   125 Babli 44a.

(38d, line 61) וְהַלָּה נוֹטֵל וְאוֹכֵל וְרִבִּי יוֹסֵי אוֹסֵר. מַאי טַעֲמָא דְּרִבִּי יוֹסֵי. מִפְּנֵי שֶׁקָּדַם נִדְרוֹ לְהֶבְקֵירוֹ. הָא הֶבְקִירוֹ לְנִדְרוֹ לֹא. בְּעוֹן קוֹמֵי רִבִּי יוֹסֵי. מִפְּנֵי שֶׁקָּדַם נִדְרוֹ לְהֶבְקֵירוֹ. מָה בֵּין שֶׁקָּדַם הֶבְקֵירוֹ לְנִדְרוֹ. אָמַר לוֹן. לֹא עָלַת עַל דַּעְתּוֹ לֶאֱסוֹר מַה שֶּׁהִבְקִיר. אָמַר רִבִּי יוֹנָה. הָכֵין קַשּׁוֹן קֳדָמוֹי. הָא הֶבְקֵר יָחִיד לֹא. וְהָא תַנִּינָן וְהַלָּה נוֹטֵל וְאוֹכֵל וְרִבִּי יוֹסֵי אוֹסֵר. אָמַר לוֹן. לֹא עָלַת עַל דַּעְתּוֹ לֶאֱסוֹר מַה שֶּׁהִבְקִיר. רִבִּי יוֹנָה רִבִּי אַבָּא רִבִּי חִייָה בְשֵׁם רִבִּי שִׁמְעוֹן בֶּן יוֹצָדָק. הַמַּבְקִיר שָׂדֵהוּ לָעֲשָׂרָה בְּנֵי אָדָם אֵינוֹ חוֹזֵר בּוֹ. אָמַר רִבִּי יוֹסֵה. אַתְיָיא כְרִבִּי מֵאִיר. רִבִּי מָנָא בָּעֵי. מָה אַתְּ אֲמָרַת. לִשְׁלֹשָׁה. לִפְנֵי שְׁלֹשָׁה. עַל דְּאַתְּ מַקְשֵׁי עַל רִבִּי מֵאִיר קַשִּׁיתָהּ עַל דְּרִבִּי יוֹסֵי. מָה אַתְּ אֲמָרַת. לָעֲשָׂרָה. לִפְנֵי עֲשָׂרָה. אָמַר לֵיהּ. הִבְקִירָהּ בִּפְנֵי שְׁנַיִם חוֹזֵר בּוֹ וְחַיָּיב בְּמַעְשְׂרוֹת. בִּפְנֵי שְׁלֹשָׁה אֵינוֹ חוֹזֵר בּוֹ וּפָטוּר מִן הַמַּעְשְׂרוֹת.

"This one can come and eat, but Rebbi Yose forbids." What is Rebbi Yose's reason? Because his vow preceded his abandonment. Therefore, not if his abandonment preceded his vow. They asked before Rebbi Yose: What is the difference if his vow preceded his abandonment[126]? He said to them, it did not occur to him to forbid what he abandoned[127]. Rebbi Jonah said, so they asked before him: That means, not if it applies to a single person[128]? But did we not state: "This one can come and eat, but Rebbi Yose forbids"? He said to them, it did not occur to him to forbid what he abandoned. Rebbi Jonah, Rebbi Abba, Rebbi Ḥiyya, in the name of Rebbi Simeon ben Joṣadaq: If somebody abandons his field to ten persons he cannot retract[129]. Rebbi Yose said, that follows Rebbi Meïr. Rebbi Mana asked: When you said, "to three," [did you not mean] "in the presence of three"? Instead of asking about Rebbi Meïr, ask about Rebbi Yose! When you said, "to ten," [did you not mean] "in the presence of ten"? He said to him, if he abandoned it before two persons, he can retract and it remains subject to tithes[130]. If he abandoned it before three persons, he cannot retract and it is free from tithes[131].

126 Why does R. Yose accept abandonment before the vow as valid when he holds that everything remains the person's own until it is picked up by somebody else?

127 It has nothing to do with property rights. A vow cannot refer to anything that was not in the vower's mind.

128 The reference is to the second half of the paragraph where it is stated that for everybody abandonment declared before three adult witnesses is immediately valid since it is a public act; even for R. Meïr an act before less than three witnesses is not valid. But in the Mishnah it is stated that no witnesses are present and nevertheless R. Meïr holds that in respect to the vow the abandonment is valid.

129 In the Babli, 45a, three people. (R. Joshua ben Levi holds that this requirement is rabbinic.)

130 If any of the persons knowing of the abandonment takes the property for himself, he cannot prove the title if the original owner reneges on his abandonment since he can support his claim only by one witness, which is not enough. Therefore, if the owner abandons the real estate and then reclaims it, it never left his potential possession and all produce grown on his field was never totally abandoned; the duty of tithing was never disestablished..

131 Any one of the three can take the real estate and has two witnesses to back up his claim. If the original owner would retake it when nobody else had taken it, he takes genuinely abandoned property and no tithes are due (cf. Note 106).

השותפין פרק חמישי

משנה א: הַשּׁוּתָּפִין שֶׁנָּדְרוּ הֲנָיָיה זֶה מִזֶּה אֲסוּרִין לִיכָּנֵס לֶחָצֵר. רַבִּי (fol. 39a) אֱלִיעֶזֶר בֶּן יַעֲקֹב אוֹמֵר זֶה נִכְנָס לְתוֹךְ שֶׁלּוֹ וְזֶה נִכְנָס לְתוֹךְ שֶׁלּוֹ. שְׁנֵיהֶן אֲסוּרִין מִלְהַעֲמִיד שָׁם רֵחַיִם וְתַנּוּר וּמִלְגַּדֵּל תַּרְנְגוֹלִין. הָיָה אֶחָד מֵהֶם מוּדָּר מֵחֲבֵירוֹ הֲנָיָיה לֹא יִכָּנֵס לֶחָצֵר. רַבִּי אֱלִיעֶזֶר בֶּן יַעֲקֹב אוֹמֵר יָכוֹל הוּא לוֹמַר לוֹ לְתוֹךְ שֶׁלִּי אֲנִי נִכְנָס וְאֵינִי נִכְנָס לְתוֹךְ שֶׁלָּךְ. כּוֹפִין אֶת הַנּוֹדֵר לִמְכּוֹר אֶת חֶלְקוֹ.

Mishnah 1: Partners[1] who mutually made vows not to have usufruct from one another are forbidden to enter the courtyard[2]. Rebbi Eliezer ben Jacob says, each one enters into what is his[3]. Both are forbidden to put up there a grindstone or an oven, or to raise chickens there[4]. If one of them made a vow not to have usufruct from the other, he cannot enter the courtyard. Rebbi Eliezer ben Jacob says, one can say to the other, I enter into my property, I do not enter into yours. One forces the one who made the vow to sell his part[5].

1 People who own houses built around a common courtyard. They are partners in the courtyard. One exits from the houses to the street only through the courtyard.

2 For the anonymous Tanna, the entire courtyard is common property; nobody can enter the courtyard without stepping into the property of both of them. Therefore, neither one can enter his courtyard without profiting from the other's property.

3 Mishnah *Baba batra* 1:6 explains that the parties of a common courtyard can force a partition if the area of the courtyard exceeds a certain minimum. As the Babli explains, 46b, R. Eliezer ben Jacob refers only to a courtyard

larger than the minimum. He holds that each square inch of the courtyard is potentially the property of one owner, only it was not determined who the actual owner is. Therefore, each of the partners can claim that he temporarily steps only onto his own property. It must be that R. Eliezer ben Jacob permits a straight walk from the entrance gate to the house door; this would be the domain belonging to the person's house in a separation of properties.

4   Everybody agrees that the common courtyard can be used for private purposes only by the consent of all owners. If the person forbidden by a vow did not object to the other using the courtyard for his private purpose, he would make him a present of monetary value.

5   According to the Babli, this statement refers to the majority position. According to the Yerushalmi, this is part of R. Eliezer ben Jacob's statement and is explained in the Halakhah.

(39a, line 34) **הלכה א**: הַשּׁוּתָּפִין שֶׁנָּדְרוּ הֲנָיָיה זֶה מִזֶּה כול׳. רַבָּנִין אָמְרִין. כָּל־טֶפַח וְטֶפַח שֶׁלַּשּׁוּתָּפִין הוּא. רִבִּי לִיעֶזֶר בֶּן יַעֲקֹב אוֹמֵר. זֶה נִכְנָס לְתוֹךְ שֶׁלּוֹ וְזֶה נִכְנָס לְתוֹךְ שֶׁלּוֹ. אִם הָיְתָה חָצֵר חֲלוּקָה פְּסֵיפָס אַף רַבָּנִין מוֹדָיֵי. עָמַד אֶחָד מֵהֶן וּמָכַר אֶת חֶלְקוֹ אַף רִבִּי אֱלִיעֶזֶר בֶּן יַעֲקֹב מוֹדֶה. הִתְנוּ בֵינֵיהֶן עַל מְנָת לְוַתֵּר בְּחֶזְקַת שׁוּתָּפִין הֵן. לֹא צוּרְכָה דְלָא הִתְנוּ בֵּינֵיהֶן עַל מְנָת לְוַתֵּר. מָה אָמַר בָּהּ רִבִּי אֱלִיעֶזֶר בֶּן יַעֲקֹב. וְהָא תַנִּינָן תַּמָּן. לוֹקֵחַ בְּיָתֵר וּמוֹכֵר בְּפָחוֹת. מָה אָמַר בָּהּ רִבִּי אֱלִיעֶזֶר בֶּן יַעֲקֹב. וְהָא תַנִּינָן תַּמָּן. לֹא יַשְׁאִילֵנוּ וְלֹא יִשְׁאַל מִמֶּנּוּ. מָה אָמַר בָּהּ רִבִּי אֱלִיעֶזֶר בֶּן יַעֲקֹב. וְהָא תַנִּינָן תַּמָּן. לֹא יִמְכּוֹר וְלֹא יִקַּח מִמֶּנּוּ. וְהָא דְּאָמַר רִבִּי שִׁמְעוֹן בֶּן יָקִים. שֶׁלֹּא יִשְׁהֵא.

Halakhah 1: "Partners who mutually made vows not to have usufruct from one another," etc. The rabbis say, every single [square] hand-breadth is common property of the partners. Rebbi Eliezer ben Jacob says, each one enters into what is his. If the courtyard was divided by pebbles[6], even the rabbis agree. If one of them went and sold his part, even Rebbi

Eliezer ben Jacob agrees[7]. If they contracted between themselves to concede[8], it is still in the hands of the partners. It is only needed if they did not contract between themselves to concede; what is the position of Rebbi Eliezer ben Jacob? And did we not state there, "he buys higher and sells lower[9]"? What is the position of Rebbi Eliezer ben Jacob? And did we not state there, "he should not lend him nor ask him for anything[10],"? What is the position of Rebbi Eliezer ben Jacob? And what Rebbi Simeon ben Yaqim said, that he should not stay long[11]?

6   Greek ψῆφος. If at some time they decide to mark the borders between the domains belonging to the different houses by rows of pebbles cemented into the ground, this amounts to a division of the common property and the rabbis will not hold that a formal contract is needed to disestablish the former common domain. (In modern Hebrew, the word means "mosaic".)

7   If one of the partners sells his part, he can no longer claim to enter into what is his and even according to R. Eliezer ben Jacob he is forbidden to set foot in the courtyard.

8   They split the common courtyard as outlined in *Baba batra* but in the contract agreed that they would not insist on excluding the other party from entering the separate domain of the other party. Then for the rabbis the split did not change anything.

9   Chapter 3, Note 147. Does R. Eliezer ben Jacob permit transactions at the regular price?

10 Chapter 4, Note 99. Since no transfer of property is involved, does R. Eliezer ben Jacob agree?

11 Chapter 4, Note 76. Does R. Eliezer ben Jacob agree that the visits have to be as short as possible?

(39a, line 44) שְׁנֵיהֶן אֲסוּרִין מִלְּהַעֲמִיד שָׁם רֵחַיִים וְתַנּוּר וּמִלְּגַדֵּל תַּרְנְגוֹלִין. נִצְרְכָה לְרִבִּי אֱלִיעֶזֶר בֶּן יַעֲקֹב. דּוּ מַתְנִיתָא הַשּׁוּתָּפִין שֶׁנָּדְרוּ הֲנָייָה זֶה מִזֶּה. מִפְּנֵי שֶׁנָּדְרוּ הֲנָייָה זֶה מִזֶּה. הָא אִם לֹא נָדְרוּ הֲנָייָה זֶה מִזֶּה סְתָמוֹ כְּמוֹתְרִין אֵילּוּ לָאֵילּוּ. אָמַר רִבִּי יִרְמְיָה. נָהֲגוּ הַשּׁוּתָּפִין לִהְיוֹת כְּמוֹתְרִין זֶה אֶת זֶה

בִּדְבָרִים הַלָּלוּ. תַּמָּן תַּנִּינָן. אִילּוּ דְבָרִים שֶׁיֵּשׁ לָהֶן חֲזָקָה. אָמַר רִבִּי אֶלְעָזָר. הַמְגַדֵּל תַּרְנְגוֹלִין בְּחָצֵר שֶׁאֵינָהּ שֶׁלּוֹ הֲרֵי זוּ חֲזָקָה. אָמַר רִבִּי יוֹסֵי. וְיָאוּת. אִם יֵשׁ לוֹ רְשׁוּת לְגַדֵּל הֲרֵי גִידֵּל. אִים אֵין לוֹ רְשׁוּת לְגַדֵּל הֲרֵי הֶחֱזִיק. רִבִּי יוֹחָנָן בְּשֵׁם רִבִּי בְּנָיָה. בְּכָל הַשּׁוּתָּפִין מְעַכְּבִין זֶה עַל זֶה חוּץ מִן הַכְּבִיסָה. מִפְּנֵי כְבוֹד בְּנוֹת יִשְׂרָאֵל. אָמַר רִבִּי מַתַּנְיָיה. הָדָא דְאַתְּ אָמַר מָקוֹם שֶׁהַנָּשִׁים מְכַבְּסוֹת. אֲבָל מָקוֹם שֶׁהָאֲנָשִׁים מְכַבְּסִין לֹא בְדָא. וְדָא דְאַתְּ אָמַר חוּץ מִן הַכְּבִיסָה בְּכָל־הֶחָצֵר. בְּרַם בְּאַרְבַּע אַמּוֹת דְּחַבְרֵיהּ לֹא מָצֵי מִימְחֵי בְיָדֵיהּ. אִם הָיָה הַמָּקוֹם מְשׁוּפָּע אֲפִילוּ בְאַרְבַּע אַמּוֹת דְּחַבְרֵיהּ מִימְחֵי הוּא בְיָדֵיהּ. דּוּ אָמַר לֵיהּ. אַתְּ שְׁפָךְ וְהוּא אָתֵי לְגַבִּי. תַּנֵּי. מְקוֹם הַתַּנּוּר מְקוֹם הַכִּירַיִים אֵין לָהֶן חֲזָקָה. עַל גַּבֵּיהֶן אֲפִילוּ כָּל־שֶׁהוּ יֵשׁ לָהֶן חֲזָקָה. אָמַר רִבִּי זְעִירָה. וּבִלְבַד קֵירוּי שֶׁמּוֹעִיל לַתַּנּוּר.

"Both are forbidden to put a grindstone or an oven up there, or to raise chickens there[4]." This is needed for Rebbi Eliezer ben Jacob[12], for what he states about "partners who mutually made vows not to have usufruct from one another." Because they mutually made vows not to have usufruct from one another, does this imply that if they had not made vows not to have usufruct from one another, they would be presumed to concede one to the other[13]? Rebbi Jeremiah said, partners have the custom to concede one to the other in these matters. There[14], we have stated: "The following establish presumption of ownership.[15]" Rebbi Eleazar said, if somebody raises chickens in a courtyard in which he does not dwell, this establishes presumption of ownership. Rebbi Yose said, this is correct. As you look at it, if he had the right to raise them, he raised them. If he had no right to raise them, he established a presumption of ownership. Rebbi Johanan in the name of Rebbi Benaiah: Partners can veto any activity of the other party in a courtyard except for washing[16], for the honor of the daughters of Israel[17]. Rebbi Mattaniah said, that is, at a place where women wash, but not at a place where men wash[18]. And what you say except for washing in the courtyard [applies to] the entire courtyard except for the four cubits of that party where one cannot hinder anything[19]. But if the place was at an incline, one can veto even within the four cubits of another party since one might say to him, you pour out and it flows down to my place[20]. It was stated: The place of an oven or a hearth does not establish a presumption of ownership, but roofing of any size on top of them establishes a presumption of ownership[21]. Rebbi Ze'ira said, only if the wall is useful for the oven.

12 While the rabbis agree, for them the statement is immaterial since both partners are forbidden entry into the courtyard.

13 If somebody wants to put up an oven or a grindstone in the courtyard, can he presume to have the permission of all inhabitants of the courtyard without asking?

14 Mishnah *Baba batra* 3:6. It is stated there that simply putting a stove, a grindstone, or chickens into a courtyard does not create a presumption of ownership, but building a foundation for the grindstone or an enclosure for the oven does.

15 In the absence of documents, a testimony of three years of undisturbed ownership together with a claim of legal acquisition (by buying, inheritance, or gift) entitles the occupant to a documentary title; cf. *Yebamot* 12, Note 29 (Mishnah *Baba batra* 3:4).

16 He disagrees with R. Jeremiah and the conclusion drawn from the formulation of the Mishnah. The same statement in the Babli, *Baba batra* 57b. The statement of R. Jeremiah does not appear in the Babli.

17 It cannot be expected that a Jewish woman would go to the river to do her washing there and be seen by everybody without shoes and with uncovered arms.

18 If men wash it is a commercial activity and that certainly needs the permission of the other dwellers in the courtyard.

19 A strip four cubits wide along the entire front of a house is private

property of the owner of the house, not common property of the partners and, as a matter of principle, the owner of the house can do there anything he wants; the mistress of the house can wash there without asking anybody.

20   That is not a matter of property rights but of torts; the injured party could claim damages.

21   In Mishnah *Baba batra* 3:6 it is asserted that only a wall of at least ten hand-breadths around an oven or a hearth does count. The text here is very close to Tosephta *Baba batra* 2:13: Putting an oven or a hearth in a courtyard does not establish a presumption of ownership, but making a roof of any size does.

(39a, line 57) רִבִּי יוֹחָנָן בְּשֵׁם רִבִּי יַנַּאי. הַשּׁוּתָפִין קוֹנִין זֶה מִזֶּה בְחָצֵר וְחַיָּיבִין זֶה בִנְיזְקֵי זֶה. אָמַר רִבִּי בּוּן בַּר כַּהֲנָא. בְּאוֹמֵר. צְבוֹר וְאַקְנֵה. אֲבָל אִם צְבוּרִין לֹא קָנָה עַד שֶׁיְּטַלְטֵל.

Rebbi Johanan in the name of Rebbi Yannai: Partners can acquire one from the other[22] and are responsible for damages inflicted by one on the other[23]. Rebbi Abun bar Cahana said, if he said, collect and acquire. But if they were collected he does not acquire unless he moves.

22   As explained in *Ševi'it* 8:1, Note 15, rabbinic practice does not recognize transfer of property by payment, but only by delivery or a symbolic act indicating delivery. Also, since anything found on a person's real estate is his, one can state that real estate acquires for its owner (cf. *Peah* 5, Note 125; *Kilaim* 8, Note 46). If there is only one owner, delivery of goods into the courtyard is legal delivery and transfer of ownership. R. Johanan asserts here that even among partners on their common real estate one may assume, following R. Eliezer ben Jacob, that the place on which some merchandise is put is at least temporarily owned by the acquiring party alone. This supports the opinion in the Babli, 46b, that practice follows R. Eliezer ben Jacob. R. Abun bar Cahana follows the opinion of the anonymous majority, that common property is not divisible, and requires an action by the acquirer, either collecting the objects or at least moving

them in a symbolic display of ownership rights.

23 This statement is taken in *Baba qama* 3:8 to show that an owner is liable for injuries on his property suffered by anybody being on the property by right or invitation.

(39a, line 62) בְּתוֹךְ שֶׁלִּי אֲנִי נִכְנָס וְלֹא בְתוֹךְ שֶׁלָּךְ. וְאַתְּ אָמַר. כּוֹפִין. לֹא עַל הָדָא אִיתְאָמְרַת אֶלָּא עַל הָדָא. בְּתוֹךְ שֶׁלַּחֲבֵירָךְ אֲנִי נִכְנָס וְלֹא לְתוֹךְ שֶׁלָּךְ. עֲלֵיהּ כּוֹפִין אֶת המוכר²⁴ שֶׁיִּמְכּוֹר אֶת חֶלְקוֹ. בְּאוֹמֵר הֲנָיָיתִי עָלֶיךָ. אֲבָל בְּאוֹמֵר. הֲנָיָיתָךְ עָלַי. לֹא בְדָא.

"I enter my property, I do not enter yours." And you say, one forces him[25]? It was not said on this, but on[26]: "I enter your partner's property, I do not enter yours." In that case one forces the [maker of the vow] to sell his part. If he says, you shall not have any usufruct from me. But not if he says, I shall not have any usufruct from you[27].

24 It seems that one should read הַנּוֹדֵר. This is the basis of the translation.

25 There seems to be no reason why R. Eliezer ben Jacob should require a sale of the property. It is clear that following the anonymous rabbis a person who by the vow of another is prevented to reach his own house can sue to remove this obstacle and force the maker of the vow to divest himself of the real estate.

26 Mishnah 2, speaking of a third person C visiting a partner B while partner A had forbidden him any use of his property.

27 There is trouble only if A forbids all his property to C but not if A forbids himself any of C's properties. Unfortunately, the word מוּדָּר admits of both interpretations. If A makes the vow, מוּדָּר בּ- means that A takes nothing from C, מוּדָּר מ- that C may have nothing from A. The Babylonian Mishnah 2 follows the first alternative, the Yerushalmi one the second.

HALAKHAH 2   555

(fol. 39a) **משנה ב**: הָיָה אֶחָד מִן הַשׁוּק מוּדָּר מֵאֶחָד מֵהֶן הֲנָיָיה לֹא יִכָּנֵס לֶחָצֵר. רְבִּי אֱלִיעֶזֶר בֶּן יַעֲקֹב אוֹמֵר יָכוֹל הוּא לוֹמַר לוֹ בְּתוֹךְ שֶׁלַּחֲבֵירָךְ אֲנִי נִכְנָס וְאֵינִי נִכְנָס לְתוֹךְ שֶׁלָּךְ.

If anyone from outside was under a vow of no usufruct from one [of the partners], he should not enter the courtyard. Rebbi Eliezer ben Jacob says, he can say to him, I enter your partner's property, I do not enter yours.

(fol. 39a) **משנה ג**: הַמּוּדָּר הֲנָיָיה מֵחֲבֵירוֹ וְיֵשׁ לוֹ מֶרְחָץ וּבֵית הַבַּד מוּשְׂכָּרִים בָּעִיר אִם יֵשׁ לוֹ בָהֶן תְּפִיסַת יָד אָסוּר אֵין לוֹ בָהֶן תְּפִיסַת יָד מוּתָּר. הָאוֹמֵר לַחֲבֵירוֹ קוֹנָם לְבֵיתְךָ שֶׁאֲנִי נִכְנָס וְשָׂדְךָ שֶׁאֲנִי לוֹקֵחַ מֵת אוֹ מְכָרָן לְאַחֵר מוּתָּר. קוֹנָם לְבַיִת זֶה שֶׁאֲנִי נִכְנָס שָׂדֶה זוֹ שֶׁאֲנִי לוֹקֵחַ מֵת אוֹ מְכָרָן לְאַחֵר אָסוּר.

Mishnah 3: If one was under a vow not to have usufruct from another and he owns a bathhouse or an olive press leased out in town; if he retains the grip of a hand[28] on them, the other one is forbidden; if he retains no grip of a hand on them, the other one is permitted. If a person says to another, a *qônām* that I shall not enter your house, or that I shall not buy your field, if the owner died or sold it, the other one is permitted. That I shall not enter this house, or that I shall not buy this field, if the owner died or sold it, the other one is forbidden.

(39a, line 34) **הלכה ב**: הָיָה אֶחָד מִן הַשׁוּק כול׳. וְלֹא תַנִּינָן כּוֹפִין. תַּנֵּי רְבִּי חִייָה. אִם הָיָה נוֹדְרָן כּוֹפִין. דּוּ אָמַר לֵיהּ. אַתְיָית קֳדָמוֹהִי עָבְדַת לֵיהּ כֵּן. תִּנְיָינָא וְעָבְדַת לֵיהּ כֵּן. מִכָּן וְאֵילָךְ אוֹ שְׁרֵי נְדְרָךְ אוֹ זְבִין חוּלְקָךְ.

Halakhah 2: "If anyone from outside was," etc. And we did not state "one forces"! Rebbi Ḥiyya stated: "If he was a frequent maker of vows, one forces him," because the other [partner] can say to him, one came to me and you did such and such to him; a second person and you did such and such to him; the third time he tells him either you undo your vow or sell your part.

(39a, line 68) כָּמָה הִיא תְפִיסַת יָד. לְמַחֲצִית וְלִשְׁלִישׁ וְלִרְבִיעַ.
What is the grip of a hand? One half, a third, or a quarter[29].

28 "Hand" here means "possession", as in Middle High German *hant*, Swiss legal German *Hand*, French (for real estate) *main*.

29 If the lessee pays a percentage of revenue or gain (in the examples between 50% and 25%), the original owner is directly profiting from the other's use of his facilities. But if the rent is a fixed sum, then no gain accrues directly to the building's owner by people using bathhouse or olive press. The latter statement is explicit in the Babli, 46b.

(39a, line 69) בֵּיתָךְ זֶה. מִשֶׁם מַה אַתָּה תוֹפְשׂוֹ. מִשֶׁם בֵּיתָךְ זֶה. נָפַל וּבְנָאוֹ הוּא. לֵית לֵיהּ. נִישְׁמְעִינָהּ מִן הָדָא. הָאוֹמֵר לְיוֹרְשָׁיו. תְּנוּ בֵית חַתְנוּת לִבְנוֹ אוֹ בֵית אַרְמְלוּת לְבִתּוֹ. וְנָפַל. יוֹרְשִׁין חַיָּיבִין לִבְנוֹתוֹ. תַּמָּן תַּגִּינָן. הָאוֹמֵר לִבְנוֹ. קוֹנָם שֶׁאַתְּ נֶהֱנֶה לִי. אִם מֵת יִירָשֶׁנּוּ. בְּחַיַּי וּבְמוֹתִי. מֵת לֹא יִירָשֶׁנּוּ. [וְהָתַגֵּי. בְּחַיַּי. אִם מֵת יִירָשֶׁנּוּ. בְּמוֹתִי. אִם מֵת יִירָשֶׁנּוּ.][30] מַה בֵּין דְּהוּא דְאָמַר חָדָא לָהוּא דְאָמַר תְּרֵיי. רַב יִרְמְיָה וְרִבִּי יוֹסֵי [בֶּן חֲנִינָה][31] תְּרֵיהוֹן אָמְרִין. קוֹנָם הֲנָייַת נְכָסַיי אִילוּ עָלַי בְּחַיַּי וּבְמוֹתִי. מִכֵּיוָן שֶׁאָמַר. אִילוּ. אֲסָרָן עָלָיו בֵּין בַּחַיִּים בֵּין לְאַחַר מִיתָה. אָמַר רִבִּי יוֹסֵי. תַּגִּינָן בִּנְדָרִים מַה דְּלֹא תַגִּינָן בִּשְׁבוּעוֹת. קוֹנָם לְבֵיתָךְ שֶׁאֵינִי נִכְנָס. שָׂדָךְ שֶׁאֵינִי לוֹקֵחַ. מֵת אוֹ שֶׁמְּכָרוֹ לְאַחֵר מוּתָּר. לְבַיִת זֶה שֶׁאֵינִי נִכְנָס. שָׂדֶה זוֹ שֶׁאֵינִי לוֹקֵחַ. מֵת אוֹ שֶׁמְּכָרוֹ לְאַחֵר אָסוּר. מִפְּנֵי שֶׁאָמַר. זֶה. הָא לֹא אָמַר. זֶה. אֲסָרוֹ[32] עָלָיו בֵּין בַּחַיִּים בֵּין לְאַחַר מִיתָה.

"This, your house," because of what do you catch him? Because of "your house," "this"[33]? If it collapsed and he himself rebuilt it, is it not "this"? Let us hear from the following: "If somebody said to his heirs, give a wedding house to my son or a widow's house to my daughter, if it collapsed, the heirs are required to rebuild it.[34]" [35]There, we have stated: "If somebody says to his son, 'a *qônām* that you can not enjoy anything from me,' if he dies, [the son] inherits[36]. 'During my lifetime and after my death,' if he dies, [the son] does not inherit.[37]" [Did we not state, 'during my lifetime', [the son] inherits; 'after my death', [the son] inherits?] What is the difference between the one who says it one by one and the one who says it by twos[38]? [39]Rav Jeremiah and Rebbi Yose [ben Hanina] both say, 'a *qônām* that I[40] cannot enjoy these my properties during my lifetime and after my death,' from the moment he said "these" he forbade to him during his lifetime and after his death[41]. Rebbi Yose said, we have stated in *Nedarim* what we did not state in *Šebuot*[42]: "A *qônām* that I shall not enter your house, or that I shall not buy your field, if the owner died or sold it, the other is permitted. That I shall not enter this house, or that I shall not buy this field, if the owner died or sold it, the other is forbidden." Because he said "this". Therefore, if he had not said "this", he would have[43] forbidden to him both during his lifetime and after his death.

30   From the parallel text in *Baba Qama* 9:14. Since *Neziqin* may be from a different editing team, it is not certain that the text is exactly what is missing here, but the question which follows indicates that it cannot have been much different.

31   From the text in *Baba Qama*, missing here. Since R. Yose ben Hanina was a younger contemporary of Rav Jeremiah but R. Yose the Amora came 4 generations after him, the reading is reasonable. In the Babli, 47a, the quote is in the name of Rava, an older

contemporary of R. Yose the Amora.

32   The ms. is vocalized אָסְרוּ, identifying ָ and ְ, as usual in Ashkenazic (Italian and German) medieval mss.

33   Rashba (*Novellae* to 46b) has a slightly enlarged text: משום ביתך או משום זה "because of 'your house' or because of 'this'?" The text as it stands is completely intelligible. A vow because of "your house" becomes void if it is no longer the other's, because of "this" is permanent.

34   Since the *baraita* does *not* say that if he said "this house" the heirs do not have to rebuild, it follows that "your house" is determining, not "this". This means that if the house collapses and he rebuilds, it is forbidden, but if it is sold, it is permitted.

35   From here to the end of the paragraph there is an approximate parallel in *Baba Qama* 9:14, source of the Mishnah.

36   Since he inherits by biblical decree (*Num.* 27:6-11), not by his father's will.

37   Cf. Chapter 2, Note 15; Babli 47a.

38   If he makes two separate vows, the first one, a *qônām* forbidding his property during his lifetime, is valid, but the second one for the time after his death is invalid since nobody can forbid to another person anything not in his possession. Why does it become valid if combined?

39   The text in *Baba Qama* switches the Mishnaiot quoted, respectively, by Rav Jeremiah and Rebbi Yose.

40   It seems that instead of עלי "for me" one has to read עליו "for him", as is clear from the rest of the sentence.

41   Both of them disagree with the position taken earlier by the editors of the Yerushalmi and assert that "this" overrides "your house". If the house collapses and he rebuilds, it is permitted, but if sold, it remains forbidden.

42   There is no comparable Mishnah in Tractate *Šebuot*. In *Baba Qama*, the text is: "We have stated in *Neziqin* what we did not state in *Nedarim*," but there, the reference is to a Mishnah in *Neziqin*, cf. Note 39. The difference is *not* a variant reading.

43   It seems that one has to read "had *not* forbidden". In *Baba Qama* this last sentence is missing; the preceding one reads: "Because he said 'these', he forbade to him both during his lifetime and after his death."

(fol. 39a) **משנה ד:** הֲרֵינִי עָלֶיךָ חֵרֶם הַמּוּדָּר אָסוּר. הֲרֵי אַתְּ עָלַי חֵרֶם הַנּוֹדֵר אָסוּר. הֲרֵינִי עָלֶיךָ וְאַתְּ עָלַי שְׁנֵיהֶן אֲסוּרִין. וּשְׁנֵיהֶן מוּתָּרִין בְּדָבָר שֶׁלְּעוֹלֵי בָבֶל וַאֲסוּרִין בְּדָבָר שֶׁלְּאוֹתָהּ הָעִיר.

"I am *ḥerem* for you[44]", the addressee is forbidden[45]. "You are for me *ḥerem*," the vower is forbidden. "I am for you and you are for me," both are forbidden. Both are permitted the institutions of the returnees from Babylonia[46] and forbidden the institutions of their own town[47].

[44] *Ḥerem* is an expression for a gift to the Temple of offerings that cannot be redeemed, *Lev.* 27:28. As a term for a vow, it is equivalent to *qorbān*.

[45] To have any usufruct from the vower's property.

[46] These are detailed in Mishnah 5. They were destined for public use and are immune against private vows.

[47] Since both of them are partners in the public institutions of the town; cf. Mishnah 1.

(39b, line 10) **הלכה ד:** הֲרֵינִי עָלֶיךָ חֵרֶם כול׳. קוֹנָם שֶׁאֵינִי נֶהֱנֶה לָךְ לִנְשְׁאַל לוֹ עָלֶיךָ. נִשְׁאַל עַל הָרִאשׁוֹן וְאֵינוֹ נִשְׁאַל עַל הַשֵּׁנִי. אִית תַּנָּיֵי תַנֵּי. נִשְׁאַל בֵּין עַל הָרִאשׁוֹן בֵּין עַל הַשֵּׁנִי. שְׁמוּאֵל בְּרֵיהּ דְּרִבִּי יוֹסֵף בֵּירִבִּי בּוּן אָמַר. כְּמָאן דְּאָמַר. לְאַחַר הָאִיסָּר. בְּרַם כְּמָאן דְּאָמַר. לְאַחַר הַנֶּדֶר. נֶדֶר שֶׁבָּטַל מִקְצָתוֹ בָּטַל כּוּלוֹ.

Halakhah 4: "'I am *ḥerem* for you", etc. 'A *qônām* that I shall not have any usufruct from you and anyone I would ask about you', he has to ask about the first but not the second. Some Tannaïm state: He has to ask both about the first and the second[48]. Samuel the son of Rebbi Joseph ben Rebbi Abun said, that follows the one who said "after the prohibition"[49]. But for the one who said "after the vow", a vow which is partially invalid is totally invalid[50].

48 If a person vows not to have anything from a certain other person and any rabbi who would dissolve this vow, if he has second thoughts and asks a rabbi to disolve the vow, there are differing opinions on whether he then has to ask a second rabbi to dissolve his vow regarding the first rabbi. In the Babli, 90a/b, two questions are raised which are not found in the Yerushalmi: (1) What means first and second; maybe first is the rabbi whom he has to approach and second the object of the vow? (2) Is it clear whether a vow can be dissolved that has not yet led to any prohibition?

49 This refers to the disagreement of R. Ismael and R. Aqiba (Chapter 3, Note 128; Halakhah 11:9, Babli 89a) whether the point in time which determines the rules is the moment the vow is made or the moment the prohibition is slated to begin. For R. Ismael, who holds that the moment of prohibition is determining, the second prohibition starts the moment the vower goes to see a rabbi. Therefore, that prohibition has to be dissolved also. But for R. Aqiba, who goes after the moment the vow was made, there is a vow only about one person and when that prohibition is lifted, the vow and the second case with it disappear.

50 Mishnah 9:6, cf. Chapter 3, Note 84.

(39b, line 15) הַנּוֹדֵר מִבְּנֵי הָעִיר וּבָא אַחֵר וְיָשַׁב שָׁם שְׁלֹשִׁים יוֹם מוּתָּר בּוֹ. מִיּוֹשְׁבֵי הָעִיר וּבָא אַחֵר וְיָשַׁב שָׁם שְׁלֹשִׁים יוֹם אָסוּר בּוֹ. קוֹנָם הֲנָייָתִי עַל בְּנֵי עִירִי. אֵינוֹ נִשְׁאַל לְזָקֵן שֶׁיֵּשׁ שָׁם. הֲנָיַית בְּנֵי עִירִי עָלַי. נִשְׁאַל לְזָקֵן שֶׁיֵּשׁ שָׁם. אִית תַּנָּיֵי תַּנֵּי אֲפִילוּ עַל קַדְמָייָתָא נִשְׁאָל. שֶׁאֵינוֹ כְּמֵפֵר נִדְרֵי עַצְמוֹ. נֶדֶר שֶׁעָרַבִים אֵין לוֹ הֵיתֵר. הַנּוֹדֵר בָּרַבִּים. אֵין לוֹ הֵיתֵר. הַמּוּדָּר הֲנָייָה מֵחֲבֵירוֹ בְּפָנָיו לֹא יִשְׁאַל לוֹ אֶלָּא בְּפָנָיו. שֶׁלֹּא בְּפָנָיו נִשְׁאָלִין לוֹ בֵּין בְּפָנָיו בֵּין שֶׁלֹּא בְּפָנָיו. רִבִּי יוֹחָנָן אָמַר. מִפְּנֵי הַבּוּשָׁה. רִבִּי יְהוֹשֻׁעַ בֶּן לֵוִי אָמַר. מִפְּנֵי הַחֲשָׁד.

[51]"A person who makes a vow 'to forbid himself the people of the town,' if another person came and dwelled there for thirty days, [the vower] is permitted to deal with him. 'From the inhabitants of the town,' if another person came and dwelled there for thirty days, [the vower] is

prohibited from dealing with him.⁵² "A *qônām* that the people of my town cannot have any usufruct from me,' he cannot ask the local rabbi⁵³. 'The usufruct of the people of my town [is forbidden] to me', he can ask the local rabbi. Some Tannaïm state, even in the first case he can ask, for it does not mean that [the rabbi] would dissolve his own vow⁵⁴. A vow of the community cannot be dissolved⁵⁵. A vow made in public cannot be dissolved⁵⁶. ⁵⁷"If somebody made a vow that another should not have usufruct from him, if the vow was made in the other's presence, he can request the vow to be dissolved only in the other's presence; if the vow was not made in the other's presence, he can request the dissolution either in the other's presence or in his absence." Rebbi Joḥanan said, because of the shame; Rebbi Joshua ben Levi said, because of the suspicion⁵⁸.

---

51 Tosephta 2:10, a slightly different version in the Babli, *Baba Batra* 8a, *Sanhedrin* 112a.

52 "People of the town" are its taxpayers. The obligation to pay local taxes starts only with a residence of 12 months. "Town dwellers" are those who have to contribute to the local welfare fund. That obligation starts after thirty days.

53 Since he is an interested party.

54 The rabbi does not have to disqualify himself since formally he is only forbidden to dissolve his own vows and it is probably embarrassing to him to deal with a person who makes that kind of vow.

55 This is generally agreed on (Babli *Giṭṭin* 36a, *Makkot* 16a); since voter rolls change continuously, it is impossible to get all people who voted for the vow together to ask for dissolution.

56 The Babli, *Giṭṭin* 36a, decides against this.

57 Tosephta 2:10.

58 R. Joḥanan feels that the maker of an inappropriate vow should be shamed, R. Joshua ben Levi requires the other party to be present lest he thought that the vower broke his vow. The Babli, 65a, disagrees and holds that the rule is biblical. Since Moses had sworn to Reuel to stay in Midian (*Ex.*

2:21), God dissolved his vow not at the Senna-bush but in Midian, with the consent of his family (*Ex.* 3:18).

(39b, line 22) וְאַתְיָין אִילֵּין פְּלוּגְוָתָא כְּאִילֵין פְּלוּגְוָתָא. דְּתַנֵּי. יוֹם הַכִּיפּוּרִים צָרִיךְ לִפְרוֹט אֶת מַעֲשָׂיו. דִּבְרֵי רִבִּי יוּדָה בֶּן בְּתֵירָה. רִבִּי עֲקִיבָה אוֹמֵר. אֵינוֹ צָרִיךְ לִפְרוֹט אֶת הַחֵטְא. אִית תַּנָּיֵי תַּגֵּי. צָרִיךְ לִפְרוֹט אֶת הַנֶּדֶר. אִית תַּנָּיֵי תַּגֵּי. אֵינוֹ צָרִיךְ לִפְרוֹט אֶת הַנֶּדֶר. חַד בַּר נָשׁ נָדַר דְּלָא מִרְוָוחָא. אָתָא לְגַבֵּי רִבִּי יוּדָן בַּר שָׁלוֹם. אָמַר לֵיהּ. מִמַּאי אִישְׁתַּבָּעַת. אָמַר לֵיהּ. דְּלָא מִרְוָוחָא. אָמַר לֵיהּ רִבִּי יוּדָן. וְכֵן בַּר נָשׁ עֲבִיד. [אָמַר לֵיהּ בְּקַבְיוֹסְטָא].[59] אָמַר. בָּרוּךְ שֶׁבָּחַר בַּתּוֹרָה וּבַחֲכָמִים שֶׁאָמְרוּ. צָרִיךְ לִפְרוֹט אֶת הַנֶּדֶר.

It turns out that one disagreement is like an other other disagreement, as it was stated: On the Day of Atonement, one has to detail one's deeds, the words of Rebbi Jehudah ben Bathyra. Rebbi Aqiba says, one does not have to detail the sin[60]. Some Tannaïm state, one has to detail the vow; some Tannaïm state, one does not have to detail the vow. A person made a vow not to earn money. He came before Rebbi Yudan bar Shalom. He asked him, what did you forswear to yourself? He said to him, not to earn money. Rebbi Yudan said to him, is there anyone doing that? He said to him, as a gambler[61]. He said, praise to Him Who chose the Torah and the Sages who said, one has to detail the vow[62].

59 Reading of the quote in Rosh (R. Asher ben Iehiel) to *Giṭṭin* 35b. In the ms. there is an erasure here, on which is written פ׳ דילמ׳ בקביוסטיסא "explanation: perhaps in gambling". The last two words are printed in the *editio princeps* but because of the Babylonian/rabbinic דילמא they cannot represent the text. (It seems that in his notes for his dictionary, J. Levy misread לח (38) for לה (35). The error was faithfully copied by the compilors of later dictionaries (Kohut, Jastrow, Krauss).)

60 *Yoma*, Yerushalmi 1:9 (45c, l. 48); Babli 86b. [There, the first author

is R. Jehudah ben Baba. In the first hand of the Munich ms. the second author is R. Jehudah; this seems to have been the reading of Maimonides (*Tešubah* 2:3) and *Tosafot Yešenim ad loc.*]

61   Perhaps Greek κυβευτής, ὁ "gambler". (In rabbinic practice, a professional gambler is inadmissible as a witness.)

62   If he had not asked, he would have dissolved the vow which did not warrant dissolution.

משנה ה: וְאֵי זֶהוּ דָבָר שֶׁלְעוֹלֵי בָבֶל. כְּגוֹן הַר הַבַּיִת וְהָעֲזָרוֹת וְהַבְּאֵר שֶׁבְּאֶמְצַע הַדֶּרֶךְ. וְאֵי זֶהוּ דָבָר שֶׁלְּאוֹתָהּ הָעִיר כְּגוֹן הָרְחָבָה וְהַמֶּרְחָץ וּבֵית הַכְּנֶסֶת וְהַתֵּיבָה וְהַסְפָרִים וְהַכּוֹתֵב חֶלְקוֹ לַנָּשִׂיא. (fol. 39a)

Mishnah 5: What are the institutions of the returnees from Babylonia? For example, the Temple Mount, the courtyards[63], and the cistern in the middle of the road[64]. What are the institutions of that town? For example, the town square, the bathhouse, the synagogue with the ark and the scrolls. And he writes his part to the Patriarch[65].

63   The Temple courtyards.
64   Traditionally made for pilgrims.
65   In the case of Mishnah 4, if each one writes over his part of the public institutions of the town to the Patriarch, both of them are permitted to walk in the town and to use its institutions.

הלכה ה: וְאֵי זֶהוּ דָבָר שֶׁלְעוֹלֵי בָבֶל כול'. כֵּינִי מַתְנִיתָא. רְחָבָה שֶׁדֶּרֶךְ הָרַבִּים מַפְסַקְתָּהּ כְּעוֹלֵי בָבֶל הִיא. חַד בַּר נָשׁ קִידֵּשׁ בְּסֵפֶר תּוֹרָה. רִבִּי שׁוֹבְתַי וְרִבִּי חֲסִידָא אַעֲלוּן עוֹבְדָא קוֹמֵי רִבִּי יוֹסֵי וְאָמַר. אֵינָהּ מְקוּדֶּשֶׁת. אָמַר רִבִּי חִזְקִיָה. אַתְּ קָרֵת אִיגַּרְתָּא וּכְתִיב בְּגַוָּהּ. וְלֹא עוֹד. אָמַר רִבִּי מָנָא. קַשִׁיתָהּ קוֹמֵי רִבִּי חִזְקִיָה. מַהוּ וְלֹא עוֹד. בְּסֵפֶר תּוֹרָה שֶׁלְיָחִיד קִידֵּשׁ. אָמַר (39b, line 29)

לוֹן. אֵינָהּ מְקוּדֶּשֶׁת. אָתָא מֵימַר לָךְ אֲפִילוּ בְסֵפֶר תּוֹרָה שֶׁלָרַבִּים קִידֵּשׁ. וְהֵינוּ וְלֹא עוֹד. אָתָא מֵימַר לָךְ אֲפִילוּ בְסֵפֶר תּוֹרָה שֶׁלַיְחִידִי קִידֵּשׁ. וְהֵינוּ אֵינָהּ מְקוּדֶּשֶׁת.

Halakhah 5: "What are the institutions of the returnees from Babylonia," etc. So is the Mishnah: A town square which is crossed by a public road is as if from the returnees from Babylonia[66]. A man used a Torah scroll for his preliminary marriage[67] to a woman. Rebbi Sabbatai and Rebbi Ḥasida brought the matter before Rebbi Yose who said, she is not married[68]. Rebbi Ḥizqiah said, you read the letter[69] and there is written in it "not only". Rebbi Mana said, I asked before Rebbi Ḥizqiah, what means "not only"? Did he marry with a Torah scroll which is private property[70]? He said to us, she is not married. That comes to tell you, even if he used the public Torah scroll[71] to marry, that is "not only". But that means, even if he used a privately owned Torah scroll to marry, that is "she is not married."

66 Tosephta 2:10. This is not an emendation of the Mishnah but an explanation: A town square which is crossed by an imperial highway is imperial, not local, property.

67 Where the man has to give his fiancee something of value; cf. *Peah* 2:3, Note 46; *Demay* 4:2, Note 19; *Yebamot* 1:1, Note 63.

68 A Torah scroll cannot serve as a marriage gift.

69 Maybe it should be: I read the letter.

70 Since a Torah scroll may be sold only if a person is in extreme difficulties (*Bikkurim* 3:7, end), it is doubtful whether monetary value was transferred. (For that reason, a modern marriage is concluded by the gift of a gold ring without a stone, whose commercial value can be easily determined.)

71 In which every member of the synagogue has partial ownership. But since only the town council backed by a vote of the entire population could

sell a Torah scroll, even if the man transferred his interest to his bride, he did not transfer disposable value.

משנה ו: רִבִּי יְהוּדָה אוֹמֵר אֶחָד כּוֹתֵב לַנָּשִׂיא וְאֶחָד כּוֹתֵב לַהֶדְיוֹט. (fol. 39a) מַה בֵּין כּוֹתֵב לַנָּשִׂיא לַכּוֹתֵב לַהֶדְיוֹט שֶׁהַכּוֹתֵב לַנָּשִׂיא אֵינוֹ צָרִיךְ לְזַכּוֹת וְהַכּוֹתֵב לַהֶדְיוֹט צָרִיךְ לוֹ לְזַכּוֹת. וַחֲכָמִים אוֹמְרִים אֶחָד זֶה וְאֶחָד זֶה צְרִיכִין לְזַכּוֹת. לֹא דִּבְּרוּ בַנָּשִׂיא אֶלָּא בַהוֹוֶה. רִבִּי יְהוּדָה אוֹמֵר אֵין אַנְשֵׁי הַגָּלִיל צְרִיכִין לִכְתּוֹב שֶׁכְּבָר כָּתְבוּ אֲבוֹתָם עַל יְדֵיהֶם.

Mishnah 6: Rebbi Jehudah says, one of them writes to the Patriarch and the other to a private person[72]. What is the difference between him who writes to the Patriarch and him who writes to a private person? The one who writes to the Patriarch does not have to perform an act of delivery[73], the one who writes to a private person has to perform an act of delivery. But the Sages say, in either case one has to perform an act of delivery. Rebbi Jehudah says, the people of Galilee do not have to write since their forefathers already wrote for them[74].

72 This is a continuation of the previous Mishnah. R. Jehudah permits either of the parties to donate their usufruct of public property to a third party even though public property is not transferable in this way.

73 In talmudic legal theory, a transfer of property is only valid if the point in time of the transfer of property rights or of claims to property is well defined. This usually is done by the buyer (or recipient) or his representative giving to the seller (or donor) or his representative a vessel (or edge of garment) to hold temporarily. In talmudic theory, Boaz took off his shoe to acquire the right to buy back Elimelekh's property and with it Ruth (by preliminary marriage) from Tob (*Ruth* 4:8). Following the

terminology of the Book of Ruth, in Babylonian/rabbinic terminology this act is called קִנְיָן "acquisition".

74 They never recognized private rights of the citizens to public property. Therefore, the vower and the subject of his vow can use public property without formalities.

(39b, line 37) **הלכה ו**: רִבִּי יְהוּדָה אוֹמֵר אֲפִילוּ אֶחָד כּוֹתֵב חֶלְקוֹ לַנָּשִׂיא כול׳. כֵּינִי מַתְנִיתָא. צָרִיךְ לִכְתּוֹב חֶלְקוֹ לַנָּשִׂיא.

Halakhah 6: "Rebbi Jehudah says, even if only one signs over his part to the Patriarch," etc. So is the Mishnah: One of them has to sign over his part to the Patriarch[75].

75 Not both of them to ordinary citizens. Cf. J. N. Epstein, מבוא לנוסח המשנה ², Jerusalem-Tel Aviv 1964, p. 361, who raises the question whether the "Patriarch" is the head of the Academy or the head of the city administration.

(fol. 39a) **משנה ז**: הַמּוּדָּר הֲנָיָיה מֵחֲבֵירוֹ וְאֵין לוֹ מַה יּאׁכַל נוֹתְנוֹ לְאַחֵר מִשֵּׁם מַתָּנָה וְהַלָּה מוּתָּר בָּהּ. מַעֲשֶׂה בְּבֵית חוֹרוֹן בְּאֶחָד שֶׁהָיָה אָבִיו מוּדָּר מִמֶּנּוּ הֲנָייָה וְהָיָה מַשִּׂיא אֶת בְּנוֹ וְאָמַר לַחֲבֵירוֹ הֲרֵי הֶחָצֵר וְהַסְּעוּדָה נְתוּנִין לָךְ בְּמַתָּנָה וְהֵן בְּפָנֶיךָ עַד שֶׁיָּבוֹא אַבָּא וְיֹאכַל עִמָּנוּ בַּסְּעוּדָה. אָמַר לוֹ אִם שֶׁלִּי הֵם הֲרֵי הֵן מוּקְדָּשִׁין לַשָּׁמַיִם. אָמַר לוֹ לֹא נָתַתִּי לָךְ אֶת שֶׁלִּי שֶׁתַּקְדִּישֵׁם לַשָּׁמַיִם. אָמַר לוֹ לֹא נָתַתָּה לִי אֶת שֶׁלָּךְ אֶלָּא שֶׁתְּהֵא אַתָּה וְאָבִיךָ אוֹכְלִים וְשׁוֹתִים וּמִתְרַצִּין זֶה לָזֶה וִיהֵא עָוֹן תָּלוּי בְּרֹאשִׁי. וּכְשֶׁבָּא דָּבָר לִפְנֵי חֲכָמִים אָמְרוּ כָּל מַתָּנָה שֶׁאֵינָהּ שֶׁאִם הִקְדִּישָׁהּ אֵינָהּ מְקוּדֶּשֶׁת אֵינָהּ מַתָּנָה.

Mishnah 7: If a person who by a vow was forbidden usufruct from another has nothing to eat, the other donates [food] as a gift to a third party and the person is permitted it[76]. It happened in Bet Ḥoron with a person whose father was by a vow forbidden usufruct from him; when he married off his son he said to a friend, here the courtyard[77] and the meal are given to you as a gift and they shall be yours until my father has come and eaten with us at the [wedding] meal. He said to him, if they are mine, they are dedicated to Heaven[78]. He said, I did not give you my property that you should dedicate it to Heaven. He said to him, you gave me your property only that you and your father should eat, drink, and be friendly with one another and let the sin hang on my head. When the case came before the Sages they said, any gift with the proviso that if [the recipient] dedicated, it was not sanctified, is no gift.

76 This was already stated in Mishnah 4:10; it is repeated as introduction to the definition of "gift".

77 His own courtyard, where the wedding takes place and his father is forbidden entry.

78 They are Temple property to be sold for the upkeep of the Temple.

(39b, line 39) **הלכה ז**: הַמּוּדָּר הֲנָייָה מֵחֲבֵירוֹ כול׳. אָמַר רְבִּי יוֹחָנָן. נִיכָּר הוּא זֶה שֶׁהוּא תַּלְמִיד חָכָם.

Halakhah 7: "If a person who by a vow was forbidden usufruct from another," etc. Rebbi Joḥanan said, it is obvious that this one was learned.

(39b, line 40) שְׁמוֹנִים זוּג שֶׁלְּתַלְמִידִים הָיוּ לוֹ לְהִלֵּל הַזָּקֵן. גָּדוֹל שֶׁבָּהֶן יוֹנָתָן בֶּן עוּזִּיאֵל. וְהַקָּטָן שֶׁבָּהֶן רַבָּן יוֹחָנָן בֶּן זַכַּאי. פַּעַם אַחַת חָלָה וְנִכְנְסוּ כּוּלָּן לְבַקְּרוֹ. עָמַד לוֹ רַבָּן יוֹחָנָן בֶּן זַכַּאי בֶּחָצֵר. אָמַר לָהֶן. הֵיכָן הוּא הַקָּטָן שֶׁבָּכֶם שֶׁהוּא אַב לְחָכְמָה וְאַב לְדוֹרוֹת. אֵין צָרִיךְ לוֹמַר הַגָּדוֹל שֶׁבָּכֶם. אָמְרוּ לוֹ. הֲרֵי הוּא בֶחָצֵר. אָמַר לָהֶן. יִכָּנֵס. כֵּיוָן שֶׁנִּכְנַס אָמַר לָהֶן. לְהַנְחִיל אוֹהֲבַי יֵשׁ וְאוֹצְרוֹתֵיהֶם אֲמַלֵּא.

[79]Hillel the Elder had eighty pairs of students. The greatest among them was Jonathan ben Uzziel, the least important Rabban Johanan ben Zakkai. Once he fell sick and all came to visit him. Rabban Johanan ben Zakkai waited in the courtyard. He said to them, where is the least important among you who is a head in wisdom and a head for generations? Unnecessary to speak of the greatest among you! They said, he is in the courtyard. He said to them, let him enter. When he entered, he said to them "to let my lovers inherit substance; their treasuries I shall fill.[80]"

79   Cf. Babli *Sukkah* 28a.   3:12.
80   *Prov.* 8:21. Cf. Mishnah *Uqeṣin*

(39b, line 46) וְאָמַר רִבִּי יוֹחָנָן. נִיכָּר הוּא זֶה שֶׁהוּא תַּלְמִיד חָכָם. אָמַר רִבִּי יוֹסֵי בֵּירִבִּי בּוּן. אָכֵין הֲוָה עוֹבְדָא. יוֹנָתָן בַּר עוּזִיאֵל הִדִּירוֹ אָבִיו מִנְּכָסָיו וְעָמַד וּכְתָבָן לְשַׁמַּי. מַה עָשָׂה שַׁמַּי. מָכַר מִקְצָת וְהִקְדִּישׁ מִקְצָת וְנָתַן לוֹ מַתָּנָה אֶת הַשְּׁאָר וְאָמַר. כָּל־מִי שֶׁיָּבוֹא וִיעַרְעֵר עַל הַמַּתָּנָה הַזֹּאת יוֹצִיא מִיַּד הַלְּקוּחוֹת וּמִיַּד הַהֶקְדֵּשׁ וְאַחַר כָּךְ יוֹצִיא מִיַּד זֶה.

"Rabbi Johanan said, it is obvious that this one was learned." Rebbi Yose ben Rebbi Abun said, that is what happened[81]: Jonathan ben Uzziel's father vowed not to let him have any usufruct from him and in his will gave his[82] part to Shammai. What did Shammai do? He sold some, gave some to the sacred fund, gave him[82] the remainder as a gift, and said: He who wants to attack this gift[83], let him first get back [the merchandise] from the buyers and from the sacred fund; after that he can get [the remainder] back from this[82] one[84].

81 The background of the last Mishnah. A similar story, with Jonathan ben Uzziel in the role given here to Shammai, is in the Babli, *Baba Batra* 133b with Shammai trying and failing to attack the method.	83 As circumventing the will of the donor.
82 Jonathan ben Uzziel.	84 If somebody wants to shield himself from an accusation of "Beth Ḥoron gift", he should give something away before giving to the person prohibited by the vow.

(39b, line 51) רִבִּי יִרְמְיָה בְּעֵי. מֵעַתָּה אֵין אָדָם נוֹתֵן מַתָּנָה לַחֲבֵירוֹ עַל מְנָת שֶׁלֹּא יַקְדִּישֶׁנָּה לַשָּׁמַיִם. כֵּינִי מַתְנִיתָא. כָּל מַתָּנָה שֶׁהִיא כְּמַתְּנַת בֵּית חוֹרוֹן שֶׁהָיְתָה בְהַעֲרָמָה שֶׁאֵינָהּ שֶׁאִם הִקְדִּישָׁהּ אֵינָהּ מְקוּדֶּשֶׁת אֵינָהּ מַתָּנָה.

Rebbi Jeremiah asked: Does this mean that nobody can give a gift to a friend on condition that he not dedicate it to Heaven[85]? So is the Mishnah: Any gift similar to that of Beth Ḥoron, which was dishonest in that if [the recipient] dedicated, it was not sanctified, is no gift[86].

85 Does such a clause invalidate any gift even if given honestly and permanently?	48a: If the end proved that the beginning was dishonest. The Babli prefers to emend the first, not the last, sentence of the Mishnah.
86 In the language of the Babli,	

הנודר מן המבושל פרק שישי

(fol. 39b) **משנה א:** הַנּוֹדֵר מִן הַמְבוּשָׁל מוּתָּר בַּצָּלִי וּבַשָּׁלוּק. אָמַר קוֹנָם תַּבְשִׁיל שֶׁאֵינִי טוֹעֵם אָסוּר בְּמַעֲשֵׂה קְדֵירָה דַק וּמוּתָּר בְּעָבֶה. וּמוּתָּר בְּבֵיצָה טְרֹמֵיטָן וּבְדַלַּעַת הָרְמוּצָה.

Mishnah 1: One who makes a vow to abstain from cooked food is permitted roasted and scalded food[1]. If one said, a *qônām* that I will not taste a cooked dish, he is forbidden fine dishes[2] and permitted thick ones[3]. Also he is permitted a soft boiled egg[4] and ash-gourd[5].

1 In rabbinic tradition, based on the Babli, שלק means "preserved by prolonged cooking" so that the food can be kept for a long time without refrigeration. But Rashba (*Novellae ad loc.*) makes a convincing argument, based on *Terumot* 10:8 (Notes 103-104), that שלק is scalding (pouring hot water over the food), not cooking in a pot.

2 Those which contain visible moisture.

3 If there is no more visible moisture and it can be eaten without bread (or today, without a fork).

4 Galen VI, 769 distinguishes kinds of eggs: ἑφθά "hard boiled", τρομητά "trembling" , i. e. with solid egg white but soft yolk, which tremble if shelled, ῥοφητά "soft", which can be sipped. In contrast to the Yerushalmi which identifies the last two kinds, the Babli (50b) on the testimony of Samuel, a medical doctor, defines a *trometa* egg as a diagnostic egg made extra hard and indigestible by alternatingly cooking and freezing until it is small and hard, can be swallowed whole, and, when excreted, examined for traces of blood from stomach or intestines.

5 Explained in the Halakhah.

HALAKHAH 1

(39c line 23) **הלכה א**: הַנּוֹדֵר מִן הַמְבוּשָׁל כול׳. מַתְנִיתָא אָמְרָה שֶׁהַשָּׁלוּק קָרוּי מְבוּשָׁל. דְּתַנִינָן. ׳ הָיָה מְבַשֵּׁל אֶת הַשְּׁלָמִים אוֹ שׁוֹלֵק. וְקַרְיָיא שֶׁהַצָּלוּי קָרוּי מְבוּשָׁל. וַיְבַשְּׁלוּ אֶת הַפֶּסַח וגו׳. אִין תֵּימַר שֶׁלֹּא כַהֲלָכָה. רִבִּי יוֹנָה בּוֹצְרָייָא אָמַר כַּמִשְׁפָּט. מַתְנִיתָא אָמְרָה שֶׁהַשָּׁלוּק קָרוּי מְבוּשָׁל. וְקַרְיָיא אָמַר שֶׁהַצָּלוּי קָרוּי מְבוּשָׁל. וְהָתַנִּינָן. הַנּוֹדֵר מִן הַמְבוּשָׁל מוּתָּר בַּצָּלִי וּבַשָּׁלוּק. אָמַר רִבִּי יוֹחָנָן. הָלְכוּ בַּנְּדָרִים אַחַר לְשׁוֹן בְּנֵי אָדָם. אָמַר רִבִּי יֹאשִׁיָּה. הָלְכוּ בַּנְּדָרִים אַחַר לְשׁוֹן תּוֹרָה. מַה נְפִיק מִבֵּינֵיהוֹן. קוֹנָם יַיִן שֶׁאֵינִי טוֹעֵם בַּחַג. עַל דַּעְתֵּיהּ דְּרִבִּי יוֹחָנָן אָסוּר בְּיוֹם טוֹב הָאַחֲרוֹן. עַל דַּעְתֵּיהּ דְּרִבִּי יֹאשִׁיָּה מוּתָּר. אַף רִבִּי יֹאשִׁיָּה מוֹדֶה שֶׁאָסוּר. לֹא אָמַר רִבִּי יֹאשִׁיָּה אֶלָּא לְחוֹמְרִין.

Halakhah 1: "One who makes a vow to abstain from cooked food," etc. [6]A Mishnah states that scalding is called cooking, as we have stated: "If he cooked the well-being offering or scalded it[7]". A verse [states] that "roasted" is called "cooked"[8]: "They cooked the *pesaḥ*" etc. If you say, against the rules, Rebbi Jonah from Bostra said, "as is the rule". A Mishnah states that scalded is called cooked, and a verse that roasted is called cooked; but did we not state: "One who makes a vow to abstain from cooked food is permitted roasted and scalded food"? Rebbi Joḥanan said, in matters of vows one follows common usage. Rebbi Joshia said, in matters of vows one follows biblical usage[9]. What is the difference between them? 'A *qônām* that I shall not taste wine on Tabernacles.' In the opinion of Rebbi Joḥanan he is forbidden on the last day of the holiday[10]. In the opinion of Rebbi Joshia, is he permitted? Also Rebbi Joshia agrees that he is prohibited. Rebbi Joshia said it only for restrictions[11].

6   This paragraph and the next are also in *Erubin* 3:1 (20d l. 21) and *Nazir* 6:11 (55c l. 18). The argument of this paragraph is also in the Babli, 49a,

where the opinion of R. Joḥanan is declared to be that of the Tanna of the Mishnah.

7 Mishnah *Nazir* 6:11. This refers to the ram which is the well-being offering of the *nazir* at the end of his period of sanctification. The verse, *Num.* 6:18, requires the Cohen to take a limb "from the cooked ram". The Mishnah accepts שָׁלוּק as cooked. Since the meat of the ram must be eaten immediately, it is clear that שלק cannot mean "to preserve by prolonged cooking".

8 *2Chr.* 35:13: "They cooked the *pesaḥ* in the fire as is the rule"; i. e., (*Ex.* 12:9) "roasted in fire". Cooked would have been "over the fire".

9 The Babli, 49a, states that R. Joshia disagrees with the Mishnah and forbids both roasted and preserved.

10 The eighth day of the fall festival which in popular consciousness is part of Tabernacles but in biblical terminology (*Num.* 29:35) is a separate holiday.

11 He requires that both in biblical Hebrew and in the vernacular the terms should denote different things.

(39c line 32) רִבִּי חִייָה בַּר בָּא אָמַר. רִבִּי יוֹחָנָן אָכַל חֲלִיטָא וְאָמַר. לֹא טָעַמִית מָזוֹן בְּהָדָא יוֹמָא. וְהָא תַּנִּינָן. הַנּוֹדֵר מִן הַמָּזוֹן מוּתָּר בְּמַיִם וּבְמֶלַח. פָּתַר לָהּ כְּרִבִּי יֹאשִׁיָּה דְּאָמַר. הִילְכוּ בִּנְדָרִים אַחַר לְשׁוֹן תּוֹרָה. וּמְנַיִין שֶׁכָּל־הַדְּבָרִים קְרוּיִין מָזוֹן. רִבִּי אָחָא בַּר עוּלָא אָמַר. וַעֲשֶׂר אֲתוֹנוֹת נוֹשְׂאוֹת בָּר וְלֶחֶם וּמָזוֹן. מַה תַּלְמוּד לוֹמַר וּמָזוֹן. אֶלָּא מִכָּן שֶׁכָּל־הַדְּבָרִים קְרוּיִין מָזוֹן.

Rebbi Ḥiyya bar Abba said, Rebbi Joḥanan ate bake-meats[12] and said, I did not taste food on that day. But did we not state[13]: "He who made a vow not to eat food is permitted water and salt"? Explain it following Rebbi Joshia, who said, in matters of vows one follows biblical usage. And from where that everything is called food? Rebbi Aḥa bar Ulla said[14]: "And ten female donkeys carrying grain, bread, and food." Why does the verse say, "and food"? From here that everything is called food.

12 Cf. *Ḥallah* 1:5, Note 164; baked goods, not bread, made in the market. An exaggerated parallel to this is in the Babli, *Berakhot* 44a.	14 Gen. 45:23; the verse implies that "food" is different from grain and bread. The Babli, *Berakhot* 35b, disagrees and defines as מזון any food made from grain.
13 *Erubin* 3:1. That Mishnah contradicts R. Joḥanan.	

(39c line 37) הַנּוֹדֵר מִן הַמְבוּשָׁל מָהוּ שֶׁיְּהֵא מוּתָּר מִן הַמְעוּשָׁן. מָהוּ שֶׁיְּהֵא מוּתָּר בִּמְטוּגָּן. מָהוּ שֶׁיְּהֵא מוּתָּר בְּתַבְשִׁיל שֶׁנִּתְבַּשֵּׁל בָּה מֵי טְבֶּרְיָה. רַבָּנִין דְּקַיְסָרִין שָׁאָלוֹן. מְעוּשָׁן מָהוּ שֶׁיְּהֵא בּוֹ מִשּׁוּם בִּישּׁוּלֵי גוֹיִם. מָהוּ שֶׁיְּהֵא בּוֹ מִשּׁוּם תַּבְשִׁילֵי שַׁבָּת. מָהוּ שֶׁיְּהֵא בּוֹ מִשּׁוּם בָּשָׂר בְּחָלָב. מָהוּ שֶׁיְּטַבֵּל לְמַעְשְׂרוֹת. הַנּוֹדֵר מִן הַמְעוּשָׁן מָהוּ שֶׁיְּהֵא מוּתָּר בְּתַבְשִׁיל. רִבִּי בָּא רַב יְהוּדָה בְּשֵׁם דְּבֵית רַב אַסִּי.[15] חֲבִיצָה אֵין בּוֹ מִשּׁוּם בִּישּׁוּלֵי גוֹיִם וְיוֹצְאִין בּוֹ מִשֵּׁם עֵירוּבֵי תַבְשִׁילִין. רִבִּי יוֹסֵי בֵּירִבִּי בּוּן בְּשֵׁם רַב חוּנָה. כָּל־אוֹכֶל שֶׁהוּא נֶאֱכָל חַי כְּמוֹת שֶׁהוּא אֵין בּוֹ מִשּׁוּם בִּישּׁוּלֵי גוֹיִם וְיוֹצְאִין בּוֹ מִשֵּׁם עֵירוּבֵי תַבְשִׁילִין.

May one who made a vow not to have anything cooked be permitted smoked? May he be permitted fried? May he be permitted anything cooked in the hot springs of Tiberias[16]? The rabbis of Caesarea asked: Is anything smoked forbidden because of Gentile cooking[17]? Is it forbidden because of cooking on the Sabbath? Is it forbidden because of meat and milk? Does it cause *ṭevel* for tithes[18]? If somebody made a vow not to have anything smoked, is he permitted cooked? Rebbi Abba, Rav Jehudah in the name of the House of Rav Assi: *Ḥabiṣ*[19] is unproblematic as Gentile cooking and is acceptable as *eruv tavšilin*. Rebbi Yose ben Rebbi Abun in the name of Rav Huna: Anything which can be eaten raw is unproblematic as Gentile cooking and is acceptable as *eruv tavšilin*[20].

15   This is the reading of the first hand in the mss. The corrector (followed by *editio princeps*) has unexplained אתי.

16   If a pot is immersed in a hot spring, is the food cooked by human action? If it is not by human action, it cannot be sanctioned.

17   In the opinion of the Yerushalmi [*Šabbat* 1 (3c l. 65), *Avodah zarah* 2:9 (41d l. 35)] it is a biblical prohibition, based on *Deut.* 2:28 to eat Gentile food which is in a state different from raw and not prepared with the help of a Jew. In the opinion of the Babli, *Avodah zarah* 37b/38a, this is a purely pharisaic-rabbinic restriction for which the verse serves as a crutch. The question now is whether hanging anything in a chimney over a smoky fire which was not lit for the purpose of cooking would be considered cooking anyhow.

18   This is always the same question. Cooking is forbidden on the Sabbath (Mishnah *Šabbat* 7:2) parallel to baking. Since baking cannot be replaced by smoking, there is a question. Similarly, it is forbidden to cook milk and meat together (*Ex.* 23:19; 34:26; *Deut.* 14:21).

Cooking untithed food makes the food forbidden until heave and tithes have been taken. {While the Mishnah (*Ma'serot* 4:1) only states that preserving by prolonged cooking creates the obligation, the formulation in the Halakhah is "fire creates the obligation". In the first formulation, preserving by smoking might be excluded, in the second it is included.} The questions are unanswered since in matters of biblical prohibitions a doubt must be resolved in a restrictive decision.

19   Arabic خَبِيص "a delicacy made from dates, cream, and starch".

20   In the Babli, *Avodah zarah* 38a, in the name of Rav, Rav Huna's teacher.

(39c line 46) הַנּוֹדֵר מִן הַמְבוּשָׁל מָהוּ שֶׁיְּהֵא מוּתָּר בְּעָבֶה. נִישְׁמְעִינָהּ מִן הָדָא. וְאָסוּר בְּמַעֲשֵׂה קְדֵירָה רַךְ²¹ וּמוּתָּר בְּעָבֶה. מָה אִם תַּבְשִׁיל שֶׁהוּא נֶאֱסָר בְּצָלוּי וּבְשָׁלוּק מוּתָּר בְּעָבֶה. מְבוּשָּׁל שֶׁהוּא מוּתָּר בְּצָלוּי וּבְשָׁלוּק אֵינוֹ דִין שֶׁיְּהֵא מוּתָּר בְּעָבֶה. וְיֵשׁ קַל וָחוֹמֶר בִּנְדָרִים. אֶלָּא כֵינִי. תַּבְשִׁיל שֶׁאָסוּר בְּצָלוּי וּבְשָׁלוּק אָסוּר בְּעָבֶה מְבוּשָּׁל. מְבוּשָּׁל שֶׁהוּא מוּתָּר בְּצָלוּי וּבְשָׁלוּק מוּתָּר בְּעָבֶה.

HALAKHAH 1   575

Reading of Rashba (*Novellae ad* 49a)[22]:

הַנּוֹדֵר מִן הַמְבוּשָׁל מָהוּ שֶׁיְּהֵא מוּתָּר בְּעָבָה. נִשְׁמְעִינָהּ מִן הָדָא. אָסוּר בְּמַעֲשֵׂה קְדֵירָה רַךְ וּמוּתָּר בְּעָבָה. מָה אִם תַּבְשִׁיל שֶׁהוּא אָסוּר בִּצְלִי וּבְשָׁלוּק מוּתָּר בְּמַעֲשֵׂה קְדֵרָה עָבֶה. מְבוּשָׁל שֶׁהוּא מוּתָּר בִּצְלִי וּבְשָׁלוּק אֵינוֹ דִין שֶׁיְּהֵא מוּתָּר בְּעָבָה. וְיֵשׁ קַל וָחוֹמֶר בִּנְדָרִים. אֶלָּא כֵינִי. תַּבְשִׁיל שֶׁהוּא בִּצְלִי וּבְשָׁלוּק אָסוּר מוּתָּר בְּעָבָה. וּמְבוּשָׁל שֶׁהוּא מוּתָּר בִּצְלִי וּבְשָׁלוּק מוּתָּר בְּעָבָה.

[23]Is one who makes a vow to abstain from cooked food permitted a thick[3] dish? Let us hear from the following: "He is forbidden soft dishes[2] and permitted thick ones[3]." Since a dish which would be forbidden roasted or scalded is permitted as a thick dish, regarding "cooked food" which permits roasted and scalded, is it not logical that he be permitted the thick dish? Are there arguments *de minore ad majus* in matters of vows[24]? But it must be so: Since a dish which is forbidden roasted or scalded is permitted as a thick dish, the cooked which is permitted roasted or scalded is permitted as a thick dish.

21   This is the reading of the Mishnah in the Babli.

22   This is a coherent text which makes sense. However, the susbstitution of צלי for צלוי indicates that the text was copied without attention to the intricacies of Yerushalmi spelling. The deviations from the ms. text are indicated by a change of typeface.

23   The translation follows the Rashba text.

24   According to R. Johanan, the meaning of vows can be ascertained only by analysis of the vernacular which is not subject to logical rules.

(39c line 52) תַּנֵּי. אָסוּר בְּהִטְרִיּוֹת רַכּוֹת. שֶׁכֵּן דֶּרֶךְ הָרוֹפֶא לוֹכַל פִּתּוֹ בָּהֶן. אָמַר רַב חִסְדָּא. אָסוּר בְּבֵיצָה מְגוּלְגֶּלֶת. שֶׁכֵּן דֶּרֶךְ הַחוֹלֶה לוֹכַל פִּתּוֹ בָהּ.

It was stated: He is forbidden soft cakes[25], since the physician frequently eats his bread with them. Rav Ḥisda said, he is forbidden a roasted[26] egg since a sick person frequently eats his bread with them.

25 Greek ἴτριον, cf. Ḥallah 1, Note 178. The dough must still be so soft that it must be put into a pitta to be eaten.

26 This usage of גלגל "to roll, make round" is documented in Mishnah (*Uqeṣin* 2:6) and Yerushalmi *Šabbat* 3:3 (6a l. 18). The Babli, 49a, has a general formulation by Abai, a student of Rav Ḥisda: Anything eaten with bread is called a dish.

(39c line 54) וּמוּתָּר בְּבֵיצָה טְרוֹמֵיטָא. רוֹפֵיטוֹן. וּבְדַלַּעַת הָרְמוּצָה. אָמַר רִבִּי חֲנִינָה כְּמִין דְּלַעַת מָרָה וְהֵן מְמַתְּקִין אוֹתָהּ בְּרִימְצָא.

"He is permitted a soft boiled egg," a soft one[4,27]. "And ash-gourd," [28]Rebbi Ḥinenah said, it is a kind of bitter gourd and they sweeten it in hot ashes.

27 It must be fluid if it cannot be eaten in a pitta, cf. the preceding Note.

28 This is from *Kilaim* 1, end of Halakhah 2, formulated in a slightly different way.

(fol. 39b) **משנה ב:** הַנּוֹדֵר מִמַּעֲשֵׂה קְדֵירָה אֵינוֹ אָסוּר אֶלָּא מִמַּעֲשֵׂה רְתַחְתָּהּ. אָמַר קוֹנָם יוֹרֵד לַקְּדֵירָה שֶׁאֵינִי טוֹעֵם אָסוּר בְּכָל־הַמִּתְבַּשְּׁלִים בַּקְּדֵירָה.

Mishnah 2: If somebody makes a vow to forbid himself anything made in a pot, he is forbidden only what is made in its heat[29]. If he said, a qônām that I shall not taste anything going into the pot, he is forbidden anything that may be cooked in any pot[30].

29 The expression "made in a pot" is restricted to cereals; cf. Babli *Berakhot* 37a.

30 Including vegetables and meat.

הלכה ב: (39c line 56) הַנּוֹדֵר מִמַּעֲשֵׂה קְדֵירָה כול׳. אֵיזוֹ הִיא מַעֲשֶׂה רוֹתְחָנָה. כְּגוֹן חִילְקָה טְרַגִּיס וְטִיסָנֵי סוֹלֶת וְאוֹרֶז זְרִיד וְעַרְסָן.

Halakhah 2: "If somebody makes a vow to forbid himself anything made in a pot," etc. What is made in its heat? For example split spelt, porridge, barley gruel[31], farina, rice, groats[32] and mashed cereal[33].

31 For these three kinds of cereal, cf. *Soṭa* 2, Notes 47-49.

32 This translation is tentative; from זרד "making branches".

33 This meaning is well established in the Babli, *Yoma* 47a, *Nedarim* 41b. According to Rashi (to *Berakhot* 37a), made from cereal split into many small pieces.

(39c line 57) מִן הַיּוֹרֵד לַקְּדֵירָה. אָסוּר בְּיוֹרֵד לַלְּפָס. מִן הַיּוֹרֵד לַלְּפָס מוּתָּר בְּיוֹרֵד לַקְּדֵירָה. שֶׁכָּל־הַיּוֹרֵד לַקְּדֵירָה יוֹרֵד לַלְּפָס וְיֵשׁ שֶׁיּוֹרֵד לַלְּפָס וְאֵינוֹ יוֹרֵד לַקְּדֵירָה. מַאי אִית לָךְ. כְּגוֹן הַחָל מִן נוּנְיָה. הַנּוֹדֵר מִן הָאָפוּי בַּתַּנּוּר אֵינוֹ אָסוּר אֶלָּא בְּפַת בִּלְבָד. מִן הַנַּעֲשִׂין בַּתַּנּוּר אָסוּר בְּכָל־הַנַּעֲשִׂין בַּתַּנּוּר.

[34][One who forbids himself] "anything going into the pot, is forbidden what goes into the frying pan[35]. From anything going into the frying pan is permitted what goes into the pot."[36] For there are things going into the frying pan which do not go into the pot. What do you have? For example, greasy[37] fish. "One who makes a vow to forbid to himself what is baked in the oven, is forbidden only bread. From what is prepared in the oven, anything is forbiddden that may be made in an oven"[36].

34 A similar text in the Babli, 51a.

35 Greek λοπάς; cf. *Peah* 8:8, Note 128.

36 Tosephta 3:2.

37 This translation is very tentative; it is based on Arabic خلم "sheep's fat". It is difficult to read one word החלמן since חֲלִימָה is a plant (cf. *Berakhot* 6:1, Note 112) and חֶלְמוֹן is egg yolk.

(fol. 39b) **משנה ג**: מִן הַכָּבוּשׁ אֵינוֹ אָסוּר אֶלָּא מִן הַכֶּבֶשׁ שֶׁלַּיָּרָק. כָּבוּשׁ שֶׁאֵינִי טוֹעֵם אָסוּר בְּכָל־הַכְּבוּשִׁים.

Mishnah 3: 'From the pickled', he is forbidden only pickled vegetables[38]. 'That I shall not taste anything pickled', he is forbidden everything pickled.

משנה ד: מִן הַשָּׁלֵק אֵינוֹ אָסוּר אֶלָּא מִן הַשָּׁלֵק שֶׁלַּבָּשָׂר דִּבְרֵי רִבִּי יְהוּדָה. שָׁלוּק שֶׁאֵינִי טוֹעֵם אָסוּר בְּכָל־הַשְּׁלָקִים.

Mishnah 4: 'From the scalded' he is forbidden only scalded meat, the words of Rebbi Jehudah[39]. 'That I shall not taste anything scalded', he is forbidden everything scalded.

משנה ה: מִן הַצָּלִי אֵינוֹ אָסוּר אֶלָּא מִן הַצָּלִי שֶׁלַּבָּשָׂר דִּבְרֵי רִבִּי יְהוּדָה. צְלִי שֶׁאֵינִי טוֹעֵם אָסוּר בְּכָל־הַצְּלוּיִים.

Mishnah 5: 'From the roast' he is forbidden only roasted meat, the words of Rebbi Jehudah. 'That I shall not taste anything roasted', he is forbidden everything roasted.

משנה ו: מִן הַמָּלִיחַ אֵינוֹ אָסוּר אֶלָּא מִן הַמָּלִיחַ שֶׁלַּדָּג. מָלִיחַ שֶׁאֵינִי טוֹעֵם אָסוּר בְּכָל־הַמְּלוּחִים.

Mishnah 6: 'From the salted' he is forbidden only salted fish. 'That I shall not taste anything salted', he is forbidden everything salted.

משנה ז: דָּג דָּגִים שֶׁאֵינִי טוֹעֵם אָסוּר בָּהֶן בֵּין גְּדוֹלִים בֵּין קְטַנִּים בֵּין מְלוּחִין בֵּין תְּפֵילִין בֵּין חַיִּין בֵּין מְבוּשָּׁלִין וּמוּתָּר בְּטָרִית טְרוּפָה וּבְצִיר. הַנּוֹדֵר

מִן הַצַּחֲנָה אָסוּר בִּטְרִית טְרוּפָה וּמוּתָּר בְּצִיר וּבְמוּרְיָיס. הַנּוֹדֵר מִטְרִית טְרוּפָה מוּתָּר בְּצִיר וּבְמוּרְיָיס.

Mishnah 7: 'That I shall not taste fish, fishes', he is forbidden them either large or small, either salted or unsalted, either raw or cooked. But he is permitted fish cake[40] and fish fluid[41]. If somebody vows not to eat anchovy[42] he is forbidden fish cake and permitted fish fluid and brine[43]. If somebody vows not to eat fish cake he is permitted[44] fish fluid and brine.

38 Normally "pickling" only vegetables. In the second sentence, anything pickled is forbidden, whether it is of the kind usually covered by the verb or not. The other Mishnaiot are treated similarly.

39 In the Babylonian Mishnah, this is missing and the entire Mishnah is anonymous. It is found in הילכות הרא״ש.

40 "Ground finely".

In the opinion of *Arukh* (s. v. טרית) and Rashi in his commentary to *Megillah* 6a the reference is to *triton*, a kind of tuna fish. This explanation is accepted by Ran (commentary to *Nedarim* 51b) who explains: "A large fish ground into fine cakes". But in *Avodah zarah* 35b, Rashi explains "small salted fish" which Lewysohn explains as Greek θρίσσα (Attic θρίττα). According to the Halakhah, both explanations might be correct, depending on a person's dialect. {טָרִית, if Greek, however, might be expected to be derived from a word beginning with *tau*, rather than *theta*. Compare Latin *tritus*, "rubbing, wearing", from *tero* "rub to pieces" forming a double expression with Hebrew טְרוּפָה "ground, finely ground with "fish" understood (E. G.). For an example of a Greek-Hebrew double expression cf. E. and H. Guggenheimer, *Notes on the Talmudic Vocabulary 5*, לשוננו לז (1973), 23-26 (in Hebrew).}

A person vowing not to eat fish intends only food recognizable as such.

41 Fluid extracted from fish by pressing.

42 Arabic صَحْنَى "small salted fish".

43 Latin *muries*, cf. *Demay* 1:3, Note 156.

44 In the Babli: "forbidden". The Mishnah mss. in the Maimonides tradition follow the Yerushalmi.

(39c line 62) **הלכה ו**: מִן הַמָּלִיחַ אֵינוֹ אָסוּר אֶלָּא בַּמָּלִיחַ שֶׁלַּדָּג כול׳. הֲווֹן בָּעֵיי מֵימַר. מָלוּחַ לְעוֹלָם. הָא לְשָׁעָה לֹא. אָמַר רִבִּי יוּדָן. מִן מָה דְתַנִּינָן. הֲרֵי עָלַי כִּבְשַׂר מָלִיחַ וּכְיֵין נֶסֶךְ. הָדָא אֲמְרָה. מָלוּחַ לְשָׁעָה מָלוּחַ הוּא. אֵי זֶהוּ מָלוּחַ לְשָׁעָה. כְּהָ דָא דְתַנֵּי. נוֹתֵן אֶת הָאֵיבָרִים עַל גַּבֵּי הַמֶּלַח וְהוֹפְכָן. אָמַר רִבִּי אַבָּא מָרִי. שַׁנְיָיא הִיא. שָׁאִים מַשְׁהֵא הוּא אוֹתָן הֵן נִמְלָחִין. מִן מָה דְּאָמַר רִבִּי חִיָּיה בַּר זַבְדָא. הַנּוֹטֵל זֵיתִים מִן הַמַּעֲטָן טוֹבֵל אַחַת אַחַת בְּמֶלַח וְאוֹכֵל. הָדָא אֲמְרָה. מָלוּחַ לְשָׁעָה מָלוּחַ הוּא.

"'From the salted' he is forbidden only salted fish," etc. [45]They wanted to say, salted for preservation, not short-term salted. Rebbi Yudan said, since we have stated: "this is for me like salted meat, like libation wine," this implies that short-term salted is called "salted". What is short-term salted? As it was stated: "He puts the limbs on the salt and turns them over." Rebbi Abba Mari said, there is a difference, for if he left them there, they would become salted meat. But which text says it? As Rebbi Ḥiyya bar Zabda said, "one who takes olives from the vat dips each single one in salt and eats it." This implies that short-term salted is called "salted".

45 This is a copy from Chapter 2:4, Notes 59-63.

(39c line 69) תַּנֵּי. רִבִּי שִׁמְעוֹן בֶּן אֶלְעָזָר אוֹמֵר. אָמַר. קוֹנָם דָּג שֶׁאֵינִי טוֹעֵם. אָסוּר בַּגְּדוֹלִים וּמוּתָּר בַּקְּטַנִּים. דָּגִים שֶׁאֵינִי טוֹעֵם. אָסוּר בֵּין בַּגְּדוֹלִים בֵּין בַּקְּטַנִּים. דָּגָה שֶׁאֵינִי טוֹעֵם. אֵינוֹ אָסוּר אֶלָּא בְכָלְכִּיד. אֵי זֶהוּ קָטָן וְאֵי זֶהוּ גָדוֹל. יַבָּא כֵּיי דָּמַר רִבִּי זְעִירָא. כָּל־נוּן דְּנָא אֲכִיל פָּחוֹת מִן לִיטְרָא כַּיְלְכִּיד אֲנָא טְעִים. וְהָכָא כֵן.

It was stated: [46]Rebbi Simeon ben Eleazar says: If he said, 'a *qônām* that I shall not taste a fish', he is forbidden large ones and permitted small ones. 'Fishes I shall not taste,' he is forbidden large and small ones. 'Fish[47] I shall not taste,' he is forbidden only sardines[48]. What is small and what is large? This is as Rebbi Ze'ira said, from any fish less than a *litra*[49] which I eat, I am tasting sardines. Here, it is the same[50].

46   A different version in the Babli, 51b; Tosephta 3:5.
47   The collective for fish, meaning fish that appear in large swarms.
48   Greek χαλκίς, -ίδος "pilchard, sardine".
49   A Roman *libra*, 345 g.
50   A fish is small if it weighs less than a Roman lb.

(39d line 1) וּמוּתָּר בִּטְרִית טְרוּפָה. הָא בִּשְׁאֵינָהּ טְרוּפָה אָסוּר. רִבִּי יִרְמְיָה אָמַר. זְעִירָה בְעֵי. לֵית הָדָא פְלִיגָא עַל רִבִּי יוֹחָנָן. דְּרִבִּי יוֹחָנָן אָמַר. הִילְכוּ בִנְדָרִים אַחַר לְשׁוֹן בְּנֵי אָדָם. לֵית אוֹרְחֵיהּ דְּבַר נָשׁ מֵימַר לְחַבְרֵיהּ. זְבִין לִי נוּן. וְהוּא זָבִין לֵיהּ כַּלְבִּיד. רִבִּי אָבִין שָׁמַע לֵיהּ מִן דְּבַתְרָהּ. הַנּוֹדֵר מִטְרִית טְרוּפָה מוּתָּר בְּצִיר וּבְמוּרְיֵיס. הָא כִּשְׁאֵינָהּ טְרוּפָה אָסוּר. רִבִּי [ ] אָמַר רִבִּי זְעוּרָה בְעֵי. לֵית הָדָא פְלִיגָא עַל רִבִּי יוֹחָנָן. דְּרִבִּי יוֹחָנָן אָמַר. הִילְכוּ בִנְדָרִים אַחַר לְשׁוֹן בְּנֵי אָדָם. לֵית אוֹרְחֵיהּ דְּבַר נָשָׁא מֵימַר לְחַבְרֵיהּ. זְבוֹן לִי טְרִי. וְהוּא זָבִין לֵיהּ צַחְנָא. תַּמָּן קַרְיָין לִיטְרִיתָא צַחְנָה.

"He is permitted fish cake"; therefore not if it is not ground. Rebbi Jeremiah said, Ze'ira[51] asked: Does this not disagree with Rebbi Johanan who said, in matters of vows one follows common usage[52] It is not the way of people that if a man says to his neighbor, sell me a fish, that he should sell him a sardine[53]. Rebbi Abin understood it from the last clause, "if somebody vows not to eat fish cake he is permitted fish fluid and brine[54]," therefore not if it is not ground? Rebbi [Jeremiah][55] said, Rebbi

Ze'ira asked: Does this not disagree with Rebbi Joḥanan who said, in matters of vows one follows common usage. It is not the way of people that if a man says to his neighbor, sell me a טְרִי, that he sells him a צַחֲנָא. There[56], they call צַחֲנָה טְרִית.

51 Almost certainly, the scribe forgot the title "Rebbi".

52 Cf. Halakhah 1, first paragraph. In the Babli 30b, 49a, 51b, and 5 times in other tractates.

53 Unspecified "fish" does not mean sardine.

54 It seems that the quote should be the sentence before the last, forbidding fish cake for the person who vows not to eat anchovy.

55 In analogy to the first version, this is the name forgotten by the scribe.

56 In Babylonia. It is asserted that there one calls צחנא what in Galilee is called טרית. The Tanna of the Mishnah is Babylonian.

(fol. 39b) **משנה ח:** הַנּוֹדֵר מִן הֶחָלָב מוּתָּר בַּקּוּם וְרִבִּי יוֹסֵי אוֹסֵר. וּמִן הַקּוּם מוּתָּר בֶּחָלָב. אַבָּא שָׁאוּל אוֹמֵר. הַנּוֹדֵר מִן הַגְּבִינָה אָסוּר בָּהּ בֵּין מְלוּחָה בֵּין טְפֵילָה.

Mishnah 8: If somebody vows not to drink milk, he is permitted curd[57] but Rebbi Yose forbids[58]. But from curd, he is permitted milk. Abba Shaul says, if he vows not to have cheese, it is forbidden to him whether salted or unsalted[59].

57 This is the definition of the Yerushalmi. The definition of Rashi and the Arukh is: the serum remaining when curd is pressed into cheese.

58 He holds that curd is colloidal milk, not cheese. But if somebody restricts his vow to curd, he certainly excludes fluid milk.

59 Even though most cheese is salted.

(39d line 10) **הלכה ח**: הַנּוֹדֵר מִן הֶחָלָב מוּתָּר בַּקּוּם כול'. מָהוּ בַּקּוּם. חַלְבָּא מְקַטְרָא. מַה טָעֲמָא דְּרִבִּי יוֹסֵי. שֵׁם אָבִיו קָרוּי עָלֶיהָ. עַל דַּעְתֵּיהּ דְּרִבִּי יוֹסֵי הַנּוֹדֵר מִן הַיַּיִן מוּתָּר בְּיַיִן מְבוּשָׁל. חַמְרָא מְבַשְּׁלָא.

"If somebody vows not to drink milk, he is permitted curd," etc. What is curd? Curdled milk. What is the reason of Rebbi Yose? The name of its father is called over it[60]. In the opinion of Rebbi Yose, is one who vows not to taste wine permitted cooked wine[61]? Cooked wine".

60 Since its name still contains the word "milk".	cooking. Since in the Aramaic vernacular it still is called wine it is forbidden.
61 Which has lost all its alcohol by	

(39d line 12) זֶה הַכְּלָל שֶׁהָיָה רִבִּי שִׁמְעוֹן אוֹמֵר מִשֵּׁם רִבִּי יְהוֹשֻׁעַ. כָּל־דָּבָר שֶׁיֵּשׁ לוֹ מַתִּירִין. כְּגוֹן טֶבֶל וּמַעֲשֵׂר שֵׁנִי וְהֶקְדֵּשׁ וְהֶחָדָשׁ. לֹא נָתְנוּ לָהֶן חֲכָמִים שִׁיעוּר אֶלָא מִין בְּמִינוֹ כָּל־שֶׁהוּא וְשֶׁלֹּא בְמִינוֹ בְּנוֹתֵן טַעַם. וְכָל־שֶׁאֵין לוֹ מַתִּירִין. כְּגוֹן תְּרוּמָה וְחַלָּה וְעָרְלָה וְכִלְאֵי הַכֶּרֶם. נָתְנוּ לָהֶן חֲכָמִים שִׁיעוּר מִין בְּמִינוֹ. שֶׁלֹּא בְמִינוֹ בְּנוֹתֵן טַעַם. אִילֵּין נְדָרִין מַה אַתְּ עֲבִיד לְהוֹן. כְּדָבָר שֶׁיֵּשׁ לוֹ מַתִּירִין אוֹ כְדָבָר שֶׁאֵין לוֹ מַתִּירִין. מִסְתַּבְּרָא מֵיעַבְדִינוֹן כְּדָבָר שֶׁיֵּשׁ לוֹ מַתִּירִין. דְּתַנִינָן תַּמָּן. שֶׁהַזָּקֵן עוֹקֵר אֶת הַנֶּדֶר מֵעִיקָּרוֹ. אָמְרוּ. אֵינוֹ עִיקְרוֹ אֶלָא מִיכָּן וּלְהַבָּא. וַדַּאי מַתְנִיתָא עֲבַד לוֹן כְּדָבָר שֶׁאֵין לוֹ מַתִּירִין. דְּתַנִינָן תַּמָּן. גִּידּוּלֵי תְרוּמָה תְרוּמָה וְגִידּוּלֵי גִידּוּלִין חוּלִין. אֲבָל טֶבֶל וּמַעֲשֵׂר רִאשׁוֹן וּסְפִיחֵי שְׁבִיעִית וּתְרוּמוֹת חוּצָה לָאָרֶץ וְהַמְדוּמָּע וְהַבִּיכּוּרִין גִּידּוּלֵיהֶן חוּלִין וְגִידּוּלֵי גִידּוּלִין הֶקְדֵּשׁ. וּמַעֲשֵׂר שֵׁנִי חוּלִין יִפְדֶּה אוֹתָן בִּזְמַן זַרְעָם. וְתַנֵּי עֲלָהּ. בַּמֶּה דְבָרִים אֲמוּרִים. בְּדָבָר שֶׁזַּרְעוֹ כָלֶה. אֲבָל בְּדָבָר שֶׁאֵין זַרְעוֹ כָלֶה גִּידּוּלֵי גִידּוּלִין אֲסוּרִין. דְּאָמַר רִבִּי זְעִירָא בְשֵׁם רִבִּי יוֹנָתָן. בָּצָל שֶׁלְּכִלְאֵי הַכֶּרֶם שֶׁעֲקָרוֹ וּשְׁתָלוֹ אֲפִילוּ הוֹסִיף כַּמָּה אָסוּר. שֶׁאֵין גִּידּוּלֵי אִיסּוּר מַעֲלִין אֶת הָאִיסּוּר. וְדָא מַתְנִיתָא עֲבַד לוֹן כְּדָבָר שֶׁיֵּשׁ לוֹ מַתִּירִין. דְּתַנִינָן תַּמָּן. שֶׁהַנּוֹדֵר

וְנִתְעָרֵב בְּאַחֵר. אִם יֵשׁ בּוֹ בְּנוֹתֵן טַעַם אָסוּר. תִּיפְתָּר מִין בְּשֶׁאֵינוֹ מִינוֹ בְּדָבָר שֶׁיֵּשׁ לוֹ מַתִּירִין.

[62]"This is the rule Rebbi Simeon declared in the name of Rebbi Joshua: For everything that may become permitted through some action, such as *ṭevel*, Second Tithe, donations to the Temple, and "new grain", the Sages did not fix any limits, but a kind with its own is forbidden in the minutest amount, a kind with a different kind if it can be tasted. But for everything that cannot become permitted through any action, such as heave, *ḥallah*, *orlah*, and *kilaim* in a vineyard, the Sages did fix as limit both a kind with itself or with a different kind if it can be tasted."

How do you treat vows[63]? As referring to something that can become permitted or to something that cannot become permitted? It seems reasonable that we treat them as referring to things that can become permitted, as we have stated there[64] "for the Elder uproots the vow from the start." They said, he only uproots for the future[65].

Certainly a Mishnah treats it as referring to something that cannot become permitted, as we have stated there[66]: "The growth from heave is heave; the growth from their growth is profane. But the growths from *ṭevel*, First Tithe, aftergrowth of the Sabbatical, heaves from outside the Land, *dema'*, and First Fruits are profane as are growths from their growths. Growths from dedicated [seeds] and Second Tithe become profane; one redeems them corresponding to the time of sowing." We have stated on this: When has this been said? Anything whose seeds disappear. But in produce whose seeds do not disappear, the growth from their growth is forbidden[67].

[68]There is a restriction on growth, as Rebbi Zeïra said in the name of Rebbi Jonathan: An onion of *kilaim* in a vineyard, taken out of the ground and replanted, stays forbidden even if it grows enormously because growth of something forbidden cannot neutralize the prohibition.

But another Mishnah treats it as something that can become permitted, as we have stated there[69]: "For if somebody vowed not to have a certain thing and it became mixed with something else, if it can be tasted it is forbidden." This explains that it was mixed with another kind, following the rules of something that can become permitted.

62 This paragraph is from *Ševi'it* 6:3, Notes 116-125; quoted in Babli 57b/58a.

63 If somebody vowed not to eat something which then became mixed with permitted food and is no longer recognizable. Is the mixture forbidden if it contains the most minute amount of forbidden material or does it become permitted if the forbidden food no langer can be tasted?

64 *Ketubot* 7:9, in a discussion of the difference between the dissolution of a vow by a rabbi for cause compared to that by the father of the vow of his not quite adult daughter. One would have expected the text to read דתני as appropriate for a *baraita*, not דתנינן תמן used for a Mishnah.

65 While the rabbi might annul the vow, he cannot annul the guilt incurred by violation of the vow before it was annulled.

66 *Terumot* 9:4, Notes 57-64; quoted in Babli, 60a.

67 Since the growth of the growth from seeds dedicated by a vow remains forbidden, a vow makes it something which admits of an act (a request for annulment) that makes it permitted.

68 *Ševi'it* 6:3, Note 126. (*Kilaim* 5:7, Note 76; *Terumot* 7:7, Note 122; *'Orlah* 1:1, Note 29; Babli *Nedarim* 57b).

69 *Nedarim* 6:9.

משנה ט: (fol. 39b) הַנּוֹדֵר מִן הַבָּשָׂר מוּתָּר בָּרוֹטֵב וּבַקְּיפָה וְרִבִּי יְהוּדָה אוֹסֵר. אָמַר רִבִּי יְהוּדָה מַעֲשֶׂה וְאָסַר עָלַי רִבִּי טַרְפוֹן בֵּיצִים שֶׁנִּתְבַּשְּׁלוּ בְּתוֹכוֹ. אָמְרוּ לוֹ וְכֵן הַדָּבָר. אֵימָתַי בִּזְמָן שֶׁיֹּאמַר בָּשָׂר זֶה עָלַי. אֲבָל הַנּוֹדֵר מִן הַדָּבָר וְנִתְעָרֵב בְּאַחֵר. אִם יֵשׁ בּוֹ בְּנוֹתֵן טַעַם אָסוּר.

Mishnah 9: If somebody vows not to eat meat, he is permitted clear bouillon and coagulated fibers[70], but Rebbi Jehudah forbids. Rebbi Jehudah said, it happened that Rebbi Tarphon forbade to me eggs that were cooked in it. They said to him, that is correct; when? If he would say, that piece of meat [is forbidden] to me[71]. In truth, if somebody forbids himself something by a vow and it became mixed with something else, if it can be tasted it is forbidden

70 The solid material which accumulates on the wall of the pot at the water's edge, which usually is scrubbed off as waste.

71 If somebody forbids for himself meat in general, food is judged by categories and eggs are not meat. But if somebody forbids a particular piece of meat, that piece is for him as if it were not kosher and it follows the rules of admixtures of forbidden ingredients as detailed in *Terumot* Chapter 10; or, as explained in the Halakhah, he forbids himself any usufruct, i. e., any taste of the forbidden food.

הלכה ט: (39d line 31) הַנּוֹדֵר מִן הַבָּשָׂר כול'. אָמַר רבי הִילָא. מִכֵּיוָן שֶׁאָמַר. זֶה. אֲסָרוֹ עָלָיו הוּא וַהֲנָייָתוֹ.

Halakhah 9: "If somebody vows not to eat meat," etc. Rebbi Hila said: The moment he said "this one", he forbade for himself it and its usufruct.

(fol. 39c) **משנה י:** הַנּוֹדֵר מִן הַיַּיִן מוּתָּר בְּתַבְשִׁיל שֶׁיֶּשׁ בּוֹ טַעַם יַיִן. אָמַר קוֹנָם יַיִן זֶה שֶׁאֵינִי טוֹעֵם וְנָפַל לְתַבְשִׁיל אִם יֶשׁ בּוֹ בְּנוֹתֵן טַעַם הֲרֵי זֶה אָסוּר.

Mishnah 10: If somebody vows not to drink wine he is permitted a dish prepared with wine. If he said, a *qônām* that I shall not taste this wine, if it fell into a dish and it can be tasted, that is forbidden.

משנה יא: הַנּוֹדֵר מִן הָעֲנָבִים מוּתָּר בַּיַּיִן מִן הַזֵּיתִים מוּתָּר בַּשֶּׁמֶן. אָמַר קוֹנָם זֵיתִים וַעֲנָבִים אִלּוּ שֶׁאֵינִי טוֹעֵם אָסוּר בָּהֶן וּבַיּוֹצֵא מֵהֶן.

Mishnah 11: If somebody vows not to eat grapes, he is permitted wine; not to eat olives, he is permitted oil. If he said, a *qônām* that I shall not taste these olives or grapes, he is forbidden them and anything coming from them[72].

---

72   These rules are all examples of the principle expounded in Halakhah 9.

(39d line 32) **הלכה יא:** הַנּוֹדֵר מִן הָעֲנָבִים כול׳. תַּנֵּי. רבי שִׁמְעוֹן בֶּן אֶלְעָזָר אוֹמֵר. קוֹנָם כָּל־דָּבָר שֶׁדַּרְכּוֹ לְאוֹכְלוֹ דֶּרֶךְ הַיּוֹצֵא לֵיאָכֵל. נָדַר בּוֹ מוּתָּר בְּיוֹצֵא מִמֶּנּוּ. נָדַר בְּיוֹצֵא מִמֶּנּוּ מוּתָּר בּוֹ. מַה אִית לָךְ. כְּגוֹן זֵיתִים וַעֲנָבִים. וְכָל־דָּבָר שֶׁדַּרְכָּן לֵיאָכֵל וְאֵין דֶּרֶךְ הַיּוֹצֵא מִמֶּנּוּ לֵיאָכֵל. נָדַר בּוֹ מוּתָּר בְּיוֹצֵא מִמֶּנּוּ. מַה אִית לָךְ. כְּגוֹן אִילֵּין תּוּתַיָּיא. וְכָל־דָּבָר שֶׁאֵין דַּרְכּוֹ לֵיאָכֵל וְדֶרֶךְ הַיּוֹצֵא מִמֶּנּוּ לֵיאָכֵל. נָדַר בּוֹ לֹא נִתְכַּוֵּון אֶלָּא בְּיוֹצֵא מִמֶּנּוּ. מַה אִית לָךְ. אָמַר רבי יוֹסֵי בֵּירבִּי בּוּן. זֵירְעוֹנֵי גִינָּה שֶׁאֵינָן נֶאֱכָלִין.

Halakhah 11: "If somebody vows not to eat grapes," etc. It was stated[73]: Rebbi Simeon ben Eleazar said, a *qônām* for anything which usually is eaten and of which some derivative is eaten; if he forbade the thing to himself by a vow, the derivative is permitted[74]. What is an example? E. g., grapes and olives. And anything which usually is eaten but no derivative of which is eaten; if he forbade the thing to himself by a vow, the derivative is permitted. What is an example? E. g., mulberries. And anything which usually is not eaten and but a derivative is eaten; if he forbade the thing to himself by a vow, he intended the derivative. What is an example? E. g., garden seeds that are not eaten[75].

73 Babli 53a, Tosephta 3:3.
74 In Babli and Tosephta: Forbidden.
75 Cf. *Kilaim* 1:1, Note 21.

(fol. 39c) **משנה יב:** הַנּוֹדֵר מִן הַתְּמָרִים מוּתָּר בִּדְבַשׁ תְּמָרִים. מִן הַסִּתְוָנִית מוּתָּר בְּחוֹמֶץ סִתְוָנִיּוֹת. רִבִּי יְהוּדָה בֶּן בְּתֵירָה אוֹמֵר כָּל־שֶׁשֵּׁם תּוֹלַדְתּוֹ קְרוּיָה עָלָיו וְנוֹדֵר מִמֶּנּוּ אָסוּר אַף בְּיוֹצֵא מִמֶּנּוּ. וַחֲכָמִים מַתִּירִין.

Mishnah 12: If somebody vows not to eat dates, he is permitted date honey; from winter grapes[76], he is permitted winter grape vinegar. Rebbi Jehudah ben Bathyra says, if he vowed to forbid to himself anything which is called by the name of its derivative[77], he also is forbidden the derivative, but the Sages permit it.

76 They are sour and can only be used for making vinegar.
77 For example dates which in *Deut*. 8:8 are called "honey". In the same verse, olives are referred to as "oil olives".

(39d line 40) **הלכה יב:** הַנּוֹדֵר מִן הַתְּמָרִים כול׳. מַאי טַעְמָא דְּרִבִּי יוֹסֵי. שֵׁם אָבִיו קָרוּי עָלָיו. מַאי טַעְמָא דְּרִבִּי יְהוּדָה בֶּן בְּתֵירָה. שֵׁם בְּנוֹ קָרוּי עָלָיו. מִסְתַּבְּרָה רִבִּי יוּדָה בֶּן בְּתֵירָה יוֹדֵי לְרִבִּי יוֹסֵי. רִבִּי יוֹסֵי לֹא יוֹדֵי לְרִבִּי יוּדָה בֶּן בְּתֵירָה. רִבִּי יוּדָה בֶּן בְּתֵירָה יוֹדֵי לְרִבִּי יוֹסֵי. שֵׁם בְּנוֹ לֹא כָּל־שֶׁכֵּן שֵׁם אָבִיו. רִבִּי יוֹסֵי לֹא יוֹדֵי לְרִבִּי יוּדָה בֶּן בְּתֵירָה. לֹא אָמַר אֶלָּא שֵׁם אָבִיו. הָא שֵׁם בְּנוֹ לֹא.

Halakhah 12: "If somebody vows not to eat dates," etc. What is the reason of Rebbi Yose? The name of its father is called over it[60]. What is the reason of Rebbi Jehudah ben Bathyra? The name of its descendant is called over it. It is reasonable that Rebbi Jehudah ben Bathyra should agree with Rebbi Yose but Rebbi Yose would not agree with Rebbi Jehudah ben Bathyra. Rebbi Jehudah ben Bathyra should agree with Rebbi Yose: The name of its descendant, so certainly also the name of its father. Rebbi Yose would not agree with Rebbi Jehudah ben Bathyra: He says only, the name of its father. This implies: not the name of its descendant.

(fol. 39c) **משנה יג:** הַנּוֹדֵר מִן הַיַּיִן מוּתָּר בְּיֵין תַּפּוּחִים. מִן הַשֶּׁמֶן מוּתָּר בְּשֶׁמֶן שׁוּמְשְׁמִין. מִן הַדְּבָשׁ מוּתָּר בִּדְבָשׁ תְּמָרִים. מִן הַחוֹמֶץ מוּתָּר בְּחוֹמֶץ סִיתְוָנִיּוֹת. מִן הַכְּרֵשִׁין מוּתָּר בְּקֶפְלוֹטוֹת. מִן הַיָּרָק מוּתָּר בְּיַרְקוֹת שָׂדֶה מִפְּנֵי שֶׁהוּא שֵׁם לְוַוי.

Mishnah 13: If somebody vows not to use wine, he is permitted apple wine. Not oil, he is permitted sesame oil. Not honey, he is permitted date honey. Not vinegar, he is permitted winter grape vinegar. Not leeks, he is permitted field leeks[78]. Of vegetables, he is permitted field vegetables[79], because that is an accompanying name[80].

78 For the relationship between כרשין, *allium porrum,* and κεφαλωτόν, *allium capitatum,* cf. *Kilaim* 1:2, Notes 42,56.

79 Vegetables grown in extensive cultivation.

80 In all examples of the Mishnah, the simple name does not cover the

composite name as product of trade. For example, if somebody buys "wine", the seller cannot fulfill his contract by delivering apple wine. The Babli, 53a, points out that in Babylonia no olive trees grow and a standard contract for "oil" there is for delivery of sesame oil; there, a vow of abstention from oil permits the use of olive oil.

(39d line 45) **הלכה יג**: הַנּוֹדֵר מִן הַיַּיִן כול'. מַתְנִיתָא מָקוֹם שֶׁאֵין קוֹרִין לְקֵפָלוֹטוֹת כְּרֵישִׁין. אֲבָל בְּמָקוֹם שֶׁקּוֹרִין לְקֵפָלוֹטוֹת כְּרֵישִׁין לֹא בְדָא. לָכֵן צְרִיכָה אֲפִילוּ בְּמָקוֹם שֶׁקּוֹרִין לְקֵפָלוֹטוֹת כְּרֵישִׁין. מִן הַכְּרֵשִׁין מוּתָּר בְּקֵפָלוֹטוֹת.

Halakhah 13: "If somebody vows not to use wine," etc. The Mishnah speaks of a place where one does not call field leeks leeks. But not at a place where one calls field leeks leeks. Just in that case it is needed[81], even a place where one calls field leeks leeks: "Not leeks, he is permitted field leeks."

81 The case of leeks is different from the other cases in the Mishnah since it is not question of a composite name but of Greek vs. Hebrew name. Therefore, at a place where *allium capitatum* is never called כרשין the assertion of the Mishnah is trivial and does not have to be stated. The Mishnah is only needed when in common speech Hebrew and Greek expressions are used interchangeably. Since this would not extend to commercial contracts, the rule of the Mishnah stands.

(39d line 49) מִן הַיָּרָק מוּתָּר בְּיַרְקוֹת שָׂדֶה מִפְּנֵי שֶׁהוּא שֵׁם לְוַוִיי. וְתַנֵּי עֲלָהּ הַנּוֹדֵר מִן הַיָּרָק בַּשְּׁבִיעִית אָסוּר בְּיַרְקוֹת הַשָּׂדֶה. תַּנְיָיתָהּ רִבִּי קְרִיסְפָּא בְשֵׁם רִבִּי חֲנִינָה בֶּן גַּמְלִיאֵל דְּאָמַר טַעְמָא. הָדָא דְאַתְּ אָמַר עַד שֶׁלֹּא הִתִּיר רִבִּי לְהָבִיא יָרָק מִחוּץ לָאָרֶץ לָאָרֶץ. אֲבָל מִשֶּׁהִתִּיר רִבִּי לְהָבִיא מִחוּצָה לָאָרֶץ לָאָרֶץ. הִיא שְׁבִיעִית הִיא שְׁאָר שְׁנֵי שָׁבוּעַ. אָמַר רִבִּי יוֹסֵי בֶּן חֲנִינָא. עוּלְשִׁין

חֲשׁוּבִין הֵן לְטַמֵּא טוּמְאַת אוֹכְלִין בַּשְּׁבִיעִית. הָדָא דְאַתְּ אָמַר עַד שֶׁלֹּא הִתִּיר רִבִּי לְהָבִיא יְרָקוֹת מֵחוּצָה לָאָרֶץ לָאָרֶץ. אֲבָל מִשֶּׁהִתִּיר רִבִּי לְהָבִיא מֵחוּצָה לָאָרֶץ לָאָרֶץ הִיא שְׁבִיעִית הִיא שְׁאָר שְׁנֵי שָׁבוּעַ.

[82]"Not vegetables, he is permitted field vegetables because this is an accompanying name." We have stated on that: "He who makes a vow to abstain from vegetables in the Sabbatical is also forbidden field vegetables." Rebbi Crispus stated the reason in the name of Rebbi Ḥanina ben Gamliel: That means, as long as Rebbi did not permit to import vegetables into the Land. But since Rebbi permitted to import into the Land there is no difference between the Sabbatical and the remaining years of the Sabbatical cycle. Rebbi Yose bar Ḥanina says, endives are important enough to become impure as food in the Seventh year. That means, as long as Rebbi did not permit to import vegetables into the Land. But since Rebbi permitted to import vegetables into the Land there is no difference between the Sabbatical and the remaining years of the Sabbatical cycle.

82   This paragraph is from *Ševi'it* 6:4, explained there in Notes 140-144.   A different version is in the Babli, 53a/b.

(39d line 58) תַּנֵּי. אֵין מְעַבְּרִין אֶת הַשָּׁנָה לֹא בַשְּׁבִיעִית וְלֹא בְּמוֹצָאֵי שְׁבִיעִית. וְאִם עִיבְּרוּהָ הֲרֵי זֶה מְעוּבֶּרֶת. רִבִּי זְעִירָא בְּשֵׁם רִבִּי אַבָּהוּ אָמַר. עַד שֶׁלֹּא הִתִּיר רִבִּי לִיקַּח יָרָק מֵחוּצָה לָאָרֶץ לָאָרֶץ. אֲבָל מִשֶּׁהִתִּיר רִבִּי לִיקַּח יָרָק מֵחוּצָה לָאָרֶץ לָאָרֶץ הִיא שְׁבִיעִית הִיא שְׁאָר שְׁנֵי שָׁבוּעַ.

[83]It was stated: "One intercalates for a year neither in a Sabbatical nor in the year after the Sabbatical; but if they intercalated it is intercalated[84]." Rebbi Ze'ira in the name of Rebbi Abbahu said: That means, as long as

Rebbi did not permit to buy vegetables for importation into the Land. But since Rebbi permitted to buy vegetables for importation into the Land there is no difference between the Sabbatical and the remaining years of the Sabbatical cycle[85].

83 From here to the end of the Halakhah, the text is from *Sanhedrin* 1:2 (18d l. 28). The tannaïtic statements are from Tosephta *Sanhedrin* 2:9-13. The entire piece is inserted here since this first paragraph refers to the preceding one. For this and the following paragraphs the reference in the Babli is *Sanhedrin* 12a. In Babli sources, before Rabban Gamliel the observant never ate imported vegetables since those might still carry lumps of impure foreign soil.

84 The lunar/solar calendar of rabbinic Judaism requires 7 additional lunar months in a 19 year period. Before the publication of the computed calendar by the fifth generation Amora R. Yose, it was the privilege of the Synhedrion to declare the intercalation (which had to be the month before the spring equinox). One tried not to extend the Sabbatical during which agricultural work was forbidden. In the year following the Sabbatical, the use of new grain was forbidden until the first sheaf of newly cut barley was presented in the Temple during the festival of unleavened bread (the 16th of Nisan in Pharisaic theory, the Sunday of the festival in Boethusian-Sadducee, and the 22nd of Nisan in Jubilee-Sadducee theory), *Lev.* 23:14; Philo *The Special Laws* II, 162 ff. Therefore, one should try to have Nisan as early as possible in such a year.

85 Therefore, the calendar computation disregards the Sabbatical. {The calendar computation is explained in the Appendix to the author's edition of *Seder Olam*, Northvale NJ 1998.}

(39d line 62) הָיָה רבִּי מֵאִיר אוֹמֵר. הֲרֵי הוּא אוֹמֵר. וְאִישׁ בָּא מִבַּעַל שָׁלִישָׁה וַיָּבֵא לְאִישׁ הָאֱלֹהִים לֶחֶם בִּיכּוּרִים וגו'. אֵין לָךְ מְבַכֵּר בְּאֶרֶץ יִשְׂרָאֵל יוֹתֵר מִבַּעַל שָׁלִישָׁה וְלֹא בִיכֵּר אֶלָּא אוֹתוֹ הַמִּין. וְהֵבִיא לְאִישׁ הָאֱלֹהִים. אֵימָתַי הֱבִיאוֹ. לְאַחַר הָעוֹמֶר. שֶׁנֶּאֱמַר תֵּן לָעָם וְיֹאכֵלוּ. הוֹאִיל וְהָיְתָה הַשָּׁנָה צְרִיכָה

לַעֲבֵּר מִפְּנֵי מָה לֹא עִיבְּרָהּ אֱלִישָׁע. אֶלָּא מְלַמֵּד שֶׁהָיוּ שְׁנֵי רְעָבוֹן וְהָיוּ הַכֹּל קוֹפְצִים לַגְּרָנוֹת.

"Rebbi Meïr used to teach: It says, 'A man came from Baal-Shalishah and brought to the man of God bread from first grain, etc[86].' At no place in the Land of Israel does produce ripen earlier than at Baal-Shalishah, and only that kind ripened early." 'He brought to the man of God,' when did he bring it? After the *'Omer* ceremony[87], since it is said: 'Give to the people to eat.' "But since the year was in need of an intercalation, why did Elisha not intercalate? This teaches you that the year was one of famine and everybody was jumping to the threshing floors[88]."

86 2K. 4:42. He brought 20 barley-grain breads. Baal-Shalisha seems to have been near Jericho.

87 The presentation of new barley, cf. Note 84.

88 All grain was sold directly from the threshing floor because of its scarcity. The Babli, *Sanhedrin* 11b/12a and Tosephta *Sanhedrin* 2:9 state outright that "one does not intercalate in a year of famine." A minority of sources in the Babli attributes the argument to Rebbi.

אֵין מְעַבְּרִין אֶת הַשָּׁנָה מִפְּנֵי הַטּוּמְאָה. רַבִּי יְהוּדָה אוֹמֵר. מְעַבְּרִין. שֶׁכֵּן מָצִינוּ בְחִזְקִיָּה שֶׁעִיבֵּר אֶת הַשָּׁנָה מִפְּנֵי הַטּוּמְאָה. שֶׁנֶּאֱמַר כִּי מַרְבִּית הָעָם וגו'. רַבִּי שִׁמְעוֹן אָמַר. אַף עַל פִּי שֶׁעִיבְּרוּ נִיסָן אֵינוֹ מְעוּבָּר אֶלָּא אֲדָר. רַבִּי שִׁמְעוֹן בֶּן יְהוּדָה בְּשֵׁם רַבִּי שִׁמְעוֹן. חִזְקִיָּה הֶעֱשִׂי לְצִיבּוּר לַעֲשׂוֹת פֶּסַח שֵׁינִי. אִית תַּנָּיֵי תַּנֵּי. מְעַבְּרִין אֶת הַשָּׁנָה מִפְּנֵי הַטּוּמְאָה. אִית תַּנָּיֵי תַּנֵּי. אֵין מְעַבְּרִין. מָאן דְּאָמַר אֵין[89] מְעַבְּרִין מִינָהּ כִּי אָכְלוּ אֶת הַפֶּסַח בְּלֹא כַּכָּתוּב. וּמָאן דְּאָמַר (אֵין)[90] מְעַבְּרִין מַה מְקַיְּיִם כִּי אָכְלוּ אֶת הַפֶּסַח. שֶׁעִיבְּרוּ אֶת נִיסָן וְאֵינוֹ מְעוּבָּר אֶלָּא אֲדָר. וְאָתְיָיא כַּיי דָּמַר רַבִּי סִימוֹן בַּר זַבְדִּי. גּוּלְגּוּלְתּוֹ שֶׁלְּאָרְנָן הַיְבוּסִי מְצָאוּ תַּחַת הַמִּזְבֵּחַ.

It was stated[91]: "One does not intercalate for a year because of impurity[92]; Rebbi Jehudah says, one does, since we find that Hezekia intercalated because of impurity, as it was said[93]: 'For most of the people, etc.' Rebbi Simeon said, even though they intercalated in Nisan, only Adar was intercalated[94]. Rebbi Simeon ben Jehudah said in the name of Rebbi Simeon, Hezekia forced the multitude to celebrate the Second Passover[95]." Some Tannaïm state: One intercalates for the year because of impurity. Some Tannaïm state: One does not intercalate. He who says, one does not intercalate, from the following[93]: "For they ate the *pesaḥ* not as it was written." How does the one who says one does intercalate, explain "for they ate the *pesaḥ*"? They intercalated in Nisan but only Adar was intercalated. This follows what Rebbi Simon bar Zavdi said, they found the skull of Ornan the Jebusite under the altar[96].

89 From the text in *Sanhedrin*, missing here.

90 In the text here, missing in *Sanhedrin*. The text in *Sanhedrin* seems to be the correct one.

91 Tosephta *Sanhedrin* 2:10-11; Babli *Sanhedrin* 12a/b. Instead of the hapax *hip'il* הָעֲשׂי לְצִיבּוּר (confirmed by the Tosephta), the parallel in *Sanhedrin* has standard rabbinic *pi'el* עִישָּׂה "he forced", which because of the disappearance of gutturals appears in the Babli as הֵשִּׂיא "counseled" (which is a correct reference to *2Chr.* 30:2).

92 One does not intercalate a 13th month to give people time to purify themselves in time for the *pesaḥ* sacrifice on the 14th of the first month.

93 *2Chr.* 30:18: Most of the people from the former Northern Kingdom were not pure (in the first month) so they ate the *pesaḥ* in the second month, not as is written.

94 R. Simeon holds that the biblical reference in *2Chr.* 30, that after the fall of Samaria Hezekia celebrated the festival in the second month is really incorrect but that he decided in Nisan that more time was needed to prepare for the sacrifices and, what is not permitted by the calendar rules, retroactively turned Nisan into Second

Adar and, therefore, the second month into the first. He prayed for divine indulgence for this breach of the rules.

95 The substitute festival for people absent or impure in the first month, available for individuals only, not for a majority of the people (*Num.* 9:9-14).

96 This explanation disagrees with R. Simeon ben Jehudah. They moved the month because the Temple was not usable in Nisan since the altar was found to be a "tent" over human bones and thus impure. The text is from *Soṭah* 5:2, Note 90.

(40a line 1) כְּתִיב בְּכָל־לְבָבוֹ הֵכִין לִדְרוֹשׁ הָאֱלֹהִים אֶל אֲבוֹתָיו וגו'. רִבִּי סִימוֹן בַּר זַבְדִּי וְרִבִּי שְׁמוּאֵל בַּר נַחְמָן. חַד אָמַר אֲפִילוּ כַּמָּה עָשָׂה לְטָהֳרַת הַקּוֹדֶשׁ לֹא יָצָא יְדֵי טָהֳרַת הַקּוֹדֶשׁ. וְחָרְנָה אָמַר. אֲפִילוּ כָּל־מַעֲשִׂים⁹⁷ טוֹבִים שֶׁעָשָׂה לֹא יָצָא כְּדֵי טָהֳרַת הַקּוֹדֶשׁ. כְּתִיב וַיָּחֵילוּ⁹⁸ בְּאֶחָד לַחוֹדֶשׁ הָרִאשׁוֹן וגו'. וּכְתִיב וּבְיוֹם שִׁשָּׁה עָשָׂר לַחוֹדֶשׁ הָרִאשׁוֹן כִּלּוּ. וַהֲלֹא לְיוֹם אֶחָד יְכוֹלִין הָיוּ לְבַעֵר כָּל־עֲבוֹדָה זָרָה שֶׁהָיְתָה שָׁם. אָמַר רִבִּי אִידִי. מִפְּנֵי צַלְמֵי כַּשְׂדִּים שֶׁחֲקוּקִים.

It is written⁹⁹: "With all his heart he prepared himself to seek God, his fathers' [God], etc." Rebbi Simon bar Zavdi and Rebbi Samuel bar Naḥman. One of them said, with all he did to purify the Temple, he did not fully establish the purity of the Temple. The other said, with all the good works he did, he did not fully do his duty for the purity of the Temple. It is written¹⁰⁰: "They started on the first of the first month." And it is written¹⁰¹: "On the sixteenth of the month they finished. Could they not have eliminated all idolatry from there in one day? Rebbi Idi said, because of Chaldean idols which were engraved.

97 From the text in *Sanhedrin*. The reading here is a singular, מעשה.

98 Reading of the text in *Sanhedrin* and in the Bible. Text here: ויכלו (וַיָּכַלּוּ

"they finished").

99 *2Chr.* 30:19: "With all his heart he prepared himself to seek God, the Eternal, his fathers' God, except for

Temple purity." Since one was discussing Hezekia, some related verses are explained.

100 *2Chr.* 29:17.

101 *2Chr.* 29:18. They needed 7 days to cleanse the Temple courtyards and 8 for the Temple building.

(40a line 7) שִׁשָּׁה דְבָרִים עָשָׂה חִזְקִיָּה מֶלֶךְ יְהוּדָה. עַל שְׁלֹשָׁה הוֹדוּ לוֹ וְעַל שְׁלֹשָׁה לֹא הוֹדוּ לוֹ. גֵּרֵר עַצְמוֹת אָבִיו וְהוֹדוּ לוֹ. כִּיתֵּת נְחַשׁ הַנְּחוֹשֶׁת וְהוֹדוּ לוֹ. גָּנַז טַבְלָה שֶׁל רְפוּאוֹת וְהוֹדוּ לוֹ. וְעַל שְׁלֹשָׁה לֹא הוֹדוּ לוֹ. סָתַם מֵימֵי גִיחוֹן הָעֶלְיוֹן וְלֹא הוֹדוּ לוֹ. קִיצֵּץ דַּלְתוֹת הַהֵיכָל וְלֹא הוֹדוּ לוֹ. עִיבֵּר נִיסָן בְּנִיסָן וְלֹא הוֹדוּ לוֹ.

[102]Six things did Ezekiah, the king of Judea, do. With three they[103] agreed, with three they did not agree. He dragged his father's bones and they agreed[104]. He smashed the bronze snake and they agreed[105]. He hid the table of medicines and they agreed[106]. With three they disagreed. He closed the upper Gihon spring and they disagreed[107]. He cut down the Temple doors[108] and they disagreed. He intercalated Nisan in Nisan[109] and they disagreed.

102 A *baraita* in Babli *Pesaḥim* 56a; quoted *Berakhot* 10b, *Sanhedrin* 47a; in most Mishnah mss. *Pesaḥim* 4:9.
103 The rabbinic authorities of the Mishnaic period.
104 He buried him in an undignified way to atone for his bad ways. The basis is the note in *2Chr.* 28:27 that Aḥaz was not buried in the kings' graves, contradicting *2K.* 16:20.

105 *2K.* 18:4.
106 According to Maimonides (Commentary to *Pesaḥim* 4:9), a book of magical remedies.
107 It seems that they did not connect *2Chr.* 32:30 with *2K.* 20:20.
108 *2K.* 18:16.
109 As explained in the preceding paragraph, following R. Simeon.

(40a line 12) אֵין מְעַבְּרִין אֶת הַשָּׁנָה קוֹדֶם רֹאשׁ הַשָּׁנָה וְאִם עִיבְּרוּהָ אֵינָהּ מְעוּבֶּרֶת. אֲבָל מִפְּנֵי הַדַּחַק[110] הִתְקִינוּ שֶׁיְּהוּ מְעַבְּרִין אוֹתָהּ אַחַר רֹאשׁ הַשָּׁנָה מִיָּד. אַף עַל פִּי כֵן אֵינוֹ מְעוּבָּר אֶלָּא אֲדָר. רִבִּי אוֹמֵר. נִיסָן לֹא נִתְעַבֵּר מִיָּמָיו. וְהָתַנִּינָן. אִם הָיָה הַחֹדֶשׁ מְעוּבָּר. [אִם בָּא לֹא בָא. רַב אָמַר תִּשְׁרֵי לֹא נִתְעַבֵּר מִיָּמָיו וְהָא תַּנִּינָן אִם הָיָה חוֹדֶשׁ מְעוּבָּר.][111] אִם הָיָה לֹא הָיָה.

One does not intercalate for a year before New Year's Day; if they did intercalate it would be invalid. But for an urgent need one may intercalate immediately after New Year's Day. Nevertheless, only Adar is intercalated.

[114]Rebbi says, Nisan never was lengthened. But did we not state: "If the New Moon appeared in time"? If it would appear, it did not appear. Rav said, Tishre was never lengthened. But did we not state: "If the month was long"? If it would be, it never was.

(40a line 16) וּכְשֶׁקִּידְּשׁוּ אֶת הַשָּׁנָה בְּאוּשָׁה בַּיּוֹם הָרִאשׁוֹן עָמַד רִבִּי יִשְׁמָעֵאל בְּנוֹ שֶׁל רִבִּי יוֹחָנָן בֶּן בְּרוֹקָה אָמַר כְּדִבְרֵי רִבִּי יוֹחָנָן בֶּן נוּרִי. אָמַר רַבָּן שִׁמְעוֹן בֶּן גַּמְלִיאֵל. לֹא הָיִינוּ נוֹהֲגִין כֵּן בְּיַבְנֶה. בַּיּוֹם הַשֵּׁינִי עָבַר רִבִּי חֲנַנְיָה בֶּן רִבִּי יוֹסֵי הַגְּלִילִי וְאָמַר כְּדִבְרֵי רִבִּי עֲקִיבָה. אָמַר רַבָּן שִׁמְעוֹן בֶּן גַּמְלִיאֵל. כֵּן הָיִינוּ נוֹהֲגִין בְּיַבְנֶה. וְהָתַנֵּי. קִידְּשׁוּהוּ בָרִאשׁוֹן וּבַשֵּׁינִי. רִבִּי זְעוּרָא בְּשֵׁם רַב חִסְדָּא אוֹתָהּ שָׁנָה נִתְקַלְקְלָה. מַה בֵּין הָרִאשׁוֹן לַשֵּׁינִי. רִבִּי בּוּן בְּשֵׁם רַב.[112] שָׁנָה הָרִאשׁוֹנָה וְשָׁנָה הַשְּׁנִיָּיה. וְהָתַנֵּי יוֹם הָרִאשׁוֹן יוֹם הַשֵּׁנִי.

"When they sanctified the year at Usha, on the first day Rebbi Ismael, the son of Rebbi Johanan ben Baroqa, led and recited following the opinion of Rebbi Johanan ben Nuri. Rabban Simeon ben Gamliel said, we did not follow this at Jabneh. On the second day, Rebbi Hananiah, the son of Rebbi Yose the Galilean led and recited following the opinion of Rebbi Aqiba. Rabban Simeon ben Gamliel said, this we did follow at Jabneh."

But does this not mean that they sanctified it on the first and the second day? Rebbi Zeïra in the name of Rav Ḥisda: That year was disorganized. What is "the first, the second"? Rebbi Abun in the name of Rav: The first year, the second year[52]! But was it not stated: the first day, the second day?

(40a line 23) קִידְּשׁוּהוּ קוֹדֶם זְמַנּוֹ אוֹ לְאַחַר עִיבּוּרוֹ יוֹם אֶחָד יָכוֹל יְהֵא מְעוּבָּר. תַּלְמוּד לוֹמַר אוֹתָם אוֹתָם אֵלֶּה הֵם [מוֹעֲדָי].[111] אֵין אֵלָּא מוֹעֲדָי. לִפְנֵי זְמַנּוֹ עֶשְׂרִים וְתִשְׁעָה יָמִים. לְאַחַר עִיבּוּרוֹ שְׁלֹשִׁים וּשְׁנַיִם. וּמְנַיִין שֶׁמְּעַבְּרִין אֶת הַשָּׁנָה עַל הַגָּלִיּוֹת שֶׁיָּצְאוּ וַעֲדַיִין לֹא הִגִּיעוּ לִמְקוֹמָן. תַּלְמוּד לוֹמַר וַיְדַבֵּר מֹשֶׁה אֶת מוֹעֲדֵי י'י אֶל בְּנֵי יִשְׂרָאֵל.[113] עֲשֵׂה אֶת הַמּוֹעֲדוֹת שֶׁיַּעֲשׂוּם כָּל־יִשְׂרָאֵל. אָמַר רִבִּי שְׁמוּאֵל בַּר נַחְמָן. וְהֵן שֶׁהִגִּיעוּ לִנְהַר פְּרָת.

If they sanctified it before its time or after its lengthening, should I assume it was lengthened? The verse says (*Lev.* 23:2) "them", "them", "these are My holidays." Before its time is not "My holidays." Before its time, the 29th day, after its lengthening, the 32nd day. From where that one intercalates for the year because of the [men of the] diaspora who set out but did not yet arrive? The verse says (*Num.* 23:44), "Moses spoke about the holidays of the Eternal to the Children of Israel". Make the holidays so they can be observed by all of Israel. Rebbi Samuel bar Naḥman said, only if they had reached the river Euphrates.

110 This is the reading in three of the four parallel texts. In *Sanhedrin*, the reading is הַדּוּחַק ; cf. the author's *The Scholar's Haggadah* (Northvale 1995) p. 298.

111 Missing here, appears in all parallels.

112 Reading of the parallel texts. Here 'ר, i. e., רִבִּי

113 In all parallels, the quote is *Lev.* 23:2.

114 This and the following

paragraphs are found in *Ševi'it* 10:2, explained there in Notes 41-55. The text is also in *Roš Haššanah* 3:1, 58c l. 51, in addition to *Sanhedrin* 1:2.

(40a line 28) אֵין מְעַבְּרִין אֶת הַשָּׁנָה אֶלָּא בִיהוּדָה. וְאִים עִיבְּרוּהָ בַּגָּלִיל מְעוּבֶּרֶת. הֵעִיד רִבִּי חֲנַנְיָה אִישׁ אוֹנוֹ. אִם אֵינָהּ יְכוּלָה לְהִתְעַבֵּר בִּיהוּדָה שֶׁמְעַבְּרִין אוֹתָהּ בַּגָּלִיל. אֵין מְעַבְּרִין אֶת הַשָּׁנָה בַּגָּלִיל. וְאִים עִיבְּרוּהָ מְעוּבֶּרֶת. אֵין מְעַבְּרִין אֶת הַשָּׁנָה בְּחוּצָה לָאָרֶץ. וְאִים עִיבְּרוּהָ אֵינָהּ מְעוּבֶּרֶת. בְּשֶׁיְּכוֹלִים לְעַבְּרָהּ בְּאֶרֶץ יִשְׂרָאֵל. אֲבָל בְּשֶׁאֵין יְכוֹלִין לְעַבְּרָהּ בְּאֶרֶץ יִשְׂרָאֵל מְעַבְּרִין אוֹתָהּ בְּחוּצָה לָאָרֶץ.

"One intercalates for a year only in Judea, but if [a month] was intercalated in Galilee it is validly intercalated. Rebbi Ḥanania from Ono testified that, if it cannot be intercalated in Judea[116], one intercalates in Galilee.[115]" One does not intercalate a year in Galilee, but if it was intercalated in Galilee it is validly intercalated. One does not intercalate a year outside the Land; if it was intercalated outside the Land it is not validly intercalated if it was possible to intercalate in the Land of Israel; but if one cannot intercalate in the Land of Israel[116], one intercalates outside the Land.

115 Tosephta *Sanhedrin* 2:13; Babli *Sanhedrin* 11b.

116 Because of war or persecution, as in the war of Bar Kokhba and its aftermath.

(40a line 34) יִרְמְיָה עִיבֵּר בְּחוּצָה לָאָרֶץ. יְחֶזְקֵאל עִיבֵּר חוּצָה לָאָרֶץ. בָּרוּךְ עִיבֵּר חוּצָה לָאָרֶץ. חֲנַנְיָה בֶּן אֲחִי רִבִּי יְהוֹשֻׁעַ עִיבֵּר בְּחוּצָה לָאָרֶץ. שָׁלַח לֵיהּ רִבִּי תְּלַת אִיגְרָן גַּבֵּי רִבִּי יִצְחָק וְרִבִּי נָתָן. בְּחָדָא כָתַב. לִקְדוּשַׁת חֲנַנְיָה. וּבְחָדָא כָתַב. גְּדָיִים שֶׁהִינַּחְתָּה נַעֲשׂוּ תַּיָּישִׁים. וּבְחָדָא כָתַב. אִם אֵין אַתְּ מְקַבֵּל עָלֶיךָ צֵא לְמִדְבַּר הָאָטָד וּתְהֵא שׁוֹחֵט וּנְחוּנְיוֹן זוֹרֵק. קַדְמִיתָא וְאִיקְרוּן. תִּינְיָיתָא

וְאִיקְרוּן. תְּלִיתִיָּיא בָּעֵי מַבְסַרְתּוּן. אָמְרִין לֵיהּ. לֵית אַתְּ יָכִיל דִּכְבָר אִיקְרְתִּנּוּן. קָם רִבִּי יִצְחָק וְקָרָא. כְּתִיב בָּאוֹרַיְתָא אֵלֶּא מוֹעֲדֵי חֲנַנְיָה בֶּן אֲחִי רִבִּי יְהוֹשֻׁעַ. אָמְרִין לֵיהּ. מוֹעֲדֵי יי. אָמַר לוֹן. גַּבָּן. קָם רִבִּי נָתָן וְאַשְׁלִים. כִּי מִבָּבֶל תֵּצֵא תוֹרָה וּדְבַר יי מִנְּהַר פְּקוֹד. אָמְרִין לֵיהּ. כִּי מִצִּיּוֹן תֵּצֵא תוֹרָה וּדְבַר יי מִרוּשָׁלַיִם. אָמַר לוֹן. גַּבָּן. אֲזַל וְקָבַל עֲלֵיהּ גַּבֵּי רִבִּי יְהוּדָה בֶּן בְּתֵירָה לִנְצִיבִין. אָמַר לֵיהּ. אֲחַרֵיהֶם אֲחַרֵיהֶם. אָמַר לֵיהּ. לִינָה יָדַע מַה שֶּׁבְּקִית תַּמָּן. מָאן מוֹדַע לִי דְאִינּוּן חַכְמִין מְחַשָּׁבָה דִכְוָתִי. מִכֵּיוָן דּוּ אָמַר. לָא חַכְמִין דִּכְוָתִי. יִשְׁמְעוּן לֵיהּ. מִכֵּיוָן דִּינוּן חַכְמִין מְחַשָּׁבָה יִשְׁמַע לְהוֹן. קָם וְרָכַב סוּסְיָיא. מִן דְּמָטָא מָטָא, הֵב דְּלָא מָטָא נוֹהֲגִין בְּקִילְקוּל.

Jeremiah intercalated outside the Land. Ezechiel intercalated outside the Land. Baruch intercalated outside the Land[117]. [118]Hanania the nephew of Rebbi Joshua[119] intercalated outside the Land. Rebbi[120] sent him three letters through Rebbi Isaac and Rebbi Nathan[121]. In one he wrote, to His holiness Hanania. And in one he wrote, the kid goats you left behind became rams. And in one he wrote, if you do not accept, go to the thistle desert, do slaughter and let Onias sprinkle[122]. After the first [letter], he honored them. After the second, he honored them. After the third, he wanted to disgrace them. They said to him, you cannot do that since you already did honor us. Rebbi Isaac rose and quoted, it is written in the Torah: These are the holidays of Hanania the nephew of Rebbi Joshua. They said to him, "the holdays of the Eternal[123]". He said to them, that is with us[124]. Rebbi Nathan rose and finished: "For from Babylonia will go Torah forth and the Eternal's word from Nahar-Peqod." They said to him, "for from Zion will Torah go forth and the Eternal's word from Jerusalem[125]". He said to them, that is with us. He went to complain about them to Rebbi Jehudah ben Bathyra at Nisibis[126]. He[127] said to him[128], follow them, follow them. He said to him[127], I do not know whom I left there. Who would tell me that they are wise to the computations as I am? If he[128] had said, they are not wise, they should listen to him. Since they are wise to the computations as he is, he[128] has to listen to them. He[127] got up and rode on a horse. Where he reached, he reached. Where he did not reach, they continued following the corrupt [calendar][129].

117 There is no biblical basis for these statements which are based on the hypothesis that the biblical calendar is identical with the rabbinical. In Talmudic tradition, Baruch ben Neriah did not follow Jeremiah to Egypt but went to Babylonia where he founded the first Babylonian academy.

118 Babli *Berakhot* 63a/b; some details there seem to be more historical.

119 His name and that of his father was Hananiah ben Hananiah, meaning that both were posthumous sons, a very unlucky reference which can be avoided by circumlocution. He supported his uncle's determined opposition to any revolt against Rome and it seems that he left Palestine at the outbreak of the Bar Kokhba revolt and founded the Academy of Nahardea, later headed by his descendant Samuel.

120 In the Babli, the identity of the head of the Academy who re-established the authority of the Palestinian Academy in fixing the calendar is not mentioned. It is to be expected that this was Rabban Simeon ben Gamliel who became head after the Hadrianic decrees were abolished, perhaps by Septimius Severus. If it was Rebbi, Hananiah must have been a centenarian.

121 In the Babli, two grandsons of priests serving in the Temple. The Tanna R. Nathan (the Babylonian) is to be dated to the time of Rabban Simeon ben Gamliel.

122 The blood of the sacrifice. A reference to the (illegitimate) Onias Temple in Egypt.

123 *Lev.* 23:4.

124 The correct verse only applies to the followers of the patriarchate in

Galilee.
125   *Is.* 2:3.
126   The representative of the autochthonous Babylonian Academy whose ancestors already were the leaders in Jerusalem 100 years before the destruction of the Temple.
127   R. Jehudah ben Bathyra.
128   Ḥanania.
129   We do not know what the material difference was in the calendar computations. There is a slight possibility that it was in the rules of moving the date of the New Year, a difference that surfaced 700 years later in the quarrel between Saadya Gaon in Baghdad and the Patriarch Meïr in Jerusalem.

(40a line 49) כְּתִיב וְאֶל יֶתֶר זִקְנֵי הַגּוֹלָה. אָמַר הַקָּדוֹשׁ בָּרוּךְ הוּא. בְּיוֹתֵר הֵן חֲבִיבִין עָלַי זִקְנֵי הַגּוֹלָה. חֲבִיבָה עָלַי כַּת קְטַנָּה שֶׁבְּאֶרֶץ יִשְׂרָאֵל מִסַּנְהֶדְרִין גְּדוֹלָה שֶׁבְּחוּצָה לָאָרֶץ. כְּתִיב הֶחָרָשׁ וְהַמַּסְגֵּר אֶלֶף. וְאַתְּ אָמַר הָכֵן. רִבִּי בְּרֶכְיָה בְשֵׁם רִבִּי חֶלְבוֹ וְרַבָּנִין. רִבִּי בְּרֶכְיָה אָמַר. הֶחָרָשׁ אֶלֶף וְהַמַּסְגֵּר אֶלֶף. וְרַבָּנִין אָמְרֵי. כּוּלְּהוֹן אֶלֶף. רִבִּי בְּרֶכְיָה בְשֵׁם רִבִּי חֶלְבוֹ אָמַר. אִילּוּ הַחֲבִירִים. וְרַבָּנִין אָמְרִין. אִינוּ הַבּוּלְוְוטִין.

It is written[130], "to the outstanding Elders of the diaspora". The Holy One, praise to Him, said: The Elders of the diaspora are very dear to me. More beloved by me is a small group in the Land of Israel than a great Synhedrion outside the Land. It is written[131]: "The craftsmen and the smiths one thousand," and you say so? Rebbi Berekhiah in the name of Rebbi Ḥelbo and the rabbis. Rebbi Berekhiah said, one thousand craftsmen and one thousand smiths. But the rabbis say, together one thousand[132]. Rebbi Berekhiah in the name of Rebbi Ḥelbo said, these are the fellows[133]; but the rabbis say, these are the councilmen[134].

130   *Jer.* 29:1.
131   *2K.* 24:16. It has been suggested from their association with the soldiers that these were the people trained in the production of weapons.
132   Modern Bible commentators

follow the rabbis.
133 The people strictly adhering to the rules of ritual purity, cf. *Introduction to Tractate Demay*, p. 349. If this is the correct interpretation, the question is who are the small group in the Land of Israel. In the Babli, *Giṭṭin* 88a, this is the only opinion mentioned.
134 Greek βουλευταί, cf. *Peah* 1:1, Note 167.

(40a line 54) רִבִּי¹³⁵ חוֹשַׁעְיָה כַּד הֲוָה מְקַבֵּל סַהֲדָיָא בְּעֵין טָב הֲוָה אָמַר לוֹן. הֱווֹן יָדְעִין כַּמָּה עֵדוּת יוֹצֵא מִפִּיכֶם. כַּמָּה שְׂכַר בָּתִּים יוֹצֵא מִפִּיכֶם. אָמַר רִבִּי אֲבִינָא. אִין כָּךְ הוּא אֲפִילוּ דִינֵי נְפָשׁוֹת. בַּת ג׳ שָׁנִים וְיוֹם אֶחָד בָּא עָלֶיהָ הֲרֵי זֶה בִסְקִילָה. נִמְלְכוּ בֵית דִּין לְעַבְּרוֹ וּבָא עָלֶיהָ אֵינָהּ בִּסְקִילָה. אָמַר רִבִּי אָבוּן. אֶקְרָא לֵאלֹהִים עֶלְיוֹן לָאֵל גּוֹמֵר עָלָי. בַּת ג׳ שָׁנִים וְיוֹם אֶחָד נִמְלְכוּ בֵית דִּין לְעַבְּרוֹ בְּתוּלִין חוֹזְרִין וְאִם לָאו אֵינָן חוֹזְרִין.

Rebbi Hoshaia, when he received witnesses at Kallirhoë¹³⁶, used to say to them: You should know the importance of the testimony that comes from your mouth, how much rent money depends on your mouths¹³⁷. Rebbi Abuna said, if it is so, it is even a matter of criminal law. If somebody sleeps with a girl three years and one day old, he is stoned¹³⁸. The Court decided to lengthen¹³⁹, if he sleeps with her he is not stoned. Rebbi Abun said: ¹⁴⁰"I am calling to Almighty God, to the God who decides¹⁴¹ with me." If a girl is three years and one day old, if the Court decided to lengthen, her hymen repairs itself, otherwise it does not repair itself¹³⁸.

135 Reading of the parallel in *Sanhedrin*. Reading here: רַ.
136 *En Ṭab, Kallirhoë* (probably Ḥamat Gader; cf. Babli *Roš Haššanah* 25a) was the place chosen in the early Amoraic period to proclaim the days of the New Moon and the intercalation of a month in a year. The witnesses testify that they have seen the new moon.
137 Since rent usually is paid by the month or the year, it makes a

difference whether a month has 29 or 30 days, or a year has 12 or 13 months.

138   If the girl was engaged to be married (*Deut.* 22:23-26), for which the minimal age of consent is 3 years and a day. The girl, as a minor, cannot be prosecuted. Any seduction of an underage girl is statutory rape, but talmudic law assumes that a girl who was raped at less than 3 years and one day is still a virgin since her hymen is supposed to repair itself. But if she was raped at the age of at least 3 years and one day she is no longer a virgin and cannot demand a virgin's portion in any marriage settlement.

139   Either a month or a year. In the first case, assume the girl was born on the 30th of a certain month. After three years, if the same month has 30 days, she is only 3 years old. But if that month is declared to have only 29 days, the 30th is the first day of her fourth year and any man committing adultery with her is stoned. Similarly, if the girl was born in Nisan then the 3rd birthday is either 12 or 13 months after the 2nd; there is a full month where the decision of the Synhedrion makes a difference in her standing in criminal law. Obviously, the same problems appear with reaching adulthood; the example of the minor was chosen because of the sermon following.

140   *Ps.* 57:3.

141   גמר is used for the vote of the judges by which a case is decided. Nature, created by God, acts as if God had voted with the majority of the judges; cf. *Midrash Tehillim* 57[1].

משנה יד: הַנּוֹדֵר מִן הַכְּרוּב אָסוּר בְּאִיסְפָּרְגוֹס מִן הָאִיסְפָּרְגוֹס מוּתָּר (fol. 39c) בַּכְּרוּב. מִן הַגְּרִיסִים אָסוּר בַּמִּקְפָּה וְרִבִּי יוֹסֵי מַתִּיר. מִן הַמִּקְפָּה מוּתָּר בַּגְּרִיסִין. מִן הַמִּקְפָּה אָסוּר בַּשּׁוּם וְרִבִּי יוֹסֵי מַתִּיר. מִן הַשּׁוּם מוּתָּר בַּמִּקְפָּה.

Mishnah 14: One who makes a vow to abstain from cabbage is forbidden cabbage shoot[142], from cabbage shoot he is permitted cabbage[143]. From groats, he is forbidden groat soup but Rebbi Yose permits it; from groat soup he is permitted groats¹⁴⁴. From soup he is forbidden garlic¹⁴⁵ but Rebbi Yose permits it; from garlic he is permitted soup.

142 Greek ἀσπαραγός "shoot of edible vegetable", used here in the restricted sense of cabbage shoot.

143 The shoot has no leaves yet; from cabbage one eats the leaves but not the shoot

144 Dry groats.

145 Which was always used to spice soup.

(40a line 60) **הלכה יד**: מַה טַעֲמָא דְּרְבִּי יוֹסֵי. שֵׁם אָבִיו קָרוּי עָלָיו. עַל דַּעְתֵּיהּ דְּרְבִּי יוֹסֵי הַנּוֹדֵר מִן הַיַּיִן מוּתָּר בְּקוֹנְדִיטוֹן.

Halakhah 14¹⁴⁶: What is Rebbi Yose's reason? Is its father's name called upon it¹⁴⁷? In the opinion of Rebbi Yose, if somebody makes a vow to abstain from wine, he is permitted spiced wine¹⁴⁸.

146 In ms. and *editio princeps*, Halakhah 14 is the next paragraph.

147 Since the name "cabbage" does not appear in *asparagos*, the vow concerning cabbage cannot extend to *asparagos*.

148 Latin *conditum (vinum)*, cf. *Berakhot* 6:5, Note 157.

(40a line 62) מִן הַכְּרוּב אָסוּר בְּאִיסְפָּרָגוֹס כּוּל׳. מִן הַגְּרִיסִין אָסוּר בְּמִקְפָּה. וְהוּא שֶׁיְּהֵא רוּבָּן גְּרִיסִין. מִן הַמִּקְפָּה אָסוּר בַּשּׁוּם. וְהוּא שֶׁיְּהֵא רוּבָּן שׁוּם. וְהָכָא אַתְּ מְהַלֵּךְ אַחַר הַטַּעַם וְכָא אַתְּ מְהַלֵּךְ אַחַר הָרוֹב.

"From cabbage, he is forbidden cabbage shoot," etc. "From groats, he is forbidden groat soup," only if most of it is groats. "From soup he is forbidden garlic," only if most of it is garlic? In that case, you go after the taste, in the other after the main ingredient¹⁴⁹.

149 Spices are forbidden as long as they can be tasted; bland food only as long as it is the main ingredient.

(fol. 39c) **משנה טו:** מִן הָעֲדָשִׁים אָסוּר בָּאֲשִׁישִׁים וְרִבִּי יוֹסֵי מַתִּיר. מִן הָאֲשִׁישִׁים מוּתָּר בָּעֲדָשִׁים.

Mishnah 15: From lentils, he is is forbidden *ašišim*, but Rebbi Yose permits. From *ašišim* he is permitted lentils.

(40a line 65) **הלכה טו:** רִבִּי יָסָא אֲזַל לְגַבֵּי רִבִּי יוֹסֵי וְאַפִּיק קוֹמוֹי טְלוֹפְחִין מְקַלְיָין וּטְחִינָן וּמְגַבְּלָן בִּדְבָשׁ וּמְטוֹגְן. אָמַר לֵיהּ. אִילֵין אִינּוּן אֲשִׁישִׁין שֶׁאָמְרוּ חֲכָמִים.

Halakhah 15: Rebbi Yasa went to Rebbi Yose who brought roasted lentils out for him, ground them, formed them into a dough with honey, and fried them. He said to him, these are the *ašišim* mentioned by the Sages.

(fol. 39c) **משנה יו:** חִיטָּה חִיטִּים שֶׁאֵינִי טוֹעֵם אָסוּר בָּהֶן בֵּין קֶמַח בֵּין פַּת. גְּרִיס גְּרִיסִין שֶׁאֵינִי טוֹעֵם אָסוּר בָּהֶן בֵּין חַיִּין בֵּין מְבוּשָּׁלִין. רִבִּי יְהוּדָה אוֹמֵר קוֹנָם גְּרִיס אוֹ חִיטָּה שֶׁאֵינִי טוֹעֵם מוּתָּר לָכוֹס חַיִּים.

Mishnah 16: 'That I shall not taste wheat or wheats: he is forbidden both flour and bread[150]. 'That I shall not taste groat or groats: he is forbidden both raw and cooked. Rebbi Jehudah says, 'a *qônām* that I shall not taste groat or wheat', he is permitted to chew them raw.

150 The interpretation of the Mishnah in the Halakhah and the Tosephta (3.7) in the name of R. Jehudah is the opposite of that given in the Babli (53b) in the name of Rabban Simeon ben Gamliel. Following R. Jehudah in *baraita*/Tosephta, חִטָּה is a singular and refers to single kernels for chewing; חִיטִים as plural refers to material for baking. R. Jehudah in the Mishnah, and Rabban Simeon ben Gamliel in the Babli, hold that the collective חִטָּה means wheat bread but the plural חִטִּים means single kernels to be chewed. Similarly, for them the collective גְּרִיס means porridge, but the plural single kernels to be chewed. According to both Talmudim, in the first part of the Mishnah the person forbade to himself both the singular-collective and the plural. Therefore, R. Jehudah, who quotes only the singular in his statement, does not disagree with the anonymous majority.

(40a line 68) **הלכה יו**: גְּרִיס גְּרִיסִין שֶׁאֵינִי טוֹעֵם כול׳. תַּנֵּי רבּי יְהוּדָה אוֹמֵר. קוֹנָם גְּרִיס שֶׁאֵינִי טוֹעֵם. אָסוּר לָכוֹס וּמוּתָּר בְּמִקְפָּה. גְּרִיסִים שֶׁאֵינִי טוֹעֵם אָסוּר בְּמִקְפָּה וּמוּתָּר לָכוֹס. חִיטָּה שֶׁאֵינִי טוֹעֵם. אָסוּר לָכוֹס וּמוּתָּר בְּפַת. חִיטִּים שֶׁאֵינִי טוֹעֵם. אָסוּר בְּפַת וּמוּתָּר לָכוֹס.

Halakhah 16: 'That I shall not taste groat or groats, etc. It was stated: "Rebbi Jehudah says, 'a *qônām* that I shall not taste a groat kernel,' he is forbidden to chew and permitted soup. 'That I shall not taste groats,' he is forbidden soup and permitted to chew. 'That I shall not taste a wheat kernel,' he is forbidden to chew and permitted bread. 'That I shall not taste wheats,' he is forbidden bread and permitted to chew.

(40a line 71) חִיטָּה וְאַתְּ אָמַר אָכֵן. אָמַר רבּי יוֹסֵי. כֵּן אוֹרְחֵיהּ דְּבַר נָשׁ מֵי חָמֵי פִּיתָּה נְקִיָּיה וּמֵימַר. בָּרוּךְ דְּבָרָא הָדֵין חִיטְּתָא.

"Wheat" and you say so? Rebbi Yose said, so is the way of people, if they see white bread they say, blessed Who created this wheat[151].

151 This is inconsistent with the preceding *baraita*; it refers to the statement of R. Jehudah in the Mishnah who sees in the collective חִישָׁה a synonym of "bread".

הנודר מן הירק פרק שביעי

(fol. 40b) **משנה א:** הַנּוֹדֵר מִן הַיָּרָק מוּתָּר בַּדִּילוּעִים. וְרִבִּי עֲקִיבָה אוֹסֵר. אָמְרוּ לוֹ לְרִבִּי עֲקִיבָה וַהֲלֹא אוֹמֵר אָדָם לִשְׁלוּחוֹ קַח לָנוּ יָרָק וְהוּא אוֹמֵר לֹא מָצָאתִי אֶלָּא דִילוּעִין. אָמַר לָהֶם כֵּן הַדָּבָר אוֹ שֶׁמָּא אוֹמֵר הוּא לֹא מָצָאתִי אֶלָּא קִטְנִית. אֶלָּא שֶׁהַדִּילוּעִין בִּכְלָל יָרָק. אָסוּר בְּפוֹל הַמִּצְרִי לַח וּמוּתָּר בַּיָּבֵשׁ.

Mishnah 1: One who makes a vow to abstain from vegetables is permitted squash, but Rebbi Aqiba forbids it. They said to Rebbi Aqiba, does it not happen that a person says to his agent, buy vegetables for us, and he says, I found only squash[1]? He said to them, that is true. Would he ever say, I found only legumes[2]? But squash is contained in the notion of "vegetable"[3]. He is forbidden fresh Egyptian beans and permitted dried ones.

1 "Vegetables" are grown in a vegetable garden and eaten raw or as a side dish. Squash is produced without irrigation and is not eaten raw. The person sent to buy vegetables will not buy squash without separate instructions.

2 Legumes (Arabic ڤُلْ) are seeds, such as peas and lentils, to be ground into flour. As the last sentence of the Mishnah makes clear, legumes not ready to be ground into flour are vegetables. The person sent to buy vegetables will never ask for permission to buy legumes.

3 The Babylonian Mishnah adds: "But legumes are not contained in the notion of 'vegetables'".

(40b line 35) **הלכה א**: הַנּוֹדֵר מִן הַיָּרָק כּוֹל׳. מִיסְבַּר סָבַר רִבִּי עֲקִיבָה מָצָאתִי וְלֹא מָצָאתִי. מֵעַתָּה הַנּוֹדֵר מִן הַבָּשָׂר יְהֵא אָסוּר בִּבְשַׂר דָּגִים וַחֲגָבִים. שֶׁכֵּן אָדָם אוֹמֵר לַחֲבֵירוֹ. קַח לָנוּ בָשָׂר. וְהוּא אוֹמֵר לַחֲבֵירוֹ. לֹא מָצָאתִי אֶלָּא דָגִים. אֶלָּא רִבִּי עֲקִיבָה סָבַר מֵימַר. הַדִּילוּעִין בִּכְלָל יָרָק. וְרַבָּנִין אָמְרִין. אֵין הַדִּילוּעִין בִּכְלָל יָרָק. אַף לְמִידַת הַדִּין כֵּן. יָרָק גִינָה זֶה מָכוּר. וְהָיוּ שָׁם דִּילוּעִין. עַל דַּעְתֵּיהּ דְּרִבִּי עֲקִיבָה מְכוּרִין. עַל דַּעְתּוֹן דְּרַבָּנִין אֵינָן מְכוּרִין. וּבְהֶבְקֵר וּבְהֶקְדֵּשׁ כֵּן.

Halakhah 1: Does Rebbi Aqiba think "I found, I did not find"[4]? Then one who forbids meat to himself should be forbidden fish and grasshopper meat since, if a man says to another, buy meat for us, he will return and say, I found only fish[5]! But Rebbi Aqiba must think that squash are vegetables, but the rabbis think that squash are not vegetables. That applies to legal situations. "The vegetables of this garden are sold;" if squash were there, they would be sold in the opinion of Rebbi Aqiba, not sold in the opinion of the rabbis. The same applies to declarations of abandonment[6] or dedications.

4   Does R. Aqiba hold that any usual substitute comes under the category of the original? The Babli, 54a, holds that this is R. Aqiba's opinion. The Babli must hold that a person sent to buy meat will not suggest fish as a substitute.

5   Fish and grasshoppers do not come under the category of "meat" since they can be cooked with milk. (Yemenite Jews used to roast grasshoppers in clay pots used for neither meat nor milk).

6   If somebody declares his vegetables as ownerless or dedicates them to the Temple, for the rabbis he does not include squash, for R. Aqiba he does.

(40b line 41) רִבִּי יַעֲקֹב בַּר אָחָא רִבִּי חִייָה בְּשֵׁם רִבִּי יוֹחָנָן. אָתָא דִיחִידָייָא דְהָכָא כִּסְתָמָא דְתַמָּן. וִיחִידָייָא דְתַמָּן כִּסְתָמָא דְהָכָא. דְּתַנֵּי. הַנּוֹדֵר מִן הַבָּשָׂר

אָסוּר בְּכָל־מִין בָּשָׂר אָסוּר[7] בְּרֹאשׁ וּבִכְרָעַיִם וּבְקָנֶה וּבְלֵב וּבְכָבֵד. וּמוּתָּר בִּבְשַׂר דָּגִים וַחֲגָבִים. וְכֵן הָיָה רַבָּן שִׁמְעוֹן בֶּן גַּמְלִיאֵל אוֹמֵר. קִרְבַּיָּיא לָאו בָּשָׂר וְאָכְלֵיהוֹן לָאו אִינָשׁ.

Rebbi Jacob bar Idi, Rebbi Ḥiyya, in the name of Rebbi Joḥanan: It turns out that the minority opinion here is the majority opinion there and vice-versa. As it was stated: "One who makes a vow to abstain from meat is forbidden all kinds of meat, is forbidden head, feet, neck, heart, and liver[8]. But he is permitted fish meat and grasshoppers[9]. In this vein, Rabban Simeon ben Gamliel said, intestines are not meat and those who eat them are not humans."

7   This is the text of the scribe of the ms. The corrector changed it to וּמוּתָּר "but he is permitted", copied by *editio princeps*. It is obvious that both "forbidden" and "permitted" was in the text before the scribe, as preserved in the Tosephta (3.5) and the Babli (54b):

הַנּוֹדֵר מִן הַבָּשָׂר אָסוּר בְּכָל־מִין בָּשָׂר אָסוּר בְּרֹאשׁ וּבְרַגְלַיִם בְּקָנֶה וּבְעוֹפוֹת. וּמוּתָּר בִּבְשַׂר דָּגִים וַחֲגָבִים. רַבָּן שִׁמְעוֹן בֶּן גַּמְלִיאֵל אוֹמֵר הַנּוֹדֵר מִן הַבָּשָׂר אָסוּר בְּכָל־מִין בָּשָׂר וּמוּתָּר בְּרֹאשׁ וּבְרַגְלַיִם וּבְקָנֶה וּבְעוֹפוֹת. וְכֵן הָיָה רַבָּן שִׁמְעוֹן בֶּן גַּמְלִיאֵל אוֹמֵר. קִרְבַּיִין לָא בָּשָׂר אָכְלֵיהוֹן לָא אִינָשׁ.

"One who makes a vow to abstain from meat is forbidden all kinds of meat, is forbidden head, feet, neck, and fowl. But he is permitted fish meat and grasshoppers. *Rabban Simeon ben Gamliel said,* one who makes a vow to abstain from meat is forbidden all kinds of meat, is *permitted* head, feet, neck, and fowl. In this vein, Rabban Simeon ben Gamliel said, intestines are not meat and those who eat them are not humans."

In this text, the expression "similarly" makes sense and the anonymous majority are inclusive as R. Aqiba is here, Rabban Simeon ben Gamliel is narrow in his definition as the rabbis are with vegetables. The Babli, 54b, simply states that R. Aqiba and Rabban Simeon ben Gamliel are on opposite sides in this discussion.

8   The Babli adds, "and fowl", cf.

Note 7.   Ḥulin 8:1, Tosephta Ḥulin 8:2.

9   This statement also in Mishnah

(40b line 46) הַכֹּל מוֹדִין בְּנוֹדֵר מִן הַדִּילוּעִין שֶׁמּוּתָּר בְּיָרָק. כְּהָדָא דְתַנֵּי. הַנּוֹדֵר מִן הָעִיקָר אָסוּר בַּתְּפִילָה. הַנּוֹדֵר מִן הַתְּפִילָה מוּתָּר בָּעִיקָר. הַנּוֹדֵר מִן הַבָּשָׂר אָסוּר בַּגִּידִים. הַנּוֹדֵר מִן הַגִּידִים מוּתָּר בַּבָּשָׂר. מַה פְּלִיגֵי. בִּדְלַעַת מִצְרִית. אֲבָל בִּדְלַעַת יְוָנִית כָּל־עַמָּא מוֹדֵיי שֶׁהוּא כְּיָרָק. רִבִּי קְרִיסְפָּא בְּשֵׁם רִבִּי יוֹחָנָן. כָּל־אִילֵּין קַרְיָיא וּכְרוּבְתָא דַאֲנָן אֲכְלִין דְּלַעַת יְוָנִית אִינּוּן. רִבִּי יוּדָה בַּר צְרָדִיָּה אוֹמֵר. קִירמוֹלִין הֵן כְּיָרָק. רִבִּי יוֹנָה וְרִבִּי יוֹסֵי בְּעֵיי. קרמולין מַהוּ שֶׁיְּהוּ חַיָּיבִין בְּמַעְשְׂרוֹת. תַּנֵּי בַּר קַפָּרָא. קרמולין פְּטוּרִין מִן הַמַּעְשְׂרוֹת. הָדָא דְאַתְּ אֲמַר עַד שֶׁלֹּא עָשׂוּ דִילוּעִין. אֲבָל אִם עָשׂוּ דִילוּעִין כְּיָרָק הֵן. הוֹרֵי רִבִּי יוֹסֵי בְּאִילֵּין עֲלֵי קָלוֹקַסְיָיה שֶׁאָסוּר לִגְמוֹת בָּהֶן מַיִם מִפְּנֵי שֶׁהַצְּבָיִין אוֹכְלִין אוֹתָן.

Everybody agrees that a person who vows to forbid gourd to himself is permitted vegetables, as it was stated: A person who makes a vow to abstain from a main object is forbidden the peripherals; if he vows from the peripherals, he is permitted the main object. One who vows to abstain from meat is forbidden sinews, he who vows to abstain from sinews is permitted meat. Where do they disagree? About Egyptian gourd. But everybody agrees that Greek gourds[10] are vegetables. Rebbi Crispus in the name of Rebbi Joḥanan: All sorts of gourd and cabbage which we eat are Greek gourds. Rebbi Jehudah bar Ṣeradia says, *qarmals*[12] are vegetables. Rebbi Jonah and Rebbi Yose asked, are *qarmals* subject to tithes? [11]Bar Qappara stated, *qarmals* are free from tithes. That is, as long as they did not form gourds; but when they formed gourds they are like vegetables. Rebbi Yose instructed that it is forbidden to sip water from colocasia leaves because they are food for deer.

10 Cf. *Kilaim* 1:5.

11 From *Ševi'it* 2:10, Notes 98-101, dealing with the rules of the Sabbatical year. The statement of Bar Qappara there is attributed to R. Jonah.

(40b line 56) הַנּוֹדֵר מִן הַיָּרָק מַהוּ שֶׁיְּהֵא מוּתָּר בְּמִינֵי אפומלייא כְּגוֹן נבעה ומסרולה ופלוליה וְקָלוֹקַסְיָה. רִבִּי יִצְחָק בֶּן חֲקוֹלָה וְרִבִּי יְהוֹשֻׁעַ בֶּן לֵוִי תְּרֵיהוֹן אָמְרִין קוֹלְקָס כְּיָרָק לְמַעְשְׂרוֹת וְלַשְּׁבִיעִית וּלְפֵיאָה וּלְכִלְאַיִם. וְלַנְּדָרִים צְרִיכָא.

Is one who makes a vow to abstain from vegetables permitted kinds of '*pvmlyy*', as, for example, *nb'h*, *msrvlh*, *plvlyh*[12], and taro[13]. [14]Rebbi Isaac ben Ḥaqolah and Rebbi Joshua ben Levi both say taro is like a vegetable for tithes, the sabbatical year, *peah*, and *kilaim*. For vows it is problematic.

12 Neither the family of plants אפומלייא nor the individual plants mentioned here have been determined, except for the last one. In Arabic, נבע is a tree from which arrows and bows are made. {Perhaps cf. Greek πωμάριον, τό, Latin *pomarium*, "orchard", as a reference to "tree fruits"? (E. G.)}

13 Colocasia, Greek κολοκασία, Arabic קלקאס. Its root is used to produce a kind of flour in Africa; hence, it is an intermediate between a vegetable and a legume. The only problem is that of vows (e. g., if a person makes a vow to abstain from vegetables), since in matters of vows one does not follow technical usage but the meaning in local dialects. Hence, there may be places where taro is commonly subsumed under vegetables and other places where it is not.

14 Text from *Peah* 1:6, Note 273.

(40b line 59) הַנּוֹדֵר מִן הַיָּרָק מַהוּ שֶׁיְּהֵא מוּתָּר בַּיָּבֵשׁ. נִשְׁמְעִינָהּ מִן הָדָא. אָסוּר בְּפוֹל מִצְרִי לַח וּמוּתָּר בַּיָּבֵשׁ. לֹא אָמַר אֶלָּא פוֹל מִצְרִי דָּבָר שֶׁיֵּשׁ לוֹ גּוֹרֶן. הָא דָבָר שֶׁאֵין לוֹ גּוֹרֶן אָסוּר אֲפִילוּ יָבֵשׁ. הַנּוֹדֵר מִן הָאֲפִינָה אָסוּר בַּקִּישּׁוּאִין וּבִדְלוּעִין וּבַאֲבַטִּיחִין וּבַמְלַפְּפוֹנִיּוֹת וְאָסוּר בְּכָל־פֵּירוֹת הָאִילָן. הַנּוֹדֵר מִן

כָּבְשָׁה מוּתָּר בִּגְדָיִים וּבְגוֹזָלִים וּבְחָלָב. וְאִם אָמַר. בְּגִידּוּלֵי שָׁנָה אָסוּר בַּכֹּל. הַנּוֹדֵר מִן הַתִּירוֹשׁ אָסוּר בְּכָל־מִינֵי מְתִיקָה וּמוּתָּר בְּיַיִן. כְּמָאן דְּאָמַר. הִילְכוּ בִנְדָרִים אַחַר לְשׁוֹן בְּנֵי אָדָם. בְּרַם כְּמָאן דְּאָמַר. הִילְכוּ בִנְדָרִים אַחַר לְשׁוֹן תּוֹרָה. הַתּוֹרָה קָרָאת אוֹתוֹ תִירוֹשׁ. תִּירוֹשְׁךָ זֶה הַיַּיִן.

If somebody makes a vow to abstain from vegetables, would he be permitted dried ones? Let us hear from the following: "He is forbidden fresh Egyptian beans and permitted dried ones." He mentioned only Egyptian beans, a kind which has a threshing floor[15]. Therefore, anything which has no threshing floor is forbidden even if dried. [16]If somebody makes a vow to abstain from bulbous plants[17] he is forbidden green melon[18], squash, water melon, sweet melon[18] and all tree fruits. If somebody makes a vow to abstain from sheep meat, he is permitted lambs, pidgeon chicks[19], and milk[20]. But if he said, which grew this year, he is forbidden all of these. [21]If somebody makes a vow to abstain from cider, he is forbidden everything sweet and permitted wine. That is, following those who say that vows are interpreted in the vernacular[22]. But following those who say, vows are interpreted in biblical Hebrew[23], the Torah used "cider" as an expression for wine; "your cider"[24], that is wine.

15   I. e., Egyptian beans are separated from their hulls and stored in quantity. A contract for delivery of Egyptian beans requires delivery of dried ones. A vegetable is permitted in dry form only if that dry form is traded as a separate kind.

16   Tosephta 4:3.

17   This translation follows S. Lieberman, *Tosefta ki-fshutah Nedarim*, p. 455.

18   Cf. *Kilaim* 1:2, Notes 38-39.

19   These have nothing to do with sheep; pigeons are only mentioned for inclusion in the next clause.

20   Sheep's milk.

21 Tosephta 4:3, Babli *Yoma* 76b.
22 R. Johanan, Halakhah 6:1; everybody's opinion in the Babli, *Yoma* 76b. It seems that in Mishnaic times, the sweetness of the cider was the determinig factor.
23 R. Joshiah, Halakhah 6:1.
24 *Deut.* 12:17, 14:23, 18:4.

משנה ב: הַנּוֹדֵר מִן הַדָּגָן אָסוּר בְּפוֹל הַמִּצְרִי יָבֵשׁ דִּבְרֵי רִבִּי מֵאִיר. וַחֲכָמִים אוֹמְרִים אֵינוֹ אָסוּר אֶלָּא בַחֲמֵשֶׁת הַמִּינִין. רִבִּי מֵאִיר אוֹמֵר הַנּוֹדֵר מִן הַתְּבוּאָה אֵינוֹ אָסוּר אֶלָּא בַחֲמֵשֶׁת הַמִּינִין אֲבָל הַנּוֹדֵר מִן הַדָּגָן אָסוּר בַּכֹּל וּמוּתָּר בְּפֵירוֹת הָאִילָן וּבְיָרָק. (fol. 40b)

Mishnah 2: One who makes a vow to abstain from flour is forbidden dry Egyptian beans[25], the words of Rebbi Meïr. But the Sages say, he is forbidden only the Five Kinds[26]. Rebbi Meïr says, one who makes a vow to abstain from produce[27] is forbidden only the Five Kinds but he who makes a vow to abstain from flour is forbidden everything[28], but permitted tree fruits[29] and vegetables.

25 Not only Egyptian beans but all legumes (Note 2) ground into flour, as explained at the end. Egyptian beans are only mentioned because of Mishnah 1.
26 Wheat, barley, spelt, foxtail, and oats; cf. *Berakhot* 6:1 (Note 89), *Kilaim* 1:1 (Notes 2,3), *Hallah* 1:1 (Note 1). Only these contain gluten which produces sour dough.
27 In Biblical language, תבואה is all agricultural produce. In rabbinic language, the word is used only for cereals.
28 Not everything but every cereal and legume.
29 Even carob fruit which sometimes is ground into a kind of flour.

(40b line 68) **הלכה ב:** הַנּוֹדֵר כו'. מַה טַעֲמָא דְּרִבִּי מֵאִיר. דְּגָנָא דְאַרְעָא. מַה טַעֲמוֹן דְּרַבָּנִין. דְּגָנָה מֵעֲבוּרָה.

"One who makes a vow," etc. What is Rebbi Meïr's reason? What the rain produces from the earth[30]. What is the reason of the rabbis? Flour is עבור[31].

30 Arabic دجن "to be dark, rainy".
31 The expression עבור is used in Jos. 5:12 to indicate grains used to make bread.

(40c line 1) תַּמָּן תַּנִּינָן. הַנּוֹדֵר מִן הַפַּת וּמִן הַתְּבוּאָה אָסוּר בָּהֶן. דִּבְרֵי רִבִּי מֵאִיר. הָא הַנּוֹדֵר מִן הַפַּת וּמִן הַתְּבוּאָה יְהֵא אָסוּר בַּכֹּל כְּרַבָּנִין. רִבִּי חִיָּיה בְשֵׁם רִבִּי יוֹחָנָן. מַתְנִיתָא אָמְרָה כֵן שֶׁהַנּוֹדֵר מִן הַדָּגָן אֵינוֹ אָסוּר אֶלָּא מֵהֶן. מָה אֲנָן קַיָּימִין. אִם בְּאוֹמֵר. פַּת תּוֹרָה.[32] מֵעַתָּה אַף הָאוֹמֵר. תְּבוּאַת תּוֹרָה סְתָם. יְהֵא אָסוּר בַּכֹּל. דִּכְתִיב וּתְבוּאַת הַכָּרֶם. אִם בְּאוֹמֵר. פַּת סְתָם. אֵין לָךְ קָרוּי פַּת סְתָם אֶלָּא חִיטִּין וּשְׂעוֹרִין בִּלְבַד. אָמַר רִבִּי יוֹסֵי. קִייַּמְתִּיהּ בְּמָקוֹם שֶׁאוֹכְלִין כָּל־פַּת. אֵין קָרוּי פַּת סְתָם אֶלָּא חֲמִשָּׁה מִינִין בִּלְבַד.

[33]He who makes a vow not to use bread or produce is forbidden them, the words of Rebbi Meïr. Therefore, is he who makes a vow not to use bread or produce forbidden everything according to the rabbis? Rebbi Ḥiyya in the name of Rebbi Joḥanan, so is the Mishnah: "He who makes a vow not to use flour is only forbidden these." How do we hold? If he uses "bread" in the biblical sense, then also if he says "produce" it is meant in the biblical sense. He should be forbidden everything since it is written (*Deut.* 22:9): "The produce of the vineyard." If he simply says "bread"; only from wheat or barley is it simply called "bread". Rebbi Yose said, I confirmed it, at a place where one eats bread from all [kinds], only from the five kinds it is simply called "bread".

32 From the text in *Ḥallah*. Here: פַּת סְתָם, which is the text in the next argument.

33 The quote is from Mishnah *Ḥallah* 1:2, the remainder from Halakhah *Ḥallah* 1:3, Notes 105, 110-112. Cf. Tosephta *Nedarim* 4:3.

(fol. 40b) **משנה ג:** הַנּוֹדֵר מִן הַכְּסוּת מוּתָּר בַּשָּׂק בַּיְרִיעָה וּבַחֲמִילָה. אָמַר קוֹנָם צֶמֶר עוֹלֶה עָלַי מוּתָּר לְכַסּוֹת בְּגִיזֵי צֶמֶר. פִּשְׁתָּן עוֹלֶה עָלַי מוּתָּר לְכַסּוֹת בָּאֲנִיצֵי פִשְׁתָּן. רִבִּי יְהוּדָה אוֹמֵר הַכֹּל לְפִי הַנּוֹדֵר. טָעַן וְהִזִּיעַ וְהָיָה רֵיחוֹ קָשֶׁה אָמַר קוֹנָם צֶמֶר וּפִשְׁתִּים עוֹלִים עָלַי מוּתָּר לְכַסּוֹת וְאָסוּר לְהַפְשִׁיל לַאֲחוֹרָיו.

Mishnah 3: One who made a vow to abstain from garments is permitted sack-cloth, carpets, and goat's hair cloth. If he said, a *qônām* that wool shall not come onto me, he is permitted to cover himself with shorn wool; that linen should not come upon me, he is permitted to cover himself with linen fibers[34]. Rebbi Jehudah says, everything refers to the vow. If he was carrying[35] and sweating and smelling badly, when he said, a *qônām* that no wool or flax should be on me, he is permitted to wear but forbidden to carry on his back.

34 It is assumed that "wool" and "linen" refer to garments made from these materials, not to the materials in themselves. R. Jehudah disagrees and describes a scenario where the opposite would be true.

35 A load of raw wool or linen.

(40c line 9) **הלכה ג:** הַנּוֹדֵר מִן הַכְּסוּת כול'. הַנּוֹדֵר מִן הַכְּסוּת מוּתָּר בַּשָּׂק בַּיְרִיעָה וּבַחֲמִילָה וּבְסִקוּרְטְיָה וּבְפָמַלְיָה. וְאָסוּר בְּפַסִיקְיָא וּבְפוּנְדָה. הַנּוֹדֵר מִן הַמַּלְבּוּשׁ אָסוּר בְּכָל־מִינֵי מַלְבּוּשׁ וּמוּתָּר בְּאֵילוּ. רִבִּי יִרְמְיָה אָמַר. רִבִּי זְעוּרָה בָּעֵי. אָמַר. קוֹנָם כְּסוּת שֶׁאֵינִי לוֹבֵשׁ לְבוּשׁ שֵׁינִי מִתְכַּסֶּה. רִבִּי שִׁמְעוֹן בֶּן

אֶלְעָזָר אוֹמֵר. אָמַר. קוֹנָם כָּל־דָּבָר שֶׁדַּרְכּוֹ לְהִתְכַּסּוֹת וְדֶרֶךְ הַיּוֹצֵא מִמֶּנּוּ לְהִתְכַּסּוֹת. כְּדַרְכּוֹ מוּתָּר בְּיוֹצֵא מִמֶּנּוּ. נָדַר בְּיוֹצֵא מִמֶּנּוּ מוּתָּר בּוֹ. מָה אִית לָךְ. כְּגוֹן אִילֵּין שְׁלָחַיָּה. כָּל־דָּבָר שֶׁדַּרְכּוֹ לְהִתְכַּסּוֹת וְאֵין דֶּרֶךְ הַיּוֹצֵא מִמֶּנּוּ לְהִתְכַּסּוֹת. נָדַר בּוֹ מוּתָּר בְּיוֹצֵא מִמֶּנּוּ. נָדַר בְּיוֹצֵא מִמֶּנּוּ אָסוּר בּוֹ. מָה אִית לָךְ. כְּגוֹן אִילֵּין סוּסְרָנָה. וְכָל־דָּבָר שֶׁאֵין דַּרְכּוֹ לְהִתְכַּסּוֹת וְדֶרֶךְ הַיּוֹצֵא מִמֶּנּוּ לְהִתְכַּסּוֹת. נָדַר בּוֹ לֹא נִתְכַּוֵּון אֶלָּא בְּיוֹצֵא מִמֶּנּוּ. מָה אִית לָךְ. אָמַר רִבִּי יוֹסֵי בֵּי רִבִּי בּוּן. כְּגוֹן הָדֵין צֶמֶר גֶּפֶן.

Halakhah 3: "One who made a vow to abstain from garments," etc. [36]One who made a vow to abstain from clothing is permitted sack-cloth, carpet, and goat's hair cloth, leather apron[37], and bandages[38]. He is forbidden fascia[39] and belt[40]. One who vows to abstain from clothing is forbidden all kinds of clothing but permitted these. Rebbi Jeremiah said, Rebbi Ze'ira asked: If one said, a *qônām* that I shall not wear a garment, that I shall not cover myself with clothing[41]? Rebbi Simeon ben Eleazar said, if he said, a *qônām* for anything that is generally used to cover oneself and a derivative of it is generally used to cover oneself; generally[42] he is permitted the derivative; if he made a vow to abstain from the derivative he is permitted the material itself. What is an example? For example, sheepskin[43]. For anything that is generally used to cover oneself but no derivative of it is generally used to cover oneself; if he vowed about it, he is permitted the derivative; if he made a vow to abstain from the derivative he is forbidden the material itself. What is an example? For example, goatskin[44]. And anything that is generally not used to cover oneself but a derivative of it is generally used to cover oneself; if he vowed about it, he intended only the derivative. What is an example? Rebbi Yose ben Rebbi Abun said, for example raw cotton[45].

36 A similar text in Tosephta 4:3; a longer list in the Babli, 55b.

37 Latin *scortea, sc. vestis*.

38 By consensus of the moderns, from Buxtorf to Lieberman, this is Latin *feminalia, -ium, n.*, which Lewis and Short translate by "bandages for upper thighs". {Compare also *femorale, -is, n.*, "covering for the thigh" (E. G.)} Maimonides (Commentary to *Kelim* 27:6) defines פמליא as a "muslin headscarf".

39 *fascia, -ae, f*. "band, bandage, breast band, diadem" (Lewis and Short).

40 Latin *funda*, cf. *Berakhot* 9:7, Note 258.

41 Is anything permitted to a person abstaining from garments and clothing? The question, more typical for R. Jeremiah than R. Ze'ira (cf. *Terumot* 10, Note 110, *Ma'serot* 3, Note 156), is not answered.

42 Usually amended to: If he vowed to abstain from the material. The emendation seems to be a corruption; the text requires an investigation of the vower's intention.

43 Sheepskin can be made into coats but wool is textile material in its own right.

44 Goat's hair is used for doormats but not usually for garments.

45 This is not usable unless freed from wood particles.

(40c line 21) כֵּינִי מַתְנִיתָא. טָעַן וְהֵזִיעַ וְאָמַר קוֹנָם צֶמֶר וּפִשְׁתִּים עוֹלִין עָלַי. אָסוּר לִלְבּוֹשׁ וּמוּתָּר לְהַפְשִׁילָן אֲחֲרָיו.

So is the Mishnah: If he was carrying and sweating; when he said, a *qônām* that no wool or flax should be on me, he is forbidden to wear them but permitted to carry them on his back[46].

46 This text seems to imply that in popular usage, עולה על was used only for garments, not for loads. In Tosephta (4:4) and Babli (55b), the text is: "If he was wearing wool, was uncomfortable, and said, a *qônām* that wool should be on me, he is forbidden to wear but permitted to carry it. If he was carrying wool and sweating; when he said, a *qônām* that no wool should be on me, he is permitted to wear it but forbidden to carry it on his back." In that version, the meaning of עולה על has to be determined by the context.

(fol. 40b) **משנה ד:** הַנּוֹדֵר מִן הַבַּיִת מוּתָּר בָּעֲלִיָּה דִּבְרֵי רִבִּי מֵאִיר. וַחֲכָמִים אוֹמְרִים עֲלִיָּה בִּכְלָל הַבַּיִת. הַנּוֹדֵר מִן הָעֲלִיָּה מוּתָּר בַּבַּיִת.

Mishnah 4: One who vows not to use the house is permitted the upper floor, the words of Rebbi Meïr; but the Sages say that the upper floor is part of the house. One who vows not to use the upper floor is permitted the house.

(40c line 22) **הלכה ד**: הַנּוֹדֵר מִן הַבַּיִת כול'. נְרָאִין דִּבְרֵי רִבִּי מֵאִיר בְּעַיִרוֹנִי.

Halakhah 4: "One who vows not to use the house," etc. The opinion of Rebbi Meïr is reasonable for a city dweller[47].

47 In rabbinic (and also modern) Hebrew, בַּיִת has two different meanings. It may mean "building" in a general sense; but applied to dwellings it usually means "appartment"; in talmudic Hebrew often "ground floor one-room appartment". In most cases in a city, two different families dwell in the "house", the ground floor, and in the upper floor. But a farmer uses the ground floor as a dwelling and the upper floor for storage; for him, "house" and upper floor form a unit. Therefore, practice has to follow R. Meïr in a city and the Sages in the countryside.

On the other hand, a mention of the upper floor certainly excludes the ground floor.

(fol. 40b) **משנה ה:** הַנּוֹדֵר מִן הַמִּיטָה מוּתָּר בַּדַּרְגֵּשׁ דִּבְרֵי רִבִּי מֵאִיר. וַחֲכָמִים אוֹמְרִים הַדַּרְגֵּשׁ בִּכְלָל הַמִּיטָה. הַנּוֹדֵר מִן הַדַּרְגֵּשׁ מוּתָּר בַּמִּיטָה.

Mishnah 5: One who vows not to use the bed[48] is permitted the couch, the words of Rebbi Meïr, but the Sages say, a couch is included in the notion of bed. One who vows not to use the couch is permitted the bed.

48 Again, "bed" can mean any appliance used to sleep on, or the particular implement called "bed" in the trade. R. Meïr assumes that the narrow meaning is understood since this is the most frequent use, but the Sages include all lexical meanings of the word.

(40c line 23) **הלכה ה**: הַנּוֹדֵר מִן הַמִּיטָה כול'. תַּנֵּי. דַּרְגֵּשׁ נִזְקֶפֶת וְאֵינָהּ נִיקֶפֶת.⁴⁹ רִבִּי שִׁמְעוֹן בֶּן אֶלְעָזָר אוֹמֵר. שׁוֹמֵט קלונטרין⁵⁰ שֶׁלָּהּ וְדַיְיוֹ. רִבִּי יוֹסָה בְּשֵׁם רִבִּי יְהוֹשֻׁעַ בֶּן לֵוִי. הֲלָכָה כְּרִבִּי שִׁמְעוֹן בֶּן אֶלְעָזָר. רִבִּי יַעֲקֹב בַּר אֲחָא בְּשֵׁם רִבִּי אִיסִי. מִיטָה שֶׁנִּקְלִיטֶיהָ עוֹלִין וְיוֹרְדִין בּוֹ שׁוֹמְטוֹ וְדָיוֹ.

"One who vows not to use the bed," etc. ⁵¹It was stated: "A *dargeš* is put upright and is not turned over. Rebbi Simeon ben Eleazar says, he removes its *qlwnṭryn* and that is enough." Rebbi Yosa in the name of Rebbi Joshua ben Levi: practice follows Rebbi Simeon ben Eleazar. Rebbi Jacob bar Aḥa in the name of Rebbi Yose, if a couch has posts which are upright and removed together with it, he takes them off and that is enough.

(40c line 27) אֵי זוֹ הִיא מִיטָה וְאֵי זֶהוּ דַרְגֵּשׁ. אָמַר רִבִּי יִרְמְיָה כָּל־שֶׁמְּסָרְגִין עַל גּוּפָהּ זוֹ הִיא הַמִּיטָה. וְשֶׁאֵין מְסָרְגִין עַל גּוּפָהּ זֶהוּ דַרְגֵּשׁ. וְהָא תַנִּינָן מִיטָה וַעֲרִיסָה מְשֶׁיְּשׁוּפָם⁵² בְּעוֹר הַדָּג. וּמְסוּרָג עַל גּוּפָהּ לְאֵי זֶה דָבָר הוּא שָׁפָהּ. אָמַר רִבִּי אֶלְעָזָר תִּיפְתָּר בְּאִילֵּין עַרְסִיָּיתָא קֵיסָרִיָּיתָא דְּאִית לָהֶן נִיקְבִין.

What is a couch and what is a *dargeš*? Rebbi Jeremiah said, one that one plaits on its body is a couch and one that one does not plait on its body is a *dargeš*. But have we not stated (*Kelim* 16:1) "Bed and crib after he rubs them with fish skin." If it is plaited on its body, why does he rub? Rebbi Eleazar said, explain it with those Caesarean cribs that have holes.

49 Both in *Berakhot* and in *Mo'ed Qaṭan*: נכסית. This has been taken as basis for the translation.

50 In *Berakhot* קלבינטרין, in *Mo'ed Qaṭan*: קלמנטרין.

51 This paragraph and the next are also in *Berakhot* 3:1 (5d l. 70) and *Mo'ed Qaṭan* 3:5, 83a l. 11; explained in *Berakhot* 3, Notes 22-35 (pp. 261-264). Both paragraphs are paralleled in the Babli, 56a/b.

52 In *Mo'ed Qaṭan*: מְשֶׁיְשִׁיפֶם.

(fol. 40b) **משנה ו**: הַנּוֹדֵר מִן הָעִיר מוּתָּר לִיכָּנֵס לִתְחוּמָהּ שֶׁלָעִיר וְאָסוּר לִיכָּנֵס לְעִיבּוּרָהּ. אֲבָל הַנּוֹדֵר מִן הַבַּיִת אָסוּר מִן הָאֲנָף וְלִפְנִים.

Mishnah 6: One who vows not to use a town is permitted to enter its domain[53] but forbidden to enter its suburbs[54]. But one who vows not to use a house is forbidden inwards from the doorpost[55].

53 The domain of a city is a rectangular area whose boundaries are 2000 cubits (one mile) from the last house in Northern, Southern, Eastern, and Western directions. A town dweller is permitted to walk in this domain on the Sabbath. Cf. *Soṭah* 5:4.

54 A house is defined as suburban if it is outside the city wall but connected to the wall by a row of houses where no two houses are more than 70 cubits apart. This also implies that the person making the vow may not approach a suburban house closer than 70 cubits.

55 While a house opening onto a common courtyard has the 4 cubits in front of its door as its proper domain which no other dweller of the courtyard may use to deposit his wares, the maker of the vow is not excluded from stepping on that domain.

(40c line 31) **הלכה ו**: הַנּוֹדֵר מִן הָעִיר כול׳. וּמְנַיִין שֶׁעִיבוּרָהּ שֶׁלָעִיר כָּעִיר. כְּתִיב וַיְהִי בִּהְיוֹת יְהוֹשֻׁעַ בִּירִיחוֹ. וְכִי בִּירִיחוֹ הָיָה. כְּתִיב וִירִיחוֹ סוֹגֶרֶת וּמְסוּגֶּרֶת וְאַתְּ אֲמַר אָכֵין. אָמַר רִבִּי יוּדָן בַּר שָׁלוֹם. בְּעִיבּוּרָהּ הָיָה. רִבִּי אָבוּן בְּשֵׁם רבי אָחָא. הֲוָה בִּירִיחוֹ.

Halakhah 6: "One who vows not to use a town," etc. From where that the suburbs of a town are like the town? It is written[56], "it happened when Joshua was in Jericho." How could he have been in Jericho? Is it not written that[57] "Jericho was closed and besieged," and you say so? Rebbi Judan bar Shalom said, he was in a suburb. Rebbi Abun in the name of Rebbi Aḥa: It happened in Jericho[58].

56 *Jos.* 5:13; this is written before the description of the conquest of Jericho. In the Babli, 56b, the argument is in the name of R. Joḥanan. Since for the Sages, the biblical meaning of a word has precedence over the meaning in the vernacular, one tries to have a biblical reference for the Sages' opinion.

57 *Jos.* 6:1: "Jericho was closed and besieged because of the Children of Israel; no one left and *no one entered*."

58 The argument does not prove anything; nobody can be sure that the editor of the book of Joshua follows a chronological order; cf. *Soṭa* 8, Note 127.

(40c line 27) רִבִּי מָנָא בָּעֵי. לֵית הָדָא פְּלִיגָא עַל דְּרִבִּי יוֹחָנָן. דְּרִבִּי יוֹחָנָן אָמַר. הִילְכוּ בִנְדָרִים אַחַר לְשׁוֹן בְּנֵי אָדָם. לֵית אוֹרְחֵיהּ דְּבַר נָשָׁא מֵיחְמֵיהּ חַבְרֵיהּ בְּפוּמָא בָּעֵי מֵימַר. בְּטִיבֶּרְיָה חַמְתֵיהּ.

Rebbi Mana asked, does this not disagree with Rebbi Joḥanan, since Rebbi Joḥanan said, in matters of vows they follow the vernacular[59]? Is it not the way of a person who sees another one outside the gate to say, I saw him in Tiberias[60]?

59 Even the Sages should not be interested in the biblical acceptation of a word if it is a matter of interpretation of a vow.

60 The common acceptation of the word is identical with the biblical.

משנה ז: (fol. 40b) קוֹנָם פֵּירוֹת הָאֵילוּ עָלַי קוֹנָם הֵן עַל פִּי אָסוּר בְּחִילוּפֵיהֶן וּבְגִידּוּלֵיהֶן. שֶׁאֲנִי אוֹכֵל שֶׁאֲנִי טוֹעֵם מוּתָּר בְּחִילוּפֵיהֶן וּבְגִידּוּלֵיהֶן בְּדָבָר שֶׁזַּרְעוֹ כָלֶה אֲבָל בְּדָבָר שֶׁאֵין זַרְעוֹ כָלֶה אֲפִילוּ גִידּוּלֵי גִידּוּלִין אֲסוּרִין.

Mishnah 7: 'These fruits shall be *qônām* for me, a *qônām* they shall be for my mouth', he is forbidden what is exchanged for them or what grows from them[61]. 'That I shall not eat, that I shall not taste,' he is permitted what is exchanged for them, or what grows from them if the seed disappears. But if the seed does not disappear[62], even second generation growth is forbidden.

61 Since he forbade himself any usufruct.

62 Defined in *Terumot* 9:6 as arum, garlic, and onion.

הלכה ז: (40c line 37) קוֹנָם פֵּירוֹת הָאֵילוּ עָלַי כוֹל׳. עַד אֵיכָן. יֵיבָא כַּיי דָמַר רִבִּי יַעֲקֹב בַּר אִידִי בְּשֵׁם רִבִּי יוֹחָנָן. עַד שָׁלֹשׁ גְּרָנוֹת אֲסוּרָה וְהָרְבִיעִית מוּתֶּרֶת. וָכָא כֵן.

Halakhah 7: 'These fruits shall be *qônām* for me,' etc. How far[63]? It comes, as Rebbi Jacob bar Idi said in the name of Rebbi Joḥanan: It is forbidden for three harvests, but the fourth is permitted. Here, it is the same.

63 How far is the growth of replanted garlic and onions forbidden if there is a vow not to eat from them. The reference is to *Terumot* 9:7, Notes 82-83, referring to growth from garlic and onions forbidden as *ṭevel*. The Babli, 57b, refers to a more lenient opinion discussed in *Terumot* 7:7, Note 121.

משנה ח: הָאוֹמֵר לְאִשְׁתּוֹ קוֹנָם מַעֲשֵׂה יָדַיִךְ עָלַי קוֹנָם הֵן לְפִי קוֹנָם (fol. 40b) הֵן עַל פִּי אָסוּר בְּחִילּוּפֵיהֶם וּבְגִידּוּלֵיהֶם. שֶׁאֲנִי אוֹכֵל שֶׁאֲנִי טוֹעֵם מוּתָּר בְּחִילּוּפֵיהֶן וּבְגִידּוּלֵיהֶן בְּדָבָר שֶׁזַּרְעוֹ כָלֶה אֲבָל בְּדָבָר שֶׁאֵין זַרְעוֹ כָלֶה אֲפִילוּ גִידּוּלֵי גִידּוּלֵיהֶן אֲסוּרִין.

Mishnah 8: If one says to his wife, a *qônām* shall be anything you work for, a *qônām* shall it be for my mouth, a *qônām* shall it be to my mouth; he is forbidden what is exchanged for it[64] or what grows from it[65]. 'That I shall not eat, that I shall not taste,' he is permitted what is exchanged for them, or what grows from them if the seed disappears. But if the seed does not disappear[62], even second generation growth is forbidden.

משנה ט: שֶׁאַתְּ עוֹשָׂה וַאֲנִי אוֹכֵל עַד הַפֶּסַח שֶׁאַתְּ עוֹשָׂה וַאֲנִי מִתְכַּסֶּה עַד הַפֶּסַח. עָשְׂתָה לִפְנֵי הַפֶּסַח מוּתָּר לָאֱכוֹל וּלְהִתְכַּסּוֹת אַחַר הַפֶּסַח.

Mishnah 9: 'What you prepare I would eat until Passover[66], what you make I would wear until Passover,' if she made before Passover, he may eat or wear after Passover.

משנה י: שֶׁאַתְּ עוֹשָׂה עַד הַפֶּסַח וַאֲנִי אוֹכֵל וְשֶׁאַתְּ עוֹשָׂה עַד הַפֶּסַח וַאֲנִי מִתְכַּסֶּה עָשְׂתָה לִפְנֵי הַפֶּסַח אָסוּר לָאֱכוֹל וּלְהִתְכַּסּוֹת אַחַר הַפֶּסַח.

Mishnah 10: 'What you prepare until Passover I would eat, what you make until Passover I would wear,' if she made before Passover, he is forbidden to eat or wear after Passover.

---

64 If the wife earned money, any usufruct of that money is forbidden to her husband.

65 If the wife planted a tree or grew agricultural produce, fruit and produce are forbidden to her husband.

66 In all the following statements it is understood that the husband said, "it shall be a *qônām* if . . .". The Babli and most independent Mishnah mss. read אֵינִי "I do not" for Yerushalmi אֲנִי "I would"; the meaning is the same.

(40c line 40) **הלכה ח:** הָאוֹמֵר לְאִשְׁתּוֹ כול'. כֵּינִי מַתְנִיתָא. מַה שֶׁאַתְּ עוֹשָׂה עַד הַפֶּסַח אֵינִי אוֹכֵל. מַה שֶׁאַתְּ עוֹשָׂה עַד הַפֶּסַח אֵינִי מִתְכַּסֶּה.

Halakhah 8: "If one says to his wife," etc. So is the Mishnah: "What you prepare until Passover I shall not eat, what you make until Passover I shall not wear".

(40c line 41) **הלכה ט,י:** מַה שֶׁאַתְּ עוֹשָׂה כול'. כֵּינִי מַתְנִיתָא. מַה שֶׁאַתְּ עוֹשָׂה עַד הַפֶּסַח אֲנִי מִתְכַּסֶּה.

Halakhah 9,10: "What you prepare," etc. So is the Mishnah: 'What you make until Passover I shall wear'[67].

67 It seems that the text intends to read Mishnah 10 before Mishnah 9 and to emphasize the positive statement in Mishnah 9. These and the following two Mishnaiot emphasize that word order does count.

(fol. 40b) **משנה יא:** שֶׁאַתְּ נֶהֱנֵית לִי עַד הַפֶּסַח אִם הוֹלֶכֶת אַתְּ לְבֵית אָבִיךְ עַד הֶחָג הָלְכָה לִפְנֵי הַפֶּסַח אֲסוּרָה בַּהֲנָיָיתוֹ עַד הַפֶּסַח. אַחַר הַפֶּסַח בְּלֹא יַחֵל דְּבָרוֹ.

Mishnah 11: 'That you provide me with usufruct until Passover if you would go to your father's house until Tabernacles[68].' If she went before Passover, she is forbidden to deliver usufruct to him until Passover, after Passover "he should not profane his word[69]."

משנה יב: שֶׁאַתְּ נֶהֱנֵית לִי עַד הֶחָג אִם הוֹלֶכֶת אַתְּ לְבֵית אָבִיךְ עַד הַפֶּסַח הָלְכָה לִפְנֵי הַפֶּסַח אֲסוּרָה בַּהֲנָיָיתוֹ עַד הֶחָג וּמוּתֶּרֶת לֵילֵךְ אַחַר הַפֶּסַח.

Mishnah 12: 'That you provide me with usufruct from you until Tabernacles if you would go to your father's house until Passover.' If she went before Passover, she is forbidden to deliver usufruct to him until Tabernacles; but she is permitted to go after Passover.

68 In the interpretation of the Babli, 15 a/b, the husband after Tabernacles makes a vow of *qônām* that his wife cannot have anything from him until Passover (in the spring) if she goes to her father's house before Tabernacles (next fall). It is obvious that if the wife goes before Passover, she is forbidden until Passover (and she should not have any usufruct from her husband now since maybe she will go afterwards). But if she goes during the six months between Passover and Tabernacles, any usufruct she had before Passover would be retroactively forbidden; therefore, he would transgress the commandment not to profane vows (by formulating his vow in a way which invites violating it) and she could be punished for violating his vow.

While this interpretation seems to fit the language of the Mishnah (and is accepted as obvious by Maimonides in his Commentary), the Yerushalmi in the Halakhah rejects the idea that the wife could be guilty because of the husband's vow and reads the Mishnah as given in the translation, that the husband forbids himself any usufruct from his wife. Therefore, he cannot have any usufruct now since she later might defy his instructions. There is no reason to think that the text of the Halakhah be corrupt.

69 *Num.* 30:3.

(40c line 43) **הלכה יא**: שֶׁאַתְּ נֶהֱנֵית לִי כול׳. וְאָסוּר לֵיהָנוֹת מִמֶּנָּה מִכְּבָר. שֶׁמָּא תֵלֵךְ אַחַר הַפֶּסַח וְנִמְצֵאת הֲנָיָיתוֹ לְמַפְרֵעַ.

Halakhah 11: "That you would have usufruct from me," etc. *He* is forbidden to have usufruct from *her* immediately, for maybe she would go after Passover and it would turn out that his having usufruct would be retroactively [forbidden].

(40c line 43) **הלכה יב**: שֶׁאַתְּ נֶהֱנֵית לִי עַד הֶחָג כול׳. וְאָסוּר לֵיהָנוֹת מִמֶּנָּה מִכְּבָר. שֶׁמָּא תֵלֵךְ אַחַר הַפֶּסַח וְנִמְצֵאת הֲנָיָיתוֹ לְמַפְרֵעַ.

Halakhah 11: "That you would have usufruct from me until Tabernacles," etc. *He* is forbidden to have usufruct from *her* immediately, for maybe she would go after Passover and it would turn out that his having usufruct would be retroactively [forbidden].

קונם יין פרק שמיני

(fol. 40c) **משנה א:** קוֹנָם יַיִן שֶׁאֵינִי טוֹעֵם הַיּוֹם אֵינוֹ אָסוּר אֶלָּא עַד שֶׁתֶּחְשַׁךְ. שַׁבָּת זוֹ אָסוּר בְּכָל־הַשַּׁבָּת וְשַׁבָּת שֶׁעָבְרָה. חֹדֶשׁ זֶה אָסוּר בְּכָל־הַחֹדֶשׁ וְרֹאשׁ חֹדֶשׁ שֶׁלְּבָא. שָׁנָה זוֹ אָסוּר בְּכָל־הַשָּׁנָה וְרֹאשׁ הַשָּׁנָה לֶעָתִיד לָבוֹא. שָׁבוּעַ זֶה אָסוּר בְּכָל־הַשָּׁבוּעַ וּשְׁבִיעִית שֶׁעָבְרָה.

משנה ב: וְאִם אָמַר יוֹם אֶחָד שַׁבָּת אַחַת חֹדֶשׁ אֶחָד שָׁנָה אַחַת אָסוּר מִיּוֹם לְיוֹם.

Mishnah 1: 'A *qônām* that I shall not taste wine today,' he is forbidden only until nightfall[1]. 'This week', he is forbidden the entire week; the Sabbath belongs to the past[2]. 'This month', he is forbidden the entire month; the day of the New Moon belongs to the future[3]. 'This year', he is forbidden the entire year; New Year's Day belongs to the future. 'This Sabbatical period', he is forbidden the entire Sabbatical period[4]; the Sabbatical year belongs to the past.

Mishnah 2: But if he said, one day, one week, one month, one year, he is forbidden from day to day[5].

1 The Tanna will not include the night with the day.

2 If he makes a vow not to drink wine this week, he is forbidden until after the coming Sabbath day since the Sabbath is the end of the week.

3 If he makes a vow not to drink wine this month he is permitted wine the first day of the New Moon.

4 The period of 7 years including the next Sabbatical year.

5 If he vows to abstain from wine for one day, he has to abstain for 24 hours from the moment of the vow. One week is counted as 7 times 24 hours from the moment of the vow, a

year is from day and hour of the vow to the same day, same hour, of the next year.

הלכה א: (40d, line 20) קוֹנָם יַיִן שֶׁאֵינִי טוֹעֵם הַיּוֹם כול׳. הָא מִשֶּׁחֲשֵׁיכָה מוּתָּר. לֵית הָדָא פְלִיגָא עַל רִבִּי יוֹחָנָן. דְּרִבִּי יוֹחָנָן אָמַר. הִילְכוּ בִנְדָרִים אַחַר לְשׁוֹן בְּנֵי אָדָם. לֵית אוֹרְחֵיהּ דְּבַר נָשָׁא מֵימַר לְחַבְרֵיהּ בְּרוּמְשָׁא. לֹא טְעָמִית כְּלוּם רוּמְשִׁית. וְאָמַר. אֶתְמוֹל. אֱמוֹר דְּבַתְרָא וְהוּא פְלִיגָא. לֵית אוֹרְחֵיהּ דְּבַר נָשָׁא מֵימַר לְחַבְרֵיהּ בְּצַפְרָא. לֹא טְעָמִית כְּלוּם רוּמְשִׁית. מֵימוֹר. יוֹם דֵּין הוּא. לֵית הוּא פְלִיגָא. יוֹם זֶה מִשַּׁבָּת זוֹ וְשַׁבָּת זוֹ מִיּוֹם זֶה. יוֹם זֶה מֵהַיּוֹם. כְּמַאן דָּמַר. הִילְכוּ בִנְדָרִים אַחַר לְשׁוֹן בְּנֵי אָדָם. בְּרַם הָכָא כְּמַאן דָּמַר. הִילְכוּ בִנְדָרִים אַחַר לְשׁוֹן תּוֹרָה. אָמַר רִבִּי יוֹנָה בּוּצְרָייָא. כֵּן אוֹרְחֵיהּ דְּבַר נָשָׁא מֵימַר לְחַבְרֵיהּ. סוֹבַר לִי הָדֵין יוֹמָא.

Halakhah 1: "'A *qônām* that I shall not taste wine today,'" etc. This implies that he is permitted at nightfall[6]. Does this not disagree with Rebbi Joḥanan, since Rebbi Joḥanan said, in matters of vows one follows common usage? It is not usual that a man should say to another in the evening, I did not eat until evening. Would he say, yesterday[7]? Refer to the following and it does disagree: It is not usual that a man should say to another in the morning, I did not eat in the evening. Would he say, the same day[8]? Does the following not disagree? This day from this week, or this week from this day[9]? What is the difference between "this day" and "today"? That is, following the opinion that in matters of vows one follows common usage. But here, one follows the opinion that in matters of vows one follows biblical usage[10]. Rebbi Jonah from Bostra said, it is the way of people to say to another, bear with me this day[11].

6   This seems to be obvious from the Mishnah. But in the Babli, 60a, Rav Jeremiah bar Abba requires that a rabbi give permission to drink wine after nightfall. The statement here has to be read as rejection of that opinion.

7 In the evening, he does not refer to the daylight hours as 'yesterday". Therefore, he should be forbidden wine until he goes to sleep.

8 This is the same argument in the reverse. A person before sunrise will refer to the evening hours of the same night as "yesterday". Therefore, the evening hours of the preceding day belong to that day in popular conscience.

9 Since everybody agrees that a week consists of 7 times 24 hours, and it consists of 7 days, it should be obvious that a day in vows should be 24 hours and the distinction made between Mishnaiot 1 and 2 seems to have no basis.

10 Which in the story of Creation defines a day by a night followed by daylight.

11 He asks him to work with him during daytime only. There is an acceptation of "day" in the vernacular which refers to daytime only.

For this meaning of the root סבר cf. *Baba Batra* 2:1 (13b line 31).

(40d, line 29) תַּמָּן תַּנִּינָן. עַד רֹאשׁ אֲדָר עַד רֹאשׁ אֲדָר הָרִאשׁוֹן. עַד סוֹף אֲדָר עַד סוֹף אֲדָר הָרִאשׁוֹן. הָדָא אָמְרָה. נִיסָן רֹאשׁ הַשָּׁנָה לִנְדָרִים. תִּשְׁרֵי רֹאשׁ הַשָּׁנָה לִנְדָרִים. שֶׁלֹּא תֹאמַר. יַעֲלֶה רֹאשׁ חֹדֶשׁ אֲדָר תַּחַת אֱלוּל וִיהֵא מוּתָּר בֶּאֱלוּל. לְפוּם כֵּן צָרַךְ מֵימַר. אָסוּר בָּהּ וּבְעִיבּוּרָהּ.

There[12], we have stated: "Until the beginning of Adar, until the beginning of the First Adar. Until the end of Adar, until the end of the First Adar[13]." Does this imply that Nisan is the beginning of the year as far as vows are concerned[14]? Tishre is the beginning of the year as far as vows are concerned. That you should not say, the beginning of Adar should compensate for Ellul and he would be permitted in Ellul[15]; therefore, it was necessary to say that "he is forbidden it and its intercalary [month]".

12 Mishnah 7: "'A *qônām* that I shall not taste wine this year,' he is forbidden the year and [an eventual] intercalary month. 'Until the beginning of Adar,' until the beginning of the First Adar. 'Until the end of Adar,' until the end of the First Adar." The main argument is about the first part of

the Mishnah.

13 Even in an intercalary year, when the Second Adar is added as the 13th month, "Adar" without a qualifier means only the month of First Adar which is part of every year. [Halakhah 7 and the Babli (63a/b), supported by the Tosephta (4:7), qualify this statement to apply only if the person making the vow did not know that the year would have a second Adar. If he knew, the vow would extend to Second Adar.]

14 Cf. Mishnah *Roš Haššanah* 1:1. Nisan is biblically counted as the first month and Tishre as the seventh, but in Second Temple practice the year always started in the fall with the first day of Tishre. One does not discuss here the problem of the several calendars of the monarchical period.

Since the Mishnah states that "he is forbidden during the year and its intercalary month", it seems that the year must be counted from Nisan since, if it were counted from Tishre, the intercalary month would be in the middle of the year and it should be obvious that the person imposes a continuous prohibition on himself.

15 If a person said, I shall not drink wine for a year, it would imply a prohibition for 12 months. But since he said, *this* year, the prohibition lasts either 12 or 13 months, as the case may be. The statement of the intercalary month is made to underline the difference between "a year" of twelve months and "this year" of possibly 13 months. If somebody says on New Year's Day of an intercalary year that he will not drink wine for *a* year, he will in effect be permitted to drink wine on the first of the coming Ellul. But for *this* year, he has to observe the additional intercalary month without compensation.

(40d, line 34) אִם אָמַר יוֹם אֶחָד שַׁבָּת אַחַת חֹדֶשׁ אֶחָד שָׁנָה אַחַת אָסוּר מִיוֹם לְיוֹם. מֵעֵת לְעֵת. תַּנֵּי מֵעֵת לְעֵת.

"If he said, one day, one week, one month, one year, he is forbidden from day to day." From hour to hour[16]. It was stated, from hour to hour.

16 To the same time on the next day (or day of the next week, next month, next year). It then is stated that a *baraita* parallels the Mishnah, explicitly mentioning "from hour to hour."

(40d, line 35) רִבִּי אָחָא רִבִּי אַבָּהוּ בְּשֵׁם רִבִּי יוֹסֵי בֶּן חֲנִינָה. אָסוּר לְאָדָם לְהִתְעַנּוֹת עַד שֵׁשׁ שָׁעוֹת בַּשַּׁבָּת. אָמַר רִבִּי יוֹסֵי. מַתְנִיתָא אָמְרָה כֵן. הָיוּ מִתְעַנִּין וְיָרְדוּ לָהֶן גְּשָׁמִים. קוֹדֶם חֲצוֹת לֹא יַשְׁלִימוּ. עַד כְּדוֹן צַפְרָא הוּא. אַחַר חֲצוֹת יַשְׁלִימוּ. שֶׁכְּבָר עָבַר רוּבּוֹ שֶׁלַּיּוֹם בִּקְדוּשָׁה.

[17]Rebbi Aḥa, Rebbi Abbahu, in the name of Rebbi Yose ben Ḥanina: On the Sabbath, a person is forbidden to fast until the sixth hour[18]. Rebbi Yose said, a Mishnah states this[19]: "If they fasted when it started to rain, before noon they should not finish," because until then it is morning; "after noon they should finish," since most of the day already was spent in holiness.

17 This text is from *Ta'aniot* 3:13.

18 Since it says (*Is.* 58:13): "You shall call the Sabbath a delight", one is forbidden to fast on the Sabbath (except if the Sabbath is preempted by the Day of Atonement). As R. Yose states, the Mishnah in *Ta'aniot* (3:13) states that a person who fasted for more than half the day is required to fast the entire day. The day between sunrise and sunset is divided into 12 equal hours with noon being the end of the sixth hour (disregarding the equation of time). At the equinox, these hours are the constant hours, 1/24th of a day. Since a person fasting until noon then would have to fast the entire day, he may not fast until noon on the Sabbath.

19 *Ta'aniot* 3:13, speaking of a fastday proclaimed in a year of draught, position of R. Eliezer. (The anonymous majority requires a full day of a fast for rain if the rain started to fall during daytime.)

(40d, line 39) מִילְתֵיהּ דְּרִבִּי יוֹחָנָן אָמְרָה. מִתְעַנִּין שָׁעוֹת. דְּרִבִּי יוֹחָנָן אָמַר. הַרְאֵינִי בְּתַעֲנִיתִי עַד דְּחָסַל פִּירְקִי. עַד דְּנֵיחְסַל פָּרָשָׁתִי. מִילְתֵיהּ דְּרִבִּי יוֹנָה אָמְרָה. מִתְעַנִּין שָׁעוֹת. רִבִּי יוֹנָה הֲוָה בְּצוֹר וְשָׁמַע דִּדְמָךְ בְּרֵיהּ דְּרִבִּי יוֹסֵי. אַף עַל גַּב דְּאָכַל גּוּבְנָה וְשָׁתָה מַיָא אַסְקֵיהּ צוֹם כָּל־הַהוּא יוֹמָא. מִילְתֵיהּ דְּרַב אָמְרָה. מִתְעַנִּין שָׁעוֹת. דְּרַב אָמַר. לֹוֶוה אָדָם תַּעֲנִיתוֹ וּפוֹרֵעַ. אָמַר לֵיהּ שְׁמוּאֵל. וְכִי נֶדֶר הוּא זֶה. נָדַר לְהִתְעַנּוֹת וְשָׁכַח וְאָכַל כְּזַיִת אִיבֵּד תַּעֲנִיתוֹ. רִבִּי

בָּא בְשֵׁם רַבָּנִין דְּתַמָּן. וְהוּא שֶׁאָמַר יוֹם סְתָם. הָא אִם אָמַר יוֹם זֶה מִתְעַנֶּה וּמַשְׁלִים. לֹא אָמַר אֶלָּא אָכַל. הָא טָעַם לֹא. רִבִּי בָּא חֲסִידָא בְשֵׁם רִבִּי זְעִירָא. הָדָא מַטְעַמִיתָה אֵין בָּהּ לֹא מִשּׁוּם בְּרָכָה וְלֹא מִשּׁוּם גֶּזֶל וְלֹא מִשּׁוּם דְּמַאי וְלֹא מִשּׁוּם הֶפְסֵק תַּעֲנִית.

The words of Rebbi Johanan imply that one may fast for hours[20], for Rebbi Johanan said, I shall fast until I finish studying this chapter, until I finish studying this text. The words of Rebbi Jonah imply that one may fast for hours, for Rebbi Jonah was in Tyre when he heard that Rebbi Yose's son had died. Even though he had eaten cheese and drunk water, he finished that day fasting. The words of Rav imply that one may fast for hours, for Rav said, one may borrow his fast day and pay back[21]. Samuel said to him, is that a vow[22]? If he had vowed to fast but forgot and ate the volume of an olive, he lost his fast day. Rebbi Abba in the name of the rabbis there[23]: That is, if he said simply "a day". But if he said "this day", he has to continue fasting until the end. He spoke only of eating; that excludes tasting[24]. Rebbi Abba Hasida in the name of Rebbi Ze'ira: Tasting does not create obligations of benediction[25], robbery[26], nor of *demay*[27], nor of the interruption of a fast day.

20 In both Talmudim, not eating is counted as a private fast only if the person fasting undertook the fast by a vow or its equivalent. From the example of R. Johanan it follows that the Yerushalmi accepts as valid a vow to fast a certain time, even if the person did eat before and will eat after the fast during daylight. It is possible that R. Jonah held that a fast can be vowed in the middle of the day, on condition that one abstain from food for the remainder of the day. The Babli (*Ta'anit* 11b/12a) seems to accept only fasts that cover the entire daylight hours of a day. The only "fast by hours" accepted in the Babli is one where a person did not eat breakfast and in the middle of the day decides to vow to spend the remainder of the day fasting (cf. Maimonides *Ta'aniot* 1:13 and its commentaries.)

HALAKHAH 1   635

21 In the Babli, *Ta'anit* 12b, this refers only to fasting full days, that one may transfer the obligation of a private fast to another date.

22 It depends on the terms of the vow. If "a day" of fast was vowed, Samuel will agree with Rav. If "this day" was vowed and the person can no longer stand his hunger, Samuel will send him to a rabbi to dissolve the vow. In the Babli, *Ta'anit* 12b, Samuel agrees with Rav in the case the person fasting can no longer stand his hunger. [The Babli, (*Ta'anit* 12b, *Šabbat* 11a), disallows the statement of Rav in case of a fast to avert the consequences of a bad dream.]

23 In Babylonia.

24 Consuming less than the volume of an average olive is not called "eating".

25 There is no obligation of a benediction for tasting a small amount; cf. *Berakhot* 6:1, Note 5. A shortened version of the statement is a *baraita* in the Babli, *Berakhot* 14a.

26 Taking such a small amount from somebody else is not robbery. (Cf. *Demay* 3:2, Note 56).

27 Even the most scrupulous may taste food from a person suspected of not tithing.

(40d, line 49) יָחִיד שֶׁגָּזַר עָלָיו תַּעֲנִית אוֹכֵל וְשׁוֹתֶה מִשֶּׁחֲשֵׁיכָה. וְאִם אָמַר. בְּתַעֲנִית צִיבּוּר. אוֹכֵל וְשׁוֹתֶה מִבְּעוֹד יוֹם. נָדַר לְהִתְעַנּוֹת וְנִמְצְאוּ יָמִים טוֹבִים וְשַׁבָּתוֹת. לוֹקֶה וְאֵינוֹ צָרִיךְ הֶיתֵּר חָכָם. נָדַר לְהִתְעַנּוֹת וְנִמְצְאוּ יָמִים הַכְּתוּבִין בִּמְגִילַת תַּעֲנִית. רִבִּי חִזְקִיָּה רִבִּי יוּדָן רִבִּי יִרְמְיָה בְּשֵׁם רִבִּי חִיָּיה בַּר בָּא. חַד אָמַר. מִתְעַנֶּה וְאֵינוֹ מַשְׁלִים. וְחָרְנָה אָמַר. לוֹקֶה וְאֵינוֹ צָרִיךְ הֶיתֵּר חָכָם. הָדָא דְאַתְּ אָמַר עַד שֶׁלֹּא בָּטְלָה מְגִילַת תַּעֲנִית. אֲבָל מִשֶּׁבָּטְלָה מְגִילַת תַּעֲנִית בָּטְלוּ כָּל־אִילּוּ. רִבִּי חֲנַנְיָה וְרִבִּי יוֹחָנָן תְּרֵיהוֹן אָמְרֵי. בָּטְלָה מְגִילַת תַּעֲנִית. רִבִּי יְהוֹשֻׁעַ בֶּן לֵוִי אָמַר. בָּטְלָה מְגִילַת תַּעֲנִית. אָמַר רִבִּי יוֹחָנָן. אֶמֶשׁ הָיִיתִי יוֹשֵׁב וְשׁוֹנֶה מַעֲשֶׂה שֶׁגָּזְרוּ תַּעֲנִית בַּחֲנוּכָה בְּלוֹד. וְאָעַל רִבִּי אֱלִיעֶזֶר וְסִיפֵּר וְרִבִּי יְהוֹשֻׁעַ וְרָחַץ. אָמַר לָהֶן רִבִּי יְהוֹשֻׁעַ. צְאוּ וְהִתְעַנּוּ עַל מַה שֶּׁהִתְעַנִּיתֶם. וְאַתְּ אָמַר. בָּטְלָה מְגִילַת תַּעֲנִית. אָמַר רִבִּי אַבָּא. אַף עַל גַּב דְּתֵימַר בָּטְלָה מְגִילַת תַּעֲנִית. חֲנוּכָּה וּפוּרִים לֹא בָּטְלוּ. מִילֵּיהוֹן דְּרַבָּנִין אָמְרִין. בָּטְלָה מְגִילַת תַּעֲנִית. רִבִּי יוֹנָתָן צַיֵּים צְיֵּים כָּל־עֲרוּבַת רֹאשׁ הַשָּׁנָה. רִבִּי אָבִין צַיֵּים צִיִּים כָּל־עֲרוּבַת סוּכּוֹת. רִבִּי זְעוּרָא צַיֵּים תְּלַת מְאָוָון דְּצוֹמִין. וְאִית דְּאָמְרֵי. תִּשְׁעַת מְאָוָון

דְּצוֹמִין. וְלֹא חָשׁ עַל מְגִילַת תַּעֲנִית. רִבִּי יַעֲקֹב בַּר אָחָא מְפַקֵּד לְסָפְרַיָּיא. אִין אָתַת אִיתָּא מִישְׁאֲלִינְכוֹן. אֵימְרוּן לָהּ. בְּכָל מִתְעַנִּין חוּץ מִשַּׁבָּתוֹת וְיָמִים טוֹבִים וְרָאשֵׁי חֳדָשִׁים וְחוּלוֹ שֶׁלַּמּוֹעֵד וַחֲנוּכָּה וּפוּרִים.

A private person who committed himself for a fast day[28], eats and drinks after nightfall. But if he said a public fast day[29], he eats and drinks only during daytime. If he made a vow to fast[30] and it turned out to fall on Sabbath days or holidays, he is whipped but does not need permission from a Sage[31]. If he made a vow to fast and it turned out to fall on days written in the Scroll of Fasts[32], Rebbi Ḥizqia and Rebbi Yudan in the name of Rebbi Ḥiyya bar Abba: One said, he fasts but does not finish, but the other one said, he is whipped but does not need permission from a Sage. That is, you say that before the scroll of fasts was abolished. But when the Scroll of Fasts was abolished, all this was abolished. Rebbi Ḥanania[33] and Rebbi Joḥanan both say that the Scroll of Fasts was abolished[34]. Rebbi Joshua ben Levi said, the Scroll of Fasts was abolished. Rebbi Joḥanan said, yesterday I was sitting and stating: "It happened that they decreed a fast day at Lod during Ḥanukka. Rebbi Eliezer went and had a haircut, Rebbi Joshua went and took a hot bath. Rebbi Joshua said to them, go and fast for what you fasted." And you say, the Scroll of Fasts was abolished? Rebbi Abba said, even though you say that the Scroll of Fasts was abolished, Ḥanukka and Purim were not abolished[35]. The acts of the rabbis imply that the Scroll of Fasts was abolished: Rebbi Jonathan fasted on the day before New Year's Day. Rebbi Abin fasted on the day before Tabernacles. Rebbi Ze'ira fasted 300 fast days, and some say 900 fast days and did not care about the Scroll of Fasts. Rebbi Jacob bar Aḥa told the scribes: If a woman comes to ask you, tell her that one may fast any day except Sabbaths, holidays, New Moons, the intermediary days of holidays, Ḥanukka, and Purim.

28   By making the vow on the day before (commonly after the afternoon prayer). A common fast is only during daytime.

29   Following the rules of the Day of Atonement which runs from evening to evening (*Lev.* 23:32).

30   And indicated the dates of the days he wanted to fast.

31   Since festive meals are required on the Sabbath or any holiday of pilgrimage by biblical law, it is sinful to make a vow to break a biblical law (which subjects to vower to punishment) even though the vow is invalid (and does not need invalidation by a rabbi).

32   The collection of *beraitot* describing the days on which in pharisaic practice fasts are forbidden. These include the days before and after holidays, Ḥanukka (a popular holiday having no biblical source since the books of Maccabees are disavowed in Jewish tradition), Purim (a biblical holiday based on the book of Esther which has no status of holiness), and a great number of days recording the ascent of the pharisaic sect to dominance in Jewish public life, in particular Temple practice. These later dates would have lost their significance with the destruction of the Temple. The last event mentioned in the Scroll of Fasts is the revocation of Hadrian's decrees by Antoninus Pius. This shows that the Scroll of Fasts is tannaïtic; its abolition was an amoraitic problem.

33   Probably a scribal error for "R. Ḥanina".

34   In the Babli, *Roš Haššanah* 18b, R. Ḥanina holds that the Scroll of Fasts was abolished, R. Joḥanan that it was not abolished (since usually Rabbis Ḥanina and Joḥanan are opposed to one another).

35   The Babli agrees, *Roš Haššanah* 19b.

(fol. 40c) **משנה ג:** עַד הַפֶּסַח אָסוּר עַד שֶׁיַּגִּיעַ עַד שֶׁיְּהֵא אָסוּר עַד שֶׁיֵּצֵא. עַד לִפְנֵי הַפֶּסַח רִבִּי מֵאִיר אוֹמֵר עַד שֶׁיַּגִּיעַ. רִבִּי יוֹסֵי אוֹמֵר עַד שֶׁיֵּצֵא.

Mishnah 3: 'Until Passover'[36], he is forbidden until it comes, 'until it be', he is forbidden until it is passed[37]. 'Until before Passover', Rebbi Meïr says, until it comes, Rebbi Yose says, until it passed[38].

36 "A *qônām* that I shall not . . . until Passover".

37 This follows the vernacular since in popular language "Passover" means "the holiday of unleaved bread" (Nisan 15-21), whereas in biblical language "Passover" is the day of slaughter of the Passover sacrifice (Nisan 14).

38 The Halakhah explains that this refers to biblical language; the difference between the two opinions is whether the prohibition ends at nightfall of Nisan 13 or 14.

(40d, line 68) **הלכה ג:** עַד הַפֶּסַח אָסוּר כול'. רִבִּי יִרְמְיָה בָּעֵי קוֹמֵי רִבִּי זְעִירָה. מִחְלְפָה שִׁיטָתֵיהּ דְּרִבִּי יוֹסֵי. תַּמָּן הוּא אוֹמֵר. עַד שֶׁיֵּצְאוּ כָל־הָקְרֵשְׁווֹת הַגְּדוֹלוֹת. עַד שֶׁיֵּצְאוּ כָל־הָקְרֵשְׁווֹת הַקְּטַנּוֹת. וָכָא הוּא אָמַר הָכֵין. אָמַר לֵיהּ. מִשֶּׁמֵּת בֶּן עַזַּאי וּבֶן זוֹמָא בָּטְלוּ הַשַּׁקְדָּנִים. לֹא עָמַד שׁוֹקֵד עַד שֶׁעָמַד יִרְמְיָה. אָמַר רִבִּי בָּא בְּרֵיהּ דְּרִבִּי חִייָה בַּר וָא. לָמָּה הוּא מְקַנְתֵּר לְהוֹן. לֹא כְּבָר קַשׁוּנְתָהּ רִבִּי אֶלְעָזָר קוֹמֵי רִבִּי יוֹחָנָן. מִחְלְפָה שִׁיטָתֵיהּ דְּרִבִּי יוֹסֵי. אָמַר לֵיהּ. לֵית הִיא מִחְלְפָה. מַתְנִיתָא הִיא מִחְלְפָה. וְתַנֵּי דְבֵית רִבִּי כֵן. עַד לִפְנֵי הַפֶּסַח. רִבִּי מֵאִיר אוֹמֵר. עַד שֶׁיֵּצֵא. רִבִּי יוֹסֵי אוֹמֵר. עַד שֶׁיַּגִּיעַ. אֲנָן בָּעֵי עַד לִפְנֵי וְאַתְּ אֲמַר אָכֵין. אָמַר רִבִּי זְעִירָא. לְשׁוֹן נִינְתִי הוּא. עַד לִפְנֵי פִיסְחָא. אָמַר רִבִּי אָבִין. הַכֹּל מוֹדִין בַּפֶּסַח שֶׁהוּא מוּתָּר. בִּפְרוֹס הַפֶּסַח. הָהֵין אָמַר. עַד שֶׁיַּגִּיעַ. וְהָהֵין אָמַר. עַד שֶׁיֵּצֵא.

Halakhah 3: " 'Until Passover', he is forbidden," etc. [39]Rebbi Jeremiah asked before Rebbi Ze'ira: The opinion of Rebbi Yose seems to be inverted. There[40], he says "until all the elder possibilities are exhausted, until all the younger possibilities are exhausted," and here, he says so? He said to him: Since Ben Azai and Ben Zoma died, the perseverers[41] disappeared; no perseverer was there until Jeremiah appeared. Rebbi Abba, son of Rebbi Ḥiyya bar Abba, said, why does he needle him[42]? Did not Rebbi Eleazar already ask before Rebbi Joḥanan, the opinion of Rebbi Yose seems to be inverted? He said to him, it is not inverted, the Mishnah is inverted, for in the House of Rebbi they stated[43]: "'Until before

Passover', Rebbi Meïr says, until it passed, Rebbi Yose says, until it comes." We ask "until before", and you say so[44]? He said to him, this is a Nabatean expression, "much[45] before Passover". Rebbi Abin said, everybody agrees that he is permitted on Passover[46]. Where do they disagree? The day before Passover. One of them says, until it comes, the other until it passed.

39 A slightly longer parallel to this paragraph is in *Qiddušin* 3:11. It is difficult to decide which version is original.

40 *Qiddušin* Mishnah 3:9-10. A father, who has the right to marry off his underage daughter without asking her consent, has two sets of daughters from two wives. He marries off an older daughter (whom the bridegroom has not yet seen) but does not remember which one. Rebbi Meïr says, all his daughters are forbidden to marry except the youngest of the younger group, since any other daughter either is married and forbidden to every man except the one with whom the father contracted, or she is the sister of the married one and forbidden to the man with whom the father contracted. Rebbi Yose holds that all are permitted to other men except the oldest of the older group, who is married to the chosen groom.

Similarly, if he married off the younger one, R. Meïr forbids all but the oldest of the older group while R. Joshua declares the youngest of the younger group to be married. It follows that R. Meïr interprets common language to mean the largest possible set whereas R. Yose holds that people always speak as definitely as possible. Therefore, in the Mishnah here, R. Yose should exclude the day of Passover and R. Meïr should include it.

41 Cf. *Soṭa* 9, Note 271.

42 Cf. *Berakhot* 2:3, Note 96.

43 The same in the Babli, 61b, in the name of Rav.

44 Who could ever think that "until before" could mean "until after"?

44 Cf. Arabic عَدّ "equal, similar, large quantity"; عِدّة "number, quantity". עד does not mean "until" here but is simply added for emphasis.

45 I. e., the festival of unleavened bread; cf. Note 39.

(fol. 40c) **משנה ד:** עַד הַקָּצִיר עַד הַבָּצִיר עַד הַמָּסִיק אֵינוֹ אָסוּר אֶלָּא עַד שֶׁיַּגִּיעַ. זֶה הַכְּלָל כָּל־שֶׁזְּמַנּוֹ קָבוּעַ אָמַר עַד שֶׁיַּגִּיעַ אָסוּר עַד שֶׁיַּגִּיעַ. אָמַר עַד שֶׁיְּהֵא אָסוּר עַד שֶׁיֵּצֵא. וְכָל־שֶׁאֵין זְמַנּוֹ קָבוּעַ בֵּין אָמַר עַד שֶׁיְּהֵא בֵּין אָמַר עַד שֶׁיַּגִּיעַ אֵינוֹ אָסוּר אֶלָּא עַד שֶׁיַּגִּיעַ.

Mishnah 4: 'Until the grain harvest, the grape harvest, the olive harvest', he is forbidden only until their time arrives. That is the principle: Everything that has a fixed time[46], if he said 'until it arrives', he is forbidden until it arrives; if he said 'until it shall be', he is forbidden until it passed. But everthing that does not have a fixed time[47], whether he said 'until it arrives' or 'until it shall be', he is forbidden only until it arrives.

46 Holidays which are fixed in the calendar.

47 Harvests which depend on the weather.

(41a, line 6) **הלכה ד:** עַד הַבָּצִיר כול׳. קָבַע זְמָן לְמִשְׁתֵּה בְנוֹ וְאָמַר. קוֹנָם יַיִן שֶׁאֵינִי טוֹעֵם עַד שֶׁיַּגִּיעַ מִשְׁתֵּה. עַד כְּמִי שֶׁזְּמַנּוֹ קָבוּעַ. אוֹ מֵאַחַר שֶׁיָּכוֹל לִדְחוֹתוֹ לְאַחַר זְמָן כְּמִי שֶׁאֵין זְמַנּוֹ קָבוּעַ.

Halakhah 4: If one fixed the time for his son's wedding and said, a *qônām* that I shall not taste wine until the wedding[48], is that as if the time was fixed? Or, since he could move the time to a later date, is it as if the time was not fixed[49]?

48 The problem really would be if he said "until the wedding takes place".

49 The question is not answered. In the opinion of R. Nissim Gerondi (Babli 61b), this means an automatic restriction; if he said "until the wedding takes place", he is forbidden to drink wine at the wedding.

(fol. 40c) **משנה ה:** עַד הַקַּיִץ עַד שֶׁיְּהֵה הַקַּיִץ עַד שֶׁיַּתְחִילוּ הָעָם לְהַכְנִיס בַּכַּלְכָּלוֹת. עַד שֶׁיַּעֲבוֹר הַקַּיִץ עַד שֶׁיַּכְפִּילוּ הַמַּקְצוּעוֹת. עַד הַקָּצִיר עַד שֶׁיַּתְחִילוּ הָעָם לִקְצוֹר קְצִיר חִטִּים אֲבָל לֹא קְצִיר שֶׁל שְׂעוֹרִים הַכֹּל לְפִי מְקוֹם נִדְרוֹ. אִם הָיָה בָהָר בָּהָר וְאִם הָיָה בַבִּקְעָה בַּבִּקְעָה.

Mishnah 5: 'Until the fig harvest[50], until there be fig harvest', until people start to bring in baskets. 'Until the fig harvest is over', until people fold their knives. 'Until the grain harvest', until people start to cut wheat but not barley[51]; everything follows the place of the vow, if made on the hills, on the hills, if made in the plain, in the plain.

50   This is the conclusion of the Halakhah. Biblically, קַיִץ, from קצה "to cut", is the harvest of any fruit ripening in the summer which is cut from the tree by a knife (and also means "summer").

51   Which is harvested in early spring.

(41a, line 9) **הלכה ה:** עַד הַקַּיִץ עַד שֶׁיְּהֵה הַקַּיִץ כול׳. כַּלְכָּלוֹת. מָה. כַּלְכָּלוֹת שֶׁלַּתְּאֵינִים. כַּלְכָּלוֹת שֶׁלָּעֲנָבִים. נִישְׁמְעִינָהּ מִן הָדָא. עַד שֶׁיְּקַפְּלוּ[52] הַמַּקְצוּעוֹת. אִית לָךְ מֵימַר. מַקְצוּעוֹת תְּאֵינִים וְלֹא מַקְצוּעוֹת עֲנָבִים. נִישְׁמְעִינָהּ מִן הָדָא. חַד טְעִין צִימּוּקִין אָעַל לִטְבֶרְיָא. שָׁאַל גַּמְלִיאֵל זוּגָא לְרִבִּי בָּא בַּר זַבְדָּא. אֲמַר לֵיהּ. אֵין כָּל־אֶרֶץ יִשְׂרָאֵל עוֹשָׂה מַשּׂוֹי אֶחָד שֶׁל צִימוּקִין. אֶלָּא כֵן אָמַר לֵיהּ. אֵין מָקוֹם בְּאֶרֶץ יִשְׂרָאֵל עוֹשָׂה מַשּׂוֹי אֶחָד שֶׁל צִימוּקִין.

Halakhah 5: 'Until the fig harvest, until there be fig harvest', etc. "baskets". Baskets of figs or baskets of raisins[53]? Let us hear from this: "Until they fold the knives". You have to say, knives for figs, not knives for raisins[54]. Let us hear from the following: [55]A load of raisins came up to Tiberias. Gamliel the twin asked Rebbi Abba bar Zavda. He said to him: All of the Land of Israel does not produce a load of raisins. [56]But so he said to him: No single place in the land of Israel produces a load of raisins[57].

52 This is the spelling in the Babylonian Mishnah and most independent Mishnah mss. קפל "to fold", כפל "to double up".

53 Raisins are transported in baskets in contrast to grapes which are harvested into vats, so as not to lose the juice flowing from injured grape berries. (Cf. Babli 61a).

54 Raisins do not need knives.

55 This text is from *Demay* 2:1, Notes 105-107.

56 In the text of *Demay*, there follows a rhetorical question: Does the entire Land of Israel not produce a load of raisins?

57 Therefore, the Mishnah must speak of the fig harvest.

(41a, line 15) עַד הַקָּצִיר. כְּתִיב. עַד כְּלוֹת קְצִיר הַשְּׂעוֹרִים וּקְצִיר הַחִטִּים וְאַתְּ אָמַר כֵּן. מַה דְהַהוּא קְרָיָיא בַּדָּרוֹם הוּא. מַתְנִיתָא בַּגָּלִיל.

"Until the grain harvest". It is written[58], "until the end of the barley harvest and the wheat harvest". That verse speaks of the South[59], the Mishnah of Galilee.

58 *Ruth* 2:23. It is clear from the narrative that there was one continuous harvest activity, the wheat harvest following the barley harvest immediately. Therefore, the Mishnah seems unjustified in denying that "harvest" cannot refer to barley harvest.

59 Bethlehem.

(41a, line 17) נָדַר מִן הַקַּיִץ בַּגָּלִיל וְיוֹרֵד לוֹ לַעֲמָקִים. אַף עַל פִּי שֶׁבִּיכֵּר קַיִץ בָּעֲמָקִים אָסוּר עַד שֶׁיְּבַכֵּר בַּגָּלִיל.

If he made a vow "until the fig harvest" in Galilee and descended into the valleys. Even though the fig harvest did start in the valleys, he is forbidden until it starts in Galilee[60].

60 Tosephta 4:7, Babli (as tannaïtic statement) 63a.

משנה ו: עַד הַגְּשָׁמִים עַד שֶׁיְּהוּ גְּשָׁמִים עַד שֶׁתֵּרֵד רְבִיעָה שְׁנִיָּה. רַבָּן שִׁמְעוֹן בֶּן גַּמְלִיאֵל אוֹמֵר עַד שֶׁיַּגִּיעַ זְמַנָּהּ שֶׁלָּרְבִיעָה. עַד שֶׁיִּפְסְקוּ הַגְּשָׁמִים עַד שֶׁיֵּצֵא נִיסָן כּוּלּוֹ דִּבְרֵי רִבִּי מֵאִיר. רִבִּי יְהוּדָה אוֹמֵר עַד שֶׁיַּעֲבוֹר הַפֶּסַח. (fol. 40c)

Mishnah 6: 'Until the rains, until there be rain,' until the second rainy spell[61]; Rabban Simeon ben Gamliel said, until the time of the second rainy spell. 'Until the rains stop', until the end of the Month of Nisan, the words of Rebbi Meïr; Rebbi Jehudah says, until after Passover[62].

61 A similar statement in Mishnah *Ševi'it* 9:7, Note 93. A rainy spell is called רביע "fertilizing" if the total amount of water is one handbreadth for R. Jehudah, 3 for R. Meïr. The time of the expected second rainy spell is given in *Ta'aniot* 1:3 (64a, l. 64), Tosephta *Ta'aniot* 1:3, Babli *Nedarim* 63a, as *Marḥešwan* 7 for R. Meïr, 17 for R. Jehudah, 23 for R. Yose.

62 The evening after Nisan 21.

הלכה ו: עַד הַגְּשָׁמִים כול'. רִבִּי זְעוּרָא בָּעֵי. אָמַר. עַד הַגֶּשֶׁם. אָסוּר עַד שֶׁיָּרַד הַגֶּשֶׁם אַחֵר. תַּמָּן תַּנִּינָן. הָאוֹמֵר. הֲרֵי עָלַי עֵצִים. לֹא יִפְחוֹת מִשְּׁנֵי גִיזְרֵי עֵצִים. רִבִּי יוֹסֵי בְּרִבִּי אָמַר רִבִּי בָּא בַר מָמָל בָּעֵי. הֲרֵי עָלַי עֵץ. מֵבִיא גִיזֶר אֶחָד. אָמַר רִבִּי לְעָזָר. מַתְנִיתָא אָמְרָה כֵן שֶׁזֶּה קָרְבָּן בִּפְנֵי עַצְמוֹ וְזֶה קָרְבָּן בִּפְנֵי עַצְמוֹ. דְּתַנִּינָן תַּמָּן. וּשְׁנַיִם בְּיָדָן שְׁנֵי גִיזְרֵי עֵצִים. כְּדֵי לְרַבּוֹת בָּעֵצִים. (41a, line 18)

Halakhah 6: "'Until the rains,'" etc. Rebbi Ze'ira asked: If one said 'until the rain', is he forbidden until another rainfall came down[63]? There[64], we have stated: "One who said, I take upon me [the obligation to bring] wood[65], should not bring less that two cut logs[66]." Rebbi Yose the important said that Rebbi Abba bar Mamal asked, if he said, I take upon me [the obligation to bring] to bring wood[67], does he bring one cut log? Rebbi Eleazar said, a Mishnah explains that each one is a separate sacrifice, as we have stated there[68]: "Two in whose hands are two cut logs." In order to increase the number of logs[69].

63 In the Babli, 62b, R. Ze'ira is quoted to declare that the singular implies that one fertilizing rain only is meant.

64 Mishnah *Šeqalim* 6:6, *Menaḥot* 106b.

65 A plural.

66 For the altar in the Temple. The logs used for the altar had to be prepared so that all branches were cut off and all worms taken out. This is the emphasis on *cut* logs.

67 Singular.

68 Mishnah *Yoma* 2:5. While for the daily morning sacrifice only one Cohen brought wood to the altar, for the evening sacrifice there were two. R. Eleazar read the Mishnah to imply that each Cohen took only one log to the altar. This would imply that a single log is an acceptable gift to the altar.

69 There were four logs brought to the altar, two by each Cohen. This certainly implies that a person vowing "a log" has in fact to bring two, and probably that the person who vows not to taste something until the rains, is forbidden until the second batch of rain showers. (The Babli seems to disagree, 63a).

(41a, line 24) תַּנֵי רִבִּי יוֹסֵי אוֹמֵר. כָּל־דָּבָר שֶׁתָּלוּי בִּרְבִיעָה עַד שֶׁתֵּרֵד רְבִיעָה שְׁנִיָּיה. וְשֶׁאֵין תָּלוּי בִּרְבִיעָה עַד שֶׁיַּגִּיעַ זְמַן רְבִיעָה. תַּנֵי. רַבָּן שִׁמְעוֹן בֶּן גַּמְלִיאֵל אוֹמֵר. שִׁבְעַת יָמִים שֶׁיָּרְדוּ בָהֶן גְּשָׁמִים וְלֹא פָסְקוּ וְיֵשׁ בָּהֶן כְּדֵי רְבִיעָה שְׁנִיָּיה. וְלָמָּה נִקְרָא שְׁמָהּ רְבִיעָה. שְׁרוֹבַעַת לָאָרֶץ.

It was stated[70]: "Rebbi Yose said, anything depending on the fertilizing rain[71], until the second fertilizing rain comes. And anything not depending on the fertilizing rain[72], until the time of the second fertilizing rain. It was stated: Rabban Simeon ben Gamliel says, if rain came down for seven days without interruption, that includes the second fertilizing rain[73]." Why is it called fertilizing? Because it fertilizes the land.

70 Tosephta *Ta'aniot* 1:4 (in the Erfurt ms.) The statements are switched in the Vienna ms. and *editio princeps*. The paragraph is from *Ševi'it* 9:7, Notes 98-101.

71 The vow mentions רביעה, the fertilizing aspect.

72 The vow mentions simply גשם

"rain".	fertilizing periods; quoted in Babli 63a.
73 That is enough for two	

משנה ז: (fol. 40c) קוֹנָם יַיִן שֶׁאֵינִי טוֹעֵם הַשָּׁנָה נִתְעַבְּרָה הַשָּׁנָה אָסוּר בָּהּ וּבְעִיבּוּרָהּ. עַד ראשׁ אֲדָר עַד ראשׁ אֲדָר הָרִאשׁוֹן. עַד סוֹף אֲדָר עַד סוֹף אֲדָר הָרִאשׁוֹן.

Mishnah 7: 'A *qônām* that I shall not taste wine this year', if the year became intercalary he is forbidden it and its intercalary month. 'Until the start of Adar', until the first of First Adar; 'until the end of Adar', until the end of First Adar[74].

משנה ח: רִבִּי יְהוּדָה אוֹמֵר אָמַר קוֹנָם יַיִן שֶׁאֵינִי טוֹעֵם עַד שֶׁיְּהֵא פֶסַח אֵינוֹ אָסוּר אֶלָּא עַד לֵיל הַפֶּסַח שֶׁלֹּא נִתְכַּוֵון זֶה אֶלָּא עַד שָׁעָה שֶׁדֶּרֶךְ בְּנֵי אָדָם לִשְׁתּוֹת יַיִן.

Mishnah 8: Rebbi Jehudah says, if one said 'a *qônām* that I shall not taste wine until Passover has come', he is forbidden only until the night of Passover since he intended only until the time everybody drinks wine[75].

משנה ט: אָמַר קוֹנָם בָּשָׂר שֶׁאֵינִי טוֹעֵם עַד הַצוֹם אֵינוֹ אָסוּר אֶלָּא עַד לֵילֵי הַצוֹם שֶׁלֹּא נִתְכַּוֵון זֶה אֶלָּא עַד שָׁעָה שֶׁדֶּרֶךְ בְּנֵי אָדָם לוֹכַל בָּשָׂר.

Mishnah 9: If one said, "a *qônām* that I shall not taste meat until the fast[76],' he is forbidden only until the evening before the fast since he intended only until the time everybody eats meat.

משנה י: רִבִּי יוֹסֵי בְּנוֹ אוֹמֵר אָמַר קוֹנָם שׁוּם שֶׁאֵינִי טוֹעֵם עַד שֶׁתְּהֵא שַׁבָּת אֵינוֹ אָסוּר אֶלָּא עַד לֵילֵי שַׁבָּת שֶׁלֹּא נִתְכַּוֵון זֶה אֶלָּא עַד שָׁעָה שֶׁדֶּרֶךְ בְּנֵי אָדָם לָאֱכוֹל שׁוּם.

Mishnah 10: His son Rebbi Yose said, if one said 'a *qônām* that I shall not taste garlic until the Sabbath,' he is forbidden only until Friday evening, since he intended only until the time everybody eats garlic[77].

74 Cf. Halakhah 1, Note 12.

75 While the essence of a festival of pilgrimage is the holiday sacrifice which is possible only during daylight hours, the holiday starts in the evening and today "Passover" means the holiday starting with sunset on Nisan 14. Cf. Note 37 and the author's *The Scholar's Haggadah* (Northvale NJ 1995), pp. 185-191.

76 "Fast" without qualification always refers to the Day of Atonement, from the evening of Tishre 9 to the evening of Tishre 10. Since he is obligated to eat in the later hours of the afternoon of Tishre 9 to prepare for the fast, he intended the vow to terminate then.

77 Cf. Mishnah 3:10.

(41a, line 28) **הלכה ז:** קוֹנָם יַיִן וכו'. רִבִּי מֵאִיר כְּדַעְתֵּיהּ וְרִבִּי יְהוּדָה כְּדַעְתֵּיהּ. דְּתַנִינָן תַּמָּן. עַד אֵימָתַי שׁוֹאֲלִין אֶת הַגְּשָׁמִים. רִבִּי יוּדָה אוֹמֵר. עַד שֶׁיַּעֲבוֹר הַפֶּסַח. רִבִּי מֵאִיר אוֹמֵר. עַד שֶׁיֵצֵא נִיסָן.

Halakhah 7: "A *qônām* wine," etc. Rebbi Meïr follows his opinion and Rebbi Jehudah follows his opinion, as we have stated there[78]: "Until when does one pray for rain? Rebbi Jehudah says, until after Passover; Rebbi Meïr says until the end of the Month of Nisan."

78 Mishnah *Ta'aniot* 1:2.

(41a, line 30) הָדָא אֲמָרָה. נִיסָן רֹאשׁ הַשָּׁנָה לִנְדָרִים. תִּשְׁרֵי רֹאשׁ הַשָּׁנָה לִנְדָרִים. שֶׁלֹּא תֹאמַר. יַעֲלֶה רֹאשׁ חֹדֶשׁ אֲדָר תַּחַת אֱלוּל וִיהֵא מוּתָּר בְּאֱלוּל. לְפוּם כָּךְ צָרַךְ מֵימַר אָסוּר בָּהּ וּבְעִיבּוּרָהּ.

[79]Does this imply that Nisan is the beginning of the year as far as vows are concerned[14]? Tishre is is the beginning of the year as far as vows are concerned. That you should not say, the beginning of Adar should compensate for Ellul and he would be permitted in Ellul[15]; therefore, it was necessary to say that "he is forbidden it and its intercalary [month]".

79 This is from Halakhah 1 and refers to Mishnah 7.

(41a, line 33) רִבִּי אָבִין בְּשֵׁם רִבִּי אִילָא. וְהוּא שֶׁנָּדַר וְאַחַר כָּךְ עִיבְּרוּ. אֲבָל אִם עִיבְּרוּ וְאַחַר כָּךְ נָדַר לֹא בְדָא. לְעִנְיָין שְׂכַר בָּתִּים לֹא שַׁנְיָיא. זֶה אוֹמֵר. אֲדָר הָרִאשׁוֹן. וְזֶה אוֹמֵר. אֲדָר הַשֵּׁינִי. יַחֲלוֹקוּ חוֹדֶשׁ הָעִיבּוּר. אִיתָא חֲמֵי. לִנְדָרִים לֵית אַתְּ חָשֵׁישׁ וּלְמָמוֹן אַתְּ חָשֵׁשׁ. אָמַר רִבִּי הִילָא. וְהֵן שֶׁעִיבְּרוּ וְאַחַר כָּךְ הִשְׂכִּיר. אֲבָל הִשְׂכִּיר וְאַחַר כָּךְ עִיבְּרוּ לֹא בְדָא. וּלְעִנְיָין שְׁטָרוֹת כּוֹתְבִין בָּאֲדָר הָרִאשׁוֹן וּבָאֲדָר הַשֵּׁינִי. אֶלָּא שֶׁכּוֹתְבִין אֲדָר הַשֵּׁינִי. תִּנְיָין. רִבִּי יוּדָה אוֹמֵר אֲדָר הַשֵּׁינִי כּוֹתֵב תָּי״ו וְדַיּוֹ.

Rebbi Abin in the name of Rebbi Hila: That is only if he vowed before they intercalated. But if they intercalated and then he vowed, that is not so[80]. Is it no different for rent of houses[81]? If one said, the First Adar, and the other one says, the Second Adar, they should split the intercalary month[82]. Come and see, for vows you have no problem but for money matters you have a problem? Rebbi Hila said, that is, if they intercalated and after that he leased. But if he leased and after that they intercalated, that is not so[83]. And in matters of documents one writes First Adar, Second Adar, only that for Second Adar one writes חניין[84]. Rebbi Jehudah says, for Second Adar one writes ת and that is enough.

80 If he knew that there would be a Second Adar and he vowed until the end of Adar, that means the end of the Second Adar. The Babli, 63a/b, differentiates between whether the vower knew that the year would have an intercalary month or whether he did not know (in the absence of a published calendar).

81 If the house was let for a year. Does this mean 12 months if at the time of the contract it was not declared that the next year would have 13 months?

82 The parties come before the court in matters of a lease that was not supported by a written contract. The owner claims to have leased the house for 12 months, the renter claims it was for a year. Monetary disputes which cannot be decided because there are no

documents are resolved by splitting the difference, Mishnah *Baba Meṣi'a* 1:1.

83 The standard lease contract for rental property is one year. In the absence of proof to the contrary, one follows the standard contract.

84 The Aramaic version; the Babli agrees in the name of R. Jehudah (63a). According to R. Jehudah, a mention of אדר ﬨ is documentary proof of a reference to Second Adar. The latter statement is missing in the Babli.

משנה יא: הָאוֹמֵר לַחֲבֵירוֹ קוֹנָם שֶׁאֲנִי נֶהֱנֶה לָךְ אִם אֵין אַתָּה בָא (fol. 40d) וְנוֹטֵל לְבָנֶיךָ כּוֹר אֶחָד שֶׁלַּחִיטִין וּשְׁתֵּי חָבִיוֹת שֶׁלַּיַיִן הֲרֵי זֶה יָכוֹל לְהָפֵר נִדְרוֹ שֶׁלֹּא עַל פִּי חָכָם וְיֹאמַר לוֹ כְּלוּם אָמַרְתָּ אֶלָּא מִפְּנֵי כְבוֹדִי זֶהוּ כְבוֹדִי. וְכֵן הָאוֹמֵר לַחֲבֵירוֹ קוֹנָם שֶׁאַתְּ נֶהֱנֶה לִי אִם אֵין אַתָּה בָא וְנוֹתֵן לִבְנִי כּוֹר אֶחָד שֶׁלַּחִיטִין וּשְׁתֵּי חָבִיוֹת שֶׁלַּיַיִן רַבִּי מֵאִיר אוֹמֵר אָסוּר עַד שֶׁיִּתֵּן וַחֲכָמִים אוֹמְרִים אַף זֶה יָכוֹל לְהָפֵר נִדְרוֹ שֶׁלֹּא עַל פִּי חָכָם וְיֹאמַר לוֹ הֲרֵי אֲנִי כְּאִילּוּ נִתְקַבַּלְתִּי.

Mishnah 11: If one says to his friend: A *qônām* that I shall not have any usufruct from you if you do not come and take for your children a *kor*[85] of wheat and two amphoras of wine, he[86] can undo his vow without referring to a Sage by saying, you did that only to honor me, that is my honor. Similarly, if one says to his friend: A *qônām* that you shall not have any usufruct from me if you do not come and give to my child a *kor* of wheat and two amphoras of wine. Rebbi Meïr says, he is forbidden until he gives, but the Sages say, this one also can undo his[87] vow without referring to a Sage by saying, it is as if I received it.

85 A volume of 30 *se'ah*, equal to Ezechiel's *bat*; 384 liter.

86 The recipient can declare that it is as if he had received the amount stipulated and by this free the vower from his vow.

87 In this case it is his own vow.

(41a, line 40) **הלכה יא**: רִבִּי חִייָה בְשֵׁם רִבִּי יוֹחָנָן. אַף הָרִאשׁוֹן בְּמַחֲלוֹקֶת. אָמַר רִבִּי זְעִירָא. בִּסְתָם חֲלוּקִין. מָה אֲנָן קַייָמִין. אִם בְּשֶׁזֶּה אָמַר מִפְּנֵי כְבוֹדוֹ וְזֶה אָמַר מִפְּנֵי כְבוֹדוֹ. הַכֹּל אָסוּר. אִם בְּשֶׁזֶּה אָמַר. מִפְּנֵי כְבוֹדִי. וְזֶה אָמַר. מִפְּנֵי כְבוֹדָךְ אָמַרְתִּי. דִּבְרֵי הַכֹּל מוּתָּר. אֶלָּא כֵן אֲנָן קַייָמִין בִּסְתָם. רִבִּי אוֹמֵר. סְתָמִין כְּמַאן דְּאָמַר. מִפְּנֵי כְבוֹדִי. וְרַבָּנִין אָמְרִין. סְתָמִין כְּמִי שֶׁזֶּה אָמַר מִפְּנֵי כְבוֹדִי. וְזֶה אָמַר. מִפְּנֵי כְבוֹדָךְ אָמַרְתִּי.

Halakhah 11: Rebbi Ḥiyya in the name of Rebbi Joḥanan: The first case also is in dispute[88]. Rebbi Ze'ira said, they disagree when it was undetermined. [89]Where do we hold? If each one of them said, because of my honor, everybody agrees that he is forbidden[90]. If one of them said, because of my honor, and the other said, I said it in your honor, everybody agrees he is permitted[91]. But we hold if it is undetermined[92]. Rebbi says, undetermined is as if [every] one said, because of my honor. But the Sages say, undetermined is as if one said, because of my honor, and the other said, I said it in your honor.

88   R. Meïr disagrees also in the first case and requires the vow to be fulfilled.

89   Most of this text is from Halakhah 3:3, Notes 94-95.

90   They cannot agree on the essence of the vow; each one insists it is made in his own honor. In that case, what either one of them says is irrelevant for the other.

91   This is the first case of the Mishnah, and R. Meïr will agree that there is no vow.

92   The maker of the vow does not indicate whether he agrees or disagrees with the interpretation of the vow by his friend. Then R. Meïr will hold that what the other party says has no influence on the vower.

(41a, line 46) רִבִּי יָסָא בָּעֵי קוֹמֵי רִבִּי יוֹחָנָן. מַתְנִיתָא דְּרַבָּן שִׁמְעוֹן בֶּן גַּמְלִיאֵל. דְּרַבָּן שִׁמְעוֹן בֶּן גַּמְלִיאֵל אָמַר. כָּל־עֲקָבָה שֶׁאֵינָה מִמֶּנָּה הֲרֵי זֶה גֵט. אָמַר לֵיהּ. שַׁנְייָא הִיא הָכָא מִפְּנֵי פְּתִיחַת נֶדֶר. אָמַר רִבִּי יוֹסֵי. וְלֹא נְדָרִים שֶׁאֵינָן צְרִיכִין

הֵיתֵר חָכָם אָנָן קַיָּימִין. אָמַר רִבִּי יוֹנָה. לֹא בִּלְבָד הַתּוֹלֶה נִדְרוֹ בְּדָבָר אָנָן קַיָּימִין. עַד כְּדוֹן הוּא דְּבָעֵי מִיתַּן לָהּ. בְּרַם הַהוּא דְּלָא בָּעֵי מִיתַּן לֵהּ יְכִיל הוּא אֲמַר לֵיהּ. לָא בְעִית אֶלָּא מִבְדְּקִינָךְ. כֵּיוָן דַּחֲמִיתָךְ מִצְטָעֵר הֲרֵי אֲנִי כְּאִילוּ נִתְקַבַּלְתִּי.

Rebbi Yasa asked before Rebbi Johanan: Is our Mishnah from Rabban Simeon ben Gamliel, since Rabban Simeon ben Gamliel says, any obstacle that is not from her side does not invalidate the bill of divorce[93]? He said to him, here it is different because of opening the vow[94]. Rebbi Yose said, but do we not deal with vows which do not need dissolution by a Sage[95]? Rebbi Jonah said, we deal not only with one who made his vow dependent on something[96]. So far it is if he wants to give him something. But in the case that he does not want to give to him[97], he can say, I wanted only to examine you; but since I saw that it gives you pain, it is as if I had received.

93 Mishnah *Giṭṭin* 7:6. A man gives his wife (who desires a divorce) a bill of divorce under the condition that she nurse his child for two years or that she serve his father for two years. If the child dies in the meantime or his father refuses to be served by her while she did nothing to make him angry, the anonymous majority holds that the condition was not satisfied and the bill of divorce invalid. But Rabban Simeon ben Gamliel holds that if she fulfilled the condition to the best of her ability, the divorce is valid. R. Yasa wanted to say, that Rabban Simeon ben Gamliel also will hold that a vow can be considered fulfilled if the second party refuses to accept the service.

94 The Mishnah starts the topic of the next Chapter, the conditions under which a vow can be invalidated. The main condition is that one find "an opening of remorse", that a person would not have made the vow had he considered certain implications of it. These considerations are irrelevant for bills of divorce.

95 The topic discussed here is not that of the next Chapter.

96 This goes back to the previous paragraph. One can extend the

argument given for the first case of the Mishnah to that of the second case and support the argument of R. Ze'ira that R. Meïr and the Sages both hold that the two cases are parallel.

97   The second case of the Mishnah, since the person from whom the other vowed usufruct is providing the argument that the intention of the vow has been fulfilled. A different interpretation is in the Babli, 24a.

(fol. 40d) **משנה יב**: הָיוּ מְסָרְבִין בּוֹ לָשֵׂאת אֶת בַּת אֲחוֹתוֹ וְאָמַר קוֹנָם שֶׁהִיא נֶהֱנֵית לִי לְעוֹלָם וְכֵן הַמְגָרֵשׁ אֶת אִשְׁתּוֹ וְאָמַר קוֹנָם אִשְׁתִּי נֶהֱנֵית לִי לְעוֹלָם הֲרֵי אֵילוּ מוּתָּרוֹת לֵיהָנוֹת לוֹ שֶׁלֹא נִתְכַּוֵּון זֶה אֶלָּא לְשֵׁם אִישׁוּת.

Mishnah 12: If they[98] were importuning him to marry his sister's daughter[99] and he said, a *qônām* if she ever has any usufruct from me, and similarly, a man who was about to divorce his wife and said, a *qônām* if my wife ever has any usufruct from me, they may have usufruct from him[100] since he intended only about matters of marriage.

98   His family.
99   Which is considered a good deed; Babli *Yebamot* 62b/63a, *Sanhedrin* 76b, based on *Is.* 58:7.
100   The man who is about to divorce his wife cannot deprive her of the payments due to her as consequence of the divorce. He only forbade to himself any future sexual relations with his wife, implying that he could not remarry her after divorce.

(41a, line 53) **הלכה יב**: הָיוּ מְסָרְבִין בּוֹ לָשֵׂאת אֶת בַּת אֲחוֹתוֹ כול׳. אָמַר רִבִּי יוֹסֵי. רִבִּי יוּדָה הִיא. דְּרִבִּי יוּדָה אָמַר. הַכֹּל לְפִי הַנֶּדֶר. וְכֵן הַמְגָרֵשׁ אֶת אִשְׁתּוֹ כול׳. אָמַר רִבִּי יוֹסֵי. רִבִּי יוּדָה הִיא. דְּרִבִּי יוּדָה אָמַר. הַכֹּל לְפִי הַנֶּדֶר.

Halakhah 12: "If they were importuning him to marry his sister's daughter," etc. Rebbi Yose said, this is Rebbi Jehudah's, since Rebbi

Jehudah said[101], "everything refers to the vow." "And similarly, a man who was about to divorce his wife." Rebbi Yose said, this is Rebbi Jehudah's, since Rebbi Jehudah said[101], "everything refers to the vow."

101 Mishnah 7:3. The state of mind of the vower decides the meaning of his vow.

משנה יג: הָיָה מְסָרֵב בַּחֲבֵירוֹ שֶׁיֹּאכַל אֶצְלוֹ אָמַר קוֹנָם לְבֵיתָךְ שֶׁאֵינִי נִכְנָס טִיפַּת צוֹנִין שֶׁאֵינִי טוֹעֵם לָךְ מוּתָּר לִיכָּנֵס לְבֵיתוֹ וְלִשְׁתּוֹת מִמֶּנּוּ צוֹנִין שֶׁלֹּא נִתְכַּוֵּון זֶה אֶלָּא לְשֵׁם אֲכִילָה וּשְׁתִיָּה. (fol. 40d)

Mishnah 13: If somebody was importuning his neighbor that he should eat at his place and that one said, a *qônām* that I shall not enter your house nor taste a drop of cold water from you, he is permitted to enter his house and to drink cold water there since he intended only about eating and drinking.

הלכה יג: הָיָה מְסָרֵב בַּחֲבֵירוֹ שֶׁיֹּאכַל אֶצְלוֹ כול'. אָמַר רִבִּי יוֹסֵי. הָדָא אָמְרָה. הָהֵן דְּמַשְׁבַּע לְחַבְרֵיהּ דְּלָא יֵיכוּל. הָהֵן אוֹכֵל וְהָהֵן עָבַר. (41a, line 53)

Halakhah 13: "If somebody was importuning his neighbor that he should eat at his place," etc. Rebbi Yose said, this implies that if one brings his neighbor to swear that he will not eat, this one may eat of that neighbor[102].

102 He may eat at his place after the dinner to which he was invited had passed without his participation. The interpretation is that of S. Lieberman (*Tosefta kiFshutah Nedarim* p. 464) who follows R. Simḥa of Dwinsk in reading חבר for עבר because of the well-documented collapse of gutturals in Galilean speech. The restriction of the vow to the one intended formal

dinner is also explicit in the Tosephta (4:8-9) (even though the scenario there is slightly different) and in Maimonides (*Hilkhot Nedarim* 8:10). The Babli does not discuss the Mishnah.

רבי אליעזר פרק תשיעי

(fol. 41a) **משנה א:** רִבִּי לִיעֶזֶר אוֹמֵר פּוֹתְחִין לְאָדָם בִּכְבוֹד אָבִיו וְאִמּוֹ. וַחֲכָמִים אוֹסְרִים. אָמַר רִבִּי צָדוֹק עַד שֶׁפּוֹתְחִין לוֹ בִּכְבוֹד אָבִיו וְאִמּוֹ יִפְתְּחוּ לוֹ בִּכְבוֹד הַמָּקוֹם אִם כֵּן אֵין נְדָרִים. מוֹדִין חֲכָמִים לְרִבִּי אֱלִיעֶזֶר בְּדָבָר שֶׁבֵּין אָדָם לְבֵין אָבִיו וְאִמּוֹ שֶׁפּוֹתְחִין לוֹ בִּכְבוֹד אָבִיו וְאִמּוֹ.

Mishnah 1: Rebbi Eliezer says, one opens[1] for a man by the honor of his father and mother, but the Sages forbid it. Rebbi Ṣadoq said, before one opens by the honor of his father and mother one should open by the honor of the Omnipresent[2]; then there are no vows[3]. The Sages agree with Rebbi Eliezer that if was a matter between a man and his father and mother[4], that one opens for him by the honor of his father and mother.

1 If a person comes to a Sage to ask about a vow, the Sage may find him "an opening of remorse" by telling him that his parents must be ashamed that their son is one of the wicked who make vows (cf. Chapter 1, Note 9).

2 Who in general does not approve of vows.

3 If the Sage said, did you really want to make a vow to be called a sinner before God, everybody would say No, and every vow would be dissolved.

4 For example, if the son forbade all usufruct from his property to his parents (*Mat.* 15:5), it is appropriate for the Sage to point out to the son that he sins against the commandment to honor father and mother.

(41b, line 36) **הלכה א:** רִבִּי אֱלִיעֶזֶר אוֹמֵר. פּוֹתְחִין לְאָדָם כּוֹל'. רַבָּנִין אָמְרִין. חֲזָקָה שֶׁאָדָם מַעֲמִיד בִּכְבוֹד אָבִיו וְאִמּוֹ. רִבִּי לִיעֶזֶר אוֹמֵר. פְּעָמִים מַעֲמִיד וּפְעָמִים אֵינוֹ מַעֲמִיד. מוֹדֶה רִבִּי לִיעֶזֶר לְאַחַר מִיתָה שֶׁאֵינוֹ מַעֲמִיד. הַכֹּל מוֹדִין בִּכְבוֹד רַבּוֹ שֶׁאֵינוֹ מַעֲמִיד. דְּתַנִּינָן וּמוֹרָא רַבָּךְ כְּמוֹרָא שָׁמַיִם.

Halakhah 1: "Rebbi Eliezer says, one opens for a man," etc. The rabbis say, a man resists the honor of his father and mother[5]. Rebbi Eliezer says, sometimes he resists, sometimes he does not resist[6]. Rebbi Eliezer agrees that after their death he does not resist[7]. Everybody agrees that nobody resists the honor of his teacher, as we stated[8]: "And the fear of your teacher shall be like the fear of Heaven."

5   It seems to be confirmed by the third sentence that one has to read "a man *does not* resist the honor of his parents." This means that if the vower is told that his vow infringes on his duty to honor his parents, he immediately will agree to rescind the vow even though he has no remorse for making the vow. Then the annulment of the vow would be illegal.

6   Then it is not sure that the avowed remorse is faked.

7   The Sage certainly cannot invoke the memory of his parents or that of his teacher.

8   Mishnah *Abot* 4:15.

(41b, line 40) אִם כֵּן אֵין נְדָרִים. לֹא יְהוּ נְדָרִים. וְהָכְתִיב וַיְדַבֵּר מֹשֶׁה אֶל רָאשֵׁי הַמַּטּוֹת. תָּלָה הַפָּרְשָׁה בְּרָאשֵׁי הַמַּטּוֹת. שֶׁיְּהוּ מַתִּירִין אֶת נִדְרֵיהֶן. אִם אוֹמֵר אַתְּ כֵּן נִמְצֵאת עוֹקֵר פָּרְשַׁת נְדָרִים מִן הַתּוֹרָה.

"Then there are no vows." Let there be no vows! But is it not written[9]: "Moses spoke to the heads of the tribes." He hung the chapter on the heads of the tribes, that they could dissolve their vows[10]. If you say so[11], it turns out that you uproot the chapter of vows from the Torah.

9   *Num.* 30:2, the start of the chapter on vows.

10   Chapter 3:1, Note 6.

11   That there should be no vows.

(41b, line 40) רִבִּי יִרְמְיָה בָּעֵי. אַתְּ אוֹמֵר. פּוֹתְחִין לוֹ בִּכְבוֹד אָבִיו וְאִמּוֹ. דְּבָרִים שֶׁבֵּינוֹ לְבֵין הַמָּקוֹם אַל יִפְתְּחוּ לוֹ בִּכְבוֹד הַמָּקוֹם. מֵעַתָּה דְּבָרִים שֶׁבֵּינוֹ לְבֵין אָבִיו וְאִמּוֹ פּוֹתְחִין לוֹ בִּכְבוֹד אָבִיו וְאִמּוֹ. וְדִכְוָותָהּ יִפְתְּחוּ לוֹ בִּכְבוֹד דְּבָרִים שֶׁבֵּינוֹ לְבֵין הַמָּקוֹם. אֵי זֶהוּ כְּבוֹד הַמָּקוֹם. כְּגוֹן סוּכָה שֶׁאֵינִי עוֹשֶׂה.

לוּלָב שֶׁאֵינִי נוֹטֵל. תְּפִילִין שֶׁאֵינִי נוֹתֵן. וְהַיְינוּ כְּבוֹד הַמָּקוֹ'ם. מִשְׁמַע לֵיהּ דְּלַנַפְשֵׁיהּ הוּא מְהַנֵּי. כְּהָדָא אִם צָדַקְתָּ מַה תִּתֶּן לוֹ. אִם חָטָאתָ מַה תִּפְעָל־בּוֹ. אָמַר רִבִּי יַנַּאי. כָּל־הַשּׁוֹמֵעַ לְיִצְרוֹ כְּאִילוּ עוֹבֵד עֲבוֹדָה זָרָה. מַאי טַעֲמָא. לֹא יִהְיֶה בְךָ אֵל זָר וְלֹא תִשְׁתַּחֲוֶה לְאֵל נֵכָר. זָר שֶׁבְּקִרְבְּךָ אַל תַּמְלִיכֵהוּ עָלֶיךָ.

Rebbi Jeremiah asked: Since you say, one opens for him by the honor of his father and mother; in things between him and the Omnipresent, one does not open for him by the honor of the Omnipresent[12]. But since in matters between him and his father and mother one opens for him by the honor of his father and mother; similarly, in things between him and the Omnipresent should one not open for him by the honor of the Omnipresent? What is the honor of the Omnipresent? For example, that I shall not make a tabernacle[13], that I shall not take a *lulab*[14], that I shall not put on phylacteries[15]. One understands that he does it for his own benefit. As in the following[16]: "If you are just, what are you giving Him?" "If you sinned, what would you do to Him?[17]" Rebbi Yannai said, one who listens to his urges is as if he worshipped idols. What is the reason? "In yourself there shall be no alien force; do not bow down to a foreign god.[18]"

12   Since this is not mentioned in the Mishnah. Since "the Omnipresent" is a name of God, the scribe inserted an apostrophe to make a later correction or erasure possible.

13   *Lev.* 23:42.

14   One of the "four kinds", *Lev.* 23:40.

15   *Ex.* 13:9,16.

16   *Job* 35:7. The reward of good deeds is purely the benefit of the doer.

17   *Job* 35:6. The mention of this verse and the sermon following are induced by the preceding quote.

18   *Ps.* 81:10. The alien forces are the evil urges in a person; they are put in parallel with idol worship. In the Babli, *Šabbat* 105b, the statement is attributed to R. Abin.

(41b, line 51) רִבִּי שִׁמְעוֹן בֶּן לָקִישׁ פָּתַח. אִילּוּ הָיִיתָ יוֹדֵעַ שֶׁהַנּוֹדֵר כְּאִילּוּ נוֹתֵן קוֹלָר עַל צַוָּארוֹ נוֹדֵר הָיִיתָ. לְקַסְטוֹרִיָּיה שֶׁהָיְתָה עוֹבֶרֶת וְרָאָה קוֹלָר פָּנוּי וְהִכְנִיסָהּ אֶת רֹאשָׁהּ לְתוֹכוֹ. לֶאֱסוֹר אִסָּר עַל נַפְשׁוֹ. כְּמָה דְאַתְּ אָמַר וְהוּא אָסוּר בַּזִּיקִים. רִבִּי יוֹנָתָן פָּתַח. אִילּוּ הָיִיתָ יוֹדֵעַ שֶׁהַנּוֹדֵר כְּבוֹנֶה בָּמָה וְהַמְקַיְּימוֹ כְּמַקְרִיב עָלָיו נוֹדֵר הָיִיתָ. וְקַשְׁיָא. עֲבוֹדָה זָרָה בִּסְקִילָה וְהַנְּדָרִים בְּלֹא תַעֲשֶׂה וְאַתְּ אָמַר אָכֵן. לֵית לָהּ אֶלָּא כַּיי דָמַר רִבִּי יַנַּאי. כָּל־הַשּׁוֹמֵעַ לְיִצְרוֹ כְּאִילּוּ עוֹבֵד עֲבוֹדָה זָרָה. רִבִּי יִצְחָק פָּתַח. אִילּוּ הָיִיתָ יוֹדֵעַ שֶׁהַנּוֹדֵר כְּאִילּוּ נוֹטֵל חֶרֶב וְדוֹקְרָהּ בְּלִיבּוֹ נוֹדֵר הָיִיתָ. יֵשׁ בּוֹטֶה כְּמַדְקְרוֹת חָרֶב. רִבִּי חֲנִינָה דְצִיפּוֹרִין בְּשֵׁם רִבִּי פִינְחָס. כְּמִדַּקֵּר אֵין כְּתִיב אֶלָּא כְּמַדְקְרוֹת חָרֶב. לְאֶחָד שֶׁנָּדַר מִן הַכִּכָּר. וַיי דְיֵיכוֹל וַיי דְּלָא יֵיכוֹל. אִין אֲכִיל עָבַר עַל נִדְרֵיהּ. אִין לָא אֲכִיל חֲטֵי עַל נַפְשֵׁיהּ. כֵּיצַד הוּא עוֹשֶׂה. הוֹלֵךְ אֵצֶל חָכָם וְהוּא מַתִּיר נִדְרוֹ. וּלְשׁוֹן חֲכָמִים מַרְפֵּא. רִבִּי דִימִי בְּשֵׁם רִבִּי יִצְחָק. לֹא דַיֶּיךָ מַה שֶּׁאָסְרָה לָךְ הַתּוֹרָה אֶלָּא שֶׁאַתָּה מְבַקֵּשׁ לֶאֱסוֹר עָלֶיךָ דְּבָרִים אֲחֵרִים. לֶאֱסוֹר אִסָּר.

Rebbi Simeon ben Laqish provided an opening: If you had known that one who makes a vow is as if he put a neck-iron[19] on his neck, would you have made the vow? It is as if a gang of prisoners[20] was passing by, he saw that there was one unused neck-iron and put his head into it! "To bind a prohibition onto himself[21]", as you say[22], "he was bound with chains."

Rebbi Jonathan[23] provided an opening: If you had known that one who makes a vow is like one who builds an idolatrous altar and one who continues in it is like one who sacrifices there, would you have made the vow? That is difficult to understand. Idolatry is a capital crime but vows are a simple prohibition; how can you say that? You have only what Rebbi Yannai said, one who listens to his urges is as if he worshipped idols.

Rebbi Isaac provided an opening: If you had known that one who makes a vow is like one who takes a sword and sticks it in his heart, would you have made the vow? "Some talk bluntly like sword piercings.²⁴" Rebbi Ḥanina from Sepphoris in the name of Rebbi Phineas: It does not say "piercing" but "sword piercings". For example, one who made a vow not to eat a loaf. Woe if he eats, woe if he does not eat. If he eats he transgresses his vow. If he does not eat he sins against himself²⁵. What can he do? He goes to a Sage who will dissolve his vow, "but the speech of Sages is healing²⁴.

Rebbi Eudaimon in the name of Rebbi Isaac: Is it not enough what the Torah forbade you that you want to forbid other things for yourself? "To forbid a prohibition²¹".

19	Cf. *Berakhot* 7:5, Note 116.	22	*Jer.* 40:1.
20	Reading with Jastrow and Krauss קַסְטוֹרִיָּיה for קַסְטוֹדִיָּיה, Latin *custodia* "watch, guard; gang of prisoners".	23	In the Babli, 22a, R. Nathan.
		24	*Prov.* 12:18.
		25	Since a person who mortifies himself is called a sinner, *Sifry Num.* 30, *Nazir* 1:5 (51c, l. 58).
21	*Num.* 30:3.		

(41b, line 62) רִבִּי יוֹחָנָן פָּתַח וְתָהֵי. וְאִילוּלֵי דוּ תְהֵא הוּ אֲתֵי. וְתָהוּת לֵהּ כְּנוֹלָד הוּא. אָמַר רִבִּי הִילָא. הַתָּהוּת מְצוּיָה. כְּהָדָא רִבִּי שִׁמְעוֹן לֹא מָצָא פֶּתַח לְנִדְרוֹ עַד שֶׁבָּא אֶחָד מִזִּקְנֵי הַגָּלִיל. אִית דְּאָמְרִין. רִבִּי שִׁמְעוֹן בֶּן אֶלְעָזָר הֲוָה נְסִיב לֵהּ מִכָּא וּמוּקִים לֵהּ הָכָא. נְסִיב לֵהּ מִכָּא וּמוּקִים לֵהּ הָכָא. עַד דְּאוּקְמֵיהּ גּוֹ שִׁמְשָׁא מַפְלֵי מָנוֹהִי. אָמְרִין לֵהּ. אִילוּ הָיִיתָ יוֹדֵעַ דְּהָהֵן סַבָּא עָבַד לָךְ כֵּן נוֹדֵר הָיִיתָ. אָמַר לוֹן. לֹא. וְשָׁרָא לֵהּ. אָמְרוּן. מְנָא לָךְ הָדָא. אָמַר לָהֶן. מְשָׁרֵת מֵאִיר הָיִיתִי בְּבָרְחוֹ שָׁנִים. וְאִית דְּאָמְרֵי. מַקְלוֹ שֶׁלָּרִבִּי מֵאִיר הָיְתָה בְיָדִי וְהִיא מְלַמֶּדֶת לִי דַּעַת.

Rebbi Joḥanan provided an opening by having second thoughts: "If it were not for that, would he have come²⁶?" Are second thoughts not something new²⁷? Rebbi Hila said, second thoughts are a common occurrence²⁸. In this kind, Rebbi Simeon²⁹ did not find an opening for his own vow until one of the Galilean Elders came; some say, that one was Rebbi Simeon ben Eleazar[30]. He took him from here and put him there; he took him from here and put him there, until finally he put him into the sun and told him to check his garments for fleas. They said to him, if you had known that this old man would treat you in such a way, would you have made the vow? He said, No. He permitted him. They asked, from where do you have this? He said to them, I was Meïr's servant both times when he fled[31], but some say, Rebbi Meïr's walking stick was in my hand and it teaches me knowledge.

26   R. Joḥanan took the fact that a person came to him to ask about a vow as proof of repentance and dissolved the vow without further inquiry.

27   In Mishnah 2, the Sages forbid to take future changes into consideration.

28   They are built into the original vow.

29   In the Babli, 22b, R. Simeon ben Rebbi.

30   One of the students of R. Meïr.

31   Most commentators want to read שנית "the second time" instead of שנים "twice" since the first time he had to flee was when he received ordination after the Bar Kokhba war when giving or receiving ordination was an act of rebellion against the Roman government and a capital crime. The reason for his second exile is not known; it is known that he died in Asia Minor (*Kilaim* 9:4, Note 128). If he left Galilee because Rabban Simeon ben Gamliel had excluded him from the Academy it was not "fleeing". It is unlikely that (1) R. Meïr had a student with him when he fled the first time, and (2) that the same student would have been with him both in his youth and in his old age.

(41b, line 70) רִבִּי יִרְמְיָה שָׁרֵי נִדְרָא וּמְקַיֵּים לֵיהּ. אִין מִשּׁוּם דְּהוּא חָשַׁשׁ לְהוּא דְשָׁרֵי לֵיהּ לָא יָדְעִין. אִין מִשּׁוּם דְּאֵין הַיֵּצֶר תָּאֵב אֶלָּא דָּבָר שֶׁאָסוּר לוֹ לָא יָדְעִין. רִבִּי יִרְמְיָה כַּד לֹא הֲוָה בָּעֵי מֵידוֹן אָמַר. עֵינַי כְהַיָּא. וְעַל פִּיהֶן יִהְיֶה כָּל־רִיב וְכָל־נָגַע. הִקִּישׁ רִיבִים לִנְגָעִים. מַה נְּגָעִים לְכָל־מַרְאֵה עֵינֵי הַכֹּהֵן. אַף רִיבִים לְכָל־מַרְאֵה עֵינֵי הַכֹּהֵן.

Rebbi Jeremiah had his vow dissolved but kept it. Whether it was because he did not trust him who dissolved it[32], we do not know. Whether it was because one has urges only for things forbidden to oneself[33], we do not know. When Rebbi Jeremiah was not in the mood to judge, he said, my eyes are weak. "Following their pronouncements shall be all quarrels and all disfiguration[34]." This compares quarrels to disfigurations[35]. Since disfigurations are "for all the Cohen sees[36]", so also quarrels are "for all the Cohen sees".

32 He was worried that the opening which another rabbi found for him was really invalid and that the other invalidated the vow only to please the head of the Academy.

33 The same argument in *Yoma* 6:4 (43c l. 21).

34 *Deut.* 21:5.

35 Different detailed discussions of this comparison are in the Babli, *Sanhedrin* 34b, and *Sifry Deut.* 208.

36 *Lev.* 13:12.

(41c, line 1) רִבִּי מָנָא נָדַר מִן חַמְרָא דַאֲבוֹהִי. אֲתָא אֲבוֹהִי סְלַק לְגַבֵּיהּ. אֲמַר לֵיהּ. אִילּוּ הָיֵית יוֹדֵעַ דַּאֲנָא מִצְטַעֵר נוֹדֵר הָיֵית. אָמַר לֵיהּ לֹא. וְשָׁרָא לֵיהּ. מַה אָנָן קַיָּימִין. אִם בְּאוֹמֵר. הֲנָייָתִי עַל אַבָּא. הָדָא הִיא דָּמַר רִבִּי יַעֲקֹב בַּר אָחָא רִבִּי שְׁמוּאֵל בַּר נַחְמָן בְּשֵׁם רִבִּי יוֹנָתָן. כּוֹפִין אֶת הַבֵּן שֶׁיִּזּוּן אֶת הָאָב. אֶלָּא כִּי נָן קַיָּימִין בְּאוֹמֵר. הֲנָיַית אַבָּא עָלַי. רִבִּי מָנָא נָדַר וּסְלַק לְגַבֵּי רִבִּי שַׁמַּי. אָמַר לֵיהּ. אִילּוּ הָיֵיתָ יוֹדֵעַ שֶׁהַבְּרִיּוֹת רַחֲקִין מִינָּךְ. דְּאַתְּ נָדְרָן. נָדַר הֲוֵיתָה. אָמַר לֵיהּ לֹא. וְשָׁרָא לֵיהּ.

Rebbi Mana made a vow away from his father's wine[37]. His father came to him and said to him, would you have made that vow if you had known that I am hurt by it? He said, no. He dissolved for him. Where do we hold? If he said, my benefit [is forbidden] to my father; is that not what Rebbi Jacob bar Aḥa, Rebbi Samuel bar Naḥman said in the name of Rebbi Jonathan: One forces the son to support his father[38]. But we must hold that he said, my father's benefit [is forbidden] to me. Rebbi Mana made a vow and came to Rebbi Shammai, who said to him, would you have made that vow if you had known that people do not want to deal with you since you are a vower? He said, no, and he dissolved for him.

37 Not to have any benefit from his father's wine. It seems that R. Mana here is R. Mana II, the colleague of R. Shammai. He was the son of R. Jonah; one has to wonder why the father appears without his name.

38 This parallels Mishnah 12; a person cannot get rid of monetary obligations by making a vow. But even if R. Mana had forbidden his own wine on R. Jonah (which seems to be excluded by the formulation of the vow), the head of the Academy certainly could buy his own wine without taking from charity and forcing the overseers of charity to have regress on his son.

(41a) **משנה ב:** וְעוֹד אָמַר רבִּי אֱלִיעֶזֶר פּוֹתְחִין בְּנוֹלָד. וַחֲכָמִים אוֹסְרִין. כֵּיצַד אָמַר קוֹנָם שֶׁאֵינִי נֶהֱנֶה לְאִישׁ פְּלוֹנִי וְנַעֲשָׂה סוֹפֵר אוֹ שֶׁהָיָה מַשִּׂיא אֶת בְּנוֹ בְקָרוֹב וְאָמַר אִילּוּ הָיִיתִי יוֹדֵעַ שֶׁהוּא נַעֲשָׂה סוֹפֵר אוֹ שֶׁהוּא מַשִּׂיא אֶת בְּנוֹ בְקָרוֹב לֹא הָיִיתִי נוֹדֵר. קוֹנָם לְבַיִת הַזֶּה אֵינִי נִכְנָס וְנַעֲשָׂה בֵית הַכְּנֶסֶת. אָמַר אִילּוּ הָיִיתִי יוֹדֵעַ שֶׁהוּא נַעֲשָׂה בֵית הַכְּנֶסֶת לֹא הָיִיתִי נוֹדֵר. רבִּי אֱלִיעֶזֶר מַתִּיר וַחֲכָמִים אוֹסְרִין.

Mishnah 2: In addition, Rebbi Eliezer said, one finds an opening in changed circumstances, but the Sages forbid it. How is this? If he said, a *qônām* that I shall not benefit from Mr. X, who then becomes a public scribe[39] or who marries off his son to one of [the vower's] relatives[40], and he said, if I had known that he will become a public scribe or marry off his son to a relative, I would not have vowed; or if he said, a *qônām* that I shall not enter this house and it was turned into a synagogue and he said, if I had known that it would become a synagogue, I would not have vowed; Rebbi Eliezer permits but the Sages prohibit[41].

39 Or any public official whose services he might need.

40 And he wants to go to the wedding feast which, according to the custom of the times, was paid for by the groom's family.

41 Since it could not have been in the vower's mind at the moment he made the vow.

הלכה ב: וְעוֹד אָמַר רִבִּי אֱלִיעֶזֶר פּוֹתְחִין בַּנּוֹלָד כול׳. רִבִּי סִימוֹן (41c, line 8) בְּשֵׁם רִבִּי יְהוֹשֻׁעַ בֶּן לֵוִי. מִמֹּשֶׁה לָמַד רִבִּי אֱלִיעֶזֶר שֶׁפָּתַח לוֹ הַקָּדוֹשׁ בָּרוּךְ הוּא בַּנּוֹלָד. אָמַר לוֹ הַקָּדוֹשׁ בָּרוּךְ הוּא. אִילוּ הָיִיתָ יוֹדֵעַ כִּי מֵתוּ כָּל־הָאֲנָשִׁים הַמְבַקְשִׁים אֶת נַפְשְׁךָ נוֹדֵר הָיִיתָ. וְכִי מֵתִים הָיוּ. וַהֲלֹא דָתָן וַאֲבִירָם הָיוּ. אֶלָּא שֶׁיָּרְדוּ מִנְּכָסֵיהֶם.

Halakhah 2: "In addition, Rebbi Eliezer said, one finds an opening in changed circumstances," etc. Rebbi Simon in the name of Rebbi Joshua ben Levi[42]: Rebbi Eliezer learned from Moses, to whom the Holy One, praise to Him, provided an opening by changed circumstances. The Holy One, praise to Him, said to him: If you had known that "all the men who want to kill you have died," would you have vowed[43]? But did they really die? Were they not Dathan and Abiram[44]? Only, they became poor[45].

42 In the Babli, 64b, Rav Ḥisda

43 The background is in *Tanḥuma Šemot* 12, *Tanḥuma Buber Šemot* 11, on *Ex.* 2:21, quoted in the Babli 65a: "Moses swore that he would dwell with the man" deriving וַיּוֹאֶל from אלה "to swear", not from יאל "to agree, to decide". (The problem naturally is that the form וַיּוֹאֶל is *qal* if derived from יאל but *hiph'il* if derived from אלה and would have to be translated "he (Reuel) made Moses swear to dwell with the man," which should require a *nota accusativi* before "Moses".) Since Moses swore in Midyan that he would stay there when he thought that he never

could return to Egypt, he had to return there to have his vow dissolved.

44 The identification of "the evil one" in *Ex.* 2:13 is in the Babli, 64b, and *Tanḥuma Šemot* 10; identifying all anonymous evildoers in *Ex.* and *Num.* with Dathan and Abiram who were called "evil ones" by Moses (*Num.* 16:26).

45 Therefore, nobody in government would listen to their calumnies. In the Babli, this is attributed to R. Simeon ben Laqish.

(41c, line 12) אָמַר רִבִּי יִרְמְיָה. הָדָא דְאַתְּ אָמַר עַד שֶׁלֹּא נָשְׂאוּ וְנָתְנוּ בַּדְּבָרִים כְּנוֹלַד הֵם. חֵיילֵיהּ דְּרִבִּי יוֹסֵי מִן הָדָא. זוֹ טָעוּת טָעָה נַחוּם הַמָּדִי. מַה טָעָה. שֶׁפָּתַח לָהֶן בְּנוֹלַד. אָמַר לָהֶן נַחוּם הַמָּדִי. אִילוּ הָיִיתֶם יוֹדְעִין שֶׁבֵּית הַמִּקְדָּשׁ עָתִיד לִיחָרֵב נוֹדְרִין הָיִיתֶם לִהְיוֹת נְזִירִין. אָמַר רִבִּי זְעוּרָה. הָכֵין הֲוָה צָרִיךְ מֵימַר לוֹן. לֹא הָיִיתֶם יוֹדְעִין שֶׁנִּיבְּאוּ לָכֶם נְבִיאִים הָרִאשׁוֹנִים בִּזְמַן שֶׁבֵּית הַמִּקְדָּשׁ קַיָּים שֶׁעָתִיד לִיחָרֵב. לֹא הֲוָה כְנוֹלַד. אָמַר רִבִּי הִילָא. עוֹד הוּא בְנוֹלַד. יְכָלִין הֲווֹן מֵימַר. יָדְעִין הֲוֵינָן אֶלָּא דַהֲוֵינָן סָבְרִין דְּמִילַּיָּיא רְחִיקִין. הֶחָזוֹן אֲשֶׁר הוּא חוֹזֶה לְיָמִים רַבִּים וּלְעִתִּים רְחוֹקוֹת הוּא נִיבָּא. וְאַתְיָיא דְּרִבִּי יִרְמְיָה כְּרִבִּי זְעִירָא וּדְרִבִּי יוֹסֵי כְּרִבִּי אִילָא.

Rebbi Jeremiah said, what you say is only that there are changed circumstances before the matter is discussed[46]. The force of Rebbi Yose[47] is from the following[48]: "That was the error of Naḥum the Mede." What was his error? That he found them an opening by changed circumstances. "Naḥum the Mede said to them: 'Would you have made a vow to become *nezirim* if you had known that the Temple would be destroyed at some future time?'" Rebbi Ze'ira said, the following he should have said to them: Did you not know that the earlier prophets had prophesied while the Temple was standing that eventually it would be destroyed? Then there are no changed circumstances. Rebbi Hila said, still it is changed circumstances. They could have said to him, we knew it, but it seemed to us that this referred to the far future[49]: "The vision he sees is for many years; for faraway times he prophesies." It turns out that Rebbi Jeremiah parallels Rebbi Ze'ira and Rebbi Yose parallels Rebbi Hila.

46 It always is possible by discussing the matter to find an aspect of changed circumstances which has not changed from the time the vow was made.

47 It is not stated what R. Yose (the Amora's) position is but the last sentence of the paragraph implies that R. Yose opposes R. Jeremiah.

48 Mishnah 5:4. When a group of *nezirim* came from Babylonia to Palestine shortly after the destruction of the Temple, he asked them whether they would have vowed to be *nezirim* had they known that the Temple would be destroyed and they would permanently be forbidden wine and grapes and contact with corpses since the termination of the state of *nazir* depends on the Temple ceremony; cf. *Num.* 6:20.

49 *Ez.* 12:27.

(41c, line 21) דְּתַגִּינָן תַּמָּן. אֵין מוֹכְרִין בֵּית הַכְּנֶסֶת אֶלָּא עַל תְּנַאי. עַד כְּדוֹן שֶׁבְּנָיָיהּ לְשֵׁם כְּנֶסֶת. בְּנָיָיהּ לְשֵׁם חָצֵר וְהִקְדִּישָׁהּ מָהוּ. נִישְׁמְעִינָהּ מִן הָדָא. קוֹנָם לְבַיִת זֶה שֶׁאֵינִי נִכְנָס. וְנַעֲשָׂה בֵּית הַכְּנֶסֶת. הָדָא אָמְרָה. שֶׁבְּנָיָיהּ לְשֵׁם חָצֵר וְהִקְדִּישָׁהּ מָהוּ. אֵימָתַי הִיא קְדוֹשָׁה. מִיַּד אוֹ בִשְׁעַת תַּשְׁמִישׁ. נִישְׁמְעִינָהּ מִן הָדָא. הָעוֹשֶׂה תֵּיבָה לְשֵׁם סֵפֶר וּמִטְפָּחוֹת לְשֵׁם סֵפֶר. עַד שֶׁלֹּא נִשְׁתַּמֵּשׁ בָּהֶן סֵפֶר מוּתָּר לְהִשְׁתַּמֵּשׁ בָּהֶן הֶדְיוֹט. מִשֶּׁנִּשְׁתַּמֵּשׁ בָּהֶן סֵפֶר אָסוּר לְהִשְׁתַּמֵּשׁ בָּהֶן הֶדְיוֹט. וּמָה אֵילּוּ שֶׁנַּעֲשׂוּ לְשֵׁם סֵפֶר אֵינָן קְדוֹשׁוֹת אֶלָּא בִשְׁעַת תַּשְׁמִישׁ. זוֹ שֶׁבְּנָיָיהּ לְשֵׁם חָצֵר לֹא כָּל־שֶׁכֵּן. אֵילוּ עֲשָׂאָן לְשֵׁם חוּלִּין וְהִקְדִּישָׁן קָדְשׁוּ.

(As)[50] we have stated there[51]: "One sells a synagogue only conditionally". [52]So far if it was built as a synagogue. How is the situation if the building was first built for profane use and then dedicated? Let us hear from the following: "A *qônām* that I shall not enter this house and it was turned into a synagogue." That implies that if it was built as a courtyard and afterwards was dedicated that it becomes holy. How? When does it become holy, immediately or when it is used? Let us hear from the following⁵³: "If somebody makes a chest for a Torah scroll, or wrappings for a Torah scroll, before they were used for a Torah scroll they may be used for private use; after they were used for a Torah scroll they may not be used for private use." Since these were made for holy use but became holy only when used, that which was built as a courtyard not so much more⁵⁴? What is the status of those if they were made for profane use and then dedicated? They become holy⁵⁵.

50   It seems that the additional ד is a scribal error since this paragraph has no connection with the previous one.

51   Mishnah *Megillah* 3:3. R. Meïr holds that a synagogue can be sold only with a clause that would let the community reacquire the building if it so chooses. The Sages permit the sale to be absolute as long as the building is not used for undignified purposes. (According to a popular tradition, the *Altneuschul* synagogue in Prague is *Al-Tnai-Schul*, a synagogue built *on condition* that on the arrival of the Messiah it could be sold without restrictions.)

52   From here on, the text is from *Megillah* 3:1 (73b l. 38).

53   Tosephta *Megillah* 2:13.

54   The same conclusion in the Babli, *Megillah* 26b.

55   The text of *Megillah* is very much condensed here.

(fol. 41a) **משנה ג:** רִבִּי מֵאִיר אוֹמֵר יֵשׁ דְּבָרִים שֶׁהֵן כְּנוֹלָד וְאֵינָן כְּנוֹלָד וַחֲכָמִים מוֹדִין לוֹ. כֵּיצַד אָמַר קוֹנָם שֶׁאֵינִי נוֹשֵׂא פְּלוֹנִית שֶׁאָבִיהָ רַע. אָמְרוּ לוֹ מֵת אוֹ שֶׁעָשָׂה תְּשׁוּבָה. קוֹנָם לְבַיִת זֶה שֶׁאֵינִי נִכְנָס שֶׁהַכֶּלֶב רַע בְּתוֹכוֹ אוֹ שֶׁהַנָּחָשׁ בְּתוֹכוֹ אָמְרוּ לוֹ מֵת הַכֶּלֶב וְנֶהֱרַג הַנָּחָשׁ הֲרֵי הֵן כְּנוֹלָד וְאֵינָן כְּנוֹלָד וַחֲכָמִים מוֹדִין לוֹ.

Mishnah 3: Rebbi Meïr says, there are things like changed circumstances which are not really changed circumstances⁵⁶, and the Sages agree with him[57]. How is this? He said, a *qônām* that I shall not marry this woman for her father is evil, and they told him that he died or that he repented; a *qônām* that I shall not enter this house because it has a bad dog inside, or a snake; they said to him the dog died, the snake was killed; these there are things like changed circumstances which are not changed circumstances, and the Sages agree with him.

56 There are changed circumstances which are admissible to annul a vow.

57 This is the reading in many Mishnah mss. and Gaonic and early rabbinic sources but not in the existing Babli mss. and the printed editions which read: The Sages do not agree with him. The *gemara* in the Babli seems to presuppose the Yerushalmi Mishnah. For details cf. *The Babylonian Talmud with variant readings, Nedarim II*, ed. M. Hershler, Jerusalem 1991, p. קנב, Note 49.

משנה ד: וְעוֹד אָמַר רִבִּי מֵאִיר פּוֹתְחִין לוֹ מִן הַכָּתוּב בַּתּוֹרָה וְאוֹמְרִים (fol. 41a) לוֹ אִילּוּ הָיִיתָ יוֹדֵעַ שֶׁאַתָּה עוֹבֵר עַל לֹא תִקּוֹם וְעַל לֹא תִטּוֹר וְעַל לֹא תִשְׂנָא אֶת אָחִיךָ בִּלְבָבֶךָ וְאָהַבְתָּ לְרֵעֲךָ כָּמוֹךָ וְחֵי אָחִיךָ עִמָּךְ שֶׁמָּא יַעֲנִי וְאֵין אַתְּ יָכוֹל לְפַרְנְסוֹ וְאָמַר אִילּוּ הָיִיתִי יוֹדֵעַ שֶׁהוּא כֵן לֹא הָיִיתִי נוֹדֵר הֲרֵי זֶה מוּתָּר.

Mishnah 4: In addition, Rebbi Meïr said, one opens for him with what is written in the Torah. One says to him[58], if you had realized that you sin against "you shall not take revenge[59]", "you shall not nurse hatred[59]", "you shall not hate your brother in your heart[60]", "you shall love your neighbor as yourself[59]", "let your brother live with you[61]", maybe he would become poor and you cannot provide for him! If he said, if I had realized this, I would not have vowed, he is permitted.

58 A person who vowed that another could not have any benefit from him.

59 Lev. 19:18.
60 Lev. 19:17.
6 Lev. 25:36.

(41c, line 30) **הלכה ג:** רִבִּי מֵאִיר אוֹמֵר יֵשׁ דְּבָרִים שֶׁהֵן כְּנוֹלָד. שְׁמוּאֵל אָמַר מִשֵּׁם גֶּדֶר טָעוּת. כְּבָר מֵת הַכֶּלֶב כְּבָר נֶהֱרַג הַנָּחָשׁ. רִבִּי אִילָא בְּשֵׁם רִבִּי לְעָזָר. מִפְּנֵי שֶׁהוּא כְּתוֹלֶה נִדְרוֹ בְּדָבָר. קוֹנָם שֶׁאֵינִי נֶהֱנֶה לְאִישׁ פְּלוֹנִי כָּל־זְמָן שֶׁהוּא לָבוּשׁ שְׁחוֹרִים. לָבַשׁ לְבָנִים מוּתָּר בּוֹ. רִבִּי זְעוּרָא בְּשֵׁם רִבִּי יוֹחָנָן. אַף הוּא אֵינוֹ צָרִיךְ הֵיתֵר חָכָם.

Halakhah 3: "Rebbi Meïr says, there are things like changed circumstances". Samuel says, because of an erroneous vow; the dog was already dead, the snake had already been killed[62]. Rebbi Hila in the name of Rebbi Eleazar, because he is like someone who makes his vow dependent on something[63]: A *qônām* that I shall have no benefit from this man as long as he wears black garments[64]. If he wore white, he would be permitted to him. Rebbi Ze'ira in the name of Rebbi Johanan: That one does not need the permission of a Sage.

62 Samuel restricts the Mishnah to the case that the dog was already dead when the vow was made. Then it is obvious that the vow would not have been made had the vower known all the facts. But if the vow was justified at the moment it was made, Samuel would deny that the death of the dog was reason enough to nullify the vow for the future.

63 They hold that the vow can be nullified at the death of the dog because the reason for the vow had been stated at the beginning. As the example shows, if the vower had said, I shall not enter the house as long as there is a bad dog there, the vow would automatically be voided at the dog's death. But because the reason was not formally stated as a condition, the vow mentioned in the Mishnah needs to be voided by a Sage.

In the Babli, 65a, the opinion of Samuel is attributed to R. Johanan and that of R. Hila to Rav Huna, with the discussion supporting Rav Huna.

64 The sign of a person engaged in sexual misbehavior; Babli *Mo'ed Qatan* 17a, *Hagigah* 16a, *Qiddušin* 40a.

(41c, line 35) כְּתִיב לֹא תִקּוֹם וְלֹא תִטּוֹר אֶת בְּנֵי עַמֶּךָ. הֵיךְ עֲבִידָה. הֲוָה מְקַטֵּעַ קוֹפָד וּמְחַת סַכִּינָא לְיָדוֹי. תַּחֲזוֹר וְתִמְחֵי לְיָדֵיהּ.

It is written: "You should not take revenge or nurse hatred against your fellow countrymen." How is that? He was cutting meat and the knife fell down on his hand. Should he go and hit his hand[65]?

וְאָהַבְתָּ לְרֵעֲךָ כָּמוֹךָ. רִבִּי עֲקִיבָה אוֹמֵר. זֶהוּ כְּלָל גָּדוֹל בַּתּוֹרָה. בֶּן עַזַּאי אוֹמֵר. זֶה סֵפֶר תּוֹלְדוֹת אָדָם זֶה כְּלָל גָּדוֹל מִזֶּה.

"You shall love your neighbor as yourself[59]". Rebbi Aqiba says, that is a great principle in the Torah. Ben Azzai says, "this is the book of the descent of man[66]" is a more important principle[67].

65 Should he punish the hand which held the knife for injuring his other hand? Since all Jews are responsible for one another (Babli *Sanhedrin* 27b), hitting one's neighbor is like hitting himself.

66 Gen. 5:1, which negates the role of race in the creation of man.

67 *Sifra Qedošim Pereq* 4(12). A fuller version is in *Gen. rabba* 24(8): Ben Azzai says, "this is the book of the descent of man" is a great principle in the Torah. Rebbi Aqiba says, "you shall love your neighbor as yourself" is a great principle in the Torah. That you should not say, since I was insulted, another should be insulted with me; since I was cursed, another should be cursed with me. Rebbi Tanḥuma (last generation of Galilean Amoraim) said, if you did this, know Whom you are insulting: "In God's image He made him."

(41c, line 38) שְׁמָא יַעֲנִי. לֹא כְנוֹלַד הוּא. אָמַר רִבִּי זְעוּרָא. עֲנִיוּת מְצוּיָה. כְּהָדָא. חַד בַּר נַשׁ הֲוָה בַּעַל דִּינֵיהּ עָתִיר. אָתָא בָּעֵי מֵידוֹן קוֹמֵי רַב. שָׁלַח רַב בַּתְרֵיהּ אָמַר. עִם הַהוּא אֲנָא בְּעֵי מֵייתֵי מֵידוֹן. כָּךְ אֵין אַתְיָין כָּל־גָּמְלַיָּיא דַּעֲרָבִיָּיא לָא טְעִינָן קוֹרְקָסַיָּיא דְּאָפוֹתֵיקִים דִּידִי. שָׁמַע וַאֲמַר. מַהוּ מִתְגָּאֶה דְּלֹא לֵיהּ. תְּהֵא פְחָתָהּ בָּהּ. מִן יַד נָפְקַת קְלֵווסִיס מִן מַלְכוּתָא דְּיֵיעוּל הוּא וּמִדְלֵיהּ לְטִימוֹן. אָמַר לֵיהּ. צְלֵי עֲלַי דּוּ נַפְשִׁי תַּחֲזוֹר. צְלֵי עֲלוֹי וְחָזַר עֲלָהּ.

"Maybe he would become poor". Are these not changed circumstances[68]? Rebbi Ze'ira said, poverty is frequent. As the following: A man had a lawsuit against a rich man. He wanted to be judged before Rav; Rav sent for [the rich man], who said: For this one I should come to court? If all the camels of Arabia came they could not carry all the leather sacks[69] containing my mortgages[70]! [Rav] heard this and said, what does this one pride himself with what is not his! There should be depreciation of it! Immediately there came a royal decree[71] that he and his property should belong to the treasury[72]. He [the rich man] said to him [Rav], pray for me that my personality[73] could be restored. He prayed, and it was restored to him.

68 And therefore excluded as argument following Mishnah 1.
69 Aramaic plural of Greek κώρυκος "leather bag".
70 Greek ὑποθήκη; cf. *Yebamot* 7:1, Note 25.
71 Greek κέλευσις "command, order".
72 Greek ταμεῖον "treasure, storage", used in the sense of the king's treasury. The mixture of Aramaic and Greek in this popular tale may be an example of "hellenistic speech"; cf. *Sota* 7:1, Note 22.
73 Lest he become a slave of the treasury.

(fol. 41b) **משנה ה:** פּוֹתְחִין לָאָדָם בִּכְתוּבַּת אִשְׁתּוֹ. מַעֲשֶׂה בְּאֶחָד שֶׁנָּדַר מֵאִשְׁתּוֹ הֲנָייָה וְהָיְתָה כְּתוּבָּתָהּ אַרְבַּע מֵאוֹת דֵּינָרִין וּבָאת לִפְנֵי רַבִּי עֲקִיבָה וְחִיְּבוֹ לִיתֵּן לָהּ כְּתוּבָּתָהּ. אָמַר לוֹ רַבִּי שְׁמוֹנֶה מֵאוֹת דֵּינָרִין הִנִּיחַ אַבָּא וְנָטַל אָחִי אַרְבַּע מֵאוֹת וַאֲנִי אַרְבַּע מֵאוֹת לֹא דַיָּיהּ שֶׁתִּיטּוֹל מָאתַיִם וַאֲנִי מָאתַיִם. אָמַר לוֹ רַבִּי עֲקִיבָה אֲפִילוּ אַתְּ מוֹכֵר שְׂעַר רֹאשָׁךְ אַתְּ נוֹתֵן לָהּ כְּתוּבָּתָהּ. אָמַר לוֹ אִילּוּ הָיִיתִי יוֹדֵעַ שֶׁהוּא כֵן לֹא הָיִיתִי נוֹדֵר וְהִתִּירוֹ רַבִּי עֲקִיבָה.

Mishnah 5: One creates an opening for a man with his wife's *ketubah*[74]. It happened that one vowed usufruct from his wife[75] whose *ketubah* was 400 denar. She[76] came before Rebbi Aqiba who obliged him to give her her *ketubah*. He said, Rebbi, my father left 800 denar. My brother took 400 and I 400, would it not be enough if she take 200[77] and I 200? Rebbi Aqiba told him, even if you have to sell the hair on your head, you will pay her *ketubah*. He said to him, if I had known that, I would not have vowed. Rebbi Aqiba freed him[78].

74 The marriage contract, here taken as technical term for the sum the groom promises to pay his wife in case of a divorce. The minimal sum for a first marriage of the woman is 200 *zuz*, defined in Mishnah *Peah* 8:8 as sufficient capital to lift its owner above the poverty level and disqualify him from public charity. The *zuz* is usually identified with the silver denarius.

75 This makes it impossible for him to live with his wife and forces him to divorce her.

76 In the Babylonian Mishnah, he came before R. Aqiba.

77 The minimum amount admissible as *ketubah*.

78 From his vow so he could remain married. One might also translate: R. Aqiba voided it [the vow]. In the Babylonian Mishnah, R. Aqiba permitted her to remain with her husband.

(41c, line 30) **הלכה ה:** פּוֹתְחִין לָאָדָם בִּכְתוּבַת אִשְׁתּוֹ כול׳. וְגוֹבִין מִן הַמְטַלְטְלִין. אָמַר רִבִּי בָּא. אַף עַל גַּב דְּתֵימַר. גּוֹבִין מִן הַמְטַלְטְלִין. אוֹמֵר לוֹ שֶׁיִּתֵּן. רִבִּי מַנִּישָׁא שָׁאַל. מַהוּ לוֹמַר לְיוֹרְשִׁין לִגְבּוֹת מִן הַמְשׁוּעְבָּדִין. אָמַר רִבִּי אַבָּא מָרִי. מַתְנִיתָא אֲמָרָהּ כֵּן שֶׁאֵין אוֹמֵר לָהֶן. דְּתַנִינָן תַּמָּן. אֶלָּא יִינָתְנוּ לְיוֹרְשִׁין. שֶׁכּוּלָּן צְרִיכִין שְׁבוּעָה וְאֵין הַיּוֹרְשִׁין צְרִיכִין שְׁבוּעָה. מַהוּ מִשְׁבְּעוֹנָהּ. תַּמָּן אֲמְרִין מִן תְּבָנָא לֹא גָבָאי וּמִן גּוּפֵיהּ גָּבָאי.

Halakhah 5: "One creates an opening for a man with his wife's *ketubah*," etc. Does one collect from movables[79]? Rebbi Abba said, even if one could say, one collects from movables, one tells him to pay⁸⁰. Rebbi Manisha asked, could one tell the heirs to collect from pledged property⁸¹? Rebbi Abba Mari said, the Mishnah says that one does not say so, as we have stated there⁸²: "It should be given to the heirs since everybody has to swear but the heirs do not have to swear." What does one make her swear? There, they say, from straw I did not collect, from his person I did collect⁸³.

79 It is talmudic theory that debts covered by a document (such as a *ketubah* or a mortgage) must be satisfied by foreclosing real estate (unless otherwise stated in the document of indebtedness). It was only after the Arab conquest, when the Jews in Babylonia had lost their real estate holdings, that the Gaonic authorities decreed that every *ketubah* must be paid in currency and/or movables. How could R. Aqiba order the man to cut off and sell his hair to pay his ex-wife since cut hair clearly is movable? (The Babli explains that the man should hand over all his real estate to his wife and sell his hair to buy food for himself.)

80 It seems that one has here a disagreement of the two Talmudim (explanation of I. Eisenstein in עמודי ירושלים *ad loc.*). The Babli sticks to its thesis that a *ketubah* is satisfied only by real estate and holds that a partially satisfied *ketubah* represents a title to all future property the ex-husband might acquire. The Yerushalmi holds that if the husband cannot satisfy his divorcee's claim with real estate, one tells him to satisfy it with any other means available.

81 If this would refer to real estate, the question would be trivial. Mortgaged or otherwise pledged property is part of the inheritance. Standard mortgages (including *ketubah*) are not on a specified piece of land but on all holdings of the debtor. If the debtor dies, the entire property comes to the heirs from whom the mortgage holder can require satisfaction under the supervision of the court.

The quote with which the question is answered shows clearly that the issue is about movables. Then it cannot be a question of mortgages other than a *ketubah*. The question is whether the court can order the heirs to honor their father's obligation to his ex-wife from movables, *to let her collect* from movables.

82 Mishnah *Ketubot* 9:2. In the Mishnah, R. Aqiba states that the heirs take all movables since any creditor would have to swear that his claim was not in any way satisfied by the deceased but the heirs take everything without oath. (R. Tarphon disagrees and would give the widow preference).

83 "There" is Babylonia. It is difficult to understand what is meant. It seems that she has to swear that her claim was not satisfied even in an indirect way.

(fol. 41b) **משנה ו:** פּוֹתְחִין בְּיָמִים טוֹבִים וּבְשַׁבָּתוֹת. בָּרִאשׁוֹנָה הָיוּ אוֹמְרִין אוֹתָן הַיָּמִים מוּתָּרִין וּשְׁאָר כָּל־הַיָּמִים אֲסוּרִין עַד שֶׁבָּא רִבִּי עֲקִיבָה וְלִימֵּד שֶׁהַנֶּדֶר שֶׁהוּתַּר מִקְצָתוֹ הוּתַּר כּוּלוֹ.

Mishnah 6: One opens about festive days and Sabbaths[84]. In earlier times, they said that these days are permitted but the rest forbidden, until Rebbi Aqiba came and taught that a vow which was partially voided is totally voided.

משנה ז: כֵּיצַד. קוֹנָם שֶׁאֵינִי נֶהֱנֶה לְכוּלְכֶם הוּתַּר אֶחָד מֵהֶן הוּתְּרוּ כוּלָּן. שֶׁאֵינִי נֶהֱנֶה לָזֶה וְלָזֶה הוּתַּר הָרִאשׁוֹן הוּתְּרוּ כוּלָּן הוּתַּר הָאַחֲרוֹן הָאַחֲרוֹן מוּתָּר וְכוּלָּן אֲסוּרִין. שֶׁאֵינִי נֶהֱנֶה לָזֶה קָרְבָּן וְלָזֶה קָרְבָּן צְרִיכִין פֶּתַח לְכָל־אֶחָד וְאֶחָד.

Mishnah 7: How is this? 'A *qônām* that I shall not benefit any one of you,' if one was permitted, all are permitted. 'That I shall not benefit this one and this one and this one,' if the first one becomes permitted, all are permitted; if the last one becomes permitted, he is permitted and the others are prohibited[85]. 'That I shall not benefit, a *qorbān* for this one, a *qorbān* for that one'; each single one needs a separate opening[86].

משנה ח: קוֹנָם יַיִן שֶׁאֵינִי טוֹעֵם שֶׁהַיַּיִן רַע לַמֵּעַיִם. אָמְרוּ לוֹ וַהֲלֹא הַמְיוּשָׁן יָפֶה לַמֵּעַיִם הוּתַּר בַּמְיוּשָׁן וְלֹא בַמְיוּשָׁן בִּלְבַד הוּתַּר אֶלָּא בְּכָל־הַיַּיִן. קוֹנָם

בְּצָל שֶׁאֵינִי טוֹעֵם שֶׁהַבָּצָל רַע לַלֵּב. אָמְרוּ לוֹ וַהֲלֹא הַכּוּפְרִי יָפֶה לַלֵּב. הוּתַּר בַּכּוּפְרִי וְלֹא בַּכּוּפְרִי בִּלְבַד הוּתַּר אֶלָּא בְּכָל־הַבְּצָלִים. מַעֲשֶׂה הָיָה וְהִתִּירוֹ רִבִּי מֵאִיר בְּכָל־הַבְּצָלִים.

Mishnah 8: 'A *qônām* that I shall not taste wine, for wine is bad for the intestines.' If they told him, but old [wine] is good for the intestines, old [wine] was permitted; not only old wine is permitted but all wines. 'A *qônām* that I shall not taste onion, for onion is bad for the heart.' If they told him, but the rural kind is good for the heart, rural [onion] was permitted; not only rural is permitted but all onions. It happened that Rebbi Meïr permitted all onions to him.

84 That the vower could not enjoy Sabbaths and holidays.

85 The *n*-th term in a sequence cannot appear before the (*n*-1)-th. If there is no (*n*-1)-th there can be no *n*-th. If he had said: all of you, *viz*., X and Y and Z, the order would have been irrelevant. Since he says, X and also Y and also Z, the later depends on the former. The Babli, 66a, notes that only R. Simeon considers this three separate vows; the Yerushalmi, which quotes R. Simeon elsewhere [e. g., *Nazir* 4:3 (53b)], does not mention it here but seemingly restricts the principle of R. Aqiba to vows declared to concern a group; cf. also Note 89.

86 While these statements all form one sentence, they represent two separate vows.

(41c, line 50) **הלכה ו**: פּוֹתְחִין בְּיָמִים טוֹבִים וּבְשַׁבָּתוֹת כול'. תַּנֵּי. הוּתַּר מִמֶּנּוּ וּלְמַטָּה מוּתָּר. מִמֶּנּוּ וּלְמַעֲלָה אָסוּר. תַּנֵּי בְשֵׁם רִבִּי נָתָן. יֵשׁ נֶדֶר שֶׁמִּקְצָתוֹ בָטֵל וּמִקְצָתוֹ קַיָּים. כֵּיצַד. נָדַר מִן הַכַּלְכָּלָה וְהָיוּ שָׁם בְּנוֹת שֶׁבַע. אָמַר. אִילּוּ הָיִיתִי יוֹדֵעַ שֶׁיֵּשׁ שָׁם בְּנוֹת שֶׁבַע לֹא הָיִיתִי נוֹדֵר. הוּתַּר בִּבְנוֹת שֶׁבַע. לֹא בִּבְנוֹת שֶׁבַע בִּלְבַד הוּתַּר אֶלָּא בְּכָל־הַכַּלְכָּלָה. אֲבָל אִם אָמַר. אִילּוּ הָיִיתִי יוֹדֵעַ שֶׁיֵּשׁ שָׁם בְּנוֹת שֶׁבַע לֹא הָיִיתִי נוֹדֵר מִבְּנוֹת שֶׁבַע. לֹא הוּתַּר אֶלָּא בִּבְנוֹת שֶׁבַע בִּלְבַד.

Halakhah 6: "One opens about festive days and Sabbaths," etc. It was stated[87]: "If one[88] was permitted, all subsequent ones are permitted, all preceding ones are forbidden." It was stated in the name of Rebbi Nathan[89]: "There exists a type of vow which may be partly voided and the rest confirmed. How is this? One made a vow [not to eat] from a fig basket which contained *benot šeba'*[90] figs. If he said, if I had known that it contained *benot šeba'* figs, I would not have made the vow, he is permitted the *benot šeba'* figs and not only these but all figs. But if he said, if I had known that it contained *benot šeba'* figs, I would not have extended my vow to *benot šeba'* figs, only *benot šeba'* figs are permitted to him."

87   Tosephta 5:1, this entered some Mishnah texts in the Babli.
88   In a series of people who should have no benefit.
89   Tosephta 5:1, quoted in the Babli, 26b/27a. There, R. Aqiba disagrees and upholds his principle while the Yerushalmi does not mention R. Aqiba and gives the impression that it accepts the position of R. Nathan.
90   Light green delicacy figs; *Ma'serot* 2:8, Note 135.

(fol. 41b) **משנה ט:** פּוֹתְחִין לָאָדָם בִּכְבוֹד עַצְמוֹ וּבִכְבוֹד בָּנָיו. אוֹמְרִים לוֹ אִילּוּ הָיִיתָ יוֹדֵעַ שֶׁלְּמָחָר אוֹמְרִין עָלֶיךָ כָּךְ הִיא וֶסְתּוֹ שֶׁלִּפְלוֹנִי מְגָרֵשׁ נָשָׁיו וְעַל בְּנוֹתֶיךָ יְהוּ אוֹמְרִים בְּנוֹת גְּרוּשָׁה הֵן מָה רָאָת אִימָּן שֶׁלָּאֵילּוּ לְהִתְגָּרֵשׁ. וְאָמַר אִילּוּ הָיִיתִי יוֹדֵעַ שֶׁהוּא כֵן לֹא הָיִיתִי נוֹדֵר הֲרֵי זֶה מוּתָּר.

Mishnah 9: One finds an opening for a man with his own honor and that of his children. One tells him[91], if you had known that tomorrow one will say of you, it is the habit of this man to divorce his wife, and about your daughters one will say, they are daughters of a divorcee, what did the mother of these do to get herself divorced? If he said, if I had known that it is so I would not have made the vow, then it is dissolved.

91 A man who made a vow which forces a divorce.

(41c, line 57) **הלכה ט:** פּוֹתְחִין לָאָדָם בִּכְבוֹד עַצְמוֹ כול'. תַּנֵּי. רִבִּי יוּדָה בֶּן בְּתֵירָה אוֹמֵר. אֵין פּוֹתְחִין לָאָדָם אֶלָּא בִּכְבוֹד עַצְמוֹ בִּלְבָד. כְּהָדָא חָדָא אִיתָּה נָדְרַת מִן בְּרַתָּהּ. אָתַת לְגַבֵּי רִבִּי יוֹחָנָן. אֲמַר לָהּ. אִילּוּ הֲוֵית יָדַעַת דִּבְרַתֵּיךְ נָסְבָה שׁוּם בִּישׁ נוֹדֶרֶת הֲוֵית. אָמְרָה. לֹא. וְשָׁרַת לָהּ. וְלֹא מַתְנִיתָא הִיא. פּוֹתְחִין לָאָדָם בִּכְבוֹד עַצְמוֹ וּבִכְבוֹד בָּנָיו. דְּלֹא תִיסְבּוֹר כְּרִבִּי יוּדָה בֶּן בְּתֵירָה.

Halakhah 9: "One finds an opening for a man about his own honor," etc. It was stated[92]: Rebbi Jehudah ben Bathyra said, one finds an opening for a man exclusively about his own honor. As the following? A woman vowed [not to have benefit] from her daughter[93]. She came to Rebbi Joḥanan who said to her, if you had known that your daughter gets a bad reputation[94], would you have made the vow? She said, no, and he permitted her. Is that not the Mishnah[95]: "One finds an opening for a man about his own honor and that of his children"? That you should not think one follows Rebbi Jehudah ben Bathyra.

92 Obviously, this is the Yerushalmi tradition. The (Babylonian) Tosephta, 5:6 attributes the text of the Mishnah to R. Jehudah ben Bathyra.

93 She did not want to be supported by her daughter.

94 People will say that she does not care for her mother.

95 Why is it worthwhile to record a decision which follows the Mishnah closely? [In the Babli (a total of 24 times) R. Joḥanan is reported to hold that an anonymous Mishnah *always* represents practice; in the Yerushalmi he holds *in general* that practice follows an anonymous Mishnah (*Yebamot* 4:11, Note 177)].

(fol. 41b) **משנה י:** קוֹנָם שֶׁאֵינִי נוֹשֵׂא אֶת פְּלוֹנִית כְּעוּרָה וַהֲרֵי הִיא נָאָה שְׁחוֹרָה וַהֲרֵי הִיא לְבָנָה קְצָרָה וַהֲרֵי הִיא אֲרוּכָּה מוּתָּר לֹא מִפְּנֵי שֶׁהִיא כְּעוּרָה וְנַעֲשֵׂית נָאָה שְׁחוֹרָה וְנַעֲשֵׂית לְבָנָה קְצָרָה וְנַעֲשֵׂית אֲרוּכָּה אֶלָּא שֶׁהַנֶּדֶר טָעוּת. מַעֲשֶׂה בְּאֶחָד שֶׁנָּדַר מִבַּת אֲחוֹתוֹ הֲנָייָה וְהִכְנִיסוּהָ לְבֵית רִבִּי יִשְׁמָעֵאל וְיִפּוּהָ. אָמַר לוֹ רִבִּי יִשְׁמָעֵאל בְּנִי לָזוֹ נָדַרְתָּ. אָמַר לוֹ לָאו וְהִתִּירוֹ רִבִּי יִשְׁמָעֵאל. בְּאוֹתָהּ שָׁעָה בָּכָה רִבִּי יִשְׁמָעֵאל וְאָמַר בְּנוֹת יִשְׂרָאֵל יָפוֹת הֵן אֶלָּא שֶׁהָעֲנִיּוּת מְנַוְּולָתָן.

Mishnah 10: "A *qônām* that I shall not marry the ugly Miss X, and she is beautiful, black and she is white, short and she is tall, he is permitted. Not because she was ugly and became beautiful[96], black and she became white, short and she became tall, but because the vow was erroneous. It happened that one[97] made a vow renouncing benefit from his sister's daughter. They brought her to Rebbi Ismael's house and gave her a beauty treatment. Rebbi Ismael asked him, did you make your vow about this one? He said no, and Rebbi Ismael dissolved it[98]. At that moment, Rebbi Ismael cried and said, the daughters of Israel are beautiful, but poverty disfigures them.

96 This would be a change of circumstances, not admissible in an annulment.

97 Being pressured by his family to marry his niece.

98 The vow.

(41c, line 62) **הלכה י:** קוֹנָם שֶׁאֵינִי נוֹשֵׂא אֶת פְּלוֹנִית כְּעוּרָה כול׳. עָשָׂה לָהּ עַיִן שֶׁלַּזָּהָב שֵׁן שֶׁלַּזָּהָב. כִּלְשׁוֹן זֶה אָמַר לוֹ. זְכֵה בְּמָה שֶׁעָלֶיהָ.

Halakhah 10: "'A *qônām* that I shall not marry the ugly Miss X,'" etc. He made her a golden eye, a golden tooth[99]. So he said to him, acquire what is on her[100].

99 The Babli, 66b, notes only that she had an ugly artificial tooth and R. Ismael replaced it by a gold tooth for which he paid himself. In the opinion of the Babli, R. Ismael denies that changed circumstances are no cause for annulment of a vow.

100 In the Tosephta, 5:6: "acquire her and her dresses".

(fol. 41b) **משנה יא:** וּכְשֶׁמֵּת רַבִּי יִשְׁמָעֵאל הָיוּ בְּנוֹת יִשְׂרָאֵל נוֹשְׂאוֹת קִינָה וְאוֹמְרוֹת בְּנוֹת יִשְׂרָאֵל אֶל רַבִּי יִשְׁמָעֵאל בְּכֶינָה. וְכֵן הוּא בְּשָׁאוּל אוֹמֵר בְּנוֹת יִשְׂרָאֵל אֶל שָׁאוּל בְּכֶינָה וגו'.

Mishnah 11: And when Rebbi Ismael died the daughters of Israel did sing a dirge and say, 'Daughters of Israel, cry about Rebbi Ismael', as it is said about Saul: 'Daughters of Israel, cry about Saul, etc.[101]'

101 "Who clothes you in crimson with ornaments, who puts a golden jewel on your garments", 2S. 1:24.

(41c, line 64) **הלכה יא:** וּכְשֶׁמֵּת רַבִּי יִשְׁמָעֵאל כול'. כְּתִיב בְּנוֹת יִשְׂרָאֵל אֶל שָׁאוּל בְּכֶינָה וגו'. רַבִּי יוּדָה וְרַבִּי נְחֶמְיָה. חַד אָמַר. בְּנוֹת יִשְׂרָאֵל מַמָּשׁ. שֶׁהָיוּ בַעֲלֵיהֶן הוֹלְכִין לַמִּלְחָמָה וְהָיָה מַעֲלֶה לָהֶן מְזוֹנוֹת. מַה תַּלְמוּד לוֹמַר. הַמַּעֲלֶה עֲדִי זָהָב עַל לְבוּשְׁכֶן. שֶׁאֵין תַּכְשִׁיט נָאֶה אֶלָּא עַל גּוּף מְעוּדָּן. וְחָרָנָה אָמַר. בְּנוֹת יִשְׂרָאֵל. בָּנִיּוֹת שֶׁבְּיִשְׂרָאֵל. סַנְהֶדְרִיּוֹת שֶׁלְּיִשְׂרָאֵל. הָיָה רוֹאֶה כַת חֲבֵירִים וּמַאֲכִילָן וּמַשְׁקָן. וּמַה תַּלְמוּד לוֹמַר. הַמַּעֲלֶה עֲדִי זָהָב עַל לְבוּשְׁכֶן. שֶׁהָיָה שׁוֹמֵעַ טַעַם הֲלָכָה מִפִּי חָכָם וּמְקַלְּסוֹ.

Halakhah 11: "And when Rebbi Ismael died," etc. It is written, ""Daughters of Israel, cry about Saul, etc." Rebbi Jehudah and Rebbi Nehemiah. One said, really daughters of Israel. For their husbands went to war and he provided them with food. Why does the verse say "who puts a golden jewel on your garments"?[102] Jewellery looks good only on a supple body[103]. The other one said, "the daughters of Israel" means the builders of Israel, the councils of Israel[104]. When he saw a group of fellows[105], he gave them to eat and drink. What does the verse mean by "who puts a golden jewel on your garments"? That he heard the reason for a practice from a Sage and praised him.

102 Is it not forbidden to any man, including the king, to give jewels to otherwise married women?
103 Having enough subcutaneous fat.
104 He bends the verse to avoid the appearance of questionable behavior, cf. Note 102.
105 Cf. Introduction to Tractate *Demay*.

נערה מאורסה פרק עשירי

(fol. 41c) **משנה א**: נַעֲרָה מְאוֹרָסָה אָבִיהָ וּבַעֲלָהּ מְפֵרִין נְדָרֶיהָ. הֵיפֵר הָאָב וְלֹא הֵיפֵר הַבַּעַל הֵיפֵר הַבַּעַל וְלֹא הֵיפֵר הָאָב אֵינוֹ מוּפָר וְאֵין צָרִיךְ לוֹמַר אִם קִייַם אֶחָד מֵהֶן.

Mishnah 1: Father and husband jointly dissolve the vows of a preliminarily married adolescent girl[1]. If the father dissolved but not the husband, or the husband but not the father, it is not dissolved; one does not have to mention whether one of them confirmed it.

1 An underage girl can be married off by her father. A woman becomes an adult in two steps. At age 12 (if she had developed two pubic hairs) she becomes an adult before the law but the father retains the right to marry her off and the right to her earnings for an additional 6 months, when she is called נַעֲרָה "adolescent girl". After these 6 months she becomes an adult, בּוֹגֶרֶת "ripe", is totally independent from her father, and has to marry on her own. The vow of a minor below age 11 is void. If she made a vow after age 11 (for a male after age 12), one has to investigate whether she understands the meaning and implications of a vow. If the investigation has a positive result, her vows are valid and, as far as vows are concerned, she has acquired the status of adolescent, even though in other legal aspects she remains a minor.

The chapter on vows states clearly that the father can dissolve his dependent daughter's vows (*Num.* 30:4-6). Similarly, the husband can dissolve the vows of his wife if she lives "in his house" (vv. 11-15). A preliminarily married girl (cf. *Peah* 6:2 Note 46; *Demay* 4:1, Note 19; *Terumot* 8:1, Note 9) remains under her father's jurisdiction until she is taken to her husband's house in the final ceremony. It is asserted that during her status as preliminarily married wife, the father can dissolve her vows since she is "in his house" and the husband is given special authority over her vows in vv. 7-9 which, therefore, are not duplicated in vv. 11-15.

The power of dissolution in any case is restricted to the day after the father or husband first was informed of the vow (vv. 6,9,13,15). But if one of them agreed to the vow within the allotted period, he can no longer object after that.

(41d line 31) **הלכה א**: נַעֲרָה מְאוֹרָסָה כול׳. כְּתִיב אִם הָיוֹ תִהְיֶה לְאִישׁ. מַה אֲנָן קַייָמִין. אִם בִּנְשׂוּאָה. כְּבָר כְּתִיב אִם בֵּית אִשָּׁהּ נָדָרָה. וְאִם בִּפְנוּיָה. כְּבָר כְּתִיב וְאִשָּׁה כִּי תִדֹּר נֶדֶר לַי׳. מַה תַּלְמוּד לוֹמַר וְאִם הָיוֹ תִהְיֶה לְאִישׁ וּנְדָרֶיהָ עָלֶיהָ. וְאֵי זוֹ זוֹ. זוֹ נַעֲרָה מְאוֹרָסָה שֶׁאָבִיהָ וּבַעֲלָהּ מְפֵירִין נְדָרֶיהָ. עַד כְּדוֹן נְדָרִים שֶׁנֶּדְרָה מִשֶּׁנִּתְאָרְסָה. נְדָרִים שֶׁנָּדְרָה עַד שֶׁלֹּא נִתְאָרְסָה. וּנְדָרֶיהָ עָלֶיהָ. לְרַבּוֹת אֶת הַנְּדָרִין שֶׁבָּא בְיָדָהּ מִבֵּית אָבִיהָ.

Halakhah 1: "An adolescent girl," etc. [2]It is written[3], "if she should be a man's". What are we speaking about? If a married one, it already is written[4] "if she vowed in her husband's house". If about an unmarried one, it already is written[5] "if she vows a vow to the Eternal". Why does the verse say[3], ""if she should be a man's with her vows on her"? That refers to the preliminarily married adolescent girl whose vows are dissolved by father and husband. So far for vows which she vowed after she was prelinimarily married. Vows which she vowed before she was prelinimarily married? "With her vows on her,[3]" to include the vows which come with her from her father's house.

2 A similar argument in the Babli, 67a/b. In both Talmudim, the argument is amoraic.

3 *Num.* 30:7. The masoretic text reads הָיוֹ.

4 *Num.* 30:11.

5 *Num.* 30:4.

(41d line 37) תַּנֵּי בְשֵׁם רִבִּי לְעָזָר. אִם הָיָה תִהְיֶה לְאִישׁ. בְּבוֹגֶרֶת אֲרוּסָה הַכָּתוּב מְדַבֵּר. חַבְרַיָּיא אָמְרֵי. יָאוּת אָמַר רִבִּי לְעָזָר. וְקַשְׁיָא עַל דְּרִבִּי לְעָזָר. מִכֵּיוָן שֶׁבָּגְרָה לֹא כְבָר יָצְאָת מֵרְשׁוּת אָבִיהָ. יְתוֹמָה שֶׁמֵּת אָבִיהָ מִי מֵיפֵר לָהּ. הַבַּעַל מֵיפֵר. וְקַשְׁיָא עַל רַבָּנִין. אִם עַד שֶׁלֹּא נִכְנְסָה לִרְשׁוּתוֹ הוּא מֵיפֵר לָהּ. נִכְנְסָה לִרְשׁוּתוֹ לֹא כָּל־שֶׁכֵּן. מַה מְקַיְּימִין רַבָּנִין וּנְדָרֶיהָ עָלֶיהָ. מָא אֲנָן קַיָּימִין. אִם בִּנְדָרִים שֶׁנָּדְרָה עַד שֶׁלֹּא נִתְאָרְסָה וְנִתְאָרְסָה. כְּבָר נִרְאָה לָאָב וְלַבַּעַל לְהָפֵר. אֶלָּא כִּי אֲנָן קַיָּימִין בְּנֶדֶר שֶׁנָּדְרָה עַד שֶׁלֹּא מֵת אָבִיהָ וּמֵת אָבִיהָ וְהִיא בוֹגֶרֶת. מְנָן לְרִבִּי לְעָזָר נַעֲרָה מְאוֹרָסָה אָבִיהָ וּבַעֲלָהּ מְפִירִין נְדָרֶיהָ. בֵּין אִישׁ לְאִשְׁתּוֹ. עַד כְּדוֹן בְּבַעַל. בֵּין אָב לְבִתּוֹ. מַה מְקַיְּימִין רַבָּנִין בֵּין אִישׁ לְאִשְׁתּוֹ. וְלֹא שְׁבֵּינָהּ לְבֵין אֲחֵרִים. בֵּין אָב לְבִתּוֹ. וְלֹא שְׁבֵּינָהּ לְבֵין אֲחֵרִים. וְלֵית לְרִבִּי לְעָזָר כֵּן. אִית לֵיהּ. כּוּלָּהּ מִתַּמָּן אִית לֵיהּ. בֵּין אִישׁ לְאִשְׁתּוֹ. וְלֹא מַה שֶּׁבֵּינָהּ לְבֵין אֲחֵרִים. בֵּין אָב לְבִתּוֹ. וְלֹא שְׁבֵּינָהּ לְבֵין אֲחֵרִים.

It was stated in the name of Rebbi Eleazar[6]: "If she should be a man's"[3], the verse speaks about a preliminarily married adult girl[7]. The colleagues say, Rebbi Eleazar says it correctly[8]. Is it not difficult for Rebbi Eleazar: Did she not leave her father's power the moment she became an adult[9]? Who may dissolve the vows of an orphan whose father had died[10]? The husband dissolves[11]. It is difficult for the rabbis: If he may dissolve before she entered his power, is it not obvious [that he may dissolve] after she entered[12]? How do the rabbis explain "with her vows on her"? What are we talking about? If about vows which she made before she was preliminarily married and she became preliminarily married, already the father and the husband had the power to dissolve[13]. But we must talk about a vow which she made before her father died, then the father died[14] and she became an adult. From where does Rebbi Eleazar obtain: "The father and the husband dissolve the vows of a preliminarily married adolescent girl.[15]" "Between a man and his wife.[16]"

That deals with the husband. The father? "Between a father and his daughter.¹⁶" How do the rabbis interpret "between a man and his wife"? Not what is between her and others. "Between a father and his daughter," not what is between her and others. Does Rebbi Eleazar not agree with this? He agrees; he understands everything from there: "Between a man and his wife", not what is between her and others¹⁷; "between a father and his daughter," not what is between her and others.

6 If the material in the first paragraph is Amoraic, R. Eleazar is the Amora, bar Pedat. If the argument is tannaïtic, he is the Tanna, ben Shamua. R. Eleazar's argument is paralleled in *Sifry Num.* 153 by R. Joshia, student of R. Ismael. The final argument in this paragraph is attributed to R. Ismael in the Babli, 68a.

7 At 12 years and 6 months (or 6 months after she developed two pubic hairs) she permanently leaves her father's *potestas*. He reads the verse as dealing with a case where there is no residual power of the father. But since vv. 11 ff. speak of the married woman, he must find a case of a preliminarily married woman free from her father.

8 His interpretation follows the wording of the verse more closely.

9 Vv. 7-8 give the husband the right to dissolve vows which preceded the marriage. But vv. 11 ff. restrict the right of the husband to vows made during the marriage (Mishnah 2). For the rabbis, the right to dissolve prior vows depends on the father's collaboration. But R. Eleazar denies any participation to the father; why should the power of the preliminarily married husband be greater than that of the fully married one?

10 If the father had arranged his daughter's preliminary marriage and then had died, the husband cannot dissolve his wife's prior vows (Mishnah 2) and, after the definitive marriage ceremony, he cannot dissolve prior vows. (The existence of undisclosed prior vows might be grounds for divorce.) An underage girl orphaned from her father can be married off by her mother and brothers, but that is only a rabbinic institution (cf. *Yebamot* 1:2, Note 118). The husband can dissolve her vows only after the definitive marriage or after she became an adult. The latter case is the one dealt with by R. Eleazar.

11 But only the vows made after

the preliminary marriage and only after she has reached adulthood.

12 Why are vv. 11 ff. needed after vv. 7-9? That is a rhetorical question since the two cases are not comparable. For the rabbis, the husband dissolves the vow of the preliminarily married minor only in conjunction with the father, but he also dissolves vows made before the marriage. Once the woman is emancipated from her father, either by completed marriage or by becoming of age, the husband dissolves alone but only vows made during the marriage.

13 If they do not exercise their powers, they get no second chance. If the girl became an adult between preliminary and definitive marriage, the father lost his right of dissolution and the husband lost it with him. If the father died between preliminary and definitive marriages, the husband alone cannot dissolve; therefore, he cannot dissolve her vow after the definitive marriage when he lives with her.

14 Before she was preliminarily married. Then the father never had any right concurrent with the husband; the husband is not hindered by the father's power.

15 Since he rejects the references given in the first paragraph.

16 *Num.* 30:17.

17 This is the topic of Chapter 11. The husband can only void vows that either involve the relations between husband and wife or "vows of deprivation" (v. 14); he can forbid his wife to mortify herself. As in Mishnah 11:13, if she had vowed not to sleep with any man, he can void his part but she remains forbidden if she should become a widow or a divorcee.

(41d line 50) וְאֵין צָרִיךְ לוֹמַר שֶׁיְּקַיְּים אֶחָד מֵהֶן. אִיתָא חֲמֵי. הֵיפֵר הָאָב אֵין מוּפָר. וְאַתְּ אֲמַר הָכֵין. לֹא עַל הָדָא אִתְאֲמָרַת אֶלָּא עַל הָדָא. הֵיפֵר הָאָב אֶת חֶלְקוֹ. לֹא הִסְפִּיק הַבַּעַל לְהָפֵר עַד שֶׁמֵּת. הָאָב מֵיפֵר חֶלְקוֹ שֶׁלַּבַּעַל. אָמַר רִבִּי נָתָן. זוֹ דִבְרֵי בֵית שַׁמַּי. אֲבָל דִּבְרֵי חֲכָמִים אֵין צוֹרֶךְ לְהָפֵר בְּשֶׁלֹּא הֵקַם. אֲבָל אִם הֵקַם אֵינוֹ יָכוֹל לְהָפֵר.

"One does not have to mention if one of them confirmed it." Come and see; if the father dissolved, it is not dissolved, and you say so[18]? Not on that it was said, but on the following: If the father dissolved his part but the husband did not have time to dissolve before he died, the father dissolves the husband's part[19]. Rebbi Nathan said, those are the words of the House of Shammai. But the statement of the Sages is that he does not need to dissolve[20] if [the husband] did not confirm it. But if [the husband] confirmed, [the father] cannot void[21].

18 Since the Mishnah stated that if only one of them dissolved, in the example given, the father, the vow is not dissolved. Why does one have to mention that it is not dissolved if one of them confirmed the vow, since confirmation implies non-dissolution!

19 While the husband cannot dissolve after the father's death (Mishnah 2), the father can dissolve alone after the husband's death (as long as the marriage is in the preliminary stage) since after the husband's death the underage daughter returns to the father's tutelage.

20 Since the husband's power has disappeared, the father's prior dissolution is sufficient.

The Babli (69a, 71a) and the Tosephta 6:3 read: "[the father] *cannot* dissolve". The Babli has a long discussion about the nature of the joint powers of dissolution. If the powers are parallel, then the dissolution by one of the parties has no influence on the other; the husband's death leaves half of the vow undissolved and undissolvable. But if the powers are joint ones, then the husband's death opens the way for the father to exercise his now unrestrained powers. There is no reason to think that the Yerushalmi makes a similar distinction.

21 Since the affirmation cannot be undone.

(41d line 55) אַתְּ אָמַר. הָאָב מֵיפֵר חֶלְקוֹ שֶׁלַּבַּעַל. בִּיקֵּשׁ לְהָקֵם אָמַר. מוּקָם לֵיךְ סְתָם. מוּקָם לֵיךְ סְתָם. מוּפָר לָךְ חֶלְקוֹ שֶׁלַּבַּעַל. פְּשִׁיטָא דָא מִילְתָא. לֹא הֵיפֵר הָאָב חֶלְקוֹ וְעָבְרָה עַל נִדְרָהּ. לוֹקָה. הֵיפֵר הָאָב וְלֹא הֵיפֵר הַבַּעַל מַהוּ שֶׁתִּלְקֶה. אוֹ מֵאַחַר שֶׁאִים יָמוּת הַבַּעַל מִתְרוֹקֶנֶת אֵצֶל הָאָב אֵינָהּ לוֹקָה. נִיחָא כְּמָאן דְּאָמַר. אֵין מִיתָה. בְּרַם כְּמָאן דְּאָמַר. יֵשׁ מִיתָה בַּהֲפָרָה. מִיתָה כַּהֲפָרָה הִיא. וְכָן מִכֵּיוָן שֶׁאֵינוֹ מֵיפֵר לָהּ וְעָבְרָה עַל נִדְרָהּ לוֹקָה. תַּנֵּי. הֵיפֵר הָאָב אֶת חֶלְקוֹ וְלֹא הִסְפִּיק הַבַּעַל עַד שֶׁמֵּת. הַבַּעַל הָאַחֲרוֹן מֵיפֵר לָהּ חֶלְקוֹ שֶׁלָּרִאשׁוֹן. אָמַר רִבִּי יוֹסֵי. מַתְנִיתָא אֲמָרָה כֵן. אָבִיהָ וּבַעֲלָהּ הָאַחֲרוֹן מְפִירִין נְדָרֶיהָ.

You say that the father dissolves the husband's part. If he wanted to confirm, he says, it is confirmed for you, without details, (it is confirmed for you, without details)[22]; the husband's part is dissolved for you[23]. The following is obvious: If the father did not dissolve his part and she violated her vow, she is whipped. If the father dissolved but the husband did not, would she be whipped[24]? Or since if the husband died and his part became void in favor of the father, would she not be whipped? This follows him who said, death does not force [dissolution][25]. But following him who said, death does force dissolution[26], and here since he did not dissolve for her and she violated her vow, she is whipped. It was stated: If the father dissolved his part but the husband died before he could dissolve[27], the last husband dissolves the part of the first one. Rebbi Yose said, a Mishnah says so: "Her father and her last husband dissolve her vows[28]".

22 It seems that this is a case of dittography, even though one could read it as: If the father confirmed without indicating what he confirmed, then the vow is legally confirmed without indication whose part was confirmed (since the confirmation by one party is absolute.)

23 In contrast, for the House of Shammai who hold that the father has to dissolve the late husband's part, the dissolution is invalid unless the father explicitly declares the husband's part dissolved.

24 Since the father may dissolve after the husband's death but the husband cannot dissolve after the father's death, it is clear that the father's power over his underage preliminarily married daugher is greater than the husband's. Is the father's power strong enough to eliminate the prohibition to violate one's vow contained in 30:3?

25 It seems that the word בַּהֲפָרָה is missing here; it was inserted in *editio princeps*.

The argument follows the Sages in the previous paragraph, who hold that the husband's death automatically voids the vow. For them, the power of the husband is secondary and the woman cannot be prosecuted.

26 The House of Shammai, who require the father explicitly to dissolve the late husband's part, imply that the hunsband's and the father's powers are equal and that partial dissolution is of no legal value.

27 And she was preliminarily married to another man on the same day (since the period of dissolution is at most 24 hours after the first person knew of the vow.). Tosephta 6:4; there the re-marriage is noted.

28 Mishnah 3.

(fol. 41c) **משנה ב**: מֵת הָאָב לֹא נִתְרוֹקְנָה רְשׁוּת לַבַּעַל. מֵת הַבַּעַל נִתְרוֹקְנָה רְשׁוּת לָאָב. בָּזֶה יִיפָּה כֹּחַ הָאָב מִכֹּחַ הַבַּעַל. בְּדָבָר אַחֵר יִיפָּה כֹּחַ הַבַּעַל מִכֹּחַ הָאָב. שֶׁהַבַּעַל מֵיפֵר בְּבֶגֶר וְהָאָב אֵינוֹ מֵיפֵר בְּבֶגֶר.

Mishnah 2: If the father died, his power is not voided in favor of the husband. If the husband died, his power is voided in favor of the father[19]. In this, He strengthened the father's power over the husband. In another matter, He strengthened the husband's power over the father since the husband dissolves in adulthood but the father does not dissolve in adulthood[1].

(41d line 63) **הלכה ב**: מֵת הָאָב לֹא נִתְרוֹקְנָה רְשׁוּת לַבַּעַל כול׳. הֲווֹן בָּעֵי מֵימַר. בְּשֶׁלֹא הֵיפֵר הָאָב חֶלְקוֹ וָמֵת וְלֹא נִתְרוֹקְנָה רְשׁוּת לַבַּעַל. נִישְׁמְעִינָהּ מִן הָדָא. דֶּרֶךְ תַּלְמִידֵי חֲכָמִים עַד שֶׁלֹּא הָיְתָה בִּתּוֹ יוֹצֵאת מֵאֶצְלוֹ אוֹמֵר לָהּ. כָּל־נְדָרִים שֶׁנָּדַרְתְּ בְּתוֹךְ בֵּיתִי הֲרֵי הֵן מוּפָרִין. הָדָא אֲמָרָה. אֲפִילוּ הֵיפֵר הָאָב חֶלְקוֹ וָמֵת לֹא נִתְרוֹקְנָה רְשׁוּת לַבַּעַל.

Halakhah 2: "If the father died, his power is not voided in favor of the husband," etc. They wanted to say that if the father had dissolved his part and died, his power is not voided in favor of the husband[29]. Let us hear from the following[30]: "The way of learned people is that, before his daughter left his house, he told her: 'Any vows which you had vowed in my house are dissolved'." This implies that if the father had dissolved his part and died, his power is not voided in favor of the husband.

29 If the girl is preliminarily married and the father dies after he had dissolved her vow but before the husband did, her vow cannot be dissolved.

30 Mishnah 4. The quote does not prove anything; the proof is from the second part of the Mishnah which requires the husband to dissolve all prior vows of his bride prior to her entering his house, i. e., as long as she still is only preliminarily married. After she enters his house, he can no longer dissolve prior vows. Since the final marriage ceremony emancipated the girl (older than three years and one day) from her father and the father's death does the same, it is concluded that the husband's power over a preliminarily married girl endures only as long as she is under her father's tutelage.

(41d line 68) מֵת הַבַּעַל נִתְרוֹקְנָה רְשׁוּת לָאָב. הָוון בָּעֵיי מֵימַר. בְּשֶׁהֵיפֵר הַבַּעַל אֶת חֶלְקוֹ. אֲבָל לֹא הֵיפֵר הַבַּעַל חֶלְקוֹ וָמֵת וְלֹא נִתְרוֹקְנָה רְשׁוּת לָאָב נִישְׁמְעִינָהּ מִן הָדָא. נָדְרָה וְהִיא אֲרוּסָה. נִתְגָּרְשָׁה בּוֹ בַיּוֹם. נִתְאָרְסָה בּוֹ בַיּוֹם. אֲפִילוּ לְמֵאָה. אָבִיהָ וּבַעֲלָהּ הָאַחֲרוֹן מֵיפֵירִין אֶת נְדָרֶיהָ. הָדָא אָמְרָה. אֲפִילוּ לֹא הֵיפֵר הַבַּעַל חֶלְקוֹ וָמֵת הַבַּעַל. נִתְרוֹקְנָה רְשׁוּת לָאָב.

"If the husband died, his power is voided in favor of the husband." They wanted to say, after the husband had dissolved his part. But if the husband had not dissolved his part when he died, the power is not voided in favor of the father. Let us hear from the following: "If she made a vow while being preliminarily married. If she was divorced on the same day, preliminarily married on the same day, even a hundred times, her father and her last husband dissolve her vows[31]." That means, even if the husband had not dissolved his part and died, his power is voided in favor of the father.

31 Mishnah 3. Since the last husband has to dissolve, it follows that the first did not. Nevertheless, the father can dissolve her vows after the first husband was eliminated by divorce (or death).

(41d line 73) מֵת הָאָב לֹא נִתְרוֹקְנָה רְשׁוּת לַבַּעַל. רִבִּי חַגַּיי בָּעֵי קוֹמֵי רִבִּי יוֹסֵה. עַד כְּדוֹן בִּנְדָרִים שֶׁנֶּדְרָה מִשֶּׁנִּתְאָרְסָה. נְדָרִים שֶׁנֶּדְרָה עַד שֶׁלֹּא תִתְאָרֵס מֵת הָאָב לֹא נִתְרוֹקְנָה רְשׁוּת לַבַּעַל. אָמַר לֵיהּ. וְכִי נְדָרִים שֶׁנֶּדְרָה עַד שֶׁלֹּא תִתְאָרֵס וְנִתְאָרְסָה לֹא כְּבָר נִרְאוּ לָאָב לַבַּעַל לְהָפֵר לָהּ. דְּתֵימַר. מֵת הָאָב לֹא נִתְרוֹקְנָה רְשׁוּת לַבַּעַל. הָדָא אֲמָרָה. אֲפִילוּ נֶדֶר שֶׁנֶּדְרָה מִשֶּׁנִּתְאָרְסָה. נֶדֶר עַד שֶׁלֹּא נִתְאָרְסָה. מֵת הָאָב נִתְרוֹקְנָה רְשׁוּת לַבַּעַל. אָמַר לֵיהּ. וְכִי נֶדֶר שֶׁנֶּדְרָה עַד שֶׁלֹּא נִתְאָרְסָה וְנִתְאָרְסָה לֹא כְּבָר נִרְאוּ לָאָב וְלַבַּעַל לְהָפֵר לָהּ. דְּתֵימַר. מֵת הַבַּעַל נִתְרוֹקְנָה רְשׁוּת לָאָב. הָדָא אֲמָרָה. אֲפִילוּ נֶדֶר שֶׁנֶּדְרָה מִשֶּׁנִּתְאָרְסָה מֵת הַבַּעַל נִתְרוֹקְנָה רְשׁוּת לָאָב.

"If the father died, his power is not voided in favor of the husband.³²" Rebbi Ḥaggai asked before Rebbi Yose. So far for vows she made after she was preliminarily married³³. Vows she made before she was preliminarily married; if the father died, was his power not voided in favor of the husband? He said to him, is it not true that vows she made before she was preliminarily married already could be dissolved by father and husband³⁴? Why do you have to say, if the father died, his power is not voided in favor of the husband? That means, even vows she made after she was preliminarily married. Vows she made before she was preliminarily married, if the father died, was his power voided in favor of the husband?³⁵ He said to him, is it not true that vows she made before she was preliminarily married already could be dissolved by father and husband? You say, "if the husband died, his power is voided in favor of the father"! That means, even vows she made after she was preliminarily married, if the husband died, his power is voided in favor of the father!

32 As R. M. Margalit points out, one would expect the quote to read: "If the husband died, his power is voided in favor of the husband."

33 Since it is a biblical decree that her vows can be voided only by the concurrent action of father and husband, we can understand that in the absence of the father, the husband has no authority. But the father was the only authority for vows preceding the preliminary marriage; why can we not say that at the father's death the husband inherits his powers?

34 Since the husband in conjunction with the father can void vows that precede the preliminary marriage, the requirement of joint action is permanent.

35 The argument is parallel to the preceding one, only this time to confirm that even for vows made after the preliminary marriage, the sole powers of dissolution belong to the father after the husband's death.

(42a line 8) שֶׁהַבַּעַל מֵיפֵר בְּבֶגֶר. מַתְנִיתָא דְּרִבִּי לָעֶזָר. דְּתַנֵּי בְּשֵׁם רִבִּי לָעֶזָר. אִם הָיֹה תִהְיֶה לְאִישׁ. בְּבוֹגֶרֶת אֲרוּסָה הַכָּתוּב מְדַבֵּר.

"Since the husband dissolves in adulthood." The Mishnah follows Rebbi Eleazar, since it was stated in the name of Rebbi Eleazar[6]: "If she should be a man's"[3], the verse speaks about a preliminarily married adult girl[7].

(fol. 41d) **משנה ג:** נָדְרָה וְהִיא אֲרוּסָה נִתְגָּרְשָׁה בּוֹ בַיּוֹם נִתְאָרְסָה בּוֹ בַיּוֹם אֲפִילוּ לְמֵאָה אָבִיהָ וּבַעֲלָהּ הָאַחֲרוֹן מְפֵרִין נְדָרֶיהָ. זֶה הַכְּלָל כָּל־שֶׁלֹּא יָצְאָת לִרְשׁוּת עַצְמָהּ שָׁעָה אַחַת אָבִיהָ וּבַעֲלָהּ הָאַחֲרוֹן מְפֵרִין נְדָרֶיהָ.

Mishnah 3: If she made a vow while preliminarily married, was divorced on the same day[36], preliminarily married on the same day, even to a hundred men[37], her father and her last husband dissolve her vows. That is the principle: as long as she did not leave her father's power for one moment[38], her father and her last husband dissolve her vows.

36 The day she told of her vow either to her husband or to her father.
37 Sequentially, each one after the previous one's divorce.
38 Either by definitive marriage or by becoming an adult.

(42a line 9) **הלכה ג**: נָדְרָה וְהִיא אֲרוּסָה כול'. אָמַר רִבִּי הִילָא. הָיָה תִהְיֶה. אֲפִילוּ מֵאָה הֲוָיוֹת אָבִיהָ וּבַעֲלָהּ הָאַחֲרוֹן מְפֵרִין נְדָרֶיהָ. אָמַר רִבִּי יוֹסֵי. מַתְנִיתָא אָמְרָה כֵן. אָבִיהָ וּבַעֲלָהּ הָאַחֲרוֹן מְפֵירִין נְדָרֶיהָ.

"If she made a vow while preliminarily married," etc. Rebbi Hila said, "being she will be"[39], even for a hundred beings, her father and her last husband dissolve her vows. Rebbi Yose said, a Mishnah says so: "Her father and her last husband dissolve her vows[28]".

39 *Num.* 30:7. "To be" applied to a woman means "to be married," *Deut.* 24:2.

(fol. 41d) **משנה ד**: דֶּרֶךְ תַּלְמִידֵי חֲכָמִים עַד שֶׁלֹּא הָיְתָה בִתּוֹ יוֹצְאָה מֵאֶצְלוֹ אוֹמֵר לָהּ. כָּל־נְדָרִים שֶׁנָּדַרְתְּ בְּתוֹךְ בֵּיתִי הֲרֵי הֵן מוּפָרִין. וְכֵן הַבַּעַל עַד שֶׁלֹּא תִיכָּנֵס לִרְשׁוּתוֹ אוֹמֵר לָהּ כָּל־נְדָרִים שֶׁנָּדַרְתְּ עַד שֶׁלֹּא תִיכָּנְסִי לִרְשׁוּתִי הֲרֵי הֵן מוּפָרִין. שֶׁמִּשֶּׁתִּיכָּנֵס לִרְשׁוּתוֹ אֵינוֹ יָכוֹל לְהָפֵר.

Mishnah 4: "The way of learned people is that, before his daughter left his house, he told her: 'Any vows which you had vowed in my house are dissolved'. Similarly, the husband tells her before she enters his domain[40]: 'Any vows which you had vowed before you enter my domain are dissolved,' for after she enters his domain he cannot dissolve[30].

משנה ה: בּוֹגֶרֶת וְשֶׁשָּׁהֲתָה שְׁנֵים עָשָׂר חֹדֶשׁ וְאַלְמָנָה שְׁלֹשִׁים יוֹם. רִבִּי אֱלִיעֶזֶר אוֹמֵר הוֹאִיל וּבַעֲלָהּ חַיָּיב בִּמְזוֹנוֹתֶיהָ יָפֵר וַחֲכָמִים אוֹמְרִים אֵין הַבַּעַל מֵיפֵר עַד שֶׁתִּיכָּנֵס לִרְשׁוּתוֹ.

Mishnah 5: An adult girl and one who had waited[41] twelve months and a widow 30 days[42], Rebbi Eliezer says, since her husband is responsible for her upkeep he may dissolve but the Sages say that the husband dissolves only after she enters his domain.

40 I. e., before the final marriage ceremony.

41 A different text of the Babylonian Mishnah is amended in the Halakhah there to the Yerushalmi text.

42 Mishnah *Ketubot 5:2* states that a girl who never was married before has 12 months after the preliminary marriage to prepare her trousseau and a widow 30 days. An adult girl, for whom the father no longer has responsibility, is supposed to have a trousseau by the twelfth month of her adulthood and can marry immediately (cf. the commentary ascribed to Rashi to the Babli, 73b, and Halakhah *Ketubot* 5:3). If the groom does not bring her into his house by the appointed time (by means of the final marriage ceremony), he nevertheless becomes resposible for her upkeep as if he were completely married.

(42a line 12) **הלכה ה**: בּוֹגֶרֶת וְשֶׁשָּׁהֲתָה שָׁנִים עָשָׂר חֹדֶשׁ כול׳. מִיסְבַּר סָבַר רִבִּי אֱלִיעֶזֶר דְּבִמְזוֹנוֹת הַדָּבָר תָּלוּי. קִידֵּשׁ אִשָּׁה עַל מְנָת לָזוּן הַבַּעַל מֵיפֵר לָהּ. נָשָׂא אִשָּׁה עַל מְנָת לָזוּן הָאָב מֵיפֵר לָהּ. דִּבְרֵי חֲכָמִים. רִבִּי יַעֲקֹב בַּר אָחָא בְּשֵׁם רִבִּי יוֹחָנָן. לְעוֹלָם אֵין הַבַּעַל מֵיפֵר עַד שֶׁתִּיכָּנֵס לִרְשׁוּתוֹ.

Halakhah 5: "An adult girl and one who had waited twelve months," etc. Rebbi Eliezer holds that the matter depends on the support. If he preliminarily married a woman on condition to support her[43], the husband dissolves for her[44]. If he completely married a woman on condition that he[45] support her, the father dissolves for her[46]. The words of the Sages? Rebbi Jacob bar Aḥa in the name of Rebbi Joḥanan: The husband never dissolves[47] before she enters his domain.

43 He agrees to support his wife from the time of the preliminary marriage.

44 Without the father's

concurrence.

45 The father.

46 Without the husband's concurrence. This paragraph has been emended by the standard commentaries to mean the opposite it says.

47 Alone.

משנה ו: שׁוֹמֶרֶת יָבָם בֵּין לְיָבָם אֶחָד בֵּין לִשְׁנֵי יְבָמִים רִבִּי אֱלִיעֶזֶר אוֹמֵר יָפֵר. רִבִּי יְהוֹשֻׁעַ אוֹמֵר לְאֶחָד אֲבָל לֹא לִשְׁנָיִם. רִבִּי עֲקִיבָה אוֹמֵר לֹא לְאֶחָד וְלֹא לִשְׁנָיִם. (fol. 41d)

Mishnah 6: If a woman was waiting for her levir[48], whether it be one or two, Rebbi Eliezer says, he shall dissolve[49]. Rebbi Joshua says, for one but not for two[50]. Rebbi Aqiba says, neither for one nor for two[51].

48 She is a widow whose husband died without issue; she waits to be married to her husband's brother; cf. *Yebamot* 4:3, Note 84. The Mishnah must speak about an underage girl who became a widow after a preliminary marriage only, and who still is under her father's jurisdiction. The question is only whether the levir may dissolve her vows in conjuction with the father, since for a woman who is emancipated from her father, either by coming of age or by final marriage, the husband can dissolve only vows made after the final marriage act.

49 All the ceremonies involved in a levirate marriage are rabbinical; by biblical law the childless sister-in-law is married only by actual intercourse (*Yebamot* 2:12, Note 12; 6:1). The rabbinic equivalent of the preliminary marriage is called "bespeaking" (*Yebamot* 2:1, Note 6). The legal power of "bespeaking" is a matter of controversy but it is certain that adultery with a "bespoken" woman is not a capital crime. While under the obligation to marry a levir, the widow by biblical law is unable to contract a valid marriage with any other man (*Yebamot* 1:1, Note 94.) For R. Eliezer, the latter fact gives any levir the status of a husband in matters of vows.

50 R. Joshua gives the right of the preliminary husband only to a single levir, even after "bespeaking". Cf.

Babli, 74a.	following Mishnah.
51 His position is explained in the	

מִשְׁנָה ז: אָמַר רִבִּי אֱלִיעֶזֶר. מָה אִם אִשָּׁה שֶׁקְּנָה הוּא לְעַצְמוֹ הֲרֵי הוּא מֵיפֵר נְדָרֶיהָ אִשָּׁה שֶׁקְּנוּ לוֹ מִן שָׁמַיִם אֵינוֹ דִין שֶׁיָּפֵר נְדָרֶיהָ. אָמַר לוֹ רִבִּי עֲקִיבָה לֹא. אִם אָמַרְתָּ בְּאִשָּׁה שֶׁקְּנָה הוּא לְעַצְמוֹ שֶׁאֵין לָאֲחֵרִים רְשׁוּת בָּהּ תֹּאמַר בְּאִשָּׁה שֶׁקְּנוּ לוֹ מִן שָׁמַיִם שֶׁיֵּשׁ לָאֲחֵרִים רְשׁוּת בָּהּ. אָמַר לוֹ רִבִּי יְהוֹשֻׁעַ. עֲקִיבָה דְּבָרֶיךָ בִּשְׁנֵי יְבָמִין מָה אַתָּה מֵשִׁיב עַל יָבָם אֶחָד. אָמַר לוֹ אֵין הַיְבָמָה גְּמוּרָה לְאִישָׁהּ כְּשֵׁם שֶׁהָאֲרוּסָה גְּמוּרָה לְבַעֲלָהּ.

Mishnah 7: Rebbi Eliezer said, if he can dissolve vows for a wife which he himself acquired, so much more that he should be able to dissolve for a wife which Heaven acquired for him. Rebbi Aqiba answered him: No. What you say is about a wife which he himself acquired, where nobody else has any authority over her; what can you say about the wife which Heaven acquired for him, where others[52] have authority over her? Rebbi Joshua said to him, Aqiba, your words apply to two levirs. What can you reply about one levir? He said to him, the sister-in-law does not belong completely to her man as the wife belongs completely to her husband[53].

52 The other brothers of the deceased husband.

53 The childless widow is unable to contract a marriage except with the levir; she does not commit adultery if she sleeps with another man before she is married by the levir. But a married woman who sleeps with another man commits a capital crime. For R. Aqiba, marriage is only a relationship whose violation is a capital crime.

מִשְׁנָה ח: הָאוֹמֵר לְאִשְׁתּוֹ כָּל־נְדָרִים שֶׁתִּדּוֹרִי מִכָּאן עַד שֶׁאָבֹא מִמָּקוֹם פְּלוֹנִי הֲרֵי הֵן קַיָּמִין לֹא אָמַר כְּלוּם. הֲרֵי הֵן מוּפָרִין רִבִּי אֱלִיעֶזֶר אוֹמֵר מוּפָר וַחֲכָמִים אוֹמְרִים אֵינוֹ מוּפָר.

Mishnah 8: If somebody says to his wife, all vows that you might vow from now until I shall return from place X shall be confirmed[54], he did not say anything; [if he says] they shall be dissolved, Rebbi Eliezer says, they are dissolved, but the Sages say, they are not dissolved.

משנה ט: אָמַר רִבִּי אֶלְעָזָר. אִם הֵיפֵר נְדָרִים שֶׁבָּאוּ לִכְלָל אָסוּר לֹא יָפֵר נְדָרִים שֶׁלֹּא בָאוּ לִכְלָל אִיאָסוּר. אָמְרוּ לוֹ הֲרֵי הוּא אוֹמֵר אִישָׁהּ יְקִימֶנּוּ וְאִישָׁהּ יְפֵרֶינּוּ. אֶת שֶׁבָּא לִכְלָל הָקֵם בָּא לִכְלָל הֵפֵר. לֹא בָא לִכְלָל הָקֵם לֹא בָא לִכְלָל הֵפֵר.

Mishnah 9: Rebbi Eliezer said, if he can dissolve vows that came under the category of prohibition[55], should he not be able to dissolve vows that did not yet come under the category of prohibition[56]? They said to him, it says[57] 'her husband may confirm them and her husband may dissolve them". What can be confirmed can be dissolved; what cannot be confirmed cannot be dissolved.

54   In his absence. Everybody agrees that an as yet nonexistent vow cannot be confirmed.

55   Vows actually made by which the wife imposes a legally enforceable prohibition on herself.

56   Vows not yet made.

57   *Num.* 30:14. The verse treats confirmation and voiding as parallels.

(42a line 16) **הלכה ו**: שׁוֹמֶרֶת יָבָם כול׳. עַל דַּעְתֵּיהּ דְּרִבִּי עֲקִיבָה מֵיפֵר לָהּ. וְהֵן דָּמַר רִבִּי אַבָּהוּ בְּשֵׁם רִבִּי יוֹחָנָן. אֲפִילוּ קִידּוּשֵׁי מֵאָה תּוֹפְשִׂין בָּהּ. מִי מֵיפֵר לָהּ. וַיִי דָּמַר רִבִּי יַעֲקֹב בְּשֵׁם רִבִּי יוֹחָנָן. מִייַעֲדָהּ לִבְנוֹ הַקָּטָן. מִי מֵיפֵר לָהּ. וַיִי דָּמַר רִבִּי יַעֲקֹב בַּר אָחָא בְּשֵׁם רִבִּי יוֹחָנָן וְרִבִּי הִילָא בְּשֵׁם רִבִּי לָעְזָר. אֲפִילוּ אָשָׁם תָּלוּי אֵין לָהּ. מִי מֵיפֵר לָהּ.

Halakhah 6: "If a woman was waiting for her levir," etc. Following Rebbi Aqiba[58], who can dissolve? For example, what Rebbi Abbahu said in the name of Rebbi Joḥanan, even a hundred *qiddušin* are valid for her[59], who dissolves? And what Rebbi Jacob[60] said in the name of Rebbi Joḥanan, he can allot her to his underage son[61], who dissolves? And what Rebbi Jacob bar Aḥa sind in the name of Rebbi Joḥanan, she does not even need a reparation offering for a possible sin[62], who dissolves?

58 For whom the right of dissolution depends on his relationship with the woman defining adultery, can the husband dissolve in questionable cases? The answers, which are not given, are obviously "no".

59 Babli *Qidduŝin* 60a; Yerushalmi *Yebamot* 3:4 (Notes 102-104), 5:1 (Note 35); *Qidduŝin* 3:1, (63c l. 71). A man gives something of value to a woman to serve as *qidduŝin* money for a preliminary marriage in a month's time. If other men also give her deferred *qidduŝin*, they all might end up preliminarily married to her and none of them can marry her. In that case, she is not bound to any one by marriage in the sense of R. Aqiba.

60 In the source of this statement, *Qidduŝin* 1:2, 59c l. 8, one reads: "R. Joḥanan said." Since there is no R. Jacob without father's name among the students of R. Joḥanan (there are R. Jacob bar Aḥa and R. Jacob bar Idi), the name has to be considered a scribal error.

61 This refers to the Hebrew slave girl (*Ex.* 21:7-11), about a situation intrinsically connected to the Jubilee year which became void with the exile of the Ten Tribes. The verse gives the master the right to marry the girl by considering the price he paid for her as *qidduŝin* money, or to give her to his son as wife without additional expenditure. If the son is a minor, she becomes his wife by biblical decree, But the wife of a minor cannot be prosecuted for adultery [*Sifra Qedoŝim Pereq* 9(11)]. Can the underage husband, biblically married to his underage wife, dissolve her vows?

62 The wife of a deaf-mute or of an insane person (at the time of marriage) is not married by biblical standards and cannot commit adultery. *Yebamot*, Babli 113a, Yerushalmi 14:1 Note 7. (The rules of reparation offerings for possible sins are in *Lev.* 5:17-19).

(42a line 21) **הלכה ז**: אָמַר רִבִּי לִיעֶזֶר כּוֹל'. אָמַר רִבִּי לִיעֶזֶר. וּמַה אִם אִשָּׁה שֶׁלֹּא הָיָה לוֹ בָהּ רְשׁוּת עַד שֶׁלֹּא נִכְנְסָה לִרְשׁוּתוֹ מִשֶּׁנִּכְנְסָה לִרְשׁוּתוֹ הוּגְמְרָה לִי.

אִשָּׁה שֶׁהָיָה לִי בָּהּ רְשׁוּת עַד שֶׁלֹּא נִכְנְסָה לִרְשׁוּתִי. מִשֶּׁנִּכְנְסָה לִרְשׁוּתִי אֵינוֹ דִין שֶׁתִּיגָּמֵר לִי. אָמַר לוֹ רִבִּי עֲקִיבָה. לֹא. אִם אָמַרְתָּ בְּאִשָּׁה שֶׁלֹּא הָיָה לָךְ בָּהּ רְשׁוּת עַד שֶׁלֹּא נִכְנְסָה לִרְשׁוּתָךְ. מִשֶּׁנִּכְנְסָה לִרְשׁוּתָךְ הוּגְמְרָה לָךְ. שֶׁכְּשֵׁם שֶׁלֹּא הָיָה לָךְ בָּהּ חֵלֶק כָּךְ לֹא הָיָה לָהּ לַאֲחֵרִים בָּהּ עִמְּךָ חֵלֶק. תֹּאמַר בְּאִשָּׁה שֶׁהָיָה לָךְ בָּהּ רְשׁוּת עַד שֶׁלֹּא נִכְנְסָה לִרְשׁוּתָךְ. מִשֶּׁנִּכְנְסָה לִרְשׁוּתָךְ הוּגְמְרָה לָךְ. שֶׁכְּשֵׁם שֶׁהָיָה לָךְ בָּהּ חֵלֶק כָּךְ הָיָה לַאֲחֵרִים עִמָּךְ בָּהּ חֵלֶק. אָמַר לוֹ רִבִּי יְהוֹשֻׁעַ. עֲקִיבָה. דְּבָרֶיךָ בִּשְׁנֵי יְבָמִין. מָה אַתָּה מֵשִׁיב עַל יָבָם אֶחָד. אָמַר לוֹ. כְּשֵׁם שֶׁלֹּא חָלַקְתָּ לָנוּ בֵּין שׁוֹמֶרֶת יָבָם אֶחָד לִשְׁנֵי יְבָמִין. בֵּין שֶׁעָשָׂה בָהּ מַאֲמָר בֵּין שֶׁלֹּא עָשָׂה בָהּ מַאֲמָר. יָכוֹל בִּנְדָרִים וּבִשְׁבוּעוֹת כֵּן. אָמַר לוֹ. אֲבָל. אָמַר לוֹ. אִילּוּ הָיִיתָ בִּימֵי רִבִּי לָעָזָר בֶּן עֲרָךְ אָמַר. אֵין מַאֲמָר קוֹנֶה קִנְיָן גָּמוּר. מוֹדֶה שֶׁאֵינוֹ מֵיפֵר לָהּ עַד שֶׁתִּיכָּנֵס לִרְשׁוּתוֹ.

Halakhah 7: "Rebbi Eliezer said," etc. [63]Rebbi Eliezer said, since a woman on whom I had no claim before she entered into my domain, becomes absolutely mine after she entered my domain, is it not logical that a woman on whom I had some claim before she entered my domain, shall become absolutely mine when she enters my domain[64]? Rebbi Aqiba told him, no. If you speak about a woman on whom you had no claim before she entered into your domain, but after she entered your domain she became absolutely yours, then just as you had no part in her so no other man had any part in her. What can you conclude about a woman on whom you had some claim before she entered your domain, and after she entered your domain she became absolutely yours, but just as you had some rights to her so others had the same rights to her[65]! Rebbi Joshua told him, Aqiba, your argument holds for two levirs. What do you respond in the case of a single levir? He said to him, just as you make no difference in the rules of one waiting for one levir or for two levirs, whether he 'bespoke' her or did not 'bespeak' her, can it not be the same for vows and oaths? He said to him, that is true[66]. He said to him, if you had lived in the times of Rebbi Eleazar ben Arakh, he would have said that 'bespeaking' does not acquire completely since he would agree that he cannot dissolve until she enters his domain[63].

63 Tosephta 6:5, Babli 74b.

64 A man has no relation to an unrelated woman. After the preliminary marriage he has the exclusive right to her and dissolves her vows (together with the father). Since he has potential rights to his childless sister-in-law, should he not have the right to dissolve her vows (together with the father) after "bespeaking"?

65 The other brothers.

66 The text in the Tosephta is different: אָמַר לוֹ. הֲבָל אִילּוּ הָיִיתָ בִּימֵי רִבִּי לָעָזָר בֶּן עֲרָךְ וְהָשֵׁבְתָ תְשׁוּבָה זוֹ. "He said to him, I am sorry that you did not live in the time of R. Eleazar ben Arakh and give him this reply" (maybe he would have changed his mind).

67 R. Eleazar ben Arakh holds that "bespeaking" has all the powers of preliminary marriage (*Yebamot* 2:1, Notes 19-20). R. Joshua notes that after R. Aqiba's argument, R. Eleazar ben Arakh could not hold that the levir has the right to dissolve vows of his underage betrothed; therefore, the parallel with *qiddušin* is necessarily incomplete. R. Joshua is seen to accept R. Aqiba's argument.

(42a line 34) הֵשִׁיב עַל דִּבְרֵי רִבִּי לִיעֶזֶר. וַהֲרֵי מִקְוֶה יוֹכִיחַ. שֶׁמַּעֲלֶה אֶת הַטְּמֵאִין מִטּוּמְאָתָן וְאֵינוֹ מַצִּיל אֶת הַטְּהוֹרִין. חָזַר רִבִּי לִיעֶזֶר וְדָנָן דִּין אַחֵר. מָה אִם בְּמָקוֹם שֶׁאֵינוֹ מֵיפֵר נִדְרֵי עַצְמוֹ עַד שֶׁלֹּא יִדּוֹר הֲרֵי הוּא מֵיפֵר נִדְרֵי אִשְׁתּוֹ עַד שֶׁלֹּא תִדּוֹר. מָקוֹם שֶׁהוּא מֵיפֵר נִדְרֵי עַצְמוֹ מִשֶּׁיִּדּוֹר אֵינוֹ דִין שֶׁיָּפֵר נִדְרֵי אִשְׁתּוֹ עַד שֶׁלֹּא תִדּוֹר. לֹא. מַה לוֹ אֵינוֹ מֵיפֵר נִדְרֵי עַצְמוֹ עַד שֶׁלֹּא יִדּוֹר. שֶׁכֵּן אִם רָצָה לְהָקֵם מוּקָם. יָפֵר נִדְרֵי אִשְׁתּוֹ מִשֶּׁתִּדּוֹר. שֶׁכֵּן אִם רָצָה לְהָקֵם אֵינוֹ מוּקָם. וְאוֹמֵר אִישָׁהּ יְקִימֶנּוּ וְאִישָׁהּ יְפֵרֶנּוּ. אֶת שֶׁבָּא לִכְלָל הָקֵם בָּא לִכְלָל הָפֵר. וְאֶת שֶׁלֹּא בָא לִכְלָל הָקֵם לֹא בָא לִכְלָל הָפֵר.

[68]"He[69] answered to the words of Rebbi Eliezer: Let the *miqweh*[70] prove it! It frees the impure from their impurities but it cannot save pure ones. Rebbi Eliezer argued another track: Since in a situation where he

cannot dissolve his own vows before he made them, he dissolves his wife's vows before she made them, in a situation where he can dissolve his own vows after he made them, would it not be logical that he could dissolve his wife's vows before she made them?[71] No! Why can he not dissolve his own vows before he made them[72]? For if he wants to confirm them, he confirms them. Could he dissolve his wife's vows after she made them, when if he wanted to confirm them, he could not confirm them?[73]" [74]"But it says[57], 'her husband may confirm them and her husband may dissolve them'. What can be confirmed can be dissolved,; what cannot be confirmed cannot be dissolved."

68   This refers to Mishnaiot 8,9. Tosephta 6:5; Babli 75b.

69   In the parallel sources: They. This is no longer part of R. Aqiba's argument, but belongs to the anonymous Sages.

70   The ritual bath cleanses from most impurities. But a pure person cannot immerse himself to become immune to future impurities.

71   It is difficult to make sense of this text. In Tosephta and Babli one reads: מָה אִם בְּמָקוֹם שֶׁאֵינוֹ מֵפֵר נִדְרֵי עַצְמוֹ מִשֶּׁנָּדַר הֲרֵי הוּא מֵיפֵר נִדְרֵי עַצְמוֹ עַד שֶׁלֹּא יִדּוֹר. מָקוֹם שֶׁמֵּפֵר נִדְרֵי אִשְׁתּוֹ מִשֶּׁנָּדְרָה אֵינוֹ דִין שֶׁיָּפֵר נִדְרֵי אִשְׁתּוֹ עַד שֶׁלֹּא תִדּוֹר. "Since he cannot dissolve his own vows after he vowed (for only a Sage can do that), but he can dissolve his own vows before he vows (by a declaration that all his future vows are null and void), then since he can dissolve his wife's vows after she vowed it is only logical that he should be able to dissolve his wife's vows before she vowed." It seems that the Yerushalmi text should follow similar lines.

72   This text contradicts the next sentence. The Tosephta reads אָמְרוּ לוֹ וּמָה מֵיפֵר נִדְרֵי עַצְמוֹ עַד שֶׁלֹּא יִדּוֹר. "They said to him, *why is it that* he can dissolve his own vows before he made them?"

73   The Tosephta reads יָפֵר נִדְרֵי אִשְׁתּוֹ עַד שֶׁלֹּא תִדּוֹר. שֶׁכֵּן אִם רָצָה לְהָקֵם אֵינוֹ מוּקָם. "Could he dissolve his wife's vows *before she made them* when if he wanted to confirm them, he could not confirm them?" (As R. Eliezer agrees in the Mishnah.)

74   Tosephta 6:6; Babli 76b.

(fol. 42b) **משנה י**: הֵפֵר נְדָרִים כָּל־הַיּוֹם. שֶׁיֵּשׁ בַּדָּבָר לְהָקֵל וּלְהַחֲמִיר. כֵּיצַד. נָדְרָה בְלֵילֵי שַׁבָּת מֵיפֵר בְּלֵילֵי שַׁבָּת וּבְיוֹם הַשַׁבָּת עַד שֶׁתֶּחְשָׁךְ. נָדְרָה עִם חֲשֵׁיכָה מֵיפֵר עַד שֶׁלֹּא תֶחְשַׁךְ שֶׁאִם לֹא הֵפֵר מִשֶּׁחֲשֵׁיכָה אֵינוֹ יָכוֹל לְהָפֵר.

The dissolution of vows may take place the entire day[75]; this can imply a lenient or a stringent implementation. How is that? If she made the vow Friday night[76], he may dissolve during the night and the next day until [the next] nightfall. If she made the vow shortly before nightfall, he dissolves until it becomes dark; for after dark he cannot dissolve.

75 The day of Creation, the night followed by daylight.

76 It could be any other night; the Mishnah informs us that dissolution of vows is permitted on the Sabbath.

(42a line 43) **הלכה י**: הֵפֵר נְדָרִים כָּל־הַיּוֹם כול'. תַּנֵּי רִבִּי יוֹסֵי בֵּירִיבִּי יוּדָה וְרִבִּי לֶעְזָר בֵּירִבִּי שִׁמְעוֹן אוֹמְרִים. הֵפֵר נְדָרִים מֵעֵת לָעֵת. מַה טַעֲמוֹן דְּרַבָּנִין. מִיּוֹם אֶל יוֹם. מַה טַעֲמֵיהּ דְּרִבִּי יוֹסֵי בֵּירִיבִּי יוּדָה. בְּיוֹם שָׁמְעוֹ. מָה מְקַיְימִין רַבָּנִין טַעֲמֵיהּ דְּרִבִּי יוֹסֵי בֵּירִיבִּי יוּדָה בְּיוֹם שָׁמְעוֹ. תִּיפָּתָּר שֶׁנָּדְרָה בִּתְחִילַת הַלַּיְלָה. מַה מְקַיֵּים רִבִּי יוֹסֵי בֵּירִיבִּי יוּדָה טַעֲמוֹן דְּרַבָּנָן מִיּוֹם אֶל יוֹם. תִּיפָּתָּר שֶׁנָּדְרָה בִּתְחִילַת לֵילֵי שַׁבָּת וְנִשְׁתַּתֵּק וְחָזַר לְדִיבּוּרוֹ. עַל דַּעְתֵּיהּ דְּרִבִּי יוֹסֵי בֵּירִיבִּי יוּדָה נוֹתְנִין לוֹ כֹּד שָׁעוֹת. עַל דַּעְתּוֹן דְּרַבָּנִין אֵין לוֹ אֶלָּא אוֹתוֹ הַיּוֹם בִּלְבַד. נִשְׁתַּתֵּק וְחָזַר לְדִיבּוּרוֹ. עַל דַּעְתֵּיהּ דְּרִבִּי יוֹסֵי בֵּירִיבִּי יוּדָה מְצָרְפִין לוֹ כֹּד שָׁעוֹת. עַל דַּעְתּוֹן דְּרַבָּנִין לְעוֹלָם הוּא מֵיפֵר וְהוֹלֵךְ עַד שֶׁיַּחֲזוֹר לְדִיבּוּרוֹ. לִפְנֵי שְׁקִיעַת הַחַמָּה שָׁעָה אַחַת. עוֹד אֵינוֹ יָכוֹל לְהָפֵר.

Halakhah 10: "The dissolution of vows may take place the entire day," etc. It was stated[77]: "Rebbi Yose ben Rebbi Jehudah and Rebbi Eleazar ben Rebbi Simeon say[78], the dissolution of vows may take place from time to time[79]." What is the reason of the rabbis? "From day to day[80]." What is the reason of Rebbi Yose ben Rebbi Jehudah? "On the day of his hearing[81]." How do the rabbis explain Rebbi Yose ben Rebbi Jehudah's reason, "on the day of his hearing"? Explain it that she made the vow on the start of the night[82]. How does Rebbi Yose ben Rebbi Jehudah explain the rabbis' reason, "from day to day"? Explain it that she made the vow at the start of Friday night[83], he became paralyzed[84], and then his power of speech returned[85]. In the opinion of Rebbi Yose ben Rebbi Jehudah one gives him 24 hours. In the opinion of the rabbis he has only that day[86]. If he became paralyzed, and later[87] his power of speech returned, in the opinion of Rebbi Yose ben Rebbi Jehudah one adds up to a total of 24 hours[88]. In the opinion of the rabbis he always can dissolve when his speech returns. But if it happened one hour[89] before sundown, he can no longer dissolve.

77 Babli 76b, 77a, *Šabbat* 157a.
78 In *Sifry Num.* 156 this is attributed to R. Simeon himself.
79 24 hours from the moment the husband is informed.
80 *Num.* 30:15.
81 *Num.* 30:6,8,13. In the Babli, 76b, and *Sifry Num.* 156, the arguments are switched: "On the *day* of his hearing" implies that at nightfall the time has run out, "from day to day" implies 24 hours.

It is not necessary to amend the Yerushalmi since Targum Pseudo-Jonathan and Rashi explain *Num.* 30:15 following the rabbis: "If her husband remains silent from the day he was informed to another day", i. e., the next night. R. Yose ben R. Jehudah will explain that "the day of his hearing" starts only with his hearing.

82 In that case, the husband has 24 hours even according to the rabbis.
83 The mention of the *start* of Friday night is problematic. It is a correction by the scribe himself and probably an insertion at the wrong place.
84 After he was informed of the vow.
85 Within 24 hours after he heard from his wife.
86 Until nightfall on Saturday, less than 24 hours.
87 Not on the same day.
88 The paralysis does not stop the clock. In this case, R. Yose ben R. Jehudah is more restrictive than the rabbis.
89 "One hour" means "a short time".

If the husband was informed of the vow shortly before sundown and before he could dissolve the vow was paralyzed at sundown, for the rabbis he had his day and when he regains his speech cannot undo the vow.

(42a line 53) מוּפָר לָךְ בַּמִּנְחָה. מוּפָר לְעוֹלָם. מוּקָם לָךְ בַּמִּנְחָה. מוּקָם לְעוֹלָם. מוּפָר לָךְ עַד הַמִּנְחָה. כְּאוֹמֵר. מוּפָר לֵיךְ מִן הַמִּנְחָה וּלְמַעֲלָה.

"It shall be dissolved at the time of the afternoon prayer," it is permanently dissolved[90]. "It shall be confirmed at the time of the afternoon prayer," it is permanently confirmed. "It shall be dissolved until the time of the afternoon prayer," it is as if he said, "it shall be dissolved starting with the time of the afternoon prayer."

90 There can be no partial confirmation or dissolution. Since he did not mention confirmation, one does not take his word to mean that the vow shall be valid until the time of the afternoon prayer; it is dissolved immediately and permanently. The same holds in the following two cases.

(42a line 55) תַּמָּן תַּנִּינָן. מְפֵירִין נְדָרִים בַּשַּׁבָּת. תַּנֵּי. בֵּין נְדָרִים שֶׁהֵן לְצוֹרֶךְ שַׁבָּת בֵּין נְדָרִים שֶׁאֵין לְצוֹרֶךְ שַׁבָּת לֹא. וְנִשְׁאָלִין נְדָרִים שֶׁהֵן לְצוֹרֶךְ שַׁבָּת. הָא שֶׁלֹּא לְצוֹרֶךְ שַׁבָּת. זָקֵן שֶׁהוּא יָכוֹל לְהָפֵר לְמָחָר. וּכְרִבִּי יוֹסֵי בֵּירִבִּי יוּדָה וּכְרִבִּי רִבִּי לְעָזָר בֵּירִבִּי שִׁמְעוֹן דְּאָמְרֵי. הֵפֵר נְדָרִים מֵעֵת לָעֵת. אֲפִילוּ נְדָרִים שֶׁהֵן לְצוֹרֶךְ שַׁבָּת לֹא יָפֵר. תִּיפְתָּר דִּבְרֵי הַכֹּל שֶׁנְּדָרָהּ בִּתְחִילַת לֵילֵי שַׁבָּת.

There[91], we have stated: "One dissolves vows on the Sabbath." It was stated[92]: Both vows that intrude on the Sabbath and vows that do not intrude on the Sabbath. "And one asks about vows that intrude on the Sabbath[91]," therefore not if there is no need for the Sabbath. The Elder can dissolve the next day[93]. Then for Rebbi Yose ben Rebbi Jehudah and Rebbi Eleazar ben Rebbi Simeon who say that the dissolution of vows is from time to time, he should not dissolve even vows that intrude on the Sabbath[94]! Explain it according to everybody, if she made the vow at the start of Friday night.

91 Mishnah *Šabbat* 24:5.
92 In the Babli, 77a, this is the result of a discussion of late Amoraïm.
93 But the husband who was informed on the Sabbath must dissolve on the Sabbath or lose his right to dissolution.
94 This argument is also made in the Babli, 77a.

(42a line 60) רְבִּי אַבָּהוּ בְשֵׁם רְבִּי יוֹחָנָן. הַבַּעַל שֶׁאָמַר. אֵין כָּאן נֶדֶר אֵין כָּאן שְׁבוּעָה. לֹא אָמַר כְּלוּם. וְזָקֵן שֶׁאָמַר. מוּפָּר לֵיךְ בָּטֵל לֵיךְ. לֹא אָמַר כְּלוּם. אֶלָּא זֶה כְּהִילְכָתוֹ וְזֶה כְּהִילְכָתוֹ. הַבַּעַל אֹמֵר. מוּפָּר לֵיךְ בָּטֵל לֵיךְ. וְהַזָּקֵן אוֹמֵר. אֵין כָּאן נֶדֶר אֵין כָּאן שְׁבוּעָה.

[95]Rebbi Abbahu in the name of Rebbi Johanan: The husband who said "there is no vow, there is no oath," did not say anything. Also the Elder who said "it is dissolved for you, it is voided for you," did not say anything. But everybody has to follow his own rules. The husband says "it is dissolved for you, it is voided for you," and the Elder says, "there is no vow, there is no oath".

95 Babli 77b, with biblical support for the change in language between dissolution and permission.

(42a line 63) אָמַר רְבִּי יוֹחָנָן. רִאשׁוֹנִים הָיוּ נִשְׁאָלִין. מַהוּ שֶׁיִּשְׁאַל אָדָם עַל הֲקָמָתוֹ. הֵיךְ עֲבִידָא. נָדְרָה אִשָּׁה וְשָׁמַע בַּעֲלָהּ וְלֹא הֵיפֵר לָהּ. פְּשִׁיטָא שֶׁאֵינוֹ מֵיפֵר[96] לָהּ לְעִנְיָין הַבַּעַל. מַהוּ שֶׁיְּפֵר לָהּ לְעִנְיָין הַזָּקֵן. מָה אֲנָן קַיָּימִין. אִם בִּנְדָרִים שֶׁבֵּינוֹ לְבֵינָהּ נִדְרֵי עַצְמוֹ[97] הֵן. אֶלָּא כִי נָן קַיָּימִין בִּנְדָרִים שֶׁבֵּינָהּ לְבֵין אֲחֵרִים. [וְלָאו מַתְנִיתָא הִיא. אַף לֹא נִדְרֵי אִשְׁתּוֹ שֶׁבֵּינָהּ לְבֵין אֲחֵרִים.[98]] וְלֹא רְבִּי יוּדָה הִיא. תַּנֵּי בְשֵׁם רְבִּי יוּדָה רְבִּי חִייָה תַּנֵּי לָהּ בְּשֵׁם חֲכָמִים.

Rebbi Joḥanan[99] said, earlier generations were asking, may a man ask about his confirmation? How is that? If his wife made a vow, her husband heard it and did not dissolve for her[100]. It is obvious that he cannot dissolve as a husband. May he dissolve as an Elder? What are we talking about? If it is about vows between him and her, these are vows of himself[101]. But we must talk about vows between her and others. [Is that not a Mishnah[102]? "Not his wife's vows between her and others!"] Is that not Rebbi Jehudah's? It was stated in the name of Rebbi Judah; Rebbi Ḥiyya stated it in the name of the Sages[103].

96 In the text quoted by Naḥmanides (*Halakhot*, 11:1) מוּפָר "it was dissolved". It is to be noted that the text quoted by Naḥmanides can be trusted to mirror the Yerushalmi text as to content but not as witness to the text; e. g., he writes Babylonian חייא, חנא for Yerushalmi חייה, תני.

98 From Naḥmanides. Ms. and *editio princeps* עֶצְמָהּ "her own", which they are in any case.

99 From Naḥmanides, missing in ms. and *editio princeps*; required by the general style of the Yerushalmi.

99 In the Babli, 79a, R. Joḥanan has a flat statement that vows confirmed by the husband can be referred to an Elder.

100 He did not dissolve in time and by inaction lost his veto power. The Yerushalmi seems to hold that a vow explicitly confirmed by the husband cannot be referred to an Elder for annulment, since it discusses only confirmation by default.

101 The husband can interfere with his wife's vows only if it touches him personally or is a vow of mortification (cf. Note 17). If it touches him personally, he certainly cannot act as an Elder in his own behalf.

102 Mishnah *Nega'im* 2:5: "A man [sitting as judge] can permit all vows except his own. R. Jehudah says, nor his wife's vows concerning others."

103 R. Ḥiyya [the older] is the great authority for the Mishnah text. According to him, one has to switch the attributions in the Mishnah and, therefore, practice has to follow what in the common Mishnah is attributed to R. Jehudah. Naḥmanides (11:1) holds that practice has to follow the Yerushalmi in this since the Babli does

not discuss the theme; Maimonides (Commentary to *Nega'im* 2:5; Code *HilkhotŠevu'ot* 6:6) disagrees and follows the majority opinion in the Mishnah.

(42a line 69) מָהוּ לְהַתִּיר נְדָרִים בַּלַּיְלָה. וּמָה אִם נֶדֶר הַבַּעַל שֶׁכָּתוּב בָּהֶן בְּיוֹם הֲרֵי הוּא מֵיפֵר בַּלַּיְלָה. נִדְרֵי זָקֵן שֶׁאֵין כָּתוּב בָּהֶן בְּיוֹם לֹא כָּל־שֶׁכֵּן. מָהוּ לְהַתִּיר עַל יְדֵי הַתּוּרְגְּמָן. נִישְׁמְעִינָה מִן הָדָא. רְבִּי בָּא בַר זוּטְרָא אִיתְעֲבִיד תּוּרְגְּמָן דְּרִבִּי יוֹחָנָן בְּחָדָא אִיתְּתָא דְלָא הֲוַת חָכְמָה סוּרִיבְטִין.

May one permit[103] vows in the night? Since vows under the husband's jurisdiction, about which "on the *day*" is written[81], he may dissolve in the night, vows under the jurisdiction of the Elder, where "on the day" is *not* written, not so much more[104]? Can one permit through an interpreter? Let us hear from the following: Rebbi Abba bar Zuṭra was made an interpreter for Rebbi Joḥanan in the case of a woman who did not know Syriac[105].

103 As stated above, this expression can only refer to the action of a Sage. In general, court actions cannot be started in the night but there are exceptions; cf. *Yebamot* 12:1, Note 40.

104 The Babli agrees, 77b, *Eruvin* 62b.

105 She spoke only Greek. In general, a judge is only competent to sit in a case if he understands all witnesses since it says "by the mouth of two witnesses", not the mouth of an interpreter (*Deut.* 19:15; *Makkot* 1:9. *Sifry Deut.* 188.)

(42a line 72) תַּנֵּי. אֵין נִשְׁאָלִין נְדָרִים אֶלָּא עֲטוּפִין וְיוֹשְׁבִין. וְהַנִּשְׁאָל יוֹשֵׁב. וְהַשּׁוֹאֵל צָרִיךְ לִהְיוֹת עוֹמֵד. מִן הָדֵין וְעָמְדוּ שְׁנֵי הָאֲנָשִׁים אֲשֶׁר לָהֶם הָרִיב. אֵין לִי עוֹמְדִין אֶלָּא נִידּוֹנִין. שׁוֹאֵל הֲלָכוֹת. אַגָּדוֹת מְנַיִין. תַּלְמוּד לוֹמַר עָמְדוּ וְעָמְדוּ. רְבִּי אָחָא בַר פַּפָּא סָלַק מִישְׁרֵי נִידְרָא דְּרִבִּי אִימִּי. אִיחֵר בַּעֲמִידָה כְּדֵי לוֹמַר. אֵין כָּאן נֶדֶר. רְבִּי מָנָא סָלַק מִישְׁרֵי נִידְרָא דְּגַמְלִיאֵל דְּקוֹנָתֵיהּ. אִיחֵר בַּעֲמִידָה כְּדֵי לוֹמַר. אֵין כָּאן נֶדֶר אֵין כָּאן שְׁבוּעָה. רְבִּי מָנָא סָלַק מִישְׁרֵי

נִידְרָא דְגַמְלִיאֵל בַּר בְּרֵיהּ. אֲמַר לֵיהּ. לָא תֵּיעַבֵּיד לִי כְּמָה דָעֲבַדְתְּ לְסַבִּי. אֶלָּא תִיב לָךְ וַאֲנָא קִיַּים לִי.

It was stated: One is asked about vows only while sitting and wrapped[106]. The one who is asked must be sitting and the one who is asking is standing; from the following[107]: "And the two people who have the dispute shall stand." "Standing" means only "being judged". That is for asking legal rules[108]. Asking about sermons from where? The verse says "shall stand, and shall stand"[109]. Rebbi Aḥa bar Pappus went to permit the vow of Rebbi Immi. He remained standing to say "there is no vow"[110]. Rebbi Mana went to permit the vow of the older Gamliel. He remained standing to say "there is no vow, there is no oath". Rebbi Mana went to permit the vow of Gamliel the grandson. He said to him, do not treat me as you treated my grandfather, but sit down and I shall remain standing[111].

106 According to the rules of court proceedings. The judges have to be seated and wrapped in their judicial robes.

107 *Deut.* 19:17.

108 The verse does not imply that the parties have to stand before the judges but that they have to remain there to be judged. The interpretation of the verse is in dispute, cf. *Ševu'ot* 4:1 (35b, l. 30 ff.), *Sanhedrin* 3:10 (21c l. 15ff.), *Yoma* 6:1 (43b l. 51 ff.); Babli *Ševu'ot* 30a; *Sifry Deut.* 190.

109 The consecutive *vaw* is interpreted as sign of an addition; to answer anything of a theological nature, the Sage has to sit. The Babli disagrees, 77b; the opinion of the Yerushalmi is quoted as that of Rabban Gamliel II.

110 Following the opinion of the Babylonian Amoraïm for the Babylonian Immi.

111 He asked him to follow the Palestinian rules.

(42b line 4) רִבִּי זְעִירָא רַב יְהוּדָה יִרְמְיָה בַּר אַבָּא בְּשֵׁם רִבִּי שְׁמוּאֵל. שְׁלֹשָׁה שֶׁיּוֹדְעִין לִפְתּוֹחַ מַתִּירִין כְּזָקֵן. סָבְרִין מֵימַר. בְּמָקוֹם שֶׁאֵין זָקֵן. רַבָּנִין

דְּקַיְסָרִין. אֲפִילוּ בְּמָקוֹם שֶׁיֵּשׁ שָׁם זָקֵן. אָמְרִין קוֹמֵי רִבִּי יָסָא. רַב הוּנָא רָאשֵׁי מַטּוֹת. מָאן אִינּוּן רָאשֵׁי מַטּוֹת. רַב הוּנָא רֹאשׁ לְרָאשֵׁי הַמַּטּוֹת.

[112]Rebbi Ze'ira, Rav Jehudah, Jeremiah bar Abba, in the name of Rebbi Samuel[113]: Three who know how to find an opening may permit like an Elder[114]. They thought, at a place where no Elder was available. The rabbis of Caesarea: Even at a place of an Elder[115]. They said before Rebbi Yasa: Rav Huna is "head of tribes"[116]. Who are the heads of tribes[117]? Rav Huna is head of the heads of tribes[118].

112 From here to the end of the Halakhah, the text also is in *Hagigah* 1:8, 76c l. 62.

113 Probably one should read: R. Ze'ira, Rav Jehudah, Rav Jeremiah bar Aha in the name of Samuel.

114 Persons who are not ordained but know the rules of invalidating vows explained in the preceding Chapters. In the Babli, 78a, R. Aha bar Jacob admits any three lay persons to invalidate vows (cf. R. Nissim Gerondi *ad loc., s. v.* אמר רב אחא בר יעקב). In *Bekhorot* 36b, the same rule is attributed to R. Hiyya bar Abin in the name of Rav Amram, a student of Samuel's student Rav Nahman.

115 Invalidation of a vow by three laymen is not infringing on the privileges of the rabbinate. The ordained rabbi has the privilege to invalidate a vow alone (Babli, 78a).

116 Who was the undisputed head of the Babylonian rabbinate and was of the family of the davidic Head of the Diaspora. He certainly had the right to invalidate vows, being of the "heads of the tribes" (*Num.* 30:2).

117 Since they are mentioned in the plural, it appears that more than one person in a generation was empowered to invalidate vows.

118 He is the head of all ordained rabbis, even though his Babylonian ordination is not complete as explained in the next paragraph.

(42b line 8) מָהוּ לִמְנוֹת זְקֵינִים לִדְבָרִים יְחִידִים. נִישְׁמְעִינָהּ מִן הָדָא. רַב מְנִיתֵיהּ רִבִּי לְהַתִּיר נְדָרִים וְלִרְאוֹת כְּתָמִים. מִן דְּדָמָךְ בְּעָא נַבֵּי בְּרֵיהּ מוּמֵי בְּכוֹרוֹת. אָמַר לֵיהּ. אֵינִי מוֹסִיף לָךְ עַל מַה שֶׁנָּתַן לָךְ אַבָּא. אָמַר רִבִּי יוֹסֵי בֵּי רִבִּי בּוּן. כּוּלָּא יְהִיב לוֹ. לָדוּן יְחִידִי וּלְהַתִּיר נְדָרִים וְלִרְאוֹת כְּתָמִים וְלִרְאוֹת

מוּמִין שֶׁבְּגָלוּי. מִן דִּדְמָךְ בְּעָא גַבֵּי בְּרֵיהּ מוּמִין שֶׁבְּסֵתֶר. אָמַר לֵיהּ. אֵינִי
מוֹסִיף לָךְ עַל מַה שֶּׁנָּתַן לָךְ אַבָּא. אַף עַל גַּב דְּתֵימַר. מְמַנִּין זְקֵינִים לִדְבָרִים
יְחִידִים. וְהוּא שֶׁיְּהֵא רָאוּי לְכָל־הַדְּבָרִים. כְּהָדָא. רִבִּי יְהוֹשֻׁעַ בֶּן לֵוִי מְנֵי
לְכָל־תַּלְמִידוֹי. וַהֲוָה מִצְטָעֵר עַל חַד דַּהֲוָה גִּבֵּי בְּעֵינֵיהּ וְלֹא הֲוָה יָכִיל מְמַנֵּיתֵיהּ.
וּמְנֵיהּ יָתֵיהּ לִדְבָרִים יְחִידִים. הָדָא אָמְרָה. הָרָאוּי לְדָבָר אֶחָד רָאוּי
לְכָל־הַדְּבָרִים. וְשֶׁאֵינוֹ רָאוּי לְכָל־הַדְּבָרִים אֲפִילוּ לְדָבָר אֶחָד אֵינוֹ רָאוּי.

May one appoint Elders for selected topics[119]? Let us hear from the following: Rebbi appointed Rav to invalidate vows and to see stains[120]. After his death, [Rav] asked his son for [permission to see] defects of firstlings. He said to him, I shall not add to what my father gave you. Rebbi Yose ben Rebbi Abun said, he gave him everything: To sit in judgment alone, to invalidate vows, to see stains, and to see outside blemishes[121]. After his death, [Rav] asked his son for [permission to see] hidden defects. He said to him, I shall not add to what my father gave you. Even though you say, one appoints Elders for selected topics, only if he is competent for everything. As the following: Rebbi Joshua ben Levi ordained all his students, but he was sorry about one who had a defect in his eye and he could not ordain him[122]; so he ordained him for selected topics[123]. That implies that one who is competent in one thing has to be competent in everything, and one who is not competent in everything cannot be declared competent in one thing[124].

119 Is it possible to give ordination without conferring all rabbinical powers on the candidate?

120 To decide whether a female genital discharge was menstrual blood or not; i. e., whether the woman would be permitted to her husband or not.

This is taken as example of his power to decide in matters of ritual prohibitions and includes permission to judge in all matters of such prohibitions.

121 In the tradition of the Babli, *Sanhedrin* 5a, Rav received full

rabbinic powers except the right to decide anything in matters of firstlings. (A firstling of cattle, sheep, or goats must be sacrificed unless it has a blemish which disqualifies it as a sacrifice. In the absence of a Temple, the firstling must graze until it develops a blemish; *Deut.* 15:19-23.) The full ordination was refused to him since his intent was to return to Babylonia and Rebbi disapproved of that. After him, all rabbis with the limited diaspora ordination received the title of "Rav".

122 Since skin lesions (wrongly translated as "leprosy", *Lev.* 13-14) must be seen with both eyes, a one-eyed or blind person could not be ordained to decide on their ritual purity.

123 For everything except matters of impurity and duties as judge.

124 The difference between the titles of "Rav" and "Rebbi" is one of circumstances, not of quality.

(42b line 8) מָהוּ לִמְנוֹת זְקֵינִים לְיָמִים. נִישְׁמְעִינָהּ מִן הָדָא. דְּרִבִּי חִייָה בַּר אַבָּא אֲתָא לְגַבֵּי רִבִּי לְעָזָר. אָמַר לֵיהּ. פַּייֵס לְרִבִּי יוּדָן נְשִׂייָא דְּיִכְתּוֹב לִי חָדָא אִיגְּרָא דְּאִיקָר דְּאֵיפוֹק לְפַרְנָסָתִי לְאַרְעָא בָּרַייְתָא. וּפַייְסֵיהּ וְכָתַב לֵיהּ. הֲרֵי שֶׁשָּׁלַחְנוּ לָכֶם אָדָם גָּדוֹל שְׁלוּחֵינוּ וּכְיוֹצֵא בָנוּ עַד שֶׁיַּגִּיעַ אֶצְלֵינוּ. רִבִּי חִזְקִיָּה רִבִּי דּוֹסְתַּי רִבִּי אַבָּא בַּר זְמִינָא וּמָטוּ בָהּ בְּשֵׁם רִבִּי דּוֹסְתַּי סַבָּא. אָכֵן כָּתַב לֵיהּ. הֲרֵי שָׁלַחְנוּ לָכֶם אָדָם גָּדוֹל. שֶׁאֵינוֹ בּוֹשׁ לוֹמַר. לֹא שְׁמַעְתִּיו.

May one appoint Elders for a fixed time? Let us hear from the following: Rebbi Hiyya bar Abba went to Rebbi Eleazar and asked him to intervene with the Patriarch Rebbi Jehudah, that the latter should write him a letter of recommendation for seeking a livelihood in a foreign country. He intervened, and [the Patriarch] wrote for him: Here we are sending you as our representative a great personality with all our powers until he shall return to us[125]. Rebbi Hizqiah, Rebbi Dositheus, Rebbi Abba bar Zamina in the name of the old Rebbi Dositheus: He wrote him the following. Here we are sending you a great personality who will not be ashamed to say "I did not learn this"[126].

125 He shall have full ordination until he returns to the Patriarch. The Babli, *Sanhedrin* 5b, has a similar story involving R. Joḥanan who similarly gave conditional ordination to Rebbi Shimen.

126 In this version, which has no parallel in the Babli, the ordination was unconditional and permanent.

(42b line 25) מַהוּ לְהַתִּיר בְּפָלוֹנָס. רִבִּי אַבָּהוּ בְשֵׁם רִבִּי יוֹחָנָן. מַתִּירִין בְּפָלוֹנָס. רִבִּי יְהוֹשֻׁעַ בֶּן לֵוִי הִתִּיר בְּפָלוֹנָס. רִבִּי הוּנָא בְשֵׁם רִבִּי יִרְמְיָה. בְּמָקוֹם שֶׁאֵין טַלִּית. אָמַר רִבִּי יוֹסֵי בֵּירִבִּי בּוּן. בִּנְדָרִים הַקַּלִּים.

May one permit wearing a coat[127]? Rebbi Abbahu in the name of Rebbi Joḥanan: One permits wearing a coat. Rebbi Joshua ben Levi permitted wearing a coat. Rebbi Huna in the name of Rebbi Jeremiah: At a place where one does not wear a toga. Rebbi Yose ben Abun said, for easy vows[128].

127 Must the rabbi always be wrapped in his robe (Note 106)? The word פלונס parallels Syriac פלימנא, פילמנא, Greek παινόλης (παιλόνης), παινόλης, Latin *paenula* "coat".

128 Those which can be permitted unquestionably, for which no argument is needed.

אילו נדרים פרק אחד עשר

משנה א: (fol. 42b) אִילוּ נְדָרִים שֶׁהוּא מֵיפֵר. דְּבָרִים שֶׁיֵּשׁ בָּהֶן עִינּוּי נֶפֶשׁ אִם אֶרְחַץ וְאִם לֹא אֶרְחַץ אִם אֶתְקַשֵּׁט וְאִם לֹא אֶתְקַשֵּׁט. אָמַר רִבִּי יוֹסֵי אֵין אִילוּ נִדְרֵי עִינּוּי נֶפֶשׁ.

Mishnah 1: These are the vows which he may dissolve: Matters connected with mortification[1]. [E. g.], "if I wash, if I do not wash; if I wear jewels, if I do not wear jewels.[2]" Rebbi Yose said, these are not vows of mortification[3].

1 In addition, he can dissolve vows impinging on their marital relations, as explained later.

2 These examples refer to conditional vows. One derives from the contract of the tribes of Gad and Reuben with Moses (*Num.* 32:29-30) that a legally valid conditional contract must spell out the conditions both positively and negatively: If I do certain things, there is a stipulated consequence; if I do not, then the consequence is stipulated not to happen (Mishnah *Qiddušin* 3:3). The vow is understood to be: A *qônām* should be a certain thing for me if I ever wash; if I do not wash, the thing shall not be *qônām*. Since not washing is mortification, the husband has the right to void the vow. If the vow had been unconditional, the husband would have no jurisdiction over it.

3 His position is explained in Mishnah 2.

משנה ב: אִילוּ הֵן נִדְרֵי עִינּוּי נֶפֶשׁ. אָמְרָה קוֹנָם פֵּירוֹת הָעוֹלָם עָלַי הֲרֵי זֶה יָכוֹל לְהָפֵר. פֵּירוֹת מְדִינָה עָלַי יָבִיא לָהּ מִמְּדִינָה אַחֶרֶת. פֵּירוֹת הַחֶנְוָנִי זֶה עָלַי אֵינוֹ יָכוֹל לְהָפֵר. אִם לֹא הָיְתָה פַּרְנָסָתוֹ אֶלָּא מִמֶּנּוּ הֲרֵי זֶה יָפֵר דִּבְרֵי רִבִּי יוֹסֵה.

Mishnah 2: The following are vows of mortification. If she said, all produce of the world is *qônām* for me, he may dissolve. The produce of this province [is *qônām*] for me, he can buy for her from another province. The produce of this grocery store [is *qônām*] for me, he cannot dissolve. If he can get the necessities of life only from that grocery[4], he may dissolve, the words of Rebbi Yose.

4 If that store is the only one which extends credit to him and he needs the credit, he can dissolve.

(42c line 1) **הלכה א**: אֵילוּ נְדָרִים שֶׁהוּא מֵיפֵר כוּל׳. כְּתִיב כָּל־נֶדֶר וְכָל־שְׁבוּעַת אִסָּר לַעֲנוֹת נָפֶשׁ. אֵין לִי אֶלָּא נְדָרִים שֶׁיֵּשׁ בָּהֶן עִינּוּי נָפֶשׁ. נְדָרִים שֶׁבֵּינוֹ לְבֵינָהּ מְנַיִין. בֵּין אִישׁ לְאִשְׁתּוֹ. עַד כְּדוֹן בְּבַעַל. בָּאָב מְנַיִין. מַה הַבַּעַל אֵינוֹ מֵיפֵר אֶלָּא נְדָרִים שֶׁיֵּשׁ בָּהֶן עִינּוּי נֶפֶשׁ וּנְדָרִים שֶׁבֵּינוֹ לְבֵינָהּ. אַף הָאָב אֵינוֹ מֵיפֵר אֶלָּא נְדָרִים שֶׁיֵּשׁ בָּהֶן עִינּוּי נֶפֶשׁ וּנְדָרִים שֶׁבֵּינוֹ לְבֵינָהּ.

Halakhah 1: "These are the vows which he can dissolve," etc. It is written[5]: "Any vow and any oath of prohibition to mortify." That covers only vows which contain mortification. Vows regarding the relations between him and her, from where? "Between a man and his wife[6]." So far the husband; the father from where? Since the husband can dissolve only vows of mortification and matters between him and her, so the father can dissolve only vows of mortification and matters between him and her[7].

5 *Num.* 30:14. The verse ends: "Her husband shall confirm it or her husband shall dissolve it."

6 *Num.* 30:17. One opinion in this Halakhah (Notes 11 ff.) and the consensus in the Babli (79b) hold that the dissolution of vows of mortification is permanent since it is expressly sanctioned by the verse but that dissolution of a vow regarding marital relations, which is the result of an indirect inference, is valid only as long

as the marriage continues. Such a dissolution would be automatically voided for the divorcee or widow. The Mishnah mentions only vows the husband can permanently dissolve.

7 This argument seems to be taken out of thin air. It is explained in *Sifry Num.* 155: V. 17 reads "These are the principles which the Eternal commanded to Moses between a husband and his wife, between a father and his daughter, in her adolescence, in her father's house." Now this verse is really an appendix to the laws governing the married wife. It is concluded that the restrictions which apply to the husband in relation with his wife in *his* house also apply to the father in relation to the adolescent daughter in *his* house.

(42c line 7) רִבִּי יַעֲקֹב בַּר אָחָא אָמַר. אִיתְפַּלְגוּן רִבִּי יוֹחָנָן וְרִבִּי שִׁמְעוֹן בֶּן לָקִישׁ. רִבִּי יוֹחָנָן אָמַר. בֵּין לִנְדָרִים בֵּין לִשְׁבוּעוֹת הַבַּעַל מֵיפֵר. רִבִּי שִׁמְעוֹן בֶּן לָקִישׁ אָמַר. לִנְדָרִים מֵיפֵר וְלֹא לִשְׁבוּעוֹת. אָמַר רִבִּי יוֹסֵי בֵּירִבִּי בּוּן. אַף בְּנִדְרֵי הַזָּקֵן פְּלִיגִין רִבִּי יוֹחָנָן וְרִבִּי שִׁמְעוֹן בֶּן לָקִישׁ. רִבִּי יוֹחָנָן אָמַר. בֵּין לִנְדָרִים בֵּין לִשְׁבוּעוֹת הַזָּקֵן מַתִּיר. וְרִבִּי שִׁמְעוֹן בֶּן לָקִישׁ אָמַר. לִנְדָרִים הַזָּקֵן מַתִּיר וְלִשְׁבוּעוֹת אֵין הַזָּקֵן מַתִּיר. וְאַתְיָיא דְּרִבִּי שִׁמְעוֹן בֶּן לָקִישׁ כְּהָדָא דְּאִיסִי. חַד בַּר נָשׁ אֲתָא מִישְׁרֵי נִדְרָא קוֹמֵי רִבִּי יוֹסֵי. מִתְעַטֵּף וְיָתִיב לֵיהּ. אָמַר לֵיהּ. מָה אִישְׁתַּבָּעַת. אָמַר לֵיהּ. אִיפּוֹפִי יִשְׂרָאֵל. לֹא עֲלָלָה לְבֵיתִי. אָמַר לֵיהּ. אִיפּוֹפִי יִשְׂרָאֵל. וְלֹא עֲלָלָה לְבֵייתָךְ.

Rebbi Jacob bar Aḥa said, Rebbi Joḥanan and Rebbi Simeon ben Laqish disagree. Rebbi Joḥanan said, the husband dissolves both vows and oaths[8]. Rebbi Simeon ben Laqish said, he dissolves vows but not oaths[9]. Rebbi Yose ben Rebbi Abun said, Rebbi Joḥanan and Rebbi Simeon ben Laqish also disagree about the vows submitted to the Elder. Rebbi Joḥanan said, the Elder permits both vows and oaths. Rebbi Simeon ben Laqish said, the Elder permits vows, the Elder does not permit oaths. That of Rebbi Simeon ben Laqish parallels that of Issi (Assi). A person came before Rebbi Yasa[10] to have his vow permitted. He asked him, what did you swear? He answered, ὦ πόποι[11] Israel, that she should not enter my house. He said to him, ὦ πόποι Israel, she shall not enter your house!

8   The heading of the paragraph, *Num.* 30:2, speaks of vows and oaths. (A vow refers to a thing, an oath implies the use of God's name.)

9   Except for v. 2, oaths are never mentioned.

10   Since Yerushalmi אִיסִי is the same as Babylonian אַסִי, the formal name should not be יוֹסֵי but יָסָה.

11   Greek πόποι is classically an exclamation of surprise, anger, pain, etc.; it is later explained as "divinities, gods". While the husband avoided using Hebrew or Aramaic expressions for God's name, the Greek in this case has the meaning of "God of Israel"; this classifies the act as an oath, which R. Yasa refused to annul. The husband swore that his wife should no longer enter his house, i. e., he forced himself to divorce her and pay her the divorce settlement.

(42c line 14) רִבִּי זְעִירָא פָּתַר מַתְנִיתָא אִילוּ נְדָרִים שֶׁמֵּיפֵר. נְדָרִים שֶׁיֵּשׁ בָּהֶן עִינּוּי נֶפֶשׁ. אִם אָרְחַץ וְאִם לֹא אָרְחַץ. אִם אֶתְקַשֵּׁט וְאִם לֹא אֶתְקַשֵּׁט. אָמַר רִבִּי יוֹסֵי. אֵין אִילוּ נִדְרֵי עִינּוּי נֶפֶשׁ אֶלָּא נְדָרִים שֶׁבֵּינוֹ לְבֵינָהּ. אִילוּ הֵן נִדְרֵי עִינּוּי נֶפֶשׁ כְּרִבִּי יוֹסֵי. כְּשֶׁאָמְרָה פֵּירוֹת הָעוֹלָם עָלַי. הֲרֵי זֶה יָפֵר. רַבָּנִין אָמְרִין. נִדְרֵי עִינּוּי נֶפֶשׁ הֵיפֵר לָהּ מוּפָר לְעוֹלָם. נְדָרִים שֶׁבֵּינוֹ לְבֵינָהּ אֵינוֹ מוּפָר אֶלָּא כָּל־זְמָן שֶׁהִיא[11] עִמּוֹ. רִבִּי יוֹסֵי אוֹמֵר. בֵּין נִדְרֵי עִינּוּי נֶפֶשׁ בֵּין נְדָרִים שֶׁבֵּינוֹ לְבֵינָהּ הֵיפֵר לָהּ מוּפָר לְעוֹלָם. וְהָא רַבָּנִין אָמְרִין. נִדְרֵי עִינּוּי נֶפֶשׁ הֵפֵר לָהּ מוּפָר לְעוֹלָם. רִבִּי יוֹסֵי אוֹמֵר. נְדָרִים שֶׁבֵּינוֹ לְבֵינָהּ הֵיפֵר לָהּ מוּפָר לְעוֹלָם. מַה בֵּינֵיהוֹן. בְּשֶׁאָמְרָה. קוֹנָם הֲנָייָתִי עָלֶיךָ אִם אֵצֵא מֵרְשׁוּתָךְ. וְיָפֵר לָהּ. בִּשְׁלֹא אָמְרָה. קוֹנָם הֲנָיַית גּוּפִי עָלֶיךָ לִכְשֶׁאֵצֵא מֵרְשׁוּתָךְ. רַבָּנִין אָמְרִין. נִדְרֵי עִינּוּי נֶפֶשׁ הֵן. רִבִּי זְעוּרָא וְרִבִּי הִילָא תְּרֵיהוֹן אָמְרִין. נְדָרִים שֶׁבֵּינוֹ לְבֵינָהּ כֵּן. עַל דַּעְתֵּיהּ דְּרִבִּי זְעוּרָא וְרִבִּי הִילָא רִבִּי יוֹסֵי וְרִבִּי יוֹחָנָן בֶּן נוּרִי שְׁנֵיהֶן אָמְרוּ דָּבָר אֶחָד. דַּתַנִּינָן תַּמָּן. רִבִּי יוֹחָנָן אָמַר. יָפֵר. שֶׁמָּא יְגָרְשֶׁנָּה וּתְהֵא אֲסוּרָה לַחֲזוֹר לוֹ.

Rebbi Ze'ira explained the Mishnah: "These are the vows which he can dissolve: Matters connected with mortification. [E. g.], 'if I wash, if I do not wash; if I shall wear jewels, if I do not wear jewels.' Rebbi Yose said, these are not vows of mortification" but vows between him and her. "The following are vows of mortification[12]" following Rebbi Yose. For example, "she said, all produce of the world is *qônām* for me, he may dissolve." The rabbis say, if he dissolves vows of mortification, they are permanently dissolved. Vows between him and her are only dissolved as long as she is married to him. Rebbi Yose says, both vows of mortification and vows between him and her, if he dissolved them they are permanently dissolved[13]. That means, the rabbis say, if he dissolves vows of mortification, they are permanently dissolved. Rebi Yose says, if he dissolves vows between him and her, they are permanently dissolved. What is the difference between them? If she said, any benefit from me shall be *qônām* for you when I leave your domain. Why can he not dissolve that? Because she did not say, any benefit from my body shall be *qônām* for you when I leave your domain[14]. Rebbi Ze'ira and Rebbi Hila, both of them say: That is the essence of vows between him and her. In the opinion of Rebbi Ze'ira, Rebbi Yose and Rebbi Joḥanan ben Nuri said the same thing since we stated there[15]: "Rebbi Joḥanan said, he shall dissolve it since maybe he would divorce her, then she would be forbidden to return to him."

12 Mishnah 11:2. In this interpretation, Mishnah 2 is the continuation of the remark of R. Yose in Mishnah 1.

13 Since R. Yose also agrees that the husband dissolves both vows of mortification and those between him and her, there must be a practical difference between the two classes of vows to make the classification important.

14 A vow between him and her is only subject to the husband's dissolution if it interferes with their marital relations. For R. Yose, he can dissolve a vow that would permanently forbid any sex with her after divorce; for the rabbis, he cannot dissolve the vow which comes into effect only after he will have lost the right of dissolution.

15 Mishnah 11:4, about a woman

who vows not to do anything he tells her to do. The rabbis hold that he does not have to dissolve the vow since by law she is required to live with him and keep house for him, and nobody can abolish his duties under the law by making a vow. R. Aqiba holds that he must dissolve the vow since she might do more for him than is legally required and then would violate her vow. R. Joḥanan ben Nuri says that he would be well advised to dissolve the vow since she would not be able to do anything for him after a divorce. This implies that the husband may dissolve now the vow regarding matters between him and her which would become effective only after a future divorce.

(42c line 28) רִבִּי הִילָא פָּתַר מַתְנִיתָא אִילוּ נְדָרִים שֶׁהוּא מֵיפֵר לָהּ. דְּבָרִים שֶׁיֵּשׁ בָּהֶן עִינּוּי נֶפֶשׁ. אִם אֶרְחַץ וְאִם לֹא אֶרְחַץ. אִם אֶתְקַשֵּׁט וְאִם לֹא אֶתְקַשֵּׁט. מָהוּ אָמַר רִבִּי יוֹסֵי אֵין אִילֵּין נְדָרִים נִדְרֵי עִינּוּי נֶפֶשׁ אֶלָא אִילוּ נְדָרִים שֶׁבֵּינוֹ לְבֵינָהּ. אִילוּ הֵן נִדְרֵי עִינּוּי נֶפֶשׁ. דִּבְרֵי הַכֹּל.

Rebbi Hila explained the Mishnah: "These are the vows which he can dissolve: Matters connected with mortification. [E. g.], 'if I wash, if I do not wash; if I wear jewels, if I do not wear jewels.'" What means "Rebbi Yose said, these vows are not vows of mortification"? They are vows between him and her. "The following are vows of mortification" is everybody's opinion[16].

16 He holds that Mishnah 2 can be read as being accepted by everybody. This implies that R. Yose does not disagree with the anonymous majority that the husband's powers of dissolution of vows between him and her are restricted to the time of their marriage. He simply disagrees with the classification of the two examples quoted in the Mishnah and holds that not washing or not wearing jewellery is not done as mortification but to spite the husband.

(42c line 28) אִם אֶרְחַץ אִם לֹא אֶרְחַץ. וְתַנֵּי כֵן. נִידְרֵי עִינּוּי נֶפֶשׁ. אִם אֶרְחַץ אִם לֹא אֶרְחַץ. אִם אֶתְקַשֵּׁט אִם לֹא אֶתְקַשֵּׁט. בֵּין עַל דַּעְתֵּיהּ דְּרִבִּי זְעִירָא בֵּין

עַל דַּעְתֵּיהּ דְּרִבִּי הִילָא מִחְלְפָה שִׁיטָתֵיהּ דְּרִבִּי יוֹסֵי. דְּתַנֵּי. מַעְיָין שֶׁלִּבְנֵי הָעִיר. הֵן וַאֲחֵרִים. הֵן קוֹדְמִין לַאֲחֵרִים. אֲחֵרִים וּבְהֶמְתָּן. אֲחֵרִים קוֹדְמִין לִבְהֶמְתָּן. כְּבִיסָתָן וְחַיֵּי אֲחֵרִים. כְּבִיסָתָן קוֹדֶמֶת לְחַיֵּי אֲחֵרִים. אָמַר רִבִּי יוֹחָנָן. מָאן תַּנָּא. כְּבִיסָה חַיֵּי נֶפֶשׁ. רִבִּי יוֹסֵה. דְּתַנֵּי. אֵין נוֹתְנִין מֵהֶן לֹא לְמִשְׁרָה וְלֹא לִכְבִיסָה. רִבִּי יוֹסֵי מַתִּיר בִּכְבִיסָה. מִחְלְפָה שִׁיטָתֵיהּ דְּרִבִּי יוֹסֵי. תַּמָּן הוּא אָמַר. אֵין רְחִיצָה חַיֵּי נֶפֶשׁ. וְכָא הוּא אָמַר. הַכְּבִיסָה חָיֵי נֶפֶשׁ. אָמַר רִבִּי מָנָא אָדָם מְנַלְגֵּל בִּרְחִיצָה וְאֵין אָדָם מְנַלְגֵּל בִּכְבִיסָה.

"If I wash, if I do not wash." It was stated[17]: "If I wash, if I do not wash; if I wear jewels, if I do not wear jewels", these are vows of mortification. Both according to Rebbi Ze'ira or according to Rebbi Hila, Rebbi Yose seems to contradict his own opinion, as [18]it was stated: "A water source belonging to the townspeople, between them and outsiders, they have precedence over outsiders. Between outsiders and their animals, the outsiders have precedence over their animals. Their washing and the lives of outsiders, their washing has precedence over the lives of outsiders." Rebbi Johanan said, who is the Tanna who said that washing is a necessity for survival? Rebbi Yose! As it was stated: "One may use it neither for steeping nor for washing. But Rebbi Yose permits it for washing." The opinions of Rebbi Yose are contradictory. There he says, washing oneself is not a necessity of life[19]. And here, he says washing one's garments is a necessity of life! Rebbi Mana said, a person might put off washing himself but nobody puts off washing his clothes.

17 In a *baraita* not otherwise recorded.

18 From here to the end of the next paragraph, the text is from *Ševi'it* 8:5, Notes 77-84.

19 "There" is the Mishnah here, where R. Yose qualifies not washing as not being a mortification.

HALAKHAH 1

(42c line 40) יְהוּדָה אִישׁ הוּצָא עֲבִיד טְמִיר בִּמְעָרְתָא תְּלָתָא יוֹמִין מֵיקוֹם עַל הָדֵין טַעֲמָא. מְנַיִין שֶׁחַיֵּי הָעִיר הַזֹּאת קוֹדְמִין לְחַיֵּי עִיר אַחֶרֶת. אָתָא לְגַבֵּי רִבִּי יוֹסֵי בֶּן חֲלַפְתָּא. אָמַר לֵיהּ. אִית לִי טְמִיר בִּמְעָרְתָא תְּלָתָא יוֹמִין מֵיקוֹם עַל הָדֵין טַעֲמָא. מְנַיִין שֶׁחַיֵּי הָעִיר הַזֹּאת קוֹדְמִין לְחַיֵּי עִיר אַחֶרֶת. קָרָא לְרִבִּי אַבָּא בְּרֵיהּ. אֲמַר לֵיהּ הָדֵין טַעֲמָא. מְנַיִין שֶׁחַיֵּי הָעִיר הַזֹּאת קוֹדְמִין לְחַיֵּי עִיר אַחֶרֶת. אָמַר לֵיהּ. תִּהְיֶינָה הֶעָרִים הָאֵלֶּא תִּהְיֶינָה עִיר וָעִיר וְאַחַר כָּךְ וּמִגְרְשֵׁיהֶם סְבִיבוֹתֵיהֶן. אָמַר לֵיהּ. מַאן גָּרַם לָךְ. דְּלֹא יְלַפְתְּ עִם חֲבֵירֶךְ.

[18]Jehudah from Huṣa hid himself in a cave for three days because he wanted to find the reason why the necessities of life of one's town have precedence over the necessities of life of another town. He came to Rabbi Yose bar Ḥalaphta and said, I was hiding in a cave for three days because I wanted to find the reason why the necessities of life of one's town have precedence over the necessities of life of another town. He called his son Rebbi Abba and asked him about the reason why the necessities of life of one's town have precedence over the necessities of life of another town. He said to him (*Num.* 35:15): "These [six] cities shall be", each town shall be, and only afterwards their surroundings around them. He [R. Yose] said to him [Jehudah from Huṣa], what did cause you [this embarassment]? That you did not study with your companions!

(42c line 47) נִיחָא אִם אֶרְחַץ. אִם לֹא אֶרְחַץ. וְתִרְחַץ. אָמַר רִבִּי מָנָא. בִּשְׁאָמְרָה. קוֹנָם הֲנָייָתִי עָלַיִךְ מִשֶּׁאֶרְחַץ אִם אֶרְחַץ. וְיָפֵר לָהּ. אָמַר רִבִּי יוֹסֵי בִּי רִבִּי בּוּן. בְּשֶׁלֹּא אָמְרָה אֶלָּא. קוֹנָם הֲנָיַית גּוּפִי עָלַיִךְ לִכְשֶׁאֶרְחַץ. וְיָכוֹף. לֹא כֵן אָמַר רַב הוּנָא. הֲנָיָיתִי עָלַיִךְ. כּוֹפָהּ וּמְשַׁמַּשְׁתּוֹ. הֲנָיָיתָךְ עָלַי. הֲרֵי זֶה יָפֵר. שַׁנְיָיא הִיא שֶׁהִיא הֲנָיָיתוֹ וַהֲנָיָיתָהּ. אָמַר רִבִּי אַבָּא מָרִי. אִם אֶרְחַץ אִם לֹא אֶרְחַץ לְעוֹלָם. אִם אֶתְקַשֵּׁט אִם לֹא אֶתְקַשֵּׁט לְעוֹלָם. רַבָּנִין דְּקַיְסָרִין בְּשֵׁם רִבִּי נָסָא. אִם אֶרְחַץ וְאִם לֹא אֶתְקַשֵּׁט. אִם אֶתְקַשֵּׁט וְאִם לֹא אֶרְחַץ.

We understand "if I wash[20]". "If I do not wash"? Let her wash! Rebbi Mana said, if she said: "Any benefit from me shall be *qônām* for you after I shall have washed myself, if I ever wash myself.[21]" Why should he not dissolve for her? Rebbi Yose ben Rebbi Abun said, only when she said, "any benefit from my body shall be *qônām* for you after I shall have washed myself.[22]" Why can he not force? Did not Rebbi Huna say, [if she vowed] any benefit from me [shall be forbidden] to you, he forces her[23] and sleeps with her. Any benefit from you [shall be forbidden] to me, he has to dissolve[24]. There is a difference because it[25] is a benefit for him and her. Rebbi Abba Mari said, If I wash [today], I shall not wash forever. If I wear jewellery [today], I shall not wear jewellery forever[26]. The rabbis of Caesarea in the name of Rebbi Nasa: If I wash I shall not wear jewellery; if I wear jewellery I shall not wash.

20 The discussion here is to understand R. Yose, who classifies the vows as being between him and her. He cannot accept the explanation given in Note 2 but it must somehow refer to marital relations. If she makes a vow not to have any relations with him if she washes, it is clear that he may dissolve the vow as one between him and her. But if she makes the vow not to have any relations with him if she does not wash, why can we not rely on her washing, as normal people do?

21 The mention of "not washing" is not an independent vow. She makes the vow not to have any relations with him if she washes and then reinforces her statement by the assertion that she will not wash.

22 It is only a vow between him and her if she makes it clear that she refers to marital intercourse.

23 He goes to court and has her declared an unruly wife; the court will deduct 7 denar from her marriage settlement per week and, if that settlement was reduced to zero, give the husband the right to claim 7 denar per week from any future inheritance or earnings (Mishnah *Ketubot* 5:7).

24 Since it is in his hand to dissolve the vow, he cannot sleep with her as long as her vow is in existence since "one does not feed a person anything

forbidden to him" (Babli 81b).

25 Sexual relations.

26 R. Abba Mari disagrees with the preceding and holds that the vow means what it says, that it is only about washing (or wearing jewellery) and not about sex. R. Yose holds that a person can go for a day without washing or wearing jewellery; therefore, the vow described in the Mishnah is neither a vow of mortification nor one between him and her; the husband has no way of interfering with that vow. It might become a vow between him and her if she should wash that day.

(42c line 54) שְׁמוּאֵל אָמַר. אָמְרָה קוֹנָם פֵּירוֹת הָעוֹלָם עָלַי. וְהָיוּ שָׁם צְבוּרִים בְּסִידָקֵי. יִקַּח לָהּ מֵהֶן. רִבִּי שִׁמְעוֹן בֶּן לָקִישׁ אָמַר. קוֹנָם פֵּירוֹת בְּנֵי זוֹ הַמְּדִינָה עָלַי. וְהָיוּ שָׁם אַכְסְנָאִין מוֹכְרִין. יִקַּח מֵהֶן.

Samuel said, if she said, all produce of the world is *qônām* for me; if there was grain heaped in the grain container[27], he may buy for her from that[28]. Rebbi Simeon ben Laqish said, "the produce of the people of this province [is *qônām*] for me, if there were strangers[29] selling there, he can buy from them.

27 The word is explained as a contraction from סִיטוֹדְקֵי, Greek σιτοδόκη "granary". The grocer sells grain from his container.

28 Samuel holds that a vow is future directed unless otherwise stated; it does not cover produce already harvested.

29 Greek ξένος "stranger, host".

(42c line 56) כְּתִיב וְכָל־נֶדֶר וְכָל־שְׁבוּעַת אִסָּר לַעֲנוֹת נָפֶשׁ. כְּגוֹן פִּילְפֵּל שֶׁאֲנִי טוֹעֶמֶת.[30] קָלוֹסְקִין שֶׁאֲנִי טוֹעֶמֶת. לֹא סוֹף דָּבָר שֶׁיֵּשׁ מֵאוֹתוֹ הַמִּין אֶלָּא אֲפִילוּ אֵין בּוֹ מֵאוֹתוֹ הַמִּין. שֶׁמָּא יָבִיא לָהּ אַחַר מֵאוֹתוֹ הַמִּין. רִבִּי יוֹחָנָן בְּשֵׁם רִבִּי יַנַּאי. הָיוּ לְפָנָיו שְׁתֵּי חֲתִיכוֹת אַחַת יָפָה וְאַחַת רָעָה. נָתְנָה עֵינֶיהָ בְּיָפָה וְנָדְרָה מִן הָרָעָה הֲרֵי זֶה יָפֵר. מִפְּנֵי מָה הוּא מֵיפֵר. חֲבֵרַיָּיא אָמְרֵי. מִפְּנֵי נִדְרֵי עִינּוּי נֶפֶשׁ שֶׁלָּהּ. רִבִּי זְעִירָא וְרִבִּי הִילָא תְּרֵיהוֹן אָמְרִין. מִפְּנֵי נִדְרֵי עִינּוּי נֶפֶשׁ שֶׁלּוֹ. רִבִּי זְעִירָא בְּשֵׁם שְׁמוּאֵל. כָּל־הַנְּדָרִים אָדָם מֵיפֵר חוּץ מֵהָאוֹמֶרֶת. הֲנָייָתִי עַל

פְּלוֹנִי. הָא הֲנָיַת פְּלוֹנִי עָלַי. יָפֵר. וְהָתַנִּינָן. קוֹנָם פֵּירוֹת חֶנְוָנִי זֶה עָלַי אֵינוֹ יָכוֹל לְהָפֵר. פָּתַר לָהּ כְּרִבִּי יוֹסֵי וַחֲלוּקִים עָלָיו. תְּתַנִּינָן תַּמָּן. אִם לֹא הָיְתָה פַרְנָסָתוֹ אֶלָּא מִמֶּנּוּ הֲרֵי זֶה יָפֵר. אָמַר רִבִּי יוֹסֵי. דּוּ מַקִּיף לָהּ. דּוּ יָב לָהּ. אָמַר רִבִּי מָנָא. דּוּ יָב לָהּ מִקָּמָא טָבָא.

It is written[30]: "Every vow and every oath of prohibition to mortify a person." For example, [a *qônām*] if I would taste peppers, if I would taste rolls[31]. Not only if that kind is available now; even if that kind is not available now, perhaps he might bring her some later on. Rebbi Joḥanan in the name of Rebbi Yannai: If there were two pieces before them, one nice and one not nice. If she desired the nice one[32] and made a vow to forbid herself the less nice one, he may dissolve that. Why can he dissolve? The colleagues say, because of her mortification[33]. Rebbi Ze'ira and Rebbi Hila both say, because of his mortification[34]. Rebbi Ze'ira in the name of Samuel: A man can dissolve all vows except if she says, any benefit from me shall [be *qônām*] for X. That means he can dissolve: Any benefit from X shall [be *qônām*] for me[35]. But did we not state: "The produce of this grocery store [is *qônām*] for me, he cannot dissolve." Explain that following Rebbi Yose and they disagree with him, for we did state there[36]: "If he can get the necessities of life only from that grocer, he may dissolve." Rebbi Yose[37] said, because he gives him credit, he delivers to him[38]. Rebbi Mana said, because he gives him good quality produce[39].

30 *Num.* 30:14.
31 In the opinion of S. Fraenkel κολλίκιον, diminutive of Greek κόλλιξ "large round bread".
32 There were two pieces of meat and she was afraid her husband would take the nicer (larger) one for himself. It is assumed that the servants cooked and brought the meal.
33 She might change her mind and opt for the smaller piece. The Babli, 82b, holds that the husband cannot

dissolve as long as she has enough not to be hungry. It does not discuss the case of a person becoming afraid of overeating.

34 Since the verse speaks only of mortification whithout indicating to whom it refers, it is implied that the husband can dissolve his wife's vow if it mortifies him.

35 The Babli, 82a, agrees with both statements.

36 Which is declared to be R. Yose's opinion.

37 The late Amora.

38 Since he would have to go hungry if he is temporarily out of cash and could not pay another grocer, this certainly is potential mortification for him.

39 R. Mana even considers it mortification if he had to take a lesser quality from another store.

משנה ג: קוֹנָם שֶׁאֵינִי נֶהֱנֶה לַבְּרִיּוֹת אֵינוֹ יָכוֹל לְהָפֵר וִיכוֹלָה הִיא (fol. 42b) לֵהָנוֹת בַּלֶּקֶט וּבַשִּׁכְחָה וּבַפֵּיאָה. קוֹנָם כֹּהֲנִים וּלְוִיִּים נֶהֱנִין לִי יִטְּלוּ עַל כָּרְחָהּ. כֹּהֲנִים אִילוּ וּלְוִיִּים אֵילוּ נֶהֱנִין לִי יִטְּלוּ אֲחֵרִים.

Mishnah 3: 'A *qônām* that I shall not have benefit from people[40]' he cannot dissolve, and she may benefit from gleanings, forgotten sheaves, and *peah*[41]. 'A *qônām* that priests and Levites can have no benefit from me'; they may take forcibly[42]. 'These priests and these Levites can have no benefit from me;' others may take.

40 "People" means everybody except her husband, who is considered to be identical with her.

41 As is pointed out in the Halakhah, these agricultural gifts to the poor, described in Tractate *Peah*, are abandoned by the farmer who has no right to give them to a poor person of his acquaintance. Therefore, the poor receive these gifts from God's bounty, not from the farmer.

42 If the person (male or female) has farming property, the vow cannot free them from the obligations which are liens on agricultural produce.

(42c line 68) **הלכה ג:** קוֹנָם שֶׁאֵינִי נֶהֱנָה לַבְּרִיוֹת כוּל'. אָמַר רִבִּי יוֹחָנָן. כֵּינִי מַתְנִיתָא. וִיכוֹלָה הִיא לֵהָנוֹת בַּלֶּקֶט וּבַשִּׁכְחָה וּבַפֵּיאָה. תַּנֵּי. וּבְמַעֲשַׂר עָנִי. לֵית כָּאן מַעֲשַׂר עָנִי. מַעֲשַׂר עָנִי נִיתָּן בִּזְכִייָה וְאִילּוּ בַעֲזִיבָה.

Halakhah 3: "'A *qônām* that I shall not have benefit from people,' etc. Rebbi Yoḥanan said, so is the Mishnah: "*And she may benefit from gleanings, forgotten sheaves, and peah*.[43]". It was stated[44]: "*And the tithe of the poor.*" The tithe of the poor is not listed here. The tithe of the poor is given as acquisition; these by abandoning[41].

43 This remark stands for a lenghty discussion in the Babli, whose Mishnah seems to read: "She may benefit from gleanings, forgotten sheaves, and peah." (Cf. The Babylonian Talmud with Variant Readings, *Nedarim* vol. 2, p. 264, Note 15.) The Babli, 83b, notes that the first sentence of the Mishnah implies that the husband is not "people". The second clause, in its version, seems to imply that the woman can eat only from gleanings etc., not from the husband, who would be part of "people" and as such entitled to dissolve the vow. R. Johanan points out that the second clause is part of the first sentence, not a stand-alone sentence: The woman may eat from her husband and, in addition, gleanings, abandoned sheaves, and *peah*.

44 Tosephta 7:4. The Babli, 84a/b, quotes verses which give the farmer the option either to distribute the tithe, then the woman is disqualified; or to abandon it on his threshing floor, then the woman may take it if she is poor.

(42c line 70) רִבִּי יוֹסֵי בֶּן חֲנִינָה אָמַר. אָדָם נוֹתֵן מַעְשְׂרוֹתָיו בְּטוֹבַת הֲנָיָיה. וְרִבִּי יוֹחָנָן אָמַר. אֵין אָדָם נוֹתֵן מַעְשְׂרוֹתָיו בְּטוֹבַת הֲנָיָיה. מַאי טַעְמָא דְּרִבִּי יוֹסֵי בֶּן חֲנִינָה. וְאִישׁ אֶת קֳדָשָׁיו לוֹ יִהְיֶה. וְרִבִּי יוֹחָנָן אָמַר. לֹא[45] יִהְיֶה. יִתְּנֵם לְכָל־מִי שֶׁיִּרְצֶה.

[46]Rebbi Yose ben Rebbi Ḥanina said, a person gives his tithes for the benefit of goodwill. Rebbi Joḥanan said, a person may not give his tithes for the benefit of goodwill. What is the reason of Rebbi Yose ben Rebbi Ḥanina? (*Num.* 5:10) "Everybody shall be the owner of his holy things."

Rebbi Johanan said " it shall not be his". May he give them to whomever he likes?

45   In the Biblical text, in *Demay*, and in the *editio princeps* here: לו. The ms. text is the only one making sense here.

46   From here to the end of the Halakhah, the text (with minor variants) is from *Demay* 6:3, explained there in Notes 59-76.

(42c line 74) מַתְנִיתָא פְּלִיגָא עַל רִבִּי יוֹסֵי בִּירְבִּי חֲנִינָה. קוֹנָם כֹּהֲנִים וּלְוִיִּם נֶהֱנִים לִי. יִטְּלוּ עַל כָּרְחוֹ. פָּתַר לָהּ בְּאוֹמֵר. אִי אֶיפְשִׁי לִיתֵּן מַתָּנוֹת כָּל־עִיקָּר. תֵּדַע שֶׁהוּא כֵן. דְּתַגֵּינָן כֹּהֲנִים אִילוּ לְוִיִּם אִילוּ נֶהֱנִין לִי. יִטְּלוּ אֲחֵרִים. מַתְנִיתָא פְּלִיגָא עַל רִבִּי יוֹחָנָן. אָמַר הוּא יִשְׂרָאֵל לְיִשְׂרָאֵל. הֵילָךְ סֶלַע זֶה וְתֵן בְּכוֹר זֶה לְבֶן בִּתִּי כֹהֵן. פָּתַר לָהּ בְּרוֹצֶה לִיתְּנוֹ לִשְׁנַיִם וּבֶן בִּתּוֹ אֶחָד מֵהֶן. אָמַר לוֹ. הֵא לָךְ סֶלַע זֶה וְתֵן כּוּלּוֹ לְבֶן בִּתִּי כֹהֵן.

A Mishnah disagrees with Rebbi Yose ben Rebbi Haninah: "A vow that no Cohanim or Levites should have any advantage from me, they should take against his will." He explains it about a person who says, I cannot possibly give them *any* gifts. You should know that this is so, since we have stated: "*These* Cohanim and Levites should [not] have any advantage from me, let others take." A *baraita* disagrees with Rebbi Johanan: "An Israel can say to another Israel, here you have a tetradrachma and give this firstling to my daughter's son, a Cohen." He explains, if he already wanted to give it to two [Cohanim] and that daughter's son was one of them; then one said, here you have a tetradrachma and give it whole to my daughter's son, a Cohen.

(42d line 3) בְּעוֹן קוֹמֵי רִבִּי זְעוּרָא. כֹּהֵן לְיִשְׂרָאֵל. רִבִּי אוֹסֵר. מָה רִבִּי יוֹסֵי אָמַר. רִבִּי חִזְקִיָּה בְּשֵׁם רִבִּי אָחָא אָמַר. הָכֵין אֲגִיבוֹן. עַל דַּעְתֵּיהּ דְּרִבִּי יוֹסֵי בַּר חֲנִינָה כֹּהֵן לְיִשְׂרָאֵל לָמָּה הוּא אָסוּר. לֹא מִפְּנֵי מַרְאִית הָעַיִן. אוֹף רִבִּי

יוֹחָנָן אִית לֵיהּ יִשְׂרָאֵל לְיִשְׂרָאֵל אָסוּר מִפְּנֵי מַרְאִית הָעַיִן. וְעוֹד מִן הָדָא. הַכֹּהֲנִים וְהַלְוִיִּם הַמְסַיְיעִין בַּגְּרָנוֹת אֵין נוֹתְנִין לָהֶן לֹא תְרוּמָה וְלֹא מַעֲשֵׂר. וְאִם נָתַן חִלֵּל. וְלֹא יְחַלְּלוּ אֶת קָדְשֵׁי בְּנֵי יִשְׂרָאֵל. וְהֵן מְחַלְּלִין אוֹתָן. יוֹתֵר מִכֵּן אָמְרוּ. תְּרוּמָתָן אֵינָן תְּרוּמָה וּמַעְשְׂרוֹתָן אֵינָן מַעֲשֵׂר וְהֶקְדֵּישָׁן אֵינָן הֶקְדֵּשׁ. וַעֲלֵיהֶן הַכָּתוּב אוֹמֵר רָאשֶׁיהָ בְּשׁוֹחַד יִשְׁפּוֹטוּ. וְהַמָּקוֹם מֵבִיא עֲלֵיהֶן שָׁלֹשׁ פּוּרְעָנִיּוֹת. הַהוּא דִכְתִיב לָכֵן בִּגְלַלְכֶם צִיּוֹן שָׂדֶה תֵחָרֵשׁ וִירוּשָׁלַיִם עִיִּין תִּהְיֶה וְהַר הַבַּיִת לְמוֹת יָעַר.

They asked before Rebbi Zeïra: a Cohen to an Israel, Rebbi forbids. What does Rebbi Yose say? Rebbi Ḥizqiah in the name of Rebbi Aḥa said, so he responded to them: In the opinion of Rebbi Yose ben Rebbi Ḥanina, why is a Cohen to an Israel forbidden, not because it looks badly? Also Rebbi Joḥanan holds that from an Israel to an Israel it is forbidden because it looks badly. In addition, because of the following, as it was stated: "Cohanim and Levites who help at the threshing floor have no right either to heave or to tithe, and if the farmer gave, it is desecrated, as it is said (*Lev.* 22:15): 'They should not desecrate the sanctified things of the Children of Israel,' but they desecrate them! In addition, they said that their heave is no heave, their tithes are no tithes, their dedications are no dedications, and about them the verse says (*Micha* 3:11): 'Their heads judge for bribes, [their priests are for hire].' The Omnipresent brings over them three catastrophies; that is what is written (*Micha* 3:12): 'Therefore, because of you Zion will be ploughed over as a field, Jerusalem will be desolate, and the Temple Mount a wooded hill.'

(42d line 13) מַתְנִיתָא פְּלִיגָא עַל רִבִּי יוֹחָנָן. הַמְקַדֵּשׁ בִּתְרוּמוֹת וּבְמַעְשְׂרוֹת וּבְמַתָּנוֹת וּבְמֵי חַטָּאת וּבְאֵפֶר חַטָּאת הֲרֵי זוּ מְקוּדֶּשֶׁת אַף עַל פִּי יִשְׂרָאֵל. פָּתַר לָהּ בִּתְרוּמָה שֶׁנָּפְלָה לוֹ מִשֶּׁל אֲבִי אִמּוֹ כֹהֵן.

A Mishnah disagrees with Rebbi Joḥanan: "If somebody marries preliminarily giving heave, tithes, 'gifts', water for sprinkling, or ashes of the red heifer, she is married, even if the groom is an Israel." He explains it with heave he inherited from his maternal grandfather, a Cohen.

(fol. 42b) **משנה ד**: קוֹנָם שֶׁאֵינִי עוֹשָׂה עַל פִּי אַבָּא וְעַל פִּי אָבִיךְ וְעַל פִּי אָחִי וְעַל פִּי אָחִיךְ אֵינוֹ יָכוֹל לְהָפֵר. שֶׁאֵינִי עוֹשָׂה עַל פִּיךָ אֵינוֹ צָרִיךְ לְהָפֵר. רַבִּי עֲקִיבָה אוֹמֵר יָפֵר שֶׁמָּא תַעֲדִיף עָלָיו יוֹתֵר מִן הָרָאוּי לוֹ. רַבִּי יוֹחָנָן בֶּן נוּרִי אָמַר יָפֵר. שֶׁמָּא יְגָרְשֶׁנָּה וּתְהֵא אֲסוּרָה לַחֲזוֹר לוֹ.

Mishnah 4: 'A *qônām* that I shall not work according to the wishes of my father, or your father, or my brother, or your brother,' he cannot dissolve. 'According to your wish,' he does not have to dissolve[47]. Rebbi Aqiba says, he has to dissolve, maybe she works more than the required minimum[48]. Rebbi Joḥanan ben Nuri said, he shall dissolve since maybe he would divorce her, then she would be forbidden to return to him.

47 Since she is obligated to keep house for him and work in the house, and nobody can annul his obligations by a vow.

48 She would be sinning if she did anything for him over the legal minimum stated in Mishnah *Ketubot* 5:5.

(42d line 15) **הלכה ד**: קוֹנָם שֶׁאֵינִי עוֹשָׂה עַל פִּי אַבָּא כול׳. תַּמָּן תַּנִּינָן. הַמַּקְדִּישׁ מַעֲשֵׂי יְדֵי אִשְׁתּוֹ הֲרֵי זוֹ עוֹשָׂה וְאוֹכֶלֶת. הַמּוֹתָר. רַבִּי מֵאִיר אוֹמֵר. הֶקְדֵּשׁ. רַבִּי יוֹחָנָן הַסַּנְדְּלָר אוֹמֵר. חוּלִין. רַבִּי שִׁמְעוֹן בֶּן לָקִישׁ אוֹמֵר. בְּמוֹתָר חָמֵשׁ סְלָעִים פְּלִיגִין. דּוּ פָתַר לָהּ בְּמַעֲלָה לָהּ מְזוֹנוֹת וְאֵינוֹ נוֹתֵן לָהּ מָעָה כֶּסֶף לְצָרְכֶיהָ. וְתַנִּינָן. אִם אֵינוֹ נוֹתֵן לָהּ מָעָה כֶּסֶף לְצָרְכֶיהָ מַעֲשֵׂה יָדֶיהָ שֶׁלָּהּ. רַבִּי יוֹחָנָן אָמַר. בְּמוֹתָר לְאַחַר מִיתָה פְלִיגִין. דּוּ פָתַר לָהּ בְּשֶׁאֵינוֹ מַעֲלֶה לָהּ מְזוֹנוֹת.

אֲבָל בְּמַעֲלֶה לָהּ מְזוֹנוֹת דִּבְרֵי הַכֹּל קִידְּשׁוּ. וְכָא אֵינוֹ יָכוֹל לְהָפֵר. רִבִּי מֵאִיר אוֹמֵר. אֵינוֹ צָרִיךְ לְהָפֵר. רִבִּי יוֹחָנָן הַסַּנְדְּלָר אוֹמֵר. שֶׁלָּהּ. רִבִּי עֲקִיבָה אוֹמֵר. שֶׁלָּהּ. רִבִּי יוֹחָנָן בֶּן נוּרִי אוֹמֵר. שֶׁלּוֹ.

Halakhah 4: "'A *qônām* that I shall not work according to the wishes of my father,' etc. There, we have stated[49]: "If somebody dedicates his wife's work, she works and eats. The excess? Rebbi Meïr says, it is dedicated; Rebbi Johanan the Alexandrian said, it is profane." Rebbi Simeon ben Laqish said, they disagree about the excess over five tetradrachmas[50]. He explains it in the case of one who supports his wife with food but does not give her an obolus for her needs[51], as we stated: "If he does not give her an obolus for her needs, what she earns is hers". Rebbi Johanan said, they disagree about the excess left after [the husband's] death; for he explains it if he does not support her with food[52]. But if he supports her with food, everybody agrees that it became dedicated[53]. And here, he cannot dissolve! Rebbi Meïr says, he does not have to dissolve[54]. Rebbi Johanan the Alexandrian said, hers. Rebbi Aqiba said, hers. Rebbi Johanan ben Nuri said, his[55].

49 Mishnah *Ketubot* 5:4. The husband dedicated the wife's income from her work to the Temple. He cannot dispose of what she needs for her livelihood. The question is only about what she earns in excess of her needs. The text of the first part of the paragraph is in *Ketubot* 5:5 in slightly extended form; the parallel discussion in the Babli *Ketubot* 58b-59a.

50 It is stated in Mishnah *Ketubot* 5:9 that the husband has to give his wife a silver obolus every week as pocket money. If he does not give it, the Mishnah states that he has lost his claim to her earnings (and his dedication is void since nobody can dedicate what is not his.) He can also require her to spin wool in the weight of 5 Judean tetradrachmas.

51 He holds that R. Meïr, who is the presumed author of an anonymous Mishnah, states that spinning the 5 tetradrachmas is for the silver obolus

she receives, and the excess of her work is for the food the husband provides. In the case considered here, the husband has no right to the value of the first 5 tetradrachma weights of her spinning but he can dedicate all the excess. R. Joḥanan the Alexandrian will hold that the 5 tetradrachmas will pay for the food and the excess for the pocket money, then the excess is the wife's property and the husband has no right to dedicate it.

52 He explains an arrangement that the wife takes neither food nor money from the husband and retains all her earnings for herself. In that case, the husband has no say about her earnings. But if she dies before him, he inherits from her and can dedicate what he wishes. (In the Babli, *Ketubot* 58b, this is Samuel's position.) R. Joḥanan the Alexandrian holds that nobody can dedicate anything not in his possession;

therefore, any disposition of his future inheritance which he makes during her lifetime is void.

53 R. Joḥanan holds that the spinning of the first 5 tetradrachmas pays for food and pocket money. Therefore, anything in excess is unincumbered property of the husband.

54 Since she is obligated, she cannot avoid an obligation by a vow.

55 R. Joḥanan the Alexandrian in *Ketubot* and R. Aqiba in *Nedarim* both hold that the excess work of the wife belongs to the wife. Therefore, R. Aqiba requires the husband to dissolve the vow lest the wife give to her husband from her earnings and break her vow. But R. Joḥanan ben Nuri holds that the excess is the husband's; therefore he only counsels the husband to dissolve to permit him to take his wife back after a divorce.

(42d line 24) רִבִּי עֲקִיבָה אוֹמֵר. יָפֵר. אָמַר רִבִּי בָּא. בְּשֶׁאָסְרָה מַעֲשֵׂה יָדֶיהָ מְלַעֲשׂוֹת עַד הֹ סְלָעִים הוּא כוֹפָהּ. מִיכָּאן וְאֵילַךְ אֵינוֹ כוֹפָהּ. שֶׁמִּתְיָירֵא שֶׁמָּא תַעֲשֶׂה יֶתֶר וְנִמְצֵאת נֶהֱנִית מִן הָאִסּוּר. לְפוּם כֵּן רִבִּי עֲקִיבָה אוֹמֵר. יָפֵר שֶׁלּוֹ. אָמַר רִבִּי הִילָא. אֵיפְשָׁר לָהּ לַעֲשׂוֹת חָמֵשׁ סְלָעִים מְצוּמְצָמוֹת. עַד הֹ סְלָעִים כּוֹפָהּ. מִיכָּן וְאֵילַךְ אֵינוֹ כוֹפָה. שֶׁמִּתְיָירֵא שֶׁמָּא תַעֲדִיף כָּל־שֶׁהוּא וְנִמְצָא נֶהֱנָה מִן הָאִסּוּר. לְפוּם כֵּן.

"Rebbi Aqiba said, he has to dissolve." Rebbi Abba said, if she forbids the yields of her work, [vowing] not to work, he can force her up to the weight of five tetradrachmas. More than that he cannot force, for he has to be afraid that she may work more and it turns out that she profits from what is forbidden[56]. Therefore, Rebbi Aqiba says, he has to dissolve his part. Rebbi Hila said, it is impossible for her to make exactly the weight of five tetradrachmas. He could force her up to the weight of five tetradrachmas; more that that he cannot force. He has to be afraid that she might be over the limit by a minute amount; then he would profit from what is forbidden[57]. Therefore...[58].

56 Since the excess is hers automatically.

57 If she thinks that she spun the weight of five tetradrachmas but in fact she made a little more, then in accepting this he would be sinning inadvertently. It is in his interest to dissolve the vow. The smallest weight measurable in talmudic theory is the *peruṭa*, $1/32$ of an obolus (about 4 mg in silver equivalent).

58 It seems that one has to insert here the text from R. Abba's argument.

(42d line 30) רִבִּי יוֹחָנָן בֶּן נוּרִי אָמַר. יָפֵר. אָמַר רִבִּי הִילָא. טַעֲמָא דְּרִבִּי יוֹחָנָן בֶּן נוּרִי שֶׁמִּתּוֹךְ שֶׁיּוֹדֵעַ שֶׁאִם מְגָרְשָׁהּ הָיָה אֲסוּרָה לַחֲזוֹר לוֹ וְאַף מַקְנִיטָתוֹ וְהוּא מְגָרְשָׁהּ.

"Rebbi Johanan ben Nuri said, he should dissolve." Rebbi Hila said, the reason of Rebbi Johanan ben Nuri is that even if he knows that if he divorces her she would be forbidden to return to him, she needles him until he divorces her[59].

59 Since R. Johanan ben Nuri holds that the excess work is the husband's and the vow would be active only after divorce, it seems that at this moment there is neither a vow of mortification nor one between him and her. How could the husband legally dissolve the vow? It seems R. Hila reads "she knows that if he divorces". He argues that it is a vow between him and her since the wife, knowing that the husband would be extremely reluctant to divorce her, could be quite unpleasant with impunity and he would suffer.

(fol. 42b) **משנה ה:** נָדְרָה אִשְׁתּוֹ וְסָבוּר שֶׁנָּדְרָה בִתּוֹ. נָדְרָה בִתּוֹ וְסָבוּר שֶׁנָּדְרָה אִשְׁתּוֹ. נָדְרָה בַנָּזִיר וְסָבוּר שֶׁנָּדְרָה בַקָּרְבָּן. נָדְרָה בַקָּרְבָּן וְסָבוּר שֶׁנָּדְרָה בַנָּזִיר. נָדְרָה מִן הַתְּאֵינִים וְסָבוּר שֶׁנָּדְרָה מִן הָעֲנָבִים. מִן הָעֲנָבִים וְסָבוּר שֶׁנָּדְרָה מִן הַתְּאֵינִים. הֲרֵי זֶה יַחֲזוֹר וְיָפֵר.

Mishnah 5: If his wife made a vow and he was under the impression that it was his daughter, or his daughter made a vow and he was under this impression that it was his wife. If she vowed to be a *nazir* and he was under the impression that she vowed a sacrifice, or if she vowed a sacrifice and he was under the impression that she vowed to be a *nazir*. If she woved to abstain from figs and he was under the impression that it was from grapes, or if from grapes and he was under the impression that it was from figs, he shall dissolve a second time[60].

משנה ו: אָמְרָה קוֹנָם תְּאֵינִים וַעֲנָבִים אִילּוּ שֶׁאֵינִי טוֹעֶמֶת קִייֵם לַתְּאֵינִים כּוּלּוֹ קִייֵם. הֵיפֵר עַל הַתְּאֵינִים אֵינוֹ מוּפָר עַד שֶׁיָּפֵר אַף לָעֲנָבִים. אָמְרָה קוֹנָם תְּאֵינִים שֶׁאֵינִי טוֹעֶמֶת וַעֲנָבִים שֶׁאֵינִי טוֹעֶמֶת הֲרֵי אִילּוּ שְׁנֵי נְדָרִים.

If she said, a *qônām* that I shall not taste these figs and grapes, if he confirmed for the figs he confirmed everything. If he dissolved for figs it is not dissolved unless he also dissolves for grapes[61]. If she said, a *qônām* that I shall not taste these figs, that I shall not taste these grapes; these are two vows.

60 Since erroneous dissolutions or confirmations are invalid, the time limit for dissolution starts to run again the moment he is informed of his error.

61 A partially confirmed vow is confirmed; a partially dissolved vow is not dissolved (Tosephta 7:4).

(42d line 32) **הלכה ו:** אָמְרָה קוֹנָם תְּאֵינִים וַעֲנָבִים אִילּוּ כוּל׳. אֲפִילוּ שָׁמַע וְשָׁתַק. אֲפִילוּ שָׁמַע וְקִייֵם.

Halakhah 6 "If she said, a *qônām* that I shall not taste these figs and grapes," etc. Even if he heard and remained silent, even if he heard and confirmed[62].

62 This refers to Mishnah 5. Even if he had erroneously confirmed the vow, once he is informed of the true situation, he may dissolve. This is explicit in the Tosephta, 7:4.

(42d line 30) אִית תַּנָּיֵי תַנֵּי. יְקִימֶינּוּ מִמֶּינוּ. וִיפִירֶנּוּ מִימֶינוּ. אִית תַּנָּיֵי תַנֵּי. יְקִימֶינּוּ כּוּלוֹ. וִיפִירֶנּוּ כּוּלוֹ. אִית תַּנָּיֵי תַנֵּי. יְקִימֶינּוּ מִימֶינוּ. וִיפִירֶנּוּ כּוּלוֹ. וְאִית תַּנָּיֵי תַנֵּי. יְקִימֶינּוּ כּוּלוֹ. וִיפִירֶנּוּ מִימֶינוּ. מַתְנִיתָא כְּמַאן דְּאָמַר. יְקִימֶינּוּ מִמֶּינוּ. וִיפִירֶנּוּ כּוּלוֹ. דְּתַנֵּי קִיֵּים לַתְּאֵינִים קִיֵּים לְכוּלוֹ. הֵפֵר לַתְּאֵינִים אֵינוֹ מוּפָר עַד שֶׁיָּפֵר אַף לָעֲנָבִים. אָמְרָה. קוֹנָם תְּאֵינָה שֶׁאֵינִי טוֹעֶמֶת וְעוֹד עֵינָב. תַּפְלוּגְתָּא דְּרִבִּי יִשְׁמָעֵאל וְרִבִּי עֲקִיבָה. דְּרִבִּי יִשְׁמָעֵאל אוֹמֵר. אַחַר הַנֶּדֶר. וְרִבִּי עֲקִיבָה אוֹמֵר. אַחַר הָאִסָּר.

Some Tannaïm state: "He shall confirm it[63]", even partially, "he shall dissolve it", even partially. Some Tannaïm state: "He shall confirm it", totally[64], "he shall dissolve it", totally. Some Tannaïm state: "He shall confirm it", even partially, "he shall dissolve it", totally. Some Tannaïm state: "He shall confirm it", totally, "he shall dissolve it", even partially. The Mishnah follows him who said, "he shall confirm it", even partially, "he shall dissolve it", totally. As we have stated: "If he confirmed for the figs he confirmed everything. If he dissolved for figs it is not dissolved unless he also dissolves for grapes."

If she said, a *qônām* that I shall not taste a fig nor a grape berry, that is a matter of difference between Rebbi Ismael and Rebbi Aqiba since Rebbi Ismael says, the vow decides, and Rebbi Aqiba says, the prohibition decides[65].

63 *Num.* 30: 14: "Her husband may confirm it or her husband may dissolve it."

The Tosephta (7:4) has a fifth version: The husband may confirm one and dissolve the other of two vows made at the same time, i. e., it is applicable to the situation described at the end of Mishnah 6.

64 The husband has only the choice to accept or to reject the wife's vow *in toto.*

65 In Halakhah 9, R. Ismael says the determining factor is the vow. A multiplicity of vows made at the same time is treated as a multiplicity; there are two separate vows in our case. R. Aqiba says that a multiplicity of prohibitions imposed at the same time are one prohibition; there is only one vow.

(fol. 42b) **משנה ז**: יוֹדֵעַ אֲנִי שֶׁיֵּשׁ נְדָרִים אֲבָל אֵינִי יוֹדֵעַ שֶׁיֵּשׁ מְפִירִין יָפֵר. יוֹדֵעַ אֲנִי שֶׁיֵּשׁ מְפִירִין אֲבָל אֵינִי יוֹדֵעַ שֶׁזֶּה נֶדֶר. רִבִּי מֵאִיר אוֹמֵר לֹא יָפֵר. וַחֲכָמִים אוֹמְרִים יָפֵר.

Mishnah 7: 'I knew that there are vows but I did not know that they can be dissolved.' 'I knew that one can dissolve but I did not realize that this was a vow.' Rebbi Meïr says, he cannot dissolve, but the Sages say, he can dissolve[66].

66 R. Meïr holds that he had his chance; if he did not use it because of his ignorance, it is his fault. The Sages hold that the time for dissolution starts only when he is instructed about the law. In the Babli, 87b/88a, R. Meïr's position is explained by his interpretation of the biblical verses.

(42d line 40) **הלכה ז**: יוֹדֵעַ אֲנִי שֶׁיֵּשׁ נְדָרִים כול'. אָמַר רִבִּי זְעִירָא. טַעֲמָא דְרִבִּי מֵאִיר עִילָּה הִיא רוֹצֶה שֶׁתִּדּוֹר וִיגָרְשֶׁנּוּ. דַּל כֵּן הָיָה לוֹ לְגָרְשָׁהּ מִשָּׁעָה רִאשׁוֹנָה.

Halakhah 7: "'I knew that there are vows,'" etc. Rebbi Ze'ira said, the reason of Rebbi Meïr: It is a subterfuge. He wants her to make vows so he can divorce her[67]. That is not so, he could have divorced her on the first occasion[68].

67 This refers to the second case, when he admits that he knew he could dissolve his wife's vows. Then he should have dissolved the vow immediately even if it was a borderline case. If it was a vow, it would be dissolved; if it was not a vow, no harm would have been done. We suspect that he wants to encourage his wife to make vows so he could claim that she always makes vows and one cannot expect from him to live with such a wife; he asks permission from the court to divorce her without payment of the *ketubah* sum (Mishnah *Ketubot* 7:6).

68 This gives the position of the Sages who note that he could have started complaining at the first vow. Therefore, they accept his words at face value.

(fol. 42b) **משנה ח**: הַמּוּדָּר הֲנָיָיה מֵחֲתָנוֹ וְהוּא רוֹצֶה לָתֵת לְבִתּוֹ מָעוֹת אוֹמֵר לָהּ הֲרֵי הַמָּעוֹת הָאִילוּ נְתוּנִים לָךְ בְּמַתָּנָה וּבִלְבַד שֶׁלֹּא יְהֵא לְבַעֲלֵיךְ רְשׁוּת בָּהֶן. אֶלָּא מַה שֶּׁאַתְּ נוֹשָׂא וְנוֹתֶנֶת בְּפִיךְ.

Mishnah 8: If a person is by a vow prevented to benefit his son-in-law but wants to give money to his daughter, he says to her: These coins are given to you as a gift on condition that your husband shall have no claim to them, except what you trade for your needs.

(42d line 42) **הלכה ח**: הַמּוּדָּר הֲנָיָיה מֵחֲתָנוֹ כול'. תַּנֵּי. וְלֹא לֵיהּ. אָמַר רִבִּי מָאן תַּנָּא. וְלֹא לֵיהּ. רִבִּי מֵאִיר. דְּרִבִּי מֵאִיר עֶבֶד יַד הָעֶבֶד כְּיַד רַבּוֹ. מִפְּנֵי שֶׁאָמַר. וְלֹא לֵיהּ. הָא אִם לֹא אָמַר. וְלֹא לֵיהּ. זָכָה הָאִשָּׁה זָכָה בַעְלָהּ.

Halakhah 8: "If a person is by a vow prevented to benefit his son-in-law," etc. It was stated[69]: "Neither do you". Rebbi said, who stated "neither do you"? Rebbi Meïr, for Rebbi Meïr makes the hand of the slave the hand of his master[70]. Because he said "neither do you." If he had not said "neither do you", if the wife acquired, the husband would have acquired.

---

69 In this version, the father cannot give his daughter an unrestricted gift. He must spell out a use; the daughter cannot save the money for an unspecified future.

70 For R. Meïr, anything the slave acquires becomes automatically his master's property. Therefore, no slave can buy his freedom from his master since he cannot have money that is not his master's. Any money needed for his manumission must be in the hand of a third party [Babli 88b; *Qiddušin* 1:3 (60a l. 26), Babli 23b; *Ma'aser Šeni* 4:4, Notes 89,96; *Ketubot* 6:1 (30c l. 46); *Eruvin* 7:6 (24c l. 62)]. Similarly, R. Meïr gives the husband property rights in everything his wife acquires. He will accept a contract in which the wife retains all her earnings while renouncing all support from her husband as a contract in which the wife acts by the husband's authorization. The majority accepts separate property both for the slave and the wife.

משנה ט: וְנֶדֶר אַלְמָנָה וּגְרוּשָׁה כֹּל אֲשֶׁר אָסְרָה עַל נַפְשָׁהּ יָקוּם עָלֶיהָ. (fol. 42b) כֵּיצַד. אָמְרָה הֲרֵינִי נְזִירָה אַחַר שְׁלֹשִׁים יוֹם אַף עַל פִּי שֶׁנִּישֵּׂאת בְּתוֹךְ שְׁלֹשִׁים יוֹם אֵינוֹ יָכוֹל לְהָפֵר. נָדְרָה וְהִיא בִּרְשׁוּת הַבַּעַל וְהֵיפֵר לָהּ. אָמְרָה הֲרֵינִי נְזִירָה לְאַחַר שְׁלֹשִׁים אַף עַל פִּי שֶׁנִּתְאַלְמְנָה אוֹ נִתְגָּרְשָׁה בְּתוֹךְ שְׁלֹשִׁים הֲרֵי זֶה מוּפָר. **משנה י**: נָדְרָה בּוֹ בַיּוֹם נִתְגָּרְשָׁה בּוֹ בַיּוֹם הֶחֱזִירָהּ בּוֹ בַיּוֹם אֵינוֹ יָכוֹל לְהָפֵר. זֶה הַכְּלָל כָּל־שֶׁיָּצְאָת לִרְשׁוּת עַצְמָהּ שָׁעָה אַחַת אֵינוֹ יָכוֹל לְהָפֵר.

Mishnah 9: "The vow of a widow or a divorcee, anything she forbids to herself shall be confirmed.[70]" How is that? If she said, I shall be a *nazir* after thirty days, even if she married within these thirty days he cannot dissolve. If she made the vow under her husband's authority and he dissolved it, if she had said, I shall be a *nazir* after thirty days, even if she should become a widow or a divorcee within the next 30 days, it remains dissolved.

Mishnah 10: If she made a vow, was on the same day divorced[71], and taken back, he cannot dissolve. This is the principle: He cannot dissolve for any one who was on her own for one moment.

---

70   *Num.* 30:10.

71   She was definitively married or was an adult. By divorce she became an independent adult. If he remarries her, even on the same day, the vow precedes the marriage and is out of the husband's power.

(42d line 42) **הלכה ח**: וְנֶדֶר אַלְמָנָה וּגְרוּשָׁה כול׳. הָדָא הִיא רבִּי יִשְׁמָעֵאל אוֹמֵר. אַחֲרֵי הַנֶּדֶר. רבִּי עֲקִיבָה אוֹמֵר. אַחֲרֵי הָאִיסָר. הָיָה נֶדֶר וְאִיסָר כְּאַחַת. הֵיךְ עֲבִידָא. אָמְרָה. הֲרֵינִי נְזִירָה לְאַחַר שְׁלֹשִׁים יוֹם. וְשָׁמַע בַּעֲלָהּ וְלֹא הֵיפֵר לָהּ וְגֵירְשָׁהּ וְהֶחֱזִירָהּ בְּתוֹךְ ל יוֹם. הַיְינוֹ נֶדֶר וְאִיסָר כְּאַחַת.

Halakhah 9: "The vow of a widow or a divorcee," etc. This refers to what Rebbi Ismael says, the vow decides; Rebbi Aqiba says, prohibition decides[72]. If vow and prohibition came together[73]? How is that? She said, I shall be a *nazir* in 30 days. Her husband heard it and did not dissolve[74]. He divorced her and remarried her within the 30 days. Is that when vow and prohibition come together[75]?

---

72   Cf. Note 65. R. Aqiba says the moment she imposed the prohibition is the decisive one; since at that time she had no husband, the vow is not under the later husband's jurisdiction. R. Ismael says that the point of activation

of the vow determines; there is no vow until after 30 days and the husband then can dissolve the vow. The Mishnah follows R. Aqiba. This interpretation of the opinions of Rebbis Aqiba and Ismael is forced by the Tosephta, 7:6, and is interpreted in this way in the Babli, 89a.

73 It is the normal case that a woman makes a vow for immediate validity. But we are looking for a case involving a divorcee.

74 For R. Aqiba, he had his chance and missed it. For R. Ismael, his inaction is irrelevant since the vow is not yet activated.

75 The Tosephta states: A widow who said: I shall be a *nazir* the moment I shall be married. R. Ismael says, the husband can dissolve (since the vow starts to be active in his domain, it is not a vow preceding the marriage). R. Aqiba says, he cannot dissolve (since the vow was made when she was a widow). In the case here, the remarriage was before the 30 days were over; for R. Ismael there is no question that the husband can dissolve the vow. For R. Aqiba the question is whether the divorce is counted to introduce a new domain, in which case he can dissolve, or is a continuation of the old, in which case he had his chance and did not use it. The question is not resolved.

(fol. 42b) **משנה יא:** תֵּשַׁע נְעָרוֹת נִדְרֵיהֶן קַיָּימִין. בּוֹגֶרֶת וְהִיא יְתוֹמָה נַעֲרָה וּבָגְרָה וְהִיא יְתוֹמָה נַעֲרָה שֶׁלֹּא בָגְרָה וְהִיא יְתוֹמָה. בּוֹגֶרֶת וּמֵת אָבִיהָ נַעֲרָה בוֹגֶרֶת וּמֵת אָבִיהָ נַעֲרָה שֶׁלֹּא בָגְרָה וּמֵת אָבִיהָ. נַעֲרָה שֶׁמֵּת אָבִיהָ וּמִשֶּׁמֵּת אָבִיהָ בָּגְרָה וְאָבִיהָ קַיָּים נַעֲרָה בוֹגֶרֶת וְאָבִיהָ קַיָּים. רִבִּי יְהוּדָה אוֹמֵר. אַף הַמַּשִּׂיא בִּתּוֹ הַקְּטַנָּה וְנִתְאַלְמְנָה אוֹ נִתְגָּרְשָׁה וְחָזְרָה אֶצְלוֹ עֲדַיִן הִיא נַעֲרָה.

Mishnah 11: The vows of nine young women[76] are confirmed: An adult who is an orphan, an adolescent who became an adult and is an orphan, an adolescent who did not become an adult but is an orphan. An adult whose father died, an adolescent who became an adult and her father died, an adolescent who did not become an adult and her father died. An adolescent whose father died and afterwards she became an adult, an adult whose father lives, an adolescent girl whose father lives. Rebbi Jehudah says, also if somebody marries off his underage daughter and she becomes widowed or divorced and returns to him, she still is an adolescent[77].

76 In this introduction to the Mishnah, נערה is used in a nontechnical term "young female", whether minor, adolescent, or of age. Later the same word is used in a more technical sense, "underage or adolescent." The principle underlying the Mishnah is very simple: The vows of an unmarried girl are not subject to dissolution if either she has no father or she is emancipated from him either by coming of age or by having been definitively married and then divorced or widowed.

77 R. Jehudah denies that an underage girl (not an adolescent) is emancipated from her father by marriage.

(42d line 48) **הלכה יא**: תֵּשַׁע נְעָרוֹת נִדְרֵיהֶן קַיָּימִין כול'. אָמַר רִבִּי יוֹחָנָן. שְׁתַּיִם הֵן. וְלָמָּה תַּנִּינָן תֵּשַׁע. בִּשְׁבִיל לְחַדֵּד אֶת הַתַּלְמִידִים. וּכְרִבִּי יוּדָה שָׁלֹשׁ.

Halakhah 11: "The vows of nine young women are confirmed," etc. Rebbi Johanan said, there are two[78]. But why did we state "two"? To train the students. And according to Rebbi Jehudah, there are three.

78 One category is the orphan and the minor or adolescent emancipated by dissolution of her marriage; the other is the adult. For R. Jehudah, the widowed or divorced minor falls in a separate category. The Bablí, 89b, holds that the nine are R. Jehudah's but that the majority recognizes the adult, the orphan, and the minor or adolescent emancipated by dissolution of her marriage.

(fol. 42b) **משנה יב:** קונָם שֶׁאֵינִי נֶהֱנִית לְאַבָּא וּלְאָבִיךָ אִם עוֹשָׂה אֲנִי עַל פִּיךָ. שֶׁאֵינִי נֶהֱנִית לָךְ אִם עוֹשָׂה אֲנִי עַל פִּי אַבָּא וְעַל פִּי אָבִיךָ הֲרֵי זֶה יָפֵר.

Mishnah 12: 'A *qônām* that I shall not take any benefit from my father, or your father, if I shall do anything for you.' '[A *qônām*] that I shall not have any benefit from you if I shall do anything for my father, or for your father.' These he can dissolve.

(42d line 50) **הלכה יב:** קונָם שֶׁאֵינִי נֶהֱנִית לְאַבָּא וּלְאָבִיךָ כול'. תַּנֵּי. רִבִּי נָתָן אוֹמֵר. לֹא יָפֵר. וַחֲכָמִים אוֹמְרִים. יָפֵר. מִפְּנֵי מָה הוּא מֵיפֵר. חַבְרַיָּיא אָמְרֵי. מִפְּנֵי עִינּוּי נֶפֶשׁ שֶׁלּוֹ. רִבִּי זְעִירָא וְרִבִּי הִילָא תְּרֵיהוֹן אָמְרִין מִפְּנֵי נִדְרֵי עִינּוּי נֶפֶשׁ שֶׁלָּהּ.

Halakhah 12: "'A *qônām* that I shall not take any benefit from my father, or your father," etc. It was stated[79]: Rebbi Nathan says, he cannot dissolve[80], but the Sages say, he can dissolve. Why can he dissolve? The colleagues say, because of his mortification[81]. Rebbi Ze'ira and Rebbi Hila say, because of her mortification[82].

79 Tosephta 7:7; cf. *Tosefta ki-Fshutah* vol. 7, p. 501; Babli 89b.
80 The reason seems to be that the vow is neither a mortification nor does it hinder marital relations. The Babli gives as reason that the husband cannot dissolve as long as his wife did not work for him because the prohibition did not start. There is no hint of that in the Yerushalmi.
81 He feels badly about the situation; that is reason enough.
82 They hold that his being hurt can never be a reason. He gets the power of dissolution because she might be hurt by this in the future.

(fol. 42b) **משנה יג:** בָּרִאשׁוֹנָה הָיוּ אוֹמְרִים שָׁלֹשׁ נָשִׁים יוֹצְאוֹת וְנוֹטְלוֹת כְּתוּבָּה. הָאוֹמֶרֶת טְמֵיאָה אֲנִי לָךְ. שָׁמַיִם בֵּינִי לְבֵינָךְ. נְטוּלָה אֲנִי מִן הַיְּהוּדִים. חָזְרוּ

לוֹמַר שֶׁלֹּא תְהֵא אִשָּׁה נוֹתֶנֶת עֵינֶיהָ בְּאַחֵר וּמְקַלְקֶלֶת עַל בַּעֲלָהּ. הָאוֹמֶרֶת טְמֵיאָה אֲנִי לָךְ תָּבִיא רְאָיָיא לִדְבָרֶיהָ. שָׁמַיִם בֵּינִי לְבֵינָךְ יַעֲשׂוּ דֶּרֶךְ בַּקָּשָׁה. נְטוּלָה אֲנִי מִן הַיְּהוּדִים יָפֵר חֶלְקוֹ וּתְהֵא מְשַׁמְּשַׁתּוֹ וּתְהֵא נְטוּלָה מִן הַיְּהוּדִים.

Mishnah 13: Earlier they said, three categories of women have to be divorced and collect their *ketubah*: The one who says, I am impure for you[83], or Heaven is between you and me[84], or I am separated from the Jews[85]. They changed to say that a woman should not be encouraged to want another man and cause trouble to her husband. If she says, I am impure for you, she should bring proof[86]. Heaven is between you and me, they should try to mediate[87]. I am separated from the Jews, he shall dissolve his part, she shall live with him and be separated from the Jews[88].

83 The wife of a Cohen who declares that she was raped without witnesses. Since the rabbinically accepted definition of a זוֹנָה (*Lev.* 21:7) is a woman who had sexual contact with a man whom she could not legally marry, and a married woman cannot marry anybody, she is forbidden to her husband who has to divorce her. Since it is not her fault, he has to pay the entire *ketubah* sum.

84 She claims that he is infertile.

85 She made a vow not to sleep with any Jew. The earlier opinion was that a woman would not make such a vow unless she suffers from vaginism and sexual relations are painful for her. Since the vow is not frivolous, she can claim her *ketubah* payment.

86 Obviously not proof beyond a reasonable doubt but to make the claim plausible.

87 As long as it is infertility, not impotence, she cannot force a divorce. The Babli, *Yebamot* 65b, holds that the rabbi shall grant the divorce and not try to keep the wife in the marriage if she claims that their financial situation is such that she needs children to care for her in her old age and the husband cannot provide the children.

88 Since she made the vow only against sleeping with Jews, not with any man in the world, one assumes that she can enjoy intercourse and only prefers Gentiles.

(42d line 53) **הלכה יג:** רִאשׁוֹנָה הָיוּ אוֹמְרִים כול'. הָא לֹא הֲבִיאָה רְאָיָיה לִדְבָרֶיהָ פְּשִׁיטָא שֶׁהִיא מוּתֶּרֶת לְבֵיתָהּ. אָמַר רִבִּי הִילָא. לֹא מִסְתַּבְּרָא אִם הָיָה חָבֵר יָחוּשׁ. וְאִם הָיָה כֹהֵן שֶׁהִיא אֲסוּרָה לוֹכַל בִּתְרוּמָה. אָתָא עוֹבְדָא קוֹמֵי רִבִּי חֲנַנְיָה חֲבֵרִין דְּרַבָּנִין וְהִתִּירָהּ לוֹכַל בִּתְרוּמָה. אָמַר רִבִּי חַגַּיי. אַבָּא יָדַע רֵישָׁא וְסֵיפָא. אִיסְטְרַטְיוֹת נִכְנְסוּ לָעִיר. וּבָאת אִשָּׁה וְאָמְרָה. אִיסְטְרַטְיוֹט חִבְּקַנִי וְהִטִּיל שִׁכְבַת זֶרַע בֵּין בִּרְכַּיי. וְהִתִּירָהּ לוֹכַל בִּתְרוּמָה. אָתָא עוֹבְדָא קוֹמֵי רִבִּי יִצְחָק בַּר טְבַלַיי בְּאִשָּׁה אַחַת שֶׁאָמְרָה. הַבַּיָּים שְׁלִי פִּיתַּנִי. אָמַר לָהּ. אֵין הַבַּיָּים אָסוּר. וַאֲסָרָהּ. הָכָא אַתְּ אָמַר. וַאֲסָרָהּ. הָכָא אַתְּ אָמַר. וְהִתִּירָהּ. תַּמָּן בָּאת לוֹסַר עַצְמָהּ וְהִתִּירָהּ. בְּרַם הָכָא בָּאת לְהַתִּיר עַצְמָהּ וַאֲסָרָהּ.

Halakhah 13: "Earlier they said," etc. That is, if she cannot bring proof for her assertion, it is obvious that she is permitted to her house[89]. Rebbi Hila said, would it not be reasonable that a fellow should be apprehensive[90], and if he was a Cohen that she should be forbidden to eat heave[91]? There came a case before Rebbi Ḥanina, the colleague of the rabbis, and he permitted her to eat heave. Rebbi Ḥaggai said, my father knew the first and the last case. Soldiers[92] entered the town. A woman came and said, a soldier[92] embraced me and ejaculated semen between my knees. He permitted her to eat heave[93]. There came a case before Rebbi Isaac bar Tevele of a woman who said, my cowhand[94] seduced[95] me. He said to her, is the cowhand not forbidden? And he forbade her. Here, you say that he forbade her. There, you say that he permitted her. There, she came to forbid herself and he permitted her. But here, she came to permit herself and he forbade her.

89 Since the later Mishnah states that she is not divorced, obviously she will be permitted to her husband.

90 A "fellow" follows the rules of purity strictly, cf. Introduction to Tractate *Demay*. R. Hila suggests that the strictly observant should follow the earlier Mishnah in this case.

91 In the Babli, 90b, this is the authoritative opinion of Rava. (There is internal and some ms. evidence that the author of this opinion is the less authoritative Rabba. In that case, the Babli would concur with the Yerushalmi that she may eat heave. But the legal tradition is to read Rava.)

92 Greek στρατιώτης, "warrior, commander".

93 Since we do not know of the incident from any other source, "the mouth which forbade" (she, who tells of the encounter with the soldier) "is the mouth which permitted" (that there was no penetration) (Mishnah *Ketubot* 2:2).

94 Reading בֵּיהֶם "the one who cares for the cattle" for ביאם because of the disappearance of guttural sounds; already noted by David Fraenckel.

95 An adult woman is guilty of adultery if she lets herself be seduced and must be divorced without payment of the *ketubah*. (Seduction of a minor is treated as rape; cf. *Soṭah* 1:1, Note 91.)

(42d line 63) שָׁמַיִם בֵּינִי לְבֵינָךְ. כַּמָּא דִשְׁמַיָּא רְחִיקִין מִן אַרְעָא כֵּן תְּהֵא הַאי אִתְּתָא רְחִיקָה מִן הַהוּא גַבְרָא. יַעֲשׂוּ דֶּרֶךְ בַּקָּשָׁה. אָמַר רַב הוּנָא. יַעֲשׂוּ סְעוּדָה וְהֵן מִתְרַגְּלִין לָבוֹא דֶּרֶךְ סְעוּדָה.

"Heaven is between you and me": as Heaven is far from earth, so this woman should be far from that man. "They should try to mediate." Rav Huna said, they should make a dinner and they will get used to be with one another by the dinner.

(42d line 67) תַּנֵּי. כָּלוּי אֲנִי מִמָּךְ. פָּרוּשׁ אֲנִי מִמָּךְ. רִבִּי יִרְמְיָה בָּעֵי. וְלָמָּה לֹא תַנִּינָן נָטוּל. אָמַר רִבִּי יוֹסֵה. וְתַנִּיתָהּ בְּסוֹפָהּ. וּנְטוּלָה אֲנִי מִן הַיְּהוּדִים.

[96]It was stated: "I am jailed away from you, I am separated away from you". Rebbi Jeremiah asked, why did one not state "taken away from"? Rebbi Yose said, that was stated at the end: "I am taken away from the Jews."

96 This is from Chapter 1, Note 74.

HALAKHAH 13   741

(42d line 67) נִתְגָּרְשָׁה. תֵּלֵךְ וְתִדְבַּק בָּעַרְבִיִּים שֶׁחָשְׁקָה נַפְשָׁהּ בָּהֶם.

If she was divorced[97], let her go and cling to the Arabs, for she loves them.

97   The woman who vowed not to sleep with Jews.

(42d line 63) תַּנֵּי. הָאִשָּׁה שֶׁנָּדְרָה בַנָּזִיר וְשָׁמַע בַּעֲלָהּ וְלֹא הֵיפֵר לָהּ. רִבִּי מֵאִיר וְרִבִּי יְהוּדָה אוֹמְרִים. הוּא נוֹתֵן אֶצְבָּעוֹ בֵּין שִׁינֶּיהָ. שֶׁכֵּן אִם רָצָה לְהָקֵם יוּקָם. אָמַר. אִי אֶפְשִׁי שֶׁתְּהֵא נְזִירָה. יוֹצִיא וְיִתֵּן כְּתוּבָּה. רִבִּי יוֹסֵי וְרִבִּי שִׁמְעוֹן אוֹמְרִין. הִיא נֶתָנָה אֶצְבָּעָהּ בֵּין שִׁינֶּיהָ. שֶׁכֵּן אִם רָצָה לְהָקֵם מוּקָם. אוֹ שֶׁאָמְרָה. אֶיפְשָׁר שֶׁאֲהֵא נְזִירָה. תֵּצֵא שֶׁלֹּא בִכְתוּבָּה. דַּל כֵּן מָה כֵן אָמְרֵי רִבִּי מֵאִיר וְרִבִּי יְהוּדָה בַּמִּשְׁנָה. וַאֲפִילוּ בַּמִּשְׁנָה הָאַחֲרוֹנָה. מִפְּנֵי מָה אֵינוֹ מֵיפֵר לָהּ. רִבִּי יוֹסֵי וְרִבִּי שִׁמְעוֹן בַּמִּשְׁנָה הָאַחֲרוֹנָה. וַאֲפִילוּ תֵּימָא בַּמִּשְׁנָה רִאשׁוֹנָה. מִפְּנֵי מָה נָדְרָה.

[98]"If a woman made a vow to be a *nazir*; her husband heard and did not dissolve it: Rebbi Meïr and Rebbi Jehudah say, he put his finger between her teeth[99], for if he wants to confirm, he can confirm. If he said, I cannot stand her being a *nazir*, he should divorce her and pay the *ketubah*. Rebbi Yose and Rebbi Simeon say, she put her finger between her teeth, for if he wants to confirm, he can confirm[100]. If she said, I can stand it to be a *nazir*, he may divorce her[101] without paying the *ketubah*." Remove this, how can Rebbi Meïr and Rebbi Jehudah say so in the Mishnah[102]? Even in the later Mishnah, why did he not dissolve? Rebbi Yose and Rebbi Simeon follow the later Mishnah[103]. But you might say, the earlier Mishnah. Why did she make the vow?

98   Tosephta *Nezirut* 3:12-13. In the Babli, *Ketubot* 71a, there is a lengthy discussion about the attribution of the statements to different authors.

99   He is to blame if she bites and hurts him.

100 She knows that she takes the risk that her husband would confirm her vow and she would be unable to serve him wine, or to cook dishes which require wine in the recipe, and that at the end she will be without her hair, so that the husband might get exasperated. (In *Ketubot* 7:2, the Yerushalmi notes that if the husband by needling his wife pushes her to make the vow, Rebbis Yose and Simeon agree that he put his finger between her teeth.)

101 If he cannot stand living with a *nezirah*.

102 It seems that the text here is somewhat defective, judging from the following parallel story. In any case, if he does not dissolve his wife's vows, the husband is responsible for all consequences.

103 In requiring the woman to repeat and affirm her statement.

Indices

Index of Biblical Quotations

Gen. 2:24	54	4:25-26	517	2:14	88,132	
3:9	265	9:20	242	4:15	359	
3:13	265	9:31	88	4:27	523	
3:14	265	13:9	468	5:1	438	
5:1	668	13:16	468	5:4	470	
6:19	376	15:1	231,232	5:15	11	
9:3	464	15:2	232	6:7	129	
12:6	272	15:28	514	6:13	320	
15:20-12	63	15:29	514	6:16	165,169	
17:1	513	19:19	271	6:18	347	
17:2	513	20:21	310	7:14	476	
21:12	510,511	20:25	406	7:16	421	
23:21	241	21:4	29	7:19	223	
24:50	271	21:7	175,695	9:22	299	
25:23	265	22:6-12	263	11:29	464	
26:12	243	22:30	464	11:32	210	
31:47	271	24:8	513	11:33	206	
34:2	275	25:10	324	12:2	514	
34:7	241	25:11	327	12:3	518	
35:22	45	25:16	331	13:2	518	
38:13	45,62	25:21	331	13:44	174	
38:25	385	28:9	289	14:5	93,102	
45:23	573	30:23	319	14:6	102	
46:4	77	30:24	319,320	14:10	530	
48:5	509	30:25	320	14:34	332	
49:10	322	30:31	320	18:16	491	
50:2	71	31:14	514	19:12	502	
50:7	71	34:16	63	19:20	28,29,102	
50:10	73	35:25	149	19:21	28,29	
				19:22	28,29	
Ex. 1:2	288	Lev. 1:6	201	20:2	176	
2:14	69	2:8	130	20:4	401	
2:21	452	2:9	130,133	20:18	233	
4:24	517	2:13	474	21:1	168	

21:2	171	5:31	36,125,158,390	Deut. 1:12	295
21:7	179,193	6:2	429	4:5	531
21:14	179	6:14	447,530	4:13	328
21:15	170,183,184	6:22	269	6:5	236
22:11	169	6:23	271	6:7	266
22:13	33	6:24	299	6:13	236,238
22:15	724	8:11	212	7:3	22
22:23	421	8:24	279	7:20	322
23:4	601	10:33	75	7:23	315
23:17	89	12:15	69	8:1	322
23:40	468	13:23	294	10:2	324
23:42	468	13:27	385	10:6	75
24:14	175	14:44	317	11:26	280
26:40	11	15:1	474	11:30	274
26:46	282	15:22	515	13:7	16
27:9	421	19:2	95,375	14:21	464
27:11	527	23:7	243	14:29	545
27:26	429	24:4	243	15:21	21
27:28	427	24:17	511	17:8	186
		24:21	379	17:11	42
Num. 5:6	11	28:23	39	19:5	11
5:10	722	30:2	422,435,482,	19:15	21,256
5:12	11,122		655	19:17	705
5:13	26,29,119,123,	30:3	429,435,439,	19:19	16
	165,198,249,254		465,470,482,627	20:2	308,311
5:14	8,179,194,198	30:4	437,680	20:3	308,314
5:15	36,79,126,122,	30:6	700	20:5	330,333
	132,179	30:7	680,690	20:6	334,337
5:16	51	30:8	700	20:7	339
5:17	91,93,98,103	30:10	734	20:9	311,348
5;18	49,51,80	30:11	680	21:1	229,261,270,
5:19	38	30:13	700		351,361
5:20	33,194	30:14	38,694,711,720,	21:2	351,361,365
5:21	55,106,264		731	21:3	365,370,375
5:22	59,83,106,111	30:15	700	21:4	379
5:23	109,110	30:17	683,711,712	21:7	269,365,382
5:24	135	30:38	75	21:8	376,384
5:25	129,130	30:40	75	21:9	387
5:26	133	32:38	78	21:18	185
5:27	59,134,390	35:4	226	22:2	518
5:28	146,156,158,	35:5	116,230	22:9	616
	183	35:30	13	21:22	173
5:29	120,179	36:8	491,492	22:14	41
5:30	42,102			22:16	174

INDEX OF BIBLICAL QUOTATIONS

22:24	175	7:25-26	478	6:7	406
24:1	11,102,256	8:30	275	7:9	406
24:2	690	8:33	278,286	13:2	511
24:5	341	8:34	269,280	15:22	350
24:8	518			22:1	144
25:5	491	Jud. 5:2	234	24:17	323
25:9	102	5:28	385		
26:5	270	13:24-25	64	2K. 4:42	593
26:12	263	14:1	61	18:4	596
26:13	265	14:4-5	62	18:16	596
26:14	216	15:20	64	20:14	296
26:16	271	16:28	64	22:11	284
27:4	290	16:31	64	23:31	321
27:8	290			24:16	602
27:11	269,279	1Sam. 2:22	47		
27:12	278	2:25	49	Is. 2:3	602
27:14	270,273	2:29	47	3:9	367
27:15	278,280,282	4:8	317	9:4	56
27:26	282	4:17	348	24:9	398
28:2	280	7:1-2	317	27:8	56
28:36	318	8:3	47	33:12	292
28:69	282	9:2	67	39:3	296
29:11	113	14:8	317	48:12	288
30:10-11	304	14:24	452	56:15	271
31:10	269	16:12	320	57:2	78
31:12	148	31:1	348	58:7	651
31:26	324,330			58:8	71
32:49	78	2Sam. 1:17-18	75	58:13	633
33:2	330	3:38	67	60:12	292
33:20	78	7:18	305	63:11	233
34:6	71	11:11	317		
36:6	45	13:23	144	Jer. 2:30	495
36:7	45	14:25	67	9:25	510
		15:4	69	10:11	272
Jos. 4:3	293	15:6	69	11:5	112
4:5	294	15:7	67	11:9	70
4:8	277,293	15:8	69	23:29	492
4:16	296	15:11	69	29:1	602
4:19	275	18:14	60	33:25	513
4:20	293	18:15	60	45:3	40
5:1	296	19:14	44		
5:12	616			Ez. 18:24	11
5:13	623	1K. 1:33	321	20:13	515
7:5	297	1:36	113	20:21	515

21:31	415	119:106	482	7:8	506
20:39	517			7:12	285
21:34	356,368	Prov. 3:18	285	7:27	56
44:15	279	3:34	62	12:1	100
		6:26	31		
Hos. 4:14	390	7:4	70	Esth. 2:2	242
9:1	242	8:21	568	3:12	72
		20:25	444		
Am. 3:7	70	23:10	187	Ezra 9:2	62
5:9	406			9:4	62
9:1	70	Job 1:1	239,241	10:8	442
		1:15	242		
Mic. 3:11	724	1:17	242	Neh. 9:8	237
3:12	724	1:20	242	9:13-14	515
7:1	391	2:10	241		
		9:7	452	Dan. 2:4	272
Ob. 1:4	513	13:15	235	4:26	144
		13:16	235	12:3	511
Hag. 2:12	219	15:18	45,241	12:7	453
2:14	219	16:11	142		
2:16	410	27:2	235	1Chr. 3:15	322
		27:5	235	21:18	220
Ps. 7:12	409	27:12	242	26:23	75
12:2	401	32:2	243		
18:13-15	315	42:15	242	2Chr. 26:5	402
25:14	32			28:12	312
55:19	69	Cant. 5:14	328	28:15	311
57:3	604			29:17-18	596
62:12	492	Ruth 2:23	642	30:18	594
68:27	233			30:19	595
72:2	76	Thr. 5:14	400	35:3	318
76:12	445	5:15	401	35:13	572
81:6	289				
95:11	483	Eccl. 2:14	349	Mat. 15:5	422,
109:22	237	5:4	444		426,654

Index of Talmudical Quotations

Babylonian Talmud

Berakhot 8b	317	50b	530	Yebamot 24b	10
28a	206	52b	318	33b	26
31b	199	66b	149	36b	187
37a	577	69b	305	38b	185
44a	573	72b	327	56b	193
63a	6031	76b	614	58a	38
		84a	542	61b	124
Šabbat 14a	107	86b	562	65b	312,738
56a	47			71b	517
80b	47	Sukkah 3a/b	332	81a	117
86a	413	28a	568	86b	279
105b	56			88b	261
121a	542	Roš Haššanah 3a	75	92a	117
132a	514	18b	637	113a	695
157a	700	19b	637		
		25b	353	Soṭah 2b	12,14,16,29
Eruhin 6b	152	27a	491	3a	8
13a	110			4a	30
23a	228	Megillah 3a	199	4b	31
56b	228	12b	56	5b	24
58b	229	14a	234,322	6a	158
62b	704	18a	266	6b	162
69b	515	18b	109	7a	40,41
				7b	42,43,45
Pesaḥim 17a	219	Ta'anit 11b	634	8a	48,51
18b	222	12b	635	8b	52,53,54,56
26a	371			9a	61
34a	139	Mo'ed Qaṭan 5a	353	10a	62,64,350
56a	596	6a	357	10b	47
68b	513	20b	242	11a	60,145
117a	232			13b	78
		Ḥagigah 3a	147	14a	242
Yoma 6b	27	10a	482,483	14b	86,128,242
21b	402	22a	214	15a	87
25a	305	24a	222	15b	93,94,95,103
47a	577			16b	102
48a	200			17a	461

17b	105	43b	335,337	23b	481
18a	102,109	44a	339	24b	494
18b	117,119,120	44b	350,359	25a	268,489
19a	127	45a	360	25b	497
19b	105,134,135,141	45b	355,362,367,368,369	28a	502
				28b	505
20b	135,142,144	46a	371,372	30b	507,508
21a	144	46b	282	31a	511
21b	152,153,155	47b	387,389,390	31b	517
22a	155	48a	402	32a	513,517
22b	237	48b	408,405,406,407	35a	450,527
23a	81,166,174			35b	527
23b	166,169,170,174,176	49b	411,413	36b	530
				37a	531
24a	179	Ketubot 9a	27	37b	387
24b	38	21b	353	38a	324
25a	124,182,185	26b	20	38b	532
26a	122,152,183,187,193,194	45a	129	39a	533
		51b	193	41b	535,577
26b	191	58b	726,727	42b	536
27a	58,123	60b	188,189	43a	544
27b	83,282	63a	31	44a	546
28a	26,32,198,200	71a	740	46b	548,553,555
28b	26	72a	24	47a	465,557
29a	209	87b	251,261	48a	569
29b	208,212,222	112a	65	49a	571,572,576
30a	212			50b	570
30b	232	Nedarim 4b	448	51b	581
31b	249	5a	439	53a	568,590
32b	261,264,265,347	9a	444	53b	607
		9b	448	54a	610
33a	268,270,403	10a	427,447,452	54b	611
33b	275,276,277	10b	452	55b	619
34a	294,296	11a	461	56b	623
34b	295	12a	435,455	57b	585,624
35b	291,293	13a	453	60a	585,630
36a	146,289	14a	435,465,466	61a	642
36b	288	14b	458	61b	639
37a	282	15a	469,627	63a	632
37b	181	16b	470	65a	561
40b	305	17a	470	67a/b	680
41a	302	19b	477	68a	682
42b	305,316	21a	484,485	69a	684
43a	331	22a	445	74a	693

74b	697	32a	20		
75b	698	57b	552	Horaiot 11b	320,
76b	698,700	91b	65		321,322
77a	700,702	111b	200,492	12a	318
77b	704	146	316,317		
78a	706			Zebaḥim 6a	530
79a	703	Šebuot 20a	487	25a	200
79b	711	20b	491	102a	133
81b	719	22a	527	118b	277
82a	721	28b	438,4997		
82b	720	29a	268,489,493	Menaḥot 19a	8
83b	722	30a	705	21a	475
84a/b	722	36a	112	72b	133
88b	733			99a	317,324
89a	507,560,735	Sanhedrin 5a	707	99b	412
90a	560	11a	405		
90b	740	11b	599,593	Bekhorot 36b	706
		12a	594	44b	200
Nazir 25a/b	174	14b	360		
		21b	16,272	Keritut 5a	319,
Giṭṭin 33b	20	27a	129		320
36a	561	30a	20,249	5b	318,320,322
68b	406	30b	20,22	6a	322
80b	117	38b	291	8b	174
90a/b	10,11	43a	175,176	11a	28
		43b	297		
Qiddushin 18a	177	45a	51	Arakhin 3a	174
23b	305	59b	511	12a	322
27b	113	63a	427	13a	277
60a	695	70a	335	29a	478
77a	171	90a	56		
78b	305	101b	305	Temura 2b	530
80b	16	112a	561	14b	69
				15b	391,392
Baba Qama 46b	185,	Makkot 11b	45	24a	160
	433	12a	230		
80a	392	16a	561	Ḥulin 2a	444
90b	353	23b	385	9b	26
116b	525			43a	102
		Aboda Zara 5a	291	82a	387
Baba Batra 8a	561	25a	75		
14b	324	27a	429	Tamid 27a	305
15a	241	36b	16		
15b	241,243,244	37b	26	Niddah 45a	193

Jerusalem Talmud

Berakhot 1:8	152	Šabbat 8:7	31	12:1	695
3:1	622	16	542	12:3,4	269
9:6	236	19:2	199	12:5	188
Peah 1:1	412,426	Erubin 3:1	571, 575	14;1	695
1:6	6153			15:3	85
6:1	539,546	5:1	228	15:5	22,389
6:3	363	Pesaḥim 7:2	9	15:7	257
6:9	364	9:1	220	16:3	367
8:8	155	Yoma 6:1	705	Ketubot 2:4	20
Demay 2:1	642	7:1	300	2:10	17,40
2:3	220	Šeqalim 3:1	474	5:1	180
6:3	723	7:1	316	7:2	742
Kilaim 1:2	576	Roš Haššanah 3:1	353	7:5	24
8:1	4953	Megillah 1:1	199	7:7	10
Ševi'it 2:10	613	1:9	521	7:9	585
6:1	418	1:11	272	13:1	47
6:3	585	3:1	665	13:2	522
6:4	591	4:1	109	Nedarim 1:1	199
8:1	553	4:11	45	3:1	268
8:5	716	Ta'aniot 3:13	633	Nazir 1:1	434, 452
9:7	644	Mo'ed Qaṭan 1:1	355		
Terumot 5:9	312	3:7	242	1:2	441
8:5	205	Ḥagigah 1:1	147	1:6	447,448
9:4	585	1:8	706	5:1	200
9:7	624			5:5	485
Ma'serot 1:1	545	Yebamot 1:1	117, 692	6;1	571
3:7	332			8:1	253
4:3	475	1:2	83,695	Giṭṭin 5:4	20
5:7	490	1:5	179	Qiddušin 1:3	461
Ma'aser Šeni 4:4	735	1:6	152	1:5	113
5:1	355	2:1	692,697	1:8	127
5:5	279	2:4	179	3:5	505
5:13	394	3:11	155	3:11	639
Ḥallah 1:2,3	617	4:3	692		
2:1	518	4:11	102,137	Baba Qama 3:7	417
Orlah 2:1	137,246	6:5	124	9:14	557
		7:5	196,197	Sanhedrin 1:2	353, 592
Bikkurim 3:7	564	8:1	199,429	Sanhedrin 1:3	359
		10:1	35		

3:9	185,433	3:0	488	3:1	403,420
3:10	20,705	4:1	705	Makkot 2:7	228,
4:1	20	4:14	461		366
6:8	51	5:4	458	Horaiot 1:3	200
8:6	124,186	6:1	251	3:7	405
Šebu'ot 3:8	472	Abodah zarah 2:9	574		

Tosephta

Hagigah 3:8	225	7:24	343	4:6	450
3:16,17	223	8:1	274,275	4:7	642
Šeqalim 1:5	357	8:2-3	296	5:1	674
Kippurim 2:15	318	8:6	293,294	6:3	684
Megillah 2:13	665	8:8	279	6:5	697,698
Ta'aniot 1:4	644	9:1	302,381	6:6	698
		11:1	75	7:4	722,729,730,
Yebamot 12:8	58	13:1	318		731
Sota 1:1	12,30,41	13:3	402,403,405	7:6	735
1:4	49	13:5,6	403,419	Nezirut 3:12-13	741
1:6	43	15:1	406	3:19	485
1:8	102	15:2	409,410	Gittin 2:7	102
2:2	119,139	15:6	401	5:4	20
2:3	141,157	15:7	400,419		
2:4	160	15:8,9	412	Sanhedrin 2:9	593
2:5	162	Nedarim 1:1	444	2:10	594
2:6	80,166,168	1:3	455	2:13	599
3:1	56	1:4	435,458	7:11	115
3:15	60,61	1:6	427	Šebuot 2:4	438
3:16	60	2:1	494		
4:1	69,145	2:7	513	Zebahim 7:6	139
4:8	78	2:8	538	Menahot 1:16	86
5:4	183	2:10	561,564	Keritut 4:3	387
6:2-4	232	3:2	577		
7:17	331	3:3	568	Tahorot 6:17	26
7:18	317	3:5	581,611	Nega'im 8:2	95,97
7:19	342	3:7	607	Niddah 2:1,2	188
7:22	344	4:3	614		

Other Talmudic Sources

Abot dR. Nathan 78, 100,318,406	65,67 Midrash Psalms 56,69	276,277,280,292,331,3 35,339,341,343,344,347,351,353,355,359,361, 382,385,406,491
Derekh Ereṣ 100		
Šemaḥot 405	Mekhilta	
Soferim 302	dR. Ismael 56, 232,234,3218,405, 406,491,	Sifry Zuṭa 30,32, 39,93,102,120,123, 175,390
Gen. rabba 45,47, 50,56,72,264,265,266,291,456	dR. Simeon bar Ioḥai 60,232,234,491	Seder Olam 69, 274, 277,318,322,411
Ex. rabba 56,70,242,289,328	Midrash Tannaïm 78, 284,344,493	Midrash 32 Rules 199 Melekhet Hamiškan 317
Lev. rabba 50,100,285	Sifra 11,28,88,89,93, 97,102,124,133,165,	
Num. rabba 30,40, 41,44,45,50,56,62,64,67,69,75,83,93,102, 105,109,112,115,120, 121,122,123,136,145, 146,149,174,249,316,390,448	169,170,171,174,176,193,206,207,222,223,283,359,361,364,514,518, 583,668,695	Pesiqta rabbati 328, 495
		Tanḥuma 30,56, 67,75,123,266,315, 328,330,451,495,663
	Sifry Num. 13,30, 32,33,39,41,43,56,75,93,109,115,123,136, 144,145,146,174,183,193,194,249,264,375,390,447,448,465,515,682, 700,705,712	Tanḥuma Buber 30,67, 75,123,266,328
Deut. rabba 44		
Cant. rabba 328, 329,330		Pseudo-Jonathan 406, 700
Ruth rabba 415		
Eccl. rabba 445		Pirqe R. Eliezer 406
Threni rabbati 75,411	Sifry Deut. 10,13, 78,102,233,265,275,	Bet Hamidrasch (Jellinek) 406
Midrash Šemuel 42,		

Index of Greek, Latin, Hebrew, and Arabic Words

ἀνδροληψία	50	γλοσσόκομον	330
ἀπόφασις	292		
ἀσπαραγός	605	διφθέρα	111
βῆμα	304	ἑλληνιστί	266
βουλευταί	603	ἐξέδρα	135
βουλή	495	ἔπαρχος	76,542

ἑφθά	570	συνωρίς	31
θεμέλιος	248	ταμεῖον	669
θυρεός	314	τετράγονον	328
		τραγός	90
ἴτριον	576	τρεῖς	90
		τρομητά	570
κάμινος	401	τρυτάνη·	295
κατάβα	266		
κέλευσις	669	φαινόλης	709
κεντρόω	47	φιάλη	91
κεφαλωτόν	589		
κοιτών	4,8	ξένος	719
κολλίκιον	720		
κολοκασία	613	ψῆφος	550
κόμμι	111		
κοσμίδιον	521	ὦ πόποι	712
κυβευτής	563		
κύριε πολὺ βρέξον	497	alica	90
κώρυκος	669		
		ballista	315
ληστής	393		
λόγχη	60	caliga	314
λοπάς	577	castra	542
		catella	52
μεσοστύλιον	489	commis	111
		conditum vinum	535,605
χάλκανθον	110	custodia	658
χρῶμα	329		
χαλκίς	581	familia	242
		fascia	619
ὁμολογῶ χαρίζεσθαί σοι	499	feminalia	619
		femorale	619
πίναξ	406,445	funda	619
πλατεῖον	25		
πραγματεία	47,408	haustrum	519
πωμάριον	613		
		magis, magida	93
ῥοφητά	570	mistarius	534
		muries	579
σάλπιγξ	315		
σιτοδόκη	719	notarius	291
στήλη	293		
στρατιώτης	740	paenula	709

pomarium	613	מעל			11
ptisana	90	מפרע			119
		מקדה			93
scortea vestis	619				
signum	315	סינר			31
tero	579	ערער			137
tormentum	315				
tragos	90				
turma	315	ختن			517
		خبيص			574
בית	620	خلم			578
גריס	607	دجن			616
זונה	738	صحنى			579
גלגל	30	عمن			489
דקל	103	معالة			11
		مغالة			11
מי חטאת	95				

Author Index

Abraham ben David, Rabad		Eisenstein, S.	20,671	Halberstam, S. Z.	95
	26,22,500,534	Elbogen, I.	301,302,	Ḥananel, R.	67
Amir, Y.	302		303	Heinemann, J.	302
Asher ben Ieḥiel, Rosh		Epstein. J. N.	304,566	Herschler, M.	666
	484,562,579	Finkelstein, L.	275,292	Jastrow, M.	499
Ashkenazi, B.	133	Fleischer, H. L.	119,120	Josephus Flavius	389
		Fraenckel, D.	49,63,65,	Julianus, Emperor	
Ben Adrat, Shelomo,			472,493,582,740		489
	Rashba	Friedman, M. A.	154		
	442,494,534,558,570	Friedmann, M.	495	Kahle, P.	99
Brand, J.	293	Fürst, J.	50	Keller, G.	423
Brichto, H. Ch.	2,3,51,51			Kohut, A.	410
Brüll, N.	495,499	Galen	570	Krauss, S.	295
Buxtorf, J.	619	Ginzburg, L.	153,409	Kutscher, E. Y.	500
		Graetz, H.	56,409		
Caro, J.	20,27,149	Guggenheimer, E.	579	Levin, B. M.	31
Cohen, M.	2,193			Levy, J.	119,220,343,412,

Levy, J. 441,562	Milgrom, J. 89	Rashi 31,32,110,360
Lieberman, S. 49,57,282, 381,499,500,521,534,614, 652	Naḥmanides 284,703 Nissim Gerondi, RAN 439,484,531,640,706	Samuel ben Meïr, Rashbam 201 Sofer, A. 21
Liss, A. 282,304		Sussman, J. 27
Maimonides 21,27,31, 72,103,107,149,36,563,634, 653,704	Philo Judaeus 3,468,592 Pliny 110	Urbach, E. E. 204
Margalit, M. 62,103, 473,493,679	Qalir, E. 56 Qimḥi, D. 64	Vidal de Tolosa 27
Meïri, M. 21		Wacholder, B. Z. 234
Meshorer, Y. 320		

Subject Index

Abandoning property	544,547	Contract language	712
Accents, dividing	270	Cooked wine	583
Action on rumor	245	Covering blood	378
Acute danger	517	Cow and calf	387
Adult	21	Criminal intent	268
Alcohol, under the influence of	336	law,	177
Altneuschul	665	standard of proof	149
Attributes of mercy	511	Crown money	479
Arukh	67,201,266,579,582		
		Damascus document	226,422,468,482
Ban	427,432,559	Dedicated animals, disabling work	371,374
Bans, priestly	474	Dedication, of one's worth	432
Bet se'ah	381	substitutes	432
Bileam	242	Descendants, of Abraham	510
Black dress	667	of Noah	510
Burden of proof	185	Desecrated, children	170
		woman	33,36
Canaanite women, prohibition	62	Divorce, document	109
Childless widow, infidelity of	178	forced by wife	24
Circumcision, valid	517	formula, invalid	464,466
City, greenbelt of	226	grounds for	11,256
levitic	226	provoked	742
limits	622	Divorcee, promiscuous	123
of gold	413	Document, certified	22
Cohen, defilement	171	Door of regret	445
Commandment, obligation of	282	Double negation	468
Condominium propertty	548,549		
Confessions, invalid	138	Eating suet	253

Elevation offering	454		283,309,371,372,374,430,462
Enclytic letters	200	new	129
Ephah	79,165	Honor father and mother	426
Eruv	332	House, suburban	622
Expiation ritual	223	Husband, and wife's sacrifices	84,85
Familia, Emperor's	501	Infertility, male	736
of a Cohen	169,184	Impotence, claim of	37
Fast of Gedaliah	435	Impurity, degrees of	206,208,
Fasting, definition	634		209,214, 225
on Sabbath	633	doubtful	26
Fellows	603	generated by human body	48,83
Festival of the sheaf	592	of fluids	217,377
Field, broken	210	or reptiles	225
Firstling	20,708	of biblical texts	107
Fiscal agent	500	Incest, Egyptian	53
Flour Offering	80,81	Indiction	500
obligatoy	89	Inference rules	223
of Cohen's wife	81	combinations	225
voluntary	165	Intercourse, definition	23,28
Food, impure	211	duration	30
invalid	211	forbidden	7
Foreclosure	671	with slave girl	28
Fourth year, fruit of	338	Israel in Egypt	242
Fundraising	285		
		Jealousy, declaration of	7
Galilean pronunciation	451	repeal	185
Gambler	563	Jethro	242
Gentile food	574	Joseph, cof'fin of	76
Gezerah šawah	93,430,462	Judge, relying on own knowledge	353
Girl, adolescent	679		
adult	691	*Ketubah*	15
age of vows	679	mortgage	154
orphaned	682	Killing, preventive	151
ripe	679	self-defense	177
underage	173,682	*Kor*	648
Grain, five kinds	615		
Gutturals, disappearance	338	Lease, oral	647
		Legumes	609
Hallel	231,233	Letters, as numerals	201
Hands, unwashed	209,217	Levirate, of accused woman	58
Ḥazan	284	Locusts, edible	610
Hemina	56	*Log*	320
Hermeneutical rules	115,199,270,277	Logical binding	167

GENERAL INDEX

Man, alone with female not his wife	15,24	Pious, foolish	150
		fake	151
Mankind, literate	291	Plural, unspecified	351
Man's house	83	Police powers	149,388
Marriage, appointed time	691	Possession, legal	558
definition	693	Priestly service	128
forbidden to Cohen	170	Profane food, in Temple	7
of deaf-mute	695	Prohibition, private	435
of insane	695	property, abandoned	544,547
of pregnant or nursing woman	186	condominium	548,549
preliminary	111	of slaves	733
preliminary "bespeaking"	695	of wife	733
preliminary delayed	505	ownerless	538
ring	564	private	553
Measure for Measure	54,56	transfer of	553,565
Mina	320	Purifications, preliminary	97,102
Minimum measure	91	sacrifice	24,87,447
Mishnah, anonymous	675	of deceased	160
Moses, burial of	78	of poor	165
oath of	561,562	service	96
Nakedness, illegitimate	10	*Qab*	56
Natural law	376	Qor'an	464
Nazir	173	*Qorbān, qônām*	422,426,450
pentatouchal	431	*Qorbān*, substitute	453
prophetic	431		
Nest	523	Rape, of virgin	604
Night, court action in	704	victim	37,193,738
Nikanor Gate	49	presumed	40
		Reading, of Prophets	301
Oath, adding to	113	of Torah	301
repeated	496	Real estate, robbed	527
vain	438,467	title to	21
Object oriented	459	Red cow	374
'Omer sacrifice	88	Refuge, cities of	366
Omnipresent	55	Reparation offering, hung	161
Oracle, priestly	402	Restrictions, multiple	364
Ordination, Babylonian	706,707		
		Sabbath domain	229,332
Parallel commandments	491	Sacrifice, disposition	530
Parallel figure	227	mushy	453
Pentecost	89	purification	29,87
Pĕ'ôlâ nouns	153	reparation	29
Perjurer, punishment	177	Sacrifices, burning of	167

intention of	166	*Toman*	56
time of	165	*Torah*	42,106
Sacrilege	527	offered to mankind	291
Šamir worm	406	original script	272
Scale disease	87,173	scroll, material	109
Scroll of Fasts	636	scroll, not proofread	109
Seah	56	scroll, selling of	564
Second tithe	215,216	sentence order	330
Self-deprivation, sinful	427	study by women	142,149,180
Sextarius	56	style	199
Sheqel, currency	481	Tree, futile	335
She-ram	183	orchard	335
Sin, actionless	427	Translators, in court	704
by cooking	576	Tribes, order of	288,289
in error	312		
intentional	29,87	Ugliness, moral	10
not prosecutable	426,434	Underage girl, marriage by father	173
of mortification	658	by mother	173
secret	297	Underage male, sex act	155
Slaughter, ritual	378	*Urna*	56
Slave, circumcized	532		
Slave girl, Hebrew	695	Voice, heavenly	403
Son, rebellious	185,336	Vow, conditional	627
Sukkah, roof of	317	confirmed	703
Status, of child	304	deferred	507,735
Stoning	52	father's power	685
		husband's power	684,688,703, 714,734
Taxes, local	561		
Teaching, for salary	529,531	multiple	731
girls	529	of *nazir*	426
Temple incense	319	of self-deprivation	426
Temple service, in impurity	27	pronounced	540
Temple gift	559	public	561
tax	474	to Heaven	426
surplus	54	vs. oath	427
Terefa	376	violation of	438
Testimony, hearsay	13		
informal	22	Water, uncovered	205
by interested party	13	*Waw* consecutive	705
valid	21	Ways of peace	434
Tevul Yom	209,210,216	Weaving	126,129,132
13 lucky number	513	Widow, underage childless	692
Toll, collectors	502	Wife, unruly	718
tariff	502	Wine, definition	336

for mourner	336	Writing, abbreviated	99
Witness, in own behalf	41	Woman, after childbirth	83,84
scheming	16	refusing to live with husband	186,188
single	13,14,250,251,253,254,258,261,262	waiting for levir	119
		weaning a baby	189
unqualified	261		

www.ingramcontent.com/pod-product-compliance
Lightning Source LLC
Chambersburg PA
CBHW031841220426

43663CB00006B/459